HOLT McDOUGAL

Literature

Grade 8

COMMON CORE

EDITION

Typeset in *The Sans* from LucasFonts.

ACKNOWLEDGMENTS

STUDENT GUIDE TO ACADEMIC SUCCESS

Robert Laidlaw: "Zoos: Myth and Reality" by Rob Laidlaw. Used by permission of the author.

Michael Hutchins: "Zoos connect us to the natural world" by Michael Hutchins, from *The Boston Globe,* November 2, 2003. Copyright © 2003 by Michael Hutchins. Used by permission of the author.

Fulcrum Publishing: "Loo-Wit, the Fire-Keeper," from *Native American Stories* by Joseph Bruchac. Copyright © 1992 by Joseph Bruchac. Reprinted by permission of Fulcrum Publishing.

Marian Reiner: "Simile: Willow and Ginkgo," from *It Doesn't Always Have to Rhyme* by Eve Merriam. Copyright © 1964, renewed © 1992 by Eve Merriam. All rights reserved. Used by permission of Marian Reiner.

Acknowledgments are continued at the back of the book, following the Index of Skills.

ART CREDITS

COVER, TITLE PAGE

top left © Brooklyn Museum/Corbis; *top right* Photo © Civil War Archive/Bridgeman Art Library; *bottom center* © Getty Images; *background* © Henry Georgi/All Canada Photos/Corbis; *bottom left* Ken Kinzie/HMH Publishers.

Art Credits are continued at the back of the book, following the Acknowledgments.

HOLT McDOUGAL

Literature

Grade 8

Janet Allen

Arthur N. Applebee

Jim Burke

Douglas Carnine

Yvette Jackson

Carol Jago

Robert T. Jiménez

Judith A. Langer

Robert J. Marzano

Mary Lou McCloskey

Donna M. Ogle

Carol Booth Olson

Lydia Stack

Carol Ann Tomlinson

Special Contributor: Kylene Beers

HOLT McDOUGAL

 HOUGHTON MIFFLIN HARCOURT

SENIOR PROGRAM CONSULTANTS

JANET ALLEN Reading and Literacy Specialist; creator of the popular "It's Never Too Late"/"Reading for Life" Institutes. Dr. Allen is an internationally known consultant who specializes in literacy work with at-risk students. Her publications include *Tools for Content Literacy; It's Never Too Late: Leading Adolescents to Lifelong Learning; Yellow Brick Roads: Shared and Guided Paths to Independent Reading; Words, Words, Words: Teaching Vocabulary in Grades 4–12;* and *Testing 1, 2, 3 . . . Bridging Best Practice and High-Stakes Assessments.* Dr. Allen was a high school reading and English teacher for more than 20 years.

ARTHUR N. APPLEBEE Leading Professor, School of Education at the University at Albany, State University of New York; Director of the Center on English Learning and Achievement. During his varied career, Dr. Applebee has been both a researcher and a teacher, working in institutional settings with children with severe learning problems, in public schools, as a staff member of the National Council of Teachers of English, and in professional education. He was elected to the International Reading Hall of Fame and has received, among other honors, the David H. Russell Award for Distinguished Research in the Teaching of English.

JIM BURKE Lecturer and Author; Teacher of English at Burlingame High School, Burlingame, California. Mr. Burke is a popular presenter at educational conferences across the country and is the author of numerous books for teachers, including *School Smarts: The Four Cs of Academic Success; The English Teacher's Companion; Reading Reminders; Writing Reminders;* and *ACCESSing School: Teaching Struggling Readers to Achieve Academic and Personal Success.* He is the recipient of NCTE's Exemplary English Leadership Award and was inducted into the California Reading Association's Hall of Fame.

DOUGLAS CARNINE Professor of Education at the University of Oregon; Director of the Western Region Reading First Technical Assistance Center. Dr. Carnine is nationally known for his focus on research-based practices in education, especially curriculum designs that prepare instructors of K–12 students. He has received the Lifetime Achievement Award from the Council for Exceptional Children and the Ersted Award for outstanding teaching at the University of Oregon. Dr. Carnine frequently consults on educational policy with government groups, businesses, communities, and teacher unions.

YVETTE JACKSON Executive Director of the National Urban Alliance for Effective Education. Nationally recognized for her work in assessing the learning potential of underachieving urban students, Dr. Jackson is also a presenter for the Harvard Principal Center and is a member of the Differentiation Faculty of the Association for Supervision and Curriculum Development. Dr. Jackson's research focuses on literacy, gifted education, and cognitive mediation theory. She designed the Comprehensive Education Plan for the New York City Public Schools and has served as their Director of Gifted Programs.

CAROL JAGO Teacher of English with thirty-two years of experience at Santa Monica High School in California; Author and nationally known Lecturer; and Past President of the National Council of Teachers of English. With varied experience in standards assessment and secondary education, Ms. Jago is the author of numerous books on education and is active with the California Association of Teachers of English, editing its scholarly journal *California English* since 1996. Ms. Jago also served on the planning committee for the 2009 NAEP Framework and the 2011 NAEP Writing Framework.

ROBERT T. JIMÉNEZ Professor of Language, Literacy, and Culture at Vanderbilt University. Dr. Jiménez's research focuses on the language and literacy practices of Latino students. A former bilingual education teacher, he is now conducting research on how written language is thought about and used in contemporary Mexico. Dr. Jiménez has received several research and teaching honors, including two Fulbright awards from the Council for the International Exchange of Scholars and the Albert J. Harris Award from the International Reading Association.

JUDITH A. LANGER Distinguished Professor at the University at Albany, State University of New York; Director of the Center on English Learning and Achievement; Director of the Albany Institute for Research in Education. An internationally known scholar in English language arts education, Dr. Langer specializes in developing teaching approaches that can enrich and improve what gets done on a daily basis in classrooms. Her publications include *Getting to Excellent: How to Create Better Schools* and *Effective Literacy Instruction: Building Successful Reading and Writing Programs.*

ROBERT J. MARZANO Senior Scholar at Mid-Continent Research for Education and Learning (McREL); Associate Professor at Cardinal Stritch University in Milwaukee, Wisconsin; President of Marzano & Associates. An internationally known researcher, trainer, and speaker, Dr. Marzano has developed programs that translate research and theory into practical tools for K–12 teachers and administrators. He has written extensively on such topics as reading and writing instruction, thinking skills, school effectiveness, assessment, and standards implementation.

DONNA M. OGLE Professor of Reading and Language at National-Louis University in Chicago, Illinois; Past President of the International Reading Association. Creator of the well-known KWL strategy, Dr. Ogle has directed many staff development projects translating theory and research into school practice in middle and secondary schools throughout the United States and has served as a consultant on literacy projects worldwide. Her extensive international experience includes coordinating the Reading and Writing for Critical Thinking Project in Eastern Europe, developing integrated curriculum for a USAID Afghan Education Project, and speaking and consulting on projects in several Latin American countries and in Asia.

CAROL BOOTH OLSON Senior Lecturer in the Department of Education at the University of California, Irvine; Director of the UCI site of the National Writing Project. Dr. Olson writes and lectures extensively on the reading/writing connection, critical thinking through writing, interactive strategies for teaching writing, and the use of multicultural literature with students of culturally diverse backgrounds. She has received many awards, including the California Association of Teachers of English Award of Merit, the Outstanding California Education Research Award, and the UC Irvine Excellence in Teaching Award.

CAROL ANN TOMLINSON Professor of Educational Research, Foundations, and Policy at the University of Virginia; Co-Director of the University's Institutes on Academic Diversity. An internationally known expert on differentiated instruction, Dr. Tomlinson helps teachers and administrators develop effective methods of teaching academically diverse learners. She was a teacher of middle and high school English for 22 years prior to teaching at the University of Virginia. Her books on differentiated instruction have been translated into eight languages.

SPECIAL CONTRIBUTOR:
KYLENE BEERS Special Consultant; Former Middle School Teacher; nationally known Lecturer and Author on reading and literacy; and former President of the National Council of Teachers of English. Dr. Beers is the nationally known author of *When Kids Can't Read: What Teachers Can Do* and co-editor of *Adolescent Literacy: Turning Promise into Practice,* as well as articles in the *Journal of Adolescent and Adult Literacy.* Former editor of *Voices from the Middle,* she is the 2001 recipient of NCTE's Richard W. Halley Award, given for outstanding contributions to middle-school literacy.

ENGLISH LEARNER SPECIALISTS

MARY LOU McCLOSKEY Past President of Teachers of English to Speakers of Other Languages (TESOL); Director of Teacher Development and Curriculum Design for Educo in Atlanta, Georgia. Dr. McCloskey is a former teacher in multilingual and multicultural classrooms. She has worked with teachers, teacher educators, and departments of education around the world on teaching English as a second and foreign language. She is author of *On Our Way to English, Voices in Literature, Integrating English,* and *Visions: Language, Literature, Content.* Her awards include the Le Moyne College Ignatian Award for Professional Achievement and the TESOL D. Scott Enright Service Award.

LYDIA STACK International ESL consultant. Her areas of expertise are English language teaching strategies, ESL standards for students and teachers, and curriculum writing. Her teaching experience includes 25 years as an elementary and high school ESL teacher. She is a past president of TESOL. Her awards include the James E. Alatis Award for Service to TESOL (2003) and the San Francisco STAR Teacher Award (1989). Her publications include *On Our Way to English; Wordways: Games for Language Learning;* and *Visions: Language, Literature, Content.*

CURRICULUM SPECIALIST

WILLIAM L. McBRIDE Curriculum Specialist. Dr. McBride is a nationally known speaker, educator, and author who now trains teachers in instructional methodologies. A former reading specialist, English teacher, and social studies teacher, he holds a Masters in Reading and a Ph.D. in Curriculum and Instruction from the University of North Carolina at Chapel Hill. Dr. McBride has contributed to the development of textbook series in language arts, social studies, science, and vocabulary. He is also known for his novel *Entertaining an Elephant,* which tells the story of a burned-out teacher who becomes re-inspired with both his profession and his life.

MEDIA SPECIALISTS

DAVID M. CONSIDINE Professor of Instructional Technology and Media Studies at Appalachian State University in North Carolina. Dr. Considine has served as a media literacy consultant to the U.S. government and to the media industry, including Discovery Communications and Cable in the Classroom. He has also conducted media literacy workshops and training for county and state health departments across the United States. Among his many publications are *Visual Messages: Integrating Imagery into Instruction,* and *Imagine That: Developing Critical Viewing and Thinking Through Children's Literature.*

LARKIN PAULUZZI Teacher and Media Specialist; trainer for the New Jersey Writing Project. Ms. Pauluzzi puts her extensive classroom experience to use in developing teacher-friendly curriculum materials and workshops in many different areas, including media literacy. She has led media literacy training workshops in several districts throughout Texas, guiding teachers in the meaningful and practical uses of media in the classroom. Ms. Pauluzzi has taught students at all levels, from Title I Reading to AP English IV. She also spearheads a technology club at her school, working with students to produce media and technology to serve both the school and the community.

LISA K. SCHEFFLER Teacher and Media Specialist. Ms. Scheffler has designed and taught media literacy and video production curriculum, in addition to teaching language arts and speech. Using her knowledge of mass communication theory, coupled with real classroom experience, she has developed ready-to-use materials that help teachers incorporate media literacy into their curricula. She has taught film and television studies at the University of North Texas and has served as a contributing writer for the Texas Education Agency's statewide viewing and representing curriculum.

TEACHER ADVISORS

These are some of the many educators from across the country who played a crucial role in the development of the tables of contents, the lesson design, and other key components of this program:

Virginia L. Alford, MacArthur High School, San Antonio, Texas

Yvonne L. Allen, Shaker Heights High School, Shaker Heights, Ohio

Dave T. Anderson, Hinsdale South High School, Darien, Illinois

Kacy Colleen Anglim, Portland Public Schools District, Portland, Oregon

Jordana Benone, North High School, Torrance, California

Patricia Blood, Howell High School, Farmingdale, New Jersey

Marjorie Bloom, Eau Gallie High School, Melbourne, Florida

Edward J. Blotzer, Wilkinsburg Junior/Senior High School, Wilkinsburg, Pennsylvania

Stephen D. Bournes, Evanston Township High School, Evanston, Illinois

Barbara M. Bowling, Mt. Tabor High School, Winston-Salem, North Carolina

Kiala Boykin-Givehand, Duval County Public Schools, Jacksonville, Florida

Laura L. Brown, Adlai Stevenson High School, Lincolnshire, Illinois

Cynthia Burke, Yavneh Academy, Dallas, Texas

Hoppy Chandler, San Diego City Schools, San Diego, California

Gary Chmielewski, St. Benedict High School, Chicago, Illinois

Delorse Cole-Stewart, Milwaukee Public Schools, Milwaukee, Wisconsin

Kathy Dahlgren, Skokie, Illinois

Diana Dilger, Rosa Parks Middle School, Dixmoor, Illinois

L. Calvin Dillon, Gaither High School, Tampa, Florida

Dori Dolata, Rufus King High School, Milwaukee, Wisconsin

Jon Epstein, Marietta High School, Marietta, Georgia

Helen Ervin, Fort Bend Independent School District, Sugar Land, Texas

Sue Friedman, Buffalo Grove High School, Buffalo Grove, Illinois

Chris Gee, Bel Air High School, El Paso, Texas

Paula Grasel, The Horizon Center, Gainesville, Georgia

Rochelle L. Greene-Brady, Kenwood Academy, Chicago, Illinois

Christopher Guarraia, Centreville High School, Clifton, Virginia

Michele M. Hettinger, Niles West High School, Skokie, Illinois

Elizabeth Holcomb, Forest Hill High School, Jackson, Mississippi

Jim Horan, Hinsdale Central High School, Hinsdale, Illinois

James Paul Hunter, Oak Park-River Forest High School, Oak Park, Illinois

Susan P. Kelly, Director of Curriculum, Island Trees School District, Levittown, New York

Beverley A. Lanier, Varina High School, Richmond, Virginia

Pat Laws, Charlotte-Mecklenburg Schools, Charlotte, North Carolina

Diana R. Martinez, Treviño School of Communications & Fine Arts, Laredo, Texas

Natalie Martinez, Stephen F. Austin High School, Houston, Texas

Elizabeth Matarazzo, Ysleta High School, El Paso, Texas

Carol M. McDonald, J. Frank Dobie High School, Houston, Texas

Amy Millikan, Consultant, Chicago, Illinois

Eileen Murphy, Walter Payton Preparatory High School, Chicago, Illinois

Lisa Omark, New Haven Public Schools, New Haven, Connecticut

Kaine Osburn, Wheeling High School, Wheeling, Illinois

Andrea J. Phillips, Terry Sanford High School, Fayetteville, North Carolina

Cathy Reilly, Sayreville Public Schools, Sayreville, New Jersey

Mark D. Simon, Neuqua Valley High School, Naperville, Illinois

Scott Snow, Sequin High School, Arlington, Texas

Jane W. Speidel, Brevard County Schools, Viera, Florida

Cheryl E. Sullivan, Lisle Community School District, Lisle, Illinois

Anita Usmiani, Hamilton Township Public Schools, Hamilton Square, New Jersey

Linda Valdez, Oxnard Union High School District, Oxnard, California

Nancy Walker, Longview High School, Longview, Texas

Kurt Weiler, New Trier High School, Winnetka, Illinois

Elizabeth Whittaker, Larkin High School, Elgin, Illinois

Linda S. Williams, Woodlawn High School, Baltimore, Maryland

John R. Williamson, Fort Thomas Independent Schools, Fort Thomas, Kentucky

Anna N. Winters, Simeon High School, Chicago, Illinois

Tonora D. Wyckoff, North Shore Senior High School, Houston, Texas

Karen Zajac, Glenbard South High School, Glen Ellyn, Illinois

Cynthia Zimmerman, Mose Vines Preparatory High School, Chicago, Illinois

Lynda Zimmerman, El Camino High School, South San Francisco, California

Ruth E. Zurich, Brown Deer High School, Brown Deer, Wisconsin

COMMON
CORE

COMMON
CORE

OVERVIEW
Student Edition

LESSONS WITH EMBEDDED COMMON CORE INSTRUCTION

COMMON
CORE

Look for the COMMON CORE symbol throughout the book. It highlights targeted objectives to help you succeed in mastering the knowledge and skills you will need for college or for a career.

© Getty Images

COMMON CORE CONTENTS

CONTENTS IN BRIEF

Online at

Log in to learn more at thinkcentral.com, where you can access most program resources in one convenient location.

LITERATURE AND READING CENTER

- Author Biographies
- *PowerNotes* Presentations with Video Trailers
- Professional Audio Recordings of Selections
- Graphic Organizers
- Analysis Frames
- NovelWise

WRITING AND GRAMMAR CENTER

- Interactive Student Models*
- Interactive Graphic Organizers*
- Interactive Revision Lessons*
- *GrammarNotes* Presentations and Practice

also available on WriteSmart CD-ROM

VOCABULARY CENTER

- *WordSharp* Interactive Vocabulary Tutor
- Vocabulary Practice Copy Masters

MEDIA AND TECHNOLOGY CENTER

- MediaScope: Media Literacy Instruction
- Digital Storytelling
- Speaking and Listening Support

RESEARCH CENTER

- Writing and Research in a Digital Age
- Citation Guide

Assessment Center

- Program Assessments
- Level Up Online Tutorials
- Online Essay Scoring

MORE TECHNOLOGY

Student One Stop
Access an electronic version of your textbook, complete with selection audio and worksheets.

Media Smart DVD-ROM
Sharpen your critical viewing and analysis skills with these in-depth interactive media studies.

COMMON CORE
UNIT 1

The Main Events
PLOT AND CONFLICT

• FICTION • DRAMA • MEDIA • INFORMATIONAL TEXT • POETRY

> ### *Vocabulary Strategies*
> Foreign words in English, *p. 48*   Reference aids, *p. 89*
> Prefixes: *com-* and *multi-, p. 64*   Latin roots: *dict, p. 121*
> Suffixes that form nouns, *p. 78*   Context Clues, *p. 134*

Through Different Eyes
CHARACTER AND POINT OF VIEW

• FICTION • MEDIA • INFORMATIONAL TEXT • POETRY

> ### Vocabulary Strategies
>
> Similes, *p. 188*   Analogies, *p. 260*
>
> Specialized vocabulary, *p. 228*   Synonyms as context clues, *p. 280*
>
> Prefixes: *fore-* and *mal-, p. 244* Multiple-meaning words, *p. 289*

The Place to Be
SETTING AND MOOD

• FICTION • INFORMATIONAL TEXT • POETRY

INFORMATIONAL TEXT: LITERARY NONFICTION

Vocabulary Strategies

Idioms, *p. 337*

Homographs, *p. 368*

Latin roots: *cred, p. 386*

Recognizing base words and affixes, *p. 408*

Prefixes: *inter-, p. 428*

COMMON
CORE

UNIT **4**

A World of Meaning
THEME AND SYMBOL

• FICTION • POETRY • DRAMA • MEDIA

Vocabulary Strategies
Reference aids, *p. 485*   Suffixes: *-ly, p. 498*

Painting with Words
POETRY

> *Vocabulary Strategies*
>
> Latin roots: *carn, p. 651*

A Unique Imprint
STYLE, VOICE, AND TONE

• FICTION • INFORMATIONAL TEXT • POETRY

> ### Vocabulary Strategies
> Multiple-meaning words, *p. 702*   Latin roots: *leg, p. 737*
> Connotation and denotation, *p. 715*   Foreign words in English, *p. 750*

Our Place in the World
HISTORY, CULTURE, AND THE AUTHOR

• FICTION • INFORMATIONAL TEXT • MEDIA • POETRY

Vocabulary Strategies

Analogies, *p. 802*   Similes, *p. 850*

Reference aids, *p. 820*

COMMON CORE

UNIT 8

Believe It or Not
FACTS AND INFORMATION

• INFORMATIONAL TEXT • MEDIA

Vocabulary Strategies

Context clues, *p. 898*   Suffixes that form adjectives, *p. 932*

Word origins, *p. 909*   Latin roots: *pend, p. 943*

Denotation and connotation, *p. 923*

State Your Case
ARGUMENT AND PERSUASION
• INFORMATIONAL TEXT • MEDIA • LITERATURE

> ### Vocabulary Strategies
>
> Greek roots: *exo, p. 998*   Related words, *p. 1021*
> Latin words: *gressus, p. 1012*   Antonyms and context clues, *p. 1029*
>   Using the dictionary, *p. 1036*

Investigation and Discovery
THE POWER OF RESEARCH

STANDARDS FOCUS
Use Reference Materials and Technology, Evaluate Sources

Research, Synthesize

Selections by Genre

TEXT ANALYSIS WORKSHOPS

SPEAKING AND LISTENING WORKSHOPS

WRITING WORKSHOPS

WriteSmart CD-ROM

MEDIA STUDY

MediaSmart DVD-ROM

VOCABULARY STRATEGIES

GRAMMAR IN CONTEXT

STUDENT GUIDE TO ACADEMIC SUCCESS

STUDENT GUIDE

© Jupiterimages/Getty Images

The Common Core for Uncommon Achievement

Carol Jago

*"If you don't know where you are going,
any road will get you there."* – Lewis Carroll

The Common Core State Standards make clear where students are going. They describe what today's children need to know and be able to do to thrive in post-secondary education and the workplace. By focusing on results — the destination — rather than on the how — the means of transportation — the Common Core allows for a variety of teaching methods and many different classroom approaches. The challenge for teachers is to turn the daily journey towards this destination into an intellectual adventure.

One way to think about the Common Core is as a kind of GPS device to situate curriculum. While some students may choose the road less traveled, the objective is fixed. When students become lost through a wrong turn, teachers recalculate the route, providing a calm and confident voice that guides all students to academic achievement and deep literacy.

Shared Responsibility for Students' Literacy Development

The Common Core State Standards insist that the responsibility for helping students achieve literacy is not the sole responsibility of the English teacher. The introduction states clearly that, "instruction in reading, writing, speaking, listening, and language (should) be a shared responsibility within the school" (4). Citing NAEP Reading assessment test specification guidelines, the Common Core recommends that 55% of what students read in grade 8 and 70% in grade 12 should be informational text. These percentages are not meant to reflect the balance of reading materials in English class alone but rather the totality of what students should be reading across the curriculum in history/social studies, science, and technical subjects as well as in English. Given the type of reading that will be required of students in college and of graduates in the workplace, this distribution is both relevant and practical.

Understanding of Other Perspectives and Cultures

The Common Core also makes clear the importance of literature in the education of America's children. "Through reading great classic and contemporary works of literature representative of a variety of periods, cultures, and worldviews, students can vicariously inhabit worlds and have experiences much different from their own" (7). Reading literature demands that readers look inward, examine their beliefs in light of new information, consider the world through different eyes, take time for reflection. Such reading is a key to student learning.

The Purpose of Exemplar Texts

To describe the quality and complexity of the works students should read at each grade level, the Common Core offers lists of "exemplar texts." While some may choose to treat the texts on these lists as required reading, such usage would represent a misunderstanding of their purpose. "The choices should serve as useful guideposts in helping educators select texts of similar complexity, quality, and range for their own classrooms. They expressly do not represent a partial or complete reading list" (Appendix B, 2). The poems, stories, novels, and nonfiction that appear on the Common Core lists are intended as models for guiding — not dictating — text selection.

The Difference Between Persuasion and Argument

The Common Core writing standards describe the types and purposes for writing that students need to master. You will find extended definitions of argument, informative/explanatory writing, and narrative writing in Appendix A. Of particular note is the distinction the Common Core draws between persuasion and argument. "When writing to persuade, writers employ a variety of persuasive strategies. One common strategy is an appeal to the credibility, character, or authority of the writer (or speaker). A logical argument, on the other hand, convinces the audience because of the perceived merit and reasonableness of the claims and proofs offered rather than either the emotions the writing evokes in the audience or the character or credentials of the writer" (24). Because of its importance for college and workplace readiness, argument holds a special place in the Common Core writing standards.

> *One way to think about the Common Core is as a kind of GPS device …*

Complex Literary and Informational Texts

Throughout the Common Core document you will notice the anchor standard, "Read and comprehend complex literary and informational texts independently and proficiently." It isn't enough for students to read with a teacher by their side. They need to be able, often with a little help from their friends or from the habits of mind they learned from their teachers, to read for themselves. They need to be able, like Huck Finn, to head out for the territory on their own. Such a journey requires confidence in one's ability to navigate uncharted waters and to overcome challenges their teachers can't foresee or even imagine. As we guide students on the academic adventure that is middle and high school, let us never forget that the path we tread is the path to intellectual freedom.

WORKS CITED

Common Core State Standards for English Language Arts and History/Social Studies, Science, & Technical Subjects. 2010.

Appendix B. Common Core State Standards for English Language Arts and History/Social Studies, Science, & Technical Subjects. 2010.

Carol Jago has taught middle and high school for over 30 years and was a member of the Common Core Initiative feedback team. She is the Past President of the National Council of Teachers of English.

Understanding the Common Core State Standards

What are the English Language Arts Common Core State Standards?

The Common Core State Standards for English Language Arts indicate what you should know and be able to do by the end of your grade level. These understandings and skills will help you be better prepared for future classes, college courses, and a career. For this reason, the standards for each strand in English Language Arts (such as reading informational text or writing) directly relate to the College and Career Readiness Anchor Standards for each strand. The Anchor Standards broadly outline the understandings and skills you should learn by the end of middle school so that you are well-prepared for high school, for college, or for a career.

How do I learn the English Language Arts Common Core State Standards?

Your textbook is closely aligned to the English Language Arts Common Core State Standards. Every time you learn a concept or practice a skill, you are working on mastery of one of the standards. Each unit, each selection, and each workshop in your textbook connects to one or more of the standards for English Language Arts listed on the following pages.

The English Language Arts Common Core State Standards are divided into five strands: Reading Literature, Reading Informational Text, Writing, Speaking and Listening, and Language.

Reading Literature (RL)

This strand concerns the literary texts you will read at this grade level: stories, drama, and poetry. The Common Core State Standards stress that you should read a range of texts of increasing complexity as you progress through middle school.

Reading Informational Text (RI)

Informational text includes a broad range of literary nonfiction, including exposition, argument, and functional text, such as personal essays, speeches, opinion pieces, memoirs, and historical and technical accounts. The Common Core State Standards stress that you will also read a range of informational texts of increasing complexity as you progress from grade to grade.

Writing (W)

The Writing strand focuses on your generating three types of texts: arguments, informative or explanatory texts, and narratives, as well as using the writing process and technology to develop and share your writing. The Common Core State Standards also emphasize research and specify that you should write routinely for both short and extended time frames.

Speaking and Listening (SL)

The Common Core State Standards focus on comprehending information presented in a variety of media and formats, on participating in collaborative discussions, and on presenting knowledge and ideas clearly.

Language (L)

The standards in the Language strand address the conventions of Standard English grammar, usage, and mechanics; knowledge of language; and vocabulary acquisition and use.

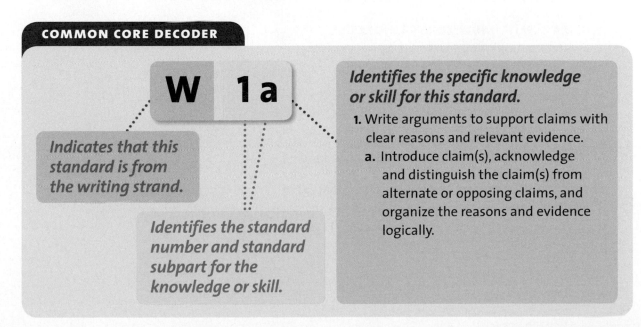

COMMON CORE DECODER

W 1 a

Indicates that this standard is from the writing strand.

Identifies the standard number and standard subpart for the knowledge or skill.

Identifies the specific knowledge or skill for this standard.

1. Write arguments to support claims with clear reasons and relevant evidence.
   a. Introduce claim(s), acknowledge and distinguish the claim(s) from alternate or opposing claims, and organize the reasons and evidence logically.

English Language Arts
Common Core State Standards

Listed below are the English Language Arts Common Core State Standards that you are required to master by the end of grade 8. To help you understand what is required of you, we have provided a summary of the concepts you will learn on your way to mastering each standard.

College and Career Readiness Anchor Standards for Reading

COMMON CORE STATE STANDARDS

KEY IDEAS AND DETAILS

1. Read closely to determine what the text says explicitly and to make logical inferences from it; cite specific textual evidence when writing or speaking to support conclusions drawn from the text.

2. Determine central ideas or themes of a text and analyze their development; summarize the key supporting details and ideas.

3. Analyze how and why individuals, events, and ideas develop and interact over the course of a text.

CRAFT AND STRUCTURE

4. Interpret words and phrases as they are used in a text, including determining technical, connotative, and figurative meanings, and analyze how specific word choices shape meaning or tone.

5. Analyze the structure of texts, including how specific sentences, paragraphs, and larger portions of the text (e.g., a section, chapter, scene, or stanza) relate to each other and the whole.

6. Assess how point of view or purpose shapes the content and style of a text.

INTEGRATION OF KNOWLEDGE AND IDEAS

7. Integrate and evaluate content presented in diverse formats and media, including visually and quantitatively, as well as in words.

8. Delineate and evaluate the argument and specific claims in a text, including the validity of the reasoning as well as the relevance and sufficiency of the evidence.

9. Analyze how two or more texts address similar themes or topics in order to build knowledge or to compare the approaches the authors take.

RANGE OF READING AND LEVEL OF TEXT COMPLEXITY

10. Read and comprehend complex literary and informational texts independently and proficiently.

Reading Standards for Literature, Grade 8 Students

COMMON CORE STATE STANDARD	WHAT IT MEANS TO YOU
KEY IDEAS AND DETAILS	
1. Cite the textual evidence that most strongly supports an analysis of what the text says explicitly as well as inferences drawn from the text.	You will use information from the text to support its main ideas—both those that are stated directly and those that are suggested.
2. Determine a theme or central idea of a text and analyze its development over the course of the text, including its relationship to the characters, setting, and plot; provide an objective summary of the text.	You will define a text's theme or main idea by analyzing its relationship to the characters, setting, and plot, as well as how it unfolds throughout the text. You will also summarize the main idea of the text without adding your own ideas or opinions.
3. Analyze how particular lines of dialogue or incidents in a story or drama propel the action, reveal aspects of a character, or provoke a decision.	You will analyze how specific events or lines of dialogue in a story or drama move the action forward or show you things about the characters.
CRAFT AND STRUCTURE	
4. Determine the meaning of words and phrases as they are used in a text, including figurative and connotative meanings; analyze the impact of specific word choices on meaning and tone, including analogies or allusions to other texts.	You will analyze specific words, phrases, and patterns of sound in the text to determine what they mean and how they contribute to the text's larger meaning.
5. Compare and contrast the structure of two or more texts and analyze how the differing structure of each text contributes to its meaning and style.	You will compare and contrast the forms of two or more texts and analyze how those forms contribute to meaning and style.
6. Analyze how differences in the points of view of the characters and the audience or reader (e.g., created through the use of dramatic irony) create such effects as suspense or humor.	You will analyze how differences between the points of view of characters and readers create effects like suspense or humor.
INTEGRATION OF KNOWLEDGE AND IDEAS	
7. Analyze the extent to which a filmed or live production of a story or drama stays faithful to or departs from the text or script, evaluating the choices made by the director or actors.	You will compare and contrast how events and information are presented in a text and a filmed or live production of the text.
8. (Not applicable to literature)	
9. Analyze how a modern work of fiction draws on themes, patterns of events, or character types from myths, traditional stories, or religious works such as the Bible, including describing how the material is rendered new.	You will recognize and analyze how an author draws from and uses historical source material.
RANGE OF READING AND LEVEL OF TEXT COMPLEXITY	
10. By the end of the year, read and comprehend literature, including stories, dramas, and poems, at the high end of grades 6–8 text complexity band independently and proficiently.	You will read and understand grade-level appropriate literary texts by the end of grade 8.

Spotlight on Common Core

RL 9 Analyze how a modern work of fiction draws on themes, patterns of events, or character types from myths, traditional stories, or religious works such as the Bible, including describing how the material is rendered new.

COMMON CORE

Literature: Analyzing Traditional Material in Modern Fiction

The Common Core State Standards require you to analyze how modern stories and novels use themes, events, and characters from myths, traditional stories, and religious works. There are certain stories that never grow old. Even if they were first written down hundreds of years ago, they still spark readers' imaginations. When modern writers use material from these stories, they try to make them new. There are four main ways writers do this:

- by telling the stories in modern language
- by giving the stories modern settings
- by telling the stories from a different point of view
- by relating the stories to current events

Throughout this book, you will read modern works based on myths and traditional stories. Study the following example.

Read the following excerpt. Then answer the question that follows.

from "Loo-Wit the Fire Keeper"
by Joseph Bruchac

In this myth, two brothers quarrel over land. The Creator takes them to a new land and gives each brother the land on one side of a river. He makes a stone bridge across the river so the people can visit each other. The stone bridge will stand, he says, as long as the people's hearts are good. After many seasons, the two peoples begin to fight again, so the Creator takes away their fire. The people grow cold and pray to the Creator. He feels sorry for them, so he goes to see an old woman named Loo-Wit. Because her heart is still good, she still has fire. The Creator asks her to share her fire. In return, he promises to give her whatever she wishes. She wants to be young and beautiful, so the Creator makes her a lovely young woman. Loo-Wit goes to the middle of the stone bridge and makes a fire. All the people come to her and get the fire they need. Once again all is peaceful until the two chiefs quarrel over Loo-Wit. They both want to marry her, but Loo-Wit can't decide between them. Once again the peoples begin to fight.

When the Creator saw the fighting he became angry. He broke down the Great Stone Bridge. He took each of the two chiefs and changed them into mountains. The chief of the Klickitat became the mountain we now know as Mount Adams. The chief of the Multnomahs became the mountain we now know as Mount Hood. Even as mountains, they continued to quarrel, throwing flames and stones at each other. In some places, the stones they threw almost blocked the river between them. That is why the Columbia River is so narrow in the place called the Dalles today.

    Loo-Wit was heartbroken over the pain caused by her beauty. She no longer wanted to be a beautiful young woman. She could no longer find peace as a human being. The Creator took pity on her and changed her into a mountain also, the most beautiful of the mountains. She was placed so that she stood between Mount Adams and Mount Hood, and she was allowed to keep the fire within herself which she had once shared on the Great Stone Bridge. Eventually, she became known as Mount St. Helens and she slept peacefully.

continued

Though she was asleep, Loo-Wit was still aware, the people said. The Creator had placed her between the two quarreling mountains to keep the peace, and it was intended that humans, too, should look at her beauty and remember to keep their hearts good, to share the land and treat it well. If we human beings do not treat the land with respect, the people said, Loo-Wit will wake up and let us know how unhappy she and the Creator have become again. So they said long before the day in the 1980s when Mount St. Helens woke again.

1. How does the author make this myth new?

LEARN HOW **Analyzing Traditional Material in Modern Fiction** To answer the question, you must compare the version of the myth you just read with the original myth. If you are not familiar with the original myth, you have to guess what it was probably like. Because myths are very old stories, you know that anything that belongs to today's world was not part of the original myth. Here are one writer's notes.

> This myth was composed by native people long ago. I know that Mount Adams, Mount Hood, and Mount St. Helens are all names given by European settlers. I can be sure that these were not the names used in the original myth. I also know that the myth was composed long before 1980, when Mount St. Helens erupted. The information about Mount St. Helens waking up is new.

Now that you have decided what is new about this retelling of the myth, ask yourself why the writer made these changes. Was he or she trying to relate the myth to current events? When you answer the question, be sure to include the work's title and author.

> 1. In "Loo-Wit, the Fire-Keeper," Joseph Bruchac updates the myth by using the new names for the mountains and referring to the eruption of Mount St. Helens in 1980.

As you read modern works based on myths and traditional stories throughout this book, guess what the original works were like and compare them with the modern works. Identify how the authors have updated the traditional material. Then ask yourself why the writer made these changes.

Reading Standards for Informational Text, Grade 8 Students

COMMON CORE STATE STANDARD	WHAT IT MEANS TO YOU
KEY IDEAS AND DETAILS	
1. Cite the textual evidence that most strongly supports an analysis of what the text says explicitly as well as inferences drawn from the text.	You will cite information from the text to support its main ideas—both those that are stated directly and those that are suggested.
2. Determine a central idea of a text and analyze its development over the course of the text, including its relationship to supporting ideas; provide an objective summary of the text.	You will determine a text's main idea by analyzing its relationship to supporting details as well as how it progresses throughout the text. You will also summarize the text as a whole without adding your own ideas or opinions.
3. Analyze how a text makes connections among and distinctions between individuals, ideas, or events (e.g., through comparisons, analogies, or categories).	You will analyze the ways in which a text groups together or separates individuals, events, and ideas.
CRAFT AND STRUCTURE	
4. Determine the meaning of words and phrases as they are used in a text, including figurative, connotative, and technical meanings; analyze the impact of specific word choices on meaning and tone, including analogies or allusions to other texts.	You will analyze specific words and phrases in the text to determine both what they mean and how they affect the text's tone and meaning as a whole.
5. Analyze in detail the structure of a specific paragraph in a text, including the role of particular sentences in developing and refining a key concept.	You will examine individual paragraphs in a text and analyze how particular sentences contribute to the whole.
6. Determine an author's point of view or purpose in a text and analyze how the author acknowledges and responds to conflicting evidence or viewpoints.	You will understand the author's point of view and analyze how the author sets his or her position apart from others.
INTEGRATION OF KNOWLEDGE AND IDEAS	
7. Evaluate the advantages and disadvantages of using different mediums (e.g., print or digital text, video, multimedia) to present a particular topic or idea.	You will evaluate the benefits and drawbacks of using visual and non-visual mediums to present information.
8. Delineate and evaluate the argument and specific claims in a text, assessing whether the reasoning is sound and the evidence is relevant and sufficient; recognize when irrelevant evidence is introduced.	You will evaluate the strength of the author's claims and reasoning and identify any faults or weaknesses in them.
9. Analyze a case in which two or more texts provide conflicting information on the same topic and identify where the texts disagree on matters of fact or interpretation.	You will compare and contrast at least two different authors' treatments of the same subject and show where they disagree on matters of fact or opinion.
RANGE OF READING AND LEVEL OF TEXT COMPLEXITY	
10. By the end of the year, read and comprehend literary nonfiction at the high end of the grades 6–8 text complexity band independently and proficiently.	You will demonstrate the ability to read and understand grade-level appropriate literary nonfiction texts by the end of grade 8.

Spotlight on Common Core

RI 9 Analyze a case in which two or more texts provide conflicting information on the same topic and identify where texts disagree on matters of fact or interpretation.

Informational Text: Comparing Texts on the Same Topic

The Common Core State Standards require you to analyze texts that give conflicting information about the same topic. You must find which information from the two texts is contradictory and where the writers interpret the same information differently. This skill will help you decide which of two conflicting texts to believe.

Throughout this book, you will be asked to analyze informational texts that present conflicting information. Study the following example:

Read the following editorial excerpts. Then answer the questions that follow.

from "Zoos: Myth and Reality"
by Rob Laidlaw

Nearly every zoo, from the smallest amateur operations to the largest professional facilities, claims to be making important contributions to conservation, usually through participation in endangered species captive propagation initiatives and public education programming. The zoo world buzzword of the moment is "conservation."

Yet, with an estimated 10,000 organized zoos worldwide, representing tens of thousands of human workers and billions of dollars in operating budgets, only a tiny percentage allocate the resources necessary to participate in captive propagation initiatives, and fewer still provide any real support in the *in situ* [at the site] protection of wildlife and their natural habitat.

from "Zoos Connect Us to the Natural World"
by Michael Hutchins

The best zoos include conservation, education, and science among their core missions, and the animals in their collections can be viewed as ambassadors for their counterparts in the wild. Many species are endangered or threatened and would have little chance of survival without human intervention. Increasingly, zoos are playing an important role in those efforts. Last year alone, AZA member institutions supported 1,400 field conservation and associated educational and scientific projects in over 80 countries worldwide. These ranged from restoring habitat for endangered Karner blue butterflies in Ohio to attempting to curb the illegal, commercial harvest of wildlife for meat in Africa to rehabilitating injured marine mammals and sea turtles and returning them to the sea.

1. Which information from the two texts is contradictory?

2. Which information do the two writers interpret differently?

Comparing Texts on the Same Topic Writers whose viewpoints differ on a topic often disagree on what information is true. Even more often, they disagree on their interpretation of information: what they believe about it, or what they think it means. To compare texts on the same topic, first identify which information in the texts is the same and which is different. For the information that is the same, ask yourself how each writer interprets the information. Take a look at one writer's answer to the questions below.

1. Which information from the two texts is contradictory?

> 1. Laidlaw says that few zoos provide any real support in protecting wildlife and natural habitat, while Hutchins says that zoos play an important role in conservation.

2. Which information do the two writers interpret differently?

> 2. Laidlaw and Hutchins both include the information that zoos have made conservation part of their mission. Laidlaw believes that zoos overall have failed, while Hutchins believes that many zoos have fulfilled their mission.

As you compare texts on the same topic throughout the book, be sure to look at which pieces of information are the same and which contradict each other. For information that is the same, ask yourself how the writers interpret the information.

College and Career Readiness Anchor Standards for Writing

COMMON CORE STATE STANDARDS

TEXT TYPES AND PURPOSES

1. Write arguments to support claims in an analysis of substantive topics or texts, using valid reasoning and relevant and sufficient evidence.

2. Write informative/explanatory texts to examine and convey complex ideas and information clearly and accurately through the effective selection, organization, and analysis of content.

3. Write narratives to develop real or imagined experiences or events using effective technique, well-chosen details, and well-structured event sequences.

PRODUCTION AND DISTRIBUTION OF WRITING

4. Produce clear and coherent writing in which the development, organization, and style are appropriate to task, purpose, and audience.

5. Develop and strengthen writing as needed by planning, revising, editing, rewriting, or trying a new approach.

6. Use technology, including the Internet, to produce and publish writing and to interact and collaborate with others.

RESEARCH TO BUILD AND PRESENT KNOWLEDGE

7. Conduct short as well as more sustained research projects based on focused questions, demonstrating understanding of the subject under investigation.

8. Gather relevant information from multiple print and digital sources, assess the credibility and accuracy of each source, and integrate the information while avoiding plagiarism.

9. Draw evidence from literary or informational texts to support analysis, reflection, and research.

RANGE OF WRITING

10. Write routinely over extended time frames (time for research, reflection, and revision) and shorter time frames (a single sitting or a day or two) for a range of tasks, purposes, and audiences.

Writing Standards, Grade 8 Students

COMMON CORE STATE STANDARD	WHAT IT MEANS TO YOU
TEXT TYPES AND PURPOSES	
1. Write arguments to support claims with clear reasons and relevant evidence.	You will write and develop arguments with clear reasons and strong evidence that include
a. Introduce claim(s), acknowledge and distinguish the claim(s) from alternate or opposing claims, and organize the reasons and evidence logically.	a. a clear organization of claims and counterclaims
b. Support claim(s) with logical reasoning and relevant evidence, using accurate, credible sources and demonstrating an understanding of the topic or text.	b. strong, accurate support for claims
c. Use words, phrases, and clauses to create cohesion and clarify the relationships among claim(s), counterclaims, reasons, and evidence.	c. use of cohesive words, phrases, and clauses to link information
d. Establish and maintain a formal style.	d. a formal style
e. Provide a concluding statement or section that follows from and supports the argument presented.	e. a strong concluding statement that summarizes the argument
2. Write informative/explanatory texts to examine a topic and convey ideas, concepts, and information through the selection, organization, and analysis of relevant content.	You will write clear, well-organized, and thoughtful informative and explanatory texts with
a. Introduce a topic clearly, previewing what is to follow; organize ideas, concepts, and information into broader categories; include formatting (e.g., headings), graphics (e.g., charts, tables), and multimedia when useful to aiding comprehension.	a. a clear introduction and organization, including headings and graphic organizers (when appropriate)
b. Develop the topic with relevant, well-chosen facts, definitions, concrete details, quotations, or other information and examples.	b. sufficient supporting details and background information
c. Use appropriate and varied transitions to create cohesion and clarify the relationships among ideas and concepts.	c. cohesive transitions to link ideas
d. Use precise language and domain-specific vocabulary to inform about or explain the topic.	d. precise language and relevant vocabulary
e. Establish and maintain a formal style.	e. a formal style
f. Provide a concluding statement or section that follows from and supports the information or explanation presented.	f. a strong conclusion that restates the importance or relevance of the topic

Writing Standards, Grade 8 Students, continued

COMMON CORE STATE STANDARD	WHAT IT MEANS TO YOU
3. Write narratives to develop real or imagined experiences or events using effective technique, relevant descriptive details, and well-structured event sequences.	You will write clear, well-structured, detailed narrative texts that
a. Engage and orient the reader by establishing a context and point of view and introducing a narrator and/or characters; organize an event sequence that unfolds naturally and logically.	**a.** draw your readers in with a clear topic that unfolds logically
b. Use narrative techniques, such as dialogue, pacing, description, and reflection, to develop experiences, events, and/or characters.	**b.** use narrative techniques to develop and expand on events and/or characters
c. Use a variety of transition words, phrases, and clauses to convey sequence, signal shifts from one time frame or setting to another, and show the relationships among experiences and events.	**c.** use a variety of transition words to clearly signal shifts between time frames or settings
d. Use precise words and phrases, relevant descriptive details, and sensory language to capture the action and convey experiences and events.	**d.** use precise words and sensory details that keep readers interested
e. Provide a conclusion that follows from and reflects on the narrated experiences or events.	**e.** have a strong conclusion that reflects on the topic

PRODUCTION AND DISTRIBUTION OF WRITING

4. Produce clear and coherent writing in which the development, organization, and style are appropriate to task, purpose, and audience. (Grade-specific expectations for writing types are defined in standards 1–3 above.)	You will produce writing that is appropriate to the task, purpose, and audience for whom you are writing.
5. With some guidance and support from peers and adults, develop and strengthen writing as needed by planning, revising, editing, rewriting, or trying a new approach, focusing on how well purpose and audience have been addressed.	With help from peers and adults, you will revise and refine your writing to address what is most important for your purpose and audience.
6. Use technology, including the Internet, to produce and publish writing and present the relationships between information and ideas efficiently as well as to interact and collaborate with others.	You will use technology to share your writing and to provide links to other relevant information.

RESEARCH TO BUILD AND PRESENT KNOWLEDGE

7. Conduct short research projects to answer a question (including a self-generated question), drawing on several sources and generating additional related, focused questions that allow for multiple avenues of exploration.	You will conduct short research projects to answer a question using multiple sources and generating topics for further research.
8. Gather relevant information from multiple print and digital sources, using search terms effectively; assess the credibility and accuracy of each source; and quote or paraphrase the data and conclusions of others while avoiding plagiarism and following a standard format for citation.	You will effectively conduct searches to gather information from different sources and assess the strength of each source, following a standard format for citation.

Writing Standards, Grade 8 Students, continued

COMMON CORE STATE STANDARD	WHAT IT MEANS TO YOU

9. Draw evidence from literary or informational texts to support analysis, reflection, and research.
 	
   • Apply *grade 8 Reading standards* to literature (e.g., "Analyze how a modern work of fiction draws on themes, patterns of events, or character types from myths, traditional stories, or religious works such as the Bible, including describing how the material is rendered new").
 	
   • Apply *grade 8 Reading standards* to literary nonfiction (e.g., "Delineate and evaluate the argument and specific claims in a text, assessing whether the reasoning is sound and the evidence is relevant and sufficient; recognize when irrelevant evidence is introduced").
	You will paraphrase, summarize, quote, and cite primary and secondary sources to support your analysis, reflection, and research.

RANGE OF WRITING **10.** Write routinely over extended time frames (time for research, reflection, and revision) and shorter time frames (a single sitting or a day or two) for a range of discipline-specific tasks, purposes, and audiences.	You will write for many different purposes and audiences both over short and extended periods of time.

Spotlight on Common Core

COMMON CORE

W 10 Write routinely over extended time frames (time for research, reflection, and revision) and shorter time frames (a single day or two) for a range of tasks, purposes, and audiences. **W 4** Produce clear and coherent writing in which the development, organization, and style are appropriate to task, purpose, and audience.

Writing: Maintaining Clarity and Coherence

The Common Core State Standards require you to write in a variety of forms and situations. For instance, you might spend a month writing a short story and only an hour writing a journal entry. No matter what your writing task, purpose, or audience, your writing will be better if you start with a plan. Here are some questions you can ask yourself to make a plan for any writing task.

• **What is my purpose for writing?**
Do I want to compare and contrast two stories, explain a cause-and-effect relationship, or persuade people to take action?

• **What is my task, or final product?**
What am I being asked to write? An editorial? A procedural explanation? A personal narrative? What length should the final product be, and in what form will I publish it?

• **Who is my audience?**
Am I writing a short story for publication in the school's online literary magazine or an editorial about funding a science magnet school to be published in the city's newspaper? What will my audience want and expect from my writing? What information does my audience need to understand my topic? What do I feel comfortable sharing with my audience? What tone and level of language will be appropriate?

• **How much time do I have to write?**
Do I have to finish my writing by tomorrow, or do I have a month to finish it? If I have an extended time frame, how can I break the task into manageable parts so that I do not find myself overwhelmed at the last minute?

- **What is my topic?**
  Has the topic been assigned or can I choose the topic myself? If I can choose the topic myself, what techniques can I use to brainstorm and then focus ideas? Can I write about the topic I have chosen in the amount of time I have, or do I need to narrow my topic? Is the topic appropriate for my audience?

Once you have a plan for your writing, it will be easier to develop your ideas clearly and coherently in a way that fits your task, purpose, and audience. Clear writing is writing that conveys ideas in a way readers can understand. You can create **clarity** in your writing by focusing on your main ideas, expressing them clearly, and choosing the most precise words. **Coherent writing** is writing in which sentences are clearly related to one another so that one idea flows smoothly into the next. You can create coherence in your writing by presenting your ideas in logical order; using transitions between ideas; and using pronouns, repeated words, and synonyms to connect ideas.

The Writing Workshops in this book give many strategies to help students become successful writers. Here are some examples of the types of strategies you'll find:

DEVELOPMENT	WHAT DOES IT LOOK LIKE?
• **Engage** your audience with an interesting introduction and memorable concluding section, such as a call to action. • **Focus** your ideas with a controlling idea, or thesis statement, that clearly states your claim. • **Support your claims** with logical reasons and relevant evidence, including facts, definitions, concrete details, quotations, and examples.	*You have probably seen the "No Skateboarding" signs all over town. Business owners put the signs up to protect themselves from liability should a skateboarder be injured on their property. However, I want to know: What's a kid to do? If we can't skateboard at the school, or the park, or in anybody's parking lot anymore, where are we supposed to skate? One recent proposal by city council member Garcia aims to answer that question. She has proposed that the city build a skate park downtown to give kids a safe, legal, fun place to skate. However, for this proposal to succeed, we need to show our support at the next city council meeting.*
ORGANIZATION	WHAT DOES IT LOOK LIKE?
• **Organize ideas logically** using relevant evidence from accurate, credible sources. • **Use transitions** to clarify the relationships among reasons and evidence and to create coherence. • **Acknowledge and respond to opposing claims,** when necessary.	*While it is true that (like other sports) skateboarding can result in injuries, skating in a well-maintained, supervised skate park is much safer than skating on the street or in a parking lot. A U.S. Consumer Safety Commission Study shows that over half of skateboarding injuries occur because of irregular surfaces. Since the riding surfaces in skate parks are usually smooth and free of rocks and pebbles, this makes them safer. In fact, according to the Canadian Amateur Skateboarding Association, only 5% of all skateboarding injuries actually occur in skate parks.*
LANGUAGE/STYLE	WHAT DOES IT LOOK LIKE?
• **Use an appropriate style and tone** (formal for academic tasks). • **Use words, phrases, and clauses to create coherence and to clarify the relationships between ideas.** • Write with correct grammar, usage, capitalization, and punctuation.	*The skate park proposed by Councilmember Garcia will be safer not only because it is a park with regular riding surfaces, but also because of the level of supervision she proposes. Garcia has proposed that the skate park be supervised by park personnel at all times and that skaters be required to wear helmets. Her proposal will prevent some skaters from endangering others by becoming unruly.*

College and Career Readiness Anchor Standards for Speaking and Listening

COMPREHENSION AND COLLABORATION

1. Prepare for and participate effectively in a range of conversations and collaborations with diverse partners, building on others' ideas and expressing their own clearly and persuasively.

2. Integrate and evaluate information presented in diverse media and formats, including visually, quantitatively, and orally.

3. Evaluate a speaker's point of view, reasoning, and use of evidence and rhetoric.

PRESENTATION OF KNOWLEDGE AND IDEAS

4. Present information, findings, and supporting evidence such that listeners can follow the line of reasoning and the organization, development, and style are appropriate to task, purpose, and audience.

5. Make strategic use of digital media and visual displays of data to express information and enhance understanding of presentations.

6. Adapt speech to a variety of contexts and communicative tasks, demonstrating command of formal English when indicated or appropriate.

Speaking and Listening Standards, Grade 8 Students

COMMON CORE STATE STANDARD	WHAT IT MEANS TO YOU
COMPREHENSION AND COLLABORATION	
1. Engage effectively in a range of collaborative discussions (one-on-one, in groups, and teacher-led) with diverse partners on grade 8 topics, texts, and issues, building on others' ideas and expressing their own clearly.	You will actively participate in a variety of discussions in which you
a. Come to discussions prepared, having read or researched material under study; explicitly draw on that preparation by referring to evidence on the topic, text, or issue to probe and reflect on ideas under discussion.	a. have read any relevant material beforehand and have come to the discussion prepared
b. Follow rules for collegial discussions and decision-making, track progress toward specific goals and deadlines, and define individual roles as needed.	b. work with others to establish goals and processes within the group
c. Pose questions that connect the ideas of several speakers and respond to others' questions and comments with relevant evidence, observations, and ideas.	c. ask questions that connect the ideas of several speakers and give relevant responses to the questions of others
d. Acknowledge new information expressed by others and, when warranted, qualify or justify their own views in light of the evidence presented.	d. recognize different perspectives and adjust your own views if necessary

Speaking and Listening Standards, Grade 8 Students, continued

COMMON CORE STATE STANDARD	WHAT IT MEANS TO YOU
2. Analyze the purpose of information presented in diverse media and formats (e.g., visually, quantitatively, orally) and evaluate the motives (e.g., social, commercial, political) behind its presentation.	You will analyze the purposes of and reasons for presenting information in different media and formats.
3. Delineate a speaker's argument and specific claims, evaluating the soundness of the reasoning and relevance and sufficiency of the evidence and identifying when irrelevant evidence is introduced.	You will evaluate a speaker's argument and identify any false reasoning or evidence.
PRESENTATION OF KNOWLEDGE AND IDEAS	
4. Present claims and findings, emphasizing salient points in a focused, coherent manner with relevant evidence, sound valid reasoning, and well-chosen details; use appropriate eye contact, adequate volume, and clear pronunciation.	You will organize and present information to your listeners in a logical sequence and engaging style that is appropriate to your task and audience.
5. Integrate multimedia and visual displays into presentations to clarify information, strengthen claims and evidence, and add interest.	You will use digital media to enhance and add interest to presentations.
6. Adapt speech to a variety of contexts and tasks, demonstrating command of formal English when indicated or appropriate.	You will adapt the formality of your speech appropriately.

Spotlight on Common Core

COMMON CORE

SL 3 Delineate a speaker's argument and specific claims, evaluating the soundness of the reasoning and relevance and sufficiency of the evidence and identifying when irrelevant evidence is introduced.

Speaking and Listening: Evaluating an Argument

The Common Core State Standards require you to delineate, or identify, the elements of a speaker's argument. These elements are the speaker's **claim,** or position on an issue or problem, and the reasons and evidence offered to support that claim. The Common Core State Standards also require you to decide whether the reasoning, or logic, used in the argument is sound and the claim is supported by sufficient relevant evidence. **Sufficient evidence** means enough facts, examples, and other details to convince you that the claim is most likely true or valid. **Relevant evidence** is evidence that actually supports the claim. **Irrelevant evidence** might be related to the issue in some way but does not back up the claim or the reasons given for adopting the claim.

In this book, you will be asked to delineate and evaluate arguments in speeches that you read, give, and hear. Studying the following example can help you do this.

Read the following draft of a short speech. Then answer the questions that follow.

Biking to School

Any middle school students who are physically able and who live within a reasonable distance from the school should consider biking to school. Riding your bike to school promotes energy conservation, physical fitness, and independence.

Energy conservation is a hot topic these days, and one way to conserve energy is to ride a bike. Bikes don't use gasoline and don't pollute the air. They are kid-powered. Even if you only live a mile from school, you are saving the gas it takes for an adult to drive two miles in the morning and two miles in the afternoon. That may not sound like much, but if you multiply that by the number of middle school kids in the United States, that's a lot of gas saved. By using kid-power to get to school, instead of gasoline, kids have the power to fight global warming!

Another thing on people's minds is childhood obesity. A startling number of middle school kids are overweight and not very physically fit. Riding a bike every day can help change that. Being physically fit is one of my goals. When you ride your bike to school, you get your heart rate up, build muscles, and burn calories. If more kids rode their bikes to school, there might be fewer problems with obesity. Kids would be healthier and happier.

The last benefit of riding your bike to school is independence. When you ride your bike to school, you are responsible for leaving early enough to arrive on time. You are also responsible for maintaining your bicycle, locking it up, and keeping track of your helmet. I have a mountain bike and the friend I ride to school with has a bmx. You have more responsibility and you also have more freedom. You can choose your route. You can ride hard or you can coast. It is up to you. I love the feeling of independence and self-confidence that biking to school on my own power gives me.

I urge all of you to talk to your parents about biking to school. If they hesitate, tell them what I have told you: biking to school will make you more independent, more physically fit, and more in harmony with the environment. Plus, it is fun!

1. What is the speaker's claim?
2. What reasons does the speaker give to support this claim?
3. Does this speech provide sufficient relevant evidence to support its argument? Explain.
4. Identify two instances of irrelevant evidence and tell why they are irrelevant.

Here are one student's answers to the questions above.

1. The speaker's claim is that middle school kids should ride their bikes to school.

2. The speaker gives three reasons for adopting this claim: riding a bike to school conserves energy, makes kids more physically fit, and promotes independence.

3. The speaker provides relevant evidence to support each claim. However, I think the speaker could have included more facts, such as statistics about how riding a bike makes you more fit. For instance, he or she might have included information about how many calories are burned for each mile that you ride a bike. Including this type of evidence would have made the argument more convincing.

4. These two sentences are irrelevant to the speaker's argument because they don't support any of the claims:
   "Being physically fit is one of my goals."
   "I have a mountain bike and the friend I ride to school with has a bmx."

People will try to persuade you of things throughout your life, in school and out. When they do, remember to evaluate their arguments and specific claims to determine whether they are supported by sufficient relevant evidence.

College and Career Readiness Anchor Standards for Language

COMMON CORE STATE STANDARDS

CONVENTIONS OF STANDARD ENGLISH

1. Demonstrate command of the conventions of standard English grammar and usage when writing or speaking.

2. Demonstrate command of the conventions of standard English capitalization, punctuation, and spelling when writing.

KNOWLEDGE OF LANGUAGE

3. Apply knowledge of language to understand how language functions in different contexts, to make effective choices for meaning or style, and to comprehend more fully when reading or listening.

VOCABULARY ACQUISITION AND USE

4. Determine or clarify the meaning of unknown and multiple-meaning words and phrases by using context clues, analyzing meaningful word parts, and consulting general and specialized reference materials, as appropriate.

College and Career Readiness Anchor Standards for Language, continued

5. Demonstrate understanding of word relationships and nuances in word meanings.

6. Acquire and use accurately a range of general academic and domain-specific words and phrases sufficient for reading, writing, speaking, and listening at the college and career readiness level; demonstrate independence in gathering vocabulary knowledge when considering a word or phrase important to comprehension or expression.

Language Standards, Grade 8 Students

COMMON CORE STATE STANDARD	WHAT IT MEANS TO YOU
CONVENTIONS OF STANDARD ENGLISH	
1. Demonstrate command of the conventions of standard English grammar and usage when writing or speaking.	You will correctly understand and use the conventions of English grammar and usage, including
a. Explain the function of verbals (gerunds, participles, infinitives) in general and their function in particular sentences.	**a.** explaining the function of verbals
b. Form and use verbs in the active and passive voice.	**b.** using verbs in both active and passive voice
c. Form and use verbs in the indicative, imperative, interrogative, conditional, and subjunctive mood.	**c.** using verbs in the indicative, imperative, interrogative, conditional, and subjunctive mood
d. Recognize and correct inappropriate shifts in verb voice and mood.	**d.** recognizing and correcting shifts in verb voice and mood
2. Demonstrate command of the conventions of standard English capitalization, punctuation, and spelling when writing.	You will correctly use the conventions of English capitalization, punctuation, and spelling, including
a. Use punctuation (commas, ellipsis, dash) to indicate a pause or break.	**a.** using different punctuation to indicate a pause or break
b. Use an ellipsis to indicate an omission.	**b.** using ellipsis to indicate when text has been left out
c. Spell correctly.	**c.** spelling correctly
KNOWLEDGE OF LANGUAGE	
3. Use knowledge of language and its conventions when writing, speaking, reading, or listening.	You will apply your knowledge of language in different contexts by
a. Use verbs in the active and passive voice and in the conditional and subjunctive mood to achieve particular effects (e.g., emphasizing the actor or the action; expressing uncertainty or describing a state contrary to fact).	**a.** choosing appropriate verb voice and mood to create different effects

Language Standards, Grade 8 Students, continued

COMMON CORE STATE STANDARD	WHAT IT MEANS TO YOU
VOCABULARY ACQUISITION AND USE	
4. Determine or clarify the meaning of unknown and multiple-meaning words and phrases based on grade 8 reading and content, choosing flexibly from a range of strategies.	You will understand the meaning of grade-level appropriate words and phrases by
a. Use context (e.g., the overall meaning of a sentence or paragraph; a word's position or function in a sentence) as a clue to the meaning of a word or phrase.	**a.** using context clues
b. Use common, grade-appropriate Greek or Latin affixes and roots as clues to the meaning of a word (e.g., *precede, recede, secede*).	**b.** using Greek or Latin roots
c. Consult general and specialized reference materials (e.g., dictionaries, glossaries, thesauruses), both print and digital, to find the pronunciation of a word or determine or clarify its precise meaning or its part of speech.	**c.** using reference materials
d. Verify the preliminary determination of the meaning of a word or phrase (e.g., by checking the inferred meaning in context or in a dictionary).	**d.** inferring and verifying the meanings of words in context
5. Demonstrate understanding of figurative language, word relationships, and nuances in word meanings.	You will understand figurative language, word relationships, and slight differences in word meanings by
a. Interpret figures of speech (e.g., verbal irony, puns) in context.	**a.** interpreting figures of speech in context
b. Use the relationship between particular words to better understand each of the words.	**b.** analyzing relationships between words
c. Distinguish among the connotations (associations) of words with similar denotations (definitions) (e.g., *bullheaded, willful, firm, persistent, resolute*).	**c.** distinguishing among words with similar definitions
6. Acquire and use accurately grade-appropriate general academic and domain-specific words and phrases; gather vocabulary knowledge when considering a word or phrase important to comprehension or expression.	You will learn and use grade-appropriate vocabulary.

Spotlight on Common Core

Vocabulary: Figures of Speech

The Common Core State Standards require you to determine the meaning of figures of speech as you read. A **figure of speech** is an imaginative way of using words to communicate meaning beyond their strict definitions. Figures of speech are used to create vibrant images, express complex ideas with just a few words, and to stir emotions.

Here's an example from the poem "Simile: Willow and Gingko," by Eve Merriam:

> The gingko forces its way through the gray concrete;
> Like a city child, it grows up in the street.

In this example, the gingko tree is not literally like a child but is being compared to a child in a type of figurative language called a simile. **Similes** use *like* or *as* to compare two unlike things.

The next two lines of the poem contain another type of figurative language that makes a comparison—a metaphor. **Metaphors** make comparisons without using *like* or *as*.

> Thrust against the metal sky,
> Somehow it survives and even thrives.

In this example, the sky is not really made out of metal; it just looks like metal. The poet uses this comparison to emphasize the hardness of the gingko's surroundings.

While you are probably familiar with similes and metaphors, there are other figures of speech that you might not know so well. One of these is verbal irony.

Verbal irony is when someone says one thing but means another. For instance, a friend of yours might say, "Thanks a lot," in response to an insult. In this example, your friend does not really mean to thank the person who insulted her. Instead, she is being ironic.

Another type of figurative language that uses humor for effect is the pun. A **pun** is a play on the multiple meanings of a word or on two different words that sound alike but have different meanings.

For instance, when the ogre in the story says, "I'd like to have you for lunch," this is a pun. He could mean "I'd like to have you *over* for lunch" or "I'd like to have you for *my* lunch."

Throughout this book, you will read poems, stories, essays, and articles that use figures of speech. You might also want to use figures of speech in your own writing. Either way, you will want to understand how they work.

LEARN HOW Interpreting Figures of Speech in Context When you come across a figure of speech, ask yourself these questions:

- Is the figure of speech comparing two things? If so, what does it compare?
- Is the figure of speech an example of verbal irony, in which one thing is said while another is meant? What is really meant?
- Is the figure of speech a play on a word or phrase that has multiple meanings or on words that sound the same? Does it create a humorous effect?

Read this paragraph and interpret each of the underlined figures of speech.

Oh, sure. I love football! Having guys who weigh about twice as much as me, run at me as fast as they can and try to knock me down is a real blast! I also appreciate having a hard pointy ball thrown at me when I'm least expecting it. Attempting to catch such a ball is another real pleasure. Especially when it is cold outside and your fingers practically snap off like twigs as the ball slams into them. It gives whole new meaning to the term *cold snap*.

Here are one student's interpretations of the figures of speech.

1. The tone and the context tell me that the writer is being ironic. He doesn't really like football. This is an example of verbal irony.
2. Again, the tone and the previous sentences tell me the writer is being ironic.
3. This figure of speech uses the comparing word like to compare fingers to twigs. This is a simile.
4. Here, the writer is playing on two meanings of snap. One meaning is a sudden change in the weather. Another meaning is when something snaps, or breaks. This is an example of a pun.

As you read the literature in this book, watch for and enjoy the figures of speech used by authors to enliven their writing.

Spotlight on Common Core

COMMON
CORE

L 3a Use verbs in the active and passive voice and in the conditional and subjunctive mood to achieve particular effects.

Grammar: Verbs

The Common Core State Standards require you to use the voices and moods of verbs that best fit your ideas.

In English, verbs have two voices, active and passive. In the **active voice**, the subject of the sentence performs the action.

> Ben broke the glass.
> I called the doctor.

In the **passive voice**, the subject of the sentence is the receiver of the action.

> The glass was broken by Ben.
> The doctor was called.

The active voice is the most straightforward way of saying something. Use the active voice when you want to sound direct and natural. But if you don't know who performed the action, or you want to de-emphasize who was performing the action, you may want to use the passive voice. In general, the passive voice is less forceful than the active voice. Use it infrequently as a way to vary your sentences.

Almost all of the verbs you use in speaking and writing are in the indicative mood, which is used to make statements of fact. However, two other moods English verbs can express are the subjunctive and conditional moods.

The **subjunctive mood** expresses a condition that is contrary to fact, a wish that has not yet been realized, or an imaginary state.

> I wish I <u>had</u> curly hair, but my hair is straight.

> If I <u>were</u> rich, I would donate money to charity.

The **conditional mood** expresses ideas that depend on something to be true.

> I never <u>could have run</u> ten miles without your encouragement.

Throughout this book, you will be required to write a variety of assignments. Whenever you write, choose the verb voices and moods that best express your ideas.

LEARN HOW Writing in the Active and Passive Voice and in the Subjunctive and Conditional Moods Now that you know what the active and passive voices and the subjunctive and conditional moods are, let's take a look at how they are formed.

Active Voice
Form the active voice by using the principal parts of a verb with an action performed by its subject.

> We <u>push</u> the buggy down the sidewalk. (infinitive)

> He <u>is pushing</u> me toward the edge of the pool. (present participle)

> She <u>pushed</u> me away from her. (past)

> They <u>have pushed</u> us to our limit. (past participle)

Passive Voice
Form the passive voice by using a form of *be* with the past participle of the verb. Because the passive voice is less direct, use it only when you want to emphasize the receiver of the action or when the doer of the action is unknown or unimportant.

> The table <u>was set</u> for the wedding reception.

> The musician <u>is interviewed</u> by the reporter.

Subjunctive Mood
The subjunctive form is identical to the past form. When you use the verb *be* in the subjunctive mood, the form is *were*, even when the subject is singular.

> If I <u>were</u> a professional football player, I would be a good role model.

> If you <u>had told</u> me you wanted to go to the zoo, we could have brought our bus passes.

Conditional Mood
The conditional mood is used to refer to an event that may or may not happen depending on another set of circumstances. This mood uses the verbs *could, would,* or *should.* Take another look at the examples from above.

> If I were a professional football player, I <u>would be</u> a good role model.

> If you had told me you wanted to go to the zoo, we <u>could have brought</u> our bus passes.

Now follow the directions to write your own sentences.

1. Write a sentence in the subjunctive mood about something you wish.
2. Write a sentence in the passive voice about something that happened at home.
3. Write a sentence using both the subjunctive and conditional mood about something that could happen at school.
4. Write a sentence in the active voice about something you do in your free time.
5. Write a sentence in the conditional mood about something or someone you rely on. Start with the word "without."

Here are one writer's sentences.

1. I wish my sister lived nearby.
2. The milk was spilled all over the floor.
3. If I made the volleyball team, I would have to stay up later to study.
4. In my free time I play soccer with my friends.
5. Without my friends, I would feel lonely.

Whenever you are asked to write throughout this book, use the active and passive voices and the subjunctive and conditional moods to accurately express your ideas.

The Power of Ideas

INTRODUCING THE ESSENTIALS

- Genres Workshop

- Reading Strategies Workshop

- Academic Vocabulary Workshop

- Writing Process Workshop

1

The Power of Ideas

What Are Life's Big Questions?

We never stop searching for answers to life's big questions. Asking questions such as the ones shown here is our way of making sense of who we are, where we're going, and how we fit into the world. While our own experiences can guide us toward answers, good literature can also help. Through reading, writing, and talking about literature, we can explore the big questions in life and gain meaningful insights into our own lives and the world.

What does it mean to BELONG?

Humans are naturally social beings. We create groups— families, friends, communities—that bind us together. But what happens when you're on the outside of a group and can't find a way in? Explore the meaning of belonging through the writing of Naomi Shihab Nye, Daniel Keyes, David Sedaris, and others. Then ask yourself: Is it always good to belong?

Why does the PAST matter?

There's an old saying: "History repeats itself"—in other words, everything that happens in the world is bound to happen again. If that's the case, then we can look to the past to help us understand conflicts and issues that challenge us in the present. In this book, you'll read about the Civil War, Paul Revere, and Harriet Tubman. Find out what we can still learn from them all these years later.

Are people basically GOOD?

In her diary, Anne Frank wrote: "...I still believe, in spite of everything, that people are truly good at heart." This sentiment is surprising, given that Anne was one of the millions of Jews who lost their lives in Nazi concentration camps during World War II. Today, we might find ourselves asking this same question. After all, war and crime are still facts of life. What do you think? Are people really good?

What's really IMPORTANT?

Some objects, such as flashy cars and diamonds, are worth a lot of money. But then there are other things—a photograph or a beautiful sunset, for instance—that are priceless. Authors such as Sandra Cisneros, Walter Dean Myers, and Joseph Bruchac all write about the things people treasure most. Reading about what others value can help you decide for yourself what's really important to *you*.

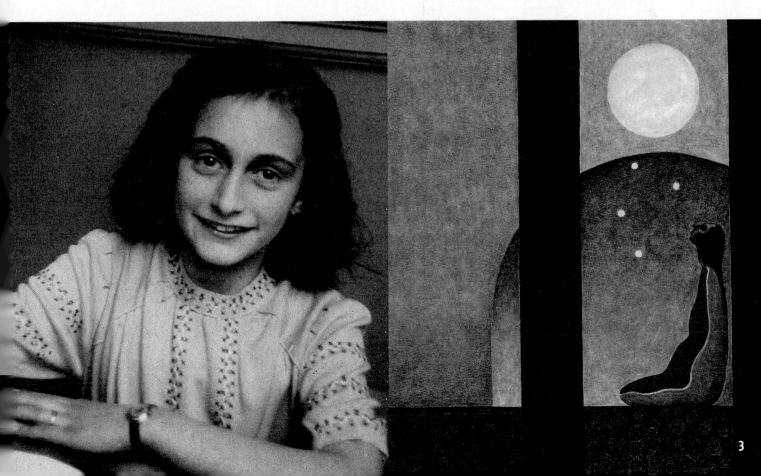

Exploring Text Types

Throughout history, people have turned to everything from ancient cave walls, fragile paper manuscripts, and up-to-the-minute blogs in search of answers to life's big questions. Exploring literature of all types can help you think about these questions—and answers—in new and exciting ways.

The Genres

COMMON CORE

Included in this workshop:
RL 1, RL 3, RI 1

What draws you to the books you read or the movies you see? Most likely, their ideas or topics appeal to you. Family relationships, competition between friends, impossible decisions—powerful ideas and topics such as these are at the heart of many literary and nonfiction texts. In fact, traditional literature and nonfiction—whether it comes from the first part of the 20th century or as far back as a centuries-old oral tradition—also address ideas and topics that are relevant to you in today's world.

In this book, you'll explore ideas in a variety of genres, or categories, of text. You'll also consider the ideas in popular media forms, such as ads and movies. First, though, familiarize yourself with the characteristics of each genre.

GENRES AT A GLANCE

STORIES
Stories are narratives about made-up events and characters.
• short stories   • novels   • novellas   • graphic novels

POETRY
Poetry is a type of literature in which words are chosen and arranged in a precise way to create certain sounds and meanings.
• odes   • sonnets   • narrative poems   • lyric poems

DRAMA
Drama is meant to be performed. Characters and conflicts are developed through dialogue and action.
• comedies   • radio plays   • historical dramas

NONFICTION
Nonfiction is writing that tells about real people, events, and places.
• autobiographies   • essays   • news articles
• biographies   • speeches   • feature articles

TYPES OF MEDIA

Media **refers to forms of communication that reach large numbers of people.**
• TV shows   • advertising   • Web sites

STORIES

Does fiction mean "fake"? Some authors dream up every element of a story, from the setting to the plot and the characters. Others may be inspired by real events and people, and build a story around them. Whether it's an original product of an author's imagination or an idea "ripped straight from the headlines," all good fiction guarantees a stirring **plot,** a vivid **setting,** and compelling **characters.** Most stories also have **themes,** or larger messages about life. Fiction usually takes one of three forms.

- A **short story** often focuses on a single event or incident. Most stories are short enough to be read without taking a break.
- A **novel** is a longer work of fiction that weaves together many different events, storylines, and characters.
- A **novella** is generally longer than a short story but shorter than a novel. Novellas usually feature a limited number of characters.

Read the Model In the novel *Slam!,* Greg Harris has just transferred from a high school in Harlem to a more academically challenging school for the arts. At his old school, Greg was the star of his basketball team. Will he still shine on the court now that he's on unfamiliar ground? As you read this excerpt, notice how Greg describes his athletic abilities. In what ways does his attitude help you to understand the idea of self-confidence?

LITERARY TERMS FOR STORIES
- plot
- conflict
- character
- setting
- theme
- narrator
- point of view

from

SLAM!

Novel by **Walter Dean Myers**

Basketball is my thing. I can hoop. Case closed. I'm six four and I got the moves, the eye, and the heart. You can take my game to the bank and wait around for the interest. With me it's not like playing a game, it's like the only time I'm being for real. Bringing the ball down the court makes me feel like
5 a bird that just learned to fly. I see my guys moving down in front of me and everything feels and looks right. Patterns come up and a small buzz comes into my head that starts to build up and I know it won't end until the ball swishes through the net. If somebody starts messing with my game it's like they're getting into my head. But if I've got the ball it's okay, because I can take care of
10 the situation. That's the word and I know it the same way I know my tag, Slam. Yeah, that's it. Slam. But without the ball, without the floorboards under my feet, without the mid-court line that takes me halfway home, you can get to me.

So when Mr. Tate, the principal at my new school, started talking about me laying low for the season until I got my grades together I was like seriously
15 turned out. The night after he talked to my moms I couldn't sleep. It wasn't the hissing of the radiator or my little brother talking in his sleep in the other bed, it was the idea of not playing ball that was bouncing crazylike through my head.

Close Read

1. Characters and conflicts are two key elements of good stories. Which characters are introduced in this excerpt? What is Greg's conflict?

2. **Exploring a Big Question** Greg's confidence springs from his "game." Other than athletic ability, what else can be a source of self-confidence?

POETRY

"Poetry: the best words in the best order." This is how British poet Samuel Taylor Coleridge summed up the goal and the struggle of writing poetry. Poets search for the perfect words and then arrange them in precise ways to achieve specific effects. The result can be both ear-catching and unforgettable.

As you know, poetry looks different on the page than fiction or nonfiction. Poems are made up of **lines,** which are often arranged into groups called **stanzas.** In some poems, the lines and stanzas reflect the rules of a particular form, such as a haiku or a sonnet. In others, there is no recognizable form; instead, the poet lets the ideas drive what the poem looks like on the page.

In poetry, sounds and language are just as important as form. Does the poem have a brisk **rhythm** or singsong **rhymes?** What sensory details help readers clearly picture what's being described? Every choice a poet makes can affect the overall meaning and sound of the poem.

Read the Model You already know what it's like to be a teenager—but how about the parent of one? As you read this poem, think about relationships, especially between parents and teenagers.

> **LITERARY TERMS FOR POETRY**
> - form
> - line
> - stanza
> - speaker
> - rhyme
> - rhythm
> - sound devices
> - imagery

Teenagers
Poem by Pat Mora

One day they disappear
into their rooms.
Doors and lips shut
and we become strangers
5   in our own home.

I pace the hall, hear whispers,
a code I knew but can't remember,
mouthed by mouths I taught to speak.

Years later the door opens.
10   I see faces I once held,
open as sunflowers in my hands. I see
familiar skin now stretched on long bodies
that move past me
glowing almost like pearls.

Close Read

1. What specific characteristics tell you that "Teenagers" is a poem, rather than a work of fiction?

2. **Exploring a Big Question** According to this poem, how do parents view their relationships with their teenaged children? How might teenagers' views differ?

DRAMA

You may use the term *drama* in everyday speech to mean something or somebody acting in a dramatic way (as in, "What a drama queen!"). In literature, though, a **drama** is any work that is written to be performed on a stage. A drama has all the elements of good fiction—plot, characters, setting, and theme. Unlike a work of fiction, however, a drama is usually divided into **scenes,** with several scenes grouped into **acts.**

A drama is primarily written as **dialogue** between characters. The playwright, or author, describes the setting, characters' movements, and props as **stage directions,** written in *italics* throughout the play. These notes represent the playwright's vision of the performance. However, a great deal is left to the imagination of the director, the actors, and readers.

Read the Model This drama takes place in Brooklyn in 1937. Fourteen-year-old Eugene has just discovered that his oldest brother, Stanley, is leaving home. Stanley is ashamed because he gambled away his paycheck, which the family relies on to make ends meet. In this excerpt, Eugene offers Stanley "his life savings" for train fare. As you read, consider what admiration means.

> **LITERARY TERMS FOR DRAMA**
> - plot
> - character
> - act
> - scene
> - stage directions
> - dialogue

from Brighton Beach Memoirs

Drama by **Neil Simon**

Eugene. You're leaving home?

Stanley. When I'm gone, you tell Aunt Blanche what happened to my salary. Then she'll know why Mom was so angry. Tell her please not to leave, because it was all my fault, not Mom's. Will you do that?

5   (*He takes the coins out of the cigar box*)

Eugene. I have eight cents' worth of stamps, if you want that too.

Stanley. Thanks. (*He picks up a small medal*) What's this?

Eugene. The medal you won for the hundred-yard dash two years ago.

Stanley. From the Police Athletic League. I didn't know you still had this.

10   **Eugene.** You gave it to me. You can have it back if you want it.

Stanley. It's not worth anything.

Eugene. It is to me.

Close Read

1. How does Eugene feel about Stanley? Cite details from the dialogue and the stage directions to support your answer.

2. **Exploring a Big Question** Think of a person you look up to or admire. If that person made a mistake, would your opinion of him or her change? Why or why not?

NONFICTION

Some works of nonfiction, such as biographies and true-life adventures, read like gripping novels. There's a key difference, though. In nonfiction, the events actually happened, and the characters are real people. Other types of nonfiction—such as news articles, manuals, and directions to a friend's house—are nothing like stories. They are sources you consult for information. Since you read all kinds of nonfiction texts daily, you should know what to expect from them.

TERMS FOR NONFICTION
- purpose
- text features
- argument
- persuasion

TYPE OF NONFICTION	CHARACTERISTICS	
AUTOBIOGRAPHY/ BIOGRAPHY The true story of a person's life, told by that person (autobiography) or by another person (biography)	• Provides details about a person's life • Written from the first-person point of view (autobiography) or from the third-person point of view (biography) • Presents the writer's own version of his or her life (autobiography) or an outside writer's research (biography)	
ESSAY A short work of nonfiction that focuses on a single subject. Common types include reflective, persuasive, and descriptive essays.	• Is intended to share a personal experience, to express feelings, to inform, to entertain, or to persuade • May be written in a **formal** style, with an academic tone • May be written in an **informal** style, with a conversational tone	Zoos: Myth and Reality Rob Laidlaw In recent years, zoos have become the target of intense public scrutiny and criticism. In response, many have tried to repackage themselves as institutions devoted to wildlife conservation, public education, and animal welfare. But most zoos fail to live up to their own **propaganda** and vast numbers of zoo animals continue to endure lives of misery and **deprivation.** Nearly every zoo, from the smallest amateur operation to the largest professional facilities, claims to be making important contributions to conservation, usually through participation in endangered species
SPEECH An oral presentation of the ideas, beliefs, or proposals of a speaker	• May be intended to share a personal experience, to express feelings, to inform, to entertain, or to persuade • Relies on powerful language, as well as the speaker's voice and gestures	
NEWS/FEATURE ARTICLES Informative writing in newspapers and magazines. **News articles** report on recent events. **Feature articles** offer in-depth coverage of human-interest topics.	• Are primarily intended to inform or entertain • Use headlines, subheadings, photographs, and graphic aids to present information • Strive to be objective and fair	**Over the Top** The True Adventures of a Volcano Chaser Renee Skelton
FUNCTIONAL TEXTS Writing that serves a practical purpose. Types include consumer documents, such as user manuals, and workplace documents, such as résumés.	• Are written to inform a specific audience (for example, employees or consumers) • Often include charts, diagrams, or other helpful graphic aids	Chicago to Kenosha

MODEL 1: BIOGRAPHY

As the cofounder and CEO of a major technology corporation, Steve Jobs helped develop some of the first user-friendly personal computers. As you read this excerpt from a biography of Jobs, keep in mind the personal quality of initiative—the ability to take action.

from
Steve Jobs: [Thinks Different]

Biography by **Ann Brashares**

At thirteen, Jobs's interest in electronics was blossoming. One day he was building an electronic counting machine, and he needed some parts. He knew he could get them from Hewlett-Packard, a giant electronics company not far from his house. Jobs looked up the phone number of Bill Hewlett, the
5   cofounder of Hewlett-Packard. Some kids would have been afraid to dial up one of the richest and most important men in California. Not Steve Jobs.

He boldly chatted with Bill Hewlett for twenty minutes, and Hewlett was so impressed and surprised by the young man that he not only gave him the parts he needed but offered him a summer job, too. That phone call taught an early
10   lesson: If you ask for what you want, you often get it.

Close Read

1. How can you tell that this excerpt is from a biography rather than an autobiography?

2. **Exploring a Big Question** Jobs was a "go-getter" even at the age of 13. What qualities do you think people must have in order to take initiative?

MODEL 2: FEATURE ARTICLE

Did you know that the first computer weighed *30 tons*? As you read this excerpt from a feature article on computer history, look for other mind-boggling facts. Also, consider the idea of progress.

WIRELESS EVOLUTION: THANK YOU ENIAC

WAY BACK WHEN, ONE COMPUTER COULD FILL AN ENTIRE MIDDLE SCHOOL CAFETERIA. TODAY, YOU CAN WEAR ONE ON YOUR BELT LOOP.

by David Santos

Far from a Handheld The first computerized "counting machine" was called ENIAC—Electronic Numerical Integrator and Computer. Completed
5   in 1946, covering three walls, standing eight feet high, and weighing 30 tons, ENIAC required 7,468 vacuum tubes and 6,000 manual switches just to get warmed up!

10   ENIAC could execute thousands of calculations in seconds. However, reprogramming it took a team of people, three days, and lots of patience.
15   ENIAC's advanced technology, even with its massive shortcomings, was critical in spurring on the decades of computer evolution that followed.

Close Read

1. What characteristics make this article different from the biography you just read?

2. **Exploring a Big Question** Think about the role technology plays in our society. What are the dangers of technological progress, or is it all positive?

TYPES OF MEDIA

The World Wide Web alerts you to breaking news. A blockbuster movie keeps you on the edge of your seat for two action-packed hours. A clever ad campaign convinces you to buy a product you probably don't need. Media messages are all around you, and they influence your beliefs and actions more than you might realize. That's why it's important to become **media literate**—to learn how to "read" all types of media messages, including the ones shown here.

TYPE OF MEDIA	CHARACTERISTICS	
FEATURE FILMS Motion pictures that use narrative elements to tell stories	• Created for entertainment and to make money • Rely on music, cinematography, sets, and actors to tell interesting stories • Are at least one hour in length	
NEWS MEDIA Accounts of current events in newspapers and magazines, as well as on television, the radio, and the Web	• Designed to inform and entertain viewers • Present information differently in each medium (TV, Web, print) • Can include bias and inaccuracies, so must be closely examined	
TV SHOWS Programs broadcast on television, including dramas, sitcoms, talk shows, documentaries, and reality shows	• Are usually created to entertain or inform • Are sponsored by advertisers who pay to market their products during commercial breaks • Use camera techniques and dramatic music to make stories more compelling • Typically last for a half hour or an hour	
ADVERTISING Paid promotion of products, services, candidates, or public service messages using print, electronic, and broadcast media	• Is designed to persuade a target audience to buy a product, use a service, or agree with an idea • Uses visuals, sound effects, and actors to persuade viewers • Is presented when and where the target audience is likely to see it	
WEB SITES Collections of "pages" on the World Wide Web. Users navigate to pages by clicking menus or hyperlinks.	• Present information through text, graphics, audio, video, animation, and interactive features • Require careful evaluation, as most Web sites are not checked for credibility	

Literature and Nonfiction Strategies

 Record your reactions and observations in your **Reader/Writer Notebook.**

❶ Ask the Right Questions

It's one thing to "get through" a text but another to really enjoy and understand it. To get the most from what you read, make sure you ask the right questions.

Where to Look	What You'll Find
Text Analysis Workshops (at the beginning of every unit)	▶ Interactive practice models and Close Read questions
Side notes and discussion questions	▶ Questions (throughout and following each selection) that focus on the analysis of literary and nonfiction elements
Analysis Frames THINK central Go to thinkcentral.com. KEYWORD: HML8-11	▶ Guided questions for analyzing different genres of text

❷ Make Connections

The conflicts and themes in literature can help you make sense of your own life. Use these tips to make connections.

- **Big Questions** Take time to think about how the big questions in this book are relevant to your life. For example, where do you think confidence comes from? Has someone you admire ever disappointed you?

- **Discussion/Journaling** Jot down your thoughts and opinions as you read, or share them with others. You might want to record
  - conflicts or events that you can relate to
  - characters who remind you of people you know
  - ideas you strongly agree or disagree with

❸ Record Your Reactions

Organize your questions, thoughts, and analysis by writing them down. Experiment with different formats to find out which works best for you.

JOURNAL

Pause as you read to record your impressions, predictions, or questions.

> *Brighton Beach Memoirs*
>
> *I wonder how Stanley's family will react when he leaves home.*
>
> *I predict that Eugene will have a hard time dealing with his brother's absence.*

GRAPHIC ORGANIZER

After reading, create a graphic organizer to help you analyze characters and events.

Eugene's Character Traits

Eager to Please Wants to help out his brother

Selfless Offers life savings

Honest Lets Stanley know the medal is important to him

Becoming an Active Reader

Are you sometimes tempted to race through your reading just to get it done? Have you ever skipped ahead a few scenes or chapters to find out what happens? While you might save time, you probably won't enjoy the experience as much. Reading actively means taking the time to ask questions, clarify, and connect to what you're reading, whether it's a message-board posting, a novel, or even a TV drama. Use these skills and strategies to stay engaged in the process.

SKILLS AND STRATEGIES FOR ACTIVE READING

Preview
Become familiar with the text before you start to read.
- Look at the title, the graphics, and subheadings.
- Skim the first paragraph to get a feel for what the text is about.

Set a Purpose
Know why you are reading.
- Ask: Am I reading for pure entertainment, information, or another reason?
- Think about how your purpose affects your approach. Should you take notes or sit back and enjoy?

Connect
Find something you can personally relate to.
- Consider whether any characters remind you of people in your life.
- Ask: If I were in this situation, would I react differently?

Use Prior Knowledge
Recall what you already know about a topic.
- Before reading, jot down what you already know.
- As you read, connect what you know to what you are learning.

Predict
Guess what's going to happen next.
- Pay attention to certain clues, such as important statements made by characters or repeated details.
- Resist the urge to read ahead.
- Ask: Was my prediction on target, or did I miss the mark?

Visualize
Get a clear mental picture of what is being described.
- Notice the author's description of characters, settings, and events.
- Use these descriptions to help you "see" what's happening like a movie in your mind.

Monitor
Check your own understanding.
- Ask **questions** like, What just happened? Why did the character do that?
- **Clarify** your understanding by rereading confusing parts.
- **Evaluate** yourself as a reader. Ask: How well am I understanding this?

Make Inferences
Make logical guesses by considering the text and your own experiences.
- Record specific details in the text about characters and events.
- Use common sense and your own experiences to help you "read between the lines."

Details in "The Winter Hibiscus"	What I Know	My Inference
Saeng is nervous about passing the driver's test.	It's easy to make mistakes when you're nervous.	Saeng's nerves probably interfered with her judgment during the test.

MODEL: SHORT STORY

This story is about a 16-year-old girl named Saeng, who has moved with her
family from Laos to the United States. The time has come for Saeng to take
her driver's test. The stakes are high because Saeng's family is counting on
her to be their sole driver. In this excerpt, David, a fellow classmate, is letting
Saeng borrow his car to take the exam. As you read, use the **Close Read**
questions to practice the skills and strategies you just learned.

from The
Winter
Hibiscus

Short story by **Minfong Ho**

"Ready?" David asked, eyebrow arched quizzically as he handed her his
car keys.
Saeng nodded. Her mouth suddenly felt dry, and she licked her lips.
"Don't forget: Step on the gas real gently. You don't want to jerk the car
5 forward the way you did last time," David said with a grin.
"I won't," Saeng said, and managed a smile.
Another car drove up, and the test instructor stepped out of it and onto
the curb in front of them. He was a pale, overweight man whose thick lips
jutted out from behind a bushy moustache. On his paunch[1] was balanced a
10 clipboard, which he was busy marking.
Finally he looked up and saw Saeng. "Miss Saeng Panouvong?" he asked,
slurring the name so much that Saeng did not recognize it as her own until she
felt David nudge her slightly.
"Y—yes, sir," Saeng answered.
15 "Your turn. Get in."
Then Saeng was behind the wheel, the paunchy man seated next to her,
clipboard on his lap.
"Drive to the end of the street and take a right," the test instructor said. He
spoke in a low, bored staccato[2] that Saeng had to strain to understand.
20 Obediently, she started up the car, careful to step on the accelerator very
slowly, and eased the car out into the middle of the street. *Check the rearview
mirror, make the hand gestures, take a deep breath,* Saeng told herself.

---

1. **paunch:** a protruding belly.
2. **staccato:** short, crisp sounds, or way of speaking.

Close Read

1. **Make Inferences** Given
David's comments in
lines 4–5, what can you
infer about Saeng and
David's relationship?

2. **Monitor** How can
you tell that Saeng is
nervous? Cite details
from lines 1–22 to
support your answer.

So far, so good. At the intersection at the end of the street, she slowed down. Two cars were coming down the cross street toward her at quite a high speed. 25 Instinctively, she stopped and waited for them both to drive past. Instead, they both stopped, as if waiting for her to proceed.

Saeng hesitated. Should she go ahead and take the turn before them or wait until they went past?

Better to be cautious, she decided, and waited, switching gears over to neutral.

30 For what seemed an interminable³ moment, nobody moved. Then the other cars went through the intersection, one after the other. Carefully, Saeng then took her turn (*turn signal, hand signal, look both ways*).

As she continued to drive down the street, out of the corner of her eye she saw the instructor mark down something on his clipboard.

35 *A mistake,* she thought. *He's writing down a mistake I just made. But what did I do wrong?* She stole a quick look at his face. It was stern but impassive. *Maybe I should ask him right now, what I did wrong,* Saeng wondered.

"Watch out!" he suddenly exclaimed. "That's a stop sign!"

Startled, Saeng jerked the car to a stop—but not soon enough. They were 40 right in the middle of the crossroads.

The instructor shook his head. An almost imperceptible⁴ gesture, but Saeng noted it with a sinking feeling in her stomach.

"Back up," he snapped.

Her heart beating hard, Saeng managed to reverse the car and back up to 45 the stop sign that she had just gone through.

"You might as well go back to where we started out," the instructor said. "Take a right here, and another right at the next intersection."

It's over, Saeng thought. *He doesn't even want to see me go up the hill or parallel park or anything. I've failed.*

50 Swallowing hard, she managed to drive the rest of the way back. In the distance she could see the big M archway outside the McDonald's restaurant, and as she approached, she noticed David standing on the opposite curb, hands on his hips, watching their approach.

With gratitude she noticed that he had somehow managed to stake out two 55 parking spaces in a row so that she could have plenty of space to swerve into place.

She breathed a deep sigh of relief when the car was safely parked. Only after she had turned off the ignition did she dare look the instructor in the face.

"How—how did I do, sir?" she asked him, hating the quaver in her own voice.

"You'll get your results in the mail next week," he said in that bored 60 monotone again, as if he had parroted the same sentence countless times. Then he must have seen the anxious, pleading look on Saeng's face, for he seemed to soften somewhat. "You stopped when you didn't need to—you had right of way⁵ at that first intersection," he said. "Then at the second intersection, when you should have stopped at the stop sign, you went right through it."

65 He shrugged. "Too bad," he mumbled. . . .

---

3. **interminable:** seeming to be without end.

4. **imperceptible:** extremely subtle; hard to notice.

5. **right of way:** customary or legal right of one car to pass in front of another.

3. **Visualize** Reread the boxed text, picturing where each car stops. Then give a short summary of what happened at the intersection. (Hint: Sketch the scene in your notebook.)

4. **Predict** Given what's happened so far, do you think Saeng will pass the test? Give a reason for your prediction.

5. **Connect** Do most people perform well under pressure, or are they more likely to make mistakes? Support your opinion.

6. **Make Inferences** What do you think Saeng might be thinking or feeling as the instructor is evaluating her performance on the test?

Strategies That Work: Reading

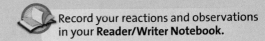 Record your reactions and observations in your **Reader/Writer Notebook.**

❶ Read Independently

The best way to become a better reader is to read as much as you can, every chance you get.

What Should I Read?	Where Should I Look?
Novels 	Get Novel Wise **THINK**central Go to **thinkcentral.com.** KEYWORD: HML8-15
Magazines **Newspapers** **Web sites** 	Every time you check your favorite Web site or leaf through the daily newspaper, you are reading. Pick up whatever interests you, and keep reading.

❷ Use Graphic Organizers

Recording your ideas in a graphic organizer can help you analyze and make sense of characters, relationships, and events. Depending on your purpose, you might use a cluster diagram, a Y-chart, or a time line.

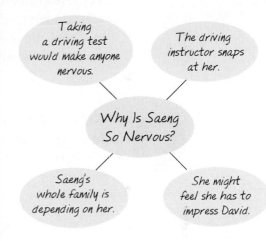

- Taking a driving test would make anyone nervous.
- The driving instructor snaps at her.
- Why Is Saeng So Nervous?
- Saeng's whole family is depending on her.
- She might feel she has to impress David.

❸ Build Your Vocabulary

Creating a personal word list in your **Reader/Writer Notebook** can help you better understand not only a specific selection but also other readings throughout your life. Use these tips to get started:

- **List difficult words.** Consider listing vocabulary words from the selections, as well as other challenging terms you encounter.
- **Go beyond the definitions.** To help you remember each word and its meaning, list synonyms and antonyms, or write a sentence using the word.
- **Try them out.** Using new words in your writing and discussions is one of the best ways to build your vocabulary.

Word	Meaning
quizzically adv. "The Winter Hibiscus," line 1	**Definition:** expressing doubt, curiosity, or confusion. **Synonyms:** curiously, questioningly **Antonyms:** knowingly, seriously **Sentence:** "So, you finished all your homework?" my mother asked *quizzically* when she saw me watching TV.

What Is Academic Vocabulary?

Even in a single day you can find yourself in different situations—chatting about the latest movie, responding to an e-mail, or giving a younger student homework help. No matter the situation, it helps to know that you have thousands of words from which to choose. However, the kinds of words you use change, depending on your purpose. With family and friends, you use informal and conversational vocabulary. In school, though, you rely on **academic vocabulary,** the language you use to talk and write about the subject matter you are studying.

Design, criteria, interpret—you may encounter academic vocabulary words such as these in all subject areas, including science, math, social studies, and language arts. Understanding and using these words correctly will help you to be successful in school and on assessments. This web shows examples of academic vocabulary words in different subject areas.

COMMON CORE

Included in this workshop:
L 4a–d, L 6

SOCIAL STUDIES
To **interpret** a map's symbols, check the legend or key.

LANGUAGE ARTS
What is the **source** of the folk tale?

WORLD HISTORY
What **motive** did the United States have for entering World War II?

ACADEMIC VOCABULARY
The language that you use to think, talk, and write about different subject areas you are studying

BIOLOGY
Research how to predict patterns of heredity.

ALGEBRA
Investigate how to solve equations with variables.

PHYSICAL SCIENCE
Technology improves the use of energy resources.

Use the following chart to become familiar with some of the academic vocabulary terms in this book. As you read, look for the activities labeled "Academic Vocabulary in Writing" and "Academic Vocabulary in Speaking." These activities provide opportunities to use academic language in your writing and discussions.

Word	Definition	Example
achieve	to accomplish or to succeed	What did Alexander the Great **achieve** in invading Persia?
bias	a preference that prevents fair decision-making	Look for evidence of **bias** in the speech.
community	all people living in the same location under the same government	A **community** of artists arose in Harlem in the 1920s.
criteria	standards or rules by which something can be judged	Be sure to use **criteria** for the evaluation.
design	to think up the plans for	**Design** a simple machine and determine its mechanical efficiency.
emphasis	special attention or effort directed toward something	Ancient Romans placed an **emphasis** on building roads.
interpret	to explain the meaning of	**Interpret** the graphical elements in the poems by E. E. Cummings.
investigate	to examine in detail	Let's **investigate** the feeding habits of manatees.
logic	correct reasoning	The **logic** of the argument is sound.
motive	emotion, desire, or need that compels one to take a certain action	What **motive** does the princess have in indicating a certain door?
perspective	a certain point of view	An author's **perspective** is often related to his or her environment.
research	close, careful study	You can **research** probability by tossing a coin.
source	the point of origin	Use a map to find the **source** of the Nile River.
style	the unique way in which something is said, done, expressed, or performed	Stephen King's **style** is quite different from Edgar Allan Poe's.
technology	science as it is applied to practical use	With the help of **technology,** ideas and information spread rapidly.

Academic Vocabulary in Action

The terms below are two examples of the academic vocabulary you will use throughout your studies. Knowing the meanings of these terms is essential for completing the activities and lessons in this book as well as mastering test items.

source *(noun)*

Defining the Word

A *source* is a thing's point of origin. You may learn about the source for details in a science report and about primary sources. When reading literature, you will often look for the source of a folk tale to discover what gives the tale its distinctive flavor.

Using the Word

Now that you know the definition of *source*, practice using the word.

- Use a chart like the one shown to identify a source you have learned about in different subject areas.

- Write a different definition for *source*, if the subject area requires a different meaning than the one you know.

- Check a dictionary or glossary to make sure your definition is correct.

Subject Area	Word	Definition
social studies	source	person or document that supplies information

technology *(noun)*

Defining the Word

The word *technology* means "science as it is applied to practical use." An architect uses technology to devise blueprints; a computer programmer might use technology—in the form of a computer—to solve a problem; and a person who is lost might use a tool of technology to figure out his or her location.

Using the Word

Once you understand the meaning of a word root, you will be able to understand the meanings of other words built on the same root. The word root *techno*, from the Greek word *tekne*, means "art, skill, or craft."

- In a chart like this one, make a list of other words you know formed from the root *techno*.

- Look up each word in a dictionary and write down its meaning.

- Write a sentence using each word.

Word	Definition	Sentence
technique	a practical method or procedure	We learned a variety of <u>techniques</u> for persuading our audience in our essays.

Strategies That Work: Vocabulary

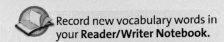

Record new vocabulary words in your **Reader/Writer Notebook.**

❶ Use Context Clues

The most important part of building your vocabulary is recognizing unfamiliar words as you read. When you encounter an unfamiliar word, look at the **context**, the words, phrases, or sentences that surround that word. Often, the context can give you important clues to the word's meaning, as in the following example:

> At first, the author's perspective seems peculiar. However, once you find out details about her life, the way she looks at the subject becomes clear.

Even if you do not know what *perspective* means, you can figure out from the surrounding context that it means "the way she looks at the subject."

❷ Clarify Word Definitions

If you cannot rely on a word's context to help you understand its meaning, consult a dictionary. A dictionary entry will also provide a word's pronunciation, parts of speech, origin, and additional meanings. When you are reading a textbook or manual, you may find definitions for unfamiliar words in a glossary at the back of the book.

fossil (fŏs′əl) *n.*: the remains of a living thing, preserved in soil or rock.

❸ Keep a Word List

List new academic terms in your **Reader/Writer Notebook.** Add to your list each time you take on a new reading assignment. In addition to listing the word and its definition, you might draw a symbol or picture to show you what the word represents or provide examples to remind you of what the word means. Challenge yourself to use words from the list in your writing and discussions. The more frequently you use the words, the easier they will be to remember.

Interactive Vocabulary
THINKcentral
Go to **thinkcentral.com.**
KEYWORD: HML8-19

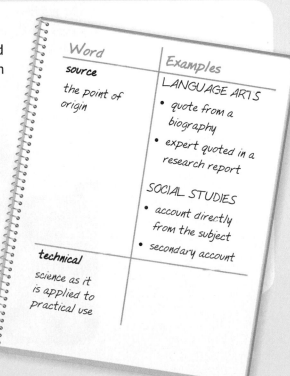

Word	Examples
source the point of origin	LANGUAGE ARTS • quote from a biography • expert quoted in a research report SOCIAL STUDIES • account directly from the subject • secondary account
technical science as it is applied to practical use	

*For a complete list of terms in this book, see the **Academic Vocabulary Glossary** on pages R118–R119.*

Expressing Ideas in Writing

Writing is a way to let others know who you are and how your mind works. Through the right words, you can express laugh-out-loud humor, inspiring thoughts, or strong opinions and then share those ideas with the world. You might be writing to your favorite musician, a teacher, an e-mail buddy, or the entire blogosphere. In each case, your words can carry an important message.

COMMON CORE

Included in this workshop:
W 4, W 5

Consider Your Options

Any work of writing starts with careful planning. Long before your polished ideas hit the page or screen, take the time to ask some basic questions about the **purpose, audience,** and **format** of your writing. Are you crafting a research paper for class or posting a short movie review to an online database? Questions like these can help you get off to a good start—and stay on track later on.

PURPOSE	AUDIENCE	FORMAT
Why am I writing?	**Who are my readers?**	**Which format will best suit my purpose and audience?**
• to entertain	• classmates	• essay • speech
• to inform or explain	• teachers	• letter • research paper
• to argue or persuade	• friends	• poem • short story
• to describe	• community members	• review • journal entry
• to express thoughts and feelings	• customer service at a company	• script • Web site
• to inspire	• Web users	• power presentation

Continue with the Process

The more you write, the more you'll understand your own process of writing. It takes practice, but eventually you will find what works best for you. As you tackle the **Writing Workshops** in this book, begin by following this basic process.

THE WRITING PROCESS

PLANNING/PREWRITING

Explore your ideas and decide what you want to write about. To get your ideas flowing, try **freewriting, listing,** or using one of the other prewriting strategies described on page 23.

WHAT DOES IT LOOK LIKE?

Ideas from *Slam!*
- passion for an activity
- what activities am I good at?
- what if I had to give up doing something I love? (possible short story idea?)

DRAFTING

Transform your prewriting efforts into a rough draft. For a formal essay, it might be helpful to **draft from an outline.** For an informal essay, **draft to discover**—in other words, let your ideas take shape as you write. If you're writing a short story, create a **story map.**

WHAT DOES IT LOOK LIKE?

Setting: High school; Midwestern town.
Characters: Judy Brack (student); Mr. Brack (Judy's dad); Mr. Valdez (basketball coach)
Conflict: Judy joins boys' basketball team without parents' approval. They want her to quit the team. Should she?

REVISING

Review your draft. Look for ways to clarify the development, organization, and style. Make sure your writing is clear and **coherent**, or easy to follow.
- Review the **rubric** (page 22).
- Ask a classmate to review your work.
- Consider trying a new approach if something simply is not working.
- **Proofread** for errors in spelling and grammar.

ASK A PEER READER

Judy scored a basket as the buzzer sounded. Her teammates cheered but she didn't feel like celebrating.

Suggestion: Add details to convey the excitement of the game. Try: "Swoosh. From the three-point line, Judy heard the familiar sound of the ball gliding through the net."

EDITING AND PUBLISHING

Review your draft. Look for ways to clarify the ideas, style, and structure of your writing.
- Use the **Proofreader's Checklist** to help you catch common mistakes.
- Let the world know your idea. Where you publish will depend on your purpose, audience, and format.

PROOFREADER'S CHECKLIST

- ☑ Revise sentence fragments and run-on sentences.
- ☑ Fix mistakes in subject-verb agreement and pronoun agreement.
- ☑ Capitalize and use punctuation marks correctly.
- ☑ Correct misspellings.

Scoring Rubric

Score	COMMON CORE TRAITS
6	• **Development** Includes a meaningful, memorable introduction; develops ideas with varied, relevant evidence; ends powerfully • **Organization** Is effectively and logically organized; uses varied transitions to create cohesion (flow) and link ideas • **Language** Uses precise language in original ways; effectively maintains an appropriate style; shows a strong command of grammar, mechanics, and spelling
5	• **Development** Has an effective introduction; develops ideas with relevant evidence; has a strong concluding section • **Organization** Is logically organized; uses transitions to create cohesion and link ideas • **Language** Uses precise language; maintains an appropriate style; has a few errors in grammar, mechanics, and spelling
4	• **Development** Has an introduction, but it could be more interesting; lacks support for one or two ideas; has an adequate concluding section • **Organization** Is logically organized, with one or two exceptions; could use a few more transitions • **Language** Generally uses precise language; has one or two lapses in style; includes a few distracting errors in grammar, mechanics, and spelling
3	• **Development** Has a superficial introduction that lacks interest; includes some unsupported ideas or irrelevant evidence; has a weak ending • **Organization** Has some flaws in organization; needs more transitions • **Language** Uses words correctly, though language is unoriginal; has frequent lapses in style; has some critical errors in grammar, mechanics, and spelling
2	• **Development** Has a weak, uninteresting introduction; does not support most ideas; ends abruptly • **Organization** Has a weak organization; lacks transitions throughout • **Language** Uses vague language and misuses some words; has an inappropriate style in many places; contains many distracting errors in grammar, mechanics, and spelling
1	• **Development** Lacks an introduction, support for ideas, and a concluding section • **Organization** Has no organization or transitions; is confusing and disconnected • **Language** Uses many words incorrectly; has an inappropriate style; has major problems with grammar, mechanics, and spelling

Strategies That Work: Writing

 Record your reactions and observations in your **Reader/Writer Notebook.**

❶ Use Prewriting Strategies

Anyone who has ever faced a blank page or screen knows how difficult the first steps can be. Try these strategies.

- **Freewrite.** Write for ten minutes, letting whatever comes to you flow without interruption.
- **Get visual.** Use a graphic organizer, such as a cluster diagram or a chart, to flesh out your ideas.
- **Brainstorm with others.** Bounce ideas off other writers for their feedback.
- **Ask big questions.** "Who was the most courageous person in history?" "Which fictional character is the most popular?" Ask fun or serious questions in search of a topic.

❷ Get Feedback from Peers

Often, it is easier to see trouble spots when the writing is not your own. When you exchange feedback with classmates, keep these guidelines in mind.

When You're the Writer	When You're the Reader
• Ask for specific feedback. Should readers comment on your ideas, look for errors, or both?	• Be respectful and positive.
• Invite your readers to offer honest feedback. Respect their opinions, even if you don't agree.	• Support your opinions with relevant observations, and give suggestions for improvement.
• Clarify their suggestions. Review them on your own, and use the suggestions most helpful to your piece.	• Ask questions to learn more about the writer's goals and ideas.
	• Don't rewrite the work yourself.

❸ Pay Attention to Details

Even minor mistakes, such as errors in grammar, punctuation, and spelling, can keep readers from taking your ideas seriously.

Use these spelling tips to make sure your writing is polished and correct.

- Review spelling rules on pages R72–R74.
- Avoid misusing commonly confused words, such as accept and except. (See page R75 for more examples.)
- Use the spell-check feature in your word-processing program or a dictionary.
- Read your draft backwards to catch mistakes your eye might miss while scanning over sentences you are very familiar with.

When Phillip wakes up, he is all alone on the island accept (except) for a member of the ship's crew and a cat. Soon, Phillip becomes blind. Overcoming that is a huge obstical (obstacles) for him.

Writing Online

THINK central

Go to **thinkcentral.com.**
KEYWORD: HML7N-23

The Main Events

UNIT 1

PLOT AND CONFLICT

- In Fiction
- In Drama
- In Media
- In Nonfiction
- In Poetry

25

What makes a STORY worth telling?

A great story can make you laugh, cry, or gasp in surprise, but one thing is for sure: you'll give it your full attention. You might even forget your own troubles as the story unfolds or gain an insight that will change the way you view your life. Something about the fabulous setting, the compelling characters, or the unusual situations presented will stay with you long after you close the book or turn away from the screen.

ACTIVITY Think about the last time you thought to yourself, "That's a great story!" With a group of classmates, discuss the following:

- What story did you think was special?

- Why did you like that story so much?

- How do your reasons for liking it compare with others' reasons for liking what they did?

Based on your discussion, come up with a list of qualities that make a story worth telling.

Find It Online!

Go to **thinkcentral.com** for the interactive version of this unit.

Preview Unit Goals

TEXT ANALYSIS	• Analyze how incidents in a story or drama propel the action, reveal aspects of a character, or provoke a decision • Identify plot stages, conflicts, and subplots • Analyze suspense
READING	• Identify and analyze sequence and cause-effect relationships • Make inferences and cite evidence to support them
WRITING AND LANGUAGE	• Write a personal narrative • Use and understand perfect and progressive tense • Maintain pronoun-antecedent agreement • Use coordinating conjunctions and semicolons correctly
SPEAKING AND LISTENING	• Present an oral narrative
VOCABULARY	• Use knowledge of word roots, base words, and affixes to understand word meaning • Use reference aids, including a dictionary and a thesaurus • Use context clues to figure out the meanings of words
ACADEMIC VOCABULARY	• affect • imply • conclude • initial • evident
MEDIA AND VIEWING	• Identify and analyze film elements; analyze a director's choices • Present a narrative

Media Smart DVD-ROM

Captivating Stories in Movies

Explore how storytelling techniques take *The Sisterhood of the Traveling Pants* from page to screen. Page 110

Text Analysis Workshop

Plot and Conflict

Will the hero save the world *and* win the girl? Can the young soldier survive the war? How will the family stay alive on the deserted island? Good stories are all around you—in novels and short stories, on television, and in movies. How do they capture your imagination and keep you riveted? Read on to find out.

Part 1: Conflict—The Fuel of a Story

A knight must slay a fierce dragon. A girl faces the consequences of betraying her friend. No matter what they're about, all good stories are fueled by conflict. A **conflict,** or a struggle between opposing forces, can be external or internal.

- An **external conflict** involves a struggle between a character and an outside force, such as another character, a force of nature, or society.

- An **internal conflict** is a struggle that takes place within a character's own mind, as he or she wrestles with difficult thoughts, feelings, or choices.

Whether it is external or internal, a conflict is what drives a story forward, from its beginning to its end. How will the characters handle the conflict? What obstacles will they face? Such questions prompt you to keep turning the pages.

Examine the different types of conflicts described in this graphic.

COMMON CORE

Included in this workshop:
RL 1 Cite the textual evidence that supports inferences drawn from the text. **RL 3** Analyze how incidents in a story propel the action.

TYPES OF CONFLICTS

External

Character vs. Character
Ling overhears Julian bragging about his malicious plan to ridicule her best friend. Angered, she confronts Julian and becomes even more incensed when he denies every word. (*Ling vs. Julian*)

External

Character vs. Force of Nature
A blinding snowstorm hits while Yoni is hiking in unfamiliar territory. Suddenly, he loses his bearings and has no idea how to find his way home. (*Yoni vs. snowstorm*)

External

Character vs. Society
The year is 1961. Sarah works in a factory at a time when workers must put in long hours and deal with dismal, even dangerous, conditions on the job. (*Sarah vs. poor working conditions*)

Internal

Character vs. Self
Hannah accepted Raj's marriage proposal against the strong wishes of her family. If she marries him, they will never speak to her again. It's one day before the wedding, and Hannah is doubting her decision. (*marry Raj and alienate her family vs. call off the wedding and lose her true love*)

MODEL 1: EXTERNAL CONFLICT

Johnny Tremain, a poor orphaned silversmith, believes he is related to the wealthy merchant Mr. Lyte. Johnny has proof—a cup engraved with the Lyte family name. How does Mr. Lyte react to the news?

from Johnny Tremain

Novel by **Esther Forbes**

"I think," said Mr. Lyte quietly, "all of you ladies and gentlemen will agree that this cup our—ah, cousin, is it?—has brought back tonight is one of this set?"

There was a murmur of assent. Johnny could hear the tiny tinkle, seemingly far away, of Miss Lavinia's spinet.[1]

5 "It is perfectly obvious that this cup now stands where it belongs. The question is how was it ever separated from its fellows?"

Johnny felt that everyone there except himself knew the answer to this question.

"In fact," the merchant's voice was as smooth as oil, "I declare this to be the
10 very cup which was stolen from me by thieves. They broke through yonder window on the twenty-third of last August. Sheriff, I order you to arrest this boy for burglary."

---

1. **spinet:** a small, compact upright piano.

Close Read

1. In your own words, describe the conflict that Johnny is facing.

2. Johnny's conflict isn't fully revealed until lines 11–12. What details earlier in the excerpt suggest that a problem is brewing?

MODEL 2: INTERNAL CONFLICT

Eva is thrilled when her friend Kenisha moves back to town. Most of the time, Kenisha is too involved with the popular crowd to acknowledge her old friend. In fact, Kenisha is only nice when she wants to copy Eva's homework. How does Eva feel after she lets Kenisha copy her work?

from *Eva* and the **Mayor**

Short story by **Jean Davies Okimoto**

Eva knew it wasn't right to copy other people's work, but it wasn't as bad as cheating on a test, and a lot of people did it. She knew that didn't make it right, but still it didn't seem like such a big sin, and besides, she wasn't the copier. The whole thing made her feel pretty mixed up.

5 She didn't know for sure if she had let Kenisha copy her work because of all that stuff Gramma Evelyn said about being nice to Kenisha or because she wanted to get in with Kenisha and be one of the cool people.

Close Read

1. What details suggest that Eva is conflicted about her decision to let Kenisha copy her homework? One detail is boxed.

2. In your opinion, is Eva overcome with guilt? Support your answer.

Part 2: Stages of Plot

To draw readers into a story and maintain their interest, a writer must do more than simply introduce an intriguing conflict. He or she has to create a plot in which every development builds upon the conflict. A **plot,** or the series of events in a story, typically includes five stages of development. In a linear plot, the order in which these stages occur follows a pattern. It's important to remember, though, that not every story follows the pattern exactly.

Take a look at the following graphic, which shows a linear structure. Notice what happens to the conflict at the different stages.

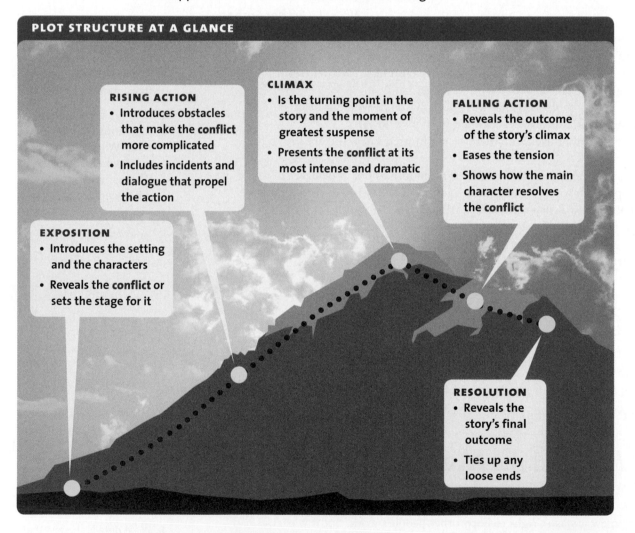

PLOT STRUCTURE AT A GLANCE

RISING ACTION
- Introduces obstacles that make the **conflict** more complicated
- Includes incidents and dialogue that propel the action

CLIMAX
- Is the turning point in the story and the moment of greatest suspense
- Presents the **conflict** at its most intense and dramatic

FALLING ACTION
- Reveals the outcome of the story's climax
- Eases the tension
- Shows how the main character resolves the **conflict**

EXPOSITION
- Introduces the setting and the characters
- Reveals the **conflict** or sets the stage for it

RESOLUTION
- Reveals the story's final outcome
- Ties up any loose ends

Of course, the plot's development does not have to follow this traditional pattern to be effective. A plot's development just needs to be suspenseful, coherent, constantly moving ahead, and satisfying. When evaluating plot development, you might want to keep those qualities in mind.

Part 3: Analyze the Text

"The Elevator" is about a boy named Martin who recently moved with his father to a new apartment. Living on the seventeenth floor, Martin has no choice but to take the elevator. The idea of the elevator terrifies him. What exactly is Martin so afraid of? Use what you've learned about plot and conflict to analyze this unsettling story.

Short story by **William Sleator**

It was an old building with an old elevator—a very small elevator, with a maximum capacity of three people. Martin, a thin twelve-year-old, felt nervous in it from the first day he and his father moved into the apartment. Of course he was always uncomfortable in elevators, afraid that they would
5 fall, but there was something especially unpleasant about this one. Perhaps its baleful[1] atmosphere was due to the light from the single fluorescent ceiling strip, bleak and dim on the dirty brown walls. Perhaps the problem was the door, which never stayed open quite long enough, and slammed shut with such ominous, clanging finality. Perhaps it was the way the mechanism
10 shuddered in a kind of exhaustion each time it left a floor, as though it might never reach the next one. Maybe it was simply the dimensions of the contraption that bothered him, so small that it felt uncomfortably crowded even when there was only one other person in it.
     Coming home from school the day after they moved in, Martin tried the
15 stairs. But they were almost as bad, windowless, shadowy, with several dark landings where the light bulbs had burned out. His footsteps echoed behind him like slaps on the cement, as though there was another person climbing, getting closer. By the time he reached the seventeenth floor, which seemed to take forever, he was winded and gasping.
20 His father, who worked at home, wanted to know why he was so out of breath. "But why didn't you take the elevator?" he asked, frowning at Martin when he explained about the stairs. Not only are you skinny and weak and bad at sports, his expression seemed to say, but you're also a coward. After that, Martin forced himself to take the elevator. He would have to get used to it, he
25 told himself, just the way he got used to being bullied at school, and always picked last when they chose teams. The elevator was an undeniable fact of life.

---

1. **baleful:** sinister; ominous.

Close Read
Exposition (lines 1–40)

1. Reread the boxed details. What do you learn about the main character Martin in the exposition?

He didn't get used to it. He remained tense in the trembling little box, his eyes fixed on the numbers over the door that blinked on and off so haltingly, as if at any moment they might simply give up. Sometimes he forced himself to look away from them, to the Emergency Stop button, or the red Alarm button. What would happen if he pushed one of them? Would a bell ring? Would the elevator stop between floors? And if it did, how would they get him out?

That was what he hated about being alone on the thing—the fear of being trapped there for hours by himself. But it wasn't much better when there were other passengers. He felt too close to any other rider, too intimate. And he was always very conscious of the effort people made *not* to look at one another, staring fixedly at nothing. Being short, in this one situation, was an advantage, since his face was below the eye level of adults, and after a brief glance they ignored him.

Until the morning the elevator stopped at the fourteenth floor, and the fat lady got on. She wore a threadbare green coat that ballooned around her; her ankles bulged above dirty sneakers. As she waddled into the elevator, Martin was sure he felt it sink under her weight. She was so big that she filled the cubicle; her coat brushed against him, and he had to squeeze into the corner to make room for her—there certainly wouldn't have been room for another passenger. The door slammed quickly behind her. And then, unlike everyone else, she did not stand facing the door. She stood with her back to the door, wheezing, staring directly at Martin.

For a moment he met her gaze. Her features seemed very small, squashed together by the loose fleshy mounds of her cheeks. She had no chin, only a great swollen mass of neck, barely contained by the collar of her coat. Her sparse red hair was pinned back by a plastic barrette. And her blue eyes, though tiny, were sharp and penetrating, boring into Martin's face.

Abruptly he looked away from her to the numbers over the door. She didn't turn around. Was she still looking at him? His eyes slipped back to hers, then quickly away. She *was* still watching him. He wanted to close his eyes; he wanted to turn around and stare into the corner, but how could he? The elevator creaked down to twelve, down to eleven. Martin looked at his watch; he looked at the numbers again. They weren't even down to nine yet. And then, against his will, his eyes slipped back to her face. She was still watching him. Her nose tilted up; there was a large space between her nostrils and her upper lip, giving her a piggish look. He looked away again, clenching his teeth, fighting the impulse to squeeze his eyes shut against her.

She had to be crazy. Why else would she stare at him this way? What was she going to do next?

She did nothing. She only watched him, breathing audibly, until the elevator reached the first floor at last. Martin would have rushed past her to get

2. Consider what you've read so far about the setting and Martin's feelings about his surroundings. What do you think the main conflict will be about?

**Close Read
Rising Action
begins** (lines 41–80)

3. What event sets the rising action in motion?

4. Martin seems to perceive the strange lady as a threat. In your opinion, is this conflict real or in his head? Support your answer.

out, but there was no room. He could only wait as she turned—reluctantly, it
70 seemed to him—and moved so slowly out into the lobby. And then he ran. He
didn't care what she thought. He ran past her, outside into the fresh air, and he
ran almost all the way to school. He had never felt such relief in his life.

He thought about her all day. Did she live in the building? He had never
seen her before, and the building wasn't very big—only four apartments
75 on each floor. It seemed likely that she didn't live there, and had only been
visiting somebody.

But if she were only visiting somebody, why was she leaving the building at
seven thirty in the morning? People didn't make visits at that time of day. Did
that mean she *did* live in the building? If so, it was likely—it was a certainty—
80 that sometime he would be riding with her on the elevator again.

He was apprehensive as he approached the building after school. In the
lobby, he considered the stairs. But that was ridiculous. Why should
he be afraid of an old lady? If he *was* afraid of her, if he let it control him, then
he was worse than all the names they called him at school. He pressed the
85 button; he stepped into the empty elevator. He stared at the lights, urging the
elevator on. It stopped on three.

At least it's not fourteen, he told himself; the person she was visiting lives
on fourteen. He watched the door slide open—revealing a green coat, a
piggish face, blue eyes already fixed on him as though she knew he'd be there.
90 It wasn't possible. It was like a nightmare. But there she was, massively real.
"Going up!" he said, his voice a humiliating squeak.

She nodded, her flesh quivering, and stepped on. The door slammed. He
watched her pudgy hand move toward the buttons. She pressed, not fourteen,
but eighteen, the top floor, one floor above his own. The elevator trembled
95 and began its ascent.[2] The fat lady watched him.

He knew she had gotten on at fourteen this morning. So why was she
on three, going up to eighteen now? The only floors *he* ever went to were
seventeen and one. What was she doing? Had she been waiting for him? Was
she riding with him on purpose?
100 But that was crazy. Maybe she had a lot of friends in the building. Or else
she was a cleaning lady who worked in different apartments. That had to be
it. He felt her eyes on him as he stared at the numbers slowly blinking on
and off—slower than usual, it seemed to him. Maybe the elevator was having
trouble because of how heavy she was. It was supposed to carry three adults,
105 but it was old. What if it got stuck between floors? What if it fell?

They were on five now. It occurred to him to press seven, get off there, and
walk the rest of the way. And he would have done it, if he could have reached
the buttons. But there was no room to get past her without squeezing against
her, and he could not bear the thought of any physical contact with her. He
110 concentrated on being in his room. He would be home soon, only another

---

2. **ascent:** the act of climbing or rising upward.

Close Read
Rising Action
continues (lines 81–174)

5. What internal conflict is
plaguing Martin in lines
81–84?

6. Tension builds as Martin
and the lady meet again.
What details in lines
88–105 help to create
suspense about what
might happen? One
detail is boxed.

minute or so. He could stand anything for a minute, even this crazy lady watching him.

Unless the elevator got stuck between floors. Then what would he do? He tried to push the thought away, but it kept coming back. He looked at her. She was still staring at him, no expression at all on her squashed little features.

When the elevator stopped on his floor, she barely moved out of the way. He had to inch past her, rubbing against her horrible scratchy coat, terrified the door would close before he made it through. She quickly turned and watched him as the door slammed shut. And he thought, *Now she knows I live on seventeen.*

"Did you ever notice a strange fat lady on the elevator?" he asked his father that evening.

"Can't say as I have," he said, not looking away from the television.

He knew he was probably making a mistake, but he had to tell somebody. "Well, she was on the elevator with me twice today. And the funny thing was, she just kept staring at me, she never stopped looking at me for a minute. You think . . . you know of anybody who has a weird cleaning lady or anything?"

"What are you so worked up about now?" his father said, turning impatiently away from the television.

"I'm not worked up. It was just funny the way she kept staring at me. You know how people never look at each other in the elevator. Well, she just kept looking at me."

"What am I going to do with you, Martin?" his father said. He sighed and shook his head. "Honestly, now you're afraid of some poor old lady."

"I'm not afraid."

"You're afraid," said his father, with total assurance. "When are you going to grow up and act like a man? Are you going to be timid all your life?"

He managed not to cry until he got to his room—but his father probably knew he was crying anyway. He slept very little.

And in the morning, when the elevator door opened, the fat lady was waiting for him.

She was expecting him. She knew he lived on seventeen. He stood there, unable to move, and then backed away. And as he did so, her expression changed. She smiled as the door slammed.

He ran for the stairs. Luckily, the unlit flight on which he fell was between sixteen and fifteen. He only had to drag himself up one and a half flights with the terrible pain in his leg. His father was silent on the way to the hospital, disappointed and annoyed at him for being such a coward and a fool.

It was a simple fracture. He didn't need a wheelchair, only a cast and crutches. But he was condemned to the elevator now. Was that why the fat lady had smiled? Had she known it would happen this way?

At least his father was with him on the elevator on the way back from the hospital. There was no room for the fat lady to get on. And even if she did, his

7. What details in lines 121–139 suggest a conflict between father and son?

8. Review your answer to question 4. Then consider the lady's behavior each time Martin sees her on the elevator. Has your answer changed? Explain.

father would see her, he would realize how peculiar she was, and then maybe
155　he would understand. And once they got home, he could stay in the apartment
for a few days—the doctor had said he should use the leg as little as possible.
A week, maybe—a whole week without going on the elevator. Riding up with
his father, leaning on his crutches, he looked around the little cubicle and felt
a kind of triumph. He had beaten the elevator, and the fat lady, for the time
160　being. And the end of the week was very far away.

"Oh, I almost forgot," his father reached out his hand and pressed nine.

"What are you doing? You're not getting off, are you?" he asked him, trying
not to sound panicky.

"I promised Terry Ullman I'd drop in on her," his father said, looking at his
165　watch as he stepped off.

"Let me go with you. I want to visit her, too," Martin pleaded, struggling
forward on his crutches.

But the door was already closing. "Afraid to be on the elevator alone?" his
father said, with a look of total scorn. "Grow up, Martin." The door slammed
170　shut.

Martin hobbled to the buttons and pressed nine, but it didn't do any good.
The elevator stopped at ten, where the fat lady was waiting for him. She
moved in quickly; he was too slow, too unsteady on his crutches to work his
way past her in time. The door sealed them in; the elevator started up.
175　　"Hello, Martin," she said, and laughed, and pushed the Stop button.

9. In lines 145–160, the story takes an unexpected turn. How might this development affect Martin's conflict?

Close Read
Climax (line 175)

10. Line 175 is the climax, or turning point, of the story. Do you think Martin is in danger? Explain your opinion.

Close Read
Falling Action and Resolution

11. The author ends this story at the climax. What is your opinion of the plot's development and of leaving the conflict unresolved? Explain.

Raymond's Run

Short Story by Toni Cade Bambara

VIDEO TRAILER **THINK** central   KEYWORD: HML8-37

What's worth the EFFORT?

Have you ever wanted something so badly you'd do anything to achieve it? If so, you've felt motivation, the drive that causes people to strive toward a goal. In the story you are about to read, a spunky young girl does what it takes to be the fastest runner in her neighborhood.

QUICKWRITE Jot down a list of things you've been willing to work for. Choose a favorite and write a short paragraph telling what motivates you.

1. Hold record for most chin-ups
2. Learn new dance

● TEXT ANALYSIS: PLOT

A **plot** is the series of events that happen in a story. When a story develops in a linear way, it progresses through the following plot stages in the order in which they are listed:

- **Exposition**—introduces the main characters, the setting, and sometimes the conflict
- **Rising action**—increases tension and builds the conflict
- **Climax**—the point of greatest interest, or the turning point in the story where the conflict begins to be resolved
- **Falling action**—shows the result of the climax and brings the story to a close
- **Resolution**—reveals the final outcome of the conflict and ties up loose ends

As you read "Raymond's Run," notice the incidents that occur at each stage of the plot.

● READING SKILL: MAKE INFERENCES

When you make an **inference** while reading, you use clues from the story and your own knowledge to guess about things the author doesn't say directly. As you read "Raymond's Run," make inferences to better understand the main character's feelings, thoughts, and ideas. Record your inferences in equations.

| Squeaky says her dad is the only one faster than she is. | + | Kids like when their parents are talented. | = | Squeaky is proud of her father. |

▲ VOCABULARY IN CONTEXT

The boldfaced words help Toni Cade Bambara tell a story about a race that's important in more ways than one. Use context clues to figure out what each word means.

1. Teams of three or four usually compete in **relay** races.
2. The talented young sprinter was considered a track **prodigy.**
3. Mai's teammate is also her good friend, or **sidekick.**
4. Ben is **liable** to get injured if he doesn't warm up before the race.
5. At the start of a race, runners **crouch** close to the ground.
6. The winner might **clutch** the blue ribbon to her chest.

 Complete the activities in your **Reader/Writer Notebook.**

Meet the Author

Toni Cade Bambara
1939–1995

Creativity and Concern
Raised in urban neighborhoods of New York and New Jersey in the 1940s and 1950s, Toni Cade spent much time daydreaming and exploring her world. Her mother encouraged her to do so. In the dedication of her award-winning novel *The Salt Eaters,* Bambara thanks her "mama . . . who in 1948, having come upon me daydreaming in the middle of the kitchen floor, mopped around me." One day, while looking through an old trunk, Toni found her great-grandmother's sketchbook. The name inscribed there was "Bambara." Impressed with her ancestor's creative drive, she decided to add that name to her own.

"A Tremendous Responsibility"
Toni Cade Bambara went on to careers as a teacher, community activist, and documentary filmmaker. She continued to write, sharing her personal concern for and understanding of the lives of African-American families and communities. She was always aware of the influence that writers, artists, and cultural workers have on others. "It's a tremendous responsibility," she said. "One's got to see what the factory worker sees, what the prisoner sees, what the welfare children see . . . in order to tell the truth and not get trapped."

Authors Online
Go to **thinkcentral.com**. KEYWORD: HML8-37

THINK central

RAYMOND'S RUN

Toni Cade Bambara

don't have much work to do around the house like some girls. My mother does that. And I don't have to earn my pocket money by hustling; George runs errands for the big boys and sells Christmas cards. And anything else that's got to get done, my father does. All I have to do in life is mind my brother Raymond, which is enough.

Sometimes I slip and say my little brother Raymond. But as any fool can see he's much bigger and he's older too. But a lot of people call him my little brother cause he needs looking after cause he's not quite right. And a lot of smart mouths got lots to say about that too, especially when George was 10 minding him. But now, if anybody has anything to say to Raymond, anything to say about his big head,[1] they have to come by me. And I don't play the dozens[2] or believe in standing around with somebody in my face doing a lot of talking. I much rather just knock you down and take my chances even if I am a little girl with skinny arms and a squeaky voice, which is how I got the name Squeaky. And if things get too rough, I run. And as anybody can tell you, I'm the fastest thing on two feet. **A**

There is no track meet that I don't win the first place medal. I used to win the twenty-yard dash when I was a little kid in kindergarten. Nowadays, it's the fifty-yard dash. And tomorrow I'm subject to run the quarter-meter 20 **relay** all by myself and come in first, second, and third. The big kids call me Mercury[3] cause I'm the swiftest thing in the neighborhood. Everybody knows that—except two people who know better, my father and me. He can beat me to Amsterdam Avenue with me having a two fire hydrant headstart and him running with his hands in his pockets and whistling. But that's private information. Cause can you imagine some thirty-five-year-old man stuffing himself into PAL shorts to race little kids? So as far as everyone's concerned, I'm

---

1. **big head:** a result of hydrocephalus, or fluid in parts of the brain, that causes enlargement of the skull.
2. **play the dozens:** exchange rhyming insults.
3. **Mercury:** in Roman mythology, the swift messenger of the gods.

Analyze Visuals ▶
From her posture and her expression, what can you **infer** about the girl in this photograph?

A **PLOT: EXPOSITION**
What have you learned about Squeaky so far?

relay (rē′lā) *n.* a race in which several team members take turns running to complete the race

the fastest and that goes for Gretchen, too, who has put out the tale that she is going to win the first-place medal this year. Ridiculous. In the second place, she's got short legs. In the third place, she's got freckles. In the first place, no one can beat me and that's all there is to it.

I'm standing on the corner admiring the weather and about to take a stroll down Broadway so I can practice my breathing exercises, and I've got Raymond walking on the inside close to the buildings, cause he's subject to fits of fantasy and starts thinking he's a circus performer and that the curb is a tightrope strung high in the air. And sometimes after a rain he likes to step down off his tightrope right into the gutter and slosh around getting his shoes and cuffs wet. Then I get hit when I get home. Or sometimes if you don't watch him he'll dash across traffic to the island in the middle of Broadway and give the pigeons a fit. Then I have to go behind him apologizing to all the old people sitting around trying to get some sun and getting all upset with the pigeons fluttering around them, scattering their newspapers and upsetting the waxpaper lunches[4] in their laps. So I keep Raymond on the inside of me, and he plays like he's driving a stage coach which is O.K. by me so long as he doesn't run me over or interrupt my breathing exercises, which I have to do on account of I'm serious about my running, and I don't care who knows it. **B**

Now some people like to act like things come easy to them, won't let on that they practice. Not me. I'll high-prance down 34th Street like a rodeo pony to keep my knees strong even if it does get my mother uptight so that she walks ahead like she's not with me, don't know me, is all by herself on a shopping trip, and I am somebody else's crazy child. Now you take Cynthia Procter for instance. She's just the opposite. If there's a test tomorrow, she'll say something like, "Oh, I guess I'll play handball this afternoon and watch television tonight," just to let you know she ain't thinking about the test. Or like last week when she won the spelling bee for the millionth time, "A good thing you got 'receive,' Squeaky, cause I would have got it wrong. I completely forgot about the spelling bee." And she'll **clutch** the lace on her blouse like it was a narrow escape. Oh, brother. But of course when I pass her house on my early morning trots around the block, she is practicing the scales on the piano over and over and over and over. Then in music class she always lets herself get bumped around so she falls accidentally on purpose onto the piano stool and is so surprised to find herself sitting there that she decides just for fun to try out the ole keys. And what do you know—Chopin's waltzes[5] just spring out of her fingertips and she's the most surprised thing in the world. A regular **prodigy.** I could kill people like that. I stay up all night studying the words for the spelling bee. And you can see me any time of day practicing running. I never walk if I can trot, and shame on Raymond if he can't keep up. But of course he does, cause if he hangs back someone's **liable** to walk up to him and get

B MAKE INFERENCES
Reread lines 31–45. How do you think Squeaky feels about taking care of her brother? Use an equation to note your inference.

clutch (klŭch) *v.* to grasp and hold tightly

prodigy (prŏd'ə-jē) *n.* a person with an exceptional talent

liable (lī'ə-bəl) *adj.* likely to

---

4. **waxpaper lunches:** sandwiches wrapped in wax paper.

5. **Chopin's** (shō'pănz') **waltzes:** music by composer Frédéric Chopin.

smart, or take his allowance from him, or ask him where he got that great big pumpkin head. People are so stupid sometimes.

70   So I'm strolling down Broadway breathing out and breathing in on counts of seven, which is my lucky number, and here comes Gretchen and her **sidekicks:** Mary Louise, who used to be a friend of mine when she first moved to Harlem from Baltimore and got beat up by everybody till I took up for her on account of her mother and my mother used to sing in the same choir when they were young girls, but people ain't grateful, so now she hangs out with the new girl Gretchen and talks about me like a dog; and Rosie, who is as fat as I am skinny and has a big mouth where Raymond is concerned and is too stupid to know that there is not a big deal of difference between herself and Raymond and that she can't afford to throw stones. So they are steady coming up

80 Broadway and I see right away that it's going to be one of those Dodge City[6] scenes cause the street ain't that big and they're close to the buildings just as we are. First I think I'll step into the candy store and look over the new comics and let them pass. But that's chicken and I've got a reputation to consider. So then I think I'll just walk straight on through them or even over them if necessary. But as they get to me, they slow down. I'm ready to fight, cause like I said I don't feature a whole lot of chit-chat, I much prefer to just knock you down right from the jump and save everybody a lotta precious time. **C**

     "You signing up for the May Day races?" smiles Mary Louise, only it's not a smile at all. A dumb question like that doesn't deserve an answer. Besides,

90 there's just me and Gretchen standing there really, so no use wasting my breath talking to shadows.

     "I don't think you're going to win this time," says Rosie, trying to signify with her hands on her hips all salty, completely forgetting that I have whupped her behind many times for less salt than that.

     "I always win cause I'm the best," I say straight at Gretchen who is, as far as I'm concerned, the only one talking in this ventriloquist-dummy routine. Gretchen smiles, but it's not a smile, and I'm thinking that girls never really smile at each other because they don't know how and don't want to know how and there's probably no one to teach us how, cause grown-up girls don't know

100 either. Then they all look at Raymond who has just brought his mule team to a standstill. And they're about to see what trouble they can get into through him.

     "What grade you in now, Raymond?"

     "You got anything to say to my brother, you say it to me, Mary Louise Williams of Raggedy Town, Baltimore."

     "What are you, his mother?" sasses Rosie.

     "That's right, Fatso. And the next word out of anybody and I'll be *their* mother too." So they just stand there and Gretchen shifts from one leg to the other and so do they. Then Gretchen puts her hands on her hips and is about to say something with her freckle-face self but doesn't. Then she walks

sidekick (sĭd'kĭk') *n.*
a close friend

C PLOT: RISING ACTION
What is the conflict between Gretchen and Squeaky?

VISUAL VOCABULARY

ventriloquist-dummy *n.*
A ventriloquist controls his or her voice and moves the mouth of a puppet, or dummy, to make it appear to be talking.

---

6. **Dodge City:** an Old West town, famous for showdowns between outlaws and lawmen.

110 around me looking me up and down but keeps walking up Broadway, and her sidekicks follow her. So me and Raymond smile at each other and he says, "Gidyap" to his team and I continue with my breathing exercises, strolling down Broadway toward the ice man on 145th with not a care in the world cause I am Miss Quicksilver[7] herself.

I take my time getting to the park on May Day because the track meet is the last thing on the program. The biggest thing on the program is the May Pole dancing, which I can do without, thank you, even if my mother thinks it's a shame I don't take part and act like a girl for a change. You'd think my mother'd be grateful not to have to make me a white organdy dress with a big
120 satin sash and buy me new white baby-doll shoes that can't be taken out of the box till the big day. You'd think she'd be glad her daughter ain't out there prancing around a May Pole getting the new clothes all dirty and sweaty and trying to act like a fairy or a flower or whatever you're supposed to be when you should be trying to be yourself, whatever that is, which is, as far as I am concerned, a poor Black girl who really can't afford to buy shoes and a new dress you only wear once a lifetime cause it won't fit next year. **D**

I was once a strawberry in a Hansel and Gretel pageant when I was in nursery school and didn't have no better sense than to dance on tiptoe with my arms in a circle over my head doing umbrella steps and being a perfect fool just
130 so my mother and father could come dressed up and clap. You'd think they'd know better than to encourage that kind of nonsense. I am not a strawberry. I do not dance on my toes. I run. That is what I am all about. So I always come late to the May Day program, just in time to get my number pinned on and lay in the grass till they announce the fifty-yard dash.

I put Raymond in the little swings, which is a tight squeeze this year and will be impossible next year. Then I look around for Mr. Pearson, who pins the numbers on. I'm really looking for Gretchen, if you want to know the truth, but she's not around. The park is jam-packed. Parents in hats and corsages and breast-pocket handkerchiefs peeking up. Kids in white dresses
140 and light-blue suits. The parkees[8] unfolding chairs and chasing the rowdy kids from Lenox[9] as if they had no right to be there. The big guys with their caps on backwards, leaning against the fence swirling the basketballs on the tips of their fingers, waiting for all these crazy people to clear out the park so they can play. Most of the kids in my class are carrying bass drums and glockenspiels[10] and flutes. You'd think they'd put in a few bongos or something for real like that. **E**

Then here comes Mr. Pearson with his clipboard and his cards and pencils and whistles and safety pins and 50 million other things he's always dropping all over the place with his clumsy self. He sticks out in a crowd because he's

D MAKE INFERENCES
Reread lines 115–126. What do you think Squeaky's relationship with her mother is like?

E MAKE INFERENCES
Reread lines 135–136. How is Squeaky's life affected by having to take care of Raymond? Think about how she might deal with Raymond next year.

---

7. **Miss Quicksilver:** a reference to how fast quicksilver (mercury) flows.

8. **parkees:** people who regularly gather in the park.

9. **Lenox:** street in Harlem in New York City.

10. **glockenspiels** (glŏk´ən-spēlz´): musical instruments with tuned metal bars played with light hammers.

150 on stilts. We used to call him Jack and the Beanstalk to get him mad. But I'm the only one that can outrun him and get away, and I'm too grown for that silliness now.

"Well, Squeaky," he says, checking my name off the list and handing me number seven and two pins. And I'm thinking he's got no right to call me Squeaky, if I can't call him Beanstalk.

"Hazel Elizabeth Deborah Parker," I correct him and tell him to write it down on his board.

"Well, Hazel Elizabeth Deborah Parker, going to give someone else a break this year?" I squint at him real hard to see if he is seriously thinking I should 160 lose the race on purpose just to give someone else a break. "Only six girls running this time," he continues, shaking his head sadly like it's my fault all

▼ **Analyze Visuals**

How does the boy in this picture **compare** with the way you imagine Raymond?

of New York didn't turn out in sneakers. "That new girl should give you a run for your money." He looks around the park for Gretchen like a periscope[11] in a submarine movie. "Wouldn't it be a nice gesture if you were . . . to ahhh . . ."

I give him such a look he couldn't finish putting that idea into words. Grownups got a lot of nerve sometimes. I pin number seven to myself and stomp away, I'm so burnt. And I go straight for the track and stretch out on the grass while the band winds up with "Oh, the Monkey Wrapped His Tail Around the Flag Pole," which my teacher calls by some other name. The man
170 on the loudspeaker is calling everyone over to the track and I'm on my back looking at the sky, trying to pretend I'm in the country, but I can't, because even grass in the city feels hard as sidewalk, and there's just no pretending you are anywhere but in a "concrete jungle" as my grandfather says. ◆

The twenty-yard dash takes all of two minutes cause most of the little kids don't know no better than to run off the track or run the wrong way or run smack into the fence and fall down and cry. One little kid, though, has got the good sense to run straight for the white ribbon up ahead so he wins. Then the second-graders line up for the thirty-yard dash and I don't even bother to turn my head to watch cause Raphael Perez always wins. He wins before he
180 even begins by psyching the runners, telling them they're going to trip on their shoelaces and fall on their faces or lose their shorts or something, which he doesn't really have to do since he is very fast, almost as fast as I am. After that is the forty-yard dash which I used to run when I was in first grade. Raymond is hollering from the swings cause he knows I'm about to do my thing cause the man on the loudspeaker has just announced the fifty-yard dash, although he might just as well be giving a recipe for angel food cake cause you can hardly make out what he's sayin for the static. I get up and slip off my sweat pants and then I see Gretchen standing at the starting line, kicking her legs out like a pro. Then as I get into place I see that ole Raymond is on line on
190 the other side of the fence, bending down with his fingers on the ground just like he knew what he was doing. I was going to yell at him but then I didn't. It burns up your energy to holler. 🅕

Every time, just before I take off in a race, I always feel like I'm in a dream, the kind of dream you have when you're sick with fever and feel all hot and weightless. I dream I'm flying over a sandy beach in the early morning sun, kissing the leaves of the trees as I fly by. And there's always the smell of apples, just like in the country when I was little and used to think I was a choo-choo train, running through the fields of corn and chugging up the hill to the orchard. And all the time I'm dreaming this, I get lighter and lighter until I'm
200 flying over the beach again, getting blown through the sky like a feather that weighs nothing at all. But once I spread my fingers in the dirt and **crouch** over the Get on Your Mark, the dream goes and I am solid again and am telling

◆ **GRAMMAR IN CONTEXT**
Line 165 is a complete sentence because it contains both a subject and a predicate. A **sentence fragment** would be missing one of these two elements.

🅕 **PLOT: RISING ACTION**
What details in this paragraph increase the excitement and tension?

crouch v. to stoop with bent knees

---

11. **periscope:** a tube with mirrors or prisms inside through which a person can see the reflection of an object at the other end.

myself, Squeaky you must win, you must win, you are the fastest thing in the world, you can even beat your father up Amsterdam if you really try. **G** And then I feel my weight coming back just behind my knees then down to my feet then into the earth and the pistol shot explodes in my blood and I am off and weightless again, flying past the other runners, my arms pumping up and down and the whole world is quiet except for the crunch as I zoom over the gravel in the track. I glance to my left and there is no one. To the right, a

210 blurred Gretchen, who's got her chin jutting out as if it would win the race all by itself. And on the other side of the fence is Raymond with his arms down to his side and the palms tucked up behind him, running in his very own style, and it's the first time I ever saw that and I almost stop to watch my brother Raymond on his first run. But the white ribbon is bouncing toward me and I tear past it, racing into the distance till my feet with a mind of their own start digging up footfuls of dirt and brake me short. Then all the kids standing on the side pile on me, banging me on the back and slapping my head with their May Day programs, for I have won again and everybody on 151st Street can walk tall for another year.

220 "In first place . . ." the man on the loudspeaker is clear as a bell now. But then he pauses and the loudspeaker starts to whine. Then static. And I lean down to catch my breath and here comes Gretchen walking back, for she's overshot the finish line too, huffing and puffing with her hands on her hips taking it slow, breathing in steady time like a real pro and I sort of like her a little for the first time. "In first place . . ." and then three or four voices get all mixed up on the loudspeaker and I dig my sneaker into the grass and stare at Gretchen who's staring back, we both wondering just who did win. I can hear old Beanstalk arguing with the man on the loudspeaker and then a few others running their mouths about what the stopwatches say. Then I hear Raymond

230 yanking at the fence to call me and I wave to shush him, but he keeps rattling the fence like a gorilla in a cage like in them gorilla movies, but then like a dancer or something he starts climbing up nice and easy but very fast. And it occurs to me, watching how smoothly he climbs hand over hand and remembering how he looked running with his arms down to his side and with the wind pulling his mouth back and his teeth showing and all, it occurred to me that Raymond would make a very fine runner. Doesn't he always keep up with me on my trots? And he surely knows how to breathe in counts of seven cause he's always doing it at the dinner table, which drives my brother George up the wall. And I'm smiling to beat the band cause if I've lost this race, or if

240 me and Gretchen tied, or even if I've won, I can always retire as a runner and begin a whole new career as a coach with Raymond as my champion. After all, with a little more study I can beat Cynthia and her phony self at the spelling bee. And if I bugged my mother, I could get piano lessons and become a star. And I have a big rep as the baddest thing around. And I've got a roomful of ribbons and medals and awards. But what has Raymond got to call his own? **H**

G MAKE INFERENCES
Why do you think Squeaky always feels this way before a race?

Language Coach

Similes A simile is a comparison using the words *like* or *as*. Reread line 220. A simile compares the voice on the loudspeaker to the sound of a bell. Would it be easy or hard to hear a voice that is "clear as a bell"?

H PLOT: CLIMAX
What decision does Squeaky make as she waits for the announcement? Note what incidents influence this decision.

◄ Analyze Visuals

What can you **infer** about how the girl in red feels about herself? Tell what clues you used to make your inference.

So I stand there with my new plans, laughing out loud by this time as Raymond jumps down from the fence and runs over with his teeth showing and his arms down to the side, which no one before him has quite mastered as a running style. And by the time he comes over I'm jumping up and down so
250 glad to see him—my brother Raymond, a great runner in the family tradition. But of course everyone thinks I'm jumping up and down because the men on the loudspeaker have finally gotten themselves together and compared notes and are announcing, "In first place—Miss Hazel Elizabeth Deborah Parker." (Dig that.) "In second place—Miss Gretchen P. Lewis." And I look over at Gretchen wondering what the "P" stands for. And I smile. Cause she's good, no doubt about it. Maybe she'd like to help me coach Raymond; she obviously is serious about running, as any fool can see. And she nods to congratulate me and then she smiles. And I smile. We stand there with this big smile of respect between us. It's about as real a smile as girls can do for each other, considering
260 we don't practice real smiling every day, you know, cause maybe we too busy being flowers or fairies or strawberries instead of something honest and worthy of respect . . . you know . . . like being people. ∽ ❶

❶ **PLOT: FALLING ACTION AND RESOLUTION**
How does Squeaky react to the announcement that she won the race?

Comprehension

COMMON CORE

RL 1 Cite the evidence that supports inferences drawn from the text.
RL 3 Analyze how incidents in a story propel the action or provoke a decision.

1. **Recall** What nickname have the big kids given Squeaky, and why?

2. **Clarify** Why does Squeaky feel the May Pole dance is a waste of time?

3. **Clarify** Describe Squeaky's reaction when she sees Raymond running parallel to her in the race.

Text Analysis

4. **Make Inferences** Review the inference equations you created as you read the story. Use these **inferences** to answer this question: Why might Squeaky react to other people the way she does? Support your answer.

5. **Compare and Contrast** What are some differences between Squeaky and Gretchen? What are some similarities?

6. **Analyze Plot** The plot of "Raymond's Run" revolves around Squeaky's desire to win the May Day race. Using a diagram like the one shown, note the events that happen at each stage of the **plot**. How is the conflict resolved?

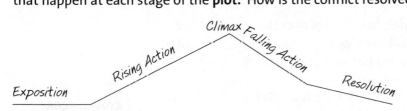

7. **Draw Conclusions** How do the events in the story change the way Squeaky views competition?

8. **Evaluate Plot** A plot should be suspenseful, coherent, well-paced, and satisfying. What is your evaluation of the plot of "Raymond's Run"? Be sure to assess the climax and resolution of the story as well as the other structural elements of the plot.

Extension and Challenge

9. **Inquiry and Research** According to Squeaky, Raymond has a "big head." Find out more about hydrocephalus, the condition he has. With the medical advances of today, is there a treatment or cure for hydrocephalus? What is known about the causes of it? Present your findings to the class.

What's worth the EFFORT?

Review the Quickwrite activity on page 36. If Squeaky were in your class, what do you think her respose to this activity would be? Make sure you explain her motivation.

Vocabulary in Context

▲ VOCABULARY PRACTICE

Answer each question to show your understanding of the vocabulary words.

1. Is a **sidekick** likely to be a friend or someone you just met?
2. If you were to **clutch** something, would you be tossing it away or holding it close?
3. Which would you expect a sports **prodigy** to be—clumsy or talented?
4. When are you more likely to **crouch**—picking a flower from the garden or reaching for a glass in the cabinet?
5. If a person is **liable** to do something, does that mean it's likely or unlikely to happen?
6. What's more important in a **relay** race—one good runner or a team effort?

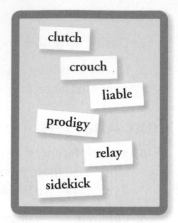

ACADEMIC VOCABULARY IN WRITING

> • affect   • conclude   • evident   • imply   • initial

How does Squeaky's attitude toward Gretchen change over the course of the story? Using at least one Academic Vocabulary word, compare Squeaky's **initial** reaction to Gretchen to her feelings toward her rival at the end of the story.

VOCABULARY STRATEGY: FOREIGN WORDS IN ENGLISH

The English language includes words from diverse languages, including French, German, Spanish, Japanese, and many others. In "Raymond's Run," Squeaky uses a foreign word when she says, "I used to win the twenty-yard dash when I was in kindergarten." *Kindergarten* is borrowed from German. Dictionary entries include a word's origin.

PRACTICE For each sentence, identify the word that comes from a foreign language. Use a dictionary to find the word's origin, and write it next to the word.

1. His directions were vague, and we got lost trying to follow them.
2. She liked to sing karaoke, but she didn't like to sing with a band.
3. When skateboarding becomes passé, he'll move on to another sport.
4. They went to see their sister perform at the rodeo.
5. He liked sauerkraut on his hotdog.

 COMMON CORE

L 6 Use accurately grade-appropriate words.

Interactive Vocabulary   **THINK** central

Go to **thinkcentral.com**.
KEYWORD: HML8-48

Language

◆ **GRAMMAR IN CONTEXT:** Avoid Sentence Fragments

Review the **Grammar in Context** anno on page 44. A **sentence fragment** is an incomplete sentence. It is missing a subject (whom or what the sentence is about), a predicate (what the subject is or does), or both. The missing part(s) must be added in order to fix, or complete, the sentence.

Original:	My brother. (*This is a sentence fragment because it is missing a predicate.*) He likes movies with a lot of action.
Revised:	My brother likes movies with a lot of action. (*This is now a complete sentence because it contains the subject "My brother" and the predicate "likes movies with a lot of action."*)

PRACTICE Decide whether the following sentence fragments in bold are missing a subject, a predicate, or both. Then combine each fragment with the sentence before it, inserting any additional words as needed.

1. The crowd gathered in the park. **For the May Day festivities.**
2. They gathered, as usual. **The regulars, or parkees.**
3. For many, the May Pole dance is the highlight. **For others, the races.**
4. I'm sure I'll win again. **Always do.**
5. He was the surprise of the day. **Squeaky's brother Raymond.**

*For more help with fragments, see page R64 in the **Grammar Handbook.***

READING-WRITING CONNECTION

Increase your understanding of "Raymond's Run" by responding to this prompt. Then use the **revising tip** to improve your writing.

WRITING PROMPT	REVISING TIP
Extended Constructed Response: Article Imagine you are a newspaper writer covering the May Day events at the park. Write a **two- or three-paragraph** article that will appear in the next day's paper. Be sure to tell where and when events took place, who participated, and what happened.	Review your article. If you have used any sentence fragments, add the missing parts to make your sentences complete.

Interactive Revision **THINK** central

Go to **thinkcentral.com**.
KEYWORD: HML8-49

COMMON CORE

L1 Demonstrate command of standard English grammar when writing. **L3** Use knowledge of language when writing. **W2** Write informative texts.

The Ransom of Red Chief
Short Story by O. Henry

Is any plan
FOOLPROOF?

COMMON CORE

RL 3 Analyze how dialogue or incidents in a story propel the action and reveal aspects of a character. **L 5b** Use the relationship between particular words to better understand each of the words.

You can make a list. You can check it twice. You can go over every last detail of a plan in your mind. But even when you think you've thought of everything, the unexpected can change the outcome in surprising, terrible, or sometimes hysterically funny ways. In the story you are about to read, the main characters have a plan for making some quick money, but things don't work out the way they had hoped.

LIST IT With a partner, plan a surprise party for a friend by making a list of what you need to do. Then, next to each item, write down something unexpected that could possibly happen to spoil that part of the plan.

Lu's Party!

| E-mail our group to invite them. | Forget to take Lu off the list. |

● TEXT ANALYSIS: CONFLICT AND RESOLUTION

A story's plot centers on **conflicts,** or struggles between opposing forces. By the end of the story, the conflicts are usually **resolved,** or settled. For example, a fight between two characters might be resolved when one character wins and one character loses. As you read "The Ransom of Red Chief," pay attention to the conflicts and note how they are resolved.

● READING STRATEGY: PREDICT

One way to monitor your understanding is by making **predictions**, or guesses about what will happen next. As you read this story, use clues from the text and your own common sense to make predictions. Keep track of whether your predictions were right, or whether you were surprised by the way events unfolded.

My Prediction	Actual Event	Correct or Surprised?
The boy will fight back when kidnapped.	Boy fights back	correct

Review: **Make Inferences**

▲ VOCABULARY IN CONTEXT

O. Henry's characters use the words listed, but the characters aren't as smart as their big vocabulary suggests. See how many words you can match with their numbered definitions.

WORD LIST		
collaborate	diatribe	provisions
commend	impudent	ransom
comply	proposition	

1. payment demanded for the release of a person or property
2. to act according to a command or request
3. verbal attack; harsh criticism
4. bold and disrespectful
5. to work together on a project
6. to praise
7. necessary supplies, especially food
8. a suggested plan

Complete the activities in your **Reader/Writer Notebook.**

Meet the Author

O. Henry
1862–1910

Unexpected Twists
The early life of O. Henry, whose real name was William Sydney Porter, was filled with ups, downs, and unexpected turns. As a young man, he held many different jobs. He clerked in his uncle's drugstore, worked as a ranch hand, and became a bank teller. Several years after leaving his position at the bank, he was convicted of having embezzled, or stolen, money from his employer. It certainly wasn't his plan to be put in jail, but that's where he found his next occupation.

A Trailblazing Storyteller
While behind bars, Porter began penning stories to help support his young daughter. Upon his release, he changed his name to O. Henry, became a fiction writer, and contributed weekly stories to newspapers. He grew into one of the country's best-loved authors. O. Henry wrote adventure stories, humorous stories, and slice-of-life tales of ordinary people. The stories often had surprise endings. Today, stories that end with an unexpected twist are said to be written in the "O. Henry style."

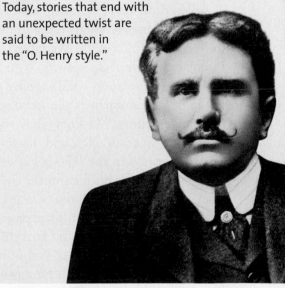

Authors Online
Go to thinkcentral.com. KEYWORD: HML8-51
THINK central

THE RANSOM OF RED CHIEF

O. HENRY

It looked like a good thing; but wait till I tell you. We were down South, in Alabama—Bill Driscoll and myself—when this kidnapping idea struck us. It was, as Bill afterward expressed it, "during a moment of temporary mental apparition";[1] but we didn't find that out till later.

There was a town down there, as flat as a flannel-cake, and called Summit, of course. It contained inhabitants of as undeleterious[2] and self-satisfied a class of peasantry as ever clustered around a Maypole.

Bill and me had a joint capital of about six hundred dollars, and we needed just two thousand dollars more to pull off a fraudulent town-lot scheme
10 in Western Illinois with. We talked it over on the front steps of the hotel. Philoprogenitiveness,[3] says we, is strong in semi-rural communities; therefore, and for other reasons, a kidnapping project ought to do better there than in the radius of newspapers that send reporters out in plain clothes to stir up talk about such things. We knew that Summit couldn't get after us with anything stronger than constables, and, maybe, some lackadaisical bloodhounds and a **diatribe** or two in the *Weekly Farmers' Budget*. So, it looked good.

We selected for our victim the only child of a prominent citizen named Ebenezer Dorset. The father was respectable and tight, a mortgage fancier and a stern, upright collection-plate passer and forecloser. The kid was a boy of ten,
20 with bas-relief[4] freckles, and hair the color of the cover of the magazine you buy at the news-stand when you want to catch a train. Bill and me figured that Ebenezer would melt down for a **ransom** of two thousand dollars to a cent. But wait till I tell you. **A**

1. **apparition** (ăp'ə-rĭsh'ən): a sudden or unusual sight.
2. **undeleterious** (ŭn-dĕl'ĭ-tîr'ē-əs): harmless.
3. **philoprogenitiveness** (fĭl'ō-prō-jĕn'ĭ-tĭv-nĕs): love for one's own children.
4. **bas-relief** (bä'rĭ-lēf'): slightly raised.

Analyze Visuals ▶
What personality **traits** might the boy in the painting possess?

diatribe (dī'ə-trīb') *n.* bitter, abusive criticism

ransom (răn'səm) *n.* payment demanded for the release of a person or property

A PREDICT
Reread lines 17–23. Based on Sam's final comment, do you think the men's plan will be successful? Add this prediction to your chart.

Illustrations by Esao Andrews.

About two miles from Summit was a little mountain, covered with a dense cedar brake.[5] On the rear elevation of this mountain was a cave. There we stored **provisions.**

One evening after sundown, we drove in a buggy past old Dorset's house. The kid was in the street, throwing rocks at a kitten on the opposite fence.

"Hey, little boy!" says Bill, "would you like to have a bag of candy and a
30 nice ride?"

The boy catches Bill neatly in the eye with a piece of brick.

"That will cost the old man an extra five hundred dollars," says Bill, climbing over the wheel.

That boy put up a fight like a welter-weight cinnamon bear; but, at last, we got him down in the bottom of the buggy and drove away. We took him up to the cave, and I hitched the horse in the cedar brake. After dark I drove the buggy to the little village, three miles away, where we had hired it, and walked back to the mountain. **B**

Bill was pasting court plaster[6] over the scratches and bruises on his features.
40 There was a fire burning behind the big rock at the entrance of the cave, and the boy was watching a pot of boiling coffee, with two buzzard tail feathers stuck in his red hair. He points a stick at me when I come up, and says:

"Ha! cursed paleface, do you dare to enter the camp of Red Chief, the terror of the plains?" **C**

"He's all right now," says Bill, rolling up his trousers and examining some bruises on his shins. "We're playing Indian. We're making Buffalo Bill's show look like magic-lantern views[7] of Palestine in the town hall. I'm Old Hank, the Trapper, Red Chief's captive, and I'm to be scalped at daybreak. By Geronimo! that kid can kick hard."

50 Yes, sir, that boy seemed to be having the time of his life. The fun of camping out in a cave had made him forget that he was a captive himself. He immediately christened me Snake-eye, the Spy, and announced that, when his braves returned from the warpath, I was to be broiled at the stake at the rising of the sun.

Then we had supper; and he filled his mouth full of bacon and bread and gravy, and began to talk. He made a during-dinner speech something like this:

"I like this fine. I never camped out before; but I had a pet 'possum once, and I was nine last birthday. I hate to go to school. Rats ate up sixteen of Jimmy Talbot's aunt's speckled hen's eggs. Are there any real Indians in these
60 woods? I want some more gravy. Does the trees moving make the wind blow? We had five puppies. What makes your nose so red, Hank? My father has lots of money. Are the stars hot? I whipped Ed Walker twice, Saturday. I don't like girls. You dassent[8] catch toads unless with a string. Do oxen make any noise?

provisions (prə-vĭzh'ənz) *n.* necessary supplies; food

COMMON CORE RL 3

B CONFLICT
Remember that a conflict can exist between characters, between characters and society, between characters and nature, or within a single character. As the plot develops, the nature of the conflict can shift, although it does not always. Who is in conflict at this point in the story?

C PREDICT
How do you think the boy will respond to being held in captivity?

---

5. **brake:** a thick grouping of trees.

6. **court plaster:** adhesive cloth for covering cuts and scratches.

7. **magic-lantern views:** slides.

8. **dassant:** dare not.

Why are oranges round? Have you got beds to sleep on in this cave? Amos Murray has got six toes. A parrot can talk, but a monkey or a fish can't. How many does it take to make twelve?" **D**

Every few minutes he would remember that he was an Indian, and pick up his stick rifle and tiptoe to the mouth of the cave to search for the scouts of the hated paleface. Now and then he would let out a war whoop that made Old
70 Hank the Trapper shiver. That boy had Bill terrorized from the start.

"Red Chief," says I to the kid, "would you like to go home?"

"Aw, what for?" says he. "I don't have any fun at home. I hate to go to school. I like to camp out. You won't take me back home again, Snake-eye, will you?"

"Not right away," says I. "We'll stay here in the cave awhile."

"All right!" says he. "That'll be fine. I never had such fun in all my life."

We went to bed about eleven o'clock. We spread down some wide blankets and quilts and put Red Chief between us. We weren't afraid he'd run away. He kept us awake for three hours, jumping up and reaching for his rifle and screeching: "Hist! pard," in mine and Bill's ears, as the fancied crackle of
80 a twig or the rustle of a leaf revealed to his young imagination the stealthy approach of the outlaw band. At last, I fell into a troubled sleep, and dreamed that I had been kidnapped and chained to a tree by a ferocious pirate with red hair.

Just at daybreak, I was awakened by a series of awful screams from Bill. They weren't yells, or howls, or shouts, or whoops, or yawps, such as you'd expect from a manly set of vocal organs—they were simply indecent, terrifying, humiliating screams, such as women emit when they see ghosts or caterpillars. It's an awful thing to hear a strong, desperate, fat man scream incontinently in a cave at daybreak.
90 I jumped up to see what the matter was. Red Chief was sitting on Bill's chest, with one hand twined in Bill's hair. In the other he had the sharp case-knife we used for slicing bacon; and he was industriously and realistically trying to take Bill's scalp, according to the sentence that had been pronounced upon him the evening before.

I got the knife away from the kid and made him lie down again. But, from that moment, Bill's spirit was broken. He laid down on his side of the bed, but he never closed an eye again in sleep as long as that boy was with us. I dozed off for a while, but along toward sun-up I remembered that Red Chief had said I was to be burned at the stake at the rising of the sun. I wasn't nervous or
100 afraid; but I sat up and leaned against a rock. **E**

"What you getting up so soon for, Sam?" asked Bill.

"Me?" says I. "Oh, I got a kind of a pain in my shoulder. I thought sitting up would rest it."

"You're a liar!" says Bill. "You're afraid. You was to be burned at sunrise, and you was afraid he'd do it. And he would, too, if he could find a match. Ain't it awful, Sam? Do you think anybody will pay out money to get a little imp like that back home?"

D PREDICT
On your chart, note whether the boy's response to captivity matches your prediction. Do you think the boy's current attitude about his captivity will make the men's plan go more smoothly?

COMMON CORE L 5b
Language Coach
Synonyms Synonyms are words that are similar in meaning. Sometimes writers include synonyms within a sentence. If you know one of the words, you can figure out the others. In the sentence that begins in line 85, which words are synonyms for *howl?*

E CONFLICT
In what way has his interaction with the boy affected Bill?

"Sure," said I. "A rowdy kid like that is just the kind that parents dote on. Now, you and the Chief get up and cook breakfast, while I go up on the top of 110 this mountain and reconnoiter."[9]

I went up on the peak of the little mountain and ran my eye over the contiguous vicinity. Over toward Summit I expected to see the sturdy yeomanry of the village armed with scythes and pitchforks beating the countryside for the dastardly kidnappers. But what I saw was a peaceful landscape dotted with one man plowing with a dun mule. Nobody was dragging the creek; no couriers dashed hither and yon, bringing tidings of no news to the distracted parents. There was a sylvan[10] attitude of somnolent sleepiness pervading that section of the external outward surface of Alabama that lay exposed to my view. "Perhaps," says I to myself, "it has not yet been 120 discovered that the wolves have borne away the tender lambkin from the fold. Heaven help the wolves!" says I, and I went down the mountain to breakfast. ◆

When I got to the cave I found Bill backed up against the side of it, breathing hard, and the boy threatening to smash him with a rock half as big as a coconut.

"He put a red-hot boiled potato down my back," explained Bill, "and then mashed it with his foot; and I boxed his ears. Have you got a gun about you, Sam?"

I took the rock away from the boy and kind of patched up the argument. "I'll fix you," says the kid to Bill. "No man ever yet struck the Red Chief but 130 what he got paid for it. You better beware!"

---

9. **reconnoiter** (rē′kə-noi′tər): to seek information about an enemy's whereabouts.
10. **sylvan** (sĭl′vən): like woods or forests.

◆ **GRAMMAR IN CONTEXT**
Reread the sentence that begins in line 115 with "Nobody was ...." Notice how the two independent clauses are separated by a semicolon. Without the semicolon, the sentence would be a **run-on sentence**.

▼ **Analyze Visuals**
Who seems to be winning the **conflict** in the painting? Tell how you know.

After breakfast the kid takes a piece of leather with strings wrapped around it out of his pocket and goes outside the cave unwinding it.

"What's he up to now?" says Bill anxiously. "You don't think he'll run away, do you, Sam?" **F**

"No fear of it," says I. "He don't seem to be much of a homebody. But we've got to fix up some plan about the ransom. There don't seem to be much excitement around Summit on account of his disappearance; but maybe they haven't realized yet that he's gone. His folks may think he's spending the night with Aunt Jane or one of the neighbors. Anyhow, he'll be missed today.
140 Tonight we must get a message to his father demanding the two thousand dollars for his return."

Just then we heard a kind of war whoop, such as David might have emitted when he knocked out the champion Goliath. It was a sling that Red Chief had pulled out of his pocket, and he was whirling it around his head.

I dodged, and heard a heavy thud and a kind of a sigh from Bill, like a horse gives out when you take his saddle off. A rock the size of an egg had caught Bill just behind his left ear. He loosened himself all over and fell in the fire across the frying pan of hot water for washing the dishes. I dragged him out and poured cold water on his head for half an hour.

150 By and by, Bill sits up and feels behind his ear and says: "Sam, do you know who my favorite Biblical character is?"

"Take it easy," says I. "You'll come to your senses presently."

"King Herod,"[11] says he. "You won't go away and leave me here alone, will you, Sam?"

I went out and caught that boy and shook him until his freckles rattled.

"If you don't behave," says I, "I'll take you straight home. Now, are you going to be good, or not?"

"I was only funning," says he, sullenly. "I didn't mean to hurt Old Hank. But what did he hit me for? I'll behave, Snake-eye, if you won't send me home,
160 and if you'll let me play the Scout today." **G**

"I don't know the game," says I. "That's for you and Mr. Bill to decide. He's your playmate for the day. I'm going away for a while, on business. Now, you come in and make friends with him and say you are sorry for hurting him, or home you go, at once." **H**

I made him and Bill shake hands, and then I took Bill aside and told him I was going to Poplar Cove, a little village three miles from the cave, and find out what I could about how the kidnapping had been regarded in Summit. Also, I thought it best to send a peremptory letter to old man Dorset that day, demanding the ransom and dictating how it should be paid.
170 "You know, Sam," says Bill, "I've stood by you without batting an eye in earthquakes, fire, and flood—in poker games, dynamite outrages, police raids, train robberies, and cyclones. I never lost my nerve yet till we kidnapped that

F MAKE INFERENCES
How do you think Bill is starting to feel about the plan to get two thousand dollars?

G PREDICT
Do you expect that the boy will behave better going forward? Add the prediction to your chart.

H CONFLICT
In what ways has the conflict changed since the beginning of the story? Note the incidents that have caused this change to occur.

---

11. **King Herod:** an ancient king of Judea who once ordered the execution of all Bethlehem boys under the age of two.

two-legged skyrocket of a kid. He's got me going. You won't leave me long with him, will you, Sam?"

"I'll be back sometime this afternoon," says I. "You must keep the boy amused and quiet till I return. And now we'll write the letter to old Dorset."

Bill and I got paper and pencil and worked on the letter while Red Chief, with a blanket wrapped around him, strutted up and down, guarding the mouth of the cave. Bill begged me tearfully to make the ransom fifteen
180 hundred dollars instead of two thousand. "I ain't attempting," says he, "to decry[12] the celebrated moral aspect of parental affection, but we're dealing with humans, and it ain't human for anybody to give up two thousand dollars for that forty-pound chunk of freckled wildcat. I'm willing to take a chance at fifteen hundred dollars. You can charge the difference up to me."

So, to relieve Bill, I acceded, and we **collaborated** a letter that ran this way:

EBENEZER DORSET, ESQ.:
We have your boy concealed in a place far from Summit. It is useless for you or the most skillful detectives to attempt to find him. Absolutely, the only terms on which you can have him restored to you are these: We demand
190 fifteen hundred dollars in large bills for his return: the money to be left at midnight at the same spot and in the same box as your reply—as hereinafter described. If you agree to these terms, send your answer in writing by a solitary messenger tonight at half-past eight o'clock. After crossing Owl Creek on the road to Poplar Cove, there are three large trees about a hundred yards apart, close to the fence of the wheat field on the right-hand side. At the bottom of the fence post, opposite the third tree, will be found a small pasteboard box.

The messenger will place the answer in this box and return immediately to Summit.
200 If you attempt any treachery or fail to **comply** with our demand as stated, you will never see your boy again.

If you pay the money as demanded, he will be returned to you safe and well within three hours. These terms are final, and if you do not accede to them no further communication will be attempted.

TWO DESPERATE MEN. ❶

I addressed this letter to Dorset and put it in my pocket. As I was about to start, the kid comes up to me and says:

"Aw, Snake-eye, you said I could play the Scout while you was gone."

"Play it, of course," says I. "Mr. Bill will play with you. What kind of a
210 game is it?"

"I'm the Scout," says Red Chief, "and I have to ride to the stockade to warn the settlers that the Indians are coming. I'm tired of playing Indian myself. I want to be the Scout."

---

collaborate
(kə-lăb′ə-rāt′) *v.* to work together on a project

comply (kəm-plī′) *v.* to act according to a command or request

❶ **PREDICT**
How do you think the boy's father will respond to the men's demands? Add the prediction to your chart.

---

12. **decry:** to criticize.

"All right," says I. "It sounds harmless to me. I guess Mr. Bill will help you foil the enemy."

"What am I to do?" asks Bill, looking at the kid suspiciously.

"You are the hoss," says Scout. "Get down on your hands and knees. How can I ride to the stockade without a hoss?"

"You'd better keep him interested," said I, "till we get the scheme going. 220 Loosen up."

Bill gets down on his all fours, and a look comes in his eye like a rabbit's when you catch it in a trap.

"How far is it to the stockade, kid?" he asks, in a husky manner of voice.

"Ninety miles," says the Scout. "And you have to hurry to get there on time. Whoa, now!"

The Scout jumps on Bill's back and digs his heels in his side.

"For Heaven's sake," says Bill, "hurry back, Sam, as soon as you can. I wish we hadn't made the ransom more than a thousand. Say, you quit kicking me or I'll get up and warm you good." **J**

230 I walked over to Poplar Cove and sat around the post office and store, talking with the chawbacons that came in to trade. One whiskerando says that he hears Summit is all upset on account of Elder Ebenezer Dorset's boy having been lost or stolen. That was all I wanted to know. I referred casually to the price of black-eyed peas, posted my letter surreptitiously and came away. The postmaster said the mail carrier would come by in an hour to take the mail on to Summit. **K**

When I got back to the cave Bill and the boy were not to be found. I explored the vicinity of the cave, and risked a yodel or two, but there was no response.

240 So I sat down on a mossy bank to await developments.

In about half an hour I heard the bushes rustle, and Bill wabbled out into the little glade in front of the cave. Behind him was the kid, stepping softly like a scout, with a broad grin on his face. Bill stopped, took off his hat and wiped his face with a red handkerchief. The kid stopped about eight feet behind him.

"Sam," says Bill, "I suppose you think I'm a renegade, but I couldn't help it. I'm a grown person with masculine proclivities and habits of self-defense, but there is a time when all systems of egotism and predominance fail. The boy is gone. I have sent him home. All is off. There was martyrs in old times,"
250 goes on Bill, "that suffered death rather than give up the particular graft they enjoyed. None of 'em ever was subjugated to such supernatural tortures as I have been. I tried to be faithful to our articles of depredation;[13] but there came a limit." **L**

"What's the trouble, Bill?" I asks him.

"I was rode," says Bill, "the ninety miles to the stockade, not barring an inch. Then, when the settlers was rescued, I was given oats. Sand ain't a

---

13. **depredation** (dĕp'rĭ-dā'shən): robbery.

Language Coach

Multiple Meaning Words Multiple Meaning Words have more than one meaning. The word *foil* in line 215 can mean "to prevent from being successful" or "a thin piece of metal." Which meaning of *foil* is correct in line 215?

J **CONFLICT**
Who seems to be winning the struggle?

K **PREDICT**
What do you think will happen now that the letter has been posted?

L **CONFLICT**
Reread lines 241–253. Bill thinks the conflict has been resolved. What details let the reader know that he is wrong?

palatable substitute. And then, for an hour I had to try to explain to him why there was nothin' in holes, how a road can run both ways and what makes the grass green. I tell you, Sam, a human can only stand so much. I takes him by the neck of his clothes and drags him down the mountain. On the way he kicks my legs black and blue from the knees down; and I've got to have two or three bites on my thumb and hand cauterized.[14]

"But he's gone"—continues Bill—"gone home. I showed him the road to Summit and kicked him about eight feet nearer there at one kick. I'm sorry we lose the ransom; but it was either that or Bill Driscoll to the madhouse."

Bill is puffing and blowing, but there is a look of ineffable peace and growing content on his rose-pink features.

"Bill," says I, "there isn't any heart disease in your family, is there?"

"No," says Bill, "nothing chronic except malaria and accidents. Why?"

"Then you might turn around," says I, "and have a look behind you."

Bill turns and sees the boy, and loses his complexion and sits down plump on the ground and begins to pluck aimlessly at grass and little sticks. For an hour I was afraid of his mind. And then I told him that my scheme was to put the whole job through immediately and that we would get the ransom and be off with it by midnight if old Dorset fell in with our **proposition.** So Bill braced up enough to give the kid a weak sort of a smile and a promise to play the Russian in a Japanese war with him as soon as he felt a little better.

I had a scheme for collecting that ransom without danger of being caught by counterplots that ought to **commend** itself to professional kidnappers. The tree under which the answer was to be left—and the money later on—was close to the road fence with big, bare fields on all sides. If a gang of constables should be watching for anyone to come for the note they could see him a long way off crossing the fields or in the road. But no, sirree! At half-past eight I was up in that tree as well hidden as a tree toad, waiting for the messenger to arrive.

Exactly on time, a half-grown boy rides up the road on a bicycle, locates the pasteboard box at the foot of the fence post, slips a folded piece of paper into it and pedals away again back toward Summit.

I waited an hour and then concluded the thing was square. I slid down the tree, got the note, slipped along the fence till I struck the woods, and was back at the cave in another half an hour. I opened the note, got near the lantern,

proposition
(prŏp′ə-zĭsh′ən) *n.*
a suggested plan

commend (kə-mĕnd′)
v. to speak highly of; to praise; to recommend

---

14. **cauterized** (kô′tə-rīzd′): burned a wound to stop bleeding.

300 and read it to Bill. It was written with a pen in a crabbed hand, and the sum and substance of it was this:

> TWO DESPERATE MEN.
> GENTLEMEN: I received your letter today by post, in regard to the ransom you ask for the return of my son. I think you are a little high in your demands, and I hereby make you a counter-proposition, which I am inclined to believe you will accept. You bring Johnny home and pay me two hundred and fifty dollars in cash, and I agree to take him off your hands. You had better come at night, for the neighbors believe he is lost, and I couldn't be responsible for what they would do to anybody they saw bringing him back.
310
>   Very respectfully,
>   EBENEZER DORSET. **M**

"Great Pirates of Penzance!" says I; "of all the **impudent**—"

But I glanced at Bill, and hesitated. He had the most appealing look in his eyes I ever saw on the face of a dumb or a talking brute.

"Sam," says he, "what's two hundred and fifty dollars, after all? We've got the money. One more night of this kid will send me to bed in Bedlam.[15] Besides being a thorough gentleman, I think Mr. Dorset is a spendthrift for making us such a liberal offer. You ain't going to let the chance go, are you?"

"Tell you the truth, Bill," says I, "this little he ewe lamb has somewhat
320 got on my nerves, too. We'll take him home, pay the ransom, and make our getaway." **N**

We took him home that night. We got him to go by telling him that his father had bought a silver-mounted rifle and a pair of moccasins for him, and we were going to hunt bears the next day.

It was just twelve o'clock when we knocked at Ebenezer's front door. Just at the moment when I should have been abstracting the fifteen hundred dollars from the box under the tree, according to the original proposition, Bill was counting out two hundred and fifty dollars into Dorset's hand.

When the kid found out we were going to leave him at home he started up
330 a howl like a calliope[16] and fastened himself as tight as a leech to Bill's leg. His father peeled him away gradually, like a porous plaster.

"How long can you hold him?" asks Bill.

"I'm not as strong as I used to be," says old Dorset, "but I think I can promise you ten minutes."

"Enough," says Bill. "In ten minutes I shall cross the Central, Southern, and Middle Western States, and be legging it trippingly for the Canadian border."

And, as dark as it was, and as fat as Bill was, and as good a runner as I am, he was a good mile and a half out of Summit before I could catch up with him. ∾ **O**

M MAKE INFERENCES
Reread the note from Ebenezer Dorset. From this passage, what can you infer about how well he knows his son?

impudent
(ĭm'pyə-dənt) *adj.* bold and disrespectful

N CONFLICT AND RESOLUTION
Who wins out in the conflict between the kidnappers and the boy's father?

O CONFLICT AND RESOLUTION
How is the conflict between the men and the boy finally resolved?

---

15. **Bedlam:** an insane asylum.
16. **calliope** (kə-lī'ə-pē'): an instrument with steam whistles.

ANECDOTE O. Henry was a master of unexpected plot twists. In the following anecdote, which was originally read on the radio, you will learn about a happy coincidence that involves an undiscovered O. Henry story.

Manuscript Found in an Attic

MARCUS ROSENBAUM

O. Henry

When I told my father that I was moving to Des Moines, he told me about the only time he'd been there. It was in the 1930s, he said, when he was the business manager of the literary magazine of Southern Methodist University in Dallas. His friend Lon Tinkle was the magazine's editor. Lon also taught English at SMU, and there was a student in his class who had a severely deformed back. It was the Depression, and the young woman came from a family that was so poor she couldn't afford the operation that would correct the problem.

Her mother, who ran a boardinghouse in Galveston, was cleaning out the attic one day when she came across an old dusty manuscript. Scribbled across the top were the words, "By O. Henry." It was a nice story, and she sent it along to her daughter at SMU, who showed it to Lon. Lon had never seen the story before, but it *sounded* like O. Henry, it had an O. Henry story line, and he knew that William Sydney Porter, aka O. Henry, had lived in Houston at one time. So it was entirely possible that the famous author had gone to the beach and stayed in the Galveston boardinghouse, had written the story while he was there, and had inadvertently left the manuscript behind. Lon showed the manuscript to my father, who contacted an O. Henry expert at Columbia University in New York. The expert said he'd like to see it, so my father got on a train and took it to him.

The expert authenticated the story as O. Henry's, and my father set out to sell it. Eventually, he found himself in Des Moines, meeting with Gardner Cowles, a top editor at the Des Moines *Register*. Cowles loved the story and bought it on the spot. My father took the proceeds to the young woman in Lon Tinkle's class. It was just enough for her to have the operation she so desperately needed—and, as far as we know, to live happily ever after.

My father never told me what the O. Henry story was about. But I doubt that it could have been better than his own story: a story about O. Henry that was an O. Henry story itself.

Comprehension

1. **Recall** Why do Sam and Bill need two thousand dollars?

2. **Clarify** Why does the boy prefer staying with Sam and Bill to going home?

3. **Represent** Reread lines 24–26 on page 54. Use the details in this paragraph to draw a simple map showing Summit, the mountain, and the cave.

COMMON CORE

RL 3 Analyze how dialogue or incidents in a story propel the action and reveal aspects of a character.

Text Analysis

4. **Predict** Look back at the chart you created as you read. Which outcomes surprised you and which did not? Tell what unexpected circumstances affected Bill and Sam's plan to get money.

5. **Analyze Conflict and Resolution** When an outcome is the opposite of what might be expected, it is said to be **ironic**. Which of the resolutions to this story's conflicts are ironic? Show your thinking in two graphic organizers like the ones shown.

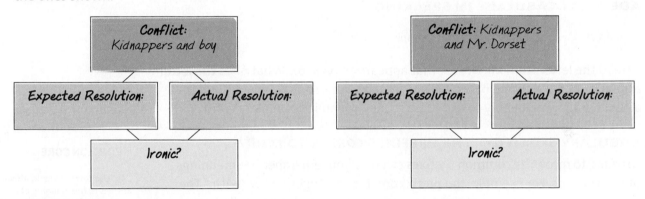

6. **Draw Conclusions** Look back at lines 8–16 on page 52. From the vocabulary Sam uses, as well as the way he presents himself and Bill to the reader at the beginning of the story, do you think the partners are typically successful in their schemes? Cite evidence to support your conclusion.

Extension and Challenge

7. **Creative Project: Music** Choose a familiar tune and rewrite the words to retell the story of "The Ransom of Red Chief." Include details that bring out the **irony** in the story.

8. **Text Criticism** O. Henry's short stories remain popular with readers in part because they often have **surprise endings.** Read the article "Manuscript Found in an Attic" on page 62. What do you think the author means when he describes it as "a story about O. Henry that was an O. Henry story itself"?

Is any plan FOOLPROOF?

What could Bill and Sam have done to make their plan more likely to succeed?

Vocabulary in Context

▲ **VOCABULARY PRACTICE**

Choose the vocabulary word that best completes each sentence.

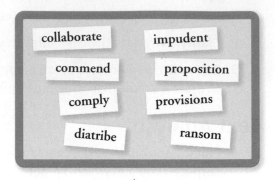

collaborate   impudent

commend   proposition

comply   provisions

diatribe   ransom

1. The kidnappers demanded a ____ before they returned the boy.
2. They had enough ____ stashed in a cave to last a week.
3. Since neither of them could complete the scheme alone, the kidnappers had to ____.
4. The worst they expected was a ____ in the local paper.
5. Red Chief was so ____, adults didn't like being around him.
6. The father did not ____ with the terms of the letter.
7. Red Chief's father had a different ____ for the kidnappers.
8. You can't ____ the parent's actions, but you can certainly understand them.

ACADEMIC VOCABULARY IN SPEAKING

| • affect   • conclude   • evident   • imply   • initial |

Reread the letter from Mr. Dorset that appears on page 61. What does the letter **imply** about how he and his neighbors feel about his son? As you discuss your answer with a partner, try to use at least one Academic Vocabulary word.

VOCABULARY STRATEGY: THE PREFIXES *com-* AND *multi-*

Learning to recognize common prefixes can help you remember the meanings of many words. For example, the prefix *com-* means "together" or "with." The vocabulary word *comply* contains this prefix, which can also be spelled *com-*, *col-*, *cor-*, or *con-*, depending on the letter that follows it. Another common prefix is *multi-*, which means "more than one."

PRACTICE Choose the word from the list that matches each numbered definition. If necessary, consult a dictionary.

| combine   communicable   concur   confirm   multipurpose   multitude |

1. transferable between persons or species; contagious
2. the condition or quality of being numerous
3. designed or used for several purposes
4. to establish that something is true
5. to be in agreement, or harmony
6. to join together

COMMON CORE

L 4b Use common Latin affixes as clues to the meaning of a word. **L 6** Use accurately grade-appropriate words.

Interactive Vocabulary   THiNK central

Go to thinkcentral.com.
KEYWORD: HML8-64

Language

♦ **GRAMMAR IN CONTEXT:** Avoid Run-On Sentences

Review the **Grammar in Context** note on page 56. A **run-on sentence**, sometimes called a run-on, is two or more sentences written as though they were a single sentence. To correct a run-on, you can

- insert an end mark and start a new sentence
- insert a **coordinating conjunction,** such as *and, but,* or *so,* after a comma
- change a comma to a **semicolon**

> *Original:* I thought Randy would win the class elections, Mary believed Ling would be the winner.
>
> *Revised:* I thought Randy would win the class elections, but Mary believed Ling would be the winner.

PRACTICE Rewrite the following sentences so that they are no longer run-ons.

1. I thought I wouldn't like being away from home, it's actually really fun.
2. I promised to behave, they threatened to send me home.
3. There weren't daily newspapers, nosy reporters wouldn't be coming around.
4. They didn't count on the boy's adventurous spirit they were surprised by it.
5. Parents worry about keeping their children safe, they don't worry about keeping people safe from their children.

For more help with run-on sentences, see page R64 in the **Grammar Handbook.**

READING-WRITING CONNECTION

YOUR TURN Demonstrate your understanding of "The Ransom of Red Chief" by responding to this prompt. Then use the **revising tip** to improve your writing.

WRITING PROMPT	REVISING TIP
Extended Constructed Response: Analysis Bill and Sam thought they had a brilliant scheme to make money, but they didn't plan for the unexpected. In **two or three paragraphs,** tell why they thought their plan would work and what they were mistaken about.	Review your analysis. If you have used any run-on sentences, correct the problem by adding appropriate punctuation or a coordinating conjunction.

Interactive Revision **THINK** central

Go to **thinkcentral.com.**
KEYWORD: HML8-65

Clean Sweep
Short Story by Joan Bauer

When does trash become
TREASURE?

⋯ **COMMON CORE**

RL 3 Analyze how dialogue or incidents in a story propel the action. **RL 5** Analyze how the structure of text contributes to its meaning.

There is an old saying, "One man's trash is another man's treasure." A scrap of cloth, a wrinkled photo, or a worn, torn book can have great value to a person if there are special memories attached. In "Clean Sweep," a girl finds out not only that a simple object can hold good memories, but also that those memories can help heal.

WEB IT What do you value that someone else might be tempted to throw away? Create a web to show some memories that are connected to that item. Expand your web by adding details that explain what makes the object special to you.

First time I met her

My Aunt Susan gave it to me.

She became my favorite aunt.

Harmonica

I got it on my 7th birthday.

My first instrument

Got me interested in guitar and bass

TEXT ANALYSIS: CONFLICTS AND SUBPLOTS

As you may recall, there are two basic kinds of conflicts.

- **External conflicts** are struggles between a character and an outside force. The outside force could be another character, society, or a force of nature.

- **Internal conflicts** are struggles within a character. This type of conflict may occur when the character has to make a difficult decision or deal with opposing feelings.

A story may develop more than one kind of conflict. Sometimes an additional conflict is worked out in a **subplot,** or minor plot.

As you read "Clean Sweep," notice how a past event causes both an internal and an external conflict. Also, see if you can spot a subplot.

READING SKILL: SEQUENCE

To follow a story, you must recognize the **sequence,** or order, of the event described. While events are often presented in the order in which they occur, sometimes the action is interrupted to present a scene from an earlier time. This scene, called a **flashback,** can help explain a character's actions. To help you figure out when events occurred, look for signal words and phrases such as these: *four years ago, moments later,* and *while.* Then keep track of the sequence of important events by recording them on a sequence chart.

Review: Predict

VOCABULARY IN CONTEXT

The boldfaced words help Joan Bauer tell about one teenager's experience with loss and familial responsibility. To see how many you know, substitute a different word or words for each.

1. The room was dark and **dingy.**
2. A **minuscule** amount of light came through the window.
3. Her sense of **propriety** kept her from interrupting him.
4. She acted calm in front of her class, but she was in **turmoil.**
5. I can't stand the **vileness** of rotten eggs.
6. It was an **aberration,** not what she usually sees.

 Complete the activities in your **Reader/Writer Notebook.**

Meet the Author

Joan Bauer
born 1951

Laughter and Life
As a child, Joan Bauer dreamed of becoming a comedian or a comedy writer when she grew up. The funny adults in her life inspired her. Her mother loved to make people laugh, and her grandmother, Nana, was a storyteller whose tales always included humor. But real life wasn't always amusing. When Joan was eight years old, her parents divorced. This and other family troubles proved devastating. However, she continued writing, finding that it helped ease her pain. Now an award-winning author, Joan Bauer admits to often drawing from these difficult life experiences while creating her touching, amusing stories.

Hope and Humor
"I want to create stories that link life's struggles with laughter," Bauer has said. "Laughter is a gift we've been given ... not just to make us feel good, but to empower us to overcome dark times." Her novels and stories are about how we can help each other by sharing both the struggle and the laughter.

Clean Sweep

Joan Bauer

"HAVE YOU EVER SEEN A DUST MITE?"

My mother always lowers her voice when she asks this; it adds to the emotional impact. Never in the four years since she's had the cleaning business has anyone ever said they've seen one. That's because the only people who have seen dust mites are scientists who put dust balls on slides and look at them under microscopes. Personally I have better things to do than look at **minuscule** animals who cause great torture among the allergic, but my mother has a photo of a dust mite blown up to ten gazillion times its size—she is holding it up now, as she always does in this part of her
10 presentation—and the two women who sit on the floral couch before her gasp appropriately and shut their eyes, because dust mites, trust me, are ugly. Think *Invasion of the Body Snatchers* meets *The Hunchback of Notre Dame*, and you're just beginning to enter into the **vileness** of this creature.

"They're everywhere," Mom says to the women. "Under the bed, on the sheets, clinging to the blinds; hiding, waiting. And at Clean Sweep," she offers quietly, but dramatically, "we *kill* them for you. We hate them even more than you do. *This* is why we're in business."

The two women look at each other and say *yes,* they want the cleaning service to start immediately.
20 Mom tells them our price. One woman, as expected, says, "That sounds a little high." People are so cheap. Everyone wants quality, no one wants to pay for it. Here's the suburban dream—to hire great workers who are such meek morons that they don't have the guts to ask for a living wage. Ⓐ

This is not my mother's problem. She holds up the dust mite enlargement to make the point. "We cost more because we know where he and his army are hiding."

Analyze Visuals ▶

What can you **conclude** about this girl's feelings toward housework?

minuscule (mĭn′ə-skyōōl′) *adj.* very small; tiny

vileness (vīl′nəs) *n.* unpleasantness; disgusting quality

Ⓐ **CONFLICTS AND SUBPLOTS**
What conflicts do the main character and her family face with each job?

She used to say "we know where he and his friends are hiding," but "army" sounds more fierce, and when you are serious about eliminating dust, you'd better let everyone know it's war.

30 "Well . . . ," the other woman says, unsure.

Mom presses in. "We suggest two cleanings per week for one month to achieve total elimination. Then weekly cleanings should do, unless you have special needs."

Special needs in the cleaning world range from cleaning out attics to detoxification[1] of teenage bedrooms. I am a specialist in cleaning rooms of kids who have just gone off to college. It takes nerves of steel. And I have them.

My brother Benjamin doesn't. To begin with, he's allergic to dust—bad news when the family business is dedicated to eliminating it. To end with, he's a devoted underachiever, in stark contrast to myself. And Benjamin knows
40 how to get out of work—he could give seminars on this. He gets the perfect look of abject[2] pain over his face, says he's not feeling too well, he's sorry, he doesn't want to be a *burden*. He talks about the pain moving across his back, down his leg, and into his ankle. Then he gets dizzy and has to sit down; lying down comes moments later after his face gets a little pale (I don't know how he does this) and his hand touches his forehead which, I swear, has small drops of sweat on it. Then he'll try to get up and help, but by this time, you feel like such a snake that a sick person is going to get sicker because of your insensitive demands that you say, no, you rest, I'll do it. **B**

This is what he's done to me today, and I'm not in the mood for the game.
50 He tells me, groaning, he'll *try* to make it to Mrs. Leonardo's today to help her pack up her attic, but he's not sure he can even sit. He's lying on the couch in misery saying if he can sit, he will try to stand, and if he attempts standing, he will attempt actual walking—Mrs. Leonardo's house being four houses down the street. I throw my book bag at him. Suggest he *crawl* to Mrs. Leonardo's house and he says, "Thanks, Katie. Just thanks." To which I reply, "Look, Benny Boy, I'm getting sick of carrying your weight around here. If you think I'm going to do your job and mine until I die, think again." Benjamin groans deep, turns off the light, closes his eyes and says his headache is cosmic and could I please go get him some aspirin. **C**
60 I don't get the aspirin. It's a big bad world out there and he needs to find it out now, at fourteen. This is what big sisters are for.

So I'm basically crabby and bitter all day; taking it out on random people. After school I have mounds of homework. You wonder what teachers are thinking—I have three hundred pages of reading in three textbooks plus a paper due on Friday. Have you ever noticed that it takes a textbook dozens of pages to say what normal people can cover fast?

Example:

What was the full impact of World War II?

SCIENCE CONNECTION

Dust mites are microscopic organisms found in house dust the world over. Some people are allergic to the feces and skin shed by the mites.

B CONFLICTS AND SUBPLOTS
How does the narrator feel about her brother's behavior? Tell how she handles it.

C SEQUENCE
Reread lines 49–51. What words or phrases show that the specific events of this story are starting now? Record the event on your chart.

---

1. **detoxification** (dē-tŏk´sə-fĭ-kā´shən): the process of removing toxic substances.

2. **abject** (ăb´jĕkt): of the most miserable kind; wretched.

Clear-cut teenage answer: We won.

70   So I'm close to dying young from excessive homework, and I have to help Mrs. Leonardo clean out her attic. She is paying big bucks for this, and, believe me, my family needs the money.

Mrs. Leonardo wants people there on time and working like ants. Ants carry their weight on their backs and are thrilled as anything to be abused. But that is the insect world; I am not one of them. I'm not in the mood to sit with her in her **dingy** attic and lug tons of garbage down the stairs and listen to her stories of how her family deserted her. I know that sounds mean, but Mrs. Leonardo is a mean person. It's easy to see why she's alone. The big joke is that when her husband died, he had a big smile on his face in the casket that he'd 80   never had in real life. The funeral director said they tried to wipe that grin off his face, but they couldn't do it.

So I'm on my knees in the dust, putting things in bags, while Mrs. Leonardo tells me about her selfish brother Horace who deserted her, and her uncaring, money-grubbing cousin Cynthia who backed out of the driveway eight years ago and never came back. She tells me how she helped them and loaned them money which they never paid back. She's going on and on about how the world is a dark, dark place. I clear my throat: "Boy, Mrs. Leonardo, you've got a lot of stuff up here. Are you sure you want to keep it all?" **D**

This is the wrong thing to say. Mrs. Leonardo's gray eyes get spitting mad and 90   she says, *well,* she's seventy-six years old and she's had a *very* interesting life and she doesn't want to throw out anything of value. I look in a box with IRS tax forms dating back to 1955.

"Mrs. Leonardo, the IRS says you only need to keep tax records from the last three years. We could dump this whole box . . ." My mother told me this.

She lunges as much as a seventy-six-year-old person can and says she isn't giving her tax records to anyone so they can steal her secrets. Like tons of thieves are out there ready to pounce on this.

But at twenty-five dollars per hour, you learn to be patient. "Think of the money," my mother always says, "and the graciousness will come." So I'm 100   taping the box and writing IMPORTANT PAPERS 1955–1963. Maybe she could turn this attic into a museum and people could walk through and learn all the things you should never hold on to.

Benjamin would have cracked under this pressure. Mrs. Leonardo is kneeling by a huge trunk, saying how the younger generation (mine) doesn't understand about manners, **propriety,** or simple human decency. Her grandniece, Veronica, walks around with her belly button showing. She pulls old clothes out of the trunk and yanks this old lace tablecloth out and just looks at it. Finally, she says she got it when she was married and she's only used it once. She waited for a special occasion and only one came—her twentieth anniversary. No 110   other occasion was special enough, and then her husband died right before

dingy (dĭn′jē) *adj.* dirty or discolored

D SEQUENCE
Reread lines 82–88. What words help signal that the narrator is returning to the main story she is telling?

propriety (prə-prī′ĭ-tē) *n.* the quality of being proper; appropriateness

their twenty-fifth anniversary and the tablecloth has been in this trunk ever since—only used once, she keeps saying—beautiful Egyptian linen. She looks kind of sad, though stiff. I say, "You could start using it now, Mrs. Leonardo," which is the wrong thing to say. She shuts that trunk and asks me just who do I think she's going to invite to dinner since everyone she's ever done anything for has either deserted her or died. **ⓔ**

I don't know how to answer a question like this. My mother didn't cover it during Clean Sweep boot camp training where I learned how to scour a bathtub that a toddler spilled ink in, how to clean pet stains from any carpet 120 known to man, how to wash windows and not leave streaks, how to open a refrigerator with year-old meat and not gag in front of the client. I pledged that the customer was always right and I, the lowly dust eliminator, was always, always wrong.

But I'm not sure what to do. If I agree with her, I'm not helping, and if I listen, I won't get the job done. The truth is, I don't like Mrs. Leonardo—so there's a big part of me that doesn't care—even though I know this is probably inhumane because she's a sad person, really. Kneeling there in the dust, surrounded by the boxes of her so-called interesting life, going on and on

ⓔ CONFLICTS AND SUBPLOTS
What causes Mrs. Leonardo to be upset with Katie?

◀ **Analyze Visuals**
What do the **details** in the picture tell you about the person or people who live here?

about people who are gone. I'm thinking about the next stage of the job—the
130 actual cleaning of the attic which is going to take two people, and I know
Benjamin will be hurled into monumental physical **aberrations** up here.

I'm tired, too, and my paper is late on King Lear who, in my opinion,
thought too much and couldn't deliver. I'm thinking about my personal life—
yes, dust eliminators have them. We have feelings; we have needs, dreams.
I'm feeling that I work too much and I wish my mom had another business
because what I do all day at school is exhausting enough without having to do
heavy lifting after school and on the weekends. I think about when my dad
died four years ago, and because of disorganization—that is, getting behind
on paying his life insurance premiums—his insurance policy was cancelled
140 and we got no insurance money when he died. He never meant to hurt us,
but it was so scary not knowing if we could keep the house mixed with all the
pain of losing him. We never got a regular time of mourning because we were
fighting to stay afloat. Mom was trying to sort through Dad's huge piles of
papers. We loved him so much, but he could never get rid of what Mom called
his "clutter demons." **F**

It took several months, but we got his papers sorted. We learned firsthand
how you get organized, clean up, and obliterate dust. We became total aces at
it; learned how widespread the problem truly is. We knew then we needed to
share what we'd learned with others who were suffering, and felt that twenty-
150 five dollars an hour was reasonable. **G**

I'm not sure if Mrs. Leonardo wants someone to help or someone to
complain to. Between you and me, I feel that listening to complaining *and*
busting dust should earn thirty-five dollars per hour. But, I'm remembering
being in our attic after my dad died; trying to go through his things. He had
a trunk that his grandfather had given him—inside were all his photos and
papers from school. I remember reading some of his essays from high school
and just crying. I couldn't throw those out. Mom said going through all that
was therapeutic[3] for me because it was like being with him, kind of. He was
forty-one years old when he died. Had a heart attack at work and was dead by
160 the time the ambulance came. **H**

Just thinking about the day makes me shaky. Over the years I've dissected
every last thing I remember about the last morning I saw him. I should have
made him breakfast—I knew how much he liked it when I did. I should have
hugged him when he went out the door, but I was on the phone with Roger
Rugsby who was my biology partner who needed me to go over my lab notes
or he would fail. I missed the bus and Dad missed his train and he took me to
school. I was late, so I hurled myself out of the car and he said, "Go get 'em,
kiddo." That's the last thing he ever said to me. But I did better than Benjamin
who overslept and didn't even see Dad that morning. **I**
170 Mrs. Leonardo leans over a trunk like the one my father had. I want to say
something encouraging to her, like, "Gee, Mrs. Leonardo, I know how hard it

---

3. **therapeutic** (thĕr′ə-pyōō′tĭk): having healing powers.

CLEAN SWEEP   **73**

aberration (ăb′ə-
rā′shən) *n.* an abnormal
alteration

F **CONFLICTS AND
SUBPLOTS**
What internal and
external conflicts does
Katie face as a result of
her dad's death?

G **SEQUENCE**
When did Katie's mother
form Clean Sweep?

H **CONFLICTS AND
SUBPLOTS**
Reread lines 153–158.
How does Katie react
while looking through
her father's things?

I **SEQUENCE**
Reread lines 161–163.
Note the phrase that lets
you know a **flashback** is
coming. When do the
events in this paragraph
take place?

must be going through all these memories," or, "I hope sorting through all this is helping you the way it helped me." Memories are the only things we have left sometimes. You can hold a photo of a person you loved who's gone, but it isn't alive. Memories—the best ones—are filled with sights, smells, love, and happiness. I try to hold some of those in my heart for my dad each day.

She goes through the trunk, stony-faced. I can't tell what she's found, can't tell if she's going to torch the contents or hold them to her heart. I lug a big bag over and throw old newspapers inside. Mrs. Leonardo stops going through
180 the trunk. She's holding something in her hands, not moving. I look at her stiff face and for a moment in the weird light of the attic, she looks like she's going to cry. But that's impossible. Then I hear a sniff and she says softly, "My mother read this book to my sister and me every night before bed."

I look at the book—a well-worn brown leather cover. Doesn't look like much. "I thought she had it," Mrs. Leonardo says sadly.

"Who had it?"

"My sister, Helen. I thought she had the book. She always wanted it."

In these situations it's best to say, "Oh."

"I thought . . . I thought I'd sent it to her after Mother died." She looks down.
190 I say, "It's hard to remember what you've done after someone important dies."

"But, she'd asked me for it. It was the one thing she'd wanted."

"Well . . ."

"I haven't talked to her since Mother died. I thought she . . ." **J**

I'm not sure how to ask this. Is Helen still alive?

I dance around it. "What do you think you should do with the book, Mrs. Leonardo?" She doesn't answer.

I try again. "Why did Helen want it so bad?"

She hands me the book. "She said these stories were her best memories of childhood." I look through it. "The Naughty Little Frog," "The Little
200 Lost Tulip," "Spanky, the Black Sheep." It's amazing what we put up with as children. But then I remember my favorite bedtime story—"Rupert, the Church Mouse"—about this little mouse who lives in a church and polishes all the stained glass windows every night before he goes to sleep so the light can come forth every morning.

"I know she lives in Vermont," Mrs. Leonardo offers. "I heard from a cousin a while ago . . ." Her voice trails off. **K**

"I think you should call her, Mrs. Leonardo."

She shakes her old head. No—she couldn't possibly.

"I think you should call her and tell her you've got the book."
210 She glares at me. "I believe we're done for today." She grabs the book from my hands, puts it back in the trunk.

"Sorry, ma'am. I didn't mean . . ."

She heads down the attic stairs.

COMMON CORE RL 3

J **CONFLICTS AND SUBPLOTS**
Like main plots, subplots often follow a linear pattern. A conflict is introduced, intensified, and resolved. A subplot may reflect on the main plot by showing how a similar conflict can play out in another situation. Reread lines 177–193. What subplot is introduced here? Tell who is involved in the subplot and what the central conflict seems to be.

K **PREDICT**
Now that she's found the book, what do you think Mrs. Leonardo might do in regard to her sister?

I tell Benjamin that I don't want to hear about his problems, that his back looks strong to me, the shooting pain in his leg will go away eventually, and his headache is just a reflection of his deep, inner **turmoil**. I say this as we're walking to Mrs. Leonardo's house.

"I think my whole left side is going numb," he whispers pitifully as we walk up her steps.

220 *"Deal with it."*

Mrs. Leonardo is waiting for us. We're late. I don't mention that having to drag a hypochondriac[4] four doors down the street takes time. Great food smells swirl from her kitchen. ⓛ

Mrs. Leonardo looks Benjamin up and down, not impressed. "You've not been here before," she says. Benjamin half smiles and rubs his tennis elbow,[5] which makes me nuts because he doesn't play tennis.

I introduce them. Tell her Benjamin is here to help with dust elimination and heavy lifting, at which point Benjamin leans painfully against the wall and closes his eyes.

230 "He's a very dedicated worker once he gets started, Mrs. Leonardo."

I jam my elbow into his side.

Okay, so we're cleaning this cavernous[6] attic like there's no tomorrow. We've got all the trunks and boxes wiped down and pushed to the far side. We're running the turbo-charged Clean Sweep Frankenstein portable vacuum that is so powerful it can suck up pets and small children if they get too close. Benjamin is wearing a dust mask over his nose and mouth—he wrote *The Terminator* over it. This boy is appropriately miserable, pulling down spiders' webs, sucking up dust mites. I can almost hear their little screams of terror. Almost, but not quite. My mother claims she can hear dust mites shrieking for mercy and uses this in her 240 presentation if she thinks potential clients can handle it. ◆

"Get the lace tablecloth from the trunk!" Mrs. Leonardo shouts from downstairs.

What's she want with that?

"And bring the book, too," she hollers impatiently.

I don't mention that we've shoved everything in the corner like she said to, that I'll have to move it all to get to the trunk, and, by the way, I'm going as fast as I can. I get the book and the lace tablecloth that's been folded in very old plastic. I look at the book—reddish brown leather—*Aunt Goody's Good Night Stories,* it's called. Benjamin comes over looking like some 250 kind of cosmic alien with his mask, takes the book, starts laughing.

"The Naughty Little Frog," he says reading. "Once upon a time there was a naughty little frog named Edmond. Edmond was so naughty that

turmoil (tûr'moil') *n.* a state of extreme confusion or agitation

ⓛ **CONFLICTS AND SUBPLOTS**
In what ways is Katie responsible for her brother?

◆ **GRAMMAR IN CONTEXT**
In line 232, notice how Joan Bauer uses the **progressive form** of the verb *to clean* to describe on ongoing action.

Language Coach
Oral Fluency In words such as *night* that contain the letter combination *ght,* the *g* and *h* are silent. Reread the sentence beginning in line 248, pronouncing *night* correctly.

---

4. **hypochondriac** (hī'pə-kŏn'drē-ăk'): a person who continually thinks he or she is ill or about to become ill.

5. **tennis elbow:** pain around the elbow, often caused from playing tennis or similar activities.

6. **cavernous** (kăv'ər-nəs): filled with caverns; like a cave.

he never, ever cleaned his lily pad. It got so dirty that his mother had to make him stay on that lily pad several times each day to—"

"You're going to have to wait for the end." I yank the book from his hands and head down the creaky attic stairs with the tablecloth. Mrs. Leonardo is in the kitchen wearing a frilly apron, stirring a pot of something that smells beyond great.

260   She turns to look at me, puts her wooden spoon down.

"Help me put it on the table," she orders.

I'm smiling a little now because I know this tablecloth's history. I'm wondering who's coming to dinner.

"Looks like you're having a party," I offer as we get the tablecloth squared perfectly on the table.

Mrs. Leonardo says nothing, sets the table for two with what looks like the good silverware, the good napkins. Then she puts the storybook in front of one of the place settings.

"My sister, you see . . ." She pauses emotionally. "Well, she's . . ."
270 coming to dinner."

"You mean the one you haven't seen for a long time?"

"I only have *one* sister."

I'm just grinning now and I tell her I hope they have the best dinner in the world.

"Well, I do too." She looks nervously out the window and says whatever work we haven't finished can be done tomorrow. "You were right about . . . calling her, Katie."

I smile brightly, wondering if she's going to offer me some of her great-smelling food to show her gratitude. She doesn't. I head up the attic stairs
280 and drag Benjamin to safety. He's sneezing like he's going to die. I take off his Terminator dust mask and lean him against a wall. Half of me wants to give Mrs. Leonardo a little hug of encouragement, but the other half warns, *Don't touch clients because they can turn on you.*

"Whatever you're cooking, Mrs. Leonardo, it sure smells good," I shout. "Your sister's going to love it." I'm not sure she hears all of that. Benjamin is into his fifth sneezing attack.

She nods from the kitchen; I push Benjamin out on the street.

"I could have died up there," he shouts, blowing his nose.

"But you didn't."

290 And I remember the book my dad would read to us when we were little about the baby animals and their parents and how each mother and father animal kissed their babies good night. That book was chewed to death, ripped, stained, and missing the last two pages, but I wouldn't give it up for anything.

We walk back home almost silently, except for Benjamin's sniffs, sneezes, and groans. People just don't understand what important things can be hiding in the dust.

Mom says that all the time in her presentation. ◆

�M SEQUENCE
What steps has Mrs. Leonardo taken to prepare for her sister's visit? Add these to your chart.

Comprehension

1. **Recall** What job does the Clean Sweep company do?

2. **Clarify** Why does Katie resent her brother?

3. **Summarize** For Katie, what makes working for Mrs. Leonardo so difficult?

COMMON CORE

RL 3 Analyze how dialogue or incidents in a story propel the action. RL 5 Analyze how the structure of text contributes to its meaning.

Text Analysis

4. **Identify Sequence** Review the chart you created as you read. Which event or events in the sequence occur as **flashbacks?** What information do you learn about Katie from the flashbacks?

5. **Examine Conflicts** Note the internal and external conflicts Katie faces after her dad's death. By the end of the story, which of these conflicts are resolved? Which are not resolved? Share your opinion of the way in which each conflict is or is not resolved.

6. **Analyze Character Motivations** Why do you think Mrs. Leonardo decided to reconnect with her sister?

7. **Analyze Subplot** Use a chart like the one shown to record details of the subplot involving Mrs. Leonardo and her sister. What does this subplot help Katie to realize? In your opinion, is the subplot a worthwhile addition to the story? Explain why or why not.

8. **Make Judgments** Reread lines 221–229 and footnote 4. Would you say that Katie's brother is a hypochondriac? Use examples from the text to support your answer.

Characters Involved: Mrs. Leonardo and her sister
Conflict:
Resolution:

Extension and Challenge

9. **SCIENCE CONNECTION** Katie's family earns a living fighting dust mites. Look back at the information about dust mites on page 70. Research more about them to find out whether they are seriously harmful to people and whether it is possible to get rid of all dust mites in a home. Is Katie's mother being honest in her presentation? Present your findings to the class.

When does trash become TREASURE?

Look again at the Web It activity on page 66. Imagine you are Katie, and her treasure is the book she mentions on page 76, lines 290–293. What good memories might Katie connect to the book?

Vocabulary in Context

▲ VOCABULARY PRACTICE

Decide whether the words in each pair are synonyms (words that mean the same) or antonyms (words that mean the opposite).

1. propriety/rudeness
2. vileness/niceness
3. dingy/shabby
4. minuscule/huge
5. aberration/sameness
6. turmoil/chaos

ACADEMIC VOCABULARY IN WRITING

> • affect   • conclude   • evident   • imply   • initial

How did the death of the narrator's father **affect** the remaining family members? In a paragraph, explain how the narrator, her mother, and her brother appear to have coped with the loss of their loved one. Use at least one Academic Vocabulary word in your response.

VOCABULARY STRATEGY: SUFFIXES THAT FORM NOUNS

A suffix is a word part that appears at the end of a root or base word to form a new word. Some suffixes, such as those in *vileness* and *aberration*, can be added to words to form nouns. The web shown includes other suffixes that have a similar meaning.

If a word seems unfamiliar, see if you can break it into a familiar root and suffix. For example, the word *embellishment* can be broken into *embellish* and *–ment,* which might help you understand that an embellishment is something that is decorated.

PRACTICE Identify the base word and suffix in each boldfaced word. Then define the nouns that have been made by adding the suffixes.

1. Winning the state championship was quite an **achievement.**
2. To make the **connection,** your flight will have to arrive on time.
3. His **performance** in the concert was superb.
4. One could see the **sadness** in their faces.
5. We have a **shortage** of paper towels in the kitchen.

⋯ COMMON CORE

L 6 Use accurately grade-appropriate words.

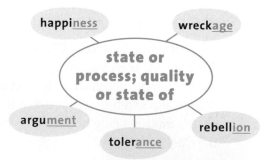

Language

◆ **GRAMMAR IN CONTEXT:** Use Progressive Form Correctly

Review the **Grammar in Context** note on page 75. When you are writing about an event that's in progress, use the progressive form of a verb.

Example: She is cleaning the attic. (*The cleaning is an ongoing action.*)

You can use the progressive form with any verb tense. Notice that the progressive form is made by using the same tense of the verb *to be* with the present participle, which is formed by using the verb stem and adding *ing*.

COMMON CORE

L1 Demonstrate command of standard English grammar when writing. **W 3b** Use dialogue to develop characters.

Tenses	▶ Examples
Present Progressive	*We are laughing.*
Past Progressive	*We were laughing.*
Future Progressive	*We will be laughing.*
Present Perfect Progressive	*We have been laughing.*
Past Perfect Progressive	*We had been laughing.*
Future Perfect Progressive	*We will have been laughing.*

PRACTICE Identify which sentences include the progressive form of the verb. Rewrite the remaining sentences using the progressive form.

1. She was sorting her father's papers.
2. She feels sad.
3. He planned a vacation they didn't get to enjoy.
4. He was loving and supportive.
5. They were thinking about getting their picture taken.

For more help with progressive form, see page R56 in the **Grammar Handbook.**

READING-WRITING CONNECTION

Increase your understanding of "Clean Sweep" by responding to this prompt. Then use the **revising tip** to improve your writing.

WRITING PROMPT	REVISING TIP
Short Constructed Response: Dialogue Reread lines 151–160. Write a **half-page of dialogue** between Katie and her mother that might have occurred while they sorted through her dad's things after his death.	Review your dialogue. Did you use the progressive form of verbs to write about events in process? If not, revise your writing.

Interactive Revision

THINK central

Go to **thinkcentral.com.**
KEYWORD: HML8-79

The Tell-Tale Heart
Short Story by Edgar Allan Poe

HISTORY | Video link at
thinkcentral.com

VIDEO TRAILER **THINK** central | KEYWORD: HML8-80

What makes you
SUSPICIOUS?

COMMON CORE

RL 4 Analyze the impact of word choices on meaning and tone.
RL 6 Analyze how differences in the points of view of the characters and the reader (e.g., created through the use of dramatic irony) create suspense.

Has something or someone ever seemed dangerous or untrustworthy to you? The feeling you had was suspicion. While suspicion might come from a misunderstanding, it can also be a warning that something is very wrong. In this story, you'll meet a man whose own suspicions are his downfall.

DISCUSS With a small group, discuss suspicious characters you've read about or seen on television shows. In what ways did these characters look or act differently from other characters? Continue your discussion by creating a list of warning signs that should make a person suspicious.

Suspicious Actions
1. Avoiding eye contact
2.

● **TEXT ANALYSIS: SUSPENSE**

Writers often "hook" readers by creating a sense of excitement, tension, dread, or fear about what will happen next. This feeling is called **suspense.** Edgar Allan Poe uses the following techniques to develop suspense:

- describing a character's anxiety or fear
- choosing vivid words to describe dramatic sights and sounds
- repeating words, phrases, or characters' actions

As you read "The Tell-Tale Heart," notice what causes you to feel suspense.

● **READING SKILL: EVALUATE NARRATOR**

Have you ever suspected someone was not telling you the truth? Just as you can't trust every person you meet, you can't believe all **narrators,** or characters who tell a story. To evaluate a narrator's **reliability,** or trustworthiness, pay attention to his or her actions, attitudes, and statements. Do any raise your suspicions? As you read "The Tell-Tale Heart," record clues that reveal whether the narrator is reliable or not.

Narrator's Reliability	
Makes Me Suspicious:	Makes Me Trust Him:
•	•
•	•

▲ **VOCABULARY IN CONTEXT**

Poe uses the following words to reveal how the main character is acting, feeling, and thinking. For each word, choose the numbered word or phrase closest in meaning.

WORD LIST				
	acute	crevice	stealthily	vehemently
	audacity	derision	stifled	vex
	conceive	hypocritical		

1. annoy
2. cautiously
3. intense
4. crack
5. deceptive
6. smothered
7. ridicule
8. think of
9. strongly
10. shameless daring

Complete the activities in your **Reader/Writer Notebook.**

Edgar Allan Poe
1809–1849

Orphan at Two
Edgar Allan Poe was born in Boston to parents who made their livings as traveling actors. When Poe was two, his father deserted the family. Less than a year later, his mother died. Edgar was raised in Virginia by family friends, the Allans. After being expelled from both the University of Virginia and the U.S. Military Academy at West Point, Poe began writing for a living.

"Madness or Melancholy"
Poe got a job as a journalist to support himself and his young wife while he worked on the stories and poems that would earn him the title "father of the modern mystery." A master of suspense, he wrote works that were often dark and full of horrifying images. Poems such as "The Raven" and short stories such as "The Pit and the Pendulum" brought him fame but no fortune. Poverty intensified his despair when his wife, Virginia, fell ill and died. Deeply depressed, Poe died two years later after being found on the streets of Baltimore. Poe's obituary stated he was a man of astonishing skill, a dreamer who walked "in madness or melancholy."

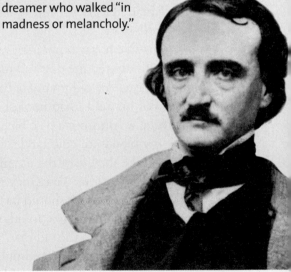

Authors Online
Go to **thinkcentral.com**. KEYWORD: HML8-81

THINK central

The Tell-Tale Heart

Edgar Allan Poe

True!—nervous—very, very dreadfully nervous I had been and am! but why *will* you say that I am mad? The disease had sharpened my senses—not destroyed—not dulled them. Above all was the sense of hearing **acute.** I heard all things in the heaven and in the earth. I heard many things in hell. How, then, am I mad? Hearken! and observe how healthily—how calmly I can tell you the whole story.

It is impossible to say how first the idea entered my brain; but once **conceived,** it haunted me day and night. Object there was none. Passion there was none. I loved the old man. He had never wronged me. He had never given 10 me insult. For his gold I had no desire. I think it was his eye! yes, it was this! He had the eye of a vulture—a pale blue eye, with a film over it. Whenever it fell upon me, my blood ran cold; and so by degrees—very gradually—I made up my mind to take the life of the old man, and thus rid myself of the eye forever.

Now this is the point. You fancy me mad. Madmen know nothing. But you should have seen *me.* You should have seen how wisely I proceeded—with what caution—with what foresight—with what dissimulation[1] I went to work! **A**

I was never kinder to the old man than during the whole week before I killed him. And every night, about midnight, I turned the latch of his door and opened it—oh, so gently! And then, when I had made an opening sufficient for my head, 20 I put in a dark lantern, all closed, closed, so that no light shone out, and then I thrust in my head. Oh, you would have laughed to see how cunningly I thrust it in! I moved it slowly—very, very slowly, so that I might not disturb the old

Illustrations by Howard Simpson.

---

1. **dissimulation** (dĭ-sĭm′yə-lā′shən): a hiding of one's true feelings.

Analyze Visuals ▶

What details in the picture help create **suspense?**

acute (ə-kyōōt′) *adj.* sharp; keen

conceive (kən-sēv) *v.* to think of

A EVALUATE NARRATOR
Reread lines 1–16. On the basis of what he plans to do, decide whether the narrator's opinion of himself makes you trust him more or less.

man's sleep. It took me an hour to place my whole head within the opening so far that I could see him as he lay upon his bed. Ha!—would a madman have been so wise as this? And then, when my head was well in the room, I undid the lantern cautiously—oh, so cautiously—cautiously (for the hinges creaked)—I undid it just so much that a single thin ray fell upon the vulture eye. And this I did for seven long nights—every night just at midnight—but I found the eye always closed; and so it was impossible to do the work; for it was not the old man who **vexed** me, but his Evil Eye. And every morning, when the day broke, I went boldly into the chamber, and spoke courageously to him, calling him by name in a hearty tone, and inquiring how he had passed the night. So you see he would have been a very profound old man, indeed, to suspect that every night, just at twelve, I looked in upon him while he slept. **B**

Upon the eighth night I was more than usually cautious in opening the door. A watch's minute hand moves more quickly than did mine. Never before that night had I *felt* the extent of my own powers—of my sagacity.[2] I could scarcely contain my feelings of triumph. To think that there I was, opening the door, little by little, and he not even to dream of my secret deeds or thoughts. I fairly chuckled at the idea; and perhaps he heard me; for he moved on the bed suddenly, as if startled. Now you may think that I drew back—but no. His room was as black as pitch with the thick darkness (for the shutters were close fastened, through fear of robbers), and so I knew that he could not see the opening of the door, and I kept pushing it on steadily, steadily.

I had my head in, and was about to open the lantern, when my thumb slipped upon the tin fastening, and the old man sprang up in the bed, crying out—"Who's there?"

I kept quite still and said nothing. For a whole hour I did not move a muscle, and in the meantime I did not hear him lie down. He was still sitting up in the bed listening,—just as I have done, night after night, hearkening to the death watches[3] in the wall. **C**

Presently I heard a slight groan, and I knew it was the groan of mortal terror. It was not a groan of pain or grief—oh, no!—it was the low, **stifled** sound that arises from the bottom of the soul when overcharged with awe. I knew the sound well. Many a night, just at midnight, when all the world slept, it has welled up from my own bosom, deepening, with its dreadful echo, the terrors that distracted me. I say I knew it well. I knew what the old man felt, and pitied him, although I chuckled at heart. I knew that he had been lying awake ever since the first slight noise, when he had turned in the bed. His fears had been ever since growing upon him. He had been trying to fancy them causeless, but could not. He had been saying to himself—"It is nothing but the wind in the chimney—it is only a mouse crossing the floor," or "it is merely a cricket which has made a single chirp." Yes, he has been trying to comfort himself with these suppositions; but he had found all in vain. *All in vain;* because Death,

vex (věks) *v.* to disturb; to annoy

B SUSPENSE
Note the actions the narrator repeats. Why does this repetition create a sense of dread?

C SUSPENSE
In what way does the characters' inaction create tension?

stifled (stī′fəld) *adj.* smothered **stifle** *v.*

---

2. **sagacity** (sə-găs′ĭ-tē): sound judgment.
3. **death watches:** deathwatch beetles—insects that make a tapping sound with their heads.

in approaching him, had stalked with his black shadow before him, and enveloped the victim. And it was the mournful influence of the unperceived shadow that caused him to feel—although he neither saw nor heard—to *feel* the presence of my head within the room.

When I had waited a long time, very patiently, without hearing him lie 70 down, I resolved to open a little—a very, very little **crevice** in the lantern. So I opened it—you cannot imagine how **stealthily,** stealthily—until, at length, a single dim ray, like the thread of the spider, shot from out the crevice and fell full upon the vulture eye.

It was open—wide, wide open—and I grew furious as I gazed upon it. I saw it with perfect distinctness—all a dull blue, with a hideous veil over it that chilled the very marrow in my bones; but I could see nothing else of the old man's face or person: for I had directed the ray as if by instinct, precisely upon the damned spot.

And now have I not told you that what you mistake for madness is but over-80 acuteness of the senses?—now, I say, there came to my ears a low, dull, quick sound, such as a watch makes when enveloped in cotton. I knew *that* sound well too. It was the beating of the old man's heart. It increased my fury, as the beating of a drum stimulates the soldier into courage. **D**

But even yet I refrained and kept still. I scarcely breathed. I held the lantern motionless. I tried how steadily I could maintain the ray upon the eye. Meantime the hellish tattoo[4] of the heart increased. It grew quicker and quicker, and louder and louder every instant. The old man's terror *must* have been extreme! It grew louder, I say, louder every moment!—do you mark me well? I have told you that I am nervous: so I am. And now at the dead hour of 90 the night, amid the dreadful silence of that old house, so strange a noise as this excited me to uncontrollable terror. Yet, for some minutes longer I refrained and stood still. But the beating grew louder, louder! I thought the heart must burst. And now a new anxiety seized me—the sound would be heard by a neighbor! The old man's hour had come! With a loud yell, I threw open the lantern and leaped into the room. He shrieked once—once only. In an instant I dragged him to the floor, and pulled the heavy bed over him. I then smiled gaily, to find the deed so far done. But, for many minutes, the heart beat on with a muffled sound. This, however, did not vex me; it would not be heard through the wall. At length it ceased. The old man was dead. I removed the 100 bed and examined the corpse. Yes, he was stone, stone dead. I placed my hand upon the heart and held it there many minutes. There was no pulsation. He was stone dead. His eye would trouble me no more. **E**

If still you think me mad, you will think so no longer when I describe the wise precautions I took for the concealment of the body. The night waned,[5] and I worked hastily, but in silence. First of all I dismembered the corpse. I cut off the head and the arms and the legs.

---

4. **hellish tattoo:** awful drumming.

5. **waned:** approached its end.

crevice (krĕv'ĭs) *n.* crack

stealthily (stĕl'thə-le) *adv.* cautiously; secretly

D EVALUATE NARRATOR
What does the narrator claim to be hearing? Decide whether you think he is correct.

E SUSPENSE
Reread lines 84–102. What is the scariest or most exciting part of this paragraph? Tell what details contribute to this feeling.

◀ **Analyze Visuals**

What can you **infer** from the character's expression in each of the three panels?

Language Coach

Syntax The way words are put together in a sentence is called syntax. Poe often uses unusual syntax. Reread line 112. What is another way to say "When I made an end of these labors"?

I then took up three planks from the flooring of the chamber, and deposited all between the scantlings.[6] I then replaced the boards so cleverly, so cunningly, that no human eye—not even *his*—could have detected anything 110 wrong. There was nothing to wash out—no stain of any kind—no blood-spot whatever. I had been too wary for that. A tub had caught all—ha! ha!

When I made an end of these labors, it was four o'clock—still dark as midnight. As the bell sounded the hour, there came a knocking at the street door. I went down to open it with a light heart,—for what had I *now* to fear?

---

6. **scantlings:** small wooden beams supporting the floor.

There entered three men, who introduced themselves, with perfect suavity,[7] as officers of the police. A shriek had been heard by a neighbor during the night: suspicion of foul play had been aroused; information had been lodged at the police office, and they (the officers) had been deputed[8] to search the premises.

120 I smiled,—for *what* had I to fear? I bade the gentlemen welcome. The shriek, I said, was my own in a dream. The old man, I mentioned, was absent in the country. I took my visitors all over the house. I bade them search—search *well*. I led them, at length, to *his* chamber. I showed them his treasures, secure, undisturbed. In the enthusiasm of my confidence, I brought chairs into the room, and desired them *here* to rest from their fatigues, while I myself, in the wild **audacity** of my perfect triumph, placed my own seat upon the very spot beneath which reposed[9] the corpse of the victim.

The officers were satisfied. My *manner* had convinced them. I was singularly at ease. They sat, and while I answered cheerily, they chatted of familiar things. But, ere long, I felt myself getting pale and wished them gone. My head

130 ached, and I fancied a ringing in my ears: but still they sat and still chatted. The ringing became more distinct:—it continued and became more distinct: I talked more freely to get rid of the feeling: but it continued and gained definitiveness—until at length, I found that the noise was *not* within my ears.

No doubt I now grew *very* pale;—but I talked more fluently, and with a heightened voice. Yet the sound increased—and what could I do? It was *a low, dull, quick sound—much such a sound as a watch makes when enveloped in cotton.* I gasped for breath—and yet the officers heard it not. I talked more quickly—more **vehemently;** but the noise steadily increased. I arose and argued about trifles, in a high key and with violent gesticulations,[10] but

140 the noise steadily increased. Why *would* they not be gone? I paced the floor to and fro with heavy strides, as if excited to fury by the observation of the men—but the noise steadily increased. What *could* I do? I foamed—I raved—I swore. I swung the chair upon which I had been sitting, and grated it upon the boards, but the noise arose over all and continually increased. It grew louder—louder—*louder!* And still the men chatted pleasantly, and smiled. Was it possible they heard not?—no, no! They heard!—they suspected!—they *knew!*—they were making a *mockery* of my horror!—this I thought, and this I think. But anything was better than this agony! Anything was more tolerable than this **derision!** I could bear those **hypocritical** smiles no longer! I felt that

150 I must scream or die!—and now—again!—hark! louder! louder! *louder!*— **F**

"Villains!" I shrieked, "dissemble[11] no more! I admit the deed!—tear up the planks!—here, here!—it is the beating of his hideous heart!" ❧

---

audacity (ô-dăs′ĭ-tē) *n.* shameless daring or boldness

vehemently (vē′ə-mənt-lē) *adv.* with intense emotion

derision (dĭ-rĭzh′ən) *n.* ridicule

hypocritical (hĭp′ə-krĭt′ĭ-kəl) *adj.* false or deceptive

F SUSPENSE
Think about the emotions that the narrator is feeling. How does Poe help the reader feel the same way?

---

7. **suavity** (swä′vĭ-tē): graceful politeness.
8. **deputed**: appointed as a representative.
9. **reposed**: rested.
10. **gesticulations** (jĕ-stĭk′yə-lā′shəns): energetic gestures of the hands or arms.
11. **dissemble**: pretend.

Comprehension

1. **Recall** Why does the narrator want to kill the old man?

2. **Clarify** Why does the narrator believe he will not be caught after murdering the old man?

3. **Summarize** How does the narrator prepare for the crime and cover up?

Text Analysis

4. **Make Inferences** Reread lines 7–13. From this passage, what do you think was the relationship between the narrator and the old man?

5. **Analyze Suspense** Which of Poe's techniques for creating suspense is most effective for you? To find out, review the following story sections. List the techniques used in each section, and then rank the sections from 1–4, with 1 being the most suspenseful.

Rank				
Lines	1–78	79–111	112–133	134–152
Techniques	1.	1.	1.	1.
	2.	2.	2.	2.

6. **Evaluate Narrator** How reliable is the narrator of the story? Should you believe what he tells you about himself? Support your answer with details from the chart you created as you read.

7. **Compare and Contrast** When readers know something a character does not, **dramatic irony** results. Contrast what you know about the narrator to what he believes about himself. What effect does this difference in perspective create? Explain.

Extension and Challenge

8. **Readers' Circle** With a group, brainstorm a list of horror stories and movies that most of you are familiar with. Choose at least two of these titles and discuss the techniques the authors or directors used to create suspense. Which of the techniques are similar to the ones Poe uses?

9. **Inquiry and Research** Do research on lie detection to find out what are the most reliable ways of finding out if someone is telling the truth. Present your findings to the class. Does what you learn change your opinion about whether the narrator is reliable?

What makes you SUSPICIOUS?

Review the list of suspicious actions you recorded on page 80. Which of these actions, if any, did the narrator exhibit while talking to the police?

COMMON CORE

RL 4 Analyze the impact of word choices on meaning and tone. **RL 6** Analyze how differences in the points of view of the characters and the reader (e.g., created through the use of dramatic irony) create suspense.

Vocabulary in Context

▲ **VOCABULARY PRACTICE**

Choose *true* or *false* for each statement.

1. It is difficult to hide a **stifled** yawn.
2. If you have the **audacity** to do something, you are bold and daring.
3. **Derision** is something you feel toward someone you respect.
4. A lion would approach its prey **stealthily.**
5. You could not hear much if you had an **acute** sense of hearing.
6. If someone **conceived** of a plan, he or she heard it from someone else.
7. A person could trip over a **crevice** in the sidewalk.
8. When a person is **hypocritical,** he is honest and true.
9. To **vex** is to delight in something.
10. If you react **vehemently** to something, you don't care much about it.

acute
audacity
conceived
crevice
derision
hypocritical
stealthily
stifled
vehemently
vex

ACADEMIC VOCABULARY IN WRITING

• affect • conclude • evident • imply • initial

At what point in "The Tell-Tale Heart" did it become **evident** to you that the narrator was mad, or insane? Write a short paragraph explaining your answer. Try to use at least one Academic Vocabulary word in your response.

VOCABULARY STRATEGY: USING REFERENCE AIDS

Choosing the perfect word can make a difference between good and great writing. One reason Poe's writing is still so popular is because of his masterful use of language. When you want to find the most accurate words to express yourself, the following reference aids can help you.

- A **thesaurus** is a reference book of **synonyms,** words with similar meanings. Most word processing software provides an electronic thesaurus tool.

  vex *verb* aggravate, annoy, bother, bug, disturb, provoke

- A **dictionary** lists synonyms after the definitions of some words.

  vex (vĕks) *v.* 1. To annoy. 2. To cause perplexity in. 3. To bring distress or suffering to. **syn** BOTHER, PUZZLE, PLAGUE, AFFLICT

PRACTICE Use a dictionary or thesaurus to find a synonym for each word. Use each synonym in a sentence that matches its distinct meaning.

1. commend   2. dupe   3. impish   4. menace

COMMON CORE

L 4c Consult reference materials (e.g., dictionaries, thesauruses) to determine a word's precise meaning.

Interactive Vocabulary
THINK central

Go to **thinkcentral.com**.
KEYWORD: HML8-89

The Hitchhiker

 Video link at
thinkcentral.com

Radio Play by Lucille Fletcher

Is seeing
BELIEVING?

Occasionally, something happens so quickly or unexpectedly, you can't be sure what you've seen. Was that a rabbit racing through the field, or was it just wind in the grass? Did you see a man hiding in the alley, or did you see only a shadow? To be convinced that something is real, you need proof, or solid evidence. In *The Hitchhiker*, a man is desperate for proof that what he's seeing can be explained.

DISCUSS Think of something you've seen that you can't explain. Maybe it was oddly shaped footprints in an empty lot, or a bright shape flying through the sky. Share your experience with a small group, and together brainstorm possible explanations. Then tell what proof you'd need to determine which explanation is the right one.

● TEXT ANALYSIS: FORESHADOWING

When a writer provides hints that suggest future events in a story, the writer is **foreshadowing.** For example, if a character says, "Whatever you do, don't open that door," you might suspect that the door will eventually be opened to create a dramatic effect. Anticipating that event can add to the story's suspense, making you more excited to find out what happens next.

As you read *The Hitchhiker*, make a chart to note events or dialogue that might foreshadow what happens later. You'll complete the chart at the end of the selection.

Foreshadowing	Events That Were Foreshadowed

● READING STRATEGY: READING A RADIO PLAY

A **radio play** is a play written for radio broadcast, which means that it is primarily meant to be heard, not seen. Since listeners can't see the actors, radio playwrights give information about the characters through

- **Dialogue,** or the words spoken by the actors
- **Stage directions,** which include instructions to the actors about how dialogue should be spoken and instructions to the crew about sounds effects

As you read *The Hitchhiker,* notice what these elements suggest about the personality and state of mind of the protagonist, or main character. Also notice what these elements suggest about the appearance and actions of the antagonist, or the force working against the main character.

▲ VOCABULARY IN CONTEXT

The words in Column A help Lucille Fletcher tell about one man's encounter with a mysterious hitchhiker. Match each word with the word or phrase in Column B that is closest in meaning.

Column A	Column B
1. lark	**a.** guarantee
2. junction	**b.** carefree adventure
3. sinister	**c.** evil
4. assurance	**d.** sameness
5. monotony	**e.** place of joining

 Complete the activities in your **Reader/Writer Notebook.**

Lucille Fletcher
1912–2000

Suspenseful Stories
As a young adult, Lucille Fletcher wanted to become a novelist. After she took her first job as a script typist and began reading scripts by other writers, she decided she wanted to write plays as well. She was successful at both. Fletcher penned more than 20 radio plays, including the well-known *Sorry, Wrong Number* and *The Hitchhiker*. In addition, she wrote several novels. Her works were suspenseful, full of mystery, and often terrifying.

BACKGROUND TO THE PLAY
Radio Plays
Though the television was invented in the 1920s, most American households did not have television sets until the late 1950s. Before then, families gathered around the radio to listen to their favorite radio plays. These plays took the form of dramas, mysteries, or comedies. Actors at the radio station read their lines into the microphone with dramatic flair. Background music helped set the mood.

Hearing Is Believing
Sound effects were an important part of a radio play. They were often produced in the radio studio. Sheet metal, shaken up and down, replicated rolling thunder. A wooden match, broken close to the microphone, sounded like a baseball bat striking a ball. Coconut halves clapped against wood imitated the sound of horses' hooves.

Author Online
THINK central
Go to thinkcentral.com.
KEYWORD: HML8-91

The HITCHHIKER

Lucille Fletcher

CAST OF CHARACTERS

Orson Welles

Ronald Adams

Adams's Mother

Voice of Hitchhiker

Mechanic

Henry, a sleepy man

Woman's Voice, Henry's wife

Girl

Operator

Long-Distance Operator

Albuquerque Operator

New York Operator

Mrs. Whitney

Welles. Good evening, this is Orson Welles . . . (*music in*) Personally I've never met anybody who didn't like a good ghost story, but I know a lot of people who think there are a lot of people who don't like a good ghost story. For the benefit of these, at least, I go on record at the outset of this evening's entertainment with the sober **assurance** that although blood may be curdled on this program none will be spilt. There's no 10 shooting, knifing, throttling, axing or poisoning here. No clanking chains, no cobwebs, no bony and/or hairy hands appearing from secret panels or, better yet, bedroom curtains. If it's any part of that dear old *phosphorescent*[1] foolishness that people who don't like ghost stories don't like, then again I promise you we haven't got it. What we do have is a thriller. If it's half as good as we think it is you can call it a shocker, and we present it proudly and without apologies. After 20 all a story doesn't have to appeal to the heart— it can also appeal to the spine. Sometimes you want your heart to be warmed—sometimes you want your spine to tingle. The tingling, it's to be hoped, will be quite audible as you listen tonight to *The Hitchhiker*—That's the name of our story, *The Hitchhiker*—

---

1. **phosphorescent** (fŏs′fə-rĕs′ənt): glowing with a cold light.

(*sound: automobile wheels humming over concrete road*)

(*music: something weird and shuddery*)

30 **Adams.** I am in an auto camp on Route Sixty-six just west of Gallup, New Mexico. If I tell it perhaps it will help me. It will keep me from going mad. But I must tell this quickly. I am not mad now. I feel perfectly well, except that I am running a slight temperature. My name is Ronald Adams. I am thirty-six years of age, unmarried, tall, dark, with a black mustache. I drive a 1940 Ford V-8, license number 6V-7989. I was born in Brooklyn. All this I know. I know that I am at

40 this moment perfectly sane. That it is not I, who has gone mad—but something else—something utterly beyond my control. But I must speak quickly. At any moment the link with life may break. This may be the last thing I ever tell on earth . . . the last night I ever see the stars. . . .

(*music in*)

Adams. Six days ago I left Brooklyn, to drive to California . . .

Mother. Goodbye, son. Good luck to you, my
50 boy . . .

Adams. Goodbye, mother. Here—give me a kiss, and then I'll go . . .

Mother. I'll come out with you to the car.

Adams. No. It's raining. Stay here at the door. Hey—what is this? Tears? I thought you promised me you wouldn't cry.

Mother. I know dear. I'm sorry. But I—do hate to see you go.

Adams. I'll be back. I'll only be on the coast three
60 months.

Mother. Oh—it isn't that. It's just—the trip. Ronald—I wish you weren't driving.

Adams. Oh—mother. There you go again. People do it every day.

Mother. I know. But you'll be careful, won't you. Promise me you'll be extra careful. Don't fall asleep—or drive fast—or pick up any strangers on the road . . .

Adams. Of course not! You'd think I was still
70 seventeen to hear you talk—

Mother. And wire me as soon as you get to Hollywood, won't you, son?

Adams. Of course I will. Now don't you worry. There isn't anything going to happen. It's just eight days of perfectly simple driving on smooth, decent, civilized roads, with a hotdog or a hamburger stand every ten miles . . . (*fade*)

(*sound: auto hum*)

(*music in*)

80 **Adams.** I was in excellent spirits. The drive ahead of me, even the loneliness, seemed like a **lark.** But I reckoned without *him.*

(*Music changes to something weird and empty.*)

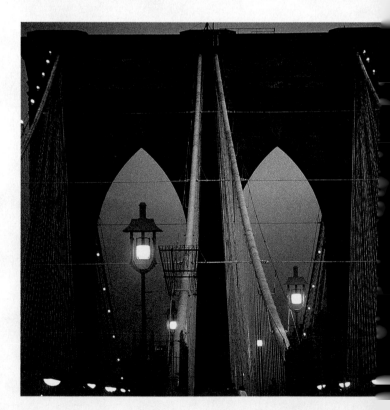

Adams. Crossing Brooklyn Bridge that morning in the rain, I saw a man leaning against the cables. He seemed to be waiting for a lift. There were spots of fresh rain on his shoulders. He was carrying a cheap overnight bag in one hand. He was thin, nondescript, with a cap pulled down
90 over his eyes. He stepped off the walk, and if I hadn't swerved, I'd have hit him.

(*sound: terrific skidding*)

(*music in*)

Adams. I would have forgotten him completely, except that just an hour later, while crossing the Pulaski Skyway over the Jersey flats, I saw him again. At least, he looked like the same person. He was standing now, with one thumb pointing west. I couldn't figure out how he'd got there, but
100 I thought probably one of those fast trucks had picked him up, beaten me to the Skyway, and let him off. I didn't stop for him. Then—late that night, I saw him again.

(*music changing*)

Adams. It was on the new Pennsylvania Turnpike between Harrisburg and Pittsburgh. It's 265 miles long, with a very high speed limit. I was just slowing down for one of the tunnels—when I saw him—standing under an arc light by the side of
110 the road. I could see him quite distinctly. The bag, the cap, even the spots of fresh rain spattered over his shoulders. He hailed me this time . . .

Voice (*very spooky and faint*). Hall-ooo . . . (*echo as through tunnel*) Hall-ooo . . . !

Adams. I stepped on the gas like a shot. That's lonely country through the Alleghenies,[2] and I had no intention of stopping. Besides, the coincidence, or whatever it was, gave me the willies.[3] I stopped at the next gas station.
120 (*sound: auto tires screeching to stop . . . horn honk*)

Mechanic. Yes, sir.

Adams. Fill her up.

Mechanic. Certainly, sir. Check your oil, sir?

Adams. No, thanks.

(*sound: gas being put into car . . . bell tinkle, et cetera*)

Mechanic. Nice night, isn't it?

Adams. Yes. It—hasn't been raining here recently, has it?

130 **Mechanic.** Not a drop of rain all week.

Adams. Hm. I suppose that hasn't done your business any harm.

Mechanic. Oh—people drive through here all kinds of weather. Mostly business, you know. There aren't many pleasure cars out on the turnpike this season of the year.

Adams. I suppose not. (*casually*) What about hitchhikers?

Mechanic (*half laughing*). Hitchhikers *here?*

140 **Adams.** What's the matter? Don't you ever see any?

Mechanic. Not much. If we did, it'd be a sight for sore eyes.

Adams. Why?

Mechanic. A guy'd be a fool who started out to hitch rides on this road. Look at it. It's 265 miles long, there's practically no speed limit, and it's a straightaway. Now what car is going to stop to pick up a guy under those conditions? Would you stop?

150 **Adams.** No. (*slowly, with puzzled emphasis*) Then you've never seen anybody?

Mechanic. Nope. Mebbe they get the lift before the turnpike starts—I mean, you know—just before the toll house—but then it'd be a mighty long ride. Most cars wouldn't want to pick up a guy for that long a ride. And you know—this is pretty lonesome country here—mountains, and woods . . . You ain't seen anybody like that, have you?

Adams. No. (*quickly*) Oh no, not at all. It was—
160 just a—technical question.

---

2. **Alleghenies** (ăl'ĭ-gā'nēz): The Allegheny Mountains, a range extending from northern Pennsylvania to western Virginia.

3. **gave me the willies:** made me nervous.

Mechanic. I see. Well—that'll be just a dollar forty-nine—with the tax . . . (*fade*)

(*sound: auto hum up*)

(*music changing*)

Adams. The thing gradually passed from my mind, as sheer coincidence. I had a good night's sleep in Pittsburgh. I did not think about the man all next day—until just outside of Zanesville, Ohio, I saw him again.

170 (*music: dark, ominous note*)

Adams. It was a bright sunshiny afternoon. The peaceful Ohio fields, brown with the autumn stubble, lay dreaming in the golden light. I was driving slowly, drinking it in, when the road suddenly ended in a detour. In front of the barrier, *he* was standing.

(*music in*)

Adams. Let me explain about his appearance before I go on. I repeat. There was nothing **sinister** about
180 him. He was as drab as a mud fence. Nor was his attitude menacing. He merely stood there, waiting, almost drooping a little, the cheap overnight bag in his hand. He looked as though he had been waiting there for hours. Then he looked up. He hailed me. He started to walk forward.

Voice (*far off*). Hall-ooo . . . Hall-ooo . . .

Adams. I had stopped the car, of course, for the detour. And for a few moments, I couldn't seem to find the new road. I knew he must be thinking
190 that I had stopped for him.

Voice (*closer*). Hall-ooo . . . Hallll . . . ooo . . .

(*sound: gears jamming . . . sound of motor turning over hard . . . nervous accelerator*)

Voice (*closer*). Halll . . . oooo . . .

Adams (*panicky*). No. Not just now. Sorry . . .

Voice (*closer*). Going to California?

(*sound: starter starting . . . gears jamming*)

Adams (*as though sweating blood*). No. Not today. The other way. Going to New York. Sorry . . .
200 sorry . . .

(*sound: car starts with squeal of wheels on dirt . . . into auto hum*)

(*music in*)

Adams. After I got the car back onto the road again, I felt like a fool. Yet the thought of picking him up, of having him sit beside me was somehow unbearable. Yet, at the same time, I felt, more than ever, unspeakably alone.

(*sound: auto hum up*)

210 **Adams.** Hour after hour went by. The fields, the towns ticked off, one by one. The lights changed. I knew now that I was going to see him again. And though I dreaded the sight, I caught myself searching the side of the road, waiting for him to appear.

(*sound: auto hum up . . . car screeches to a halt . . . impatient honk two or three times . . . door being unbolted*)

Sleepy Man's Voice. Yep? What is it? What do you
220 want?

Adams (*breathless*). You sell sandwiches and pop here, don't you?

Voice (*cranky*). Yep. We do. In the daytime. But we're closed up now for the night.

Adams. I know. But—I was wondering if you could possibly let me have a cup of coffee—black coffee.

Voice. Not at this time of night, mister. My wife's the cook and she's in bed. Mebbe further down
230 the road—at the Honeysuckle Rest . . .

(*sound: door squeaking on hinges as though being closed*)

Adams. No—no. Don't shut the door. (*shakily*) Listen—just a minute ago, there was a man standing here—right beside this stand—a suspicious looking man . . .

Woman's Voice (*from distance*). Hen-ry? Who is it, Hen-ry?

Henry. It's nobuddy, mother. Just a feller thinks he
240 wants a cup of coffee. Go back into bed.

Adams. I don't mean to disturb you. But you see, I was driving along—when I just happened to look—and there he was . . .

Henry. What was he doing?

Adams. Nothing. He ran off—when I stopped the car.

Henry. Then what of it? That's nothing to wake a man in the middle of his sleep about. (*sternly*) Young man, I've got a good mind to turn you over
250 to the sheriff.

Adams. But—I—

Henry. You've been taking a nip, that's what you've been doing. And you haven't got anything better to do than to wake decent folk out of their hard-earned sleep. Get going. Go on.

Adams. But—he looked as though he were going to rob you.

Henry. I ain't got nothin' in this stand to lose. Now—on your way before I call out Sheriff
260 Oakes. (*fades*)

(*sound: auto hum up*)

Adams. I got into the car again and drove on slowly. I was beginning to hate the car. If I could have found a place to stop . . . to rest a little. But I was in the Ozark Mountains of Missouri now. The few resort places there were closed. Only an occasional log cabin, seemingly deserted, broke the **monotony** of the wild wooded landscape. I *had* seen him at that roadside stand; I knew I
270 would see him again—perhaps at the next turn of the road. I knew that when I saw him next, I would run him down . . .

(*sound: auto hum up*)

Adams. But I did not see him again until late next afternoon . . .

(*sound: of railroad warning signal at crossroads*)

Adams. I had stopped the car at a sleepy little **junction** just across the border into Oklahoma—to let a train pass by—when he appeared, across
280 the tracks, leaning against a telephone pole.

(*sound: distant sound of train chugging . . . bell ringing steadily*)

Adams (*very tense*). It was a perfectly airless, dry day. The red clay of Oklahoma was baking under the south-western sun. Yet there were spots of fresh rain on his shoulders. I couldn't stand that. Without thinking, blindly, I started the car across the tracks.

(*sound: train chugging closer*)

290 **Adams.** He didn't even look up at me. He was staring at the ground. I stepped on the gas hard, veering the wheel sharply toward him. I could

hear the train in the distance now, but I didn't care. Then something went wrong with the car. It stalled right on the tracks.

(*sound: Train chugging closer. Above this sound of car stalling.*)

Adams. The train was coming closer. I could hear its bell ringing, and the cry of its whistle. Still
300 he stood there. And now—I knew that he was beckoning—beckoning me to my death.

(*sound: Train chugging close. Whistle blows wildly. Then train rushes up and by with pistons going, et cetera.*)

Adams. Well—I frustrated him that time. The starter had worked at last. I managed to back up. But when the train passed, he was gone. I was all alone in the hot dry afternoon.

(*sound: Train retreating. Crickets begin to sing.*)
310 (*music in*)

Adams. After that, I knew I had to do something. I didn't know who this man was or what he wanted of me. I only knew that from now on, I must not let myself be alone on the road for one moment.

(*sound: Auto hum up. Slow down. Stop. Door opening.*)

Adams. Hello, there. Like a ride?

Girl. What do you think? How far you going?

320 **Adams.** Amarillo . . . I'll take you to Amarillo.

Girl. Amarillo, Texas.

Adams. I'll drive you there.

Girl. Gee!

(*sound: Door closes—car starts.*)

(*music in*)

Girl. Mind if I take off my shoes? My dogs⁴ are killing me.

Adams. Go right ahead.

Girl. Gee, what a break this is. A swell car, a decent
330 guy, and driving all the way to Amarillo. All I been getting so far is trucks.

Adams. Hitchhike much?

Girl. Sure. Only it's tough sometimes, in these great open spaces, to get the breaks.

Adams. I should think it would be. Though I'll bet if you get a good pick-up in a fast car, you can get to places faster than—say, another person, in another car?

Girl. I don't get you.

340 **Adams.** Well, take me, for instance. Suppose I'm driving across the country, say, at a nice steady clip of about 45 miles an hour. Couldn't a girl like you, just standing beside the road, waiting for lifts, beat me to town after town—provided she got picked up every time in a car doing from 65 to 70 miles an hour?

Girl. I dunno. Maybe she could and maybe she couldn't. What difference does it make?

Adams. Oh—no difference. It's just a—crazy idea
350 I had sitting here in the car.

Girl (*laughing*). Imagine spending your time in a swell car thinking of things like that!

Adams. What would you do instead?

Girl (*admiringly*). What would I do? If I was a good-looking fellow like yourself? Why—I'd just *enjoy* myself—every minute of the time. I'd sit back, and relax, and if I saw a good-looking girl along the side of the road . . . (*sharply*) Hey! Look out!

Adams (*breathlessly*). Did you see him too?

360 **Girl.** See who?

Adams. That man. Standing beside the barbed wire fence.

Girl. I didn't see—anybody. There wasn't nothing, but a bunch of steers—and the barbed wire fence. What did you think you was doing? Trying to run into the barbed wire fence?

Adams. There was a man there, I tell you . . . a thin gray man, with an overnight bag in his hand. And I was trying to—run him down.

370 **Girl.** Run him down? You mean—kill him?

---

4. **dogs:** a slang term for feet.

Adams. He's a sort of—phantom. I'm trying to get rid of him—or else prove that he's real. But (*desperately*) you say you didn't see him back there? You're sure?

Girl. I didn't see a soul. And as far as that's concerned, mister . . .

Adams. Watch for him the next time, then. Keep watching. Keep your eyes peeled on the road. He'll turn up again—maybe any minute now.

380 (*excitedly*) There. Look there—

(*sound: Auto sharply veering and skidding. Girl screams.*)

(*sound: Crash of car going into barbed wire fence. Frightened lowing[5] of steer.*)

Girl. How does this door work? I—I'm gettin' outta here.

Adams. Did you see him that time?

Girl (*sharply*). No. I didn't see him that time. And personally, mister, I don't expect never to see him.

390 All I want to do is to go on living— and I don't see how I will very long driving with you—

Adams. I'm sorry. I—I don't know what came over me. (*frightened*) Please—don't go . . .

Girl. So if you'll excuse me, mister—

Adams. You can't go. Listen, how would you like to go to California? I'll drive you to California.

Girl. Seeing pink elephants all the way? No thanks.

Adams (*desperately*). I could get you a job there. You wouldn't have to be a waitress. I have friends

400 there—my name is Ronald Adams—You can check up.

(*sound: door opening*)

Girl. Uhn-hunh. Thanks just the same.

Adams. Listen. Please. For just one minute. Maybe you think I am half cracked. But this man. You see, I've been seeing this man all the way across the country. He's been following me. And if you could only help me—stay with me—until I reach the coast—

410 **Girl.** You know what I think you need, big boy? Not a girl friend. Just a good dose of sleep. . . . There, I got it now.

(*sound: door opens . . . slams*)

Adams. No. You can't go.

Girl (*screams*). Leave your hands offa me, do you hear! Leave your—

Adams. Come back here, please, come back.

(*sound: struggle . . . slap . . . footsteps running away on gravel . . . lowing of steer*)

420 **Adams.** She ran from me, as though I were a monster. A few minutes later, I saw a passing truck pick her up. I knew then that I was utterly alone.

(*sound: lowing of steer up*)

Adams. I was in the heart of the great Texas prairies. There wasn't a car on the road after the truck went by. I tried to figure out what to do, how to get hold of myself. If I could find a place to rest. Or even, if I could sleep right here in the car for a few hours, along the side of the road . . .

430 I was getting my winter overcoat out of the back seat to use as a blanket, (Hall-ooo) when I saw him coming toward me, (Hall-ooo), emerging from the herd of moving steer . . .

Voice. Hall-ooo . . . Hall-oooo . . .

(*sound: auto starting violently . . . up to steady hum*)

(*music in*)

Adams. I didn't wait for him to come any closer. Perhaps I should have spoken to him then, fought it out then and there. For now he began

440 to be everywhere. Whenever I stopped, even for a moment—for gas, for oil, for a drink of pop, a cup of coffee, a sandwich—he was there.

(*music faster*)

Adams. I saw him standing outside the auto camp in Amarillo that night, when I dared to slow down. He was sitting near the drinking fountain in a little camping spot just inside the border of New Mexico.

---

5. **lowing:** mooing.

(music faster)

450 **Adams.** He was waiting for me outside the Navajo Reservation, where I stopped to check my tires. I saw him in Albuquerque[6] where I bought 12 gallons of gas . . . I was afraid now, afraid to stop. I began to drive faster and faster. I was in lunar landscape now—the great arid mesa country of New Mexico. I drove through it with the indifference of a fly crawling over the face of the moon.

(music faster)

460 **Adams.** But now he didn't even wait for me to stop. Unless I drove at 85 miles an hour over those endless roads—he waited for me at every other mile. I would see his figure, shadowless, flitting before me, still in its same attitude, over the cold and lifeless ground, flitting over dried-up rivers, over broken stones cast up by old glacial upheavals, flitting in the pure and cloudless air . . .

(music strikes sinister note of finality.)

470 **Adams.** I was beside myself when I finally reached Gallup, New Mexico, this morning. There is an auto camp here—cold, almost deserted at this time of year. I went inside, and asked if there was a telephone. I had the feeling that if only I could speak to someone familiar, someone that I loved, I could pull myself together.

(sound: nickel put in slot)

Operator. Number, please?

Adams. Long distance.

480 **Operator.** Thank you.

(sound: return of nickel; buzz)

Long-Distance Opr. This is long distance.

Adams. I'd like to put in a call to my home in Brooklyn, New York. I'm Ronald Adams. The number is Beechwood 2-0828.

Long-Distance Opr. Thank you. What is your number?

---

6. **Albuquerque** (ăl′bə-kûr′kē): a city in central New Mexico.

Adams. 312.

Albuquerque Opr. Albuquerque.

490 **Long-Distance Opr.** New York for Gallup. (*pause*)

New York Opr. New York.

Long-Distance Opr. Gallup, New Mexico calling Beechwood 2-0828. (*fade*)

Adams. I had read somewhere that love could banish demons. It was the middle of the morning. I knew Mother would be home. I pictured her, tall, white-haired, in her crisp house-dress, going about her tasks. It would be enough, I thought, merely to hear the even calmness of her voice . . .

500 **Long-Distance Opr.** Will you please deposit three dollars and 85 cents for the first three minutes? When you have deposited a dollar and a half, will you wait until I have collected the money?

(*sound: clunk of six coins*)

Long-Distance Opr. All right, deposit another dollar and a half.

(*sound: clunk of six coins*)

Long-Distance Opr. Will you please deposit the remaining 85 cents.

510 (*sound: clunk of four coins*)

Long-Distance Opr. Ready with Brooklyn—go ahead please.

Adams. Hello.

Mrs. Whitney. Mrs. Adams' residence.

Adams. Hello. Hello—Mother?

Mrs. Whitney (*very flat and rather proper . . . dumb, too, in a frizzy sort of way*). This is Mrs. Adams' residence. Who is it you wished to speak to, please?

Adams. Why—who's this?

520 **Mrs. Whitney.** This is Mrs. Whitney.

Adams. Mrs. Whitney? I don't know any Mrs. Whitney. Is this Beechwood 2-0828?

Mrs. Whitney. Yes.

Adams. Where's my mother? Where's Mrs. Adams?

Mrs. Whitney. Mrs. Adams is not at home. She is still in the hospital.

Adams. The hospital!

Mrs. Whitney. Yes. Who is this calling, please? Is it 530 a member of the family?

Adams. What's she in the hospital for?

Mrs. Whitney. She's been prostrated[7] for five days. Nervous breakdown. But who is this calling?

Adams. Nervous breakdown? But—my mother was never nervous . . .

Mrs. Whitney. It's all taken place since the death of her oldest son, Ronald.

Adams. Death of her oldest son, Ronald . . . ? Hey—what is this? What number is this?

540 **Mrs. Whitney.** This is Beechwood 2-0828. It's all been very sudden. He was killed just six days ago in an automobile accident on the Brooklyn Bridge.

Long-Distance Opr. (*breaking in*). Your three minutes are up, sir. (*silence*) Your three minutes are up, sir. (*pause*) Your three minutes are up, sir. (*fade*) Sir, your three minutes are up. Your three minutes are up, sir.

Adams (*in a strange voice*). And so, I am sitting here in this deserted auto camp in Gallup, New 550 Mexico. I am trying to think. I am trying to get hold of myself. Otherwise, I shall go mad . . . Outside it is night—the vast, soulless night of New Mexico. A million stars are in the sky. Ahead of me stretch a thousand miles of empty mesa, mountains, prairies—desert. Somewhere among them, he is waiting for me. Somewhere I shall know who he is, and who . . . I . . . am . . .

(*music up*)

---

7. **prostrated:** in a state of mental collapse.

Comprehension

1. **Recall** What is Ronald Adams's original destination?

2. **Clarify** Why does the repeated sight of the hitchhiker give Adams "the willies"?

3. **Clarify** What does Adams learn about his mother at the end of the play?

Text Analysis

4. **Make Inferences** What kind of relationship did Ronald Adams have with his mother? Cite evidence to support your answer.

● 5. **Examine Foreshadowing** Now that you've read the play, is there anything you'd like to change or add to the first column of your foreshadowing chart? Make the adjustments and complete the second column. Which use of foreshadowing most increased your sense of suspense?

● 6. **Analyze the Radio Play** Reread lines 171–208. What do the stage directions and dialogue tell you about the hitchhiker's appearance and actions? What do these elements tell you about Adams' feelings and actions? Cite specific details in your answer.

7. **Draw Conclusions** Who do you think the hitchhiker is? Give proof from the play to support your conclusion.

8. **Compare Across Texts** What are some similarities and differences between the characters, settings, and structures of "The Tell-Tale Heart" and *The Hitchhiker*? Present your answers in a Venn diagram.

"The Tell-Tale Heart"   The Hitchhiker

Extension and Challenge

9. **Creative Project: Drama** With a small group, choose a scene from *The Hitchhiker* that you think is especially suspenseful. Practice performing the scene, remembering to include sound effects and to follow stage directions. Then perform for the class. Afterward, explain why your group chose the scene you did.

Is seeing BELIEVING?

If you were Adam, would you have believed your eyes, or trusted that the hitchhiker you kept seeing was real? Explain.

COMMON CORE

RL 3 Analyze how particular lines of dialogue or incidents in a story propel the action, reveal aspects of a character, or provoke a decision. **RL 5** Compare and contrast the structure of two or more texts.

Language

◆ **GRAMMAR IN CONTEXT:** Maintain Pronoun Antecedent Agreement

An antecedent is the noun or pronoun to which a pronoun refers. For example, in the following sentence, the pronoun *their* refers to the antecedent *they*: *They took their seats at the café.* Be sure to use singular pronouns with singular antecedents and plural pronouns with plural antecedents. Pair antecedents ending in *one, thing,* or *body* with singular pronouns, such as *he, her, she,* or *his.* In the revised sentence, notice how the pronouns (in yellow) and the antecedent (in green) **agree in number.**

> *Original:* Adams would ask just about anyone whether they had seen the hitchhiker.
>
> *Revised:* Adams would ask just about anyone whether he or she had seen the hitchhiker.

PRACTICE Correct the pronoun antecedent error in each sentence.

1. Adams first saw someone holding their bag on the bridge.
2. Everyone thought Adams was crazy because they could never see the hitchhiker.
3. Adams's scary story would make anybody fear for their life.
4. Nobody could have suspected that they got a ride from a dead man!

For more help with pronoun-antecedent agreement, see page R52 in the ***Grammar Handbook.***

READING-WRITING CONNECTION

YOUR TURN

Show your understanding of *The Hitchhiker* by responding to this prompt. Then use the **revising tip** to improve your writing.

WRITING PROMPT	REVISING TIP
Short Constructed Response: Evaluation The play opens with Adams telling the listeners, "I am not mad." On the basis of what you learn in the rest of the play, do you agree with his assessment? Write a **one-paragraph evaluation** of Adams's sanity.	Review your paragraph. Does each pronoun agree with its antecedent? If not, revise your writing.

COMMON CORE

L1 Demonstrate command of standard English grammar when writing. **W1** Write arguments to support claims with clear reasons and relevant evidence.

Interactive Revision **THINK** central

Go to <u>thinkcentral.com</u>.
KEYWORD: HML8-103

Hoot

Novel by Carl Hiaasen

COMMON CORE

RL 10 Read and comprehend
literature.

Meet Carl Hiaasen

Carl Hiaasen (hī′ə-sən) is a Florida native. He is an award-winning reporter and longtime columnist for the *Miami Herald*, as well as being the author of numerous mystery novels for adults. *Hoot* is his first young adult novel.

Much of Hiaasen's writing reflects his love of the outdoors. The heroes in his novels are often protectors of the environment. The villains represent corporate greed and abuse of nature. A reviewer once noted that Hiaasen "displays no mercy for anyone perceived as being responsible for defiling his home environment."

Try a Mystery Novel

What makes a book a **mystery novel?** First, you need a crime or unexplained event. There will be various clues left behind and possible motives for what happened. Suspense will build as further clues are revealed. Characters in the story will try to solve the mystery, but you, as the reader, might figure it out before they do. You can never be too sure of the answer, though—there might be a plot twist that changes everything.

Reading Fluency refers to how easily and well you read. Fluent readers read smoothly, accurately, and with feeling. To improve your reading fluency, it helps to practice reading aloud. When reading aloud, be sure to group words into meaningful phrases that sound like natural speech.

Read a Great Book

Roy Eberhardt didn't know what he was in for when his family moved from Bozeman, Montana, to Coconut Cove, Florida. He's getting bullied on the bus, but he's used to that. In fact, since his family moves around a lot, he's encountered enough bullies to consider himself "an expert on the breed." It's the stuff that he isn't used to that makes his new home seem strange. For starters, he spies a barefoot boy sprinting alongside the school bus at a speed that would put track stars in state-of-the-art running shoes to shame. Then there's the big, threatening girl who knows too much about him and won't tell him how. Roy needs to find some answers to his questions, but it won't be easy.

from

HOOT

"Are there any other schools around here?" Roy asked Garrett.

"Why? You sick of this one already?" Garrett cackled and plunged a spoon into a lump of clammy apple crisp.

"No way. The reason I asked, I saw this weird kid today at one of the bus stops. Except he didn't get on the bus, and he's not here at school," Roy said, "so I figured he must not go to Trace."

"I don't know *anyone* who doesn't go to Trace," Garrett said. "There's a Catholic school up in Fort Myers, but that's a long ways off. Was he wearing a uniform, this kid? Because the nuns make everybody wear 10 uniforms."

"No, he definitely wasn't in a uniform."

"You're sure he was in middle school? Maybe he goes to Graham," Garrett suggested. Graham was the public high school nearest to Coconut Cove.

Roy said, "He didn't look big enough for high school."

"Maybe he was a midget." Garrett grinned and made a funny noise with one of his cheeks.

"I don't think so," said Roy.

"You said he was weird."

20 "He wasn't wearing any shoes," Roy said, "and he was running like crazy."

"Maybe somebody was after him. Did he look scared?"

"Not really."

Garrett nodded. "High school kid. Betcha five bucks."

To Roy, that still didn't make sense. Classes at Graham High started fifty-five minutes earlier than the classes at Trace; the high school kids were off the streets long before the middle school buses finished their routes.

"So he was skippin' class. Kids skip all the time," Garrett said.

30 "You want your dessert?"

Roy pushed his tray across the table. "You ever skip school?"

"Uh, yeah," Garrett said sarcastically. "Buncha times."

"You ever skip alone?"

Garrett thought for a moment. "No. It's always me and my friends."

"See. That's what I mean."

"So maybe the kid's just a psycho. Who cares?"

"Or an outlaw," said Roy.

Garrett looked skeptical. "An outlaw? You mean like Jesse James?"

"No, not exactly," Roy said, though there *had* been something wild

40 in that kid's eyes.

Garrett laughed again. "An outlaw—that's rich, Eberhardt. You got a seriously whacked imagination."

"Yeah," said Roy, but already he was thinking about a plan. He was determined to find the running boy.

❧

The next morning, Roy traded seats on the school bus to be closer to the front door. When the bus turned onto the street where he had seen the running boy, Roy slipped his backpack over his shoulders and

scouted out the window, waiting. Seven rows back, Dana Matherson
was tormenting a sixth grader named Louis. Louis was from Haiti and
50 Dana was merciless.

As the bus came to a stop at the intersection, Roy poked his head
out the window and checked up and down the street. Nobody was
running. Seven kids boarded the bus, but the strange shoeless boy
was not among them.

❧

It was the same story the next day, and the day after that. By Friday,
Roy had pretty much given up. He was sitting ten rows from
the door, reading an X-Man comic, as the bus turned the familiar
corner and began to slow down. A movement at the corner of his eye
made Roy glance up from his comic book—and there he was on the
60 sidewalk, running again! Same basketball jersey, same grimy shorts,
same black-soled feet.

As the brakes of the school bus wheezed, Roy grabbed his backpack
off the floor and stood up. At that instant, two big sweaty hands
closed around his neck.

"Where ya goin', cowgirl?"

"Lemme go," Roy rasped, squirming to break free.

The grip on his throat tightened. He felt Dana's ashtray breath on
his right ear: "How come you don't got your boots on today? Who ever
heard of a cowgirl wearing Air Jordans?"

70 "They're Reeboks," Roy squeaked.

The bus had stopped, and the students were starting to board.
Roy was furious. He had to get to the door fast, before the driver closed
it and the bus began to roll.

But Dana wouldn't let go, digging his fingers into Roy's windpipe.
Roy was having trouble getting air, and struggling only made it
worse.

"Look at you," Dana chortled from behind, "red as a tomato!"

Roy knew the rules against fighting on the bus, but he couldn't think
of anything else to do. He clenched his right fist and brought it up

80 blindly over his shoulder, as hard as he could. The punch landed
on something moist and rubbery.

There was a gargled cry; then Dana's hands fell away from Roy's
neck. Panting, Roy bolted for the door of the bus just as the last
student, a tall girl with curly blond hair and red-framed eyeglasses,
came up the steps. Roy clumsily edged past her and jumped to
the ground.

"Where do you think you're going?" the girl demanded.

"Hey, wait!" the bus driver shouted, but Roy was already a blur.

The running boy was way ahead of him, but Roy figured he could
90 stay close enough to keep him in sight. He knew the kid couldn't go
at full speed forever.

He followed him for several blocks—over fences, through shrubbery,
weaving through yapping dogs and lawn sprinklers and hot tubs.
Eventually Roy felt himself tiring. This kid is amazing, he thought.
Maybe he's practicing for the track team.

Once Roy thought he saw the boy glance over his shoulder, as if he
knew he was being pursued, but Roy couldn't be certain. The boy was
still far ahead of him, and Roy was gulping like a beached trout. His
shirt was soaked and perspiration poured off his forehead, stinging
100 his eyes.

The last house in the subdivision was still under construction, but
the shoeless boy dashed heedlessly through the lumber and loose nails.
Three men hanging drywall stopped to holler at him, but the boy never
broke stride. One of the same workers made a one-armed lunge at Roy
but missed.

Suddenly there was grass under his feet again—the greenest,
softest grass that Roy had ever seen. He realized that he was on a
golf course, and that the blond kid was tearing down the middle of
a long, lush fairway.

110 On one side was a row of tall Australian pines, and on the other side
was a milky man-made lake. Roy could see four brightly dressed figures
ahead, gesturing at the barefoot boy as he ran by.

Roy gritted his teeth and kept going. His legs felt like wet cement,
and his lungs were on fire. A hundred yards ahead, the boy cut sharply

to the right and disappeared into the pine trees. Roy doggedly aimed himself for the woods.

An angry shout echoed, and Roy noticed that the people in the fairway were waving their arms at him, too. He kept right on running. Moments later there was a distant glint of sunlight on
120 metal, followed by a muted *thwack*. Roy didn't actually see the golf ball until it came down six feet in front of him. He had no time to duck or dive out of the way. All he could do was turn his head and brace for the blow.

The bounce caught him squarely above the left ear, and at first it didn't even hurt. Then Roy felt himself swaying and spinning as a brilliant gout of fireworks erupted inside his skull. He felt himself falling for what seemed like a long time, falling as softly as a drop of rain on velvet.

When the golfers ran up and saw Roy facedown in the sand trap,
130 they thought he was dead. Roy heard their frantic cries but he didn't move. The sugar-white sand felt cool against his burning cheeks, and he was very sleepy. ❧

Keep Reading

Roy has gone from reading mysteries to being right in the middle of one. But the barefoot boy is just one of the mysteries in Roy's new hometown, where reptile wranglers are listed in the phone book because you just might find an alligator in your toilet. While Roy is trying to find out who the strange boy is, the Coconut Cove Public Safety Department has another mystery on its hands. Someone is sabotaging the construction of a pancake house, and no one knows why. Keep reading to see how the mystery unfolds.

from **The Sisterhood of the Traveling Pants**

Film Clip on **Media Smart** DVD-ROM

How do GREAT stories begin?

COMMON CORE

RL 7 Analyze a filmed production, evaluating the choices made by the director.

Quite often, a popular book is made into a major motion picture. Fans of the book form long lines at theaters, eager to experience big-screen portrayals of gripping moments they know so well. What movie versions of books have you enjoyed? What made those movies worthwhile? Prepare to watch a clip from a movie that's based on a well-loved novel. You'll explore what filmmakers do to draw you into the plot of a movie.

Background

A Perfect Fit The novel *The Sisterhood of the Traveling Pants* is about four lifelong best friends who are about to spend their first summer apart. Before their vacations begin, these girls make an amazing discovery. A pair of jeans purchased in a thrift shop fits each one of them perfectly. To stay connected that summer, they agree to mail the jeans to each other. This book's popularity led to sequels to the novel as well as a movie. The scene you'll watch occurs fairly early in the movie and focuses on Carmen, who is about to visit her dad.

Media Literacy: Plot in Movies

The **exposition** stage of a story is the part that introduces the characters, setting, and conflict. Movies unfold in a similar way, introducing the characters and their struggles. For a movie director, the first steps in developing a plot are to show characters' relationships and predicaments, and to make viewers like you care about these characters. Filmmakers position the characters and the camera in certain ways to help you to follow and react to what's happening.

HOW DIRECTORS TELL THEIR STORIES

Directors position characters to portray relationships.

To show how characters relate to each other in a scene, directors use **blocking,** the arrangement of the characters within a film frame.

Directors position the camera to reveal how what's happening affects the characters.

A **close-up shot** is a detailed view of a character or an object. Close-ups can reveal a character's personality and often hint at a character's emotions or thoughts. **Medium shots** show a character from the waist up. This type of shot can capture movements that reveal a character's behavior.

Directors try to stir viewers' emotions.

Directors not only want you to understand what's happening in a story but to get you emotionally involved. They want you to follow the plot complications closely and to make you wonder about the outcome.

STRATEGIES FOR VIEWING

▶ Notice how close or how far apart characters stand to one another. Their positions may offer clues about their relationships or their emotions.

▶ To watch for what might be revealed in close-up or medium shots, ask yourself:
- What reactions or thoughts can I infer from a character's facial expressions?
- What does a character's body language tell me about how he or she feels about what's happening?

▶ As you watch a conflict unfold in a scene, ask yourself:
- How am I reacting to what's happening?
- What does the director do to make me care about what will happen?
- What is the mood of the music? Is it upbeat? Sad? How is it affecting me?

Media Smart DVD-ROM

- **Film:** *The Sisterhood of the Traveling Pants*
- **Director:** Ken Kwapis
- **Genre:** Drama
- **Running Time:** 2.5 minutes

Viewing Guide for
The Sisterhood of the Traveling Pants

The scene you'll watch focuses on Carmen, who has just arrived to spend the summer with her dad. First, watch the clip to follow what's happening in the scene. Then view the clip a few times to spot techniques that convey the conflict and encourage viewers to connect to the characters. Answer these questions to help you analyze the clip.

NOW VIEW

FIRST VIEWING: Comprehension

1. **Recall** Carmen surprises her dad with her grades. What is the surprise Carmen's dad reveals to her?

2. **Clarify** What is shown from outside of the moving car that gets Carmen's attention?

CLOSE VIEWING: Media Literacy

3. **Analyze Character** How do the filmmakers show Carmen's excitement at spending the summer with her father?

4. **Analyze Blocking** This image of the three characters is an example of how a director can position characters in a film frame to signal character relationships. Through blocking, what is the director communicating to viewers about Carmen's relationship to the others?

5. **Analyze Techniques** One song plays throughout the scene. What effect do you think the song is intended to have on you?

6. **Evaluate Techniques** The scene focuses on two characters having a conversation that leads to a tense moment. How well do the filmmakers set the stage for a conflict that will develop as the movie progresses? Base your opinion on these elements:

   - the details about the characters that are delivered through dialogue
   - the shots the filmmakers use to make the characters' emotions visible
   - your own emotional reactions to what happens in the scene

Write or Discuss

Analyze Film You've viewed a clip from *The Sisterhood of the Traveling Pants* to look at how directors portray characters and conflicts. Now put yourself in the shoes of the movie's director. How might the scene be different if it focused less on Carmen and more on her dad and his news? Write a short description of this new version. Think about

- which character would have more close-ups
- how viewers might sympathize more with him
- how the music might differ

COMMON CORE

RL 7 Analyze a filmed production, evaluating the choices made by the director.

Media Tools THINK central
Go to **thinkcentral.com**.
KEYWORD: HML8-113

Produce Your Own Media

Create a Storyboard A **storyboard** is a device filmmakers use to plan the shooting of a movie. A storyboard can serve as a visual map and is made up of a few images and brief descriptions. Choose an important scene from a novel you've recently read or any of the stories from this unit. With a partner, make a storyboard that portrays a conflict.

HERE'S HOW Use these as tips for creating your storyboard:

- Make your storyboard simple rather than beautiful. Draw or sketch the images, making sure they're easy to understand.
- Within the six separate frames, include close-ups or medium shots that reveal a character's reactions or emotions.
- Show shots that reveal a conflict. Show how at least one character reacts.
- Underneath each frame, write out a specific description or a line of dialogue.

STUDENT MODEL

"Runners, take your places at the starting line!"

Medium shot of Squeaky getting ready

Close-up shot of Raymond watching

Medium shot of Squeaky running

Medium shot of Raymond running

Medium shot of squeaky winning the race

Tech Tip

Use a word processing program to type the descriptions or dialogue for the storyboard.

My First Free Summer

Memoir by Julia Alvarez

When is it time to LEAVE?

COMMON CORE

RI 1 Cite the textual evidence that supports an analysis of what the text says explicitly. RI 3 Analyze how a text makes connections among individuals, ideas, and events.

Even under the best of circumstances, leaving someone or something behind can be difficult. Familiar people and places often provide us with a sense of safety and security. In the memoir you are about to read, Julia Alvarez faces the pain of leaving her homeland, even as she realizes the dangers of staying.

QUICKWRITE Reflect on times when you have had to leave a special person or place. Choose one experience and write a journal entry that explores your feelings about leaving. Were you looking forward to moving on? What were you worried about?

● TEXT ANALYSIS: MEMOIR

A **memoir** is a form of autobiographical writing in which a writer describes important events in his or her life. Most memoirs

- use the first-person point of view
- are true accounts of actual events
- describe conflicts faced by the writer
- include the writer's feelings about events or issues

As you read, look for places where Julia Alvarez shares her feelings about the historic events taking place in the Dominican Republic.

● READING SKILL: RECOGNIZE CAUSE AND EFFECT

Events are often related by **cause and effect,** which means that one event brings about the other. The first event is the **cause,** and what follows is the **effect.** Sometimes, one cause can have many effects. Asking questions about cause and effect relationships can help you understand important turning points, because you'll be aware of the consequences of events and actions.

As you read, chart the effects that the political struggle in Alvarez's homeland had on her life.

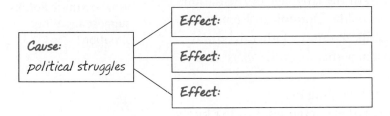

▲ VOCABULARY IN CONTEXT

Alvarez uses the vocabulary words to help describe a traumatic childhood experience. See how many you know. Make a chart like the one shown. Put each word in the appropriate column.

WORD LIST			
contradiction	replete	unravel	
interrogation	summon		

Know Well	Think I Know	Don't Know at All

 Complete the activities in your **Reader/Writer Notebook.**

Julia Alvarez
born 1950

Where Is Home?
Julia Alvarez emigrated from the Dominican Republic to the United States when she was ten. Her father had taken part in an underground plot against dictator Rafael Trujillo (rä-fä′yəl trōō-hē′yō), so the family's safety was in jeopardy. Although Alvarez and her family escaped, she found it difficult being cut off from her homeland and adjusting to a new country. Books offered Alvarez a world where she did not feel alone. Through writing, she could begin to connect her two cultures. She likes to quote another poet in saying, "Language is the only homeland."

A Poet First
Poetry first drew Alvarez to writing. After receiving degrees in literature and writing, she spent 13 years teaching poetry at several universities. *Homecoming,* a book of her poems, was published in 1984. Since then, Alvarez has gone on to write in a variety of genres, including fiction for both children and adults.

BACKGROUND TO THE MEMOIR
A Brutal Dictator
The people of the Dominican Republic suffered under the brutal dictatorship of Rafael Trujillo and his supporters for 31 years (from 1930–1961). Under his rule, masses of people were slaughtered for "crimes" as minor as not hanging his portrait in their homes. Many brave Dominicans, including Alvarez's father, tried to overthrow this government. Those caught faced terrible consequences.

Author Online
THINK central

Go to **thinkcentral.com.**
KEYWORD: HML8-115

My First FREE Summer

Julia Alvarez

I never had summer—I had summer school. First grade, summer school. Second grade, summer school. Thirdgradesummerschoolfourthgradesummerschool. In fifth grade, I vowed I would get interested in fractions, the presidents of the United States, Mesopotamia; I would learn my English.

That was the problem. English. My mother had decided to send her children to the American school so we could learn the language of the nation that would soon be liberating us. For thirty years, the Dominican Republic had endured a bloody and repressive dictatorship.[1] From my father, who was involved in an underground plot, my mother knew that *los américanos*[2] had
10 promised to help bring democracy to the island.

"You have to learn your English!" Mami kept scolding me.

"But why?" I'd ask. I didn't know about my father's activities. I didn't know the dictator was bad. All I knew was that my friends who were attending Dominican schools were often on holiday to honor the dictator's birthday, the dictator's saint day, the day the dictator became the dictator, the day the dictator's oldest son was born, and so on. They marched in parades and visited the palace and had their picture in the paper.

Meanwhile, I had to learn about the pilgrims with their funny witch hats, about the 50 states and where they were on the map, about Dick and Jane[3] and
20 their tame little pets, Puff and Spot, about freedom and liberty and justice for all—while being imprisoned in a hot classroom with a picture of a man wearing a silly wig hanging above the blackboard. And all of this learning I had to do in that impossibly difficult, rocks-in-your-mouth language of English! **A**

---

1. **dictatorship** (dĭk-tā'tər-shĭp'): a government under an absolute ruler, or dictator.
2. *los américanos* (lōs ə-mĕr'ĭ-kä'nōs) *Spanish:* the Americans.
3. **Dick and Jane:** characters in a children's reading textbook.

Analyze Visuals ▶

Look at the girl's expression, posture, and clothing, as well as the window she leans near. What do these **details** suggest about her situation?

A CAUSE AND EFFECT
What effect does Mr. Alvarez's political involvement have on Julia's life? Include this in your chart.

Detail of *The Stillness of an Afternoon* (2003), Bo Bartlett. Oil on panel, 18½″ × 21″. Courtesy of the artist and P.P.O.W. Gallery, New York.

Somehow, I managed to scrape by. Every June, when my prospects looked iffy, Mami and I met with the principal. I squirmed in my seat while they arranged for my special summer lessons.

"She is going to work extra hard. Aren't you, young lady?" the principal would quiz me at the end of our session.

My mother's eye on me, I'd murmur, "Yeah."

30 "Yes, what?" Mami coached.

"Yes." I sighed. "Sir."

It's a wonder that I just wasn't thrown out, which was what I secretly hoped for. But there were extenuating circumstances,[4] the grounds on which the American school stood had been donated by my grandfather. In fact, it had been my grandmother who had encouraged Carol Morgan to start her school. The bulk of the student body was made up of the sons and daughters of American diplomats and business people, but a few Dominicans—most of them friends or members of my family—were allowed to attend.

"You should be grateful!" Mami scolded on the way home from our 40 meeting. "Not every girl is lucky enough to go to the Carol Morgan School!"

In fifth grade, I straightened out. "Yes, ma'am!" I learned to say brightly. "Yes, sir!" To wave my hand in sword-wielding swoops so I could get called on with the right answer. What had changed me? Gratitude? A realization of my luckiness? No, sir! The thought of a fun summer? Yes, ma'am! I wanted to run with the pack of cousins and friends in the common yard that connected all our properties. To play on the trampoline and go off to *la playa*[5] and get brown as a berry. I wanted to be free. Maybe American principles had finally sunk in!  **B**

The summer of 1960 began in bliss: I did not have to go to summer school! *Attitude much improved. Her English progressing nicely. Attentive and cooperative* 50 *in classroom.* I grinned as Mami read off the note that accompanied my report card of Bs.

But the yard **replete** with cousins and friends that I had dreamed about all year was deserted. Family members were leaving for the United States, using whatever connections they could drum up. The plot had **unraveled.** Every day there were massive arrests. The United States had closed its embassy and was advising Americans to return home.

My own parents were terrified. Every night black Volkswagens blocked our driveway and stayed there until morning. "Secret police," my older sister whispered.

60 "Why are they secret if they're the police?" I asked.

"Shut up!" my sister hissed. "Do you want to get us all killed?"

Day after day, I kicked a deflated beach ball around the empty yard, feeling as if I'd been tricked into good behavior by whomever God put in charge of the lives of 10-year-olds. I was bored. Even summer school would have been better than this! **C**

SOCIAL STUDIES CONNECTION

Dictator Trujillo established the SIM (Military Intelligence Service), a secret police force that spied on fellow Dominicans and engaged in torture and murder at Trujillo's request.

B MEMOIR
What does freedom mean to Alvarez at this point in her life?

replete (rĭ-plēt′) *adj.* abundantly supplied

unravel (ŭn-răv′əl) *v.* to undo; come apart

C CAUSE AND EFFECT
What's causing Alvarez to have a boring summer?

---

4. **extenuating circumstances** (ĭk-stĕn′yōō-ā′tĭng sûr′kəm-stăn′səs): a situation or condition that provides an excuse for an action.

5. *la playa* (lä plä′yä) *Spanish:* the beach.

One day toward the end of the summer, my mother **summoned** my sisters and me. She wore that too-bright smile she sometimes pasted on her terrified face.

"Good news, girls! Our papers and tickets came! We're leaving for the United States!"

70 Our mouths dropped. We hadn't been told we were going on a trip anywhere, no less to some place so far away.

I was the first to speak up. "But why?"

My mother flashed me the same look she used to give me when I'd ask why I had to learn English.

I was about to tell her that I didn't want to go to the United States, where summer school had been invented and everyone spoke English. But my mother lifted a hand for silence. "We're leaving in a few hours. I want you all to go get ready! I'll be in to pack soon." The desperate look in her eyes did not allow for **contradiction.** We raced off, wondering how to fit the contents of our

80 Dominican lives into four small suitcases. **D**

Our flight was scheduled for that afternoon, but the airplane did not appear. The terminal filled with soldiers, wielding machine guns, checking papers, escorting passengers into a small **interrogation** room. Not everyone returned.

"It's a trap," I heard my mother whisper to my father.

This had happened before, a cat-and-mouse game[6] the dictator liked to play. Pretend that he was letting someone go, and then at the last minute, their family and friends conveniently gathered together—wham! The secret police would haul the whole clan away.

Of course, I didn't know that this was what my parents were dreading.

90 But as the hours ticked away, and afternoon turned into evening and evening into night and night into midnight with no plane in sight, a light came on in my head. If the light could be translated into words, instead, they would say: Freedom and liberty and justice for all . . . I knew that ours was not a trip, but an escape. We had to get to the United States. **E**

The rest of that night is a blur. It is one, then two the next morning. A plane lands, lights flashing. We are walking on the runway, climbing up the stairs into the cabin. An American lady wearing a cap welcomes us. We sit down, ready to depart. But suddenly, soldiers come on board. They go seat by seat, looking at our faces. Finally, they leave, the door closes, and with a powerful

100 roar, we lift off and I fall asleep.

Next morning, we are standing inside a large, echoing hall as a stern American official reviews our documents. What if he doesn't let us in? What if we have to go back? I am holding my breath. My parents' terror has become mine.

He checks our faces against the passport pictures. When he is done, he asks, "You girls ready for school?" I swear he is looking at me.

"Yes, sir!" I speak up.

The man laughs. He stamps our papers and hands them to my father. Then, wonderfully, a smile spreads across his face. "Welcome to the United States," he says, waving us in. ∽

---

6. **cat-and-mouse game:** cruel, playful game to torment another.

summon (sŭm'ən)
v. to send for; call

contradiction
(kŏn'trə-dĭk'shən) *n.*
a denial; an expression
that is opposite to

D CAUSE AND EFFECT
Why is Alvarez's family
leaving for the United
States on such short
notice? Mark this in
your chart.

interrogation
(ĭn-tĕr'ə-gā'shən) *n.*
an official or formal
questioning

E MEMOIR
Reread lines 89–94.
What changes have
occurred in Alvarez's
thinking about the
Dominican Republic
and the United States?

Comprehension

1. **Recall** Why was Alvarez allowed to attend the American school?

2. **Clarify** What happened at the airport as the Alvarez family waited for the plane?

COMMON CORE

RI 1 Cite the textual evidence that supports an analysis of what the text says explicitly. **RI 3** Analyze how a text makes connections among individuals, ideas, and events.

Text Analysis

3. **Interpret Memoir** What do you think the title of the memoir means? Consider the possible meanings of the word "free." Cite evidence from the selection to support your interpretation.

4. **Analyze Personality Traits** Choose three words or phrases to describe Alvarez as a child. Include them in a web like the one shown. Expand the web by providing specific examples from the memoir that support each description.

> curious
>
> "But why?" I'd ask, "But why?"
>
> Young Alvarez

5. **Analyze Perspective** Although the events depicted in the memoir take place when Alvarez was a child, she writes about the experience many years later. Find at least two examples from the selection that show her adult perspective, or view on the topic. What does she know as an adult that she didn't know at the time?

6. **Generalize About Cause and Effect** Review the chart you created as you read. On the basis of the information you collected, make a general statement about how political events affected Alvarez's personal life.

Extension and Challenge

7. SOCIAL STUDIES CONNECTION Research one of the following topics to find out more about the Dominican Republic during Trujillo's rule. Present your findings in a poster.

   - The 14th of June Movement
   - "The Butterflies"
   - Trujillo's assassination

When is it time to LEAVE?

By the end of the memoir, Alvarez's feelings about leaving her homeland have changed. Why does she now feel differently?

Vocabulary in Context

▲ **VOCABULARY PRACTICE**

Choose the word from the list that is the best substitute for each boldfaced word or phrase.

1. Julia had hoped her summer would be **filled** with free time and fun.
2. Her plans for a carefree summer were soon to **come apart.**
3. When Julia's mother spoke, there was no room for **disagreement.**
4. Officials started to **call** the passengers for questioning.
5. The **questioning** took place in a small room.

contradiction

interrogation

replete

summon

unravel

ACADEMIC VOCABULARY IN WRITING

• affect   • conclude   • evident   • imply   • initial

Write a paragraph explaining the challenges that led the Alvarez family to **conclude** that they had to leave the Domincan Republic. Use at least one Acacademic Vocabulary word in your response.

⋯ **COMMON CORE**

L 4b Use Latin roots as clues to the meaning of a word.

VOCABULARY STRATEGY: THE LATIN ROOT *dict*

The vocabulary word *contradiction* contains the Latin root *dict* (also spelled *dic*), which means "say" or "speak." Your understanding of this root can help you to figure out the meaning of other words formed from *dict*.

PRACTICE Look up each word that appears in the web. Then decide which word best completes each sentence. Be ready to explain how the meaning of the root is reflected in each word.

1. The jury stated its findings by announcing the _____.
2. To say that someone has done something wrong is to _____ him.
3. The ruler with absolute power will ____ the laws of the land.
4. Were you able to _____, or tell in advance, what would happen?
5. Her precise way of speaking showed that she had wonderful _____.

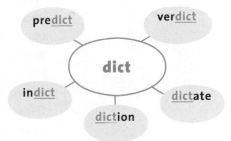

pre<u>dict</u>   ver<u>dict</u>

dict

in<u>dict</u>   <u>dict</u>ate

<u>dict</u>ion

Interactive Vocabulary THINK central

Go to thinkcentral.com.
KEYWORD: HML8-121

The Great Rat Hunt

HISTORY Video link at
<u>thinkcentral.com</u>

Memoir by Laurence Yep

When is it OK to be
SCARED?

COMMON CORE

RI 3 Analyze how a text makes connections among individuals, ideas, and events. **RI 5** Analyze the structure of a text.

A spider. A roller coaster. A hurricane. We're all scared of something. Even so, it can be hard to admit to being afraid. If your friends think it's fun to jump off the high dive, you might not want them to know that heights frighten you. In the selection you are about to read, Laurence Yep tells about a time he tried to overcome his fear in order to impress his father.

SURVEY What scares you and your classmates? Find out by conducting an informal survey. On your own, jot down three or four of your fears. Then meet with a small group, combine your lists, and tally the results. Which fears are most common? Which surprised you? Create a list of the suggestions you think are most effective.

What Scares You?	
Fears	Number of People
1. Heights	))))
2. Thunder	))
3. The dark	)))
4.	

● **TEXT ANALYSIS: CONFLICT IN NONFICTION**

In the memoir you're about to read, Laurence Yep relates an event from his childhood. To tell this real-life story, he uses some of the same literary elements that appear in his award-winning fiction. For example, the narrative centers around **conflicts,** or struggles between opposing forces. As you read "The Great Rat Hunt," identify the conflicts the young Laurence Yep faces.

● **READING SKILL: IDENTIFY CHRONOLOGICAL ORDER**

Memoirs are often organized in **chronological order,** which means that events are presented in the order in which they happened. To make sure you know when each event occurs, follow these steps:

- Identify individual events taking place.
- Look for words and phrases that signal order, such as *before, after, first, next, then, while, the next day,* or *an hour and a half later.*

As you read, keep track of the chronology in a chart. Use parallel boxes when two actions occur at the same time.

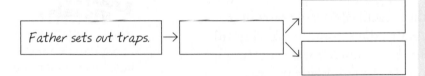

Father sets out traps. →

▲ **VOCABULARY IN CONTEXT**

The boldfaced words help Laurence Yep relate a story from his childhood. To see how many you know, substitute a different word or phrase for each one.

1. **barricade** the doorway
2. **rationalize** a bad habit
3. **wince** in pain
4. **perpetual** motion
5. an **improvised** comedy skit
6. known for his quiet **reserve**
7. **vigilant** watchdog
8. the **ravage** caused by the flood
9. embarrassed by my **ineptitude**
10. spoken to me **brusquely**

Complete the activities in your **Reader/Writer Notebook.**

Laurence Yep
born 1948

A Man of Accomplishment
Laurence Yep has said that he approaches American culture as "somewhat of a stranger." Born in San Francisco, California, Yep was always surrounded by people of various backgrounds, none quite like his own. He was raised in an African-American community and commuted to a bilingual school in Chinatown. There, his classmates teased him for not knowing Chinese. Yep began submitting his work to magazines when a high school English teacher made publishing a story a requirement for getting an A in the class. He became a published author at 18 and went on to publish dozens of stories, as well as earning a college degree and a PhD. Many of the main conflicts in his works involve feeling like an outsider.

A Father's Pride
Yep's writing has gained him numerous awards, including more than ten for his book *Dragonwings*—a book that, like many of his more recent works, explores Chinese mythology. Yep's success as a writer greatly pleased his father, who displayed his son's writing medals and plaques "in lieu of athletic accomplishments."

Authors Online
Go to **thinkcentral.com.** KEYWORD: HML8-123
THINK central

The Great Rat Hunt

Laurence Yep

Analyze Visuals ▶
What can you **infer** about the relationship between the man and the boy in this painting?

I had asthma[1] when I was young, so I never got to play sports much with my father. While my brother and father practiced, I could only sit in bed, propped up by a stack of pillows. As I read my comic books, I heard them beneath our apartment window. In the summer, it was the thump of my brother's fastball into my father's mitt. In the fall, it was the smack of a football. In the winter, it was the airy bounce of a basketball.

Though my father had come from China when he was eight, he had taken quickly to American games. When he and Mother were young, they had had the same dances and sports leagues as their white schoolmates—but kept
10 separate in Chinatown. (He had met Mother when she tripped him during a co-ed basketball game at the Chinatown Y.)

Father was big as a teenager and good at sports. In fact, a social club in Chinatown had hired him to play football against social clubs in other Chinatowns. There he was, a boy playing against grown men.

During a game in Watsonville, a part-time butcher had broken Father's nose. It never properly healed, leaving a big bump at the bridge. There were other injuries too from baseball, basketball, and tennis. Each bump and scar on his body had its own story, and each story was matched by a trophy or medal.

20 Though he now ran a grocery store in San Francisco, he tried to pass on his athletic skills to my older brother Eddy and me. During the times I felt well, I tried to keep up with them, but my lungs always failed me. **A**

A CONFLICT
How does Yep's asthma affect his relationship with his father and brother?

---

1. **asthma** (ăz′mə): a lung disease that at times makes breathing difficult.

Illustrations by Jan Peng Wang.

When I had to sit down on the curb, I felt as if I had let my father down. I'd glance up anxiously when I felt his shadow over me; but he looked neither angry nor disgusted—just puzzled, as if he could not understand why my lungs were not like his.

"S-s-sorry." I panted.

"That's okay." He squatted and waved his hat, trying to fan more air at me. In the background, Eddy played catch with himself, waiting impatiently for
30 the lessons to begin again. Ashamed, I would gasp. "Go on . . . and play."

And Father and Eddy would start once more while I watched, doomed to be positively un-American, a weakling, a **perpetual** spectator, an outsider. Worse, I felt as if Eddy were Father's only true son. **B**

And then came the day when the rat invaded our store. It was Eddy who first noticed it while we were restocking the store shelves. I was stacking packages of pinto beans when Eddy called me. "Hey, do you know what this is?" He waved me over to the cans of soup. On his palm lay some dark drops. "Is it candy?"

Father came out of the storeroom in the rear of our store. Over his back, he
40 carried a huge hundred pound sack of rice. He let it thump to the floor right away. "Throw that away."

"What is it, Father?" I asked.

"Rat droppings," he said. "Go wash your hands."

"Yuck." Eddy flung the droppings down.

While Eddy washed his hands, I helped Father get rid of the evidence. Then he got some wooden traps from a shelf and we set them out.

However, the traps were for mice and not for rats. The rat must have gotten a good laugh while it stole the bait and set off the springs. **C**

Then Father tried poison pellets, but the rat avoided them all. It even left a
50 souvenir right near the front door.

Father looked grim as he cleaned it up. "I'm through fooling around." **D**

So he called up his exterminator[2] friend, Pete Wong, the Cockroach King of Chinatown. While Pete fumigated[3] the store, we stayed with my Aunt Nancy over on Mason, where the cable cars kept me up late. They always rang their bells when they rounded the corner. Even when they weren't there, I could hear the cable rattling in its channel beneath the street. It was OK, though, because my cousin Jackie could tell stories all night.

The next day, when we went back home, Father searched around the store, sniffing suspiciously for deadly chemicals. Mother went upstairs to our
60 apartment over the store to get our electric fan. **E**

She came right back down empty-handed. "I think he's moved up there. I could hear him scratching behind the living room walls."

Father stared at the ceiling as if the rat had gone too far. "Leave it to me," he said. He fished his car keys from his pocket.

---

2. **exterminator** (ĭk-stûr′mə-nā′tər): a person whose job it is to get rid of insects or rodents.

3. **fumigated** (fyo͞o′mĭ-gāt′d): used smoke or fumes to kill rodents or insects.

perpetual
(pər-pĕch′o͞o-əl) *adj.* continuing without interruption

B CONFLICT
Reread lines 28–33. Why does Yep feel "un-American" and "as if Eddy were Father's only true son"?

C CONFLICT
What **external conflict** is the Yep family facing?

D CHRONOLOGICAL ORDER
Describe Father's first two attempts to catch the rat. Add them to your chart.

E CHRONOLOGICAL ORDER
Reread lines 52–60. What words make clear the order in which events occurred? Add the events to your chart.

"Where are you going?" Mother asked.

Father, though, was a man of few words. He preferred to speak by his actions. "I'll be back soon."

An hour and a half later he returned with a rifle. He held it up for the three of us to examine. "Isn't it a beaut? Henry Loo loaned it to me." Henry Loo was 70 a pharmacist and one of Father's fishing buddies.

Mother frowned. "You can't shoot that cannon off in my house."

"It's just a twenty-two." Father tugged a box of cartridges out of his jacket pocket. "Let's go, boys."

Mother sucked in her breath sharply. "Thomas!"

Father was surprised by Mother's objection. "They've got to learn sometime."

Mother turned to us urgently. "It means killing. Like buying Grandpop's chickens. But you'll be the ones who have to make it dead."

"It's not the same," Father argued. "We won't have to twist its neck."

80 Buying the chicken was a chore that everyone tried to avoid at New Year's when Mother's father insisted on it. To make sure the chicken was fresh, we had to watch the poulterer[4] kill it. And then we had to collect the coppery-smelling blood in a jar for a special dish that only Mother's father would eat. For a moment, I felt queasy.

"You're scaring the boys," Father scolded her.

Mother glanced at him over her shoulder. "They ought to know what they're getting into."

didn't believe in killing—unless it was a bug like a cockroach. However, I felt different when I saw a real rifle—the shiny barrel, the faint smell of oil, 90 the decorated wooden stock. I **rationalized** the hunt by telling myself I was not murdering rabbits or deer, just a mean old rat—like a furry kind of cockroach.

"What'll it be, boys?" Father asked.

Taking a deep breath, I nodded my head. "Yes, sir."

Father turned expectantly to Eddy and raised an eyebrow.

From next to me, though, Eddy murmured, "I think I'll help Mother." He wouldn't look at me.

Father seemed just as shocked as Mother and I. "Are you sure?"

Eddy drew back and mumbled miserably. "Yes, sir."

Mother gave me a quick peck on the cheek. "I expect you to still have ten 100 toes and ten fingers when you finish."

As we left the store, I felt funny. Part of me felt triumphant. For once, it was Eddy who had failed and not me. And yet another part of me wished I were staying with him and Mother. **G**

Father said nothing as we left the store and climbed the back stairs. As I trailed him, I thought he was silent because he was disappointed: He would rather have Eddy's help than mine.

---

4. **poulterer** (pōl'tər-ər): a person who sells domestic fowls, such as chickens, turkeys, ducks, or geese.

Language Coach

Oral Fluency When the letters *ph* appear at the beginning of a word, they combine to form an *f* sound, as in the word *pharmacist.* Reread lines 68–70, pronouncing *pharmacist* correctly.

rationalize
(răsh'ə-nə-līz') *v.* to make explanations for one's behavior

G CONFLICT
Reread lines 88–103. Why is Yep torn between staying with his mother and going to help his father?

At the back door of our apartment, he paused and said **brusquely,** "Now for some rules. First, never, never aim the rifle at anyone."

I listened as attentively as I had the disastrous times he'd tried to teach me
110 how to dribble, or catch a football, or handle a pop foul. "I won't." I nodded earnestly.

Father pulled a lever near the middle of the gun. "Next, make sure the rifle is empty." He let me inspect the breech.⁵ There was nothing inside.

"Yes, sir," I said and glanced up at him to read his mood. Because Father used so few words, he always sounded a little impatient whenever he taught me a lesson. However, it was hard to tell this time if it was genuine irritation or his normal **reserve.** **G**

He merely grunted. "Here. Open this." And he handed me the box of cartridges.

120 I was so nervous that the cartridges clinked inside the box when I took it. As I fumbled at the lid, I almost felt like apologizing for not being Eddy.

Now, when I got edgy, I was the opposite of Father: I got talkier. "How did you learn how to hunt?" I asked. "From your father?"

My father rarely spoke of his father, who had died before I was born. He **winced** now as if the rat had just nipped him. "My old man? Nah. He never had the time. I learned from some of my buddies in Chinatown."⁶ He held out his hand.

I passed him a cartridge. "What did you hunt? Bear?"

"We shot quail." Father carefully loaded the rifle.

130 I was uncomfortable with the idea of shooting the cute little birds I saw in cartoons. "You did?"

He clicked the cartridge into the rifle. "You have to be tough in this world, boy. There are going to be some times when nobody's around to help—like when I first came to America."

That was a long speech for Father. "You had your father." His mother had stayed back in China, because in those days, America would not let her accompany her husband. ◆

"He was too busy working." Father stared back down the stairs as if each step were a year. "When I first came here, I got beaten up by the white kids.
140 And when the white kids weren't around, there were the other Chinese kids."

I furrowed my forehead in puzzlement. I handed him another cartridge. "But they were your own kind."

He loaded the rifle steadily as I gave him the ammunition. "No, they weren't. The boys born here, they like to give a China-born a hard time. They thought I'd be easy pickings. But it was always a clean fight. No knives. No guns. Just our feet and fists. Not like the punks nowadays." He snapped the last cartridge into the rifle. "Then I learned how to play their games, and I made them my friends." He said the last part with pride. **H**

---

5. **breech:** the part of a gun behind the barrel.

6. **Chinatown:** the name given to some neighborhoods in which there is a large Chinese population with prominent Chinese cultural influence.

brusquely (brŭsk'lē) *adv.* in an abrupt, sudden manner

reserve (rĭ-zûrv') *n.* self-restraint in the way one looks or acts

G CONFLICT
How does Yep think his father sees him?

wince (wĭns) *v.* to flinch or shrink in pain or distress

◆ GRAMMAR IN CONTEXT
In lines 135–137, Lawrence Yep uses the **past perfect tense** when he writes "His mother had stayed back in China...."

H CHRONOLOGICAL ORDER
What action is taking place at the same time the father is talking about his past?

And suddenly I began to understand all the trophies and medals in our
150 living room. They were more than awards for sports. Each prize was a sign
that my father belonged to America—and at the same time, to Chinatown.
And that was why he tried so hard now to teach sports to Eddy and me.

When I finally understood what sports really meant to my father, it only
magnified the scale of my **ineptitude.** "I'm not good at fighting." As I closed
the lid on the box of ammunition, I thought I ought to prepare him for future
disappointments. "I'm not much good at anything."

Careful to keep the rifle pointed away from me, Father unlocked the door.
"I said you have to be tough, not stupid. No reason to get a beat-up old mug[7]
like mine."

160 I shook my head, bewildered. "What's wrong with your face?"

Father seemed amused. He stepped away from the door and jerked his head
for me to open it. "It's nothing that a steamroller couldn't fix."

"But you have an interesting face," I protested as I grabbed the doorknob.

"Are you blind, boy? This mug isn't ever going to win a beauty contest." He
chuckled. "I've been called a lot of names in my time, but never 'interesting.'
You've got a way with words."

▲ **Analyze
Visuals**

How would you describe
the **mood** of this
painting? Tell what
elements of the image
contribute to the mood.

ineptitude
(ĭn-ĕp'tĭ-tood') *n.*
clumsiness; lack of
competence

The doorknob was cold in my hand. "I do?"

Father adjusted his grip on the rifle. "I wouldn't buy any real estate from you." And he gave me an encouraging grin. "Now let's kill that rat."

170   When I opened the door, our home suddenly seemed as foreign to me as Africa. At first, I felt lonely—and a little scared. Then I heard Father reassure me, "I'm with you, boy."

Feeling more confident, I crept through the kitchen and into the living room. Father was right behind me and motioned me to search one half of the room while he explored the other. When I found a hole in the corner away from the fireplace, I caught Father's eye and pointed.

He peered under a chair with me and gave me an approving wink. "Give me a hand," he whispered.

In silent cooperation, we moved the chair aside and then shifted the
180   sofa over until it was between us and the rat hole. Bit by bit, Father and I constructed an upholstered **barricade**. I couldn't have been prouder if we'd built a whole fort together.

Father considerately left the lighter things for me to lift, and I was grateful for his thoughtfulness. The last thing I wanted was to get asthma now from overexertion. When we were done, Father got his rifle from the corner where he had left it temporarily.

As we crouched down behind our **improvised** wall, Father rested the rifle on it. "We'll take turns watching."

"Yes, sir," I said, peering over the barrier. There wasn't so much as a whisker
190   in the hole.

While I scanned the hole with intense radar eyes, Father tried to make himself comfortable by leaning against the sofa. It made me feel important to know Father trusted me; and I was determined to do well. In the center of the living room wall was the fireplace, and on its mantel stood Father's trophies like ranks of soldiers reminding me to be **vigilant**.

We remained in companionable silence for maybe three quarters of an hour. Suddenly, I saw something flicker near the mouth of the hole. "Father," I whispered. ❶

Father popped up alertly and took his rifle. Squeezing one eye shut, he
200   sighted on the rat hole. His crouching body grew tense. "Right." He adjusted his aim minutely. "Right. Take a breath," he recited to himself. "Take up the slack. Squeeze the trigger." Suddenly, he looked up, startled. "Where'd it go?"

As the gray shape darted forward, I could not control my panic. "It's coming straight at us."

The rifle barrel swung back and forth wildly as Father tried to aim. "Where?"

I thought I could see huge teeth and beady, violent eyes. The teeth were the size of daggers and the eyes were the size of baseballs, and they were getting bigger by the moment. It was the rat of all rats. "Shoot it!" I yelled.

barricade (băr'ĭ-kād') *n.* a structure that blocks passage

improvised (ĭm'prə-vīzd') *adj.* to put together with little preparation or planning **improvise** *v.*

vigilant (vĭj'ə-lənt) *adj.* watchful; alert

❶ **CONFLICT**
Reread line 196. Compare the "companionable silence" Yep describes here with an earlier statement, "I thought he was silent because he was disappointed." Why does Yep view the silence differently the second time?

210 "Where?" Father shouted desperately.

My courage evaporated. All I could think of was escape. "It's charging." Springing to my feet, I darted from the room.

"Oh, man," Father said, and his footsteps pounded after me.

In a blind panic, I bolted out of the apartment and down the back stairs and into the store. **J**

"Get the SPCA[8]. I think the rat's mad," Father yelled as he slammed the door behind him.

Mother took the rifle from him. "I'd be annoyed too if someone were trying to shoot me."

220 "No." Father panted. "I mean it's rabid."[9] We could hear the rat scurrying above us in the living room. It sounded as if it were doing a victory dance.

Mother made Father empty the rifle. "You return that to Henry Loo tomorrow," she said. "We'll learn to live with the rat."

As she stowed the rifle in the storeroom, Father tried to regather his dignity. "It may have fleas," he called after her.

Now that my panic was over, I suddenly became aware of the enormity of what I had done. Father had counted on me to help him, and yet I had run, leaving him to the **ravages** of that monster. I was worse than a failure. I was a coward. I had deserted Father right at the time he needed me most. I wouldn't
230 blame him if he kicked me out of his family.

It took what little nerve I had left to look up at my father. At that moment, he seemed to tower over me, as grand and remote as a monument. "I'm sorry," I said miserably.

He drew his eyebrows together as he clinked the shells in his fist. "For what?"

It made me feel even worse to have to explain in front of Eddy. "For running," I said wretchedly.

He chuckled as he dumped the cartridges into his shirt pocket. "Well, I ran too. Sometimes it's smart to be scared."

240 "When were you ever scared?" I challenged him.

He buttoned his pocket. "Plenty of times. Like when I came to America. They had to pry my fingers from the boat railing."

It was the first time I'd ever heard my father confess to that failing. "But you're the best at everything."

"Nobody's good at everything." He gave his head a little shake as if the very notion puzzled him. "Each of us is good at some things and lousy at others. The trick is to find something that you're good at."

I thought again of the mantel where all of Father's sports trophies stood. Eddy gave every promise of collecting just as many, but I knew I would be
250 lucky to win even one.

"I'm lousy at sports," I confessed.

---

8. **SPCA:** Society for the Prevention of Cruelty to Animals.

9. **rabid:** affected by the viral disease rabies.

J CHRONOLOGICAL ORDER
How much time do you think passes from when Yep and his father begin their rat hunt until they give up? Explain your reasoning.

ravage (răv′ĭj) *n.* serious damage or destruction

Language Coach

Homophones
Homophones are words that sound alike but have different meanings and spellings. The words *won* and *one* are homophones. Which of the two words is used in line 250? Tell what it means.

His eyes flicked back and forth, as if my face were a book open for his inspection. He seemed surprised by what he read there.

Slowly his knees bent until we were looking eye to eye. "Then you'll find something else," he said and put his arm around me. My father never let people touch him. In fact, I hardly ever saw him hug Mother. As his arm tightened, I felt a real love and assurance in that embrace. **K**

Shortly after that, the rat left as mysteriously as it had come. "I must've scared it off," Father announced.

260 Mother shook her head. "That rat laughed itself to death."

Father disappeared into the storeroom: and for a moment we all thought Mother had gone too far. Then we heard the electric saw that he kept back there. "What are you doing?" Mother called.

He came back out with a block of wood about two inches square. He was carefully sandpapering the splinters from the edges. "Maybe some day we'll find the corpse. Its head ought to look real good over the fireplace."

Mother was trying hard to keep a straight face. "You can't have a trophy head unless you shoot it."

"If it died of laughter like you said, then I killed it," he insisted proudly.

270 "Sure as if I pulled the trigger." He winked at me. "Get the varnish out for our trophy will you?"

I was walking away when I realized he had said "our." I turned and said, "That rat was doomed from the start." I heard my parents both laughing as I hurried away. ⌒

K **CONFLICT**
How has Yep's relationship with his father changed since the beginning of the story?

Comprehension

1. **Recall** How do Laurence and his brother differ?

2. **Recall** What compliment does Laurence's father give him?

3. **Clarify** What happens to the rat at the end of the selection?

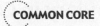

COMMON CORE

RI 3 Analyze how a text makes connections among individuals, ideas, and events. **RI 5** Analyze the structure of a text.

Text Analysis

4. **Identify Chronological Order** Review the chart you made as you read. Does it contain all the important events of the selection? If not, add them now. Then use your chart to tell what happened right before Father ran out of the apartment. What happened right after?

5. **Examine Conflict** In a conflict map like the one shown, note one of the selection's most important conflicts and the events that lead to its **resolution,** or outcome.

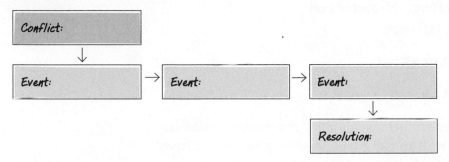

6. **Analyze Characters** Even though Yep was scared, he still agreed to help his father capture the rat. What do you learn about Yep from his actions?

7. **Compare and Contrast** Compare Yep's feelings about his role in the family in the beginning of the selection with his feelings at the end. How are they different?

8. **Interpret Meaning** Reread lines 270–271. What do you think it means that Yep's father uses the word "our" to refer to the trophy?

Extension and Challenge

9. **Creative Project: Drama** With two other classmates, rehearse a dramatic reading of the rat-hunt scene. Have one student play the role of Father, one student play the role of Yep, and one student act as the narrator. Perform your reading for the class.

When is it OK to be SCARED?

Yep's father says, "Sometimes it's smart to be scared." Do you think the encounter with the rat was one of those times, or is Yep's father just trying to make himself and his son feel better? Explain your answer.

Vocabulary in Context

▲ VOCABULARY PRACTICE

For each item, choose the word that differs most in meaning from the other words.

1. (a) justify, (b) rationalize, (c) multiply, (d) explain
2. (a) improvised, (b) ad-libbed, (c) invented, (d) practiced
3. (a) openness, (b) modesty, (c) reserve, (d) coolness
4. (a) destruction, (b) ravage, (c) construction, (d) ruin
5. (a) keen, (b) inattentive, (c) observant, (d) vigilant
6. (a) ineptitude, (b) awkwardness, (c) incompetence, (d) gracefulness
7. (a) finite, (b) infinite, (c) constant, (d) perpetual
8. (a) abruptly, (b) gruffly, (c) brusquely, (d) kindly
9. (a) walkway, (b) barricade, (c) fence, (d) obstruction
10. (a) flinch, (b) wince, (c) strut, (d) cringe

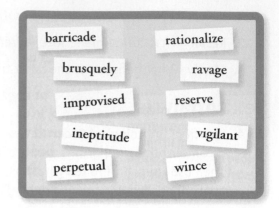

barricade   rationalize
brusquely   ravage
improvised   reserve
ineptitude   vigilant
perpetual   wince

ACADEMIC VOCABULARY IN SPEAKING

• affect   • conclude   • evident   • imply   • initial

Reread lines 132–159. What do Yep's father's words **imply** about what it means to be tough? Discuss the question with a small group. Together, arrive at an answer that uses at least one Academic Vocabulary word.

VOCABULARY STRATEGY: CONTEXT CLUES

Context clues are words and phrases in a text that suggest the definition of an unfamiliar word. For example, an author might restate or define an unfamiliar word, as in this sentence: *It was a farcical, ridiculous idea.* An author might also compare an unfamiliar word to something that is familiar: *The workers were as expendable as week-old newspaper.*

PRACTICE Use context clues in each sentence to help you determine the meaning of the underlined word.

1. The <u>iridescent</u> tail feathers spread like a rainbow behind the bird's back.
2. He <u>jostled</u> the other passengers, pushing them aside as he moved toward the door.
3. Her <u>azure</u> eyes sparkled like bits of cloudless sky.
4. She was <u>contrite</u>, sorry for all the trouble she had caused.

:···: **COMMON CORE**

L 4a Use context (e.g., a word's position or function in a sentence) as a clue to the meaning of a word.
L 5b Use the relationship between words to better understand each of the words.

Interactive Vocabulary **THINK** central
Go to **thinkcentral.com**.
KEYWORD: HML8-134

Language

◆ **GRAMMAR IN CONTEXT:** Use Past Perfect Tense Correctly

COMMON CORE

L1 Demonstrate command of standard English grammar when writing. **W 2** Write explanatory texts.

The tense of a verb indicates the time of the action or the state of being. There are six verb tenses, each expressing a range of time.

The **past perfect tense** shows that an action or condition in the past came before another past action or condition. For an example of how Lawrence Yep uses the past perfect tense to make the order of events clear, review the **Grammar in Context** note on page 128. For another example of the past perfect tense, see the sentence below:

> *Example:*   She had decided not to go, so he sailed without her.

To form the past perfect tense, combine the verb *had* with the past participle.

Past Perfect	▶	*Singular*	▶	*Plural*
had+past participle		I had left you had left he/she/it had left		we had left you had left they had left laughing.

PRACTICE For each sentence, make the order of events as clear as possible by choosing the best tense of the verb in parentheses.

1. Before she left, she (wrote, had written) to her cousins so they knew she was coming.
2. His first year in the United States, he (wants, had wanted) to avoid trouble.
3. By the time he started high school, he (became, had become) a highly respected athlete.
4. Now that he is a father, he (encourages, had encouraged) his sons to play a variety of sports.
5. They (felt, had felt) happy when they had pleased him.

*For more help with verb tenses, see page R56 in the **Grammar Handbook**.*

READING-WRITING CONNECTION

YOUR TURN
Broaden your understanding of "The Great Rat Hunt" by responding to this prompt. Then use the **revising tip** to improve your writing.

WRITING PROMPT	**REVISING TIP**
Extended Constructed Response: Comparison Both Laurence Yep and his father felt like outsiders. In **two or three paragraphs,** compare their experiences, including the conflicts each person faced and how he dealt with them.	Review your work. Make sure you have used past perfect tense to describe any past actions or conditions that come before other past actions or conditions.

Interactive Revision
THINK central
Try it at thinkcentral.com.
KEYWORD: HML8-135

Paul Revere's Ride

Poem by Henry Wadsworth Longfellow

VIDEO TRAILER **THINK** central KEYWORD: HML8-136

When does truth become LEGEND?

COMMON CORE

RL 4 Determine the meaning of words and phrases as they are used in a text. **RL 5** Analyze how the structure of [a] text contributes to its meaning. **RL 10** Read and comprehend poems.

George Washington was an amazing leader, but did he really never, ever lie? When highly regarded people are famous for long enough, they sometimes become legends, and the stories about them are exaggerated. You're about to read a poem featuring one such person.

DISCUSS In a small group, come up with a list of people you consider legendary. Think about sports heroes, performers, and historical figures. What do these people have in common? Why do you think they became legends? Share your ideas with the class.

TEXT ANALYSIS: NARRATIVE POETRY

You've read fictional stories, true stories, and stories presented dramatically. Now you're about to read a **narrative poem,** which is a poem that tells a story. Like a short story, a narrative poem has the following elements:

- a **plot,** or series of events that center on a conflict faced by a main character
- a **setting,** the time and place(s) where the story occurs; setting is usually established in the exposition stage of the plot
- **character(s),** or the individual or individuals who take part in the action

As you read "Paul Revere's Ride," notice how Longfellow uses story elements to describe Paul Revere's adventures.

Review: Suspense

READING SKILL: PARAPHRASE

Have you ever explained a complex idea using easier language, or retold a story in your own words? Restating complete information in simpler terms is called **paraphrasing.** A good paraphrase includes all of the main ideas and supporting details of the original source and is usually just as long, or longer. Paraphrasing challenging passages can help you better understand them. As you read "Paul Revere's Ride," use a chart like the one shown to paraphrase parts of the poem, such as the following lines, that may be difficult to understand:

Original: *Meanwhile, his friend through alley and street Wanders and watches, with eager ears . . .*

Paraphrase: *At the same time, his friend walks through quiet streets and alleys, looking and listening carefully.*

Line Numbers	Paraphrase

 Complete the activities in your **Reader/Writer Notebook.**

Henry Wadsworth Longfellow
1807–1882

An Accomplished Teenager
When he was just 14, Henry Wadsworth Longfellow was accepted into Bowdoin College in Maine. He did well in his studies and had nearly 40 poems published before he graduated. He learned French, Italian, and Spanish and translated famous literary works into English.

World Fame
After traveling in Europe, Longfellow returned to teach at Harvard University. He continued to write poetry that explored many important American themes. Works such as *The Song of Hiawatha* and *Tales of a Wayside Inn,* which includes "Paul Revere's Ride," brought American history to the attention of readers around the world. Though the death of his wife in 1861 made Longfellow deeply depressed, he remained extraordinarily kind, courteous, and generous. He never refused to give an autograph or welcome visitors who sometimes lingered around his house, hoping for a glimpse of the famous author.

BACKGROUND TO THE POEM

By 1775, many American colonists had begun to rebel against the British government's interference in their affairs. On the night of April 18, British troops left Boston, heading to Concord to arrest the rebel leaders and seize their weapons stockpile. Hoping to warn the rebel leaders of the British advance, Paul Revere, along with William Dawes and Dr. Samuel Prescott, set off on a ride that would make Revere a legend.

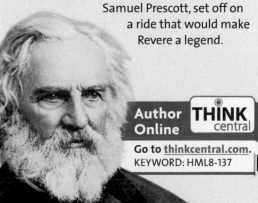

Author Online
THINK central
Go to thinkcentral.com.
KEYWORD: HML8-137

Paul Revere's Ride

Henry Wadsworth Longfellow

Listen, my children, and you shall hear
Of the midnight ride of Paul Revere,
On the eighteenth of April, in Seventy-five;
Hardly a man is now alive
5 Who remembers that famous day and year.

He said to his friend, "If the British march
By land or sea from the town to-night,
Hang a lantern aloft in the belfry arch
Of the North Church tower as a signal light,—
10 One if by land, and two if by sea;
And I on the opposite shore will be,
Ready to ride and spread the alarm
Through every Middlesex[1] village and farm,
For the country folk to be up and to arm." Ⓐ

Analyze Visuals ▶

What **mood** does this painting convey?

Ⓐ **NARRATIVE POETRY**
According to the first two stanzas, where does the poem take place?

---

1. **Middlesex:** a county in eastern Massachusetts—the setting of the first battle of the Revolutionary War on April 19, 1775.

Illustration by Christopher Bing.

15 Then he said "Good-night!" and with muffled oar
Silently rowed to the Charlestown shore,
Just as the moon rose over the bay,
Where swinging wide at her moorings[2] lay
The *Somerset,* British man-of-war;[3]
20 A phantom ship, with each mast and spar[4]
Across the moon like a prison bar,
And a huge black hulk, that was magnified
By its own reflection in the tide. **B**

Meanwhile, his friend through alley and street
25 Wanders and watches, with eager ears,
Till in the silence around him he hears
The muster of men at the barrack door,
The sound of arms, and the tramp of feet,
And the measured tread of the grenadiers,[5]
30 Marching down to their boats on the shore.

B NARRATIVE POETRY
What is the **conflict** being described?

---

2. **moorings:** the place where the ship is docked.
3. **man-of-war:** a warship, often a large sailing ship, bearing cannons and other guns.
4. **spar:** a pole supporting a ship's sail.
5. **grenadiers** (grĕn'ə-dîrz'): British foot soldiers.

Then he climbed the tower of the Old North Church,
By the wooden stairs, with stealthy tread,[6]
To the belfry chamber overhead,
And startled the pigeons from their perch
35 On the somber[7] rafters, that round him made
Masses and moving shapes of shade,—
By the trembling ladder, steep and tall,
To the highest window in the wall,
Where he paused to listen and look down
40 A moment on the roofs of the town
And the moonlight flowing over all. **C**

Beneath, in the churchyard, lay the dead,
In their night encampment on the hill,
Wrapped in silence so deep and still
45 That he could hear, like a sentinel's[8] tread,
The watchful night-wind, as it went
Creeping along from tent to tent,
And seeming to whisper, "All is well!"
A moment only he feels the spell
50 Of the place and the hour, and the secret dread
Of the lonely belfry and the dead;
For suddenly all his thoughts are bent
On a shadowy something far away,
Where the river widens to meet the bay,—
55 A line of black that bends and floats
On the rising tide like a bridge of boats. **D**

Meanwhile, impatient to mount and ride,
Booted and spurred, with a heavy stride
On the opposite shore walked Paul Revere.
60 Now he patted his horse's side,
Now he gazed at the landscape far and near,
Then, impetuous,[9] stamped the earth,
And turned and tightened his saddle girth;[10]
But mostly he watched with eager search

C **PARAPHRASE**
Reread lines 31–41.
Paraphrase this stanza,
remembering to include
all details in your own
words. Add this to your
chart.

D **SUSPENSE**
Reread lines 52–56.
What words or phrases
does the writer use in
this passage to create a
feeling of suspense?

---

6. **stealthy tread:** quiet footsteps.
7. **somber:** gloomy.
8. **sentinel:** a guard or sentry.
9. **impetuous** (ĭm-pĕch'oo-əs): acting suddenly, on impulse.
10. **saddle girth:** the strap attaching a saddle to a horse's body.

65　The belfry tower of the Old North Church,
　　As it rose above the graves on the hill,
　　Lonely and spectral[11] and somber and still.
　　And lo! as he looks, on the belfry's height
　　A glimmer, and then a gleam of light!
70　He springs to the saddle, the bridle he turns,
　　But lingers and gazes, till full on his sight
　　A second lamp in the belfry burns. **E**

　　A hurry of hoofs in a village street,
　　A shape in the moonlight, a bulk in the dark,
75　And beneath, from the pebbles, in passing, a spark
　　Struck out by a steed flying fearless and fleet;
　　That was all! And yet, through the gloom and the light,
　　The fate of a nation was riding that night;
　　And the spark struck out by that steed, in his flight,
80　Kindled the land into flame with its heat.
　　He has left the village and mounted the steep,
　　And beneath him, tranquil and broad and deep,
　　Is the Mystic,[12] meeting the ocean tides;
　　And under the alders[13] that skirt its edge,
85　Now soft on the sand, now loud on the ledge,
　　Is heard the tramp of his steed as he rides. **F**

　　It was twelve by the village clock,
　　When he crossed the bridge into Medford town.
　　He heard the crowing of the cock,
90　And the barking of the farmer's dog,
　　And felt the damp of the river fog,
　　That rises after the sun goes down.

　　It was one by the village clock,
　　When he galloped into Lexington.
95　He saw the gilded weathercock
　　Swim in the moonlight as he passed,
　　And the meeting-house windows, black and bare,
　　Gaze at him with a spectral glare,
　　As if they already stood aghast[14]
100　At the bloody work they would look upon.

E NARRATIVE POETRY
Who are the **characters** in this narrative poem?

F PARAPHRASE
Reread the lines 73–80. What's happening in this passage? Paraphrase the passage and add it to your chart.

Language Coach

Personification Giving human qualities to something that is not human is called personification. In lines 97–100, the meeting-house windows are described as being able to look at things. What does the poet expect they will see?

---

11. **spectral:** ghostly.

12. **Mystic:** a short river flowing into Boston Harbor.

13. **alder:** tree of the birch family.

14. **aghast:** (ə-găst′): terrified.

It was two by the village clock,
When he came to the bridge in Concord town.
He heard the bleating[15] of the flock,
And the twitter of birds among the trees,
105 And felt the breath of the morning breeze
Blowing over the meadow brown.
And one was safe and asleep in his bed
Who at the bridge would be first to fall,
Who that day would be lying dead,
110 Pierced by a British musket ball.

You know the rest. In the books you have read
How the British Regulars[16] fired and fled,—
How the farmers gave them ball for ball,
From behind each fence and farmyard wall,
115 Chasing the redcoats down the lane,
Then crossing the fields to emerge again
Under the trees at the turn of the road,
And only pausing to fire and load. **G**

So through the night rode Paul Revere;
120 And so through the night went his cry of alarm
To every Middlesex village and farm,—
A cry of defiance, and not of fear,
A voice in the darkness, a knock at the door,
And a word that shall echo for evermore!
125 For, borne on the night-wind of the Past,
Through all our history, to the last,
In the hour of darkness and peril[17] and need,
The people will waken and listen to hear
The hurrying hoof-beats of that steed,
130 And the midnight message of Paul Revere.

G NARRATIVE POETRY
What is the **climax** of
the plot? Give reasons
for your answer.

---

15. **bleating:** the cry of sheep.

16. **British Regulars:** members of Great Britain's
standing army.

17. **peril:** danger.

Comprehension

1. **Recall** How many lanterns were hung in the belfry of the Old North Church? What do they signify?

2. **Summarize** In your own words, describe what Paul Revere hoped to accomplish with his late-night ride.

3. **Represent** Reread lines 37–56. Draw what you think Revere's friend sees from the bell tower.

COMMON CORE

RL 4 Determine the meaning of words and phrases as they are used in a text. RL 5 Analyze how the structure of [a] text contributes to its meaning. RL 10 Read and comprehend poems.

Text Analysis

● 4. **Analyze Narrative Poetry** In a chart like the one shown, note the story elements in "Paul Revere's Ride." Then tell the main conflict and how it is resolved.

● 5. **Understand Paraphrasing** Now that you've read the whole poem, review the paraphrases you wrote in your chart as you read. Did you capture the correct meaning in each case? If not, revise your paraphrases.

	"Paul Revere's Ride"
Setting	
Characters	
Main Plot Events	• •

● 6. **Analyze Suspense** How did Longfellow create tension and excitement in the poem? Consider the way he used **language, rhythm, rhyme,** and **repetition.** Cite specific details to support your answer.

7. **Evaluate Sensory Details** "Paul Revere's Ride" is full of descriptive language that appeals to the senses. List two or three images that you find most striking. Why did you choose these?

Extension and Challenge

8. SOCIAL STUDIES CONNECTION Paul Revere did more in his life than ride to warn the colonists that the British army was on its way. Find out where he lived, what he did for a living, and about his involvement in the "Sons of Liberty" before and during the American Revolution. Share your findings with the class.

When does truth become LEGEND?

Reread lines 119–130. On the basis of this stanza, why do you think Paul Revere became an American legend?

Use with "Paul Revere's Ride," page 138.

COMMON CORE

RI 1 Cite the evidence that supports an analysis of what the text says explicitly. **RI 9** Analyze a case in which two or more texts provide conflicting information on the same topic and identify where the texts disagree.

The Other Riders
History Article

What's the Connection?

The poem you just read celebrates Paul Revere, but did you know he was not the only brave rider on the eve of the Revolutionary War? The following article tells about two equally important but lesser-known heroes: William Dawes and Samuel Prescott. Connect the information in the article and the spirit of the poem to create your own impression of what happened on a historic night.

Standards Focus: Take Notes

When you're trying to make logical connections between texts, it's often a good idea to **take notes** on the texts as you read. Writing down important facts and ideas can help you remember them and see relationships between them.

Here are some tips for note-taking:

• First, preview the text by looking at its title and any subheadings, topic sentences, and graphic aids to determine its topic and main ideas.

• Next, decide how to organize your notes. For a single text, you might use the subheadings to create a simple outline. To make connections between texts, you might want to collect information in a graphic organizer like the one shown.

• As you take notes, paraphrase the main ideas and record only the most important facts and details under the appropriate headings. When you paraphrase main ideas, note them down in the order in which they appear in the texts. Be sure to include the names, dates, and terms that are necessary for a full understanding of the material.

For help taking notes on the following article and the preceding poem, use a graphic organizer like the one started here.

	from "Paul Revere's Ride"	from "The Other Riders"	Similarities and Differences
Main Participants			
Main Events			

The Other Riders

PBS

Late on the night of April 18, 1775, Boston patriot Joseph Warren learned of a British military operation planned for the next day. To warn John Hancock and Samuel Adams, who were across the Charles River in Lexington, Warren dispatched two riders, Paul Revere and William Dawes. Revere's ride has been celebrated in poems and textbooks, but
10 Dawes's role was at least as important.

William Dawes (unknown), attributed to John Johnston. Oil on canvas, 35″ × 29″. © Collection of the Evanston Historical Society, Evanston, Illinois.

Rumors of a March on Concord

On the night of April 18, 1775, rumors of a planned British action to seize ammunition in the town of Concord raced through Boston. Word reached William Dawes, a tanner, who told Paul Revere—who had heard about it from two others already. The two men received orders from Dr. Joseph Warren to ride to inform the leaders of the Provincial Congress of the developments.

Sneaking Past Guards

Dawes's route led him to the British guards at the gate of Boston Neck—the narrowest part of the isthmus—as he rode south out of the
20 city. A naturally witty and friendly man, Dawes had spent numerous afternoons sneaking in and out of the city without being stopped. He would disguise himself as a peddler, smuggling gold coins disguised as buttons that he wore sewn on his coat. Dawes also befriended any British guards who seemed amicable. On the historic night, one of his buddies was on duty. When the guard opened the gate for some British soldiers, Dawes slipped through with them. **A**

Spreading the Word

On his ride west, Dawes alerted more riders, who in turn rallied companies from neighboring towns: Dedham, Needham, Framingham, Newton and Watertown. Avoiding trouble, Dawes made good time and
30 caught up to Revere in Lexington just after midnight. After notifying Hancock and Adams, Dawes and Revere set out for Concord together,

Internet

FOCUS ON FORM
You are about to read a **history article,** a nonfiction article about real events and people of historical importance.

Language Coach

Word Definitions The word *isthmus* refers to the narrow strip of land connecting two larger bodies of land. Reread the sentence that begins in line 19. Was there any way to leave Boston without passing through the isthmus?

A TAKE NOTES
At this point in the article, who are the main participants in the events described? Make sure to note their names.

Back   Forward   Stop   Refresh   Home   Search   Favorites   Mail   Print

B HISTORY ARTICLE
History articles often
contain maps, timelines,
and other graphic aids
to help you track the
details presented in the
text. As you read this
article, follow Revere's,
Dawes's, and Prescott's
progress on this map.

C TAKE NOTES
What surprising fact
do you learn from this
section? Be sure to add
this to your notes.

D HISTORY ARTICLE
This history article
primarily tells about the
true story of the people
and events of April 18,
1775. What does the
additional information
in this last section help
you understand?

joined by Dr. Samuel Prescott,
a Concord resident who had
been visiting a girlfriend.

A Clever Escape

Revere, riding in front, ran into
a British roadblock. Dawes and
Prescott were captured before
they could be warned. As the
British tried to lead them into a
40 meadow, Prescott signaled that
they should make their escape,
and all three rode off. Back on
the road towards Lexington,
Dawes realized that his horse
was too tired to outrun the Redcoats. As he pulled up in the yard of a
house, he reared his horse and shouted, "I've got two of them—surround
them!" His trick succeeded in scaring off his pursuers, although he fell
from his horse and lost his watch.

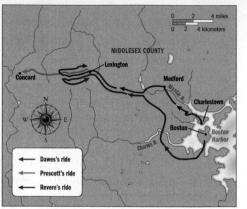

This map of eastern Massachusetts shows
the route of each rider. **B**

Prescott Warns Concord

Prescott, the local, rode off toward Concord through fields and creek beds
50 that he knew, quickly outdistancing his would-be captors. It was Prescott
who warned the town of Concord of the impending British march. **C**

So Forgotten It's Funny

Over the years, Dawes's relative anonymity has become something
of a joke. In 1896, Helen F. Moore published a parody of Longfellow's
famous poem about the historic night, entitled "The Midnight Ride
of William Dawes," one verse of which reads:

> 'Tis all very well for the children to hear
> Of the midnight ride of Paul Revere;
> But why should my name be quite forgot,
> Who rode as boldly and well, God wot?
> 60   Why should I ask? The reason is clear—
> My name was Dawes and his Revere.

A cartoon in the early 1960s turned on the same humor, namely that
"Dawes" was a name less suited for rhyming than "Revere" (in that
comic strip, Longfellow is stuck on "Listen my children while I pause,
to tell the ride of William Dawes" when his wife suggests using the
name of that other rider). **D**

Internet

Comprehension

1. **Recall** Who was sent to warn John Hancock and Samuel Adams about a British military operation?

2. **Clarify** What kind of person was William Dawes?

3. **Clarify** What "near miss" did the riders encounter as they rode to Concord?

Text Analysis

4. **Use Your Notes** Use your notes to create a timeline of the historic events that occurred on the night of April 18, 1775.

5. **Understand a History Article** Now that you've read this history article, what do you think are the main points the author wants to make about the events of April 18, 1775?

COMMON CORE

RI 1 Cite the evidence that supports an analysis of what the text says explicitly. **RI 9** Analyze a case in which two or more texts provide conflicting information on the same topic and identify where the texts disagree. **W 2** Write explanatory texts.

Read for Information: Compare and Contrast

WRITING PROMPT

How does the information in "The Other Riders" match up with the story told in "Paul Revere's Ride"? In a paragraph, compare and contrast the legend in the poem with the true account of that night as it is presented in the historical article.

Remember that when you **compare and contrast,** you identify the ways in which two or more things are alike and different. Then follow these steps:

1. If you haven't already done so, fill in your chart with the main participants and events discussed in the poem and the article.

2. Note the similarities and differences between the two accounts in the last column of the chart. For example, your paraphrases might reveal that both texts follow the same logical order.

3. In a sentence, make a general statement about the similarities and differences in the accounts. Support your statement with evidence from the texts.

	from "Paul Revere's Ride"	from "The Other Riders"	Similarities and Differences
Main Participants			
Main Events			

Personal Narrative

Like the characters in this unit, you have played a part in many memorable events. Now you have a chance to write about experiences that are important to you. In this workshop, you will learn how to write a personal narrative that engages readers through the use of vivid details.

 Complete the workshop activities in your **Reader/Writer Notebook**.

WRITE WITH A PURPOSE

WRITING TASK

Write a **personal narrative** in which you attempt to entertain a specific audience by telling about a meaningful experience from your own life.

Idea Starters
- a childhood adventure
- going to a family reunion
- your first day in a new place
- winning or losing a big game

THE ESSENTIALS

Here are some common purposes, audiences, and formats for a personal narrative.

PURPOSES	AUDIENCES	FORMATS
• to entertain the people who read it • to share reflections on a meaningful event	• classmates and teacher • parents • club members • friends • Web users	• essay for class • speech • blog posting • journal entry • school newspaper column • documentary • podcast

COMMON CORE TRAITS

1. DEVELOPMENT OF IDEAS

- provides an **engaging introduction**
- uses techniques such as **dialogue, description,** and **reflection** to develop the events
- provides a **conclusion** that reflects on events

2. ORGANIZATION OF IDEAS

- uses appropriate **transitions** to convey **sequence**
- uses effective **pacing** to develop the narrative

3. LANGUAGE FACILITY AND CONVENTIONS

- establishes and maintains a **point of view**
- includes **precise language, relevant descriptive details,** and **sensory language**
- punctuates **verbs in a series** and corrects **run-on sentences**
- employs correct **grammar, usage,** and **spelling**

Writing Online

THINK central

Go to **thinkcentral.com**.
KEYWORD: HML8N-148

Planning/Prewriting

COMMON CORE W 3a–e Write narratives to develop real or imagined experiences or events using effective technique, relevant descriptive details, and well-structured event sequences.
W 5 Develop and strengthen writing as needed by planning.

Getting Started

CHOOSE A TOPIC

Use the Idea Starters on page 148 to help you recall some memorable experiences that you enjoy telling people about. Focus on experiences that have remained important to you over time. Choose the one that you think would be most interesting for you to write about and for your audience to read about.

► ASK YOURSELF:

- What specific, relevant details do I remember about the experience?
- What does the experience reveal about me or someone else?
- Why might reading about this experience be engaging or important to other people?
- Am I comfortable sharing my thoughts about the experience with readers?

THINK ABOUT AUDIENCE AND PURPOSE

Before you begin your draft, think about your **audience** and your **purpose** for writing. This will help you choose relevant descriptive details, determine what background information is necessary to orient readers, and decide what ideas to emphasize.

► ASK YOURSELF:

- Who will read my narrative? What information will they need to understand my story?
- Why am I writing about this experience? Do I want to make my audience laugh—or cry? Do I want them to understand something about me or the world we live in?

GATHER DETAILS

As you decide what experience you will write about, gather relevant descriptive details you want to include—sights, sounds, smells, sensations. Think like a newspaper reporter and remember the questions reporters use to make sure they've covered the important facts in a story: *Who? What? When? Where? Why? How?* For example:

- *Who* was involved in the experience, and what did he or she say?
- *What* happened, and in what order did events occur?
- *When* did I have this experience?
- *Where* did the events happen?
- *Why* did the events happen? What set them in motion?
- *How* did I feel about the events at the time, and how do I feel now? *How* do I want my readers to feel about my experience?

► WHAT DOES IT LOOK LIKE?

Who?	myself; runner who beat me in first race; coach
What?	pushed myself to succeed in running; nearly won first race; made varsity team
When?	eighth grade
Where?	cross-country course; school cafeteria (awards ceremony)
Why?	I was motivated to become the only middle-school student on the varsity team.
How?	I felt proud of myself. I want readers to see that trying one's best is even more important than actually reaching a goal.

Planning/Prewriting *continued*

Getting Started

WRITE A STATEMENT OF MEANING

In a personal narrative, you reflect on decisions you've made or actions you've taken as well as the consequences of those decisions and actions. You want your audience to understand why the experience you're describing was significant in your life. Consider what the experience means to you and write a brief, direct statement of its meaning. This statement will help you focus your narrative.

▶ WHAT DOES IT LOOK LIKE?

> This experience was significant to me because I learned that the most important thing is to do your best.

PLAN YOUR NARRATIVE

When planning your narrative, remember to organize an event sequence that unfolds naturally and logically. The clearest way to structure your narrative is in **chronological order**—the order in which events occurred. Also remember to think about effective **pacing**, or the smooth flow of events from one to the next. Avoid focusing on unnecessary and irrelevant details.

▶ WHAT DOES IT LOOK LIKE?

> 1. I decided this would be the year I'd achieve success as a runner.
> 2. I trained hard for the first race, so that I would make the varsity team.
> 3. In the race, I ran as fast as I could, and only one runner kept up.
> 4. The other runner at first fell behind but caught up with me at the end.
> 5. After a long season, I won a varsity letter and met my goal.

PEER REVIEW Briefly describe to a peer the experience you plan to write about, and explain to him or her what makes it meaningful to you. Then ask: What kinds of details could I include to help my audience understand the importance of the experience? What background information could I include to help orient my audience?

 YOUR TURN In your *Reader/Writer Notebook,* record possible experiences to write about and choose one. Use a chart like the one on page 149 to help you record details about the experience. Next, write a statement about what the experience means and plan the events you want to include in your narrative. Then review your plan, asking yourself which details you should emphasize and what you could add or remove to make your narrative more effective. Remember to keep in mind your purpose and audience.

Drafting

COMMON CORE

W 4 Produce clear and coherent writing in which the development, organization, and style are appropriate to task, purpose, and audience.
L 2a Use punctuation to indicate a pause or break.

The following chart shows how to organize a draft of an effective personal narrative.

Organizing a Personal Narrative

INTRODUCTION

- Begin with an engaging first sentence using your **natural voice**—the words and phrases you would use when telling the story to your friends.
- Use the **first-person point of view;** refer to yourself with the pronouns *I, me,* and *my*.
- Establish context by including details about when and where the experience took place.

▼

BODY

- Develop a logical event sequence, using **transitional words, phrases,** and **clauses** such as *first, next,* and *then* to guide readers.
- Use **sensory language** to help readers experience the action.
- Include your **reflections,** or your thoughts and feelings, as the events unfold.
- Use effective **pacing** to keep events moving smoothly in your narrative.

▼

CONCLUDING SECTION

- Provide a **conclusion** that reveals why the experience is meaningful to you.
- **Reflect** on your experience and how what you learned might apply to readers' lives.

GRAMMAR IN CONTEXT: PUNCTUATING VERBS IN A SERIES

Use action verbs throughout your personal narrative to make events come alive for your readers. Follow these rules for punctuating a series of verbs.

Rule	Example
Separate more than two verbs in a series with commas.	*I drank, ate, and slept running that year.*
Commas are not needed if all the verbs in a series are joined by *and, or,* or *nor*.	*I lifted weights and jumped rope and ran sprints every day.* *I didn't know whether to laugh or dance or shout when I won the race.*

YOUR TURN Write a draft of your personal narrative based on the structure outlined above. As you write, make sure you correctly punctuate verbs in a series.

Revising

When you revise, your goal is to make your personal narrative more engaging and meaningful. The questions, tips, and strategies in the chart below will help you revise, rework, and improve your draft.

PERSONAL NARRATIVE

Ask Yourself	Tips	Revision Strategies
1. Does my introduction engage readers and help set the scene?	▶ **Highlight** interesting statements. **Circle** details that show the setting.	▶ **Add** an attention-getting question or statement. **Add** details about where and when the event took place.
2. Are events in chronological order?	▶ **Number** the events.	▶ **Rearrange** events, as necessary. **Add** transitions to link events.
3. Are the details describing people, places, and events relevant and precise?	▶ **Circle** sensory details. In the margin, **note** which senses they appeal to.	▶ **Elaborate** with additional descriptions and sensory details, if necessary. **Delete** irrelevant details.
4. Does my narrative provide enough background information to orient readers?	▶ **Bracket** passages that might be unclear to someone who knows little about your topic.	▶ **Elaborate** on ideas that might be confusing or unfamiliar to some people in your audience. **Add** background information as needed.
5. Does the pacing keep events moving smoothly?	▶ **Box** sentences that slow the pace of the narrative.	▶ **Delete** unnecessary details to improve the pace of your narrative.
6. Have I included my reflections about events in my narative?	▶ **Put a check mark** next to statements of your feelings and thoughts.	▶ **Add** specific details about feelings and thoughts as needed.
7. Does my conclusion reveal why the experience is meaningful?	▶ **Underline** your statement about why the experience is meaningful.	▶ **Add** a statement that explains why the experience is important to you.

 YOUR TURN

PEER REVIEW Review your draft with a peer. Answer each question on the chart above to see how you could both improve or rework your personal narratives, and whether you should consider a new approach. Be sure to take notes about what your partner suggests.

W 3d Use relevant descriptive details and sensory language. **W 5** Develop and strengthen writing as needed by revising, editing, rewriting, or trying a new approach, focusing on how well purpose and audience have been addressed.

ANALYZE A STUDENT DRAFT

Read this student's draft and the comments on it as a model for revising your own personal narrative.

Today Is the Day

by Alex Bloom, Gray Middle School

❶ "This is going to be the year for me," I thought. To achieve the standards I set for myself, I worked out every spare minute. As the season progressed, I focused even more on my running, securing a position on the school's track team. But I wanted more. Determined to be the only varsity cross-country runner from middle school, I pushed myself the extra mile. I made running part of my daily routine. I drank, ate, and slept running. I was determined to be prepared to win the first race of the year.

❷ Bang! The race began. "I can do this," I thought. I quickly passed most of the racers from the other teams, putting myself in the front of the pack. My hair blew from side to side in the wind, and my uniform was no longer neat. I sped past the rest of the racers, leaving them behind. Only one runner stayed with me throughout the race. We flew around every turn with speed and precision, competing, challenging each other. He fell back as I powered up the hill, I moved ahead, gaining distance. I turned into the final corner.

> Alex establishes his **first-person point of view** right away and maintains it throughout the narrative.

> **Precise details** help capture the action and forward movement of the race. However, Alex could add **descriptive details** and **sensory language** to help readers really picture the race.

LEARN HOW Add Descriptive Details and Sensory Language Alex might add **descriptive details** and **sensory language** to make the race even more vivid to the reader. By helping readers picture the race, he will engage them in his narrative and make it more entertaining for them to read. Alex inserted some details, shown in blue.

ALEX'S REVISION TO PARAGRAPH ❷

Bang! The race began. "I can do this," I thought. I quickly passed most of the racers from the other teams, putting myself in the front of the pack. My *long* hair blew from side to side in the wind, and my uniform was *bright red* no longer *drenched in sweat.* neat. I sped past the rest of the racers, leaving them behind. Only one *, a gangly freshman,* runner stayed with me throughout the race.

❸   I stepped carefully on the uneven surface, hoping not to twist my ankle. "I want to win this race," I thought. I used every bit of energy left in my exhausted body, but the other runner suddenly appeared right behind me. I guess you could call it a photo finish because we crossed the finish line neck and neck, but he won by inches. Then it hit me. It didn't matter if I won or not because I tried my hardest.

> After writing the **climax** of the narrative, Alex reflects on what it means.

❹   The season ended. An awards ceremony was held in the school cafeteria. The coach called everybody's name, and then he finally called mine. "This is the moment," I thought. "This is the moment of truth." I received a varsity letter, reaching the goal I had set. I was also named the Outstanding Middle School Runner of the Year. Proud of myself, I thought, "I did my best this year, and next year I'll do even better."

> This paragraph needs some **transitions** to connect the ideas.

> The final sentence of the narrative helps reveal the **significance** of Alex's experience.

LEARN HOW **Add Transitions** In the final paragraph of his draft, Alex jumps from the end of the season to an awards ceremony. Readers may be confused by these abrupt changes in time and place. Did the season end immediately after Alex's big race? After the race, did the team go directly to the school cafeteria for the awards ceremony?

Alex can fix this problem by adding **transitional words, phrases,** or **clauses** that signal shifts from one time frame or setting to another. In a narrative, transitions that indicate time order are especially helpful. Examples include *before, after, then, later, the following week,* and *eventually.* Alex added transitions in his last paragraph to make the passage of time clear.

ALEX'S REVISION TO PARAGRAPH ❹

After many more races,   I was excited when I went to the   *later that month. Soon*
     ~~The season ended.~~ An awards ceremony ~~was held~~ in the school cafeteria.
The coach called everybody's name, and then he finally called mine.

YOUR TURN   Use the revision strategies chart, feedback from your peers and teacher, and the two "Learn How" lessons to revise your narrative or try a new approach. Evaluate how well you have achieved the characteristics of a good personal narrative and fulfilled your purpose.

Editing and Publishing

COMMON CORE

W 3c Use transition words, phrases, and clauses to convey sequence.
W 5 Strengthen writing by revising, editing, rewriting, or trying a new approach.
L 1 Demonstrate command of standard English grammar and usage when writing.

In the editing stage, you review your writing to look for errors in grammar, usage, spelling, and punctuation. Such mistakes can distract your audience from focusing on what's important—your personal narrative.

GRAMMAR IN CONTEXT: CORRECTING RUN-ON SENTENCES

As you review your writing, pay attention to places where one thought runs into another. You may need to fix a **run-on sentence,** which is actually two or more sentences written as if they were one. There are several ways to correct a run-on sentence.

> **Run-on sentence:** *I like to run I joined the track team.*

Make two sentences. ▶	*I like to run. I joined the track team.*
Use a semicolon. ▶	*I like to run; I joined the track team.*
Add a conjunction. ▶	*I like to run, so I joined the track team.*

In the second paragraph of his draft, Alex's writing was not clear because he had a run-on sentence. Alex decided to break it into two sentences.

> *He fell back as I powered up the hill, I moved ahead, gaining distance.*
>
> [Alex had used a comma to run together two complete sentences. By changing the comma to a period, he fixed the run-on.]

PUBLISH YOUR WRITING

Share your personal narrative with an audience.
- Give a copy of your narrative to friends, family members, and classmates. If you wish, add photographs or illustrations to your narrative.
- Present your narrative orally to a group.
- Submit your narrative to an online literary magazine.
- Post your narrative on your personal Web page.

YOUR TURN Correct any errors in your narrative. As you proofread, look carefully for run-on sentences and fix the punctuation. Also, correct any errors in punctuating a series of verbs. Then publish your final narrative for others to enjoy.

Scoring Rubric

Use the rubric below to evaluate your personal narrative from the Writing Workshop or your response to the on-demand writing task on the next page.

PERSONAL NARRATIVE

SCORE	COMMON CORE TRAITS
6	• **Development** Has an engaging introduction that orients readers; develops events with strong dialogue and description; provides a strong conclusion • **Organization** Establishes a natural and logical sequence of events; uses effective pacing and transitions to convey sequence • **Language** Maintains a clear point of view; uses relevant descriptive details and vivid sensory language; shows a command of conventions
5	• **Development** Has an effective introduction; develops events with dialogue and description; provides a conclusion that sums up the narrative • **Organization** Has a logical sequence of events; uses mostly effective pacing and some transitions to signal shifts in time • **Language** Maintains a point of view; includes relevant descriptive details and some sensory language; has a few errors in conventions
4	• **Development** Has an introduction, but doesn't provide context; could use more dialogue or description to develop events; provides an adequate conclusion • **Organization** Has a logical sequence of events but needs more transitions • **Language** Mostly maintains a point of view; needs more descriptive details and sensory language; includes a few distracting errors in conventions
3	• **Development** Has an introduction, but needs more development; needs more dialogue and description; lacks a strong conclusion • **Organization** Has a confusing sequence due to unnecessary events; has a slow pace at times; needs more transitions to convey sequence • **Language** Has some lapses in point of view; lacks effective descriptive details and sensory language; has some major errors in conventions
2	• **Development** Lacks an effective introduction and fails to develop events • **Organization** Includes distracting events; has choppy pacing • **Language** Lacks a clear point of view; mostly lacks details and sensory language; has many errors in conventions
1	• **Development** Has no introduction; lacks descriptive details; ends abruptly • **Organization** Has no transitions and an unclear sequence of events • **Language** Has no clear point of view, no effective details or sensory language; has major errors in conventions

Preparing for Timed Writing

 COMMON CORE **W 10** Write routinely over shorter time frames for a range of tasks, purposes, and audiences.

1. ANALYZE THE TASK   5 MIN

Read the task carefully. Then read it again, underlining or circling the words that tell the type of writing, the topic, the purpose, and the audience.

> **WRITING TASK**   ✓Type of Writing   ✓Purpose   ✓Audience
>
> Write a <u>personal narrative</u> that will <u>entertain your</u> (classmates) by relating a
> <u>significant personal experience</u>. Use descriptive details and sensory language to describe
> the experience, and tell readers why the experience is still meaningful to you.
> ↳Topic

2. PLAN YOUR RESPONSE   10 MIN

First, think of some personal experiences that you feel comfortable writing about. Choose the most meaningful of those experiences as the topic of your narrative. Then use a graphic organizer to help you take notes.

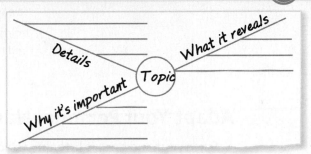

3. RESPOND TO THE TASK   20 MIN

Using your notes, begin drafting your narrative. Follow these guidelines:
- In the introduction, grab the reader's attention with an interesting opener, and set the scene with sensory details.
- In the body, relate the events of your experience in a clear order, usually chronological.
- In the conclusion, reflect on why the experience is meaningful to you.
- Remember to use a consistent first-person point of view.

4. IMPROVE YOUR RESPONSE   5–10 MIN

Revising Go back to the key aspects of the task. Have you used descriptive details and sensory language? Have you used transitions to guide the reader? Do you use effective pacing to keep events moving smoothly?

Proofreading Check your narrative to correct errors in grammar, spelling, punctuation, and capitalization. Make sure that your paper and any edits are legible.

Checking Your Final Copy Before you turn in your narrative, look at it once more to catch any errors you may have missed.

Presenting an Oral Narrative

You tell stories all the time—when you tell friends about what you did over the weekend or share something funny that happened at home. In this workshop, you will turn a true story, or a personal narrative, into an oral presentation.

 Complete the workshop activities in your **Reader/Writer Notebook.**

SPEAK WITH A PURPOSE	COMMON CORE TRAITS
TASK Adapt your written narrative into an **oral narrative.** After you have practiced delivering your narrative, present it to your class.	**A STRONG ORAL NARRATIVE . . .** • focuses on a single meaningful experience • contains well-chosen details that allow listeners to visualize the people, settings, and events • has a clear sequence of events that allows listeners to easily follow the story • holds listeners' attention through effective verbal and nonverbal techniques

COMMON CORE

SL 4 Present claims and findings in a focused, coherent manner; use appropriate eye contact, adequate volume, and clear pronunciation.
SL 6 Adapt speech, demonstrating command of formal English when appropriate.

Adapt Your Personal Narrative

Since your audience is listening to your narrative, not reading it, they have only one chance to understand it. Use these tips to help you develop an engaging, coherent, or easy-to-follow, oral presentation your listeners will enjoy.

• **Background Information** Include extra information your listeners might need to understand your narrative.

• **Realistic Dialogue** Try to re-create the actual words of the people involved.

• **Specific Action** Describe events directly and clearly. Stick to the most salient, or important, events.

• **Word Choice** Use precise language to describe people, settings, and things. Use correct formal English, as appropriate, to help you deliver your message clearly. Choose words that will be familiar to your audience.

• **Sensory Details** Select words that appeal to one or more of the five senses.

• **Organization** Organize your story in chronological order. Use transitional words, phrases, and clauses to help listeners follow your story.

• **Conclusion** Sum up your personal narrative by sharing with listeners why your experience was memorable, fun, scary, or eye-opening.

• **Make Notes** Make your notes brief and easy to read. This way you'll be able to glance at them and hold your focus without losing eye contact with your audience as you speak.

THINK central
Speaking & Listening Online
Go to **thinkcentral.com**.
KEYWORD: HML8-158

Deliver Your Personal Narrative

ENGAGE YOUR AUDIENCE

Acting out information, rather than depending solely on your words, is an effective—and often more interesting—way to communicate ideas. **Verbal techniques,** the manner in which you use your voice, and **nonverbal techniques,** the manner in which you use your body, can help you get your message across. For example, instead of telling your audience that a character is angry, you can show them by using facial expressions (such as scowling or glaring), raising the pitch of your voice to a shrill level, or changing the tone of your voice to sound irritated.

Before you deliver your personal narrative, practice your delivery techniques. Look at the chart below for tips.

Ways to Communicate Ideas

VERBAL TECHNIQUES	NONVERBAL TECHNIQUES
Volume No matter how loudly or softly you speak, be sure your audience can understand you.	**Facial Expressions** Smiling or frowning, looking puzzled or surprised can help you convey your meaning.
Rate Speak fast enough not to bore your listeners and slowly enough that they can follow your presentation.	**Gestures** Pointing, reaching, or banging can add emphasis to what you say, but be careful not to gesture needlessly.
Pitch Qualities of pitch, or modulation—such as high, low, shrill, musical, or rumbling—can help clarify your meaning.	**Posture** Whether you stand straight or slouch can influence the way your audience reacts to what you say.
Tone Your attitude toward what you are saying, such as amused, angry, or serious, should be clear from the tone of your voice.	**Appearance** You may want to dress more formally for a serious presentation or wear casual clothes for a humorous one.

YOUR TURN

As a Speaker Practice your presentation in front of a mirror, using the verbal and nonverbal techniques described above. Then deliver your speech to a friend. Consider your friend's feedback as you practice and improve your presentation.

As a Listener Evaluate your friend's delivery of his or her personal narrative. Listen carefully to make sure you can follow the story, and identify any places that seem unclear. Note whether your friend's volume, pace, and gestures are effective for his or her audience and purpose.

159

Assessment Practice

DIRECTIONS Read the selections and answer the questions that follow.

The Invaders   *by Jack Ritchie*

1   None of them left the ship on the first day of its arrival, but I knew that they would be watching carefully for signs of human life.

2   The skies were dark with scudding clouds, and the cold wind moved high in the trees. Thin snow drifted slowly to the ground.

3   From the cover of the forest, I now watched as a small, heavily armed group of them left the large craft. When they reached the edge of the woods, they hesitated for a few moments and then moved cautiously forward.

4   I had seen them before and I knew that in appearance, at least, they were not monsters. They looked very much like us. There were some differences, of course, but all in all, we were really quite similar to them.

5   I met them first when I was almost a boy and I had been without caution. I approached them and they seemed friendly, but then suddenly they seized me and carried me off in their strange ship.

6   It was a long journey to their land and when our ship made a landing, I was shown about and exhibited as though I were some kind of animal.

7   I saw their cities, and I was shown plants and animals completely strange to me. I learned to wear their clothing and even to eat their food.

8   They taught me to communicate in their strange and difficult tongue until I could, at times, even think in their language.

9   I had almost given up the hope of ever seeing my home again, but they one day put me back on one of their ships and told me that they were returning me because they wished to establish friendly relations with my people. But by now, I knew enough of them to know that this was not true. However, I nodded and smiled and watched for my opportunity to escape.

10 When the ship landed, I went out with the first search party. It was near evening and as the darkness gathered, I edged away from them and finally I fled into the blackness and safety of the forest.

11 They came after me, of course, but I was hidden deep in the woods where they could not find me.

12 Finally they gave up and I watched their ship become smaller and finally disappear, and I hoped fervently that they would never return.

13 But now they were back again.

14 I felt a coldness inside of me as I watched them moving slowly through the trees. They seemed somehow different from the others who had been here before. It was not so much in their appearance as in the air about them—the way they walked, the way they looked about with speculating eyes.

15   Slowly and instinctively, I realized that this time they were not here on just
another raid for a captive or two.

16   This time they had come to stay.

17   What could we do now? Could we lure them deeper into the forest and kill
them? Could we take their weapons and learn how to use them?

18   No, I thought despairingly. There were so many more of the invaders on
the ship. And more weapons. They would come out and hunt us down like
animals. They would hunt us down and kill us all.

19   I sighed. We must find out what it was that they wanted this time and
whatever it might be, we must learn to adjust and to hope for the best.

20   But I still retreated silently before them, afraid to approach. I watched them
search the ground ahead of them and knew they were looking for footprints,
for some signs of life. But there was not yet enough snow on the ground to
track us down.

21   Their strangely colored eyes glanced about warily. They were cautious, yes.

22   They could be a cruel race, I knew. I had seen with my own eyes how they
treated their animals and even their own kind.

23   I sighed again. Yes, we could be cruel, too. In this respect we could not
claim to be superior to the invaders.

24   They paused now in a clearing, their eyes gleaming beneath their helmets.

25   It was time for me to approach them.

26   I took a deep breath and stepped into the open.

27   Their weapons quickly pointed at me.

28   "Welcome," I said.

29   They stared at me, and then one of them turned to their bearded leader. "It
appears that this savage can speak some English, Captain Standish."

30   "Welcome," I said again. But I wondered what they would do to my land
and my people now.

Reading Comprehension

Use "The Invaders" to answer questions 1–14.

1. What event happens first in the story?
   A. The invaders look at the ground for footprints.
   B. The invaders leave the ship and enter the woods.
   C. The narrator thinks about attacking the invaders.
   D. The narrator steps into view and greets the invaders.

2. In the exposition of the story, you learn that —
   A. the narrator speaks English
   B. the invaders are cruel people
   C. Captain Standish is a leader
   D. the weather is cold and snowy

3. In paragraph 1 the author develops suspense by using the phrase —
   A. *first day of its arrival*
   B. *I knew that they would be watching*
   C. *None of them left the ship*
   D. *signs of human life*

4. The conflict the narrator struggles with is —
   A. choosing whether to return with the invaders to their country
   B. deciding which response to the invaders will be best for his people
   C. sharing food with the invaders or hiding it from them
   D. betraying his people by helping the invaders find what they want

5. The conflict not resolved at the end of the story is —
   A. what will happen between the invaders and the narrator's people
   B. how the narrator will decide to communicate with the invaders
   C. whether the invaders can make their way off the ship and into the forest
   D. if the narrator will choose to stay hidden from the invaders

6. The rising action begins when the narrator says —
   A. *They looked very much like us* (paragraph 4)
   B. *I learned to wear their clothing and even to eat their food* (paragraph 7)
   C. *But now they were back again* (paragraph 13)
   D. *Yes, we could be cruel, too* (paragraph 23)

7. In paragraph 18 the narrator is losing hope because —
   A. he fears his people are outnumbered and will be killed
   B. his hiding places in the snowy forest are too visible
   C. he thinks that the invaders are looking for another captive
   D. his footprints might lead the invaders to his people

8. The flashback begins when the narrator says —
   A. *I met them first when I was almost a boy and I had been without caution* (paragraph 5)
   B. *But by now, I knew enough of them to know that this was not true* (paragraph 9)
   C. *There were so many more of the invaders on the ship* (paragraph 18)
   D. *But I still retreated silently before them, afraid to approach them* (paragraph 20)

9. The flashback reveals that the narrator —

    A. carefully watched the invaders when they left their ship

    B. was captured as a child by invaders and taken to their land

    C. grew to believe that invaders had friendly intentions

    D. had many habits in common with the invaders

10. The climax of the story occurs when the narrator —

    A. steps out and speaks to the invaders

    B. hides from the invaders in the woods

    C. returns home after being held captive

    D. hears the invaders talk to their leader

11. The narrator hides from the new invaders because —

    A. he distrusts the invaders and is trying to decide what to do

    B. other people are coming to help him

    C. he wants to surprise the invaders from a well-protected location

    D. a search party is looking for him

12. Which phrase from the story helps you figure out when an event occurs?

    A. *There were some differences . . .*

    B. *It was a long journey . . .*

    C. *I could at times . . .*

    D. *They paused now . . .*

13. The narrator rejects the idea of attacking the invaders because —

    A. the strangers have enough people and weapons to harm the local people

    B. the strangers are peaceful and hope to do good deeds

    C. neither the strangers nor the local people want to have a fight

    D. the narrator can speak the strangers' language

14. During the falling action, you discover that the invaders —

    A. arrive on a large ship

    B. have strangely colored eyes

    C. are led by an English captain

    D. mistreat their animals and each other

SHORT CONTRUCTED RESPONSE
Write two or three sentences to answer each question.

15. Identify one technique the author uses to create suspense. Give an example from the text to support your choice.

16. In the flashback, what steps does the narrator take to escape the invaders?

Write a paragraph to answer this question.

17. Reread paragraphs 15–19. What does the narrator realize about the invaders? Explain how this realization helps him to resolve his conflict.

Vocabulary

Use your knowledge of context clues and the Latin word root definitions to answer the following questions.

1. The Latin word *habere* means "to hold" or "to see." In paragraph 6, what does the word *exhibited* mean?

   A. Made to work hard

   B. Presented in public

   C. Held captive in a prison

   D. Soothed with kind words

2. The Latin word *stabilis* means "firm." In paragraph 9, what does the word *establish* mean?

   A. To end quickly

   B. To damage beyond repair

   C. To bring about using trickery

   D. To set up and make solid

3. The Latin word *fervere* means "to boil." In paragraph 12, what does the word *fervently* mean?

   A. In a dreamy way

   B. For a long time

   C. With great emotion

   D. While cooking

4. The Latin word *speculare* means "to observe." In paragraph 14, what does the word *speculating* mean?

   A. Creating a new object

   B. Thinking about or guessing

   C. Taking a risk in the hope of gain

   D. Accepting something as true

5. Read the dictionary entry below for the word *craft*.

   craft (krăft) *noun* **1.** A boat, ship, or aircraft. **2.** Skill in doing or making something. **3.** An occupation or trade. *Verb* **1.** To make by hand. **Synonyms:** *noun:* vehicle, talent, profession, trickery; *verb:* create.

   Which definition represents the meaning of the word *craft* as it is used in paragraph 3?

   A. Definition noun 1

   B. Definition noun 2

   C. Definition noun 3

   D. Definition verb 1

6. In which sentence is the word *craft* used as a verb?

   A. She learned her craft from her father, who was a carpenter.

   B. The fine workmanship revealed the sculptor's craft.

   C. He tried to craft a set of bookshelves for the library.

   D. The small craft was tossed about by the rough waves.

7. Which synonym would best replace the word *craft* in the following sentence?

   The singer demonstrated her <u>craft</u> through her performance in the opera.

   A. Profession

   B. Talent

   C. Trickery

   D. Vehicle

Revising and Editing

DIRECTIONS Read this paragraph and answer the questions that follow.

---

(1) When the Pilgrims first landed at Plymouth in 1620, everyone had their dream of a better life. (2) They had been agreeing that they should work together to build a common house for meetings and religious services. (3) People's lives became difficult though, especially because there was a shortage of food. (4) Nobody knew whether they would survive. (5) In fact, many settlers died during his first winter in the colony. (6) The Native American Squanto helped everyone who remained find where they could fish and trap animals for food. (7) The Native Americans' willingness to share their knowledge of agriculture helped the Pilgrims survive in the new land. (8) Today the national holiday of Thanksgiving recalls the Pilgrims' celebration of their first harvest in Plymouth.

---

1. The meaning of sentence 1 can be improved by changing *their* to —
   A. theirs
   B. its
   C. his or her
   D. they

2. What change, if any, should be made in sentence 2?
   A. Change *had been agreeing* to **will agree**
   B. Change *had been agreeing* to **agreed**
   C. Change *had been agreeing* to **agrees**
   D. Make no change

3. What change, if any, should be made in sentence 3?
   A. Change *became* to **will become**
   B. Change *became* to **are becoming**
   C. Change *became* to **will be becoming**
   D. Make no change

4. The meaning of sentence 4 can be improved by changing *they* to —
   A. he or she
   B. them
   C. his or her
   D. its

5. The meaning of sentence 5 can be improved by changing *his* to —
   A. their
   B. its
   C. his or her
   D. her

6. The meaning of sentence 6 can be improved by changing *they* to —
   A. it
   B. its
   C. their
   D. he or she

Ideas for Independent Reading

Which questions from Unit 1 made an impression on you? Continue exploring them with these books.

COMMON CORE

RL 10 Read and comprehend literature.

What's worth the effort?

The Circuit: Stories from the Life of a Migrant Child
by Francisco Jiménez

In the 1940s, Francisco and his family crossed the Mexican border. Together they worked picking crops in California, struggling to make a life and a permanent home in a new country.

Dancing at the Odinochka
by Kirkpatrick Hill

Erinia and her family live on a small trading post in Russian America. Life is hard, but Erinia is happy. When America buys the territory, life changes. Will the Pavaloffs be able to survive?

Lord of the Deep
by Graham Salisbury

This summer, 13-year-old Mikey is the youngest deckhand in the marina. He soon realizes that working on his stepdad's boat is complicated. When two customers ask for "special" treatment, Mikey has to decide where his loyalty lies.

Is seeing believing?

The Kite Rider
by Geraldine McCaughrean

In thirteenth-century China, Hayou works as a kite rider. It's a terrifying job, but as he soars through the clouds he sometimes sees his father's spirit. Can these sightings give Hayou the wisdom and courage to save his mother and himself?

Sorceress
by Celia Rees

Agnes grew up on a Mohawk reservation in upstate New York. When she starts dreaming of a 17th-century ancestor, she goes home to her Aunt M for help. Is Agnes going crazy, or is someone trying to tell her secrets of her family's past?

The True Confessions of Charlotte Doyle
by Avi

At only 13, Charlotte is a perfect young lady. When she's on a ship traveling to America, she swears she will never leave her cabin, but by the end of the voyage she's been accused of murder, tried, and found guilty.

When is it OK to be scared?

Code Orange
by Caroline B. Cooney

Mitty panics when he remembers his biology paper. He grabs some old medical books from his mother's office and finds an envelope of smallpox scabs from 1912. Has Mitty just unleashed a deadly virus on New York City?

A Girl Named Disaster
by Nancy Farmer

Nhamo isn't even 12 when she's forced to marry a cruel man with three wives. Her grandmother convinces her to run away, and Nhamo must find her way from Mozambique to Zimbabwe on her own.

The Rag and Bone Shop
by Robert Cormier

A little girl has been murdered. Trent, an expert interrogator, is brought to Monument, Massachusetts to meet the 12-year-old suspect, Jason Dorrant. If Trent can get the boy's confession it'll make his career, but is Jason really guilty?

Get Novel Wise

THINK central

Go to **thinkcentral.com**.
KEYWORD: HML8-166

Through Different Eyes

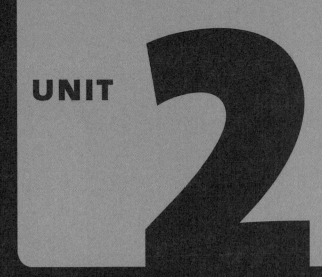

CHARACTER AND POINT OF VIEW

- In Fiction
- In Media
- In Nonfiction
- In Poetry

167

What brings a CHARACTER to life?

A great character might start out as a few words jotted on a page or as a lump of clay squeezed between an artist's fingers. How can these humble beginnings result in a person—or a dog, a rabbit, or a robot—who can seem as familiar as your best friend? A skilled creator knows how to add layers of details that make someone who doesn't even exist in real life seem like someone you've known forever.

ACTIVITY Can you bring a character to life? Follow these steps to give it a try:

- Look through magazines and find a picture of someone or something that looks like he, she, or it could be an interesting character.

- Invent a life for that character. Think about things like where the character lives, what the character cares about most, and how he, she, or it responds to triumphs and challenges.

- Introduce your character to your group. Which of the details you provide most help your classmates feel like they know the person or creature you've invented?

Find It Online!
THINK central

Go to **thinkcentral.com** for the interactive version of this unit.

Preview Unit Goals

TEXT ANALYSIS
- Analyze differences in points of view and the effects they create
- Analyze how dialogue or incidents in a story reveal aspects of a character
- Identify and analyze sound devices and their impact on meaning
- Determine the central idea of a text and its relationship to supporting ideas

READING
- Infer characters' motivations
- Identify scope of ideas and information in different texts

WRITING AND LANGUAGE
- Write a critical review
- Identify and use comparative and superlative forms correctly
- Form and use verb moods correctly
- Identify and use verb tenses correctly

SPEAKING AND LISTENING
- Produce a debate

VOCABULARY
- Use context as a clue to the meaning of a word
- Use knowledge of base words and affixes to determine the meanings of words

ACADEMIC VOCABULARY
- appropriate
- motive
- assess
- role
- intelligence

MEDIA AND VIEWING
- Analyze a filmed production, evaluating the choices made by the director and actors

Media Smart DVD-ROM

Memorable Characters in Movies

Find out how filmmakers developed the unforgettable main character in *Whale Rider*. Page 262

Text Analysis Workshop

Character and Point of View

For a story to really resonate, it must have characters you can care about, relate to, understand, or even love to hate. How do writers create characters that trigger these kinds of reactions? How does *who* tells the story affect your feelings? In this workshop, you'll look closely at characterization and point of view, two techniques that help shape your reactions and opinions.

COMMON CORE

Included in this workshop:
RL 1 Cite textual evidence to support inferences drawn from the text.
RL 3 Analyze how lines of dialogue or incidents in a story reveal aspects of a character. **RL 6** Analyze how differences in the points of view of the characters and the audience or reader create effects.

Part 1: Point of View

Point of view—the vantage point from which a story is told—can affect your understanding of characters and events. Point of view is created by a writer's choice of **narrator,** the voice that tells the story. The narrator may be a character in the story or an outside observer.

This chart describes three points of view. You'll notice that all the examples focus on two students vying to win a school election. In each example, how does the choice of narrator influence your impressions of the characters?

POINT OF VIEW		EXAMPLE
FIRST-PERSON *The narrator* • is a main or minor character in the story • uses the pronouns *I* and *me* • shares his or her **subjective,** or personal, view of other characters and events • doesn't know the thoughts, feelings, and opinions of other characters		Nervously, I eyed Gwen, my competition in the election, and flashed her a gracious smile. Believe me—I wasn't feeling very gracious. After Gwen began her speech, I relaxed. What kind of campaign speech is *that?* I thought. There's no way I'll lose now!
THIRD-PERSON LIMITED *The narrator* • is not a character in the story but an outside observer • zooms in on the thoughts, feelings, and opinions of one character		Devin had trouble wiping the smile off his face as he listened to Gwen fumble through her speech. For a brief moment, he felt a wave of sympathy for Gwen. Then Devin forgot about his opponent and started planning his acceptance speech in his head.
THIRD-PERSON OMNISCIENT *The narrator* • is not a character in the story but an outside observer whose observations can be **objective,** or unbiased. • is "all knowing"—that is, he or she has access to the thoughts, feelings, and opinions of all the characters		Feeling confident and superior, Devin gave his opponent, Gwen, a genuine smile as she walked past him. Though Gwen returned Devin's smile, she was suspicious of his kindness. He's probably gloating over my mistakes, Gwen thought angrily.

MODEL 1: FIRST-PERSON

Emily, the young narrator of this novel, is visiting her sick grandmother, Ola. Emily and Ola have spent the entire day together trying on Ola's old hats and scarves. In this excerpt, Emily describes their special relationship.

from Toning the Sweep

Novel by **Angela Johnson**

Ola and I lie on our backs in the kitchen, scarves and hats everywhere. I look over at the night-light by the table. It's the only light in the room now. Ola's eyes are closed, but I don't think she's asleep.

5 I have always loved my grandmother, but I know that she is a strange woman. I know that not too many of my friends would spend an evening trying on hats with their grandmothers. A few years ago they would have. Now most of them don't even admit that they like their grandparents, though they do.

I'm clueless about how to be cool. I've always told my friends that I like
10 my grandmother. Since most of them only get a glimpse of who she is by the books and strange things she sends through the mail, I think secretly they think she's cool. That makes up for me being clueless, I guess.

Close Read

1. One sentence that reflects the first-person point of view has been boxed. Identify another one.

2. Suppose Emily's grandmother was the narrator of this novel. How might that change what you learn about the woman and her granddaughter?

MODEL 2: THIRD-PERSON OMNISCIENT

The narrator of this story shares the thoughts of more than one character. Alfonso is thrilled when Sandra agrees to go on a bike ride with him. Before his date, Alfonso breaks the chain on his bike. Will his brother help him out?

from Broken Chain

Short story by **Gary Soto**

"Come on, man, let me use it," Alfonso pleaded. "Please, Ernie, I'll do anything."

Although Ernie could see Alfonso's desperation, he had plans with his friend Raymundo. They were going to catch frogs at the Mayfair canal. He felt sorry for
5 his brother, and gave him a stick of gum to make him feel better, but there was nothing he could do. The canal was three miles away, and the frogs were waiting.

Alfonso took the stick of gum, placed it in his shirt pocket, and left the bedroom with his head down. . . .

At four he decided to get it over with and started walking to Sandra's house,
10 trudging slowly, as if he were waist-deep in water. Shame colored his face. How could he disappoint his first date? She would probably laugh.

Close Read

1. How does Ernie feel about Alfonso's predicament? How does Alfonso himself feel? Cite details to support your answers.

2. Suppose the narrator had not revealed Ernie's thoughts in lines 3–6. How might this affect your impression of Ernie?

Part 2: Character Traits and Motivation

As a reader, you can't help but have strong reactions to the people you meet on the page. Did you know that writers use different methods of characterization to create these responses in you? Read on to find out exactly how writers develop lifelike characters with distinct traits and motivations.

CHARACTER TRAITS

Loyal, outgoing, lazy—you might use words like these to describe people in your life. You may not realize it, but you learn about people's qualities, or **traits,** by observing the way they look, talk, and act. For example, a new neighbor probably wouldn't introduce herself by saying, "Hi! I'm outgoing." Instead, you would infer this trait by noticing her big smile and confident voice.

Like people, characters in literature have unique personalities and traits. Sometimes, a narrator will directly tell you what a character is like. More often, you have to infer a character's traits the same way you would a person's—by considering his or her appearance and behavior, for instance.

Writers show you what their characters are like by using the following **indirect methods of characterization.** Look at this graphic, noting the descriptions of the girl Madeleine. What traits can you infer?

PHYSICAL APPEARANCE
Descriptions of a character's looks, clothing, body language, and facial expressions
Madeleine walked stiffly toward her new locker, a solemn expression glued to her face.

OTHER CHARACTERS
Presentation of others' impressions of the character and their interactions or relationships with him or her
Madeleine's classmates smirked and laughed as she walked by. Not only was she unfriendly, they concluded, but she took herself way too seriously.

SPEECH, THOUGHTS, AND ACTIONS
Presentation of a character's speech patterns, habits, talents, opinions, and interactions with others
This was Madeleine's third move in five years, and she was sick of starting over. This time, she vowed to keep to herself. No longer would she waste any energy trying to fit in.

MODEL 1: CHARACTERIZATION

The narrator of this story takes the 8:12 train to work every day; he sees the same commuters and sits in the same corner seat. Today, however, he notices a stranger on the platform. What do you learn about the stranger from this brief excerpt?

from **Galloping Foxley**

Short story by **Roald Dahl**

The stranger was standing plumb in the middle of the platform, feet apart and arms folded, looking for all the world as though he owned the whole place. He was a biggish, thickset man, and even from behind he somehow managed to convey a powerful impression of arrogance and oil. Very
5 definitely, he was not one of us. He carried a cane instead of an umbrella, his shoes were brown instead of black, the grey hat was cocked at a ridiculous angle, and in one way and another there seemed to be an excess of silk and polish about his person. More than this I did not care to observe.

Close Read

1. What methods of characterization has the author used to describe the stranger?

2. What kind of person do you think the stranger is? Cite specific details that affected your impression of him.

MODEL 2: CHARACTER TRAITS

Sopeap is a Cambodian teenager whose family recently moved to the United States. One day, a classmate walks into her family's store, lugging a green armchair. How does Sopeap respond to the classmate's request for help?

from **The Green Armchair**

Short story by **Minfong Ho**

Thomas Ramsey. For an awful moment she thought she had said his name out loud, but then realized it had only been in her mind.
Sopeap forced a smile. "Sure," she said, pleasantly surprised by how casual, how American, she sounded. "Be right with you."
5 "Hey, aren't you in my history class?" he asked.
"Algebra," she said quietly. At least he recognized her. She had long since noticed him, intrigued by the aloof, easy banter he carried on with his classmates, as if he were looking at them from the wrong end of a telescope. A bit of a loner, and liking it that way. *Sort of like me*, she had sometimes
10 thought, clutching onto her solitude as tightly as she held her textbooks. . . .

Close Read

1. How would you describe Thomas? Identify at least two details in this excerpt that influenced your impression of him.

2. Reread the boxed descriptions of Sopeap's thoughts and feelings. What do these descriptions suggest about her traits?

CHARACTER MOTIVATION

Why did the boy decide to volunteer at the animal shelter? What prompted the woman to risk her life for a stranger? A big part of understanding characters is analyzing their **motivations,** or the reasons behind their actions. For instance, did the boy volunteer at the shelter because of his passion for animals or because he has a crush on someone who works there? Think about what each motivation might suggest about the boy's traits.

To uncover a character's motivation, you often have to look for details in the story. As you read, consider the following:

- the narrator's direct comments about a character's motivation

- a character's actions, thoughts, and values

- your own understanding of the emotions—love, greed, ambition, jealousy—that drive human behavior

In this story, 17-year-old Mike finally decides to visit his grandmother in the nursing home. What factors are motivating his actions?

from # The Moustache

Short story by **Robert Cormier**

⌐. . . I told my mother I'd go, anyway. I hadn't seen my grandmother since she'd been admitted to Lawnrest. Besides, the place is located on the Southwest Turnpike, which meant I could barrel along in my father's new Le Mans. My ambition was to see the speedometer hit 75.⌐ Ordinarily, I used the
5   old station wagon, which can barely stagger up to 50.
   Frankly, I wasn't too crazy about visiting a nursing home. They reminded me of hospitals, and hospitals turn me off. I mean, the smell of ether makes me nauseous, and I feel faint at the sight of blood. And as I approached Lawnrest—which is a terrible cemetery kind of name, to begin with—I was
10 sorry I hadn't avoided the trip. Then I felt guilty about it. I'm loaded with guilt complexes. Like driving like a madman after promising my father to be careful. Like sitting in the parking lot, looking at the nursing home with dread and thinking how I'd rather be with Cindy. Then I thought of all the Christmas and birthday gifts my grandmother had given me, and I got out of
15 the car, guilty as usual.

Close Read

1. Reread the boxed text. What is the narrator's initial motivation for visiting his grandmother?

2. The narrator has second thoughts about his visit once he's in the parking lot. What eventually motivates him to go inside?

3. Consider the two motivating factors that influence the narrator's actions. What do they tell you about him?

Part 3: Analyze the Text

Meet Gene, a high school student in Mrs. Tibbetts' second-period class. Gene and his fellow classmates have just found out that Mrs. Tibbetts is taking the advanced English class to a poetry reading. What happens when Mrs. Tibbetts unexpectedly extends the invitation to Gene's class? Read on to find out.

from
I GO ALONG

Short story by **Richard Peck**

Since it's only the second period of the day, we're all feeling pretty good. Also it's a Tuesday, a terrible TV night. Everybody in the class puts up their hands. I mean everybody. Even Marty Crawshaw, . . . And Pink Hohenfield, who's in class today for the first time this month. I put up mine. I go along.

5   Mrs. Tibbetts looks amazed. She's never seen this many hands up in our class. She's never seen anybody's hand except Darla's. . . .

   But then she sees we have to be putting her on. So she just says, "Anyone who would like to go, be in the parking lot at five-thirty. And eat first. No eating on the bus."

10   Mrs. Tibbetts can drive the school bus. Whenever she's taking the advanced class anywhere, she can go to the principal for the keys. She can use the bus anytime she wants to, unless the coach needs it.

   Then she opens her attendance book, and we tune out. And at five-thirty that night I'm in the parking lot. I have no idea why. Needless to say, I'm the

15 only one here from second period. Marty Crawshaw and Pink Hohenfield will be out on the access highway about now, at 7-Eleven, sitting on their hoods. Darla couldn't make it either. Right offhand I can't think of anybody who wants to ride a school bus thirty miles to see a poet. Including me.

   The advanced-English juniors are milling around behind school. I'm still

20 in my car, and it's almost dark, so nobody sees me.

   Then Mrs. Tibbetts wheels the school bus in. She's got the amber fogs flashing, and you can see the black letters along the yellow side: CONSOLIDATED SCHOOL DIST. She swings in and hits the brakes, and the doors fly open. The advanced class starts to climb aboard. They're

25 more orderly than us, but they've got their groups too. . . . I'm settling behind my dashboard. The last kid climbs the bus.

   And I seem to be sprinting across the asphalt. I'm on the bus, and the door's hissing shut behind me. When I swing past the driver's seat, I don't look at Mrs. Tibbetts, and she doesn't say anything. I wonder where I'm supposed to sit.

30   They're still milling around in the aisle, but there are plenty of seats. I find an empty double and settle by the window, pulling my ball cap down in front. It doesn't take us long to get out of town, not in this town. When we go past 7-Eleven, I'm way down in the seat with my hand shielding my face on the window side. Right about then, somebody sits down next to me. I flinch.

Close Read

1. From what point of view is this story told? Explain how you can tell.

2. Reread the boxed sentences. What do they suggest about Gene's character traits?

3. How would this excerpt be different if Mrs. Tibbetts were the narrator?

4. Examine lines 32–34. Why do you think Gene hides when the bus passes the 7–Eleven?

5. Consider Gene's actions and body language in lines 27–34. Based on these details, what can you infer about his personality?

The Treasure of Lemon Brown

Short Story by Walter Dean Myers

VIDEO TRAILER **THiNK** central | KEYWORD: HML8-176

What do you CHERISH?

COMMON CORE

RL 1 Cite textual evidence to support inferences drawn from the text. RL 3 Analyze how lines of dialogue and incidents in a story reveal aspects of a character or provoke a decision.
RL 6 Analyze how differences in the points of view of the characters and the audience or reader create effects.

Think of what you most cherish, or hold dear. Is it worth a lot of money, or is it valuable because of a memory that is important only to you? For example, a photograph of a favorite friend or relative wouldn't bring much money at an auction, but the memories it holds might make it one of the first things you'd save if your home were on fire. In "The Treasure of Lemon Brown," a boy's encounter with an old blues musician helps him discover what he treasures most.

LIST IT Make a list of three to five things that you cherish. They might be tangible (things you can touch, such as a pair of jeans or a pet) or intangible (things you cannot touch, such as a memory or an idea like freedom). Explain why these things are important to you.

TEXT ANALYSIS: THIRD-PERSON POINT OF VIEW

In the **third-person omniscient point of view**, the narrator is an outside observer who can see into the minds of all the characters. A **third-person limited** narrator is also an outside observer, but this point of view focuses on what one character sees, thinks, and feels. Look at the following example:

Report cards were due in a week, and Greg had been hoping for the best.

In this sentence, the narrator tells the reader how Greg feels about the report card he's about to receive.

As you read, pay attention to how much the narrator allows you to know about each character's thoughts and feelings.

READING SKILL: INFER CHARACTERS' MOTIVATIONS

To fully understand the characters in a story, you need to think about their **motivations,** or the reasons for their actions. Sometimes a narrator will actually state a character's motives, but more often you need to **infer,** or guess, them. To infer a character's motives, notice his or her reactions, thoughts, and statements, and ask yourself what you would feel or want in that situation. Also, recall times when you were in a similar situation or behaved similarly.

As you read, note details about the characters and inferences about their motives on a chart like the one here.

Details About Character	What I Infer About Motives
Greg's father lectures Greg about his poor effort in math.	Greg's father wants him to succeed in life.

▲ VOCABULARY IN CONTEXT

Walter Dean Myers uses the boldfaced words to tell the story of Lemon Brown. To see how many of the words you know, substitute a different word or phrase for each one.

1. The door was **ajar** and let in a small amount of light.
2. There was a **tremor** in his voice as he told the sad tale.
3. The silence was **ominous** and scary.
4. He would **commence** his trip when the rain stopped.
5. Years of hard work left him with **gnarled** hands.
6. The hallway was dark, so he moved **tentatively.**

 Complete the activities in your **Reader/Writer Notebook.**

Meet the Author

Walter Dean Myers
born 1937

Contest to Career
Walter Dean Myers was born to a large family in West Virginia. After his mother died, his father could no longer care for all the children. Myers grew up with foster parents in New York City. A speech impediment made it difficult for him to speak, so he began writing poetry and stories with the encouragement of a teacher who thought writing would help him express himself. Still, he didn't think he could earn a living as an author. After unhappily working as a post-office clerk and a messenger, Myers saw an advertisement for a children's book-writing contest. He had never written for young people, but he won the contest and began a highly successful writing career.

Writing His Life
Myers frequently draws on his own experience in his writing. Many of his characters belong to low-income families and deal with urban problems. He has also written biographies of prominent African Americans, including Malcolm X and Muhammad Ali. Myers has said, "As a black writer, I want to talk about my people." But the characters he creates and the issues he addresses have universal appeal.

BACKGROUND TO THE STORY
Harlem
"The Treasure of Lemon Brown" takes place in Harlem, the neighborhood in which Myers grew up in New York City. Since about 1910, it has been one of the largest African-American communities in the United States.

Author Online

Go to **thinkcentral.com.**
KEYWORD: HML8-177

THE TREASURE OF LEMON BROWN

Walter Dean Myers

The dark sky, filled with angry, swirling clouds, reflected Greg Ridley's mood as he sat on the stoop[1] of his building. His father's voice came to him again, first reading the letter the principal had sent to the house, then lecturing endlessly about his poor efforts in math.

"I had to leave school when I was 13," his father had said, "that's a year younger than you are now. If I'd had half the chances that you have, I'd . . ."

Greg had sat in the small, pale green kitchen listening, knowing the lecture would end with his father saying he couldn't play ball with the Scorpions. He had asked his father the week before, and his father had said it depended on his

10 next report card. It wasn't often the Scorpions took on new players, especially 14-year-olds, and this was a chance of a lifetime for Greg. He hadn't been allowed to play high school ball, which he had really wanted to do, but playing for the Community Center team was the next best thing. Report cards were due in a week, and Greg had been hoping for the best. But the principal had ended the suspense early when she sent that letter saying Greg would probably fail math if he didn't spend more time studying. **A**

"And you want to play *basketball?*" His father's brows knitted over deep brown eyes. "That must be some kind of a joke. Now you just get into your room and hit those books."

20 That had been two nights before. His father's words, like the distant thunder that now echoed through the streets of Harlem, still rumbled softly in his ears.

---

1. **stoop:** a porch or staircase at the entrance of a building.

Analyze Visuals ▶

This collage was created by Walter Dean Myers's son. What can you **infer** about Harlem from the details in this image?

A POINT OF VIEW
Whose thoughts and feelings is the **narrator** describing?

Illustrations by Christopher Myers.

It was beginning to cool. Gusts of wind made bits of paper dance between the parked cars. There was a flash of nearby lightning, and soon large drops of rain splashed onto his jeans. He stood to go upstairs, thought of the lecture that probably awaited him if he did anything except shut himself in his room with his math book, and started walking down the street instead. Down the block there was an old tenement that had been abandoned for some months. Some of the guys had held an impromptu checker tournament there the week
30 before, and Greg had noticed that the door, once boarded over, had been slightly **ajar.**

Pulling his collar up as high as he could, he checked for traffic and made a dash across the street. He reached the house just as another flash of lightning changed the night to day for an instant, then returned the graffiti-scarred building to the grim shadows. He vaulted over the outer stairs and pushed **tentatively** on the door. It was open, and he let himself in.

The inside of the building was dark except for the dim light that filtered through the dirty windows from the streetlamps. There was a room a few feet from the door, and from where he stood at the entrance, Greg could see
40 a squarish patch of light on the floor. He entered the room, frowning at the musty smell. It was a large room that might have been someone's parlor at one time. Squinting, Greg could see an old table on its side against one wall, what looked like a pile of rags or a torn mattress in the corner, and a couch, with one side broken, in front of the window.

He went to the couch. The side that wasn't broken was comfortable enough, though a little creaky. From this spot he could see the blinking neon sign over the bodega[2] on the corner. He sat a while, watching the sign blink first green then red, allowing his mind to drift to the Scorpions, then to his father. His father had been a postal worker for all Greg's life, and was proud of it, often
50 telling Greg how hard he had worked to pass the test. Greg had heard the story too many times to be interested now. **B**

For a moment Greg thought he heard something that sounded like a scraping against the wall. He listened carefully, but it was gone.

Outside the wind had picked up, sending the rain against the window with a force that shook the glass in its frame. A car passed, its tires hissing over the wet street and its red tail lights glowing in the darkness.

Greg thought he heard the noise again. His stomach tightened as he held himself still and listened intently. There weren't any more scraping noises, but he was sure he had heard something in the darkness—something breathing!
60 He tried to figure out just where the breathing was coming from; he knew it was in the room with him. Slowly he stood, tensing. As he turned, a flash of lightning lit up the room, frightening him with its sudden brilliance. He saw nothing, just the overturned table, the pile of rags and an old newspaper on the floor. Could he have been imagining the sounds? He continued listening,

---

2. **bodega** (bō-dä′gə): a small grocery store.

ajar (ə-jär′) *adj.* partially open

tentatively (tĕn′tə-tĭv-lē) *adv.* uncertainly or hesitantly

B INFER CHARACTERS' MOTIVATIONS
Reread lines 25–27 and 48–51. From Greg's thoughts, what would you infer are his reasons for not going home?

but heard nothing and thought that it might have just been rats. Still, he thought, as soon as the rain let up he would leave. He went to the window and was about to look out when he heard a voice behind him.

"Don't try nothin' 'cause I got a razor here sharp enough to cut a week into nine days!"

70   Greg, except for an involuntary **tremor** in his knees, stood stock still. The voice was high and brittle, like dry twigs being broken, surely not one he had ever heard before. There was a shuffling sound as the person who had been speaking moved a step closer. Greg turned, holding his breath, his eyes straining to see in the dark room.

The upper part of the figure before him was still in darkness. The lower half was in the dim rectangle of light that fell unevenly from the window. There were two feet, in cracked, dirty shoes from which rose legs that were wrapped in rags.

"Who are you?" Greg hardly recognized his own voice.

"I'm Lemon Brown," came the answer. "Who're you?"

80   "Greg Ridley."

"What you doing here?" The figure shuffled forward again, and Greg took a small step backward.

"It's raining," Greg said.

"I can see that," the figure said.

The person who called himself Lemon Brown peered forward, and Greg could see him clearly. He was an old man. His black, heavily wrinkled face was surrounded by a halo of crinkly white hair and whiskers that seemed to separate his head from the layers of dirty coats piled on his smallish frame. His pants were bagged to the knee, where they were met with rags that went
90   down to the old shoes. The rags were held on with strings, and there was a rope around his middle. Greg relaxed. He had seen the man before, picking through the trash on the corner and pulling clothes out of a Salvation Army box. There was no sign of the razor that could "cut a week into nine days." **C**

"What are you doing here?" Greg asked.

"This is where I'm staying," Lemon Brown said. "What you here for?"

"Told you it was raining out," Greg said, leaning against the back of the couch until he felt it give slightly.

"Ain't you got no home?"

"I got a home," Greg answered.

100   "You ain't one of them bad boys looking for my treasure, is you?" Lemon Brown cocked his head to one side and squinted one eye. "Because I told you I got me a razor."

"I'm not looking for your treasure," Greg answered, smiling. "*If* you have one."

"What you mean, *if* I have one," Lemon Brown said. "Every man got a treasure. You don't know that, you must be a fool!"

"Sure," Greg said as he sat on the sofa and put one leg over the back. "What do you have, gold coins?"

"Don't worry none about what I got," Lemon Brown said. "You know who I am?"

tremor (trĕm'ər) *n.* nervous trembling

C POINT OF VIEW
How does knowing Greg's thoughts and actions affect your impression of Lemon Brown?

Language Coach

Oral Fluency Notice that the author uses italics in lines 103–104 to show that the characters emphasize the word *if* in their dialogue. Now read these lines aloud with this word emphasized.

◄ Analyze Visuals

How does the man in the picture **compare** with the way you imagine Lemon Brown?

110   "You told me your name was orange or lemon or something like that."

"Lemon Brown," the old man said, pulling back his shoulders as he did so, "they used to call me Sweet Lemon Brown." **D**

"Sweet Lemon?" Greg asked.

"Yessir. Sweet Lemon Brown. They used to say I sung the blues³ so sweet that if I sang at a funeral, the dead would **commence** to rocking with the beat. Used to travel all over Mississippi and as far as Monroe, Louisiana, and east on over to Macon, Georgia. You mean you ain't never heard of Sweet Lemon Brown?"

D INFER CHARACTERS' MOTIVATIONS

Why does the man pull back his shoulders as he tells Greg his name?

commence (kə-měns′) *v.* to begin

---

3. **blues:** a style of music developed from southern African-American songs.

"Afraid not," Greg said. "What . . . what happened to you?"

"Hard times, boy. Hard times always after a poor man. One day I got tired,
120 sat down to rest a spell and felt a tap on my shoulder. Hard times caught up with me."

"Sorry about that."

"What you doing here? How come you didn't go on home when the rain come? Rain don't bother you young folks none."

"Just didn't." Greg looked away.

"I used to have a knotty-headed boy just like you." Lemon Brown had half walked, half shuffled back to the corner and sat down against the wall. "Had them big eyes like you got. I used to call them moon eyes. Look into them moon eyes and see anything you want."

130 "How come you gave up singing the blues?" Greg asked.

"Didn't give it up," Lemon Brown said. "You don't give up the blues; they give you up. After a while you do good for yourself, and it ain't nothing but foolishness singing about how hard you got it. Ain't that right?"

"I guess so."

"What's that noise?" Lemon Brown asked, suddenly sitting upright.

Greg listened, and he heard a noise outside. He looked at Lemon Brown and saw the old man was pointing toward the window.

Greg went to the window and saw three men, neighborhood thugs, on the stoop. One was carrying a length of pipe. Greg looked back toward Lemon
140 Brown, who moved quietly across the room to the window. The old man looked out, then beckoned frantically for Greg to follow him. For a moment Greg couldn't move. Then he found himself following Lemon Brown into the hallway and up darkened stairs. Greg followed as closely as he could. They reached the top of the stairs, and Greg felt Lemon Brown's hand first lying on his shoulder, then probing down his arm until he finally took Greg's hand into his own as they crouched in the darkness. **E**

"They's bad men," Lemon Brown whispered. His breath was warm against Greg's skin.

"Hey! Rag man!" a voice called. "We know you in here. What you got up
150 under them rags? You got any money?"

Silence.

"We don't want to have to come in and hurt you, old man, but we don't mind if we have to."

Lemon Brown squeezed Greg's hand in his own hard, **gnarled** fist.

There was a banging downstairs and a light as the men entered. They banged around noisily, calling for the rag man.

"We heard you talking about your treasure." The voice was slurred. "We just want to see it, that's all."

"You sure he's here?" One voice seemed to come from the room with the sofa.

160 "Yeah, he stays here every night."

"There's another room over there; I'm going to take a look. You got that flashlight?"

E INFER CHARACTERS' MOTIVATIONS
Why does Lemon Brown hold Greg's hand?

gnarled (närld) *adj.* roughened, as from age or work

"Yeah, here, take the pipe too."

Greg opened his mouth to quiet the sound of his breath as he sucked it in uneasily. A beam of light hit the wall a few feet opposite him, then went out.

"Ain't nobody in that room," a voice said. "You think he gone or something?"

"I don't know," came the answer. "All I know is that I heard him talking about some kind of treasure. You know they found that shopping bag lady with that money in her bags."

"Yeah. You think he's upstairs?"

"HEY, OLD MAN, ARE YOU UP THERE?"

Silence.

"Watch my back. I'm going up."

There was a footstep on the stairs, and the beam from the flashlight danced crazily along the peeling wallpaper. Greg held his breath. There was another step and a loud crashing noise as the man banged the pipe against the wooden banister. Greg could feel his temples throb as the man slowly neared them. Greg thought about the pipe, wondering what he would do when the man reached them—what he *could* do. **F**

Then Lemon Brown released his hand and moved toward the top of the stairs. Greg looked around and saw stairs going up to the next floor. He tried waving to Lemon Brown, hoping the old man would see him in the dim light and follow him to the next floor. Maybe, Greg thought, the man wouldn't follow them up there. Suddenly, though, Lemon Brown stood at the top of the stairs, both arms raised high above his head.

"There he is!" a voice cried from below.

"Throw down your money, old man, so I won't have to bash your head in!"

Lemon Brown didn't move. Greg felt himself near panic. The steps came closer, and still Lemon Brown didn't move. He was an eerie sight, a bundle of rags standing at the top of the stairs, his shadow on the wall looming over him. Maybe, the thought came to Greg, the scene could be even eerier.

Greg wet his lips, put his hands to his mouth and tried to make a sound. Nothing came out. He swallowed hard, wet his lips once more and howled as evenly as he could.

"What's that?"

As Greg howled, the light moved away from Lemon Brown, but not before Greg saw him hurl his body down the stairs at the men who had come to take his treasure. There was a crashing noise, and then footsteps. A rush of warm air came in as the downstairs door opened, then there was only an **ominous** silence. **G**

Greg stood on the landing. He listened, and after a while there was another sound on the staircase.

"Mr. Brown?" he called.

"Yeah, it's me," came the answer. "I got their flashlight."

Greg exhaled in relief as Lemon Brown made his way slowly back up the stairs.

"You O.K.?"

"Few bumps and bruises," Lemon Brown said.

COMMON CORE RL 6

F POINT OF VIEW
When a story has a third-person limited narrator, readers may feel that they are "looking over the shoulder" of the **point-of-view character.** This effect helps readers become emotionally involved in that character's experiences. Reread lines 174–179. If the narrator's point of view was not limited to Greg, would this passage be as suspenseful? Why or why not?

ominous (ŏm'ə-nəs) *adj.* threatening

G POINT OF VIEW
Reread lines 196–200. How would this passage be different if you knew what Lemon Brown was thinking?

"I think I'd better be going," Greg said, his breath returning to normal. "You'd better leave, too, before they come back." **H**

210   "They may hang around outside for a while," Lemon Brown said, "but they ain't getting their nerve up to come in here again. Not with crazy old rag men and howling spooks. Best you stay awhile till the coast is clear. I'm heading out West tomorrow, out to east St. Louis."

"They were talking about treasures," Greg said. "You *really* have a treasure?"

"What I tell you? Didn't I tell you every man got a treasure?" Lemon Brown said. "You want to see mine?"

"If you want to show it to me," Greg shrugged.

"Let's look out the window first, see what them scoundrels be doing," Lemon Brown said.

220   They followed the oval beam of the flashlight into one of the rooms and looked out the window. They saw the men who had tried to take the treasure sitting on the curb near the corner. One of them had his pants leg up, looking at his knee.

"You sure you're not hurt?" Greg asked Lemon Brown.

"Nothing that ain't been hurt before," Lemon Brown said. "When you get as old as me all you say when something hurts is 'Howdy, Mr. Pain, sees you back again.' Then when Mr. Pain see he can't worry you none, he go on mess with somebody else."

Greg smiled.

230   "Here, you hold this." Lemon Brown gave Greg the flashlight.

He sat on the floor near Greg and carefully untied the strings that held the rags on his right leg. When he took the rags away, Greg saw a piece of plastic. The old man carefully took off the plastic and unfolded it. He revealed some yellowed newspaper clippings and a battered harmonica. ◆

"There it be," he said, nodding his head. "There it be."

Greg looked at the old man, saw the distant look in his eye, then turned to the clippings. They told of Sweet Lemon Brown, a blues singer and harmonica player who was appearing at different theaters in the South. One of the clippings said he had been the hit of the show, although not the headliner. 240 All of the clippings were reviews of shows Lemon Brown had been in more than 50 years ago. Greg looked at the harmonica. It was dented badly on one side, with the reed holes on one end nearly closed.

"I used to travel around and make money for to feed my wife and Jesse— that's my boy's name. Used to feed them good, too. Then his mama died, and he stayed with his mama's sister. He growed up to be a man, and when the war come he saw fit to go off and fight in it. I didn't have nothing to give him except these things that told him who I was, and what he come from. If you know your pappy did something, you know you can do something too. **I**

"Anyway, he went off to war, and I went off still playing and singing. 250 'Course by then I wasn't as much as I used to be, not without somebody to make it worth the while. You know what I mean?"

H INFER CHARACTERS' MOTIVATIONS
What may be motivating Greg to want to leave now?

◆ GRAMMAR IN CONTEXT
Reread lines 231–234. Notice that the author consistently uses **past-tense verbs** to describe actions in the story.

I INFER CHARACTERS' MOTIVATIONS
Reread lines 243–248. Why does Lemon Brown give his son his old newspaper clippings and harmonica?

"Yeah," Greg nodded, not quite really knowing.

"I traveled around, and one time I come home, and there was this letter saying Jesse got killed in the war. Broke my heart, it truly did.

"They sent back what he had with him over there, and what it was is this old mouth fiddle and these clippings. Him carrying it around with him like that told me it meant something to him. That was my treasure, and when I give it to him he treated it just like that, a treasure. Ain't that something?"

"Yeah, I guess so," Greg said. **J**

260 "You *guess* so?" Lemon Brown's voice rose an octave as he started to put his treasure back into the plastic. "Well, you got to guess 'cause you sure don't know nothing. Don't know enough to get home when it's raining."

"I guess . . . I mean, you're right."

"You O.K. for a youngster," the old man said as he tied the strings around his leg, "better than those scalawags⁴ what come here looking for my treasure. That's for sure."

"You really think that treasure of yours was worth fighting for?" Greg asked. "Against a pipe?"

"What else a man got 'cepting what he can pass on to his son, or his
270 daughter, if she be his oldest?" Lemon Brown said. "For a big-headed boy you sure do ask the foolishest questions."

Lemon Brown got up after patting his rags in place and looked out the window again.

"Looks like they're gone. You get on out of here and get yourself home. I'll be watching from the window so you'll be all right."

Lemon Brown went down the stairs behind Greg. When they reached the front door the old man looked out first, saw the street was clear and told Greg to scoot on home.

"You sure you'll be O.K.?" Greg asked.

280 "Now didn't I tell you I was going to east St. Louis in the morning?" Lemon Brown asked. "Don't that sound O.K. to you?"

"Sure it does," Greg said. "Sure it does. And you take care of that treasure of yours."

"That I'll do," Lemon said, the wrinkles about his eyes suggesting a smile. "That I'll do."

The night had warmed and the rain had stopped, leaving puddles at the curbs. Greg didn't even want to think how late it was. He thought ahead of what his father would say and wondered if he should tell him about Lemon Brown. He thought about it until he reached his stoop, and decided against
290 it. Lemon Brown would be O.K., Greg thought, with his memories and his treasure.

Greg pushed the button over the bell marked Ridley, thought of the lecture he knew his father would give him, and smiled. ⌇ **K**

---

4. **scalawags** (skăl'ə-wăgz'): rascals.

Comprehension

1. **Recall** How does Greg meet Lemon Brown?

2. **Recall** How does Lemon Brown scare off the intruders?

3. **Clarify** Why does Lemon Brown cherish his treasure?

Text Analysis

● 4. **Examine Third-Person Point of View** Whose sights, thoughts, and feelings does the narrator present? Explain how the story might be different if readers knew more about the thoughts of the other characters.

5. **Understand Events** How do Greg's feelings toward Lemon Brown change over time? In a graphic like the one shown, note important events from the story. Under each event, tell how Greg feels about Lemon Brown at that point.

Greg hears
Lemon Brown

Greg sees
Lemon Brown

scared

relieved

● 6. **Infer Characters' Motivations** Review your chart of inferences to recall why Lemon Brown gave his son his "treasure." What does Lemon Brown's story help Greg realize about his own father? Support your answer.

7. **Analyze Dialect** One way writers create realistic characters is to include the characters' **dialect,** the language spoken by people in a particular place or group. Find three examples of Lemon Brown's dialect. Explain how his language contributes to your understanding of his character.

8. **Draw Conclusions About Characters** In fiction, a character may be either static or dynamic. **Static** characters experience little change over the course of a story. **Dynamic** characters change and grow during a story. Which characters in this story are static? Which are dynamic? Explain.

Extension and Challenge

9. **Readers' Circle** Discuss with a small group of classmates what makes a good role model and in what ways Lemon Brown is a role model for Greg.

10. **Inquiry and Research** Lemon Brown describes singing the blues as "singing about how hard you got it." Research the blues and find some representative songs. Is Lemon Brown's description of the blues accurate? Play parts of the songs for the class and talk about the kind of life the songs suggest.

What do you CHERISH?

How has reading this story influenced your thoughts about the things that are most valuable to you?

COMMON CORE

RL1 Cite textual evidence to support inferences drawn from the text. **RL3** Analyze how lines of dialogue and incidents in a story reveal aspects of a character or provoke a decision. **RL6** Analyze how differences in the points of view of the characters and the audience or reader create effects.

Vocabulary Practice

▲ VOCABULARY PRACTICE

Synonyms are words that have the same meaning. **Antonyms** are words that have the opposite meaning. Explain the meaning of the words in each pair and then decide whether they are synonyms or antonyms.

1. tentatively/cautiously
2. ominous/haunting
3. gnarled/smooth
4. ajar/open
5. tremor/stillness
6. commence/stop

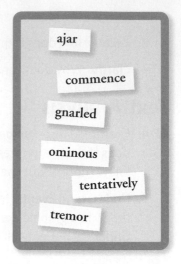

ajar

commence

gnarled

ominous

tentatively

tremor

ACADEMIC VOCABULARY IN WRITING

> • appropriate • assess • intelligence • motive • role

Write a paragraph in which you **assess** the value of Lemon Brown's "treasure." Discuss what it is worth to him and what it would be worth to the boys who try to steal it from him. Use at least one of the Academic Vocabulary words in your response.

VOCABULARY STRATEGY: SIMILES

Similes compare two things that are not alike using the words *like* or *as*. In this selection, Lemon Brown's voice is said to be "high and brittle, **like** dry twigs being broken." Understanding the literal meaning of a simile will help you infer its figurative meaning—in this example, the sound of Lemon Brown's voice.

Similes can also provide a context clue to help you figure out the meaning of an unfamiliar or ambiguous word. If you know the sound of dry twigs being broken, you understand what the word *brittle* means.

PRACTICE First pay attention to the literal meaning of each simile. Then use your understanding to infer its figurative meaning. Use it as a context clue to help you define the boldfaced word.

1. The windows were as **murky** as the muddy waters of the Mississippi.
2. Like a mule unwilling to move, the **obstinate** child held his ground.
3. As she danced across the stage, she looked as **nimble** as a graceful deer.
4. The **persistent** detective looked for clues like a dog sniffing out a bone.
5. Their friendship was becoming as **tenuous** as a fraying rope.

COMMON CORE

L 5a Interpret figures of speech in context. **L 6** Acquire and use accurately academic words; gather vocabulary knowledge when considering a word important to comprehension and expression.

Interactive Vocabulary **THINK** central

Go to thinkcentral.com.
KEYWORD: HML8-188

Language

◆ **GRAMMAR IN CONTEXT:** Use Correct Verb Tense

COMMON CORE

L1 Demonstrate command of the conventions of standard English grammar and usage when writing.

Review the **Grammar in Context** note on page 185. **Verb tense** indicates the time that an action or condition takes place—whether in the **past, present,** or **future.** In your writing, use the same verb tense to describe actions that take place at the same time, and change the verb tense when an action or condition happens at a different time.

Original: I always have a good time when I went to the beach. Last week, I swim and collect seashells. (Have *and* went *are in two different tenses.* Swim *and* collect *are present tense.*)

Revised: I always have a good time when I go to the beach. Last week, I swam and collected seashells. (*In the first sentence, both verbs need to be in the present tense. In the second sentence, the action is happening in the past, so the verbs should be in the past tense.*)

PRACTICE Choose the correct verb tenses in the following paragraph.

I (meet, met, will meet) an old blues musician earlier tonight. He (carries, carried, will carry) a harmonica around in his pocket every day because it reminds him of his son. He (helps, helped, will help) me realize that I should treasure people in my life more. I (work, worked, will work) harder in school to make you proud.

*For more help with verb tenses, see page R56 in the **Grammar Handbook.***

READING-WRITING CONNECTION

YOUR TURN   Increase your appreciation of "The Treasure of Lemon Brown" by responding to this prompt. Then use the **revising tip** to improve your writing.

WRITING PROMPT	REVISING TIP
Short Constructed Response: Description Imagine that a friend of yours had to find Lemon Brown in a crowd. What would you tell your friend to look for? Write a **one-paragraph description** of Lemon Brown that includes details about his appearance and the treasure he cherishes.	Review your description. Have you used the same verb tense to describe actions that take place at the same time? If not, revise.

Interactive Revision   **THINK** central

Go to **thinkcentral.com**.
KEYWORD: HML8-189

Blues: A National Treasure

- Timeline
- History Article
- Feature Article

Use with "The Treasure of Lemon Brown," page 178.

What's the Connection?

In "The Treasure of Lemon Brown," you met a blues musician, but do you know what blues music is? Where it came from? The other kinds of music it inspired? The selections that follow will tell you about all that and more.

Standards Focus: Identify Scope

Scope refers to a work's range, or breadth, of coverage. In general, the fewer people, places, events, and ideas a work covers, the narrower its scope. For example, the "The Treasure of Lemon Brown" has a narrow scope because it covers just a few key interactions between a couple of characters on a single rainy evening. A story or article with a broad scope might introduce many people or events or cover a long period of time.

    To identify how wide or narrow the scope of a selection is, consider how the writer covers the following:

- **People**—How many people are introduced? How well do you get to know them?

- **Places**—How many places, or settings, are described? How much do you get to know about them?

- **Events**—How many events are covered? How much time do these events span? How much do you learn about them?

- **Topic**—What is the topic? How many aspects of it are discussed?

As you read the selections that follow, keep track of your answers to these questions. Then, use your answers to estimate each selection's scope.

	Timeline	History Article	Feature Article
How many people does it introduce? How well do you get to know them?			
How many places does it describe?			
How many events does it cover? How much time do they span?			
What is the topic? How many aspects of it are discussed?			

COMMON CORE

RI 1 Cite textual evidence that most strongly supports an analysis of what the text says. **RI 9** Analyze two or more texts on the same topic.

Timeline: Evolution of the Blues Ⓐ

The blues emerged as a new form of music in the 20th century, but its roots date back to the music created by enslaved African Americans.

🎵	THE BLUES	AFRICAN-AMERICAN HISTORY
1910s	**1912** W. C. Handy writes the first blues song. He later becomes known as "the father of the blues."	**The Great Migration** Many African Americans leave the South in search of greater opportunity in Northern cities.
1920s	**1923** Ma Rainey, "the mother of the blues," releases her first album.	**The Harlem Renaissance** African-American music, art, and writing thrive in Harlem, New York.
1930s	**1933** Billie Holiday is discovered; she becomes one of the most famous jazz singers of all time. Her style is characteristic of the blues.	**The Great Depression** African Americans, along with the population as a whole, experience massive unemployment.
1940s	**1943** Blues musician Muddy Waters moves to Chicago, which becomes the center of a new style of blues.	**World War II** More than one million African Americans serve in the military despite widespread segregation and discrimination.
1950s	**1954** Elvis Presley records his first song. Influenced by blues and country music, he becomes known as "the king of rock and roll."	**A Landmark Court Case** In 1954, racial segregation in schools is declared unconstitutional in *Brown* v. *Board of Education.*
1960s	**1962** The Rolling Stones form. Influenced by the blues, the band creates a new hard-rock style that inspires countless bands to follow.	**The Civil Rights Movement** Congress passes the Civil Rights Act, which makes racial discrimination illegal in public places.
1970s to present	**1973** Kool Herc begins to DJ in the Bronx. He is seen as the father of hip-hop, a musical style that has blues roots and is known for rapping and instrumental "beats." Ⓑ	**Struggles and Accomplishments** Though racial tensions still exist, African Americans gain broader economic opportunity than they had in previous decades.

Ⓕ **OCUS ON FORM**
A **timeline** is a graphic aid that identifies key events during a certain time period. Labels usually tell the specific time in which notable events occurred.

Ⓐ **TIMELINE**
Preview the timeline's title and headings. Based on these, what kinds of events will the timeline include?

Ⓑ **IDENTIFY SCOPE**
What period of time does the entire timeline cover?

File Edit View Tools Help

Back Forward Stop Refresh Home Search Favorites Mail Print

MUDDY WATERS   MA RAINEY   W. C. HANDY   BESSIE SMITH

Basic Blues:
An American Art Form

W.C. Handy knew about music.
The composer, cornet player, and orchestra leader had traveled a lot, and he had encountered many different types of music along the way. But while waiting for a train late one night, Handy discovered a style of music unlike anything he had ever heard or played: the blues.

The legend goes like this: One night in 1903, Handy arrived at a train station in Tutwiler, Mississippi, to find that his train was about nine hours behind schedule. His companion on the platform was a raggedly dressed fellow with a guitar. The man had an odd style of playing. He slid the back of a knife
10   blade up and down the guitar's strings, creating a warbling sound. As he sang, he repeated an odd refrain—"goin' where the Southern cross the Dog"—which meant nothing to Handy. It turned out that the guitar-playing fellow was a traveling musician headed to a town called Moorhead, which was located at the intersection of two railroads, the Southern and the Yellow Dog. Handy was so intrigued by the musician's unique style and lyrics that he decided to put something similar down on paper. In the years to come, Handy would be known as the "Father of the Blues."

The American blues that Handy heard that night had its roots in the soulful songs of enslaved African Americans, which in turn were influenced by the call-
20   and-response style of singing found in Africa. Field hollers, work songs, and

Internet

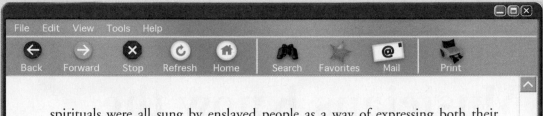

spirituals were all sung by enslaved people as a way of expressing both their suffering and their dreams. After the Civil War, some solo musicians in the South adapted these sounds into songs they sang while accompanying themselves on guitar. The term "the blues" goes back to the 18th century, when being sad or depressed meant that you were experiencing the "blue devils." Since many of the songs were about emotional pain and loss, the name fit.

    In 1912, Handy became one of the first composers to release sheet music for a blues song, "Memphis Blues." In 1920, Mamie Smith, a vaudeville performer, became the first African American to record a blues record. "Crazy Blues" sold
30 75,000 copies in its first month. Such "race records," as they were called, were originally marketed to African-American consumers, but by the end of the 1920s, both African-American and white listeners were snapping up copies of blues recordings from such artists as Ma Rainey and Bessie Smith. Blues artists went from doing informal performances in taverns to large-scale stage performances in theaters and nightclubs, and blues musicians were no longer a phenomenon of the South alone. **C**

    Throughout the first half of the 20th century, many African Americans began relocating to the North, looking for a better life with more opportunity. When they moved to cities like Chicago and Detroit, they brought blues music with
40 them. Blues musicians at the time invented new ways to play the blues as a means of reflecting the changes they had experienced. One artist, Muddy Waters, traded in his acoustic guitar for an electric one and added new instruments such as an upright bass, drums, and a harmonica. The new blues was livelier, gave folks something to dance to, and paved the way for rhythm and blues and rock and roll.

    Waters's style of "electrified blues" was popular until the early 1950s. But then rock and roll took over the American airwaves. This could have been the end of the blues, but starting in the 1960s, a new wave of white musicians from England and the United States revived interest with their own versions
50 of classic blues tunes. Groups like the Rolling Stones, Cream, and Led Zeppelin brought the blues back to the forefront of the American music scene. However, some blues musicians resented the success of these white musicians, who were gaining fortune and fame using the sounds of lesser-known African-American musicians. **D**

    In recent years, new artists such as Jonny Lang, Shemekia Copeland, and Susan Tedeschi have contributed their own styles to the evolution of blues music. These new artists have managed to keep the genre fresh, while at the same time paying tribute to generations of past musicians who taught the United States—and the world—how to sing the blues.

C IDENTIFY SCOPE
How many people has the writer mentioned so far? Note how much you learn about each one of them.

D IDENTIFY SCOPE
Over what period of time do the events in this paragraph take place?

Reprinted from **The New York Times**

SUNDAY, MARCH 21, 2004   B16

Musicians Know the Blues Firsthand

Andrew Jacobs

No one ever said the blues was any way to make a living. . . . Broke even in good times, Little Freddie King survived by playing juke joints in New Orleans until old age left his body broken. Deprived of a steady income, he went without dentures or glasses, and one night, a heavy rain brought down the ceiling of his
10 bedroom.

Without an audience for his quirky style of music, Haskel "Whistling Britches" Thompson ended up in a Winston-Salem homeless shelter. . . .

"These people are our culture, our folk musicians, and no one is looking after them," said the bluesman Taj Mahal. "We're always putting our hands over our heart and saying the
20 Pledge of Allegiance and honoring Davy Crockett, yet we're allowing these people and their music to fall through the cracks."

In the 1980s, Tim Duffy came to a similar realization. As a student studying folklore at the University of North Carolina, he grew obsessed with preserving the sounds of these unheralded musicians. But as he
30 traveled the rural South with recording equipment, he grew even more troubled by the poverty that left many artists without instruments and too strapped for heating oil or medicine.

"Their music ended up in archives but the problem is no one gets to hear it," said Mr. Duffy, who lives in Hillsborough, N.C. "And the recordings don't put food on their
40 table, it doesn't get them a gig."

Over the last two decades, Mr. Duffy, 41, has turned his passion into a nonprofit organization, the Music Maker Foundation, which is part recording company, part artist management service, and part social welfare agency. For those able to perform, the foundation promotes roots music and offers artists a touring career;
50 for those too old or sickly, he sends monthly checks that average $100.

When unexpected hardships strike, as in the case of Little Freddie King's collapsing ceiling, Mr. Duffy provides emergency cash. . . .

The foundation also puts CDs into the hands of men like Cootie Stark, a blind guitarist from Greenville, S.C., who had never had his music recorded
60 until he met Mr. Duffy at age 68. Mr. Stark, now 77, has since taken to the stages of Lincoln Center, the Rockport Rhythm and Blues Festival at Newport, and other concert venues. He earns about $8,000 a year selling his CDs.

"It should have happened 45 years ago, but I finally got a break," he said. **E**

E IDENTIFY SCOPE
What is this article about? What time period does it focus on? Jot this information in your chart.

Comprehension

1. **Recall** Who became known as "the father of the blues" and why?

2. **Summarize** In a few sentences, summarize what gave rise to electrified blues.

3. **Clarify** Reread lines 15–23 in "Musicians Know the Blues Firsthand." What is Taj Mahal pointing out here?

Text Analysis

● 4. **Compare Scope** Which of the three selections has the narrowest scope? How do the scopes of the other two selections compare? Use the chart you made as you read to give reasons for your answers.

● 5. **Draw Conclusions About a Timeline** Why do you suppose a timeline called "Evolution of the Blues" includes key events in African-American history?

COMMON CORE

RI 1 Cite textual evidence that most strongly supports an analysis of what the text says. **RI 9** Analyze two or more texts on the same topic. **W 9** Draw evidence from literary or informational texts to support analysis, reflection, and research.

Read for Information: Evaluate Sources for Usefulness

WRITING PROMPT

Imagine you have chosen one of the following topics for a report:

- the birth of blues music and how blues has changed over the years
- important events in African-American history
- the life of blues musicians

Explain which selection you would use as a source of information for this topic and why. If more than one selection would be useful to you, be sure to explain what each would provide.

To answer this prompt, first identify the topic you would want to focus on. Then follow these steps:

1. Using the chart you filled in, consider the focus of each selection you just read. What kinds of information does each selection provide?

Topic of Report: _____	
Selection I Would Use	Why I Would Use It

2. In a chart like the one shown, identify the topic you picked, the selection(s) you would use for a report on that topic, and a brief explanation as to why the selection(s) would be useful to you.

Flowers for Algernon
Short Story by Daniel Keyes

from Charly
Screenplay by Stirling Silliphant

When is it better not to KNOW?

COMMON CORE

RL 3 Analyze how lines of dialogue and incidents in a story reveal aspects of a character.
RL 5 Compare and contrast the structure of two or more texts and analyze how the differing structure of each text contributes to its meaning and style.
RL 6 Analyze how differences in the points of view of the characters and the audience or reader create effects.

As young children, we want to know everything: why the sky is blue, how computers work, why people can talk but dogs can't. Humans have a natural thirst for knowledge. But as we grow up, we sometimes find there are things it's not necessary, or even desirable, to know. In the short story you are about to read, a man learns that knowledge can bring with it some unpleasant truths.

DISCUSS If it were possible, would you want to see what the future holds for you in ten years, even if you couldn't change it? Discuss this question with a small group. Consider the benefits of knowing what your life will be like, as well as the potential negatives.

● **TEXT ANALYSIS: CHARACTER TRAITS**

Like real people, literary characters have distinct personal qualities known as **character traits.** A reader must often infer these traits based on the characters' words, actions, and appearances. Character traits can lead to conflict in a story and influence how the conflict is resolved.

In "Flowers for Algernon," the main character undergoes a dramatic transformation. As you read, use a Y-chart to note which of his character traits change and which stay the same.

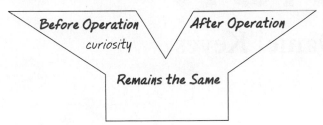

Before Operation
curiosity

After Operation

Remains the Same

Review: **Point of View**

● **READING SKILL: EXAMINE STRUCTURE**

The **structure** of a text is the way the paragraphs and events are arranged. The text of "Flowers for Algernon" takes the form of letters and journal entries. These help the author to

- reveal the thoughts and feelings of the main character
- remind readers that this character is changing daily
- make the story seem as if it is a true account

As you read, notice the dates, lengths, and language of the letters and journal entries and consider how these affect your understanding of the story.

▲ **VOCABULARY IN CONTEXT**

Try to figure out what each boldfaced word means in the context of its sentence.

1. The doctor had a **specialization** in brain development.
2. The research findings created a **sensation** at the conference.
3. Will you **refute** the results, or do you believe them, too?
4. His understanding is **proportional** to his intelligence.
5. His long work hours could **impair** his social life.
6. They laughed at his **absurd** moves when dancing.

Complete the activities in your **Reader/Writer Notebook.**

Daniel Keyes
born 1927

Wondering, What If?
Daniel Keyes started his career as an English teacher. A struggling student once approached him and said, "I want to be smart." Keyes wondered what would happen if science discovered a way to increase a person's intelligence, and he explored the idea in "Flowers for Algernon." He later expanded the story into a novel, published in 1966.

Stirling Silliphant
1918-1996

Screenwriter
Stirling Silliphant's career included winning the Academy Award for best screenplay in 1968. Known for action-filled scripts, he showed the range of his abilities by writing the screenplay for *Charly* (1969), based on the novel *Flowers for Algernon.*

BACKGROUND TO THE STORY

IQ In "Flowers for Algernon," the main character takes tests to measure his IQ, or intelligence quotient. IQ is a number that is thought to provide a measurement of a person's intelligence. IQ tests involve memory, reasoning, and numerical ability. Intelligence tests were once considered to be a reliable measure, but today, questions remain about the accuracy of such tests.

Authors Online
Go to **thinkcentral.com.** KEYWORD: HML8-197

Flowers *for* Algernon

Daniel Keyes

progris riport 1—martch 5 1965

Dr. Strauss says I shud rite down what I think and evrey thing that happins to me from now on. I dont know why but he says its importint so they will see if they will use me. I hope they use me. Miss Kinnian says maybe they can make me smart. I want to be smart. My name is Charlie Gordon. I am 37 years old and 2 weeks ago was my brithday. I have nuthing more to rite now so I will close for today.

progris riport 2—martch 6

I had a test today. I think I faled it. and I think that maybe now they wont use me. What happind is a nice young man was in the room and he had some white cards with ink spillled all over them. He sed Charlie what do you see on
10 this card. I was very skared even tho I had my rabits foot in my pockit because when I was a kid I always faled tests in school and I spillled ink to. **A**

I told him I saw a inkblot. He said yes and it made me feel good. I thot that was all but when I got up to go he stopped me. He said now sit down Charlie we are not thru yet. Then I dont remember so good but he wantid me to say what was in the ink. I dint see nuthing in the ink but he said there was picturs there other pepul saw some picturs. I coudnt see any picturs. I reely tryed to see. I held the card close up and then far away. Then I said if I had my glases I coud see better I usally only ware my glases in the movies or TV but I said they are in the closit in the hall. I got them. Then I said let me see that card
20 agen I bet Ill find it now.

Analyze Visuals ▶

What is the **mood** of this illustration? Tell how the colors and brush strokes help create that mood.

A CHARACTER TRAITS
What can you **infer** about Charlie's abilities and personality?

Illustration by Sylvia Chesley Smith.
All other illustrations by Todd Davidson.

I tryed hard but I still coudnt find the picturs I only saw the ink. I told him maybe I need new glases. He rote somthing down on a paper and I got skared of faling the test. I told him it was a very nice inkblot with littel points all around the eges. He looked very sad so that wasnt it. I said please let me try agen. Ill get it in a few minits becaus Im not so fast somtimes. Im a slow reeder too in Miss Kinnians class for slow adults but I'm trying very hard.

He gave me a chance with another card that had 2 kinds of ink spillled on it red and blue.

He was very nice and talked slow like Miss Kinnian does and he explained
30 it to me that it was a *raw shok.* He said pepul see things in the ink. I said show me where. He said think. I told him I think a inkblot but that wasnt rite eather. He said what does it remind you—pretend somthing. I closd my eyes for a long time to pretend. I told him I pretned a fowntan pen with ink leeking all over a table cloth. Then he got up and went out.

I dont think I passd the *raw shok* test. **B**

progris report 3—martch 7

Dr Strauss and Dr Nemur say it dont matter about the inkblots. I told them I dint spill the ink on the cards and I coudnt see anything in the ink. They said that maybe they will still use me. I said Miss Kinnian never gave me tests like that one only spelling and reading. They said Miss Kinnian told that I was her
40 bestist pupil in the adult nite scool becaus I tryed the hardist and I reely wantid to lern. They said how come you went to the adult nite scool all by yourself Charlie. How did you find it. I said I askd pepul and sumbody told me where I shud go to lern to read and spell good. They said why did you want to. I told them becaus all my life I wantid to be smart and not dumb. But its very hard to be smart. They said you know it will probly be tempirery. I said yes. Miss Kinnian told me. I dont care if it herts. **C**

Later I had more crazy tests today. The nice lady who gave it me told me the name and I asked her how do you spellit so I can rite it in my progris riport. THEMATIC APPERCEPTION TEST.[1] I dont know the frist 2 words but I
50 know what *test* means. You got to pass it or you get bad marks. This test lookd easy becaus I coud see the picturs. Only this time she dint want me to tell her the picturs. That mixd me up. I said the man yesterday said I shoud tell him what I saw in the ink she said that dont make no difrence. She said make up storys about the pepul in the picturs.

I told her how can you tell storys about pepul you never met. I said why shud I make up lies. I never tell lies any more becaus I always get caut.

She told me this test and the other one the raw-shok was for getting personalty. I laffed so hard. I said how can you get that thing from inkblots and fotos. She got sore and put her picturs away. I dont care. It was sily. I gess
60 I faled that test too.

---

1. **Thematic Apperception** (thĭ-măt'ik ăp'ər-sĕp'shən) **Test:** test for analyzing personality on the basis of stories people make up about a series of pictures.

B EXAMINE STRUCTURE
In what ways are Charlie's journal entries unique?

C CHARACTER TRAITS
What do lines 41–46 tell you about Charlie's desire to change?

Language Coach

Informal Language
Notice that Charlie misspells many words in lines 55–60. To understand these misspelled words, try reading them aloud. Also, look for clues to their meaning in the surrounding words.

Later some men in white coats took me to a difernt part of the hospitil and gave me a game to play. It was like a race with a white mouse. They called the mouse Algernon. Algernon was in a box with a lot of twists and turns like all kinds of walls and they gave me a pencil and a paper with lines and lots of boxes. On one side it said START and on the other end it said FINISH. They said it was *amazed*[2] and that Algernon and me had the same *amazed* to do. I dint see how we could have the same *amazed* if Algernon had a box and I had a paper but I dint say nothing. Anyway there wasnt time because the race started.

One of the men had a watch he was trying to hide so I woudnt see it so
70 I tryed not to look and that made me nervus.

Anyway that test made me feel worser than all the others because they did it over 10 times with difernt *amazeds* and Algernon won every time. I dint know that mice were so smart. Maybe thats because Algernon is a white mouse. Maybe white mice are smarter then other mice. **D**

progris riport 4—Mar 8

Their going to use me! Im so exited I can hardly write. Dr Nemur and Dr Strauss had a argament about it first. Dr Nemur was in the office when Dr Strauss brot me in. Dr Nemur was worryed about using me but Dr Strauss told him Miss Kinnian rekemmended me the best from all the people who she was teaching. I like Miss Kinnian becaus shes a very smart teacher. And she said
80 Charlie your going to have a second chance. If you volenteer for this experament you mite get smart. They dont know if it will be perminint but theirs a chance. Thats why I said ok even when I was scared because she said it was an operashun. She said dont be scared Charlie you done so much with so little I think you deserv it most of all.

So I got scaird when Dr Nemur and Dr Strauss argud about it. Dr Strauss said I had something that was very good. He said I had a good *motor-vation*.[3] I never even knew I had that. I felt proud when he said that not every body with an eye-q[4] of 68 had that thing. I dont know what it is or where I got it
90 but he said Algernon had it too. Algernons *motor-vation* is the cheese they put in his box. But it cant be that because I didnt eat any cheese this week.

Then he told Dr Nemur something I dint understand so while they were talking I wrote down some of the words.

He said Dr Nemur I know Charlie is not what you had in mind as the first of your new brede of intelek** (coudnt get the word) superman. But most people of his low ment** are host** and uncoop** they are usualy dull apath** and hard to reach. He has a good natcher hes intristed and eager to please. **E**

Dr Nemur said remember he will be the first human beeng ever to have his intelijence trippled by surgicle meens.

D POINT OF VIEW
Because this story is told in the **first-person point of view,** you learn about Charlie's thought process directly from him. What do you learn about his mental capacity?

E CHARACTER TRAITS
What have you learned about Charlie through the comments of Miss Kinnian and the doctors?

Dr Strauss said exakly. Look at how well hes lerned to read and write for his
low mentel age its as grate an acheve** as you and I lerning einstines therey of
vity⁵ without help. That shows the intenss motor-vation. Its comparat a
tremen** achev** I say we use Charlie. **F**

I dint get all the words and they were talking to fast but it sounded like
Dr Strauss was on my side and like the other one wasnt.

Then Dr Nemur nodded he said all right maybe your right. We will use
Charlie. When he said that I got so exited I jumped up and shook his hand for
being so good to me. I told him thank you doc you wont be sorry for giving
me a second chance. And I mean it like I told him. After the operashun Im
gonna try to be smart. Im gonna try awful hard.

progris ript 5—Mar 10

Im skared. Lots of people who work here and the nurses and the people who
gave me the tests came to bring me candy and wish me luck. I hope I have
luck. I got my rabits foot and my lucky penny and my horse shoe. Only a black
cat crossed me when I was comming to the hospitil. Dr Strauss says dont be
supersitis Charlie this is sience. Anyway Im keeping my rabits foot with me.

I asked Dr Strauss if Ill beat Algernon in the race after the operashun and
he said maybe. If the operashun works Ill show that mouse I can be as smart
as he is. Maybe smarter. Then Ill be abel to read better and spell the words
good and know lots of things and be like other people. I want to be smart like
other people. If it works perminint they will make everybody smart all over the
wurld. **G**

They dint give me anything to eat this morning. I dont know what that
eating has to do with getting smart. Im very hungry and Dr Nemur took away
my box of candy. That Dr Nemur is a grouch. Dr Strauss says I can have it
back after the operashun. You cant eat befor a operashun . . .

Progress Report 6—Mar 15

The operashun dint hurt. He did it while I was sleeping. They took off the
bandijis from my eyes and my head today so I can make a PROGRESS
REPORT. Dr Nemur who looked at some of my other ones says I spell
PROGRESS wrong and he told me how to spell it and REPORT too. I got
to try and remember that.

I have a very bad memary for spelling. Dr Strauss says its ok to tell about
all the things that happin to me but he says I shoud tell more about what I feel
and what I think. When I told him I dont know how to think he said try.
All the time when the bandijis were on my eyes I tryed to think. Nothing
happened. I dont know what to think about. Maybe if I ask him he will tell
me how I can think now that Im suppose to get smart. What do smart people
think about. Fancy things I suppose. I wish I knew some fancy things alredy.

F CHARACTER TRAITS
Which of Charlie's traits
convince Dr. Strauss
to use him in the
experiment?

G CHARACTER TRAITS
What hopes does Charlie
have for the operation?

---

5. **einstines therey of **vity:** Charlie's way of writing *Einstein's theory of relativity,* the theory of space
   and time developed by Albert Einstein.

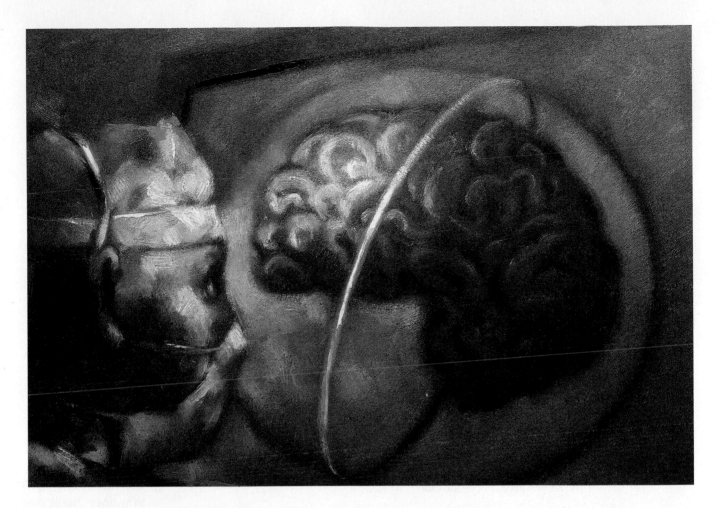

Progress Report 7—mar 19

Nothing is happining. I had lots of tests and different kinds of races with Algernon. I hate that mouse. He always beats me. Dr Strauss said I got to play those games. And he said some time I got to take those tests over again. Thse
140 inkblots are stupid. And those pictures arc stupid too. I like to draw a picture of a man and a woman but I wont make up lies about people.

I got a headache from trying to think so much. I thot Dr Strauss was my frend but he dont help me. He dont tell me what to think or when Ill get smart. Miss Kinnian dint come to see me. I think writing these progress reports are stupid too. **H**

Progress Report 8—Mar 23

Im going back to work at the factery. They said it was better I shud go back to work but I cant tell anyone what the operashun was for and I have to come to the hospitil for an hour evry night after work. They are gonna pay me mony every month for lerning to be smart.

▲ **Analyze Visuals**

What is the **connection** between this illustration and what happens to Charlie?

H **EXAMINE STRUCTURE**

In what ways is the March 19 progress report different from the other reports so far? Think about its length and language.

150 Im glad Im going back to work because I miss my job and all my frends and all the fun we have there.

Dr Strauss says I shud keep writing things down but I dont have to do it every day just when I think of something or something speshul happins. He says dont get discoridged because it takes time and it happins slow. He says it took a long time with Algernon before he got 3 times smarter then he was before. Thats why Algernon beats me all the time because he had that operashun too. That makes me feel better. I coud probly do that *amazed* faster than a reglar mouse. Maybe some day Ill beat Algernon. Boy that would be something. So far Algernon looks like he mite be smart perminent.

160 *Mar 25* (I dont have to write PROGRESS REPORT on top any more just when I hand it in once a week for Dr Nemur to read. I just have to put the date on. That saves time)

We had a lot of fun at the factery today. Joe Carp said hey look where Charlie had his operashun what did they do Charlie put some brains in. I was going to tell him but I remembered Dr Strauss said no. Then Frank Reilly said what did you do Charlie forget your key and open your door the hard way. That made me laff. Their really my friends and they like me.

Sometimes somebody will say hey look at Joe or Frank or George he really pulled a Charlie Gordon. I dont know why they say that but they always laff.
170 This morning Amos Borg who is the 4 man at Donnegans used my name when he shouted at Ernie the office boy. Ernie lost a packige. He said Ernie for godsake what are you trying to be a Charlie Gordon. I dont understand why he said that. I never lost any packiges. ❶

Mar 28 Dr Straus came to my room tonight to see why I dint come in like I was suppose to. I told him I dont like to race with Algernon any more. He said I dont have to for a while but I shud come in. He had a present for me only it wasnt a present but just for lend. I thot it was a little television but it wasnt. He said I got to turn it on when I go to sleep. I said your kidding why shud I turn it on when Im going to sleep. Who ever herd of a thing like that. But he said if I want to get
180 smart I got to do what he says. I told him I dint think I was going to get smart and he put his hand on my sholder and said Charlie you dont know it yet but your getting smarter all the time. You wont notice for a while. I think he was just being nice to make me feel good because I dont look any smarter.

Oh yes I almost forgot. I asked him when I can go back to the class at Miss Kinnians school. He said I wont go their. He said that soon Miss Kinnian will come to the hospitil to start and teach me speshul. I was mad at her for not comming to see me when I got the operashun but I like her so maybe we will be frends again.

Mar 29 That crazy TV kept me up all night. How can I sleep with something
190 yelling crazy things all night in my ears. And the nutty pictures. Wow. I dont know what it says when Im up so how am I going to know when Im sleeping.

❶ **CHARACTER TRAITS**
Why does Charlie think these men are his friends? Note whether he is a good judge of character at this point.

Dr Strauss says its ok. He says my brains are lerning when I sleep and that will help me when Miss Kinnian starts my lessons in the hospitl (only I found out it isnt a hospitil its a labatory. I think its all crazy. If you can get smart when your sleeping why do people go to school. That thing I dont think will work. I use to watch the late show and the late late show on TV all the time and it never made me smart. Maybe you have to sleep while you watch it.

PROGRESS REPORT 9—April 3

Dr Strauss showed me how to keep the TV turned low so now I can sleep. I dont hear a thing. And I still dont understand what it says. A few times I play it over
200 in the morning to find out what I lerned when I was sleeping and I dont think so. Miss Kinnian says Maybe its another langwidge or something. But most times it sounds american. It talks so fast faster than even Miss Gold who was my teacher in 6 grade and I remember she talked so fast I coudnt understand her.

I told Dr Strauss what good is it to get smart in my sleep. I want to be smart when Im awake. He says its the same thing and I have two minds. Theres the *subconscious* and the *conscious*[6] (thats how you spell it). And one dont tell the other one what its doing. They dont even talk to each other. Thats why I dream. And boy have I been having crazy dreams. Wow. Ever since that night TV. The late late late late late show.
210 I forgot to ask him if it was only me or if everybody had those two minds.

(I just looked up the word in the dictionary Dr Strauss gave me. The word is *subconscious. adj. Of the nature of mental operations yet not present in consciousness; as, subconscious conflict of desires.*) There's more but I still dont know what it means. This isnt a very good dictionary for dumb people like me.

Anyway the headache is from the party. My frends from the factery Joe Carp and Frank Reilly invited me to go with them to Muggsys Saloon for some drinks. I dont like to drink but they said we will have lots of fun. I had a good time.

Joe Carp said I shoud show the girls how I mop out the toilet in the factory
220 and he got me a mop. I showed them and everyone laffed when I told that Mr Donnegan said I was the best janiter he ever had because I like my job and do it good and never come late or miss a day except for my operashun.

I said Miss Kinnian always said Charlie be proud of your job because you do it good.

Everybody laffed and we had a good time and they gave me lots of drinks and Joe said Charlie is a card when hes potted.[7] I dont know what that means but everybody likes me and we have fun. I cant wait to be smart like my best frends Joe Carp and Frank Reilly. **J**

I dont remember how the party was over but I think I went out to buy a
230 newspaper and coffe for Joe and Frank and when I came back there was no one

J POINT OF VIEW
How does hearing about the party from Charlie's **point of view** affect your reaction to his coworkers?

---

6. **the subconscious** (sŭb-kŏn'shəs) **and the conscious** (kŏn'shəs): psychological terms. *Subconscious* refers to mental activity a person is not aware of; *conscious* refers to mental activity of which a person is aware.

7. **Charlie is a card when he's potted:** Charlie is funny when he's drunk.

their. I looked for them all over till late. Then I dont remember so good but I think I got sleepy or sick. A nice cop brot me back home. Thats what my landlady Mrs Flynn says.

But I got a headache and a big lump on my head and black and blue all over. I think maybe I fell but Joe Carp says it was the cop they beat up drunks some times. I don't think so. Miss Kinnian says cops are to help people. 240 Anyway I got a bad headache and Im sick and hurt all over. I dont think Ill drink anymore.

April 6 I beat Algernon! I dint even know I beat him until Burt the tester told me. Then the second time I lost because I got so exited I fell off the chair before I finished. But after that I beat him 8 more times. I must be getting smart to beat a smart mouse like Algernon. But I dont *feel* smarter.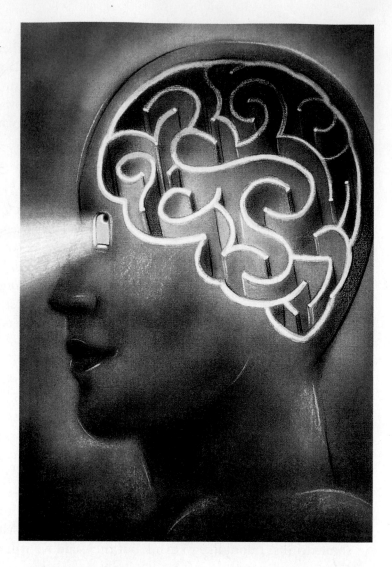

I wanted to race Algernon some more but 250 Burt said thats enough for one day. They let me hold him for a minit. Hes not so bad. Hes soft like a ball of cotton. He blinks and when he opens his eyes their black and pink on the eges.

I said can I feed him because I felt bad to beat him and I wanted to be nice and make frends. Burt said no Algernon is a very specshul mouse with an operashun like mine, and he was the first of all the animals to stay smart so long. He told me 260 Algernon is so smart that every day he has to solve a test to get his food. Its a thing like a lock on a door that changes every time Algernon goes in to eat so he has to lern something new to get his food. That made me sad because if he coudnt lern he woud be hungry.

I dont think its right to make you pass a test to eat. How woud Dr Nemur like it to have to pass a test every time he wants to eat. I think Ill be frends with Algernon. **L**

April 9 Tonight after work Miss Kinnian was at the laboratory. She looked like she was glad to see me but scared. I told her dont worry Miss Kinnian Im not smart yet and she laffed. She said I have confidence in you Charlie the way 270 you struggled so hard to read and right better than all the others. At werst you will have it for a littel wile and your doing somthing for sience.

K EXAMINE STRUCTURE
Note the date on this journal entry. What significant changes have happened in the story since the first entries one month ago?

L CHARACTER TRAITS
In lines 249–266, what does Charlie's treatment of Algernon reveal about his character?

We are reading a very hard book. I never read such a hard book before. Its called *Robinson Crusoe* about a man who gets merooned on a dessert Iland. Hes smart and figers out all kinds of things so he can have a house and food and hes a good swimmer. Only I feel sorry because hes all alone and has no frends. But I think their must be somebody else on the iland because theres a picture with his funny umbrella looking at footprints. I hope he gets a frend and not be lonly.

April 10 Miss Kinnian teaches me to spell better. She says look at a word and
280 close your eyes and say it over and over until you remember. I have lots of truble with *through* that you say *threw* and *enough* and *tough* that you dont say *enew* and *tew*. You got to say *enuff* and *tuff*. Thats how I use to write it before I started to get smart. Im confused but Miss Kinnian says theres no reason in spelling.

Apr 14 Finished *Robinson Crusoe*. I want to find out more about what happens to him but Miss Kinnian says thats all there is. *Why*

Apr 15 Miss Kinnian says Im lerning fast. She read some of the Progress Reports and she looked at me kind of funny. She says Im a fine person and Ill show them all. I asked her why. She said never mind but I shoudnt feel bad if
290 I find out that everybody isnt nice like I think. She said for a person who god gave so little to you done more then a lot of people with brains they never even used. I said all my frends are smart people but there good. They like me and they never did anything that wasnt nice. Then she got something in her eye and she had to run out to the ladys room. Ⓜ

Apr 16 Today, I lerned, the *comma*, this is a comma (,) a period, with a tail, Miss Kinnian, says its importent, because, it makes writing, better, she said, sombeody, coud lose, a lot of money, if a comma, isnt, in the, right place, I dont have, any money, and I dont see, how a comma, keeps you, from losing it,
     But she says, everybody, uses commas, so Ill use, them too,

300 *Apr 17* I used the comma wrong. Its punctuation. Miss Kinnian told me to look up long words in the dictionary to lern to spell them. I said whats the difference if you can read it anyway. She said its part of your education so now on Ill look up all the words Im not sure how to spell. It takes a long time to write that way but I think Im remembering. I only have to look up once and after that I get it right. Anyway thats how come I got the word *punctuation* right. (Its that way in the dictionary). Miss Kinnian says a period is punctuation too, and there are lots of other marks to lern. I told her I thot all the periods had to have tails but she said no.
     You got to mix them up, she showed? me" how. to mix! them(up,. and
310 now; I can! mix up all kinds" of punctuation, in! my writing? There, are lots! of rules? to lern; but Im gettin'g them in my head.

Ⓜ **CHARACTER TRAITS**
What can you **infer** about Miss Kinnian from her conversation with Charlie?

One thing I? like about, Dear Miss Kinnian: (thats the way it goes in a business letter if I ever go into business) is she, always gives me' a reason" when—I ask. She's a gen'ius! I wish! I cou'd be smart" like, her;

(Punctuation, is; fun!)

April 18 What a dope I am! I didn't even understand what she was talking about. I read the grammar book last night and it explanes the whole thing. Then I saw it was the same way as Miss Kinnian was trying to tell me, but I didn't get it. I got up in the middle of the night, and the whole thing
320 straightened out in my mind.

Miss Kinnian said that the TV working in my sleep helped out. She said I reached a plateau. Thats like the flat top of a hill.

After I figgered out how punctuation worked, I read over all my old Progress Reports from the beginning. Boy, did I have crazy spelling and punctuation! I told Miss Kinnian I ought to go over the pages and fix all the mistakes but she said, "No, Charlie, Dr. Nemur wants them just as they are. That's why he let you keep them after they were photostated, to see your own progress. You're coming along fast, Charlie."

That made me feel good. After the lesson I went down and played with
330 Algernon. We don't race any more.

April 20 I feel sick inside. Not sick like for a doctor, but inside my chest it feels empty like getting punched and a heartburn at the same time.

I wasn't going to write about it, but I guess I got to, because its important. Today was the first time I ever stayed home from work.

Last night Joe Carp and Frank Reilly invited me to a party. There were lots of girls and some men from the factory. I remembered how sick I got last time I drank too much, so I told Joe I didn't want anything to drink. He gave me a plain coke instead. It tasted funny, but I thought it was just a bad taste in my mouth.

340 We had a lot of fun for a while. Joe said I should dance with Ellen and she would teach me the steps. I fell a few times and I couldn't understand why because no one else was dancing besides Ellen and me. And all the time I was tripping because somebody's foot was always sticking out.

Then when I got up I saw the look on Joe's face and it gave me a funny feeling in my stomack. "He's a scream," one of the girls said. Everybody was laughing.

Frank said, "I ain't laughed so much since we sent him off for the newspaper that night at Muggsy's and ditched him."

"Look at him. His face is red."
350 "He's blushing. Charlie is blushing."

"Hey, Ellen, what'd you do to Charlie? I never saw him act like that before."

I didn't know what to do or where to turn. Everyone was looking at me and laughing and I felt naked. I wanted to hide myself. I ran out into the street and

I threw up. Then I walked home. It's a funny thing I never knew that Joe and Frank and the others liked to have me around all the time to make fun of me.

Now I know what it means when they say "to pull a Charlie Gordon." I'm ashamed. **N**

PROGRESS REPORT 10

April 21 Still didn't go into the factory. I told Mrs. Flynn my landlady to call and tell Mr. Donnegan I was sick. Mrs. Flynn looks at me very funny lately
360 like she's scared of me.

I think it's a good thing about finding out how everybody laughs at me. I thought about it a lot. It's because I'm so dumb and I don't even know when I'm doing something dumb. People think it's funny when a dumb person can't do things the same way they can.

Anyway, now I know I'm getting smarter every day. I know punctuation and I can spell good. I like to look up all the hard words in the dictionary and I remember them. I'm reading a lot now, and Miss Kinnian says I read very fast. Sometimes I even understand what I'm reading about, and it stays in my mind. There are times when I can close my eyes and think of a page and it all
370 comes back like a picture.

Besides history, geography, and arithmetic, Miss Kinnian said I should start to learn a few foreign languages. Dr. Strauss gave me some more tapes to play while I sleep. I still don't understand how that conscious and unconscious mind works, but Dr. Strauss says not to worry yet. He asked me to promise that when I start learning college subjects next week I wouldn't read any books on psychology—that is, until he gives me permission. **O**

I feel a lot better today, but I guess I'm still a little angry that all the time people were laughing and making fun of me because I wasn't so smart. When I become intelligent like Dr. Strauss says, with three times my I.Q. of 68, then
380 maybe I'll be like everyone else and people will like me and be friendly.

I'm not sure what an *I.Q.* is. Dr. Nemur said it was something that measured how intelligent you were—like a scale in the drugstore weighs pounds. But Dr. Strauss had a big arguement with him and said an I.Q. didn't weigh intelligence at all. He said an I.Q. showed how much intelligence you could get, like the numbers on the outside of a measuring cup. You still had to fill the cup up with stuff.

Then when I asked Burt, who gives me my intelligence tests and works with Algernon, he said that both of them were wrong (only I had to promise not to tell them he said so). Burt says that the I.Q. measures a lot of different
390 things including some of the things you learned already, and it really isn't any good at all.

So I still don't know what I.Q. is except that mine is going to be over 200 soon. I didn't want to say anything, but I don't see how if they don't know *what* it is, or *where* it is—I don't see how they know *how much* of it you've got.

Dr. Nemur says I have to take a *Rorshach Test* tomorrow. I wonder what *that* is.

N CHARACTER TRAITS
Why is Charlie ashamed now? Why wasn't he ashamed a couple of weeks ago?

O POINT OF VIEW
How might your understanding of Charlie's progress be different if you knew what others were thinking?

April 22 I found out what a *Rorshach* is. It's the test I took before the operation—the one with the inkblots on the pieces of cardboard. The man who gave me the test was the same one.

400   I was scared to death of those inkblots. I knew he was going to ask me to find the pictures and I knew I wouldn't be able to. I was thinking to myself, if only there was some way of knowing what kind of pictures were hidden there. Maybe there weren't any pictures at all. Maybe it was just a trick to see if I was dumb enough to look for something that wasn't there. Just thinking about that made me sore at him.

"All right, Charlie," he said, "you've seen these cards before, remember?"

"Of course I remember."

The way I said it, he knew I was angry, and he looked surprised. "Yes, of course. Now I want you to look at this one. What might this be? What do you
410 see on this card? People see all sorts of things in these inkblots. Tell me what it might be for you—what it makes you think of."

I was shocked. That wasn't what I had expected him to say at all. "You mean there are no pictures hidden in those inkblots?"

He frowned and took off his glasses. "What?"

"Pictures. Hidden in the inkblots. Last time you told me that everyone could see them and you wanted me to find them too."

He explained to me that the last time he had used almost the exact same words he was using now. I didn't believe it, and I still have the suspicion that he misled me at the time just for the fun of it. Unless—I don't know any
420 more—could I have been *that* feeble-minded?

We went through the cards slowly. One of them looked like a pair of bats tugging at something. Another one looked like two men fencing with swords. I imagined all sorts of things. I guess I got carried away. But I didn't trust him any more, and I kept turning them around and even looking on the back to see if there was anything there I was supposed to catch. While he was making his notes, I peeked out of the corner of my eye to read it. But it was all in code that looked like this:

WF+A DdF-Ad orig. WF-A SF+obj

The test still doesn't make sense to me. It seems to me that anyone could
430 make up lies about things that they didn't really see. How could he know I wasn't making a fool of him by mentioning things that I didn't really imagine? Maybe I'll understand it when Dr. Strauss lets me read up on psychology. **P**

April 25 I figured out a new way to line up the machines in the factory, and Mr. Donnegan says it will save him ten thousand dollars a year in labor and increased production. He gave me a $25 bonus.

I wanted to take Joe Carp and Frank Reilly out to lunch to celebrate, but Joe said he had to buy some things for his wife, and Frank said he was meeting his cousin for lunch. I guess it'll take a little time for them to get

P CHARACTER TRAITS
How is Charlie's second experience with the Rorschach test different from his first experience?

used to the changes in me. Everybody seems to be frightened of me. When I went over to Amos Borg and tapped him on the shoulder, he jumped up in the air.

People don't talk to me much any more or kid around the way they used to. It makes the job kind of lonely.

April 27 I got up the nerve today to ask Miss Kinnian to have dinner with me tomorrow night to celebrate my bonus.

At first she wasn't sure it was right, but I asked Dr. Strauss and he said it was okay. Dr. Strauss and Dr. Nemur don't seem to be getting along so well. They're arguing all the time. This evening when I came in to ask Dr. Strauss about having dinner with Miss Kinnian, I heard them shouting. Dr. Nemur was saying that it was *his* experiment and *his* research, and Dr. Strauss was shouting back that he contributed just as much, because he found me through Miss Kinnian and he performed the operation. Dr. Strauss said that someday thousands of neurosurgeons[8] might be using his technique all over the world.

Dr. Nemur wanted to publish the results of the experiment at the end of this month. Dr. Strauss wanted to wait a while longer to be sure. Dr. Strauss said that Dr. Nemur was more interested in the Chair of Psychology at Princeton[9] than he was in the experiment. Dr. Nemur said that Dr. Strauss was nothing but an opportunist who was trying to ride to glory on *his* coattails.

When I left afterwards, I found myself trembling. I don't know why for sure, but it was as if I'd seen both men clearly for the first time. I remember hearing Burt say that Dr. Nemur had a shrew of a wife who was pushing him all the time to get things published so that he could become famous. Burt said that the dream of her life was to have a big shot husband.

Was Dr. Strauss really trying to ride on his coattails?

April 28 I don't understand why I never noticed how beautiful Miss Kinnian really is. She has brown eyes and feathery brown hair that comes to the top of her neck. She's only thirty-four! I think from the beginning I had the feeling that she was an unreachable genius—and very, very old. Now, every time I see her she grows younger and more lovely. ◆

◆ **GRAMMAR IN CONTEXT**
Reread lines 477–478. Notice that Charlie uses the **comparative form** ("younger" and "more lovely") to compare his current impression of Miss Kinnian with his earlier impression of her.

---

8. **neurosurgeons** (nŏŏr′ō-sûr′jənz): doctors who perform surgery on the brain and nervous system.

9. **Chair of Psychology at Princeton:** head of the psychology department at Princeton University.

We had dinner and a long talk. When she said that I was coming along so
480 fast that soon I'd be leaving her behind, I laughed.

"It's true, Charlie. You're already a better reader than I am. You can read
a whole page at a glance while I can take in only a few lines at a time. And
you remember every single thing you read. I'm lucky if I can recall the main
thoughts and the general meaning."

"I don't feel intelligent. There are so many things I don't understand."

She took out a cigarette and I lit it for her. "You've got to be a *little* patient.
You're accomplishing in days and weeks what it takes normal people to do in
half a lifetime. That's what makes it so amazing. You're like a giant sponge
now, soaking things in. Facts, figures, general knowledge. And soon you'll
490 begin to connect them, too. You'll see how the different branches of learning
are related. There are many levels, Charlie, like steps on a giant ladder that
take you up higher and higher to see more and more of the world around you.

"I can see only a little bit of that, Charlie, and I won't go much higher
than I am now, but you'll keep climbing up and up, and see more and more,
and each step will open new worlds that you never even knew existed." She
frowned. "I hope . . . I just hope to God—"

"What?"

"Never mind, Charles. I just hope I wasn't wrong to advise you to go into
this in the first place."

500 I laughed. "How could that be? It worked, didn't it? Even Algernon is
still smart."

We sat there silently for a while and I knew what she was thinking about as
she watched me toying with the chain of my rabbit's foot and my keys. I didn't
want to think of that possibility any more than elderly people want to think
of death. I *knew* that this was only the beginning. I knew what she meant
about levels because I'd seen some of them already. The thought of leaving her
behind made me sad.

I'm in love with Miss Kinnian. ⓠ

PROGRESS REPORT 11

April 30 I've quit my job with Donnegan's Plastic Box Company. Mr.
510 Donnegan insisted that it would be better for all concerned if I left. What did
I do to make them hate me so?

The first I knew of it was when Mr. Donnegan showed me the petition.
Eight hundred and forty names, everyone connected with the factory, except
Fanny Girden. Scanning the list quickly, I saw at once that hers was the only
missing name. All the rest demanded that I be fired.

Joe Carp and Frank Reilly wouldn't talk to me about it. No one else would
either, except Fanny. She was one of the few people I'd known who set her
mind to something and believed it no matter what the rest of the world

ⓠ **CHARACTER TRAITS**
What new aspects of
Charlie's personality are
revealed in this scene
with Miss Kinnian?

proved, said or did—and Fanny did not believe that I should have been fired. She had been against the petition on principle and despite the pressure and threats she'd held out.

"Which don't mean to say," she remarked, "that I don't think there's something mighty strange about you, Charlie. Them changes. I don't know. You used to be a good, dependable, ordinary man—not too bright maybe, but honest. Who knows what you done to yourself to get so smart all of a sudden. Like everybody around here's been saying, Charlie, it's not right."

"But how can you say that, Fanny? What's wrong with a man becoming intelligent and wanting to acquire knowledge and understanding of the world around him?"

She stared down at her work and I turned to leave. Without looking at me, she said: "It was evil when Eve listened to the snake and ate from the tree of knowledge. It was evil when she saw that she was naked. If not for that none of us would ever have to grow old and sick, and die." [10]

Once again now I have the feeling of shame burning inside me. This intelligence has driven a wedge between me and all the people I once knew and loved. Before, they laughed at me and despised me for my ignorance and dullness; now, they hate me for my knowledge and understanding. What in God's name do they want of me?

They've driven me out of the factory. Now I'm more alone than ever before . . .

▼ **Analyze Visuals**

What might the flask in this illustration **symbolize?**

May 15 Dr. Strauss is very angry at me for not having written any progress reports in two weeks. He's justified because the lab is now paying me a regular salary. I told him I was too busy thinking and reading. When I pointed out that writing was such a slow process that it made me impatient with my poor handwriting, he suggested that I learn to type. It's much easier to write now because I can type nearly seventy-five words a minute. Dr. Strauss continually reminds me of the need to speak and write simply so that people will be able to understand me.

I'll try to review all the things that happened to me during the last two weeks. Algernon and I were presented to the *American Psychological Association* sitting in convention

10. **It was evil . . . die:** a reference to the biblical story of Adam and Eve (Genesis 2–3).

with the *World Psychological Association* last Tuesday. We created quite a **sensation.** Dr. Nemur and Dr. Strauss were proud of us.

560   I suspect that Dr. Nemur, who is sixty—ten years older than Dr. Strauss— finds it necessary to see tangible results of his work. Undoubtedly the result of pressure by Mrs. Nemur.

    Contrary to my earlier impressions of him, I realize that Dr. Nemur is not at all a genius. He has a very good mind, but it struggles under the specter of self-doubt. He wants people to take him for a genius. Therefore, it is important for him to feel that his work is accepted by the world. I believe that Dr. Nemur was afraid of further delay because he worried that someone else might make a discovery along these lines and take the credit from him.

    Dr. Strauss on the other hand might be called a genius, although I feel that
570 his areas of knowledge are too limited. He was educated in the tradition of narrow **specialization;** the broader aspects of background were neglected far more than necessary—even for a neuro-surgeon.

    I was shocked to learn that the only ancient languages he could read were Latin, Greek, and Hebrew, and that he knows almost nothing of mathematics beyond the elementary levels of the calculus of variations.[11] When he admitted this to me, I found myself almost annoyed. It was as if he'd hidden this part of himself in order to deceive me, pretending—as do many people I've discovered—to be what he is not. No one I've ever known is what he appears to be on the surface.

580   Dr. Nemur appears to be uncomfortable around me. Sometimes when I try to talk to him, he just looks at me strangely and turns away. I was angry at first when Dr. Strauss told me I was giving Dr. Nemur an inferiority complex.[12] I thought he was mocking me and I'm oversensitive at being made fun of.

    How was I to know that a highly respected psycho-experimentalist like Nemur was unacquainted with Hindustani[13] and Chinese? It's **absurd** when you consider the work that is being done in India and China today in the very field of his study.

    I asked Dr. Strauss how Nemur could **refute** Rahajamati's attack on his method and results if Nemur couldn't even read them in the first place. That
590 strange look on Dr. Strauss' face can mean only one of two things. Either he doesn't want to tell Nemur what they're saying in India, or else—and this worries me—Dr. Strauss doesn't know either. I must be careful to speak and write clearly and simply so that people won't laugh. **Ⓡ**

May 18 I am very disturbed. I saw Miss Kinnian last night for the first time in over a week. I tried to avoid all discussions of intellectual concepts and to keep the conversation on a simple, everyday level, but she just stared at me blankly and asked me what I meant about the mathematical variance equivalent in Dorbermann's *Fifth Concerto*.

---

11. **calculus** (kǎl′kyə-ləs) **of variations:** a branch of higher mathematics.

12. **inferiority complex:** feelings of worthlessness.

13. **Hindustani** (hǐn′dŏŏ-stä′nē): a group of languages used in India.

sensation (sĕn-sā′shən) *n.* a state of great interest and excitement

specialization (spĕsh′ə-lǐ-za′shən) *n.* a focus on a particular area of study

absurd (əb-sûrd′) *adj.* ridiculously unreasonable

refute (rĭ-fyōōt′) *v.* to prove as false

Ⓡ EXAMINE STRUCTURE
What do the length and language of the May 15 progress report reveal about Charlie's intelligence? Think about how this report differs from those in March and April.

When I tried to explain she stopped me and laughed. I guess I got angry,
600 but I suspect I'm approaching her on the wrong level. No matter what I try
to discuss with her, I am unable to communicate. I must review Vrostadt's
equations on *Levels of Semantic Progression*. I find that I don't communicate
with people much any more. Thank God for books and music and things I
can think about. I am alone in my apartment at Mrs. Flynn's boarding house
most of the time and seldom speak to anyone. **S**

May 20 I would not have noticed the new dishwasher, a boy of about sixteen,
at the corner diner where I take my evening meals if not for the incident of the
broken dishes.

They crashed to the floor, shattering and sending bits of white china under
610 the tables. The boy stood there, dazed and frightened, holding the empty tray
in his hand. The whistles and catcalls from the customers (the cries of "hey,
there go the profits!" . . . "*Mazeltov!*" . . . and "well, *he* didn't work here very
long . . ." which invariably seems to follow the breaking of glass or dishware in
a public restaurant) all seemed to confuse him.

When the owner came to see what the excitement was about, the boy cowered
as if he expected to be struck and threw up his arms as if to ward off the blow.

"All right! All right, you dope," shouted the owner, "don't just stand there!
Get the broom and sweep that mess up. A broom . . . a broom, you idiot!
It's in the kitchen. Sweep up all the pieces."

620 The boy saw that he was not going to be punished. His frightened
expression disappeared and he smiled and hummed as he came back with
the broom to sweep the floor. A few of the rowdier customers kept up the
remarks, amusing themselves at his expense.

"Here, sonny, over here there's a nice piece behind you . . ."

"C'mon, do it again . . ."

"He's not so dumb. It's easier to break 'em than to wash 'em . . ."

As his vacant eyes moved across the crowd of amused onlookers, he slowly
mirrored their smiles and finally broke into an uncertain grin at the joke
which he obviously did not understand.

630 I felt sick inside as I looked at his dull, vacuous smile, the wide, bright eyes
of a child, uncertain but eager to please. They were laughing at him because
he was mentally retarded.

And I had been laughing at him too.

Suddenly, I was furious at myself and all those who were smirking at him.
I jumped up and shouted, "Shut up! Leave him alone! It's not his fault he can't
understand! He can't help what he is! But for God's sake . . . he's still a human
being!" **T**

The room grew silent. I cursed myself for losing control and creating a
scene. I tried not to look at the boy as I paid my check and walked out without
640 touching my food. I felt ashamed for both of us.

S CHARACTER TRAITS
How has Charlie's
attitude toward
socializing changed?

T CHARACTER TRAITS
Why does Charlie
defend the dishwasher?
Tell what you can **infer**
about his personality
based on his behavior.

How strange it is that people of honest feelings and sensibility, who would not take advantage of a man born without arms or legs or eyes—how such people think nothing of abusing a man born with low intelligence. It infuriated me to think that not too long ago I, like this boy, had foolishly played the clown.

And I had almost forgotten.

I'd hidden the picture of the old Charlie Gordon from myself because now that I was intelligent it was something that had to be pushed out of my mind. But today in looking at that boy, for the first time I saw what I had been. *I was* 650 *just like him!*

Only a short time ago, I learned that people laughed at me. Now I can see that unknowingly I joined with them in laughing at myself. That hurts most of all.

I have often reread my progress reports and seen the illiteracy, the childish naïveté, the mind of low intelligence peering from a dark room, through the keyhole, at the dazzling light outside. I see that even in my dullness I knew that I was inferior, and that other people had something I lacked—something denied me. In my mental blindness, I thought that it was somehow connected with the ability to read and write, and I was sure that if I could get those skills I would automatically have intelligence too.

660 Even a feeble-minded man wants to be like other men.

A child may not know how to feed itself, or what to eat, yet it knows of hunger.

This then is what I was like. I never knew. Even with my gift of intellectual awareness, I never really knew.

This day was good for me. Seeing the past more clearly, I have decided to use my knowledge and skills to work in the field of increasing human intelligence levels. Who is better equipped for this work? Who else has lived in both worlds? These are my people. Let me use my gift to do something for them. **U**

Tomorrow, I will discuss with Dr. Strauss the manner in which I can work in 670 this area. I may be able to help him work out the problems of widespread use of the technique which was used on me. I have several good ideas of my own.

There is so much that might be done with this technique. If I could be made into a genius, what about thousands of others like myself? What fantastic levels might be achieved by using this technique on normal people? On *geniuses?*

There are so many doors to open. I am impatient to begin.

PROGRESS REPORT 12

May 23 It happened today. Algernon bit me. I visited the lab to see him as I do occasionally, and when I took him out of his cage, he snapped at my hand. I put him back and watched him for a while. He was unusually disturbed and vicious.

680 *May 24* Burt, who is in charge of the experimental animals, tells me that Algernon is changing. He is less cooperative; he refuses to run the maze any more; general motivation has decreased. And he hasn't been eating. Everyone is upset about what this may mean.

U INTERNAL CONFLICT
An **internal conflict** is a struggle that occurs within a character. Reread lines 641–668. As Charlie thinks about his past behavior, he feels angry at the people who used to make fun of him, and he also feels ashamed of the way he played along with them. What new character trait or traits are revealed in this passage? How do they help Charlie resolve conflicted feelings about his past?

May 25 They've been feeding Algernon, who now refuses to work the shifting-lock problem. Everyone identifies me with Algernon. In a way we're both the first of our kind. They're all pretending that Algernon's behavior is not necessarily significant for me. But it's hard to hide the fact that some of the other animals who were used in this experiment are showing strange behavior.

Dr. Strauss and Dr. Nemur have asked me not to come to the lab any more. I know what they're thinking but I can't accept it. I am going ahead with my
690 plans to carry their research forward. With all due respect to both of these fine scientists, I am well aware of their limitations. If there is an answer, I'll have to find it out for myself. Suddenly, time has become very important to me.

May 29 I have been given a lab of my own and permission to go ahead with the research. I'm on to something. Working day and night. I've had a cot moved into the lab. Most of my writing time is spent on the notes which I keep in a separate folder, but from time to time I feel it necessary to put down my moods and my thoughts out of sheer habit.

I find the *calculus of intelligence* to be a fascinating study. Here is the place for the application of all the knowledge I have acquired. In a sense it's the
700 problem I've been concerned with all my life.

▼ **Analyze Visuals**
In what way does this illustration **represent** the actions Charlie describes in his May 29 entry?

May 31 Dr. Strauss thinks I'm working too hard. Dr. Nemur says I'm trying to cram a lifetime of research and thought into a few weeks. I know I should rest, but I'm driven on by something inside that won't let me stop. I've got to find the reason for the sharp regression in Algernon. I've got to know *if* and *when* it will happen to me.

June 4

LETTER TO DR. STRAUSS (*copy*)

Dear Dr. Strauss:

710
    Under separate cover I am sending you a copy of my report entitled, "The Algernon-Gordon Effect: A Study of Structure and Function of Increased Intelligence," which I would like to have you read and have published.

    As you see, my experiments are completed. I have included in my report all of my formulae, as well as mathematical analysis in the appendix. Of course, these should be verified.

    Because of its importance to both you and Dr. Nemur (and need I say to myself, too?) I have checked and rechecked my results a dozen times in the hope of finding an error. I am sorry to say the results must stand. Yet for the sake of science, I am grateful for the little bit that I here add to the knowledge of the function of the human mind and of the laws governing
720
the artificial increase of human intelligence.

    I recall your once saying to me that an experimental *failure* or the *disproving* of a theory was as important to the advancement of learning as a success would be. I know now that this is true. I am sorry, however, that my own contribution to the field must rest upon the ashes of the work of two men I regard so highly.

Yours truly,
Charles Gordon 🆅

encl.: rept.

June 5 I must not become emotional. The facts and the results of my
730
experiments are clear, and the more sensational aspects of my own rapid climb cannot obscure the fact that the tripling of intelligence by the surgical technique developed by Dr.'s Strauss and Nemur must be viewed as having little or no practical applicability (at the present time) to the increase of human intelligence.

    As I review the records and data on Algernon, I see that although he is still in his physical infancy, he has regressed mentally. Motor activity[14] is **impaired;** there is a general reduction of glandular activity; there is an accelerated loss of coordination.

    There are also strong indications of progressive amnesia.[15]

    As will be seen by my report, these and other physical and mental
740
deterioration syndromes can be predicted with statistically significant results by the application of my formula.

🆅 EXAMINE STRUCTURE
What is different about the June 4 entry? Tell what you learn about Charlie and his future from this section.

impair (ĭm-pâr') *v.* to weaken; damage

---

14. **motor activity:** movement produced by use of the muscles.

15. **progressive amnesia** (prə-grĕs'ĭv ăm-nē'zhə): a steadily worsening loss of memory.

The surgical stimulus to which we were both subjected has resulted in an intensification and acceleration of all mental processes. The unforeseen development, which I have taken the liberty of calling the *Algernon-Gordon Effect*, is the logical extension of the entire intelligence speed-up. The hypothesis here proven may be described simply in the following terms: Artificially increased intelligence deteriorates at a rate of time directly **proportional** to the quantity of the increase.

I feel that this, in itself, is an important discovery.

750   As long as I am able to write, I will continue to record my thoughts in these progress reports. It is one of my few pleasures. However, by all indications, my own mental deterioration will be very rapid.

I have already begun to notice signs of emotional instability and forgetfulness, the first symptoms of the burn-out.

June 10 Deterioration progressing. I have become absent-minded. Algernon died two days ago. Dissection shows my predictions were right. His brain had decreased in weight and there was a general smoothing out of cerebral convolutions as well as a deepening and broadening of brain fissures.[16]

I guess the same thing is or will soon be happening to me. Now that it's
760 definite, I don't want it to happen.

I put Algernon's body in a cheese box and buried him in the back yard.
I cried. Ⓦ

June 15 Dr. Strauss came to see me again. I wouldn't open the door and I told him to go away. I want to be left to myself. I have become touchy and irritable. I feel the darkness closing in. It's hard to throw off thoughts of suicide. I keep telling myself how important this introspective journal will be.

It's a strange sensation to pick up a book that you've read and enjoyed just a few months ago and discover that you don't remember it. I remembered how great I thought John Milton was, but when I picked up *Paradise Lost* I couldn't
770 understand it at all. I got so angry I threw the book across the room.

I've got to try to hold on to some of it. Some of the things I've learned. Oh, God, please don't take it all away.

June 19 Sometimes, at night, I go out for a walk. Last night I couldn't remember where I lived. A policeman took me home. I have the strange feeling that this has all happened to me before—a long time ago. I keep telling myself I'm the only person in the world who can describe what's happening to me.

June 21 Why can't I remember? I've got to fight. I lie in bed for days and I don't know who or where I am. Then it all comes back to me in a flash.

proportional
(prə-pôr′shə-nəl) *adj.*
having a constant relation in degree or number

Ⓦ **EXAMINE STRUCTURE**
What does Charlie's language in the June 10 entry tell you about what is happening to his intelligence? Think about how this might affect Charlie's attitude toward Algernon's death.

---

16. **cerebral convolutions** (sĕr′ə-brəl kŏn′-və-lōō′shən) . . . **brain fissures** (fĭsh′ərz): cerebral convolutions are ridges or folds on the brain's surface; fissures are grooves that divide the brain into sections.

Fugues[17] of amnesia. Symptoms of senility—second childhood. I can watch
780 them coming on. It's so cruelly logical. I learned so much and so fast. Now
my mind is deteriorating rapidly. I won't let it happen. I'll fight it. I can't help
thinking of the boy in the restaurant, the blank expression, the silly smile,
the people laughing at him. No—please—not that again . . . ⊗

June 22 I'm forgetting things that I learned recently. It seems to be following
the classic pattern—the last things learned are the first things forgotten. Or is
that the pattern? I'd better look it up again. . . .

I reread my paper on the *Algernon-Gordon Effect* and I get the strange feeling
that it was written by someone else. There are parts I don't even understand.

Motor activity impaired. I keep tripping over things, and it becomes
790 increasingly difficult to type.

June 23 I've given up using the typewriter completely. My coordination is bad.
I feel that I'm moving slower and slower. Had a terrible shock today. I picked
up a copy of an article I used in my research, Krueger's *Uber psychische
Ganzheit,* to see if it would help me understand what I had done. First I
thought there was something wrong with my eyes. Then I realized I could
no longer read German. I tested myself in other languages. All gone.

June 30 A week since I dared to write again. It's slipping away like sand through
my fingers. Most of the books I have are too hard for me now. I get angry with
them because I know that I read and understood them just a few weeks ago.

800 I keep telling myself I must keep writing these reports so that somebody
will know what is happening to me. But it gets harder to form the words and
remember spellings. I have to look up even simple words in the dictionary now
and it makes me impatient with myself.

Dr. Strauss comes around almost every day, but I told him I wouldn't see or
speak to anybody. He feels guilty. They all do. But I don't blame anyone.
I knew what might happen. But how it hurts.

July 7 I don't know where the week went. Todays Sunday I know because I
can see through my window people going to church. I think I stayed in bed
all week but I remember Mrs. Flynn bringing food to me a few times. I keep
810 saying over and over Ive got to do something but then I forget or maybe its
just easier not to do what I say Im going to do.

I think of my mother and father a lot these days. I found a picture of
them with me taken at a beach. My father has a big ball under his arm and
my mother is holding me by the hand. I dont remember them the way they
are in the picture. All I remember is my father drunk most of the time and
arguing with mom about money.

---

17. **fugues** (fyo͞ogz): psychological states where people seem to act consciously but later have no memory
of the action.

He never shaved much and he used to scratch my face when he hugged me. My mother said he died 820 but Cousin Miltie said he heard his mom and dad say that my father ran away with another woman. When I asked my mother she slapped my face and said my father was dead. I dont think I ever found out which was true but I dont care much. (He said he was going to take me to see cows on a farm once but he never did. He never kept his 830 promises . . .)

July 10 My landlady Mrs Flynn is very worried about me. She says the way I lay around all day and dont do anything I remind her of her son before she threw him out of the house. She said she doesnt like loafers. If Im sick its one thing, but if Im a loafer thats another thing and she wont have it. I told her I think 840 Im sick.

I try to read a little bit every day, mostly stories, but sometimes I have to read the same thing over and over again because I dont know what it means. And its hard to write. I know I should look up all the words in the dictionary but its so hard and Im so tired all the time.

Then I got the idea that I would 850 only use the easy words instead of the long hard ones. That saves time. I put flowers on Algernons grave about once a week. Mrs Flynn thinks Im crazy to put flowers on a mouses grave but I told her that Algernon was special.

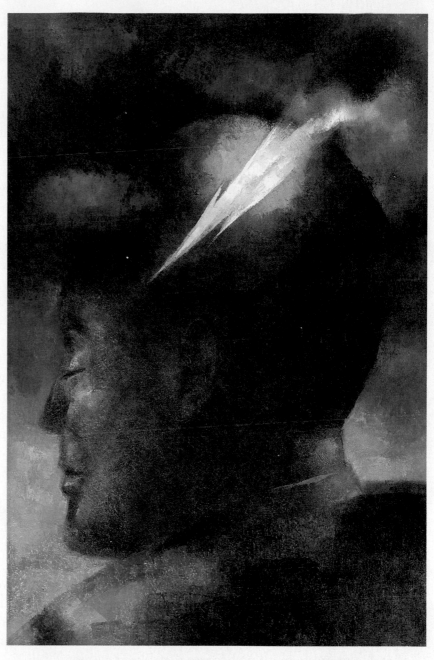

▲ **Analyze Visuals**
What can you **infer** about what is happening to the man in the picture?

July 14 Its sunday again. I dont have anything to do to keep me busy now because my television set is broke and I dont have any money to get it fixed. (I think I lost this months check from the lab. I dont remember)

I get awful headaches and asperin doesnt help me much. Mrs Flynn knows Im really sick and she feels very sorry for me. Shes a wonderful woman whenever someone is sick.

860 *July 22* Mrs Flynn called a strange doctor to see me. She was afraid I was going to die. I told the doctor I wasnt too sick and that I only forget sometimes. He asked me did I have any friends or relatives and I said no I dont have any. I told him I had a friend called Algernon once but he was a mouse and we used to run races together. He looked at me kind of funny like he thought I was crazy.

   He smiled when I told him I used to be a genius. He talked to me like I was a baby and he winked at Mrs Flynn. I got mad and chased him out because he was making fun of me the way they all used to.

July 24 I have no more money and Mrs Flynn says I got to go to work somewhere and pay the rent because I havent paid for over two months. I dont
870 know any work but the job I used to have at Donnegans Plastic Box Company. I dont want to go back there because they all knew me when I was smart and maybe they'll laugh at me. But I dont know what else to do to get money.

July 25 I was looking at some of my old progress reports and its very funny but I cant read what I wrote. I can make out some of the words but they dont make sense.

   Miss Kinnian came to the door but I said go away I dont want to see you. She cried and I cried too but I wouldnt let her in because I didnt want her to laugh at me. I told her I didn't like her any more. I told her I didn't want to be smart any more. Thats not true. I still love her and I still want to be smart but
880 I had to say that so shed go away. She gave Mrs. Flynn money to pay the rent. I dont want that. I got to get a job.

   Please . . . please let me not forget how to read and write . . . **Y**

July 27 Mr. Donnegan was very nice when I came back and asked him for my old job of janitor. First he was very suspicious but I told him what happened to me then he looked very sad and put his hand on my shoulder and said Charlie Gordon you got guts.

   Everybody looked at me when I came downstairs and started working in the toilet sweeping it out like I used to. I told myself Charlie if they make fun of you dont get sore because you remember their not so smart as you once thot
890 they were. And besides they were once your friends and if they laughed at you that doesnt mean anything because they liked you too.

   One of the new men who came to work there after I went away made a nasty crack he said hey Charlie I hear your a very smart fella a real quiz kid. Say something intelligent. I felt bad but Joe Carp came over and grabbed him by the shirt and said leave him alone you lousy cracker or Ill break your neck. I didnt expect Joe to take my part so I guess hes really my friend.

   Later Frank Reilly came over and said Charlie if anybody bothers you or trys to take advantage you call me or Joe and we will set em straight. I said thanks Frank and I got choked up so I had to turn around and go into the
900 supply room so he wouldnt see me cry. Its good to have friends.

Y EXAMINE STRUCTURE
Compare the July 25 progress report to those from previous months. How does it help you understand what has happened to Charlie?

July 28 I did a dumb thing today I forgot I wasnt in Miss Kinnians class at the adult center any more like I use to be. I went in and sat down in my old seat in the back of the room and she looked at me funny and she said Charles. I dint remember she ever called me that before only Charlie so I said hello Miss Kinnian Im redy for my lesin today only I lost my reader that we was using. She startid to cry and run out of the room and everybody looked at me and I saw they wasnt the same pepul who use to be in my class.

Then all of a suddin I rememberd some things about the operashun and me getting smart and I said holy smoke I reely pulled a Charlie Gordon that time.

910 I went away before she come back to the room.

Thats why Im going away from New York for good. I dont want to do nothing like that agen. I dont want Miss Kinnian to feel sorry for me. Evry body feels sorry at the factery and I dont want that eather so Im going someplace where nobody knows that Charlie Gordon was once a genus and now he cant even reed a book or rite good.

Im taking a cuple of books along and even if I cant reed them Ill practise hard and maybe I wont forget every thing I lerned. If I try reel hard maybe Ill be a littel bit smarter then I was before the operashun. I got my rabits foot and my luky penny and maybe they will help me.

920 If you ever reed this Miss Kinnian dont be sorry for me Im glad I got a second chanse to be smart becaus I lerned a lot of things that I never even new were in this world and Im grateful that I saw it all for a littel bit. I dont know why Im dumb agen or what I did wrong maybe its becaus I dint try hard enuff. But if I try and practis very hard maybe Ill get a littl smarter and know what all the words are. I remember a littel bit how nice I had a feeling with the blue book that has the torn cover when I red it. Thats why Im gonna keep trying to get smart so I can have that feeling agen. Its a good feeling to know things and be smart. I wish I had it rite now if I did I woud sit down and reed all the time. Anyway I bet Im the first dumb person in the

930 world who ever found out somthing importent for sience. I remember I did somthing but I dont remember what. So I gess its like I did it for all the dumb pepul like me. **❷**

Goodbye Miss Kinnian and Dr. Strauss and evreybody. And P.S. please tell Dr Nemur not to be such a grouch when pepul laff at him and he woud have more frends. Its easy to make frends if you let pepul laff at you. Im going to have lots of frends where I go.

P.P.S. Please if you get a chanse put some flowrs on Algernons grave in the bak yard . . . ❧

❷ CHARACTER TRAITS
What does Charlie's attitude toward his experience suggest about the kind of person he is?

CHARLY [1]

STIRLING SILLIPHANT

> **CHARACTERS**
> **Charlie**   **Dr. Strauss**   **Dr. Nemur**   **Alice Kinnian**

Charlie. Boy!

(*He straightens, looks at* Dr. Nemur *and* Dr. Strauss *who stand at one end of the cage.* Alice Kinnian *is just to one side of* Charlie *in a laboratory around which cages containing mice, rats, and monkeys are arranged. Here and there in the background lab assistants are at work.* Dr. Strauss *reaches in a piece of cheese, rewards the mouse.*)

10 **Dr. Strauss.** Well, Charlie, what do you think of Algernon?

Charlie (*grinning*). Pretty fancy name for a mouse!

Dr. Strauss. Algernon's a pretty special mouse.

(Charlie *turns back to the cage, rubs the tip of his fingers along the mesh and baby-talks to the mouse.* Algernon *twitches its nose and waggles its whiskers.*)

(*favoring* Dr. Nemur)

20 **Dr. Nemur** (*to* Alice). How much does Charlie understand about the operation?

Alice Kinnian. Charlie?

(Charlie *looks up.*)

Charlie. Yeh?

Alice Kinnian. What do you remember about the operation we discussed? The reason I brought you here?

---

1. **Charly:** The screenwriter might have chosen to misspell Charlie's name as "Charly" to convey the main character's struggle with spelling.

Movie still from the 1969 film *Charly*

(Charlie *straightens, looks the two doctors straight in the eye—this is his big moment—and the* words *come now, tumbling.*)

Charlie. All my life I wantid to be smart not dumb. It's very hard to be smart. It's—kind of—slow. I mean, I *try*—but it's—slow. Even when I learn something in Miss Kinnian's class at the Training Center where I try the hardest it's slow—and I ferget. I used to think maybe it's because I talk to myself a lot—you know, I say, hey, Charlie—and stuff like that—but that don't slow me down—because I don't listen to myself.

(*He stops, out of breath, discovers that* Alice—*and the two doctors—still seem to expect more from him.*)

Charlie. Oh—the operashun! The operashun will make me smart. (*a beat—then to* Alice) Is that what you told me?

Alice Kinnian (*softly*). We *hope* it will, Charlie. But nobody knows for sure. Anyway . . . (*looking at the doctors*) . . . the doctors have to talk to a lot of other people too—before they decide who'll be the first to have this operation.

(*favoring* Dr. Strauss)

Dr. Strauss. Charlie . . . how would you like to race Algernon?

Charlie (*grinning*). Sure, but . . . (*He looks down at the cage.*)

Charlie. I can't fit in there.

(Dr. Strauss *hands* Charlie *a long metal rod.*)

Dr. Strauss. We call this an electric stylus.

(*She guides* Charlie's *hand holding the stylus into the open space between the walls of a maze which sits next to* Algernon's *cage on the long bench before which they stand.*)

Dr. Strauss. When I say START—move the pencil along this line until you come to . . . that place there—the FINISH. If you move the wrong way, you'll get a shock.

(*She causes* Charlie's *hand to touch the wall of a cul-de-sac.* Charlie *reacts.*)

Dr. Strauss. Did that hurt?

Charlie. Naw.

Dr. Strauss. That shock is a signal . . . it tells you to back up the stylus and go down another row.

Alice Kinnian. You understand, Charlie?

(Charlie *nods reassuringly, smiles broadly. This is FUN.* Dr. Nemur *moves* Algernon *from the finish box to the start box.*)

Dr. Strauss. Ready?

(Charlie, *eager to begin, nods. He holds up his left hand, exhibiting the rabbit's foot.* Alice *smiles at him reassuringly.*)

Dr. Strauss. Start.

(Dr. Strauss *waits until she sees that* Charlie *has already begun to guide the stylus, then she lifts the hatch and releases* Algernon. *Camera shots alternate between* Charlie *and* Algernon *as each "runs" his race.* Charlie's *race is hardly run—it is actually one shock after another, one bafflement piled on top another, one dead end after another—then all too quickly* Algernon's *telltale victory squeak is heard.* Charlie *looks over at* Algernon *in the finish box.* Dr. Strauss *is feeding him a small piece of cheese. Close-up on* Charlie *as he considers what has just happened. He looks up at* Alice, *who is smiling reassuringly.* Dr. Nemur's *face is without expression.* Charlie *brings the stylus out of the maze. He shrugs.*)

Charlie. Anybody so stoopid even a little mouse can beat him you sure don't want to give *him* no operashun. I don't blame you!

(*He puts down the stylus, leans closer to the cage, and smiles in wonder at* Algernon.)

Charlie. I dint know mice was so smart.

Comprehension

1. **Recall** What type of operation does Charlie undergo?

2. **Clarify** Why does Charlie decide to leave New York at the end of the story?

3. **Clarify** In *Charly*, what is the purpose of the electric stylus?

Text Analysis

● 4. **Identify Character Traits** If you haven't done this yet, fill in the bottom of your Y-chart with traits that Charlie showed throughout the story. Use notes on your chart to support your answer.

5. **Understand Plot Elements** The technique of hinting about something that will occur later in a story is called **foreshadowing**. Explain how Algernon's death is an example of this technique.

● 6. **Examine Structure** This story covers a period of five months. Analyze the progress reports from each of these months to determine the change in Charlie's abilities. Track your results on a graph like the one shown. How quickly did Charlie Gordon's intelligence rise and fall?

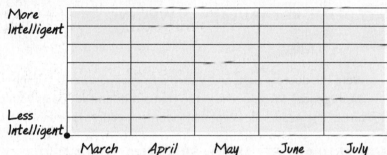

7. **Analyze Parallel Episodes** A **parallel episode** is a repeated element in a story's plot. For example, Charlie races Algernon both before he has the operation and after. Identify at least three other parallel episodes in this story. What is the purpose of repeating these elements? In your opinion, are these parallel episodes good additions to the structure of the story? Give reasons for your answer.

8. **Compare Texts** Think about the ways that the short story and the screenplay present the scene in which Charlie meets Algernon. What are the similarities and differences? Consider the amount of detail each selection provides.

Extension and Challenge

9. **Text Criticism** A literary critic wrote that "Flowers for Algernon" has "one of the most perfect and perfectly controlled narrative arcs in the entire history of the short story...." A **narrative arc** is the shape a story's plot takes as it slowly rises, reaches a high point, and then falls to reach a resolution. What do you think the critic meant by this comment?

When is it better not to KNOW?

Would Charlie have been better off if he had never gained the knowledge he did? Consider how he feels at different points in the story.

COMMON CORE

RL 3 Analyze how lines of dialogue and incidents in a story reveal aspects of a character. **RL 5** Compare and contrast the structure of two or more texts and analyze how the differing structure of each text contributes to its meaning and style. **RL 6** Analyze how differences in the points of view of the characters and the audience or reader create effects. **RL 7** Analyze the extent to which a filmed production of a story stays faithful to or departs from the text.

Vocabulary in Context

▲ VOCABULARY PRACTICE

Show that you understand the boldfaced words. Decide if each statement is true or false.

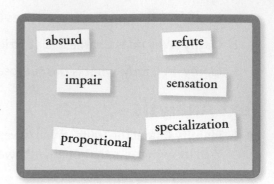

1. Something that causes a **sensation** is not of much interest.
2. A **specialization** means a little knowledge about a lot of things.
3. If something is **absurd,** it's unusual or ridiculous.
4. To **refute** something is to agree with it wholeheartedly.
5. Lack of sleep can **impair** your ability to stay alert.
6. When two things are **proportional,** they are not at all related to each other.

ACADEMIC VOCABULARY IN WRITING

   • appropriate   • assess   • intelligence   • motive   • role

Were the doctors right to try such a risky experiment to improve Charlie's **intelligence**? Write a paragraph that states and supports your opinion. Use at least one of the Academic Vocabulary words in your response.

VOCABULARY STRATEGY: SPECIALIZED VOCABULARY

Many of the words used in this selection are specialized terms that relate to the study of psychology. Knowing the meanings of these words can help you understand more about this field of study. When you come across a word that you do not know, try to use context clues to help you figure out its meaning. Use a dictionary or a specialized dictionary for that field of study to find the exact meaning.

⋯ **COMMON CORE**

L 4a Use context as a clue to the meaning of a word. **L 4c** Consult general and specialized reference materials to find the pronunciation of a word or determine or clarify its precise meaning. **L 6** Acquire and use domain-specific words.

PRACTICE Match the word in the first column with its definition in the second column. Use a dictionary if you need help.

1. hypothesis
2. syndrome
3. regression
4. introspective

a. symptoms that characterize a disease or disorder
b. a return to a less developed condition
c. an assumption used as the basis for research
d. examining one's own thoughts, feelings, and sensations

Interactive Vocabulary **THINK**central

Go to thinkcentral.com.
KEYWORD: HML8-228

Language

◆ **GRAMMAR IN CONTEXT:** Compare Correctly

Review the **Grammar in Context** note on page 211. The **comparative form** of a modifier is used to compare only two people or things. For most one-syllable modifiers, add *-er* (brighter, closer) to form the comparative. For most modifiers with two or more syllables, use the word *more* (more important, more easily).

The **superlative form** is used to compare three or more people or things. For most one-syllable modifiers, add *-est* (brightest, closest). For most modifiers with two or more syllables, use the word *most* (most important, most easily).

> *Example:* Dr. Strauss is closer to being a genius than Dr. Nemur. (*Two things are being compared, and* close *has one syllable.*)

> *Example:* Even the most intelligent person in the world must be unhappy sometimes. (*More than two things are being compared, and* intelligent *hus more than one syllable.*)

PRACTICE Choose the correct form to complete each sentence.

1. Charlie Gordon becomes (smarter, more smart) than he was before.
2. Dr. Strauss and Dr. Nemur might be the (brightest, most bright) doctors in their field, but they do not always make good decisions.
3. At first, Charlie is (more content, contenter) at his job than at the lab.
4. Miss Kinnian is the person (more, most) worried about Charlie's well-being.

For more help with comparative and superlative forms, see page R58 in the **Grammar Handbook.**

READING-WRITING CONNECTION

YOUR TURN Explore the issues raised in "Flowers for Algernon" by responding to this prompt. Then use the **revising tip** to improve your writing.

WRITING PROMPT	REVISING TIP
Extended Constructed Response: Reflection After reading this story, do you think having knowledge makes a person happier, kinder, or generally better? Write a **two- or three-paragraph response,** citing as evidence two or more characters.	Review your response. Have you used any comparative or superlative modifiers? If not, revise your writing.

◌ **COMMON CORE**

W 1b Write arguments to support claims with logical reasoning and relevant evidence. **L1** Demonstrate command of standard English grammar and usage when writing.

Interactive Revision THINK central

Go to **thinkcentral.com**.
KEYWORD: HML8-229

Rules of the Game

Short Story by Amy Tan

VIDEO TRAILER **THINK** central   KEYWORD: HML8-230

Video link at
thinkcentral.com

Can allies be
OPPONENTS?

COMMON CORE

RL 1 Cite textual evidence to support inferences drawn from the text. **RL 6** Analyze how differences in the points of view of the characters and the audience or reader create effects.

Family, friends, coaches—these are people who usually want the best for you. Then why can it feel like they're always giving you a hard time? Understanding people's good intentions can be challenging, and it may even feel like your supporters aren't on your side. In "Rules of the Game," find out why a young girl sees her mother—who is her biggest fan—as her main opponent.

QUICKWRITE Think of one or two people in your life who want you to be the best you can be. Then write a brief journal entry about your relationship with them. In what ways does their support help you? In what ways does their support make things harder for you?

● TEXT ANALYSIS: FIRST-PERSON POINT OF VIEW

When a writer uses the **first-person point of view,** the narrator is a character in the story—usually the main character. A story is told in the first-person point of view when the narrator

- describes people and events as he or she experiences them
- uses the pronouns *I* and *me* to talk about himself or herself
- doesn't know what other characters are thinking and feeling

As you read, notice how the narrator's **subjective,** or personal, observations affect your understanding of the selection.

● READING SKILL: DRAW CONCLUSIONS

In reading and in life, you often have to **draw conclusions,** or make logical judgments, about things that are not directly stated. Follow these steps to draw a conclusion:

- Gather evidence from the literature.
- Consider your own experience and knowledge.
- Make a judgment that combines both.

As you read, use a chart like the one shown to help you form conclusions about Waverly's relationship with her mother.

Evidence	My Thoughts	Conclusion
Mrs. Jong scolds Waverly for crying out for salted plums.	I know parents try to teach their kids how to behave.	Mrs. Jong wants Waverly to learn self-control.

Review: **Visualize**

▲ VOCABULARY IN CONTEXT

Amy Tan uses the words listed to help her describe one girl's conflicts with her mother. In your Reader/Writer Notebook, write a sentence for each of the vocabulary words. Use a dictionary or the definitions in the following selection pages to help you.

WORD LIST		
adversary	impart	pungent
benefactor	malodorous	retort
concession	ponder	tactic
foresight		

 Complete the activities in your **Reader/Writer Notebook.**

Meet the Author

Amy Tan
born 1952

Change of Heart
The daughter of Chinese immigrants, Amy Tan grew up in California having little interest in her heritage. When she was a teenager, her father and older brother died. Their deaths devastated her, and her rocky relationship with her mother became worse. Tan's mother wanted her to become a doctor or a concert pianist, but Tan became a business writer instead. She later turned to fiction writing, which helped her express her emotions about her family and embrace her Chinese heritage as an important part of her identity.

Mother-Daughter Ties
Tan wrote "Rules of the Game" for a writing workshop in 1985. She later used it as part of her first novel, *The Joy Luck Club,* which is a series of interconnected stories about four Chinese mothers and their Chinese-American daughters. Tan's family stories have inspired her writing. She once said of her mother, "My books have amounted to taking her stories—a gift to me—and giving them back to her."

BACKGROUND TO THE STORY
An Old Game Lives On
Although the game of chess is hundreds of years old, competitive chess remains a popular pastime today. A special class of players strives for the title of grand master, which only the top 0.02% of tournament players worldwide earn. A player must accumulate at least 2,500 points in tournament play to be recognized as a grand master by the World Chess Federation.

Author Online
THINK central
Go to **thinkcentral.com.**
KEYWORD: HML8-231

Rules of the Game

Amy Tan

I was six when my mother taught me the art of invisible strength. It was a strategy for winning arguments, respect from others, and eventually, though neither of us knew it at the time, chess games.

"Bite back your tongue," scolded my mother when I cried loudly, yanking her hand toward the store that sold bags of salted plums. At home, she said, "Wise guy, he not go against wind. In Chinese we say, Come from South, blow with wind—poom!—North will follow. Strongest wind cannot be seen."

The next week I bit back my tongue as we entered the store with the forbidden candies. When my mother finished her shopping, she quietly
10 plucked a small bag of plums from the rack and put it on the counter with the rest of the items. **Ⓐ**

My mother **imparted** her daily truths so she could help my older brothers and me rise above our circumstances. We lived in San Francisco's Chinatown. Like most of the other Chinese children who played in the back alleys of restaurants and curio shops,[1] I didn't think we were poor. My bowl was always full, three five-course meals every day, beginning with a soup full of mysterious things I didn't want to know the names of.

We lived on Waverly Place, in a warm, clean, two-bedroom flat that sat above a small Chinese bakery specializing in steamed pastries and dim sum.[2]

---

1. **curio shops:** shops that sell curious or unusual objects.
2. **dim sum:** small portions of a variety of Chinese foods and dumplings.

Analyze Visuals ▶

Note which **details** of this photograph are in focus and which are blurry. What effect does this have on you, the viewer?

Ⓐ POINT OF VIEW
Identify who is telling this story. What has she suggested about her relationship with her mother so far?

impart (ĭm-pärt') *v.* to make known; reveal

20 In the early morning, when the alley was still quiet, I could smell fragrant red beans as they were cooked down to a pasty sweetness. By daybreak, our flat was heavy with the odor of fried sesame balls and sweet curried chicken crescents. From my bed, I would listen as my father got ready for work, then locked the door behind him, one-two-three clicks.

At the end of our two-block alley was a small sandlot playground with swings and slides well-shined down the middle with use. The play area was bordered by wood-slat benches where old-country people sat cracking roasted watermelon seeds with their golden teeth and scattering the husks to an impatient gathering of gurgling pigeons. The best playground, however, was 30 the dark alley itself. It was crammed with daily mysteries and adventures. My brothers and I would peer into the medicinal herb shop, watching old Li[3] dole out onto a stiff sheet of white paper the right amount of insect shells, saffron-colored seeds, and **pungent** leaves for his ailing customers. It was said that he once cured a woman dying of an ancestral curse that had eluded the best of American doctors. Next to the pharmacy was a printer who specialized in gold-embossed wedding invitations and festive red banners. **B**

Farther down the street was Ping Yuen[4] Fish Market. The front window displayed a tank crowded with doomed fish and turtles struggling to gain footing on the slimy green-tiled sides. A hand-written sign informed tourists, 40 "Within this store, is all for food, not for pet." Inside, the butchers with their bloodstained white smocks deftly gutted the fish while customers cried out their orders and shouted, "Give me your freshest," to which the butchers always protested, "All are freshest." On less crowded market days, we would inspect the crates of live frogs and crabs which we were warned not to poke, boxes of dried cuttlefish, and row upon row of iced prawns, squid, and slippery fish. The sanddabs made me shiver each time; their eyes lay on one flattened side and reminded me of my mother's story of a careless girl who ran into a crowded street and was crushed by a cab. "Was smash flat," reported my mother.

At the corner of the alley was Hong Sing's, a four-table café with a recessed 50 stairwell in front that led to a door marked "Tradesmen." My brothers and I believed the bad people emerged from this door at night. Tourists never went to Hong Sing's, since the menu was printed only in Chinese. A Caucasian man with a big camera once posed me and my playmates in front of the restaurant. He had us move to the side of the picture window so the photo would capture the roasted duck with its head dangling from a juice-covered rope. After he took the picture, I told him he should go into Hong Sing's and eat dinner. When he smiled and asked me what they served, I shouted, "Guts and duck's feet and octopus gizzards!" Then I ran off with my friends, shrieking with laughter as we scampered across the alley and hid in the entryway grotto[5] of the China Gem 60 Company, my heart pounding with hope that he would chase us. **C**

pungent (pŭn'jənt) *adj.* sharp or intense

B VISUALIZE
Reread lines 25–36. What words help you picture the neighborhood?

C POINT OF VIEW
Reread lines 49–60. What do the narrator's words and actions tell you about her attitude toward taking risks?

---

3. **Li** (lē).

4. **Ping Yuen** (bǐng yü'ĕn).

5. **grotto** (grŏt'ō): an artificial structure made to resemble a cave or cavern.

My mother named me after the street that we lived on: Waverly Place Jong, my official name for important American documents. But my family called me Meimei,[6] "Little Sister." I was the youngest, the only daughter. Each morning before school, my mother would twist and yank on my thick black hair until she had formed two tightly wound pigtails. One day, as she struggled to weave a hard-toothed comb through my disobedient hair, I had a sly thought.

I asked her, "Ma, what is Chinese torture?" My mother shook her head. A bobby pin was wedged between her lips. She wetted her palm and smoothed the hair above my ear, then pushed the pin in so that it nicked sharply against my scalp.

"Who say this word?" she asked without a trace of knowing how wicked I was being. I shrugged my shoulders and said, "Some boy in my class said Chinese people do Chinese torture."

"Chinese people do many things," she said simply. "Chinese people do business, do medicine, do painting. Not lazy like American people. We do torture. Best torture." **D**

My older brother Vincent was the one who actually got the chess set. We had gone to the annual Christmas party held at the First Chinese Baptist Church at the end of the alley. The missionary ladies had put together a Santa bag of gifts donated by members of another church. None of the gifts had names on them. There were separate sacks for boys and girls of different ages.

---

6. **Meimei** (mā'mā).

One of the Chinese parishioners had donned a Santa Claus costume and a stiff paper beard with cotton balls glued to it. I think the only children who thought he was the real thing were too young to know that Santa Claus was not Chinese. When my turn came up, the Santa man asked me how old I was. I thought it was a trick question; I was seven according to the American formula and eight by the Chinese calendar. I said I was born on March 17, 1951. That seemed to satisfy him. He then solemnly asked if I had been a very, very good girl this year and did I believe in Jesus Christ and obey my parents. I knew the only answer to that. I nodded back with equal solemnity. ◆

Having watched the other children opening their gifts, I already knew that the big gifts were not necessarily the nicest ones. One girl my age got a large coloring book of biblical characters, while a less greedy girl who selected a smaller box received a glass vial of lavender toilet water. The sound of the box was also important. A ten-year-old boy had chosen a box that jangled when he shook it. It was a tin globe of the world with a slit for inserting money. He must have thought it was full of dimes and nickels, because when he saw that it had just ten pennies, his face fell with such undisguised disappointment that his mother slapped the side of his head and led him out of the church hall, apologizing to the crowd for her son who had such bad manners he couldn't appreciate such a fine gift.

As I peered into the sack, I quickly fingered the remaining presents, testing their weight, imagining what they contained. I chose a heavy, compact one that was wrapped in shiny silver foil and a red satin ribbon. It was a twelve-pack of Life Savers and I spent the rest of the party arranging and rearranging the candy tubes in the order of my favorites. My brother Winston chose wisely as well. His present turned out to be a box of intricate plastic parts; the instructions on the box proclaimed that when they were properly assembled he would have an authentic miniature replica of a World War II submarine.

Vincent got the chess set, which would have been a very decent present to get at a church Christmas party, except it was obviously used and, as we discovered later, it was missing a black pawn and a white knight. My mother graciously thanked the unknown **benefactor,** saying, "Too good. Cost too much." At which point, an old lady with fine white, wispy hair nodded toward our family and said with a whistling whisper, "Merry, merry Christmas."

When we got home, my mother told Vincent to throw the chess set away. "She not want it. We not want it," she said, tossing her head stiffly to the side with a tight, proud smile. My brothers had deaf ears. They were already lining up the chess pieces and reading from the dog-eared instruction book. **E**

I watched Vincent and Winston play during Christmas week. The chessboard seemed to hold elaborate secrets waiting to be untangled. The chessmen were more powerful than Old Li's magic herbs that cured ancestral curses. And my brothers wore such serious faces that I was sure something was at stake that was greater than avoiding the tradesmen's door to Hong Sing's.

"Let me! Let me!" I begged between games when one brother or the other would sit back with a deep sigh of relief and victory, the other annoyed, unable

◆ **GRAMMAR IN CONTEXT**
Notice that the verb *nodded* in the last sentence of line 91 is in the indicative mood. The **mood** of a verb conveys the status of the action or condition it describes. The **indicative** mood is used to make statements.

benefactor
(bĕn′ə-făk′tər) *n.* a person who gives monetary or other aid

E DRAW CONCLUSIONS
Why does Mrs. Jong want Vincent to throw away his chess set?

to let go of the outcome. Vincent at first refused to let me play, but when I offered my Life Savers as replacements for the buttons that filled in for the missing pieces, he relented. He chose the flavors: wild cherry for the black pawn and peppermint for the white knight. Winner could eat both.

As our mother sprinkled flour and rolled out small doughy circles for the steamed dumplings that would be our dinner that night, Vincent explained the rules, pointing to each piece. "You have sixteen pieces and so do I. One king and queen, two bishops, two knights, two castles, and eight pawns. The pawns can only move forward one step, except on the first move. Then they can move two. But they can only take men by moving crossways like this, except in the beginning, when you can move ahead and take another pawn."

"Why?" I asked as I moved my pawn. "Why can't they move more steps?"

"Because they're pawns," he said.

"But why do they go crossways to take other men? Why aren't there any women and children?"

"Why is the sky blue? Why must you always ask stupid questions?" asked Vincent. "This is a game. These are the rules. I didn't make them up. See. Here. In the book." He jabbed a page with a pawn in his hand. "Pawn. P-A-W-N. Pawn. Read it yourself."

My mother patted the flour off her hands. "Let me see book," she said quietly. She scanned the pages quickly, not reading the foreign English symbols, seeming to search deliberately for nothing in particular.

"This American rules," she concluded at last. "Every time people come out from foreign country, must know rules. You not know, judge say, Too bad, go back. They not telling you why so you can use their way go forward. They say, Don't know why, you find out yourself. But they knowing all the time. Better you take it, find out why yourself." She tossed her head back with a satisfied smile.

I found out about all the whys later. I read the rules and looked up all the big words in a dictionary. I borrowed books from the Chinatown library. I studied each chess piece, trying to absorb the power each contained.

I learned about opening moves and why it's important to control the center early on; the shortest distance between two points is straight down the middle. I learned about the middle game and why **tactics** between two **adversaries** are like clashing ideas; the one who plays better has the clearest plans for both attacking and getting out of traps. I learned why it is essential in the endgame to have **foresight,** a mathematical understanding of all possible moves, and patience; all weaknesses and advantages become evident to a strong adversary and are obscured to a tiring opponent. I discovered that for the whole game one must gather invisible strengths and see the endgame before the game begins.

I also found out why I should never reveal "why" to others. A little knowledge withheld is a great advantage one should store for future use. That is the power of chess. It is a game of secrets in which one must show and never tell.

I loved the secrets I found within the sixty-four black and white squares. I carefully drew a handmade chessboard and pinned it to the wall next to my

 SOCIAL STUDIES CONNECTION
Waverly's mother might be suggesting something larger about American rules. Between the years 1882 and 1965, Chinese immigration to the U.S. was restricted. Those who were let into the country were not granted the same rights as other Americans.

tactic (tăk′tĭk) *n.* a maneuver to achieve a goal

adversary (ăd′vər-sĕr′ē) *n.* an opponent

foresight (fôr′sīt) *n.* perception of the significance of events before they have occurred

bed, where at night I would stare for hours at imaginary battles. Soon I no longer lost any games or Life Savers, but I lost my adversaries. Winston and Vincent decided they were more interested in roaming the streets after school in their Hopalong Cassidy cowboy hats. **F**

On a cold spring afternoon, while walking home from school, I detoured through the playground at the end of our alley. I saw a group of old men, two seated across a folding table playing a game of chess, others smoking pipes, eating peanuts, and watching. I ran home and grabbed Vincent's

180 chess set, which was bound in a cardboard box with rubber bands. I also carefully selected two prized rolls of Life Savers. I came back to the park and approached a man who was observing the game.

"Want to play?" I asked him. His face widened with surprise and he grinned as he looked at the box under my arm.

"Little sister, been a long time since I play with dolls," he said, smiling benevolently. I quickly put the box down next to him on the bench and displayed my **retort.**

Lau Po,[7] as he allowed me to call him, turned out to be a much better player than my brothers. I lost many games and many Life Savers. But over the

190 weeks, with each diminishing roll of candies, I added new secrets. Lau Po gave me the names. The Double Attack from the East and West Shores. Throwing Stones on the Drowning Man. The Sudden Meeting of the Clan. The Surprise from the Sleeping Guard. The Humble Servant Who Kills the King. Sand in the Eyes of Advancing Forces. A Double Killing Without Blood.

---

7. **Lau Po** (lou bō).

F POINT OF VIEW
What do Waverly's descriptions of her thoughts and actions reveal about her?

retort (rĭ-tôrt') *n.* a quick, sharp, witty reply

◀ **Analyze Visuals**
How does the angle at which this photograph was taken affect what you first notice in the picture?

There were also the fine points of chess etiquette. Keep captured men in neat rows, as well-tended prisoners. Never announce "Check"[8] with vanity, lest someone with an unseen sword slit your throat. Never hurl pieces into the sandbox after you have lost a game, because then you must find them again, by yourself, after apologizing to all around you. By the end of the summer, Lau Po had taught me all he knew, and I had become a better chess player.

A small weekend crowd of Chinese people and tourists would gather as I played and defeated my opponents one by one. My mother would join the crowds during these outdoor exhibition games.[9] She sat proudly on the bench, telling my admirers with proper Chinese humility, "Is luck." **G**

A man who watched me play in the park suggested that my mother allow me to play in local chess tournaments. My mother smiled graciously, an answer that meant nothing. I desperately wanted to go, but I bit back my tongue. I knew she would not let me play among strangers. So as we walked home I said in a small voice that I didn't want to play in the local tournament. They would have American rules. If I lost, I would bring shame on my family. **H**

"Is shame you fall down nobody push you," said my mother.

During my first tournament, my mother sat with me in the front row as I waited for my turn. I frequently bounced my legs to unstick them from the cold metal seat of the folding chair. When my name was called, I leapt up. My mother unwrapped something in her lap. It was her *chang,* a small tablet of red jade which held the sun's fire. "Is luck," she whispered, and tucked it into my dress pocket. I turned to my opponent, a fifteen-year-old boy from Oakland. He looked at me, wrinkling his nose.

As I began to play, the boy disappeared, the color ran out of the room, and I saw only my white pieces and his black ones waiting on the other side. A light wind began blowing past my ears. It whispered secrets only I could hear.

"Blow from the South," it murmured. "The wind leaves no trail." I saw a clear path, the traps to avoid. The crowd rustled. "Shhh! Shhh!" said the corners of the room. The wind blew stronger. "Throw sand from the East to distract him." The knight came forward ready for the sacrifice. The wind hissed, louder and louder. "Blow, blow, blow. He cannot see. He is blind now. Make him lean away from the wind so he is easier to knock down."

"Check," I said, as the wind roared with laughter. The wind died down to little puffs, my own breath.

My mother placed my first trophy next to a new plastic chess set that the neighborhood Tao society had given to me. As she wiped each piece with a soft cloth, she said, "Next time win more, lose less."

"Ma, it's not how many pieces you lose," I said. "Sometimes you need to lose pieces to get ahead."

G DRAW CONCLUSIONS
Why does Waverly start winning more chess games?

H POINT OF VIEW
Reread lines 208–211. How are Waverly's thoughts and words different from each other? What does this tell you about her?

---

8. **check:** a move in chess that places an opponent's king under direct attack.

9. **exhibition games:** public showings or demonstrations.

"Better to lose less, see if you really need."

At the next tournament, I won again, but it was my mother who wore the triumphant grin.

"Lost eight pieces this time. Last time was eleven. What I tell you? Better
240 off lose less!" I was annoyed, but I couldn't say anything. **❶**

I attended more tournaments, each one farther away from home. I won all games, in all divisions. The Chinese bakery downstairs from our flat displayed my growing collection of trophies in its window, amidst the dust-covered cakes that were never picked up. The day after I won an important regional tournament, the window encased a fresh sheet cake with whipped-cream frosting and red script saying, "Congratulations, Waverly Jong, Chinatown Chess Champion." Soon after that, a flower shop, headstone engraver, and funeral parlor offered to sponsor me in national tournaments. That's when my mother decided I no longer had to do the dishes. Winston and Vincent had to do my chores.

250 "Why does she get to play and we do all the work?" complained Vincent.

"Is new American rules," said my mother. "Meimei play, squeeze all her brains out for win chess. You play, worth squeeze towel."

By my ninth birthday, I was a national chess champion. I was still some 429 points away from grand-master status, but I was touted as the Great American Hope, a child prodigy and a girl to boot. They ran a photo of me in *Life* magazine next to a quote in which Bobby Fischer[10] said, "There will never be a woman grand master." "Your move, Bobby," said the caption.

The day they took the magazine picture I wore neatly plaited braids clipped with plastic barrettes trimmed with rhinestones. I was playing in a large high
260 school auditorium that echoed with phlegmy coughs and the squeaky rubber knobs of chair legs sliding across freshly waxed wooden floors. Seated across from me was an American man, about the same age as Lau Po, maybe fifty. I remember that his sweaty brow seemed to weep at my every move. He wore a dark, **malodorous** suit. One of his pockets was stuffed with a great white kerchief on which he wiped his palm before sweeping his hand over the chosen chess piece with great flourish.

In my crisp pink-and-white dress with scratchy lace at the neck, one of two my mother had sewn for these special occasions, I would clasp my hands under my chin, the delicate points of my elbows poised lightly on the table in the
270 manner my mother had shown me for posing for the press. I would swing my patent leather shoes back and forth like an impatient child riding on a school bus. Then I would pause, suck in my lips, twirl my chosen piece in midair as if undecided, and then firmly plant it in its new threatening place, with a triumphant smile thrown back at my opponent for good measure.

I no longer played in the alley of Waverly Place. I never visited the playground where the pigeons and old men gathered. I went to school, then directly home to learn new chess secrets, cleverly concealed advantages, more escape routes.

---

10. **Bobby Fischer:** a well-known chess player who, at 15, was the world's youngest grand master.

❶ DRAW CONCLUSIONS
Why does Waverly feel she can't correct her mother?

Language Coach

Informal Language In the dialogue in lines 251–252, notice grammatical errors such as missing pronouns and verbs that do not agree with their subjects. The author intentionally included these errors to reflect Mrs. Jong's struggle with the English language. Rewrite the dialogue in standard English.

malodorous
(măl-ō'dər-əs) *adj.*
having a bad odor

But I found it difficult to concentrate at home. My mother had a habit of standing over me while I plotted out my games. I think she thought of herself as my protective ally. Her lips would be sealed tight, and after each move I made, a soft "Hmmmmph" would escape from her nose.

"Ma, I can't practice when you stand there like that," I said one day. She retreated to the kitchen and made loud noises with the pots and pans. When the crashing stopped, I could see out of the corner of my eye that she was standing in the doorway. "Hmmmph!" Only this one came out of her tight throat. **J**

My parents made many **concessions** to allow me to practice. One time I complained that the bedroom I shared was so noisy that I couldn't think. Thereafter, my brothers slept in a bed in the living room facing the street. I said I couldn't finish my rice; my head didn't work right when my stomach was too full. I left the table with half-finished bowls and nobody complained. But there was one duty I couldn't avoid. I had to accompany my mother on Saturday market days when I had no tournament to play. My mother would proudly walk with me, visiting many shops, buying very little. "This my daughter Wave-ly Jong," she said to whoever looked her way.

One day, after we left a shop I said under my breath, "I wish you wouldn't do that, telling everybody I'm your daughter." My mother stopped walking. Crowds of people with heavy bags pushed past us on the sidewalk, bumping into first one shoulder, then another.

"Aiii-ya. So shame be with mother?" She grasped my hand even tighter as she glared at me.

I looked down. "It's not that, it's just so obvious. It's just so embarrassing."

"Embarrass you be my daughter?" Her voice was cracking with anger.

"That's not what I meant. That's not what I said."

"What you say?"

I knew it was a mistake to say anything more, but I heard my voice speaking. "Why do you have to use me to show off? If you want to show off, then why don't you learn to play chess." **K**

My mother's eyes turned into dangerous black slits. She had no words for me, just sharp silence.

I felt the wind rushing around my hot ears. I jerked my hand out of my mother's tight grasp and spun around, knocking into an old woman. Her bag of groceries spilled to the ground.

"Aii-ya! Stupid girl!" my mother and the woman cried. Oranges and tin cans careened down the sidewalk. As my mother stooped to help the old woman pick up the escaping food, I took off.

I raced down the street, dashing between people, not looking back as my mother screamed shrilly, "Meimei! Meimei!" I fled down an alley, past dark curtained shops and merchants washing the grime off their windows. I sped into the sunlight, into a large street crowded with tourists examining trinkets and souvenirs. I ducked into another dark alley, down another street, up another alley. I ran until it hurt and I realized I had nowhere to go, that I was not running from anything. The alleys contained no escape routes.

J POINT OF VIEW
Reread lines 278–285. How does knowing only Waverly's point of view affect your impression of her mother?

concession (kən-sĕsh′ən) *n.* the act of yielding or conceding

K DRAW CONCLUSIONS
Why is Waverly embarrassed by her mother's behavior?

My breath came out like angry smoke. It was cold. I sat down on an upturned plastic pail next to a stack of empty boxes, cupping my chin with my hands, thinking hard. I imagined my mother, first walking briskly down one street or another looking for me, then giving up and returning home to await my arrival. After two hours, I stood
330 up on creaking legs and slowly walked home.

The alley was quiet and I could see the yellow lights shining from our flat like two tiger's eyes in the night. I climbed the sixteen steps to the door, advancing quietly up each so as not to make any warning sounds. I turned the knob; the door was locked. I heard a chair moving, quick steps, the locks turning—click! click! click!—and then the door opened.

"About time you got home," said Vincent.
340 "Boy, are you in trouble."

He slid back to the dinner table. On a platter were the remains of a large fish, its fleshy head still connected to bones swimming upstream in vain escape. Standing there waiting for my punishment, I heard my mother speak in a dry voice.

"We not concerning this girl. This girl not have concerning for us."

Nobody looked at me. Bone chopsticks clinked against the insides of bowls being emptied into hungry mouths.

I walked into my room, closed the door, and lay down on my bed. The
350 room was dark, the ceiling filled with shadows from the dinnertime lights of neighboring flats.

In my head, I saw a chessboard with sixty-four black and white squares. Opposite me was my opponent, two angry black slits. She wore a triumphant smile. "Strongest wind cannot be seen," she said.

Her black men advanced across the plane, slowly marching to each successive level as a single unit. My white pieces screamed as they scurried and fell off the board one by one. As her men drew closer to my edge, I felt myself growing light. I rose up into the air and flew out the window. Higher and higher, above the alley, over the tops of tiled roofs, where I was gathered up
360 by the wind and pushed up toward the night sky until everything below me disappeared and I was alone.

I closed my eyes and **pondered** my next move. ◥

▲ **Analyze Visuals**
What is the **mood** of this photograph?

L VISUALIZE
Reread lines 331–338. What **images** help you picture Waverly's walk home?

ponder (pŏn´dər) *v.* to think or consider carefully

Comprehension

1. **Recall** How does Waverly's family get a chess set?

2. **Clarify** What does Waverly learn from the old man in the park?

3. **Clarify** What events cause Waverly to run away from her mother at the market?

COMMON CORE

RL 1 Cite textual evidence to support inferences drawn from the text. RL 6 Analyze how differences in the points of view of the characters and the audience or reader create effects.

Text Analysis

4. **Visualize** What scene in this story can you picture most vividly? Reread that part of the selection, noting at least three words or phrases that help you visualize the people, places, or events.

5. **Compare and Contrast** Use a Venn diagram like the one shown to compare and contrast Waverly before she learns chess and after she learns chess. How does she change? How does she stay the same?

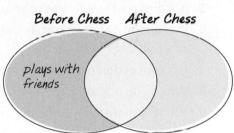

Before Chess   After Chess

plays with friends

6. **Analyze First-Person Point of View** How would "Rules of the Game" be different if you knew what Waverly's mother was thinking?

7. **Draw Conclusions** Review the chart you made as you read. Why does Waverly view her mother as her opponent? Use evidence from the story and your own ideas to support your conclusion.

8. **Evaluate Conflict** Give one or two reasons why Waverly and her mother might be in conflict with each other. Do you think they treat each other fairly? Explain.

Extension and Challenge

9. **Text Criticism** Amy Tan once mentioned in an interview that even though "Rules of the Game" is fiction and she never played chess, it is the closest she has come to describing her own life with her mother. She spoke of the "invisible force" her mother taught her. Tan uses the image of the wind throughout the story to represent this invisible force. Look for specific passages in the story in which Tan writes about the wind. With a small group, discuss the wind's effect on Waverly and her chess game.

10. **SOCIAL STUDIES CONNECTION** What challenges did Chinese immigrants face when they moved to the United States in the 1940s and 1950s, as Waverly's mother probably did? Research what it was like for newly arrived people to find jobs and housing and how the government responded to immigration from China. Share your findings with the class.

Can allies be OPPONENTS?

Do you think that Waverly and her mother will soon end their quarrel and become allies again? Why or why not?

Vocabulary in Context

▲ VOCABULARY PRACTICE

Answer each question to show your understanding of the vocabulary words.

adversary · malodorous · benefactor · ponder · concession · pungent · foresight · retort · impart · tactic

1. Is a **retort** a high-pitched sound or a sharp reply?
2. When you **ponder,** do you think carefully or wander around a pond?
3. Which is an **adversary**—an opponent or an advisor?
4. Would a **tactic** help you more in playing sports or watching a movie?
5. Is a **pungent** smell faint or sharp?
6. If a person has **foresight,** is she likely to make a mistake or avoid one?
7. Is a **concession** more like giving in or letting loose?
8. When you **impart** something, do you hide it or reveal it?
9. What is more likely to be **malodorous**—flowers or garbage?
10. Is a **benefactor** someone who gives money or takes it away?

ACADEMIC VOCABULARY IN SPEAKING

· appropriate · assess · intelligence · motive · role

Is it **appropriate** for Mrs. Jong to show off her daughter in public? Explain why or why not in a paragraph in a discussion with your classmates. Use at least one of the Academic Vocabulary words in your response.

VOCABULARY STRATEGY: THE PREFIXES *fore-* AND *mal-*

The prefixes *fore-* and *mal-* are used in the vocabulary words *foresight* and *malodorous.* The prefix *fore-* means "in front" or "before," and the prefix *mal-* means "bad" or "badly."

PRACTICE Decide which prefix, *fore-* or *mal-,* should be added to each word to make it match the definition provided.

1. _____ **cast:** to predict the weather conditions in advance
2. _____ **content:** dissatisfied with existing conditions
3. _____ **function:** to function improperly
4. _____ **arm:** part of the arm between the wrist and elbow
5. _____ **word:** a preface or introductory note in a book
6. _____ **practice:** improper treatment of a patient

COMMON CORE

L 4b Use common, grade-appropriate affixes as clues to the meaning of a word.
L 6 Acquire and use accurately academic words; gather vocabulary knowledge when considering a word important to comprehension and expression.

Interactive Vocabulary **THINK** central

Go to thinkcentral.com.
KEYWORD: HML8-244

Language

◆ **GRAMMAR IN CONTEXT: Use Verb Moods**

COMMON CORE

L 1c Form and use verbs in the indicative, imperative, interrogative, conditional, and subjunctive mood.

Review the **Grammar in Context** note on page 236. The **mood** of a verb conveys the status of the action or condition it describes. The five possible moods of a verb are indicative, imperative, interrogative, conditional, and subjunctive.

The **indicative** mood is used to make a statement.

> *Example:* Waverly **plays** chess.

The **imperative** mood is used to make a command or a request.

> *Example:* **Play** chess.

The **interrogative** mood is used to ask a question.

> *Example:* **Will** you **take** your turn already?

The **conditional** mood is used to refer to an event that may or may not happen depending on another set of circumstances. It uses *would, could,* or *should.*

> *Example:* If she lost the tournament, she **would bring** shame to her family.

The **subjunctive** mood is used to express a wish or recommendation, an imaginary state, or a condition contrary to fact. The subjunctive form is identical to the past form. The subjunctive of *be* is *were*—even when the subject is singular.

> *Examples:* She wished she **were** a better player.
> As if it **were** the wind, her mind **would whisper** chess strategies.
> As if Waverly **were** not there, everyone just ignored her.

PRACTICE Identify the mood of the boldfaced verbs in the following sentences.

1. Waverly **learns** the rules of chess.
2. "**Want to play?**" she asks Lau Po.
3. After that, if she came to the park, Lau Po **would play** with her.
4. As if she **were** the chess champion, Mrs. Jong **would swell** with pride.
5. Waverly's mother tells her, "Next time, **win** more, **lose** less."

READING-WRITING CONNECTION

Explore Mrs. Jong's thoughts and feelings by responding to this prompt. Then use the **revising tip** to improve your writing.

WRITING PROMPT	REVISING TIP
Extended Constructed Response: Point of View If Waverly's mother were telling the story, what might she say? In **two or three paragraphs**, retell from Waverly's mother's point of view the scenes in which Waverly runs away from the market and then returns home.	Review your response. Have you used the subjunctive mood? If not, revise.

Interactive Revision

THINK central

Go to thinkcentral.com.
KEYWORD: HML8N-245

The Medicine Bag

Video link at
thinkcentral.com

Short Story by Virginia Driving Hawk Sneve

Who Are You Today, María?

Vignette by Judith Ortiz Cofer

VIDEO TRAILER THINK central   KEYWORD: HML8-246

What shows others WHO we are?

COMMON CORE

RL1 Cite textual evidence to support inferences drawn from the text. RL3 Analyze how dialogue or incidents in a story reveal aspects of character.

The clothes we wear, the way we speak, and the traditions we follow are just a few of the ways we show others who we are. Our families and our heritage can also play important roles in shaping our identity, which is how we see ourselves and how we want others to see us. In the stories you are about to read, two young people must decide which parts of their identities they want to share with the world.

PICTURE IT Create a collage or drawing that reflects your identity. Think of ways to visually represent your background, the beliefs that are important you, and the meaningful activities and relationships in your life.

TEXT ANALYSIS: CENTRAL CHARACTER

Short stories usually focus on one **central character.** The plot and central conflict of the story generally revolve around this person. As you read each of the following stories, get to know the central character just as you would get to know a real person. Ask questions like these:

- Where does the character live, and how does that place affect him or her?

- With whom does the character have important relationships? What conflicts develop in these relationships?

- What is the character's social background or cultural heritage? How does the character feel about who he or she is?

READING STRATEGY: SET A PURPOSE FOR READING

In this lesson, your **purpose** for reading is to compare two central characters. As you read, begin filling in a chart like the one shown. You will be asked to add to this chart later.

	Martin	María
How does his or her environment affect him or her?		
What is his or her relationship with grandparent like?		
What is his or her attitude toward cultural heritage?		

VOCABULARY IN CONTEXT

The words in the box help tell two stories of family relationships. Match each numbered word or phrase with a vocabulary word.

WORD LIST	authentic	conspiracy	sheepishly
	commotion	descendant	unseemly

1. excitement
2. improper
3. son or daughter
4. not fake
5. scheme
6. timidly

Complete the activities in your **Reader/Writer Notebook.**

Virginia Driving Hawk Sneve
born 1933

Sioux Storyteller
Born at the height of the Great Depression, Virginia Driving Hawk Sneve grew up on the Rosebud Sioux reservation in South Dakota. Since her parents often had to leave the reservation to find work, Sneve spent a great deal of time with her grandmothers, whose tales inspired many of her books. Sneve has said that her goal in writing is to present accurate portrayals of Native American life. "The Medicine Bag" describes a tradition in which Native American boys create medicine bags, small pouches that hold items of religious significance and that symbolize the wearer's transition to adulthood.

Judith Ortiz Cofer
born 1952

A Rich Identity
Judith Ortiz Cofer was born in Puerto Rico, but she spent much of her childhood in New Jersey after her father joined the U.S. Navy. When her father was at sea, the family returned to Puerto Rico for extended visits with Cofer's grandmother. At times, Cofer felt that she did not fit in either culture— American or Puerto Rican. She uses her writing to explore the difficulties and rewards of her dual identity.

Authors Online
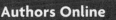
Go to **thinkcentral.com**. KEYWORD: HML8-247

The Medicine Bag

Virginia Driving Hawk Sneve

My kid sister Cheryl and I always bragged about our Sioux grandpa, Joe Iron Shell. Our friends, who had always lived in the city and only knew about Indians from movies and TV, were impressed by our stories. Maybe we exaggerated and made Grandpa and the reservation sound glamorous, but when we'd return home to Iowa after our yearly summer visit to Grandpa we always had some exciting tale to tell.

We always had some **authentic** Sioux article to show our listeners. One year Cheryl had new moccasins that Grandpa had made. On another visit he gave me a small, round, flat, rawhide drum which was decorated with a painting of
10 a warrior riding a horse. He taught me a real Sioux chant to sing while I beat the drum with a leather-covered stick that had a feather on the end. Man, that really made an impression. **A**

We never showed our friends Grandpa's picture. Not that we were ashamed of him, but because we knew that the glamorous tales we told didn't go with the real thing. Our friends would have laughed at the picture, because Grandpa wasn't tall and stately like TV Indians. His hair wasn't in braids, but hung in stringy, gray strands on his neck and he was old. He was our great-grandfather, and he didn't live in a tipi, but all by himself in a part log, part tar-paper shack on the Rosebud Reservation in South Dakota. So when Grandpa
20 came to visit us, I was so ashamed and embarrassed I could've died.

There are a lot of yippy poodles and other fancy little dogs in our neighborhood, but they usually barked singly at the mailman from the safety of their own yards. Now it sounded as if a whole pack of mutts were barking together in one place. **B**

Analyze Visuals ▶

What **details** of the man's face tell you the most about him?

authentic (ô-thĕn′tĭk) *adj.* having a verifiable origin; not counterfeit

A CENTRAL CHARACTER
Why did the narrator and his sister exaggerate when they talked about their grandfather?

B CENTRAL CHARACTER
What **conclusions** can you draw about the narrator's neighborhood?

Detail of *They Moved Them* (1991), David Behrens.
Oil glazing, 9¼″ × 14½″. © David Behrens.

I got up and walked to the curb to see what the **commotion** was. About a block away I saw a crowd of little kids yelling, with the dogs yipping and growling around someone who was walking down the middle of the street.

I watched the group as it slowly came closer and saw that in the center of the strange procession was a man wearing a tall black hat. He'd pause now and 30 then to peer at something in his hand and then at the houses on either side of the street. I felt cold and hot at the same time as I recognized the man. "Oh, no!" I whispered. "It's Grandpa!"

I stood on the curb, unable to move even though I wanted to run and hide. Then I got mad when I saw how the yippy dogs were growling and nipping at the old man's baggy pant legs and how wearily he poked them away with his cane. "Stupid mutts," I said as I ran to rescue Grandpa.

When I kicked and hollered at the dogs to get away, they put their tails between their legs and scattered. The kids ran to the curb where they watched me and the old man.

40 "Grandpa," I said and felt pretty dumb when my voice cracked. I reached for his beat-up old tin suitcase, which was tied shut with a rope. But he set it down right in the street and shook my hand.

"*Hau,*[1] *Takoza,* Grandchild," he greeted me formally in Sioux.

All I could do was stand there with the whole neighborhood watching and shake the hand of the leather-brown old man. I saw how his gray hair straggled from under his big black hat, which had a drooping feather in its crown. His rumpled black suit hung like a sack over his stooped frame. As he shook my hand, his coat fell open to expose a bright-red, satin shirt with a beaded bolo tie under the collar. His getup wasn't out of place on the reservation, but it sure 50 was here, and I wanted to sink right through the pavement. **C**

"Hi," I muttered with my head down. I tried to pull my hand away when I felt his bony hand trembling, and looked up to see fatigue in his face. I felt like crying. I couldn't think of anything to say so I picked up Grandpa's suitcase, took his arm, and guided him up the driveway to our house.

Mom was standing on the steps. I don't know how long she'd been watching, but her hand was over her mouth and she looked as if she couldn't believe what she saw. Then she ran to us.

"Grandpa," she gasped. "How in the world did you get here?"

She checked her move to embrace Grandpa and I remembered that such 60 a display of affection is **unseemly** to the Sioux and would embarrass him.

"*Hau,* Marie," he said as he shook Mom's hand. She smiled and took his other arm.

As we supported him up the steps the door banged open and Cheryl came bursting out of the house. She was all smiles and was so obviously glad to see Grandpa that I was ashamed of how I felt.

"Grandpa!" she yelled happily. "You came to see us!"

---

1. *Hau Sioux:* hello.

commotion (kə-mō′shən)
n. a disturbance

SOCIAL STUDIES CONNECTION

The Rosebud Reservation in South Dakota

C CENTRAL CHARACTER
How does Martin feel about his grandfather's outfit?

unseemly (ŭn-sēm′lē)
adj. inappropriate

Grandpa smiled and Mom and I let go of him as he stretched out his arms to my 10-year-old sister, who was still young enough to be hugged.

"*Wicincala*,[2] little girl," he greeted her and then collapsed.

70 He had fainted. Mom and I carried him into her sewing room, where we had a spare bed.

After we had Grandpa on the bed Mom stood there helplessly patting his shoulder.

"Shouldn't we call the doctor, Mom?" I suggested, since she didn't seem to know what to do.

"Yes," she agreed with a sigh. "You make Grandpa comfortable, Martin."

I reluctantly moved to the bed. I knew Grandpa wouldn't want to have Mom undress him, but I didn't want to, either. He was so skinny and frail that his coat slipped off easily. When I loosened his tie and opened his shirt collar,
80 I felt a small leather pouch that hung from a thong around his neck. I left it alone and moved to remove his boots. The scuffed old cowboy boots were tight and he moaned as I put pressure on his legs to jerk them off. **D**

I put the boots on the floor and saw why they fit so tight. Each one was stuffed with money. I looked at the bills that lined the boots and started to ask about them, but Grandpa's eyes were closed again.

Mom came back with a basin of water. "The doctor thinks Grandpa is suffering from heat exhaustion," she explained as she bathed Grandpa's face. Mom gave a big sigh, "*Oh hinh*, Martin. How do you suppose he got here?"

We found out after the doctor's visit. Grandpa was angrily sitting up in bed
90 while Mom tried to feed him some soup.

"Tonight you let Marie feed you, Grandpa," spoke my dad, who had gotten home from work just as the doctor was leaving. "You're not really sick," he said as he gently pushed Grandpa back against the pillows. "The doctor said you just got too tired and hot after your long trip."

Grandpa relaxed, and between sips of soup, he told us of his journey. Soon after our visit to him Grandpa decided that he would like to see where his only living **descendants** lived and what our home was like. Besides, he admitted **sheepishly**, he was lonesome after we left.

I knew everybody felt as guilty as I did—especially Mom. Mom was all
100 Grandpa had left. So even after she married my dad, who's a white man and teaches in the college in our city, and after Cheryl and I were born, Mom made sure that every summer we spent a week with Grandpa.

I never thought that Grandpa would be lonely after our visits, and none of us noticed how old and weak he had become. But Grandpa knew and so he came to us. He had ridden on buses for two and a half days. When he arrived in the city, tired and stiff from sitting for so long, he set out, walking, to find us. **E**

He had stopped to rest on the steps of some building downtown and a policeman found him. The cop, according to Grandpa, was a good man who

D CENTRAL CHARACTER
Reread lines 77–82. Which details in these lines indicate that Martin is uneasy around his grandfather?

descendant (dĭ-sĕn'dənt) *n.* a person whose descent can be traced to an individual or group

sheepishly (shē'pĭsh-lē) *adv.* meekly; with embarrassment

E CENTRAL CHARACTER
Reread lines 99–106. What do you learn about Martin's relationship with his grandfather?

---

2. *Wicincala* Sioux: girl.

took him to the bus stop and waited until the bus came and told the driver to
110 let Grandpa out at Bell View Drive. After Grandpa got off the bus, he started
walking again. But he couldn't see the house numbers on the other side when
he walked on the sidewalk so he walked in the middle of the street. That's
when all the little kids and dogs followed him.

I knew everybody felt as bad as I did. Yet I was proud of this 86-year-old
man, who had never been away from the reservation, having the courage to
travel so far alone. **F**

"You found the money in my boots?" he asked Mom.

"Martin did," she answered, and roused herself to scold. "Grandpa, you
shouldn't have carried so much money. What if someone had stolen it from you?"

120 Grandpa laughed. "I would've known if anyone tried to take the boots off
my feet. The money is what I've saved for a long time—a hundred dollars—for
my funeral. But you take it now to buy groceries so that I won't be a burden to
you while I am here."

"That won't be necessary, Grandpa," Dad said. "We are honored to
have you with us and you will never be a burden. I am only sorry that we
never thought to bring you home with us this summer and spare you the
discomfort of a long trip."

Grandpa was pleased. "Thank you," he answered. "But do not feel bad
that you didn't bring me with you for I would not have come then. It was
130 not time." He said this in such a way that no one could argue with him. To
Grandpa and the Sioux, he once told me, a thing would be done when it was
the right time to do it and that's the way it was.

"Also," Grandpa went on, looking at me, "I have come because it is soon
time for Martin to have the medicine bag."

We all knew what that meant. Grandpa thought he was going to die and he
had to follow the tradition of his family to pass the medicine bag, along with
its history, to the oldest male child.

"Even though the boy," he said still looking at me, "bears a white man's
name, the medicine bag will be his."

140 I didn't know what to say. I had the same hot and cold feeling that I had
when I first saw Grandpa in the street. The medicine bag was the dirty
leather pouch I had found around his neck. "I could never wear such a
thing," I almost said aloud. I thought of having my friends see it in gym
class, at the swimming pool, and could imagine the smart things they would
say. But I just swallowed hard and took a step toward the bed. I knew I
would have to take it. **G**

But Grandpa was tired. "Not now, Martin," he said, waving his hand in
dismissal, "it is not time. Now I will sleep."

So that's how Grandpa came to be with us for two months. My friends kept
150 asking to come see the old man, but I put them off. I told myself that I didn't
want them laughing at Grandpa. But even as I made excuses I knew it wasn't
Grandpa that I was afraid they'd laugh at.

F CENTRAL CHARACTER
What is Martin's attitude toward his grandfather's journey?

G CENTRAL CHARACTER
How does Martin feel about receiving the medicine bag?

Nothing bothered Cheryl about bringing her friends to see Grandpa. Every day after school started there'd be a crew of giggling little girls or round-eyed little boys crowded around the old man on the patio, where he'd gotten in the habit of sitting every afternoon.

Grandpa would smile in his gentle way and patiently answer their questions, or he'd tell them stories of brave warriors, ghosts, animals, and the kids listened in awed silence. Those little guys thought Grandpa was great.

160 Finally, one day after school, my friends came home with me because nothing I said stopped them. "We're going to see the great Indian of Bell View Drive," said Hank, who was supposed to be my best friend. "My brother has seen him three times so he oughta be well enough to see us." **H**

When we got to my house Grandpa was sitting on the patio. He had on his red shirt, but today he also wore a fringed leather vest that was decorated with beads. Instead of his usual cowboy boots he had solidly beaded moccasins on his feet that stuck out of his black trousers. Of course, he had his old black hat on—he was seldom without it. But it had been brushed and the feather in the beaded headband was proudly erect, its tip a brighter white. His hair lay in

170 silver strands over the red shirt collar.

I stared just as my friends did and I heard one of them murmur, "Wow!"

Grandpa looked up and when his eyes met mine they twinkled as if he were laughing inside. He nodded to me and my face got all hot. I could tell that he had known all along I was afraid he'd embarrass me in front of my friends.

"*Hau, hoksilas,* boys," he greeted and held out his hand.

My buddies passed in a single file and shook his hand as I introduced them. They were so polite I almost laughed. "How, there, Grandpa," and even a "How-do-you-do, sir."

"You look fine, Grandpa," I said

180 as the guys sat on the lawn chairs or on the patio floor.

"*Hanh,* yes," he agreed. "When I woke up this morning it seemed the right time to dress in the good clothes. I knew that my grandson would be bringing his friends."

"You guys want some lemonade or something?" I offered. No one answered. They were listening to

190 Grandpa as he started telling how he'd killed the deer from which his vest was made.

Grandpa did most of the talking while my friends were there. I was so proud of him and amazed at how respectfully quiet my buddies

H **CENTRAL CHARACTER**
What bothers Martin about bringing his friends home to meet his grandfather?

▼ **Analyze Visuals**
Compare this picture of a medicine bag to the way you imagine the medicine bag in the story. How is it similar?

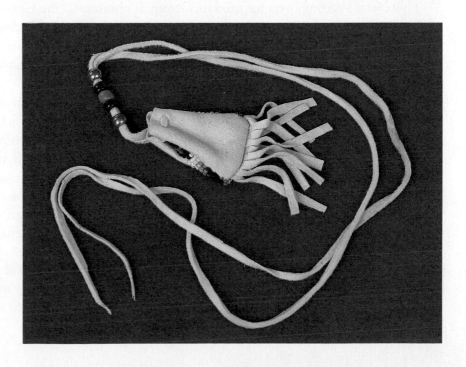

were. Mom had to chase them home at supper time. As they left they shook Grandpa's hand again and said to me:

"Martin, he's really great!"

200 "Yeah, man! Don't blame you for keeping him to yourself."

"Can we come back?" **I**

But after they left, Mom said, "No more visitors for a while, Martin. Grandpa won't admit it, but his strength hasn't returned. He likes having company, but it tires him."

That evening Grandpa called me to his room before he went to sleep. "Tomorrow," he said, "when you come home, it will be time to give you the medicine bag."

I felt a hard squeeze from where my heart is supposed to be and was scared, but I answered, "OK, Grandpa."

210 All night I had weird dreams about thunder and lightning on a high hill. From a distance I heard the slow beat of a drum. When I woke up in the morning I felt as if I hadn't slept at all. At school it seemed as if the day would never end and, when it finally did, I ran home. **J**

Grandpa was in his room, sitting on the bed. The shades were down and the place was dim and cool. I sat on the floor in front of Grandpa, but he didn't even look at me. After what seemed a long time he spoke.

"I sent your mother and sister away. What you will hear today is only for a man's ears. What you will receive is only for a man's hands." He fell silent and I felt shivers down my back.

220 "My father in his early manhood," Grandpa began, "made a vision quest to find a spirit guide for his life. You cannot understand how it was in that time, when the great Teton Sioux were first made to stay on the reservation. There was a strong need for guidance from *Wakantanka,* the Great Spirit. But too many of the young men were filled with despair and hatred. They thought it was hopeless to search for a vision when the glorious life was gone and only the hated confines of a reservation lay ahead. But my father held to the old ways.

"He carefully prepared for his quest with a purifying sweat bath and then he went alone to a high butte³ top to fast and pray. After three days he received 230 his sacred dream—in which he found, after long searching, the white man's iron. He did not understand his vision of finding something belonging to the white people, for in that time they were the enemy. When he came down from the butte to cleanse himself at the stream below, he found the remains of a campfire and the broken shell of an iron kettle. This was a sign which reinforced his dream. He took a piece of the iron for his medicine bag, which he had made of elk skin years before, to prepare for his quest.

"He returned to his village, where he told his dream to the wise old men of the tribe. They gave him the name *Iron Shell,* but neither did they understand the

I CENTRAL CHARACTER
Why is Martin proud of his grandfather?

J CENTRAL CHARACTER
How have Martin's feelings about receiving the medicine bag changed?

Language Coach

Etymology The history of a word is its etymology. The words *quest* and *question* both come from the Latin verb *quaerere,* which means "to ask or seek." Use this etymology and context clues to help you figure out the meaning of *quest* in line 220.

---

3. **butte** (byōōt): an abruptly rising hill with sloping sides and a flat top.

meaning of the dream. This first Iron Shell kept the piece of iron with him at all
240 times and believed it gave him protection from the evils of those unhappy days.

"Then a terrible thing happened to Iron Shell. He and several other young
men were taken from their homes by the soldiers and sent far away to a white
man's boarding school. He was angry and lonesome for his parents and the young
girl he had wed before he was taken away. At first Iron Shell resisted the teachers'
attempts to change him and he did not try to learn. One day it was his turn to
work in the school's blacksmith shop. As he walked into the place he knew that
his medicine had brought him there to learn and work with the white man's iron.

"Iron Shell became a blacksmith and worked at the trade when he returned to
the reservation. All of his life he treasured the medicine bag. When he was old,
250 and I was a man, he gave it to me, for no one made the vision quest any more."

Grandpa quit talking and I stared in disbelief as he covered his face with his
hands. His shoulders were shaking with quiet sobs and I looked away until he
began to speak again.

"I kept the bag until my son, your mother's father, was a man and had to
leave us to fight in the war across the ocean. I gave him the bag, for I believed
it would protect him in battle, but he did not take it with him. He was afraid
that he would lose it. He died in a faraway place." **K**

Again Grandpa was still and I felt his grief around me.

"My son," he went on after clearing his throat, "had only a daughter and it
260 is not proper for her to know of these things."

He unbuttoned his shirt, pulled out the leather pouch, and lifted it over his
head. He held it in his hand, turning it over and over as if memorizing how it
looked.

"In the bag," he said as he opened it and removed two objects, "is the
broken shell of the iron kettle, a pebble from the butte, and a piece of the
sacred sage." He held the pouch upside down and dust drifted down.

"After the bag is yours you must put a piece of prairie sage within and never
open it again until you pass it on to your son." He replaced the pebble and the
piece of iron and tied the bag.

270 I stood up, somehow knowing I should. Grandpa slowly rose from the bed
and stood upright in front of me holding the bag before my face. I closed my
eyes and waited for him to slip it over my head. But he spoke.

"No, you need not wear it." He placed the soft leather bag in my right hand
and closed my other hand over it. "It would not be right to wear it in this time
and place where no one will understand. Put it safely away until you are again
on the reservation. Wear it then, when you replace the sacred sage."

Grandpa turned and sat again on the bed. Wearily he leaned his head
against the pillow. "Go," he said. "I will sleep now."

"Thank you, Grandpa," I said softly and left with the bag in my hands.

280 That night Mom and Dad took Grandpa to the hospital. Two weeks later
I stood alone on the lonely prairie of the reservation and put the sacred sage
in my medicine bag. 〜 **L**

K CENTRAL
CHARACTER
What is Martin learning
about his heritage?

L CENTRAL
CHARACTER
What does Martin's
return to the reservation
suggest about his
attitude toward his
heritage?

Who Are You Today, María?

Judith Ortiz Cofer

Abuela[1] knocks on my bedroom door. She has come to my room this
morning to watch me choose my outfit for Who You Are Day at school.
This is a day when we are allowed to dress in clothes that we think tell the
world who we really are. (Within reason, our principal warned—no extremes
will be tolerated. I hope that her definition of the word *extreme* is the same as
my friend Whoopee's. Nothing that she will put on this morning has ever been
seen on this planet, much less at school.)

Abuela makes herself comfortable on my bed as I put on my costume of
myself made up of pieces of my life. I thought about my Who You Are Day
10 outfit a lot. Mr. Golden told us in English class to think about our choices:
are you going to walk around as a joke or as a poem? I have a suspicion that
our teachers have allowed us this chance to dress up as ourselves for a reason.
Our school is already a united nations, a carnival, and a parade all at once.
There are students from dozens of different countries, and we do not always
get along. Most of us are too shy to talk to others outside our little circles, and
so misunderstandings come up. The principal has tried almost everything.
The Who You Are Day is another of her crazy ideas to get us to communicate.
In each of my classes, the teacher said, let us know something about what has
made you who you are by what you wear to school tomorrow. It all sounds like
20 a **conspiracy** to me. But I like dressing up so I do not complain like the boys
have been doing. Most of them hate the idea! Ⓜ

Abuela looks at my choices hanging on the door and shakes her head,
smiling, like she did when we went to see *Cats*. It is a smile that says, I do not
understand, but if it is important to María, I will bear it the best I can. She is
elegant even at 7:00 A.M. in her embroidered silk robe and red velvet slippers.
She has wrapped a shawl over her shoulders because she is always cold in our
cueva,[2] as she calls the apartment. The shawl was handmade by her mother
and it is Abuela's most prized possession. As a little girl, I liked to put it over

---

Analyze Visuals ▶
Based on the **details**
in this painting, what
impression do you get
of the girl?

conspiracy
(kən-spîr′ə-sē) *n.* an
agreement to perform
together an illegal or
wrongful act

Ⓜ **CENTRAL
CHARACTER**
What can you **infer**
about the community in
which María lives?

---

1. **Abuela** (ä-bwā′lä) *Spanish:* grandmother.

2. *cueva* (kwâ′vä) *Spanish:* cave.

Frida (2004), María Sanchez.
Acrylic on canvas. C. Perez
Collection. © María Sanchez.

my head because the pattern of sequins made a night sky full of stars and
30 because it smelled like Abuela. **N**

Abuela sips from her cup of café con leche[3] as she watches me.

I feel a little strange about being in my underwear in front of her and go
in my closet with my choices, which are:

My mother's red skirt that she wore when she had a part in a musical play
on the Island. I have played dress-up with it since I was five years old, but it
finally fits me perfectly. It is the kind of skirt that opens like an umbrella when
you turn in circles.

A top I sewed together from an old sari[4] Uma's mother was going to throw
away. It is turquoise blue with silver edges.

40 And finally, over my sari, I will wear my father's sharkskin[5] suit jacket—it's
big on me but I can roll up the sleeves. It is what he likes to wear when he
sings at rent parties. Under the light, it changes colors and seems to come alive
as the design shifts and moves. Papi says it is great for dancing; you don't even
need a partner.

And finally, tall platform shoes we found buried deep in Whoopee's closet,
circa 1974, she told me. Whoopee collects antique shoes to go with her science
fiction outfits. It is a fashion statement; she will tell anyone who asks. No one
knows what the statement means, and that is just fine with Whoopee.

When I part the clothes in my closet and come out like an actor in a play,
50 Abuela's eyes open wide. Before she can say anything, I point to each piece of
my outfit and say a name: Mami, Papi, Uma, and Whoopee.

Abuela's face changes as she begins to understand the meaning of my
fashion statement.

"Ahora sé quién eres, María, y quién puedes ser, si quieres. Ven acá, mi amor."
Abuela says that she knows who I am and who I may be if I choose.
I have heard those words before but I don't remember when or where. Abuela
embraces me and kisses my face several times. This is a Puerto Rican thing.
It goes on for a while. I close my eyes to wait it out and I suddenly inhale a
familiar scent. When I open my eyes, I see a starry sky. Abuela has put her
60 shawl over my head.

"Algo mío para tu día de ser quien eres, mi hija," she tells me. *Something of
mine for your day of being who you are.* She is letting me borrow her mother's
beautiful shawl! **O**

All day at school, I feel elegant. Whenever anyone tries to make fun of my
costume, I think of the words my grandmother quoted to me: *I know who you
are and who you may be if you choose.* And when I go into Mr. Golden's class
and his eyes ask me, *Who are you today, María?* I will say by the way I walk in,
head held high, that today I am a poem. ❧

---

3. **café con leche** (kă-fā' kŏn lĕch'ā) *Spanish:* coffee with milk.
4. **sari** (sä'rē): a traditional Indian women's garment.
5. **sharkskin**: a synthetic fabric with a smooth, shiny surface.

N CENTRAL
CHARACTER
What can you
infer about María's
relationship with her
grandmother?

O CENTRAL
CHARACTER
Reread lines 55–63. What
is María's attitude toward
her grandmother's
Puerto Rican customs
and clothing?

Comprehension

1. **Recall** In "The Medicine Bag," why does Martin's grandfather come to visit?

2. **Recall** What does the medicine bag contain?

3. **Represent** Create a sketch of María in her Who You Are Day outfit. Make sure your sketch reflects the details in the selection.

Text Analysis

4. **Make Inferences** In "The Medicine Bag," how do Martin's mother, father, and sister each feel about Grandpa? Cite details from the story to support your answer.

● 5. **Draw Conclusions About a Central Character** How are Martin's feelings about his grandfather and his Sioux heritage affected by the kind of neighborhood he lives in?

6. **Interpret Ideas** In "Who Are You Today, María?" what do you think María's English teacher means in line 11 when he asks, "are you going to walk around as a joke or as a poem"?

● 7. **Compare and Contrast Characters** Compare Martin's relationship with Grandpa to María's relationship with Abuela. Which relationship creates more conflict within the central character? Explain.

8. **Analyze Theme** What message about identity does each story contain?

Comparing Characters

● 9. **Set a Purpose for Reading** Now that you've read both stories, finish filling in your chart. Then add the final question and answer it, too.

	Martin	María
How does his or her environment affect him or her?		
What is his or her relationship with grandparent like?		
What is his or her attitude toward cultural heritage?		
Does the character change in any way? Explain.		

What shows others **WHO** we are?

How has reading these two selections influenced your ideas about your own identity?

COMMON CORE

RL 1 Cite textual evidence to support inferences drawn from the text. **RL 3** Analyze how dialogue or incidents in a story reveal aspects of character.

Vocabulary in Context

▲ VOCABULARY PRACTICE

For each item, choose the word that differs most in meaning from the other words. Refer to a dictionary if you need help.

1. (a) uprising, (b) commotion, (c) calmness, (d) racket
2. (a) unseemly, (b) crude, (c) rude, (d) proper
3. (a) phony, (b) factual, (c) real, (d) authentic
4. (a) heir, (b) descendant, (c) parent, (d) child
5. (a) shyly, (b) self-consciously, (c) sheepishly, (d) boldly
6. (a) conspiracy, (b) loyalty, (c) plot, (d) trickery

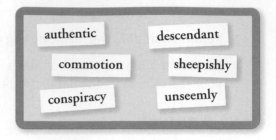

authentic   descendant
commotion   sheepishly
conspiracy   unseemly

ACADEMIC VOCABULARY IN WRITING

• appropriate   • assess   • intelligence   • motive   • role

What is Joe Iron Shell's **motive** for coming to visit Martin's family in Iowa? Write a paragraph in response to this question, using at least one of the Academic Vocabulary words.

VOCABULARY STRATEGY: ANALOGIES

An **analogy** is a relationship between pairs of words. To complete an analogy, identify the relationship between the words in the first pair. The second pair of words must relate to each other in the same way. For example, if the first pair describes a function, the second pair should also describe a function. If the first pair of words describes an object, the second pair should describe an object, too.

Analogies are often written as follows—pen : paper :: chalk : blackboard. If the analogy is read aloud, you would say, "pen **is to** paper **as** chalk **is to** blackboard."

PRACTICE Choose a word from the box to complete each analogy.

hard   slice   slippery   fasten

1. pebble : smooth :: oil : _____
2. scissors : cut :: stapler : _____
3. kitten: soft :: baseball : _____
4. wrench : tighten :: knife : _____

> **COMMON CORE**
>
> **L 5b** Use the relationship between particular words to better understand each of the words.
> **L 6** Acquire and use accurately academic words; gather vocabulary knowledge when considering a word important to comprehension and expression.

Interactive Vocabulary   **THINK** central

Go to **thinkcentral.com**.
KEYWORD: HML8-260

Writing for Assessment

COMMON CORE RL 1, W 9, W 9a

1. READ THE PROMPT

In writing assessments, you will often be asked to compare and contrast main characters from different selections.

> In four or five paragraphs, compare and contrast the main characters in "The Medicine Bag" and "Who Are You Today, María?" Consider the environments they came from, their relationships with their grandparents, and their attitudes toward their cultural heritage. In your conclusion, explain whether the characters change in any important ways. Support your response with details from the two stories.

◄ **STRATEGIES IN ACTION**

1. *I need to discuss the* **similarities and differences** *between the two characters.*

2. *I need to* **give examples** *to show how the characters' environments, relationships, and heritage are* **alike** *or* **different.**

3. *In the conclusion, I need to* **describe** *whether the characters change, and if so, how.*

2. PLAN YOUR WRITING

Review the chart you filled out on page 259. Use the chart to help you identify the characters' similarities and differences. Then think about how you will set up the body of your essay.

- Do you want to compare the characters' environments in one paragraph, relationships with their grandparents in the next paragraph, and attitudes toward their cultural heritage in a third paragraph?

- Do you want to describe the characters in separate paragraphs and then discuss their similarities and differences in a third paragraph?

Once you have decided on an organization, create an outline. Then write a thesis statement that describes the main idea or purpose of your essay.

> I. Introduction
> II. Environments they came from
> III. Relationships with grandparents
> IV. Attitudes toward cultural heritage
> V. Conclusion

3. DRAFT YOUR RESPONSE

Introduction Provide the titles and authors of both selections as well as a sentence telling what each is about. Include your thesis statement.

Body Discuss characters' similarities and differences, using your outline as a guide. Support your ideas with evidence from the text.

Conclusion Remind readers of your thesis statement. End by noting whether either character changed in any important way.

Revision Make sure your essay answers the question in the writing prompt.

from **Whale Rider**

Film Clip on **Media 🎞 Smart** DVD-ROM

What puts a
CHARACTER in focus?

COMMON CORE

RL 7 Analyze a filmed production, evaluating the choices made by the director or actors.

Think about your favorite fictional characters. What is it that draws you to them? Is it the things they say, the way they behave, the lives they lead? As you read about or watch these characters, perhaps you imagine how you would act if you were in their shoes. In this lesson, you'll view two clips from *Whale Rider* to explore the tools filmmakers use to create believable characters.

Background

Out with the Old In *Whale Rider,* a young native New Zealand girl named Paikea, or Pai, must challenge the old ways of her tribe to fulfill her destiny. For over 1,000 years, Paikea's tribe has been ruled by a male. The current chief is Koro, Paikea's grandfather. When Paikea's father refuses his rightful place as chief, Koro must decide who will take his place. Although Paikea is descended from the chief, Koro doesn't believe a girl can lead.

Koro starts a school to train the young men of the tribe in the old ways of their people. He will choose one among them to succeed him. You'll watch the conflict that arises between the determined Paikea and her stubborn grandfather when she tries to join the school.

Media Literacy: Characters in Movies

The best books and movies develop characters that feel like real people. You laugh with them and cry with them. You're drawn into their stories and you truly care what happens to them. An author provides detail and background through descriptive passages to develop his or her characters. A filmmaker has to rely on his or her camera work, the performances of the actors, and the skills of the film editor to create true-to-life characters.

FILMMAKING TECHNIQUES	STRATEGIES FOR VIEWING
Camera Shots • A **close-up shot** provides a detailed view of a person or object. • A **long shot** provides a wide view of a scene. It can show distance between characters and establish location. • A **reaction shot** shows a person react to what occurred in the previous shot.	• Notice how close-ups focus on facial expressions. Ask yourself what the character might be feeling. • Watch how long shots can reveal relationships. A shot of two people standing apart can show emotional distance. A long shot of one character can single him or her out from a group. • Watch for reaction shots. What does the character's response to an event say about his or her feelings?
Performance • **Physical appearance,** including height, weight, hairstyle, and clothing • **Behavior,** including **facial expressions** and **body language** • **Dialogue,** both what the character says and how he or she says it	• Pay attention to how a main character's appearance provides clues about his or her personality. • Watch a character's posture and facial expressions. These can convey feelings, reactions, or self-image. • Listen to the dialogue. Is the character's tone of voice happy, calm, or angry? What does speech reveal about a character's background and intelligence?
Editing **Editing** is the process of choosing and arranging shots in a sequence. Filmmakers combine the shots they've filmed to create an overall effect on the audience.	• Notice the different types of shots the editor uses. How do they reflect the emotion of the scene? • Watch for reaction shots that are edited into a scene. How do they reveal characters' thoughts and feelings? • Notice how long each shot stays on the screen. How does shot length change as emotion rises in a scene?

Viewing Guide for
Whale Rider

In these scenes, Koro, the chief, starts to teach the tribe's traditions to the boys of the village. You'll see what happens when Paikea attempts to join the school. As you watch, notice how the director's choice of shots, the actors' performances, and the editing work together to create memorable characters. Pay special attention to the techniques that are used when the emotion rises. Use the questions to analyze the scenes. You may want to view the clips more than once.

NOW VIEW

FIRST VIEWING: Comprehension

1. **Recall** Why doesn't Koro get angry when the boy hits him in the back with his stick?

2. **Clarify** Paikea doesn't say a single word to her grandfather in these scenes. How does she defy his wishes without speaking?

CLOSE VIEWING: Media Literacy

3. **Identify Film Technique** A **long shot** is used to show Paikea's loneliness when she walks away from the group in the beginning of these clips. Find another example from the clips of how the director separates Paikea from the group.

4. **Analyze Shots** Why do you think the director chose to show **reaction shots** of the grandmother when Paikea defies Koro?

5. **Analyze Editing** Even though these scenes are short, they cover several days in Paikea's life. Cite evidence from the clips that tell you the scenes took place over more than one day.

6. **Compare Characters** Even though Koro and Paikea are at odds throughout these scenes, they are similar in many ways. Compare the two characters by listing descriptive traits of each in a Venn diagram. As a starting point, think of the qualities of a chief that Koro mentions in the scenes: strength, courage, intelligence, and leadership.

Koro   Paikea

Both

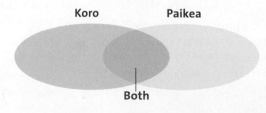

Write or Discuss

Evaluate Film In this lesson, you learned some of the techniques filmmakers use to create believable characters. Think about Paikea's predicament. She believes she can be a leader, but she has to defy her grandfather to prove it. Write a paragraph describing how the filmmaking techniques you learned were used in the scene. In your opinion, were the filmmakers successful in making Paikea into a believable character? Think about

- the types of shots the filmmakers use
- the appearance and performance of the actor playing Paikea
- the editing of the scene

Produce Your Own Media

Plan a Scene Imagine you're a movie director. You're planning a scene that is designed to show the relationship between two characters. Create a shot-by-shot description of a two-person scene. You can choose a scene from a story you've read or create your own. Your description should include a brief overall description of what happens in the scene, a list of shots describing what happens in each, and a sketch of each shot.

HERE'S HOW Use these tips to help you plan your scene:

- Remember that conflict drives a story. Consider creating a scene in which your two characters are in a disagreement.
- Include any dialogue that will be spoken in your description of each shot.
- Identify each type of shot you will use. **Close-up shots** are perfect for capturing facial expressions in **reaction shots. Long shots** work better for showing body language and distance between characters.

STUDENT MODEL

Scene description: Koro has called a tribe meeting. He tells Paikea to sit in the back because she is a girl. Paikea defies him, refusing to move to the back. Koro kicks her out of the meeting.

Long shot of Koro and other tribe members: Koro stands and says to Paikea, "What did I say?"

Close-up shot of Paikea: She refuses to move.

Reaction shot of Paikea's grandmother: She looks proudly on at Paikea's determined stand.

COMMON CORE

RL 7 Analyze a filmed production, evaluating the choices made by the director or actors. **W 3b** Use narrative techniques, such as dialogue, pacing, description, to develop events and characters.

Media Tools

THINK central

Go to **thinkcentral.com**.
KEYWORD: HML8-265

Tech Tip

If a camera is available, shoot photographs of your classmates acting out your scene in place of the sketches.

from **Harriet Tubman: Conductor on the Underground Railroad**

Biography by Ann Petry

When is a RISK worth taking?

COMMON CORE

RI 1 Cite the textual evidence that most strongly supports an analysis of what the text says explicitly. **RI 3** Analyze how a text makes connections between individuals, ideas, or events.

Some people risk their lives needlessly looking for a thrill. Others hold themselves back from accomplishment because they are afraid to take a chance. How can you be sure when it's right to put your safety or reputation on the line? In the biography you are about to read, you will meet a woman who took enormous risks to help others because she believed all people have the right to freedom.

QUICKWRITE Think about a time when you took a risk. In a brief paragraph, describe the risk and why you took it. What were the results? Looking back, was the risk worth taking?

● TEXT ANALYSIS: CHARACTERIZATION

Whether they are describing fictional characters or real people, skillful writers can make you feel as if you've met the person you're reading about. To bring figures to life in this way, writers use the following methods of **characterization:**

- describing the person's physical appearance
- presenting the person's own thoughts, speech, and actions
- revealing other people's reactions to the person
- directly commenting on the person

As you read, pay attention to the methods Ann Petry uses to create a portrait of the biography's subject, Harriet Tubman.

● READING STRATEGY: ASK QUESTIONS

Have you ever found yourself reading without fully understanding the words in front of you? If so, pause and ask yourself **questions** about confusing parts. When you read to find the answers, you will probably find that more information stays with you.

As you read this biography, take time to note places where you become confused or lose track of ideas. Use a chart like the one shown to record your questions and their answers.

My Questions	Answers
How does Harriet Tubman avoid getting caught?	

▲ VOCABULARY IN CONTEXT

The boldfaced words help Ann Petry tell about one of Harriet Tubman's journeys for freedom. Try to figure out what each word means in the context of its sentence.

1. After days of wear, his shirt was wrinkled and **disheveled.**
2. A good leader can **instill** a feeling of confidence in others.
3. Music can often **evoke** a pleasant memory.
4. Days on their feet made them long to **linger** at each stop.
5. She used clever stories to **cajole** them to take risks.
6. His **sullen** attitude discouraged others in the group.
7. Her positive attitude helped **dispel** their fears.
8. Her **eloquence** helped convince them to follow her.

Complete the activities in your **Reader/Writer Notebook.**

Meet the Author

Ann Petry
1908–1997

Making History Speak
The descendant of a runaway slave from Virginia, Ann Petry grew up in a comfortable middle-class household in Old Saybrook, Connecticut. Hers was the only African-American family in town. Despite her father's respected position as the town's pharmacist, Petry experienced racism growing up. Much of her writing describes the struggles of African Americans against prejudice in New England and in Harlem, where she moved in the 1930s. After Petry had a daughter of her own, she became interested in writing for young readers. In addition to her biography of Harriet Tubman, Petry wrote four other books for young people and four books for adults. She said that writing about the lives of real people helped her "make history speak across the centuries." She wanted to remind readers of the important contributions that African-American men and women have made to American history.

BACKGROUND TO THE BIOGRAPHY
The Underground Railroad
In the period before and during the Civil War, many people enslaved in the South fled north to freedom using a secret network of escape routes known as the Underground Railroad. The "conductors" on the Underground Railroad were brave men and women who provided the escaping people with food, hiding places, and guidance to the next "station." Harriet Tubman was one of the most famous of these conductors.

Author Online **THINK** central
Go to thinkcentral.com.
KEYWORD: HML8-267

Harriet Tubman:

CONDUCTOR ON THE UNDERGROUND RAILROAD

Ann Petry

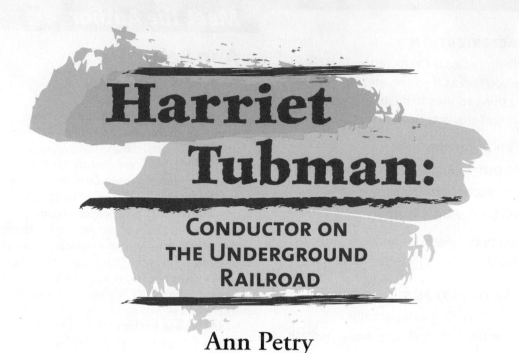

The Railroad Runs to Canada

Along the Eastern Shore of Maryland, in Dorchester County, in Caroline County, the masters kept hearing whispers about the man named Moses, who was running off slaves. At first they did not believe in his existence. The stories about him were fantastic, unbelievable. Yet they watched for him. They offered rewards for his capture. **A**

They never saw him. Now and then they heard whispered rumors to the effect that he was in the neighborhood. The woods were searched. The roads were watched. There was never anything to indicate his whereabouts. But a few days afterward, a goodly number of slaves would be gone from the

10 plantation. Neither the master nor the overseer had heard or seen anything unusual in the quarter.[1] Sometimes one or the other would vaguely remember having heard a whippoorwill call somewhere in the woods, close by, late at night. Though it was the wrong season for whippoorwills. **B**

Sometimes the masters thought they had heard the cry of a hoot owl, repeated, and would remember having thought that the intervals between the low moaning cry were wrong, that it had been repeated four times in succession instead of three. There was never anything more than that to suggest that all was not well in the quarter. Yet when morning came, they invariably discovered that a group of the finest slaves had taken to their heels.

20 Unfortunately, the discovery was almost always made on a Sunday. Thus a whole day was lost before the machinery of pursuit could be set in motion. The posters offering rewards for the fugitives could not be printed until Monday.

---

1. **quarter:** the area in which enslaved people lived.

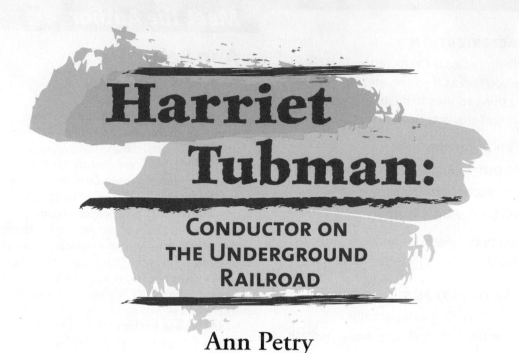

Analyze Visuals ▶
What **symbols** do you notice in this painting?

A ASK QUESTIONS
What are you wondering about Moses?

B CHARACTERIZATION
Reread lines 6–13. What does the author tell you about Moses' actions?

Harriet Tubman (1945), William H. Johnson. Oil on paperboard, sheet, 29⅜″ × 23⅜″. Smithsonian American Art Museum, Washington, D.C.

The men who made a living hunting for runaway slaves were out of reach, off in the woods with their dogs and their guns, in pursuit of four-footed game, or they were in camp meetings saying their prayers with their wives and families beside them. C

Harriet Tubman could have told them that there was far more involved in this matter of running off slaves than signaling the would-be runaways by imitating the call of a whippoorwill, or a hoot owl, far more involved than a matter of waiting for a clear night when the North Star was visible.

In December, 1851, when she started out with the band of fugitives that she planned to take to Canada, she had been in the vicinity of the plantation for days, planning the trip, carefully selecting the slaves that she would take with her.

She had announced her arrival in the quarter by singing the forbidden spiritual—"Go down, Moses, 'way down to Egypt Land"[2]—singing it softly outside the door of a slave cabin, late at night. The husky voice was beautiful even when it was barely more than a murmur borne[3] on the wind. D

Once she had made her presence known, word of her coming spread from cabin to cabin. The slaves whispered to each other, ear to mouth, mouth to ear,

---

2. **"Go down, Moses, 'way down to Egypt Land":** a line from an African-American folk song.

3. **borne:** carried.

C ASK QUESTIONS
Why does Moses choose Saturday night to help enslaved people escape?

D ASK QUESTIONS
What is Harriet Tubman's relationship to Moses?

▼ **Analyze Visuals**
Consider the colors, shapes, and figures in this painting. What **mood** do they convey?

Through Forest, Through Rivers, Up Mountains (1967), Jacob Lawrence. Tempera, gouache and pencil on paper, 15 11/16″ × 26⅞″. Smithsonian Institution, Hirshhorn Museum and Sculpture Garden. © 2007 The Jacob and Gwendolyn Lawrence Foundation, Seattle/Artists Rights Society (ARS), New York.

"Moses is here." "Moses has come." "Get ready. Moses is back again." The ones who had agreed to go North with her put ashcake and salt herring in an old bandanna, hastily tied it into a bundle, and then waited patiently for the signal that meant it was time to start.

There were eleven in this party, including one of her brothers and his wife. It was the largest group that she had ever conducted, but she was determined that more and more slaves should know what freedom was like.

She had to take them all the way to Canada. The Fugitive Slave Law[4] was no longer a great many incomprehensible words written down on the country's
50 lawbooks. The new law had become a reality. It was Thomas Sims, a boy, picked up on the streets of Boston at night and shipped back to Georgia. It was Jerry and Shadrach, arrested and jailed with no warning.

She had never been in Canada. The route beyond Philadelphia was strange to her. But she could not let the runaways who accompanied her know this. As they walked along she told them stories of her own first flight, she kept painting vivid word pictures of what it would be like to be free. **E**

But there were so many of them this time. She knew moments of doubt when she was half-afraid, and kept looking back over her shoulder, imagining that she heard the sound of pursuit. They would certainly be pursued. Eleven
60 of them. Eleven thousand dollars' worth of flesh and bone and muscle that belonged to Maryland planters. If they were caught, the eleven runaways would be whipped and sold South, but she—she would probably be hanged. ◆

They tried to sleep during the day but they never could wholly relax into sleep. She could tell by the positions they assumed, by their restless movements. And they walked at night. Their progress was slow. It took them three nights of walking to reach the first stop. She had told them about the place where they would stay, promising warmth and good food, holding these things out to them as an incentive to keep going. **F**

When she knocked on the door of a farmhouse, a place where she and her
70 parties of runaways had always been welcome, always been given shelter and plenty to eat, there was no answer. She knocked again, softly. A voice from within said, "Who is it?" There was fear in the voice.

She knew instantly from the sound of the voice that there was something wrong. She said, "A friend with friends," the password on the Underground Railroad.

The door opened, slowly. The man who stood in the doorway looked at her coldly, looked with unconcealed astonishment and fear at the eleven **disheveled** runaways who were standing near her. Then he shouted, "Too many, too many. It's not safe. My place was searched last week. It's not safe!"
80 and slammed the door in her face.

She turned away from the house, frowning. She had promised her passengers food and rest and warmth, and instead of that, there would be

---

4. **Fugitive Slave Law:** a law by which enslaved people who escaped could be recovered by their owners.

E CHARACTERIZATION
What do Tubman's words to the runaways tell you about her?

◆ GRAMMAR IN CONTEXT
Notice in line 61 that the author begins a sentence with the **dependent clause** "If they were caught."

F ASK QUESTIONS
What questions do you have about the journey?

disheveled (dĭ-shĕv′əld)
adj. messy; untidy

hunger and cold and more walking over the frozen ground. Somehow she would have to **instill** courage into these eleven people, most of them strangers, would have to feed them on hope and bright dreams of freedom instead of the fried pork and corn bread and milk she had promised them.

They stumbled along behind her, half-dead for sleep, and she urged them on, though she was as tired and as discouraged as they were. She had never been in Canada but she kept painting wondrous word pictures of what it would be like. She managed to **dispel** their fear of pursuit, so that they would not become hysterical, panic-stricken. Then she had to bring some of the fear back, so that they would stay awake and keep walking though they drooped with sleep.

Yet during the day, when they lay down deep in a thicket, they never really slept, because if a twig snapped or the wind sighed in the branches of a pine tree, they jumped to their feet, afraid of their own shadows, shivering and shaking. It was very cold, but they dared not make fires because someone would see the smoke and wonder about it.

She kept thinking, eleven of them. Eleven thousand dollars' worth of slaves. And she had to take them all the way to Canada. Sometimes she told them about Thomas Garrett, in Wilmington. She said he was their friend even though he did not know them. He was the friend of all fugitives. He called them God's poor. He was a Quaker[5] and his speech was a little different from that of other people. His clothing was different, too. He wore the wide-brimmed hat that the Quakers wear.

She said that he had thick white hair, soft, almost like a baby's, and the kindest eyes she had ever seen. He was a big man and strong, but he had never used his strength to harm anyone, always to help people. He would give all of them a new pair of shoes. Everybody. He always did. Once they reached his house in Wilmington, they would be safe. He would see to it that they were.

She described the house where he lived, told them about the store where he sold shoes. She said he kept a pail of milk and a loaf of bread in the drawer of his desk so that he would have food ready at hand for any of God's poor who should suddenly appear before him, fainting with hunger. There was a hidden room in the store. A whole wall swung open, and behind it was a room where he could hide fugitives. On the wall there were shelves filled with small boxes—boxes of shoes—so that you would never guess that the wall actually opened.

While she talked, she kept watching them. They did not believe her. She could tell by their expressions. They were thinking, New shoes, Thomas Garrett, Quaker, Wilmington—what foolishness was this? Who knew if she told the truth? Where was she taking them anyway?

That night they reached the next stop—a farm that belonged to a German. She made the runaways take shelter behind trees at the edge of the fields before she knocked at the door. She hesitated before she approached the door, thinking, suppose that he, too, should refuse shelter, suppose— Then she

instill (ĭn-stĭl′) *v.*
to supply gradually

dispel (dĭ-spĕl′) *v.*
to drive away

○ SOCIAL STUDIES
   CONNECTION

Free states
Slave states

In the years leading up to the Civil War, the United States was bitterly divided about slavery. Many enslaved people in the South escaped all the way to Canada to reach freedom.

---

5. **Quaker:** a member of a religious group called the Society of Friends.

thought, Lord, I'm going to hold steady on to You and You've got to see me through—and knocked softly. **G**

She heard the familiar guttural voice say, "Who's there?"

She answered quickly, "A friend with friends."

He opened the door and greeted her warmly. "How many this time?" he asked.

130 "Eleven," she said and waited, doubting, wondering.

He said, "Good. Bring them in."

He and his wife fed them in the lamplit kitchen, their faces glowing, as they offered food and more food, urging them to eat, saying there was plenty for everybody, have more milk, have more bread, have more meat.

They spent the night in the warm kitchen. They really slept, all that night and until dusk the next day. When they left, it was with reluctance. They had all been warm and safe and well-fed. It was hard to exchange the security offered by that clean warm kitchen for the darkness and the cold of a December night.

"Go On or Die"

140   **H**arriet had found it hard to leave the warmth and friendliness, too. But she urged them on. For a while, as they walked, they seemed to carry in them a measure of contentment; some of the serenity and the cleanliness of that big warm kitchen **lingered** on inside them. But as they walked farther and farther away from the warmth and the light, the cold and the darkness entered into them. They fell silent, **sullen,** suspicious. She waited for the moment when some one of them would turn mutinous. It did not happen that night.

    Two nights later she was aware that the feet behind her were moving slower and slower. She heard the irritability in their voices, knew that soon someone 150 would refuse to go on.

    She started talking about William Still and the Philadelphia Vigilance Committee.[6] No one commented. No one asked any questions. She told them the story of William and Ellen Craft and how they escaped from Georgia. Ellen was so fair that she looked as though she were white, and so she dressed up in a man's clothing and she looked like a wealthy young planter. Her husband, William, who was dark, played the role of her slave. Thus they traveled from Macon, Georgia, to Philadelphia, riding on the trains, staying at the finest hotels. Ellen pretended to be very ill—her right arm was in a sling, and her right hand was bandaged, because she was supposed to have 160 rheumatism. Thus she avoided having to sign the register at the hotels for she could not read or write. They finally arrived safely in Philadelphia, and then went on to Boston. **H**

    No one said anything. Not one of them seemed to have heard her.

G **CHARACTERIZATION**
What do Tubman's thoughts suggest about the way she deals with hardship?

linger (lĭng′gər) *v.* to remain or stay longer

sullen (sŭl′ən) *adj.* showing silent resentment; sulky

H **ASK QUESTIONS**
Why does Tubman tell stories of how other enslaved people escaped?

---

6. **Philadelphia Vigilance Committee:** fundraising organization that helped people who escaped enslavement.

She told them about Frederick Douglass,[7] the most famous of the escaped slaves, of his **eloquence,** of his magnificent appearance. Then she told them of her own first vain effort at running away, **evoking** the memory of that miserable life she had led as a child, reliving it for a moment in the telling.

But they had been tired too long, hungry too long, afraid too long, footsore too long. One of them suddenly cried out in despair, "Let me go back. It is 170 better to be a slave than to suffer like this in order to be free."

She carried a gun with her on these trips. She had never used it—except as a threat. Now as she aimed it, she experienced a feeling of guilt, remembering that time, years ago, when she had prayed for the death of Edward Brodas, the Master, and then not too long afterward had heard that great wailing cry that came from the throats of the field hands, and knew from the sound that the Master was dead.

One of the runaways said, again, "Let me go back. Let me go back," and stood still, and then turned around and said, over his shoulder, "I am going back."

She lifted the gun, aimed it at the despairing slave. She said, "Go on with us 180 or die." The husky low-pitched voice was grim. **❶**

He hesitated for a moment and then he joined the others. They started walking again. She tried to explain to them why none of them could go back to the plantation. If a runaway returned, he would turn traitor, the master and the overseer would force him to turn traitor. The returned slave would disclose the stopping places, the hiding places, the cornstacks they had used with the full knowledge of the owner of the farm, the name of the German farmer who had fed them and sheltered them. These people who had risked their own security to help runaways would be ruined, fined, imprisoned.

She said, "We got to go free or die. And freedom's not bought with dust." **❶**

190 This time she told them about the long agony of the Middle Passage[8] on the old slave ships, about the black horror of the holds, about the chains and the whips. They too knew these stories. But she wanted to remind them of the long hard way they had come, about the long hard way they had yet to go. She told them about Thomas Sims, the boy picked up on the streets of Boston and sent back to Georgia. She said when they got him back to Savannah, got him in prison there, they whipped him until a doctor who was standing by watching said, "You will kill him if you strike him again!" His master said, "Let him die!"

Thus she forced them to go on. Sometimes she thought she had become nothing but a voice speaking in the darkness, **cajoling,** urging, threatening. 200 Sometimes she told them things to make them laugh, sometimes she sang to them, and heard the eleven voices behind her blending softly with hers, and then she knew that for the moment all was well with them.

She gave the impression of being a short, muscular, indomitable woman who could never be defeated. Yet at any moment she was liable to be seized by one of those curious fits of sleep, which might last for a few minutes or for hours.

---

eloquence (ĕl′ə-kwəns) *n.* an ability to speak powerfully and persuasively

evoke (ĭ-vōk′) *v.* to call forth; to summon

❶ CHARACTERIZATION
Why does Tubman take such a drastic action? Consider what this tells you about her character.

❶ CHARACTERIZATION
How does Tubman's statement reflect her attitude about the journey?

cajole (kə-jōl′) *v.* to urge gently; to coax

---

7. **Frederick Douglass:** African-American leader who worked to end slavery.

8. **Middle Passage:** sea route along which enslaved Africans were transported to the Americas.

Even on this trip, she suddenly fell asleep in the woods. The runaways, ragged, dirty, hungry, cold, did not steal the gun as they might have, and set off by themselves, or turn back. They sat on the ground near her and waited patiently until she awakened. They had come to trust her implicitly, totally. They, too, 210 had come to believe her repeated statement, "We got to go free or die." She was leading them into freedom, and so they waited until she was ready to go on. **K**

Finally, they reached Thomas Garrett's house in Wilmington, Delaware. Just as Harriet had promised, Garrett gave them all new shoes, and provided carriages to take them on to the next stop.

By slow stages they reached Philadelphia, where William Still hastily recorded their names, and the plantations whence they had come, and something of the life they had led in slavery. Then he carefully hid what he had written, for fear it might be discovered. In 1872 he published this record

K CHARACTERIZATION
What do the runaways' actions tell you about Tubman?

An Underground Railroad (1967), Jacob Lawrence. Gouache and tempera on paper, 14¼″ × 13″. © 2007 The Jacob and Gwendolyn Lawrence Foundation, Seattle/Artists Rights Society (ARS), New York.

◄ **Analyze Visuals**
What can you **infer** about the people in the painting?

in book form and called it *The Underground Railroad*. In the foreword to his
220 book he said: "While I knew the danger of keeping strict records, and while
I did not then dream that in my day slavery would be blotted out, or that the
time would come when I could publish these records, it used to afford me
great satisfaction to take them down, fresh from the lips of fugitives on the
way to freedom, and to preserve them as they had given them." **L**

William Still, who was familiar with all the station stops on the
Underground Railroad, supplied Harriet with money and sent her and her
eleven fugitives on to Burlington, New Jersey.

Harriet felt safer now, though there were danger spots ahead. But the biggest
part of her job was over. As they went farther and farther north, it grew colder;
230 she was aware of the wind on the Jersey ferry and aware of the cold damp in
New York. From New York they went on to Syracuse, where the temperature
was even lower.

In Syracuse she met the Reverend J. W. Loguen, known as "Jarm" Loguen.
This was the beginning of a lifelong friendship. Both Harriet and Jarm Loguen
were to become friends and supporters of Old John Brown.[9]

From Syracuse they went north again, into a colder, snowier city—
Rochester. Here they almost certainly stayed with Frederick Douglass, for he
wrote in his autobiography:

> On one occasion I had eleven fugitives at the same time under my roof,
240 and it was necessary for them to remain with me until I could collect
sufficient money to get them to Canada. It was the largest number I ever
had at any one time, and I had some difficulty in providing so many with
food and shelter, but, as may well be imagined, they were not very fastidious
in either direction, and were well content with very plain food, and a strip
of carpet on the floor for a bed, or a place on the straw in the barnloft.

Late in December, 1851, Harriet arrived in St. Catharines, Canada West (now
Ontario), with the eleven fugitives. It had taken almost a month to complete this
journey; most of the time had been spent getting out of Maryland.

That first winter in St. Catharines was a terrible one. Canada was a strange
250 frozen land, snow everywhere, ice everywhere, and a bone-biting cold the like of
which none of them had ever experienced before. Harriet rented a small frame
house in the town and set to work to make a home. The fugitives boarded with
her. They worked in the forests, felling trees, and so did she. Sometimes she took
other jobs, cooking or cleaning house for people in the town. She cheered on
these newly arrived fugitives, working herself, finding work for them, finding
food for them, praying for them, sometimes begging for them. **M**

Often she found herself thinking of the beauty of Maryland, the mellowness
of the soil, the richness of the plant life there. The climate itself made for an
ease of living that could never be duplicated in this bleak, barren countryside.

---

9. **Old John Brown:** anti-slavery leader who was executed.

L ASK QUESTIONS
What do you want to know about the people who help the escapees?

Language Coach

Word Definitions
The word *fastidious* means "difficult to please." Reread lines 241–245. What were the fugitives not fastidious about?

M CHARACTERIZATION
How does Tubman help the fugitives?

Harriet and the Promised Land No. 15: Canada Bound (1967), Jacob Lawrence. Gouache and tempera on paper, 16½″ × 28¼″. The University of Michigan Museum of Art. © 2007 The Jacob and Gwendolyn Lawrence Foundation, Seattle/Artists Rights Society (ARS), New York.

▲ **Analyze Visuals**
What **details** do you notice in this painting that portray the escapees' journey?

260　In spite of the severe cold, the hard work, she came to love St. Catharines, and the other towns and cities in Canada where black men lived. She discovered that freedom meant more than the right to change jobs at will, more than the right to keep the money that one earned. It was the right to vote and to sit on juries. It was the right to be elected to office. In Canada there were black men who were county officials and members of school boards. St. Catharines had a large colony of ex-slaves, and they owned their own homes, kept them neat and clean and in good repair. They lived in whatever part of town they chose and sent their children to the schools.

　　When spring came she decided that she would make this small Canadian
270　city her home—as much as any place could be said to be home to a woman who traveled from Canada to the Eastern Shore of Maryland as often as she did.

　　In the spring of 1852, she went back to Cape May, New Jersey. She spent the summer there, cooking in a hotel. That fall she returned, as usual, to Dorchester County, and brought out nine more slaves, conducting them all the way to St. Catharines, in Canada West, to the bone-biting cold, the snow-covered forests—and freedom.

　　She continued to live in this fashion, spending the winter in Canada, and the spring and summer working in Cape May, New Jersey, or in Philadelphia. She made two trips a year into slave territory, one in the fall and another in
280　the spring. She now had a definite crystallized purpose, and in carrying it out, her life fell into a pattern which remained unchanged for the next six years. ∿ Ⓝ

Ⓝ **CHARACTERIZATION**
What does the way Tubman lives her life tell you about her?

LETTER Frederick Douglass, a vocal African-American statesman and journalist, had a very different style of leadership than Harriet Tubman did. Douglass wrote the following letter when the first biography of Tubman was about to be published.

August 29, 1868

Dear Harriet:

I am glad to know that the story of your eventful life has been written by a kind lady, and that the same is soon to be published. You ask for what you do not need when you call upon me for a word of commendation.[1] I need such words from you far more than you can need them from me, especially where your superior labors and devotion to the cause of the lately enslaved of our land are known as I know them. The difference between us is very marked. Most that I have done and suffered in the service of our cause has been in public, and I have received much encouragement at every step of the way. You, on the other hand, have labored in a private way. I have wrought in the day—you in the night. I have had the applause of the crowd and the satisfaction that comes of being approved by the multitude, while the most that you have done has been witnessed by a few trembling, scarred, and footsore bondmen and women, whom you have led out of the house of bondage, and whose heartfelt "God bless you" has been your only reward. The midnight sky and the silent stars have been the witnesses of your devotion to freedom and of your heroism. Excepting John Brown—of sacred memory—I know of no one who has willingly encountered more perils and hardships to serve our enslaved people than you have. Much that you have done would seem improbable to those who do not know you as I know you. It is to me a great pleasure and a great privilege to bear testimony to your character and your works, and to say to those to whom you may come, that I regard you in every way truthful and trustworthy.

Your friend,

Fred. Douglass

Frederick Douglass

---

1. **commendation** (kŏm'ən-dā'shən): an expression of praise or recommendation.

Comprehension

1. **Recall** What is the purpose of Harriet Tubman's trips to Maryland?

2. **Clarify** Why does the man at the first stop on the Underground Railroad turn away the group of runaways?

3. **Summarize** How does life for the runaways change in Canada?

Text Analysis

● 4. **Examine Questions** Review the chart of questions and answers you made as you read. Which questions added the most to your understanding of the selection? Why?

● 5. **Examine Characterization** Review the four methods of **characterization.** Which method of characterization does Petry use the most in her biography? Tell what you learn about Tubman through this method.

6. **Analyze a Character** Complete a character map for Harriet Tubman like the one shown. Then create a one-sentence description of her.

7. **Make Judgments** Read the "Letter to Harriet Tubman" by Frederick Douglass. Why does Douglass believe that Harriet Tubman is "superior" to him? Decide why Douglass might have felt this way, and support your opinion with details from the biography and the letter.

COMMON CORE

RI 1 Cite the textual evidence that most strongly supports an analysis of what the text says explicitly. **RI 3** Analyze how a text makes connections between individuals, ideas, or events. **W 9** Draw evidence from informational texts to support analysis, reflection, and research.

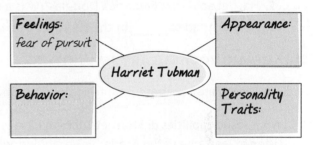

Extension and Challenge

8. **Readers' Circle** Based on the information in the selection, would you have been willing to trust Harriet Tubman with your life? Discuss which of Tubman's qualities make her a good leader and why you might be hesitant to follow her.

9. 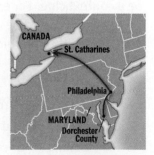 **SOCIAL STUDIES CONNECTION** Because the Fugitive Slave Law allowed slave owners to recover enslaved people who escaped, Harriet Tubman led escapees on Underground Railroad routes to Canada, where they reached freedom. Research more about the approximately 18 other trips to Canada that Tubman led and present your findings to the class. Consider what continued to motivate her to risk her life to help others.

Harriet Tubman's route from Maryland to Canada

When is a RISK worth taking?

How has reading this selection affected your thoughts about taking risks in life?

Vocabulary in Context

▲ **VOCABULARY PRACTICE**

Choose the word from the list that makes the most sense in each sentence.

1. Harriet had to make sure that they didn't _____ too long in any one place.
2. She had to work hard to _____ a sense of hope.
3. At times, it was difficult for Harriet to _____ feelings of despair.
4. When she saw the _____ looks on people's faces, she knew it was time for another encouraging story.
5. When they arrived at a destination, they were hungry and their appearance was _____.
6. Harriet often had to _____ the fugitives into moving toward their next stop.
7. Harriet said that Frederick Douglass was a man of great _____.
8. Harriet tried to _____ in the fugitives a sense of responsibility.

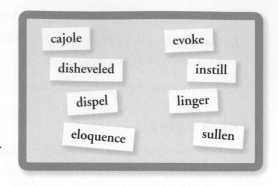

cajole   evoke

disheveled   instill

dispel   linger

eloquence   sullen

ACADEMIC VOCABULARY IN WRITING

> • appropriate   • assess   • intelligence   • motive   • role

What responsibilities did Harriet Tubman have in the Underground Railroad? Using at least one of the Academic Vocabulary words, write a paragraph describing her **role**.

VOCABULARY STRATEGY: SYNONYMS AS CONTEXT CLUES

Context clues are often found in the words and sentences that surround an unfamiliar, ambiguous, or novel word. These clues can help you figure out the meaning of the word. A **synonym,** or a word that has a similar definition, can be a context clue. For example, a sentence from the selection refers to "a voice speaking in the darkness, cajoling, urging. . . ." If you know the word *urging,* you can figure out what *cajoling* means because they are synonyms.

PRACTICE Identify the synonyms of each boldfaced word. Then define the word.

1. They had come to trust her **implicitly,** just as they believed in her totally.
2. She was considered **indomitable** because of her undefeatable spirit.
3. Harriet longed for **contentment.** Like most, she wanted to feel ease and happiness. However, she would never be satisfied until the journey ended.
4. The group was not **fastidious** or fussy about what they ate or where they slept.
5. In the end, the lure of freedom was its own **incentive.** It was the reason to endure the hardship.
6. The escape was unimaginable, and the journey almost **incomprehensible.**

COMMON CORE

L 4a Use context (e.g., the overall meaning of a sentence or paragraph) as a clue to the meaning of a word. **L 5b** Use the relationship between particular words to better understand each of the words.

Interactive Vocabulary **THINK** central

Go to **thinkcentral.com.**
KEYWORD: HML8-280

Language

COMMON CORE

L1 Demonstrate command of the conventions of standard English grammar and usage when writing.

◆ **GRAMMAR IN CONTEXT:** Avoid Clauses as Fragments

Review the **Grammar in Context** note on page 271. A clause is a group of words that contains a subject and a verb. An **independent,** or **main, clause** expresses a complete thought and can stand alone as a sentence. A **dependent,** or **subordinate, clause** cannot. Dependent clauses begin with words such as *although, before, because, so that, when, while,* and *that.* To avoid a sentence fragment, join a dependent clause (shown in yellow) to an independent clause, which will be the **main clause** in the combined sentence.

> *Original:* Harriet Tubman was willing to take risks. Because she wanted everyone to be free.

> *Revised:* Harriet Tubman was willing to take risks because she wanted everyone to be free.

PRACTICE Find four fragments in the following paragraph. Then fix the fragments by combining independent and dependent clauses.

> Harriet Tubman would be hanged. If slaveholders caught her. Tubman was willing to kill. So that the Underground Railroad would remain a secret. It made Tubman happy. When former slaves had the right to vote. Although her work was dangerous. She did not ask for any reward.

*For more help with clauses, see page R62 in the **Grammar Handbook**.*

READING-WRITING CONNECTION

YOUR TURN Demonstrate your understanding of "Harriet Tubman: Conductor on the Underground Railroad" by responding to this prompt. Then use the **revising tip** to improve your writing.

WRITING PROMPT	REVISING TIP
Extended Constructed Response: Write a Character Sketch You learned about Harriet Tubman from the way Ann Petry characterized her. Now it's your turn to describe this historic figure for an elementary school audience. Write a **two- or three-paragraph character sketch** that uses various methods of characterization to capture the personality of Harriet Tubman.	Review your character sketch. Have you included any sentences that combine a dependent clause with an independent clause? If not, revise.

Interactive Revision

THINK central

Go to **thinkcentral.com**.
KEYWORD: HML8-281

The Mysterious Mr. Lincoln
Biography by Russell Freedman

Video link at
thinkcentral.com

What are the signs of
GREATNESS?

COMMON CORE

RI 2 Identify a central idea of a text and analyze its development over the course of the text, including its relationship to supporting ideas. **RI 3** Analyze how a text makes connections between individuals, ideas, or events. **RI 5** Analyze in detail the structure of a specific paragraph in a text, including the role of particular sentences in developing and refining a key concept.

People can be noticed for a variety of reasons. A brilliant mind, confident personality, strong work ethic, or generous spirit can make someone shine. When people use these qualities to improve the world and inspire others, they are said to have greatness. The biography you are about to read describes the complicated personality—and extraordinary leadership—of one of the greatest U.S. presidents, Abraham Lincoln.

WEB IT Think of two or three people you consider to have qualities of greatness. You can include public figures, friends, or family members. For each person, create a web like the one shown to show the qualities that make him or her great. Then compare your web with your classmates' webs. What qualities come up more than once?

continued in the face of threats

bravery

Martin Luther King Jr.

● TEXT ANALYSIS: BIOGRAPHY

Real people often inspire fascinating pieces of writing. A true account of a person's life that's written by someone else is called a **biography.** Writers of biographies

- use the third-person point of view
- present facts and opinions from a variety of sources
- provide an interpretation of a person's character

As you read this biography, watch for ways Russell Freedman highlights President Lincoln's strengths and weaknesses.

● READING SKILL: IDENTIFY MAIN IDEAS AND DETAILS

Nonfiction writing is usually organized around **main ideas,** which are the most important ideas a writer wants to convey about a topic. The writer develops the main ideas through **supporting details,** which can include

- **facts:** statements that can be proven
- **anecdotes:** brief stories that reveal important points
- **quotations:** direct statements from relevant people

Sometimes writers state their main ideas clearly, often at the beginning or end of paragraphs. Other times, you must **infer** the main ideas from the details provided. As you read, note the main ideas and details on a rough outline like the one shown.

> I. Lincoln had a distinctive, changing appearance.
>   A. Tall with long legs
>   B.
> II.

▲ VOCABULARY IN CONTEXT

The following phrases could have been headlines at the time Abraham Lincoln lived. Replace each boldfaced term with a word or words that means something similar.

1. Southern States **Denounce** the War
2. A **Melancholy** Nation Faces Civil War
3. Soldiers **Defy** the Odds
4. Lincoln to **Patronize** Local Business
5. Exhausted Generals Grow **Listless** as War Rages On
6. Senators **Meddle** in Lincoln's War Plans

 Complete the activities in your **Reader/Writer Notebook.**

Meet the Author

Russell Freedman
born 1929

The Art of Nonfiction
Russell Freedman's father worked for a publishing company and often brought authors home to have dinner with the family. "I wanted to be like them," Freedman says. To improve his writing skills, he got a job as a news reporter. His interest in writing biographies started when he learned about a blind 16-year-old boy who had invented a Braille typewriter. Fascinated by the boy's story, Freedman wrote his first book, *Teenagers Who Made History* (1961). When asked why he specializes in writing nonfiction for young readers, Freedman says he enjoys the challenge of conveying "the spirit and essence of a life."

BACKGROUND TO THE BIOGRAPHY
Abraham Lincoln
Despite being born into a poor family with few opportunities, Abraham Lincoln managed to educate himself. He became a successful lawyer and state politician, but he had even greater ambitions. In 1860, he achieved them; he won the presidency. He steered the country through the long and bloody Civil War (1861–1865), which resulted in an end to slavery in the United States. In April 1865, Lincoln was assassinated by John Wilkes Booth, a southerner who wanted slavery to continue. Lincoln has held an enduring fascination for historians who often find new facets of his personality to examine. As Russell Freedman has pointed out, "Every ten years Lincoln changes character dramatically."

Author Online THINK central
Go to **thinkcentral.com.**
KEYWORD: HML8-283

The *Mysterious* Mr. Lincoln

Russell Freedman

"If any personal description of me is thought desirable, it may be said, I am, in height, six feet, four inches, nearly; lean in flesh, weighing, on average, one hundred and eighty pounds dark complexion, with coarse black hair and grey eyes—no other marks or brands recollected."

Abraham Lincoln wasn't the sort of man who could lose himself in a crowd. After all, he stood six feet four inches tall, and to top it off, he wore a high silk hat.

His height was mostly in his long bony legs. When he sat in a chair, he seemed no taller than anyone else. It was only when he stood up that he towered above other men.

At first glance, most people thought he was homely. Lincoln thought so too, referring once to his "poor, lean, lank face." As a young man he was sensitive about his gawky looks, but in time, he learned to laugh at himself. When a
10 rival called him "two-faced" during a political debate, Lincoln replied: "I leave it to my audience. If I had another face, do you think I'd wear this one?" **A**

According to those who knew him, Lincoln was a man of many faces. In repose,[1] he often seemed sad and gloomy. But when he began to speak, his expression changed. "The dull, **listless** features dropped like a mask," said a Chicago newspaperman. "The eyes began to sparkle, the mouth to smile, the whole countenance[2] was wreathed in animation, so that a stranger would have said 'Why, this man, so angular and solemn a moment ago, is really handsome!'" **B**

---

1. **repose** (rĭ-pōz'): the act of resting.
2. **countenance** (koun'tə-nəns): the face; expression of the face.

Analyze Visuals ▶

Look at this photograph of Lincoln. How would you **describe** the expression on his face?

A **MAIN IDEAS AND DETAILS**
Reread lines 7–11. What type of detail does the author use to help convey Lincoln's appearance? Add this to your outline.

listless (lĭst'lĭs) *adj.* lacking energy

B **BIOGRAPHY**
Who thinks Lincoln is "a man of many faces"? Tell how you know this.

Lincoln was the most photographed man of his time, but his friends insisted
20 that no photo ever did him justice. It's no wonder. Back then, cameras required
long exposures. The person being photographed had to "freeze" as the seconds
ticked by. If he blinked an eye, the picture would be blurred. That's why Lincoln
looks so stiff and formal in his photos. We never see him laughing or joking.

Artists and writers tried to capture the "real" Lincoln that the camera
missed, but something about the man always escaped them. His changeable
features, his tones, gestures, and expressions, seemed to **defy** description.

Today it's hard to imagine Lincoln as he really was. And he never cared to
reveal much about himself. In company he was witty and talkative, but he rarely
betrayed his inner feelings. According to William Herndon, his law partner, he
30 was "the most secretive—reticent—shut-mouthed man that ever lived."

In his own time, Lincoln was never fully understood even by his closest friends.
Since then, his life story has been told and retold so many times, he has become
as much a legend as a flesh-and-blood human being. While the legend is based on
truth, it is only partly true. And it hides the man behind it like a disguise. **C**

The legendary Lincoln is known as Honest Abe, a humble man of the
people who rose from a log cabin to the White House. There's no doubt that
Lincoln was a poor boy who made good. And it's true that he carried his
folksy manners and homespun speech to the White House with him. He said
"howdy" to visitors and invited them to "stay a spell." He greeted diplomats
40 while wearing carpet slippers, called his wife "mother" at receptions, and told
bawdy[3] jokes at cabinet meetings.

Lincoln may have seemed like a common man, but he wasn't. His friends
agreed that he was one of the most ambitious people they had ever known.
Lincoln struggled hard to rise above his log-cabin origins, and he was proud
of his achievements. By the time he ran for president he was a wealthy man,
earning a large income from his law practice and his many investments. As for
the nickname Abe, he hated it. No one who knew him well ever called him
Abe to his face. They addressed him as Lincoln or Mr. Lincoln.

Lincoln is often described as a sloppy dresser, careless about his appearance. In
50 fact, he **patronized** the best tailor in Springfield, Illinois, buying two suits a year.
That was at a time when many men lived, died, and were buried in the same suit.

It's true that Lincoln had little formal "eddication," as he would have
pronounced it. Almost everything he "larned" he taught himself. All his life he
said "thar" for *there,* "git" for *get,* "kin" for *can.* Even so, he became an eloquent
public speaker who could hold a vast audience spellbound, and a great writer
whose finest phrases still ring in our ears. He was known to sit up late into the
night, discussing Shakespeare's plays with White House visitors. **D**

He was certainly a humorous man, famous for his rollicking stories. But he
was also moody and **melancholy,** tormented by long and frequent bouts of
60 depression. Humor was his therapy. He relied on his yarns,[4] a friend observed,
to "whistle down sadness."

---

3. **bawdy** (bô'dē): vulgar.

4. **yarn:** an entertaining tale.

Language Coach

Idioms An idiom is a phrase that has a meaning different from its individual words. The phrase "do justice to" means "treat fairly or with full appreciation." What is the author suggesting with this idiom in line 20?

defy (dĭ-fī') *v.* to boldly oppose or resist

C MAIN IDEAS AND DETAILS
What is the main idea in this paragraph? Add it to your outline.

patronize (pā'trə-nīz') *v.* to go to as a customer

D MAIN IDEAS AND DETAILS
Note the details about Lincoln's words and actions. What main idea do they support?

melancholy (mĕl'ən-kŏl'ē) *adj.* sad; depressed

He had a cool, logical mind, trained in the courtroom, and a practical, commonsense approach to problems. Yet he was deeply superstitious, a believer in dreams, omens, and visions. **E**

We admire Lincoln today as an American folk hero. During the Civil War, however, he was the most unpopular president the nation had ever known. His critics called him a tyrant, a hick, a stupid baboon who was unfit for his office. As commander in chief of the armed forces, he was **denounced** as a bungling amateur who **meddled** in military affairs he knew nothing about. But he also

70 had his supporters. They praised him as a farsighted statesman, a military mastermind who engineered the Union victory.

Lincoln is best known as the Great Emancipator, the man who freed the slaves. Yet he did not enter the war with that idea in mind. "My paramount object in this struggle *is* to save the Union," he said in 1862, "and is *not* either to save or destroy slavery." As the war continued, Lincoln's attitude changed. Eventually he came to regard the conflict as a moral crusade to wipe out the sin of slavery.

No black leader was more critical of Lincoln than the fiery abolitionist[5] writer and editor Frederick Douglass. Douglass had grown up as a slave.

80 He had won his freedom by escaping to the North. Early in the war, impatient with Lincoln's cautious leadership, Douglass called him "preeminently the white man's president, entirely devoted to the welfare of white men." Later, Douglass changed his mind and came to admire Lincoln. Several years after the war, he said

90 this about the sixteenth president:

"His greatest mission was to accomplish two things: first, to save his country from dismemberment and ruin; and, second, to free his country from the great crime of slavery. . . . taking him for all in all, measuring the tremendous magnitude of the work before him, considering the necessary means to

100 ends, and surveying the end from the beginning, infinite wisdom has seldom sent any man into the world better fitted for his mission than Abraham Lincoln." ∾

Allan Pinkerton, President Abraham Lincoln, and Major General John A. McClernand at Antietam Battle Site, Maryland. October 3, 1862.

---

5. **abolitionist** (ăb'ə-lĭsh'ə-nĭst): one who advocated the end of slavery.

E **BIOGRAPHY**
Which of the qualities described would you expect a great leader to have, and which would you not?

denounce (dĭ-nouns') *v.* to condemn; to criticize

meddle (mĕd'l) *v.* to intrude or interfere

THE MYSTERIOUS MR. LINCOLN　**287**

Comprehension

1. **Recall** According to the author, why does Abraham Lincoln look "so stiff and formal" in photographs?

2. **Recall** What was Lincoln's original reason for entering into the Civil War?

3. **Clarify** What caused Frederick Douglass to change his opinion of Lincoln?

Text Analysis

4. **Identify Main Ideas and Details** Review the outline you filled in as you read. Based on the main ideas and details you noted, what do you think is the overall main idea of the selection?

5. **Analyze Characterization** One method of characterization is to present the way a person talks. Review the quotations from Lincoln that Freedman includes in this biography. In what way do Lincoln's words add to your understanding of his character? Cite one or two specific quotations to support your answer.

6. **Make Judgments** What signs of greatness did Lincoln exhibit in his life? Support your response with evidence from the text.

7. **Evaluate Biography** List the strengths and weaknesses of Lincoln in a chart like the one shown. In your opinion, does the author provide a balanced portrait of his subject? Explain.

Strengths	Weaknesses
sense of humor	

COMMON CORE

RI 2 Identify a central idea of a text and analyze its development over the course of the text, including its relationship to supporting ideas. **RI 3** Analyze how a text makes connections between individuals, ideas, or events. **RI 5** Analyze in detail the structure of a specific paragraph in a text, including the role of particular sentences in developing and refining a key concept.

Extension and Challenge

8. **Readers' Circle** People often say that Abraham Lincoln would have a difficult time winning an election today. Why do you think they say that? Discuss the question with your group. Then decide whether or not you agree. Support your opinion with examples from the biography.

9. **SOCIAL STUDIES CONNECTION** In 1922, President Harding dedicated the Lincoln Memorial, a magnificent structure built in Washington D.C. to honor Abraham Lincoln. Research the memorial to find out what is included within it and what it stands for.

Lincoln Memorial

What are the signs of GREATNESS?

Review your response to the activity on page 282. What qualities did Lincoln have in common with the people you consider to be great?

Vocabulary in Context

▲ **VOCABULARY PRACTICE**

For each sentence, choose the vocabulary word that has a similar meaning to the boldfaced word or phrase.

1. It's easy now, after the fact, to say that you **condemn** the awful crime.
2. I **shop regularly at** the corner grocery.
3. Why must you always **interfere** in things that are not your business?
4. He thought it was wrong to **oppose** his parents.
5. That particular music made them feel **sad.**
6. Because he felt so **tired,** he began taking vitamins.

defy

denounce

listless

meddle

melancholy

patronize

ACADEMIC VOCABULARY IN SPEAKING

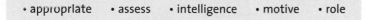

• appropriate   • assess   • intelligence   • motive   • role

How **appropriate** is Frederick Douglass's remark that "infinite wisdom has seldom sent any man into the world better fitted for his mission than Abraham Lincoln"? Use at least one of the Academic Vocabulary words in your response.

VOCABULARY STRATEGY: MULTIPLE-MEANING WORDS

Many English words have more than one meaning. The vocabulary word *patronize* is one of these words. In the selection, *patronize* means "to visit as a customer," but another definition is "to treat in a condescending manner." You can usually figure out which meaning the writer intended by looking at the **context** in which the word appears.

PRACTICE Each boldfaced word below has multiple meanings. Read the sentence and figure out the meaning of the boldfaced word based on context clues. Use a dictionary to check your answer. Then find another meaning for the word and use the word in a new sentence.

1. My grandmother knit a sweater using yellow **yarn.**
2. I can **sink** the basketball in the net even when I'm nervous.
3. The **pipe** below the sink was rusty from age.
4. When I am hungry, I **gorge** myself on pancakes and eggs.

⋮ **COMMON CORE**

L 4a Use context (e.g., a word's position or function in a sentence) as a clue to the meaning of a word. **L 6** Acquire and use accurately academic words; gather vocabulary knowledge when considering a word important to comprehension and expression.

Interactive Vocabulary THINK central

Go to **thinkcentral.com.**
KEYWORD: HML8-289

Barbara Frietchie
Poem by John Greenleaf Whittier

John Henry
Traditional Poem

Is it ever right to
GIVE UP?

COMMON CORE

RL 1 Cite textual evidence to support inferences drawn from the text. **RL 3** Analyze how dialogue or incidents reveal aspects of character. **RL 4** Analyze the impact of specific word choices on meaning.

Think of a time when you kept trying something without success. Did you get discouraged, or did the experience make you try harder? When some of us might give up, other people find the strength to persevere. In the poems you are about to read, you will meet two characters who refuse to take no for an answer.

QUICKWRITE Think of a situation in which you gave up doing something—perhaps playing an instrument or being on a team. Write a brief paragraph explaining the positive and negative consequences of your decision.

● TEXT ANALYSIS: CHARACTERIZATION IN POETRY

The two works you are about to read are **narrative poems,** which means they tell a story. Like short stories, narrative poems always feature characters. Poets can bring their characters to life, or **characterize** them, in just a few words. A telling image, a carefully chosen scrap of dialogue, or a striking detail can suggest a great deal about a character's traits, behavior, and values.

As you read "Barbara Frietchie" and "John Henry," pay attention to what the poets' language suggests about the characters. Then note information about each main character in the appropriate part of a graphic like the one shown.

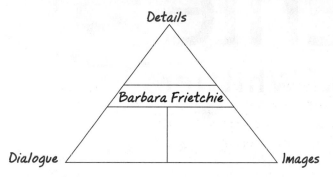

Details

Barbara Frietchie

Dialogue   Images

● READING SKILL: RECOGNIZE SOUND DEVICES

One way that narrative poems differ from short stories is the extent to which they use **sound devices** to add meaning and interest. The three Rs of sound devices are

- **Rhyme:** the repetition of sounds at the ends of words

  Over the mountains winding <u>down</u>,
  Horse and foot, into Frederick <u>town</u>.

- **Rhythm:** the pattern of stressed and unstressed syllables in the lines of a poem

  She leáned fár oút on thě window-síll

- **Repetition:** repeated sounds, words, or phrases that are used for emphasis

  You must be a steel driving man like me,
  You must be a steel driving man like me.

Reading a poem aloud can help you appreciate the sound devices. As you read "Barbara Frietchie" and "John Henry," notice the effect the devices have on the sound and sense of the poem.

 Complete the activities in your **Reader/Writer Notebook.**

Meet the Author

John Greenleaf Whittier
1807–1892

Fiery Abolitionist
Although John Greenleaf Whittier had little formal schooling, he was naturally drawn to poetry. His career began in 1826 when a newspaper published one of his poems, which his sister had submitted without his knowledge. William Lloyd Garrison, a noted abolitionist, was the newspaper's editor, and his passion for ending slavery affected Whittier. Whittier's poems about the evils of slavery were published in 1846 under the title *Voices of Freedom.*

BACKGROUND TO THE POEMS

"Barbara Frietchie" and the Civil War
As an abolitionist, John Greenleaf Whittier strongly supported the Union side in the Civil War. He wrote "Barbara Frietchie" to honor a legendary act of courage. Barbara Frietchie was a citizen of Frederick, Maryland, who was fiercely loyal to the Union. According to legend, as Confederate soldiers marched through the town, she defiantly waved a Union flag.

John Henry
It is not known if John Henry actually existed, but the character may have been based on a real steel driver in the early 1870s. Steel drivers used hammers and steel drills to pound holes into mountains. Then explosives blasted deeper into the mountains to create tunnels for railroads. The speed and efficiency of machines like steam drills eventually threatened the livelihood of steel drivers. John Henry's story is often sung as a ballad.

Author Online
THINK central
Go to **thinkcentral.com.**
KEYWORD: HML8-291

Barbara Frietchie

John Greenleaf Whittier

Up from the meadows rich with corn,
Clear in the cool September morn,

The clustered spires of Frederick stand
Green-walled by the hills of Maryland.

5 Round about them orchards sweep,
Apple and peach tree fruited deep,

Fair as the garden of the Lord
To the eyes of the famished rebel horde,[1]

On that pleasant morn of the early fall
10 When Lee[2] marched over the mountain wall;

Over the mountains winding down,
Horse and foot, into Frederick town. **A**

Analyze Visuals ▶

This union flag flew during the Civil War. What **conclusions** can you draw about why the flag looks the way it does?

A SOUND DEVICES
Which sound devices do you notice in lines 1–12?

---

1. **horde:** a large group or crowd.
2. **Lee:** a general for the Confederate army during the Civil War.

Forty flags with their silver stars,
Forty flags with their crimson bars,

15 Flapped in the morning wind: the sun
Of noon looked down, and saw not one.

Up rose old Barbara Frietchie then,
Bowed with her fourscore years and ten;[3]

Bravest of all in Frederick town,
20 She took up the flag the men hauled down.

In her attic window the staff she set,
To show that one heart was loyal yet. **B**

Up the street came the rebel tread,
Stonewall Jackson[4] riding ahead.

25 Under his slouched hat left and right
He glanced; the old flag met his sight.

"Halt!"—the dust-brown ranks stood fast.
"Fire!"—out blazed the rifle-blast.

It shivered the window, pane and sash;
30 It rent[5] the banner with seam and gash.

Quick, as it fell, from the broken staff
Dame Barbara snatched the silken scarf. **C**

She leaned far out on the window-sill,
And shook it forth with a royal will.

35 "Shoot, if you must, this old gray head,
But spare your country's flag," she said.

B CHARACTERIZATION
Reread lines 17–22.
What do you learn
about Barbara Frietchie?

C SOUND DEVICES
A poet's use of words
that almost rhyme,
but not quite, is called
slant rhyme. Reread
lines 29–36 and find an
example of two lines
that end with a slant
rhyme. Tell what effect
this has on your reading
of the poem.

---

3. **fourscore years and ten:** ninety years.

4. **Stonewall Jackson:** a general for the Confederate army
during the Civil War.

5. **rent:** tore apart.

A shade of sadness, a blush of shame,
Over the face of the leader came;

The nobler nature within him stirred
40 To life at that woman's deed and word;

"Who touches a hair of yon gray head
Dies like a dog! March on!" he said. **D**

All day long through Frederick street
Sounded the tread of marching feet:

45 All day long that free flag tost
Over the heads of the rebel host. **E**

Ever its torn folds rose and fell
On the loyal winds that loved it well;

And through the hill-gaps sunset light
50 Shone over it with a warm good-night.

Barbara Frietchie's work is o'er,
And the Rebel rides on his raids no more.

Honor to her! and let a tear
Fall, for her sake, on Stonewall's bier.[6]

55 Over Barbara Frietchie's grave,
Flag of Freedom and Union, wave!

Peace and order and beauty draw
Round thy symbol of light and law;

And ever the stars above look down
60 On thy stars below in Frederick town!

D CHARACTERIZATION
In lines 35–42, what traits and behavior does Barbara Frietchie display that make Stonewall Jackson feel shame?

E SOUND DEVICES
Reread lines 43–46. What does the **repetition** emphasize about the events in Frederick?

---

6. **bier** (bîr): a stand on which a coffin is placed before a burial.

John Henry

Traditional

When John Henry was a little boy,
Sitting upon his father's knee,
His father said, "Look here, my boy,
You must be a steel driving man like me,
5 You must be a steel driving man like me." **F**

John Henry went up on the mountain,
Just to drive himself some steel.
The rocks was so tall and John Henry so small,
He said lay down hammer and squeal,
10 He said lay down hammer and squeal.

John Henry had a little wife,
And the dress she wore was red;
The last thing before he died,
He said, "Be true to me when I'm dead,
15 Oh, be true to me when I'm dead."

John Henry's wife ask him for fifteen cents,
And he said he didn't have but a dime,
Said, "If you wait till the rising sun goes down,
I'll borrow it from the man in the mine,
20 I'll borrow it from the man in the mine."

John Henry started on the right-hand side,
And the steam drill started on the left.
He said, "Before I'd let that steam drill beat me down,
I'd hammer my fool self to death,
25 Oh, I'd hammer my fool self to death." **G**

F SOUND DEVICES
What part of John Henry's life does the **repetition** in lines 4–5 emphasize?

G CHARACTERIZATION
How would you describe John Henry's attitude?

The steam drill started at half-past six,
John Henry started the same time.
John Henry struck bottom at half-past eight,
And the steam drill didn't bottom till nine,
30 And the steam drill didn't bottom till nine.

John Henry said to his captain,
"A man, he ain't nothing but a man,
Before I'd let that steam drill beat me down,
I'd die with the hammer in my hand,
35 Oh, I'd die with the hammer in my hand."

John Henry said to his shaker, [1]
"Shaker, why don't you sing just a few more rounds?
And before the setting sun goes down,
You're gonna hear this hammer of mine sound,
40 You're gonna hear this hammer of mine sound."

John Henry hammered on the mountain,
He hammered till half-past three,
He said, "This big Bend Tunnel on the C. & O. road [2]
Is going to be the death of me,
45 Lord! is going to be the death of me."

John Henry had a little baby boy,
You could hold him in the palm of your hand.
The last words before he died,
"Son, you must be a steel driving man,
50 Son, you must be a steel driving man." **H**

John Henry had a little woman,
And the dress she wore was red,
She went down the railroad track and never come back,
Said she was going where John Henry fell dead,
55 Said she was going where John Henry fell dead.

John Henry hammering on the mountain,
As the whistle blew for half-past two,
The last word I heard him say,
"Captain, I've hammered my insides in two,
60 Lord, I've hammered my insides in two." **I**

H CHARACTERIZATION
Why do you think it is important to John Henry that his son follows in his footsteps?

I SOUND DEVICES
Read lines 56–57 aloud with a natural **rhythm**. Which syllables are stressed?

---

1. **shaker:** the person who holds the steel drill for the steel driving man and shakes the drill to remove it from the rock.

2. **big Bend . . . road:** Construction work on the Big Bend Tunnel on the Chesapeake & Ohio Railroad in West Virginia took place from 1870 to 1873.

COMIC STRIP John Henry has been the subject of ballads, children's books, feature films, and more. In this comic, cartoonist John Steventon shows one of the ways he's been inspired by this American folk hero.

SECTION B   THE STAR JOURNAL   B4

Cartoon Tribute to
John Henry

John Henry was a childhood hero of mine, and he was probably one of the biggest influences on who I am and how I live my life. To me, the legend and the man are the same; I still see him as a regular guy who was confident in himself and who never, ever gave up. When he needed a job, he went and got one, convincing the boss that he was the right man for it. And when that job of Steel Driving Man was threatened by automation, he challenged that Steam Drill to a contest and won. Sure, he died in the process, but that just adds to his legend. The point is, he said he would win and did, against all odds. What a role model for young and old alike!

Comprehension

1. **Recall** What causes Barbara Frietchie to hold a flag out her window?

2. **Clarify** Why does John Henry have a contest with the steam drill?

Text Analysis

3. **Make Inferences** Reread lines 23–42 of "Barbara Frietchie." Why do you think Stonewall Jackson decides to protect the woman who defied him?

4. **Interpret Symbol** What do you think John Henry's victory over the steam drill **symbolizes,** or stands for beyond its usual meaning?

5. **Analyze Couplets** "Barbara Frietchie" is written in **couplets,** rhymed pairs of lines that usually have the same or a similar number of syllables. Think about the characteristics of these couplets and the effect they help create. Then tell what purpose couplets serve in the poem.

6. **Analyze Ballad** "John Henry" is a **ballad,** a poem that tells a story and was originally meant to be sung. What elements of the poem make it songlike?

7. **Compare and Contrast** Using a Venn diagram like the one shown, compare and contrast the characters of Barbara Frietchie and John Henry. Are they more similar or different?

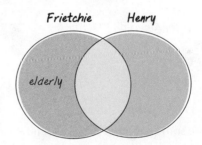

Frietchie   Henry

elderly

8. **Analyze Characterization** Review the character maps you created as you read. Based on the information you collected, describe each character in detail. What are they like? What do they believe in?

9. **Evaluate Sound Devices** Read several stanzas of each poem aloud. For each poem, tell whether you think the **rhythm, rhyme,** or **repetition** affects the meaning most. Explain your answer.

10. **Compare Texts** In the "Cartoon Tribute to John Henry," how does Bobby's encounter with Dr. Dampflok parallel John Henry's experience in the poem?

Extension and Challenge

11. **Readers' Circle** Why do you think Barbara Frietchie and John Henry captured the American imagination? Think about why Americans value the traits these characters display in the poems.

Is it ever right to GIVE UP?

Considering the outcome, do you think John Henry was right to persevere at his work on the railroad? Explain.

COMMON CORE

RL 1 Cite textual evidence to support inferences drawn from the text. **RL 3** Analyze how dialogue or incidents reveal aspects of character. **RL 4** Analyze the impact of specific word choices on meaning.

Writing Workshop
ARGUMENT

Critical Review

"That's not how I pictured her character." You may have made a remark like this after watching a film based on a familiar story or novel. In this workshop, you will write an argument in which you explain why a movie adaptation of literature does or does not live up to the original, supporting your opinion with reasons and evidence.

 Complete the workshop activities in your **Reader/Writer Notebook**.

WRITE WITH A PURPOSE

WRITING TASK

Write a **critical review** of a movie based on a favorite story. Evaluate the effectiveness of the choices the director and actors made about how to portray the plot, setting, and characters. Draw a conclusion about whether the film version is as good as or better than the literature.

Idea Starters
- *Flowers for Algernon / Charly*
- *Holes*
- *Little Women*
- *The Blind Side*

THE ESSENTIALS

Here are some common purposes, audiences, and formats for writing a critical review.

PURPOSES	AUDIENCES	FORMATS
• to compare a film version of a story to the original text • to convince others to agree with your evaluation of a movie	• classmates and teacher • friends and family members • newspaper readers • Web users	• essay for class • movie review in school or local newspaper • online movie review • class debate

COMMON CORE TRAITS

1. DEVELOPMENT OF IDEAS
- includes an **introduction** that presents a **claim**, or position
- provides **clear reasons** and **relevant evidence** to support the claim
- addresses **opposing claims**, or different views
- offers a **conclusion** that follows from the argument presented

2. ORGANIZATION OF IDEAS
- **organizes** reasons and evidence in a **logical way**
- uses **transitions**, such as *however* and *for example*, to show relationships among claim, reasons, and evidence

3. LANGUAGE FACILITY AND CONVENTIONS
- maintains a **formal style** appropriate for an academic essay
- uses the **subjunctive mood** to achieve particular effects
- employs correct **grammar, mechanics,** and **spelling**

Writing Online
Go to **thinkcentral.com**.
KEYWORD: HML8N-300

Planning/Prewriting

COMMON CORE W 1a–e Write arguments to support claims with clear reasons and relevant evidence. W 5 Develop writing by planning. W 9a (RL 1, 7) Cite textual evidence; analyze the extent to which a filmed production stays faithful to the text.

Getting Started

CHOOSE A MOVIE

List movies you have seen that are based on stories you have read. If you need help, look at the Idea Starters on page 300. Then choose the movie on your list to which you have the strongest positive or negative reaction. Jot down brief notes about what you like or don't like about the film, including differences between the film and the original text. Consider elements such as the portrayal of the characters, the setting, the plot, the ending, and the filmmaking techniques.

▶ the movie _Charly_, based on _Flowers for Algernon_

What I Like	What I Dislike
• same basic plot as in story	• the ending, which is different from the story
• the actors who play the characters	• the way Charlie appears violent at times
• new character of the landlady and her dog	• movie is confusing in parts

STATE YOUR CLAIM AND REASONS

Review your list of what you like and don't like about the movie. Overall, do you think the film is better or worse than the original text? State your opinion as your **claim,** or position. Then return to your list. Identify the major reasons why you think as you do. These reasons must relate to your claim and support it. If you have difficulty identifying reasons to support your claim, you may need to rephrase it or try a new approach. For example, reverse your original opinion to see if you can come up with more or better reasons.

▶ **Claim:** The movie _Charly_, based on _Flowers for Algernon_ by Daniel Keyes, does not live up to the story.

Reason 1: Charlie is portrayed as having a dark, or violent side.

Reason 2: The ending happens too abruptly.

Reason 3: Some of the scenes are confusing.

THINK ABOUT AUDIENCE AND PURPOSE

Your **purpose** in this argument is to convince your **audience** to agree with your claim. To accomplish this purpose you need to first identify who will be reading your review. Then you need to choose the reasons that will be most convincing to those readers. Finally, you should think about how much your audience already knows about the movie and original text, and how much you will need to tell them.

▶ **ASK YOURSELF:**

- Who will read my argument?
- If my audience has not seen the movie, what do they need to know about its plot, characters, and other elements in order to follow my argument?
- What details do I need to include about the story upon which the movie is based?

Planning/Prewriting *continued*

Getting Started

GATHER YOUR EVIDENCE

To make your reasons convincing, you need to support them with **evidence**. When you are presenting a critical review of a movie, your evidence includes quotations; examples of events or characters' actions; and description of setting, actors' expressions, or special techniques used by the filmmaker. Watch the movie again; this time, record details that support your reasons.

- **quotations**—"Whenever you feel like telling me to go, just let me know."
- **example**—Charlie smashes into bumper cars filled with children.
- **description**—The director includes a quick series of images that shows Charlie riding a motorcycle, growing a beard, and spending time with "hippies."

▶ **WHAT DOES IT LOOK LIKE?**

Reasons	Evidence
In the movie, Charlie has a dark, violent side that contradicts his gentleness in the story.	• shows anger in bumper car scene, slamming into children's cars
The ending is underdeveloped.	• shows Charlie alone in his room and then back in the park playing with the children and laughing
Some parts are confusing and distracting.	• director's technique of showing quick series of images, for example, when Charlie "finds himself"

CONSIDER OPPOSING CLAIMS

When you write your argument, you must anticipate what **opposing claims,** or different opinions, your readers might have about the movie. To convince readers of your claim, you should offer **counterclaims,** or reasons that address their views while showing that your position is more valid.

▶ **WHAT DOES IT LOOK LIKE?**

Opposing Claim: The director's technique of inserting quick series of images to fill in detail about Charlie after his surgery is helpful.

Counterclaim: The images don't have a clear connection to the rest of the movie and they are confusing.

PEER REVIEW Review your claim and reasons with a peer. Discuss evidence in support of each reason. Then ask: Have I anticipated valid opposing views of my audience? Are my counterclaims convincing? If not, how else might I address these opposing views?

 YOUR TURN In your *Reader/Writer Notebook,* state your claim and your reasons. Then gather your evidence in a chart similar to the one on page 302 making sure to use various types of details. Finally, list possible opposing views and your counterclaims.

Drafting

The following chart shows how to organize your draft to create a clear and coherent critical review.

COMMON CORE — W 4 Produce clear and coherent writing appropriate to task, purpose, and audience. L1 Demonstrate command of the conventions of standard English grammar and usage.

Organizing Your Critical Review

INTRODUCTION

- Use a challenging **question** or insightful **comment** to catch the audience's attention.
- Give the title of the movie, the title and author of the story upon which it is based, and necessary **background information** about plot and character.
- State your opinion in a strong **claim**.

▼

BODY

- Present your reasons in **logical order**, such as order of importance.
- Support each reason with **evidence**, including quotations, examples, and descriptions.
- Identify possible **opposing claims** and explain your **counterclaims** to each.
- Use **transitions**, such as *in addition, in contrast,* and *finally,* to show the **relationships** among the claim, reasons, evidence, opposing claims, and counterclaims.
- Maintain a **formal style** by avoiding slang and using correct grammar.

▼

CONCLUDING SECTION

- **Restate your claim** and summarize your **reasons**. Include a recommendation for your audience.

GRAMMAR IN CONTEXT: USING *WHO* AND *WHOM*

The relative pronouns *who* and *whom* are used in adjective clauses to connect the clause back to the person being described. To help you decide whether to use *who* or *whom*, follow these rules:

Rule	Example
Use **who** as the subject of a verb in an independent or adjective clause.	▶ *The actor* **who** *plays Charlie in the movie is very talented.* [**Who** is the subject of the verb **plays** in the adjective clause.]
Use **whom** as the object of a verb or preposition in an independent or adjective clause.	▶ *Alice Kinnian is a person for whom Charlie has strong feelings.* [**Whom** is the object of the preposition **for** in the adjective clause.]

YOUR TURN Develop a draft of your argument, following the plan outlined in the chart above. Use the relative pronouns *who* or *whom* in clauses that help to describe actors, characters, or other people associated with the film.

Revising

When you revise, you examine your essay to see where you can improve the clarity of your language, the development of your ideas, and the logic of your organization. In this step, you may find that you need to rewrite some parts extensively in order to achieve your purpose, which is to convince your audience to agree with your claim. Use the chart shown to help you revise where necessary.

ARGUMENT

Ask Yourself	Tips	Revision Strategies
1. Does the introduction grab my audience's attention?	▶ **Underline** the sentence that captures your audience's attention.	▶ **Add** a direct quotation, a question, or a comment to interest the audience.
2. Does my introduction provide necessary background information?	▶ **Highlight** the title of the movie, the title of the story, and the author's name. **Underline** details that summarize plot.	▶ **Add** details to answer general questions such as "Who is the main character?" and "What happens to him or her?"
3. Does my introduction have a strong claim?	▶ **Bracket** the claim. Ask a peer to read it and restate your position.	▶ **Reword** the claim to clearly state your position on the movie you have chosen.
4. Are there at least two reasons that support my claim? Is each reason supported by at least one piece of relevant evidence?	▶ **Number** each reason. **Draw arrows** from the evidence to the reason.	▶ **Add** clear reasons that support the claim. **Insert** quotations, examples, or descriptions to support each reason.
5. Have I included transitions to show clear relationships among my ideas?	▶ **Highlight** words, phrases, and clauses that connect your claim, reasons, evidence, opposing claims, and counterclaims.	▶ **Add** transitions, such as *for example, also,* and *as a result* to connect sentences and paragraphs.
6. Does my concluding section follow logically from the argument presented and restate my claim and reasons?	▶ **Bracket** your claim and restatement of your reasons.	▶ **Insert** sentences restating your claim and summarizing your reasons.

YOUR TURN

PEER REVIEW Working with a peer, review your drafts together. Answer each question in the chart to identify which parts of your draft need to be reworked or where you should try a new approach.

COMMON CORE W 1d Maintain a formal style.
W 5 Strengthen writing by revising, editing, rewriting, or trying a new approach.

ANALYZE A STUDENT DRAFT

Read this student's draft and the comments about it as a model for revising your own critical review.

Charly—Two Stars Out of Five
by Etta Smith, Horseheads Free Academy

❶   Is it worse to have something and lose it than never to have had it at all? That's the question asked by the movie *Charly* as well as by the story upon which the movie is based, *Flowers for Algernon* by Daniel Keyes. In both the movie and the story, the main character Charlie starts out with below normal intelligence. Then he has experimental surgery that turns him into a super genius, but only for a limited time. It's an interesting, moving plot, and the movie is faithful to the story in many ways. However, some of the director's choices make the movie ultimately less emotionally satisfying than the story.

❷   The actor playing Charlie Gordon skillfully portrays him before and after the surgery. But the director has chosen to add some scenes in the movie that show a dark side of Charlie that grows along with his intelligence. For example, when Charlie becomes frustrated over his lack of progress after the surgery, he storms out of the clinic. He is then seen in a bumper car, intentionally slamming into the other cars driven by children. Later in the film, Charlie attacks Alice Kinnian, for whom he has strong romantic feelings. You just feel like saying "Hey, man! Where's your head at?" In contrast, in the story, Charlie remains sweet and childlike even as his intelligence increases. He tells his diary that he loves Alice Kinnian, but he does not force himself on her. The director's vision might be more dramatic to watch, but it makes Charlie's character less endearing.

> Etta includes the **title** of the text that the movie is based on, the **author**, and the basic **plot** of the movie.

> Etta concludes her first paragraph with a statement of her **claim**.

> Etta identifies her first major **reason** in support of her claim.

> Here, Etta fails to **maintain her formal style**. Instead, she uses slang and nonstandard sentence structure.

LEARN HOW Maintain a Formal Style In the middle of Etta's second paragraph, she switches from writing in a formal style to writing the way she might talk to her friends. To maintain the consistency of a style appropriate for a formal critical review, she completely rewrote the sentence.

ETTA'S REVISION TO PARAGRAPH ❷

Later in the film, Charlie, unable to control his strong feelings for Alice Kinnian, attacks her. ~~You just feel like saying "Hey, man! Where's your head at?"~~ *He does no real harm, but the violence of the scene is disturbing.*

3   The abruptness of the ending is unsatisfying as well. After Charlie realizes he cannot stop the loss of his intelligence, Alice Kinnian comes to see him. She says, "Whenever you feel like telling me to go, just let me know . . . I'll leave." He replies immediately, "Leave. Please leave." The next scene shows Charlie back on the playground, acting like the children there. By choosing not to show Charlie's awareness of each phase of his decline, the director prevents the audience from feeling Charlie's despair. That decision weakens the power of the story.

> Etta identifies her second reason and **supports** it with a description of the scene and some dialogue.

4   Some viewers might argue that the director's technique of inserting quick series of images to fill in detail about Charlie after his surgery is helpful. These images don't have a clear connection to the rest of the movie, and they cause confusion.

> Etta mentions but does not **address an opposing claim**, which weakens her argument.

5   In spite of these flaws, the movie *Charly* is worth seeing. The audience doesn't experience Charlie's triumphs and tragedies as fully as in the story. They see a dark side of him. But, they also come away with some important ideas to think about, such as the pain of growth and of loss. See the movie if you can; read the story because you must.

> Etta's **concluding section** restates the claim and adds a recommendation to her audience.

LEARN HOW   Address Opposing Claims   While Etta acknowledges an opposing claim and responds to it, she doesn't provide enough support for her counterclaim. When she revised this paragraph of her argument, she included more details that show why the opposing claim is not valid.

ETTA'S REVISION TO PARAGRAPH 4

    Some viewers might argue that the director's technique of inserting quick series of images to fill in detail about Charlie after his surgery is helpful. These images don't have a clear connection to the rest of the movie, and they cause confusion.

These viewers might say that the blur of shots of Charlie on a motorcycle, Charlie with a beard, Charlie without one, and Charlie hanging out with "hippies" works to show his rebellious period. But it is not clear how long this episode lasts, where it takes place, or even whether it is real or in Charlie's mind.

YOUR TURN   Use feedback from your peers and your teacher as well as the two "Learn How" lessons to revise your critical review. Evaluate how well you maintain a formal style, connect your ideas, and convince your audience to agree with your opinion.

Editing and Publishing

COMMON CORE W 5 Strengthen writing as needed by editing. L 1c–d Form verbs in the conditional and subjunctive mood; correct inappropriate shifts in verb mood. L 3a Use verbs in the conditional and subjunctive mood to achieve particular effects.

In the editing stage, it is important to proofread your essay. You don't want mistakes to weaken the impact of your critical review.

GRAMMAR IN CONTEXT: SUBJUNCTIVE MOOD

Verbs in the **conditional mood** refer to events that may or may not happen, depending on another set of circumstances. *(If I'm free, I would like to attend.)* Verbs in the **subjunctive mood** express uncertainty, a state that is contrary to fact, or a wish or regret. *(I wish I were free to attend.)* Most commonly, the verb *were* is used to indicate the subjunctive mood and follows both singular and plural subjects.

Tips	*Examples*
Use the subjunctive mood in clauses that follow *wish, as if, if* (if the state is contrary to fact or not real).	Charlie **wishes** he <u>were</u> able to read. Dr. Nemur acted **as if** Algernon <u>were</u> still healthy.
Use the subjunctive mood to achieve particular effects in your writing.	Charlie often wondered what his life would be like if he were "normal." (thoughtful) Alice Kinnian wished that she were able to hold back time. (wistful)
Avoid shifts in mood.	**Incorrect:** If I **was** to recommend a movie and suggest you see it, it would be <u>Charly</u>. **Correct:** If I **were** to recommend a movie and suggest you see it, it would be <u>Charly</u>.

When editing, Etta fixed any errors in the subjunctive mood that she found.

... the courage of people like Charlie, a man who makes the best of what he has even though he wishes he ~~was~~ smarter.
          ↑
           were

PUBLISH YOUR WRITING

Share your review with an audience.
- Participate in a debate of the merits or flaws of your movie.
- Submit your critical review to your school newspaper.
- Post excerpts of your critical review on the Web.

YOUR TURN Proofread your review, checking for places where you can use the conditional or subjunctive mood to achieve a certain effect. Choose the publishing option that will best reach your intended audience.

Scoring Rubric

Use the rubric below to evaluate your critical review from the Writing Workshop or your response to the on-demand writing task on the next page.

CRITICAL REVIEW

SCORE	COMMON CORE TRAITS
6	• **Development** Asserts a strong claim; supports the claim with compelling reasons and relevant evidence; thoroughly addresses opposing claims with convincing counterclaims; ends with a powerful conclusion • **Organization** Presents reasons and evidence gracefully and in a logical order; effectively uses transitions to show relationships among ideas • **Language** Consistently maintains a formal style; shows a strong command of conventions
5	• **Development** States a strong claim; supports the claim with clear reasons and relevant evidence; addresses opposing claims with adequate counterclaims; concludes with a restatement of claim and reasons • **Organization** Presents reasons and evidence in a clear order; uses transitions to show relationships among the claim, reasons, evidence, opposing claim, and counterclaim • **Language** Maintains a formal style; has a few errors in conventions
4	• **Development** States a sufficient claim; supports the claim with reasons and evidence; includes an opposing claim and counterclaim; has an adequate conclusion • **Organization** Presents most ideas and details clearly; includes some transitions but could use more • **Language** Mostly maintains a formal style; includes a few distracting errors in conventions
3	• **Development** States a claim; provides some reasons and evidence but needs more; identifies an opposing claim but does not adequately respond to it; has a weak conclusion • **Organization** Presents reasons and evidence in a way that is somewhat confusing; needs more transitions • **Language** Often lapses into an informal style; has several errors in conventions
2	• **Development** Has a weak claim; offers unclear reasons; needs more evidence; does not acknowledge opposing claims; has a weak concluding section • **Organization** Arranges reasons and evidence in a confusing way; uses few transitions • **Language** Uses an informal style; has many distracting errors in conventions
1	• **Development** Lacks a claim; offers unclear reasons, little evidence, and no opposing claim or counterclaim; has no concluding section • **Organization** Has no organization; lacks transitions • **Language** Lacks a formal style; has major problems with grammar, mechanics, and spelling

Preparing for Timed Writing

COMMON CORE

W 10 Write routinely over shorter time frames for a range of tasks, purposes, and audiences.

1. ANALYZE THE TASK   5 MIN

Read the writing task carefully. Then read it again, underlining words that tell the topic, audience, and purpose. Circle the type of writing you are being asked to do.

> **WRITING TASK**   *Audience*   *Type of Writing*
>
> For your school newspaper, write a (critical review) of a novel you have read or a recently released movie you have seen. Convince readers to read the book or see the movie by including relevant reasons and specific evidence to support your claim.
>
> *Topic*   *Purpose*

2. PLAN YOUR RESPONSE   10 MIN

Choose a book or movie that is your favorite. List reasons why you think people should read the book or see the movie. Support each reason with evidence. Consider opinions that others might have. Decide what counterclaims you will develop to address possible opposing claims.

Movie or Book Title	
Reason 1	Evidence
Reason 2	Evidence
Opposing Claim	
Counterclaim	

3. RESPOND TO THE TASK   20 MIN

As you write, keep these guidelines in mind:

- In the introduction, capture your audience's attention, identify the movie or book, give background information, and state your claim.
- In each body paragraph, provide a reason for your opinion and support it with examples, events, quotations, or other details from the work.
- Acknowledge a possible opposing claim and then offer a counterclaim.
- Develop a concluding section that flows logically from your previous paragraphs.

4. IMPROVE YOUR RESPONSE   5–10 MIN

Revising Review key aspects of your essay. Is your claim clearly stated? Do you support it with convincing reasons and evidence? Do you address an opposing claim?
Proofreading Neatly correct any errors in grammar, spelling, and mechanics.
Checking Your Final Copy Before you turn in your essay, read it once more to catch any errors you may have missed and to make any finishing touches.

Technology Workshop

Producing a Critics' Debate

When you discuss with friends the pros and cons of various gaming systems, you are having a debate. A **debate** is a discussion in which opposing sides of a question are argued. Participants in a debate express their views and listen respectfully to those of others, often gaining new insights on the issue.

 Complete the workshop activities in your **Reader/Writer Notebook.**

PRODUCE WITH A PURPOSE	COMMON CORE TRAITS
TASK Plan and film a **critics' debate** about a specific movie that you and another classmate have seen. You will state and support your claim about the movie's merits or drawbacks.	**PARTICIPANTS IN AN EFFECTIVE DEBATE . . .** • state a clear claim; defend it with reasons and evidence • respond to new information with questions or thoughtful comments • delineate, or trace, the claim and reasons in other speakers' arguments • maintain eye contact, appropriate volume, and clear pronunciation

Planning a Critics' Debate

COMMON CORE

W 6 Use technology to present ideas. **SL 1a–e** Engage in collaborative discussions; come to discussions prepared. **SL 3** Delineate a speaker's argument and specific claims. **SL 4** Present claims and findings in a coherent manner; use appropriate eye contact, adequate volume, and clear pronunciation.

A critics' debate is a way to share opinions about a movie, literary work, or even a concert. Follow these suggestions to plan your debate before filming it:

- **Organize Groups** Pair up with a classmate who viewed the same movie and has some different opinions on it. Include in your group one or two other classmates who will moderate the debate and film it.

- **Establish Rules** Together, decide the order of speakers and the length of time each will have. Review points of debate etiquette, such as using a firm, clear voice when stating the claim and reasons, listening respectfully to the other speaker, responding appropriately and politely, and maintaining eye contact.

- **Prepare for the Debate** Clarify the responsibilities of each group member, giving them time to prepare if needed.

  - **Speakers** should outline their claim, reasons, and evidence on note cards. When listening to other speakers, they should take notes.

  - The **moderator** will introduce the speakers and topic, provide necessary background on the film, keep track of time, and bring the debate to a close.

  - The **director** will film the debate. In advance, he or she should check the video equipment, become familiar with its operation, and plan a stage set.

- **Rehearse** Have speakers and the moderator do a walk-through of the debate. The director should do a sound and light check.

Media Tools

THINK central

Go to **thinkcentral.com.**
KEYWORD: HML8N-310

Producing the Debate

Filming the debate has the advantage of allowing a wider audience to view it. In addition, participants can review the film to evaluate their own performances and improve the quality of their speaking skills in the future.

GETTING STARTED

Follow these guidelines to produce an effective critics' debate:

Filming	Editing
• Set up a site for the debate in advance, such as a cleared area of the classroom with two podiums. • During the debate, focus mostly on whoever is speaking, but include some cutaway reaction shots of the other person nodding or disagreeing nonverbally. • Be sure to film the moderator's introduction and closing remarks. • Include some long shots to allow viewers to see all of the participants as well as the setting. • Invite classmates to act as a studio audience.	• Cut dead air time or prolonged pauses by speakers that detract from the momentum of the debate. • Insert short clips of the movie being discussed to help illustrate important points. Check the terms of use to make sure you are honoring the movie's copyright. • Invite other students to view the debate and share feedback before making final edits.

YOUR TURN Present and film your debate, following the suggestions on these pages. Then watch it critically in your group. Discuss strengths and weaknesses of each participant's delivery as well as ways in which the final product could be improved by more sophisticated filming or editing techniques.

Assessment Practice

ASSESS
Taking this practice test will help you assess your knowledge of these skills and determine your readiness for the Unit Test.

REVIEW
After you take the practice test, your teacher can help you identify any standards you need to review.

COMMON CORE

RL 1 Cite textual evidence to support inferences drawn from the text. **RL 3** Analyze how lines of dialogue reveal aspects of a character. **RL 6** Analyze how differences in the points of view of the characters and the audience or reader create effects. **L 1c** Form and use verbs in the indicative, imperative, interrogative, conditional, and subjunctive mood. **L 4a** Use context as a clue to the meaning of a word. **L 4b** Use common, grade-appropriate affixes as clues to the meaning of a word.

DIRECTIONS Read the selections and answer the questions that follow.

from A Year Down Yonder

by Richard Peck

1   As the train pulled out behind me, there came Grandma up the platform steps. My goodness, she was a big woman. I'd forgotten. And taller still with her spidery old umbrella held up to keep off the sun of high noon. A fan of white hair escaped the big bun on the back of her head. She drew nearer till she blotted out the day.

2   You couldn't call her a welcoming woman, and there wasn't a hug in her. She didn't put out her arms, so I had nothing to run into.

3   Nobody had told Grandma that skirts were shorter this year. Her skirttails brushed her shoes. I recognized the dress. It was the one she put on in hot weather to walk uptown in. Though I was two years older, two years taller than last time, she wasn't one for personal comments. The picnic hamper quivered, and she noticed. "What's in there?"

4   "Bootsie," I said. "My cat."

5   "Hoo-boy," Grandma said. "Another mouth to feed." Her lips pleated. "And what's that thing?" She nodded to my other hand.

6   "My radio." But it was more than a radio to me. It was my last touch with the world.

7   "That's all we need." Grandma looked skyward. "More noise."

8   She aimed one of her chins down the platform. "That yours?" She meant the trunk. It was the footlocker Dad had brought home from the Great War.

9   "Leave it," she said. "They'll bring it to the house." She turned and trudged away, and I was supposed to follow. I walked away from my trunk, wondering if I'd ever see it again. It wouldn't have lasted long on the platform in Chicago. Hot tongs wouldn't have separated me from Bootsie and my radio.

10 The recession of thirty-seven had hit Grandma's town harder than it had hit Chicago. Grass grew in the main street. Only a face or two showed in the window of The Coffee Pot Café. Moore's Store was hurting for trade. Weidenbach's bank looked to be just barely in business.

11 On the other side of the weedy road, Grandma turned the wrong way, away from her house. Two old slab-sided dogs slept on the sidewalk. Bootsie knew because she was having a conniption in the hamper. And my radio was getting heavier. I caught up with Grandma.

12 "Where are we going?"

13 "Going?" she said, the picture of surprise. "Why, to school. You've already missed pretty nearly two weeks."

Practice Test THINK central

Take it at thinkcentral.com.
KEYWORD: HML8N-312

from Luke Baldwin's Vow

by Morley Callaghan

1   That summer when twelve-year-old Luke Baldwin came to live with his Uncle Henry in the house on the stream by the sawmill, he did not forget that he had promised his dying father he would try to learn things from his uncle; so he used to watch him very carefully.

2   Uncle Henry, who was the manager of the sawmill, was a big, burly man weighing more than two hundred and thirty pounds, and he had a rough-skinned, brick-colored face. He looked like a powerful man, but his health was not good. He had aches and pains in his back and shoulders which puzzled the doctor. The first thing Luke learned about Uncle Henry was that everybody had great respect for him. The four men he employed in the sawmill were always polite and attentive when he spoke to them. His wife, Luke's Aunt Helen, a kindly, plump, straightforward woman, never argued with him. "You should try and be like your Uncle Henry," she would say to Luke. "He's so wonderfully practical. He takes care of everything in a sensible, easy way."

3   Luke used to trail around the sawmill after Uncle Henry, not only because he liked the fresh, clean smell of the newly cut wood and the big piles of sawdust, but because he was impressed by his uncle's precise, firm tone when he spoke to the men.

4   Sometimes Uncle Henry would stop and explain to Luke something about a piece of timber. "Always try and learn the essential facts, son," he would say. "If you've got the facts, you know what's useful and what isn't useful, and no one can fool you."

5   He showed Luke that nothing of value was ever wasted around the mill. Luke used to listen, and wonder if there was another man in the world who knew so well what was needed and what ought to be thrown away. Uncle Henry had known at once that Luke needed a bicycle to ride to his school, which was two miles away in town, and he bought him a good one. He knew that Luke needed good, serviceable clothes. He also knew exactly how much Aunt Helen needed to run the house, the price of everything, and how much a woman should be paid for doing the family washing. In the evenings Luke used to sit in the living room watching his uncle making notations in a black notebook which he always carried in his vest pocket, and he knew that he was assessing the value of the smallest transaction that had taken place during the day.

Reading Comprehension

Use "A Year Down Yonder" to answer questions 1–6.

1. You can tell that this story is told from the first person point of view because the narrator —

   A. is a minor character in the story who reveals some information

   B. is an outside observer rather than a character in the story

   C. reveals the grandmother's and the girl's thoughts

   D. uses the pronouns *I* and *me* to refer to herself

2. The author brings Grandma's character to life mainly by revealing —

   A. the townspeople's opinions of Grandma

   B. Grandma's own thoughts about her granddaughter

   C. the granddaughter's reactions to Grandma

   D. a detailed description of Grandma's life

3. The narrator makes you aware that Grandma is not a sentimental person when she says —

   A. *My goodness, she was a big woman.*

   B. *She drew nearer till she blotted out the day.*

   C. *You couldn't call her a welcoming woman, and there wasn't a hug in her.*

   D. *She aimed one of her chins down the platform.*

4. Grandma can best be described as —

   A. easygoing

   B. generous

   C. no-nonsense

   D. self-important

5. Which character trait do the narrator and her grandmother seem to share?

   A. Determination

   B. Idealism

   C. Lightheartedness

   D. Talkativeness

6. The narrator brings her radio with her because she —

   A. is afraid that her radio will be taken

   B. thinks that people in Grandma's town don't have radios

   C. does not want to make friends in Grandma's town

   D. thinks she will be in an isolated place

Use "Luke Baldwin's Vow" to answer questions 7–12.

7. You can tell this excerpt is told from a third-person limited point of view because the narrator —

   A. is a main character in the story

   B. tells about the thoughts and feelings of all of the characters

   C. is outside the story and tells what one character sees, thinks, and feels

   D. describes his or her own thoughts

8. The story's point of view helps you understand —

   A. the importance of sawmills

   B. what Aunt Helen thinks about her husband

   C. that nothing of value should be wasted

   D. what Luke learns from his uncle

9. Luke watches his uncle carefully because —

   A. he is new to the family and wants to make a good impression

   B. he promised his father he would try to learn things from his uncle

   C. Uncle Henry knows more about what is needed than anyone else Luke has met

   D. the family wants Luke to succeed as a worker at the sawmill

10. Which method of characterization is used in paragraph 2 to describe Uncle Henry?

    A. A description of his speech patterns

    B. Another character's opinion of him

    C. Uncle Henry's own thoughts about life

    D. The author's direct comments about him

11. Uncle Henry's words and actions in paragraph 4 show him to be a —

    A. patient teacher

    B. strict boss

    C. fun-loving relative

    D. dishonest businessman

12. From the description of Uncle Henry in this excerpt, you can infer he is —

    A. unconcerned about the feelings of others

    B. very shy and forgetful about business dealings

    C. careful and smart in his work and personal business

    D. confident that he has good health and will live a long time

Use both selections to answer question 13.

13. The granddaughter and Luke can both be described as —

    A. cheerful

    B. confused

    C. observant

    D. spoiled

SHORT CONSTRUCTED RESPONSE
Write two or three sentences to answer each question.

14. Reread paragraph 3 in the excerpt from *A Year Down Yonder*. What can you infer about the grandmother from this description?

15. Reread paragraph 3 in the excerpt from "Luke Baldwin's Vow." What motivates Luke to follow Uncle Henry around the sawmill?

Write a paragraph to answer this question.

16. Describe two ways in which Peck brings Grandma's character to life and Callaghan brings Uncle Henry's character to life. Give examples from the excerpts to support your answer.

GO ON ➡

Vocabulary

Use context clues and your knowledge of multiple-meaning words to answer the following questions.

1. Which meaning of the word *trail* is used in paragraph 3 of "Luke Baldwin's Vow"?

   "Luke used to <u>trail</u> around the sawmill after Uncle Henry. . . ."
   - **A.** Stream along
   - **C.** Follow behind
   - **B.** Drag heavily
   - **D.** Track closely

2. Which meaning of the word *platform* is used in paragraph 1 of *A Year Down Yonder*?

   ". . . there came Grandma up the <u>platform</u> steps."
   - **A.** A statement of principles
   - **B.** A place for discussion
   - **C.** A device for drilling
   - **D.** A raised surface

3. Which meaning of the word *trunk* is used in paragraph 9 of *A Year Down Yonder*?

   "I walked away from my <u>trunk</u>, wondering if I would ever see it again."
   - **A.** A storage compartment
   - **B.** A piece of luggage
   - **C.** A tree stem
   - **D.** The center of the body

4. Which meaning of the word *trade* is used in paragraph 10 of *A Year Down Yonder*?

   "Moore's Store was hurting for <u>trade</u>."
   - **A.** The customers of a business
   - **B.** An exchange of one thing for another
   - **C.** An occupation that requires skilled training
   - **D.** The people who work in a certain kind of business

Use context clues and your knowledge of prefixes to answer the following questions.

5. One meaning of the prefix *re-* is "again." What does the word *recognize* mean in paragraph 3 of *A Year Down Yonder*?

   "I <u>recognized</u> the dress."
   - **A.** Learned from someone else
   - **B.** Had forgotten once more
   - **C.** Could not remember
   - **D.** Knew from before

6. One meaning of the prefix *im-* is "on." What does the word *imposition* mean in this sentence about *A Year Down Yonder*?

   She felt she was an <u>imposition</u> on her Grandmother.
   - **A.** A relief
   - **B.** A great joy
   - **C.** A burden
   - **D.** A surprise

7. One meaning of the prefix *trans-* is "transfer." What does the word *transaction* mean as used in paragraph 5 of "Luke Baldwin's Vow"?

   ". . . he knew that he was assessing the value of the smallest <u>transaction</u> that had taken place during the day."
   - **A.** A sudden burst of activity
   - **B.** A business agreement or exchange
   - **C.** An immigration to a new land
   - **D.** The distribution of the business profits

Revising and Editing

DIRECTIONS Read this passage and answer the questions that follow.

> (1) On October 29, 1929, the stock market will crash, sending the United States into an economic depression. (2) Because it was the most devastating depression ever to afflict the country, it would be called the Great Depression. (3) Herbert Hoover, the president at the time, will refuse to provide direct federal relief to the poor. (4) Americans are furious about Hoover's lack of action, and in 1932, the country elected Franklin D. Roosevelt as the new president. (5) Roosevelt was more willing than Hoover to provide aid. (6) He supplied immediate relief to the poor and aid to farms and businesses. (7) Although a lot of people remained unemployed, their circumstances could be better than they had been before.

1. What change, if any, should be made in sentence 1?

   A. Change *will crash* to **is crashing**

   B. Change *will crash* to **crashed**

   C. Change *will crash* to **will be crashing**

   D. Make no change

2. What change, if any, should be made in sentence 2?

   A. Change *Because it was* to **If it were**

   B. Change *would be* to **was**

   C. Change *would be* to **were**

   D. Make no change

3. What change, if any, should be made in sentence 3?

   A. Change *will refuse* to **refused**

   B. Change *will refuse* to **will be refusing**

   C. Change *will refuse* to **is refusing**

   D. Make no change

4. What change, if any, should be made in sentence 4?

   A. Change *are* to **will be**

   B. Change *are* to **were**

   C. Change *are* to **have been**

   D. Make no change

5. What change, if any, should be made in sentence 6?

   A. Change *supplied* to **supplies**

   B. Change *immediate relief* to **most immediate relief**

   C. Add a comma after *farms*

   D. Make no change

6. What change, if any, should be made in sentence 7?

   A. Change *remained* to **remains**

   B. Change *could* to **should**

   C. Change *could be* to **were**

   D. Make no change

Ideas for Independent Reading

Which questions from Unit 2 made an impression on you?
Continue exploring them with these books.

COMMON CORE

RL 10 Read and comprehend literature. **RI 10** Read and comprehend literary nonfiction.

What do you cherish?

A Thief in the House of Memory
by Tim Wynne-Jones

Declan barely remembers his mother, but this year the memories have started coming back. Sometimes he thinks he can see and hear her in his old house. Can Declan recall his "real" mom and still trust his dad?

Hope Was Here
by Joan Bauer

Hope and her aunt are starting over again—this time at a diner in small-town Wisconsin. When G.T., the owner, decides to run for mayor even though he has a terminal illness, Hope gets sucked into the campaign.

Song of the Trees
by Mildred D. Taylor

Times are tough for Cassie Logan and her family. They don't even have enough to eat. But when someone offers to buy the trees that have whispered outside of her window for as long as she can remember, Cassie knows she must protect them.

What shows others who we are?

I, Juan de Pareja
by Elizabeth Borton de Treviño

A man named Juan de Pareja is enslaved in Spain during the 1600s. By watching his owner, a famous artist, Juan learns to paint—a skill forbidden to slaves. If he reveals his true talent, will he be celebrated, or punished?

Stargirl
by Jerry Spinelli

Leo knows Stargirl is different from the rest of Mica High. She has a pet rat and a ukulele and at basketball games she cheers for the other team. When Leo falls in love with her, he likes her just the way she is—at first.

An Innocent Soldier
by Josef Holub

Adam is only 16 when he's forced to serve in Napoleon's army in the place of his employer's son. He is trapped in freezing Russia with a sick lieutenant his own age. Slowly the two boys become friends, but will they survive?

What are the signs of greatness?

The Voice that Challenged a Nation: Marian Anderson and the Struggle for Equal Rights
by Russell Freedman

Marian Anderson was an acclaimed singer, but there were some segregated concert halls that wouldn't let her perform. She helped to erase these barriers.

Sir Walter Raleigh and the Quest for El Dorado
by Marc Aronson

Walter Ralegh was a favorite courtier of Queen Elizabeth. After her death, he tried to regain his glory by returning to South America in search of El Dorado, the fabled city of gold.

Summerland
by Michael Chabon

Ethan is the worst ballplayer in the league. He's called Dog Boy because "he's always hoping for a walk." Surprised when a mysterious talent scout chooses him to help save Summerland, the home of baseball, Ethan hopes he's up for the task.

Get Novel Wise

THINK central

Go to **thinkcentral.com.**
KEYWORD: HML8-318

The Place to Be

UNIT

3

SETTING AND MOOD

- In Fiction
- In Nonfiction
- In Poetry

Where can
IMAGINATION
take you?

Close your eyes and picture a place you've always wanted to visit. Maybe you're diving down to a sunken ship, swimming slowly through the murky waters. Maybe you're in the locker room of your favorite team on the night they won the world championship. Wherever you are, your imagination is what takes you there. Good writers know how to spark your imagination and transport you to faraway places or times.

ACTIVITY

- With a partner, make a list called "Stories That Have Taken Me Places." In it, include at least four books, stories, or movies with settings that made you feel you had visited another time or place.

- Make another list called "Places I'd Like to Visit." Include at least four settings you'd like to explore.

- Then question others to see if any of the places you'd like to visit are featured in their "Stories That Have Taken Me Places" list. What can your classmates tell you about the places you want to go?

Find It Online!
THiNK central

Go to **thinkcentral.com** for the interactive version of this unit.

PUFFIN CLASSICS
JULES VERNE

JOURNEY TO THE CENTRE of THE EARTH

Preview Unit Goals

TEXT ANALYSIS	• Determine a theme or central idea of a text and analyze its relationship to the characters and setting • Identify and analyze mood • Analyze how differences in points of view create effects • Compare how authors achieve their purposes in two nonfiction texts
READING	• Develop strategies for reading, including predicting, connecting, and setting a purpose for reading • Infer characters' motivations • Read and analyze a primary source • Read science fiction
WRITING AND LANGUAGE	• Write a comparison-contrast essay • Use ellipses and dashes correctly
SPEAKING AND LISTENING	• Create a story discussion blog
VOCABULARY	• Use context as a clue to the meaning of a word • Interpret figures of speech in context • Use common Latin roots and affixes to determine the meanings of words
ACADEMIC VOCABULARY	• circumstance • emerge • predominant • rely • technology

Text Analysis Workshop

Setting and Mood

Suppose you are immersed in a story about ten castaways stranded on an island. What makes the story such a page-turner? At first, you might credit the intriguing conflicts and characters. However, the setting and the atmosphere may also be responsible for drawing you in. The perilous terrain, the raging storms, the lurking wildlife—details like these can transport you to the world that a writer describes. Read on to find out how setting and mood can make you feel as if you are there.

Part 1: Setting

You know that the **setting** of a story is the time and place in which the action occurs. The time can be a particular time of day, season, year, or historical period. The place can be anywhere—from a Civil War battlefield to Mars.

A writer reveals a setting by describing details of that time and place, such as clothing, hair styles, household objects, or even lifestyles. These details often reflect the customs of a region, era, or society.

In some stories, the details of a setting do more than create a backdrop for events. As this chart shows, a setting can affect how characters live and what they do, value, and believe. It can even create conflicts that they must endure.

COMMON CORE

Included in this workshop:
RL 1 Cite textual evidence to support inferences drawn from the text. **RL 4** Determine the meaning of words and phrases as they are used in a text, including figurative and connotative meanings; analyze the impact of specific word choices.

ROLE OF SETTING	EXAMPLE	
Setting can affect characters by • determining the jobs and living conditions available to them • influencing their values, beliefs, and emotions	Small-town rural life had taken its toll on Garrett. He was sick of being around people who had no intention of finishing school or exploring the world. Garrett was determined to do more with his life than settle for a job on his family's farm.	
Setting can create conflicts by • exposing the characters to dangerous weather or natural disasters • making the characters live through difficult time periods, events, or situations, such as poverty or war	The flood had ravaged their home beyond repair and destroyed their personal belongings. For the Tilak family, the loss was devastating. It would take months, even years, for them to rebuild their lives.	

MODEL 1: SETTING AND CHARACTERS

For Sun-hee's entire life, Korea has been under the rule of the Japanese emperor, who has, by law, forbidden the practicing of Korean customs. When World War II breaks out, life becomes even more difficult for the people of Korea. While no battles are fought on Korean soil, Japanese soldiers patrol the streets, and school classes are replaced by war drills.

from When My Name Was *Keoko* Novel by **Linda Sue Park**

It seemed as if the war would never end. Day after day of too much hard work, not enough food, constant exhaustion—and no chance to make or do anything beautiful. If a war lasts long enough, is it possible that people would completely forget the idea of beauty? That they'd only be able to do what they needed to survive and would no longer remember how to make and enjoy beautiful things?

5

I was determined not to let this happen to me. At school every day, while I was working with my hands, I let my mind float away to think of something beautiful.

Close Read

1. How has the war affected people's daily lives?

2. Reread the boxed text. How does the narrator fear a long-lasting war could shape people's attitude toward their surroundings?

MODEL 2: SETTING AND CONFLICT

In this science fiction novel, a chain of volcanic explosions has caused ash to seep into the atmosphere. Miles and his family live in Minneapolis, where the air has become increasingly murky.

from Memory Boy Novel by **Will Weaver**

"I'm not leaving," Sarah said, jerking away from me. "Everybody's going to die anyway, so why can't we die in our own house?" She plopped down onto the lawn. Pale pumice[1] puffed up around her and hung in the air like a ghostly double. That was the weird thing about the volcanic ash; it had been falling softly, softly falling, for over two years now—and sometimes it was almost beautiful. Tonight the rock flour suspended in the air made a wide, furry-white halo around the moon. Its giant, raccoon-like eyeball stared down and made the whole neighborhood look X-rayed.

"Nobody's going to die," I said. "Though if we stay in the city, we might," I muttered to myself.

5

10

Close Read

1. Find two details that help you to understand the effects of the volcanic explosions on Minneapolis.

2. How do Sarah and Miles each view the conflict that the setting has created for their family?

---

1. **pumice:** a powdery substance that comes from volcanic glass.

Part 2: Mood

The way a writer describes a setting can make you feel as if "you are there," whether "there" is a war-torn country or a city threatened by volcanic explosions. Like setting, mood is responsible for prompting this reaction in you.

Mood is the feeling or atmosphere that a writer creates for readers. A mood can be described as *exciting, somber, terrifying, cheerful, carefree,* or something else. To identify the mood in a work of literature, notice the following elements.

- **Descriptions of Setting** Does the story take place in an abandoned house on a stormy night or on a crowded beach during the summer? The writer's choice of setting and the words he or she uses to describe it can create a mood.

- **Imagery** Writers use **imagery**—language that appeals to your senses of sight, hearing, smell, taste, or touch—to affect your emotions and establish a mood. For instance, images such as *squeals of laughter* and *a rainbow of beach umbrellas* help to convey a cheerful mood.

- **Descriptions of Characters' Speech or Feelings** Pay attention to what the characters say, think, or feel about the setting and the conflict. Are they scared, joyful, or depressed? The characters' reactions often reflect the mood the writer is trying to create.

Examine this graphic. Notice how these three elements work together to create a terrifying mood.

DESCRIPTIONS OF SETTING
The forest at the edge of town was even more ominous at night. There wasn't a house or store within two miles. So far, no one in Jake's class had been brave enough to explore it.

IMAGERY
He walked hesitantly, leaves crunching under his feet. Bare trees hovered over him, casting armlike shadows across his path. His heart hammered in his chest as he inched forward.

CHARACTERS' SPEECH OR FEELINGS
Jake couldn't believe he accepted the dare. "What was I thinking?" he muttered to himself, stopping suddenly when he heard approaching footsteps. Fear paralyzed him.

MODEL 1: COMPARING MOOD

Set in New England during the Civil War years, *Little Women* follows the lives of the four March sisters. This excerpt describes the day on which Meg, the oldest sister, is to get married. As you read, pay attention to the descriptions of the setting and the roses.

from *Little Women*

Novel by **Louisa May Alcott**

The June roses over the porch were awake bright and early on that morning, rejoicing with all their hearts in the cloudless sunshine, like friendly little neighbors, as they were. Quite flushed with excitement were their ruddy faces, as they swung in the wind, whispering to one another what they had
5 seen; for some peeped in at the dining-room windows, where the feast was spread, some climbed up to nod and smile at the sisters, as they dressed the bride, others waved a welcome to those who came and went on various errands in garden, porch and hall, and all, from the rosiest full-blown flower to the palest baby-bud, offered their tribute of beauty and fragrance to the gentle
10 mistress who had loved and tended them so long.

Close Read

1. In the boxed text, the roses are described as if they were human. What details help you understand the roses' "feelings" about the wedding?

2. What imagery is used to describe the setting?

3. How would you describe the mood of this scene?

MODEL 2: COMPARING MOOD

The mood of this scene is dramatically different from the one you identified in the *Little Women* excerpt. As you read this passage, look closely at the descriptions that help to create this different mood.

from **MAX**

Short story by **Chaim Potok**

That night it stormed, and a school bus turned slowly into our small street from the main road, one block away. Our new house was only two blocks from my school, and yellow school buses went up and down the street mornings and afternoons. But never during the night! Now the bus moved
5 carefully along the rain-drenched asphalt, and about fifty feet from our house, it picked up speed. Lying in my bed, I heard the revving of the engine and stepped quickly to the window—in time to see the bus skid from the street and mount the curb, barely missing our sycamore tree. It advanced solemnly, ponderously, as if in slow motion. . . .

Close Read

1. In what ways is this setting different from the one described in *Little Women*?

2. Consider the boxed examples of imagery, as well as the descriptions of the setting. How would you describe the mood?

Part 3: Analyze the Text

Now, you'll use what you've learned about setting and mood to analyze the following two novel excerpts. In each, the main character is seeing his or her new home for the first time.

The first excerpt is from *Journey to Topaz*, which is about a Japanese-American family being moved to an internment camp, or holding facility, during World War II. How will life change for Yuki and her family?

from Journey to TOPAZ

Novel by **Yoshiko Uchida**

The eager hopeful voices on the bus died down and soon stopped altogether. Mother said nothing more and Yuki herself grew silent. At the western rim of the desert they could see a tall range of mountains, but long before they reached their sheltering shadows the buses made a sharp left
5 turn, and there in the midst of the desert, they came upon rows and rows of squat tar-papered barracks sitting in a pool of white dust that had once been the bottom of a lake. They had arrived at Topaz, the Central Utah War Relocation Center, which would be their new home.

Ken turned to look at Yuki. "Well, here we are," he said dryly. "This is
10 beautiful Topaz."

The minute Yuki stepped off the bus, she felt the white powdery dust of the desert engulf her like a smothering blanket. The Boy Scout Drum and Bugle Corp had come out to welcome the incoming buses, but now they looked like flour-dusted cookies that had escaped from a bakery.

15 Yuki coughed while one of the team of doctors inspected her throat and then she ran quickly to talk to Emi while Ken finished registering the family.

"We've been assigned to Block 7, Barrack 2, Apartment C," she informed her. "Try to get the room next door."

Emi nodded. "OK, I'll tell Grandma," she said, for they both knew that if
20 anybody could manage such an arrangement, Grandma could.

A boy about Ken's age offered to take them out to their new quarters. He had come in one of the earlier contingents and already knew his way around the big, sprawling barrack city.

"It's a mile square," he explained as they started toward Block 7, and like a
25 guide on a tour he told them all he knew about Topaz.

"There're forty-two blocks and each block has twelve barracks with a mess hall and a latrine-washroom in the center," he pointed out. "When the barracks are all finished and occupied, we'll be the fifth largest city in Utah."

"Imagine!" Mother said.

30 It sounded impressive, but Yuki thought she had never seen a more dreary place in all her life. There wasn't a single tree or a blade of grass to break the monotony of the sun-bleached desert.

Close Read

1. Where does this scene take place? Find three details that reveal the setting.

2. What conflicts has the setting created for the characters?

3. Reread the boxed lines, which reveal Yuki's first impression of her new home. Which word best describes the mood of this scene?

   a. hopeful
   b. bleak
   c. threatening

Now read this excerpt from the novel *The House of Dies Drear.* Thomas Small and his family are driving across states toward their new house, which is rumored to have a long, interesting history. During the Civil War years, the house was owned by an abolitionist who hid fugitive slaves there. How will Thomas react when he sees his new home for the first time?

from THE HOUSE *of* DIES DREAR

Novel by **Virginia Hamilton**

Thomas did not wake in time to see the Ohio River. Mr. Small was glad he didn't, for through the gloom of mist and heavy rain, most of its expanse was hidden. What was visible looked much like a thick mud path, as the sedan crossed over it at Huntington.

5 Thomas lurched awake a long time after. The car went slowly; there was hardly any rain now. His mother spoke excitedly, and Thomas had to shake his head rapidly in order to understand what she was saying.

"Oh dear! My heavens!" Mrs. Small said. "Why it's huge!"

Mr. Small broke in eagerly, turning around to face Thomas. You've waited
10 a long time," he said. "Take a good look, son. There's our new house!"

Thomas looked carefully out of his window. He opened the car door for a few seconds to see better, but found the moist air too warm and soft. The feel of it was not nice at all, and he quickly closed the door. He could see well enough out of the window, and what he saw made everything inside him grow
15 quiet for the first time in weeks. It was more than he could have dreamed.

The house of Dies Drear loomed out of mist and murky sky, not only gray and formless, but huge and unnatural. It seemed to crouch on the side of a hill high above the highway. And it had a dark, isolated look about it that set it at odds with all that was living.

20 A chill passed over Thomas. He sighed with satisfaction. The house of Dies Drear was a haunted place, of that he was certain.

"Well," Mr. Small said, "what do you think of it, Thomas?"

"It must be the biggest house anyone ever built," Thomas said at last. "And to think—it's our new house! Papa, let's get closer, let's go inside!"

Close Read

1. What clues in the text could help you determine the location of the Small family's new house?

2. What images in lines 16–19 help you to visualize the Small's new house?

3. Pay attention to Thomas's thoughts and speech in lines 11–24. How does he feel about the setting? Support your answer.

4. Review your answers to the preceding two questions. How would you describe the mood of the scene when Thomas first sees the house?

The Drummer Boy of Shiloh

HISTORY | Video link at
thinkcentral.com

Short Story by Ray Bradbury

Does every
CONTRIBUTION
count?

◌ COMMON CORE

RL 1 Cite textual evidence to
support inferences drawn from
the text. RL 2 Determine a
theme of a text and analyze its
relationship to the characters
and setting. RL 3 Analyze how
particular lines of dialogue
or incidents in a story propel
the action, reveal aspects
of a character, or provoke a
decision. RL 4 Determine the
meaning of words and phrases
as they are used in a text,
including figurative meanings;
analyze the impact of specific
word choices on meaning and
tone, including allusions to
other texts.

When there are 12 people on the team, and you're not even a starter,
you might think that staying for extra practice doesn't matter. But
one good assist can make the difference between victory and defeat.
In sports, as in many areas of life, every contribution counts. You are
about to read a short story in which a young drummer boy learns that
even he can make a difference.

CHART IT Think of a situation in which one person's contribution affects
the outcome. What would happen if that person didn't do his or her
part? Create a cause-and-effect chain like the one shown.

Cause	Effect/Cause	Effect
Alicia forgets to practice her solo for the concert. →	→	

● TEXT ANALYSIS: SETTING

The **setting** of a story is the time and place in which events occur. Setting is particularly important in **historical fiction,** which features real places and events from the past and might also include characters based on real people. To give readers a sense of the past, writers of historical fiction

- refer to historically significant events
- recreate details and customs that help readers see, hear, and smell what life was like at a different time

As you read, notice the details Bradbury uses to capture a Civil War encampment the night before a battle. Consider which of these details may have been customs of that time or place.

● READING SKILL: INFER CHARACTER'S MOTIVATIONS

In this story, a drummer boy's chance conversation with his general profoundly affects the boy. To understand the impact of this conversation, keep track of what the boy feels and his **motivations,** or the reasons for his feelings and actions. Sometimes the narrator will tell you these motivations outright. More often, you will need to make **inferences,** or logical guesses based on story information and your own knowledge and experience. As you read, use a chart to keep track of these inferences.

Details from the Story	What I Know from Experience	Inference

Review: Monitor

▲ VOCABULARY IN CONTEXT

These words help Ray Bradbury convey what it was like to fight in the Civil War. To see how many you know, match each numbered word or phrase with the word closest in meaning.

WORD LIST	askew	muted	solemn
	legitimately	resolute	strew

1. muffled
2. serious
3. to one side
4. lawfully
5. determined
6. scatter

 Complete the activities in your **Reader/Writer Notebook.**

Ray Bradbury
born 1920

An Idea Man
Fans often ask Ray Bradbury, "Where do you get your ideas?" Bradbury says that he often wakes up with a great idea and immediately turns it into a story. He has written nearly 600 short stories—showing his fans that he's not short on ideas.

More than a Science-Fiction Writer
Because much of his work explores the effect of scientific development on human lives, Ray Bradbury is often called a science-fiction writer; however, he doesn't accept this label, and he actually avoids some of the most common technological conveniences. For example, Bradbury does not drive a car or own a computer. In addition to science fiction, he's written plays, mysteries, fantasies, realistic stories and novels, and various types of nonfiction—much of it on an old-fashioned typewriter.

BACKGROUND TO THE STORY
A "Deeply Felt" Story
One morning over 40 years ago, Bradbury read in the paper about an actor whose great-grandfather was known as the drummer boy of Shiloh. Struck by the phrase, Bradbury rushed to his typewriter and wrote the first draft of this story in one day. Later, he researched the Civil War and revised the story to make it historically accurate. He says it's one of the most "deeply felt" stories he's ever written. The Battle of Shiloh, upon which this story is based, took place in April, 1862, in southwestern Tennessee. This major battle was the bloodiest yet seen in the U.S.

Author Online
THINK central
Go to **thinkcentral.com.**
KEYWORD: HML8-329

329

THE
Drummer Boy
OF Shiloh

Ray Bradbury

In the April night, more than once, blossoms fell from the orchard trees and lit with rustling taps on the drumskin. At midnight a peach stone left miraculously on a branch through winter, flicked by a bird, fell swift and unseen, struck once, like panic, which jerked the boy upright. In silence he listened to his own heart ruffle away, away, at last gone from his ears and back in his chest again.

After that, he turned the drum on its side, where its great lunar[1] face peered at him whenever he opened his eyes. **A**

His face, alert or at rest, was **solemn.** It was indeed a solemn time and a
10 solemn night for a boy just turned fourteen in the peach field near the Owl Creek not far from the church at Shiloh.

". . . thirty-one, thirty-two, thirty-three . . ."

Unable to see, he stopped counting.

Beyond the thirty-three familiar shadows, forty thousand men, exhausted by nervous expectation, unable to sleep for romantic dreams of battles yet unfought, lay crazily **askew** in their uniforms. A mile yet farther on, another army was **strewn** helter-skelter, turning slow, basting themselves with the thought of what they would do when the time came: a leap, a yell, a blind plunge their strategy, raw youth their protection and benediction.[2]

20 Now and again the boy heard a vast wind come up, that gently stirred the air. But he knew what it was, the army here, the army there, whispering to itself in the dark. Some men talking to others, others murmuring to themselves, and all so quiet it was like a natural element arisen from south or north with the motion of the earth toward dawn.

---
1. **lunar** (lo͞o′nər): of or relating to the moon.
2. **benediction** (bĕn′ĭ-dĭk′shən): a blessing.

A **INFER MOTIVES**
Note the boy's reaction when the peach pit strikes the drum. Why do you think he reacted that way?

solemn (sŏl′əm) *adj.* deeply serious

askew (ə-skyo͞o′) *adj.* to one side; awry

strew (stro͞o) *v.* to spread here and there; scatter

The Musician, Dale Gallon.
Courtesy of Gallon Historical Art,
Gettysburg, Pennsylvania.

Letter from Home, Mort Künstler. © Mort Künstler, Inc. www.mkunstler.com.

◀ **Analyze Visuals**
Based on this image, what can you **conclude** about what life was like in a Civil War army camp?

What the men whispered the boy could only guess, and he guessed that it was: Me, I'm the one, I'm the one of all the rest won't die. I'll live through it. I'll go home. The band will play. And I'll be there to hear it.

Yes, thought the boy, that's all very well for them, they can give as good as they get!

30 For with the careless bones of the young men harvested by night and bindled[3] around campfires were the similarly strewn steel bones of their rifles, with bayonets[4] fixed like eternal lightning lost in the orchard grass. **B**

Me, thought the boy, I got only a drum, two sticks to beat it, and no shield.

There wasn't a man-boy on this ground tonight did not have a shield he cast, riveted or carved himself on his way to his first attack, compounded of remote but nonetheless firm and fiery family devotion, flag-blown patriotism and cocksure immortality strengthened by the touchstone[5] of very real gunpowder, ramrod, minnieball and flint.[6] But without these last the boy felt his family move yet farther off away in the dark, as if one of those great prairie-burning

B SETTING
Reread lines 30–32. What **details** help you to imagine this particular time and place?

---

3. **bindled:** fastened or wrapped by encircling, as with a belt.

4. **bayonets** (bā'ə-nĕts'): blades adapted to fit the muzzle end of a rifle; used in close combat.

5. **touchstone:** a reference point against which other things are compared or measured.

6. **ramrod, minnieball, and flint:** items used to fire a rifle.

40 trains had chanted them away never to return, leaving him with this drum which was worse than a toy in the game to be played tomorrow or some day much too soon. **C**

The boy turned on his side. A moth brushed his face, but it was peach blossom. A peach blossom flicked him, but it was a moth. Nothing stayed put. Nothing had a name. Nothing was as it once was.

If he lay very still, when the dawn came up and the soldiers put on their bravery with their caps, perhaps they might go away, the war with them, and not notice him lying small here, no more than a toy himself. **D**

"Well, by God, now," said a voice.
50 The boy shut up his eyes, to hide inside himself, but it was too late. Someone, walking by in the night, stood over him.

"Well," said the voice quietly, "here's a soldier crying *before* the fight. Good. Get it over. Won't be time once it all starts."

And the voice was about to move on when the boy, startled, touched the drum at his elbow. The man above, hearing this, stopped. The boy could feel his eyes, sense him slowly bending near. A hand must have come down out of the night, for there was a little rat-tat as the fingernails brushed and the man's breath fanned his face.

"Why, it's the drummer boy, isn't it?"
60 The boy nodded, not knowing if his nod was seen. "Sir, is that *you?*" he said.

"I assume it is." The man's knees cracked as he bent still closer.

He smelled as all fathers should smell, of salt sweat, ginger tobacco, horse and boot leather, and the earth he walked upon. He had many eyes. No, not eyes, brass buttons that watched the boy. **E**

He could only be, and was, the General.

"What's your name, boy?" he asked.

"Joby," whispered the boy, starting to sit up.

"All right, Joby, don't stir." A hand pressed his chest gently, and the boy relaxed. "How long you been with us, Joby?"
70 "Three weeks, sir."

"Run off from home or joined **legitimately**, boy?"

Silence.

"Damn-fool question," said the General. "Do you shave yet, boy? Even more of a damn-fool. There's your cheek, fell right off the tree overhead. And the others here not much older. Raw, raw, damn raw, the lot of you. You ready for tomorrow or the next day, Joby?"

"I think so, sir."

"You want to cry some more, go on ahead. I did the same last night."

"*You,* sir?"
80 "God's truth. Thinking of everything ahead. Both sides figuring the other side will just give up, and soon, and the war done in weeks, and us all home. Well, that's not how it's going to be. And maybe that's why I cried."

C MONITOR
Reread lines 34–42. Do you understand what the man-boys' shields represent? If not, reread this paragraph slowly and refer to the footnotes.

D INFER MOTIVES
What feelings is the boy experiencing? Why might he feel this way? Include your answers in your chart, along with the clues that help you infer them.

E SETTING
Reread lines 62–64. What do the **descriptive details** about the General suggest about how men lived in the 1800s?

legitimately
(lə-jǐt′ə-mǐt-lē) *adv.*
lawfully

"Yes, sir," said Joby.

The General must have taken out a cigar now, for the dark was suddenly filled with the Indian smell of tobacco unlit as yet, but chewed as the man thought what next to say.

"It's going to be a crazy time," said the General. "Counting both sides, there's a hundred thousand men, give or take a few thousand out there tonight, not one as can spit a sparrow off a tree, or knows a horse clod from a minnieball. Stand up, bare the breast, ask to be a target, thank them and sit down, that's us, that's them. We should turn tail and train four months, they should do the same. But here we are, taken with spring fever and thinking it blood lust, taking our sulphur with cannons instead of with molasses[7] as it should be, going to be a hero, going to live forever. And I can see all of them over there nodding agreement, save the other way around. It's wrong, boy, it's wrong as a head put on hind side front and a man marching backward through life. It will be a double massacre if one of their itchy generals decides to picnic his lads on our grass. More innocents will get shot out of pure Cherokee enthusiasm than ever got shot before. Owl Creek was full of boys splashing around in the noonday sun just a few hours ago. I fear it will be full of boys again, just floating, at sundown tomorrow, not caring where the tide takes them." **F**

The General stopped and made a little pile of winter leaves and twigs in the darkness, as if he might at any moment strike fire to them to see his way through the coming days when the sun might not show its face because of what was happening here and just beyond.

The boy watched the hand stirring the leaves and opened his lips to say something, but did not say it. The General heard the boy's breath and spoke himself.

"Why am I telling you this? That's what you wanted to ask, eh? Well, when you got a bunch of wild horses on a loose rein somewhere, somehow you got to bring order, rein them in. These lads, fresh out of the milkshed, don't know what I know, and I can't tell them: men actually die, in war. So each is his own army. I got to make *one* army of them. And for that, boy, I need you."

"Me!" The boy's lips barely twitched.

"Now, boy," said the General quietly, "you are the heart of the army. Think of that. You're the heart of the army. Listen, now."

And, lying there, Joby listened.

And the General spoke on.

If he, Joby, beat slow tomorrow, the heart would beat slow in the men. They would lag by the wayside.[8] They would drowse in the fields on their muskets.[9] They would sleep forever, after that, in those same fields, their hearts slowed by a drummer boy and stopped by enemy lead.

SOCIAL STUDIES CONNECTION

The Battle of Shiloh took place near Shiloh Church, on the banks of Owl Creek.

F SETTING
What do you learn about the Civil War from the General's **dialogue?**

COMMON CORE RL 4

Language Coach

Metaphors Writers use metaphors to compare two things without using *like* or *as*. When a metaphor continues for several lines or sentences, it is called an **extended metaphor**. In your own words, explain the extended metaphor in lines 116–122.

---

7. **taking our sulphur with cannons instead of with molasses:** sulphur was an ingredient in gunpowder that was used to fire cannons; at that time sulphur was also used as a tonic or medical treatment. Molasses is a thick, brown syrup, used to mask the unpleasant taste of medicines.

8. **lag by the wayside:** fall behind.

9. **musket:** shoulder gun with a long barrel.

But if he beat a sure, steady, ever faster rhythm, then, then their knees
would come up in a long line down over that hill, one knee after the other, like
a wave on the ocean shore! Had he seen the ocean ever? Seen the waves rolling
in like a well-ordered cavalry charge to the sand? Well, that was it, that's what
he wanted, that's what was needed! Joby was his right hand and his left. He
gave the orders, but Joby set the pace!

So bring the right knee up and the right foot out and the left knee up and
130 the left foot out. One following the other in good time, in brisk time. Move
the blood up the body and make the head proud and the spine stiff and the
jaw **resolute.** Focus the eye and set the teeth, flare the nostrils and tighten the
hands, put steel armor all over the men, for blood moving fast in them does
indeed make men feel as if they'd put on steel. He must keep at it, at it! Long
and steady, steady and long! Then, even though shot or torn, those wounds got
in hot blood—in blood he'd helped stir—would feel less pain. If their blood
was cold, it would be more than slaughter, it would be murderous nightmare
and pain best not told and no one to guess. **G**

The General spoke and stopped, letting his breath slack off. Then, after a
140 moment, he said, "So there you are, that's it. Will you do that, boy? Do you
know now you're general of the army when the General's left behind?"

The boy nodded mutely.

"You'll run them through for me then, boy?"

"Yes, sir."

"Good. And, God willing, many nights from tonight, many years from
now, when you're as old or far much older than me, when they ask you what
you did in this awful time, you will tell them—one part humble and one part
proud—'I was the drummer boy at the battle of Owl Creek,' or the Tennessee
River, or maybe they'll just name it after the church there. 'I was the drummer
150 boy at Shiloh.' Good grief, that has a beat and sound to it fitting for Mr.
Longfellow.[10] 'I was the drummer boy at Shiloh.' Who will ever hear those
words and not know you, boy, or what you thought this night, or what you'll
think tomorrow or the next day when we must get up on our legs and *move!*" **H**

The general stood up. "Well, then. God bless you, boy. Good night."

"Good night, sir."

And, tobacco, brass, boot polish, salt sweat and leather, the man moved
away through the grass.

Joby lay for a moment, staring but unable to see where the man had gone.
He swallowed. He wiped his eyes. He cleared his throat. He settled himself.
160 Then, at last, very slowly and firmly, he turned the drum so that it faced up
toward the sky.

He lay next to it, his arm around it, feeling the tremor, the touch, the **muted**
thunder as, all the rest of the April night in the year 1862, near the Tennessee
River, not far from the Owl Creek, very close to the church named Shiloh,
the peach blossoms fell on the drum. ∾

resolute (rĕz'ə-lo͞ot') *adj.*
firm or determined

G MONITOR
Reread lines 119–138.
To make sure you
understand it,
summarize the General's
advice to Joby.

COMMON CORE RL 4

H MONITOR
An **allusion** is a reference
to a famous person,
place, event, or work
of literature. In lines
150–151 Bradbury makes
an allusion to the poet
Henry Wadsworth
Longfellow. When you
come across an allusion
in a text, pause to
consider why it was
made. If there is a
footnote to help explain
the allusion as there is
here, read the footnote
before continuing to
read the story. How does
this footnote about
Longfellow help you to
understand the allusion?

muted (myo͞o'tĭd) *adj.*
muffled; softened

---

10. **Longfellow:** Henry Wadsworth Longfellow (1807–1882), popular American author of "Paul Revere's
Ride" and *The Song of Hiawatha.*

Comprehension

1. **Recall** At the beginning of the story, what does Joby guess that the men were whispering about?

2. **Clarify** What causes the General to stop and talk with Joby?

3. **Clarify** According to the General, why was he telling Joby his thoughts about the war?

Text Analysis

● 4. **Infer Character's Motivations** Review the chart in which you noted inferences about Joby's feelings and motivations. Share your inferences about Joby's feelings both before and after the General talks with him. How does the General affect Joby? Be sure to cite reasons and evidence to support your inferences.

● 5. **Examine Setting** In a chart, jot down descriptive details of the story's setting. Then decide which details reveal customs of the story's time and place and tell what you think they reveal.

Descriptive Details	Customs of Time and Place?
blossoms falling	

● 6. **Recognize Relevance of Setting to Meaning** One of the questions Bradbury explores in this story is "What makes a person brave?" How does the setting Bradbury chose help him to explore this question? What answer does he find?

7. **Evaluate Historical Fiction** The information about the Civil War that is found in the story can also be found in numerous works of nonfiction. Tell whether you think Bradbury's use of **historical fiction** is an effective way to learn about the kinds of people who fought in the Civil War. Cite evidence to support your opinion.

Extension and Challenge

8. **SOCIAL STUDIES CONNECTION** Conduct some research about Johnny Clem, a real drummer boy at the Battle of Shiloh, or about another hero or battle of the American Civil War. Share your findings with your classmates.

Does every CONTRIBUTION count?

There was no clear winner in the Battle of Shiloh, and nearly 24,000 lives were lost. Given this outcome, do you think the General still would have told Joby that his contribution mattered? Discuss your answer in a small group.

COMMON CORE

RL1 Cite textual evidence to support inferences drawn from the text. RL2 Determine a theme of a text and analyze its relationship to the characters and setting. RL3 Analyze how particular lines of dialogue or incidents in a story propel the action, reveal aspects of a character, or provoke a decision. W8 Gather relevant information from multiple print and digital sources.

Vocabulary in Context

▲ VOCABULARY PRACTICE

For each item, choose the word that differs most in meaning from the other words.

1. (a) legally, (b) legitimately, (c) lawfully, (d) illegally
2. (a) askew, (b) tidy, (c) crooked, (d) awry
3. (a) softened, (b) muted, (c) harsh, (d) indistinct
4. (a) scatter, (b) arrange, (c) jumble, (d) strew
5. (a) bright, (b) heavy, (c) solemn, (d) glum
6. (a) paralyzed, (b) strong, (c) persistent, (d) resolute

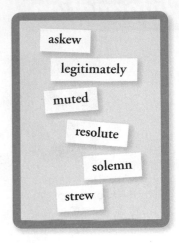

ACADEMIC VOCABULARY IN WRITING

• circumstance • emerge • predominant • rely • technology

If you were the drummer boy, how would you describe the soldiers' camp and the **predominant** mood there? Write a one-paragraph journal entry using at least one Academic Vocabulary word in your entry.

VOCABULARY STRATEGY: IDIOMS

An idiom is an expression in which the meaning of the entire phrase is different from the meaning of the individual words in it. For example, in the story, the General says that the marching soldiers would "lag by the wayside" if Joby beat his drum too slowly. The General meant that the soldiers would fall behind. Today we use the phrase "fall by the wayside" to mean the same thing.

You won't be familiar with every idiom you encounter. Sometimes analyzing the literal meaning of an idiom will help you infer its figurative meaning. When that doesn't work, use **context clues**. Also, idioms appear in some dictionaries.

PRACTICE First analyze each idiom for its literal and figurative meaning. If necessary, use context clues to determine what each idiom means.

1. My old computer finally **bit the dust;** it had been working poorly for weeks.
2. Amanda wanted to continue arguing with her sister, but she decided to **leave well enough alone.**
3. I've always been a good dancer, so learning the routine was **a piece of cake.**
4. After signing up for four after-school activities, Max realized that he had **bitten off more than he could chew.**
5. I'm bringing my umbrella, because it's **raining cats and dogs** out there.
6. Maria **let the cat out of the bag** and told Lamar about the surprise party.

COMMON CORE

L 5a Interpret figures of speech in context. L 5b Use the relationship between particular words to better understand each of the words.

Interactive Vocabulary
THiNK central
Go to thinkcentral.com.
KEYWORD: HML8-337

Use with "The Drummer Boy of Shiloh," page 330.

COMMON CORE

RI 1 Cite textual evidence to support inferences drawn from the text. **RI 3** Analyze how a text makes connections among and distinctions between individuals, ideas, or events. **W 8** Gather relevant information from multiple print sources.

Civil War Journal

 HISTORY   Video link at thinkcentral.com

Journal

What's the Connection?

Historical fiction such as "The Drummer Boy of Shiloh" can give you an idea about what it was like during the Civil War, but reading about the time period from someone who was actually there can be even more revealing. Louisa May Alcott, who wrote the famous novel *Little Women*, kept a journal during the war years.

Standards Focus: Read a Primary Source

One of the best ways to learn about past events is through **primary sources,** materials that were written or made by people who took part in the events. Journals, photographs, and even personal letters are all examples of primary sources. When you study them, you get direct knowledge, rather than someone else's interpretation, of people, places, and events.

When gathering information from a primary source, it's important to consider what the source is and how its form might limit or affect what it conveys. For example, a business letter is not likely to contain colorful details or gossip. You should also think about other factors that would have shaped the source's contents, such as when and where it was created, for whom, and the creator's position in society.

As you read Alcott's journal entries, keep these considerations in mind. Also note what her journal entries tell you about life during the Civil War. Completing a chart such as the one started here can help.

What is the form and purpose of this text?	The text is a journal. It was most likely written to reflect on experiences.
Who was its author? What do you know about her?	Louisa May Alcott; she was the author of <u>Little Women</u> and other novels.
When and where was it written?	
What do you already know about life at that time and place?	
Who was its intended audience?	
What does this document reveal about life at the time it was written?	

Civil War Journal

Portrait of the author

Louisa May Alcott

F OCUS ON FORM
A **journal** is a personal record of thoughts, activities, observations, and feelings. It usually consists of separate, dated entries that appear in chronological order.

1861 Ⓐ

April.—War declared with the South, and our Concord company went to Washington. A busy time getting them ready, and a sad day seeing them off; for in a little town like this we all seem like one family in times like these. At the station the scene was very dramatic, as the brave boys went away perhaps never to come back again.

I've often longed to see a war, and now I have my wish. I long to be a man; but as I can't fight, I will content myself with working for those who can. . . .

1862 Ⓑ

September, October.—War news bad. Anxious faces, beating hearts, and busy minds.

10   I like the stir in the air, and long for battle like a warhorse when he smells powder. The blood of the Mays is up!

November.—Thirty years old. Decided to go to Washington as a nurse if I could find a place. Help needed, and I love nursing, and *must* let out my pent-up energy in some new way. Winter is always a hard and a dull time, and if I am away there is one less to feed and warm and worry over.

Ⓐ **JOURNAL**
Preview the journal entries' headings. In what years were they written?

Ⓑ **READ A PRIMARY SOURCE**
What do you already know about the times in which these entries were written? Add this information to your chart.

I want new experiences, and am sure to get 'em if I go. So I've sent in my name, and bide my time writing tales, to leave all snug behind me, and mending up my old clothes,—for nurses don't need nice things, thank Heaven!

Patients in a military hospital, 1865 **C**

C VIEW A PRIMARY SOURCE

What do you learn about Civil War hospitals from this photograph?

December.—On the 11th I received a note from Miss H[annah] M. Stevenson
20 telling me to start for Georgetown next day to fill a place in the Union Hotel Hospital. Mrs. Ropes of Boston was matron, and Miss Kendall of Plymouth was a nurse there, and though a hard place, help was needed. I was ready, and when my commander said "March!" I marched. Packed my trunk, and reported in B[oston] that same evening.

We had all been full of courage till the last moment came; then we all broke down. I realized that I had taken my life in my hand, and might never see them all again. I said, "Shall I stay, Mother?" as I hugged her close. "No, go! and the Lord be with you!" answered the Spartan woman; and till I turned the corner she bravely smiled and waved her wet handkerchief on the doorstep. Shall I ever see
30 that dear old face again?

So I set forth in the December twilight, with May and Julian Hawthorne as escort, feeling as if I was the son of the house going to war.

D READ A PRIMARY SOURCE

Reread lines 33–38. How does Alcott spend her last day in Boston? What do her activities suggest about her needs and values?

Friday, the 12th, was a very memorable day, spent in running all over Boston to get my pass, etc., calling for parcels, getting a tooth filled, and buying a veil,— my only purchase. A. C. gave me some old clothes, the dear Sewalls money for myself and boys, lots of love and help; and at 5 P.M., saying "good-by" to a group of tearful faces at the station, I started on my long journey, full of hope and sorrow, courage and plans. **D**

A most interesting journey into a new world full of stirring sights and sounds,
40 new adventures, and an evergrowing sense of the great task I had undertaken.

I said my prayers as I went rushing through the country white with tents, all
alive with patriotism, and already red with blood.

A solemn time, but I'm glad to live in it; and am sure it will do me good
whether I come out alive or dead.

All went well, and I got to Georgetown one evening very tired. Was kindly
welcomed, slept in my narrow bed with two other roommates, and on the morrow
began my new life by seeing a poor man die at dawn, and sitting all day between
a boy with pneumonia and a man shot through the lungs. A strange day, but I did
my best; and when I put mother's little black shawl round the boy while he sat up
50 panting for breath, he smiled and said, "You are real motherly, ma'am." I felt as
if I was getting on. The man only lay and stared with his big black eyes, and made
me very nervous. But all were well behaved; and I sat looking at the twenty strong
faces as they looked back at me,—hoping that I looked "motherly" to them; for
my thirty years made me feel old, and the suffering round me made me long to
comfort every one. . . . **E**

1863

January.—I never began the year in a stranger place than this; five hundred miles
from home, alone among strangers, doing painful duties all day long, & leading a
life of constant excitement in this greathouse surrounded by 3 or 4 hundred men
in all stages of suffering, disease & death. Though often home sick, heart sick &
60 worn out, I like it—find real pleasure in comforting tending & cheering these poor
souls who seem to love me, to feel my sympathy though unspoken, & acknowledge
my hearty good will in spite of the ignorance, awkwardness, & bashfulness which
I cannot help showing in so new & trying a situation. The men are docile, respectful,
& affectionate, with but few exceptions; truly lovable & manly many of them. John
Suhre a Virginia blacksmith is the prince of patients, & though what we call a
common man, in education & condition, to me is all that I could expect or ask
from the first gentleman in the land. Under his plain speech & unpolished manner
I seem to see a noble character, a heart as warm & tender as a woman's, a nature
fresh & frank as any child's. He is about thirty, I think, tall & handsome, mortally
70 wounded & dying royally, without reproach, repining, or remorse. Mrs. Ropes &
myself love him & feel indignant that such a man should be so early lost, for
though he might never distinguish himself before the world, his influence &
example cannot be without effect, for real goodness is never wasted.

Mon 4th—I shall record the events of a day as a sample of the days I
spend—

Up at six, dress by gas light, run through my ward & fling up the windows
though the men grumble & shiver; but the air is bad enough to breed a pestilence
& as no notice is taken of our frequent appeals for better ventilation I must do what
I can. Poke up the fire, add blankets, joke, coax, & command; but continue to
80 open doors & windows as if life depended on it; mine does, & doubtless many

E JOURNAL
Reread lines 45–55. How does Alcott spend her first day as a nurse? What does she hope and feel?

another, for a more perfect pestilence-box than this house I never saw—cold, damp, dirty, full of vile odors from wounds, kitchens, wash rooms, & stables. No competent head, male or female, to right matters, & a jumble of good, bad, & indifferent nurses, surgeons & attendants to complicate the Chaos still more.

After this unwelcome progress through my stifling ward I go to breakfast with what appetite I may; find the inevitable fried beef, salt butter, husky bread & washy coffee; listen to the clack of eight women & a dozen men; the first silly, stupid or possessed of but one idea, the last absorbed in their breakfast & themselves to a degree that is both ludicrous and provoking, for all the dishes are
90 ordered down the table *full* & returned *empty;* the conversation is entirely among themselves & each announces his opinion with an air of importance that frequently causes me to choke in my cup or bolt my meals with undignified speed lest a laugh betray to these pompous beings that a "child's among them takin notes." Till noon I trot, trot, giving out rations, cutting up food for helpless "boys," washing faces, teaching my attendants how beds are made or floors swept, dressing wounds, taking Dr. Fitz Patrick's orders, (privately wishing all the time that he would be more gentle with my big babies,) dusting tables, sewing bandages, keeping my tray tidy, rushing up & down after pillows, bed linen, sponges, books & directions, till it seems as if I would joyfully pay down all I
100 possess for fifteen minutes rest.

At twelve the big bell rings & up comes dinner for the boys who are always ready for it & never entirely satisfied. Soup, meat, potatoes & bread is the bill of fare. Charley Thayer the attendant travels up & down the room serving out the rations, saving little for himself yet always thoughtful of his mates & patient as a woman with their helplessness. When dinner is over some sleep, many read, & others want letters written. This I like to do for they put in such odd things & express their ideas so comically I have great fun interiorly while as grave as possible exteriorly. A few of the men word their paragraphs well & make excellent letters. John's was the best of all I wrote. The answering of letters from friends
110 after some one has died is the saddest & hardest duty a nurse has to do.

Supper at five sets every one to running that can run & when that flurry is over all settle down for the evening amusements which consist of newspapers, gossip, Drs last round, & for such as need them the final doses for the night. At nine the bell rings, gas is turned down & day nurses go to bed.

Night nurses go on duty, & sleep & death have the house to themselves. . . . ■

My work is changed to night watching or half night & half day, from twelve to twelve. I like it as it leaves me time for a morning run which is what I need to keep well, for bad air, food, water, work & watching are getting to be too much for me. I trot up & down the streets in all directions, some times to the Heights,
120 then half way to Washington, again to the hill over which the long trains of army wagons are constantly vanishing & ambulances appearing. That way the fighting lies, & I long to follow.

■ **READ A PRIMARY SOURCE**
What do you learn about hospital conditions and the nurses' routine activities?

Comprehension

1. **Recall** When war is declared, how do the people of Concord respond?

2. **Summarize** Review Alcott's 1861 and 1862 journal entries. Then, in a few sentences, summarize why Alcott wants to serve as a nurse.

Text Analysis

3. **Gather Information from a Primary Source** Reread lines 64–73. Which of John Suhre's qualities does Alcott find most notable? Tell what you learn about her values from her opinions about this soldier.

4. **Identify Characteristics of a Journal** If you had stumbled across the original, handwritten version of this journal in a drawer, what characteristics of it would help you identify it as a journal?

COMMON CORE

RI 1 Cite textual evidence to support inferences drawn from the text. **RI 3** Analyze how a text makes connections among and distinctions between individuals, ideas, or events. **W 8** Gather relevant information from multiple print sources. **W 9** Draw evidence from literary or informational texts to support analysis, reflection, and research.

Read for Information: Draw a Conclusion

WRITING PROMPT

By synthesizing historical details from Bradbury's story, your lesson text, and Alcott's journal, you have expanded your ideas about the Civil War. Now draw a **conclusion**—that is, a judgment or belief—about one of the Civil War topics listed here. Then, in a paragraph, state your conclusion and support it with sound reasoning and evidence.

- being a nurse in a military hospital
- Civil War soldiers
- Civil War military hospitals

To answer this prompt, first pick a topic. Then follow these steps:

1. Jot down ideas and information about it.

2. Based on this information, reach a conclusion about the topic.

3. Pick out strong support for your conclusion from Alcott's journal, Bradbury's historical fiction, and/or the lesson text.

4. State your conclusion in a topic sentence. Then present your reasons and evidence for arriving at that conclusion.

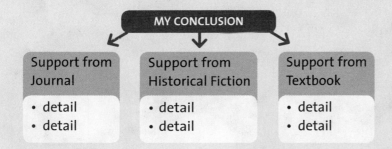

MY CONCLUSION

Support from Journal	Support from Historical Fiction	Support from Textbook
• detail • detail	• detail • detail	• detail • detail

Hallucination
Short Story by Isaac Asimov

from **Ellis Island and I**
Personal Essay by Isaac Asimov

Science Wonder Stories
Magazine Cover

VIDEO TRAILER **THiNK** central   KEYWORD: HML8-344

How do you find your PURPOSE?

COMMON CORE

RL 1 Cite textual evidence to support inferences drawn from the text. **RL 2** Determine a theme or central idea of a text and analyze its relationship to the setting.

Maybe you've heard about a pop star who began performing onstage at the age of three, or about a writer who published her first poem in grade school. But most of us have to search, question, and take a few wrong turns before we find out how to put our talents to their best use. In the story you are about to read, a 15-year-old boy discovers his purpose by traveling to a rather unusual place.

The literary selection that follows explores a boy's efforts to figure out his purpose. After you read "Hallucination" you'll read an expository selection in which Asimov reveals how he found his purpose. Then you will examine a visual that may well have been one of Asimov's early sources of inspiration.

● TEXT ANALYSIS: SETTING

As you probably recall, the time and place in which a story occurs is called the **setting.** The setting often determines the characters' values, beliefs, customs, and actions. For example, the Civil War setting of "The Drummer Boy of Shiloh" helps to explain why the main character believes it is his duty to march into battle with only a drum. As you read "Hallucination," look for ways the story's setting influences the characters' values and beliefs.

● READING STRATEGY: READING SCIENCE FICTION

Science fiction stories are narratives that typically involve fantastical settings, characters, or events. However, they are not necessarily just entertaining fantasies. Writers of science fiction often use their stories to comment upon emerging technologies, contemporary society, and human nature.

As you read this story, keep track of the technologies, customs, and beliefs that are commonplace. Then consider what Asimov might be saying about current technology, society, or human nature by making these elements ordinary in this future world. Jot your ideas next to each custom or other detail you list.

Details	What Asimov Might Be Saying
A Central Computer decides people's careers, and the characters just accept that.	• People want big decisions made for them. • Computers may one day run our lives.

Review: Infer Characters' Motivations

▲ VOCABULARY IN CONTEXT

The boldfaced words help Isaac Asimov tell the story of a boy who discovers his purpose despite opposition. Use context clues to figure out what each word means, and then write a synonym or phrase that means the same.

1. He held a strong **conviction** that something wasn't right.
2. The boy wasn't **insolent;** he tried hard to be respectful.
3. It's difficult to **refrain** from doing something that you enjoy.
4. Losing this game could **diminish** our chances for the finals.
5. Those in **opposition** to the plan were told to keep quiet.
6. She overcame her **inertia** and began seeking a cure.

 Complete the activities in your **Reader/Writer Notebook.**

Meet the Author

Isaac Asimov

1920–1992

Candy as Inspiration
A candy store had an unlikely influence on Isaac Asimov's life and work. The store was a family operation owned by Asimov's father. The new science fiction magazines sold in the store sparked young Asimov's interest in science fiction.

Science Fact and Science Fiction
Asimov grew up to combine his interests in both science and science fiction. He earned a PhD in biochemistry and was a well-respected contributor to the field of robotics, the study of robot technology. He was also famous for his dedication to his writing. He often spent 12-hour days in front of his typewriter, and he was able to type more than 90 words per minute. In addition to fiction, Asimov wrote books on a wide variety of topics, including science, math, history, and poetry. In all, Asimov wrote over 450 books, totaling over seven million words.

BACKGROUND TO THE STORY
Society at the Time
"Hallucination" was first published in 1985. In the two decades before its publication, people in the United States were losing faith in the government and growing concerned about the environment. At the same time, great advances were being made in space exploration and computer technology. The developments in computer technology would soon lead to the widespread use of computers in government and business operations—and, eventually, to the development of the personal computer.

Author Online
THINK central
Go to **thinkcentral.com.**
KEYWORD: HML8-345

345

HALLUCINATION

ISAAC ASIMOV

PART ONE

Sam Chase arrived on Energy Planet on his fifteenth birthday.

It was a great achievement, he had been told, to have been assigned there, but he wasn't at all sure he felt that at the moment.

It meant a three-year separation from Earth and from his family, while he continued a specialized education in the field, and that was a sobering thought. It was not the field of education in which he was interested, and he could not understand why Central Computer had assigned him to this project, and that was downright depressing. **A**

He looked at the transparent dome overhead. It was quite high, perhaps a

10 thousand meters high, and it stretched in all directions farther than he could clearly see. He asked, "Is it true that this is the only Dome on the planet, sir?"

The information-films he had studied on the spaceship that had carried him here had described only one Dome, but they might have been out-of-date.

Donald Gentry, to whom the question had been addressed, smiled. He was a large man, a little chubby, with dark brown, good-natured eyes, not much hair, and a short, graying beard.

He said, "The only one, Sam. It's quite large, though, and most of the housing facilities are underground, where you'll find no lack of space. Besides, once your basic training is done, you'll be spending most of your time in space.

20 This is just our planetary base." **B**

Analyze Visuals ▶

What can you **infer** from this photograph about where the story will take place?

A INFER MOTIVES
Why might the Central Computer's assignment have depressed Sam?

B SETTING
What have you learned so far about where and when the story takes place?

"I see, sir," said Sam, a little troubled.

Gentry said, "I am in charge of our basic trainees so I have to study their records carefully. It seems clear to me that this assignment was not your first choice. Am I right?"

Sam hesitated, and then decided he didn't have much choice but to be honest about it. He said, "I'm not sure that I'll do as well as I would like to in gravitational engineering."

"Why not? Surely the Central Computer, which evaluated your scholastic record and your social and personal background can be trusted in its 30 judgments. And if you do well, it will be a great achievement for you, for right here we are on the cutting edge of a new technology."

"I know that, sir," said Sam. "Back on Earth, everyone is very excited about it. No one before has ever tried to get close to a neutron star and make use of its energy."

"Yes?" said Gentry. "I haven't been on Earth for two years. What else do they say about it? I understand there's considerable **opposition?**"

His eyes probed the boy.

Sam shifted uneasily, aware he was being tested. He said, "There are people on Earth who say it's all too dangerous and might be a waste of money."

40 "Do you believe that?"

"It might be so, but most new technologies have their dangers and many are worth doing despite that. This one is, I think." **C**

"Very good. What else do they say on Earth?"

Sam said, "They say the Commander isn't well and that the project might fail without him." When Gentry didn't respond, Sam said, hastily, "That's what they say."

Gentry acted as though he did not hear. He put his hand on Sam's shoulder and said, "Come, I've got to show you to your Corridor, introduce you to your roommate, and explain what your initial duties will be." As they walked 50 toward the elevator that would take them downward, he said, "What was your first choice in assignment, Chase?"

"Neurophysiology,[1] sir."

"Not a bad choice. Even today, the human brain continues to be a mystery. We know more about neutron stars than we do about the brain, as we found out when this project first began."

"Oh?"

"Indeed! At the start, various people at the base—it was much smaller and more primitive then—reported having experienced hallucinations.[2] They never caused any bad effects, and after a while, there were no further reports. We 60 never found out the cause."

Sam stopped, and looked up and about again, "Was that why the Dome was built, Dr. Gentry?"

---

opposition (ŏp′ə-zĭsh′ən) *n.* the act of opposing or resisting

C READING SCIENCE FICTION
Reread lines 28–42. How are career decisions made in this future world?

VISUAL VOCABULARY

corridor (kôr′ĭ-dôr′) *n.* a narrow hallway, often with rooms opening onto it.

---

1. **neurophysiology** (nŏŏr′ō-fĭz′ē-ŏl′ə-jē): the study of the functions of the nervous system.

2. **hallucination** (hə-lōō′sə-nā′shən): a perception of objects that don't really exist.

"No, not at all. We needed a place with a completely Earth-like environment, for various reasons, but we haven't isolated ourselves. People can go outside freely. There are no hallucinations being reported now."

Sam said, "The information I was given about Energy Planet is that there is no life on it except for plants and insects, and that they're harmless."

"That's right, but they're also inedible, so we grow our own vegetables, and keep some small animals, right here under the Dome. Still, we've found
70 nothing hallucinogenic about the planetary life."

"Anything unusual about the atmosphere, sir?"

Gentry looked down from his only slightly greater height and said, "Not at all. People have camped in the open overnight on occasion and nothing has happened. It is a pleasant world. There are streams but no fish, just algae and water-insects. There is nothing to sting you or poison you. There are yellow berries that look delicious and taste terrible but do no other harm. The weather's pretty nearly always good. There are frequent light rains and it is sometimes windy, but there are no extremes of heat and cold." **D**

"And no hallucinations anymore, Dr. Gentry?"
80 "You sound disappointed," said Gentry, smiling.

Sam took a chance. "Does the Commander's trouble have anything to do with the hallucinations, sir?"

The good nature vanished from Gentry's eyes for a moment, and he frowned. He said, "What trouble do you refer to?"

Sam flushed and they proceeded in silence.

Sam found few others in the Corridor he had been assigned to, but Gentry explained it was a busy time at the forward station, where the power system was being built in a ring around the neutron star—the tiny object less than ten miles across that had all the mass of a normal star, and a magnetic
90 field of incredible power.

It was the magnetic field that would be tapped. Energy would be led away in enormous amounts and yet it would all be a pinprick, less than a pinprick, to the star's rotational energy, which was the ultimate source. It would take billions of years to bleed off all that energy, and in that time, dozens of populated planets, fed the energy through hyperspace, would have all they needed for an indefinite time.

Sharing his room was Robert Gillette, a dark-haired, unhappy-looking young man. After cautious greetings had been exchanged, Robert revealed the fact that he was sixteen and had been "grounded" with a broken arm, though
100 the fact didn't show since it had been pinned internally.

Robert said, ruefully, "It takes a while before you learn to handle things in space. They may not have weight, but they have **inertia** and you have to allow for that."

D **READING SCIENCE FICTION**
Reread lines 66–78. Consider the planet's name and the mission of the people stationed on it. What might Asimov be saying about our energy supply and the way we are using it? Add these details and your ideas to your chart.

inertia (ĭ-nûr'shə) *n.* resistance to motion, action, or change

Sam said, "They always teach you that in—" He was going to say that it was taught in fourth-grade science, but realized that would be insulting, and stopped himself.

Robert caught the implication, however, and flushed. He said, "It's easy to know it in your head. It doesn't mean you get the proper reflexes, till you've practiced quite a bit. You'll find out."

110   Sam said, "Is it very complicated to get to go outside?"

"No, but why do you want to go? There's nothing there."

"Have you ever been outside?"

"Sure," but he shrugged, and volunteered nothing else.

Sam took a chance. He said, very casually, "Did you ever see one of these hallucinations they talk about?"

Robert said, "*Who* talks about?"

Sam didn't answer directly. He said, "A lot of people used to see them, but they don't anymore. Or so they say."

"So *who* say?"

120   Sam took another chance. "Or if they see them, they keep quiet about them."

Robert said gruffly, "Listen, let me give you some advice. Don't get interested in these—whatever they are. If you start telling yourself you see—uh—something, you might be sent back. You'll lose your chance at a good education and an important career." **E**

Robert's eyes shifted to a direct stare as he said that.

E **INFER MOTIVES**
Why doesn't Robert want to talk about the hallucinations? Why do you suppose Sam is so interested in them?

◀ **Analyze Visuals**
What words would you use to describe the **setting** pictured here?

Sam shrugged and sat down on the unused bunk. "All right for this to be my bed?"

"It's the only other bed here," said Robert, still staring. "The bathroom's to your right. There's your closet, your bureau. You get half the room. There's
130 a gym here, a library, a dining area." He paused and then, as though to let bygones be bygones,[3] said, "I'll show you around later."

"Thanks," said Sam. "What kind of a guy is the Commander?"

"He's aces. We wouldn't be here without him. He knows more about hyperspatial technology than anyone, and he's got pull with the Space Agency, so we get the money and equipment we need."

Sam opened his trunk and, with his back to Robert, said casually, "I understand he's not well."

"Things get him down. We're behind schedule, there are cost overruns, and things like that. Enough to get anyone down."

140 "Depression, huh? Any connection, you suppose, with—"

Robert stirred impatiently in his seat, "Say, why are you so interested in all this?"

"Energy physics isn't really my deal. Coming here—"

"Well, here's where you are, mister, and you better make up your mind to it, or you'll get sent home, and then you won't be anywhere. I'm going to the library."

Sam remained in the room alone, with his thoughts.

It was not at all difficult for Sam to get permission to leave the Dome. The Corridor-Master didn't even ask the reason until after he had checked him off.
150 "I want to get a feel for the planet, sir."

The Corridor-Master nodded. "Fair enough, but you only get three hours, you know. And don't wander out of sight of the Dome. If we have to look for you, we'll find you, because you'll be wearing this," and he held out a transmitter which Sam knew had been tuned to his own personal wavelength, one which had been assigned him at birth. "But if we have to go to that trouble, you won't be allowed out again for a pretty long time. And it won't look good on your record, either. You understand?"

It won't look good on your record. Any reasonable career these days had to include experience and education in space, so it was an effective warning. No
160 wonder people might have stopped reporting hallucinations, even if they saw them. **F**

Even so, Sam was going to have to take his chances. After all, the Central Computer *couldn't* have sent him here just to do energy physics. There was nothing in his record that made sense out of that.

As far as looks were concerned, the planet might have been Earth, some part of Earth anyway, some place where there were a few trees and low bushes and lots of tall grass.

---

3. **let bygones be bygones:** decide to forget past disagreements.

Language Coach

Idioms An idiom can be a word that has a meaning different from its dictionary definition. For example, although *deal* can mean "agreement," in line 143, Sam uses it to mean "favorite thing." Reread Sam's statement with this meaning in mind.

F READING SCIENCE FICTION
Reread lines 151–159 and identify two more routine practices that occur in this future world. What might Asimov be saying about the present by making these practices commonplace in the future?

There were no paths and with every cautious step, the grass swayed, and tiny flying creatures whirred upward with a soft, hissing noise of wings.

170   One of them landed on his finger and Sam looked at it curiously. It was very small and, therefore, hard to see in detail, but it seemed hexagonal, bulging above and concave below. There were many short, small legs so that when it moved it almost seemed to do so on tiny wheels. There were no signs of wings till it suddenly took off, and then four tiny, feathery objects unfurled. **G**

     What made the planet different from Earth, though, was the smell. It wasn't unpleasant, it was just different. The plants must have had an entirely different chemistry from those on Earth; that's why they tasted bad and were inedible. It was just luck they weren't poisonous.

     The smell **diminished** with time, however, as it saturated Sam's nostrils.
180 He found an exposed bit of rocky ledge he could sit on and considered the prospect. The sky was filled with lines of clouds, and the Sun was periodically obscured, but the temperature was pleasant and there was only a light wind. The air felt a bit damp, as though it might rain in a few hours.

     Sam had brought a small hamper with him and he placed it in his lap and opened it. He had brought along two sandwiches and a canned drink so that he could make rather a picnic of it.

     He chewed away and thought: Why should there be hallucinations?

     Surely those accepted for a job as important as that of taming a neutron star would have been selected for mental stability. It would be surprising to have
190 even one person hallucinating, let alone a number of them. Was it a matter of chemical influences on the brain?

     They would surely have checked that out.

     Sam plucked a leaf, tore it in two and squeezed. He then put the torn edge to his nose cautiously, and took it away again. A very acrid, unpleasant smell. He tried a blade of grass. Much the same.

     Was the smell enough? It hadn't made him feel dizzy or in any way peculiar. **H**

     He used a bit of his water to rinse off the fingers that had held the plants and then rubbed them on his trouser leg. He finished his sandwiches slowly, and tried to see if anything else might be considered unnatural about the planet.
200   All that greenery. There ought to be animals eating it, rabbits, cows, whatever. Not just insects, innumerable insects, or whatever those little things might be, with the gentle sighing of their tiny feathery wings and the very soft crackle of their munch, munch, munchings of leaves and stalks. **I**

     What if there were a cow—a big, fat cow—doing the munching? And with the last mouthful of his second sandwich between his teeth, his own munching stopped.

     There was a kind of smoke in the air between himself and a line of hedges. It waved, billowed, and altered: a very thin smoke. He blinked his eyes, then shook his head, but it was still there.

G SETTING
What creatures are part of this setting? How does Sam react to them?

diminish (dĭ-mĭn′ĭsh′) *v.* to become smaller or less

H INFER MOTIVES
Why do you suppose Sam rips and then sniffs a leaf and a blade of grass?

I SETTING
What strikes Sam as strange about the planet?

210 He swallowed hastily, closed his lunch box, and slung it over his shoulder by its strap. He stood up.

He felt no fear. He was only excited—and curious.

The smoke was growing thicker, and taking on a shape. Vaguely, it looked like a cow, a smoky, insubstantial shape that he could see through. Was it a hallucination? A creation of his mind? He had just been thinking of a cow.

Hallucination or not, he was going to investigate.

With determination, he stepped toward the shape.

PART TWO

Sam Chase stepped toward the cow outlined in smoke on the strange, far planet on which his education and career were to be advanced.

220 He was convinced there was nothing wrong with his mind. It was the "hallucination" that Dr. Gentry had mentioned, but it was no hallucination. Even as he pushed his way through the tall rank[4] grasslike greenery, he noted the silence, and knew not only that it was no hallucination, but what it really *was*.

The smoke seemed to condense and grow darker, outlining the cow more sharply. It was as though the cow were being painted in the air.

Sam laughed, and shouted, "Stop! Stop! Don't use me. I don't know a cow well enough. I've only seen pictures. You're getting it all wrong." **J**

It looked more like a caricature[5] than a real animal and, as he cried out, the outline wavered and thinned. The smoke remained but it was as though an 230 unseen hand had passed across the air to erase what had been written.

Then a new shape began to take form. At first, Sam couldn't quite make out what it was intended to represent, but it changed and sharpened quickly. He stared in surprise, his mouth hanging open and his hamper bumping emptily against his shoulder blade.

The smoke was forming a human being. There was no mistake about it. It was forming accurately, as though it had a model it could imitate, and of course it did have one, for Sam was standing there.

It was becoming Sam, clothes and all, even the outline of the hamper and the strap over his shoulder. It was another Sam Chase.

240 It was still a little vague, wavering a bit, insubstantial, but it firmed as though it were correcting itself, and then, finally, it was steady.

It never became entirely solid. Sam could see the vegetation dimly through it, and when a gust of wind caught it, it moved a bit as if it were a tethered balloon. **K**

But it was real. It was no creation of his mind. Sam was sure of that.

But he couldn't just stand there, simply facing it. Diffidently, he said, "Hello, there."

J INFER MOTIVES
Why do you suppose Sam feels free to laugh and criticize whoever—or whatever—is making the "cow"?

K SETTING
Do you think that what Sam sees is a real part of the planet, or is it a hallucination?

---

4. **rank:** yielding an excessive crop.

5. **caricature** (kăr′ĭ-kə-chŏŏr′): a comic or exaggerated picture.

Somehow, he expected the Other Sam to speak, too, and, indeed, its mouth opened and closed, but no sound came out. It might just have been imitating
250 the motion of Sam's mouth.

Sam said, again, "Hello, can you speak?"

There was no sound but his own voice, and yet there was a tickling in his mind, a **conviction** that they could communicate.

Sam frowned. What made him so sure of that? The thought seemed to pop into his mind.

He said, "Is this what has appeared to other people, human people—my kind—on this world?"

No answering sound, but he was quite sure what the answer to his question was. This had appeared to other people, not necessarily in their own shape, but
260 *something*. And it hadn't worked.

What made him so sure of *that?* Where did these convictions come from in answer to his questions?

Yes, of course, they *were* the answers to his questions. The Other Sam was putting thoughts into his mind. It was adjusting the tiny electric currents in his brain cells so that the proper thoughts would arise.

He nodded thoughtfully at *that* thought, and the Other Sam must have caught the significance of the gesture, for it nodded, too.

It had to be so. First a cow had formed, when Sam had thought of a cow, and then it had shifted when Sam had said the cow was imperfect. The Other
270 Sam could grasp his thoughts somehow, and if it could grasp them, then it could modify them, too, perhaps.

Was this what telepathy[6] was like, then? It was not like talking. It was having thoughts, except that the thoughts originated elsewhere and were not created entirely of one's own mental operations. But how could you tell your own thoughts from thoughts imposed from outside?

Sam knew the answer to that at once. Right now, he was unused to the process. He had never had practice. With time, as he grew more skilled at it, he would be able to tell one kind of thought from another without trouble.

In fact, he could do it now, if he thought about it. Wasn't he carrying
280 on a conversation in a way? He was wondering, and then knowing. The wondering was his own question, the knowing was the Other Sam's answer. Of course it was.

There! The "of course it was," just now, was an answer.

"Not so fast, Other Sam," said Sam, aloud. "Don't go too quickly. Give me a chance to sort things out, or I'll just get confused."

He sat down suddenly on the grass, which bent away from him in all directions.

The Other Sam slowly tried to sit down as well.

conviction (kən-vĭk′shən)
n. a strong belief

---

6. **telepathy** (tə-lĕp′ə-thē): communication directly from one person's mind to another.

Sam laughed. "Your legs are bending in the wrong place."

290   That was corrected at once. The Other Sam sat down, but remained very stiff from the waist up.

"Relax," said Sam.

Slowly, the Other Sam slumped, flopping a bit to one side, then correcting that.

Sam was relieved. With the Other Sam so willing to follow his lead, he was sure good will was involved. It was! Exactly!

"No," said Sam. "I said, not so fast. Don't go by my thoughts. Let me speak out loud, even if you can't hear me. *Then* adjust my thoughts, so I'll know it's an adjustment. Do you understand?"

300   He waited a moment and was then sure the Other Sam understood.

Ah, the answer had come, but not right away. Good!

"Why do you appear to people?" asked Sam.

He stared earnestly at the Other Sam, and knew that the Other Sam wanted to communicate with people, but had failed.

No answer to that question had really been required. The answer was obvious. But then, *why* had they failed?

He put it in words. "Why did you fail? You are successfully communicating with me."

▲ **Analyze Visuals**

What details in this picture help you **visualize** the Other Sam?

Sam was beginning to learn how to understand the alien manifestation.[7] It was as if his mind were adapting itself to a new technique of communication, just as it would adapt itself to a new language. Or was Other Sam influencing Sam's mind and teaching him the method without Sam even knowing it was being done?

Sam found himself emptying his mind of immediate thoughts. After he asked his question, he just let his eyes focus at nothing and his eyelids droop, as though he were about to drop off to sleep, and then he knew the answer. There was a little clicking, or something, in his mind, a signal that showed him something had been put in from outside.

He now knew, for instance, that the Other Sam's previous attempts at communication had failed because the people to whom it had appeared had been frightened. They had doubted their own sanity. And because they feared, their minds . . . tightened. Their minds would not receive. The attempts at communication gradually diminished, though they had never entirely stopped.

"But you're communicating with me," said Sam.

Sam was different from all the rest. He had not been afraid.

"Couldn't you have made them not afraid first? Then talked to them?"

It wouldn't work. The fear-filled mind resisted all. An attempt to change might damage. It would be wrong to damage a thinking mind. There had been one such attempt, but it had not worked. **Ⓛ**

"'What is it you are trying to communicate, Other Sam?'"

A wish to be left alone. *Despair!*

Despair was more than a thought; it was an emotion; it was a frightening sensation. Sam felt despair wash over him intensely, heavily—and yet it was not part of himself. He felt despair on the surface of his mind, keenly, but underneath it, where his own mind was, he was free of it.

Sam said, wonderingly, "It seems to me as though you're giving up. Why? We're not interfering with you?"

Human beings had built the Dome, cleared a large area of all planetary life and substituted their own. And once the neutron star had its power station— once floods of energy moved outward through hyperspace to power-thirsty worlds—more power stations would be built and still more. Then what would happen to *Home*. (There must be a name for the planet that the Other Sam used but the only thought Sam found in his mind was *Home* and, underneath that, the thought: *ours—ours—ours—*)

This planet was the nearest convenient base to the neutron star. It would be flooded with more and more people, more and more Domes, and their Home would be destroyed. **Ⓜ**

"But you could change our minds if you had to, even if you damaged a few, couldn't you?"

COMMON CORE RL 1

Ⓛ SETTING
Remember that a story's setting, which includes the place, time, and culture, often influences the values, beliefs, and behavior of the story's characters. Reread lines 319–329 and explain how the setting has affected communication between the characters.

Ⓜ SETTING
What aspect of the setting makes humans such a threat to the planet's inhabitants?

---

7. **manifestation** (măn′ə-fĕ-stā′shən): an indication of the presence of something.

350   If they tried, people would find them dangerous. People would work out what was happening. Ships would approach, and from a distance, use weapons to destroy the life on Home, and then bring in People-life instead. This could be seen in the people's minds. People had a violent history; they would stop at nothing.

"But what can I do?" said Sam. "I'm just an apprentice. I've just been here a few days. What can I do?" 🄽

Fear. Despair.

There were no thoughts that Sam could work out, just the numbing layer of fear and despair.

360   He felt moved. It was such a peaceful world. They threatened nobody. They didn't even hurt minds when they could. 🄾

It wasn't their fault they were conveniently near a neutron star. It wasn't their fault they were in the way of expanding humanity.

He said, "Let me think."

He thought, and there was the feeling of another mind watching. Sometimes his thoughts skipped forward and he recognized a suggestion from outside.

There came the beginning of hope. Sam felt it, but wasn't certain.

He said doubtfully, "I'll try."

370   He looked at the time-strip[8] on his wrist and jumped a little. Far more time had passed than he had realized. His three hours were nearly up. "I must go back now," he said.

He opened his lunch hamper and removed the small thermos of water, drank from it thirstily, and emptied it. He placed the empty thermos under one arm. He removed the wrappings of the sandwich and stuffed it in his pocket.

The Other Sam wavered and turned smoky. The smoke thinned, dispersed and was gone.

Sam closed the hamper, swung its strap over his shoulder again and turned

380 toward the Dome.

His heart was hammering. Would he have the courage to go through with his plan? And if he did, would it work?

When Sam entered the Dome, the Corridor-Master was waiting for him and said, as he looked ostentatiously at his own time-strip, "You shaved it rather fine, didn't you?"

Sam's lips tightened and he tried not to sound **insolent**. "I had three hours, sir."

"And you took two hours and fifty-eight minutes."

"That's less than three hours, sir."

390   "Hmm." The Corridor-Master was cold and unfriendly. "Dr. Gentry would like to see you."

🄽 **INFER MOTIVES**
What do you suppose Sam is feeling right now? Why?

🄾 **SETTING**
What have you learned about the beings who inhabit this planet?

Language Coach
Word Definitions The verb *shave* can mean "to remove hair" or "to trim something closely." Which meaning of *shave* is being used in lines 384–385?

insolent (ĭn′sə-lənt) *adj.* insulting; arrogant

---

8. **time-strip:** watch.

"Yes, sir. What for?"

"He didn't tell me. But I don't like you cutting it that fine your first time out, Chase. And I don't like your attitude either, and I don't like an officer of the Dome wanting to see you. I'm just going to tell you once, Chase—if you're a troublemaker, I won't want you in this Corridor. Do you understand?"

"Yes, sir. But what trouble have I made?"

"We'll find that out soon enough." Ⓟ

400   Sam had not seen Donald Gentry since their one and only meeting the day the young apprentice had reached the Dome. Gentry still seemed good natured and kindly, and there was nothing in his voice to indicate anything else. He sat in a chair behind his desk, and Sam stood before it, his hamper still bumping his shoulder blade.

Gentry said, "How are you getting along, Sam? Having an interesting time?"

"Yes, sir," said Sam.

"Still feeling you'd rather be doing something else, working somewhere else?"

Sam said, earnestly, "No, sir. This is a good place for me."

"Because you're interested in hallucinations?"

"Yes, sir."

410   "You've been asking others about it, haven't you?"

"It's an interesting subject to me, sir."

"Because you want to study the human brain?"

"Any brain, sir."

"And you've been wandering about outside the Dome, haven't you?"

"I was told it was permitted, sir."

"It is. But few apprentices take advantage of that so soon. Did you see anything interesting?"

Sam hesitated, then said, "Yes, sir."

"A hallucination?"

420   "No, sir." He said it quite positively.

Gentry stared at him for a few moments, and there was a kind of speculative hardening of his eyes. "Would you care to tell me what you did see? Honestly."

Sam hesitated again. Then he said, "I saw and spoke to an inhabitant of this planet, sir."

"An intelligent inhabitant, young man?"

"Yes, sir."

Gentry said, "Sam, we had reason to wonder about you when you came. The Central Computer's report on you did not match our needs, though it was favorable in many ways, so I took the opportunity to study you that first 430 day. We kept our collective eye on you, and when you left to wander about the planet on your own, we kept you under observation."

"Sir," said Sam, indignantly. "That violates my right of privacy."

Right margin:

Ⓟ INFER MOTIVES
Why do you think the Corridor-Master believes that Sam is a troublemaker?

"Yes, it does, but this is a most vital project and we are sometimes driven to bend the rules a little. We saw you talking with considerable animation for a substantial period of time."

"I just told you I was, sir."

"Yes, but you were talking to *nothing,* to empty air. You were experiencing a hallucination, Sam!"

▼ **Analyze Visuals**
What do the details in the photograph suggest about this man's **character?**

PART THREE

440 **S**am Chase was speechless. A hallucination? It couldn't be a hallucination. Less than half an hour ago, he had been speaking to the Other Sam, had been experiencing the thoughts of the Other Sam. He knew exactly what had happened then, and he was still the same Sam Chase he had been during that conversation and before. He put his elbow over his lunch hamper as though it were a connection with the sandwiches he had been eating when the Other Sam had appeared. ◆

He said, with what was almost a stammer, "Sir—Dr. Gentry—it wasn't a hallucination. It was real."

◆ **GRAMMAR IN CONTEXT**
In line 441, Asimov inserts the prepositional phrase "of the Other Sam" to identify whose thoughts Sam had been having. Without this properly placed modifier, the originator of "the thoughts" would not be clear.

Gentry shook his head. "My boy, I saw you talking with animation to nothing at all. I didn't hear what you said, but you were talking. Nothing 450 else was there except plants. Nor was I the only one. There were two other witnesses, and we have it all on record."

"On record?"

"On a television cassette. Why should we lie to you, young man? This has happened before. At the start it happened rather frequently. Now it happens only very rarely. For one thing, we tell the new apprentices of the hallucinations at the start, as I told you, and they generally avoid the planet until they are more acclimated, and then it doesn't happen to them."

"You mean you scare them," blurted out Sam, "so that it's not likely to happen. And they don't tell you if it does happen. But I wasn't scared." **Q**

460 Gentry shook his head. "I'm sorry you weren't, if that was what it would have taken you to keep from seeing things."

"I wasn't seeing things. At least, not things that weren't there."

"How do you intend to argue with a television cassette, which will show you staring at nothing?"

"Sir, what I saw was not opaque. It was smoky, actually; foggy, if you know what I mean."

"Yes, I do. It looked as a hallucination might look, not as reality. But the television set would have seen even smoke."

"Maybe not, sir. My mind must have been focused to see it more clearly. It 470 was probably less clear to the camera than to me."

"It focused your mind, did it?" Gentry stood up, and he sounded rather sad. "That's an admission of hallucination. I'm really sorry, Sam, because you are clearly intelligent, and the Central Computer rated you highly, but we can't use you."

"Will you be sending me home, sir?"

"Yes, but why should that matter? You didn't particularly want to come here."

"I want to stay here *now*."

"But I'm afraid you cannot."

"You can't just send me home. Don't I get a hearing?" **R**

480 "You certainly can, if you insist, but in that case, the proceedings will be official and will go on your record, so that you won't get another apprenticeship anywhere. As it is, if you are sent back unofficially, as better suited to an apprenticeship in neurophysiology, you might get that, and be better off, actually, than you are now."

"I don't want that. I want a hearing—before the Commander."

"Oh, no. Not the Commander. He can't be bothered with that."

"It *must* be the Commander," said Sam, with desperate force, "or this Project will fail." **S**

Q READING SCIENCE FICTION
Reread lines 448–457. What do you find out about the authorities' activities? What is Asimov suggesting about his own present-day government?

R INFER MOTIVES
Why do you suppose Sam asks for a hearing?

S SETTING
Why does Sam so badly want to stay on Energy Planet?

"Unless the Commander gives you a hearing? Why do you say that? Come,
490 you are forcing me to think that you are unstable in ways other than those
involved with hallucinations."

"Sir." The words were tumbling out of Sam's mouth now. "The Commander
is ill—they know that even on Earth—and if he gets too ill to work, this
Project will fail. I did not see a hallucination and the proof is that I know why
he is ill and how he can be cured."

"You're not helping yourself," said Gentry.

"If you send me away, I tell you the Project will fail. Can it hurt to let me
see the Commander? All I ask is five minutes."

"Five minutes? What if he refuses?"

500 "*Ask* him, sir. Tell him that I say the same thing that caused his depression
can remove it."

"No, I don't think I'll tell him that. But I'll ask him if he'll see you."

The Commander was a thin man, not very tall. His eyes were a deep blue
and they looked tired.

His voice was very soft, a little low-pitched, definitely weary.

"You're the one who saw the hallucination?"

"It was not a hallucination, Commander. It was real. So was the one *you*
saw, Commander." If that did not get him thrown out, Sam thought, he might
have a chance. He felt his elbow tightening on his hamper again. He still had
510 it with him.

The Commander seemed to wince. "The one *I* saw?"

"Yes, Commander. It said it had hurt one person. They had to try with you
because you were the Commander, and they . . . did damage."

The Commander ignored that and said, "Did you ever have any mental
problems before you came here?"

"No, Commander. You can consult my Central Computer record."

Sam thought: *He* must have had problems, but they let it go because he's a
genius and they had to have him.

Then he thought: Was that my own idea? Or had it been put there?

520 The Commander was speaking. Sam had almost missed it. He said, "What
you saw can't be real. There is no intelligent life-form on this planet."

"Yes, sir. There is."

"Oh? And no one ever discovered it till you came here, and in three days
you did the job?" The Commander smiled very briefly. "I'm afraid I have no
choice but to—"

"Wait, Commander," said Sam, in a strangled voice. "We know about the
intelligent life-form. It's the insects, the little flying things."

"You say the insects are intelligent?"

Language Coach

Euphemism A euphemism is a word or phrase that is used in place of a more offensive or unpleasant word or phrase. In dialogue, a pause indicated by "…" may come before a euphemism. Identify the euphemism in line 513 and tell why Sam may have used it.

"Not an individual insect by itself, but they fit together when they want to,
530 like little jigsaw pieces. They can do it in any way they want. And when they
do, their nervous systems fit together, too, and build up. A lot of them *together*
are intelligent."

The Commander's eyebrows lifted. "That's an interesting idea, anyway.
Almost crazy enough to be true. How did you come to that conclusion,
young man?"

"By observation, sir. Everywhere I walked, I disturbed the insects in the
grass and they flew about in all directions. But once the cow started to form,
and I walked toward it, there was nothing to see or hear. The insects were
gone. They had gathered together in front of me and they weren't in the grass
540 anymore. That's how I knew."

"You talked with a cow?"

"It was a cow at first, because that's what I thought of. But they had it
wrong, so they switched and came together to form a human being—*me*."

"You?" And then, in a lower voice, "Well, that fits anyway."

"Did you see it that way, too, Commander?"

The Commander ignored that. "And when it shaped itself like you, it could
talk as you did? Is that what you're telling me?"

"No, Commander. The talking was in my mind."

"Telepathy?"

SETTING
Reread lines 529–532.
How do the insects
communicate with
humans?

550 "Sort of."

"And what did it say to you, or think to you?"

"It wanted us to **refrain** from disturbing this planet. It wanted us not to take it over." Sam was all but holding his breath. The interview had lasted more than five minutes already, and the Commander was making no move to put an end to it, to send him home.

"Quite impossible."

"Why, Commander?"

"Any other base will double and triple the expense. We're having enough trouble getting grants as it is. Fortunately, it is all a hallucination, young man,
560 and the problem does not arise." He closed his eyes, then opened them and looked at Sam without really focusing on him. "I'm sorry, young man. You will be sent back—officially." ⓤ

Sam gambled again. "We can't afford to ignore the insects, Commander. They have a lot to give us."

The Commander had raised his hand halfway as though about to give a signal. He paused long enough to say, "Really? What do they have that they can give us?"

"The one thing more important than energy, Commander. An understanding of the brain."
570 "How do you know that?"

Analyze Visuals ▲

In what ways is the setting captured by this photo different from how you pictured Energy Planet? In what ways is it similar?

refrain (rĭ-frān′) v. to hold oneself back; to stop

ⓤ **SETTING**
Why is it so important to the Commander to remain on the planet?

"I can demonstrate it. I have them here." Sam seized his hamper and swung it forward onto the desk.

"What's that?"

Sam did not answer in words. He opened the hamper, and a softly whirring, smoky cloud appeared.

The Commander rose suddenly and cried out. He lifted his hand high and an alarm bell sounded.

Through the door came Gentry, and others behind him. Sam felt himself seized by the arms, and then a kind of stunned and motionless silence prevailed 580 in the room.

The smoke was condensing, wavering, taking on the shape of a Head, a thin head, with high cheekbones, a smooth forehead and receding hairline. It had the appearance of the Commander.

"I'm seeing things," croaked the Commander.

Sam said, "We're all seeing the same thing, aren't we?" He wriggled and was released.

Gentry said in a low voice, "Mass hysteria." **V**

"No," said Sam, "it's real." He reached toward the Head in midair, and brought back his finger with a tiny insect on it. He flicked it and it could just 590 barely be seen making its way back to its companions.

No one moved.

Sam said, "Head, do you see the problem with the Commander's mind?"

Sam had the brief vision of a snarl in an otherwise smooth curve, but it vanished and left nothing behind. It was not something that could be easily put into human thought. He hoped the others experienced that quick snarl. Yes, they had. He knew it.

The Commander said, "There is no problem."

Sam said, "Can you adjust it, Head?"

Of course, they could not. It was not right to invade a mind.

600 Sam said, "Commander, give permission."

The Commander put his hands to his eyes and muttered something Sam did not make out. Then he said, clearly, "It's a nightmare, but I've been in one since—Whatever must be done, I give permission." **W**

Nothing happened.

Or nothing seemed to happen.

And then slowly, little by little, the Commander's face lit in a smile.

He said, just above a whisper, "Astonishing. I'm watching a sun rise. It's been cold night for so long, and now I feel the warmth again." His voice rose high. "I feel wonderful."

610 The Head deformed at that point, turned into a vague, pulsing fog, then formed a curving, narrowing arrow that sped into the hamper. Sam snapped it shut.

V READING SCIENCE FICTION
Reread lines 578–587. How does Gentry explain the group's experience? What might his response suggest about government officials?

W INFER MOTIVES
What prompts the Commander to give his permission for the invasion?

He said, "Commander, have I your permission to restore these little insect-things to their own world?"

"Yes, yes," said the Commander, dismissing that with a wave of his hand. "Gentry, call a meeting. We've got to change all our plans."

Sam had been escorted outside the Dome by a stolid guard and had then been confined to his quarters for the rest of the day.

It was late when Gentry entered, stared at him thoughtfully, and said, 620 "That was an amazing demonstration of yours. The entire incident has been fed into the Central Computer and we now have a double project— neutron-star energy and neurophysiology. I doubt that there will be any question about pouring money into this project now. And we'll have a group of neurophysiologists arriving eventually. Until then you're going to be working with those little things and you'll probably end up the most important person here."

Sam said, "But will we leave their world to them?"

Gentry said, "We'll have to if we expect to get anything out of them, won't we? The Commander thinks we're going to build elaborate settlements in orbit 630 about this world and shift all operations to them except for a skeleton crew in this Dome to maintain direct contact with the insects—or whatever we'll decide to call them. It will cost a great deal of money, and take time and labor, but it's going to be worth it. No one will question that." ⊗

Sam said, "Good!"

Gentry stared at him again, longer and more thoughtfully than before.

"My boy," he said, "it seems that what happened came about because you did not fear the supposed hallucination. Your mind remained open, and that was the whole difference. Why was that? Why weren't you afraid?"

Sam flushed. "I'm not sure, sir. As I look back on it, though, it seemed to 640 me I was puzzled as to why I was sent here. I had been doing my best to study neurophysiology through my computerized courses, and I knew very little about astrophysics. The Central Computer had my record, all of it, the full details of everything I had ever studied and I couldn't imagine why I had been sent here.

"Then, when you first mentioned the hallucinations, I thought, 'That must be it. I was sent here to look into it.' I just made up my mind that was the thing I had to do. I had no *time* to be afraid, Dr. Gentry. I had a problem to solve and I—I had faith in the Central Computer. It wouldn't have sent me here, if I weren't up to it."

650 Gentry shook his head. "I'm afraid I wouldn't have had that much faith in that machine. But they say faith can move mountains, and I guess it did in this case." ∾

⊗ **SETTING**
Reread lines 619–633. If the Commander's plans are accepted, what will change on Energy Planet?

PERSONAL ESSAY Much like Sam Chase in "Hallucination," Isaac Asimov found his purpose in a place far from where he was born. When Asimov was three, he and his parents emigrated from Russia to the U.S. His father never fully mastered English, and both father and son wanted the boy to succeed at reading and writing.

from
Ellis Island and I
Isaac Asimov

Only in one point did we clash in this matter of reading, and that was over the newsstand in the candy store. I wanted to read the magazines and my father was unalterably opposed. He felt that I would be reading trash and contaminating what he obviously was beginning to think was going to be a first-class mind.

For a while all my arguments fell on deaf ears, and then I discovered science-fiction magazines, which I took surreptitious peeks at while my father was taking his afternoon nap. In particular, I found one called *Science Wonder Stories,* and I pointed out to my father that since the stories were about science, they were bound to be educational.

It was a good time to attack, for my mother was pregnant with what turned out to be
10 my younger brother, and my father was feeling as though he had a lot more on his mind than questions over whether I could read a magazine or not. He gave in.

That started me, at the age of nine, on my career as a science-fiction reader. By the time I was eleven, I felt that I just could not get enough science fiction from the magazines (there were only three, and they came out only once a month), and it struck me that I might write my own.

I didn't quite write science fiction at first, but I managed to get to it when I was fifteen, and by the time I was eighteen I sold a story to one of the magazines and was off and running.

I cannot say how things would have been for me had I not come into the United
20 States as an immigrant. I can't go back and live life over under changed circumstances. Still, as I think about it, it seems to me I needed something to rise above.

To be brief, I'm glad I came here—and I'm glad I had to come here. Life might have been too easy for me if my ancestors had beat me to the punch and had come here on the Mayflower.

Comprehension

1. **Recall** Why does Sam succeed in communicating with the life forms on Energy Planet?

2. **Recall** Why does the Other Sam feel despair?

3. **Clarify** Why does Sam bring his lunch box to his meeting with the Commander?

COMMON CORE

RL 1 Cite textual evidence to support inferences drawn from the text. **RL 2** Determine a theme or central idea of a text and analyze its relationship to the setting.

Text Analysis

4. **Analyze Setting** How does the setting of "Hallucination" affect the plot of the story? Use examples from the selection to support your answer.

5. **Interpret Science Fiction** As you may recall, writers of science fiction often comment on present society by writing about the future. Use the chart you kept while reading to identify one message about contemporary culture Asimov might have been communicating with "Hallucination." Cite evidence from the story to support your interpretation.

6. **Compare Characters' Motivations** Think back to your reading of "The Drummer Boy of Shiloh" on page 330. Although the setting is different from that of "Hallucination," both selections feature teenaged main characters who face big challenges. In a chart like the one shown, compare and contrast these characters' motivations for taking on the challenge they face.

	Joby's	Sam's	Similarities and Differences
Motivations			

Extension and Challenge

7. **Text Criticism** Isaac Asimov once wrote that, for science fiction writers, "each year sees possible plots destroyed" as real-life technology and information catches up with the imaginary. With a group, discuss whether this means that science fiction written many years ago is no longer relevant. "Hallucination" was written in the last century. Do its messages still hold up today?

8. **Readers' Circle** Read the selection "Ellis Island and I" on page 366, taking note of the young Isaac Asimov's personality traits. What characteristics do Asimov and Sam Chase share? How did each young man realize his purpose? Share your ideas with a group.

How do you find your PURPOSE?

Would you like to live in a society in which a Central Computer like the one in "Hallucination" identified each person's career, or purpose, in life? Why or why not?

Vocabulary in Context

▲ **VOCABULARY PRACTICE**

Decide whether the words in each pair are synonyms (words that mean the same) or antonyms (words that mean the opposite).

1. refrain/persist
2. opposition/resistance
3. inertia/activity
4. diminish/decrease
5. insolent/insulting
6. conviction/doubt

conviction

diminish

inertia

insolent

opposition

refrain

ACADEMIC VOCABULARY IN WRITING

> • circumstance   • emerge   • predominant   • rely   • technology

Imagine you are the Commander, writing a report about the new information that has **emerged** since Sam's arrival on Energy Planet and how this information has changed your **circumstances**. Use two or more Academic Vocabulary words to write your one-paragraph report.

VOCABULARY STRATEGY: HOMOGRAPHS

Homographs are words that are spelled the same but have different meanings, origins, and sometimes pronunciations. The vocabulary word *refrain* is a homograph. Notice the following two different definitions of *refrain*:

refrain¹ (rĭ-frān') *v.* to hold oneself back; restrain

refrain² (rĭ-frān') *n.* a phrase or verse repeated at intervals in a poem or song

If you see a word used in a way that is unfamiliar to you, check the dictionary. You'll know a word is a homograph if there are two separate entries for the word.

PRACTICE Use a dictionary to find two or three homographs for each listed word. Note the origin of each word. Then write sentences that show the differences in meaning for each.

1. row
2. well
3. sound
4. fine
5. wind
6. found

COMMON CORE

L 4c Consult general and specialized reference materials to find the pronunciation of a word or determine or clarify its precise meaning or its part of speech.
L 4d Verify the preliminary determination of the meaning of a word or phrase (e.g., checking inferred meaning in a dictionary).

Interactive Vocabulary **THINK** central

Go to **thinkcentral.com**.
KEYWORD: HML8-368

Language

◆ **GRAMMAR IN CONTEXT:** Avoid Misplaced Modifiers

A **prepositional phrase** consists of a preposition, such as *above, at, for, from, with,* or *on;* its object (a noun or pronoun); and any modifiers of the object.

COMMON CORE

L1 Demonstrate command of the conventions of standard English grammar and usage when writing.

> *Example:* The massive dome stretched in all directions.
>
> preposition   modifier   object

When you use a prepositional phrase in your writing, place it close to the word it modifies. Otherwise, you may end up confusing your readers.

> *Original:* From the grass, I saw thousands of tiny insects flying.
> (*Who or what was in the grass?*)

> *Revised:* I saw thousands of tiny insects flying from the grass.
> (*The insects were in the grass.*)

PRACTICE Move each misplaced prepositional phrase to the correct place.

1. I wondered why I had been sent to this planet with my background.
2. The smells are different from Earth's smells on this planet.
3. The shape began to look like me in the smoke.
4. The Commander sat in his office behind a desk.

*For more help with misplaced modifiers, see page R59 in the **Grammar Handbook.***

READING-WRITING CONNECTION

Broaden your understanding of "Hallucination" by responding to this prompt. Then use the **revising tip** to improve your writing.

WRITING PROMPT	REVISING TIP
Extended Constructed Response: Letter Suppose Sam wrote home to describe his experience on Energy Planet. How would he explain how he found his purpose there? Write a **one-page letter** from Sam to his parents. Be sure your letter is based on facts from the story.	Review your letter. If you have any misplaced modifiers, move them to the correct places.

Interactive Revision

THINK central

Go to thinkcentral.com.
KEYWORD: HML8-369

MAGAZINE COVER All magazine covers are carefully planned to communicate a message about what's inside. To figure out what this magazine cover suggests about its contents, examine visual elements such as the title, the relative sizes of the words, and the illustration. The questions to the right will help you.

COMMON CORE

SL 2 Analyze the purpose of information presented in diverse media and formats.

1. **ANALYZE VISUALS**
   Which word in the magazine title is larger than the others? What does this word suggest about the contents of the magazine?

2. **ANALYZE VISUALS**
   What message does this illustration send about the nature of the stories inside? Consider the setting and characters the artist portrays.

Assessment Practice: Short Constructed Response

LITERARY TEXT: "HALLUCINATION"

Assessments often require you to answer questions that focus on particular passages from a text selection. To strengthen your close-reading skills, read the **short constructed response question** on the left and use the strategies on the right to answer it.

> Reread lines 636–652. How is the value of keeping an open mind reinforced by the events and conversations in "Hallucination"? Support your answer with evidence from the text.

◀ **STRATEGIES IN ACTION**

1. Read the passage closely before reaching a conclusion.
2. Look for evidence from the selection that supports your conclusion. Evidence may take the form of a **direct quotation**, a **paraphrase**, or a specific **synopsis**.

NONFICTION TEXT: FROM "ELLIS ISLAND AND I"

Assessments often expect you to draw conclusions from a nonfiction text. Practice this skill by answering the following **short constructed response question.**

> What is one good way to find your ideal career or purpose in life? Use evidence from the text to support your answer.

◀ **STRATEGIES IN ACTION**

1. Reread the selection to learn how the author found his career.
2. Restate what you have learned as a conclusion that answers the question.
3. Support your conclusion with specific details from the selection.

COMPARING LITERARY AND NONFICTION TEXTS

Tests sometimes ask you to make connections between literary and nonfiction texts. Practice this valuable skill by answering the **constructed response question** below.

> How is the idea that you should pursue your interests supported in both "Hallucination" and the selection from "Ellis Island and I"? Support your answer with evidence from both texts.

◀ **STRATEGIES IN ACTION**

1. Consider what happens when Sam pursues his interests in "Hallucination" and what happens when Asimov pursues what he loves.
2. Write an answer to the question that is supported by both selections.
3. Include details from both selections to support your conclusion.

The Monkey's Paw
Short Story by W. W. Jacobs

Are you SUPERSTITIOUS?

Many people say they aren't superstitious. But those same people might own a lucky charm or get nervous on Friday the 13th. Usually these superstitions are harmless, but sometimes they can interfere with a person's life. In the selection you are about to read, curiosity about the power of an unusual object brings unexpected consequences.

DISCUSS What kinds of superstitious behaviors do you or people you know believe in? In a small group, brainstorm a list of common superstitions. Then discuss which you think are harmless, and which might cause problems or interfere with someone's life. Share your findings with the class.

● TEXT ANALYSIS: MOOD

Mood is the feeling or atmosphere the writer creates for the reader. There are as many moods as there are emotions—cheerful, gloomy, anxious. Writers create mood through

- the choice of **setting,** including time and place
- **imagery**—descriptions that appeal to the reader's senses
- conversations between characters

As you read "The Monkey's Paw," notice how the story makes you feel and which words or passages make you feel that way.

● READING SKILL: IDENTIFY TYPE OF NARRATOR

You have learned that a **narrator** is the voice that tells a story. A third-person narrator is not a character in the story, but, rather, an outside voice. Now you will learn that a third-person narrator may be objective or subjective. An **objective narrator** reports events in a factual way, without sharing any characters' hidden thoughts or feelings. A **subjective narrator** recounts events with a character's thoughts, feelings, and observations.

As you read "The Monkey's Paw," try to determine whether it is told by an objective narrator or a subjective one. Use a chart to record the narrator's observations.

Event	Narrator's Description

Review: **Predict**

▲ VOCABULARY IN CONTEXT

Choose the word that best completes each sentence.

WORD LIST	compensation	fate	peril
	credulity	grimace	resignation

1. The old woman's ____ allowed the stranger to trick her.
2. My creepy neighbor wanted ____ for his broken window.
3. The sailors faced great ____ as the storm approached.
4. His ____ scared the children.
5. Tom sighed with ____ upon realizing he was lost.
6. Had she not been saved, she could have met a terrible ____.

 Complete the activities in your **Reader/Writer Notebook.**

Meet the Author

W. W. Jacobs
1863–1943

Bored at the Bank
William Wymark Jacobs grew up on the docks of London, where his father worked as a wharf manager. As a young man, Jacobs was employed at a bank, a job he hated, calling it his "days of captivity." To pass the time, he began writing humorous short stories of ships and sailors. Eventually, he began publishing his stories in magazines and soon became one of the most popular and respected writers of his time.

A Frightening Classic
Though most of Jacobs's stories were humorous, he is most famous for his horror classic "The Monkey's Paw," which has been adapted numerous times for the stage, film, and television. The story's "steady, relentlessly building tension" makes it one of the most widely read horror stories in history.

BACKGROUND TO THE STORY
The British in India
Like most of Jacobs's stories, "The Monkey's Paw" is set in Britain. One of the characters is an officer in the British Army and served in India during the British occupation of the country. The British first arrived in India in the 1600s, when the British East India Company established trading. Their role changed dramatically after the Sepoy Mutiny of 1857–1858, in which Indian soldiers of the British Army revolted. From then on, the British government controlled India through a system of governors and military outposts. As a result, young men went to India to serve in the army. British rule of India ended in 1947, and today, India is an independent nation.

Author Online
THINK central
Go to **thinkcentral.com.**
KEYWORD: HML8-373

373

THE MONKEY'S PAW

W. W. Jacobs

I

Without, the night was cold and wet, but in the small parlor of Laburnum Villa the blinds were drawn and the fire burned brightly. Father and son were at chess; the former, who possessed ideas about the game involving radical changes, putting his king into such sharp and unnecessary **perils** that it even provoked comment from the white-haired old lady knitting placidly by the fire.

"Hark at the wind," said Mr. White, who, having seen a fatal mistake after it was too late, was amiably[1] desirous of preventing his son from seeing it.

"I'm listening," said the latter, grimly surveying the board as he stretched
10 out his hand. "Check."

"I should hardly think that he'd come tonight," said his father, with his hand poised over the board.

"Mate," replied the son.

"That's the worst of living so far out," bawled Mr. White, with sudden and unlooked-for violence; "of all the beastly, slushy, out-of-the-way places to live in, this is the worst. Pathway's a bog,[2] and the road's a torrent.[3] I don't know what people are thinking about. I suppose because only two houses in the road are let,[4] they think it doesn't matter." **A**

"Never mind, dear," said his wife soothingly; "perhaps you'll win the
20 next one."

---

1. **amiably** (ā'mē-ə-blē): in a friendly way.
2. **bog:** a swamp.
3. **torrent** (tôr'ənt): a swift-flowing stream.
4. **let:** rented.

Analyze Visuals ▶

What can you **infer** about the object in the photograph? Note the clues you use to make your inference.

peril (pĕr'əl) *n.* danger

A MOOD
Reread lines 1–18. Note words and phrases that describe the **setting.** What feelings do these suggest?

Mr. White looked up sharply, just in time to intercept a knowing glance between mother and son. The words died away on his lips, and he hid a guilty grin in his thin gray beard.

"There he is," said Herbert White, as the gate banged loudly and heavy footsteps came toward the door.

The old man rose with hospitable haste, and opening the door, was heard condoling[5] with the new arrival. The new arrival also condoled with himself, so that Mrs. White said, "Tut, tut!" and coughed gently as her husband entered the room, followed by a tall, burly man, beady of eye and rubicund of visage.[6]

30 "Sergeant-Major Morris," he said, introducing him.

The sergeant-major shook hands, and taking the proffered seat by the fire, watched contentedly while his host brought out drinks and stood a small copper kettle on the fire.

He began to talk, the little family circle regarding with eager interest this visitor from distant parts, as he squared his broad shoulders in the chair and spoke of wild scenes and doughty[7] deeds; of wars and plagues and strange peoples.

"Twenty-one years of it," said Mr. White, nodding at his wife and son. "When he went away, he was a slip of a youth in the warehouse. Now look 40 at him."

"He don't look to have taken much harm," said Mrs. White politely.

"I'd like to go to India myself," said the old man, "just to look round a bit, you know."

"Better where you are," said the sergeant-major, shaking his head. He put down the empty glass, and sighing softly, shook it again.

"I should like to see those old temples and fakirs and jugglers," said the old man. "What was that you started telling me the other day about a monkey's paw or something, Morris?"

"Nothing," said the soldier hastily. "Leastways nothing worth hearing."

50 "Monkey's paw?" said Mrs. White curiously.

"Well, it's just a bit of what you might call magic, perhaps," said the sergeant-major off-handedly.

His three listeners leaned forward eagerly. The visitor absent-mindedly put his empty glass to his lips and then set it down again. His host filled it for him.

"To look at," said the sergeant-major, fumbling in his pocket, "it's just an ordinary little paw, dried to a mummy."

He took something out of his pocket and proffered it. Mrs. White drew back with a **grimace,** but her son, taking it, examined it curiously. **B**

60 "And what is there special about it?" inquired Mr. White as he took it from his son, and having examined it, placed it upon the table.

---

5. **condoling** (kən-dōl'ing): expressing sympathy.

6. **rubicund** (rōō'bǐ-kənd) **of visage** (vǐz'ǐj): with a ruddy complexion.

7. **doughty** (dou'tē): brave.

VISUAL VOCABULARY

fakir (fə-kîr') *n.* a Muslim or Hindu holy man

B **IDENTIFY TYPE OF NARRATOR**
Have you learned anything about the characters that a keen observer could not have learned? If so, jot down what you have learned. If not, make a mental note of that fact.

grimace (grĭm'ĭs) *n.* a facial expression of pain or disgust

"It had a spell put on it by an old fakir," said the sergeant-major, "a very holy man. He wanted to show that **fate** ruled people's lives, and that those who interfered with it did so to their sorrow. He put a spell on it so that three separate men could each have three wishes from it."

His manner was so impressive that his hearers were conscious that their light laughter jarred somewhat.

"Well, why don't you have three, sir?" said Herbert White cleverly.

70 The soldier regarded him in the way that middle age is wont to regard presumptuous youth. "I have," he said quietly, and his blotchy face whitened.

"And did you really have the three wishes granted?" asked Mrs. White.

"I did," said the sergeant-major, and his glass tapped against his strong teeth.

"And has anybody else wished?" persisted the old lady.

"The first man had his three wishes. Yes," was the reply; "I don't know what the first two were, but the third was for death. That's how I got the paw."

His tones were so grave that a hush fell upon the group.

"If you've had your three wishes, it's no good to you now, then, Morris," said the old man at last. "What do you keep it for?"

The soldier shook his head. "Fancy, I suppose," he said slowly. "I did have
80 some idea of selling it, but I don't think I will. It has caused enough mischief already. Besides, people won't buy. They think it's a fairy tale, some of them; and those who do think anything of it want to try it first and pay me afterward."

"If you could have another three wishes," said the old man, eyeing him keenly, "would you have them?"

"I don't know," said the other. "I don't know."

He took the paw, and dangling it between his forefinger and thumb, suddenly threw it upon the fire. White, with a slight cry, stooped down and snatched it off.

"Better let it burn," said the soldier solemnly.

90 "If you don't want it, Morris," said the other, "give it to me."

"I won't," said his friend doggedly. "I threw it on the fire. If you keep it, don't blame me for what happens. Pitch it on the fire again like a sensible man." **C**

The other shook his head and examined his new possession closely. "How do you do it?" he inquired.

"Hold it up in your right hand and wish aloud," said the sergeant-major, "but I warn you of the consequences."

"Sounds like the *Arabian Nights*,"⁸ said Mrs. White, as she rose and began to set the supper. "Don't you think you might wish for four pairs of hands for me?"

100 Her husband drew the talisman⁹ from his pocket, and then all three burst into laughter as the sergeant-major, with a look of alarm on his face, caught him by the arm.

"If you must wish," he said gruffly, "wish for something sensible." **D**

---

8. *Arabian Nights:* a famous collection of Asian stories.

9. **talisman** (tăl′ĭs-mən): an object thought to have magical powers.

fate (fāt) *n.* a power that is thought to determine the course of events

C MOOD
What feeling do you get from the **dialogue** between the Whites and Sergeant-Major Morris?

D PREDICT
What, if anything, do you think Mr. White will wish for?

Mr. White dropped it back in his pocket, and placing chairs, motioned his friend to the table. In the business of supper the talisman was partly forgotten, and afterward the three sat listening in an enthralled fashion to a second installment of the soldier's adventures in India.

"If the tale about the monkey's paw is not more truthful than those he has been telling us," said Herbert, as the door closed behind their guest, just in

110 time for him to catch the last train, "we shan't make much out of it."

"Did you give him anything for it, Father?" inquired Mrs. White, regarding her husband closely.

"A trifle," said he, coloring slightly. "He didn't want it, but I made him take it. And he pressed me again to throw it away."

"Likely," said Herbert, with pretended horror. "Why, we're going to be rich, and famous, and happy. Wish to be an emperor, Father, to begin with; then you can't be henpecked."

He darted round the table, pursued by the maligned Mrs. White armed with an antimacassar.[10]

120 Mr. White took the paw from his pocket and eyed it dubiously. "I don't know what to wish for, and that's a fact," he said slowly. "It seems to me I've got all I want."

"If you only cleared the house, you'd be quite happy, wouldn't you?" said Herbert, with his hand on his shoulder. "Well, wish for two hundred pounds, then; that'll just do it."

His father, smiling shamefacedly at his own **credulity,** held up the talisman, as his son, with a solemn face, somewhat marred by a wink at his mother, sat down at the piano and struck a few impressive chords.

"I wish for two hundred pounds," said the old man distinctly.

130 A fine crash from the piano greeted the words, interrupted by a shuddering cry from the old man. His wife and son ran toward him.

"It moved," he cried, with a glance of disgust at the object as it lay on the floor. "As I wished, it twisted in my hand like a snake." **E**

"Well, I don't see the money," said his son, as he picked it up and placed it on the table, "and I bet I never shall."

"It must have been your fancy, father," said his wife, regarding him anxiously.

He shook his head. "Never mind, though; there's no harm done, but it gave me a shock all the same."

They sat down by the fire again. Outside, the wind was higher than ever,

140 and the old man started nervously at the sound of a door banging upstairs. A silence unusual and depressing settled upon all three, which lasted until the old couple rose to retire for the night. **F**

"I expect you'll find the cash tied up in a big bag in the middle of your bed," said Herbert, as he bade them good-night, "and something horrible squatting up on top of the wardrobe[11] watching you as you pocket your ill-gotten gains."

---

10. **antimacassar** (ăn′tĭ-mə-kăs′ər): a cloth placed over an arm or back of a chair.

11. **wardrobe:** a piece of furniture that serves as a closet.

credulity (krĭ-dōō′lĭ-tē) *n.* a disposition to believe too readily

E PREDICT
What do you think will happen as a result of Mr. White's first wish? Why?

F MOOD
Reread lines 130–142. Note the **imagery** in these lines. To what senses does it appeal? Explain how it contributes to the mood.

He sat alone in the darkness, gazing at the dying fire, and seeing faces in it. The last face was so horrible and so simian[12] that he gazed at it in amazement. It got so vivid that, with a little uneasy laugh, he felt on the table for a glass containing a little water to throw over it. His hand grasped the monkey's paw, 150 and with a little shiver he wiped his hand on his coat and went up to bed. **G**

II

In the brightness of the wintry sun next morning as it streamed over the breakfast table he laughed at his fears. There was an air of prosaic[13] wholesomeness about the room which it had lacked on the previous night, and the dirty, shriveled little paw was pitched on the sideboard[14] with a carelessness which betokened no great belief in its virtues.[15]

▲ **Analyze Visuals**
What do you see in the fire? How does this **compare** to what Herbert sees?

G **IDENTIFY TYPE OF NARRATOR**
What have you just learned about Mr. White? Would this have come from an **objective** or **subjective narrator?**

---

12. **simian** (sĭm′ē-ən): monkey- or ape-like.

13. **prosaic** (prō-zā′ĭk): ordinary.

14. **sideboard:** a piece of furniture used to store linens and dishes.

15. **virtues:** powers.

"I suppose all old soldiers are the same," said Mrs. White. "The idea of our listening to such nonsense! How could wishes be granted in these days? And if they could, how could two hundred pounds hurt you, father?"

"Might drop on his head from the sky," said the frivolous[16] Herbert.

160 "Morris said the things happened so naturally," said his father, "that you might if you so wished attribute it to coincidence."

"Well, don't break into the money before I come back," said Herbert as he rose from the table. "I'm afraid it'll turn you into a mean, avaricious[17] man, and we shall have to disown you."

His mother laughed, and following him to the door, watched him down the road; and returning to the breakfast table, was very happy at the expense of her husband's credulity. All of which did not prevent her from scurrying to the door at the postman's knock, when she found that the post brought a tailor's bill.

170 "Herbert will have some more of his funny remarks, I expect, when he comes home," she said, as they sat at dinner.

"I dare say," said Mr. White, "but for all that, the thing moved in my hand; that I'll swear to."

"You thought it did," said the old lady soothingly.

"I say it did," replied the other. "There was no thought about it; I had just— What's the matter?"

His wife made no reply. She was watching the mysterious movements of a man outside, who, peering in an undecided fashion at the house, appeared to be trying to make up his mind to enter. In mental connection with the two

180 hundred pounds, she noticed that the stranger was well dressed, and wore a silk hat of glossy newness. Three times he paused at the gate, and then walked on again. The fourth time he stood with his hand upon it, and then with sudden resolution flung it open and walked up the path. Mrs. White at the same moment placed her hands behind her, and hurriedly unfastening the strings of her apron, put that useful article of apparel beneath the cushion of her chair.

She brought the stranger, who seemed ill at ease, into the room. He gazed at her furtively, and listened in a preoccupied fashion as the old lady apologized for the appearance of the room, and her husband's coat, a garment which he usually reserved for the garden. She then waited patiently for him to broach his

190 business, but he was at first strangely silent. **H**

"I—was asked to call," he said at last, and stooped and picked a piece of cotton from his trousers. "I come from Maw and Meggins."

The old lady started. "Is anything the matter?" she asked breathlessly. "Has anything happened to Herbert? What is it? What is it?"

Her husband interposed. "There, there, mother," he said hastily. "Sit down, and don't jump to conclusions. You've not brought bad news, I'm sure, sir;" and he eyed the other wistfully.

---

16. **frivolous** (frĭv′ə-ləs): inappropriately silly.

17. **avaricious** (ăv′ə-rĭsh′əs): greedy.

Language Coach

Prefixes A prefix is a word part added to the beginning of a word to form a new word. For example, in line 164 you will find the word *disown*, which contains the prefix *dis-*, meaning "to undo, do the opposite, or free from." Based on the meaning of this prefix, what do you think *disown* means?

H **PREDICT**
Reread lines 177–190. Why do you think the man comes to see the Whites?

"I'm sorry—" began the visitor.

"Is he hurt?" demanded the mother wildly.

200 The visitor bowed in assent. "Badly hurt," he said quietly, "but he is not in any pain."

"Oh!" said the old woman, clasping her hands. "Thank goodness for that! Thank—"

She broke off suddenly as the sinister meaning of the assurance dawned upon her and she saw the awful confirmation of her fears in the other's averted face. She caught her breath, and turning to her slower-witted husband, laid her trembling old hand upon his. There was a long silence. **I**

"He was caught in the machinery," said the visitor at length in a low voice.

"Caught in the machinery," repeated Mr. White, in a dazed fashion, "yes."

210 He sat staring blankly out at the window, and taking his wife's hand between his own, pressed it as he had been wont to do in their old courting days nearly forty years before.

"He was the only one left to us," he said, turning gently to the visitor. "It is hard."

The other coughed, and rising, walked slowly to the window. "The firm wished me to convey their sincere sympathy with you in your great loss," he said, without looking round. "I beg that you will understand I am only their servant and merely obeying orders."

There was no reply; the old woman's face was white, her eyes staring, and
220 her breath inaudible; on the husband's face was a look such as his friend the sergeant might have carried into his first action.

"I was to say that Maw and Meggins disclaim all responsibility," continued the other. "They admit no liability at all, but in consideration of your son's services, they wish to present you with a certain sum as **compensation**." ◆

Mr. White dropped his wife's hand, and rising to his feet, gazed with a look of horror at his visitor. His dry lips shaped the words, "How much?"

"Two hundred pounds," was the answer.

Unconscious of his wife's shriek, the old man smiled faintly, put out his hands like a sightless man, and dropped, a senseless heap, to the floor. **J**

III

230 In the huge new cemetery, some two miles distant, the old people buried their dead, and came back to a house steeped in shadow and silence. It was all over so quickly that at first they could hardly realize it, and remained in a state of expectation as though of something else to happen—something else which was to lighten this load, too heavy for old hearts to bear.

But the days passed, and expectation gave place to **resignation**—the hopeless resignation of the old, sometimes miscalled apathy. Sometimes they hardly exchanged a word, for now they had nothing to talk about, and their days were long to weariness.

I MOOD
Think about the news the stranger reveals during his conversation with the Whites. What emotions do you feel as a result of this news?

◆ GRAMMAR IN CONTEXT
In line 222, W. W. Jacobs correctly makes the verb *disclaim* plural in number to agree with its compound subject, "Maw and Meggins."

compensation
(kŏm′pən-sā′shən) *n.* something, such as money, received as payment

J PREDICT
Did your prediction about what would result from Mr. White's first wish come true?

resignation
(rĕz′ĭg-nā′shən) *n.* acceptance of something that is inescapable

It was about a week after that the old man, waking suddenly in the night,
240 stretched out his hand and found himself alone. The room was in darkness,
and the sound of subdued weeping came from the window. He raised himself
in bed and listened.

"Come back," he said tenderly. "You will be cold."

"It is colder for my son," said the old woman, and wept afresh.

The sound of her sobs died away on his ears. The bed was warm, and his
eyes heavy with sleep. He dozed fitfully, and then slept until a sudden wild cry
from his wife awoke him with a start.

"*The paw!*" she cried wildly. "The monkey's paw!"

He started up in alarm. "Where? Where is it? What's the matter?"

250 She came stumbling across the room toward him. "I want it," she said
quietly. "You've not destroyed it?" **K**

"It's in the parlor, on the bracket," he replied, marveling. "Why?"

She cried and laughed together, and bending over, kissed his cheek.

"I only just thought of it," she said hysterically. "Why didn't I think of it
before? Why didn't *you* think of it?"

"Think of what?" he questioned.

"The other two wishes," she replied rapidly. "We've only had one."

"Was not that enough?" he demanded fiercely.

"No," she cried triumphantly; "we'll have one more. Go down and get it
260 quickly, and wish our boy alive again."

The man sat up in bed and flung the bedclothes from his quaking limbs.
"You are mad!" he cried, aghast.

"Get it," she panted; "get it quickly, and wish—Oh, my boy, my boy!"

Her husband struck a match and lit the candle. "Get back to bed," he said
unsteadily. "You don't know what you are saying."

"We had the first wish granted," said the old woman feverishly; "why not
the second?"

"A coincidence," stammered the old man.

"Go and get it and wish," cried his wife, quivering with excitement.

270 He went down in the darkness, and felt his way to the parlor, and then to
the mantelpiece. The talisman was in its place, and a horrible fear that the
unspoken wish might bring his mutilated son before him ere he could escape
from the room seized upon him, and he caught his breath as he found that he
had lost the direction of the door. His brow cold with sweat, he felt his way
round the table, and groped along the wall until he found himself in the small
passage with the unwholesome thing in his hand. **L**

Even his wife's face seemed changed as he entered the room. It was white
and expectant, and to his fears seemed to have an unnatural look upon it. He
was afraid of her.

280 "*Wish!*" she cried, in a strong voice.

"It is foolish and wicked," he faltered.

"*Wish!*" repeated his wife.

He raised his hand. "I wish my son alive again." **M**

K PREDICT
What do you think
Mrs. White plans to
do with the paw?

L MOOD
Reread lines 270–276.
What **imagery** does the
author use to establish
the mood in this
paragraph?

M PREDICT
Do you think the Whites'
wish will be granted?
Note the clues that
influence your answer.

The talisman fell to the floor, and he regarded it fearfully. Then he sank trembling into a chair as the old woman, with burning eyes, walked to the window and raised the blind.

He sat until he was chilled with the cold, glancing occasionally at the figure of the old woman peering through the window. The candle-end, which had burned below the rim of the china candlestick, was throwing pulsating shadows 290 on the ceiling and walls, until, with a flicker larger than the rest, it expired.

◀ **Analyze Visuals**

Describe the **mood** of this photograph. What details contribute to this mood?

The old man, with an unspeakable sense of relief at the failure of the talisman, crept back to his bed, and a minute or two afterward the old woman came silently and apathetically beside him.

Neither spoke, but lay silently listening to the ticking of the clock. A stair creaked, and a squeaky mouse scurried noisily through the wall. The darkness was oppressive, and after lying for some time gathering up his courage, he took the box of matches, and striking one, went downstairs for a candle.

At the foot of the stairs the match went out, and he paused to strike another; and at the same moment a knock, so quiet and stealthy as to be
300 scarcely audible, sounded on the front door. **N**

The matches fell from his hand. He stood motionless, his breath suspended until the knock was repeated. Then he turned and fled swiftly back to his room, and closed the door behind him. A third knock sounded through the house.

"*What's that?*" cried the old woman, starting up.

"A rat," said the old man in shaking tones— "a rat. It passed me on the stairs."

His wife sat up in bed listening. A loud knock resounded through the house.

"It's Herbert!" she screamed. "It's Herbert!"

She ran to the door, but her husband was before her, and catching her by the arm, held her tightly.

310 "What are you going to do?" he whispered hoarsely.

"It's my boy; it's Herbert!" she cried, struggling mechanically. "I forgot it was two miles away. What are you holding me for? Let go. I must open the door."

"Don't let it in," cried the old man, trembling.

"You're afraid of your own son," she cried, struggling. "Let me go. I'm coming, Herbert; I'm coming."

There was another knock, and another. The old woman with a sudden wrench broke free and ran from the room. Her husband followed to the landing, and called after her appealingly as she hurried downstairs. He heard the chain rattle back and the bottom bolt drawn slowly and stiffly from the
320 socket. Then the old woman's voice, strained and panting.

"The bolt," she cried loudly. "Come down. I can't reach it."

But her husband was on his hands and knees groping wildly on the floor in search of the paw. If he could only find it before the thing outside got in. A perfect fusillade[18] of knocks reverberated through the house, and he heard the scraping of a chair as his wife put it down in the passage against the door. He heard the creaking of the bolt as it came slowly back, and at the same moment he found the monkey's paw, and frantically breathed his third and last wish.

The knocking ceased suddenly, although the echoes of it were still in the house. He heard the chair drawn back, and the door opened. A cold wind
330 rushed up the staircase, and a long loud wail of disappointment and misery from his wife gave him courage to run down to her side, and then to the gate beyond. The streetlamp flickering opposite shone on a quiet and deserted road. **O**

---

18. **fusillade** (fyo͞o'sə-läd'): discharge from many guns; a rapid outburst.

N MOOD
Reread lines 294–300. What sounds help create the mood in these paragraphs?

COMMON CORE RL 6

O IDENTIFY THE NARRATOR
As you may recall, an **objective narrator** reports what he or she could have gathered from observation. A **subjective narrator** shares details that could only be known if he or she were inside the character's head. Reread lines 298–332 to determine whether the narrator is objective or subjective. Explain your answer.

Comprehension

1. **Recall** How does Mr. White get the monkey's paw?

2. **Recall** What power is the monkey's paw supposed to have?

3. **Clarify** Why does Sergeant-Major Morris throw the paw onto the fire?

Text Analysis

4. **Make Inferences** At the end of the story, why did the knocking stop so suddenly? Explain.

5. **Examine Predictions** Review the chart you created as you read. Did most of your predictions come true? Looking back at the places where your predictions were wrong, notice how W. W. Jacobs tried to surprise readers by giving false clues about what would happen.

6. **Analyze Mood** How would you describe this story's mood? Include your answer at the top of a chart like the one shown. Then provide examples of setting descriptions, conversations, and imagery that are relevant to the creation of this mood.

Mood:		
Setting Descriptions:	Conversations:	Imagery:

7. **Analyze Type of Narrator** Think back over the thoughts and emotions that were described by the narrator. For the most part, which type of narrator appears to be telling this story, an objective narrator or a subjective one? Which type of narrator actually recounts the story? Explain.

Extension and Challenge

8. **Reader's Circle** Consider what would have happened if Mrs. White had opened the door before her husband made the final wish. Would you have liked to find out what was on the other side of the door? Or is it better for you as a reader not to know? In a small group, discuss your thoughts about the ending of "The Monkey's Paw."

Are you SUPERSTITIOUS?

Reread lines 160–161 of the story. Are you more inclined to believe in superstitions or coincidence? Why?

COMMON CORE

RL 4 Determine the meaning of words and phrases as they are used in a text, including figurative and connotative meanings. **RL 6** Analyze how differences in points of view create effects.

Vocabulary in Context

▲ **VOCABULARY PRACTICE**

Choose the word in each group that is most nearly opposite in meaning to the boldfaced word.

1. **peril:** (a) safety, (b) risk, (c) hazard
2. **credulity:** (a) simplicity, (b) doubt, (c) openness
3. **resignation:** (a) respect, (b) resistance, (c) acceptance
4. **compensation:** (a) consideration, (b) reward, (c) loss
5. **fate:** (a) choice, (b) destiny, (c) luck
6. **grimace:** (a) frown, (b) scowl, (c) grin

ACADEMIC VOCABULARY IN WRITING

- circumstance • emerge • predominant • rely • technology

Why do you suppose writers so often **rely** on stormy weather and night time to create a fearful or suspenseful mood? Use at least one Academic Vocabulary word to write a one-paragraph answer.

VOCABULARY STRATEGY: THE LATIN ROOT *cred*

The vocabulary word *credulity* contains the Latin root *cred,* meaning "to believe" or "to trust." A number of commonly used English words are formed using *cred*. To figure out the meanings of unfamiliar words containing *cred,* use your knowledge of the root as well as any context clues provided.

PRACTICE Choose a word from the web to complete each of the following sentences. Use context clues or, if necessary, consult a dictionary.

1. A person must get the proper _____ before he or she is able to teach.
2. Sharon didn't approve of the club's _____, so she didn't join.
3. I gave no _____ to his story, which changed each time he told it.
4. The violinist received several rounds of applause after her _____ performance.
5. They hoped to _____ the candidate by focusing on his lack of experience.

COMMON CORE

L 4b Use common, grade-appropriate Latin roots as clues to the meaning of a word.

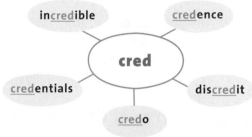

Language

◆ **GRAMMAR IN CONTEXT: Maintain Subject-Verb Agreement**

A **compound subject** is made up of two or more subjects joined by a conjunction, such as *and, or,* or *nor.* The conjunction determines whether you should use a singular or plural verb. If a compound subject is joined by *and,* then it usually takes a plural verb. If a compound subject is joined by *or* or *nor,* then the verb should agree in number with the part closest to it.

> *Original:*   Neither Mr. White nor the two men before him finds happiness.
>
> *Revised:*   Neither Mr. White nor the two men before him find happiness. (*The plural verb* find *is correct because the plural noun* men *is closer to it.*)

PRACTICE   Choose the verb form that agrees with each compound subject.

1. Mr. and Mrs. White (has, have) different feelings about the paw.
2. Neither the paw nor the wishes (has, have) any effect on fate.
3. Herbert and his father (like, likes) to play chess.
4. Either fate or several coincidences (lead, leads) to Herbert's death and the company's compensation.

For more help with subject-verb agreement with compound subjects, see page R65 in the **Grammar Handbook.**

READING-WRITING CONNECTION

Broaden your understanding of "The Monkey's Paw" by responding to this prompt. Then use the **revising tip** to improve your writing.

WRITING PROMPT	REVISING TIP
Short Constructed Response: Analysis If someone offered you a monkey's paw and claimed that it had the power to grant three wishes, would you use it? Write **one paragraph** explaining how you would respond to such an offer. Use details from the story to support your response.	Review your paragraph to make sure the verbs agree in number with the subjects. Pay special attention to verbs with compound subjects. If you find any subject-agreement errors, correct them.

COMMON CORE

L1 Demonstrate command of the conventions of standard English grammar and usage when writing.

Interactive Revision   THINK central

Go to **thinkcentral.com**.
KEYWORD: HML8-387

Roll of Thunder, Hear My Cry

COMMON CORE

RL 10 Read and comprehend literature.

Historical Novel by Mildred D. Taylor

Other Books by Mildred D. Taylor

- *The Gold Cadillac*
- *The Land*
- *Let the Circle Be Unbroken*
- *The Road to Memphis*

Meet Mildred D. Taylor

Mildred D. Taylor's personal exposure to segregation and bigotry has had a strong influence on her writing. Though Taylor was born in Mississippi, her family moved to the North when she was only three months old. Her father did not want his children to grow up in the racially segregated South. In the Ohio town where she was raised, Taylor was often the only African-American student in her class.

The Taylors returned to the South once a year, however, to visit relatives. The family tradition of sharing stories around bonfires led Taylor to imagine herself as a storyteller. Her father was considered one of the best storytellers in the family, and Taylor credits him for her success: "Without his teachings, without his words, my words would not have been."

Try a Historical Novel

Roll of Thunder, Hear My Cry takes place in Mississippi in the 1930s. Blending fictional characters and events with facts about real places, people, and occurrences, Taylor's **historical novel** creates a vivid picture of what life is like for an African-American family trying to remain united while their community is torn apart.

Reading Fluency refers to how easily and well you read. Good readers read smoothly, accurately, and with feeling. To improve your reading fluency, read a passage several times. Your goal in silent reading is to make sense of the writer's words and ideas. To improve your reading fluency, it helps to practice reading aloud. When reading aloud, think about your purpose for reading a text. Be sure to group words into meaningful phrases that sound like natural speech.

Read a Great Book

Cassie Logan and her three brothers—Christopher-John, Stacey, and Little Man—often find themselves struggling to understand why some of the white people in their community treat them so badly. But after the Logan kids pull a prank on the white school's bus driver out of revenge for his mistreatment of them, they soon realize that their actions could have very serious consequences.

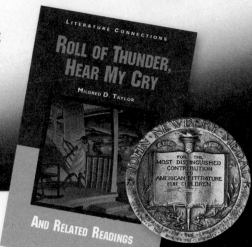

from

Roll of THUNDER, Hear My Cry

The room grew quiet again, except for the earthy humming of Big Ma's rich alto voice, the crackle of the hickory fire, and the patter of rain on the roof. Engrossed in a mystery, I was startled when the comfortable sounds were shattered by three rapid knocks on the side door.

Rising quickly, Mama went to the door and called, "Who is it?"

"It's me, ma'am," came a man's gravelly voice. "Joe Avery."

Mama opened the door and Mr. Avery stepped dripping into the room.

"Why, Brother Avery," Mama said, "what are you doing out on a
10 night like this? Come on in. Take off your coat and sit by the fire. Stacey, get Mr. Avery a chair."

"No'm," said Mr. Avery, looking rather nervously over his shoulder into the night. "I ain't got but a minute." He stepped far enough into the room so that he could close the door, then nodded to the rest of us. "Evenin', Miz Caroline, how you t'night?"

"Oh, I'll do, I reckon," said Big Ma, still ironing. "How's Miz Fannie?"

"She's fine," he said without dwelling on his wife. "Miz Logan . . . uh, I come to tell you somethin' . . . somethin' important—Mr. Morrison here?"

Mama stiffened. "David. You heard something about David?"

"Oh, no'm," replied Mr. Avery hastily. "Ain't heard nothin' 'bout yo' husband, ma'am."

Mama regarded him quizzically.

"It's . . . it's them again. They's ridin' t'night."

Mama, her face pale and frightened, glanced back at Big Ma; Big Ma held her iron in midair.

"Uh . . . children," Mama said, "I think it's your bedtime."

"But, Mama—" we chorused in protest, wanting to stay and hear who was riding.

"Hush," Mama said sternly. "I said it was time to go to bed. Now go!"

Groaning loudly enough to voice our displeasure, but not loudly enough to arouse Mama's anger, we stacked our books upon the study table and started toward the boys' room.

"Cassie, I said go to bed. That's not your room."

"But, Mama, it's cold in there," I pouted. Usually, we were allowed to build small fires in the other rooms an hour before bedtime to warm them up.

"You'll be warm once you're under the covers. Stacey, take the flashlight with you and light the lantern in your room. Cassie, take the lamp from the desk with you."

I went back and got the kerosene lamp, then entered my bedroom, leaving the door slightly ajar.

"Close that door, Cassie!"

Immediately, the door was closed.

I put the lamp on the dresser, then silently slid the latch off the outside door and slipped onto the wet front porch. I crossed to the boys' room. Tapping lightly, I whispered, "Hey, let me in."

The door creaked open and I darted in. The room was bathed in darkness.

"What they say?" I asked.

"Shhhhh!" came the answer.

I crept to the door leading into Mama's room and huddled beside the boys.

The rain softened upon the roof and we could hear Mama asking, "But why? Why are they riding? What's happened?"

"I don't rightly know," said Mr. Avery. "But y'all knows how they is. Anytime they thinks we steppin' outa our *place,* they feels like they gotta stop us. You know what some of 'em done to the Berrys." He paused,
60 then went on bitterly, "It don't take but a little of nothin' to set them devilish night men off."

"But somethin' musta happened," Big Ma said. "How you know 'bout it?"

"All's I can tell ya, Miz Caroline, is what Fannie heard when she was leavin' the Grangers' this evenin'. She'd just finished cleanin' up the supper dishes when Mr. Granger come home with Mr. Grimes—ya know, that white school's bus driver—and two other mens. . . ."

A clap of deafening thunder drowned Mr. Avery's words, then the rain quickened and the conversation was lost.
70 I grabbed Stacey's arm. "Stacey, they're coming after *us!*"

"What!" squeaked Christopher-John.

"Hush," Stacey said harshly. "And Cassie, let go. That hurts."

"Stacey, somebody musta seen and told on us," I persisted.

"No . . ." Stacey replied unconvincingly. "It couldn't be."

"Couldn't be?" cried Christopher-John in a panic. "Whaddaya mean it couldn't be?"

"Stacey," said Little Man excitedly, "whaddaya think they gonna do to us? Burn us up?"

"Nothin'!" Stacey exclaimed, standing up suddenly. "Now why don't
80 y'all go to bed like y'all s'pose to?"

We were stunned by his attitude. He sounded like Mama and I told him so.

He collapsed in silence by the door, breathing hard, and although I could not see him, I knew that his face was drawn and that his eyes had taken on a haggard look. I touched his arm lightly. "Ain't no call to go blaming yourself," I said. "We all done it."

"But I got us into it," he said listlessly.

"But we all wanted to do it," I comforted.

"Not me!" denied Christopher-John. "All I wanted to do was eat my
90 lunch!"

"Shhhhh," hissed Little Man. "I can hear 'em again."

"I'd better go tell Mr. Morrison," Mr. Avery was saying. "He out back?"

"I'll tell him," said Mama.

We could hear the side door open and we scrambled up.

"Cassie, get back to your room quick," Stacey whispered. "They'll probably come check on us now."

"But what'll we do?"

"Nothin' now, Cassie. Them men probably won't even come near here."

"Ya really believe that?" asked Christopher-John hopefully.

100 "But shouldn't we tell Mama?" I asked.

"No! We can't ever tell nobody!" declared Stacey adamantly. "Now go on, hurry!"

Footsteps neared the door. I dashed onto the porch and hastened back to my own room, where I jumped under the bedcovers with my clothes still on. Shivering, I pulled the heavy patchwork quilts up to my chin.

A few moments later Big Ma came in, leaving the door to Mama's room open. Knowing that she would be suspicious of such an early surrender to sleep, I sighed softly and, making sleepy little sounds, turned onto my stomach, careful not to expose my shirt sleeves.

110 Obviously satisfied by my performance, Big Ma tucked the covers more closely around me and smoothed my hair gently. Then she stooped and started fishing for something under our bed.

I opened my eyes. Now what the devil was she looking for down there? While she was searching, I heard Mama approaching and I closed my eyes again.

"Mama?"

"Stacey, what're you doing up?"

"Let me help."

"Help with what?"

120 "With . . . with whatever's the matter."

Mama was silent a moment, then said softly, "Thank you, Stacey, but Big Ma and I can handle it."

"But Papa told me to help you!"

"And you do, more than you know. But right now you could help me most by going back to bed. It's a school day tomorrow, remember?"

"But, Mama—"

"If I need you, I'll call you. I promise."

I heard Stacey walk slowly away, then Mama whispering in the doorway, "Cassie asleep?"

130   "Yeah, honey," Big Ma said. "Go on and sit back down. I'll be out in a minute."

Then Big Ma stood up and turned down the wick of the kerosene lamp. As she left the room, my eyes popped open again and I saw her outlined in the doorway, a rifle in her hands. Then she closed the door and I was left to the darkness.

For long minutes I waited, wide awake, wondering what my next move should be. Finally deciding that I should again consult with the boys, I swung my legs over the edge of the bed, but immediately had to swing them back again as Big Ma reentered the room. She passed the

140 bed and pulled a straight-backed chair up to the window. Parting the curtains so that the blackness of the night mixed with the blackness of the room, she sat down without a sound.

I heard the door to the boys' room open and close and I knew that Mama had gone in. I waited for the sound of the door opening again, but it did not come. Soon the chill of the cotton sheets beneath me began to fade and as Big Ma's presence lulled me into a security I did not really feel, I fell asleep.

When I awoke, it was still nightly dark. "Big Ma?" I called. "Big Ma, you there?" But there was no reply from the chair by the window.

150 Thinking that Big Ma had fallen asleep, I climbed from the bed and felt my way to her chair.

She wasn't there. ❧

Keep Reading

You've just gotten a sense of the tense situation the Logan family is in. As one of the few landowning African-American families in the community, the Logans face resentment from many of their white neighbors. Will they be able to hold on to their land through these tough times? Continue reading *Roll of Thunder, Hear My Cry* to find out.

Going Where I'm Coming From
Memoir by Naomi Shihab Nye

Can you BELONG
in two places?

⋯ **COMMON CORE**

RI 1 Cite textual evidence to support inferences drawn from the text. **RI 3** Analyze how a text makes connections among individuals, ideas, or events. **RI 4** Determine the meaning of words and phrases as they are used in a text, including figurative meanings.

Have you ever heard someone say, "This is where I belong"? What is it about a place that makes you feel a sense of belonging? If you spend a lot of time in two different places, such as home and your best friend's house, you may feel equally comfortable in both. The author of the memoir you are about to read discovered that during a year of being away from the United States, she developed a sense of belonging in her new home as well.

QUICKWRITE Think of one or two places where you feel a sense of belonging. What kinds of things make you feel that way—the people, the food, the sights and sounds, the routine? Record your thoughts in your journal.

● TEXT ANALYSIS: SETTING IN NONFICTION

You might think of **setting,** the time and place in which events occur, as an element of fiction. But setting can be important in nonfiction, too. For example, details about people's customs, beliefs, and day-to-day life are all important to setting. In a memoir, a writer might discuss how these aspects of her childhood home influenced the adult she became.

As you read "Going Where I'm Coming From," notice how the author's values and beliefs are shaped by her experiences in her father's homeland.

● READING STRATEGY: CONNECT

Sometimes the experiences of people you read about will remind you of events from your own life. When you relate the content of literature to your own experience, you are **connecting** with what you read. By making connections, you can gain new insights into your life and the lives of others around you.

As you read the selection, compare Naomi Shihab Nye's thoughts and experiences with your own. How does this help you better understand her feelings? Take notes in a chart like the one shown.

Author's Experiences	My Experiences	Insights
She doesn't feel love for her grandmother the first time she meets her.	I felt shy around my grandmother the first time I visited her in China.	Even family bonds can take time to develop.

▲ VOCABULARY IN CONTEXT

Nye uses the boldfaced words to help tell her story of living in a new land. Use the context of the numbered sentences to figure out what each word means.

1. The fabric contained a complex and **intricate** design.
2. Mom allowed me to join the team with the **stipulation** that I keep my grades up.
3. In a **valiant** act of bravery, I entered my new classroom.
4. Her father often talked about what it was like to **emigrate** from Mexico to the United States.

 Complete the activities in your **Reader/Writer Notebook.**

Meet the Author

Naomi Shihab Nye
born 1952

Combining Cultures
Naomi Shihab Nye learned about both Palestinian and American cultures as she was growing up; her mother was born in the United States and her father was born in Palestine. She says that when the other Girl Scouts brought iced cupcakes for treats, she brought dates, apricots, and almonds. In the mid-1960s, Nye and her family moved to a home just outside of Jerusalem. Nye has said that her year there "altered my perception of the universe irrevocably." "Going Where I'm Coming From" is one of many works she's written about her experiences there.

Building Bridges
In her poetry, novels, and essays, Nye encourages people from different cultures to learn to relate to each other. She believes that writers who belong to more than one culture can "build bridges between worlds."

BACKGROUND TO THE MEMOIR
A City Among Valleys
Jerusalem is an ancient Middle Eastern city located between the Mediterranean Sea and the Dead Sea. Surrounded by valleys, Jerusalem experiences warm, dry summers and cool winters. Also known as The Holy City, Jerusalem is home to over 700,000 people from a variety of national, religious, and socioeconomic backgrounds. Today, Jerusalem is the capital of the State of Israel. One of the most ancient sections of Jerusalem, the Old City, is divided into four quarters: Armenian, Christian, Jewish, and Muslim.

Author Online
THINK central
Go to **thinkcentral.com.**
KEYWORD: HML8-395

395

Going Where I'm Coming From

Naomi Shihab Nye

S hortly after we arrived in Jerusalem, our relatives came to see us at a hotel. Sitti, our grandmother, was very short. She wore a long, thickly embroidered Palestinian dress, had a musical, high-pitched voice and a low, guttural laugh. She kept touching our heads and faces as if she couldn't believe we were there. I had not yet fallen in love with her. Sometimes you don't fall in love with people immediately, even if they're your own grandmother. Everyone seemed to think we were all too thin.

We moved into a second-story flat in a stone house eight miles north of the city, among fields and white stones and wandering sheep. My brother was enrolled 10 in the Friends Girls School and I was enrolled in the Friends Boys School in the town of Ramallah a few miles farther north—it all was a little confused. But the Girls School offered grades one through eight in English and high school continued at the Boys School. Most local girls went to Arabic-speaking schools after eighth grade.

I was a freshman, one of seven girl students among two hundred boys, which would cause me problems a month later. I was called in from the schoolyard at lunchtime, to the office of our counselor who wore shoes so pointed and tight her feet bulged out pinkly on top. **Ⓐ**

"You will not be talking to them anymore," she said. She rapped on the desk 20 with a pencil for emphasis.

"To whom?"

"All the boy students at this institution. It is inappropriate behavior. From now on, you will speak only with the girls."

Jerusalem (1984), Tamam Al-Akhal. Palestine.
Oil on canvas, 50 cm × 70 cm. Private collection.

Analyze Visuals ▶

What do the colors in this painting suggest about the **setting?**

Ⓐ **SETTING IN NONFICTION**
Reread lines 1–18. What details help you understand what life was like in Jerusalem?

"But there are only six other girls! And I like only one of them!" My friend was Anna, from Italy, whose father ran a small factory that made matches. I'd visited it once with her. It felt risky to walk the aisles among a million filled matchboxes. Later we visited the factory that made olive oil soaps and stacked them in giant pyramids to dry.

"No, thank you," I said. "It's ridiculous to say that girls should only talk to girls. Did I say anything bad to a boy? Did anyone say anything bad to me? They're my friends. They're like my brothers. I won't do it, that's all."

The counselor conferred with the headmaster[1] and they called a taxi. I was sent home with a little paper requesting that I transfer to a different school. The charge: insolence. My mother, startled to see me home early and on my own, stared out the window when I told her.

My brother came home from his school as usual, full of whistling and notebooks. "Did anyone tell you not to talk to girls?" I asked him. He looked at me as if I'd gone goofy. He was too young to know the troubles of the world. He couldn't even imagine them. **B**

"You know what I've been thinking about?" he said. "A piece of cake. That puffy white layered cake with icing like they have at birthday parties in the United States. Wouldn't that taste good right now?" Our mother said she was thinking about mayonnaise. You couldn't get it in Jerusalem. She'd tried to make it and it didn't work. I felt too gloomy to talk about food.

My brother said, "Let's go let Abu Miriam's chickens out." That's what we always did when we felt sad. We let our fussy landlord's red-and-white chickens loose to flap around the yard happily, puffing their wings. Even when Abu Miriam shouted and waggled his cane and his wife waved a dishtowel, we knew the chickens were thanking us.

My father went with me to the St. Tarkmanchatz Armenian School, a solemnly ancient stone school tucked deep into the Armenian Quarter of the Old City of Jerusalem. It was another world in there. He had already called the school officials on the telephone and tried to enroll me, though they didn't want to. Their school was for Armenian students only, kindergarten through twelfth grade. Classes were taught in three languages: Armenian, Arabic and English, which was why I needed to go there. Although most Arab students at other schools were learning English, I needed a school where classes were actually taught in English—otherwise I would have been staring out the windows triple the usual amount.

The head priest wore a long robe and a tall cone-shaped hat. He said, "Excuse me, please, but your daughter, she is not an Armenian, even a small amount?"

"Not at all," said my father. "But in case you didn't know, there is a **stipulation** in the educational code books of this city that says no student may be rejected solely on the basis of ethnic background, and if you don't accept her, we will alert the proper authorities."

They took me. But the principal wasn't happy about it. The students, however, seemed glad to have a new face to look at. Everyone's name ended in *-ian,*

---

1. **headmaster:** principal of a private school.

B CONNECT
Note Nye's reaction to the school's rule about boys and girls. How do you respond to rules you think are unfair?

SOCIAL STUDIES CONNECTION

Jerusalem was built around 3000 B.C. Its original name, *Urr Salem,* meant "the land of peace."

stipulation
(stĭp′yə-lā′shən) *n.* the act of laying down a condition or agreement

the beautiful, musical Armenian ending—Boghossian, Minassian, Kevorkian, Rostomian. My new classmates started calling me Shihabian. We wore uniforms, navy blue pleated skirts for the girls, white shirts, and navy sweaters. I waited

70 during the lessons for the English to come around, as if it were a channel on television. While other students were on the other channels, I scribbled poems in the margins of my pages, read library books, and wrote a lot of letters filled with exclamation points. All the other students knew all three languages with three entirely different alphabets. How could they carry so much in their heads? I felt humbled by my ignorance. One day I felt so frustrated in our physics class—still another language—that I pitched my book out the open window. The professor made me go collect it. All the pages had let loose at the seams and were flapping free into the gutters along with the white wrappers of sandwiches. **C**

Every week the girls had a hands-and-fingernails check. We had to keep our
80 nails clean and trim, and couldn't wear any rings. Some of my new friends would invite me home for lunch with them, since we had an hour-and-a-half break and I lived too far to go to my own house.

Their houses were a thousand years old, clustered beehive-fashion behind ancient walls, stacked and curled and tilting and dark, filled with pictures of unsmiling relatives and small white cloths dangling crocheted² edges. We ate spinach pies and white cheese. We dipped our bread in olive oil, as the Arabs did. We ate small sesame cakes, our mouths full of crumbles. They taught me to say "I love you" in Armenian, which sounded like *yes-kay-see-goo-see-rem*. I felt I had left my old life entirely. **D**

90 Every afternoon I went down to the basement of the school where the kindergarten class was having an Arabic lesson. Their desks were pint-sized, their full white smocks tied around their necks. I stuffed my fourteen-year-old self in beside them. They had rosy cheeks and shy smiles. They must have thought I was a very slow learner.

More than any of the lessons, I remember the way the teacher rapped the backs of their hands with his ruler when they made a mistake. Their little faces puffed up with quiet tears. This pained me so terribly I forgot all my words. When it was my turn to go to the blackboard and write in Arabic, my hand shook. The kindergarten students whispered hints to me from the front row, but I couldn't understand them. We learned horribly useless phrases: "Please hand me the
100 bellows³ for my fire." I wanted words simple as tools, simple as *food* and *yesterday* and *dreams*. The teacher never rapped my hand, especially after I wrote a letter to the city newspaper, which my father edited, protesting such harsh treatment of young learners. I wish I had known how to talk to those little ones, but they were just beginning their English studies and didn't speak much yet. They were at the same place in their English that I was in my Arabic.

From the high windows of St. Tarkmanchatz, we could look out over the Old City, the roofs and flapping laundry and television antennas, the pilgrims and churches and mosques, the olivewood prayer beads and fragrant *falafel*⁴ lunch

C CONNECT
Reread lines 69–78. Think of a time when you felt frustrated In class. What did you do to solve the problem?

D SETTING IN NONFICTION
What details help you to picture the Armenian houses and to understand Armenian customs?

---

2. **crocheted** (krō-shād′): needlework made by looping thread with a hooked needle.

3. **bellows** (bĕl′ōz): an apparatus used for producing a strong current of air.

4. *falafel* (fə-lä′fəl): fried balls of ground, spiced chickpeas.

stands, the **intricate** interweaving of cultures and prayers and songs and holidays.
110 We saw the barbed wire separating Jordan from Israel then, the bleak, uninhabited strip of no-man's land reminding me how little education saved us after all. People who had differing ideas still came to blows, imagining fighting could solve things. Staring out over the quiet roofs of afternoon, I thought it so foolish. I asked my friends what they thought about it and they shrugged.

"It doesn't matter what we think about it. It just keeps happening. It happened in Armenia too,[5] you know. Really, really bad in Armenia. And who talks about it in the world news now? It happens everywhere. It happens in *your* country one by one, yes? Murders and guns. What can we do?" **E**

---

5. **It happened in Armenia, too:** Refers to the Armenian massacres of 1915–1923. In response to Russia's use of Armenian troops against the Ottomans in World War I, the Ottoman empire ordered the deportation of 1.75 million Armenians. During the deportation, around a million Armenians were killed or died of starvation.

intricate (ĭn'trĭ-kĭt) *adj.* elaborate

E **CONNECT**
Think of a serious conversation you have had with friends. Based on how you felt afterward, how do you think Nye might have felt after having this conversation?

The Olive Tree (2005), Ismail Shammout. Palestine. Oil on canvas, 60 cm × 80 cm. Private collection.

◀ **Analyze Visuals**
What can you **infer** about this family from the way they are posed in this painting?

Sometimes after school, my brother and I walked up the road that led past
120 the crowded refugee camp of Palestinians who owned even less than our modest
relatives did in the village. The little kids were stacking stones in empty tin cans
and shaking them. We waved our hands and they covered their mouths and
laughed. We wore our beat-up American tennis shoes and our old sweatshirts
and talked about everything we wanted to do and everywhere else we wished
we could go.

"I want to go back to Egypt," my brother said. "I sort of feel like I missed it.
Spending all that time in bed instead of exploring—what a waste."

"I want to go to Greece," I said. "I want to play a violin in a symphony
orchestra in Austria." We made up things. I wanted to go back to the United
130 States most of all. Suddenly I felt like a patriotic citizen. One of my friends,
Sylvie Markarian, had just been shipped off to Damascus, Syria to marry a man
who was fifty years old, a widower. Sylvie was exactly my age—we had turned
fifteen two days apart. She had never met her future husband before. I thought
this was the most revolting thing I had ever heard of. "Tell your parents no
thank you," I urged her. "Tell them you *refuse*."

Sylvie's eyes were liquid, swirling brown. I could not see clearly to the bottom
of them.

"You don't understand," she told me. "In United States you say no. We don't
say no. We have to follow someone's wishes. This is the wish of my father. Me, I
140 am scared. I never slept away from my mother before. But I have no choice. I am
going because they tell me to go." She was sobbing, sobbing on my shoulder. And
I was stroking her long, soft hair. After that, I carried two fists inside, one for Sylvie
and one for me. **F**

Most weekends my family went to the village to sit with the relatives. We sat
and sat and sat. We sat in big rooms and little rooms, in circles, on chairs or on
woven mats or brightly covered mattresses piled on the floor. People came in and
out to greet my family. Sometimes even donkeys and chickens came in and out.
We were like movie stars or dignitaries.[6] They never seemed to get tired of us.

My father translated the more interesting tidbits of conversation, the funny
150 stories my grandmother told. She talked about angels and food and money and
people and politics and gossip and old memories from my father's childhood,
before he **emigrated** away from her. She wanted to make sure we were going to
stick around forever, which made me feel very nervous. We ate from mountains of
rice and eggplant on large silver trays—they gave us little plates of our own since
it was not our custom to eat from the same plate as other people. We ripped the
giant wheels of bread into triangles. Shepherds passed through town with their
flocks of sheep and goats, their long canes and cloaks, straight out of the Bible.
My brother and I trailed them to the edge of the village, past the lentil fields to
the green meadows studded with stones, while the shepherds pretended we weren't
160 there. I think they liked to be alone, unnoticed. The sheep had differently colored
dyed bottoms, so shepherds could tell their flocks apart. **G**

---

6. **dignitaries** (dĭg′nĭ-tĕr′ēz): people of high rank or position.

COMMON CORE RI 4, L 5a

Language Coach

Figures of Speech
When words are used
to express something
other than their
usual meaning, they
are called figures of
speech. For example,
a *modest* person is
usually someone who
is "not boastful" or "not
showy." However, that
is not what Nye means
when she describes her
relatives as modest.
Explain what "modest
relatives" most likely
means in lines 119–121.
Think about Nye's
comparison between
the Palestinians and her
relatives.

F **SETTING IN
NONFICTION**
Note Nye's reaction to
her friend's problem.
In what ways is she
being affected by
her experiences in
Jerusalem?

emigrate (ĕm′ĭ-grāt′) *v.*
to leave one country and
settle in another

G **SETTING IN
NONFICTION**
Reread lines 144–161.
What details help create
a sense of place?

In Jerusalem (1997), Ismail Shammout. Palestine. Oil on canvas, 50 cm × 60 cm. Private collection.

During these long, slow, smoke-stained weekends—the men still smoked cigarettes a lot in those days, and the old *taboon,* my family's mounded bread-oven, puffed billowy clouds outside the door—my crying jags began. I cried without any warning, even in the middle of a meal. My crying was usually noiseless but dramatically wet—streams of tears pouring down my cheeks, onto my collar or the back of my hand.

Everything grew quiet.

Someone always asked in Arabic, "What is wrong? Are you sick? Do you wish 170 to lie down?"

My father made **valiant** excuses in the beginning. "She's overtired," he said. "She has a headache. She is missing her friend who moved to Syria. She is homesick just now."

My brother stared at me as if I had just landed from Planet X.

Analyze Visuals ▲

Nye describes the "stony splendor" of Jerusalem. How does this painting fit that description?

valiant (văl′yənt) *adj.* brave

Worst of all was our drive to school every morning, when our car came over the rise in the highway and all Jerusalem lay sprawled before us in its golden, stony splendor pockmarked with olive trees and automobiles. Even the air above the city had a thick, religious texture, as if it were a shining brocade[7] filled with broody incense. I cried hardest then. All those hours tied up in school lay just
180 ahead. My father pulled over and talked to me. He sighed. He kept his hands on the steering wheel even when the car was stopped and said, "Someday, I promise you, you will look back on this period in your life and have no idea what made you so unhappy here."

"I want to go home." It became my anthem. "This place depresses me. It weighs too much. . . . I hate the way people stare at me here." Already I'd been involved in two street skirmishes with boys who stared a little too hard and long. I'd socked one in the jaw and he socked me back. I hit the other one straight in the face with my purse. **H**

"You could be happy here if you tried just a little harder," my father said.
190 "Don't compare it to the United States all the time. Don't pretend the United States is perfect. And look at your brother—he's not having any problems!" ◆

"My brother is eleven years old."

I had crossed the boundary from uncomplicated childhood when happiness was a good ball and a horde of candy-coated Jordan almonds. **I**

One problem was that I had fallen in love with four different boys who all played in the same band. Two of them were even twins. I never quite described it to my parents, but I wrote reams and reams of notes about it on loose-leaf paper that I kept under my sweaters in my closet.

Such new energy made me feel reckless. I gave things away. I gave away my
200 necklace and a whole box of shortbread cookies that my mother had been saving. I gave my extra shoes away to the gypsies. One night when the gypsies camped in a field down the road from our house, I thought about their mounds of white goat cheese lined up on skins in front of their tents, and the wild *oud*[8] music they played deep into the black belly of the night, and I wanted to go sit around their fire. Maybe they could use some shoes.

I packed a sack of old loafers that I rarely wore and walked with my family down the road. The gypsy mothers stared into my shoes curiously. They took them into their tent. Maybe they would use them as vases or drawers. We sat with small glasses of hot, sweet tea until a girl bellowed from deep in her throat, threw
210 back her head, and began dancing. A long bow thrummed across the strings. The girl circled the fire, tapping and clicking, trilling a long musical wail from deep in her throat. My brother looked nervous. He was remembering the belly dancer in Egypt, and her scarf. I felt invisible. I was pretending to be a gypsy. My father stared at me. Didn't I recognize the exquisite oddity of my own life when I sat right in the middle of it? Didn't I feel lucky to be here? Well, yes I did. But sometimes it was hard to be lucky.

---

7. **brocade** (brō-kād′): a heavy fabric with a raised design.

8. ***oud*** (ōōd): a musical instrument resembling a lute.

H SETTING IN NONFICTION
Reread lines 175–188. What is it about Jerusalem that makes Nye feel sad and angry?

COMMON CORE L 2a

◆ GRAMMAR IN CONTEXT
A dash can be used to indicate a very abrupt break in thought. In line 191, the dash is used to indicate a pause that adds emphasis to the statement "he's not having any problems!"

I CONNECT
Which of your own experiences can help you understand what Nye is feeling?

When we left Jerusalem, we left quickly. Left our beds in our rooms and our car in the driveway. Left in a plane, not sure where we were going. The rumbles of fighting with Israel had been growing louder and louder. In the barbed-wire no-man's land visible from the windows of our house, guns cracked loudly in the middle of the night. We lived right near the edge. My father heard disturbing rumors at the newspaper that would soon grow into the infamous Six Day War of 1967. We were in England by then, drinking tea from thin china cups and scanning the newspapers. Bombs were blowing up in Jerusalem. We worried about the village. We worried about my grandmother's dreams, which had been getting worse and worse, she'd told us. We worried about the house we'd left, and the chickens, and the children at the refugee camp. But there was nothing we could do except keep talking about it all.

My parents didn't want to go back to Missouri because they'd already said goodbye to everyone there. They thought we might try a different part of the country. They weighed the virtues of different states. Texas was big and warm. After a chilly year crowded around the small gas heaters we used in Jerusalem, a warm place sounded appealing. In roomy Texas, my parents bought the first house they looked at. My father walked into the city newspaper and said, "Any jobs open around here?"

I burst out crying when I entered a grocery store—so many different kinds of bread. **J**

A letter on thin blue airmail paper reached me months later, written by my classmate, the bass player in my favorite Jerusalem band. "Since you left," he said, "your empty desk reminds me of a snake ready to strike. I am afraid to look at it. I hope you are having a better time than we are."

Of course I was, and I wasn't. *Home* had grown different forever. *Home* had doubled. Back *home* again in my own country, it seemed impossible to forget the place we had just left: the piercing call of the *muezzin*[9] from the mosque[10] at prayer time, the dusky green tint of the olive groves, the sharp, cold air that smelled as deep and old as my grandmother's white sheets flapping from the line on her roof. What story hadn't she finished?

Our father used to tell us that when he was little, the sky over Jerusalem crackled with meteors and shooting stars almost every night. They streaked and flashed, igniting the dark. Some had long golden tails. For a few seconds, you could see their whole swooping trail lit up. Our father and his brothers slept on the roof to watch the sky. "There were so many of them, we didn't even call out every time we saw one."

During our year in Jerusalem, my brother and I kept our eyes cast upwards whenever we were outside at night, but the stars were different since our father was a boy. Now the sky seemed too orderly, stuck in place. The stars had learned where they belonged. Only people on the ground kept changing. ❧

J SETTING IN NONFICTION
Reread lines 217–237. How is Texas different from Jerusalem?

---

9. *muezzin* (myōō-ĕz'ĭn): a crier who calls the Muslim faithful to prayer.
10. **mosque** (mŏsk): a Muslim house of worship.

My Father and the Figtree

Naomi Shihab Nye

For other fruits my father was indifferent.
He'd point at the cherry trees and say,
"See those? I wish they were figs."
In the evenings he sat by our beds
5 weaving folktales like vivid little scarves.
They always involved a figtree.
Even when it didn't fit, he'd stick it in.
Once Joha was walking down the road
and he saw a figtree.
10 Or, he tied his camel to a figtree and went to sleep.
Or, later when they caught and arrested him,
his pockets were full of figs.

At age six I ate a dried fig and shrugged.
"That's not what I'm talking about!" he said,
15 "I'm talking about a fig straight from the earth—
gift of Allah!—on a branch so heavy
it touches the ground.
I'm talking about picking the largest, fattest,
    sweetest fig
in the world and putting it in my mouth."
20 (Here he'd stop and close his eyes.)

Years passed, we lived in many houses,
none had figtrees.
We had lima beans, zucchini, parsley, beets.
"Plant one!" my mother said,
25 but my father never did.
He tended garden half-heartedly, forgot to water,
let the okra get too big.
"What a dreamer he is. Look how many
things he starts and doesn't finish."

30 The last time he moved, I had a phone call,
my father, in Arabic, chanting a song
I'd never heard. "What's that?"
He took me out to the new yard.
There, in the middle of Dallas, Texas,
35 a tree with the largest, fattest,
sweetest figs in the world.
"It's a figtree song!" he said,
plucking his fruits like ripe tokens,
emblems, assurance
40 of a world that was always his own.

Comprehension

1. **Recall** Why was it necessary for Naomi Shihab Nye to attend the Armenian school after being expelled from her first school?

2. **Clarify** Reread lines 130–143. Why was the author angry about her friend being sent to Damascus?

3. **Clarify** Why did the family leave Jerusalem?

Text Analysis

4. **Make Connections** Look at the chart you filled in as you read. Which two connections best help you understand what the author experienced in Jerusalem? Explain.

5. **Examine Setting** Use a web diagram to identify descriptive details that help convey the setting of this selection. Then expand your web to include insights on how this setting affected the author.

6. **Analyze Memoir** At what point in the selection does the author become aware of a sense of belonging in Jerusalem? Support your answer with examples from the memoir.

7. **Compare Literary Works** Nye's father encouraged her to try to be happy in Jerusalem and to learn to appreciate the "exquisite oddity" of her life. What does the poem "My Father and the Figtree" on page 405 reveal about her father's feelings toward living in different places?

COMMON CORE

RI 1 Cite textual evidence to support inferences drawn from the text. RI 3 Analyze how a text makes connections among individuals, ideas, or events.

Web diagram:
- girls marry young
- customs and beliefs
- landscape
- 1960s Jerusalem
- day-to-day life

Extension and Challenge

8. **SOCIAL STUDIES CONNECTION** Learn more about Jerusalem—its history, geographical setting, and culture. Present your information in the form of a colorful poster.

Can you **BELONG** in two places?

Now that you have discovered the sorts of things that help Nye feel a sense of belonging, what else might you add to your list of things that help you feel at home?

Vocabulary in Context

▲ **VOCABULARY PRACTICE**

Show that you understand the vocabulary words by deciding whether each statement is true or false.

1. A **valiant** action is a coward's way out.
2. If a pattern is **intricate,** it has a complicated design.
3. If you are given a **stipulation,** a condition of some kind is involved.
4. People who **emigrate** live in the same country their whole lives.

emigrate

intricate

stipulation

valiant

ACADEMIC VOCABULARY IN WRITING

| • circumstance | • emerge | • predominant | • rely | • technology |

Have you ever moved to a new country? If not, imagine what it might be like to live without the **technology** you take for granted now, or to be unable to understand the language. Write a paragraph describing this experience, using two or more Academic Vocabulary words.

VOCABULARY STRATEGY: RECOGNIZING BASE WORDS AND AFFIXES

To understand an unfamiliar word with affixes (prefixes and suffixes), it helps to identify the base word first. Look within the word for a word that is familiar to you, though the spelling might be different. For example, in the word *emigrate,* you might notice the base word *migrate.* In cases where you do not recognize a base word, you may need to use context clues to figure out the meaning.

PRACTICE Define each boldfaced word. Then give the base word and affixes. Use a dictionary if necessary.

1. The heavy rainfall was causing **erosion** of the soil.
2. He admired the professor for her **wisdom** and knowledge.
3. The most difficult part of the journey was the **navigation** of the river rapids.
4. It was her turn in the **rotation** to take the dog for a walk.
5. Did she accept his **proposal** of marriage?

⋯ **COMMON CORE**

L 4b Use common, grade-appropriate Greek or Latin affixes as clues to the meaning of a word. **L 6** Acquire and use accurately academic words.

Interactive Vocabulary **THINK** central

Go to thinkcentral.com.
KEYWORD: HML8-408

Language

◆ **GRAMMAR IN CONTEXT:** Use Ellipses and Dashes

Review the **Grammar in Context** note on page 403. Besides the period and comma, there are two punctuation marks that are particularly useful for indicating a pause or a break in thought: an ellipsis and a dash.

An **ellipsis** is a set of three spaced periods (. . . , not ...) preceded and followed by a space—except when it is used at the end of a sentence. At the end of a sentence, include a period before it.

> *Example:* Naomi was a freshman at Friends Boys School . . . one of seven girl students among two hundred boys.

An ellipsis may also be used to show that something has been left out of a quotation.

> *Example:* "It's ridiculous to say that girls should only talk to girls. . . . I won't do it, that's all."

A **dash** (—) can be used to indicate a very abrupt break in thought.

> *Example:* In England they scanned the newspapers for news of Jerusalem—were bombs going off?

Dashes are also used for adding information to a statement.

> *Example:* One day I felt so frustrated in our physics class—still another language—that I pitched my book out the open window.

PRACTICE Revise the following sentence according to each set of instructions. Use at least one ellipsis or dash as appropriate in each revision.

Naomi Shihab Nye learned about two cultures as she was growing up.

1. Insert *daughter of an American mother and a Palestinian father* after "Nye."
2. Insert *Palestinian and U.S.* after "cultures."
3. Add *a year in Palestine altering her perceptions forever* after "up."
4. Punctuate the sentence as a quotation, but leave out "as she was growing up" and indicate that there is an omission.

For *more help with ellipses and dashes, see page R50 in the* **Grammar Handbook.**

READING-WRITING CONNECTION

Increase your understanding of Nye's memoir by responding to this prompt. Then use the **revising tip** to improve your writing.

COMMON CORE

L 2a Use punctuation (ellipsis, dash) to indicate a pause or break.

WRITING PROMPT	**REVISING TIP**
Extended Constructed Response: Letter When in Jerusalem, Nye wrote letters to her friends in the U.S. What do you think she said about life in her new country? Write a **two- or three-paragraph letter** that she might have sent.	Review your letter to make sure that you have used ellipsis and dashes correctly when you wished to indicate a pause or break in thought.

Interactive Revision

THINK central

Go to **thinkcentral.com**. KEYWORD: HML8N-409

The Story of an Eyewitness
Magazine Article by Jack London

HISTORY — Video link at thinkcentral.com

Letter from New Orleans: Leaving Desire
Magazine Article by Jon Lee Anderson

VIDEO TRAILER — THINK central — KEYWORD: HML8-410

What is the role of a
WITNESS?

COMMON CORE

RI 1 Cite textual evidence to support inferences drawn from the text. RI 6 Determine an author's purpose in a text.

When events such as natural disasters, crimes, and wars occur, it's important that a witness describe what happened so that others can learn from these events. Witnesses have played an important role in reporting everything from local sports to the events in your history textbook. The authors of the accounts you are about to read each witnessed natural disasters. Their writing allowed people from around the world to share in their experiences.

ROLE-PLAY Picture the tornadoes, floods, and snow storms you have seen in the news. Imagine that one of these disasters has just struck your community. With a partner, role-play an evening news broadcast on the disaster. Decide who will be the news reporter and who will be the eyewitness. Then conduct an interview. Remember that your audience will want to know what the disaster looked, sounded, and felt like, as well as how people got hurt or stayed safe.

● TEXT ANALYSIS: AUTHOR'S PURPOSE

Writers usually write for one or more of these purposes: to express thoughts or feelings, to inform or explain, to persuade, or to entertain. The authors of the following articles have the same basic purpose for writing: to inform readers about a disaster. However, each has a different, more specific purpose, too. London wants to show how widespread the devastation is. Anderson wants to create empathy for the victims. As you read their accounts, notice how the authors present and develop the ideas in the articles to achieve their purposes.

● READING STRATEGY: SET A PURPOSE FOR READING

When you **set a purpose** for reading, you identify what you want to accomplish as you read. Your purpose for reading the following articles is to compare and contrast how each author achieves his purpose. As you read the first account, begin filling in the chart.

	"The Story of an Eyewitness"	"Letter from New Orleans: Leaving Desire"
What is the writer's specific purpose?		
How much of the disaster area does the writer cover?		
Which events and people does the writer focus on?		
Which details and images have a big impact on you?		

▲ VOCABULARY IN CONTEXT

In your Reader/Writer Notebook, write a sentence for each of the vocabulary words. Use a dictionary or the definitions in the following selection pages to help you.

WORD LIST		
compel	intermittently	menace
disconcert	lavishly	vigilantly

Complete the activities in your **Reader/Writer Notebook**.

Meet the Authors

Jack London
1876–1916

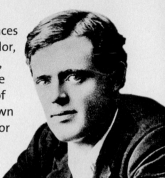

Nature Enthusiast
Inspired by his experiences as an outdoorsman, sailor, and war correspondent, Jack London became the most popular novelist of his time. He is still known throughout the world for *The Call of the Wild* and *The Sea Wolf*.

Jon Lee Anderson
born 1957

Investigative Journalist
Jon Lee Anderson always wanted to be an explorer. Now, as a correspondent for *The New Yorker*, he travels around the world reporting on war, politics, and international affairs.

BACKGROUND TO THE ARTICLES

San Francisco Earthquake
At 5:12 A.M. on April 18, 1906, a massive earthquake shook San Francisco, setting in motion events that would eventually destroy most of the city. Historians estimate that around 3,000 people died and 250,000 people were left homeless.

Hurricane Katrina
Hurricane Katrina hit the Gulf Coast on the morning of August 29, 2005. New Orleans suffered some of the worst damage of the Gulf Coast cities. Heavy flooding there destroyed entire neighborhoods, forced thousands of people to flee the city, and stranded many others in dangerous and unsanitary conditions until they, too, could get out.

Authors Online
Go to **thinkcentral.com**. KEYWORD: HML8-411

THINK central

411

The Story of an Eyewitness

JACK LONDON

People on Russian Hill look toward San Francisco's downtown.

Analyze Visuals ▶

How much of San Francisco is captured in this image? Based on this photograph, make a **prediction** about how much of the disaster area the writer is going to cover.

Upon receipt of the first news of the earthquake, Collier's *telegraphed to Mr. Jack London—who lives only forty miles from San Francisco—requesting him to go to the scene of the disaster and write the story of what he saw. Mr. London started at once, and he sent the following dramatic description of the tragic events he witnessed in the burning city.*

The earthquake shook down in San Francisco hundreds of thousands of dollars worth of walls and chimneys. But the conflagration[1] that followed burned up hundreds of millions of dollars' worth of property. There is no estimating within hundreds of millions the actual damage wrought. Not in history has a modern imperial city been so completely destroyed.

---

1. **conflagration** (kŏn'flə-grā'shən): a large destructive fire.

San Francisco is gone. Nothing remains of it but memories and a fringe of dwelling houses on its outskirts. Its industrial section is wiped out. Its business section is wiped out. Its social and residential section is wiped out. The factories and warehouses, the great stores and newspaper buildings, the
10 hotels and the palaces of the nabobs,[2] are all gone. Remains only the fringe of dwelling houses on the outskirts of what was once San Francisco. **A**

Within an hour after the earthquake shock the smoke of San Francisco's burning was a lurid[3] tower visible a hundred miles away. And for three days and nights this lurid tower swayed in the sky, reddening the sun, darkening the day, and filling the land with smoke.

On Wednesday morning at a quarter past five came the earthquake. A minute later the flames were leaping upward. In a dozen different quarters south of Market Street, in the working-class ghetto, and in the factories, fires started. There was no opposing the flames. There was no organization,
20 no communication. All the cunning adjustments of a twentieth century city had been smashed by the earthquake. The streets were humped into ridges and depressions, and piled with the debris of fallen walls. The steel rails were twisted into perpendicular and horizontal angles. The telephone and telegraph systems were disrupted. And the great water-mains had burst. All the shrewd contrivances[4] and safeguards of man had been thrown out of gear by thirty seconds' twitching of the earth-crust.

The Fire Made Its Own Draft

By Wednesday afternoon, inside of twelve hours, half the heart of the city was gone. At that time I watched the vast conflagration from out on the bay. It was dead calm. Not a flicker of wind stirred. Yet from every side wind was
30 pouring in upon the city. East, west, north, and south, strong winds were blowing upon the doomed city. The heated air rising made an enormous vacuum. Thus did the fire of itself build its own colossal chimney through the atmosphere. Day and night this dead calm continued, and yet, near to the flames, the wind was often half a gale, so mighty was the vacuum.

Wednesday night saw the destruction of the very heart of the city. Dynamite was **lavishly** used, and many of San Francisco's proudest structures were crumbled by man himself into ruins, but there was no withstanding the onrush of the flames. Time and again successful stands were made by the fire-fighters, and every time the flames flanked[5]
40 around on either side or came up from the rear, and turned to defeat

---

2. **nabobs** (nā'bŏbz'): people of wealth and prominence.
3. **lurid** (lŏŏr'ĭd): glowing with the glare of fire through a haze.
4. **contrivances** (kən-trī'vən-sĕz): acts of clever planning.
5. **flanked** (flăngk'd): placed at the side of.

A AUTHOR'S PURPOSE
How much of the city is Jack London describing in this paragraph?

Language Coach
Denotation Denotation is a word's dictionary meaning. The word *draft* has many meanings, including "a current of air," "a cold, indoor breeze," "an order to join the armed forces," "a preliminary sketch or plan," and "the act of pulling something." Which meaning do you think the author intends in the subheading here?

lavishly (lăv'ĭsh-lē) *adv.* extravagantly

the hard-won victory. An enumeration[6] of the buildings destroyed would be a directory of San Francisco. An enumeration of the buildings undestroyed would be a line and several addresses. An enumeration of the deeds of heroism would stock a library and bankrupt the Carnegie medal fund. An enumeration of the dead will never be made. All vestiges[7] of them were destroyed by the flames. The number of the victims of the earthquake will never be known. South of Market Street, where the loss of life was particularly heavy, was the first to catch fire. **B**

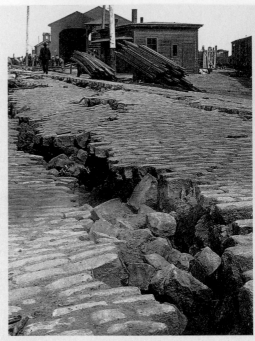

A street along San Francisco's waterfront, cracked during the earthquake

B AUTHOR'S PURPOSE
What aspects of the disaster is London describing?

Remarkable as it may seem, Wednesday night while the whole city crashed and roared into ruin, was a quiet night. There were no crowds. There was no shouting and yelling. There was no hysteria, no disorder. I passed Wednesday night in the path of the advancing flames, and in all those terrible hours I saw not one woman who wept, not one man who was excited, not one person who was in the slightest degree panic stricken.

Before the flames, throughout the night, fled tens of thousands of homeless ones. Some were wrapped in blankets. Others carried bundles of bedding and dear household treasures. Sometimes a whole family was harnessed to a carriage or delivery wagon that was weighted down with their possessions. Baby buggies, toy wagons, and go-carts were used as trucks, while every other person was dragging a trunk. Yet everybody was gracious. The most perfect courtesy obtained. Never in all San Francisco's history were her people so kind and courteous as on this night of terror.

A Caravan of Trunks

All night these tens of thousands fled before the flames. Many of them, the poor people from the labor ghetto, had fled all day as well. They had left their homes burdened with possessions. Now and again they lightened up, flinging out upon the street clothing and treasures they had dragged for miles. **C**

C AUTHOR'S PURPOSE
So far, has London described individuals or crowds? Jot this down in your chart. Why might he have made that choice?

---

6. **enumeration** (ĭ-nōō′mə-rā′shŭn): the act of counting or listing one by one.
7. **vestiges** (věs′tĭj-əs): visible signs that something once existed.

They held on longest to their trunks, and over these trunks many a strong man broke his heart that night. The hills of San Francisco are steep, 80 and up these hills, mile after mile, were the trunks dragged. Everywhere were trunks with across them lying their exhausted owners, men and women. Before the march of the flames were flung picket lines of soldiers. And a block at a time, as the flames advanced, these pickets retreated. One of their tasks was to keep the trunk-pullers moving. The exhausted creatures, stirred on by the **menace** of bayonets,[8] would arise and struggle up the steep pavements, pausing from weakness every five or ten feet.

Often, after surmounting a heart-breaking hill, they would find another wall of flame advancing upon them at right angles and be **compelled** to change anew the line of their retreat. In the end, completely played out, 90 after toiling for a dozen hours like giants, thousands of them were compelled to abandon their trunks. Here the shopkeepers and soft members of the middle class were at a disadvantage. But the working-men dug holes in vacant lots and backyards and buried their trunks.

The Doomed City

At nine o'clock Wednesday evening I walked down through the very heart of the city. I walked through miles and miles of magnificent buildings and towering skyscrapers. Here was no fire. All was in perfect order. The police patrolled the streets. Every building had its watchman at the door. And yet it was doomed, all of it. There was no water. The dynamite was giving out. And at right angles two different conflagrations were sweeping down upon it. **D**

100 At one o'clock in the morning I walked down through the same section. Everything still stood intact. There was no fire. And yet there was a change. A rain of ashes was falling. The watchmen at the doors were gone. The police had been withdrawn. There were no firemen, no fire-engines, no men fighting with dynamite. The district had been absolutely abandoned. I stood at the corner of Kearney and Market, in the very innermost heart of San Francisco. Kearney Street was deserted. Half a dozen blocks away it was burning on both sides. The street was a wall of flame. And against this wall of flame, silhouetted sharply, were two United States cavalrymen sitting on their horses, calmly watching. That was all. 110 Not another person was in sight. In the intact heart of the city, two troopers sat [on] their horses and watched. **E**

Spread of the Conflagration

Surrender was complete. There was no water. The sewers had long since been pumped dry. There was no dynamite. Another fire had broken out

---

8. **bayonets** (bā′ə-nĕts′): blades that fit on the end of rifles and are used as weapons.

menace (mĕn′ĭs) *n.* a possible danger; threat

compel (kəm-pĕl′) *v.* to pressure by force

D AUTHOR'S PURPOSE
Reread lines 94–95. What time of day is it when London is making his observations? As you continue reading, look for other references to the time.

E AUTHOR'S PURPOSE
Why might London have chosen to describe the same section of downtown twice?

further uptown, and now from three sides conflagrations were sweeping down. The fourth side had been burned earlier in the day. In that direction stood the tottering walls of the Examiner Building, the burned-out Call Building, the smoldering ruins of the Grand Hotel, and the gutted, devastated, dynamited Palace Hotel.

The following will illustrate the sweep of the flames and the inability of men to calculate their spread. At eight o'clock Wednesday evening I passed through Union Square. It was packed with refugees. Thousands of them had gone to bed on the grass. Government tents had been set up, supper was being cooked, and the refugees were lining up for free meals.

At half past one in the morning three sides of Union Square were in flames. The fourth side, where stood the great St. Francis Hotel, was still holding out. An hour later, ignited from top and sides the St. Francis was flaming heavenward. Union Square, heaped high with mountains of trunks, was deserted. Troops, refugees, and all had retreated.

A Fortune for a Horse!

It was at Union Square that I saw a man offering a thousand dollars for a team of horses. He was in charge of a truck piled high with trunks from some hotel. It had been hauled here into what was considered safety, and the horses had been taken out. The flames were on three sides of the Square and there were no horses.

Also, at this time, standing beside the truck, I urged a man to seek safety in flight. He was all but hemmed in by several conflagrations. He was an old man and he was on crutches. Said he: "Today is my birthday. Last night I was worth thirty thousand dollars. I bought some delicate fish and other things for my birthday dinner. I have had no dinner, and all I own are these crutches."

I convinced him of his danger and started him limping on his way. An hour later, from a distance, I saw the truck-load of trunks burning merrily in the middle of the street.

On Thursday morning at a quarter past five, just twenty-four hours after the earthquake, I sat on the steps of a small residence on Nob Hill. With me sat Japanese, Italians, Chinese, and negroes—a bit of the cosmopolitan flotsam⁹ of the wreck of the city. All about were the palaces of the nabob pioneers of Forty-nine.¹⁰ To the east and south at right angles, were advancing two mighty walls of flame.

---

9. **flotsam** (flŏt′səm): floating wreckage after a ship has sunk.
10. **pioneers of Forty-nine:** reference to the pioneers who came to San Francisco during the California gold rush in 1849.

Troops walk east along Market Street as the Call Building burns in the distance.

◀**Analyze
Visuals**
Which **detail** from this
photograph best helps
you understand the
devastation to the city?

150   I went inside with the owner of the house on the steps of which I sat. He
was cool and cheerful and hospitable. "Yesterday morning," he said, "I was
worth six hundred thousand dollars. This morning this house is all I have
left. It will go in fifteen minutes. He pointed to a large cabinet. "That is my
wife's collection of china. This rug upon which we stand is a present. It cost
fifteen hundred dollars. Try that piano. Listen to its tone. There are few like
it. There are no horses. The flames will be here in fifteen minutes." **F**

    Outside the old Mark Hopkins residence a palace was just catching fire.
The troops were falling back and driving the refugees before them. From
every side came the roaring of flames, the crashing of walls, and the
detonations of dynamite.

The Dawn of the Second Day

160   I passed out of the house. Day was trying to dawn through the smoke-pall.[11]
A sickly light was creeping over the face of things. Once only the sun broke
through the smoke-pall, blood-red, and showing a quarter its usual size.
The smoke-pall itself, viewed from beneath, was a rose color that pulsed and
fluttered with lavender shades. Then it turned to mauve and yellow and dun.[12]
There was no sun. And so dawned the second day on stricken San Francisco.

    An hour later I was creeping past the shattered dome of the City Hall.
Than it there was no better exhibit of the destructive force of the
earthquake. Most of the stone had been shaken from the great dome,
leaving standing the naked framework of steel. Market Street was piled
170 high with the wreckage, and across the wreckage lay the overthrown pillars
of the City Hall shattered into short crosswise sections.

F **AUTHOR'S PURPOSE**
Reread lines 129–155.
What do you notice
about how these
people are described?
What impact do the
comments from the
anonymous wealthy
man have on you?

---

11. **pall** (pôl): a covering that darkens or covers.
12. **dun** (dŭn): dull brownish gray.

This section of the city, with the exception of the Mint and the Post-Office, was already a waste of smoking ruins. Here and there through the smoke, creeping warily under the shadows of tottering walls, emerged occasional men and women. It was like the meeting of the handful of survivors after the day of the end of the world.

Beeves Slaughtered and Roasted

On Mission Street lay a dozen steers, in a neat row stretching across the street just as they had been struck down by the flying ruins of the earthquake. The fire had passed through afterward and roasted them.
180 The human dead had been carried away before the fire came. At another place on Mission Street I saw a milk wagon. A steel telegraph pole had smashed down sheer through the driver's seat and crushed the front wheels. The milk cans lay scattered around.

All day Thursday and all Thursday night, all day Friday and Friday night, the flames still raged on.

Friday night saw the flames finally conquered, though not until Russian Hill and Telegraph Hill had been swept and three-quarters of a mile of wharves and docks had been licked up. **G**

The Last Stand

The great stand of the fire-fighters was made Thursday night on Van Ness
190 Avenue. Had they failed here, the comparatively few remaining houses of the city would have been swept. Here were the magnificent residences of the second generation of San Francisco nabobs, and these, in a solid zone, were dynamited down across the path of the fire. Here and there the flames leaped the zone, but these fires were beaten out, principally by the use of wet blankets and rugs. **H**

San Francisco, at the present time, is like the crater of a volcano, around which are camped tens of thousands of refugees. At the Presidio[13] alone are at least twenty thousand. All the surrounding cities and towns are jammed with the homeless ones, where they are being cared for by the relief
200 committees. The refugees were carried free by the railroads to any point they wished to go, and it is estimated that over one hundred thousand people have left the peninsula on which San Francisco stood. The government has the situation in hand, and, thanks to the immediate relief given by the whole United States, there is not the slightest possibility of a famine. The bankers and business men have already set about making preparations to rebuild San Francisco. **I**

---

13. **Presidio** (prĭ-sē′dē-ō′): a historic military post in San Francisco.

G AUTHOR'S PURPOSE
What is the main event London tracked from beginning to end?

H AUTHOR'S PURPOSE
How much do you learn about what took place Thursday and Friday?

I AUTHOR'S PURPOSE
What information about the disaster does London provide in this last paragraph?

LETTER FROM NEW ORLEANS

Leaving Desire
Jon Lee Anderson

◀ **Analyze
Visuals**
This photo shows
Lionel Petrie, a man
trapped in the flooding
that occurred after
Hurrican Katrina hit,
climbing down into
the floodwaters. What
questions come to
mind as you look at this
image?

When I first saw Lionel Petrie, he was standing on the second-story
porch of his house, at the junction of Desire Street and North
Bunny Friend, in the Ninth Ward of New Orleans. The house was built
of wood, with white siding and peach trim. Petrie, an African-American
with salt-and-pepper hair and a mustache, appeared to be in his sixties. A
large Akita[1] was standing next to him, ears perked **vigilantly**. The two of
them looked out from across the fenced-in expanse of the front yard. Petrie
was clearly an organized man: a painter's ladder was dangling from the
railing of the porch, and a clutch of orange life vests hung within reach of
10 a fibreglass canoe that was tethered to the house. The canoe bobbed on the
surface of the stinking black water that filled the street and had engulfed
most of the first floor of the house. The spiked parapet of a wrought-
iron fence poked up about eight inches above the waterline, etching out a
formal square that separated the house from the street. **Ⓐ**

vigilantly
(vĭj′ə-lənt-lē) *adv.* in
a state of alertness;
watchfully

Ⓐ AUTHOR'S PURPOSE
What is this paragraph
about? Note the kind of
details provided about
the subject.

---

1. **Akita** (ä-kē′tə): a breed of Japanese hunting dog.

COMMON CORE L4

Language Coach

Multiple Meaning Words Multiple meaning words have more than one meaning. For example, *flush* may mean "to redden," "next to or closely alongside," or "to clean by pouring water through something." Which meaning of *flush* makes the most sense in line 17?

B AUTHOR'S PURPOSE
What do you learn about Petrie's situation and his attitude toward it?

Petrie's house was different from those of his neighbors, most of which were small brick row houses, or rundown clapboard houses that had deep porches flush with the street. His was set far back in the lot, and had a self-possessed air about it. Near the fence, in what must have been the driveway, the hoods of two submerged cars and a truck could be seen.

I was seated in the back of a four-person Yamaha WaveRunner that was piloted by Shawn Alladio, an energetic woman in her forties, with long blond hair, from Whittier, California. Eight days had passed since Hurricane Katrina made landfall, and Alladio was out on a search for trapped survivors and for what rescuers were calling "holdouts"—residents who didn't want to leave their homes—in one of the poorest and worst-hit parts of the city, the Ninth Ward, in eastern New Orleans.

Alladio maneuvered the WaveRunner so that we were alongside Petrie's fence, and, after calling out a greeting to him, she asked him if he wanted to leave; he waved politely in response, but shook his head. She told him that the floodwater was toxic and that he would soon become sick. He said something in reply, but we couldn't hear him because of the rumble of the WaveRunner's idling engine. Alladio turned the ignition key off.

Petrie explained that his wife and son and daughter had left the city by car, heading for Baton Rouge, the day before Katrina hit. He didn't know where his family was now, and, if he left, they wouldn't know where he was. He said that he intended to wait for them to come back, and for the waters to go down.

Alladio told him that the authorities were not allowing people to return to this part of New Orleans, and that it might be a month before the waters receded. He listened carefully, nodded, and replied that he had stocks of food and some water; that he'd be all right—he'd wait. He patted his dog's head. "Thank you, but I'll be fine," he said. Alladio tried again. "I can promise you that you will *not* see your family if you stay here," she told him; it was much likelier that he would pass out and die from the fumes from the water. **B**

He asked whether she would promise that he would be able to join his family.

Alladio paused, and said to me quietly, "I can't promise him that. If I turn him over to the authorities, like the other evacuees, he could end up anywhere in the country."

Turning back to Petrie, she asked, "If I drive you to Baton Rouge myself, will you come with me?"

"You would take me yourself?" he asked.

"Yes," she said. "I promise. Today, when I am done with my work, I will take you there."

Petrie took a step back on his porch. He raised his head thoughtfully and asked, "Can I take my dog with me?"

420 UNIT 3: SETTING AND MOOD

"Oh, God," Alladio said under her breath. "I hate this." Then she said to him, "I am so sorry, Mr. Petrie, but, no, they won't allow us to take out animals. You will have to leave him here."

60 Petrie gripped the railing of the porch and leaned over again, in a kind of slow, sustained forward lurch, his head down. Then he nodded and said, "O.K."

Alladio told Petrie to prepare a small bag with his essential belongings, to say goodbye to his dog and, if he wanted, put out some food and water for him. She would be back in an hour to pick him up; in the meantime, she needed to see if there were more people who needed evacuating. He said, "O.K.," and waved, and went back inside the house. The dog followed him. **C**

A lladio had arrived in New Orleans on Saturday, September 3rd, with a team of California rescue workers and a small flotilla[2] of donated
70 WaveRunners. She and her team were loosely attached to a task force sent by the State of California, but were mostly on their own. We had met at a staging area underneath an elevated section of Interstate 10. As I arrived, evacuees were being brought out of the water to a slightly raised stretch of land where railroad tracks ran under the highway. A boat came up and deposited an elderly black couple. Rescuers carried the woman, who was wearing a denim skirt, a T-shirt, and gold earrings, and sat her down on a fallen telephone pole. She rocked back and forth, with one hand raised, and murmured, "I just want to tell you—thank you, Jesus." Her husband walked over unsteadily to join her. They had stayed at home until just
80 before the hurricane, and then gone to their church. As the water rose, they took refuge in the choir loft. They stayed there for eight days, drinking the water the storm washed in. "We were down to our last two crackers," she said. Another man was brought over, shaking, and speaking incoherently. The only words I could make out were "I'm still alive."

After putting on chest waders to protect ourselves from the fetid[3] floodwaters—which Alladio warned me were "really gnarly"—we set off by boat from Interstate 10. . . .

We passed cargo yards, electrical pylons,[4] and houses with tar-paper roofs that had water halfway up the windows, and other houses that
90 were completely submerged. When we came to the intersection of Louisa Street and Higgins Boulevard, the street signs were at eye level and the traffic lights were barely above the surface of the water. We passed a house with a shattered plate-glass window. Peering down into the living room,

C AUTHOR'S PURPOSE
Reread lines 50–67. What does the conversation between Alladio and Petrie reveal about the kind of person Alladio is?

---

2. **flotilla** (flō-tĭl'ə): a small fleet of ships.

3. **fetid** (fĕt'ĭd): having an offensive odor.

4. **electrical pylons** (pī'lŏnz'): steel towers supporting electrical wires.

I saw a sofa floating near a framed photo of Muhammad Ali standing triumphantly over Sonny Liston. At a community swimming pool, a lifeguard seat poked just above the waters. We passed a rowboat carrying two white men and being towed by a black man with dreadlocks, up to his neck in water. Later, we saw them again; all three were in the boat now, and were paddling with broken street signs.

100   It was a clear, hot day, and the floodwater smelled strongly of oil and raw sewage, and stung the eyes. There were other smells, from islands of rotting garbage, and, **intermittently,** as elsewhere in the city, the smell of death. Helicopters had been clattering overhead all morning, some of them dumping buckets of water on house fires that had broken out everywhere. Scudding[5] columns of brown and gray smoke shot up from half a dozen points around the city. The towers of downtown New Orleans were visible in the distance. **D**

A New Orleans neighborhood lies under several feet of water.

Until the nineteenth century, the Ninth Ward was a swamp, and, even after it became home to a black and immigrant white community, and
110 was drained (in that order), it was periodically devastated by flooding. During Hurricane Betsy, in 1965, it was hit harder than most of the city, and was underwater for days. The neglect of the Ninth Ward by the city government was notorious; well into the twentieth century, it lacked adequate sewers and clean water. The Norman Rockwell image that the Ninth Ward inspired was that of the first grader Ruby Bridges, a tiny black

---

5. **scudding** (skŭ'dĭng): skimming along swiftly.

girl in a white dress, who was led to school by federal marshals past jeering white crowds—a chapter in a violent desegregation struggle that divided the city in the nineteen-sixties. In the next decades, many of the white residents of the Ninth Ward left; by the time Katrina hit, almost all the
120 students in the school that Ruby Bridges integrated were black.

At 2037 Desire, a block past Petrie's home, three people stood on the second-floor porch of a large wooden house: a bulky young woman in a white blouse, with dyed orange hair, and tattoos on one arm; a young man with copper skin in a lilac polo shirt . . . and an old man who was bare-chested except for a pair of red suspenders. The ground floor was flooded and a sign above it said, "Winner Supermarket—ATM Inside." Alladio hailed them and repeated the argument that she had made to Petrie. The young man said that his name was Theron Green, and that he and his father, Alfred Green, the old man, and his fiancée—Trinell Sanson, the tattooed woman—
130 were fine, and were planning to stay. They also had a friend inside the house, they said. Theron Green spoke in a thick local accent, and his eyes were alert and suspicious. He was clearly anxious for us to leave. "We feel comfortable, safe in our own house here," he said. "Anyway, I don't want no looters coming here." Alladio told him that there would soon be forced evacuations, but Green was adamant. "I'll wait till they force me out, then," he said. Trinell Sanson said, "We're fine. If it gets too bad, we'll catch the helicopter.". . .

Alladio warned me not to get spattered by the floodwater. "The people who have been in this are going to get sick," she said. The Environmental Protection Agency had teams out taking water samples to check for toxins,
140 and the rumor—apparently unfounded—was that entire districts were so contaminated that they would have to be razed, along with hundreds of thousands of vehicles. The people who lived there might not realize it, she said, "but once they leave they are never going to see their homes again.". . .

When we returned to Petrie's house, he was packed and waiting for us on the second-floor porch, dressed in slacks, a fresh unbuttoned shirt over a T-shirt, and a Marine Corps baseball cap. He leaned down to his dog, took both its ears in his hands and caressed them, and then told the dog to go inside. Petrie climbed into the canoe and began paddling over to us. The dog reemerged on the balcony, appearing **disconcerted** and watchful.
150 Petrie did not look back. He came alongside the fence and we helped him first with a bag and then with a little black case that he said had his wife's Bible in it. "I know she'd want me to bring that," he said. He climbed onto the WaveRunner behind me. Alladio gave the vessel a little power, and we began moving off. **E**

disconcert (dĭs′kən-sûrt′) *v.* to ruffle; to frustrate by throwing into disorder

E AUTHOR'S PURPOSE What event has this article focused on so far? Jot this down as well as any powerful details or images.

As we made our way down Desire, Petrie looked around him at the devastation, his neighbors' houses submerged in water. He said, "Oh, my God. I had no idea."

I asked him why he hadn't left earlier. "You tell yourself that the waters are going to recede, and when they don't one day you say maybe they will
160 the next," he answered.

The waters had subsided somewhat after the initial surge, he said. Then he had noticed, as the days went by, that there was an ebb and flow to them, as if a tide were moving in and out. To his mind, the city had become part of Lake Pontchartrain. He had heard on the radio about the levees breaking. When the electricity went out, he had listened to the radio each night, but had turned it off after a little while, to save his batteries.

As we spoke, he seemed to be trying to make sense of his own reaction to the catastrophe. He had understood logically that he was stranded and in danger, and yet he had decided that his first priority was to remain and
170 prepare the house for his family's return: "Pretty crazy, huh? I even started repairing my roof." About a third of the roof had been torn away by the hurricane, and he had worked for several days patching it up while the city lay underwater. . . .

When we passed Theron Green's house, he and his father and his fiancée waved and smiled at Petrie. . . .

Petrie told me that he was worried about his aunt Willa Mae Butler: "She's about eighty-two, and lives on Bartholomew Street. I'm worried that she's dead, because this time she said she wasn't going."

As we travelled slowly back toward Interstate 10, avoiding debris and
180 downed electrical lines, Petrie began calling out landmarks. He had lived in the neighborhood his entire life. As a child, he had lived on Louisa Street. He pointed to a building that he said was the primary school he had attended from kindergarten through eighth grade. . . . **F**

By now, he was reconciled to his rescue. "I think the good Lord sent you to me," he said. "I am looking forward to seeing my wife!" Her name was Mildred. He was sixty-four and Mildred was sixty-one. They had married when she was seventeen and he was twenty. "Everyone said we wouldn't last, but we've been together forty-five years, and this is the first time we have been apart.". . .

190 After we landed, Shawn Alladio went out on one more tour of the neighborhood to see if there was anyone else to bring in. While we waited for her to return, Petrie and I sat in my rented van in the shade under Interstate 10. Nearby, rescuers stripped down and washed in solutions of water and bleach. . . .

F AUTHOR'S PURPOSE
How much of New Orleans is this article covering? Tell how you know.

A man crosses a flooded New Orleans street.

◀ **Analyze Visuals**
What **details** in this photograph help you understand how deep the water is?

COMMON CORE RI 6

G **AUTHOR'S PURPOSE**
What do you learn about Petrie in this paragraph? Recall the four basic purposes for writing: to express ideas or feelings, to inform or explain, to persuade, or to entertain. Which of these purposes do these details help Anderson achieve? How do they help him achieve his secondary purpose of creating empathy for a disaster victim?

Petrie told me about his own children. Lionel, his namesake, forty-three years old, had been in the Marine Corps for fifteen years and served in the first Gulf War. He had been an aviation mechanic, but when he got out he couldn't get a job, so he went back to school, at the University of New Orleans, where he was pursuing an undergraduate degree when the hurricane arrived. Lionel owned two houses, one just blocks away from Petrie's, which he rented out. Petrie's second son, Bruce, who was thirty-eight, had also been a marine, had an accounting degree, and worked as a shelter supervisor for Girls and Boys Town. Bruce had driven out of the city with his wife and children before Katrina. Petrie smiled when he spoke of his daughter, Crystal, who was twenty-one. She was studying nursing in New Orleans. Lionel had driven her and their mother out of the city. **G**

Petrie hadn't gone to college; he got hired at a shipyard right after high school. After a couple of years, he decided to train as a welder. "For a year, I went to welders' school from 8 A.M. to noon and worked at American Marine from 6 P.M. until 6 A.M. Got my certificate as a certified welder around 1962. I went to several places looking for a job as a welder, but never got hired." When, in 1965, Petrie went to apply for a job at Equitable Equipment, near his home, he saw white welders being hired even as he was told that the only openings were for laborers. He contacted the local N.A.A.C.P. and filed a complaint with the newly formed Equal Employment Opportunity Commission. "They took an interest in my case, and I was the first black to be hired as a skilled worker by Equitable," he said. "I would sit down to eat my lunch and the white guys would go

sit somewhere else. I didn't care—I was just there to do my job." After
220 working for a decade at Equitable, and then at Kaiser Aluminum until
1983, when it shut down its Louisiana operations, he decided to set up his
own business, Petrie Iron and Construction. He didn't have insurance,
though, and he figured that he'd lost everything.

L ater that evening, Alladio drove Petrie and me to Baton Rouge in a
rented pickup, towing her WaveRunner behind her. She had been told
that forced evacuations would begin soon, and that the operation would
shift toward law enforcement. She was leaving the next day. **H**

In his exhaustion, Petrie had not been able to remember any telephone
numbers, but, as we drove along, cell-phone numbers for his son Bruce and
230 his daughter came back to him. I handed him my phone, and a minute
later I heard him say, "They're in Memphis!"

When he hung up, he said that his wife and daughter were staying in
Memphis at a cousin's house. Lionel had already found some temporary
factory work. Bruce was staying with his wife's family, in Kentucky. Willa
Mae Butler, Petrie's aunt, was alive and in Texas. Bruce was going to look
on the Internet for a flight for his father from Baton Rouge to Memphis.

A little while later, as we drove into the night, Petrie said reflectively,
"I don't know if I want to go back to New Orleans—seeing it how it was,
I don't think I do." He doubted, from what he had seen, that much of
240 it could ever be rebuilt. "The first thing I picture now is the water I saw
when I was coming out," he said.

A few minutes afterward, Bruce called back to say that the next available
flight was in three days' time. Alladio suggested that we try the Greyhound
station instead. It was already late when we arrived at the scruffy little
bus station in Baton Rouge, full of refugees from New Orleans. I joined a
long line of people waiting for information and tickets. Half an hour later,
it had barely moved. A man and a woman were arguing, and when the
stationmaster called for passengers for Houston, I heard the man tell her, "I
don't care what you say—I'm getting on that bus." After he left, the woman
250 leaned against a pillar and wiped her eyes. A tall man with a stack of religious
tracts was reciting Psalms from memory, and a woman made subdued sounds
of agreement or said, "That's right," in a rhythmic cadence. Two policemen
patrolled the station; there were a number of young men who looked street-
wise and seemed to be loitering among the waiting passengers.

Around midnight, Bruce called again. He had resolved to drive down
from Kentucky to get his father. He would leave shortly with his wife,
Donna. Lionel Petrie would wait for them in the Greyhound station. Bruce
thought that if he and Donna took turns driving they could make the trip
in twelve hours. They were there by noon the next day. **I**

H AUTHOR'S PURPOSE
What information do
you get about Alladio?

I AUTHOR'S PURPOSE
Over what span of time
did the events in this
account take place?

Comprehension

1. **Recall** How much of San Francisco does Jack London say was destroyed by the earthquake and the fire that came afterward?

2. **Clarify** What span of time does London's account cover?

3. **Clarify** Why is Lionel Petrie reluctant to leave his home?

COMMON CORE

RI 1 Cite textual evidence to support inferences drawn from the text. **RI 6** Determine an author's purpose in a text.

Text Analysis

4. **Analyze Author's Purpose** For one selection, state the author's specific purpose, and identify three aspects of the selection that help to achieve it.

5. **Evaluate Objectivity** An **objective** report is one that is fair, neutral, and evenhanded. Do you think that Jack London's account is objective? Cite evidence from the text to support your opinion.

6. **Make Judgments** The authorities forced thousands of people to leave behind their pets during the evacuation of New Orleans. Was it right to ask people to abandon their pets? Why or why not?

7. **Evaluate Accounts** Think about the two articles you have just read. Which account do you think is more powerful? Explain your opinion.

Comparing Accounts

8. **Set a Purpose for Reading** Now that you've read both articles, finish filling in your chart. Then add the final question, and answer it, too.

	"The Story of an Eyewitness"	"Letter from New Orleans: Leaving Desire"
What is the writer's specific purpose?	To show how widespread the devastation is.	
How much of the disaster area does the writer cover?		
Which events and people does the writer focus on?		
Which details and images have a big impact on you?		
How does the author achieve his purpose?		

What is the role of a WITNESS?

Based on the accounts you just read, what do you think an eyewitness to a disaster should pay attention to and report on?

Vocabulary in Context

▲ VOCABULARY PRACTICE

Answer each question to show your understanding of the vocabulary words.

1. Would a **lavishly** decorated home be simple or elegant?
2. Is a **menace** something to avoid or to look forward to?
3. If you **disconcert** people, do you confuse them or calm them?
4. If you **compel** people to do something, are you forcing them or inviting them?
5. Would a person who watches **vigilantly** be alert or distracted?
6. Which sound would be heard **intermittently**—thunder or a steady siren?

compel
disconcert
intermittently
lavishly
menace
vigilantly

ACADEMIC VOCABULARY IN WRITING

- circumstance - emerge - predominant - rely - technology

Imagine you volunteered to help in New Orleans after the hurricane. Using at least two Academic Vocabulary words, describe the **circumstances** you might have encountered there.

VOCABULARY STRATEGY: THE PREFIX *inter-*

A prefix is a word part attached to the beginning of a base word or root word. When a prefix is added, a new word is formed. The vocabulary word *intermittently* contains the prefix *inter-*, which means "between," added to the Latin word meaning "to let go." If you know the meaning of a prefix, it can help you figure out the meaning of an unfamiliar word, especially if you consider the word's context.

PRACTICE The boldfaced words all contain the prefix *inter-*. Use your knowledge of this prefix and the base word to write a definition for each word. Remember to use context clues or a dictionary if you need help.

1. The twins looked so similar, they could be **interchanged** and no one would know.
2. The puzzle pieces **interlock** so that they won't come apart.
3. An **international** commission was established to study world hunger.
4. I have to pass the **intermediate** course before I can move on to the advanced level.
5. We took the **interstate** highway on our drive from New York to Ohio.

COMMON CORE

L 4b Use common, grade-appropriate Latin affixes as clues to the meaning of a word.
L 6 Acquire and use accurately academic words; gather vocabulary knowledge when considering a word important to comprehension and expression.

Interactive Vocabulary **THINK** central

Go to **thinkcentral.com**.
KEYWORD: HML8-428

Writing for Assessment

1. READ THE PROMPT

The two articles you've just read cover similar subjects in different ways. In writing assessments, you might be asked to compare such texts.

> "The Story of an Eyewitness" and "Letter from New Orleans: Leaving Desire" are both eyewitness accounts of natural disasters, but they are written to achieve different goals. State the specific purpose of each account. Then, in four or five paragraphs, contrast the ways each author achieves his purpose. Use details from the articles to show the differences in how people, places, and events are covered.

◄ STRATEGIES IN ACTION

1. I need to **identify the specific purpose** of each article.

2. I need to **state the differences** in each author's disaster coverage.

3. I need to **support my statement with examples** of the authors' coverage of people, places, and events.

2. PLAN YOUR WRITING

To identify each author's specific purpose, refer to the instruction on page 411. To recall the ways each covers the disaster, review the chart you completed. In a thesis statement, identify three differences in their disaster coverage. Then think about how you will set up the body of your response.

- Option A: In one paragraph, describe the scope of the first article's coverage of people, places, and events. In the next paragraph, describe the other article's coverage.

- Option B: In one paragraph, contrast the way each article covers people. In the next paragraph, contrast the way each covers places. In the third, contrast the number of events covered.

I. Introduction
II. First article's coverage
III. Second article's coverage
IV. Conclusion

Once you have decided on your approach, create an outline to organize your details.

3. DRAFT YOUR RESPONSE

Introduction Provide the titles and authors of both articles, a brief description of what each article is about, a statement of each author's specific purpose, and your thesis statement.

Body With your outline as a guide, discuss the differences in each writers' coverage of people, places, and events.

Conclusion Restate your thesis statement, and leave your reader with a final thought about the role that purpose plays in each of these articles.

Revision Double-check to make sure your thesis statement clearly presents the ideas you develop in your body paragraphs.

Mi Madre
Poem by Pat Mora

Canyon de Chelly
Poem by Simon J. Ortiz

What gifts does the EARTH provide?

COMMON CORE

RL 4 Analyze the impact of specific word choices on meaning. **RL 6** Analyze how differences in points of view create effects.

It's not hard to appreciate nature when you're taking a walk on a sunny day or swimming at a scenic beach. But the earth gives us many gifts that we may not always recognize. The gas that warms our homes, the concrete we use to pave our sidewalks, even the paper we write on—these things are all precious resources provided to us by the earth. The poets whose works you're about to read share their appreciation for the earth's gifts through words.

LIST IT The earth's resources can be used in multiple ways. In a small group, choose one of the resources shown, and brainstorm at least five ways we can use it. Did you discover any new uses for these resources? Share your list with the class.

dirt   trees
plants   water
rocks   wind
sunlight

TEXT ANALYSIS: IMAGERY

The use of description that makes something seem real or easy to imagine is called **imagery.** Poets create imagery by using words and phrases that appeal to our senses of sight, hearing, smell, taste, and touch. Paying attention to imagery can enable you to "experience" a poem as if you were there. For example, look at the following lines from "Mi Madre":

I say tease me.
She sprinkles raindrops in my face on a sunny day.

The image "sprinkles raindrops" appeals to the sense of touch, while "sunny day" appeals to the sense of sight. If you combine these images in your mind, you can almost share in this scene. As you read "Mi Madre" and "Canyon de Chelly," use a word web to keep track of these and other examples of imagery.

READING SKILL: UNDERSTAND SPEAKER

In poetry, the **speaker** is the voice that "talks" to the reader and relates the ideas presented in the poem from a specific point of view. It is important to understand that the speaker is not the same as the poet. For example, a poet may choose to write about a subject from the perspective of a child. In that case, the ideas that are expressed are those of the child, not necessarily the poet. As you read "Mi Madre" and "Canyon de Chelly," look for clues that will help you decide who each speaker is and how he or she feels about the subject of the poem.

Meet the Authors

Pat Mora
born 1942

Literacy Advocate
The granddaughter of Mexican immigrants, Pat Mora realized early in her writing career that her cultural heritage was "a source of pride." Her books celebrate family, the desert in which she grew up, and the Mexican-American experience. Her children's books frequently feature Latino characters, because she believes that children of all backgrounds should see themselves reflected in the books they read.

Simon J. Ortiz
born 1941

Native New Mexican
Raised on New Mexico's Acoma Pueblo, Simon Ortiz is regarded as one of today's greatest Native-American writers. His work frequently focuses on having a sense of place. "You have to have it," Ortiz says. "Otherwise you are drifting." Ortiz hopes that all people can learn from his poetry. "I tell you about me and my world," he says, "so you may be able to see yourself."

BACKGROUND TO THE POEMS
Arizona's Canyon de Chelly (pronounced *sha*) is home to a Navajo tribal community that has preserved this sacred land for centuries. The canyon, now a national park, is known for its stunning landscapes, tribal artifacts, and rock paintings.

THINK central

Authors Online
Go to thinkcentral.com. KEYWORD: HML8-431

Complete the activities in your **Reader/Writer Notebook.**

431

Mi Madre[1]

Pat Mora

I say feed me.
She serves red prickly pear on a spiked cactus.

I say tease me.
She sprinkles raindrops in my face on a sunny day.

5 I say frighten me.
She shouts thunder, flashes lightning. **A**

I say comfort me.
She invites me to lay on her firm body.

I say heal me.
10 She gives me *manzanilla, orégano, dormilón.*[2]

I say caress me.
She strokes my skin with her warm breath. **B**

I say make me beautiful.
She offers turquoise for my fingers, a pink blossom for my hair. **C**

15 I say sing to me.
She chants lonely women's songs of femaleness.

I say teach me.
She endures: glaring heat
            numbing cold
20   frightening dryness.

She: the desert
She: strong mother.

---

1. **Mi Madre** (mē mä'drā) *Spanish*: my mother.
2. *manzanilla, orégano, dormilón* (măn'zə-nē'yə, ə-rĕg'ə-nō', dôr-mē-lŏn') *Spanish*: sweet-smelling herbs that can be used to make home medicines.

Analyze Visuals ▶

Compare this painting with your own mental image of the desert. Are the images similar or different?

A IMAGERY
Reread lines 1–6. To what senses do these images appeal? Record your answers in your word web.

B IMAGERY
Reread lines 11–12. What feelings does this image suggest?

C SPEAKER
What type of person is the speaker? How do you know?

Prickly Pear, Isabel Bronson Cartwright. Oil on canvas. Private collection. © Peter Harholt/SuperStock.

Canyon de Chelly

Simon J. Ortiz

Lie on your back on stone,
the stone carved to fit
the shape of yourself.
Who made it like this,
5 knowing that I would be along
in a million years and look
at the sky being blue forever?

My son is near me. He sits
and turns on his butt
10 and crawls over to stones,
picks one up and holds it,
and then puts it into his mouth.
The taste of stone.
What is it but stone,
15 the earth in your mouth.
You, son, are tasting forever. **D**

Analyze Visuals ▶

Is this a photograph or a painting? Tell what led you to your answer, and why others might **conclude** differently.

D SPEAKER
What do you know about the speaker of this poem?

We walk to the edge of cliff
and look down into the canyon.
On this side, we cannot see
20 the bottom cliff edge but looking
further out, we see fields,
sand furrows, cottonwoods.
In winter, they are softly gray.
The cliffs' shadows are distant,
25 hundreds of feet below;
we cannot see our own shadows.
The wind moves softly into us.
My son laughs with the wind;
he gasps and laughs. **E**

30 We find gray root, old wood,
so old, with curious twists
in it, curving back into curves,
juniper, piñon, or something
with hard, red berries in spring.
35 You taste them, and they are sweet
and bitter, the berries a delicacy
for bluejays. The plant rooted
fragilely into a sandy place
by a canyon wall, the sun bathing
40 shiny, pointed leaves.

My son touches the root carefully,
aware of its ancient quality.
He lays his soft, small fingers on it
and looks at me for information.
45 I tell him: wood, an old root,
and around it, the earth, ourselves. **F**

E IMAGERY
Reread lines 27–29.
Add the images in these
lines to your web. What
emotions do these
images suggest?

F SPEAKER
Reread lines 41–46. Why
do you think the speaker
brings his son to the
canyon?

Comprehension

1. **Recall** In "Mi Madre," how does the desert heal the speaker?

2. **Recall** In "Canyon de Chelly," what two things does the speaker's son taste?

3. **Represent** Reread lines 13–14 from "Mi Madre" and lines 17–22 from "Canyon de Chelly." Choose one of these groups of lines and sketch the image created in your mind.

:::: **COMMON CORE**

RL 4 Analyze the impact of specific word choices on meaning.
RL 6 Analyze how differences in points of view create effects.

Text Analysis

4. **Interpret Poem** In "Mi Madre," the speaker refers to the desert as a "strong mother." How is the desert in the poem like a mother?

5. **Make Inferences** Reread the first three lines of "Canyon de Chelly." To whom do you think the speaker is talking? Why do you think so?

6. **Compare and Contrast Speakers** Using a Y-chart like the one shown, fill in the top part with what you know about each speaker's relationship to the earth. Include the gifts he or she receives from it and how he or she feels about it. How are these relationships similar? Then cross out the similarities and write them in the bottom part.

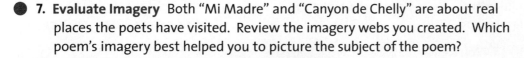

"Mi Madre" "Canyon de Chelly"

Similarities

7. **Evaluate Imagery** Both "Mi Madre" and "Canyon de Chelly" are about real places the poets have visited. Review the imagery webs you created. Which poem's imagery best helped you to picture the subject of the poem?

Extension and Challenge

8. **Creative Project: Poetry** Think of a place in the outdoors that you enjoy. Jot down notes about how the place looks, smells, feels, sounds, or tastes. Then write a poem about the place. Be sure to include **imagery** that appeals to at least three of the five senses.

9. **SOCIAL STUDIES CONNECTION** The Navajo, or Diné, make up the largest Native American nation in the United States. Research their history and traditions, including their preservation of Canyon de Chelly as a national landmark. Share your findings with a group.

What gifts does the EARTH provide?

Now that you have read the poems, what other gifts might you add to your list?

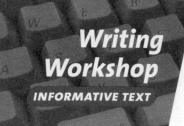

Writing Workshop
INFORMATIVE TEXT

Comparison-Contrast Essay

In Unit 3 and in your own life, you have encountered people and situations that can be compared. Identifying similarities and differences between two subjects can help you understand both of them more clearly. In this workshop, you will write a comparison-contrast essay that examines how two subjects are alike and different.

 Complete the workshop activities in your **Reader/Writer Notebook.**

WRITE WITH A PURPOSE

WRITING TASK

Write a **comparison-contrast essay** in which you describe the similarities and differences between two subjects, such as fictional characters, real people, places, or events.

Idea Starters
- two literary characters who confront similar conflicts
- two friends, siblings, or other relatives
- family rituals from two cultures
- the first and last days of school
- your neighborhood and a friend's

THE ESSENTIALS

Here are some common purposes, audiences, and formats for comparison-contrast writing.

PURPOSES	AUDIENCES	FORMATS
• to understand two subjects better	• classmates and teacher	• essay for class
	• friends	• friendly letter or e-mail
• to inform others about two subjects	• community members	• review in a newsletter or newspaper
• to decide between two choices	• Web users	• blog
	• customers	• product review Web site

COMMON CORE TRAITS

1. DEVELOPMENT OF IDEAS
- clearly **introduces the subjects** being compared and contrasted
- includes a **controlling idea** that identifies similarities and differences
- develops each point with **relevant, well-chosen facts, details, quotations,** and **examples**
- has a **concluding section** that follows from and supports the ideas presented

2. ORGANIZATION OF IDEAS
- **organizes** similarities and differences in a logical way
- uses **transitions** to link ideas and create cohesion

3. LANGUAGE FACILITY AND CONVENTIONS
- maintains a **formal style**
- uses **precise language** and **domain-specific vocabulary**
- uses parallel **sentence structures**
- employs **correct grammar, usage, spelling,** and **punctuation**

Writing Online

THINK central

Go to **thinkcentral.com.**
KEYWORD: HML8N-438

Planning/Prewriting

 COMMON CORE **W 2a–f** Write informative/explanatory texts to examine and convey ideas, concepts, and information. **W 5** Develop and strengthen writing as needed by planning.

Getting Started

CHOOSE YOUR SUBJECTS

You will find it easiest to **compare** and **contrast** two people, places, events, or characters that you have an interest in or know well. Use the Idea Starters on page 438 to help you list possible subjects for your essay. Make sure that you can identify both similarities and differences between each pair of subjects.

▶ **WHAT DOES IT LOOK LIKE?**

- my cousin's town and mine
- my two dogs
- two main characters: Joby from "The Drummer Boy of Shiloh" and Sam from "Hallucination"
  — really different lives and situations
  — some of the same traits

THINK ABOUT AUDIENCE AND PURPOSE

After you choose your subjects, consider your **purpose** and **audience**. These two considerations will affect every decision you make, from how much background information to include to which similarities and differences to explore.

▶ **ASK YOURSELF:**

- Who is my audience and what subjects will they find interesting?
- What background information will my audience need to understand my points?
- Will I need to define any **domain-specific**, or specialized, **vocabulary** so that my readers can follow my writing?

NOTE SIMILARITIES AND DIFFERENCES

Use a graphic organizer, such as a Venn diagram, to record similarities and differences between your subjects. If you have trouble thinking of interesting, important similarities and differences, try a new approach by choosing two new subjects.

▶ **WHAT DOES IT LOOK LIKE?**

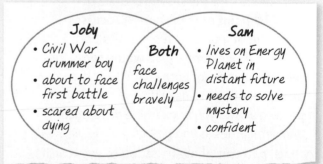

Joby
- Civil War drummer boy
- about to face first battle
- scared about dying

Both
face challenges bravely

Sam
- lives on Energy Planet in distant future
- needs to solve mystery
- confident

STATE YOUR CONTROLLING IDEA

Review the similarities and differences that you have identified. What do they help you understand about your subjects? What new insight have you gained? Express this understanding in a **controlling idea**, or thesis statement. This sentence should identify your two subjects and your main idea.

▶ **WHAT DOES IT LOOK LIKE?**

Subjects: Joby from "The Drummer Boy of Shiloh" and Sam from "Hallucination"

Main idea: They both face challenges with courage.

Controlling idea: Although Joby and Sam, the main characters of these stories, live on different planets during different centuries, both successfully face tremendous challenges.

Planning/Prewriting *continued*

COLLECT EVIDENCE

To help your audience understand your subjects more clearly, you need to illustrate their differences and similarities with relevant, well-chosen evidence that strongly supports your ideas. **Evidence** can be details, examples, facts, and quotations. For example, explaining how Joby took the general's words to heart shows how brave he was in the face of war.

▶ **WHAT DOES IT LOOK LIKE?**

> **Major similarity:** Both boys face challenges bravely.
>
> **Support:** After talking to the general, Joby feels braver. He waits to march into battle calmly. He turns his drum back up.
>
> **Support:** Sam uses his intelligence to solve the mystery of the hallucinations. He keeps an open mind to help him understand the insects.

ORGANIZE YOUR IDEAS

There are two methods for organizing a logical and coherent comparison-contrast essay:

- **Subject-by-subject organization**—Presents all the points about one subject and then all the points about the other subject. For example, you would discuss the appearance, personality, and actions of one character. Then you would move on to describe those same points for the second character.
- **Point-by-point organization**—Discusses one point at a time, as it applies to both subjects. For example, you would compare the appearances of both characters, then their personalities, and finally their actions. This pattern allows you to examine differences and similarities as you go along.

Try both patterns of organization to see which works better for the content of your essay.

▶ **ORGANIZATIONAL PATTERNS FOR A COMPARISON-CONTRAST ESSAY**

> **Subject by Subject**
> Subject A
>   1. Discussion of first point
>   2. Discussion of second point
> Subject B
>   1. Discussion of first point
>   2. Discussion of second point

> **Point by Point**
> Point 1: Discussion of Subject A
>   Discussion of Subject B
> Point 2: Discussion of Subject A
>   Discussion of Subject B

PEER REVIEW Share with a classmate a key point and the evidence you will use to support it. Ask: What additional support might I need to back up my point?

YOUR TURN In your *Reader/Writer Notebook,* identify your subjects. Then complete a Venn diagram similar to the one on page 439, identifying key similarities and differences between your two subjects. Write a controlling idea and collect the evidence that most strongly supports your ideas. Then choose an organizational pattern.

Drafting

COMMON CORE   **W 4** Produce clear and coherent writing appropriate to task, purpose, and audience. **W 9a (RL 1)** Cite textual evidence that most strongly supports an analysis. **L 3** Use knowledge of language and its conventions when writing.

The following chart shows how to organize your draft effectively.

Organizing Your Comparison-Contrast Essay

INTRODUCTION

- Capture your audience's attention with a lively "hook," such as an interesting quotation.
- State your main idea in a **controlling idea** that highlights the points of comparison and contrast.

▼

BODY

- **Organize** your similarities and differences in subject-by-subject or point-by-point order.
- Use appropriate and varied **transitions,** such as *in addition to, also, however,* and *unlike,* to clarify similarities and differences between subjects and create cohesion.
- Establish and maintain a **formal style** by avoiding casual language and contractions.
- Support key points with well-chosen **examples, facts,** or **quotations.**

▼

CONCLUDING SECTION

- Summarize the similarities and differences you discussed.
- Explain why the subjects are important to you.

GRAMMAR IN CONTEXT: PARALLEL STRUCTURE

One way to make sure that your audience can clearly follow your key points is to use parallel structure. **Parallel structure** is the use of more than one word, phrase, or sentence with the same grammatical form. Read the examples in the chart. Not only are sentences that use parallel structure clearer to understand, but they also flow more smoothly.

Mixed Structure	*Parallel Structure*
Sam is <u>confident</u> and <u>has determination</u>.	Sam is <u>confident</u> and <u>determined</u>.
There's not much he can do except worry and wait for <u>morning to come</u> and <u>the beginning of the battle</u>.	There's not much he can do except worry and wait for <u>morning to come</u> and <u>battle to begin</u>.

YOUR TURN   Develop a first draft of your essay, following the plan outlined in the chart above. As you write, use your knowledge of parallel structure to link related ideas so that you make them easier to understand.

Revising

The revising stage allows you to make changes to your draft that will improve its content and organization. Your goal is to determine if you have shown your audience how your two subjects are alike and different, and why they are important to you. This chart can help you revise or rewrite your draft.

COMPARISON-CONTRAST ESSAY

Ask Yourself	Tips	Revision Strategies
1. Does the introduction grab the audience's attention?	▶ **Put stars** next to questions, quotations, or details that would interest the audience.	▶ **Add** a surprising or interesting detail to the beginning of the introduction. **Rearrange** sentences to place the most attention-grabbing sentence first.
2. Does the introduction have a clear controlling idea?	▶ **Underline** the controlling idea. **Ask a peer** to read it and summarize the main idea of your essay.	▶ **Add** a controlling idea, or **rewrite** the existing controlling idea to more precisely describe the main idea of your essay.
3. Does the essay discuss several similarities or differences? Do they support the controlling idea?	▶ **Write an S** over ways in which the subjects are similar; **write a D** over their differences.	▶ **Eliminate** similarities or differences that do not support the controlling idea. **Add** others that do.
4. Is each key point supported with relevant, well-chosen evidence?	▶ **Circle** evidence that supports each similarity or difference.	▶ **Add** evidence as needed to strongly support each similarity or difference.
5. Does the essay have a logical and coherent organization?	▶ In the margin, **label** the organization as subject-by-subject or point-by-point. **Write 1** above each point about the first subject and **2** above each point about the second subject.	▶ If necessary, **try** a new approach to achieve a more logical organizational pattern.
6. Does the concluding section show why the subjects are important to the writer?	▶ **Put a check mark** next to the sentences that explain the subjects' significance.	▶ **Add** an explanation, if necessary. **Revise** your concluding section to clarify the importance of your subjects.

 YOUR TURN

PEER REVIEW Exchange essays with a classmate. Provide a brief comment sheet, referring to revision strategies from the chart that might help improve the essay. Point out parts that may need to be revisited or reworked.

ANALYZE A STUDENT DRAFT

COMMON CORE

W 5 Develop and strengthen writing as needed by revising, editing, rewriting, or trying a new approach, focusing on how well purpose and audience have been addressed.

Read this student's draft and the comments about it. Use it as a model for revising your own comparison-contrast essay.

Different Worlds, Similar Challenges

by Tyler Kurcewski, West Fairview Intermediate School

1   I am comparing the main characters of the short stories "The Drummer Boy of Shiloh" by Ray Bradbury and "Hallucination" by Isaac Asimov. Although these characters, Joby and Sam, live on different planets during different centuries, they both successfully face tremendous challenges.

2   The situations that these characters encounter are quite different, at least on the outside. Joby is a drummer boy in the army during the Civil War. His unit is camped on the field near where the battle will take place the next day. As a drummer boy, he could be hurt or even killed in the battle. In contrast, Sam, the main character of "Hallucination," is on a futuristic planet somewhere in the universe. He has been sent there by the Central Computer. His own life is not in danger, but he must solve the mystery of the hallucinations if the project is to succeed.

3   The way they handle their problems is also very different at first. Joby seems weak and frightened. He's afraid to die and lies crying in the dark. There's not much he can do except worry and wait for morning to come and battle to begin. Unlike Joby, Sam is confident and determined. He ignores the assignment he's been sent to work on and investigates the hallucinations on his own.

> Tyler's first sentence simply states the titles and authors of the stories he will compare. To make his introduction more interesting, he needs to add an **attention grabber.**

> Tyler ends his introduction with a strong **controlling idea.**

> For his essay, Tyler has chosen a **point-by-point organization.**

LEARN HOW   **Use Attention Grabbers to Add Interest**   Tyler's first sentence states his purpose, but it does not necessarily make the audience want to read further. To interest his readers, Tyler needs to add an **attention grabber,** such as a telling quotation, a thought-provoking question, or a universal statement. Notice how Tyler rewrote his introduction below.

TYLER'S REVISION TO PARAGRAPH 1

Nobody ever said life was easy. In fact, it's really about proving that you can face challenges.

    ~~I am comparing~~ the main characters of the short stories "The Drummer Boy of Shiloh" by Ray Bradbury and "Hallucination" by Isaac Asimov. *demonstrate this point*

❹   By the end of the stories, though, both Joby and Sam face their challenges with courage. The general stops to talk to Joby, telling him that he is "the heart of the army." This encouragement changes Joby's attitude. Turning his drum to face the sky shows that he is no longer afraid of the sound of falling peach blossoms that earlier reminded him of bullets. He knows he will march calmly and bravely into battle. Sam, too, thinks about stuff. He uses his brains to communicate with the planet's insect-like things and realizes that "previous attempts at communication had failed because the people . . . had been frightened." He does well in the end.

❺   The two characters in "The Drummer Boy of Shiloh" and "Hallucination" live in different times and places. They have different personalities and appear to be dealing with different problems. However, they are very much alike in the ways that count. Both Joby and Sam learn to face the challenges in their lives. Their courage inspires us. It teaches us to face our own challenges, whatever it is.

> To show the audience Joby's change of heart, Tyler includes well-chosen **examples** and a **quotation** from the story.

> Tyler's explanation of Sam's conflict is somewhat vague. He needs to use more **precise language** to convey his meaning.

LEARN HOW **Use Precise Language** Although Tyler is very familiar with his subject, his audience may not be. For example, the audience may wonder what "stuff" Sam is thinking about. To help them understand exactly what he means, Tyler must replace some of his vague words with more precise terms and phrases. In his revision, he also replaces weak verbs with more powerful ones.

TYLER'S REVISION TO PARAGRAPH ❹

Sam, too, ~~thinks about stuff.~~ *confronts his problem.* He uses his ~~brains~~ *almost superhuman intelligence* to communicate with the planet's insect-like ~~things~~ *creatures* and realizes that "previous attempts at communication had failed because the people . . . had been frightened." He ~~does well in the end.~~ *discovers the mystery behind the hallucinations, helps to cure the Commander, and saves the power station.*

YOUR TURN   Use feedback from your peers and your teacher as well as the two "Learn How" lessons to revise or rewrite your essay. Evaluate whether your work achieves the purpose of a comparison-contrast essay and maintains a formal style for its audience.

Editing and Publishing

COMMON CORE W 2d Use precise language. W 5 Develop and strengthen writing as needed by revising, editing, and rewriting. L 1 Demonstrate command of standard English grammar and usage when writing. L 2c Spell correctly.

When you edit, you look over your essay to make sure there are no mistakes, such as grammar or usage errors. Also, be sure to check your spelling after doing a word-processing spell-check. Though a spell-checker is useful, it can miss spelling errors that result in real words, such as misspelling *from* as *form*. These types of errors diminish the quality of your work.

GRAMMAR IN CONTEXT: PRONOUN-ANTECEDENT AGREEMENT

An **antecedent** is the noun or pronoun to which a pronoun refers. For instance, in the following sentence, the pronoun *their* refers to the antecedent *they: They walked their dog around the neighborhood.* Pair singular pronouns with singular antecedents. Pair plural pronouns with plural antecedents.

As Tyler proofread his essay, he realized that his pronouns did not always agree with their antecedents in number. His revisions in blue show how he fixed the problem.

Their courage inspires us. It teaches us to face our

own challenges, whatever ~~it is~~ they are.

[*Courage* is the antecedent of *it*. Both are singular and agree in number. However, the antecedent *challenges* (plural) does not agree with *it* (singular). Tyler fixed this error by replacing *it is* with *they are*.]

PUBLISH YOUR WRITING

Share your comparison-contrast essay with an audience.
- Create a photo essay, inserting photographs or other illustrations into your text. Display your essay on a bulletin board.
- Develop your essay into an article for an appropriate school or community publication.
- Create a discussion **blog,** or Web log, on which you discuss the similarities and differences you highlighted in your essay. Invite other classmates to participate in the discussion.

 YOUR TURN Correct any errors in your essay by carefully proofreading it. Identify and fix any capitalization, punctuation, and spelling errors. Make sure that your pronouns have clear antecedents and agree with them in number. Then publish your final essay where your audience is likely to see it.

Scoring Rubric

Use the rubric below to evaluate your comparison-contrast essay from the Writing Workshop or your response to the on-demand task on the next page.

COMPARISON-CONTRAST ESSAY

SCORE	COMMON CORE TRAITS
6	• **Development** Clearly introduces the subjects being compared and contrasted; states an effective controlling idea; strongly supports similarities and differences with relevant, well-chosen evidence; ends strongly and insightfully • **Organization** Arranges ideas in a clear, logical order; effectively uses appropriate and varied transitions to link ideas and create cohesion • **Language** Consistently maintains a formal style; effectively uses precise language; shows a strong command of conventions
5	• **Development** Competently introduces the subjects being compared and contrasted; states a clear controlling idea; supports most similarities and differences with relevant, well-chosen evidence; ends strongly • **Organization** Arranges ideas logically; uses appropriate transitions to link ideas • **Language** Maintains a formal style; uses precise language; has a few errors in conventions
4	• **Development** Sufficiently introduces the subjects being compared and contrasted; states a controlling idea; could choose better evidence to support similarities and differences; has a satisfactory concluding section • **Organization** Arranges ideas fairly logically; could vary transitions more • **Language** Mostly maintains a formal style; needs more precise language at times; includes a few distracting errors in conventions
3	• **Development** States a controlling idea but lacks a clear introduction; lacks enough relevant, well-chosen evidence; has an adequate concluding section • **Organization** Has some organizational flaws; needs more transitions to link ideas • **Language** Frequently lapses into an informal style; uses some vague language; has some critical errors in conventions
2	• **Development** Has a weak introduction and controlling idea; lacks relevant, well-chosen evidence; has a weak concluding section • **Organization** Has organizational flaws; lacks transitions throughout • **Language** Uses informal style and vague language; has many errors in conventions
1	• **Development** Has no introduction, controlling idea, and evidence; ends abruptly • **Organization** Has no organization or transitions • **Language** Uses an inappropriate style and vague words; has major problems with conventions

Preparing for Timed Writing

 COMMON CORE W 10 Write routinely over shorter time frames for a range of tasks, purposes, and audiences.

1. ANALYZE THE TASK   5 MIN

Read the task carefully. Then read it again, underlining words that tell the topic, the audience, and the purpose.

WRITING TASK

Purpose

Topic

Write a review for your school newspaper that compares and contrasts two musicians, bands, artists, movies, books, or other subjects in which the members of your school community might be interested. Include relevant details and examples to support your points.

Audience

2. PLAN YOUR RESPONSE   10 MIN

Once you have chosen your subjects, ask yourself: What do I want to show by comparing and contrasting these subjects? Then identify the similarities and differences that will help you make your point. List all that you can think of, and then select the two or three that are most important.

Subject A	Subject B
Both:	

3. RESPOND TO THE TASK   20 MIN

As you draft your essay, keep these guidelines in mind:
- Write a controlling idea that establishes which subjects you are comparing or contrasting and why.
- Decide on an organizational pattern (either subject-by-subject or point-by-point) and use it consistently throughout your essay.
- In the concluding section, restate your major points and clearly explain why these subjects are important to you.

4. IMPROVE YOUR RESPONSE   5-10 MIN

Revising Go back over key aspects of the essay. Is your introduction engaging? Do you offer significant similarities and differences backed up by relevant examples? Do you tell why these subjects are meaningful to you?

Proofreading Correct errors in grammar, spelling, punctuation, and capitalization. Make sure your edits are neat and the essay is legible.

Checking Your Final Copy Before you turn in your essay, read it one more time to catch any errors you may have missed and to apply any finishing touches.

Technology Workshop

Creating a Story Discussion Blog

Discussing or writing about elements of short stories can help you appreciate them more fully. A **blog,** or Web log, enables you to share your ideas with a broader audience and benefit from others' insights into various literary texts.

 Complete the workshop activities in your **Reader/Writer Notebook.**

PRODUCE WITH A PURPOSE

TASK

Create a **blog** in which you and your classmates share ideas about characters, themes, and other elements of literary texts that you have read. With a team, plan and build your blog. Then add posts, or messages, to spark discussion among your online community.

COMMON CORE TRAITS

A STRONG CLASS BLOG . . .

- presents content that encourages discussion
- maintains a respectful tone
- uses a structure that allows for easy navigation
- integrates multimedia and visual displays
- has coherent posts that pose questions, offer responses, and connect ideas

---

COMMON CORE

W 6 Use technology to produce and publish writing. **SL 1a–d** Engage in collaborative group discussions. **SL 4** Present claims and findings in a focused, coherent manner. **SL 5** Integrate multimedia and visual displays into presentations.

Plan and Produce the Blog

The following guidelines can help you create your blog:

- **Decide on your topics.** Think about stories you've read recently that were interesting, challenging, or meaningful. Collaborate with your team to decide which stories to discuss in your blog. Provide enough choices to encourage your readers to participate, but not too many to keep track of.

- **Determine your discussion threads.** Create a separate discussion thread—chain of related posts—for each story. Use labels to indicate what readers should expect.

- **Map out your home page.** Decide how your home page should look and what information it should include. Create a sketch of your home page, visually representing how users will link to each thread.

- **Define roles.** Plan an agenda with the work divided equally. One person might research Web sites that can host your blog. Another might create a logo for the home page. Make sure any images you plan to include are not copyrighted. In addition, each person should be responsible for writing the first post within one thread. Track your progress by setting specific deadlines.

- **Build the blog.** With the assistance of your school technology coordinator, produce and publish your blog using the Web site you chose.

Media Tools

THINK central

Go to **thinkcentral.com**.
KEYWORD: HML8-448

Participate in an Online Discussion

Discussing stories in a blog is different from writing an essay about them. Here are some tips for participating in a meaningful online discussion:

- **Clearly state your main idea.** At the beginning of each post, present your most salient, or important, point. Then support it with relevant evidence, sound reasoning, and well-chosen details. If appropriate, you may want to add multimedia or visuals to strengthen your claims and findings. End by posing a question to encourage others to share their opinions, interpretations, or ideas.

- **Make it easy to read.** Use text features, such as bullets or numbered lists, in your post. Boldface key points. This will keep your ideas organized and make the post easier to read.

- **Use a respectful tone.** Your audience cannot see you face-to-face and observe your reactions to their ideas. That is why it is important to be courteous. You don't have to agree with every idea proposed, but you should show that you are open to other perspectives. Use the points that others make as a springboard for deeper analysis of the subject.

- **Keep the discussion focused.** Check the threads frequently and respond to new questions as soon as possible. Respond to others' questions with relevant evidence, observations, and ideas. If a post reveals an idea or point of view that you never considered, acknowledge the new information in a comment. This will help keep the discussion going.

- **Invite other classmates into your blogosphere.** Send e-mails with your blog link to other classmates. Try to generate excitement and different points of view.

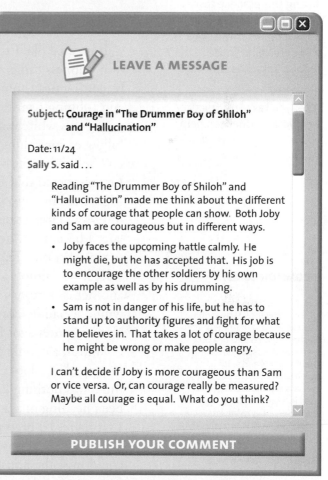

LEAVE A MESSAGE

Subject: Courage in "The Drummer Boy of Shiloh" and "Hallucination"

Date: 11/24
Sally S. said . . .

Reading "The Drummer Boy of Shiloh" and "Hallucination" made me think about the different kinds of courage that people can show. Both Joby and Sam are courageous but in different ways.

- Joby faces the upcoming battle calmly. He might die, but he has accepted that. His job is to encourage the other soldiers by his own example as well as by his drumming.

- Sam is not in danger of his life, but he has to stand up to authority figures and fight for what he believes in. That takes a lot of courage because he might be wrong or make people angry.

I can't decide if Joby is more courageous than Sam or vice versa. Or, can courage really be measured? Maybe all courage is equal. What do you think?

PUBLISH YOUR COMMENT

YOUR TURN

With your team, plan and produce a blog, using the guidelines on these pages. Once you have launched your blog, take turns posting messages several times a week. After a few weeks, evaluate what you might add or change to make your blog more user-friendly and current.

Assessment Practice

DIRECTIONS Read the two selections and the viewing and representing piece.
Then answer the questions that follow.

from Year of the Black Pony

by Walt Morey

1   It seemed like I traveled a long time hunched down inside my coat. A kind
of numbness came over me and I just sat there. Then I began to think I should
be getting near home. I tried to fight myself into alertness by shaking my head
and rubbing a mitten across my face. The house, the barn, should be coming
out of this white wall at me any minute. At least I should hit a fence I could
follow or something familiar.

2   The driving push of the storm kept clawing at me. I felt drowsy and dull.
I remembered that I'd heard this was the first indication of freezing. That
frightened me into becoming more alert. I considered getting off and walking
to restore circulation. But if I did I wouldn't be able to get on again. Sometime
later I became aware that something had changed. I stopped Lucifer and tried
to reason it out. Then I knew. The wind was no longer hitting me on the right
side. It was almost at my back. Had the wind shifted or were we heading in
another direction? Had I unconsciously turned Lucifer to get away from the
wind, or had he done it? Had whatever happened just taken place or was it
some minutes ago? I decided to retrace my tracks to see if I'd turned.

3   Within a couple of hundred feet the tracks were filled with blowing snow.
I stopped and looked about completely awake now. In a few feet I could see
there was nothing familiar, nothing to give me a clue as to which direction I'd
been heading or was headed now. I put the storm on my right side again. Then
I sat there. I'd been traveling with the storm almost at my back for some time.
So even if I was now headed in the right direction I was so far off course I
could miss the house as much as half a mile or even a mile. That could be fatal.
I was confused. In this freezing, savage storm I was utterly lost.

4   For a minute I almost panicked and whipped Lucifer up to drive him
straight into the storm and ride and ride. All I could think was that I was
going to freeze to death. I remember stories of people getting lost between the
house and barn and freezing to death. Then I got hold of myself. The only way
I'd get out of this alive was to keep my head. I had probably the best horse in
the valley under me. Frank had said that if I got lost wandering around Lucifer
would bring me home. Cats and dogs and horses had that homing instinct.
But if I let Lucifer have his head could he find his way in this storm? And
would he go to our place or back to his old home at Fletcher's? It didn't matter,
I decided, just so he got someplace where there was shelter.

5   I tied the reins around his neck, then lay down flat along his back to get all the warmth I could from his body, put my arms around his neck, and said, "It's up to you, Lucifer. Let's go. Take us home, boy."

6   Lucifer turned partially into the wind and started off as if he knew exactly where he was going.

7   I lost track of time. I began to wonder if I was beginning to freeze because I didn't seem quite so cold, or was the heat from the pony's body getting through to me. I was conscious of the constant rhythm of his walking, the cut of the wind and the endless driving snow. Sometimes I lifted my head to try to spot something familiar. I recognized nothing. I passed brush clumps almost buried by drifting snow, crossed several shallow gullies, and once skirted a low hill. They were all strange. Finally I put my head down, shut my eyes, and gave myself completely into my pony's keeping. He plodded straight ahead never faltering. How long we traveled that way I don't know. I began to wonder, vaguely, if he, too, was wandering in a circle, lost. Then I was aware he'd stopped. I raised my head and we were right in front of the barn.

from Never Get Lost on the Trail
by Joanne Meszoly

**Follow these simple steps to get back on track
if you lose your bearings on a trail outing.**

1   Some people are blessed with an innate directional sense; blindfold them and drop them off in the woods, and they'll find their way out in no time. Others become disoriented in shopping malls.

2   Horses (and dogs, if one's along for the ride) usually have excellent senses of direction, but turning all the directional decisions over to your horse when you're lost is risky. The path he chooses toward home may not be easily negotiated, and rough terrain may force him to head the wrong way; even horses can get lost and discouraged. "Horses do have a homing instinct, but home may not be where you parked your trailer, says Montana wilderness rider Dan Aadland. "In snowstorms and in flatter parts of the country, horses have saved lives by getting people home. But in the backcountry, your horse may not get you to the trailhead."

3   The best strategy when lost on the trail is to turn around and head back the way you came. "Your horse has done you one big favor," says Aadland. "He's made some tracks getting you where you are. Unless it's a loop where

GO ON ➡

it's essential that you complete it, you can probably backtrack. "Turning around on a trail may trigger your horses's mental compass, and he may help you decide which path to choose at trail junctions.

4 **Prevention:** Not getting lost comes down to good planning and taking some general safety measures. Before you set out, tell someone where you are going—the trail name/color code (if so-marked) or the general direction you plan to ride—as well as the estimated length of time you'll be away. This routine practice could be a life-saver if you're injured while riding alone and have to wait for help. Carrying a map, a compass, or a global positioning system (GPS) receiver also greatly reduces your likelihood of becoming lost. Practice map-reading skills and familiarize yourself with the navigational tools before setting out.

5 "Many of the new GPS tools are not difficult to use," says California competitive trail-riding judge Jamie Dieterich. "It's like a visual bread-crumb trail, and you can follow your way back home. "However you keep track of your position, look frequently behind you to take a "mental picture of the terrain, especially at intersections and forks. Note any landmarks that will jog your memory when you return to them. Also count how many right- or left-hand turns you make as you go along. Remember, it's the rearview going out that becomes the return vista.

6 Some hunters, hikers, and riders mark trails and trail intersections with surveyor's tape as they go along, but it's a practice that spoils the wilderness unless the tape is removed on the way back. "I can see having the tape in your trail kit," says Aadland. "If someone's hurt, you may need it to mark the trail, but when it's used frequently and left all over the place, it's unsightly."

7 **Trail tip:** If riding after sunset disorients you, dismount and lead your horse. Rely on natural light, when possible, rather than a flashlight. "It takes about 20 minutes to develop your night vision" says Aadland, "but you lose it in just a second by striking a match or turning on a light. If you must use a light to study a map, close one eye to speed the return of your night vision."

Training Tip of the Month: The Role of Praise and Reward

HORSE
INTELLIGENCE

The Magazine for Smart Horse Owners

REGULAR FEATURES

First-Person Report
My Horse Communicates with Dogs

FEATURED THIS MONTH
How Your Horse Finds Its Way Home
The Homing Instinct in Action
Does Your Horse Run Away?

Vet's Corner
Those Worrisome Hooves!

Reading Comprehension

Use "Year of the Black Pony" (pp. 450–451) to answer questions 1–8.

1. The event described in this excerpt takes place in a —
   A. landscaped suburban community with grassy yards
   B. large city park with trees and meadows
   C. tropical forest with dense undergrowth
   D. farming area with pastures and barns

2. By setting the episode over an unknown period of time, the author shows that the —
   A. horse wants to live
   B. storm has become more severe
   C. narrator has become disoriented
   D. region is very large

3. In paragraph 3, the narrator says, "In a few feet I could see there was nothing familiar, nothing to give me a clue as to which direction I'd been heading or was headed now." That statement creates a mood of —
   A. calmness
   B. fearfulness
   C. happiness
   D. weariness

4. In paragraph 4, the phrase "keep my head" means —
   A. ask questions
   B. become lost
   C. stay calm
   D. turn around

5. In paragraph 4, the phrase "have his head" means —
   A. get something to eat
   B. wander aimlessly
   C. turn around
   D. go where he wants

6. In paragraph 5, the narrator says, "Take us home, boy." What mood is created by this statement?
   A. Carefree
   B. Hopeful
   C. Somber
   D. Weary

7. Which image appeals to the reader's sense of touch?
   A. *blowing snow* (paragraph 3)
   B. *fight myself into alertness* (paragraph 1)
   C. *this white wall* (paragraph 1)
   D. *heat from the pony's body* (paragraph 7)

8. By using the phrase "kept clawing at me" in paragraph 2, the narrator creates an image of the storm as —
   A. alive
   B. peaceful
   C. serious
   D. wet

**Use "Never Get Lost on the Trail"
(pp. 451–452) to answer questions 9–14.**

9. The Latin word *negōtiārī* means "to transact business." In paragraph 2, what does the word *negotiated* mean?

"The path he chooses toward home may not be easily <u>negotiated</u> . . ."

A. Transferred to

B. Settled with

C. Traveled over

D. Suggested to

10. The Latin word *vidēre* means "to see" or "to look." In paragraph 5, what does the word *vista* mean?

"Remember, it's the rearview going out that becomes the return <u>vista</u>."

A. Mirror

B. Trip

C. View

D. Vision

11. Based on this article, you can conclude that when you rely on a horse's homing instinct, you will —

A. always get home safely

B. take the longest route home

C. take a chance

D. retrace your route

12. Based on this article, you can conclude that when people are going to go on a trail ride, they should —

A. not be concerned about getting lost

B. worry about getting lost

C. take plenty of water

D. plan ahead and take precautions

13. The author most likely wrote this article to —

A. show that getting lost is easy

B. explain ways to prevent getting lost

C. describe how to use a GPS

D. compare a horse to a GPS

14. The author uses information in paragraph 5 to —

A. show why bread crumbs make a good reminder

B. illustrate why planning ahead is very important

C. describe the advantages of a GPS

D. show easy ways to keep track of your route

Use both selections to answer questions 15–16.

15. Which conclusion about a horse's homing instinct is supported by information in both selections?

A. A horse can always find its way home.

B. Horses' homing instincts have saved lives.

C. A GPS is more reliable than a horse's homing instinct.

D. A horse's homing instinct is not always reliable.

16. Which line from "Never Get Lost on the Trail" applies to the final decision the narrator made in "Year of the Black Pony"?

A. *Turning around on a trail may trigger your horse's mental compass, and he may help you decide which path to choose . . .*

B. *Practice map-reading skills and familiarize yourself with the navigational tools before you set out.*

C. *If riding after sunset disorients you, dismount and lead your horse.*

D. *In snowstorms and flatter parts of the country, horses have saved lives by getting people home.*

GO ON

Use the visual representation on page 453 to answer questions 17–18.

17. Why is the word "Intelligence" larger than the word "Horse" on the cover of the magazine?

    A. To show that horses are smarter than other animals

    B. To emphasize how smart horses are

    C. To encourage readers to choose intelligent horses as pets

    D. To indicate that the magazine is about the intelligence of horses

18. Showing a horse going somewhere by itself on the cover suggests that the magazine articles focus on —

    A. horse shows

    B. diseases of horses

    C. horses' inborn abilities

    D. costs of horse ownership

SHORT CONSTRUCTED RESPONSE

Write a short constructed response to each question using text evidence to support your answer.

19. What do you think is the turning point in this excerpt from *Year of the Black Pony*? Support your answer with evidence from the selection.

20. What is the most important advice given in the article "Never Get Lost on the Trail"? Use evidence from the text to support your response.

Write a short constructed response to the following question using text evidence from both selections to support your answer.

21. How is the importance of problem-solving supported in both *Year of the Black Pony* and "Never Get Lost on the Trail"? Support your answer with evidence from **both** selections.

Revising and Editing

DIRECTIONS Read this passage and answer the questions that follow.

(1) People regarded the cat in ancient Egypt as a sacred animal. (2) Of grain cats were the protectors, killing any animals that might eat this staple of Egyptian diet. (3) Anyone who purposely or accidentally killed a cat was put to death. (4) Egyptians so revered the animal that many Egyptian goddesses took the form of a cat. (5) Mafdet, Sekhmet, and Bastet is examples of ancient Egyptian cat goddesses. (6) Neither Mafdet nor Sekhmet were quite as celebrated as Bastet, though. (7) Beauty, fertility, and motherhood was three of the qualities for which Egyptians worshipped Bastet. (8) In the city of Bubastis, Egyptians would hold a yearly festival to celebrate her. (9) In Bubastis and Memphis, large cemeteries were devoted to the burial of mummified cats.

1. What is the BEST way to improve the placement of modifiers in sentence 1?
   A. The cat people regarded in ancient Egypt as a sacred animal.
   B. People regarded in ancient Egypt the cat as a sacred animal.
   C. In ancient Egypt people regarded the cat as a sacred animal.
   D. The cat as a sacred animal the people regarded in ancient Egypt.

2. What is the BEST way to improve the placement of modifiers in sentence 2?
   A. Cats were of grain the protectors, killing any animal that might eat of Egyptian diet this staple.
   B. Of grain cats were the protectors, killing any animal of Egyptian diet that might eat this staple.
   C. Cats were the protectors of grain, killing any animal that might eat of Egyptian diet this staple.
   D. Cats were the protectors of grain, killing any animal that might eat this staple of Egyptian diet.

3. What change, if any, should be made in sentence 5?
   A. Change *is* to **was**
   B. Change *is* to **has been**
   C. Change *is* to **are**
   D. Make no change

4. What change, if any, should be made in sentence 6?
   A. Change *were* to **was**
   B. Change *were* to **am**
   C. Change *were* to **have been**
   D. Make no change

5. What change, if any, should be made in sentence 7?
   A. Change *was* to **were**
   B. Change *was* to **has been**
   C. Change *was* to **am**
   D. Make no change

STOP

Ideas for Independent Reading

Which questions from Unit 3 made an impression on you?
Continue exploring them with these books.

COMMON CORE

RL 10 Read and comprehend
literature. **RI 10** Read and
comprehend literary nonfiction.

How do you find your purpose?

The Boxer
by Kathleen Karr

In 1880s New York, 15-year-old
Johnny is the one who has to
work to feed his family. One
night he sees a sign promising
five dollars to anyone willing
to fight, and suddenly he's a
boxer. Will he win enough
to get his family out of the
tenements?

Full Tilt
by Neal Shusterman

Focused, steady Blake has had
one purpose his whole life:
to keep his impulsive brother
Quinn out of trouble. When
Quinn steals Blake's ticket for
a mysterious carnival, Blake
goes to save his brother—
again. But maybe Blake is
the one who needs help.

Olive's Ocean
by Kevin Henkes

Soon after Olive's death,
Martha is given a page from
Olive's journal. The two girls
were never friends, but when
Martha realizes they had a lot
in common, she begins to see
life differently. She spends
the summer at the ocean,
trying to fulfill Olive's dream.

What is the role of a witness?

Run, Boy, Run
by Uri Orlev

Srulik is only eight when he
manages to escape from
the Nazi-controlled ghetto
into the Polish countryside.
His father tells him he must
forget who he is and do
anything necessary to fit in
and survive. But forgetting
comes at a cost.

Iqbal
by Francesco D'Adamo

Everything changes at the
carpet factory when 13-year-
old Iqbal is chained to a loom
next to Fatima. Iqbal tells the
children their owner will never
release them, but he promises
to escape. If Iqbal does get
free, should he try to help his
friends and risk recapture?

Fish
by L. S. Matthews

Tiger's family moved from
their home country to a
drought-stricken village to run
a clinic. They stay until the
civil war forces them to leave,
but the borders have closed,
and only a treacherous trip
over the mountains will bring
them to safety.

What gifts does the earth provide?

Four Wings and a Prayer
by Sue Halpern

Every fall, millions of
butterflies form an orange
and black wave that rolls
down from Canada or New
York all the way to Mexico.
Every spring a new generation
of butterflies returns to their
parents' homes. How do the
butterflies know where to go?

Saving the Planet and Stuff
by Gail Gauthier

As an intern at an
environmental magazine
in Vermont, Michael must
live without a car, TV, or air
conditioning. He thinks about
quitting, but instead he stays
and learns about business,
composting, and himself.

Tofu and T. rex
by Greg Leitich Smith

Freddie was protesting
the treatment of her new
school's mascot, a live bull,
when the football field
caught fire. She's been sent
back to Chicago to live with
her cousin and grandfather.
Can a vegetarian survive life
with two meat-eaters?

Get Novel Wise **THINK** central

Go to **thinkcentral.com**.
KEYWORD: HML8-458

A World of Meaning

THEME AND SYMBOL

- In Fiction
- In Poetry
- In Drama
- In Media

459

What are life's hidden MESSAGES?

What's the best story you've ever read? Chances are you enjoyed the story not just for its characters or plot but for its theme, or message about life and human nature. All great stories have a theme, whether it's about the value of friendship, the bonds of a family's love, or the triumph of good over evil. A story's characters grow and change because of what they learn through their experiences. As the characters learn these life lessons, you as a reader grow, too.

ACTIVITY You may not have given it much thought, but your favorite movies have probably offered you valuable messages. Recall a movie that you love, and then answer these questions to help you identify its theme.

- What lessons, if any, do the characters learn?
- If there is a battle or struggle, who wins and who loses? Why?
- What did you learn from this movie that you can apply to your own life?

Find It Online! THINK central

Go to thinkcentral.com for the interactive version of this unit.

Preview Unit Goals

TEXT ANALYSIS
- Identify and interpret symbols
- Determine and analyze theme
- Determine, analyze, and compare universal themes

READING
- Make inferences and draw conclusions
- Synthesize information and make generalizations
- Read a drama

WRITING AND LANGUAGE
- Write a short story
- Use participles and participle phrases
- Use the active voice

SPEAKING AND LISTENING
- Collaborate to produce a video

VOCABULARY
- Use reference aids to find synonyms

- Use knowledge of root words and affixes to determine meanings of words

ACADEMIC VOCABULARY
- comment
- community
- criteria
- perspective
- technique

MEDIA AND VIEWING
- Identify and analyze the elements of a documentary
- Evaluate the effectiveness of different media
- Create a visual timeline

Media ◼ Smart DVD-ROM

Messages in Documentaries

See a meaningful life unfold in the Academy Award-winning documentary, *Anne Frank Remembered.* Page 578

Theme and Symbol

What makes a story memorable? Long after you've forgotten the names of the characters and the events of the plot, you'll likely remember the theme—the big idea at the heart of the story. A **theme** is a message about life or human nature that a writer wants you to understand. In this unit, you'll discover that themes in literature can give you insights into events, issues, and relationships in your life.

Part 1: What's the Big Idea?

COMMON CORE

Included in this workshop:
RL 1 Cite evidence that supports inferences drawn from the text.
RL 2 Determine a theme of a text and analyze its development, including its relationship to the characters, setting, and plot; provide a summary of the text.

Friendship, war, and family are subjects that people of all ages and in all parts of the world think about. Writers explore and comment on these topics, too—in their writing. Some writers present themes that only apply to a particular time, place, or situation. Others explore **recurring themes**, or messages that appear repeatedly in literature. Some recurring themes are considered **universal themes** because they address big ideas so fundamental to human existence and true for most people that they recur in the literature of many time periods and cultures. For example, "Good will triumph over evil" is a universal theme.

Whether it is universal or one of a kind, a theme is often communicated through different elements in a story, such as the characters, setting, and plot. A writer may also use symbols to hint at a theme. A **symbol** is an object, activity, place, or person that stands for something beyond itself. Notice how the theme is communicated in the following example.

THEME
LIVE IN THE PRESENT, NOT THE PAST.

Character

The main character is **14-year-old Eva,** who has recently moved with her family to a new city. **Sullen and angry,** Eva desperately misses her friends back home.

Setting

Eva can't stand the thought of exploring an **unfamiliar city** and an **intimidating school.** Being in this new setting reminds her of what she left behind.

Symbol

Eva shuts herself in her room all day, looking through old yearbooks and e-mailing her friends. **Eva's room symbolizes the past,** where she remains trapped and isolated from the world.

Plot and Conflict

Eva gets upset when her parents suggest that she make new friends. She also feels hurt when **her friends don't e-mail very often.**

Resolution: Eventually, Eva realizes that she must move on. While she can hold onto the past in her memories, she has to live in the present.

MODEL: THEME AND SYMBOL

Alfred is a high-school dropout who is barely staying out of trouble with the law. One night after getting beaten up, he steps into a gym to see if he can join the neighborhood boxing club. As he talks to Mr. Donatelli, the gym owner, about the challenges of training as a fighter, Alfred realizes Mr. Donatelli may be talking about more than just boxing.

from

THE CONTENDER

Novel by **Robert Lipsyte**

"How far did you go in school?"

"Eleventh grade."

"What happened?"

"I quit."

5 "Why?"

"Didn't seem like any reason to stay."

"What makes you think you won't quit here too?"

Alfred swallowed. He suddenly wished he hadn't come up the steps, that he was somewhere else, anywhere. He thought of the cave.

10 "Well?"

"I want to be somebody."

"Everybody is somebody."

"Somebody special. A champion."

Donatelli's thin lips tightened. "Everybody wants to be a champion. That's 15 not enough. You have to start by wanting to be a contender, the man coming up, the man who knows there's a good chance he'll never get to the top, the man who's willing to sweat and bleed to get up as high as his legs and his brains and his heart will take him. That must sound corny to you."

"No."

20 "It's the climbing that makes the man. Getting to the top is an extra reward."

"I want to try."

Donatelli shrugged. "Boxing is a dying sport. People aren't much interested anymore. They want easy things like television, bowling, car rides. Get yourself a good job. Finish high school. Go at night if you have to."

25 "I'll try hard."

"Talk it over with your parents."

"I don't have any. I live with my aunt."

The pale blue eyes came around again. They seemed softer now. But the voice was still cold and flat. "It's not easy trying to become a contender. It's never any 30 fun in the beginning. It's hard work, you'll want to quit at least once every day. If you quit before you really try, that's worse than never starting at all."

Close Read

1. Reread the boxed text. What conflict is set up?

2. What is Alfred's goal? What does Mr. Donatelli think about that goal?

3. Given what Mr. Donatelli says in lines 14–20, what do you think boxing might symbolize to him?

4. Reread lines 29–31. What lesson might Alfred learn from training as a boxer? State this lesson as a theme.

Part 2: Identifying Theme

Sometimes the theme of a story is stated directly by the narrator or a character. More often, the theme is implied, which means you have to do some digging to uncover it. It helps to look closely at the characters, the plot, and other clues when you're trying to identify a story's theme. The questions in the chart, as well as these reminders, can help you discover the message.

- The theme is not the topic of a story, but the writer's message *about* the topic. While a topic can be described in a word or two, it can take one or two sentences to express a theme. For example, "first impressions" is a topic. "First impressions aren't always right" is a theme.

- Some works of literature have multiple themes, but one may stand out more than the others.

- Different people can interpret the same story differently.

CLUES TO THEME

TITLE
The title of a story can suggest an important idea or symbol. Ask:

- What in the story does the title refer to?

- What idea or symbol does the title highlight?

- Could the title have more than one meaning?

CHARACTERS
Characters can influence theme by how they act or what they learn. Ask:

- What do the main character's actions and thoughts tell you about him or her?

- How does the character change?

- What lessons does the character learn?

PLOT AND CONFLICT
A story revolves around conflicts that are central to the theme. Ask:

- What conflicts do the characters face?

- How are the conflicts resolved?

SETTING
Setting can connect to a theme because of what it means to the characters or to readers. Ask:

- How does the setting affect the characters or influence their actions?

- What might the setting represent to readers?

IMPORTANT STATEMENTS
The narrator or a character may make statements that hint at the theme. Ask:

- What key statements are made in the story?

- Could any statement be reworded as an overall theme?

SYMBOLS
A symbol can convey a theme because of what it means to the main character. Ask:

- Does anything seem to stand for something beyond itself?

- What might the symbol mean to the main character? What might it represent to readers?

Part 3: Analyze the Text

Connie is not crazy about spending time with her Puerto Rican grandmother—her *abuela*. What lesson will Connie learn when her grandmother comes to visit? As you read, use what you've learned to uncover the theme of this story.

Abuela INVENTS THE Zerø

Short story by **Judith Ortiz Cofer**

"You made me feel like a zero, like a nothing," she says in Spanish, *un cero, nada*. She is trembling, an angry little old woman lost in a heavy winter coat that belongs to my mother. And I end up being sent to my room, like I was a child, to think about my grandmother's idea of math.

5   It all began with Abuela coming from the Island[1] for a visit—her first time in the United States. My mother and father paid her way here so that she wouldn't die without seeing snow, though if you asked me, and nobody has, the dirty slush in this city is not worth the price of a ticket. But I guess she deserves some kind of award for having had ten kids and survived to tell

10 about it. My mother is the youngest of the bunch. Right up to the time when we're supposed to pick up the old lady at the airport, my mother is telling me stories about how hard times were for la familia on la isla,[2] and how *la abuela* worked night and day to support them after their father died of a heart attack. I'd die of a heart attack too if I had a troop like that to support. Anyway, I

15 had seen her only three or four times in my entire life, whenever we would go for somebody's funeral. I was born here and I have lived in this building all my life. But when Mami says, "Connie, please be nice to Abuela. She doesn't have too many years left. Do you promise me, Constancia?"—when she uses my full name, I know she means business. So I say, "Sure." Why wouldn't I be

20 nice? I'm not a monster, after all.

    So we go to Kennedy[3] to get la abuela and she is the last to come out of the airplane, on the arm of the cabin attendant, all wrapped up in a black shawl. He hands her over to my parents like she was a package sent airmail. It is January, two feet of snow on the ground, and she's wearing a shawl over a thin

25 black dress. That's just the start.

    Ønce home, she refuses to let my mother buy her a coat because it's a waste of money for the two weeks she'll be in *el Polo Norte*, as she calls New Jersey, the North Pole. So since she's only four feet eleven inches tall, she walks around in my mother's big black coat looking ridiculous. I try to walk

30 far behind them in public so that no one will think we're together. I plan to

---

1. **the Island:** Puerto Rico.
2. **la familia on la isla:** the family on the island.
3. **Kennedy:** John F. Kennedy International Airport.

Close Read

1. Examine the title of the story and reread the first paragraph. What symbol do you predict will be central to the theme?

2. Reread the boxed details, in which Connie shares her thoughts about her grandmother. Based on these details, how would you describe Connie?

3. What conflicts do you think might arise for Connie during her grandmother's visit?

stay very busy the whole time she's with us so that I won't be asked to take her anywhere, but my plan is ruined when my mother comes down with the flu and Abuela absolutely *has* to attend Sunday mass. . . . My father decides that he should stay home with my mother and that I should escort la abuela
35 to church. He tells me this on Saturday night as I'm getting ready to go out to the mall with my friends.

"No way," I say.

I go for the car keys on the kitchen table: he usually leaves them there for me on Friday and Saturday nights. He beats me to them.

40 "No way," he says, pocketing them and grinning at me.

Needless to say, we come to a compromise very quickly. I do have a responsibility to Sandra and Anita, who don't drive yet. There is a Harley-Davidson fashion show at Brookline Square that we *cannot* miss.

"The mass in Spanish is at ten sharp tomorrow morning, *entiendes?*" My
45 father is dangling the car keys in front of my nose and pulling them back when I try to reach for them. He's really enjoying himself.

"I understand. Ten o'clock. I'm out of here." I pry his fingers off the key ring. He knows that I'm late, so he makes it just a little difficult. Then he laughs. I run out of our apartment before he changes his mind. I have no idea
50 what I'm getting myself into.

*S*unday morning I have to walk two blocks on dirty snow to retrieve the car. I warm it up for Abuela as instructed by my parents, and drive it to the front of our building. My father walks her by the hand in baby steps on the slippery snow. The sight of her little head with a bun on top of it sticking
55 out of that huge coat makes me want to run back into my room and get under the covers. I just hope that nobody I know sees us together. I'm dreaming, of course. The mass is packed with people from our block. It's a holy day of obligation and everyone I ever met is there.

I have to help her climb the steps, and she stops to take a deep breath after
60 each one, then I lead her down the aisle so that everybody can see me with my bizarre grandmother. If I were a good Catholic, I'm sure I'd get some purgatory[4] time taken off for my sacrifice. She is walking as slow as Captain Cousteau[5] exploring the bottom of the sea, looking around, taking her sweet time. Finally she chooses a pew, but she wants to sit in the *other* end. It's like
65 she had a spot picked out for some unknown reason, and although it's the most inconvenient seat in the house, that's where she has to sit. So we squeeze by all the people already sitting there, saying, "Excuse me, please, *con permiso,* pardon me," getting annoyed looks the whole way. By the time we settle in, I'm drenched in sweat. I keep my head down like I'm praying so as not to see
70 or be seen. She is praying loud, in Spanish, and singing hymns at the top of her creaky voice.

---

4. **purgatory:** spiritual place in which souls purify themselves of sin before going to heaven.

5. **Captain Cousteau:** Jacques Yves Cousteau (zhäk ēv kōō-stō′) (1910–1997), a French underwater explorer, film producer, and author.

Close Read

4. How would you describe Connie's attitude toward and treatment of her grandmother? Support your answer.

I ignore her when she gets up with a hundred other people to go take communion.[6] I'm actually praying hard now—that this will all be over soon. But the next time I look up, I see a black coat dragging around and around
75 the church, stopping here and there so a little gray head can peek out like a periscope on a submarine. There are giggles in the church, and even the priest has frozen in the middle of a blessing, his hands above his head like he is about to lead the congregation in a set of jumping jacks.

I realize to my horror that my grandmother is lost. She can't find her way
80 back to the pew. I am so embarrassed that even though the woman next to me is shooting daggers at me with her eyes, I just can't move to go get her. I put my hands over my face like I'm praying, but it's really to hide my burning cheeks. I would like for her to disappear. I just know that on Monday my friends, and my enemies, in the barrio[7] will have a lot of senile-grandmother
85 jokes to tell in front of me. I am frozen to my seat. So the same woman who wants me dead on the spot does it for me. She makes a big deal out of getting up and hurrying to get Abuela.

*T*he rest of the mass is a blur. All I know is that my grandmother kneels the whole time with her hands over *her* face. She doesn't speak to me on the
90 way home, and she doesn't let me help her walk, even though she almost falls a couple of times.

When we get to the apartment, my parents are at the kitchen table, where my mother is trying to eat some soup. They can see right away that something is wrong. Then Abuela points her finger at me like a judge passing a sentence
95 on a criminal. She says in Spanish, "You made me feel like a zero, like a nothing." Then she goes to her room.

I try to explain what happened. "I don't understand why she's so upset. She just got lost and wandered around for a while," I tell them. But it sounds lame, even to my own ears. My mother gives me a look that makes me cringe and goes in to
100 Abuela's room to get her version of the story. She comes out with tears in her eyes.

"Your grandmother says to tell you that of all the hurtful things you can do to a person, the worst is to make them feel as if they are worth nothing."

I can feel myself shrinking right there in front of her. But I can't bring myself to tell my mother that I think I understand how I made Abuela feel. I
105 might be sent into the old lady's room to apologize, and it's not easy to admit you've been a jerk—at least, not right away with everybody watching. So I just sit there not saying anything.

My mother looks at me for a long time, like she feels sorry for me. Then she says, "You should know, Constancia, that if it wasn't for this old woman whose
110 existence you don't seem to value, you and I would not be here."

That's when *I'm* sent to *my* room to consider a number I hadn't thought much about—until today.

---

6. **communion:** the part of a Christian service in which bread and wine are consumed in memory of Christ's sacrifice.

7. **barrio:** Spanish-speaking community or neighborhood.

Close Read

5. Why do you think the author chose a church as the setting for this scene? How might she want you to react to Connie's behavior there?

6. Summarize what Connie has learned from the conflict with her grandmother. Where on this page do you see this lesson directly stated as a theme?

7. What new understanding of the word *zero* does Connie now have? What understanding do you have of the story's title?

Gil's Furniture Bought & Sold
Anecdote by Sandra Cisneros

What makes something
PRICELESS ?

COMMON CORE

RL 1 Cite textual evidence that supports inferences drawn from the text. **RL 4** Determine the meaning of words and phrases as they are used in a text, including figurative and connotative meanings.

Perhaps you've heard a painting or antique described as **priceless.** In many cases, this means that the item is worth so much money that the amount can't be guessed at. But sometimes an object is priceless because it is worth more than money to the person who owns it. The anecdote you are about to read is a short account of a priceless object turning up in an unexpected place.

QUICKWRITE Describe your most prized possession and tell why it is special to you. Then consider if there are any circumstances under which you might give away or sell this object.

● TEXT ANALYSIS: SYMBOL

When you see an American flag, you probably think of more than the fabric it's made of and its pattern of stars and stripes. The flag represents something much bigger—the United States of America. When a person, place, or thing stands for something beyond itself, it is called a **symbol.** For example, a sunrise can symbolize a new beginning.

The technique of using symbols in writing is called **symbolism.** When a writer often relies on symbolism in his or her works, symbolism can be considered a defining element of the writer's style. It is, for example, a defining element of Sandra Cisneros's style.

To recognize and interpret the symbol Cisneros uses in "Gil's Furniture Bought & Sold," ask yourself these questions:

- What object appears repeatedly or is described more fully than other objects?

- How do the characters react to this object?

- What big ideas does the story address, and how might this object relate to them?

● READING SKILL: MAKE INFERENCES

Skilled readers know they must "read between the lines" to make logical guesses about what a writer means but does not say directly. This process is called **making inferences,** and it can help you to understand the characters in a story. Follow these steps to make an inference:

- Gather details or evidence from the story.

- Consider your own experience and knowledge.

- Form an opinion based on both.

As you read, use a chart like the one shown to make inferences about the three characters in the selection.

Details from Story	What I Know	Inference About Character

Complete the activities in your **Reader/Writer Notebook.**

Meet the Author

Sandra Cisneros
born 1954

A Bilingual Beginning
Sandra Cisneros grew up in Chicago, the only daughter in a Mexican-American family with seven children. She spoke English to her mother and Spanish to her father, and she even thought the two languages were the same when she was very young. She was fascinated with the sound of words, especially those found in fairy tales and fantasy stories, such as *Alice in Wonderland.* The strange and fancy words in the pages of these books were quite different from those she heard every day at home and in her poor neighborhood. Cisneros dreamed of escaping her neighborhood and becoming a writer. She credits her mother with helping her achieve this goal.

"I've Followed My Gut and My Heart"
In order to earn a living, Cisneros decided she should work as an English teacher and write in her free time. The poetry and short fiction she produced revealed her unique voice, created from the influences of Latino and American culture. Her first novel, *The House on Mango Street,* was published in 1984 and helped make her a best-selling author. Her work often deals with struggles, such as alienation, poverty, and dual cultural loyalties. Cisneros's stories and poems have won many awards. She has said of her success, "In everything I've done in my life, including all the choices I've made as a writer, I've followed my gut and my heart."

Author Online
THINK central
Go to thinkcentral.com.
KEYWORD: HML8-469

Gil's Furniture BOUGHT & SOLD

Sandra Cisneros

There is a junk store. An old man owns it. We bought a used refrigerator from him once, and Carlos sold a box of magazines for a dollar. The store is small with just a dirty window for light. He doesn't turn the lights on unless you got money to buy things with, so in the dark we look and see all kinds of things, me and Nenny. Tables with their feet upside-down and rows and rows of refrigerators with round corners and couches that spin dust in the air when you punch them and a hundred T.V.'s that don't work probably. Everything is on top of everything so the whole store has skinny aisles to walk through. You can get lost easy. **A**

10   The owner, he is a black man who doesn't talk much and sometimes if you didn't know better you could be in there a long time before your eyes notice a pair of gold glasses floating in the dark. Nenny who thinks she is smart and talks to any old man, asks lots of questions. Me, I never said nothing to him except once when I bought the Statue of Liberty for a dime. **B**

    But Nenny, I hear her asking one time how's this here and the man says, This, this is a music box, and I turn around quick thinking he means a *pretty* box with flowers painted on it, with a ballerina inside. Only there's nothing like that where this old man is pointing, just a wood box that's old and got a big brass record in it with holes. Then he starts it up and all sorts of things
20 start happening. It's like all of a sudden he let go a million moths all over the dusty furniture and swan-neck shadows and in our bones. It's like drops of water. Or like marimbas only with a funny little plucked sound to it like if you were running your fingers across the teeth of a metal comb.

    And then I don't know why, but I have to turn around and pretend I don't care about the box so Nenny won't see how stupid I am. But Nenny, who is stupider, already is asking how much and I can see her fingers going for the quarters in her pants pocket. **C**

    This, the old man says shutting the lid, this ain't for sale. ꙮ

Analyze Visuals ▶

Look at the way objects are arranged in the store pictured on page 471. What can you **infer** about what it would be like to shop there?

A MAKE INFERENCES
Why do you think the narrator and Nenny shop at a junk store?

B MAKE INFERENCES
Reread lines 10–14. What can you assume about each character's personality from the details in this paragraph?

C SYMBOL
How do the narrator and Nenny react to the music box?

Comprehension

1. **Recall** What item did the narrator's family buy from the junk store in the past?

2. **Clarify** Why is it sometimes hard to know that the owner is in the store?

3. **Summarize** In your own words, describe the appearance of the junk store.

Text Analysis

4. **Make Inferences** Review the chart you created as you read the anecdote. Based on these inferences, why do you think each character reacted to the music box the way he or she did? Give details from the anecdote to support your answer.

5. **Interpret a Symbol** What does the music box **symbolize?** Explain why you think so.

6. **Draw Conclusions** What do you think the narrator means when she says, "I have to turn around and pretend I don't care about the box so Nenny won't see how stupid I am"? Consider what this tells you about her personality.

7. **Compare and Contrast Characters** Using a Venn diagram like the one shown, compare and contrast the narrator and Nenny. As you fill in the diagram, note how they interact with the storeowner.

Narrator   Nenny

8. **Evaluate a Setting** A story's **setting** can affect your expectations about what is going to happen. Reread lines 1–9. In what ways is the junk store an appropriate setting for the characters to discover something priceless? In what ways is the setting surprising?

Extension and Challenge

9. **Creative Project: Art** Think about the description of the junk store and the various items for sale there. Then make a collage of items you would expect to find in the store. You can cut out pictures from magazines and newspapers or include your own sketches.

What makes something PRICELESS?

Why do you think the owner of the junk shop considers the music box to be priceless? Support your answer with details from the anecdote.

COMMON CORE

RL 1 Cite textual evidence that supports inferences drawn from the text. **RL 4** Determine the meaning of words and phrases as they are used in a text, including figurative and connotative meanings.

Language

◆ **GRAMMAR IN CONTEXT:** Maintain Subject-Verb Agreement

You may recall that subjects and verbs must agree in number. That rule remains true even when a subject and a verb have a **prepositional phrase** between them. The subject of a sentence is never found in a prepositional phrase. If you are having a problem deciding whether to use a singular or plural verb in a sentence that contains a prepositional phrase, mentally block out the phrase. This will help you determine what the subject of the sentence is and whether it needs a singular or plural verb.

> *Example:*   The items in the junk shop are too numerous to count.
> (*The subject is* items, *not* shop, *so the sentence needs the plural verb* are.)

PRACTICE Choose the verb form that agrees with the subject in each sentence.

1. A box of books (was, were) one item that got sold to the owner of the store.
2. Refrigerators in the aisle (create, creates) a problem.
3. The owner's impression of the kids (are, is) that they aren't actually going to buy anything.
4. A handful of quarters (are, is) all that Nenny has to spend.

*For more help with subject-verb agreement, see page R65 in the **Grammar Handbook**.*

READING-WRITING CONNECTION

Show your understanding of the characters in "Gil's Furniture Bought & Sold" by responding to this prompt. Then use the **revising tip** to improve your writing.

WRITING PROMPT	REVISING TIP
Short Constructed Response: Dialogue Imagine what the narrator and Nenny talked about after they left the junk store. Write a **half-page dialogue** that captures what they may have said. Be sure to use language that matches the personalities of the characters.	Review your dialogue. Do all your subjects and verbs agree in number, even if a prepositional phrase comes between them? If not, revise your writing.

◌ **COMMON CORE**

L1 Demonstrate command of standard English grammar when writing. **W 3b** Use narrative techniques such as dialogue to develop characters.

Interactive Revision **THINK** central

Go to **thinkcentral.com**.
KEYWORD: HML8-473

Pandora's Box
Greek Myth Retold by Louis Untermeyer

Loo-Wit, the Fire-Keeper
Native American Myth Retold by Joseph Bruchac

VIDEO TRAILER **THINK** central   KEYWORD: HML8-474

Why do we WANT what we don't have?

COMMON CORE

RL 1 Cite the textual evidence that most supports inferences drawn from the text. **RL 2** Determine a theme of a text and analyze its development. **RL 9** Analyze themes, patterns of events, or character types from myths.

She's in the school chorus, but she wishes she could be in the band. He has plenty of shoes, but he still wants a pair like his friend has. Why does it seem like we always want what we don't have? In the myths you're about to read, people who aren't satisfied with what they've got make trouble for everyone.

DISCUSS When you want what you don't have, what problems might that cause? What, if any, benefits might result? Discuss these questions with your group. Try to come up with at least one positive and one negative effect of desiring things that are out of reach.

● TEXT ANALYSIS: THEME

Writers often share with their readers messages about life or human nature—for example, love may come when you least expect it. This type of message is called a **theme.** Writers can either state a theme directly or allow readers to figure it out on their own. To infer the theme of the myths you're about to read, look at important details or symbols.

● READING STRATEGY: READING A MYTH

Thousands of years ago, before anyone had microscopes or even books, people explained the world through stories called **myths.** Most myths

- were passed along through word of mouth
- feature gods or other supernatural beings who often show such human characteristics as anger and love
- reveal the consequences of human errors
- explain how something came to be

Although myths from various cultures share these basic features, they often differ in detail, style, or purpose. As you read, use a chart like the one shown to compare and contrast the ancient Greek myth "Pandora's Box" with the Native American myth "Loo-Wit, the Fire Keeper."

	Pandora's Box	Loo-Wit, the Fire-Keeper
What qualities does the supreme god have? What role does he play?		
What does the myth explain?		

▲ VOCABULARY IN CONTEXT

The boldfaced words help tell the story of Pandora. Using context clues, try to figure out what each word means.

1. The gods **adorn** her with special gifts.
2. She could no longer **restrain** her curiosity.
3. Zeus' **subtle** punishment was not immediately obvious.
4. Her beauty and charm helped **ensnare** his attention.

Complete the activities in your **Reader/Writer Notebook.**

Louis Untermeyer
1885–1977

Jeweler and Writer
For years Louis Untermeyer worked in his family's jewelry business, only turning to writing, lecturing, and teaching in his late 30s. Untermeyer edited many poetry anthologies that became popular textbooks in schools. He also became a respected translator, adapting myths and stories for the contemporary American audience.

Joseph Bruchac
born 1942

Native American Storyteller
Joseph Bruchac is a poet, writer, storyteller, and musician whose works reflect his Native American ancestry. He is the author or co-author of more than 70 books for children. He has said that, "communication, clarity, and honesty have been my hope. If, along the way, I have given people a better and fuller picture of Native peoples and cultures then I am very pleased."

Authors Online
Go to **thinkcentral.com**. KEYWORD: HML8-475

Pandora's BOX

Retold by Louis Untermeyer

Prometheus had thought about mankind with such sympathy that he had dared to steal the needed fire from Olympus,[1] and for this he was grievously punished by Zeus.[2] But the lord of Olympus did not think this cruelty was enough. Prometheus had a brother, Epimetheus, and though he was harmless and slow-witted, Zeus extended his displeasure to him. He did not punish Epimetheus as brutally as he had done his brother; he had a more **subtle** plan. It was a scheme which would not only affect Epimetheus but also the whole race of human beings whom Prometheus had dared to help and who were living happily and untroubled. **A**

10   Zeus ordered Hephaestus, the smith and artisan of the gods, to make a woman out of the materials of earth. Hephaestus took some river clay that had flakes of gold in it and began to make a lovely girl. In with the clay he mixed the fragrance of a river rose, the sweetness of Hymettus[3] honey, the smoothness of a silver dolphin, the voices of larks and lake-water, the color of sunrise on snow, the warmth of a sunny morning in May. Then he summoned

---

1. **Olympus** (ə-lĭm'pəs): home of the mythical Greek gods.
2. **Zeus** (zo͞os): father of the Greek gods; ruler of the heavens. **Prometheus,** a lesser god, gave humans fire against Zeus's will. Furious, Zeus condemned Prometheus to be chained to a rock for eternity.
3. **Hymettus** (hī-mĕt'əs): a mountain ridge near Athens, Greece.

Analyze Visuals ▶

Based on the woman's expression and body language, what can you **infer** about her attitude toward the box?

subtle (sŭt'l) *adj.* slight; difficult to detect

A **READING A MYTH**
What human characteristics does Zeus have? Add this information to your chart.

Pandora, Helen Stratton. From *A Book of Myths* by Jean Lang. © Edwin Wallace/Mary Evans Picture Library.

the Four Winds to breathe life into the new creation. Finally he called upon the goddesses to complete the work and grant the glowing figure a touch of their own powers.

"Hephaestus has given her beauty," said Aphrodite,[4] "but I shall make
20 her more beautiful by adding the spark of love. It will shine in her eyes, and everyone that looks on her will be enchanted."

"I shall make her wise," said Athene.[5] "She shall be able to choose between false and true, between what men value and what she must know is worthless."

"I shall make her a woman, a puzzle to every man," said Hera, the wife of Zeus. "I shall make her a real woman, for I shall give her the gift of curiosity." **B**

Smiling, the goddesses **adorned** her, and when Zeus beheld her grace, her garland of gold, and the glory of her endowments, he was as charmed as though he had been a mortal. "We will call her Pandora," he said, "Pandora,
30 the All-Gifted. She shall become the bride of Epimetheus. But she shall not go empty-handed. She shall bring with her a casket, a box of magic as her dowry.[6] And Hermes, my messenger, shall conduct her to earth."

Epimetheus could not understand why the gods had become concerned about him. He was dazzled by Hermes, and it was some time before he could believe that the exquisite creature brought by the messenger god was meant for him. Even after Hermes departed in a flashing cloud and Pandora stood blushing beside him, he was perturbed. He remembered how often his brother Prometheus had warned him, "Do not trust the gods. And beware especially of Zeus and anything he may send you." However, when Pandora looked in his
40 eyes and smiled, he was, as Aphrodite had predicted, enchanted and **ensnared**. Yet, even as he took her in his arms, he cautioned her.

"We have reason to fear the gods," said Epimetheus, "and also their gifts," he added, pointing to the casket.

"But this is my dowry," murmured Pandora. "Zeus himself filled it with magic as a present for us. See how beautifully it is carved and painted. Look at the silver hinges and the great gold clasp that fastens it." **C**

"Keep it well fastened," said Epimetheus, "otherwise I shall never rest easy. I do not know what the casket may contain, and I do not want to know. Promise me one thing. Never open the box. It is, I grant, a beautiful thing, too
50 beautiful to destroy, and we will keep it. But hide it. Put it not only out of your sight but out of your mind. Then we shall both be content."

Happy that she could keep her dowry, Pandora put it under the bed and turned to her husband with love. And so for a long time nothing disturbed their married life and their continual joy in each other.

But, though Pandora benefited from the goddesses' gifts of beauty and wisdom, the gift of Hera had not been given in vain. For quite a while,

B READING A MYTH
What supernatural beings were involved in the creation of Pandora?

adorn (ə-dôrn′) v. to enhance or decorate

ensnare (ĕn-snâr′) v. to take or catch in something

C THEME
What can you **infer** about the contents of the box based on Zeus' desire for revenge?

---

4. **Aphrodite** (ăf′rə-dī′tē): Greek goddess of love and beauty.

5. **Athene** (ə-thē′nē): Greek goddess of wisdom; sometimes spelled *Athena*.

6. **dowry** (dou′rē): money or property a bride brings to a marriage.

Pandora **restrained** her curiosity about the wonderful casket. But with the passing of time she could not help wondering what it might contain. After all, it was *her* dowry, and she had a right to see what the greatest of the gods had
60 conferred upon her. Then, ashamed of her weakness, she put the idea from her, and thought only of her delight in her home with Epimetheus.

One day, however, the curiosity, so long stifled, overmastered her. "I shall only lift the lid," she said to herself, "and snatch a moment's glimpse of what may be inside. No matter what I see, I won't touch a thing. Surely there can be no harm in that." **D**

Anxiously, as though she were being watched, she tiptoed to her room. Gently getting down on her hands and knees, she drew the casket from under the bed. Half fearfully and half eagerly she lifted the lid. It was only a moment and the lid was up only an inch, but in that moment a swarm of horrible
70 things flew out. They were noisome,[7] abominably colored, and evil-looking, for they were the spirits of all that was evil, sad, and hurtful. They were War and Famine, Crime and Pestilence, Spite and Cruelty, Sickness and Malice, Envy, Woe, Wickedness, and all the other disasters let loose in the world.

Hearing Pandora's scream, Epimetheus rushed in. But it was too late. He and Pandora were set upon and stung, and the evil spirits flew off to attack the rest of mankind. **E**

"It is all my fault," cried Pandora. "If I had thought more about your warning and less about my own desires, I could have controlled my curiosity."

"The fault is mine," said Epimetheus. "I should have burned the box." Then
80 he added, for the poison of Malice was already taking effect, "After all, you are what you are—only a woman—and what else could one expect of a woman."

Disconsolate[8] that she had brought so harmful a dowry to Epimetheus as well as to all other men and women, Pandora wept. It was hours before she let her husband comfort her. Finally, after she grew quiet, they heard a faint sound inside the box.

"Lift the lid again," said Epimetheus. "I think you have released the worst. Perhaps something else, something better, is still there."

He was right. At the bottom of the box was a quivering thing. Its body was small; its wings were frail; but there was a radiance about it. Somehow Pandora
90 knew what it was, and she took it up, touched it carefully, and showed it to Epimetheus. "It is Hope," she said.

"Do you think it will live?" asked Epimetheus.

"Yes," answered Pandora. "I am sure it will. Somehow I know that it will outlive War and Sickness and all the other evils. And," she added, watching the shining thing rise and flutter about the room, "it will never leave us for long. Even if we lose sight of it, it will be there." **F**

She was no longer downhearted as Hope spread its wings and went out into the world. ∾

---

7. **noisome** (noi'som): offensive.

8. **disconsolate** (dĭs-kŏn'sə-lĭt): gloomy.

restrain (rĭ-strān') *v.*
to hold back; to control

D READING A MYTH
What prompts Pandora to look inside the box?

COMMON CORE RL 9

E READING A MYTH
Recall that one purpose of a **myth** is to explain how something came to be. A myth might explain a natural occurrence, such as a tidal wave; a physical landmark, such as a mountain or river; or a part of the human condition, such as falling in love. In your chart, note what this myth explains. In which of the above categories does the explanation fit?

F THEME
How does the winged creature relate to the other things in the box?

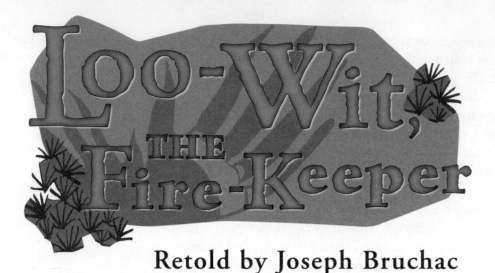

Loo-Wit, the Fire-Keeper

Retold by Joseph Bruchac

When the world was young, the Creator gave everyone all that was needed to be happy.

The weather was always pleasant. There was food for everyone and room for all the people. Despite this, though, two brothers began to quarrel over the land. Each wanted to control it. It reached a point where each brother gathered together a group of men to support his claim. Soon it appeared there would be war.

The Creator saw this and was not pleased. He waited until the two brothers were asleep one night and then carried them to a new country. There a beautiful river flowed and tall mountains rose into the clouds. He woke them
10 just as the sun rose and they looked out from the mountaintop to the land below. They saw what a good place it was. It made their hearts good.

"Now," the Creator said, "this will be your land." Then he gave each of the brothers a bow and a single arrow. "Shoot your arrow into the air," the Creator said. "Where your arrow falls will be the land of you and your people, and you shall be a great chief there." **G**

The brothers did as they were told. The older brother shot his arrow. It arched over the river and landed to the south in the valley of the Willamette River.[1] There is where he and his people went, and they became the Multnomahs.[2] The younger brother shot his arrow. It flew to the north of the
20 great river. He and his people went there and became the Klickitats.[3]

Then the Creator made a Great Stone Bridge across the river. "This bridge," the Creator said, "is a sign of peace. You and your peoples can visit each other by crossing over this bridge. As long as you remain at peace, as long as your hearts are good, this bridge will stand."

Illustrations by Eili-Kaija Kuusniemi/i2i art.

Analyze Visuals ▶

What do you notice when you **compare** the two people?

COMMON CORE RL 1

G **READING A MYTH**
You can infer the personalities of mythical gods by looking at what they do, what they say, and what others say about them. What does the Creator's response to the humans' quarrels tell you about him? Compare and contrast his attitude toward humans with Zeus's.

---

1. **Valley of the Willamette River:** a 30-mile-wide valley in Oregon, home today to a majority of Oregon's people.

2. **Multnomahs** (mult - no′ mes): Native American group who lived in the area where Portland, Oregon, currently stands.

3. **Klickitats:** Native American group whose ancestral lands were situated north of the Columbia River in Washington.

For many seasons the two peoples remained at peace. They passed freely back and forth across the Great Stone Bridge. One day, though, the people to the north looked south toward the Willamette and said, "Their lands are better than ours." One day, though, the people to the south looked north toward the Klickitats and said, "Their lands are more beautiful than ours." Then, once again, the people began to quarrel. **H**

The Creator saw this and was not pleased.

The people were becoming greedy again. Their hearts were becoming bad. The Creator darkened the skies and took fire away. Now the people grew cold. The rains of autumn began and the people suffered greatly.

"Give us back fire," they begged. "We wish to live again with each other in peace."

Their prayers reached the Creator's heart. There was only one place on Earth where fire still remained. An old woman named Loo-Wit had stayed out of the quarreling and was not greedy. It was in her lodge only that fire still burned. So the Creator went to Loo-Wit.

"If you will share your fire with all the people," the Creator said, "I will give you whatever you wish. Tell me what you want."

"I want to be young and beautiful," Loo-Wit said.

"That is the way it will be," said the Creator. "Now take your fire to the Great Stone Bridge above the river. Let all the people come to you and get fire. You must keep the fire burning there to remind people that their hearts must stay good." **I**

The next morning, the skies grew clear and the people saw the sun rise for the first time in many days. The sun shone on the Great Stone Bridge and there the people saw a young woman as beautiful as the sunshine itself. Before her, there on the bridge, burned a fire. The people came to the fire and ended their quarrels. Loo-Wit gave each of them fire. Now their homes again became warm and peace was everywhere.

One day, though, the chief of the people to the north came to Loo-Wit's fire. He saw how beautiful she was and wanted her to be his wife. At the same time, the chief of the people to the south also saw Loo-Wit's beauty. He, too, wanted to marry her. Loo-Wit could not decide which of the two she liked better. Then the chiefs began to quarrel. Their peoples took up the quarrel and fighting began.

When the Creator saw the fighting he became angry. He broke down the Great Stone Bridge. He took each of the two chiefs and changed them into mountains. The chief of the Klickitat became the mountain we now know as Mount Adams. The chief of the Multnomahs became the mountain we now know as Mount Hood.[4] Even as mountains, they continued to quarrel, throwing flames and stones at each other. In some places, the stones they threw almost blocked the river between them. That is why the Columbia River[5] is so narrow in the place called the Dalles today. **J**

---

4. **Mount Adams:** the second highest mountain in the state of Washington; **Mount Hood:** the highest mountain in Oregon. Both mountains are volcanoes and part of the Cascade Volcanic Arc.

5. **Columbia River:** the largest river in the Pacific Northwest. It forms much of the border between Washington and Oregon.

H THEME
The Creator says the Great Stone Bridge is a sign of peace. Do the people stay peaceful? Explain why or why not.

I THEME
Do you think the people's hearts will "stay good"? Explain why or why not.

J READING A MYTH
What does this myth explain? Note the answer in your chart. Tell why this myth might have been told by people who live in the area that is now Oregon and Washington.

Loo-Wit was heartbroken over the pain caused by her beauty. She no longer wanted to be a beautiful young woman. She could no longer find peace as a human being. The Creator took pity on her and changed her into a mountain also, the most beautiful of the mountains. She was placed so that she stood
70 between Mount Adams and Mount Hood, and she was allowed to keep the fire within herself which she had once shared on the Great Stone Bridge. Eventually, she became known as Mount St. Helens[6] and she slept peacefully. **K**

Though she was asleep, Loo-Wit was still aware, the people said. The Creator had placed her between the two quarreling mountains to keep the peace, and it was intended that humans, too, should look at her beauty and remember to keep their hearts good, to share the land and treat it well. If we human beings do not treat the land with respect, the people said, Loo-Wit will wake up and let us know how unhappy she and the Creator have become again. So they said long before the day in the 1980s when Mount St. Helens
80 woke again.

K **READING A MYTH**
According to this myth, how did Mount St. Helens come to be?

---

6. **Mount St. Helens:** an active volcano in Washington that erupted in 1980, killing 57 people and destroying hundreds of homes, bridges, highways, and railways.

Comprehension

1. **Recall** In "Pandora's Box," why does Zeus punish Epimetheus?

2. **Represent** Create a drawing that represents what happens when Pandora opens the box.

3. **Clarify** In "Loo-Wit, the Fire-Keeper," why is Loo-Wit the only person on Earth whose fire still burns?

Text Analysis

4. **Interpret a Line** Reread lines 25–26 of "Pandora's Box." Why does having curiosity make Pandora "real"?

5. **Draw Conclusions** According to the myth "Loo-Wit, the Fire-Keeper," what might have caused Mount St. Helens to erupt in the 1980s?

● 6. **Identify Themes** What is the theme of each myth? Write your answer in a chart like the one shown. Then list details or specific quotations that helped you identify each myth's message about life or human nature.

Theme of "Pandora's Box":	Details:
Theme of "Loo-Wit, the Fire-Keeper":	Details:

● 7. **Compare and Contrast Myths** Review the chart you made as you read. Based on the information you collected, identify one or more elements the myths have in common. Explain one or more significant differences between the myths.

Extension and Challenge

8. **SOCIAL STUDIES CONNECTION** The phrase "Pandora's box" is widely used in the English language to describe an action that can have many negative consequences. Research why the atomic bomb developed by the United States has been called a "Pandora's box," and explain the connection to the myth. Present your findings to the class.

A mushroom cloud rises into the sky after a 1954 test of a nuclear device.

Why do we what WANT we don't have?

The Creator gave each chief plenty. Why do you think each man wanted what the other had?

COMMON CORE

RL 1 Cite the textual evidence that most supports inferences drawn from the text. **RL 2** Determine a theme of a text and analyze its development. **RL 9** Analyze themes, patterns of events, or character types from myths.

Vocabulary in Context

▲ **VOCABULARY PRACTICE**

Choose the word from the list that makes the most sense in each sentence.

1. Zeus had a ____ plan for Epimetheus.
2. The goddesses wanted to ____ Pandora with gold garlands.
3. Aphrodite predicted that Pandora would ____ Epimetheus.
4. Epimetheus warned Pandora to ____ her interest in the casket.

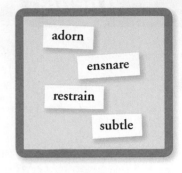

adorn

ensnare

restrain

subtle

ACADEMIC VOCABULARY IN WRITING

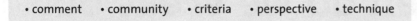

  • comment   • community   • criteria   • perspective   • technique

In a paragraph, **comment** on whose punishment was more just, Zeus's punishment of Epimetheus and all men and women or the Creator's punishment of the two brothers and their people. Use at least one Academic Vocabulary word in your response.

VOCABULARY STRATEGY: USING REFERENCE AIDS

Synonyms are words with similar meanings. For example, a synonym for *restrain* is *stifle*. When you're writing, you can use the following reference aids to help you find a more precise or powerful word to express an idea:

- a **thesaurus**—a book that lists words related to each other in meaning. An electronic thesaurus tool is also found on many word processing programs.

    restrain *verb* check, detain, stifle, suppress

- a **dictionary**—a book that lists words in alphabetical order and gives their definitions, syllabications, pronunciations, and parts of speech. Synonyms are listed after the definition of some words.

    re•strain (rĭ-strān′) *v.* **-strained, -strain•ing, -strains** to hold back or keep in check; control: *couldn't restrain the tears.* **syn** CHECK, DETAIN, STIFLE, SUPPRESS

PRACTICE Use a reference aid to find a synonym for each word. Note the synonym as well as the reference aid you used to find it. Then use each synonym in a sentence that matches its shade of meaning.

1. frail   2. methodical   3. scheme   4. invigorate

:: **COMMON CORE**

L 4c–d Consult general reference materials (e.g., dictionaries, thesauruses) to clarify a word's precise meaning; verify the preliminary determination of the meaning of a word or phrase.

Interactive Vocabulary **THINK** central

Go to **thinkcentral.com.**
KEYWORD: HML8-485

The Old Grandfather and His Little Grandson
Russian Folk Tale Retold by Leo Tolstoy

The Wise Old Woman
Japanese Folk Tale Retold by Yoshiko Uchida

How well do we treat our ELDERS?

COMMON CORE

RL 2 Determine a theme of a text and analyze its development, including its relationship to the plot and characters; provide a summary of the text. **RL 5** Compare and contrast the structure of two texts and analyze how the structure of each text contributes to its meaning.

Think about all the things the elderly people you know have done in their long lives. They've probably cared for their families, made contributions on the job or in the community, and witnessed events that are now part of history. Do you think they get the respect they deserve from younger generations? The two folk tales you are about to read explore reasons why our elders have earned special treatment.

LIST IT Create a list of three to five things that you can do to honor the wisdom and experience of someone from an older generation. Remember that a small gesture can have a big impact.

1. Visit an elderly neighbor
2.
3.

TEXT ANALYSIS: UNIVERSAL THEME

Almost every culture has its **folk tales,** simple stories passed down through generations by word of mouth. Folk tales typically express a **universal theme,** a message about life or human nature that is so fundamental to human existence that it is true for all people of all time periods and cultures.

The two folk tales in this lesson express a similar universal theme. To identify this theme, pay attention to the characters, their actions, and the consequences of their actions.

READING STRATEGY: SET A PURPOSE FOR READING

In this lesson, your **purpose for reading** is to compare two folk tales and to identify the universal theme they share. To do this, as you read take notes in a chart like the one shown. Later on, you will be asked to do more with this chart.

	"The Old Grandfather and His Little Grandson"	"The Wise Old Woman"
Who are the important characters, and what are their qualities?	elderly character: unkind characters: other characters:	elderly character: unkind characters: other characters:
How is the elderly character mistreated?		
What motivates characters to stop this mistreatment?		

▲ VOCABULARY IN CONTEXT

In "The Wise Old Woman," Yoshiko Uchida uses these words to describe a cruel lord and the people who suffer under his rule. Test your knowledge of each word by matching it with the numbered term closest in meaning.

> **WORD LIST**   arrogant   bewilderment   deceive   haughtily

1. proudly   **2.** superior   **3.** astonishment   **4.** mislead

 Complete the activities in your **Reader/Writer Notebook.**

Leo Tolstoy
1828–1910

Russian Novelist
Russian writer Leo Tolstoy wanted to produce literature that would help people adopt simple, religious lives. Tolstoy created some of the world's best-known novels, including *War and Peace* and *Anna Karenina*. He also wrote short stories, dramas, essays, and adaptations. As he grew older, Tolstoy imposed increasingly strict rigors on himself in order to live what he saw as a good life. He became isolated from his wife and 13 children. In 1910, while escaping his family by train, Tolstoy developed pneumonia and died. His works live on as literary classics.

Yoshiko Uchida
1921–1992

Japanese-American Author
The daughter of Japanese immigrants, Yoshiko Uchida grew up in California feeling different from her white classmates. This difference became more obvious after the bombing of Pearl Harbor in 1941, when Uchida and her family were sent to an internment camp. Uchida wrote many books for children that drew on her experience. She said, "I want to dispel the stereotypic image still held by many non-Asians about the Japanese and write about them as real people."

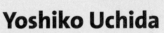

Authors Online
Go to **thinkcentral.com.** KEYWORD: HML8-487

THINK central

The Old Grandfather and His Little Grandson

Retold by Leo Tolstoy

The grandfather had become very old. His legs would not carry him, his eyes could not see, his ears could not hear, and he was toothless. When he ate, bits of food sometimes dropped out of his mouth. His son and his son's wife no longer allowed him to eat with them at the table. He had to eat his meals in the corner near the stove.

One day they gave him his food in a bowl. He tried to move the bowl closer; it fell to the floor and broke. His daughter-in-law scolded him. She told him that he spoiled everything in the house and broke their dishes, and she said that from now on he would get his food in a wooden dish. The old man sighed
10 and said nothing. **Ⓐ**

A few days later, the old man's son and his wife were sitting in their hut, resting and watching their little boy playing on the floor. They saw him putting together something out of small pieces of wood. His father asked him, "What are you making, Misha?"

The little grandson said, "I'm making a wooden bucket. When you and Mamma get old, I'll feed you out of this wooden dish."

The young peasant and his wife looked at each other and tears filled their eyes. They were ashamed because they had treated the old grandfather so meanly, and from that day they again let the old man eat with them at the
20 table and took better care of him. **Ⓑ**

Analyze Visuals ▶
How does color affect the **mood** of this picture?

Ⓐ UNIVERSAL THEME
How do the man and his wife treat the grandfather?

Ⓑ UNIVERSAL THEME
What have the man and his wife realized about themselves?

Beggar and a Boy (1903), Pablo Picasso. Oil on canvas, 125 cm × 92 cm. Pushkin Museum, Moscow. © Bridgeman Art Library. © 2007 Estate of Pablo Picasso/Artists Rights Society (ARS), New York.

THE WISE OLD WOMAN

RETOLD BY YOSHIKO UCHIDA

Many long years ago, there lived an **arrogant** and cruel young lord who ruled over a small village in the western hills of Japan.

"I have no use for old people in my village," he said **haughtily.** "They are neither useful nor able to work for a living. I therefore decree[1] that anyone over seventy-one must be banished[2] from the village and left in the mountains to die."

"What a dreadful decree! What a cruel and unreasonable lord we have," the people of the village murmured. But the lord fearfully punished anyone who disobeyed him, and so villagers who turned seventy-one were tearfully carried
10 into the mountains, never to return.

Gradually there were fewer and fewer old people in the village and soon they disappeared altogether. Then the young lord was pleased.

"What a fine village of young, healthy and hard-working people I have," he bragged. "Soon it will be the finest village in all of Japan." **C**

arrogant (ăr′ə-gənt) *adj.* displaying a sense of self-importance

haughtily (hô′tə-lē) *adv.* proudly; scornfully

Analyze Visuals ▶

How would you describe the **setting** shown in this picture?

C UNIVERSAL THEME
Why does the young lord decide that old people must be banished?

---

1. **decree** (dĭ-krē′): to make an order; an order that has the force of law.
2. **banished:** forced to leave a country or a place.

山中の里

THE WISE OLD WOMAN　**491**

Now there lived in this village a kind young farmer and his aged mother. They were poor, but the farmer was good to his mother, and the two of them lived happily together. However, as the years went by, the mother grew older, and before long she reached the terrible age of seventy-one.

"If only I could somehow **deceive** the cruel lord," the farmer thought.
20 But there were records in the village books and every one knew that his mother had turned seventy-one.

Each day the son put off telling his mother that he must take her into the mountains to die, but the people of the village began to talk. The farmer knew that if he did not take his mother away soon, the lord would send his soldiers and throw them both into a dark dungeon to die a terrible death.

"Mother—" he would begin, as he tried to tell her what he must do, but he could not go on.

Then one day the mother herself spoke of the lord's dread decree. "Well, my son," she said, "the time has come for you to take me to the mountains.
30 We must hurry before the lord sends his soldiers for you." And she did not seem worried at all that she must go to the mountains to die.

"Forgive me, dear mother, for what I must do," the farmer said sadly, and the next morning he lifted his mother to his shoulders and set off on the steep path toward the mountains. Up and up he climbed, until the trees clustered close and the path was gone. There was no longer even the sound of birds, and they heard only the soft wail of the wind in the trees. The son walked slowly, for he could not bear to think of leaving his old mother in the mountains. On and on he climbed, not wanting to stop and leave her behind. Soon, he heard his mother breaking off small twigs from the trees
40 that they passed.

"Mother, what are you doing?" he asked.

"Do not worry, my son," she answered gently. "I am just marking the way so you will not get lost returning to the village."

The son stopped. "Even now you are thinking of me?" he asked, wonderingly.

The mother nodded. "Of course, my son," she replied. "You will always be in my thoughts. How could it be otherwise?"

At that, the young farmer could bear it no longer. "Mother, I cannot leave you in the mountains to die all alone," he said. "We are going home and no matter what the lord does to punish me, I will never desert you again." **D**

50 So they waited until the sun had set and a lone star crept into the silent sky. Then in the dark shadows of night, the farmer carried his mother down the hill and they returned quietly to their little house. The farmer dug a deep hole in the floor of his kitchen and made a small room where he could hide his mother. From that day, she spent all her time in the secret room and the farmer carried meals to her there. The rest of the time, he was careful to work in the fields and act as though he lived alone. In this way, for almost two years, he kept his mother safely hidden and no one in the village knew that she was there.

deceive (dĭ-sēv') *v.* to cause to believe what is not true; to mislead

🌐 **SOCIAL STUDIES CONNECTION**

Japan is a string of several thousand islands off the east coast of the continent of Asia. Much of Japan consists of hills and mountains.

D UNIVERSAL THEME
Why does the son decide to disobey the decree even though he might be punished?

Analyze Visuals ▶

Based on this picture, what can you **conclude** about the journey up the mountain?

The Moon and the Abandoned Old Woman (1891), Yoshitoshi. © Asian Art & Archaeology, Inc./Corbis.

Moon, Tsukioka Yoshitoshi. From the *Snow, Moon and Flower* Series. © Christie's Images Ltd.

Then one day there was a terrible commotion among the villagers for Lord
60 Higa of the town beyond the hills threatened to conquer their village and
make it his own.

"Only one thing can spare you," Lord Higa announced. "Bring me a box
containing one thousand ropes of ash and I will spare your village."

The cruel young lord quickly gathered together all the wise men of his
village. "You are men of wisdom," he said. "Surely you can tell me how to meet
Lord Higa's demands so our village can be spared."

But the wise men shook their heads. "It is impossible to make even one rope
of ash, sire," they answered. "How can we ever make one thousand?"

"Fools!" the lord cried angrily. "What good is your wisdom if you cannot
70 help me now?"

And he posted a notice in the village square offering a great reward of gold
to any villager who could help him save their village.

But all the people in the village whispered, "Surely, it is an impossible thing,
for ash crumbles at the touch of the finger. How could anyone ever make
a rope of ash?" They shook their heads and sighed, "Alas, alas, we must be
conquered by yet another cruel lord."

The young farmer, too, supposed that this must be, and he wondered what
would happen to his mother if a new lord even more terrible than their own
came to rule over them.

80 When his mother saw the troubled look on his face, she asked, "Why are
you so worried, my son?"

▲ **Analyze Visuals**

What **details** about the man's appearance affect your impression of his personality?

Language Coach

Antonyms Antonyms are words that are opposite in meaning. The word *fools*, which appears in line 69, means the opposite of *wise men*, which appears in line 64. What does the word *fools* mean?

So the farmer told her of the impossible demand made by Lord Higa if the village was to be spared, but his mother did not seem troubled at all. Instead she laughed softly and said, "Why, that is not such an impossible task. All one has to do is soak ordinary rope in salt water and dry it well. When it is burned, it will hold its shape and there is your rope of ash! Tell the villagers to hurry and find one thousand pieces of rope."

The farmer shook his head in amazement. "Mother, you are wonderfully wise," he said, and he rushed to tell the young lord what he must do. **E**

90 "You are wiser than all the wise men of the village," the lord said when he heard the farmer's solution, and he rewarded him with many pieces of gold. The thousand ropes of ash were quickly made and the village was spared.

In a few days, however, there was another great commotion in the village as Lord Higa sent another threat. This time he sent a log with a small hole that curved and bent seven times through its length, and he demanded that a single piece of silk thread be threaded through the hole. "If you cannot perform this task," the lord threatened, "I shall come to conquer your village."

The young lord hurried once more to his wise men, but they all shook their heads in **bewilderment**. "A needle cannot bend its way through such curves," 100 they moaned. "Again we are faced with an impossible demand."

"And again you are stupid fools!" the lord said, stamping his foot impatiently. He then posted a second notice in the village square asking the villagers for their help.

Once more the young farmer hurried with the problem to his mother in her secret room.

"Why, that is not so difficult," his mother said with a quick smile. "Put some sugar at one end of the hole. Then, tie an ant to a piece of silk thread and put it in at the other end. He will weave his way in and out of the curves to get to the sugar and he will take the silk thread with him."

110 "Mother, you are remarkable!" the son cried, and he hurried off to the lord with the solution to the second problem.

Once more the lord commended the young farmer and rewarded him with many pieces of gold. "You are a brilliant man and you have saved our village again," he said gratefully.

But the lord's troubles were not over even then, for a few days later Lord Higa sent still another demand. "This time you will undoubtedly fail and then I shall conquer your village," he threatened. "Bring me a drum that sounds without being beaten."

"But that is not possible," sighed the people of the village. "How can anyone 120 make a drum sound without beating it?"

This time the wise men held their heads in their hands and moaned, "It is hopeless. It is hopeless. This time Lord Higa will conquer us all."

E UNIVERSAL THEME
What do you learn about the old woman from the way she solves the village's problem?

bewilderment
(bĭ-wĭl′dər-mənt) *n.* the state of being confused or astonished

The young farmer hurried home breathlessly. "Mother, Mother, we must solve another terrible problem or Lord Higa will conquer our village!" And he quickly told his mother about the impossible drum.

His mother, however, smiled and answered, "Why, this is the easiest of them all. Make a drum with sides of paper and put a bumblebee inside. As it tries to escape, it will buzz and beat itself against the paper and you will have a drum that sounds without being beaten." **F**

130   The young farmer was amazed at his mother's wisdom. "You are far wiser than any of the wise men of the village," he said, and he hurried to tell the young lord how to meet Lord Higa's third demand.

When the lord heard the answer, he was greatly impressed. "Surely a young man like you cannot be wiser than all my wise men," he said. "Tell me honestly, who has helped you solve all these difficult problems?"

The young farmer could not lie. "My lord," he began slowly, "for the past two years I have broken the law of the land. I have kept my aged mother hidden beneath the floor of my house, and it is she who solved each of your problems and saved the village from Lord Higa."

140   He trembled as he spoke, for he feared the lord's displeasure and rage. Surely now the soldiers would be summoned to throw him into the dark dungeon. But when he glanced fearfully at the lord, he saw that the young ruler was not angry at all. Instead, he was silent and thoughtful, for at last he realized how much wisdom and knowledge old people possess.

"I have been very wrong," he said finally. "And I must ask the forgiveness of your mother and of all my people. Never again will I demand that the old people of our village be sent to the mountains to die. Rather, they will be treated with the respect and honor they deserve and share with us the wisdom of their years." **G**

150   And so it was. From that day, the villagers were no longer forced to abandon their parents in the mountains, and the village became once more a happy, cheerful place in which to live. The terrible Lord Higa stopped sending his impossible demands and no longer threatened to conquer them, for he too was impressed. "Even in such a small village there is much wisdom," he declared, "and its people should be allowed to live in peace."

And that is exactly what the farmer and his mother and all the people of the village did for all the years thereafter. ⌒⌒

COMMON CORE RL 2

F **UNIVERSAL THEME**
Stories can communicate the same universal theme in different ways. For example, the elderly characters in these folk tales don't share the same qualities. The old grandfather is nearly helpless. The old woman is perceived as solving problems. Why do you think the old woman is able to solve all the problems created by Lord Higa's demands?

G **UNIVERSAL THEME**
What lesson does the young lord learn?

Comprehension

1. **Recall** In "The Old Grandfather and His Little Grandson," whose action shames the couple into treating the grandfather better?

2. **Recall** In "The Wise Old Woman," what is the young lord's decree?

Text Analysis

3. **Analyze Motives** In "The Old Grandfather," why do you think the son and his wife react so negatively to the grandfather's accident?

● 4. **Interpret Theme** Summarize the role of the farmer's mother in this story. In what way does the title of "The Wise Old Woman" reflect the theme of the folktale?

5. **Evaluate Parallel Episodes** In folk tales, events often happen in threes. There may be three wishes or three tasks, for example. These repeated events are called **parallel episodes.** Find the parallel episodes in "The Wise Old Woman." What do these parallel episodes contribute to the folk tale?

Comparing Universal Theme

● 6. **Set a Purpose for Reading** Finish filling in your chart. Then add the question about universal theme to your chart and write your answer.

	"The Old Grandfather and His Little Grandson"	"The Wise Old Woman"
Who are the important characters, and what are their qualities?	elderly character. unkind characters. other characters.	elderly character. unkind characters. other characters.
How is the elderly character mistreated?		
What motivates characters to stop this mistreatment?		
What is the universal theme?		

How well do we treat our ELDERS?

Do you think our culture treats elderly people well, or poorly? Explain your answer.

RL 2 Determine a theme of a text and analyze its development, including its relationship to the plot and characters; provide a summary of the text. RL 5 Compare and contrast the structure of two texts and analyze how the structure of each text contributes to its meaning.

Vocabulary in Context

▲ **VOCABULARY PRACTICE**

Choose the word in each group that is most nearly opposite in meaning to the boldfaced word.

1. **haughtily:** (a) snobbishly, (b) modestly, (c) indifferently
2. **bewilderment:** (a) understanding, (b) confusion, (c) shock
3. **arrogant:** (a) smug, (b) humble, (c) aloof
4. **deceive:** (a) outsmart, (b) scam, (c) guide

ACADEMIC VOCABULARY IN SPEAKING

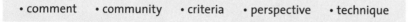

- comment   • community   • criteria   • perspective   • technique

The young lord owes the villagers an apology and an explanation. Give a speech from his **perspective**, explaining what he has learned. Use at least one Academic Vocabulary word in the speech.

VOCABULARY STRATEGY: THE SUFFIX -*ly*

A suffix is a word part that can be added to the end of a root or base word. Sometimes a suffix is used to change a word's part of speech. For example, when the suffix -*ly* is added to the end of the word *haughty*, it forms the adverb *haughtily*. When an adjective ends in -*y*, as *haughty* does, the *y* changes to *i* before -*ly* is added.

PRACTICE Change each boldfaced adjective to an adverb by adding the suffix -*ly*. Then rephrase each sentence so it makes sense.

1. In the beginning of the story, the young lord was **cruel.**
2. The **tearful** son had to take his mother into the mountains.
3. The **angry** lord asked the villagers for help.
4. The old woman was **happy** to provide her son with the answers.

COMMON CORE

L 2c Spell correctly. **L 4b** Use Latin affixes as clues to the meaning of a word.

Interactive Vocabulary **THINK** central

Go to **thinkcentral.com**.
KEYWORD: HML8-498

Writing for Assessment

COMMON CORE RL 2, W 2, W 2a–b, f

1. READ THE PROMPT

In writing assessments, you will often be asked to compare and contrast two works that share a similar theme.

> The folk tales "The Old Grandfather and His Little Grandson" and "The Wise Old Woman" express the same universal theme in different ways. In four to five paragraphs, compare and contrast the ways in which the folk tales convey their message. Support your judgments with references to both texts.

◄ **STRATEGIES IN ACTION**

1. I have to make sure I understand the **message** expressed by these folk tales.

2. I need to identify the **similarities and differences** in how the tales get the message across.

3. I should support my ideas using **information** from the two tales.

2. PLAN YOUR WRITING

Review your chart to identify the universal theme and the way each folk tale expresses it. Then think about how you will set up the body of your response.

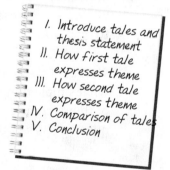

I. Introduce tales and thesis statement
II. How first tale expresses theme
III. How second tale expresses theme
IV. Comparison of tales
V. Conclusion

- Option A: In one paragraph, describe how the universal theme is conveyed in the first folk tale; in the next paragraph, describe how this theme is conveyed in the second folk tale; in a third paragraph, discuss similarities and differences.

- Option B: In one paragraph, compare the elderly characters; in a second paragraph, compare the mistreatment of the elderly characters; in a third paragraph, compare the motivations for ending the mistreatment.

Once you have decided on the organization, outline your essay. Then write a thesis statement that describes the main idea of your essay.

3. DRAFT YOUR RESPONSE

Introduction Give the titles and authors of the tales. Provide a sentence telling what each tale is about. State the universal theme and include your thesis statement.

Body Using your outline as a guide, discuss how each folk tale conveys the universal theme. Use details from the tales to support your ideas.

Conclusion End each essay by restating the universal theme and your thesis statement. Explain whether the values conveyed by these tales are still important.

Revision Make sure you clearly identify the tale you are discussing in each paragraph.

My Mother Pieced Quilts
Poem by Teresa Palomo Acosta

quilting
Poem by Lucille Clifton

What gives MEANING to simple things?

Is there a song that reminds you of a particular time or place in your life? Perhaps there is a food that makes you think of a special person or holiday. Simple things like these can have a unique meaning when they represent something more. In the poems you are about to read, you'll see how simple things can have personal significance.

SURVEY Take an informal survey of five to ten classmates to find out what simple things have the most meaning for them. What types of things come up most often? As a class, create an answer to the question "What gives meaning to simple things?"

TEXT ANALYSIS: SYMBOL IN POETRY

Symbols are people, places, and things that stand for something beyond themselves. Writers often use them to convey complex ideas in a few words. For example, in the poems you are about to read, quilts and quilting represent something more significant than an object or activity. To understand these symbols, use the following tips:

- Think about the big ideas each line or stanza expresses. Ask: *What message about families, art, or other big topics is the poem communicating?*

- Pay attention to the poet's word choice. Ask: *Which words have positive associations? Which have negative associations?*

- Notice how the symbol relates to the big ideas in the poem. Ask: *In what way do quilts or quilting help convey the poem's message?*

Use graphics like the ones shown to write down clues that help you understand each symbol. You'll finish filling in the graphics later.

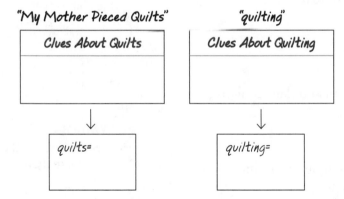

"My Mother Pieced Quilts"

Clues About Quilts

quilts=

"quilting"

Clues About Quilting

quilting=

READING SKILL: DRAW CONCLUSIONS

You often must **draw conclusions** to understand the message a poet is trying to share. A conclusion is a belief you arrive at or a logical judgment you make by combining your inferences about the poem with your personal knowledge and experience.

To help you draw a conclusion, you can fill in a statement like this: "I believe _____ because _____ and _____." For example, "I believe the daughter respects her mother because she seems awed by her mother's talent and because I know from experience how important adult role models are." As you read "My Mother Pieced Quilts" and "quilting," fill in your own statements to draw conclusions about the value of quilting.

 Complete the activities in your **Reader/Writer Notebook**.

Meet the Authors

Teresa Palomo Acosta
born 1949

Women's Advocate
Teresa Palomo Acosta grew up in central Texas, where she enjoyed listening to her grandfather tell colorful stories about her family's history in Mexico and Texas. Acosta's work as a writer springs from her desire to tell stories about people who don't usually appear in literature. In particular, she writes about the lives and struggles of Mexican-American women in the past and present. Widely recognized for her efforts in support of women, she's been named an Outstanding Woman in the Arts.

Lucille Clifton
born 1936

Creating Beautiful Poems
Lucille Clifton grew up in the state of New York and was the first in her family to finish high school and attend college. Her poetry often deals with her African-American roots and having strength through difficult times. She believes writing poetry explores what it means to be human. "Poetry doesn't have to be pretty," she said, "but it must be beautiful." Clifton has won many awards for her work, including the National Book Award and an Emmy Award.

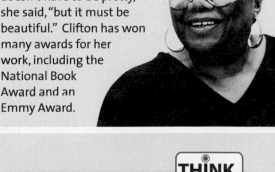

Authors Online
Go to **thinkcentral.com**. KEYWORD: HML8-501

THINK central

My Mother Pieced Quilts

Teresa Palomo Acosta

they were just meant as covers
in winters
as weapons
against pounding january winds

5 but it was just that every morning I awoke to these
october ripened canvases
passed my hand across their cloth faces
and began to wonder how you pieced
all these together
10 these strips of gentle communion cotton and flannel nightgowns
wedding organdies
dime store velvets **Ⓐ**

how you shaped patterns square and oblong and round
positioned
15 balanced
then cemented them
with your thread
a steel needle
a thimble

20 how the thread darted in and out
galloping along the frayed edges, tucking them in
as you did us at night
oh how you stretched and turned and re-arranged
your michigan spring faded curtain pieces
25 my father's santa fe work shirt
the summer denims, the tweeds of fall **Ⓑ**

Analyze Visuals ▶

What recognizable objects can you find in this quilt? Tell what each might **symbolize** to the quilt maker.

Ⓐ SYMBOL
In what ways are the quilts more than covers?

Ⓑ DRAW CONCLUSIONS
How does the mother's skill in making the quilt mirror her role in the family?

American Childhood (1995), Jane Burch Cochran.
Fabric, beads, buttons, paint, baby dress, gloves, 53" × 42".

in the evening you sat at your canvas
—our cracked linoleum floor the drawing board
me lounging on your arm
30 and you staking out the plan:
whether to put the lilac purple of easter against the red plaid
    of winter-going-
into-spring
whether to mix a yellow with blue and white and paint the
35 corpus christi noon when my father held your hand
whether to shape a five-point star from the
somber black silk you wore to grandmother's funeral **C**

you were the river current
carrying the roaring notes
40 forming them into pictures of a little boy reclining
a swallow flying
you were the caravan master at the reins
driving your threaded needle artillery[1] across the mosaic[2]
    cloth bridges
45 delivering yourself in separate testimonies.[3]

oh mother you plunged me sobbing and laughing
into our past
into the river crossing at five
into the spinach fields
50 into the plainview cotton rows
into tuberculosis wards
into braids and muslin[4] dresses
sewn hard and taut to withstand the thrashings of twenty-five years **D**

stretched out they lay
55 armed/ready/shouting/celebrating

knotted with love
the quilts sing on **E**

C SYMBOL
Reread lines 31–37.
What parts of life do
the fabrics in the quilt
represent?

D DRAW CONCLUSIONS
Think about the images
the **speaker** uses as she
describes her mother. What
is the speaker's attitude
toward her mother?

E SYMBOL
What does the **speaker**
mean when she says "the
quilts sing on"? Consider
how the quilt represents
the family itself.

---

1. **artillery** (är-tĭl′ə-rē): large weapons that are operated by crews.
2. **mosaic** (mō-zā′ĭk): a picture or design created when small colored pieces of stone
   or tile are set into a surface.
3. **testimonies** (tĕs′tə-mō′nēz): declarations.
4. **muslin** (mŭz′lĭn): sturdy cotton fabric.

Quilting

Lucille Clifton

Crossing Borders (1995), Deidre Scherer. Fabric and thread. © Deidre Scherer.

somewhere in the unknown world
a yellow eyed woman
sits with her daughter
quilting.

5 some other where
alchemists[1] mumble over pots.
their chemistry stirs
into science. their science
freezes into stone. **F**

10 in the unknown world
the woman
threading together her need
and her needle
nods toward the smiling girl
15 *remember*
this will keep us warm. **G**

how does this poem end?
   do the daughters' daughters quilt?
   do the alchemists practice their tables?
20   do the worlds continue spinning
   away from each other forever?

---

1. **alchemist** (ăl′kə-mĭst)**:** a chemist who tries to turn metals into gold.

▲ **Analyze Visuals**
What might the gesture in this picture **symbolize?**

F DRAW CONCLUSIONS
Does the **speaker** present the place where the alchemists are in a positive or negative way? Tell what words in this stanza make you think so.

G SYMBOL
How is the world where the mother and daughter quilt different from the alchemists' world?

Comprehension

1. **Recall** What were the quilts in "My Mother Pieced Quilts" meant for?

2. **Recall** In "My Mother Pieced Quilts," what does the mother consider doing with the black silk from the grandmother's funeral?

3. **Summarize** Describe the alchemists' work in "quilting."

Text Analysis

4. **Visualize** In "My Mother Pieced Quilts," the poet uses vivid language to create a picture of the fabrics, patterns, and colors of the quilts. What three descriptive phrases best help you visualize the quilts?

5. **Clarify a Line** In "quilting," the mother threads together "her need and her needle." What need might quilting fulfill for the mother? Think about why it's important for her to share the experience with her daughter.

6. **Interpret a Question** In "quilting," the poem ends with the following question: "do the worlds continue spinning away from each other forever?" Think about how the worlds are contrasted in the poem. Why might they be moving apart? Explain your answer.

● 7. **Analyze Symbols** Finish filling in your graphics with any additional clues to the meanings of "quilts" and "quilting" in the two poems. In "My Mother Pieced Quilts," what do the quilts symbolize? In "quilting," what does the act of quilting symbolize? Write the answers in your graphic.

● 8. **Draw Conclusions** In a chart like the one shown, list examples from the poems of the practical, creative, and social reasons for quilting. Based on this list, what can you conclude about the value in making quilts?

	Reasons for Quilting
Practical	
Creative	
Social	

COMMON CORE

RL 1 Cite the textual evidence that supports inferences drawn from the text. **RL 4** Determine the meaning of words and phrases as they are used in a text.

Extension and Challenge

9. **Creative Project: Art** If you were to make a quilt to represent your life, what would it look like? Think about the fabrics, colors, and designs you would choose and their meaning to you. Then make a collage of your quilt.

What gives **MEANING** to simple things?

If the speaker of "My Mother Pieced Quilts" were asked what gives her bed covers meaning, what might she say?

Language

You can make your writing interesting by varying your sentences. Using participles at the beginning of some sentences can help you add variety.

A **participle** is a verb form that acts as an adjective. A **participial phrase** consists of a participle plus its modifiers and complements. There are two kinds of participles. Present participles usually end in *-ing*. Past participles usually end in *-ed* or *-en*. Each of them can be used at the beginning of a sentence. In the examples below, notice how two sentences are combined to create one sentence that opens with a participle or participial phrase.

Original:	The girl smiles. She hands her mother the thread.
Revised:	Smiling, the girl hands her mother the thread.

Original:	The mother passed the quilt down to her daughter. The quilt was a family heirloom.
Revised:	Passed down from mother to daughter, the quilt was a family heirloom.

PRACTICE Combine each pair of sentences to create one sentence that opens with a participle or participial phrase.

1. My mother worked every night. She made three quilts a year.
2. We look at the patches. We are reminded of our past.
3. I complained. I made excuses not to help her sew.
4. My mother sewed. She talked about her own childhood.
5. I treasure the quilts I have. I want to make some for my children.

For more help with participles, see page R61 in the **Grammar Handbook***.*

READING-WRITING CONNECTION

Delve deeper into "My Mother Pieced Quilts" by responding to this prompt. Then use the **revising tip** to improve your writing.

WRITING PROMPT	REVISING TIP
Extended Constructed Response: Speech Imagine a museum has decided to show the quilts described in "My Mother Pieced Quilts." The speaker of the poem has been asked to discuss her mother's work. Write a **one-page speech** in which the speaker explains to the audience how the quilts were created and what they mean to her.	Review your speech. Have you varied your sentence openings? If not, add interest to your writing by beginning at least one sentence with a participle or participial phrase.

COMMON CORE

L1 Demonstrate command of standard English grammar when writing. **L1a** Explain the function of participles. **W2** Write explanatory texts.

Interactive Revision **THINK** central

Go to **thinkcentral.com**.
KEYWORD: HML8-507

The Diary of Anne Frank

HISTORY   Video link at
thinkcentral.com

Drama by Frances Goodrich and Albert Hackett

VIDEO TRAILER **THINK** central   KEYWORD: HML8-508

What IMPACT will you have on the world?

COMMON CORE

RL 2 Determine a theme of a text and analyze its development, including its relationship to the characters, setting, and plot. **RL 10** Read and comprehend dramas.

Everyone makes an impact on the world in some way. National leaders or sports heroes may inspire millions, while the rest of us can influence a smaller circle of friends and family through our actions, our beliefs, or our commitments. Whether you make your mark quietly or boldly, a life well lived can be a guide to others. In the play you're about to read, a young girl doesn't realize that the thoughts she expresses in her diary will later influence readers all over the world.

QUICKWRITE People of all ages make important contributions to the world. What impact do you now have on others? What impact do you hope to have later in your life? Write your ideas in a brief journal entry. Think about how education and life experience might affect your goals for the future.

● **TEXT ANALYSIS: THEME**

The play you are about to read is based on a diary written by Anne Frank, a teenager who spent more than two years hiding from the Nazis. When Anne's diary was published, readers around the world were profoundly touched that, despite all she had been through, she still believed people were good at heart.

When the playwrights adapted Anne's diary, they used her belief in the essential goodness of people as one of the work's **themes,** or messages about life. As you read, notice how Anne's thoughts and feelings, as well as the characters, setting, and plot, work together to express this theme.

● **READING STRATEGY: READING A DRAMA**

In a drama, a playwright must communicate all the information about the characters through **dialogue,** or words spoken by the actors, and **stage directions,** or directions to the crew and actors. This can be challenging when the protagonist (the main character) is going through internal changes, or when an antagonist (a force in opposition to the protagonist) is something other than a character. As you read, notice how Goodrich and Hackett meet this challenge. In a chart like the one shown, note important information you learn about Anne and about the Nazi occupation.

Information About Anne	Information About Nazi Occupation

▲ **VOCABULARY IN CONTEXT**

The following words help the playwrights capture Anne's experiences. To see how many you know, try to match each word from the list with the word or phrase closest in meaning.

WORD LIST	apprehension	fortify	remorse
	disgruntled	indignantly	unabashed
	foreboding	pandemonium	

1. wild uproar   4. angrily   7. bold
2. displeased   5. strengthen   8. sorrow
3. worry   6. sinking feeling

Complete the activities in your **Reader/Writer Notebook.**

Meet the Authors

Frances Goodrich
1890–1984

Albert Hackett
1900–1995

From Comedies to Drama

Screenwriting team Frances Goodrich and Albert Hackett were a married couple known for their upbeat comedies and musicals. In the late 1940s, they began working on a drama that would take eight years to complete. Their play, *The Diary of Anne Frank*, was based on Anne Frank's diary entries. As part of their research, the couple traveled to Amsterdam to interview Anne's father and to see the family's hiding place. Their play adaptation won a Pulitzer Prize in 1956.

BACKGROUND TO THE PLAY
Anne Frank's Diary

Anne Frank and her family were Jewish citizens of Germany. When the Nazi party, led by Adolf Hitler, came to power in 1933, the Nazis blamed the country's problems on the Jews. Jews were stripped of their rights. Many were eventually sent to concentration camps, where more than 6 million died in what became known as the Holocaust. The Franks moved to the Netherlands to escape persecution, but the Nazis invaded that country in 1940. In order to survive, Anne's family went into hiding when she was 13 years old. They hid in attic rooms behind Mr. Frank's office, and several other Jews joined them. In this "Secret Annex," Anne kept a diary about her life in hiding. More than two years later, the group's worst fears came true when the Nazis found them. Everyone who had been living there was sent to concentration camps. Anne's diary was discovered later.

Authors Online   **THINK** central
Go to **thinkcentral.com.**
KEYWORD: HML8-509

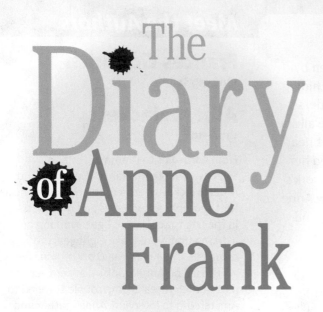

The Diary of Anne Frank

FRANCES GOODRICH AND ALBERT HACKETT

CHARACTERS

SECRET ANNEX RESIDENTS

Anne Frank	Mrs. Frank	Mrs. Van Daan
Margot Frank	Peter Van Daan	Mr. Dussel
Mr. Frank	Mr. Van Daan	

WORKERS IN MR. FRANK'S BUSINESS

Miep Gies (mēp gēs)
Mr. Kraler (krä′lər)

The Time. *July 1942–August 1944, November 1945*
The Place. *Amsterdam, the Netherlands*

The scene remains the same throughout the play. It is the top floor of a warehouse and office building in Amsterdam, Holland. The sharply peaked roof of the building is outlined against a sea of other rooftops, stretching away into the distance. Nearby is the belfry of a church tower, the Westertoren, whose carillon rings out the hours. Occasionally faint sounds float up from below: the voices of children playing in the street, the tramp of marching feet, a boat whistle from the canal.

The three rooms of the top floor and a small attic space above are exposed to our view. The largest of the rooms is in the center, with two small rooms,
slightly raised, on either side. On the right is a bathroom, out of sight. A narrow steep flight of stairs at the back leads up to the attic. The rooms are sparsely furnished with a few chairs, cots, a table or two. The windows are painted over, or covered with makeshift blackout curtains. In the main room there is a sink, a gas ring for cooking and a wood-burning stove for warmth.

The room on the left is hardly more than a closet. There is a skylight in the sloping ceiling. Directly under this room is a small steep stairwell, with steps leading down to a door. This is the only entrance from the building below. When the door is opened we see that it has been concealed on the outer side by a bookcase attached to it.

The Diary of Anne Frank, starring Natalie Portman as Anne, ran on Broadway at the Music Box Theatre from December 1997 to June 1998.

ACT ONE
Scene 1

The curtain rises on an empty stage. It is late afternoon November, 1945.

The rooms are dusty, the curtains in rags. Chairs and tables are overturned.

The door at the foot of the small stairwell swings open. Mr. Frank *comes up the steps into view. He is a gentle, cultured European in his middle years. There is still a trace of a German accent in his speech.*

He stands looking slowly around, making a
10 *supreme effort at self-control. He is weak, ill. His clothes are threadbare.*

After a second he drops his rucksack on the couch and moves slowly about. He opens the door to one of the smaller rooms, and then abruptly closes it again, turning away. He goes to the window at the back, looking off at the Westertoren as its carillon strikes the hour of six, then he moves restlessly on.

From the street below we hear the sound of a barrel organ and children's voices at play. There is a
20 *many-colored scarf hanging from a nail.* Mr. Frank *takes it, putting it around his neck. As he starts back for his rucksack, his eye is caught by something lying on the floor. It is a woman's white glove. He holds it in his hand and suddenly all of his self-control is gone. He breaks down, crying.*

We hear footsteps on the stairs. Miep Gies *comes up, looking for* Mr. Frank. Miep *is a Dutch girl of about twenty-two. She wears a coat and hat, ready to go home. She is pregnant. Her attitude toward*
30 Mr. Frank *is protective, compassionate.*

Miep. Are you all right, Mr. Frank?

Mr. Frank (*quickly controlling himself*). Yes, Miep, yes.

Miep. Everyone in the office has gone home . . . It's after six. (*then pleading*) Don't stay up here, Mr. Frank. What's the use of torturing yourself like this?

Mr. Frank. I've come to say good-bye . . . I'm leaving here, Miep.

40 **Miep.** What do you mean? Where are you going? Where?

Mr. Frank. I don't know yet. I haven't decided.

Miep. Mr. Frank, you can't leave here! This is your home! Amsterdam is your home. Your business is here, waiting for you . . . You're needed here . . . Now that the war is over, there are things that . . .

Mr. Frank. I can't stay in Amsterdam, Miep. It has too many memories for me. Everywhere there's something . . . the house we lived in . . . the
50 school . . . that street organ playing out there . . . I'm not the person you used to know, Miep. I'm a bitter old man. (*breaking off*) Forgive me. I shouldn't speak to you like this . . . after all that you did for us . . . the suffering . . .

Miep. No. No. It wasn't suffering. You can't say we suffered. (*As she speaks, she straightens a chair which is overturned.*)

Mr. Frank. I know what you went through, you and Mr. Kraler. I'll remember it as long as I live.
60 (*He gives one last look around.*) Come, Miep.

(*He starts for the steps, then remembers his rucksack, going back to get it.*)

Miep (*hurrying up to a cupboard*). Mr. Frank, did you see? There are some of your papers here. (*She brings a bundle of papers to him.*) We found them in a heap of rubbish on the floor after . . . after you left.

Mr. Frank. Burn them.

(*He opens his rucksack to put the glove in it.*)

70 **Miep.** But, Mr. Frank, there are letters, notes . . .

Mr. Frank. Burn them. All of them.

Miep. Burn *this*?

(*She hands him a paperbound notebook.*)

Mr. Frank (*quietly*). Anne's diary. (*He opens the diary and begins to read.*) "Monday, the sixth of July, nineteen forty-two." (*to* Miep) Nineteen

forty-two. Is it possible, Miep? . . . Only three years ago. (*As he continues his reading, he sits down on the couch.*) "Dear Diary, since you and I are
80 going to be great friends, I will start by telling you about myself. My name is Anne Frank. I am thirteen years old. I was born in Germany the twelfth of June, nineteen twenty-nine. As my family is Jewish, we emigrated to Holland when Hitler came to power."

(*As* Mr. Frank *reads on, another voice joins his, as if coming from the air. It is* Anne's Voice.)

Mr. Frank and Anne. "My father started a business, importing spice and herbs. Things went well for
90 us until nineteen forty. Then the war came, and the Dutch capitulation, followed by the arrival of the Germans. Then things got very bad for the Jews."

(Mr. Frank's Voice *dies out.* Anne's Voice *continues alone. The lights dim slowly to darkness. The curtain falls on the scene.*)

Anne's Voice. You could not do this and you could not do that. They forced Father out of his business. We had to wear yellow stars.[1] I had to
100 turn in my bike. I couldn't go to a Dutch school any more. I couldn't go to the movies, or ride in an automobile, or even on a streetcar, and a million other things. But somehow we children still managed to have fun. Yesterday Father told me we were going into hiding. Where, he wouldn't say. At five o'clock this morning Mother woke me and told me to hurry and get dressed. I was to put on as many clothes as I could. It would look too suspicious if we walked along carrying suitcases.
110 It wasn't until we were on our way that I learned where we were going. Our hiding place was to be upstairs in the building where Father used to have his business. Three other people were coming in with us . . . the Van Daans and their son Peter . . . Father knew the Van Daans but we had never met them . . .

(*During the last lines the curtain rises on the scene. The lights dim on.* Anne's Voice *fades out.*)

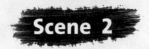

It is early morning, July, 1942. The rooms are
120 *bare, as before, but they are now clean and orderly.*

Mr. Van Daan, *a tall, portly man in his late forties, is in the main room, pacing up and down, nervously smoking a cigarette. His clothes and overcoat are expensive and well cut.*

Mrs. Van Daan *sits on the couch, clutching her possessions, a hatbox, bags, etc. She is a pretty woman in her early forties. She wears a fur coat over her other clothes.*

Peter Van Daan *is standing at the window of the*
130 *room on the right, looking down at the street below. He is a shy, awkward boy of sixteen. He wears a cap, a raincoat, and long Dutch trousers, like "plus fours." At his feet is a black case, a carrier for his cat.*

The yellow Star of David is conspicuous on all of their clothes.

Mrs. Van Daan (*rising, nervous, excited*). Something's happened to them! I know it!

Mr. Van Daan. Now, Kerli!

Mrs. Van Daan. Mr. Frank said they'd be here
140 at seven o'clock. He said . . .

Mr. Van Daan. They have two miles to walk. You can't expect . . .

Mrs. Van Daan. They've been picked up. That's what's happened. They've been taken . . .

(Mr. Van Daan *indicates that he hears someone coming.*)

Mr. Van Daan. You see?

(Peter *takes up his carrier and his schoolbag, etc., and goes into the main room as* Mr. Frank *comes*
150 *up the stairwell from below.* Mr. Frank *looks much younger now. His movements are brisk, his manner confident. He wears an overcoat and carries his hat and a small cardboard box. He crosses to the* Van Daans, *shaking hands with each of them.*)

Mr. Frank. Mrs. Van Daan, Mr. Van Daan, Peter. (*then, in explanation of their lateness*) There were

---

1. **yellow stars:** the six-pointed Stars of David that the Nazis ordered all Jews to wear for identification.

too many of the Green Police[2] on the streets . . . we had to take the long way around.

(*Up the steps come* Margot Frank, Mrs. Frank, Miep [*not pregnant now*] *and* Mr. Kraler. *All of them carry bags, packages, and so forth. The Star of David is conspicuous on all of the* Franks' *clothing.* Margot *is eighteen, beautiful, quiet, shy.* Mrs. Frank *is a young mother, gently bred, reserved. She, like* Mr. Frank, *has a slight German accent.* Mr. Kraler *is a Dutchman, dependable, kindly.*

As Mr. Kraler *and* Miep *go upstage to put down their parcels,* Mrs. Frank *turns back to call* Anne.)

Mrs. Frank. Anne?

(Anne *comes running up the stairs. She is thirteen, quick in her movements, interested in everything, mercurial in her emotions. She wears a cape, long wool socks and carries a schoolbag.*)

Mr. Frank (*introducing them*). My wife, Edith. Mr. and Mrs. Van Daan (Mrs. Frank *hurries over, shaking hands with them.*) . . . their son, Peter . . . my daughters, Margot and Anne.

(Anne *gives a polite little curtsy as she shakes* Mr. Van Daan's *hand. Then she immediately starts off on a tour of investigation of her new home, going upstairs to the attic room.* Miep *and* Mr. Kraler *are putting the various things they have brought on the shelves.*)

Mr. Kraler. I'm sorry there is still so much confusion.

Mr. Frank. Please. Don't think of it. After all, we'll have plenty of leisure to arrange everything ourselves.

Miep (*to* Mrs. Frank). We put the stores of food you sent in here. Your drugs are here . . . soap, linen here.

Mrs. Frank. Thank you, Miep.

Miep. I made up the beds . . . the way Mr. Frank and Mr. Kraler said. (*She starts out.*) Forgive me. I have to hurry. I've got to go to the other side of town to get some ration books[3] for you.

Mrs. Van Daan. Ration books? If they see our names on ration books, they'll know we're here.

Mr. Kraler. There isn't anything . . .

Miep. Don't worry. Your names won't be on them. (*as she hurries out*) I'll be up later. } *Together*

Mr. Frank. Thank you, Miep.

Mrs. Frank (*to* Mr. Kraler). It's illegal, then, the ration books? We've never done anything illegal.

Mr. Frank. We won't be living here exactly according to regulations. (*As* Mr. Kraler *reassures* Mrs. Frank, *he takes various small things, such as matches, soap, etc., from his pockets, handing them to her.*)

Mr. Kraler. This isn't the black market,[4] Mrs. Frank. This is what we call the white market . . . helping all of the hundreds and hundreds who are hiding out in Amsterdam.

(*The carillon is heard playing the quarter-hour before eight.* Mr. Kraler *looks at his watch.* Anne *stops at the window as she comes down the stairs.*)

Anne. It's the Westertoren!

Mr. Kraler. I must go. I must be out of here and downstairs in the office before the workmen get here. (*He starts for the stairs leading out.*) Miep or I, or both of us, will be up each day to bring you food and news and find out what your needs are. Tomorrow I'll get you a better bolt for the door at the foot of the stairs. It needs a bolt that you can throw yourself and open only at our signal. (*to* Mr. Frank) Oh . . . You'll tell them about the noise?

Mr. Frank. I'll tell them.

Mr. Kraler. Good-bye then for the moment. I'll come up again, after the workmen leave.

Mr. Frank. Good-bye, Mr. Kraler.

Mrs. Frank (*shaking his hand*). How can we thank you? (*The others murmur their good-byes.*)

---

2. **Green Police:** the Nazi police who wore green uniforms.

3. **ration books:** books of stamps or coupons issued by the government in wartime. With these coupons, people could purchase scarce items, such as food, clothing, and gasoline.

4. **black market:** a system for selling goods illegally, in violation of rationing and other restrictions.

Mr. Kraler. I never thought I'd live to see the day when a man like Mr. Frank would have to go into hiding. When you think—(*He breaks off, going out. Mr. Frank follows him down the steps, bolting the door after him. In the interval before he returns, Peter goes over to Margot, shaking hands with her. As Mr. Frank comes back up the steps, Mrs. Frank questions him anxiously.*)

240 **Mrs. Frank.** What did he mean, about the noise?

Mr. Frank. First let us take off some of these clothes. (*They all start to take off garment after garment. On each of their coats, sweaters, blouses, suits, dresses, is another yellow Star of David. Mr. and Mrs. Frank are underdressed quite simply. The others wear several things, sweaters, extra dresses, bathrobes, aprons, nightgowns, etc.*)

Mr. Van Daan. It's a wonder we weren't arrested, walking along the streets . . . Petronella with a fur 250 coat in July . . . and that cat of Peter's crying all the way.

Anne (*as she is removing a pair of panties*). A cat?

Mrs. Frank (*shocked*). Anne, please!

Anne. It's all right. I've got on three more. (*She pulls off two more. Finally, as they have all removed their surplus clothes, they look to* Mr. Frank, *waiting for him to speak.*)

Mr. Frank. Now. About the noise. While the men are in the building below, we must have complete 260 quiet. Every sound can be heard down there, not only in the workrooms, but in the offices too. The men come at about eight-thirty, and leave at about five-thirty. So, to be perfectly safe, from eight in the morning until six in the evening we must move only when it is necessary, and then in stockinged feet. We must not speak above a whisper. We must not run any water. We cannot use the sink, or even, forgive me, the w.c.[5] The pipes go down through the workrooms. It would be heard. No 270 trash . . . (*Mr. Frank stops abruptly as he hears the sound of marching feet from the street below. Everyone is motionless, paralyzed with fear. Mr. Frank goes*

quietly into the room on the right to look down out of the window. Anne runs after him, peering out with him. The tramping feet pass without stopping. The tension is relieved. Mr. Frank, followed by Anne, returns to the main room and resumes his instructions to the group.) . . . No trash must ever be thrown out which might reveal that someone is living up 280 here . . . not even a potato paring. We must burn everything in the stove at night. This is the way we must live until it is over, if we are to survive.

(*There is silence for a second.*)

Mrs. Frank. Until it is over.

Mr. Frank (*reassuringly*). After six we can move about . . . we can talk and laugh and have our supper and read and play games . . . just as we would at home. (*He looks at his watch.*) And now I think it would be wise if we all went to our 290 rooms, and were settled before eight o'clock. Mrs. Van Daan, you and your husband will be upstairs. I regret that there's no place up there for Peter. But he will be here, near us. This will be our common room, where we'll meet to talk and eat and read, like one family.

Mr. Van Daan. And where do you and Mrs. Frank sleep?

Mr. Frank. This room is also our bedroom.

Mrs. Van Daan. That isn't right. We'll 300 sleep here and you take the room upstairs. ⎤
⎟ *Together*
Mr. Van Daan. It's your place. ⎦

Mr. Frank. Please. I've thought this out for weeks. It's the best arrangement. The only arrangement.

Mrs. Van Daan (*to* Mr. Frank). Never, never can we thank you. (*then to* Mrs. Frank) I don't know what would have happened to us, if it hadn't been for Mr. Frank.

Mr. Frank. You don't know how your husband 310 helped me when I came to this country . . . knowing no one . . . not able to speak the language. I can never repay him for that. (*going to* Van Daan) May I help you with your things?

---

5. **w.c.:** water closet; toilet.

Mr. Van Daan. No. No. (*to* Mrs. Van Daan) Come along, *liefje.*[6]

Mrs. Van Daan. You'll be all right, Peter? You're not afraid?

Peter (*embarrassed*). Please, Mother.

(*They start up the stairs to the attic room above.*
320 Mr. Frank *turns to* Mrs. Frank.)

Mr. Frank. You too must have some rest, Edith. You didn't close your eyes last night. Nor you, Margot.

Anne. I slept, Father. Wasn't that funny? I knew it was the last night in my own bed, and yet I slept soundly.

Mr. Frank. I'm glad, Anne. Now you'll be able to help me straighten things in here. (*to* Mrs. Frank *and* Margot) Come with me . . . You and Margot rest in this room for the time being. (*He picks up*
330 *their clothes, starting for the room on the right.*)

Mrs. Frank. You're sure . . . ? I could help . . . And Anne hasn't had her milk . . .

Mr. Frank. I'll give it to her. (*to* Anne *and* Peter) Anne, Peter . . . it's best that you take off your shoes now, before you forget. (*He leads the way to the room, followed by* Margot.)

Mrs. Frank. You're sure you're not tired, Anne?

Anne. I feel fine. I'm going to help Father.

Mrs. Frank. Peter, I'm glad you are to be with us.

340 **Peter.** Yes, Mrs. Frank.

(Mrs. Frank *goes to join* Mr. Frank *and* Margot.)

(*During the following scene* Mr. Frank *helps* Margot *and* Mrs. Frank *to hang up their clothes. Then he persuades them both to lie down and rest. The Van Daans in their room above settle themselves. In the main room* Anne *and* Peter *remove their shoes. Peter takes his cat out of the carrier.*)

Anne. What's your cat's name?

Peter. Mouschi.[7]

350 **Anne.** Mouschi! Mouschi! Mouschi! (*She picks up the cat, walking away with it. To* Peter.) I love cats.

I have one . . . a darling little cat. But they made me leave her behind. I left some food and a note for the neighbors to take care of her . . . I'm going to miss her terribly. What is yours? A him or a her?

Peter. He's a tom. He doesn't like strangers.

(*He takes the cat from her, putting it back in its carrier.*)

Anne (__unabashed__). Then I'll have to stop being
360 a stranger, won't I? Is he fixed?

Peter (*startled*). Huh?

Anne. Did you have him fixed?

Peter. No.

Anne. Oh, you ought to have him fixed—to keep him from—you know, fighting. Where did you go to school?

Peter. Jewish Secondary.

Anne. But that's where Margot and I go! I never saw you around.

370 **Peter.** I used to see you . . . sometimes . . .

Anne. You did?

Peter. . . . in the school yard. You were always in the middle of a bunch of kids. (*He takes a penknife from his pocket.*)

Anne. Why didn't you ever come over?

Peter. I'm sort of a lone wolf. (*He starts to rip off his Star of David.*)

Anne. What are you doing?

Peter. Taking it off.

380 **Anne.** But you can't do that. They'll arrest you if you go out without your star.

(*He tosses his knife on the table.*)

Peter. Who's going out?

Anne. Why, of course! You're right! Of course we don't need them any more. (*She picks up his knife and starts to take her star off.*) I wonder what our friends will think when we don't show up today?

Peter. I didn't have any dates with anyone.

---

6. *liefje* (lēf'yə) *Dutch:* little darling.
7. **Mouschi** (mōō'shē)

Anne. Oh, I did. I had a date with Jopie to go and
390 play ping-pong at her house. Do you know Jopie
de Waal?[8]

Peter. No.

Anne. Jopie's my best friend. I wonder what
she'll think when she telephones and there's no
answer? . . . Probably she'll go over to the house . . .
I wonder what she'll think . . . we left everything
as if we'd suddenly been called away . . . breakfast
dishes in the sink . . . beds not made . . . (*As she
pulls off her star, the cloth underneath shows clearly*
400 *the color and form of the star.*) Look! It's still there!
(Peter *goes over to the stove with his star.*) What're
you going to do with yours?

Peter. Burn it.

Anne (*She starts to throw hers in, and cannot.*) It's
funny, I can't throw mine away. I don't know why.

Peter. You can't throw . . . ? Something they
branded you with . . . ? That they made you wear
so they could spit on you?

Anne. I know. I know. But after all, it *is* the Star
410 of David, isn't it?

(*In the bedroom, right,* Margot *and* Mrs. Frank
are lying down. Mr. Frank *starts quietly out.*)

Peter. Maybe it's different for a girl.

(Mr. Frank *comes into the main room.*)

Mr. Frank. Forgive me, Peter. Now let me see.
We must find a bed for your cat. (*He goes to a
cupboard.*) I'm glad you brought your cat. Anne
was feeling so badly about hers. (*getting a used
small washtub*) Here we are. Will it be comfortable
420 in that?

Peter (*gathering up his things*). Thanks.

Mr. Frank (*opening the door of the room on the left*).
And here is your room. But I warn you, Peter, you
can't grow any more. Not an inch, or you'll have
to sleep with your feet out of the skylight. Are you
hungry?

Peter. No.

Mr. Frank. We have some bread and butter.

Peter. No, thank you.

430 **Mr. Frank.** You can have it for luncheon then.
And tonight we will have a real supper . . .
our first supper together.

Peter. Thanks. Thanks.

(*He goes into his room. During the following scene
he arranges his possessions in his new room.*)

Mr. Frank. That's a nice boy, Peter.

Anne. He's awfully shy, isn't he?

Mr. Frank. You'll like him, I know.

Anne. I certainly hope so, since he's the only boy
440 I'm likely to see for months and months.

(Mr. Frank *sits down, taking off his shoes.*)

Mr. Frank. Annele,[9] there's a box there. Will you
open it? (*He indicates a carton on the couch.* Anne
*brings it to the center table. In the street below there
is the sound of children playing.*)

Anne (*as she opens the carton*). You know the way
I'm going to think of it here? I'm going to think
of it as a boarding house. A very peculiar summer
boarding house, like the one that we—(*She breaks
450 off as she pulls out some photographs.*) Father! My
movie stars! I was wondering where they were!
I was looking for them this morning . . . and
Queen Wilhelmina! How wonderful!

Mr. Frank. There's something more. Go on.
Look further. (*He goes over to the sink, pouring
a glass of milk from a thermos bottle.*)

Anne (*pulling out a pasteboard-bound book*).
A diary! (*She throws her arms around her father.*)
I've never had a diary. And I've always longed for
460 one. (*She looks around the room.*) Pencil, pencil,
pencil, pencil. (*She starts down the stairs.*) I'm
going down to the office to get a pencil.

Mr. Frank. Anne! No! (*He goes after her, catching
her by the arm and pulling her back.*)

Anne (*startled*). But there's no one in the
building now.

---

8. **Jopie de Waal** (yō'pē də väl')

9. **Annele/Anneke:** a nickname for Anne.

Mr. Frank. It doesn't matter. I don't want you ever to go beyond that door.

Anne (*sobered*). Never . . . ? Not even at nighttime, when everyone is gone? Or on Sundays? Can't I go down to listen to the radio?

Mr. Frank. Never. I am sorry, Anneke. It isn't safe. No, you must never go beyond that door.

(*For the first time* Anne *realizes what "going into hiding" means.*)

Anne. I see.

Mr. Frank. It'll be hard, I know. But always remember this, Anneke. There are no walls, there are no bolts, no locks that anyone can put on your mind. Miep will bring us books. We will read history, poetry, mythology. (*He gives her the glass of milk.*) Here's your milk. (*With his arm about her, they go over to the couch, sitting down side by side.*) As a matter of fact, between us, Anne, being here has certain advantages for you. For instance, you remember the battle you had with your mother the other day on the subject of overshoes? You said you'd rather die than wear overshoes. But in the end you had to wear them? Well now, you see, for as long as we are here you will never have to wear overshoes! Isn't that good? And the coat that you inherited from Margot, you won't have to wear that any more. And the piano! You won't have to practice on the piano. I tell you, this is going to be a fine life for you!

(Anne's *panic is gone.* Peter *appears in the doorway of his room, with a saucer in his hand. He is carrying his cat.*)

Peter. I . . . I . . . I thought I'd better get some water for Mouschi before . . .

Mr. Frank. Of course.

(*As he starts toward the sink the carillon begins to chime the hour of eight. He tiptoes to the window at the back and looks down at the street below. He turns to* Peter, *indicating in pantomime that it is too late.* Peter *starts back for his room. He steps on a creaking board. The three of them are frozen for a minute in fear. As* Peter *starts away again,* Anne *tiptoes over*

to him and pours some of the milk from her glass into the saucer for the cat. Peter *squats on the floor, putting the milk before the cat.* Mr. Frank *gives* Anne *his fountain pen, and then goes into the room at the right. For a second* Anne *watches the cat, then she goes over to the center table, and opens her diary.*

In the room at the right, Mrs. Frank *has sat up quickly at the sound of the carillon.* Mr. Frank *comes in and sits down beside her on the settee, his arm comfortingly around her.*

Upstairs, in the attic room, Mr. *and* Mrs. Van Daan *have hung their clothes in the closet and are now seated on the iron bed.* Mrs. Van Daan *leans back exhausted.* Mr. Van Daan *fans her with a newspaper.*

Anne *starts to write in her diary. The lights dim out, the curtain falls.*

In the darkness Anne's Voice *comes to us again, faintly at first, and then with growing strength.*)

Anne's Voice. I expect I should be describing what it feels like to go into hiding. But I really don't know yet myself. I only know it's funny never to be able to go outdoors . . . never to breathe fresh air . . . never to run and shout and jump. It's the silence in the nights that frightens me most. Every time I hear a creak in the house, or a step on the street outside, I'm sure they're coming for us. The days aren't so bad. At least we know that Miep and Mr. Kraler are down there below us in the office. Our protectors, we call them. I asked Father what would happen to them if the Nazis found out they were hiding us. Pim said that they would suffer the same fate that we would . . . Imagine! They know this, and yet when they come up here, they're always cheerful and gay as if there were nothing in the world to bother them . . . Friday, the twenty-first of August, nineteen forty-two. Today I'm going to tell you our general news. Mother is unbearable. She insists on treating me like a baby, which I loathe. Otherwise things are going better. The weather is . . .

(*As* Anne's Voice *is fading out, the curtain rises on the scene.*)

Scene 3

It is a little after six o'clock in the evening, two months later.

Margot is in the bedroom at the right, studying. Mr. Van Daan is lying down in the attic room above.

The rest of the "family" is in the main room. Anne and Peter sit opposite each other at the center table, where they have been doing their lessons. Mrs. Frank
560 *is on the couch. Mrs. Van Daan is seated with her fur coat, on which she has been sewing, in her lap. None of them are wearing their shoes.*

Their eyes are on Mr. Frank, waiting for him to give them the signal which will release them from their day-long quiet. Mr. Frank, his shoes in his hand, stands looking down out of the window at the back, watching to be sure that all of the workmen have left the building below.

After a few seconds of motionless silence,
570 Mr. Frank *turns from the window.*

Mr. Frank (*quietly, to the group*). It's safe now. The last workman has left. (*There is an immediate stir of relief.*)

Anne (*Her pent-up energy explodes.*) WHEE!

Mrs. Frank (*startled, amused*). Anne!

Mrs. Van Daan. I'm first for the w.c. (*She hurries off to the bathroom. Mrs. Frank puts on her shoes and starts up to the sink to prepare supper. Anne sneaks Peter's shoes from under the table and hides them*
580 *behind her back. Mr. Frank goes in to Margot's room.*)

Mr. Frank (*to Margot*). Six o'clock. School's over.

(*Margot gets up, stretching. Mr. Frank sits down to put on his shoes. In the main room Peter tries to find his.*)

Peter (*to Anne*). Have you seen my shoes?

Anne (*innocently*). Your shoes?

Peter. You've taken them, haven't you?

Anne. I don't know what you're talking about.

Peter. You're going to be sorry!

590 **Anne.** Am I? (Peter *goes after her.* Anne, *with his shoes in her hand, runs from him, dodging behind her mother.*)

Mrs. Frank (*protesting*). Anne, dear!

Peter. Wait till I get you!

Anne. I'm waiting! (Peter *makes a lunge for her. They both fall to the floor.* Peter *pins her down, wrestling with her to get the shoes.*) Don't! Don't! Peter, stop it. Ouch!

Mrs. Frank. Anne! . . . Peter!

600 (*Suddenly* Peter *becomes self-conscious. He grabs his shoes roughly and starts for his room.*)

Anne (*following him*). Peter, where are you going? Come dance with me.

Peter. I tell you I don't know how.

Anne. I'll teach you.

Peter. I'm going to give Mouschi his dinner.

Anne. Can I watch?

Peter. He doesn't like people around while he eats.

Anne. Peter, please.

610 **Peter.** No! (*He goes into his room.* Anne *slams his door after him.*)

Mrs. Frank. Anne, dear, I think you shouldn't play like that with Peter. It's not dignified.

Anne. Who cares if it's dignified? I don't want to be dignified.

(Mr. Frank *and* Margot *come from the room on the right.* Margot *goes to help her mother.* Mr. Frank *starts for the center table to correct* Margot's *school papers.*)

620 **Mrs. Frank** (*to Anne*). You complain that I don't treat you like a grownup. But when I do, you resent it.

Anne. I only want some fun . . . someone to laugh and clown with . . . After you've sat still all day and hardly moved, you've got to have some fun. I don't know what's the matter with that boy.

Mr. Frank. He isn't used to girls. Give him a little time.

Anne. Time? Isn't two months time? I could cry. 630 (*catching hold of* Margot) Come on, Margot . . . dance with me. Come on, please.

Margot. I have to help with supper.

Anne. You know we're going to forget how to dance . . . When we get out we won't remember a thing.

(*She starts to sing and dance by herself.* Mr. Frank *takes her in his arms, waltzing with her.* Mrs. Van Daan *comes in from the bathroom.*)

Mrs. Van Daan. Next? (*She looks around as she starts* 640 *putting on her shoes.*) Where's Peter?

Anne (*as they are dancing*). Where would he be!

Mrs. Van Daan. He hasn't finished his lessons, has he? His father'll kill him if he catches him in there with that cat and his work not done. (Mr. Frank *and* Anne *finish their dance. They bow to each other with extravagant formality.*) Anne, get him out of there, will you?

Anne (*at* Peter's *door*). Peter? Peter?

Peter (*opening the door a crack*). What is it?

650 **Anne.** Your mother says to come out.

Peter. I'm giving Mouschi his dinner.

Mrs. Van Daan. You know what your father says. (*She sits on the couch, sewing on the lining of her fur coat.*)

Peter. For heaven's sake, I haven't even looked at him since lunch.

Mrs. Van Daan. I'm just telling you, that's all.

Anne. I'll feed him.

Peter. I don't want you in there.

660 **Mrs. Van Daan.** Peter!

Peter (*to* Anne). Then give him his dinner and come right out, you hear? (*He comes back to the table.* Anne *shuts the door of* Peter's *room after her and disappears behind the curtain covering his closet.*)

Mrs. Van Daan (*to* Peter). Now is that any way to talk to your little girl friend?

Peter. Mother . . . for heaven's sake . . . will you please stop saying that?

Mrs. Van Daan. Look at him blush! Look at him!

670 **Peter.** Please! I'm not . . . anyway . . . let me alone, will you?

Mrs. Van Daan. He acts like it was something to be ashamed of. It's nothing to be ashamed of, to have a little girl friend.

Peter. You're crazy. She's only thirteen.

Mrs. Van Daan. So what? And you're sixteen. Just perfect. Your father's ten years older than I am. (*to* Mr. Frank) I warn you, Mr. Frank, if this war lasts much longer, we're going to be related and then . . .

680 **Mr. Frank.** *Mazeltov!*[10]

Mrs. Frank (*deliberately changing the conversation*). I wonder where Miep is. She's usually so prompt.

(*Suddenly everything else is forgotten as they hear the sound of an automobile coming to a screeching stop in the street below. They are tense, motionless in their terror. The car starts away. A wave of relief sweeps over them. They pick up their occupations again.* Anne *flings open the door of* Peter's *room, making a dramatic entrance. She is dressed in* Peter's *clothes.* 690 Peter *looks at her in fury. The others are amused.*)

Anne. Good evening, everyone. Forgive me if I don't stay. (*She jumps up on a chair.*) I have a friend waiting for me in there. My friend Tom. Tom Cat. Some people say that we look alike. But Tom has the most beautiful whiskers, and I have only a little fuzz. I am hoping . . . in time . . .

Peter. All right, Mrs. Quack Quack!

Anne (*outraged—jumping down*). Peter!

Peter. I heard about you . . . How you talked 700 so much in class they called you Mrs. Quack Quack. How Mr. Smitter made you write a composition . . . "'Quack, quack,' said Mrs. Quack Quack."

---

10. **Mazeltov!** (mä′zəl tôf′) *Hebrew:* Congratulations!

Anne. Well, go on. Tell them the rest. How it was so good he read it out loud to the class and then read it to all his other classes!

Peter. Quack! Quack! Quack . . . Quack . . . Quack . . .

(Anne *pulls off the coat and trousers*.)

710 **Anne.** You are the most intolerable, insufferable boy I've ever met!

(*She throws the clothes down the stairwell.* Peter *goes down after them*.)

Peter. Quack, quack, quack!

Mrs. Van Daan (*to* Anne). That's right, Anneke! Give it to him!

Anne. With all the boys in the world . . . Why I had to get locked up with one like you! . . .

Peter. Quack, quack, quack, and from now on stay 720 out of my room!

(*As* Peter *passes her,* Anne *puts out her foot, tripping him. He picks himself up, and goes on into his room*.)

Mrs. Frank (*quietly*). Anne, dear . . . your hair. (*She feels* Anne's *forehead*.) You're warm. Are you feeling all right?

Anne. Please, Mother. (*She goes over to the center table, slipping into her shoes*.)

Mrs. Frank (*following her*). You haven't a fever, have you?

730 **Anne** (*pulling away*). No. No.

Mrs. Frank. You know we can't call a doctor here, ever. There's only one thing to do . . . watch carefully. Prevent an illness before it comes. Let me see your tongue.

Anne. Mother, this is perfectly absurd.

Mrs. Frank. Anne, dear, don't be such a baby. Let me see your tongue. (*As* Anne *refuses,* Mrs. Frank *appeals to* Mr. Frank.) Otto . . . ?

Mr. Frank. You hear your mother, Anne. (Anne 740 *flicks out her tongue for a second, then turns away*.)

Mrs. Frank. Come on—open up! (*as* Anne *opens her mouth very wide*) You seem all right . . . but perhaps an aspirin . . .

Mrs. Van Daan. For heaven's sake, don't give that child any pills. I waited for fifteen minutes this morning for her to come out of the w.c.

Anne. I was washing my hair!

Mr. Frank. I think there's nothing the matter with our Anne that a ride on her bike, or a 750 visit with her friend Jopie de Waal wouldn't cure. Isn't that so, Anne?

(Mr. Van Daan *comes down into the room. From outside we hear faint sounds of bombers going over and a burst of ack-ack*.)

Mr. Van Daan. Miep not come yet?

Mrs. Van Daan. The workmen just left, a little while ago.

Mr. Van Daan. What's for dinner tonight?

Mrs. Van Daan. Beans.

760 **Mr. Van Daan.** Not again!

Mrs. Van Daan. Poor Putti! I know. But what can we do? That's all that Miep brought us.

(Mr. Van Daan *starts to pace, his hands behind his back.* Anne *follows behind him, imitating him*.)

Anne. We are now in what is known as the "bean cycle." Beans boiled, beans en casserole, beans with strings, beans without strings . . .

(Peter *has come out of his room. He slides into his place at the table, becoming immediately absorbed* 770 *in his studies*.)

Mr. Van Daan (*to* Peter). I saw you . . . in there, playing with your cat.

Mrs. Van Daan. He just went in for a second, putting his coat away. He's been out here all the time, doing his lessons.

Mr. Frank (*looking up from the papers*). Anne, you got an excellent in your history paper today . . . and very good in Latin.

Anne (*sitting beside him*). How about algebra?

780 **Mr. Frank.** I'll have to make a confession. Up until now I've managed to stay ahead of you in algebra. Today you caught up with me. We'll leave it to Margot to correct.

Anne. Isn't algebra *vile*, Pim!

Mr. Frank. Vile!

Margot (*to* Mr. Frank). How did I do?

Anne (*getting up*). Excellent, excellent, excellent, excellent!

Mr. Frank (*to* Margot). You should have used the subjunctive here . . .

Margot. Should I? . . . I thought . . . look here . . . I didn't use it here . . . (*The two become absorbed in the papers.*)

Anne. Mrs. Van Daan, may I try on your coat?

Mrs. Frank. No, Anne.

Mrs. Van Daan (*giving it to* Anne). It's all right . . . but careful with it. (Anne *puts it on and struts with it.*) My father gave me that the year before he died. He always bought the best that money could buy.

Anne. Mrs. Van Daan, did you have a lot of boy friends before you were married?

Mrs. Frank. Anne, that's a personal question. It's not courteous to ask personal questions.

Mrs. Van Daan. Oh I don't mind. (*to* Anne) Our house was always swarming with boys. When I was a girl we had . . .

Mr. Van Daan. Oh, God. Not again!

Mrs. Van Daan (*good-humored*). Shut up! (*Without a pause, to* Anne. Mr. Van Daan *mimics* Mrs. Van Daan, *speaking the first few words in unison with her.*) One summer we had a big house in Hilversum. The boys came buzzing round like bees around a jam pot. And when I was sixteen! . . . We were wearing our skirts very short those days and I had good-looking legs. (*She pulls up her skirt, going to* Mr. Frank.) I still have 'em. I may not be as pretty as I used to be, but I still have my legs. How about it, Mr. Frank?

Mr. Van Daan. All right. All right. We see them.

Mrs. Van Daan. I'm not asking you. I'm asking Mr. Frank.

Peter. Mother, for heaven's sake.

Mrs. Van Daan. Oh, I embarrass you, do I? Well, I just hope the girl you marry has as good. (*then to* Anne) My father used to worry about me, with so many boys hanging round. He told me, if any of them gets fresh, you say to him . . . "Remember, Mr. So-and-So, remember I'm a lady."

Anne. "Remember, Mr. So-and-So, remember I'm a lady." (*She gives* Mrs. Van Daan *her coat.*)

Mr. Van Daan. Look at you, talking that way in front of her! Don't you know she puts it all down in that diary?

Mrs. Van Daan. So, if she does? I'm only telling the truth!

(Anne *stretches out, putting her ear to the floor, listening to what is going on below. The sound of the bombers fades away.*)

Mrs. Frank (*setting the table*). Would you mind, Peter, if I moved you over to the couch?

Anne (*listening*). Miep must have the radio on.

(Peter *picks up his papers, going over to the couch beside* Mrs. Van Daan.)

Mr. Van Daan (*accusingly, to* Peter). Haven't you finished yet?

Peter. No.

Mr. Van Daan. You ought to be ashamed of yourself.

Peter. All right. All right. I'm a dunce. I'm a hopeless case. Why do I go on?

Mrs. Van Daan. You're not hopeless. Don't talk that way. It's just that you haven't anyone to help you, like the girls have. (*to* Mr. Frank) Maybe you could help him, Mr. Frank?

Mr. Frank. I'm sure that his father . . . ?

Mr. Van Daan. Not me. I can't do anything with him. He won't listen to me. You go ahead . . . if you want.

Mr. Frank (*going to* Peter). What about it, Peter? Shall we make our school coeducational?

Mrs. Van Daan (*kissing* Mr. Frank). You're an angel, Mr. Frank. An angel. I don't know why I didn't meet you before I met that one there.

Here, sit down, Mr. Frank . . . (*She forces him down on the couch beside* Peter.) Now, Peter, you listen to Mr. Frank.

Mr. Frank. It might be better for us to go into Peter's room. (Peter *jumps up eagerly, leading the way.*)

Mrs. Van Daan. That's right. You go in there, Peter.
870 You listen to Mr. Frank. Mr. Frank is a highly educated man. (*As* Mr. Frank *is about to follow* Peter *into his room,* Mrs. Frank *stops him and wipes the lipstick from his lips. Then she closes the door after them.*)

Anne (*on the floor, listening*). Shh! I can hear a man's voice talking.

Mr. Van Daan (*to* Anne). Isn't it bad enough here without your sprawling all over the place? (Anne *sits up.*)

880 **Mrs. Van Daan** (*to* Mr. Van Daan). If you didn't smoke so much, you wouldn't be so bad-tempered.

Mr. Van Daan. Am I smoking? Do you see me smoking?

Mrs. Van Daan. Don't tell me you've used up all those cigarettes.

Mr. Van Daan. One package. Miep only brought me one package.

Mrs. Van Daan. It's a filthy habit anyway. It's a good time to break yourself.

890 **Mr. Van Daan.** Oh, stop it, please.

Mrs. Van Daan. You're smoking up all our money. You know that, don't you?

Mr. Van Daan. Will you shut up? (*During this,* Mrs. Frank *and* Margot *have studiously kept their eyes down. But* Anne, *seated on the floor, has been following the discussion interestedly.* Mr. Van Daan *turns to see her staring up at him.*) And what are you staring at?

Anne. I never heard grownups quarrel before.
900 I thought only children quarreled.

Mr. Van Daan. This isn't a quarrel! It's a discussion. And I never heard children so rude before.

Anne (*rising,* **_indignantly_**). I, rude!

Mr. Van Daan. Yes!

Mrs. Frank (*quickly*). Anne, will you get me my knitting? (Anne *goes to get it.*) I must remember, when Miep comes, to ask her to bring me some more wool.

Margot (*going to her room*). I need some hairpins
910 and some soap. I made a list. (*She goes into her bedroom to get the list.*)

Mrs. Frank (*to* Anne). Have you some library books for Miep when she comes?

Anne. It's a wonder that Miep has a life of her own, the way we make her run errands for us. Please, Miep, get me some starch. Please take my hair out and have it cut. Tell me all the latest news, Miep.

(*She goes over, kneeling on the couch beside* Mrs. Van Daan.) Did you know she was engaged? His name is Dirk, and Miep's afraid the Nazis will ship him off to Germany to work in one of their war plants. That's what they're doing with some of the young Dutchmen . . . they pick them up off the streets—

Mr. Van Daan (*interrupting*). Don't you ever get tired of talking? Suppose you try keeping still for five minutes. Just five minutes. (*He starts to pace again. Again* Anne *follows him, mimicking him.* Mrs. Frank *jumps up and takes her by the arm up to the sink, and gives her a glass of milk.*)

Mrs. Frank. Come here, Anne. It's time for your glass of milk.

Mr. Van Daan. Talk, talk, talk. I never heard such a child. Where is my . . . ? Every evening it's the same, talk, talk, talk. (*He looks around.*) Where is my . . . ?

Mrs. Van Daan. What're you looking for?

Mr. Van Daan. My pipe. Have you seen my pipe?

Mrs. Van Daan. What good's a pipe? You haven't got any tobacco.

Mr. Van Daan. At least I'll have something to hold in my mouth! (*opening* Margot's *bedroom door*) Margot, have you seen my pipe?

Margot. It was on the table last night. (Anne *puts her glass of milk on the table and picks up his pipe, hiding it behind her back.*)

Mr. Van Daan. I know. I know. Anne, did you see my pipe? . . . Anne!

Mrs. Frank. Anne, Mr. Van Daan is speaking to you.

Anne. Am I allowed to talk now?

Mr. Van Daan. You're the most aggravating . . . The trouble with you is, you've been spoiled. What you need is a good old-fashioned spanking.

Anne (*mimicking* Mrs. Van Daan). "Remember, Mr. So-and-So, remember I'm a lady." (*She thrusts the pipe into his mouth, then picks up her glass of milk.*)

Mr. Van Daan (*restraining himself with difficulty*). Why aren't you nice and quiet like your sister Margot? Why do you have to show off all the time? Let me give you a little advice, young lady. Men don't like that kind of thing in a girl. You know that? A man likes a girl who'll listen to him once in a while . . . a domestic girl, who'll keep her house shining for her husband . . . who loves to cook and sew and . . .

Anne. I'd cut my throat first! I'd open my veins! I'm going to be remarkable! I'm going to Paris . . .

Mr. Van Daan (*scoffingly*). Paris!

Anne. . . . to study music and art.

Mr. Van Daan. Yeah! Yeah!

Anne. I'm going to be a famous dancer or singer . . . or something wonderful. (*She makes a wide gesture, spilling the glass of milk on the fur coat in* Mrs. Van Daan's *lap.* Margot *rushes quickly over with a towel.* Anne *tries to brush the milk off with her skirt.*)

Mrs. Van Daan. Now look what you've done . . . you clumsy little fool! My beautiful fur coat my father gave me . . .

Anne. I'm so sorry.

Mrs. Van Daan. What do you care? It isn't yours . . . So go on, ruin it! Do you know what that coat cost? Do you? And now look at it! Look at it!

Anne. I'm very, very sorry.

Mrs. Van Daan. I could kill you for this. I could just kill you! (Mrs. Van Daan *goes up the stairs, clutching the coat.* Mr. Van Daan *starts after her.*)

Mr. Van Daan. Petronella . . . *liefje! Liefje!* . . . Come back . . . the supper . . . come back!

Mrs. Frank. Anne, you must not behave in that way.

Anne. It was an accident. Anyone can have an accident.

Mrs. Frank. I don't mean that. I mean the answering back. You must not answer back. They are our guests. We must always show the greatest courtesy to them. We're all living under terrible tension. (*She stops as* Margot *indicates that* Van Daan *can hear. When he is gone, she continues.*) That's why we must control ourselves . . . You don't hear Margot getting into arguments with them, do you? Watch Margot. She's always courteous with them. Never familiar. She keeps her distance. And they respect her for it. Try to be like Margot.

Anne. And have them walk all over me, the way they do her? No, thanks!

Mrs. Frank. I'm not afraid that anyone is going to walk all over you, Anne. I'm afraid for other people, that you'll walk on them. I don't know what happens to you, Anne. You are wild, self-willed. If I had ever talked to my mother as you talk to me . . .

Anne. Things have changed. People aren't like that any more. "Yes, Mother." "No, Mother." "Anything you say, Mother." I've got to fight things out for myself! Make something of myself!

Mrs. Frank. It isn't necessary to fight to do it. Margot doesn't fight, and isn't she . . . ?

Anne (*violently rebellious*). Margot! Margot! Margot! That's all I hear from everyone . . . how wonderful Margot is . . . "Why aren't you like Margot?"

Margot (*protesting*). Oh, come on, Anne, don't be so . . .

Anne (*paying no attention*). Everything she does is right, and everything I do is wrong! I'm the goat around here! . . . You're all against me! . . . And you worst of all!

(*She rushes off into her room and throws herself down on the settee, stifling her sobs.* Mrs. Frank *sighs and starts toward the stove.*)

Mrs. Frank (*to* Margot). Let's put the soup on the stove . . . if there's anyone who cares to eat. Margot, will you take the bread out? (Margot *gets the bread from the cupboard.*) I don't know how we can go on living this way . . . I can't say a word to Anne . . . she flies at me . . .

Margot. You know Anne. In half an hour she'll be out here, laughing and joking.

Mrs. Frank. And . . . (*She makes a motion upwards, indicating the* Van Daans.) . . . I told your father it wouldn't work . . . but no . . . no . . . he had to ask them, he said . . . he owed it to him, he said. Well, he knows now that I was right! These quarrels! . . . This bickering!

Margot (*with a warning look*). Shush. Shush.

(*The buzzer for the door sounds.* Mrs. Frank *gasps, startled.*)

Mrs. Frank. Every time I hear that sound, my heart stops!

Margot (*starting for* Peter's *door*). It's Miep. (*She knocks at the door.*) Father?

(Mr. Frank *comes quickly from* Peter's *room.*)

Mr. Frank. Thank you, Margot. (*as he goes down the steps to open the outer door*) Has everyone his list?

Margot. I'll get my books. (*giving her mother a list*) Here's your list. (Margot *goes into her and* Anne's *bedroom on the right.* Anne *sits up, hiding her tears, as* Margot *comes in.*) Miep's here.

(Margot *picks up her books and goes back.* Anne *hurries over to the mirror, smoothing her hair.*)

Mr. Van Daan (*coming down the stairs*). Is it Miep?

Margot. Yes. Father's gone down to let her in.

Mr. Van Daan. At last I'll have some cigarettes!

Mrs. Frank (*to* Mr. Van Daan). I can't tell you how unhappy I am about Mrs. Van Daan's coat. Anne should never have touched it.

Mr. Van Daan. She'll be all right.

Mrs. Frank. Is there anything I can do?

Mr. Van Daan. Don't worry.

(*He turns to meet* Miep. *But it is not* Miep *who comes up the steps. It is* Mr. Kraler, *followed by* Mr. Frank. *Their faces are grave.* Anne *comes from the bedroom.* Peter *comes from his room.*)

Mrs. Frank. Mr. Kraler!

Mr. Van Daan. How are you, Mr. Kraler?

Margot. This is a surprise.

Mrs. Frank. When Mr. Kraler comes, the sun begins to shine.

Mr. Van Daan. Miep is coming?

Mr. Kraler. Not tonight.

(Kraler *goes to* Margot *and* Mrs. Frank *and* Anne, *shaking hands with them.*)

Mrs. Frank. Wouldn't you like a cup of coffee? . . . Or, better still, will you have supper with us?

Mr. Frank. Mr. Kraler has something to talk over with us. Something has happened, he says, which demands an immediate decision.

Mrs. Frank (*fearful*). What is it?

(Mr. Kraler *sits down on the couch. As he talks he takes bread, cabbages, milk, etc., from his briefcase, giving them to* Margot *and* Anne *to put away.*)

Mr. Kraler. Usually, when I come up here, I try to bring you some bit of good news. What's the use of telling you the bad news when there's nothing that you can do about it? But today something has happened . . . Dirk . . . Miep's Dirk, you know, came to me just now. He tells me that he has a Jewish friend living near him. A dentist. He says he's in trouble. He begged me, could I do anything for this man? Could I find him a hiding place? . . . So I've come to you . . . I know it's a terrible thing to ask of you, living as you are, but would you take him in with you?

Mr. Frank. Of course we will.

Mr. Kraler (*rising*). It'll be just for a night or two . . . until I find some other place. This happened so suddenly that I didn't know where to turn.

Mr. Frank. Where is he?

Mr. Kraler. Downstairs in the office.

Mr. Frank. Good. Bring him up.

Mr. Kraler. His name is Dussel . . . Jan Dussel.

Mr. Frank. Dussel . . . I think I know him.

Mr. Kraler. I'll get him. (*He goes quickly down the steps and out.* Mr. Frank *suddenly becomes conscious of the others.*)

Mr. Frank. Forgive me. I spoke without consulting you. But I knew you'd feel as I do.

Mr. Van Daan. There's no reason for you to consult anyone. This is your place. You have a right to do exactly as you please. The only thing I feel . . . there's so little food as it is . . . and to take in another person . . .

(Peter *turns away, ashamed of his father.*)

Mr. Frank. We can stretch the food a little. It's only for a few days.

Mr. Van Daan. You want to make a bet?

Mrs. Frank. I think it's fine to have him. But, Otto, where are you going to put him? Where?

Peter. He can have my bed. I can sleep on the floor. I wouldn't mind.

Mr. Frank. That's good of you, Peter. But your room's too small . . . even for *you*.

Anne. I have a much better idea. I'll come in here with you and Mother, and Margot can take Peter's room and Peter can go in our room with Mr. Dussel.

Margot. That's right. We could do that.

Mr. Frank. No, Margot. You mustn't sleep in that room . . . neither you nor Anne. Mouschi has caught some rats in there. Peter's brave. He doesn't mind.

Anne. Then how about *this?* I'll come in here with you and Mother, and Mr. Dussel can have my bed.

Mrs. Frank. No. No. *No!* Margot will come in here with us and he can have her bed. It's the only way. Margot, bring your things in here. Help her, Anne.

(Margot *hurries into her room to get her things.*)

Anne (*to her mother*). Why Margot? Why can't I come in here?

Mrs. Frank. Because it wouldn't be proper for Margot to sleep with a . . . Please, Anne. Don't argue. Please. (Anne *starts slowly away.*)

Mr. Frank. (*to* Anne). You don't mind sharing your room with Mr. Dussel, do you, Anne?

Anne. No. No, of course not.

Mr. Frank. Good. (Anne *goes off into her bedroom,* 1160 *helping* Margot. Mr. Frank *starts to search in the cupboards.*) Where's the cognac?

Mrs. Frank. It's there. But, Otto, I was saving it in case of illness.

Mr. Frank. I think we couldn't find a better time to use it. Peter, will you get five glasses for me?

(Peter *goes for the glasses.* Margot *comes out of her bedroom, carrying her possessions, which she hangs behind a curtain in the main room.* Mr. Frank *finds the cognac and pours it into the five* 1170 *glasses that* Peter *brings him.* Mr. Van Daan *stands looking on sourly.* Mrs. Van Daan *comes downstairs and looks around at all the bustle.*)

Mrs. Van Daan. What's happening? What's going on?

Mr. Van Daan. Someone's moving in with us.

Mrs. Van Daan. In here? You're joking.

Margot. It's only for a night or two . . . until Mr. Kraler finds him another place.

Mr. Van Daan. Yeah! Yeah!

1180 (Mr. Frank *hurries over as* Mr. Kraler *and* Dussel *come up.* Dussel *is a man in his late fifties, meticulous, finicky . . . bewildered now. He wears a raincoat. He carries a briefcase, stuffed full, and a small medicine case.*)

Mr. Frank. Come in, Mr. Dussel.

Mr. Kraler. This is Mr. Frank.

Dussel. Mr. Otto Frank?

Mr. Frank. Yes. Let me take your things. (*He takes the hat and briefcase, but* Dussel *clings* 1190 *to his medicine case.*) This is my wife Edith . . .

Mr. and Mrs. Van Daan . . . their son, Peter . . . and my daughters, Margot and Anne. (Dussel *shakes hands with everyone.*)

Mr. Kraler. Thank you, Mr. Frank. Thank you all. Mr. Dussel, I leave you in good hands. Oh . . . Dirk's coat.

(Dussel *hurriedly takes off the raincoat, giving it to* Mr. Kraler. *Underneath is his white dentist's jacket, with a yellow Star of David on it.*)

1200 **Dussel** (*to* Mr. Kraler). What can I say to thank you . . . ?

Mrs. Frank (*to* Dussel). Mr. Kraler and Miep . . . They're our life line. Without them we couldn't live.

Mr. Kraler. Please. Please. You make us seem very heroic. It isn't that at all. We simply don't like the Nazis. (*to* Mr. Frank, *who offers him a drink*) No, thanks. (*then going on*) We don't like their methods. We don't like . . .

1210 **Mr. Frank** (*smiling*). I know. I know. "No one's going to tell us Dutchmen what to do with our damn Jews!"

Mr. Kraler (*to* Dussel). Pay no attention to Mr. Frank. I'll be up tomorrow to see that they're treating you right. (*to* Mr. Frank) Don't trouble to come down again. Peter will bolt the door after me, won't you, Peter?

Peter. Yes, sir.

Mr. Frank. Thank you, Peter. I'll do it.

1220 **Mr. Kraler.** Good night. Good night.

Group. Good night, Mr. Kraler. We'll see you tomorrow, (*etc., etc.*)

(Mr. Kraler *goes out with* Mr. Frank. Mrs. Frank *gives each one of the "grownups" a glass of cognac.*)

Mrs. Frank. Please, Mr. Dussel, sit down.

(Mr. Dussel *sinks into a chair.* Mrs. Frank *gives him a glass of cognac.*)

Dussel. I'm dreaming. I know it. I can't believe my eyes. Mr. Otto Frank here! (*to* Mrs. Frank)
1230 You're not in Switzerland then? A woman told

me . . . She said she'd gone to your house . . . the door was open, everything was in disorder, dishes in the sink. She said she found a piece of paper in the wastebasket with an address scribbled on it . . . an address in Zurich. She said you must have escaped to Zurich.

Anne. Father put that there purposely . . . just so people would think that very thing!

Dussel. And you've been here all the time?

1240 **Mrs. Frank.** All the time . . . ever since July.

(Anne *speaks to her father as he comes back.*)

Anne. It worked, Pim . . . the address you left! Mr. Dussel says that people believe we escaped to Switzerland.

Mr. Frank. I'm glad . . . And now let's have a little drink to welcome Mr. Dussel. (*Before they can drink,* Mr. Dussel *bolts his drink.* Mr. Frank *smiles and raises his glass.*) To Mr. Dussel. Welcome. We're very honored to have you with us.

1250 **Mrs. Frank.** To Mr. Dussel, welcome.

(*The* Van Daans *murmur a welcome. The "grown-ups" drink.*)

Mrs. Van Daan. Um. That was good.

Mr. Van Daan. Did Mr. Kraler warn you that you won't get much to eat here? You can imagine . . . three ration books among the seven of us . . . and now you make eight.

(Peter *walks away, humiliated. Outside a street organ is heard dimly.*)

1260 **Dussel** (*rising*). Mr. Van Daan, you don't realize what is happening outside that you should warn me of a thing like that. You don't realize what's going on . . . (*As* Mr. Van Daan *starts his characteristic pacing,* Dussel *turns to speak to the others.*) Right here in Amsterdam every day hundreds of Jews disappear . . . They surround a block and search house by house. Children come home from school to find their parents gone. Hundreds are being deported . . . people
1270 that you and I know . . . the Hallensteins . . . the Wessels . . .

Mrs. Frank (*in tears*). Oh, no. No!

Dussel. They get their call-up notice . . . come to the Jewish theatre on such and such a day and hour . . . bring only what you can carry in a rucksack. And if you refuse the call-up notice, then they come and drag you from your home and ship you off to Mauthausen.[11] The death camp!

1280 **Mrs. Frank.** We didn't know that things had got so much worse.

Dussel. Forgive me for speaking so.

Anne (*coming to* Dussel). Do you know the de Waals? . . . What's become of them? Their daughter Jopie and I are in the same class. Jopie's my best friend.

Dussel. They are gone.

Anne. Gone?

Dussel. With all the others.

1290 **Anne.** Oh, no. Not Jopie!

(*She turns away, in tears.* Mrs. Frank *motions to* Margot *to comfort her.* Margot *goes to* Anne, *putting her arms comfortingly around her.*)

Mrs. Van Daan. There were some people called Wagner. They lived near us . . . ?

Mr. Frank (*interrupting, with a glance at* Anne). I think we should put this off until later. We all have many questions we want to ask . . . But I'm sure that Mr. Dussel would like to get settled 1300 before supper.

Dussel. Thank you. I would. I brought very little with me.

Mr. Frank (*giving him his hat and briefcase*). I'm sorry we can't give you a room alone. But I hope you won't be too uncomfortable. We've had to make strict rules here . . . a schedule of hours . . . We'll tell you after supper. Anne, would you like to take Mr. Dussel to his room?

Anne (*controlling her tears*). If you'll come with 1310 me, Mr. Dussel? (*She starts for her room.*)

Dussel (*shaking hands with each in turn*). Forgive me if I haven't really expressed my gratitude to all of you. This has been such a shock to me. I'd always thought of myself as Dutch. I was born in Holland. My father was born in Holland, and my grandfather. And now . . . after all these years . . . (*He breaks off.*) If you'll excuse me.

(Dussel *gives a little bow and hurries off after* Anne. Mr. Frank *and the others are subdued.*)

1320 **Anne** (*turning on the light*). Well, here we are.

(Dussel *looks around the room. In the main room* Margot *speaks to her mother.*)

Margot. The news sounds pretty bad, doesn't it? It's so different from what Mr. Kraler tells us. Mr. Kraler says things are improving.

Mr. Van Daan. I like it better the way Kraler tells it.

(*They resume their occupations, quietly.* Peter *goes off into his room. In* Anne's *room,* Anne *turns to* Dussel.)

1330 **Anne.** You're going to share the room with me.

Dussel. I'm a man who's always lived alone. I haven't had to adjust myself to others. I hope you'll bear with me until I learn.

Anne. Let me help you. (*She takes his briefcase.*) Do you always live all alone? Have you no family at all?

Dussel. No one. (*He opens his medicine case and spreads his bottles on the dressing table.*)

Anne. How dreadful. You must be terribly lonely.

1340 **Dussel.** I'm used to it.

Anne. I don't think I could ever get used to it. Didn't you even have a pet? A cat, or a dog?

Dussel. I have an allergy for fur-bearing animals. They give me asthma.

Anne. Oh, dear. Peter has a cat.

Dussel. Here? He has it here?

Anne. Yes. But we hardly ever see it. He keeps it in his room all the time. I'm sure it will be all right.

---

11. **Mauthausen** (mout'hou'zən): a Nazi concentration camp in Austria.

Dussel. Let us hope so.

1350 (*He takes some pills to **fortify** himself.*)

Anne. That's Margot's bed, where you're going to sleep. I sleep on the sofa there. (*indicating the clothes hooks on the wall*) We cleared these off for your things. (*She goes over to the window.*) The best part about this room . . . you can look down and see a bit of the street and the canal. There's a houseboat . . . you can see the end of it . . . a bargeman lives there with his family . . . They have a baby and he's just beginning to walk and
1360 I'm so afraid he's going to fall into the canal some day. I watch him . . .

Dussel (*interrupting*). Your father spoke of a schedule.

Anne (*coming away from the window*). Oh, yes. It's mostly about the times we have to be quiet. And times for the w.c. You can use it now if you like.

Dussel (*stiffly*). No, thank you.

Anne. I suppose you think it's awful, my talking about a thing like that. But you don't know
1370 how important it can get to be, especially when you're frightened . . . About this room, the way Margot and I did . . . she had it to herself in the afternoons for studying, reading . . . lessons, you know . . . and I took the mornings. Would that be all right with you?

Dussel. I'm not at my best in the morning.

Anne. You stay here in the mornings then. I'll take the room in the afternoons.

Dussel. Tell me, when you're in here, what
1380 happens to me? Where am I spending my time? In there, with all the people?

Anne. Yes.

Dussel. I see. I see.

Anne. We have supper at half past six.

Dussel (*going over to the sofa*). Then, if you don't mind . . . I like to lie down quietly for ten minutes before eating. I find it helps the digestion.

Anne. Of course. I hope I'm not going to be too much of a bother to you. I seem to be able to get
1390 everyone's back up.

(Dussel *lies down on the sofa, curled up, his back to her.*)

Dussel. I always get along very well with children. My patients all bring their children to me, because they know I get on well with them. So don't you worry about that.

(Anne *leans over him, taking his hand and shaking it gratefully.*)

Anne. Thank you. Thank you, Mr. Dussel.

1400 (*The lights dim to darkness. The curtain falls on the scene.* Anne's Voice *comes to us faintly at first, and then with increasing power.*)

Anne's Voice. . . . And yesterday I finished Cissy Van Marxvelt's latest book. I think she is a first-class writer. I shall definitely let my children read her. Monday the twenty-first of September, nineteen forty-two. Mr. Dussel and I had another battle yesterday. Yes, Mr. Dussel! According to him, nothing, I repeat . . .
1410 nothing, is right about me . . . my appearance, my character, my manners. While he was going on at me I thought . . . sometime I'll give you such a smack that you'll fly right up to the ceiling! Why is it that every grownup thinks he knows the way to bring up children? Particularly the grownups that never had any. I keep wishing that Peter was a girl instead of a boy. Then I would have someone to talk to. Margot's a darling, but she takes everything too seriously.
1420 To pause for a moment on the subject of Mrs. Van Daan. I must tell you that her attempts to flirt with Father are getting her nowhere. Pim, thank goodness, won't play.

(*As she is saying the last lines, the curtain rises on the darkened scene.* Anne's Voice *fades out.*)

It is the middle of the night, several months later. The stage is dark except for a little light which comes through the skylight in Peter's *room.*

Everyone is in bed. Mr. *and* Mrs. Frank *lie on* 1430 *the couch in the main room, which has been pulled out to serve as a makeshift double bed.*

Margot *is sleeping on a mattress on the floor in the main room, behind a curtain stretched across for privacy. The others are all in their accustomed rooms.*

From outside we hear two drunken soldiers singing "Lili Marlene." A girl's high giggle is heard. The sound of running feet is heard coming closer and then fading in the distance. Throughout the 1440 *scene there is the distant sound of airplanes passing overhead.*

A match suddenly flares up in the attic. We dimly see Mr. Van Daan. *He is getting his bearings. He comes quickly down the stairs, and goes to the cupboard where the food is stored. Again the match flares up, and is as quickly blown out. The dim figure is seen to steal back up the stairs.*

There is quiet for a second or two, broken only by the sound of airplanes, and running feet on the 1450 *street below.*

Suddenly, out of the silence and the dark, we hear Anne *scream.*

Anne (*screaming*). No! No! Don't . . . don't take me!

(*She moans, tossing and crying in her sleep. The other people wake, terrified.* Dussel *sits up in bed, furious.*)

Dussel. Shush! Anne! Anne, for God's sake, shush!

Anne (*still in her nightmare*). Save me! Save me!

(*She screams and screams.* Dussel *gets out of bed,* 1460 *going over to her, trying to wake her.*)

Dussel. For God's sake! Quiet! Quiet! You want someone to hear?

(*In the main room* Mrs. Frank *grabs a shawl and pulls it around her. She rushes in to* Anne, *taking her in her arms.* Mr. Frank *hurriedly gets up, putting on his overcoat.* Margot *sits up, terrified.* Peter's *light goes on in his room.*)

Mrs. Frank (*to* Anne, *in her room*). Hush, darling, hush. It's all right. It's all right. (*over her shoulder* 1470 *to* Dussel) Will you be kind enough to turn on the light, Mr. Dussel? (*back to* Anne) It's nothing, my darling. It was just a dream.

(Dussel *turns on the light in the bedroom.* Mrs. Frank *holds* Anne *in her arms. Gradually* Anne *comes out of her nightmare, still trembling with horror.* Mr. Frank *comes into the room, and goes quickly to the window, looking out to be sure that no one outside had heard* Anne's *screams.* Mrs. Frank *holds* Anne, *talking softly to her. In* 1480 *the main room* Margot *stands on a chair, turning on the center hanging lamp. A light goes on in the* Van Daan's *room overhead.* Peter *puts his robe on, coming out of his room.*)

Dussel (*to* Mrs. Frank, *blowing his nose*). Something must be done about that child, Mrs. Frank. Yelling like that! Who knows but there's somebody on the streets? She's endangering all our lives.

Mrs. Frank. Anne, darling.

Dussel. Every night she twists and turns. I don't 1490 sleep. I spend half my night shushing her. And now it's nightmares!

(Margot *comes to the door of* Anne's *room, followed by* Peter. Mr. Frank *goes to them, indicating that everything is all right.* Peter *takes* Margot *back.*)

Mrs. Frank (*to* Anne). You're here, safe, you see? Nothing has happened. (*to* Dussel) Please, Mr. Dussel, go back to bed. She'll be herself in a minute or two. Won't you, Anne?

Dussel (*picking up a book and a pillow*). Thank 1500 you, but I'm going to the w.c. The one place where there's peace! (*He stalks out.* Mr. Van Daan, *in underwear and trousers, comes down the stairs.*)

Mr. Van Daan (*to* Dussel). What is it? What happened?

Dussel. A nightmare. She was having a nightmare!

Mr. Van Daan. I thought someone was murdering her.

Dussel. Unfortunately, no.

(*He goes into the bathroom. Mr. Van Daan* goes
1510 *back up the stairs. Mr. Frank, in the main room, sends* Peter *back to his own bedroom.*)

Mr. Frank. Thank you, Peter. Go back to bed.

(Peter *goes back to his room. Mr. Frank* follows him, *turning out the light and looking out the window. Then he goes back to the main room, and gets up on a chair, turning out the center hanging lamp.*)

Mrs. Frank (*to* Anne). Would you like some water? (Anne *shakes her head.*) Was it a very bad dream? Perhaps if you told me . . . ?

1520 **Anne.** I'd rather not talk about it.

Mrs. Frank. Poor darling. Try to sleep then. I'll sit right here beside you until you fall asleep. (*She brings a stool over, sitting there.*)

Anne. You don't have to.

Mrs. Frank. But I'd like to stay with you . . . very much. Really.

Anne. I'd rather you didn't.

Mrs. Frank. Good night, then. (*She leans down to kiss* Anne. Anne *throws her arm up over her face,*
1530 *turning away.* Mrs. Frank, *hiding her hurt, kisses* Anne*'s arm.*) You'll be all right? There's nothing that you want?

Anne. Will you please ask Father to come.

Mrs. Frank (*after a second*). Of course, Anne dear. (*She hurries out into the other room.* Mr. Frank *comes to her as she comes in.*) *Sie verlangt nach Dir!*[12]

Mr. Frank (*sensing her hurt*). Edith, *Liebe, schau . . .*[13]

Mrs. Frank. *Es macht nichts! Ich danke dem lieben*
1540 *Herrgott, dass sie sich wenigstens an Dich wendet, wenn sie Trost braucht! Geh hinein, Otto, sie ist ganz hysterisch vor Angst.*[14] (*as* Mr. Frank *hesitates*) *Geh zu ihr.*[15] (*He looks at her for a second and then goes to get a cup of water for* Anne. Mrs. Frank *sinks down on the bed, her face in her hands, trying to keep from sobbing aloud.* Margot *comes over to her, putting her arms around her.*) She wants nothing of me. She pulled away when I leaned down to kiss her.

Margot. It's a phase . . . You heard Father . . .
1550 Most girls go through it . . . they turn to their fathers at this age . . . they give all their love to their fathers.

Mrs. Frank. You weren't like this. You didn't shut me out.

Margot. She'll get over it . . . (*She smooths the bed for* Mrs. Frank *and sits beside her a moment as* Mrs. Frank *lies down. In* Anne*'s room* Mr. Frank *comes in, sitting down by* Anne. Anne *flings her arms around him, clinging to him. In the distance*
1560 *we hear the sound of ack-ack.*)

Anne. Oh, Pim. I dreamed that they came to get us! The Green Police! They broke down the door and grabbed me and started to drag me out the way they did Jopie.

Mr. Frank. I want you to take this pill.

Anne. What is it?

Mr. Frank. Something to quiet you.

(*She takes it and drinks the water. In the main room* Margot *turns out the light and goes back*
1570 *to her bed.*)

Mr. Frank (*to* Anne). Do you want me to read to you for a while?

---

12. **Sie verlangt nach Dir** (zē fer-längt′ näкн dîr) *German*: She is asking for you.

13. **Liebe, schau** (lē′bə shou′) *German*: Dear, look.

14. **Es macht . . . vor Angst** (ĕs mäкнt′ nĭ́кнts′! ĭ́кн dängk′ə dām lē′bən hĕr′gôt′, däs zē zĭ́кн vān′ĭ́кн-shtənz än dĭ́кн′ vĕn′dət, vĕn zē trôst′ brouкнt′! gā hĭn-īn′, ôt′tô, zē ĭst gänts hü-stĕr′ĭ́sh fôr ängst′) *German*: It's all right. I thank dear God that at least she turns to you when she needs comfort. Go in, Otto; she is hysterical with fear.

15. **Geh zu ihr** (gā′ tsōō îr′) *German*: Go to her.

Anne. No. Just sit with me for a minute. Was I awful? Did I yell terribly loud? Do you think anyone outside could have heard?

Mr. Frank. No. No. Lie quietly now. Try to sleep.

Anne. I'm a terrible coward. I'm so disappointed in myself. I think I've conquered my fear . . . I think I'm really grown-up . . . and then something happens . . . and I run to you like a baby . . . I love you, Father. I don't love anyone but you.

Mr. Frank (*reproachfully*). Annele!

Anne. It's true. I've been thinking about it for a long time. You're the only one I love.

Mr. Frank. It's fine to hear you tell me that you love me. But I'd be happier if you said you loved your mother as well . . . She needs your help so much . . . your love . . .

Anne. We have nothing in common. She doesn't understand me. Whenever I try to explain my views on life to her she asks me if I'm constipated.

Mr. Frank. You hurt her very much just now. She's crying. She's in there crying.

Anne. I can't help it. I only told the truth. I didn't want her here . . . (*then, with sudden change*) Oh, Pim, I was horrible, wasn't I? And the worst of it is, I can stand off and look at myself doing it and know it's cruel and yet I can't stop doing it. What's the matter with me? Tell me. Don't say it's just a phase! Help me.

Mr. Frank. There is so little that we parents can do to help our children. We can only try to set a good example . . . point the way. The rest you must do yourself. You must build your own character.

Anne. I'm trying. Really I am. Every night I think back over all of the things I did that day that were wrong . . . like putting the wet mop in Mr. Dussel's bed . . . and this thing now with Mother. I say to myself, that was wrong. I make up my mind, I'm never going to do that again. Never!

Of course I may do something worse . . . but at least I'll never do *that* again! . . . I have a nicer side, Father . . . a sweeter, nicer side. But I'm scared to show it. I'm afraid that people are going to laugh at me if I'm serious. So the mean Anne comes to the outside and the good Anne stays on the inside, and I keep on trying to switch them around and have the good Anne outside and the bad Anne inside and be what I'd like to be . . . and might be . . . if only . . . only . . . (*She is asleep. Mr. Frank watches her for a moment and then turns off the light, and starts out. The lights dim out. The curtain falls on the scene.* Anne's Voice *is heard dimly at first, and then with growing strength.*)

Anne's Voice. . . . The air raids are getting worse. They come over day and night. The noise is terrifying. Pim says it should be music to our ears. The more planes, the sooner will come the end of the war. Mrs. Van Daan pretends to be a fatalist. What will be, will be. But when the planes come over, who is the most frightened? No one else but Petronella! . . . Monday, the ninth of November, nineteen forty-two. Wonderful news! The Allies have landed in Africa. Pim says that we can look for an early finish to the war. Just for fun he asked each of us what was the first thing we wanted to do when we got out of here. Mrs. Van Daan longs to be home with her own things, her needle-point chairs, the Beckstein piano her father gave her . . . the best that money could buy. Peter would like to go to a movie. Mr. Dussel wants to get back to his dentist's drill. He's afraid he is losing his touch. For myself, there are so many things . . . to ride a bike again . . . to laugh till my belly aches . . . to have new clothes from the skin out . . . to have a hot tub filled to overflowing and wallow in it for hours . . . to be back in school with my friends . . .

(*As the last lines are being said, the curtain rises on the scene. The lights dim on as* Anne's Voice *fades away.*)

Scene 5

It is the first night of the Hanukkah[16] celebration. Mr. Frank is standing at the head of the table on which is the Menorah.[17] He lights the Shamos, or servant candle, and holds it as he says the blessing. Seated listening is all of the "family," dressed in their best. The men wear hats, Peter *wears his cap.*

Mr. Frank (*reading from a prayer book*). "Praised be Thou, oh Lord our God, Ruler of the universe, who has sanctified us with Thy commandments
1660 and bidden us kindle the Hanukkah lights. Praised be Thou, oh Lord our God, Ruler of the universe, who has wrought wondrous deliverances for our fathers in days of old. Praised be Thou, oh Lord our God, Ruler of the universe, that Thou has given us life and sustenance and brought us to this happy season." (Mr. Frank *lights the one candle of the Menorah as he continues.*) "We kindle this Hanukkah light to celebrate the great and wonderful deeds wrought through
1670 the zeal with which God filled the hearts of the heroic Maccabees, two thousand years ago. They fought against indifference, against tyranny and oppression, and they restored our Temple to us. May these lights remind us that we should ever look to God, whence cometh our help." Amen. [Pronounced O-mayn.]

All. Amen.

(Mr. Frank *hands* Mrs. Frank *the prayer book.*)

Mrs. Frank (*reading*). "I lift up mine eyes unto
1680 the mountains, from whence cometh my help. My help cometh from the Lord who made heaven and earth. He will not suffer thy foot to be moved. He that keepeth thee will not slumber. He that keepeth Israel doth neither slumber nor sleep. The Lord is thy keeper. The Lord is thy shade upon thy right hand. The sun shall not smite thee by day,

nor the moon by night. The Lord shall keep thee from all evil. He shall keep thy soul. The Lord shall guard thy going out and thy coming in, from this
1690 time forth and forevermore." Amen.

All. Amen.

(Mrs. Frank *puts down the prayer book and goes to get the food and wine.* Margot *helps her.* Mr. Frank *takes the men's hats and puts them aside.*)

Dussel (*rising*). That was very moving.

Anne (*pulling him back*). It isn't over yet!

Mrs. Van Daan. Sit down! Sit down!

Anne. There's a lot more, songs and presents.

Dussel. Presents?

1700 **Mrs. Frank.** Not this year, unfortunately.

Mrs. Van Daan. But always on Hanukkah everyone gives presents . . . everyone!

Dussel. Like our St. Nicholas' Day.[18] (*There is a chorus of "no's" from the group.*)

Mrs. Van Daan. No! Not like St. Nicholas! What kind of a Jew are you that you don't know Hanukkah?

Mrs. Frank (*as she brings the food*). I remember particularly the candles . . . First one, as we have
1710 tonight. Then the second night you light two candles, the next night three . . . and so on until you have eight candles burning. When there are eight candles it is truly beautiful.

Mrs. Van Daan. And the potato pancakes.

Mr. Van Daan. Don't talk about them!

Mrs. Van Daan. I make the best *latkes*[19] you ever tasted!

Mrs. Frank. Invite us all next year . . . in your own home.

1720 **Mr. Frank.** God willing!

Mrs. Van Daan. God willing.

---

16. **Hanukkah** (hä'nə-kə): a Jewish holiday, celebrated in December and lasting eight days.

17. **Menorah** (mə-nôr'ə): a candleholder with nine branches, used in the celebration of Hanukkah.

18. **St. Nicholas's Day:** December 6, the day that Christian children in the Netherlands receive gifts.

19. **latkes** (lät'kəz): potato pancakes.

Margot. What I remember best is the presents we used to get when we were little . . . eight days of presents . . . and each day they got better and better.

Mrs. Frank (*sitting down*). We are all here, alive. That is present enough.

Anne. No, it isn't. I've got something . . .

(*She rushes into her room, hurriedly puts on a little* 1730 *hat improvised from the lamp shade, grabs a satchel bulging with parcels and comes running back.*)

Mrs. Frank. What is it?

Anne. Presents!

Mrs. Van Daan. Presents!

Dussel. Look!

Mr. Van Daan. What's she got on her head?

Peter. A lamp shade!

Anne (*She picks out one at random*). This is for Margot. (*She hands it to* Margot, *pulling her to* 1740 *her feet.*) Read it out loud.

Margot (*reading*).

"You have never lost your temper.
You never will, I fear,
You are so good.
But if you should,
Put all your cross words here."

(*She tears open the package.*)

A new crossword puzzle book! Where did you get it?

1750 **Anne.** It isn't new. It's one that you've done. But I rubbed it all out, and if you wait a little and forget, you can do it all over again.

Margot (*sitting*). It's wonderful, Anne. Thank you. You'd never know it wasn't new.

(*From outside we hear the sound of a streetcar passing.*)

Anne (*with another gift*). Mrs. Van Daan.

Mrs. Van Daan (*taking it*). This is awful . . . I haven't anything for anyone . . . I never 1760 thought . . .

Mr. Frank. This is all Anne's idea.

Mrs. Van Daan (*holding up a bottle*). What is it?

Anne. It's hair shampoo. I took all the odds and ends of soap and mixed them with the last of my toilet water.

Mrs. Van Daan. Oh, Anneke!

Anne. I wanted to write a poem for all of them, but I didn't have time. (*offering a large box to* Mr. Van Daan) Yours, Mr. Van Daan, is *really* 1770 something . . . something you want more than anything. (*as she waits for him to open it*) Look! Cigarettes!

Mr. Van Daan. Cigarettes!

Anne. Two of them! Pim found some old pipe tobacco in the pocket lining of his coat . . . and we made them . . . or rather, Pim did.

Mrs. Van Daan. Let me see . . . Well, look at that! Light it, Putti! Light it.

(Mr. Van Daan *hesitates.*)

1780 **Anne.** It's tobacco, really it is! There's a little fluff in it, but not much.

(*Everyone watches intently as* Mr. Van Daan *cautiously lights it. The cigarette flares up. Everyone laughs.*)

Peter. It works!

Mrs. Van Daan. Look at him.

Mr. Van Daan (*spluttering*). Thank you, Anne. Thank you.

(Anne *rushes back to her satchel for another* 1790 *present.*)

Anne (*handing her mother a piece of paper*). For Mother, Hanukkah greeting. (*She pulls her mother to her feet.*)

Mrs. Frank (*She reads.*) "Here's an I.O.U. that I promise to pay. Ten hours of doing whatever you say. Signed, Anne Frank." (Mrs. Frank, *touched, takes* Anne *in her arms, holding her close.*)

Dussel (*to* Anne). Ten hours of doing what you're told? *Anything* you're told?

1800 **Anne.** That's right.

Dussel. You wouldn't want to sell that, Mrs. Frank?

Mrs. Frank. Never! This is the most precious gift I've ever had!

(*She sits, showing her present to the others.* Anne *hurries back to the satchel and pulls out a scarf, the scarf that* Mr. Frank *found in the first scene.*)

Anne (*offering it to her father*). For Pim.

Mr. Frank. Anneke . . . I wasn't supposed to have 1810 a present! (*He takes it, unfolding it and showing it to the others.*)

Anne. It's a muffler . . . to put round your neck . . . like an ascot, you know. I made it myself out of odds and ends . . . I knitted it in the dark each night, after I'd gone to bed. I'm afraid it looks better in the dark!

Mr. Frank (*putting it on*). It's fine. It fits me perfectly. Thank you, Annele.

(Anne *hands* Peter *a ball of paper, with a string* 1820 *attached to it.*)

Anne. That's for Mouschi.

Peter (*rising to bow*). On behalf of Mouschi, I thank you.

Anne (*hesitant, handing him a gift*). And . . . this is yours . . . from Mrs. Quack Quack. (*as he holds it gingerly in his hands*) Well . . . open it . . . Aren't you going to open it?

Peter. I'm scared to. I know something's going to jump out and hit me.

1830 **Anne.** No. It's nothing like that, really.

Mrs. Van Daan (*as he is opening it*). What is it, Peter? Go on. Show it.

Anne (*excitedly*). It's a safety razor!

Dussel. A what?

Anne. A razor!

Mrs. Van Daan (*looking at it*). You didn't make that out of odds and ends.

Anne (*to Peter*). Miep got it for me. It's not new. It's second-hand. But you really do need a razor

1840 now.

Dussel. For what?

Anne. Look on his upper lip . . . you can see the beginning of a mustache.

Dussel. He wants to get rid of that? Put a little milk on it and let the cat lick it off.

Peter (*starting for his room*). Think you're funny, don't you.

Dussel. Look! He can't wait! He's going in to try it!

1850 **Peter.** I'm going to give Mouschi his present! (*He goes into his room, slamming the door behind him.*)

Mr. Van Daan (*disgustedly*). Mouschi, Mouschi, Mouschi.

(*In the distance we hear a dog persistently barking. Anne brings a gift to Dussel.*)

Anne. And last but never least, my roommate, Mr. Dussel.

Dussel. For me? You have something for me? 1860 (*He opens the small box she gives him.*)

Anne. I made them myself.

Dussel (*puzzled*). Capsules! Two capsules!

Anne. They're ear-plugs!

Dussel. Ear-plugs?

Anne. To put in your ears so you won't hear me when I thrash around at night. I saw them advertised in a magazine. They're not real ones . . . I made them out of cotton and candle wax. Try them . . . See if they don't work . . . 1870 see if you can hear me talk . . .

Dussel (*putting them in his ears*). Wait now until I get them in . . . so.

Anne. Are you ready?

Dussel. Huh?

Anne. Are you ready?

Dussel. Good God! They've gone inside! I can't get them out! (*They laugh as* Mr. Dussel *jumps about, trying to shake the plugs out of his ears. Finally he gets them out. Putting them away.*)

1880 Thank you, Anne! Thank you!

Mr. Van Daan. A real Hanukkah!

Mrs. Van Daan. Wasn't it cute of her?

Mrs. Frank. I don't know when she did it.

Margot. I love my present.

} *Together*

Anne (*sitting at the table*). And now let's have the song, Father . . . please . . . (*to Dussel*) Have you heard the Hanukkah song, Mr. Dussel? The song is the whole thing! (*She sings.*) "Oh, Hanukkah! 1890 Oh Hanukkah! The sweet celebration . . ."

Mr. Frank (*quieting her*). I'm afraid, Anne, we shouldn't sing that song tonight. (*to Dussel*) It's a song of jubilation, of rejoicing. One is apt to become too enthusiastic.

Anne. Oh, please, please. Let's sing the song. I promise not to shout!

Mr. Frank. Very well. But quietly now . . . I'll keep an eye on you and when . . .

(*As Anne starts to sing, she is interrupted by* Dussel, 1900 *who is snorting and wheezing.*)

Dussel (*pointing to Peter*). You . . . You! (Peter *is coming from his bedroom, ostentatiously holding a bulge in his coat as if he were holding his cat, and*

dangling Anne's present before it.) How many times . . . I told you . . . Out! Out!

Mr. Van Daan (*going to* Peter). What's the matter with you? Haven't you any sense? Get that cat out of here.

Peter (*innocently*). Cat?

1910 **Mr. Van Daan.** You heard me. Get it out of here!

Peter. I have no cat. (*Delighted with his joke, he opens his coat and pulls out a bath towel. The group at the table laugh, enjoying the joke.*)

Dussel (*still wheezing*). It doesn't need to be the cat . . . his clothes are enough . . . when he comes out of that room . . .

Mr. Van Daan. Don't worry. You won't be bothered any more. We're getting rid of it.

Dussel. At last you listen to me. (*He goes off into*
1920 *his bedroom.*)

Mr. Van Daan (*calling after him*). I'm not doing it for you. That's all in your mind . . . all of it! (*He starts back to his place at the table.*) I'm doing it because I'm sick of seeing that cat eat all our food.

Peter. That's not true! I only give him bones . . . scraps . . .

Mr. Van Daan. Don't tell me! He gets fatter every day! Damn cat looks better than any of us. Out
1930 he goes tonight!

Peter. No! No!

Anne. Mr. Van Daan, you can't do that! That's Peter's cat. Peter loves that cat.

Mrs. Frank (*quietly*). Anne.

Peter (*to* Mr. Van Daan). If he goes, I go.

Mr. Van Daan. Go! Go!

Mrs. Van Daan. You're not going and the cat's not going! Now please . . . this is Hanukkah . . . Hanukkah . . . this is the time to celebrate . . .
1940 What's the matter with all of you? Come on, Anne. Let's have the song.

Anne (*singing*). "Oh, Hanukkah! Oh, Hanukkah! The sweet celebration."

Mr. Frank (*rising*). I think we should first blow out the candle . . . then we'll have something for tomorrow night.

Margot. But, Father, you're supposed to let it burn itself out.

Mr. Frank. I'm sure that God understands
1950 shortages. (*before blowing it out*) "Praised be Thou, oh Lord our God, who hast sustained us and permitted us to celebrate this joyous festival."

(*He is about to blow out the candle when suddenly there is a crash of something falling below. They all freeze in horror, motionless. For a few seconds there is complete silence. Mr. Frank slips off his shoes. The others noiselessly follow his example. Mr. Frank turns out a light near him. He motions to Peter to turn off the center lamp. Peter tries to reach it,*
1960 *realizes he cannot and gets up on a chair. Just as he is touching the lamp he loses his balance. The chair goes out from under him. He falls. The iron lamp shade crashes to the floor. There is a sound of feet below, running down the stairs.*)

Mr. Van Daan (*under his breath*). God Almighty! (*The only light left comes from the Hanukkah candle. Dussel comes from his room. Mr. Frank creeps over to the stairwell and stands listening. The dog is heard barking excitedly.*) Do you hear
1970 anything?

Mr. Frank (*in a whisper*). No. I think they've gone.

Mrs. Van Daan. It's the Green Police. They've found us.

Mr. Frank. If they had, they wouldn't have left. They'd be up here by now.

Mrs. Van Daan. I know it's the Green Police. They've gone to get help. That's all. They'll be back!

Mr. Van Daan. Or it may have been the Gestapo,[20]
1980 looking for papers . . .

---

20. **Gestapo** (gə-stä′pō): the Nazi secret police force, known for its terrorism and brutality.

Mr. Frank (*interrupting*). Or a thief, looking for money.

Mrs. Van Daan. We've got to do something . . . Quick! Quick! Before they come back.

Mr. Van Daan. There isn't anything to do. Just wait.

(Mr. Frank *holds up his hand for them to be quiet. He is listening intently. There is complete silence as they all strain to hear any sound from below.*

1990 *Suddenly* Anne *begins to sway. With a low cry she falls to the floor in a faint. Mrs. Frank goes to her quickly, sitting beside her on the floor and taking her in her arms.*)

Mrs. Frank. Get some water, please! Get some water!

(Margot *starts for the sink.*)

Mr. Van Daan (*grabbing* Margot). No! No! No one's going to run water!

Mr. Frank. If they've found us, they've found us.
2000 Get the water. (Margot *starts again for the sink.* Mr. Frank, *getting a flashlight*) I'm going down.

(Margot *rushes to him, clinging to him.* Anne *struggles to consciousness.*)

Margot. No, Father, no! There may be someone there, waiting . . . It may be a trap!

Mr. Frank. This is Saturday. There is no way for us to know what has happened until Miep or Mr. Kraler comes on Monday morning. We cannot live with this uncertainty.

2010 **Margot.** Don't go, Father!

Mrs. Frank. Hush, darling, hush. (Mr. Frank *slips quietly out, down the steps and out through the door below.*) Margot! Stay close to me.

(Margot *goes to her mother.*)

Mr. Van Daan. Shush! Shush!

(Mrs. Frank *whispers to* Margot *to get the water.* Margot *goes for it.*)

Mrs. Van Daan. Putti, where's our money? Get our money. I hear you can buy the Green Police

2020 off, so much a head. Go upstairs quick! Get the money!

Mr. Van Daan. Keep still!

Mrs. Van Daan (*kneeling before him, pleading*). Do you want to be dragged off to a concentration camp? Are you going to stand there and wait for them to come up and get you? Do something, I tell you!

Mr. Van Daan (*pushing her aside*). Will you keep still! (*He goes over to the stairwell to listen.* Peter
2030 *goes to his mother, helping her up onto the sofa. There is a second of silence, then* Anne *can stand it no longer.*)

Anne. Someone go after Father! Make Father come back!

Peter (*starting for the door*). I'll go.

Mr. Van Daan. Haven't you done enough?

(*He pushes* Peter *roughly away. In his anger against his father* Peter *grabs a chair as if to hit him with it, then puts it down, burying his face in his hands.*
2040 Mrs. Frank *begins to pray softly.*)

Anne. Please, please, Mr. Van Daan. Get Father.

Mr. Van Daan. Quiet! Quiet!

(Anne *is shocked into silence.* Mrs. Frank *pulls her closer, holding her protectively in her arms.*)

Mrs. Frank (*softly, praying*). "I lift up mine eyes unto the mountains, from whence cometh my help. My help cometh from the Lord who made heaven and earth. He will not suffer thy foot to be moved . . . He that keepeth thee will not slumber . . ." (*She*
2050 *stops as she hears someone coming. They all watch the door tensely.* Mr. Frank *comes quietly in.* Anne *rushes to him, holding him tight.*)

Mr. Frank. It was a thief. That noise must have scared him away.

Mrs. Van Daan. Thank God.

Mr. Frank. He took the cash box. And the radio. He ran away in such a hurry that he didn't stop to shut the street door. It was swinging wide open. (*A breath of relief sweeps over them.*) I think it would be good to have some light.

Margot. Are you sure it's all right?

Mr. Frank. The danger has passed. (Margot *goes to light the small lamp.*) Don't be so terrified, Anne. We're safe.

Dussel. Who says the danger has passed? Don't you realize we are in greater danger than ever?

Mr. Frank. Mr. Dussel, will you be still!

(Mr. Frank *takes* Anne *back to the table, making her sit down with him, trying to calm her.*)

Dussel (*pointing to* Peter). Thanks to this clumsy fool, there's someone now who knows we're up here! Someone now knows we're up here, hiding!

Mrs. Van Daan (*going to* Dussel). Someone knows we're here, yes. But who is the someone? A thief! A thief! You think a thief is going to go to the Green Police and say . . . I was robbing a place the other night and I heard a noise up over my head? You think a thief is going to do that?

Dussel. Yes. I think he will.

Mrs. Van Daan (*hysterically*). You're crazy! (*She stumbles back to her seat at the table.* Peter *follows protectively, pushing* Dussel *aside.*)

Dussel. I think some day he'll be caught and then he'll make a bargain with the Green Police . . . if they'll let him off, he'll tell them where some Jews are hiding!

(*He goes off into the bedroom. There is a second of appalled silence.*)

Mr. Van Daan. He's right.

Anne. Father, let's get out of here! We can't stay here now . . . Let's go . . .

Mr. Van Daan. Go! Where?

Mrs. Frank (*sinking into her chair at the table*). Yes. Where?

Mr. Frank (*rising, to them all*). Have we lost all faith? All courage? A moment ago we thought that they'd come for us. We were sure it was the end. But it wasn't the end. We're alive, safe. (Mr. Van Daan *goes to the table and sits.* Mr. Frank *prays.*) "We thank Thee, oh Lord our God, that in Thy infinite mercy Thou hast again seen fit to spare us." (*He blows out the candle, then turns to* Anne.) Come on, Anne. The song! Let's have the song! (*He starts to sing.* Anne *finally starts falteringly to sing, as* Mr. Frank *urges her on. Her voice is hardly audible at first.*)

Anne (*singing*). "Oh, Hanukkah! Oh, Hanukkah! The sweet . . . celebration . . ." (*As she goes on singing, the others gradually join in, their voices still shaking with fear.* Mrs. Van Daan *sobs as she sings.*)

Group. "Around the feast . . . we . . . gather
In complete . . . jubilation . . .
Happiest of sea . . . sons
Now is here.
Many are the reasons for good cheer."

(Dussel *comes from the bedroom. He comes over to the table, standing beside* Margot, *listening to them as they sing.*)

"Together
We'll weather
Whatever tomorrow may bring."

(*As they sing on with growing courage, the lights start to dim.*)

"So hear us rejoicing
And merrily voicing
The Hanukkah song that we sing.
Hoy!"

(*The lights are out. The curtain starts slowly to fall.*)

"Hear us rejoicing
And merrily voicing
The Hanukkah song that we sing."

(*They are still singing, as the curtain falls.*)
The Curtain Falls.

DIARY ENTRY Anne Frank's diary entries give readers an intimate understanding of what was going through her mind while she was in hiding. This entry from December 1943 describes her conflicting emotions about life in the Annex.

28   2

Friday, December 24, 1943

Dear Kitty,

As I've written you many times before, moods have a tendency to affect us quite a bit here, and in my case it's been getting worse lately. *"Himmelhoch jauchzend, zu Tode betrübt"*[1] certainly applies to me. I'm "on top of the world" when I think of how fortunate we are and compare myself to other Jewish children, and "in the depths of despair" when, for example, Mrs. Kleiman comes by and talks about Jopie's hockey club, canoe trips, school plays and afternoon teas with friends.

I don't think I'm jealous of Jopie, but I long to have a really good time for once and to laugh so hard it hurts. We're stuck in this house like lepers, especially during winter and the Christmas and New Year's holidays. Actually, I shouldn't even be writing this, since it makes me seem so ungrateful, but I can't keep everything to myself, so I'll repeat what I said at the beginning: "Paper is more patient than people."

Whenever someone comes in from outside, with the wind in their clothes and the cold on their cheeks, I feel like burying my head under the blankets to keep from thinking, "When will we be allowed to breathe fresh air again?" I can't do that—on the

contrary, I have to hold my head up high and put a bold face on things, but the thoughts keep coming anyway. Not just once, but over and over.

Believe me, if you've been shut up for a year and a half, it can get to be too much for you sometimes. But feelings can't be ignored, no matter how unjust or ungrateful they seem. I long to ride a bike, dance, whistle, look at the world, feel young and know that I'm free, and yet I can't let it show. Just imagine what would happen if all eight of us were to feel sorry for ourselves or walk around with the discontent clearly visible on our faces. Where would that get us? . . .

Yours, Anne

1. ***"Himmelhoch jauchzend, zu Tode betrübt":*** A famous line from Goethe: "On top of the world, or in the depths of despair."

Comprehension

1. **Recall** How do the people in the Annex get food and other supplies?

2. **Recall** Why do some of the people in the Annex complain about Anne?

3. **Clarify** Why does Mr. Frank say that the loud air raids should be music to the ears of those hiding in the attic?

COMMON CORE

RL 2 Determine a theme of a text and analyze its development, including its relationship to the characters, setting, and plot. RL 10 Read and comprehend dramas.

Text Analysis

4. **Interpret a Character's Words** What does Anne mean when she writes in her diary, "Paper is more patient than people"? Cite specific examples from the play that explain Anne's attitude.

5. **Understand Conflicts** A conflict in literature is a struggle between two opposing forces. An **external conflict** is a struggle between a character and society, another character, or a force of nature. An **internal conflict** is a struggle within a character's mind. In a chart like the one shown, include the external and internal conflicts you notice so far in the play. Circle the one or two conflicts you think are the main ones.

External Conflicts	Internal Conflicts

6. **Identify Subplot** A **subplot** is an additional, or secondary, plot in a work of literature. The subplot contains its own conflict, often separate from the main conflicts of the story. What is one subplot that has been introduced in Act One?

7. **Analyze Theme** "Good triumphs over evil" has been a common theme in literature. A similar message is a major theme in this play: people are basically good at heart. Which characters help to develop that theme? Which characters, circumstances, or events appear to contradict it?

8. **Analyze a Drama** Review the chart in which you've been noting information about Anne and the Nazi occupation. Based on what you've learned through dialogue and stage directions, describe Anne's personality. What effect has the Nazi occupation had on her family's life?

Extension and Challenge

9. **Readers' Circle** Review the diary entry included on page 544. Anne admits she sometimes feels like burying her head under the blankets. Yet she holds her head up high and puts a "bold face on things." What impact do you think her behavior had on those around her? Discuss this question with a small group.

ACT TWO
Scene 1

In the darkness we hear Anne's Voice, *again reading from the diary.*

Anne's Voice. Saturday, the first of January, nineteen forty-four. Another new year has begun and we find ourselves still in our hiding place. We have been here now for one year, five months and twenty-five days. It seems that our life is at a standstill.

The curtain rises on the scene. It is late afternoon.
10 *Everyone is bundled up against the cold. In the main room* Mrs. Frank *is taking down the laundry which is hung across the back.* Mr. Frank *sits in the chair down left, reading.* Margot *is lying on the couch with a blanket over her and the many-colored knitted scarf around her throat.* Anne *is seated at the center table, writing in her diary.* Peter, Mr. *and* Mrs. Van Daan, *and* Dussel *are all in their own rooms, reading or lying down.*

As the lights dim on, Anne's Voice *continues,*
20 *without a break.*

Anne's Voice. We are all a little thinner. The Van Daans' "discussions" are as violent as ever. Mother still does not understand me. But then I don't understand her either. There is one great change, however. A change in myself. I read somewhere that girls of my age don't feel quite certain of themselves. That they become quiet within and begin to think of the miracle that is taking place in their bodies. I think that what is happening
30 to me is so wonderful . . . not only what can be seen, but what is taking place inside. Each time it has happened I have a feeling that I have a sweet secret. (*We hear the chimes and then a hymn being played on the carillon outside.*) And in spite of any pain, I long for the time when I shall feel that secret within me again.

(*The buzzer of the door below suddenly sounds. Everyone is startled,* Mr. Frank *tiptoes cautiously to the top of the steps and listens. Again the buzzer*
40 *sounds, in* Miep's *V-for-Victory signal.*)

Mr. Frank. It's Miep! (*He goes quickly down the steps to unbolt the door.* Mrs. Frank *calls upstairs to the Van Daans and then to* Peter.)

Mrs. Frank. Wake up, everyone! Miep is here! (Anne *quickly puts her diary away.* Margot *sits up, pulling the blanket around her shoulders.* Mr. Dussel *sits on the edge of his bed, listening,* **disgruntled.** Miep *comes up the steps, followed by* Mr. Kraler. *They bring flowers, books, newspapers,*
50 *etc.* Anne *rushes to* Miep, *throwing her arms affectionately around her.*) Miep . . . *and* Mr. Kraler . . . What a delightful surprise!

Mr. Kraler. We came to bring you New Year's greetings.

Mrs. Frank. You shouldn't . . . you should have at least one day to yourselves. (*She goes quickly to the stove and brings down teacups and tea for all of them.*)

Anne. Don't say that, it's so wonderful to see them!
60 (*sniffing at* Miep's *coat*) I can smell the wind and the cold on your clothes.

Miep (*giving her the flowers*). There you are. (*then to* Margot, *feeling her forehead*) How are you, Margot? . . . Feeling any better?

Margot. I'm all right.

Anne. We filled her full of every kind of pill so she won't cough and make a noise. (*She runs into her room to put the flowers in water.* Mr. *and* Mrs. Van Daan *come from upstairs. Outside there is the sound*
70 *of a band playing.*)

Mrs. Van Daan. Well, hello, Miep. Mr. Kraler.

Mr. Kraler (*giving a bouquet of flowers to* Mrs. Van Daan). With my hope for peace in the New Year.

Peter (*anxiously*). Miep, have you seen Mouschi? Have you seen him anywhere around?

Miep. I'm sorry, Peter. I asked everyone in the neighborhood had they seen a gray cat. But they said no.

(Mrs. Frank *gives* Miep *a cup of tea.* Mr. Frank
80 *comes up the steps, carrying a small cake on a plate.*)

Mr. Frank. Look what Miep's brought for us!

Mrs. Frank (*taking it*). A cake!

Mr. Van Daan. A cake! (*He pinches* Miep's *cheeks gaily and hurries up to the cupboard.*) I'll get some plates.

(Dussel, *in his room, hastily puts a coat on and starts out to join the others.*)

Mrs. Frank. Thank you, Miepia. You shouldn't have done it. You must have used all of your sugar
90 ration for weeks. (*giving it to* Mrs. Van Daan) It's beautiful, isn't it?

Mrs. Van Daan. It's been ages since I even saw a cake. Not since you brought us one last year. (*without looking at the cake, to* Miep) Remember? Don't you remember, you gave us one on New Year's Day? Just this time last year? I'll never forget it because you had "Peace in nineteen forty-three" on it. (*She looks at the cake and reads.*) "Peace in nineteen forty-four!"

100 **Miep.** Well, it has to come sometime, you know. (*as* Dussel *comes from his room*) Hello, Mr. Dussel.

Mr. Kraler. How are you?

Mr. Van Daan (*bringing plates and a knife*). Here's the knife, *liefje.* Now, how many of us are there?

Miep. None for me, thank you.

Mr. Frank. Oh, please. You must.

Miep. I couldn't.

Mr. Van Daan. Good! That leaves one . . . two . . . three . . . seven of us.

110 **Dussel.** Eight! Eight! It's the same number as it always is!

Mr. Van Daan. I left Margot out. I take it for granted Margot won't eat any.

Anne. Why wouldn't she!

Mrs. Frank. I think it won't harm her.

Mr. Van Daan. All right! All right! I just didn't want her to start coughing again, that's all.

Dussel. And please, Mrs. Frank should cut the cake.

Mr. Van Daan. What's the difference?

120 **Mrs. Van Daan.** It's not Mrs. Frank's cake, is it, Miep? It's for all of us. } *Together*

Dussel. Mrs. Frank divides things better.

Mrs. Van Daan (*going to* Dussel). What are you trying to say?

Mr. Van Daan. Oh, come on! Stop wasting time! } *Together*

Mrs. Van Daan (*to* Dussel). Don't I always give everybody exactly the same? Don't I?

Mr. Van Daan. Forget it, Kerli.

130 **Mrs. Van Daan.** No. I want an answer! Don't I?

Dussel. Yes. Yes. Everybody gets exactly the same . . . except Mr. Van Daan always gets a little bit more.

(Mr. Van Daan *advances on* Dussel, *the knife still in his hand.*)

Mr. Van Daan. That's a lie!

(Dussel *retreats before the onslaught of the* Van Daans.)

Mr. Frank. Please, please! (*then to* Miep) You see
140 what a little sugar cake does to us? It goes right to our heads!

Mr. Van Daan (*handing* Mrs. Frank *the knife*). Here you are, Mrs. Frank.

Mrs. Frank. Thank you. (*then to* Miep *as she goes to the table to cut the cake*) Are you sure you won't have some?

Miep (*drinking her tea*). No, really, I have to go in a minute.

(*The sound of the band fades out in the distance.*)

150 **Peter** (*to* Miep). Maybe Mouschi went back to our house . . . they say that cats . . . Do you ever get over there . . . ? I mean . . . do you suppose you could . . . ?

Miep. I'll try, Peter. The first minute I get I'll try. But I'm afraid, with him gone a week . . .

Dussel. Make up your mind, already someone has had a nice big dinner from that cat!

(Peter *is furious, inarticulate. He starts toward* Dussel *as if to hit him.* Mr. Frank *stops him.*
160 Mrs. Frank *speaks quickly to ease the situation.*)

Mrs. Frank (*to* Miep). This is delicious, Miep!

Mrs. Van Daan (*eating hers*). Delicious!

Mr. Van Daan (*finishing it in one gulp*). Dirk's in luck to get a girl who can bake like this!

Miep (*putting down her empty teacup*). I have to run. Dirk's taking me to a party tonight.

Anne. How heavenly! Remember now what everyone is wearing, and what you have to eat and everything, so you can tell us tomorrow.

170 **Miep.** I'll give you a full report! Good-bye, everyone!

Mr. Van Daan (*to* Miep). Just a minute. There's something I'd like you to do for me. (*He hurries off up the stairs to his room.*)

Mrs. Van Daan (*sharply*). Putti, where are you going? (*She rushes up the stairs after him, calling hysterically.*) What do you want? Putti, what are you going to do?

Miep (*to* Peter). What's wrong?

Peter (*his sympathy is with his mother*). Father says
180 he's going to sell her fur coat. She's crazy about that old fur coat.

Dussel. Is it possible? Is it possible that anyone is so silly as to worry about a fur coat in times like this?

Peter. It's none of your darn business . . . and if you say one more thing . . . I'll, I'll take you and I'll . . . I mean it . . . I'll . . .

(*There is a piercing scream from* Mrs. Van Daan *above. She grabs at the fur coat as* Mr. Van Daan
190 *is starting downstairs with it.*)

Mrs. Van Daan. No! No! No! Don't you dare take that! You hear? It's mine! (*Downstairs* Peter *turns away, embarrassed, miserable.*) My father gave me that! You didn't give it to me. You have no right. Let go of it . . . you hear?

(Mr. Van Daan *pulls the coat from her hands and hurries downstairs.* Mrs. Van Daan *sinks to the floor, sobbing. As* Mr. Van Daan *comes into the main room the others look away, embarrassed for him.*)

200 **Mr. Van Daan** (*to* Mr. Kraler). Just a little—discussion over the advisability of selling this coat. As I have often reminded Mrs. Van Daan, it's very selfish of her to keep it when people outside are in such desperate need of clothing . . . (*He gives the coat to* Miep.) So if you will please to sell it for us? It should fetch a good price. And by the way, will you get me cigarettes. I don't care what kind they are . . . get all you can.

Miep. It's terribly difficult to get them, Mr. Van
210 Daan. But I'll try. Good-bye.

(*She goes.* Mr. Frank *follows her down the steps to bolt the door after her.* Mrs. Frank *gives* Mr. Kraler *a cup of tea.*)

Mrs. Frank. Are you sure you won't have some cake, Mr. Kraler?

Mr. Kraler. I'd better not.

Mr. Van Daan. You're still feeling badly? What does your doctor say?

Mr. Kraler. I haven't been to him.

220 **Mrs. Frank.** Now, Mr. Kraler! . . .

Mr. Kraler (*sitting at the table*). Oh, I tried. But you can't get near a doctor these days . . . they're so busy. After weeks I finally managed to get one on the telephone. I told him I'd like an appointment . . . I wasn't feeling very well. You know what he answers . . . over the telephone . . . Stick out your tongue! (*They laugh. He turns to* Mr. Frank *as* Mr. Frank *comes back.*) I have some contracts here . . . I wonder if you'd look over
230 them with me . . .

Mr. Frank (*putting out his hand*). Of course.

Mr. Kraler (*He rises.*) If we could go downstairs . . . (Mr. Frank *starts ahead,* Mr. Kraler *speaks to the others.*) Will you forgive us? I won't keep him but a minute. (*He starts to follow* Mr. Frank *down the steps.*)

Margot (*with sudden **foreboding***). What's happened? Something's happened! Hasn't it, Mr. Kraler?

(Mr. Kraler *stops and comes back, trying to reassure*
240 Margot *with a pretense of casualness.*)

Mr. Kraler. No, really. I want your father's advice . . .

Margot. Something's gone wrong! I know it!

Mr. Frank (*coming back, to* Mr. Kraler). If it's something that concerns us here, it's better that we all hear it.

Mr. Kraler (*turning to him, quietly*). But . . . the children . . . ?

250 **Mr. Frank.** What they'd imagine would be worse than any reality.

(*As* Mr. Kraler *speaks, they all listen with intense* **apprehension.** Mrs. Van Daan *comes down the stairs and sits on the bottom step.*)

Mr. Kraler. It's a man in the storeroom . . . I don't know whether or not you remember him . . . Carl, about fifty, heavy-set, near-sighted . . . He came with us just before you left.

Mr. Frank. He was from Utrecht?

Mr. Kraler. That's the man. A couple of weeks ago,
260 when I was in the storeroom, he closed the door and asked me . . . how's Mr. Frank? What do you hear from Mr. Frank? I told him I only knew there was a rumor that you were in Switzerland. He said he'd heard that rumor too, but he thought I might know something more. I didn't pay any attention to it . . . but then a thing happened yesterday . . . He'd brought some invoices to the office for me to sign. As I was going through them, I looked up. He was standing staring at the bookcase . . . your
270 bookcase. He said he thought he remembered a door there . . . Wasn't there a door there that used to go up to the loft? Then he told me he wanted more money. Twenty guilders[1] more a week.

Mr. Van Daan. Blackmail!

Mr. Frank. Twenty guilders? Very modest blackmail.

Mr. Van Daan. That's just the beginning.

Dussel (*coming to* Mr. Frank). You know what I think? He was the thief who was down there that night. That's how he knows we're here.

280 **Mr. Frank** (*to* Mr. Kraler). How was it left? What did you tell him?

Mr. Kraler. I said I had to think about it. What shall I do? Pay him the money? . . . Take a chance on firing him . . . or what? I don't know.

Dussel (*frantic*). For God's sake don't fire him! Pay him what he asks . . . keep him here where you can have your eye on him.

Mr. Frank. Is it so much that he's asking? What are they paying nowadays?

290 **Mr. Kraler.** He could get it in a war plant. But this isn't a war plant. Mind you, I don't know if he really knows . . . or if he doesn't know.

Mr. Frank. Offer him half. Then we'll soon find out if it's blackmail or not.

Dussel. And if it is? We've got to pay it, haven't we? Anything he asks we've got to pay!

Mr. Frank. Let's decide that when the time comes.

Mr. Kraler. This may be all my imagination. You get to a point, these days, where you suspect
300 everyone and everything. Again and again . . . on some simple look or word, I've found myself . . .

(*The telephone rings in the office below.*)

Mrs. Van Daan (*hurrying to* Mr. Kraler). There's the telephone! What does that mean, the telephone ringing on a holiday?

Mr. Kraler. That's my wife. I told her I had to go over some papers in my office . . . to call me there when she got out of church. (*He starts out.*) I'll offer him half then. Good-bye . . . we'll hope for
310 the best!

(*The group call their good-byes half-heartedly.* Mr. Frank *follows* Mr. Kraler, *to bolt the door below. During the following scene,* Mr. Frank *comes back up and stands listening, disturbed.*)

Dussel (*to* Mr. Van Daan). You can thank your son for this . . . smashing the light! I tell you, it's just a question of time now. (*He goes to the window at the back and stands looking out.*)

Margot. Sometimes I wish the end would come
320 . . . whatever it is.

Mrs. Frank (*shocked*). Margot!

(Anne *goes to* Margot, *sitting beside her on the couch with her arms around her.*)

Margot. Then at least we'd know where we were.

---

1. **guilders** (gĭl′dərz): the basic monetary unit of the Netherlands at the time.

Mrs. Frank. You should be ashamed of yourself! Talking that way! Think how lucky we are! Think of the thousands dying in the war, every day. Think of the people in concentration camps.

Anne (*interrupting*). What's the good of that?
330 What's the good of thinking of misery when you're already miserable? That's stupid!

Mrs. Frank. Anne!

(*As Anne goes on raging at her mother, Mrs. Frank tries to break in, in an effort to quiet her.*)

Anne. We're young, Margot and Peter and I! You grownups have had your chance! But look at us . . . If we begin thinking of all the horror in the world, we're lost! We're trying to hold onto some kind of ideals . . . when everything . . .
340 ideals, hopes . . . everything, are being destroyed! It isn't our fault that the world is in such a mess! We weren't around when all this started! So don't try to take it out on us!

(*She rushes off to her room, slamming the door after her. She picks up a brush from the chest and hurls it to the floor. Then she sits on the settee, trying to control her anger.*)

Mr. Van Daan. She talks as if we started the war! Did we start the war? (*He spots* Anne's *cake. As he*
350 *starts to take it,* Peter *anticipates him.*)

Peter. She left her cake. (*He starts for* Anne's *room with the cake. There is silence in the main room.* Mrs. Van Daan *goes up to her room, followed by* Van Daan. Dussel *stays looking out the window.* Mr. Frank *brings* Mrs. Frank *her cake. She eats it slowly, without relish.* Mr. Frank *takes his cake to* Margot *and sits quietly on the sofa beside her.* Peter *stands in the doorway of* Anne's *darkened room, looking at her, then makes a little movement to let*
360 *her know he is there.* Anne *sits up, quickly, trying to hide the signs of her tears.* Peter *holds out the cake to her.*) You left this.

Anne (*dully*). Thanks.

(Peter *starts to go out, then comes back.*)

Peter. I thought you were fine just now. You know just how to talk to them. You know just how to say it. I'm no good . . . I never can think . . . especially when I'm mad . . . That Dussel . . . when he said that about Mouschi . . . someone eating him . . . all
370 I could think is . . . I wanted to hit him. I wanted to give him such a . . . a . . . that he'd . . . That's what I used to do when there was an argument at school . . . That's the way I . . . but here . . . And an old man like that . . . it wouldn't be so good.

Anne. You're making a big mistake about me. I do it all wrong. I say too much. I go too far. I hurt people's feelings . . .

(Dussel *leaves the window, going to his room.*)

Peter. I think you're just fine . . . What I want to say . . . if it wasn't for you around here, I don't know. What I mean . . .

(Peter *is interrupted by* Dussel's *turning on the light.* Dussel *stands in the doorway, startled to see* Peter. Peter *advances toward him forbiddingly.* Dussel *backs out of the room.* Peter *closes the door on him.*)

Anne. Do you mean it, Peter? Do you really mean it?

Peter. I said it, didn't I?

Anne. Thank you, Peter!

(*In the main room* Mr. *and* Mrs. Frank *collect the dishes and take them to the sink, washing them.* Margot *lies down again on the couch.* Dussel, *lost, wanders into* Peter's *room and takes up a book, starting to read.*)

Peter (*looking at the photographs on the wall*). You've got quite a collection.

Anne. Wouldn't you like some in your room? I could give you some. Heaven knows you spend enough time in there . . . doing heaven knows what . . .

Peter. It's easier. A fight starts, or an argument . . . I duck in there.

Anne. You're lucky, having a room to go to. His lordship is always here . . . I hardly ever get a minute alone. When they start in on me, I can't duck away. I have to stand there and take it.

Peter. You gave some of it back just now.

Anne. I get so mad. They've formed their opinions . . . about everything . . . but we . . . we're still trying to find out . . . We have problems here that no other people our age have ever had. And just as you think you've solved them, something comes along and bang! You have to start all over again.

Peter. At least you've got someone you can talk to.

Anne. Not really. Mother . . . I never discuss anything serious with her. She doesn't understand. Father's all right. We can talk about everything . . . everything but one thing. Mother. He simply won't talk about her. I don't think you can be really intimate with anyone if he holds something back, do you?

Peter. I think your father's fine.

Anne. Oh, he is, Peter! He is! He's the only one who's ever given me the feeling that I have any sense. But anyway, nothing can take the place of school and play and friends of your own age . . . or near your age . . . can it?

Peter. I suppose you miss your friends and all.

Anne. It isn't just . . . (*She breaks off, staring up at him for a second.*) Isn't it funny, you and I? Here we've been seeing each other every minute for almost a year and a half, and this is the first time we've ever really talked. It helps a lot to have someone to talk to, don't you think? It helps you to let off steam.

Peter (*going to the door*). Well, any time you want to let off steam, you can come into my room.

Anne (*following him*). I can get up an awful lot of steam. You'll have to be careful how you say that.

Peter. It's all right with me.

Anne. Do you mean it?

Peter. I said it, didn't I?

(*He goes out.* Anne *stands in her doorway looking after him. As* Peter *gets to his door he stands for a minute looking back at her. Then he goes into his room.* Dussel *rises as he comes in, and quickly passes him, going out. He starts across for his room.* Anne *sees him coming, and pulls her door shut.* Dussel *turns back toward* Peter's *room.* Peter *pulls his door shut.* Dussel *stands there, bewildered, forlorn.*

The scene slowly dims out. The curtain falls on the scene. Anne's Voice *comes over in the darkness . . . faintly at first, and then with growing strength.*)

Anne's Voice. We've had bad news. The people from whom Miep got our ration books have been arrested. So we have had to cut down on our food. Our stomachs are so empty that they rumble and make strange noises, all in different keys. Mr. Van Daan's is deep and low, like a bass fiddle. Mine is high, whistling like a flute. As we all sit around waiting for supper, it's like an orchestra tuning up. It only needs Toscanini[2] to raise his baton and we'd be off in the Ride of the Valkyries.[3] Monday, the sixth of March, nineteen forty-four. Mr. Kraler is in the hospital. It seems he has ulcers. Pim says we are his ulcers. Miep has to run the business and us too. The Americans have landed on the southern tip of Italy. Father looks for a quick finish to the war. Mr. Dussel is waiting every day for the warehouse man to demand more money. Have I been skipping too much from one subject to another? I can't help it. I feel that spring is coming. I feel it in my whole body and soul. I feel utterly confused. I am longing . . . so longing . . . for everything . . . for friends . . . for someone to talk to . . . someone who understands . . . someone young, who feels as I do . . .

470

(As these last lines are being said, the curtain rises on the scene. The lights dim on. Anne's Voice fades out.)

Scene 2

It is evening, after supper. From outside we hear the sound of children playing. The "grownups," with the exception of Mr. Van Daan, *are all in the main room.* Mrs. Frank *is doing some mending,* Mrs. Van Daan *is reading a fashion magazine.* Mr. Frank *is going over business accounts.* Dussel, *in his dentist's jacket, is pacing up and down, impatient to get into his bedroom.* Mr. Van Daan *is upstairs working on a piece of embroidery in an embroidery frame.*

480

490

In his room Peter *is sitting before the mirror, smoothing his hair. As the scene goes on, he puts on his tie, brushes his coat and puts it on, preparing himself meticulously for a visit from* Anne. *On his wall are now hung some of* Anne's *motion picture stars.*

In her room Anne *too is getting dressed. She stands before the mirror in her slip, trying various ways of dressing her hair.* Margot *is seated on the sofa, hemming a skirt for* Anne *to wear.*

In the main room Dussel *can stand it no longer. He comes over, rapping sharply on the door of his and* Anne's *bedroom.*

500

Anne (*calling to him*). No, no, Mr. Dussel! I am not dressed yet. (Dussel *walks away, furious, sitting down and burying his head in his hands.* Anne *turns to* Margot.) How is that? How does that look?

Margot (*glancing at her briefly*). Fine.

Anne. You didn't even look.

Margot. Of course I did. It's fine.

Anne. Margot, tell me, am I terribly ugly?

Margot. Oh, stop fishing.

510

Anne. No. No. Tell me.

Margot. Of course you're not. You've got nice eyes . . . and a lot of animation, and . . .

Anne. A little vague, aren't you?

(She reaches over and takes a brassière out of Margot's *sewing basket. She holds it up to herself, studying the effect in the mirror. Outside,* Mrs. Frank, *feeling sorry for* Dussel, *comes over, knocking at the girls' door.)*

Mrs. Frank (*outside*). May I come in?

520

Margot. Come in, Mother.

Mrs. Frank (*shutting the door behind her*). Mr. Dussel's impatient to get in here.

Anne (*still with the brassière*). Heavens, he takes the room for himself the entire day.

Mrs. Frank (*gently*). Anne, dear, you're not going in again tonight to see Peter?

Anne (*dignified*). That is my intention.

Mrs. Frank. But you've already spent a great deal of time in there today.

530

Anne. I was in there exactly twice. Once to get the dictionary, and then three-quarters of an hour before supper.

Mrs. Frank. Aren't you afraid you're disturbing him?

Anne. Mother, I have some intuition.

---

2. **Toscanini** (tŏs′kə-nē′nē): Arturo Toscanini, a famous Italian orchestral conductor.

3. **Ride of the Valkyries** (văl-kîr′ēz): a moving passage from an opera by Richard Wagner, a German composer.

Mrs. Frank. Then may I ask you this much, Anne. Please don't shut the door when you go in.

Anne. You sound like Mrs. Van Daan! (*She throws the brassière back in* Margot's *sewing basket and picks up her blouse, putting it on.*)

540 **Mrs. Frank.** No. No. I don't mean to suggest anything wrong. I only wish that you wouldn't expose yourself to criticism . . . that you wouldn't give Mrs. Van Daan the opportunity to be unpleasant.

Anne. Mrs. Van Daan doesn't need an opportunity to be unpleasant!

Mrs. Frank. Everyone's on edge, worried about Mr. Kraler. This is one more thing . . .

Anne. I'm sorry, Mother. I'm going to Peter's
550 room. I'm not going to let Petronella Van Daan spoil our friendship.

(Mrs. Frank *hesitates for a second, then goes out, closing the door after her. She gets a pack of playing cards and sits at the center table, playing solitaire. In* Anne's *room* Margot *hands the finished skirt to* Anne. *As* Anne *is putting it on,* Margot *takes off her high-heeled shoes and stuffs paper in the toes so that* Anne *can wear them.*)

Margot (*to* Anne). Why don't you two talk in the
560 main room? It'd save a lot of trouble. It's hard on Mother, having to listen to those remarks from Mrs. Van Daan and not say a word.

Anne. Why doesn't she say a word? I think it's ridiculous to take it and take it.

Margot. You don't understand Mother at all, do you? She can't talk back. She's not like you. It's just not in her nature to fight back.

Anne. Anyway . . . the only one I worry about is you. I feel awfully guilty about you.

570 (*She sits on the stool near* Margot, *putting on* Margot's *high-heeled shoes.*)

Margot. What about?

Anne. I mean, every time I go into Peter's room, I have a feeling I may be hurting you. (Margot

shakes her head.) I know if it were me, I'd be wild. I'd be desperately jealous, if it were me.

Margot. Well, I'm not.

Anne. You don't feel badly? Really? Truly? You're not jealous?

580 **Margot.** Of course I'm jealous . . . jealous that you've got something to get up in the morning for . . . But jealous of you and Peter? No.

(Anne *goes back to the mirror.*)

Anne. Maybe there's nothing to be jealous of. Maybe he doesn't really like me. Maybe I'm just taking the place of his cat . . . (*She picks up a pair of short white gloves, putting them on.*) Wouldn't you like to come in with us?

Margot. I have a book.

590 (*The sound of the children playing outside fades out. In the main room* Dussel *can stand it no longer. He jumps up, going to the bedroom door and knocking sharply.*)

Dussel. Will you please let me in my room!

Anne. Just a minute, dear, dear Mr. Dussel. (*She picks up her Mother's pink stole and adjusts it elegantly over her shoulders, then gives a last look in the mirror.*) Well, here I go . . . to run the gauntlet.[4] (*She starts out, followed by* Margot.)

600 **Dussel** (*as she appears—sarcastic*). Thank you so much.

(Dussel *goes into his room.* Anne *goes toward* Peter's *room, passing* Mrs. Van Daan *and her parents at the center table.*)

Mrs. Van Daan. My God, look at her! (Anne *pays no attention. She knocks at* Peter's *door.*) I don't know what good it is to have a son. I never see him. He wouldn't care if I killed myself. (Peter *opens the door and stands aside for* Anne *to come in.*) Just a minute,
610 Anne. (*She goes to them at the door.*) I'd like to say a few words to my son. Do you mind? (Peter *and* Anne *stand waiting.*) Peter, I don't want you staying up till all hours tonight. You've got to have your sleep. You're a growing boy. You hear?

---

4. **to run the gauntlet:** to endure a series of troubles or difficulties.

Mrs. Frank. Anne won't stay late. She's going to bed promptly at nine. Aren't you, Anne?

Anne. Yes, Mother . . . (*to* Mrs. Van Daan) May we go now?

Mrs. Van Daan. Are you asking me? I didn't know
620 I had anything to say about it.

Mrs. Frank. Listen for the chimes, Anne dear.

(*The two young people go off into* Peter's room, *shutting the door after them.*)

Mrs. Van Daan (*to* Mrs. Frank). In my day it was the boys who called on the girls. Not the girls on the boys.

Mrs. Frank. You know how young people like to feel that they have secrets. Peter's room is the only place where they can talk.

630 **Mrs. Van Daan.** Talk! That's not what they called it when I was young.

(Mrs. Van Daan *goes off to the bathroom.* Margot *settles down to read her book.* Mr. Frank *puts his papers away and brings a chess game to the center table. He and* Mrs. Frank *start to play. In* Peter's *room,* Anne *speaks to* Peter, *indignant, humiliated.*)

Anne. Aren't they awful? Aren't they impossible? Treating us as if we were still in the nursery.

(*She sits on the cot.* Peter *gets a bottle of pop and*
640 *two glasses.*)

Peter. Don't let it bother you. It doesn't bother me.

Anne. I suppose you can't really blame them . . . they think back to what *they* were like at our age. They don't realize how much more advanced we are . . . When you think what wonderful discussions we've had! . . . Oh, I forgot. I was going to bring you some more pictures.

Peter. Oh, these are fine, thanks.

Anne. Don't you want some more? Miep just
650 brought me some new ones.

Peter. Maybe later. (*He gives her a glass of pop and, taking some for himself, sits down facing her.*)

Anne (*looking up at one of the photographs*). I remember when I got that . . . I won it. I bet Jopie that I could eat five ice-cream cones. We'd all been playing ping-pong . . . We used to have heavenly times . . . we'd finish up with ice cream at the Delphi, or the Oasis, where Jews were allowed . . . there'd always be a lot of boys . . .
660 we'd laugh and joke . . . I'd like to go back to it for a few days or a week. But after that I know I'd be bored to death. I think more seriously about life now. I want to be a journalist . . . or something. I love to write. What do you want to do?

Peter. I thought I might go off some place . . . work on a farm or something . . . some job that doesn't take much brains.

Anne. You shouldn't talk that way. You've got the most awful inferiority complex.

670 **Peter.** I know I'm not smart.

Anne. That isn't true. You're much better than I am in dozens of things . . . arithmetic and algebra and . . . well, you're a million times better than I am in algebra. (*with sudden directness*) You like Margot, don't you? Right from the start you liked her, liked her much better than me.

Peter (*uncomfortably*). Oh, I don't know.

(*In the main room* Mrs. Van Daan *comes from the bathroom and goes over to the sink, polishing*
680 *a coffee pot.*)

Anne. It's all right. Everyone feels that way. Margot's so good. She's sweet and bright and beautiful and I'm not.

Peter. I wouldn't say that.

Anne. Oh, no, I'm not. I know that. I know quite well that I'm not a beauty. I never have been and never shall be.

Peter. I don't agree at all. I think you're pretty.

Anne. That's not true!

690 **Peter.** And another thing. You've changed . . . from at first, I mean.

Anne. I have?

Peter. I used to think you were awful noisy.

Anne. And what do you think now, Peter? How have I changed?

Peter. Well . . . er . . . you're . . . quieter.

(*In his room* Dussel *takes his pajamas and toilet articles and goes into the bathroom to change.*)

Anne. I'm glad you don't just hate me.

700 **Peter.** I never said that.

Anne. I bet when you get out of here you'll never think of me again.

Peter. That's crazy.

Anne. When you get back with all of your friends, you're going to say . . . now what did I ever see in that Mrs. Quack Quack.

Peter. I haven't got any friends.

Anne. Oh, Peter, of course you have. Everyone has friends.

710 **Peter.** Not me. I don't want any. I get along all right without them.

Anne. Does that mean you can get along without me? I think of myself as your friend.

Peter. No. If they were all like you, it'd be different.

(*He takes the glasses and the bottle and puts them away. There is a second's silence and then* Anne *speaks, hesitantly, shyly.*)

Anne. Peter, did you ever kiss a girl?

720 **Peter.** Yes. Once.

Anne (*to cover her feelings*). That picture's crooked. (Peter *goes over, straightening the photograph.*) Was she pretty?

Peter. Huh?

Anne. The girl that you kissed.

Peter. I don't know. I was blindfolded. (*He comes back and sits down again.*) It was at a party. One of those kissing games.

Anne (*relieved*). Oh. I don't suppose that really

730 counts, does it?

Peter. It didn't with me.

Anne. I've been kissed twice. Once a man I'd never seen before kissed me on the cheek when he picked me up off the ice and I was crying. And the other was Mr. Koophuis, a friend of Father's who kissed my hand. You wouldn't say those counted, would you?

Peter. I wouldn't say so.

Anne. I know almost for certain that Margot

740 would never kiss anyone unless she was engaged to them. And I'm sure too that Mother never touched a man before Pim. But I don't know . . . things are so different now . . . What do you think? Do you think a girl shouldn't kiss anyone except if she's engaged or something? It's so hard to try to think what to do, when here we are with the whole world falling around our ears and you think . . . well . . . you don't know what's going to happen tomorrow and . . . What do you think?

750 **Peter.** I suppose it'd depend on the girl. Some girls, anything they do's wrong. But others . . . well . . . it wouldn't necessarily be wrong with them. (*The carillon starts to strike nine o'clock.*) I've always thought that when two people . . .

Anne. Nine o'clock. I have to go.

Peter. That's right.

Anne (*without moving*). Good night.

(*There is a second's pause, then* Peter *gets up and moves toward the door.*)

760 **Peter.** You won't let them stop you coming?

Anne. No. (*She rises and starts for the door.*) Sometime I might bring my diary. There are so many things in it that I want to talk over with you. There's a lot about you.

Peter. What kind of things?

Anne. I wouldn't want you to see some of it. I thought you were a nothing, just the way you thought about me.

Peter. Did you change your mind, the way I

770 changed my mind about you?

Anne. Well . . . You'll see . . .

(*For a second* Anne *stands looking up at* Peter, *longing for him to kiss her. As he makes no move she turns away. Then suddenly* Peter *grabs her awkwardly in his arms, kissing her on the cheek.* Anne *walks out dazed. She stands for a minute, her back to the people in the main room. As she regains her poise she goes to her mother and father and* Margot, *silently kissing them. They murmur their good nights to her. As she*

780 *is about to open her bedroom door, she catches sight of* Mrs. Van Daan. *She goes quickly to her, taking her face in her hands and kissing her first on one cheek and then on the other. Then she hurries off into her room.* Mrs. Van Daan *looks after her, and then looks over at* Peter's *room. Her suspicions are confirmed.*)

Mrs. Van Daan (*She knows.*) Ah hah!

(*The lights dim out. The curtain falls on the scene. In the darkness* Anne's Voice *comes faintly at first and then with growing strength.*)

790 **Anne's Voice.** By this time we all know each other so well that if anyone starts to tell a story, the rest can finish it for him. We're having to cut down still further on our meals. What makes it worse, the rats have been at work again. They've carried off some of our precious food. Even Mr. Dussel wishes now that Mouschi was here. Thursday, the twentieth of April, nineteen forty-four. Invasion fever is mounting every day. Miep tells us that people outside talk of nothing else. For myself,
800 life has become much more pleasant. I often go to Peter's room after supper. Oh, don't think I'm in love, because I'm not. But it does make life more bearable to have someone with whom you can exchange views. No more tonight. P.S. . . . I must be honest. I must confess that I actually live for the next meeting. Is there anything lovelier than to sit under the skylight and feel the sun on your cheeks and have a darling boy in your arms? I admit now that I'm glad the Van Daans had a son and not a
810 daughter. I've outgrown another dress. That's the third. I'm having to wear Margot's clothes after all. I'm working hard on my French and am now reading *La Belle Nivernaise.*

(*As she is saying the last lines—the curtain rises on the scene. The lights dim on, as* Anne's Voice *fades out.*)

Scene 3

It is night, a few weeks later. Everyone is in bed. There is complete quiet. In the Van Daans' *room a match flares up for a moment and then is quickly put out.* Mr. Van Daan, *in bare feet, dressed in underwear*
820 *and trousers, is dimly seen coming stealthily down the stairs and into the main room, where* Mr. *and* Mrs.

Frank *and* Margot *are sleeping. He goes to the food safe and again lights a match. Then he cautiously opens the safe, taking out a half-loaf of bread. As he closes the safe, it creaks. He stands rigid.* Mrs. Frank *sits up in bed. She sees him.*

Mrs. Frank (*screaming*). Otto! Otto! *Komme schnell!* [5]

(*The rest of the people wake, hurriedly getting up.*)

Mr. Frank. *Was ist los? Was ist passiert?* [6]

830 (Dussel, *followed by* Anne, *comes from his room.*)

Mrs. Frank (*as she rushes over to* Mr. Van Daan). *Er stiehlt das Essen!* [7]

Dussel (*grabbing* Mr. Van Daan). You! You! Give me that.

Mrs. Van Daan (*coming down the stairs*). Putti . . . Putti . . . what is it?

Dussel (*his hands on* Van Daan's *neck*). You dirty thief . . . stealing food . . . you good-for-nothing . . .

840 **Mr. Frank.** Mr. Dussel! For God's sake! Help me, Peter!

(Peter *comes over, trying, with* Mr. Frank, *to separate the two struggling men.*)

Peter. Let him go! Let go!

(Dussel *drops* Mr. Van Daan, *pushing him away. He shows them the end of a loaf of bread that he has taken from* Van Daan.)

Dussel. You greedy, selfish . . . !

(Margot *turns on the lights.*)

850 **Mrs. Van Daan.** Putti . . . what is it?

(*All of* Mrs. Frank's *gentleness, her self-control, is gone. She is outraged, in a frenzy of indignation.*)

Mrs. Frank. The bread! He was stealing the bread!

Dussel. It was you, and all the time we thought it was the rats!

Mr. Frank. Mr. Van Daan, how could you!

Mr. Van Daan. I'm hungry.

Mrs. Frank. We're all of us hungry! I see the children getting thinner and thinner. Your own son Peter . . . 860 I've heard him moan in his sleep, he's so hungry. And you come in the night and steal food that should go to them . . . to the children!

Mrs. Van Daan (*going to* Mr. Van Daan *protectively*). He needs more food than the rest of us. He's used to more. He's a big man.

(Mr. Van Daan *breaks away, going over and sitting on the couch.*)

Mrs. Frank (*turning on* Mrs. Van Daan). And you . . . you're worse than he is! You're a mother, 870 and yet you sacrifice your child to this man . . . this . . . this . . .

Mr. Frank. Edith! Edith!

(Margot *picks up the pink woolen stole, putting it over her mother's shoulders.*)

Mrs. Frank (*paying no attention, going on to* Mrs. Van Daan). Don't think I haven't seen you! Always saving the choicest bits for him! I've watched you day after day and I've held my tongue. But not any longer! Not after this! Now I want him to go! 880 I want him to get out of here!

Mr. Frank. Edith!

Mr. Van Daan. Get out of here? ⎫
Mrs. Van Daan. What do you mean? ⎬ *Together*

Mrs. Frank. Just that! Take your things and get out!

Mr. Frank (*to* Mrs. Frank). You're speaking in anger. You cannot mean what you are saying.

Mrs. Frank. I mean exactly that!

(Mrs. Van Daan *takes a cover from the* Franks' *bed, pulling it about her.*)

890 **Mr. Frank.** For two long years we have lived here, side by side. We have respected each other's rights . . . we have managed to live in peace. Are we now going to throw it all away? I know this will never happen again, will it, Mr. Van Daan?

---

5. *Komme schnell!* (kôm'e shněl') *German:* Come quickly!

6. *Was ist los? Was ist passiert?* (väs ĭst lôs'? väs ĭst päsērt'?) *German:* What's the matter? What has happened?

7. *Er stiehlt das Essen!* (ĕr shtēlt' däs ěs'ən) *German:* He is stealing food!

Mr. Van Daan. No. No.

Mrs. Frank. He steals once! He'll steal again!

(Mr. Van Daan, *holding his stomach, starts for the bathroom. Anne* puts her arms around him, helping him up the step.)

900 **Mr. Frank.** Edith, please. Let us be calm. We'll all go to our rooms . . . and afterwards we'll sit down quietly and talk this out . . . we'll find some way . . .

Mrs. Frank. No! No! No more talk! I want them to leave!

Mrs. Van Daan. You'd put us out, on the streets?

Mrs. Frank. There are other hiding places.

Mrs. Van Daan. A cellar . . . a closet. I know. And we have no money left even to pay for that.

910 **Mrs. Frank.** I'll give you money. Out of my own pocket I'll give it gladly. (*She gets her purse from a shelf and comes back with it.*)

Mrs. Van Daan. Mr. Frank, you told Putti you'd never forget what he'd done for you when you came to Amsterdam. You said you could never repay him, that you . . .

Mrs. Frank (*counting out money*). If my husband had any obligation to you, he's paid it, over and over.

Mr. Frank. Edith, I've never seen you like this

920 before. I don't know you.

Mrs. Frank. I should have spoken out long ago.

Dussel. You can't be nice to some people.

Mrs. Van Daan (*turning on Dussel*). There would have been plenty for all of us, if *you* hadn't come in here!

Mr. Frank. We don't need the Nazis to destroy us. We're destroying ourselves.

(*He sits down, with his head in his hands. Mrs. Frank* goes to Mrs. Van Daan.)

930 **Mrs. Frank** (*giving* Mrs. Van Daan *some money*). Give this to Miep. She'll find you a place.

Anne. Mother, you're not putting *Peter* out. Peter hasn't done anything.

Mrs. Frank. He'll stay, of course. When I say I must protect the children, I mean Peter too.

(Peter *rises from the steps where he has been sitting.*)

Peter. I'd have to go if Father goes.

(Mr. Van Daan *comes from the bathroom. Mrs. Van Daan* hurries to him and takes him to the couch.
940 *Then she gets water from the sink to bathe his face.*)

Mrs. Frank (*while this is going on*). He's no father to you . . . that man! He doesn't know what it is to be a father!

Peter (*starting for his room*). I wouldn't feel right. I couldn't stay.

Mrs. Frank. Very well, then. I'm sorry.

Anne (*rushing over to* Peter). No, Peter! No! (Peter *goes into his room, closing the door after him. Anne* turns back to her mother, crying.) I don't care
950 about the food. They can have mine! I don't want it! Only don't send them away. It'll be daylight soon. They'll be caught . . .

Margot (*putting her arms comfortingly around* Anne). Please, Mother!

Mrs. Frank. They're not going now. They'll stay here until Miep finds them a place. (*to* Mrs. Van Daan) But one thing I insist on! He must never come down here again! He must never come to this room where the food is stored! We'll divide
960 what we have . . . an equal share for each! (Dussel *hurries over to get a sack of potatoes from the food safe. Mrs. Frank* goes on, to Mrs. Van Daan.) You can cook it here and take it up to him.

(Dussel *brings the sack of potatoes back to the center table.*)

Margot. Oh, no. No. We haven't sunk so far that we're going to fight over a handful of rotten potatoes.

Dussel (*dividing the potatoes into piles*). Mrs. Frank,
970 Mr. Frank, Margot, Anne, Peter, Mrs. Van Daan, Mr. Van Daan, myself . . . Mrs. Frank . . .

(*The buzzer sounds in* Miep's *signal.*)

Mr. Frank. It's Miep! (*He hurries over, getting his overcoat and putting it on.*)

Margot. At this hour?

Mrs. Frank. It is trouble.

Mr. Frank (*as he starts down to unbolt the door*). I beg you, don't let her see a thing like this!

Mr. Dussel (*counting without stopping*). . . . Anne,
980 Peter, Mrs. Van Daan, Mr. Van Daan, myself . . .

Margot (*to* Dussel). Stop it! Stop it!

Dussel. . . . Mr. Frank, Margot, Anne, Peter, Mrs. Van Daan, Mr. Van Daan, myself, Mrs. Frank . . .

Mrs. Van Daan. You're keeping the big ones for yourself! All the big ones . . . Look at the size of that! . . . And that! . . .

(Dussel *continues on with his dividing.* Peter, *with his shirt and trousers on, comes from his room.*)

Margot. Stop it! Stop it!

990 (*We hear* Miep's *excited voice speaking to* Mr. Frank *below.*)

Miep. Mr. Frank . . . the most wonderful news! . . . The invasion has begun!

Mr. Frank. Go on, tell them! Tell them!

(Miep *comes running up the steps, ahead of* Mr. Frank. *She has a man's raincoat on over her nightclothes and a bunch of orange-colored flowers in her hand.*)

Miep. Did you hear that, everybody? Did you hear
1000 what I said? The invasion has begun! The invasion!

(*They all stare at* Miep, *unable to grasp what she is telling them.* Peter *is the first to recover his wits.*)

Peter. Where?

Mrs. Van Daan. When? When, Miep?

Miep. It began early this morning . . .

(*As she talks on, the realization of what she has said begins to dawn on them. Everyone goes crazy. A wild demonstration takes place.* Mrs. Frank *hugs* Mr. Van Daan.)

1010 **Mrs. Frank.** Oh, Mr. Van Daan, did you hear that?

(Dussel *embraces* Mrs. Van Daan. Peter *grabs a frying pan and parades around the room, beating on it, singing the Dutch National Anthem.* Anne *and* Margot *follow him, singing, weaving in and out among the excited grownups.* Margot *breaks away to take the flowers from* Miep *and distribute them to everyone. While this* **pandemonium** *is going on*

Mrs. Frank *tries to make herself heard above the excitement.*)

1020 **Mrs. Frank** (*to* Miep). How do you know?

Miep. The radio . . . The B.B.C.! They said they landed on the coast of Normandy!

Peter. The British?

Miep. British, Americans, French, Dutch, Poles, Norwegians . . . all of them! More than four thousand ships! Churchill spoke, and General Eisenhower! D-Day they call it!

Mr. Frank. Thank God, it's come!

Mrs. Van Daan. At last!

1030 **Miep** (*starting out*). I'm going to tell Mr. Kraler. This'll be better than any blood transfusion.

Mr. Frank (*stopping her*). What part of Normandy did they land, did they say?

Miep. Normandy . . . that's all I know now . . . I'll be up the minute I hear some more! (*She goes hurriedly out.*)

Mr. Frank (*to* Mrs. Frank). What did I tell you? What did I tell you?

(Mrs. Frank *indicates that he has forgotten to bolt*
1040 *the door after* Miep. *He hurries down the steps.* Mr. Van Daan, *sitting on the couch, suddenly breaks into a convulsive sob. Everybody looks at him, bewildered.*)

Mrs. Van Daan (*hurrying to him*). Putti! Putti! What is it? What happened?

Mr. Van Daan. Please. I'm so ashamed.

(Mr. Frank *comes back up the steps.*)

Dussel. Oh, for God's sake!

Mrs. Van Daan. Don't, Putti.

1050 **Margot.** It doesn't matter now!

Mr. Frank (*going to* Mr. Van Daan). Didn't you hear what Miep said? The invasion has come! We're going to be liberated! This is a time to celebrate!

(*He embraces* Mrs. Frank *and then hurries to the cupboard and gets the cognac and a glass.*)

Mr. Van Daan. To steal bread from children!

Mrs. Frank. We've all done things that we're ashamed of.

1060 **Anne.** Look at me, the way I've treated Mother . . . so mean and horrid to her.

Mrs. Frank. No, Anneke, no.

(Anne *runs to her mother, putting her arms around her.*)

Anne. Oh, Mother, I was. I was awful.

Mr. Van Daan. Not like me. No one is as bad as me!

Dussel (*to* Mr. Van Daan). Stop it now! Let's be happy!

Mr. Frank (*giving* Mr. Van Daan *a glass of cognac*).
1070 Here! Here! *Schnapps! L'chaim!*[8]

(Van Daan *takes the cognac. They all watch him. He gives them a feeble smile.* Anne *puts up her fingers in a V-for-Victory sign. As* Van Daan *gives an answering V-sign, they are startled to hear a loud sob from behind them. It is* Mrs. Frank, *stricken with* **remorse**. *She is sitting on the other side of the room.*)

Mrs. Frank (*through her sobs*). When I think of the terrible things I said . . .

1080 (Mr. Frank, Anne, *and* Margot *hurry to her, trying to comfort her.* Mr. Van Daan *brings her his glass of cognac.*)

Mr. Van Daan. No! No! You were right!

Mrs. Frank. That I should speak that way to you! . . . Our friends! . . . Our guests! (*She starts to cry again.*)

Dussel. Stop it, you're spoiling the whole invasion!

(*As they are comforting her, the lights dim out. The curtain falls.*)

1090 **Anne's Voice** (*faintly at first and then with growing strength*). We're all in much better spirits these days. There's still excellent news of the invasion. The best part about it is that I have a feeling that friends are coming. Who knows? Maybe I'll be back in school by fall. Ha, ha! The joke is on us! The warehouse man doesn't know a thing and we are paying him all that money! . . . Wednesday,

the second of July, nineteen forty-four. The invasion seems temporarily to be bogged down.
1100 Mr. Kraler has to have an operation, which looks bad. The Gestapo have found the radio that was stolen. Mr. Dussel says they'll trace it back and back to the thief, and then, it's just a matter of time till they get to us. Everyone is low. Even poor Pim can't raise their spirits. I have often been downcast myself . . . but never in despair. I can shake off everything if I write. But . . . and that is the great question . . . will I ever be able to write well? I want to so much. I want to go
1110 on living even after my death. Another birthday has gone by, so now I am fifteen. Already I know what I want. I have a goal, an opinion.

(*As this is being said—the curtain rises on the scene, the lights dim on, and* Anne's Voice *fades out.*)

Scene 4

It is an afternoon a few weeks later . . . Everyone but Margot *is in the main room. There is a sense of great tension.*

Both Mrs. Frank *and* Mr. Van Daan *are nervously pacing back and forth,* Dussel *is standing*
1120 *at the window, looking down fixedly at the street below.* Peter *is at the center table, trying to do his lessons.* Anne *sits opposite him, writing in her diary.* Mrs. Van Daan *is seated on the couch, her eyes on* Mr. Frank *as he sits reading.*

The sound of a telephone ringing comes from the office below. They all are rigid, listening tensely. Mr. Dussel *rushes down to* Mr. Frank.

Dussel. There it goes again, the telephone! Mr. Frank, do you hear?

1130 **Mr. Frank** (*quietly*). Yes. I hear.

Dussel (*pleading, insistent*). But this is the third time, Mr. Frank! The third time in quick succession! It's a signal! I tell you it's Miep, trying to get us! For some reason she can't come to us and she's trying to warn us of something!

---

8. *Schnapps!* (shnäps) *German:* Brandy! *L'chaim!* (lə ĸHä'yĭm) *Hebrew:* To life!

Mr. Frank. Please. Please.

Mr. Van Daan (*to* Dussel). You're wasting your breath.

Dussel. Something has happened, Mr. Frank.
1140 For three days now Miep hasn't been to see us! And today not a man has come to work. There hasn't been a sound in the building!

Mrs. Frank. Perhaps it's Sunday. We may have lost track of the days.

Mr. Van Daan (*to* Anne). You with the diary there. What day is it?

Dussel (*going to* Mrs. Frank). I don't lose track of the days! I know exactly what day it is! It's Friday, the fourth of August. Friday, and not a man at
1150 work. (*He rushes back to* Mr. Frank, *pleading with him, almost in tears.*) I tell you Mr. Kraler's dead. That's the only explanation. He's dead and they've closed down the building, and Miep's trying to tell us!

Mr. Frank. She'd never telephone us.

Dussel (*frantic*). Mr. Frank, answer that! I beg you, answer it!

Mr. Frank. No.

Mr. Van Daan. Just pick it up and listen. You don't
1160 have to speak. Just listen and see if it's Miep.

Dussel (*speaking at the same time*). For God's sake . . . I ask you.

Mr. Frank. No. I've told you, no. I'll do nothing that might let anyone know we're in the building.

Peter. Mr. Frank's right.

Mr. Van Daan. There's no need to tell us what side you're on.

Mr. Frank. If we wait patiently, quietly, I believe that help will come.

1170 (*There is silence for a minute as they all listen to the telephone ringing.*)

Dussel. I'm going down. (*He rushes down the steps.* Mr. Frank *tries ineffectually to hold him.* Dussel *runs to the lower door, unbolting it. The telephone stops ringing.* Dussel *bolts the door and comes slowly back*

up the steps.*) Too late. (Mr. Frank *goes to* Margot *in* Anne's *bedroom.*)

Mr. Van Daan. So we just wait here until we die.

Mrs. Van Daan (*hysterically*). I can't stand it! I'll
1180 kill myself! I'll kill myself!

Mr. Van Daan. For God's sake, stop it!

(*In the distance, a German military band is heard playing a Viennese waltz.*)

Mrs. Van Daan. I think you'd be glad if I did! I think you want me to die!

Mr. Van Daan. Whose fault is it we're here? (Mrs. Van Daan *starts for her room. He follows, talking at her.*) We could've been safe somewhere . . . in America or Switzerland. But no! No! You
1190 wouldn't leave when I wanted to. You couldn't leave your things. You couldn't leave your precious furniture.

Mrs. Van Daan. Don't touch me!

(*She hurries up the stairs, followed by* Mr. Van Daan. Peter, *unable to bear it, goes to his room.* Anne *looks after him, deeply concerned.* Dussel *returns to his post at the window.* Mr. Frank *comes back into the main room and takes a book, trying to read.* Mrs. Frank *sits near the sink, starting to peel*
1200 *some potatoes.* Anne *quietly goes to* Peter's *room, closing the door after her.* Peter *is lying face down on the cot.* Anne *leans over him, holding him in her arms, trying to bring him out of his despair.*)

Anne. Look, Peter, the sky. (*She looks up through the skylight.*) What a lovely, lovely day! Aren't the clouds beautiful? You know what I do when it seems as if I couldn't stand being cooped up for one more minute? I *think* myself out. I think myself on a walk in the park where I used to go with
1210 Pim. Where the jonquils and the crocus and the violets grow down the slopes. You know the most wonderful part about *thinking* yourself out? You can have it any way you like. You can have roses and violets and chrysanthemums all blooming at the same time . . . It's funny . . . I used to take it all for granted . . . and now I've gone crazy about everything to do with nature. Haven't you?

Peter. I've just gone crazy. I think if something doesn't happen soon . . . if we don't get out of here . . . I can't stand much more of it!

Anne (*softly*). I wish you had a religion, Peter.

Peter. No, thanks! Not me!

Anne. Oh, I don't mean you have to be Orthodox[9] . . . or believe in heaven and hell and purgatory and things . . . I just mean some religion . . . it doesn't matter what. Just to believe in something! When I think of all that's out there . . . the trees . . . and flowers . . . and seagulls . . . when I think of the dearness of you, Peter . . . and the goodness of the people we know . . . Mr. Kraler, Miep, Dirk, the vegetable man, all risking their lives for us every day . . . When I think of these good things, I'm not afraid any more . . . I find myself, and God, and I . . .

(*Peter interrupts, getting up and walking away.*)

Peter. That's fine! But when I begin to think, I get mad! Look at us, hiding out for two years. Not able to move! Caught here like . . . waiting for them to come and get us . . . and all for what?

Anne. We're not the only people that've had to suffer. There've always been people that've had to . . . sometimes one race . . . sometimes another . . . and yet . . .

Peter. That doesn't make me feel any better!

Anne (*going to him*). I know it's terrible, trying to have any faith . . . when people are doing such horrible . . . But you know what I sometimes think? I think the world may be going through a phase, the way I was with Mother. It'll pass, maybe not for hundreds of years, but some day . . . I still believe, in spite of everything, that people are really good at heart.

Peter. I want to see something now . . . Not a thousand years from now! (*He goes over, sitting down again on the cot.*)

Anne. But, Peter, if you'd only look at it as part of a great pattern . . . that we're just a little minute in the life . . . (*She breaks off.*) Listen to us, going at each other like a couple of stupid grownups! Look at the sky now. Isn't it lovely? (*She holds out her hand to him. Peter takes it and rises, standing with her at the window looking out, his arms around her.*) Some day, when we're outside again, I'm going to . . .

(*She breaks off as she hears the sound of a car, its brakes squealing as it comes to a sudden stop. The people in the other rooms also become aware of the sound. They listen tensely. Another car roars up to a screeching stop. Anne and Peter come from Peter's room. Mr. and Mrs. Van Daan creep down the stairs. Dussel comes out from his room. Everyone is listening, hardly breathing. A doorbell clangs again and again in the building below. Mr. Frank starts quietly down the steps to the door. Dussel and Peter follow him. The others stand rigid, waiting, terrified.*

In a few seconds Dussel comes stumbling back up the steps. He shakes off Peter's help and goes to his room. Mr. Frank bolts the door below, and comes slowly back up the steps. Their eyes are all on him as he stands there for a minute. They realize that what they feared has happened. Mrs. Van Daan starts to whimper. Mr. Van Daan puts her gently in a chair, and then hurries off up the stairs to their room to collect their things. Peter goes to comfort his mother. There is a sound of violent pounding on a door below.)

Mr. Frank (*quietly*). For the past two years we have lived in fear. Now we can live in hope.

(*The pounding below becomes more insistent. There are muffled sounds of voices, shouting commands.*)

Men's Voices. *Auf machen! Da drinnen! Auf machen! Schnell! Schnell! Schnell! etc., etc.*[10]

(*The street door below is forced open. We hear the heavy tread of footsteps coming up. Mr. Frank gets two school bags from the shelves, and gives one to Anne and the other to Margot. He goes to get a bag for Mrs. Frank. The sound of feet coming up grows*

---

9. **Orthodox:** Orthodox Jews who strictly observe Jewish laws and traditions.

10. **Auf machen! . . . Schnell!** (ouf′ mäzкн′ən! dä drĭn′ən! ouf′ mäкн′ən! shnĕl! shnĕl! shnĕl!) *German:* Open up! Inside there! Open up! Quick! Quick! Quick!

louder. Peter *comes to* Anne, *kissing her good-bye, then he goes to his room to collect his things. The* 1300 *buzzer of their door starts to ring.* Mr. Frank *brings* Mrs. Frank *a bag. They stand together, waiting. We hear the thud of gun butts on the door, trying to break it down.*

Anne *stands, holding her school satchel, looking over at her father and mother with a soft, reassuring smile. She is no longer a child, but a woman with courage to meet whatever lies ahead.*

The lights dim out. The curtain falls on the scene. We hear a mighty crash as the door is shattered. 1310 *After a second* Anne's Voice *is heard.)*

Anne's Voice. And so it seems our stay here is over. They are waiting for us now. They've allowed us five minutes to get our things. We can each take a bag and whatever it will hold of clothing. Nothing else. So, dear Diary, that means I must leave you behind. Good-bye for a while. P.S. Please, please, Miep, or Mr. Kraler, or anyone else. If you should find this diary, will you please keep it safe for me, because some day 1320 I hope . . .

(Her voice stops abruptly. There is silence. After a second the curtain rises.)

Scene 5

It is again the afternoon in November, 1945. The rooms are as we saw them in the first scene. Mr. Kraler *has joined* Miep *and* Mr. Frank. *There are coffee cups on the table. We see a great change in* Mr. Frank. *He is calm now. His bitterness is gone. He slowly turns a few pages of the diary. They are blank.*

Mr. Frank. No more. *(He closes the diary and puts it* 1330 *down on the couch beside him.)*

Miep. I'd gone to the country to find food. When I got back the block was surrounded by police . . .

Mr. Kraler. We made it our business to learn how they knew. It was the thief . . . the thief who told them.

(Miep goes up to the gas burner, bringing back a pot of coffee.)

Mr. Frank *(after a pause).* It seems strange to say this, that anyone could be happy in a 1340 concentration camp. But Anne was happy in the camp in Holland where they first took us. After two years of being shut up in these rooms, she could be out . . . out in the sunshine and the fresh air that she loved.

Miep *(offering the coffee to* Mr. Frank). A little more?

Mr. Frank *(holding out his cup to her).* The news of the war was good. The British and Americans were sweeping through France. We felt sure 1350 that they would get to us in time. In September we were told that we were to be shipped to Poland . . . The men to one camp. The women to another. I was sent to Auschwitz. They went to Belsen. In January we were freed, the few of us who were left. The war wasn't yet over, so it took us a long time to get home. We'd be sent here and there behind the lines where we'd be safe. Each time our train would stop . . . at a siding, or a crossing . . . we'd all get out and go from 1360 group to group . . . Where were you? Were you at Belsen? At Buchenwald? At Mauthausen? Is it possible that you knew my wife? Did you ever see my husband? My son? My daughter? That's how I found out about my wife's death . . . of Margot, the Van Daans . . . Dussel. But Anne . . . I still hoped . . . Yesterday I went to Rotterdam. I'd heard of a woman there . . . She'd been in Belsen with Anne . . . I know now.

(He picks up the diary again, and turns the pages 1370 *back to find a certain passage. As he finds it we hear* Anne's Voice.)

Anne's Voice. In spite of everything, I still believe that people are really good at heart.

(Mr. Frank slowly closes the diary.)

Mr. Frank. She puts me to shame. *(They are silent.)* *The Curtain Falls.*

After Reading

Comprehension

1. **Recall** Who was stealing the bread in the Annex?

2. **Summarize** Why does the man from the storeroom request extra money?

Text Analysis

3. **Make Inferences** Mrs. Van Daan doesn't need her fur coat in the attic. Why does she react so strongly when Mr. Van Daan wants to sell it?

4. **Analyze Plot** What was the play's climax, or the point of highest tension? Use a graphic to note the events that happen at each stage of the play's plot.

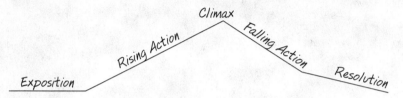

5. **Interpret a Drama** Review the chart you made as you read. Anne grew up under the Nazi occupation. In your opinion, how did life in the attic affect her personality? How did life in the attic affect the personality of Mr. Van Daan?

6. **Evaluate a Drama** Reread lines 73–118 in Act One and 1308–1330 in Act Two. According to the stage directions, what is taking place on the stage at these times? Explain how this staging allows the playwrights to convey information that might not be revealed if all dialogue occurred only between characters.

7. **Evaluate Theme** At the end of Act Two, Anne shares with Peter her ideas about the tragic events they have been hearing about. She says, "I think the world may be going through a phase . . . . It'll pass." How do Anne's ideas illustrate the theme of the play? How does Peter react to her ideas?

Extension and Challenge

8. **Creative Project: Drama** With a small group, choose a scene that supports the play's theme and practice acting it out. When you perform for the class, explain why you chose the scene you did.

9. **SOCIAL STUDIES CONNECTION** Many Jews in Europe tried to save themselves when the Nazis came to power. Research one of the following people to find out how he or she survived: Yettie Mendels, Erika Van Hesteren, Alfred Lessing, and Joseph Heinrich.

What IMPACT will you have on the world?

Review the quickwrite activity on page 508. What effect has reading *The Diary of Anne Frank* had on the way you answer the questions?

COMMON CORE

RL 2 Determine a theme of a text and analyze its development, including its relationship to the characters, setting, and plot. R 10 Read and comprehend dramas.

Language

◆ **GRAMMAR IN CONTEXT: Capitalize Correctly**

Review the stage directions in lines 1–30 on page 512. Notice how the words *European, German,* and *Dutch* are capitalized. Languages, nationalities, ethnicities, political parties, and religions should always be capitalized. Here are some examples:

Languages—English, Spanish, Russian, Chinese

Countries and Nationalities—Mexico, Canada, Irish, South African

Ethnicities—Hispanic, Native American, Caucasian, Asian

Political Parties—Democrats, Republicans, Socialists, Nazis

Religions—Judaism, Islam, Christianity, Buddhism

> *Example:*   Although the Franks lived in Holland, their first language was German.

PRACTICE Rewrite the following sentences, correcting any errors in capitalization. A sentence may contain more than one error.

1. Not all germans wanted the nazis to be in control.
2. For many europeans, it was dangerous to practice judaism.
3. Because they were jewish, the Franks fled to holland to escape persecution.
4. Anne Frank's diary was translated into many languages, including english.

*For more help with capitalization, see page R51 in the **Grammar Handbook.***

READING-WRITING CONNECTION

Increase your understanding of *The Diary of Anne Frank* by responding to this prompt. Then use the **revising tip** to improve your writing.

WRITING PROMPT	REVISING TIP
Extended Constructed Response: Explanation Why do you think Anne Frank's diary has made an impact on countless readers around the world? Write **two or three paragraphs** explaining why readers might identify with Anne and draw inspiration from her life.	Review your writing. Have you correctly capitalized all languages, nationalities, ethnicities, political parties, and religions? If not, make the appropriate corrections.

COMMON CORE

L 2 Demonstrate command of capitalization when writing.
W 2 Write explanatory texts.

Interactive Revision **THINK** central

Go to **thinkcentral.com**.
KEYWORD: HML8-567

Beyond *The Diary of Anne Frank*

Video link at
thinkcentral.com

- Newspaper Article, page 569
- Interview, page 571

Use with *The Diary of Anne Frank,* page 510.

COMMON CORE

RI 1 Cite the textual evidence that supports what the text says explicitly. **RI 3** Analyze how a text makes connections among individuals, ideas, or events. **RI 9** Analyze a case in which two or more texts provide information on the same topic.

What's the Connection?

In *The Diary of Anne Frank,* you learned what life in hiding was like for Anne and her family. Now you will read accounts from two Holocaust survivors that will tell you more about Anne, Nazi-occupied Amsterdam, and the concentration camp where the Franks were sent.

Standards Focus: Synthesize

Reading a play, diary, or book about a topic can teach you a great deal. However, you can seldom get a complete picture from any one source. To fully understand something, you have to **synthesize,** or connect facts, details, and ideas from different sources in order to form new ideas about the topic.

In this lesson, you will synthesize what you have already learned from *The Diary of Anne Frank* and one of Anne's diary entries (page 544) with information and impressions from two more sources. Your goal is to develop a fuller picture of what life was like for Jewish families in Nazi-occupied Amsterdam and in the Bergen-Belsen concentration camp.

To begin, use a chart like the one shown to record what you've learned from the play and from Anne's diary entry. Then read the next selections to add to your knowledge and fill in gaps in your understanding. Continue filling in the chart with what you learn about life under the Nazis.

	Life for a Jewish Family Hiding in Amsterdam	Life for a Jewish Family Living Openly in Amsterdam	Life in a German Concentration Camp	Impressions of Anne Frank
The Diary of Anne Frank & Anne's December 1943 diary entry				
"A Diary from Another World"				
from The Last Seven Months of Anne Frank				

A Diary from Another World

Gerda Weissmann Klein

"On Friday, June 12, I woke up at 6 A.M. and—small wonder—it was my birthday. I received a warm welcome from my cat and masses of things from Mummy and Daddy . . ."

Any 13-year-old girl could have written that on her birthday. As it happens these words appear in a diary which was one of the "masses of things" and in which Anne Frank wrote: "I hope I shall be able to confide in you completely, as I have never been able to do in anyone before . . ."

She thought that what she would write in her diary would be for her eyes alone, so she committed her innermost thoughts to it. She thought that perhaps in the very distant future—when she might have children, or even grandchildren, that they might on a rainy afternoon find their grandmother's old diary. . . .

Alas, Anne Frank died as a young girl, for no other reason than that she was Jewish. The Nazis invaded Holland, as they did most other European countries, and anyone who loved freedom and equality and was free of prejudice became an enemy of the Nazi regime. . . .

I visited Anne Frank's house the other day. Actually, I visited it twice—once alone at night when it was tightly closed, the inside shrouded in darkness. It conveyed then the eerie feeling of a tomb in which Anne's unfulfilled dreams had been dreamed during many lonely nights. . . .

Then I returned during the daytime, as the sun shone brightly and the carillon[1] from the nearby clock tower, of which Anne had written, was just playing a merry tune. In the bright sunlight, I heard music playing, saw boats moving on the canal and observed people walking by.

Across the canal I noticed a boutique, saw some young people looking at sweaters. Two kids in jeans rode on bicycles. Life was going on, even as it must have gone on while she lived there. **A**

1. **carillon** (kăr′ə-lŏn′): set of tuned bells in a tower.

Front of Anne Frank House, Amsterdam, the Netherlands

A **SYNTHESIZE**
What are Gerda Weissmann Klein's impressions of Anne Frank's house and neighborhood?

Actually, I found it sadder during the daytime, for the night at least seemed to shut out the rest of the world, whereas during the day everything revolved around the silent, subdued girl who so desperately wanted to be a part of that stream of life.

60   What did she think about in those tiny rooms where shutters had to be closed in the daytime? She tells us that often the heat became oppressive from the tiny stove on which the families cooked their meals. We know that the toilet could not be flushed in the daytime, lest the neighbors would be alerted to the existence of the hiding place.

70   What did Anne Frank think about as she sat on her bed during those perilous days looking at the pictures of American movie stars and a picture of a chimpanzee's birthday party which still hangs there today?

Her diary tells us that she thought not of fame, nor wealth, nor greatness. She thought rather how much she would want to run downstairs into the tiny 80 garden where sunflowers now bloom against the fence, instead of having to glimpse them from far above.

She thought of touching them and running through a meadow in the spring, of buying an ice cream cone from a vendor on a hot summer afternoon.

She thought of ordinary things, such as going to school with other kids. She thought of dressing up and being 90 able to go to the movies.

In short, she thought of all the things which millions of kids do every day and find boring. But to Anne, who occasionally dared to climb to the roof to see the sky and the patch of world below, that world was as remote as the evening star. **B**

This is the legacy she left us, the understanding of things all of us take 100 for granted. Through understanding, let us assure that all people everywhere can live in freedom so that a book like *The Diary of Anne Frank* will never be written again as a true story.

B SYNTHESIZE
Reread lines 76–97. What new insights about Anne's thoughts do you get from this article?

Anne Frank's diary

Hannah Elisabeth
Pick-Goslar and
Anne Frank

The Last Seven Months of Anne Frank

Interview with Hannah Elisabeth Pick-Goslar

Willy Lindwer

Mr. Frank's factory, Opekta, produced a substance for making jam. My mother always got the old packages as a gift. Soon after school let out, my mother sent me to the Franks' house to get the scale because she wanted to make jam. It was a beautiful day.

I went as usual to the Franks' house and rang and rang and rang, [10] but no one opened the door. I didn't know why no one answered. I rang again, and finally, Mr. Goudsmit, a tenant, opened the door. **C**

"What do you want? What have you come for?" he asked in astonishment.

"I've come to borrow the scale."

"Don't you know that the entire Frank family has gone to [20] Switzerland?"

I didn't know anything about it. "Why?" I asked.

He didn't know either.

This was a bolt out of the blue. Why had they gone to Switzerland? The only connection the Frank family had with Switzerland was that Otto Frank's mother lived there.

30 But later it appeared that, in fact, the family had always reckoned that it would get worse for Jews. They had been preparing for a whole year to go into hiding. We didn't know anything about this. You can't talk about something like that. Because if anyone talked, then the whole affair would go amiss. . . .

I believe that Anne was the first girlfriend that I lost. It was, of course, 40 very frightening, but we began to get used to the idea. When I went back to school after the summer, fewer children came to class every day.

We stayed in Amsterdam almost a full year longer, until June 20, 1943, and all this time things were getting worse and worse. Jews had to wear a yellow star. We had an *Ausweis* (an identification card), with a large "J" 50 on it—for Jew. People were stopped on the street: "May I see your *Ausweis?*" If you were Jewish, you were taken away and you never returned home. And a mother waiting for her child would ask herself: Where is my child? Have they taken her away? . . . **D**

So far, my family had been lucky insofar as we were able to buy South 60 American citizenship through an uncle in Switzerland. We were expatriates. That's why it was

D SYNTHESIZE
After the Franks went into hiding, what happened to other Jews in Amsterdam?

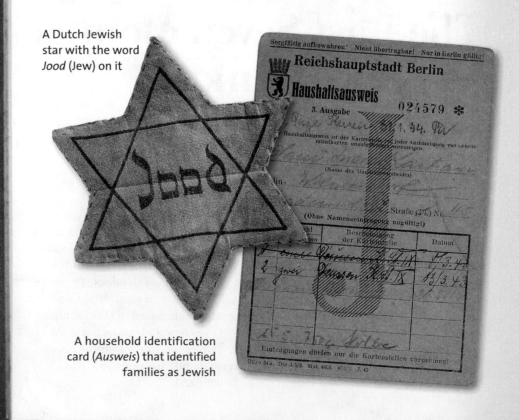

A Dutch Jewish star with the word *Jood* (Jew) on it

A household identification card (*Ausweis*) that identified families as Jewish

possible. We got passports from Paraguay. Laughing, my father said, "You'd better know something about Paraguay in case they ask." So I learned the name of the capital, Asunción. I didn't know anything else, but no one ever asked me
70 anything.

Because of these passports we could still go out for a while longer without trembling in fear, but you never knew what would happen tomorrow. . . .

So we continued to live, with little to eat and with a great deal of fear, but at least we were at home. In October, my mother died during
80 childbirth. The baby was born dead. That was in Anne's diary. Someone told Anne that our baby had died, but not that my mother had died too. They probably didn't have the heart to tell her. . . . **E**

Everything went along fine until June 20, 1943, when there was the big roundup in Amsterdam-South. On that day, the Germans started

90 something new. At five o'clock in the morning while everyone was asleep they blocked off all the southern part of Amsterdam. They went from door to door, rang, and asked:

"Do Jews live here?"

"Yes."

"You have fifteen minutes; take a backpack, put a few things in it, and get outside quickly."

100 That was our neighborhood, so we had to pack too. A passport no longer helped. We had a quarter of an hour, and we had to go with them. . . .

So we were taken to Westerbork. My father ended up in a very large barracks. My sister and I were put in an orphanage, where, they said, there was more to eat. My father had
110 known the director of the orphanage when he was in Germany. My little sister wasn't there very long. She became seriously ill and had to have operations on both ears. She was in the hospital for almost the entire time that we were in Westerbork. . . .

Language Coach

Word Definitions The word *barracks* in line 107 means "a building or group of buildings used for temporary housing." Do you think the writer's father shared the barracks with few or many people?

E **SYNTHESIZE**
Reread lines 58–85. What strategies did Jews living openly use to survive? What hardships did they endure?

```
  5                 3 September        4 · Blatt
  JUDENTRANSPORT AUS DEN NIEDERLANDEN - LAGER WESTERBORK

                       Haeftlinge

  301.✓Engers        Isidor — ✓30.4. 93-  Kaufmann
  302✓ Engers        Leonard   15.6. 20-  Lamdarbeiter
  303✓ Franco        Manfred - ✓1.5.  05-  Verleger
  304. Frank         Arthur    22.8. 81   Kaufmann
  305. Frank ×       Isaac    ✓29.11.87   Installateur
  306. Frank         Margot   ·16.2. 26   ohne
  307. Frank    ✓    Otto     ✓12.5. 89   Kaufmann
  308.✓ Frank-Hollaender Edith 16.1. 00   ohne
  309. Frank         Anneliese 12.6. 29   ohne
  310. v.Franck      Sara —    27.4. 02-  Typistin
  311. Franken       Rozanna   16.5. 96-  Landarbeiter
  312.✓ Franken-Weyand Johanna 24.12.96✓  Landbauer
  313. Franken       Hermann - ✓12.5.34   ohne
  314. Franken       Louis     10.8. 17-  Gaertner
  315. Franken  R    Rosalina  29.3. 27   Landbau
  316. Frankfort     Alex      14.11.19-  Dr.i.d.Oekonomie
```

The Franks' names on a transport list from the Westerbork transit camp

F SYNTHESIZE
Reread lines 148–162.
What is the relationship
between this incident
and the **theme** of the
play?

On February 15, 1944, we were transported to Bergen-Belsen. . . . When we arrived, our clothes weren't 120 taken away and families weren't separated. My father and my sister stayed with me. We slept in different places, but we could see each other every evening. The trip took—I don't remember precisely—two or three days to get to Bergen-Belsen. . . .

In Bergen-Belsen, it was very cold in the winter. We soon found that out. Because we had been arrested in 130 June we hadn't thought about winter clothes. Especially me, a young girl, who had to do her own packing. But what I had brought, I kept.

My sister had a large bandage on her head because she had had surgery on her ears in Westerbork. The first day we arrived in Bergen-Belsen, I got jaundice. The policy of the Germans was: whoever got sick 140 had to go to the hospital; otherwise, all the others could be infected. I didn't know what to do with my little sister. My father was confined in another barracks and I couldn't take her to him. He also had to work, so that wouldn't have worked out.

So there I was and didn't know what to do. This situation showed me 150 that there were very special people in that camp. I told an old lady that I was at my wits' end: "Tomorrow morning, I have to go to the hospital and my little sister is sick."

Two hours later, a woman came, who said, "My name is Abrahams. Mrs. Lange told me that you were here and that you don't know what to do with your sister. I have seven 160 children; give her to me; then we'll just have one more little child with us." **F**

And that's how it worked out. The next morning her daughter, who seemed to be about my age, came and took the little girl with her. Meanwhile, my father was able to visit me. We were together with that family until the end. To this day we 170 have stayed on friendly terms with them. . . .

One day, we looked in the direction where there hadn't been any barracks and saw that tents had suddenly appeared there. . . . Then a barbed-wire fence was built through the middle of the camp and filled with straw so that we couldn't see the other side. But we were, of course, 180 very close to each other, because the camp wasn't large. All those people from the tents were taken to the barracks on the other side. In spite of the German guards on the high watchtowers, we tried to make contact. . . .

One of my acquaintances, an older woman, came up to me one day. "Do you know, there are some Dutch 190 people there. I spoke to Mrs. Van Daan." The woman had known her from before, and she told me that Anne was there. She knew that I knew Anne.

"Go over to the barbed-wire fence and try to talk to her." And, of course, I did. In the evening, I stood by the barbed-wire fence and began to call out. And quite by chance Mrs. 200 Van Daan was there again. I asked her, "Could you call Anne?"

She said, "Yes, yes, wait a minute, I'll go to get Anne. I can't get Margot; she is very, very ill and is in bed."

Language Coach

Idiom An idiom is a word or phrase that has a meaning that is different than its individual words. The phrase "at my wits' end" that appears in line 152 is an idiom. It means the writer didn't know what to do. What problem did she need to solve?

THIS IS THE SITE OF
THE INFAMOUS BELSEN CONCENTRATION CAMP
Liberated by the British on 15 apri 1945.

10,000 UNBURIED DEAD WERE FOUND HERE.
ANOTHER 13,000 HAVE SINCE DIED,
ALL OF THEM VICTIMS OF THE
GERMAN NEW ORDER IN EUROPE,
AND AN EXAMPLE OF NAZI KULTUR.

A sign posted by the British army outside the Bergen-Belsen concentration camp

But naturally I was much more interested in Anne, and I waited there a few minutes in the dark.

Anne came to the barbed-wire fence—I couldn't see her. The fence and the straw were between us. There wasn't much light. Maybe I saw her shadow. It wasn't the same Anne. She was a broken girl. I probably was, too, but it was so terrible. She immediately began to cry, and she told me, "I don't have any parents anymore."

I remember that with absolute certainty. That was terribly sad, because she couldn't have known anything else. She thought that her father had been gassed right away. But Mr. Frank looked very young and healthy, and of course the Germans didn't know how old everybody was who they wanted to gas, but selected them on the basis of their appearance. Someone who looked healthy had to work, but another who might even be younger, but who was sick or looked bad, went directly to the gas chamber. **G**

I always think, if Anne had known that her father was still alive, she

G SYNTHESIZE
What happened to Jewish people in the concentration camps who looked healthy? What happened to those who were sick or looked ill?

might have had more strength to survive, because she died very shortly before the end—only a few days before [liberation]. But maybe it was all predestined.

240   So we stood there, two young girls, and we cried. I told her about my mother. She hadn't known that; she only knew that the baby had died. And I told her about my little sister. I told her that my father was in the hospital. He died two weeks later; he was already very sick. She told me that Margot was seriously ill and she told me about going into hiding
250 because I was, of course, extremely curious.

"But what are you doing here? You were supposed to be in Switzerland, weren't you?" And then she told me what had happened. That they didn't go to Switzerland at all and why they had said that; so that everyone should think that they had gone to her grandmother's.

260   Then she said, "We don't have anything at all to eat here, almost nothing, and we are cold; we don't have any clothes and I've gotten very thin and they shaved my hair." That was terrible for her. She had always been very proud of her hair. It may have grown back a bit in the meantime, but it certainly wasn't the long hair she'd had before, which she playfully curled
270 around her fingers. It was much worse for them than for us. I said, "They didn't take away our clothes." That was our first meeting. **H**

Then for the first time—we had already been in the camp for more than a year; we arrived in February 1944, and this was February 1945— we received a very small Red Cross

package: my sister, my father, and I.
280 A very small package, the size of a book, with *knäckebrot* (Scandinavian crackers), and a few cookies. You can't imagine how little that was. My son always says, "But Mama, that was something really very special." But in those days we really collected everything, half a cookie, a sock, a glove—anything that gave a little warmth or something to eat. My
290 friends also gave me something for Anne. I certainly couldn't have thrown a large package over the barbed-wire fence; not that I had one, but that wouldn't have been possible at all.

We agreed to try to meet the next evening at eight o'clock—I believe I still had a watch. And, in fact, I succeeded in throwing the package
300 over.

But I heard her screaming, and I called out, "What happened?"

And Anne answered, "Oh, the woman standing next to me caught it, and she won't give it back to me."

Then she began to scream.

I calmed her down a bit and said, "I'll try again but I don't know if I'll be able to." We arranged to meet
310 again, two or three days later, and I was actually able to throw over another package. She caught it; that was the main thing.

After these three or four meetings at the barbed-wire fence in Bergen-Belsen, I didn't see her again, because the people in Anne's camp were transferred to another section in Bergen-Belsen. That happened
320 around the end of February. **I**

That was the last time I saw Anne alive and spoke to her.

H SYNTHESIZE
What do you learn about Anne's circumstances from this first meeting?

I SYNTHESIZE
By the end of this account, what have you learned about life in Bergen-Belsen?

Comprehension

1. **Recall** For what occasion does Anne Frank receive her diary?

2. **Summarize** Briefly describe Hannah Elisabeth Pick-Goslar's experiences in Bergen-Belsen before she reconnects with Anne.

Text Analysis

3. **Evaluate a Source** Gerda Weissmann Klein, the author of "A Diary from Another World," is Jewish. When she was 15, Nazis invaded her home country, Poland. She was forced to work as a slave laborer in German factories. Her entire family was killed in the Holocaust. What effect does Klein's background have on the way you view the information in the article?

4. **Analyze an Interview** Pick-Goslar has a unique view of Anne. Explain why that is. What new information about Anne and her family do you learn from Pick-Goslar's account?

5. **Synthesize** What were the physical and emotional effects of living in a Nazi-occupied country as a Jew? What survival techniques allowed people to withstand the hardships they did? Refer to the chart you filled in as you read, and support your answer with evidence from at least three selections.

COMMON CORE

RI 1 Cite the textual evidence that supports what the text says explicitly. **RI 3** Analyze how a text makes connections among individuals, ideas, or events. **RI 9** Analyze a case in which two or more texts provide information on the same topic. **W 2** Write explanatory texts. **W 2b** Develop the topic with facts, details, quotations, or other information and examples.

Read for Information: Make a Generalization

WRITING PROMPT

Identify an important life lesson you take away from these Jewish families' experiences. Support your response with evidence from the selections.

To respond to this prompt, you will have to make a generalization. A **generalization** is a broad statement about a topic that follows logically from solid evidence. To arrive at your generalization, follow these steps:

1. Review the information you gathered in your chart, jotting down any general statements about life or human nature.

2. Pick the most convincing statement you have jotted down and rephrase it as a life lesson. To do this, begin with a phrase such as "It is human nature to ..."

3. Review the evidence for your generalization to make sure it comes from more than one source and supports your statement.

4. In a paragraph, state the life lesson you've identified. Then present evidence from two or more texts to support this generalization.

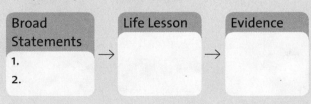

Broad Statements	Life Lesson	Evidence
1.		
2.		

from **Anne Frank Remembered**
Film Clip on **Media Smart** DVD-ROM

Can films make
HISTORY fresh?

◌ **COMMON CORE**

RI 7 Evaluate the advantages and disadvantages of using different mediums to present a topic.

Have you ever wanted to meet a famous figure from **history?** We can learn the facts about a famous person's life, but we can't know what it would be like to sit down and talk to him or her. In this lesson, you'll watch a biographical documentary about Anne Frank. You'll explore how the filmmakers try to bring you into Anne's world and give you a sense of what she was really like.

Background

Behind the Symbol Anne Frank's diary has sold over 31 million copies in approximately 67 languages. She has become an enduring symbol of the tragedy of the Holocaust. But behind that symbol was a real girl, a teenager trapped for two years in a small hiding place with seven other people.

Anne Frank Remembered is a documentary that explores the life and death of the girl behind the symbol. The film takes viewers inside the Franks' hidden annex, revealing what it was like to live in such cramped quarters. It also tells the story of Anne's diary, and how her private thoughts became the book that has touched readers throughout the world.

Media Literacy: Documentary

A **documentary** is a nonfiction film that often presents social, political, or historical subject matter. Famous historical figures make good subjects for documentaries, because the filmmakers can tell the story of both the individual and the time period. To create a documentary, filmmakers often gather **primary sources,** firsthand information such as diaries, photographs, and eyewitness accounts. They then combine these materials with **voice-over narration** and, often, a **re-enactment** of scenes or settings to re-create the times for viewers.

FEATURES OF A DOCUMENTARY

Footage is recorded material that gives information about a subject. It includes film clips, photographs, news reports, and interviews. Footage from a particular time period can show viewers what life was like back then.

Voice-over narration is the voice of an unseen speaker that is heard in a documentary. The voice-over tells the subject's story and explains the footage. **Primary sources,** such as diary entries, can also be read as part of the voice-over narration.

Re-enactment is the re-creation of key events or important settings. Filmmakers shoot scenes or settings using sets, props, actors, and costumes. They try to re-create the subject's story as realistically as possible.

STRATEGIES FOR VIEWING

- Identify the different types of **footage.** Notice how the filmmakers combine primary source footage with footage they shoot themselves, such as interviews and re-enactments, to tell the whole story.
- Think about the purpose of the **voice-over narration.** Different narrators can present different sides of someone's personality.
- Notice the type of information you learn from any **re-enactments.** Re-enactments are often used in historical documentaries. Think about why the filmmakers might have chosen to present the information in this way.

Viewing Guide for

Anne Frank Remembered

You'll view three clips from *Anne Frank Remembered.* They reveal the Franks' secret annex in Amsterdam, the story of the publication of the diary, and the only known moving footage of Anne Frank. As you view the clips, think about how the documentary features add a freshness to her story. You'll hear two different **voice-over narrators.** Notice the different types of information you learn from each. Watch for different types of **footage** and any **re-enactment** of setting the film provides. Before answering these questions, you may want to view the clip more than once.

NOW VIEW

FIRST VIEWING: Comprehension

1. **Recall** After Otto Frank had such trouble getting Anne's diary published, what finally caused a publisher to step forward?

2. **Clarify** Give two examples of **primary source** material used in the clips you viewed.

CLOSE VIEWING: Media Literacy

3. **Examine the Visuals** Think about the **re-enactment** of the setting of the secret annex. Why do you think the filmmakers show the food and furniture fading away to leave empty rooms?

4. **Analyze Voice-over Narration** Think about the different types of information the two **voice-over narrators** provide. Why might the filmmakers have decided to use two narrators rather than one?

5. **Determine Filmmakers' Purpose** The clip of Anne Frank standing at the window is from the end of the documentary. What effect do you think the filmmakers intended this clip to have on viewers?

Write or Discuss

Compare the Texts Think about the impression you had of Anne Frank from the play you read. Now think about the documentary clips you viewed. Write a brief comparison of the Anne you read about in the play and the Anne described in the film. Which is most effective at going beyond the symbol and revealing what you believe to be the real Anne Frank? Think about the following:

- the documentary footage of the actual secret annex where the Franks hid
- how the play portrays Anne's personality
- the footage of Anne at the window, and the voice-over reading of her diary

Produce Your Own Media

Create a Visual Timeline When filmmakers plan a biographical documentary, they look closely at their subject's entire life story. They decide what events to include in the documentary and what to leave out. Imagine you're planning a documentary about a friend's life. Choose five or six events in that person's life, and create a visual timeline depicting these events. Your timeline should include a photograph or drawing and a caption for each event.

HERE'S HOW Here are a few suggestions for preparing your visual timeline:

- Start by choosing the events you want to show. Choose the most exciting and interesting things that have happened to your friend.
- Collect or take photographs to illustrate each event. You might want to have your friend **re-enact** a favorite event, such as a time he or she won a contest.
- Write a brief sentence for each picture that describes the event depicted.
- Arrange your pictures on a board in chronological order.

STUDENT MODEL

Age 1 — Joel celebrates his first birthday.

Age 6 — At age six, a new friend enters Joel's life. He names the puppy Buster.

Age 10 — After a rough start, Joel finds his way at Frontier Middle School.

Age 11 — He takes second at the spelling bee, after missing the "h" in "gherkin."

Age 13 — Joel's competitive nature shows through, both on the mantel . . .

Age 13 — . . . and on the basketball court.

COMMON CORE

RI 7 Evaluate the advantages and disadvantages of using different mediums to present a topic.

Media Tools

THINK central

Go to **thinkcentral.com**.
KEYWORD: HML8-581

Tech Tip

If available, use a computer software program to present your timeline.

Writing Workshop

NARRATIVE

Short Story

What did you like best about the stories you read in this unit—the characters, the suspense, or maybe the satisfying endings? In this workshop, you will weave your own tale of adventure, mystery, triumph, or woe.

 Complete the workshop activities in your **Reader/Writer Notebook.**

WRITE WITH A PURPOSE

WRITING TASK

Write a **short story** with an interesting plot that will entertain an audience of children, teenagers, or adults.

Idea Starters
- a middle-school student travels back in time
- a lonely girl discovers a new side of herself
- two former friends compete for a prize
- a family adopts an unusual pet

THE ESSENTIALS

Here are some common purposes, audiences, and formats for fictional writing.

PURPOSES	AUDIENCES	FORMATS
• to entertain readers • to express a general idea or insight about life	• classmates and teacher • parents • storytelling festival • writing group • judges of short story contest • Web users	• story for class • oral presentation • story for school literary magazine • blog post • video • podcast

COMMON CORE TRAITS

1. DEVELOPMENT OF IDEAS
- introduces and develops a **conflict**
- introduces and develops a **narrator** and **characters**
- uses **dialogue** and **description** to develop events
- ends with a **conclusion,** or **resolution** of the conflict
- uses events and characters to reveal a **theme,** or message about life

2. ORGANIZATION OF IDEAS
- develops a **sequence of events** that unfolds naturally and logically
- uses **pacing** to develop the plot

3. LANGUAGE FACILITY AND CONVENTIONS
- establishes and maintains a **point of view**
- uses **precise words** and **phrases, relevant descriptive details,** and **sensory language**
- uses effective **sentence structures**
- employs **correct grammar, mechanics,** and **spelling**

Writing Online

THINK central

Go to **thinkcentral.com**.
KEYWORD: HML8N-582

Planning/Prewriting

COMMON CORE

W 3a–e Write narratives to develop real or imagined experiences or events using effective technique, relevant descriptive details, and well-structured event sequences. **W 5** Develop and strengthen writing as needed by planning.

Getting Started

CHOOSE A STORY IDEA

Although a story is a work of fiction, the characters and events should seem real. You can make up a story based on people and places you know.

▶ **ASK YOURSELF:**
- What types of people do I know well who would make good characters?
- What are some experiences I know about that might make an interesting story?

THINK ABOUT AUDIENCE AND PURPOSE

As you plan your story, keep in mind your **purpose** and **audience.** Remember that your audience should dictate the style of writing you use. **Style** is the way you use words to express ideas or describe things.

▶ **ASK YOURSELF:**
- Who will read my story? What style of writing would engage these readers?
- What audience would be entertained by my story?
- Do I want my audience to be inspired or to do or feel something in particular?

PLAN CHARACTERS

Think about how your characters look, act, and sound. As you develop your characters, write down **precise words** and **phrases** that give your readers a clear picture of your characters' **traits,** or qualities. Avoid describing characters with vague words, such as "cool" or "interesting." Use specific, relevant **descriptive details** and **sensory language** to really bring the characters to life.

▶ **WHAT DOES IT LOOK LIKE?**

Character: Martak		
Appearance	Personality	Others' Reactions
wears futuristic clothing	serious, businesslike	supervisor treats him with respect

PLAN POINT OF VIEW

Think about who will tell your story. A **first-person narrator** is a character in the story and refers to himself or herself as *I* or *me*. A **third-person narrator** is someone outside the story who describes the characters as *he, she,* or *they*. Once you decide on a narrator, establish and maintain the same point of view throughout the story.

▶ **TIPS:**
- A first-person narrator can give a very personal perspective on story events. Make sure to describe the narrator's thoughts and feelings about the events.
- A third-person narrator is not directly involved in the events of the story. If your third-person narrator is omniscient, or all-seeing, you can describe the thoughts and feelings of all the characters in the story.

Planning/Prewriting *continued*

Getting Started

DECIDE ON A SETTING

Your setting can give readers a lot of information. The setting tells about your characters (for example, a mansion indicates wealth) and can even play a role in the conflict (for example, a character may struggle to survive in a desert).

▶ ASK YOURSELF:

- When and where does the story take place? Over how much time?
- What role, if any, does the setting play in the conflict?
- How can I describe the setting using sensory language to create a distinct mood?

PLAN YOUR PLOT

After you've decided on your characters and setting, create a story map that outlines your plot. Make sure your plot includes these basic elements:

- a **conflict,** or struggle, that will drive the action of your story
- **rising action,** a series of related events set in motion by the conflict
- a **climax,** or most exciting point, when something happens that reveals how the conflict will end
- a **resolution,** or outcome, showing how things work out

Most of the events in your story should be presented in **chronological order,** or the order in which they happen. If your plot is well planned, the events should unfold naturally and logically.

▶ WHAT DOES IT LOOK LIKE?

> **Characters:**
> Martak, Martak's supervisor, Johnny, Johnny's parents
>
> **Setting:**
> a laboratory in space; Johnny's yard
>
> **Conflict:** Martak decides to end an experiment, but this means destroying a whole planet.
>
> **Event 1:** In lab, Martak tells his supervisor that they should end an experiment.
>
> **Event 2:** In yard, Johnny plays in a sandbox.
>
> **Event 3:** Supervisor agrees with Martak.
>
> **Event 4:** Johnny's mother calls him in.
>
> **Event 5 (climax):** Johnny sees a large star getting bigger; his parents scream.
>
> **Resolution:** In lab, Martak watches a sphere burning on his monitor.

PEER REVIEW Using your story map, give an oral summary of your story to a classmate. Then ask: Does my story make sense? How can I better engage and orient my readers?

YOUR TURN In your *Reader/Writer Notebook,* plan your story. Use a chart like the one on page 583 to develop your story's characters. Then create a story map. Exchange plans with a classmate. Think about what he or she says and then revise your plan, keeping in mind your purpose and audience.

Drafting

W 4 Produce clear and coherent writing appropriate to task, purpose, and audience. **L 1b** Form and use verbs in the active and passive voice. **L 3a** Use verbs in the active and passive voice to achieve particular effects.

The following chart shows how to draft an effective short story.

Organizing Your Short Story

EXPOSITION

- Open with a sentence or an intriguing piece of dialogue that will **engage** your audience.
- Establish the **point of view** and introduce the **conflict, characters,** and **setting**.

▼

RISING ACTION AND CLIMAX

- Create a **sequence of events** that leads toward the **climax.**
- Use **transitions,** such as *finally* or *later,* to convey sequence and signal shifts in time or setting.
- Use verbs in the active voice to move your plot forward and establish effective **pacing.**
- Develop characters and show action through **dialogue, description,** and **reflection.**

▼

RESOLUTION

- Show how the **resolution** of the conflict affects the characters.
- Reveal a **theme,** or message about life, in your conclusion.

GRAMMAR IN CONTEXT: USING THE ACTIVE VOICE

A verb in the **active voice** describes an action performed by the subject. A verb in the **passive voice** describes an action received by its subject, using a form of the verb *be*.

Type of Voice	Example
active voice ▶	Johnny **gazed on** his mostly finished sand castle.
passive voice ▶	The mostly finished sand castle **was gazed on** by Johnny.

Above, the active voice is direct and natural, while the passive voice is awkward. However, if you do not want the person performing the action to be known, or if you want to emphasize the subject receiving the action, the passive voice can be effective.

> The sand castle **had been abandoned** and **would soon be washed away** by the rising tide.

YOUR TURN Develop a draft of your story. Use the active voice to achieve a direct and forceful effect in your writing. Use the passive voice to accomplish a more subtle effect.

Revising

When you revise, your goal is to improve your draft by looking for places where you can add details about the characters, include dialogue, or further develop your plot to make your story more entertaining for your audience. The chart below will help you revise, rewrite, and improve your draft.

SHORT STORY

Ask Yourself	Tips	Revision Strategies
1. Does the story have a well-developed plot? Do the events build to a climax? Is the main conflict resolved?	▶ **Place a check mark** next to each element: conflict, rising action, climax, and resolution.	▶ **Add or elaborate** on plot elements as necessary. **Delete** events that do not help move the story toward its climax.
2. Are main characters complex and convincing? Does the story establish a specific, believable setting?	▶ **Underline** descriptive details and dialogue that reveal character traits. **Draw an arrow** to details that describe the setting.	▶ **Add** relevant descriptive details about appearance, personality, or background. **Add** dialogue and actions that develop character, if needed. **Elaborate** on the setting by adding details.
3. Does the pace keep the plot moving?	▶ **Highlight** sentences that slow the story's pace.	▶ **Delete** unnecessary details and **add** strong verbs to quicken the pace.
4. Are events arranged in a natural and logical sequence? Are transitions used to show order?	▶ **Number** the major events. **Put a star** next to transitional words, phrases, and clauses.	▶ **Rearrange** events that are out of order. **Add** a variety of transitional words, phrases, and clauses, such as *before*, *after*, or *during*, to show the order of events.
5. Is the point of view established and maintained throughout the story?	▶ **Circle** pronouns that show whether the point of view is first or third person.	▶ **Change** pronouns or details that shift the point of view.
6. Does the story reveal a theme?	▶ **Underline** clues that suggest an important idea about life or human nature.	▶ **Add** details or sentences that clarify and reflect on the theme.

 YOUR TURN *PEER REVIEW* Exchange stories with a classmate. Read your classmate's story once for enjoyment. Then reread it, and use the chart above to suggest revisions and identify areas where a new approach might be necessary.

COMMON CORE

W 3b Use narrative techniques, such as dialogue. **W 5** Develop and strengthen writing as needed by revising, editing, rewriting, or trying a new approach, focusing on how well purpose and audience have been addressed.

ANALYZE A STUDENT DRAFT

Read this student's draft. Notice the comments on its strengths as well as the suggestions for improvement.

Experiment 023681

by Peter Leary, Athens Academy

❶ "They're still regressing," said Martak, as he raised his head from the viewing screen, disappointment shadowing his face. "I can't support the continued funding of Experiment 023681. We have others which work much better."

❷ "Very well," rumbled the deep voice of Martak's supervisor. "It's too bad, though. They seemed so promising."

❸ "I know. Disappointing, isn't it?" commented Martak. "But living conditions are horrible, they insist on killing each other in these petty little things called 'wars,' and look at their life span: on the outside, ninety-five of their 'years'!"

❹ "I agree. Permission granted to terminate Experiment 023681."

❺ Johnny gazed on his mostly finished sand castle, feeling a four-year-old's pride. He knew it was getting dark, so he scooped quickly.

❻ Martak looked at the small mass of swirling blues, greens, and whites on his monitor.

> The fact that the "experiment" is mysterious creates **suspense**—a feeling of growing tension for the reader. Dialogue conveys information about the **setting, characters,** and **conflict.**

> Peter uses extra space between paragraphs to show a shift to another character and setting.

> The action returns to the first setting. Peter could use **dialogue** here to make clear what is happening at this point in the story.

LEARN HOW Use Dialogue to Develop Plot Sometimes **dialogue** is the best way to reveal what is happening in a story. In Peter's draft, Martak looks at his monitor, and then (on page 588) the action returns to Johnny and his mother. Peter added the following dialogue to his revised draft in order to make clear what is going on with Martak.

PETER'S REVISION TO PARAGRAPH ❻

Martak looked at the small mass of swirling blues, greens, and whites

on his monitor. ⌄ *He entered his access code.*

"Request?" questioned a tinny voice.

"Terminate Experiment 023681."

"Request confirmed."

❼   "John, come in the house!" his mother shouted from the porch.

❽   "I'm coming, Mom, he responded. Ambling to the porch, he glanced behind him at the sky. "Mommy, come look. There's a star that's getting bigger.

❾   His mother screamed to come inside, away from the door and the windows. His dad screamed, "Invaders!" Johnny stood entranced by the light that now seemed to shine on his house.

❿   Martak watched as the small, perfect sphere was engulfed in yellow flame. The flame slowly turned orange, then red, then finally settled into a black cloud, which died, leaving behind only dust. He sighed and turned to the next experiment.

> Peter further develops the second setting and its characters. He can make the story more engaging for his readers by building **suspense**.

> The story reaches a **climax** as Johnny's parents scream. Peter provides a clear **resolution** by returning to Martak, whose monitor reveals what has happened to Johnny's planet.

LEARN HOW Develop Suspense with Effective Pacing Peter does a good job of capturing his readers' interest with an unusual story that quickly switches back and forth between two very different settings. He can make his story even more engaging by increasing **suspense,** or the tension readers feel as they wonder what will happen next. One way that a writer can increase suspense is to emphasize that time is passing and that very soon something terrible may happen. By slowing down the pace before a major event, Peter can prolong the suspense and build the anticipation of readers. Peter added a short scene, shown in blue, to increase suspense.

PETER'S REVISION TO PARAGRAPH ❼

"John, come in the house!" his mother shouted from the porch.

Johnny sighed and dropped his shovel as he trudged toward his house. He knew his mother meant it when she said "John."

He looked up at the darkening sky, and saw the first stars.

"Now, John," said his mother sternly.

"I'm coming, Mom, he responded. Ambling to the porch, he glanced behind him at the sky. "Mommy, come look. There's a star that's getting bigger.

YOUR TURN Use the revision strategies chart, feedback from your peers and teacher, and the two "Learn How" lessons to help you revise your story. Evaluate whether you have met all the requirements of a good short story. If necessary, try a new approach in order to better fulfill your main purpose.

Editing and Publishing

W 3b Use narrative techniques, such as dialogue and pacing. **W 5** Develop and strengthen writing as needed by revising, editing, or trying a new approach. **L 2** Demonstrate command of capitalization, punctuation, and spelling.

In the editing stage, you review your writing to make sure that it is free of grammar, usage, spelling, capitalization, and punctuation errors before you prepare your final draft to share with your audience.

GRAMMAR IN CONTEXT: PUNCTUATING DIALOGUE

In a short story, dialogue—the words spoken by characters—reveals what characters are like and also helps move the plot along. It's important to use correct punctuation so that readers will know what each character says. **Quotation marks** are used to enclose a character's exact words.

> *"Very well," rumbled the deep voice of Martak's supervisor. "It's too bad, though. They seemed so promising."*
>
> *"I know. Disappointing, isn't it?" commented Martak.*

[Dialogue is usually separated from the rest of the sentence by a **comma.** However, if the speaker's words are a question or an exclamation, use a **question mark** or an exclamation point instead of a comma.]

As Peter edited his story, he realized that he had made some errors in punctuation. To clarify what his character Johnny said, he added quotation marks around Johnny's dialogue.

> *"I'm coming, Mom," he responded. Ambling to the porch, he glanced behind him at the sky. "Mommy, come look. There's a star that's getting bigger."*

PUBLISH YOUR WRITING

Share your short story with an audience.

- Submit your story to your school's literary magazine or to an online literary magazine.
- Enter your work in a short story contest.
- Adapt your story as a video and make it available in a podcast.

 YOUR TURN Correct any errors in your story. As you proofread, look closely to make sure that any dialogue spoken by your characters is punctuated correctly and enclosed in quotation marks. Check your capitalization and spelling, as well. Then publish your final story for others to enjoy.

Scoring Rubric

Use the rubric below to evaluate your short story from the Writing Workshop or your response to the on-demand writing task on the next page.

SHORT STORY

SCORE	COMMON CORE TRAITS
6	• **Development** Effectively and engagingly introduces, develops, and resolves a conflict; develops characters and events with strong dialogue and description; reveals and reflects on a significant theme • **Organization** Effectively establishes a natural and logical sequence of events; uses effective pacing and transitions • **Language** Consistently maintains a clear point of view; uses many relevant descriptive details; shows a strong command of conventions
5	• **Development** Effectively introduces, develops, and resolves a conflict; develops characters and events with dialogue and description; reveals a significant theme • **Organization** Has a natural and logical sequence of events; uses mostly effective pacing and transitions • **Language** Maintains a clear point of view; includes relevant descriptive details; has a few errors in conventions
4	• **Development** Introduces, develops, and resolves a conflict; could use more dialogue or description to develop characters and events; reveals a theme • **Organization** Has a generally logical sequence with some unnecessary events, resulting in ineffective pacing; uses some transitions that don't make sense • **Language** Usually maintains a point of view; needs more descriptive details; includes a few distracting errors in conventions
3	• **Development** Introduces and resolves a conflict, but needs more development; needs more dialogue and description; suggests a theme • **Organization** Has a confusing sequence due to unnecessary events; has a slow pace at times; needs more transitions to convey sequence • **Language** Has some lapses in point of view; has some major errors in conventions
2	• **Development** Introduces a conflict but does not develop or resolve it; lacks enough dialogue and description; presents no clear theme • **Organization** Has too many events and an uneven pace; lacks transitions throughout • **Language** Changes point of view; mostly lacks details; has many errors in conventions
1	• **Development** Has no conflict; lacks dialogue, description, reflection, and theme • **Organization** Has no apparent organization • **Language** Has no clear point of view or details; has major conventions problems

Preparing for Timed Writing

COMMON CORE **W 10** Write routinely over shorter time frames for a range of tasks, purposes, and audiences.

1. ANALYZE THE TASK   5 MIN

Read the task carefully. Then read it again, underlining the words that tell the type of writing, the topic, the purpose, and the audience.

> **WRITING TASK**   *Type of writing*   *Topic*
>
> Write a <u>fictional or personal narrative</u> about <u>someone trying something new</u> that will <u>entertain your classmates</u>. Make sure the characters and setting are believable. Use relevant descriptive details to describe events that lead to the resolution of a conflict.
>
> *Purpose and audience*

2. PLAN YOUR RESPONSE   10 MIN

Brainstorm examples of people (real or imagined) either going to a new place or trying a new food, skill, or activity. Which of these topics do you know well enough to write about in detail? After you choose an idea for your narrative, make a chart to organize your details.

Setting:
Characters:
Conflict:
Events:
Resolution:

3. RESPOND TO THE TASK   20 MIN

Using your notes about setting, characters, and conflict, begin drafting your narrative. As you write, keep the following points in mind:

- Start writing, even if you're not sure how to begin. You can always go back and strengthen the beginning of your narrative later.
- Maintain one point of view throughout the story. Will one of the characters tell the story, or will an all-knowing narrator tell the story? Personal narratives always use the first-person point of view.
- Bring your characters to life using realistic dialogue and actions.

4. IMPROVE YOUR RESPONSE   5–10 MIN

Revising Check your draft against the task. Does your narrative explain the conflict? Are your characters and setting believable? Does the pace keep the action moving?

Proofreading Check your story to correct errors in grammar, spelling, punctuation, and capitalization. Make sure all your edits are neat, and erase any stray marks.

Checking Your Final Copy Before you turn in your narrative, read it once more to catch any errors you may have missed.

Technology Workshop

Producing a Video

You may have seen movies based on books that you've read. Producing a video is a fun way to present a story in a different form and share it with new audiences.

 Complete the workshop activities in your **Reader/Writer Notebook**.

PRODUCE WITH A PURPOSE	COMMON CORE TRAITS
TASK Adapt your short story or a story from the unit into a **video**. With a team of classmates, plan and produce the video and present it to your class.	**A STRONG VIDEO . . .** • engages the audience • tells a story that is easy to follow • includes multimedia, such as sound effects, narration, onscreen text, and visuals • has a variety of camera shots and angles

COMMON CORE

W 6 Use technology to produce and publish writing. **SL 1a–b** Come to discussions prepared; define individual roles. **SL 5** Integrate multimedia and visual displays into presentations. **SL 6** Adapt speech to a variety of contexts and tasks.

Plan the Video

Follow these guidelines as you plan your video:

• **Define roles.** Meet with your team to discuss the tasks that need to be completed. Assign jobs, such as writing the script, operating cameras and lights, designing sets and costumes, acting as characters, and directing the actors.

• **Write a script.** Prepare to meet with your team by reading the story and thinking about how you can turn it into a script. Turning a story into a script almost always involves adding dialogue. It may also mean adding a narrator who supplies background information. A script includes stage directions and ideas for music and sound effects (sometimes abbreviated as *SFX*). As you write, don't hesitate to cut or add scenes from the original story. Your video should tell a well-paced story that your audience can easily follow.

• **Create a storyboard.** Plan your video by making a storyboard. Use a comic strip format with a simple sketch of each shot in a scene. Under each sketch, make brief notes about dialogue, sound effects, and any other types of multimedia.

• **Find a location for shooting.** Decide where and when you will shoot your video. Get permission to use the space, if necessary.

• **Rehearse your scenes.** Plan at least one rehearsal so the actors can practice saying their lines on set. The actors will need to adapt their speech to fit the context of the story. For example, an angry character would speak in an aggravated tone. If the script uses formal English, the actors will need to avoid casual language.

Media Tools

THiNK central

Go to **thinkcentral.com**.
KEYWORD: HML8-592

Produce the Video

When you're ready to put your plan into action, follow these guidelines:

- **Shoot the footage.** Include different kinds of camera shots to tell a story that is both interesting and easy to follow. This chart describes various camera shots and the effects you can create with them. See page R89 for more information about camera shots and camera angles.

TYPE OF CAMERA SHOT	EFFECTS
Close-up shot—shows a close view of a person or an object	Creates emotion by making viewers feel as if they know the character; focuses viewers' attention on an important detail
Medium shot—shows a slightly wider view than a close-up, such as a character from the waist up	Captures movements that reveal a character's behavior
Long shot—gives a wide view of a scene, showing the full figures of people and their surroundings	Allows viewers to see the "big picture"; shows the relationship between characters and the environment

- **Use your storyboard.** Your storyboard is the roadmap for creating your video. Refer to it often to make sure you shoot all the footage you will need.

- **Wrap it up.** Use editing software to put your scenes in the right order and to create pacing that matches the feel of the story. Quick cuts generate a sense of action and excitement. Longer cuts create drama and allow viewers to reflect on the dialogue between characters.

- **Show your masterpiece.** Screen your video for your class and invited guests. If you wish, hold a comments-and-questions session afterward to get audience feedback.

- **Adapt your video into a podcast.** A **podcast** is a digital file that others can download from the Web and play. Using appropriate software, convert your video to a format that will work as a podcast. Be sure to get permission for any words, images, or audio that you did not create yourself. Then upload your final product using a free podcasting subscription service.

YOUR TURN Plan and produce a video using the guidelines on these pages. Present your video to an audience and consider people's feedback. Decide if you want to make any changes to the video. Then convert your video into a podcast and post it on the Web.

Assessment Practice

DIRECTIONS Read the selection and answer the questions that follow.

A Blind Man Catches a Bird
by Alexander McCall Smith

1   A young man married a woman whose brother was blind. The young man was eager to get to know his new brother-in-law and so asked him if he would like to go hunting with him.

2   "I cannot see," the blind man said. "But you can help me see when we are out hunting together. We can go."

3   The young man led the blind man off into the bush. At first they followed a path that he knew and it was easy for the blind man to tag on behind the other. After a while, though, they went off into thicker bush, where the trees grew closely together and there were many places for animals to hide. The blind man now held on to the arm of his sighted brother-in-law and told him many things about the sounds that they heard around them. Because he had no sight, he had a great ability to interpret the noises made by animals in the bush.

4   "There are warthogs around," he would say, "I can hear their noises over there."

5   Or: "That bird is preparing to fly. Listen to the sound of its wings unfolding."

6   To the brother-in-law, these sounds were meaningless, and he was most impressed at the blind man's ability to understand the bush although it must have been for him one great darkness.

7   They walked on for several hours, until they reached a place where they could set their traps. The blind man followed the other's advice, and put his trap in a place where birds might come for water. The other man put his trap a short distance away, taking care to disguise it so that no bird would know that it was there. He did not bother to disguise the blind man's trap, as it was hot and he was eager to get home to his new wife. The blind man thought that he had disguised his trap, but he did not see that he failed to do so and any bird could tell there was a trap there.

8   They returned to their hunting place the next day. The blind man was excited at the prospect of having caught something, and the young man had to tell him to keep quiet, or he would scare all of the animals away. Even before they reached the traps, the blind man was able to tell that they had caught something.

9   "I can hear birds," he said. "There are birds in the traps."

10   When he reached his trap, the young man saw that he had caught a small bird. He took it out of the trap and put it in a pouch that he had brought with him. Then the two of them walked towards the blind man's trap.

11   "There is a bird in it," he said to the blind man. "You have caught a bird too."

12   As he spoke, he felt himself filling with jealousy. The blind man's bird was marvelously colored, as if it had flown through a rainbow and been stained by the colors. The feathers from a bird such as that would make a fine present for his new wife, but the blind man had a wife too, and she would also want the feathers.

13   The young man bent down and took the blind man's bird from the trap. Then quickly substituting his own bird, he passed it to the blind man and put the colored bird into his own pouch.

14   "Here is your bird," he said to the blind man. "You may put it in your pouch."

15   The blind man reached out for the bird and took it. He felt it for a moment, his fingers passing over the wings and the breast. Then, without saying anything, he put the bird into his pouch and began the trip home.

16   On their way home, the two men stopped to rest under a broad tree. As they sat there, they talked about many things. The young man was impressed with the wisdom of the blind man, who knew a great deal, although he could see nothing at all.

17   "Why do people fight with one another?" he asked the blind man. It was a question which had always troubled him and he wondered if the blind man could give him an answer.

18   The blind man said nothing for a few moments, but it was clear to the young man that he was thinking. Then the blind man raised his head, and it seemed to the young man as if the unseeing eyes were staring right into his soul. Quietly he gave his answer.

19   "Men fight because they do to each other what you have just done to me."

20   The words shocked the young man and made him ashamed. He tried to think of a response, but none came. Rising to his feet, he fetched his pouch, took out the brightly colored bird and gave it back to the blind man.

21   The blind man took the bird, felt it over with his fingers, and smiled.

22   "Do you have any other questions for me?" he asked.

23   "Yes," said the young man. "How do men become friends after they have fought?"

24   The blind man smiled again.

25   "They do what you have just done," he said. "That's how they become friends again."

Reading Comprehension

Use "A Blind Man Catches a Bird" to answer questions 1–12.

1. The overall theme of the story is —
   A. people cheat others because it makes them feel smart
   B. people should rely more on their hearing than on their sight
   C. true friendship depends on respect and fairness
   D. hunting is a good way to learn about animal behavior

2. Which quotation conveys one of the story's themes?
   A. *At first they followed a path that he knew and it was easy for the blind man to tag on behind the other.* (paragraph 3)
   B. *The blind man followed the other's advice, and put his trap in a place where birds might come for water.* (paragraph 7)
   C. *When he reached his trap, the young man saw that he had caught a small bird.* (paragraph 10)
   D. *The young man was impressed with the wisdom of the blind man, who knew a great deal, although he could see nothing at all.* (paragraph 16)

3. The hunting trip could be a symbol of the —
   A. wisdom of a person who is blind
   B. search for what is important in life
   C. human struggle to control nature
   D. difficulty of living without sight

4. The sounds in the bush are meaningless to the young man because —
   A. his ability to see limits his ability to hear
   B. he cannot speak the language of the animals
   C. a thick growth of trees muffles every sound
   D. the blind man is talking in a loud voice

5. The disguised trap might symbolize the young man's —
   A. carelessness
   B. deceitfulness
   C. foolishness
   D. laziness

6. From the two questions he asks the blind man in paragraphs 17 and 23, you can conclude that the young man is —
   A. trying to understand human nature
   B. having problems with his new wife
   C. testing the blind man's intelligence
   D. looking for something to argue about

7. Which theme is suggested by the blind man's thoughts about why people fight?
   A. Dishonesty ruins people's relationships.
   B. Friends must be willing to forgive.
   C. People should think before they speak.
   D. Compromise will solve most problems.

8. Which quality might the blind man symbolize?
   A. Courage
   B. Jealousy
   C. Strength
   D. Wisdom

9. You can conclude that the young man is eager to please his new wife when he —

   A. does not help the blind man disguise his bird trap

   B. is impressed that the blind man can understand animals' sounds

   C. steals the colorful bird so that she can have the feathers

   D. asks his brother-in-law why people fight

10. Reread paragraphs 17 through 20. You can conclude that the young man is shocked at the response to his question because he —

    A. thinks the blind man doesn't know that he cheated him

    B. expects the blind man to politely ignore his question

    C. knows the blind man doesn't understand his question

    D. believes that he has a right to take the beautiful bird

11. To the men in the story, the colorful bird symbolizes —

    A. bad luck

    B. a valued prize

    C. a happy memory

    D. broken promises

12. You can conclude that the young man gives the colorful bird to the blind man because he wants to —

    A. avoid an argument

    B. restore their friendship

    C. show his generosity

    D. please his new wife

SHORT CONSTRUCTED RESPONSE
Write two or three sentences to answer each question.

13. Even though he doesn't know how to set a trap, the blind man catches a beautiful bird. What conclusion can you draw from that incident?

14. What might the blindness in the story symbolize? In what ways are the two characters blind?

Write a paragraph to answer this question.

15. Explain the connection between one symbol and one theme in the story.

GO ON

Vocabulary

Use your knowledge of context clues and the thesaurus entries to answer the following questions.

---

tag *verb.* call, identify, brand, label, follow, trail, chase

1. Which word is a synonym for the word *tag* in paragraph 3?
   - A. Call
   - B. Chase
   - C. Follow
   - D. Identify

---

distance *noun.* space, coldness, separation, gap, length, remoteness

2. Which word is a synonym for the word *distance* in paragraph 7?
   - A. Coldness
   - B. Length
   - C. Remoteness
   - D. Separation

---

prospect *noun.* customer, chance, hope, possibility, scene, view

3. Which word is a synonym for the word *prospect* in paragraph 8?
   - A. Customer
   - B. Possibility
   - C. Scene
   - D. View

Use context clues and your knowledge of suffixes to answer the following questions.

4. What does the word *ability* mean in paragraph 3?

"Because he had no sight, he had a great <u>ability</u> to interpret the noises made by animals in the bush."

- A. Desire
- B. Feeling
- C. Intelligence
- D. Talent

5. What does the word *meaningless* mean in paragraph 6?

"To the brother-in-law, these sounds were <u>meaningless</u>, . . ."

- A. Easily overlooked
- B. Beautifully melodic
- C. Not worth listening to
- D. Impossible to understand

6. What does the word *marvelously* mean in paragraph 12?

"The blind man's bird was <u>marvelously</u> colored, as if it had flown through a rainbow and been stained by the colors."

- A. In a lighthearted manner
- B. With a reddish tint
- C. In a way that causes wonder
- D. With unattractive colors

Revising and Editing

DIRECTIONS **Read this passage and answer the questions that follow.**

(1) South Africa's current population has a rich heritage. (2) The population descends from African, Asian, and european settlers. (3) More than 1,500 years ago, members of the Bantu language group settled the transvaal region of South Africa. (4) The Dutch settled in 1652. (5) They were the first Europeans in South Africa. (6) Dutch was the dominant language spoken throughout the 1700s. (7) Later, English and Afrikaans became the official language of South Africa. (8) Today, the government recognizes 11 official languages. (9) The Zulu, the xhosa, and the Sotho are just some of the African ethnic groups who speak these languages. (10) The constitution encourages respect for many of the other languages spoken in the country.

1. What is the BEST way to combine sentences 1 and 2 using a participle?

   A. Descending from African, Asian, and European settlers, South Africa's current population reflects this rich heritage.

   B. South Africa's current population descends from African, Asian, and European settlers.

   C. South Africa's current population reflects a rich heritage of Africans, Asians, and Europeans.

   D. Settling, Africans, Asians, and Europeans came to South Africa.

2. What change, if any, should be made in sentence 2?

   A. Change *African* to **african**

   B. Change *Asian* to **asian**

   C. Change *european* to **European**

   D. Make no change

3. What change, if any, should be made in sentence 3?

   A. Change *Bantu* to **bantu**

   B. Change *language group* to **Language Group**

   C. Change *transvaal* to **Transvaal**

   D. Make no change

4. What is the BEST way to combine sentences 5 and 6 using a participle?

   A. In 1652, the Dutch became the first Europeans to settle in South Africa.

   B. The first Europeans in South Africa were the Dutch.

   C. The Dutch were the first Europeans in South Africa, settling in 1652.

   D. Firstly, the Dutch settled in South Africa in 1652.

5. What change, if any, should be made in sentence 7?

   A. Change *English* to **english**

   B. Change *Afrikaans* to **afrikaans**

   C. Change *language* to **Language**

   D. Make no change

6. What change, if any, should be made in sentence 9?

   A. Change *Sotho* to **sotho**

   B. Change *Zulu* to **zulu**

   C. Change *xhosa* to **Xhosa**

   D. Make no change

STOP

Ideas for Independent Reading

Which questions from Unit 4 made an impression on you?
Continue exploring them with these books.

COMMON CORE

RL 10 Read and comprehend literature. **RI 10** Read and comprehend literary nonfiction.

Is curiosity a gift or a curse?

East
by Edith Pattou

Rose was born curious. When a white bear shows up and asks her to go with him so her family can prosper, teenaged Rose agrees. She doesn't realize that living with a bear is only the beginning of a longer journey.

Mable Riley: A Reliable Record of Humdrum, Peril, and Romance
by Marthe Jocelyn

The year is 1901, and Mable hopes she'll have an adventure when she moves away with her sister. At first, life remains boring. But everything changes when Mable meets the neighbor.

The Thief Lord
by Cornelia Funke

Prosper and Bo have run away to Venice to escape their aunt and uncle. They are taken in by the Thief Lord, a masked boy who leads a band of children. When the Thief Lord accepts a mysterious assignment, the adventures of the band get complicated.

How well do we treat our elders?

The Cay
by Theodore Taylor

Phillip and his mother escape the German invasion of Curaçao on a freighter, but the boat is torpedoed. Phillip wakes up on a life raft with a cat and a West Indian named Timothy. Will Phillip be able to survive with only an old man for support?

A Step from Heaven
by An Na

Young Ju is only four when her family moves to the U.S. from Korea. At first, everyone is happy, but then her parents start fighting again. Young Ju has been raised to respect her elders, but she knows that sometimes her father isn't right. What should she do?

The Not-So-Star-Spangled Life of Sunita Sen
by Mitali Perkins

When Sunita's grandparents visit from India, her life changes. For one thing, she can't have boys over anymore. She has to find a way to accept her family and still fit in.

What impact will you have on the world?

The Book Thief
by Markus Zusak

Liesel is a little girl the first time she meets Death in Nazi Germany. The second time, she's a book thief, stealing books and reading them to anyone who needs to listen. Later, she writes her own story. This is the book Death wants you to hear.

The Merlin Conspiracy
by Diana Wynne Jones

Roddy and Grundo are just teenagers in the Royal Court. No one but an outsider will believe them when they warn of a conspiracy against the king. Can three young magicians win a battle to keep the magic in the multiverse?

Be the Difference: A Beginner's Guide to Changing the World
by Danny Seo

At 12, Danny Seo inspired thousands of students to join him in an environmental movement. Ten years later, he wrote this book. Read his advice about how teenagers can improve the world.

Get Novel Wise

THiNK central

Go to **thinkcentral.com**.
KEYWORD: HML8-600

Painting with Words

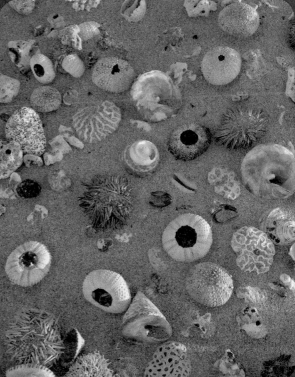

POETRY

What makes a POEM?

Have you ever tried to write a poem? If so, you probably had to think about what a poem is. Is it lines that rhyme? Pictures painted with words? Toe-tapping rhythms? A poem can be all of these things—or none of them.

ACTIVITY Poetry is everywhere—in our favorite songs, the nursery rhymes we read as children, and even in some television commercials. With a partner, make a list of poems that you have read or heard. Then answer the following questions:

• Did you find poetry in any unexpected places?

• What do these poems have in common?

• How do the words create mental pictures?

• Do these poems rhyme, or have rhythm?

Once you've answered these questions, see if you can define a poem.

Find It Online!
THINK central

Go to thinkcentral.com for the interactive version of this unit.

602

COMMON CORE

Preview Unit Goals

TEXT ANALYSIS	• Identify and analyze figurative language • Analyze the impact of word choice on meaning • Identify and analyze sound devices • Identify, analyze, and compare rhyme schemes • Identify and compare themes • Identify and analyze rhythm and meter and their effects • Compare poetic form and structure
READING	• Make inferences • Paraphrase lines in poetry • Identify and compare treatment
WRITING AND LANGUAGE	• Write an online feature article • Use commas correctly • Correct inappropriate shifts in verb voice
SPEAKING AND LISTENING	• Use multimedia elements to clarify information
VOCABULARY	• Use knowledge of Latin roots to help determine word meaning
ACADEMIC VOCABULARY	• attitude • create • emphasis • mental • style

UNIT 5
Text Analysis Workshop

Appreciating Poetry

The poet Robert Frost once said that a poem "begins in delight and ends in wisdom." While many poems are entertaining, a poem can also have the power to change how you see the world. Whether it follows a set pattern or bends all the rules, each poem uses language in a new way to communicate its message.

Part 1: The Basics

COMMON CORE

Included in this workshop:
RL 4 Determine the meaning of words and phrases, including figurative and connotative meanings; analyze the impact of word choices on meaning and tone.
RL 5 Compare and contrast texts and analyze how the differing structure of each text contributes to its meaning and style.

What do you see when you look at a poem? One difference between a poem and a short story is the **form,** or the structure of the writing. All poems are broken up into **lines.** The length of each line and where it breaks, or ends, contribute to the poem's meaning and sound. Lines often appear in groups, or **stanzas.** The stanzas work together to convey the overall message of the poem.

Some poems follow the rules of a traditional form. For example, a poem might have a specific number of lines and stanzas or a regular pattern of rhythm and rhyme. Other poems are unconventional, with no recognizable patterns. A poet might even choose to use incorrect grammar or spelling to create a particular sound or to emphasize meaning.

Just as a story has a narrator, a poem has a voice that "talks" to readers. This voice, or **speaker,** is sometimes a fictional character rather than the poet.

Take a look at the following poems. Which is traditional? Which is unconventional? Which one has a distinct speaker?

EXAMPLE 1

from "The Geese"
Poem by **Richard Peck**

My father was the first to hear
The passage of the geese each fall,
Passing above the house so near
He'd hear within his heart their call.

And then at breakfast time he'd say:
"The geese were heading south last
   night,"
For he had lain awake till day,
Feeling his earthbound soul take flight.

EXAMPLE 2

from "Street Corner Flight"
Poem by **Norma Landa Flores**

From this side . . .
   of their concrete barrio
   two small boys hold
      fat white pigeons
trapped in their trembling hands.

Then,
 gently,
   not disturbing
      their powers of flight,
         release them
into the air.

604 UNIT 5: POETRY

MODEL 1: TRADITIONAL FORM

In this traditional poem, the speaker reflects on the return of night at the end of a day. Read it aloud to help you identify the characteristics of its form.

from

Good-Night

Poem by **Robert Louis Stevenson**

When the bright lamp is carried in,
The sunless hours again begin;
O'er all without, in field and lane,
The haunted night returns again.

5 Now we behold the embers flee
About the firelit hearth; and see
Our faces painted as we pass,
Like pictures, on the window-glass.

Close Read

1. How many lines are in each stanza?

2. In the first stanza, rhyming pairs are highlighted. Identify the rhyming words in the second stanza. What pattern do you see?

MODEL 2: FREE VERSE

In this unconventional poem—called a **free verse** poem—the poet lets the ideas drive where each line breaks and when each stanza ends.

That Day

Poem by
David Kherdian

Just once
my father stopped on the way
into the house from work
and joined in the softball game
5 we were having in the street,
and attempted to play in *our*
game that *his* country had never
known.

Just once
10 and the day stands out forever
in my memory
as a father's living gesture
to his son,
that in playing even the fool
15 or clown, he would reveal
that the lines of their lives
were sewn from a tougher fabric
than the son had previously known.

Close Read

1. How does the form of this poem differ from that of "Good-Night"?

2. Notice the short lengths of the boxed lines. What might the poet be trying to emphasize by isolating and repeating this phrase?

3. What do you learn about the speaker of this poem?

Part 2: Poetic Elements

Like different colors of paint or the notes on a musical scale, language can be arranged to create a desired effect. For example, short, choppy lines can produce a fast-paced pounding beat, while long, rhythmic lines can create a soothing melody. Poets manipulate the words and lines in their writing, fully conscious of how their work will sound when read aloud and how it will make readers feel. Sound devices, imagery, and figurative language are important tools of the trade.

SOUND DEVICES

Poets choose words not only for their meaning, but also for their sounds. The sound of a word or line can help emphasize meaning or create a musical quality. Here are some examples of sound devices poets use.

SOUND DEVICES	EXAMPLE

RHYTHM
 the pattern of stressed (´) and unstressed (˘) syllables in each line. A regular pattern of rhythm is called **meter**.
	"Afternoon on a Hill"
	 Poem by **Edna St. Vincent Millay**
	
	 I will be the gladdest thing *a*
	     Under the sun! *b*
	 I will touch a hundred flowers *c*
	     And not pick one. *b*

RHYME
 the repetition of sounds at the ends of words, as in sun and one. Rhyme scheme is the pattern that the end-rhyming words follow. To identify rhyme scheme, assign a letter to each sound, as shown here.
	I will look at cliffs and clouds *d*
	     With quiet eyes, *e*
	 Watch the wind bow down the grass, *f*
	     And the grass rise. *e*

REPETITION
 the use of a word, phrase, line, or sound more than once, such as the repeated use of the phrase *I will*
	And when lights begin to show *g*
	     Up from the town, *h*
	 I will mark which must be mine, *i*
	     And then start down! *h*

ALLITERATION the repetition of consonant sounds at the beginning of words, such as the *m* in *mark*, *must*, and *mine*	
ASSONANCE the repetition of vowel sounds in words that don't end with the same consonant, such as the *ow* sound in *bow* and *down*	

MODEL 1: RHYTHM AND RHYME

Read this traditional poem aloud, listening for its rhythm and rhyme.

Stopping by Woods on a Snowy Evening

Poem by **Robert Frost**

Whose woods these are I think I know.
His house is in the village, though;
He will not see me stopping here
To watch his woods fill up with snow.

5　My little horse must think it queer
To stop without a farmhouse near
Between the woods and frozen lake
The darkest evening of the year.

He gives his harness bells a shake
10　To ask if there is some mistake
The only other sound's the sweep
Of easy wind and downy flake.

The woods are lovely, dark and deep,
But I have promises to keep,
15　And miles to go before I sleep,
And miles to go before I sleep.

Close Read

1. Stressed (ˊ) and unstressed (˘) syllables are marked in the first stanza. Read the second stanza out loud. Does it follow the same pattern as the first stanza?

2. The end rhymes in the first stanza are highlighted. Examine the end rhymes in the other stanzas to figure out the rhyme scheme.

MODEL 2: ALLITERATION AND REPETITION

This unconventional poem uses alliteration and repetition to help emphasize meaning. Make sure to read the lines all the way across.

from **Chrysalis** *Diary*

Poem by **Paul Fleischman**

November 13:

Cold told me
to fasten my feet
to this branch,

5　　　　　　　　to dangle upside down
　　　　　　　　from my perch,

to shed my skin,

and I have obeyed.

　　　　　　　　to cease being a caterpillar
　　　　　　　　and I have obeyed.

Close Read

1. The alliteration in the boxed line helps to create a sense of the caterpillar's strong grip. Find another example of alliteration.

2. What does the repetition in the last line help emphasize?

3. Who is the speaker of the poem?

IMAGERY AND FIGURATIVE LANGUAGE

In addition to sound devices, poets use **imagery,** or language that appeals to one or more of your senses—sight, hearing, smell, taste, and touch. Vivid images help readers more clearly understand what a poet describes. In "Stopping by Woods on a Snowy Evening," for example, images like "the sweep / Of easy wind and downy flake" help you visualize the scene and hear the sounds of winter.

One way poets create imagery is by using **figurative language,** or imaginative descriptions that are not literally true. The following are common types of figurative language:

- **Simile:** a comparison of two things using the word *like* or *as*

- **Metaphor:** a comparison of two things that does not include the word *like* or *as*

- **Extended metaphor:** a metaphor that extends over several lines, stanzas, or an entire poem

- **Personification:** a description of an object, animal, or idea as if it has human qualities and emotions

Notice how these examples of figurative language help you picture ordinary things in new ways.

SIMILE

The sun spun like
a tossed coin.
It whirled on the azure sky,
it clattered into the horizon,
it clicked in the slot,
and neon-lights popped
and blinked "Time expired,"
as on a parking meter.

—"Sunset"
by Oswald Mbuyiseni Mtshali

METAPHOR

In the pond in the park
all things are doubled:
Long buildings hang and
wriggle gently. Chimneys
are bent legs bouncing
on clouds below.

—from "Water Picture"
by May Swenson

PERSONIFICATION

When I opened the door
I found the vine leaves
speaking among themselves in abundant
whispers.
        My presence made them
hush their green breath,
embarrassed, the way
humans stand up, buttoning their jackets,
acting as if they were leaving anyway, as if
the conversation had ended
just before you arrived.

—from "Aware"
by Denise Levertov

Part 3: Analyze the Text

In "Lineage," Margaret Walker uses many different poetic elements to describe the speaker's admiration for her ancestors. Using what you've learned in this workshop, analyze the form, sound devices, and language in this poem. Notice how all these elements work together to communicate a powerful message.

Poem by **Margaret Walker**

My grandmothers were strong.
They followed plows and bent to toil.
They moved through fields sowing seed.
They touched earth and grain grew.
5 They were full of sturdiness and singing.
My grandmothers were strong.

My grandmothers are full of memories
Smelling of soap and onions and wet clay
With veins rolling roughly over quick hands
10 They have many clean words to say.
My grandmothers were strong.
Why am I not as they?

Close Read

1. What is traditional about the form of this poem?

2. One example of alliteration is boxed. Find two more examples.

3. The poem's first line is repeated two more times and helps to emphasize an important message. How is strength defined in the poem?

4. Find four images that help you picture the grandmothers. What sense does each image appeal to?

5. How would you describe the speaker of this poem? Think about the qualities she admires in her grandmothers and how she sees herself in relation to them.

Simile: Willow and Ginkgo
Poem by Eve Merriam

Introduction to Poetry
Poem by Billy Collins

VIDEO TRAILER **THINK** central KEYWORD: HML8-610

How can WORDS create pictures?

COMMON CORE

RL 4 Determine the meaning of words and phrases, including figurative meanings; analyze the impact of word choices on meaning and tone. **RL 5** Analyze the structure of text.

Have you ever seen the movie version of a book you've already read? Then you probably have had the experience of being surprised when a character didn't look the way you had pictured him or her. Words can create such distinct and powerful images that what you imagine while reading can seem as "real" as what you see. The poems you are about to read might help you see words themselves in a fresh, new way.

QUICKWRITE Choose a photograph from a magazine. Try to think of the way the pictured item might feel, sound, smell, or taste, in addition to how it appears. In a brief paragraph, create a vivid description of the image. Read your paragraph to a partner and ask which words best help him or her picture what you're describing. Then show the image.

POETIC FORM: STANZA

Many poems are divided into **stanzas,** or groupings of two or more lines that form a unit. In poetry, a stanza serves a similar purpose to a paragraph in prose. Stanzas may be used to separate ideas, add emphasis, or create a certain appearance on the page.

TEXT ANALYSIS: METAPHOR AND SIMILE

Have you ever heard an expression that didn't mean exactly what it said? The expression probably contained figurative language. **Figurative language** consists of words used in an imaginative way to communicate meaning beyond their strict definitions. The following are three types of figurative language:

- **Similes** use *like* or *as* to compare two unlike things. For example: *The frozen lake is like glass.*

- **Metaphors** make comparisons without the word *like* or *as.* For example: *All the world is a stage.*

- **Extended metaphors** extend over several lines, stanzas, or an entire poem.

As you read the following poems, look for examples of metaphors and similes and note how the poets use them to reveal a **tone,** or attitude; present vibrant images; or express complex ideas with a few words.

READING STRATEGY: VISUALIZE

One way to help yourself enjoy the richness of a poem is to take the time to **visualize** the words, or form pictures in your mind. To visualize, pay attention to details that help you imagine how something looks, sounds, smells, feels, or even tastes. Combine these details with your own knowledge and experiences. As you read these poems, keep track of what you visualize in a chart like the one shown.

What I Visualize	Words and Phrases That Helped
dark, jerky lines	"crude sketch"

 Complete the activities in your **Reader/Writer Notebook.**

Meet the Authors

Eve Merriam
1916–1992

Always a Poet
Eve Merriam began writing poetry when she was about eight years old, and she never considered any other career. "It's like . . . oxygen," she said, "when I hear rhymes and word play." Although at times during her life she was forced to take other jobs, she continued writing poetry. Her first collection of poetry for adults, *Family Circle,* won the 1946 Yale Younger Poets Prize. Later in her career, Merriam focused on writing poetry for children.

Billy Collins
born 1941

America's Most Popular Poet
In the United States, even the top poets can be unknown to most of the public. Billy Collins, however, is well known and well loved. His rise to fame began when Collins became a regular guest on radio programs, where his humor and welcoming manner won him a loyal following. He has since become one of the best-selling poets of his generation and regularly attracts standing-room-only crowds to his poetry readings. When he served as the Poet Laureate of the United States from 2001 to 2003, he created the 180 Project, which provided high schools across the country with poems to be read along with daily announcements. His goal was to make poetry part of everyday life for young people.

Authors Online
Go to **thinkcentral.com.** KEYWORD: HML8-611

THINK central

611

Simile: *Willow and Ginkgo*

Eve Merriam

The willow is like an etching,
Fine-lined against the sky.
The ginkgo is like a crude sketch,
Hardly worthy to be signed.

5 The willow's music is like a soprano,
Delicate and thin.
The ginkgo's tune is like a chorus
With everyone joining in.

The willow is sleek as a velvet-nosed calf;
10 The ginkgo is leathery as an old bull.
The willow's branches are like silken thread;
The ginkgo's like stubby rough wool. **A**

The willow is like a nymph with streaming hair;
Wherever it grows, there is green and gold and fair.
15 The willow dips to the water,
Protected and precious, like the king's favorite daughter.

The ginkgo forces its way through gray concrete;
Like a city child, it grows up in the street.
Thrust against the metal sky,
20 Somehow it survives and even thrives. **B**

My eyes feast upon the willow,
But my heart goes to the ginkgo.

Analyze Visuals ▶

What **motif,** or repeated element, do you notice in this image?

A **METAPHOR AND SIMILE**
In lines 9–12, what similes are used to describe the willow? What similes describe the ginkgo?

B **STANZA**
Why do you think the poet started a new stanza at line 17?

Light–1 (1992), Atsuko Kato.
Oil on board, 100 cm × 70 cm.

Introduction *to* Poetry

BILLY COLLINS

Wednesday 6: Rain, slowly clearing eastwards (2001), Ben McLaughlin. Oil on board, 20.3 cm × 20.3 cm. Private collection. © Bridgeman Art Library.

I ask them to take a poem
and hold it up to the light
like a color slide

or press an ear against its hive. **C**

5 I say drop a mouse into a poem
and watch him probe his way out,

or walk inside the poem's room
and feel the walls for a light switch.

I want them to waterski
10 across the surface of a poem
waving at the author's name on the shore.

But all they want to do
is tie the poem to a chair with rope
and torture a confession out of it. **D**

15 They begin beating it with a hose
to find out what it really means.

C **VISUALIZE**
Reread lines 1–4.
What words help you
visualize what the poet
describes? To which
senses do the details
appeal?

D **METAPHOR AND SIMILE**
In lines 12–14, what
extended metaphor is
used to describe the
poem?

Comprehension

1. **Recall** In "Simile: Willow and Ginkgo," which tree does the speaker think is more beautiful?

2. **Recall** What does the speaker in "Introduction to Poetry" want readers to do on the surface of a poem?

Text Analysis

3. **Visualize** Review the chart you made as you read. Select two examples that were especially effective in helping you make visualizations. What words helped you "see" images in your mind?

4. **Identify Simile and Metaphor** For each poem, identify as many figurative comparisons as you can. In a chart like the one shown, list what is being described and what it is compared to. Then identify whether the comparison is a simile or a metaphor.

COMMON CORE

RL 4 Determine the meaning of words and phrases, including figurative meanings; analyze the impact of word choices on meaning and tone. **RL 5** Analyze the structure of text.

"Introduction to Poetry"			
Line(s)	What Is Being Described	What It Is Compared To	Simile or Metaphor
2–3	poem	color slide	simile

5. **Interpret a Line** Reread the last two lines of "Simile: Willow and Ginkgo." Why do you think the speaker's "heart goes to the ginkgo"? Support your answer with words and phrases from the poem.

6. **Compare Stanzas** Look back at the stanzas in "Introduction to Poetry." How are the poem's stanzas alike? How are they different? Consider their length as well as their content.

7. **Analyze Metaphors to Interpret a Poem** In the first five stanzas of "Introduction to Poetry," Collins uses metaphors to convey how he would like readers to relate to a poem. In the last two stanzas, he uses an extended metaphor to communicate what he thinks most readers want to do with a poem. Identify the items to which Collins likens a poem in lines 1–11. Then, in your own words, restate his message.

Extension and Challenge

8. **Creative Project: Poem** Write your own poem about reading poetry. Include at least one **metaphor** and one **simile**.

How can WORDS create pictures?

Which words in the two poems created the most vivid images for you?

the lesson of the moth
Poem by Don Marquis

Identity
Poem by Julio Noboa

Does BEAUTY matter?

COMMON CORE

RL 1 Cite the textual evidence that supports inferences drawn from the text.
RL 4 Determine the meaning of words and phrases as they are used in a text; analyze the impact of specific word choices on meaning. **RL 5** Analyze how structure contributes to meaning.

What is our standard of beauty? A recent study found that people judged the beauty of strangers differently than they judged the beauty of people they knew. With strangers, people took into account only physical appearance. With familiar faces, the participants considered characteristics such as intelligence, courage, and dependability. The speakers in the poems you're about to read have their own ideas about beauty.

SURVEY Survey your classmates to find out what five or six characteristics they think make someone beautiful. List the ten answers that were given most often, and then separate them into internal and external characteristics. According to your survey, is beauty only skin deep?

● POETIC FORM: FREE VERSE

It is often said that to write poetry, you first have to learn the rules—then you can break them. **Free verse** is poetry that "breaks the rules" because it does not contain regular patterns of rhythm or rhyme. However, writers of free verse often use repetition and other sound devices to emphasize meaning. As you read, notice the way the poems sound like everyday speech.

● TEXT ANALYSIS: SPEAKER

In a poem, the voice that "talks" to the reader is called the **speaker.** Readers often assume that the speaker and the poet are the same, but this is not always true. The speaker may be a character created by the poet. For example, the speaker in "the lesson of the moth" is a cockroach named Archy. As you read each poem, use clues from the text to infer the speaker's identity.

● READING SKILL: CLARIFY MEANING

Poets use line breaks, stanzas, and punctuation to help emphasize ideas. For example, look at how the punctuation and line and stanza breaks in the first stanza of "Identity" affect meaning.

Let them be as flowers,
always watered, fed, guarded, admired,
but harnessed to a pot of dirt.

In the first two lines, commas cause you to pause and linger on words that are associated with positive feelings. However, the third line, which ends with a period, abruptly undercuts these comforting words. Because the stanza ends with this line, it emphasizes that the speaker sees confinement where others see beauty. As you study each poem, think about how the line breaks, stanzas, and punctuation affect the way you read and understand it. Use a graphic organizer like the one shown to note these elements and the effects they create.

Elements	Used?	Effects
line and stanza breaks	yes	separate positive and negative ideas
commas		
end marks (question marks, periods, etc.)		

 Complete the activities in your **Reader/Writer Notebook.**

Meet the Authors

Don Marquis
1878–1937

Talented Newsman
Don Marquis published novels and worked as a screenwriter, but he was mainly a newspaper writer. A daily column in the *New York Evening Sun* led Marquis to create a character called Archy the cockroach, who helped Marquis see life from a different perspective. "the lesson of the moth" is one of many poems Marquis wrote in the voice of Archy. Marquis pretended that Archy wrote his verses on a typewriter during the night. Marquis explained the lack of capitalization in the poems by saying that Archy never learned to use the shift key. Although Marquis's poems are mainly remembered for their humor, they also allowed him to comment on society.

Julio Noboa
born 1949

Poet and Educator
Julio Noboa was born in the Bronx. He credits his Puerto Rican father and a high-school English teacher with encouraging him to write. Noboa wrote "Identity" when he was in the eighth grade. The poem was inspired by Noboa's feelings after a breakup with a girlfriend, an experience that he says encouraged him to think "about what's really important to me." Noboa is now a college professor.

Authors Online
Go to **thinkcentral.com**. KEYWORD: HML8-617

the lesson of the moth

Don Marquis

i was talking to a moth
the other evening
he was trying to break into
an electric light bulb
5 and fry himself on the wires **A**

why do you fellows
pull this stunt i asked him
because it is the conventional[1]
thing for moths or why
10 if that had been an uncovered
candle instead of an electric
light bulb you would
now be a small unsightly cinder[2]
have you no sense **B**

15 plenty of it he answered
but at times we get tired
of using it
we get bored with the routine

Analyze Visuals ▶

What might the light
bulb **symbolize?**

A SPEAKER
What are your first
impressions of the
speaker?

B CLARIFY MEANING
Imagine that this stanza
was punctuated like
regular text. Where
would the punctuation
appear?

---

1. **conventional:** customary; usual; accepted.
2. **cinder:** a piece of burned material.

and crave beauty
20 and excitement
fire is beautiful
and we know that if we get
too close it will kill us
but what does that matter
25 it is better to be happy
for a moment
and be burned up with beauty
than to live a long time
and be bored all the while
30 so we wad all our life up
into one little roll
and then we shoot the roll
that is what life is for
it is better to be a part of beauty
35 for one instant and then to cease to
exist than to exist forever
and never be a part of beauty
our attitude toward life
is to come easy go easy
40 we are like human beings
used to be before they became
too civilized to enjoy themselves **C**

and before i could argue him
out of his philosophy
45 he went and immolated[3] himself
on a patent[4] cigar lighter
i do not agree with him
myself i would rather have
half the happiness and twice
50 the longevity[5] **D**

but at the same time i wish
there was something i wanted
as badly as he wanted to fry himself

—archy

C FREE VERSE
In what ways do the
lines in this stanza
sound like the way
people really talk? In
what ways do they
sound different?

D SPEAKER
In what way does
the speaker compare
himself to the moth?

---

3. **immolated** (ĭm′ə-lātd′): killed as a sacrifice.

4. **patent** (păt′nt): patented; covered by a lawful
grant that gives the inventor the exclusive right
to manufacture an item for a certain time period.

5. **longevity** (lŏn-jĕv′ĭ-tē): length of life.

IDENTITY

Julio Noboa

The Mountain (1991), Albert Herbert. Oil on canvas, 50.8 cm × 61 cm. Private collection. © Bridgeman Art Library.

Let them be as flowers,
always watered, fed, guarded, admired,
but harnessed to a pot of dirt.

I'd rather be a tall, ugly weed,
5 clinging on cliffs, like an eagle
wind-wavering above high, jagged rocks. **E**

To have broken through the surface of stone
to live, to feel exposed to the madness
of the vast, eternal sky.
10 To be swayed by the breezes of an ancient sea,
carrying my soul, my seed beyond the mountains
    of time
or into the abyss[1] of the bizarre.

I'd rather be unseen, and if,

then shunned[2] by everyone
15 than to be a pleasant-smelling flower,
growing in clusters in the fertile valley
where they're praised, handled, and plucked
by greedy, human hands. **F**

I'd rather smell of musty, green stench
20 than of sweet, fragrant lilac.
If I could stand alone, strong and free,
I'd rather be a tall, ugly weed.

E SPEAKER
Reread lines 1–6. How does the speaker's view of himself or herself contrast with the way the speaker views "them"?

F CLARIFY MEANING
Reread lines 13–18, paying attention to the commas. What effect do they have on the way you read this stanza?

---

1. **abyss:** a seemingly bottomless space.
2. **shunned:** deliberately avoided; shut out.

Comprehension

1. **Recall** According to "the lesson of the moth," why do moths fly toward light?

2. **Represent** Create a sketch that shows the differences between the flower and the weed described in "Identity." Make sure your sketch reflects at least two specific details from the poem.

Text Analysis

● 3. **Make Inferences** What does the **speaker** learn about himself in "the lesson of the moth"? Support your response with evidence from the poem.

4. **Examine Stanza** In "the lesson of the moth," how does the poet use **stanzas** to help you follow the conversation between the cockroach and the moth?

5. **Analyze Metaphor** What kind of person does the speaker in "Identity" want to be? What kind of person does he not want to be?

● 6. **Clarify Meaning** Refer to the charts you created as you read. For each poem, tell whether the line breaks, the stanzas, or the punctuation did the most to help you understand the poem's meaning. Explain what and how that element helped you understand.

7. **Compare and Contrast Views** In "the lesson of the moth," what is the moth's attitude about the price of beauty? In "Identity," what is the speaker's attitude about the price of beauty? Explain whether you think their views are more similar or more different.

● 8. **Evaluate Free Verse** Use a chart like the one shown to list examples of rhyme, repetition, or other sound devices, such as **alliteration** (the repetition of consonant sounds at the beginning of words). What images or ideas do these devices emphasize?

	"the lesson of the moth"	"Identity"
Rhyme		
Repetition		
Sound Devices		

Extension and Challenge

9. **SCIENCE CONNECTION** How do the qualities of real cockroaches and moths correspond to the poetic creations Don Marquis presents in "the lesson of the moth"? Research to find out about each creature's habits and life span. Display your findings in a poster, and be ready to explain how the poem does—or does not—relate to reality.

Cockroach

Does **BEAUTY** matter?

How has reading these poems influenced your thoughts about beauty?

COMMON CORE

RL 1 Cite the textual evidence that supports inferences drawn from the text. **RL 4** Determine the meaning of words and phrases as they are used in a text; analyze the impact of specific word choices on meaning. **RL 5** Analyze how structure contributes to meaning.

Language

◆ GRAMMAR IN CONTEXT: Use Commas Correctly

COMMON CORE

L 2a Use punctuation (comma) to indicate a pause or break.
W 10 Write over shorter time frames.

By using commas properly to indicate a pause, you can avoid confusing your readers. When writing a sentence that lists **items in a series,** insert a comma after every item except the last one. (A series consists of three or more items.) Also insert a comma between two or more **adjectives** of equal rank that modify the same noun.

> *Original:* Both the moth in "the lesson of the moth" and the speaker in "Identity" find beauty in unusual surprising places.

> *Revised:* Both the moth in "the lesson of the moth" and the speaker in "Identity" find beauty in unusual, surprising places.

PRACTICE Insert commas where needed in the following sentences.

1. The moth would rather take risks get injured and die young than be bored.
2. He thinks that the dangerous exciting heat of fire is beautiful.
3. I wouldn't mind being unseen shunned and alone like a weed.
4. Unlike flowers, weeds are strong free and independent.

*For more help with using commas correctly, see page R49 in the **Grammar Handbook.***

READING-WRITING CONNECTION

 Continue to explore the meaning of "the lesson of the moth" and "Identity" by responding to this prompt. Then use the **revising tip** to improve your writing.

WRITING PROMPT	REVISING TIP
Short Constructed Response: Paragraph Choose one of the "characters" from the poems— Archy, the moth, or the speaker in "Identity." Write **a paragraph** answering the question, "Does beauty matter?" from the point of view of this character.	Review your response. Have you used commas correctly in a series or between adjectives of equal rank that modify the same noun? If not, revise.

Interactive Revision **THINK** central

Go to **thinkcentral.com**.
KEYWORD: I IML8-623

It's all I have to bring today—
Poem by Emily Dickinson

We Alone HISTORY Video link at
thinkcentral.com
Poem by Alice Walker

Can you be RICH without money?

•••• COMMON CORE

RL 2 Determine a theme
of a text and analyze its
development. **RL 4** Determine
the meaning of words and
phrases as they are used in
a text; analyze the impact
of specific word choices on
meaning.

If you hear that people are wealthy, you probably think they have a
lot of money. Perhaps you imagine that they own expensive things
like jewels, antiques, and designer goods. But does wealth always
have to refer to material objects? The poets whose works you are
about to read would like us to find riches in more common places.

QUICKWRITE What types of non-material things do you consider part
of your wealth? Family? Friends? Pets? With a small group, discuss
the everyday things that can lend richness to your life.

TEXT ANALYSIS: RECURRING THEME

You already know that the message of a literary work is called the theme. When the same message is found in different works, it is called a **recurring theme.** The following poems were written in different centuries by poets of different cultures and backgrounds, but they express a similar idea: common things should be considered valuable. As you read, notice how each poet develops this recurring theme. Pay attention to

- the speaker's feelings and beliefs
- important statements the speaker makes
- images and details that stand out
- repeated words and phrases

READING STRATEGY: SET A PURPOSE FOR READING

Your **purpose for reading** the two poems is to compare the way the poets communicate the recurring theme. After you've read the poems once, go back and read them again. This time, take notes in a chart like the one shown.

Recurring Theme: Common things should be considered valuable.		
	"It's all I have to bring today "	"We Alone"
What strong feelings or beliefs does the speaker express?		
Which images and details stand out?		
Which words and phrases are repeated?		

![notebook icon] Complete the activities in your **Reader/Writer Notebook.**

Meet the Authors

Emily Dickinson
1830–1886

An Unsung Talent
In 1862, Emily Dickinson read an announcement in a magazine asking for the work of new poets. Dickinson sent several of her poems to the editor, asking him if her work "breathed." The editor thought she had talent, but he didn't like her use of rhythm, and he asked her to correct her punctuation and capitalization. Dickinson chose to keep her poems in a box, unchanged. After she died, her sister found this wealth of poems and had them published. Dickinson is now considered one of America's greatest poets.

Alice Walker
born 1944

Ground-Breaker
Alice Walker was born in a small town in Georgia where her part-Cherokee mother and African-American father worked as tenant farmers. Although the family did not have much money, Walker's parents made sure there were always books in the house. Walker began writing at around age eight. She also made up many stories that she never put on paper, because she feared her brothers might find them and make fun of her. Today, Walker is a world-renowned author. She was the first African-American woman to win the Pulitzer Prize in fiction.

Authors Online
Go to **thinkcentral.com.** KEYWORD: HML8-625

It's all I have to bring today—

Emily Dickinson

It's all I have to bring today—
This, and my heart beside—
This, and my heart, and all the fields—
And all the meadows wide—
5 Be sure you count—should I forget
Some one the sum could tell—
This, and my heart, and all the Bees
Which in the Clover dwell. **A**

Analyze Visuals ▶

How might you feel if you were in the **setting** depicted in this picture?

A **RECURRING THEME**
What images of nature do you find in the poem?

We Alone

Alice Walker

We alone can devalue gold
by not caring
if it falls or rises
in the marketplace.
5 Wherever there is gold
there is a chain, you know,
and if your chain
is gold
so much the worse
10 for you. **B**

Feathers, shells
and sea-shaped stones
are all as rare.

This could be our revolution:
15 To love what is plentiful
as much as
what is scarce. **C**

Analyze Visuals ▶

To what objects does the light draw attention?

B **RECURRING THEME**
How does the speaker feel about the value of gold?

C **RECURRING THEME**
Reread lines 14–17 and paraphrase the speaker's statement.

Comprehension

1. **Recall** In "It's all I have to bring today—," what does the speaker bring?

2. **Recall** According to the speaker in "We Alone," how can people decrease the value of gold?

3. **Recall** In "We Alone," what items in nature are as rare as gold?

Text Analysis

4. **Visualize** What mental pictures did you create as you read "It's all I have to bring today—"? Describe how you visualized the speaker, the setting, and the situation in this poem.

5. **Interpret Poetry** In "It's all I have to bring today—," the word *this* is repeated in lines 2, 3, and 7. What do you think *this* might refer to—the speaker, the poem, or something else? Support your ideas.

6. **Analyze Symbol** A **symbol** is a person, place, or thing that stands for something beyond itself. In "We Alone," what ideas does the chain represent? Support your response.

7. **Draw Conclusions** Reread the last stanza of "We Alone." What are some "plentiful" things that we should love as much as or more than the scarce things?

● 8. **Evaluate Theme** Which poem more clearly expresses the theme that common things should be considered valuable? Support your answer with details.

Comparing Theme

● 9. **Set a Purpose for Reading** Now that you've read both poems, finish filling in your chart. Then start thinking about the similarities and differences in how the poems express the theme.

Recurring Theme: Common things in life should be considered valuable.		
	"It's all I have to bring today—"	"We Alone"
What strong feelings or beliefs does the speaker express?	She offers only her heart and nature's beauty.	The worth of gold is determined by people.
Which images and details stand out?		
Which words and phrases are repeated?		

Can you be RICH without money?

Do you think the speakers of these poems feel wealthy? Explain your answer.

COMMON CORE

RL 2 Determine a theme of a text and analyze its development. **RL 4** Determine the meaning of words and phrases as they are used in a text; analyze the impact of specific word choices on meaning.

Writing for Assessment

COMMON CORE RL 1, RL 2, W 2, W 2a–b, f

1. READ THE PROMPT

You've just read two poems that express similar ideas about wealth. In writing assessments, you will often be asked to compare literary selections that differ in some ways but share a recurring theme.

> "It's all I have to bring today—" and "We Alone" express this theme: common things should be considered valuable. In four or five paragraphs, compare and contrast how this theme is expressed in the poems. Focus on the speakers, images, and use of repetition in each poem. Support your judgments with references to both texts.

◀ **STRATEGIES IN ACTION**

1. *I should make sure I understand how each poem expresses the* **message.**
2. *I need to identify the* **similarities and differences** *in how the poems develop the message.*
3. *I must support my ideas using* **quotations** *from the poems.*

2. PLAN YOUR WRITING

Review your chart, thinking about the way each poem conveys the theme. Make sure you can cite words and phrases to support your notes. Then think about how you will set up your response.

- Option A: In one paragraph, describe how the recurring theme is developed in the first poem; in the next paragraph, describe how this theme is developed in the second poem; in a third paragraph, discuss similarities and differences in how the poems develop the theme.

- Option B: In one paragraph, compare how the speakers contribute to the theme; in a second paragraph, compare the use of imagery; in a third paragraph, compare the use of repetition.

Now, outline your essay. Then write a thesis statement that describes your main idea.

> I. Introduce poems and thesis statement
> II. How Emily Dickinson develops theme
> III. How Alice Walker develops theme
> IV. Compare and contrast elements
> V. Conclusion

3. DRAFT YOUR RESPONSE

Introduction Include the titles and the poets' names. State the theme and your thesis.

Body Using your outline and the details in your chart, describe how each poem develops the recurring theme. Include details from the poems to support your ideas.

Conclusion End your essay by restating the recurring theme and your thesis. Include a final thought about why this theme is important.

Revision Make sure the poem details you cite truly support your ideas. Gather additional support from the poems if necessary.

Speech to the Young
Speech to the Progress-Toward
Poem by Gwendolyn Brooks

Mother to Son
Poem by Langston Hughes

What is good
ADVICE?

COMMON CORE

RL1 Cite the evidence that supports inferences drawn from the text. **RL4** Determine the meaning of words and phrases as they are used in text; analyze the impact of specific word choices on meaning and tone.

Suggestions about how to improve your grades or how to approach the new guy at school can be welcome, but how do you know if it's good advice? Sometimes it depends on who gives it. Is it someone who has been there and learned from his or her own experience? Is it someone who cares about you or has a stake in the outcome? In the two poems you are about to read, the speakers share what they have learned with a younger generation.

DISCUSS Imagine you need to bring up your grade in science class. In a small group, brainstorm a list of three people you would ask for advice on how to improve your study habits and grade, and tell why you consider these people a good source for advice.

{ 38 } ADVICE

stella says....

Dear Stella,
My best friend isn't speaking to me anymore, and I don't know why. We've been friends since kindergarten, but lately, she ignores me and spends all her time with these other girls who are more popular than me. I really want to be friends with her again, but I don't know how to get her to like me. What should I do?
—Confused, 14

632

Dear Confused
That

● POETIC FORM: LYRIC POETRY

If you're a poet and you want to share your deepest feelings on a topic such as love, death, or the power of nature, what kind of poem would you write? A good choice would be a **lyric poem.** The purpose of a lyric poem is to express personal thoughts and feelings. To achieve this purpose, lyric poems have the following characteristics. They

- are short
- have a single speaker who expresses personal thoughts and feelings
- focus on a single, strong idea

● TEXT ANALYSIS: SOUND DEVICES

Writers use sound devices to create a musical quality and to call attention to certain words. **Alliteration** is the repetition of consonant sounds at the beginning of words. Notice the repeated *w* sound in the following example:

When the wind whispers

Another sound device based on repetition is **assonance,** in which a vowel sound is repeated in two or more syllables.

Poetry is old, ancient, goes back far.

As you read the following poems, notice the alliteration and assonance, and think about the effect of these sound devices.

● READING SKILL: MAKE INFERENCES

As you try to understand the speakers and the advice they give in these two poems, look for clues that hint at their experiences, attitudes, and personality. Combine these clues with your own knowledge or experience to **make inferences,** logical guesses about what the poet doesn't state directly. Use inference equations like the one shown to record your inferences about the speakers.

The title of the poem is "Speech to the Young."	+	Older people like to give advice.	=	Speaker is an older person.

Complete the activities in your **Reader/Writer Notebook.**

Meet the Authors

Gwendolyn Brooks
1917–2000

Young Talent
As a budding young poet, Gwendolyn Brooks went to hear Langston Hughes give a speech at her church. Brooks's mother insisted that she show some of her work to Hughes. He read her poems on the spot and told her she had talent. "That did mean a lot to a sixteen-year-old girl," Brooks later said. Brooks went on to achieve great fame as a poet. She used her own money to fund literary awards for young writers.

Langston Hughes
1902–1967

World Traveler
Langston Hughes was voted "class poet" at his high school in Cleveland, Ohio. After graduation, Hughes visited his father, who was living in Mexico. During the trip, Hughes wrote "The Negro Speaks of Rivers." It remains one of his best-known works. Hughes continued to see the world, traveling extensively in Africa and Europe. The poetry he sent home helped build his literary reputation. Hughes described the people he wrote about as "beaten and baffled, but determined not to be wholly beaten." Some African-American critics disapproved of his choice of subject matter, but Hughes felt that "the masses of our people had as much in their lives to put into books as did those more fortunate ones."

Authors Online

Go to **thinkcentral.com.** KEYWORD: HML8-633

Speech to the Young Speech to the Progress-Toward

(Among them Nora and Henry III)

Gwendolyn Brooks

Say to them,
say to the down-keepers,
the sun-slappers,
the self-soilers,
5 the harmony-hushers,
"Even if you are not ready for day
it cannot always be night."
You will be right.
For that is the hard home-run. **A**

10 Live not for battles won.
Live not for the-end-of-the-song.
Live in the along. **B**

Analyze Visuals ▶

What can you **infer** about the relationship between the girl and the woman in the picture?

A SOUND DEVICES
How many examples of **alliteration** can you find in the first stanza?

B MAKE INFERENCES
What attitude does the speaker express in lines 10–12?

New Dreams (2002), Ernest Crichlow. Lithograph, 24¾″ × 16¾″. Photo by Maureen Turci, Mojo Portfolio. Courtesy of the Estate of Ernest Crichlow.

Mother *to* Son

Langston Hughes

Lady, Ernest Crichlow. Etching, 22″ × 18″. Photo by Maureen Turci, Mojo Portfolio. Courtesy of the Estate of Ernest Crichlow.

Well, son, I'll tell you:
Life for me ain't been no crystal stair.
It's had tacks in it,
And splinters,
5 And boards torn up,
And places with no carpet on the floor—
Bare.
But all the time
I'se been a-climbin' on,
10 And reachin' landin's,
And turnin' corners,
And sometimes goin' in the dark
Where there ain't been no light.
So boy, don't you turn back. **C**
15 Don't you set down on the steps
'Cause you finds it's kinder hard.
Don't you fall now—
For I'se still goin', honey,
I'se still climbin',
20 And life for me ain't been no crystal stair. **D**

▲ **Analyze Visuals**
What personality **traits** would you expect the woman in the painting to have?

C SOUND DEVICES
Notice the **assonance** created by the use of the long *o* sound in lines 12–14. What words contain this sound?

D LYRIC POETRY
What is the main idea the speaker is expressing about her life?

Comprehension

1. **Recall** In "Speech to the Young," what does the speaker tell the young to say?

2. **Recall** What two things does the speaker in "Speech to the Young" say we should *not* live for?

3. **Represent** Create a sketch of the stairway described by the speaker in "Mother to Son."

Text Analysis

4. **Interpret Meaning** What does the speaker in "Speech to the Young" mean by "Even if you are not ready for the day/it cannot always be night"?

5. **Examine Dialect** In "Mother to Son," words such as *ain't* and *kinder* are examples of **dialect,** the particular way language is used in a certain place or by a certain group of people. Dialect is an important element of Langston Hughes's style. What does Hughes's use of dialect help you to understand about the speaker?

6. **Identify Figurative Language** What **metaphor** is used throughout "Mother to Son"? What does it tell you about the mother's life and how she has responded to it?

7. **Make Inferences About the Speakers** In your own words, describe how you picture the speaker in each poem. Use the inference equations you made as you read to help you.

8. **Analyze Sound Devices** For each poem, use a chart like the one shown to record the instances of **alliteration** and **assonance.** Which poem makes greater use of these sound devices?

"Speech to the Young"	
Alliteration	Assonance
say/sun-slappers/self-soilers	

9. **Analyze Lyric Poetry** Review the relationship between the purpose and characteristics of lyric poems on page 633. Next, think about each poet's message. Then explain why each poet's choice to use a lyric poem as his or her form was an appropriate one.

Extension and Challenge

10. **Creative Project: Poetry** Write a short poem in which the speaker explains a lesson learned from life.

What is good ADVICE?

Which speaker's advice do you think is best? Why?

COMMON CORE

RL 1 Cite the evidence that supports inferences drawn from the text. **RL 4** Determine the meaning of words and phrases as they are used in text; analyze the impact of specific word choices on meaning and tone.

On the Grasshopper and Cricket
Poem by John Keats

Ode on Solitude
Poem by Alexander Pope

VIDEO TRAILER **THINK** central KEYWORD: HML8-638

When does FORM matter?

COMMON CORE

RL 4 Determine the meaning of words and phrases as they are used in a text; analyze the impact of specific word choices on meaning and tone. **RL 5** Compare and contrast the structure of two or more texts.

"Bend from the waist." "Lift your chin." "Hold your arms like this." Learning almost any new skill—swinging a bat or a tennis racket, swimming and diving, cartwheeling or dancing—involves learning form. In the poems you are about to read, two of the most well-respected poets in the English language use traditional poetic forms to create meaning.

LIST IT Make a list of activities that involve form. Rank them in order of which requires the most attention to form.

1. Ballroom dancing
2. Baseball
3. Writing
4. Painting

● POETIC FORM: TRADITIONAL FORMS

The poems that follow are examples of two traditional **forms,** or types. Both are **lyric poems,** or short poems in which a speaker expresses personal thoughts and feelings.

- "On the Grasshopper and Cricket" is a **sonnet**—a lyric poem with a specific structure that always includes 14 lines and set patterns of **rhyme** and **rhythm.**

- "Ode on Solitude" is an **ode,** a type of lyric poem that characteristically deals with an important topic.

● TEXT ANALYSIS: RHYME SCHEME

Rhyme scheme is the pattern of rhyming words at the ends of a poem's lines. You can use letters to identify rhyme scheme. Write the letter *a* next to the first rhyming word and all words that rhyme with it. Then write the letter *b* next to the second rhyming word and the words that rhyme with it, and so on.

Happy the man, whose wish and <u>care</u>	a
A few paternal acres <u>bound</u>,	b
Content to breathe his native <u>air</u>	a
In his own <u>ground</u>.	b

The letter *a* identifies all the words at the ends of lines that rhyme with *care*. The letter *b* indicates all the words that rhyme with *bound*. After your first reading of each of these poems, read it a second time and note the rhyme scheme in a chart.

"On the Grasshopper and Cricket"	
Line	Rhyme Scheme
1	a
2	

● READING STRATEGY: PARAPHRASE

Since these poems use language in a way that is seldom heard today, they can be challenging to read. To make sure you understand the poems, **paraphrase** them, or restate in your own words.

As you read the poems, look for punctuation marks that show where a thought begins and ends. Then check your understanding by paraphrasing the idea. If you still find a thought difficult to "translate," reread the lines slowly and use the context and a dictionary to decode important words you don't know.

 Complete the activities in your **Reader/Writer Notebook.**

Meet the Authors

John Keats
1795–1821

A Short, Creative Life
John Keats lost both parents when he was a child. His guardian wanted him to be a doctor, but when Keats went to London to study, he met a group of young writers and abandoned medicine for poetry. He was remarkably creative, writing four of his most famous poems in a single month. In 1818, Keats's brother died of tuberculosis. The following year, Keats began to show the same symptoms and soon became too ill to write. He died at the age of 25. In his three-year writing career, Keats created a body of work whose quality is greater than that of Shakespeare or Wordsworth at the same age.

Alexander Pope
1688–1744

Living on Poetry
Alexander Pope suffered from poor health his whole life. In addition, he was Catholic, which at that time meant that he could not attend a university. None of this stopped him from his studies. Pope mostly educated himself, learning Latin and Greek. His translations were so successful they made Pope the first English poet able to live off of his work. He is famous for his poetry, essays, and satires. Lines from his essays—such as "To err is human, to forgive, divine"—have become part of the English language.

Authors Online
Go to **thinkcentral.com**. KEYWORD: HML8-639

THINK central

ON THE Grasshopper AND Cricket

John Keats

The poetry of earth is never dead:
   When all the birds are faint with the hot sun,
   And hide in cooling trees, a voice will run
From hedge to hedge about the new-mown mead; **Ⓐ**
5 That is the Grasshopper's—he takes the lead
   In summer luxury,—he has never done
   With his delights; for when tired out with fun
He rests at ease beneath some pleasant weed.
The poetry of earth is ceasing never:
10   On a lone winter evening, when the frost
     Has wrought[1] a silence, from the stove there shrills
The Cricket's song, in warmth increasing ever,
   And seems to one in drowsiness half lost,
     The Grasshopper's among some grassy hills. **Ⓑ**

Ⓐ RHYME SCHEME
How would you describe the rhyme scheme in lines 1–4? Note that *mead* is a shortened form of *meadow,* so is pronounced mĕd.

Ⓑ PARAPHRASE
How would you paraphrase lines 10–12? Now read lines 13–14. What does the cricket's song remind the speaker of?

Analyze Visuals ▶

What **mood** does this image suggest?

---

1. **wrought** (rôt): made; produced.

Ode on Solitude

Alexander Pope

Barn at Cove, Oregon (2005), Gary Ernest Smith. Oil on canvas, 30″ × 40″.

> Happy the man whose wish and care
>   A few paternal[1] acres bound,
> Content to breathe his native[2] air,
>   In his own ground.
>
> 5 Whose herds with milk, whose fields with bread,
>   Whose flocks supply him with attire,
> Whose trees in summer yield him shade,
>   In winter fire. **C**
>
> Blest, who can unconcern'dly find
> 10   Hours, days, and years slide soft away,
> In health of body, peace of mind,
>   Quiet by day,
>
> Sound sleep by night; study and ease,
>   Together mixt; sweet recreation;
> 15 And Innocence, which most does please
>   With meditation.
>
> Thus let me live, unseen, unknown,
>   Thus unlamented[3] let me die,
> Steal from the world, and not a stone
> 20   Tell where I lie. **D**

---

1. **paternal** (pə-tûr′nəl): received from a father.
2. **native:** being one's own because of one's birthplace.
3. **unlamented** (ŭn-lə-mĕnt′ĕd): not missed; not mourned for.

C PARAPHRASE
In the second stanza, what do the speaker's herds, fields, flocks, and trees provide for him?

COMMON CORE RL 4, RL 5

D TRADITIONAL FORMS
Odes are usually written in a serious **tone,** or attitude toward a subject. The poet may praise nature or an abstract quality, or pay tribute to a person or event. Which words and phrases in lines 17–20 reflect Pope's serious attitude toward his subject?

Comprehension

1. **Recall** In "On the Grasshopper and Cricket," which insect represents summer? Which insect represents winter?

2. **Recall** Name three of the things that, according to the speaker in "Ode on Solitude," make man happy.

COMMON CORE

RL 4 Determine the meaning of words and phrases as they are used in a text; analyze the impact of specific word choices on meaning and tone. **RL 5** Compare and contrast the structure of two or more texts.

Text Analysis

3. **Examine Imagery** You remember that **imagery** consists of words or phrases that appeal to the senses. Use a web to record imagery from "On the Grasshopper and Cricket." To which senses does the poet appeal?

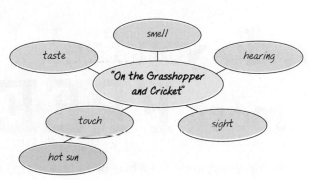

4. **Identify Soft Rhyme** Sometimes a poet cannot find words that fit a poem's rhyme scheme *and* express the correct meaning. In such a case, a poet might use a **soft rhyme,** words that share one or more sounds but do not actually rhyme. What example of a soft rhyme do you find in "Ode on Solitude"?

5. **Paraphrase Poetry** Choose two especially challenging lines from each poem and "translate" them in your own words. What does each paraphase help you to understand about the poem?

6. **Understand Traditional Forms** According to the bulleted definitions on page 639, what purpose and characteristics of its form does each poem show?

7. **Compare and Contrast Rhyme Scheme** Look back at the chart you made for each poem's rhyme scheme. Which poem's rhyme scheme is more complex? Explain.

Extension and Challenge

8. **Readers' Circle** Alexander Pope wrote the first draft of "Ode on Solitude" around 1700. How do you think the speaker's idea of happiness might be different if the poem were rewritten today? Explain.

When does FORM matter?

Which of these poems seems more influenced by its form? Explain why.

One More Round
Poem by Maya Angelou

Not My Bones
Poem by Marilyn Nelson

When do you feel most FREE?

COMMON CORE

RL 4 Determine the meaning of words and phrases as they are used in a text; analyze the impact of word choices on meaning and tone.
RL 9 Analyze how a modern work draws on themes or patterns from traditional stories or religious works, including how the material is rendered new.

Riding a skateboard or a bike or a horse makes many people feel physically free. Reading a book can liberate the mind to explore the universe. Watching fireworks on the Fourth of July might remind us that we live in a country of many freedoms. The following poems convey the feelings of those who have found freedom at long last.

QUICKWRITE When have you felt most free? Think of two or three times and either describe them or sketch them in your journal. Try to explain why these situations gave you a sense of freedom.

● TEXT ANALYSIS: WORD CHOICE

To express complicated thoughts and feelings in just a few lines, poets must make every word count. So a poet's **word choice,** or use of words, is particularly important. For example, in "Not My Bones," Marilyn Nelson writes, "the soul runs free. It roams the night sky's mute geometry." Why did she choose these words when she could have written, "The soul flies among the stars in the sky"? Perhaps because the words *mute geometry* suggest a quiet order to the universe.

As you read, look for other interesting, unusual, or striking words. Record your thoughts on a chart like the one shown.

Striking Words	Why Poet Might Have Chosen
mute geometry	to suggest a quiet, planned universe

Review: Sound Devices

▇ READING STRATEGY: READ POETRY

Poets and writers sometimes draw on traditional songs, stories, or themes in their work. By doing so, they can explore the ways the present is similar to or different from the past.

For example, the poem "One More Round" is based on work songs historically sung by enslaved African Americans. These songs feature the following characteristics:

- A call and response pattern, in which a leader sings a verse and other workers respond with a chorus
- A strong rhythm, to help workers pace themselves
- Lyrics that often express feelings or frustrations

As you read "One More Round," notice how Maya Angelou uses these traditional elements to create something new.

▲ VOCABULARY IN CONTEXT

The following words help poet Marilyn Nelson explain how an enslaved person can find freedom. To see how many you know, use the words to complete the sentences.

> **WORD LIST**   converge   cosmic   essential   incarnation

1. Abolitionist groups _____ to fight slavery.
2. Some believe that each soul has more than one _____.
3. Freedom of speech is _____ to a democracy.
4. Astronomers' work is to understand the _____ order.

Complete the activities in your **Reader/Writer Notebook.**

Meet the Authors

Maya Angelou
born 1928

Silence to Star
At the age of seven, Maya Angelou went through a difficult time and stopped talking for five years. A family friend not only taught her the importance of the spoken word but also encouraged her to write. Since then, Angelou has written poetry, autobiographies, plays, screenplays, children's books, and even a cookbook. As her fame has grown, she has become an important public figure, mixing with presidents, television and movie stars, and other internationally recognized artists.

Marilyn Nelson
born 1946

Early Promise
Marilyn Nelson's sixth-grade teacher predicted that she would become a famous writer. The teacher was right. Nelson's books of poetry have won many awards, including the Newbery Honor. The poem "Not My Bones" comes from *Fortune's Bones: The Manumission Requiem,* which Nelson wrote to honor the memory of Fortune, an enslaved person who died in 1798. She was commissioned to write the book by the Mattatuck Museum in Connecticut after the descendents of Fortune's owners donated his skeleton to the institution. Nelson has said she is motivated by the desire "to talk about finding pride . . . in people who triumphed over slavery."

Authors Online
Go to **thinkcentral.com**. KEYWORD: HML8-645

THINK central

One More Round

Maya Angelou

There ain't no pay beneath the sun
As sweet as rest when a job's well done.
I was born to work up to my grave
But I was not born
5 To be a slave.

One more round
And let's heave it down,
One more round
And let's heave it down.

10 Papa drove steel and Momma stood guard,
I never heard them holler 'cause the work was hard.
They were born to work up to their graves
But they were not born
To be worked-out slaves. **Ⓐ**

15 One more round
And let's heave it down,
One more round
And let's heave it down.

Brothers and sisters know the daily grind,[1]
20 It was not labor made them lose their minds.
They were born to work up to their graves
But they were not born
To be worked-out slaves.

Ⓐ **WORD CHOICE**
Reread the third stanza.
What words stand out
to you? Note what these
words and phrases make
you think of and then
add them to your chart.

---

1. **grind:** a labor-intensive routine.

Aspiration (1936), Aaron Douglas. Oil on canvas, 60″ × 60″. © Fine Arts Museums of San Francisco.

One more round
25 And let's heave it down,
One more round
And let's heave it down.

And now I'll tell you my Golden Rule,[2]
I was born to work but I ain't no mule.
30 I was born to work up to my grave
But I was not born
To be a slave.

One more round
And let's heave it down,
35 One more round
And let's heave it down. **B**

▲ **Analyze Visuals**
What **symbols** do you see in this painting?

B READ POETRY
If this poem were a work song, which stanzas would be the verses, sung by the leader? Which stanzas would be the chorus?

---

2. **Golden Rule:** the biblical teaching that one should behave towards others as one wants others to behave towards oneself.

NOT MY BONES

Marilyn Nelson

Fortune (2001), William B. Westwood.
© William B. Westwood.

I was not this body,
I was not these bones.
This skeleton was just my
temporary home.
5 Elementary molecules[1] **converged** for a breath,
then danced on beyond my individual death.
And I am not my body,
I am not my body.

We are brief **incarnations,**
10 we are clouds in clothes.
We are water respirators,
we are how earth knows.
I bore[2] light passed on from an original flame;
while it was in my hands it was called by my name.
15 But I am not my body,
I am not my body. **C**

converge (kən-vûrj′) *v.* to come together in one place; meet

incarnation
(ĭn′-kär-nā′-shən) *n.* a bodily form

C WORD CHOICE
Reread lines 3–6. What are they saying about our physical bodies? What words in lines 9–14 suggest the same ideas? Add these to your chart.

---

1. **elementary molecules:** the smallest, most basic particles of substances.
2. **bore:** carried; transported.

You can own a man's body,
but you can't own his mind.
That's like making a bridle
20 to ride on the wind.
I will tell you one thing, and I'll tell you true:
Life's the best thing that can happen to you.
But you are not your body,
you are not your body.

25 You can own someone's body,
but the soul runs free.
It roams the night sky's
mute geometry.
You can murder hope, you can pound faith flat,
30 but like weeds and wildflowers, they grow right back.
For you are not your body,
you are not your body.

You are not your body,
you are not your bones.
35 What's **essential** about you
is what can't be owned.
What's essential in you is your longing to raise
your itty-bitty voice in the **cosmic** praise.
For you are not your body,
40 you are not your body. **D**

Well, I woke up this morning just so glad to be free,
glad to be free, glad to be free.
I woke up this morning in restful peace.
For I am not my body,
45 I am not my bones.
I am not my body,
glory hallelujah, not my bones,
I am not my bones. **E**

essential (ĭ-sĕn′shəl) *adj.*
having the qualities that
give something its true
identity

cosmic (kŏz′mik) *adj.*
universal; infinitely large

COMMON CORE RL 4

D **WORD CHOICE**
When poets choose
a word, they consider
the way it sounds,
the way it affects the
rhythm of a line, and
sometimes even the
way it looks on the page.
They also consider the
word's **connotation**, or
the feelings and ideas
associated with the
word that go beyond
its basic definition. In
line 38, Marilyn Nelson
chooses to use the
word *itty-bitty* instead
of *small*. How does her
choice affect the line's
meaning, rhythm, and
tone?

E **SOUND DEVICES**
What lines in this poem
have been most often
repeated?

Comprehension

1 **Recall** In "One More Round," what is the speaker's "Golden Rule"?

2. **Recall** According to the speaker in "Not My Bones," what happens when hope is murdered and faith is pounded flat?

Text Analysis

● 3. **Interpret Poetry** Enslaved African Americans could not express themselves freely. Note the lines in "One More Round" that would have been dangerous to voice in a traditional work song. By expressing these once-forbidden sentiments in a traditional form, what might Maya Angelou be saying about the past and the present?

4. **Make Inferences** Why does the speaker in "Not My Bones" feel that a person's mind and soul cannot be owned?

5. **Analyze Repetition** For each poem, identify the two phrases or sections that are repeated most frequently and write them in a chart like the one shown. Complete the chart by noting how these repeated words contribute to the poem's meaning.

Repeated phrases	Effect on Poem's Meaning
1	
2	

● 6. **Compare Word Choice** Review the charts you made as you read the poems. Make a generalization, or overall statement, about each poet's word choice. What is different about the words chosen for each poem?

7. **Draw Conclusions** Do you think the people mentioned in "One More Round" would agree with the speaker of "Not My Bones" that "you are not your body"? Explain why or why not.

Extension and Challenge

8. **Creative Project: Music** Work with a small group to create a song from "One More Round." Practice reading the poem aloud, using desks, pencils, or other classroom materials as drums to keep the rhythm. Perform your piece for the class.

When do you feel most FREE?

Which poem's theme do you think conveys a greater sense of freedom? Support your response with details from the poem.

COMMON CORE

RL 4 Determine the meaning of words and phrases as they are used in a text; analyze the impact of word choices on meaning and tone. **RL 9** Analyze how a modern work draws on themes or patterns from traditional stories or religious works, including how the material is rendered new.

Vocabulary in Context

▲ **VOCABULARY PRACTICE**

Choose the letter of the word that means the same, or nearly the same, as the boldfaced word.

1. two streams **converge**: (a) rise, (b) separate, (c) meet, (d) flow
2. **cosmic** ideas: (a) fascinating, (b) universal, (c) mistaken, (d) weird
3. **essential** elements: (a) dissimilar, (b) toxic, (c) similar, (d) basic
4. a brief **incarnation**: (a) meeting, (b) lifetime, (c) quarrel, (d) vacation

ACADEMIC VOCABULARY IN WRITING

> • attitude • create • emphasis • mental • style

Both of the speakers of the poems you have read have strong opinions on what freedom means. Write a paragraph about one speaker's **attitude** toward freedom. Use at least one of the Academic Vocabulary words in your response.

VOCABULARY STRATEGY: THE LATIN ROOT *carn*

The vocabulary word *incarnation* comes from the Latin root *carn*, which means "flesh." *Carn* (combined with other word parts) appears in a number of English words. To determine the meaning of a word that contains this root, use context clues—the words and sentences around the word—as well as your knowledge of the root's meaning.

PRACTICE Choose the word from the web that best completes each sentence. Be ready to explain how the root *carn* helps to give each word its meaning.

1. Tyrannosaurus Rex was a huge _____ that devoured other dinosaurs.
2. The wolf is a _____ mammal that lives and hunts in a pack.
3. Drunk drivers cause _____ on U.S. highways.
4. Molars are _____ teeth, because they are adapted for chewing meat.

converge

cosmic

essential

incarnation

COMMON CORE

l 4h Use Latin roots as clues to the meaning of a word.

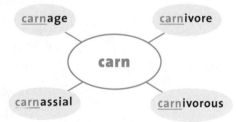

carnage   carnivore

carn

carnassial   carnivorous

Interactive Vocabulary THINK central

Go to **thinkcentral.com**.
KEYWORD: HML8-651

Fortune's Bones
Book Excerpt

What's the Connection?

The poem "Not My Bones" was inspired by the real life of Fortune, an enslaved person. Now learn more about this man and about what happened to his bones after he died.

Standards Focus: Identify Treatment

Three writers know they have to write about the first day of middle school. One writer writes a funny newspaper column about an embarrassing moment she had when she started sixth grade. Another writer describes the first day of sixth grade in a letter to his grandmother. A third writer creates an e-mail that gives students tips on how to find their way around the new middle school. How can such a variety of writings come from the same topic? It's because writers can handle the same subject matter in very different ways.

The way a topic is handled is called its **treatment.** The writer's purpose, or reason for writing, helps determine a work's treatment. So does the form the writing takes and the tone, or attitude the writer expresses about the topic. In order to identify a writer's treatment, ask yourself the following questions:

- **What form does the writing take?** For example, is it a newspaper column, a personal letter, or a business memo?

- **For what purpose(s) is the selection written?** Is it written to entertain, to express ideas and feelings, to inform, or to persuade? If there is more than one purpose, which is primary?

- **What is the writer's tone, or attitude toward the subject?** For example, the tone of a selection might be described as mocking, optimistic, or respectful.

In the following selection, the topic is Fortune's life and legacy. As you read, identify the author's treatment of this topic by completing a chart such as the one begun here.

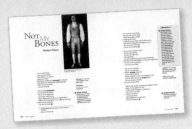

Use with "Not My Bones,"
page 648.

COMMON CORE

RI 3 Analyze how a text makes connections among and distinctions between individuals, ideas, or events. **RI 6** Determine an author's point of view or purpose in a text.

"Fortune's Bones"	
What form does the writing take?	author notes
For what purpose(s) is the selection written? What is the writer's primary purpose?	
What is the writer's tone?	

from Fortune's Bones

Notes by Pamela Espeland

F OCUS ON FORM
You're about to read the notes that accompany "Not My Bones" and Marilyn Nelson's other poems about Fortune. These **notes** provide facts and additional information about Fortune's life and his bones.

Before Fortune was bones in a Connecticut museum, he was a husband, a father, a baptized Christian, and a slave.

His wife's name was Dinah. His sons were Africa and Jacob. His daughters were Mira and Roxa. He was baptized in an Episcopal church, which did not make him free. His master was Dr. Preserved Porter, a physician who specialized in setting broken bones.

They lived in Waterbury, Connecticut, in the late 1700s. Dr. Porter had a 75-acre farm, which Fortune probably ran. He planted and harvested corn, rye, potatoes, onions, apples, buckwheat, oats, and hay. He cared for the cattle
10 and hogs.

Unlike many slaves, who owned little or nothing and were often separated from their families, Fortune owned a small house near Dr. Porter's home. He and Dinah and their children lived together. **Ⓐ**

When Dr. Porter died in 1803, he left an estate that was worth about $7,000— a lot of money for the time. The estate included Fortune's widow, Dinah, and their son Jacob. Fortune had died in 1798.

According to Connecticut's Act of Gradual Emancipation, children born to enslaved parents after March 1, 1784, were to be freed when they reached age 21. Jacob was 18. By law, he could be enslaved for another three years.
20 In Dr. Porter's will, he left Dinah to his wife, Lydia. He gave Jacob to his daughter Hannah. **Ⓑ**

No one knows what happened to Africa, Mira, and Roxa.

Ⓐ TREATMENT
Based on the number of facts you have learned already, what would you **infer** is the author's **purpose** for writing these notes?

Ⓑ NOTES
What facts about slavery in the northern United States do you learn from these notes?

A sculptor used information about Fortune's bones to create this reconstruction of Fortune's face.

C TREATMENT
How would you describe the author's **tone** as she talks about Fortune?

D TREATMENT
Does the author's tone remain the same as she talks about what happened to Fortune's bones? If not, describe her tone now.

E TREATMENT
Reread lines 60–62. What impact do these statements have on you? Based on their impact, what would you guess is another purpose for writing these author notes? Explain.

Most slaves who died in Waterbury in the 1700s were buried in one of the town's cemeteries. When Fortune died, he wasn't buried. Instead, Dr. Porter preserved Fortune's skeleton to further the study of human anatomy.

Dr. Porter had been a bonesetter for many years, but he'd never had a skeleton to study. He had two sons who were also doctors. They could learn from the skeleton, too.

Fortune was about 60 at the time of his death and, in spite of his injuries,
30 in relatively good health. His skeleton was sturdy and complete. . . . C

Four more generations of Porters became physicians, and the skeleton stayed in the family. Porter children, grandchildren, and great-grandchildren used it to learn the names of the bones. This was their earliest medical training.

Sally Porter Law McGlannan, the last Porter doctor, remembered playing with the skeleton as a young girl. . . . Another family member, Leander Law, once brought part of Fortune's skeleton to a college physiology class.

At some point—no one knows exactly when—"Larry" was written on the skull. Fortune's name was forgotten for nearly a century.

Over the years, the skeleton was lost and found. It was boarded up in an attic,
40 then discovered by a crew of workers hired to renovate an old building.

In 1933, Sally Porter Law McGlannan gave the bones to the Mattatuck Museum. The museum sent the bones to Europe to be assembled for display. The skeleton hung in a glass case in the museum for decades, fascinating adults and frightening children.

Many stories were invented about the skeleton. Some said that "Larry" was a Revolutionary War hero—maybe even George Washington. Some said he fell to his death. Some said he drowned. Some said he was killed trying to escape. Some thought he had been hanged.

One Waterbury resident remembers, "Larry was the thing to see when you
50 go to the museum. I don't think anybody ever envisioned that this was truly a human being." D

In 1970, the skeleton, still called "Larry," was taken out of its case and put into storage. Times had changed. The museum now believed that displaying the skeleton was disrespectful. It wasn't just a bunch of bones. It was the remains of someone's son, maybe someone's father.

The skeleton rested for more than 25 years. Then, in the 1990s, historians searched local records and found a slave named Fortune. Archaeologists and anthropologists studied the bones, which started giving up their secrets. The bones told how Fortune labored, suffered, and died: A quick, sudden injury,
60 like whiplash, may have snapped a vertebra in his neck. He did not drown or fall from a cliff. He was not hanged.

But he was free. E

Comprehension

1. **Recall** Where did Fortune live?

2. **Recall** Who gave Fortune's skeleton to the museum? What was her relationship to Fortune?

3. **Clarify** How did the museum learn how Fortune died?

Text Analysis

● 4. **Identify Treatment** Review the chart you completed as you read. In your own words, describe the author's treatment of Fortune's life and legacy.

● 5. **Evaluate Notes** Reread "Not My Bones" on pages 648–649. Compare the understanding of Fortune that you get from this poem with the understanding of him that you get from the accompanying notes. What might be the strengths of a book that combines poems with historical notes?

COMMON CORE

RI 3 Analyze how a text makes connections among and distinctions between individuals, ideas, or events. **RI 6** Determine an author's point of view or purpose in a text. **RI 9** Analyze a case in which two texts provide information on the same topic.

Read for Information: Compare Treatments

WRITING PROMPT

In a paragraph, compare and contrast the treatment of Fortune's life and legacy on pages 653–654 with Marilyn Nelson's treatment of the same subject in her poem "Not My Bones."

Remember that when you **compare and contrast,** you identify the ways in which two or more things are alike and different. To get started,

1. Reread the poem, noting its form, purpose(s), and speaker's tone. You might also note its overall message or its impact on you as a reader.

2. Identify the similarities and differences between the treatment of Fortune in the notes and the poem.

3. In a sentence, make a general statement about these similarities and differences. Support your statement with specific details. Then draw a conclusion about the differences you have noticed.

Author Notes	Poem
Form _____	Form _____
Purpose(s) _____	Purpose(s) _____
_____	_____
Tone _____	Tone _____

Similarities	Differences
• _____	• _____
• _____	• _____
• _____	• _____

General Statement
_____
_____

Boots of Spanish Leather
Poem by Bob Dylan

from The Song of Hiawatha
Poem by Henry Wadsworth Longfellow

When do poems tell a STORY?

COMMON CORE

RL 2 Determine a central idea of a text; provide an objective summary of the text. **RL 4** Analyze the impact of specific word choices on meaning and tone, including analogies or allusions to other texts. **RL 5** Compare the structure of two texts and analyze how structure contributes to meaning and style.

When you hear the word *story*, you might think of plots that unfold in short stories, novels, or movies. But some of the first stories that people told to each other took on the form of poetry. Ever since, some writers have used the stanzas, rhythm, and rhyme of poetry to tell about characters, setting, and conflict. The following two works are examples of stories told in poetic form.

DISCUSS Think of a poem or song you know that tells a story. For your group, summarize the story in your own words. How many of your classmates can guess the original work?

POETIC FORM: NARRATIVE POETRY

The two poems that follow are examples of specific types of **narrative poetry,** or poetry whose purpose is to tell a story.

- "Boots of Spanish Leather" is a **ballad,** a narrative poem that is meant to be sung and focuses on a single tragic event.
- *The Song of Hiawatha* is an **epic,** a long narrative poem about the life of a hero whose actions reflect the values of the group he or she belongs to.

Like all narrative poems, ballads and epics contain characters, plot, and setting.

TEXT ANALYSIS: RHYTHM AND METER

One way that poetry differs from prose is the extent to which it features rhythm and meter. **Rhythm** is the pattern of stressed (ˊ) and unstressed (˘) syllables in a line of poetry. Narrative poetry often has a regular, repeated pattern of rhythm, which is called **meter.**

Rhythm and meter create the overall tempo or pace of a poem. They give poems their musical sound and help poets to emphasize certain words or phrases. For example, notice the soothing, regular rhythm in the following lines from *The Song of Hiawatha:*

Bý the shóres ŏf Gítchĕ Gúmĕe,

Bý thĕ shíning Bíg-Sĕa-Wátĕr,

As you read the poems, listen for the way rhythm and meter create emphasis and add a musical effect.

READING STRATEGY: SUMMARIZE

When you **summarize,** you briefly retell the main ideas and most important details of a piece of writing in your own words. Summarizing narrative poetry can help you make sure you understand the characters' feelings, thoughts, and actions. As you read each poem, use a graphic organizer like the one shown to help you summarize each stanza or section.

Stanza/Section	Main Idea	Detail(s)
1	A woman lives in the forest by the water.	Her name is Nokomis.

Complete the activities in your **Reader/Writer Notebook.**

Bob Dylan
born 1941

A Poet of His Times
In the 1960s, Bob Dylan burst onto the folk music scene in New York City. He became famous as the voice of his generation. But the young man, who was born Robert Zimmerman in a Minnesota mining town, was not content to be labeled. He disappointed many of his early fans when he began to play rock music. He confused others when he left the rock scene to pursue a religious path. And all the while, drawing from both classic literature and traditional American music, he wrote lyrics widely recognized as important poems.

Henry Wadsworth Longfellow
1807–1882

American Legend
Henry Wadsworth Longfellow introduced American landscapes, history, and culture to a wide readership. *The Song of Hiawatha* was one of the first literary works in English to portray Native Americans respectfully. The real Hiawatha was a Native American chief credited with helping to make peace among warring tribes. Longfellow's hero was a combination of this historical figure and other people the poet learned about through researching the traditions of various Native American groups.

Authors Online

Go to **thinkcentral.com.** KEYWORD: HML8-657

Boots of Spanish Leather

Bob Dylan

Oh, I'm sailin' away my own true love,
I'm sailin' away in the morning.
Is there something I can send you from across the sea,
From the place that I'll be landing?

5 No, there's nothin' you can send me, my own true love,
There's nothin' I wish to be ownin'.
Just carry yourself back to me unspoiled,
From across that lonesome ocean. Ⓐ

Oh, but I just thought you might want something fine
10 Made of silver or of golden,
Either from the mountains of Madrid[1]
Or from the coast of Barcelona.[2]

Oh, but if I had the stars from the darkest night
And the diamonds from the deepest ocean,
15 I'd forsake[3] them all for your sweet kiss,
For that's all I'm wishin' to be ownin'. Ⓑ

That I might be gone a long time
And it's only that I'm askin',
Is there something I can send you to remember me by,
20 To make your time more easy passin'.

---

1. **Madrid** (mə-drĭd): the capital of Spain, located in the central part
   of the country.
2. **Barcelona** (bär'-sə-lōnə): a northeastern Spanish city, located on the
   Mediterranean Sea coast.
3. **forsake** (fôr-sāk'): to give up (something that was formerly precious).

Analyze Visuals ▶

What is the **mood** of this painting? Explain how the colors contribute to that mood.

Ⓐ **NARRATIVE POETRY**
Reread the first two stanzas. What do you know about the speaker in the first stanza? Who is the speaker in the second?

Ⓑ **SUMMARIZE**
What is this speaker's attitude toward the offered gift?

La Promenade en Mer (1988), Jean Plichart. Copper engraving. © SuperStock.

Oh, how can, how can you ask me again,
It only brings me sorrow.
The same thing I want from you today,
I would want again tomorrow. **C**

25 I got a letter on a lonesome day,
It was from her ship a-sailin',
Saying I don't know when I'll be comin' back again,
It depends on how I'm a-feelin'.

Well, if you, my love, must think that-a-way,
30 I'm sure your mind is roamin'.
I'm sure your heart is not with me,
But with the country to where you're goin'.

So take heed, take heed of the western wind,
Take heed of the stormy weather.
35 And yes, there's something you can send back to me,
Spanish boots of Spanish leather. **D**

C NARRATIVE POETRY
What is the **conflict** between the two speakers, or characters?

D RHYTHM AND METER
Reread lines 33–36 aloud. Which words are emphasized by the repetition and rhythm?

THE Song OF Hiawatha

Henry Wadsworth Longfellow

By the shores of Gitche Gumee,
By the shining Big-Sea-Water,
Stood the wigwam of Nokomis,
Daughter of the Moon, Nokomis.
5 Dark behind it rose the forest,
Rose the black and gloomy pine trees,
Rose the firs with cones upon them;
Bright before it beat the water,
Beat the clear and sunny water,
10 Beat the shining Big-Sea-Water. **E**
    There the wrinkled old Nokomis
Nursed the little Hiawatha,
Rocked him in his linden¹ cradle,
Bedded soft in moss and rushes,
15 Safely bound with reindeer sinews;
Stilled his fretful wail by saying,
"Hush! the Naked Bear will hear thee!"
Lulled him into slumber, singing,
"Ewa-yea! my little owlet!
20 Who is this, that lights the wigwam?
With his great eyes lights the wigwam?
Ewa-yea! my little owlet!"
    Many things Nokomis taught him
Of the stars that shine in heaven;
25 Showed him Ishkoodah, the comet,

Analyze Visuals ▶
What is the attitude of the person in this painting?

E NARRATIVE POETRY
What is the **setting** of this poem?

---

1. **linden** (lĭn′dən): made of wood from a linden tree.

Communion, Joe Geshick. © Joe Geshick.

Ishkoodah, with fiery tresses;[2]
Showed the Death-Dance of the spirits,
Warriors with their plumes and war-clubs,
Flaring far away to northward
30 In the frosty nights of Winter;
Showed the broad white road in heaven,
Pathway of the ghosts, the shadows,
Running straight across the heavens,
Crowded with the ghosts, the shadows. **F**

35   At the door on summer evenings
Sat the little Hiawatha;
Heard the whispering of the pine-trees,
Heard the lapping of the waters,
Sounds of music, words of wonder;
40 "Minne-wawa!" said the pine-trees,
"Mudway-aushka!" said the water.
    Saw the firefly, Wah-wah-taysee,
Flitting through the dusk of evening,
With the twinkle of its candle
45 Lighting up the brakes[3] and bushes,
And he sang the song of children,
Sang the song Nokomis taught him:
"Wah-wah-taysee, little firefly,
Little, flitting, white-fire insect,
50 Little, dancing, white-fire creature,
Light me with your little candle,
Ere upon my bed I lay me,
Ere in sleep I close my eyelids!" **G**
    Saw the moon rise from the water
55 Rippling, rounding from the water,
Saw the flecks and shadows on it,
Whispered, "What is that, Nokomis?"
And the good Nokomis answered:
"Once a warrior, very angry,
60 Seized his grandmother, and threw her
Up into the sky at midnight;
Right against the moon he threw her;
'Tis her body that you see there."
    Saw the rainbow in the heaven,
65 In the eastern sky, the rainbow,
Whispered, "What is that, Nokomis?"

F SUMMARIZE
Each new section of this poem begins with an indented line. What is the main idea of this section? Add it to your chart.

G RHYTHM AND METER
Read lines 42–53 aloud, tapping your pencil to their rhythm. Is the rhythm regular?

---

2. **tresses:** long locks or ringlets of hair.

3. **brakes:** areas overgrown with dense bushes; thickets.

And the good Nokomis answered:
"'Tis the heaven of flowers you see there
All the wildflowers of the forest,
70 All the lilies of the prairie,
When on earth they fade and perish,
Blossom in that heaven above us."
　　When he heard the owls at midnight,
Hooting, laughing in the forest,
75 "What is that?" he cried in terror,
"What is that," he said, "Nokomis?"
And the good Nokomis answered:
"That is but the owl and owlet,
Talking in their native language,
80 Talking, scolding at each other." **H**
　　Then the little Hiawatha
Learned of every bird its language,
Learned their names and all their secrets:
How they built their nests in Summer,
85 Where they hid themselves in Winter;
Talked with them whene'er he met them,
Called them "Hiawatha's Chickens."
　　Of all beasts he learned the language,
Learned their names and all their secrets:
90 How the beavers built their lodges,
Where the squirrels hid their acorns,
How the reindeer ran so swiftly,
Why the rabbit was so timid,
Talked with them whene'er he met them,
95 Called them "Hiawatha's Brothers." **I**
　　Then Iagoo, the great boaster,
He the marvelous storyteller,
He the traveler and the talker,
He the friend of old Nokomis,
100 Made a bow for Hiawatha;
From a branch of ash he made it,
From an oak bough made the arrows,
Tipped with flint,[4] and winged with feathers
And the cord he made of deerskin.
105　　Then he said to Hiawatha:
"Go, my son, into the forest,
Where the red deer herd together.

H NARRATIVE POETRY
Nokomis, Hiawatha's grandmother, raises him as her own. What kind of relationship do the woman and boy seem to have?

I SUMMARIZE
Reread lines 81–95. What does Hiawatha learn in this section?

---

4. **flint:** a hard, gray or black quartz.

Deer Spirit Helper, Joe Geshick. Oil. © Joe Geshick.

Kill for us a famous roebuck,
Kill for us a deer with antlers!"
110   Forth into the forest straightway
All alone walked Hiawatha
Proudly, with his bow and arrows;
And the birds sang round him, o'er him,
"Do not shoot us, Hiawatha!"
115 Sang the robin, the Opechee,
Sang the bluebird, the Owaissa,
"Do not shoot us, Hiawatha!"
    Up the oak tree, close beside him,
Sprang the squirrel, Adjidaumo,
120 In and out among the branches,
Coughed and chattered from the oak tree,
Laughed, and said between his laughing,
"Do not shoot me, Hiawatha!"
    And the rabbit from his pathway
125 Leaped aside, and at a distance
Sat erect upon his haunches,
Half in fear and half in frolic,
Saying to the little hunter,
"Do not shoot me, Hiawatha!"
130   But he heeded⁵ not, nor heard them,
For his thoughts were with the red deer;
On their tracks his eyes were fastened,

▲ **Analyze Visuals**
What does the painting suggest about the relationship between people and animals?

---

5. **heeded:** listened to and considered; paid attention to.

Leading downward to the river,
To the ford across the river,
135 And as one in slumber walked he.
　　Hidden in the alder bushes,
There he waited till the deer came,
Till he saw two antlers lifted,
Saw two eyes look from the thicket,
140 Saw two nostrils point to the windward,
And a deer came down the pathway,
Flecked with leafy light and shadow.
And his heart within him fluttered,
Trembled like the leaves above him,
145 Like the birch leaf palpitated,
As the deer came down the pathway. **J**
　　Then, upon one knee uprising,
Hiawatha aimed an arrow;
Scarce a twig moved with his motion,
150 Scarce a leaf was stirred or rustled,
But the wary roebuck started,
Stamped with all his hooves together,
Listened with one foot uplifted,
Leaped as if to meet the arrow;
155 Ah! the singing, fatal arrow,
Like a wasp it buzzed and stung him!
　　Dead he lay there in the forest,
By the ford across the river,
Beat his timid heart no longer;
160 But the heart of Hiawatha
Throbbed and shouted and exulted,[6]
As he bore the red deer homeward,
And Iagoo and Nokomis
Hailed his coming with applauses.
165 　　From the red deer's hide Nokomis
Made a cloak for Hiawatha,
From the red deer's flesh Nokomis
Made a banquet to his honor.
All the village came and feasted,
170 All the guests praised Hiawatha,
Called him Strong-Heart, Soan-ge-taha!
Called him Loon-Heart, Mahn-go-taysee! **K**

J RHYTHM AND METER
The meter Longfellow uses in this poem is called **trochaic tetrameter.** In a trochaic meter, a stressed syllable is followed by an unstressed syllable. The term *tetrameter* means that this pattern is repeated four times in each line of poetry. Reread lines 136–146. How does the powerful beat of the trochaic tetrameter help convey the suspense of a hunt?

K NARRATIVE POETRY
What **conflict** does Hiawatha face? How is it resolved?

---

6. **exulted** (ĭg-zŭltd'): rejoiced; felt jubilant and triumphant.

Comprehension

1. **Recall** What does the speaker who is left behind in "Boots of Spanish Leather" want at the beginning of the poem? at the end?

2. **Recall** Who raises Hiawatha?

3. **Clarify** What does the village celebrate at the end of *The Song of Hiawatha*?

Text Analysis

4. **Summarize Poetry** Look back at the graphic organizers you made as you read. Which stanzas or sections contain the most important information? Summarize each poem in a few sentences.

5. **Identify Onomatopoeia** When the sound of a word, such as *splat*, suggests its meaning, this technique is called **onomatopoeia**. Find three examples of onomatopoeia in *The Song of Hiawatha*.

6. **Compare and Contrast Narrative Forms** Review the purpose and characteristics of a ballad and epic described on page 657. Then explain why "Boots of Spanish Leather" qualifies as a ballad and "The Song of Hiawatha" qualifies as an epic.

7. **Examine Rhythm and Meter** Copy lines 31–34 of *The Song of Hiawatha* and mark the stressed and unstressed syllables as in the example on page 657. What pattern does the rhythm follow? Note whether the rest of the poem follows the same rhythm or different ones.

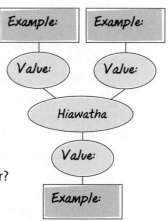

8. **Draw Conclusions about an Epic** The heroes in epic poems often represent values important to the culture they come from. What values does Hiawatha stand for? Note them on a graphic like the one shown. Also give examples that support each value.

COMMON CORE

RL 2 Determine a central idea of a text; provide an objective summary of the text. **RL 4** Analyze the impact of specific word choices on meaning and tone, including analogies or allusions to other texts. **RL 5** Compare the structure of two texts and analyze how structure contributes to meaning and style.

Extension and Challenge

9. **Text Criticism** In his diary, Longfellow wrote, "I have at length hit upon a plan for a poem on the American Indians which seems to me the right one, and the only. It is to weave together their beautiful traditions into a whole. . . ." Do you think it was a good idea for him to blend different tribal traditions to create his epic? With a group, discuss the value of this poem.

When do poems tell a STORY?

Did the stories these poems told satisfy you in the same way a good short story does? Explain your answer, making sure to evaluate elements such as character development, plot development, and conflict resolution.

Language

◆ **GRAMMAR IN CONTEXT:** Add Suffixes Correctly

When adding suffixes to words that end in *y*, sometimes you need to change the spelling of the root word. Follow these guidelines for adding suffixes correctly.

The letter before the final *y* is a vowel: Do not change the *y* when you add a suffix (*joy + -ful = joyful*).

The letter before the final *y* is a consonant: In most cases, change the *y* to *i* (*rely + -able = reliable*).

The suffix is *–ing*: Do not change the *y*, even if the letter before it is a consonant (*satisfy + -ing = satisfying*).

If you are unsure of a word's spelling, check a dictionary.

PRACTICE Spell each of the following words, including the suffix that is given.

1. employ + -able
2. silly + -ness
3. modify + -ing
4. envy + -able
5. sway + -ing
6. defy + -ance

*For more help with suffixes, see page R69 in the **Grammar Handbook**.*

READING-WRITING CONNECTION

Increase your appreciation of "Boots of Spanish Leather" and *The Song of Hiawatha* by responding to this prompt. Then use the **revising tip** to improve your writing.

WRITING PROMPT	REVISING TIP
Extended Constructed Response: Short Story Choose one of these poems and rewrite it as a **one- or two-page short story** that would appeal to teenagers today. Change or add details about the setting, characters, and conflict. Consider using dialogue to make the events seem real.	Review your short story. If you have added any suffixes to root words that end in *y*, make sure you have spelled them correctly.

COMMON CORE

L 2c Spell correctly. **W 3** Write narratives to develop imagined experiences or events.

Interactive Revision   THINK central

Go to **thinkcentral.com**.
KEYWORD: HML8-667

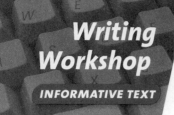

Writing Workshop
INFORMATIVE TEXT

Online Feature Article

In this unit, you discovered that poetry can be found in unexpected places. To learn more about poetry or a related topic, you could access the World Wide Web's vast network of sites. Now, you will add to this network by publishing an **online feature article**—an informative piece of writing on an interesting topic or trend.

 Complete the workshop activities in your **Reader/Writer Notebook.**

WRITE WITH A PURPOSE

WRITING TASK

Write an **online feature article** about a topic, person, or event that interests you.

Idea Starters
- a musician or athlete you admire
- poetry slams
- sightseeing locations in a favorite city or town
- a current event or issue in the news
- ideas for volunteering

THE ESSENTIALS

Here are some common purposes, audiences, and formats for informative/explanatory writing.

PURPOSES	AUDIENCES	FORMATS
• to inform readers about a subject	• classmates and teacher	• news or magazine article
• to better understand a subject	• community members	• encyclopedia article
• to develop and maintain an online readership	• friends on a social networking site	• wiki article
	• Web users with an interest in your subject	• blog
		• podcast

COMMON CORE TRAITS

1. DEVELOPMENT OF IDEAS
- begins with a compelling **introduction** that states a clear **controlling idea**
- supports the topic with **evidence** such as **relevant facts** and **quotations**
- provides a **concluding section** that supports the information

2. ORGANIZATION OF IDEAS
- **organizes** information into **logical categories**
- includes **formatting, multimedia, links**, and **graphics** to support the information
- uses **transitions** to connect ideas

3. LANGUAGE FACILITY AND CONVENTIONS
- establishes and maintains a **formal style**
- uses **precise language** and **domain-specific vocabulary**
- uses verbs in the **active voice** and **passive voice** effectively
- employs correct **grammar, mechanics,** and **spelling**

Writing Online

THINK central

Go to **thinkcentral.com.**
KEYWORD: HML8N-668

Planning/Prewriting

 COMMON CORE **W 2a–f** Write informative/explanatory texts to examine a topic. **W 5** Develop and strengthen writing by planning. **W 6** Use technology to produce and publish writing.

Getting Started

CHOOSE A TOPIC

Brainstorm topic ideas that interest you and might interest others, such as the Idea Starters on the previous page. Once you've chosen a topic, do a quick online search to confirm that there is enough information about it. Make sure that your topic isn't so broad that you can't write a short article about it. Frame your topic in the form of a focused **research question** to help guide your research, planning, and writing.

▶ **TIPS FOR GENERATING TOPIC IDEAS:**

- Visit school and community Web sites for popular topics of conversation.
- Consider activities, sports, or hobbies that you take part in outside of school.
- Look for interesting topics in the news.
- Read blogs or wikis that your teachers or classmates recommend.

THINK ABOUT AUDIENCE AND PURPOSE

As you plan your article, consider your **audience** and **purpose**. Understanding your audience will help you consider what information to include in your article, as well as where to publish your final product. Consider online forums and community Web sites that are popular with your audience and are approved by your teacher.

▶ **ASK YOURSELF:**

- Who will be most interested in my topic?
- How much does my audience know about my topic?
- What **background information** should I include?
- What **domain-specific,** or specialized, terms might be unfamiliar to my audience?
- Where will I publish, or post, my article?

FIND SOURCES AND COLLECT EVIDENCE

Look for reputable sources on the Web and in your school and local libraries. Choose **credible** sources, with information that is written or reviewed by experts. Newspapers, magazines, and Web sites maintained by universities or government offices are a good place to start.

Once you've chosen sources, start collecting interesting information—evidence that answers your research question. Jot down **quotations, facts,** and **examples** that are related to your topic. Make note of any helpful **graphics** and **multimedia** elements that you find. Confirm the accuracy of the information you find by locating it in more than one reliable source. In your notes, record which source provided each piece of evidence.

▶ **WHAT DOES IT LOOK LIKE?**

Evidence	Source
Videos of teens performing at poetry slams. Maybe I can link to one as part of my article.	Web site: Youth Speaks http://youthspeaks.org/ voice/brave-new-voices/ bnv-on-hbo/
"Slam is engineered for the audience. . . . Slam is designed for the audience to react vocally and openly to all aspects of the show slam . . ."	Web site: Poetry Slam, Inc http://www.poetryslam. com

Planning/Prewriting *continued*

Getting Started

DRAFT A CONTROLLING IDEA

Your **controlling idea,** or thesis statement, should precisely identify what you wish your audience to learn about your topic. Review your sources and evidence for the answers to your research question; these answers will serve as the basis for your controlling idea. Remember to continue to modify and refine your controlling idea as you write your draft and revise it.

▶ **WHAT DOES IT LOOK LIKE?**

Poetry slams are reviving the popularity of poetry through the use of powerful performances, competition, and audience participation.

GENERATE A STORYBOARD

Create a **storyboard** to map out the contents of your article, as well as its layout and navigation.

- Limit each screen to two or three paragraphs of text.
- Use text features, such as **headings** and **links,** to organize your information and make it easier for users to read and navigate.
- Plan how you will use **multimedia** and where you will include links to other sources.
- Try not to overcrowd each screen.

▶ **WHAT DOES IT LOOK LIKE?**

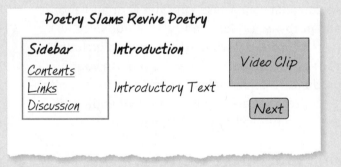

PEER REVIEW Share your controlling idea and supporting evidence with a classmate. Exchange storyboards and ask: Does my article seem easy to navigate? Is the organization clear?

YOUR TURN List possible research questions in your *Reader/Writer Notebook.* Focus on the question that interests you the most and that you can find enough information about. Gather your sources, organize your evidence, and then draft your controlling idea. Create a storyboard to plan your article.

Drafting

COMMON CORE

W 4 Produce clear and coherent writing appropriate to task, purpose, and audience.
L 2 Demonstrate command of the conventions of standard English capitalization, punctuation, and spelling.
L 2 b Use an ellipsis to indicate an omission.

The following chart shows a structure for organizing an online feature article.

Organizing Your Online Feature Article

INTRODUCTION

- Grab your audience's attention with a **compelling quotation, question**, or **anecdote**.
- Provide your audience with important **background information**. Define **domain-specific terms**.
- Include the **controlling idea** you drafted earlier.
- Establish a **formal writing style** by adopting a neutral tone and using precise language.

▼

BODY

- Organize your main ideas into logical categories, using **formatting** and **links.**
- Include **facts, details, quotations,** and **multimedia** to support your ideas.
- Use **varied transitions,** such as *also, although, however,* and *what's more,* to link ideas and create cohesion for a smooth flow.
- Document the source of each idea. See pages 1078–1091 for information on citations.

▼

CONCLUDING SECTION

- Restate your controlling idea and explain the importance of your topic.

GRAMMAR IN CONTEXT: PUNCTUATING QUOTATIONS

Incorporating quotations into your article gives your writing more depth and authority. When using quotations, follow these guidelines:

- Place quotation marks at the beginning and end of someone else's words.
- Integrate short quotations into your own sentences, using phrases such as *one participant said*.
- Use ellipses to indicate that you've omitted words from the quotation.
- Put the author's last name and page number of the quotation in parentheses at the end of the sentence. If you note the author within the sentence, include only the page number.
- If the quotation is online, link to the original source.

> Marc Kelly Smith, author of <u>Stage a Poetry Slam</u>, explains that the competitive part of poetry slams is what makes them so popular. The idea of poets engaged in a "battle against one another like wrestlers vying for a championship belt" adds a very different element to poetry (<u>xv</u>).

YOUR TURN Develop the first draft of your article. Integrate quotations, using proper punctuation and citation formats. Add multimedia and links when appropriate.

Revising

Revising, rewriting, and trying new approaches are essential parts of the writing process. The following chart will help you identify the weak parts of your draft and decide on the best improvements.

ONLINE FEATURE ARTICLE

Ask Yourself	Tips	Revision Strategies
1. **Does my introduction grab my readers' attention?**	▶ **Highlight** attention-grabbing quotations, questions, or facts.	▶ **Add** a compelling question, quotation, or fact to engage your audience.
2. **Is my controlling idea clear and appropriate for my audience and purpose?**	▶ **Place a check mark** next to your controlling idea.	▶ **Add** a controlling idea if one is missing. **Rework** your existing controlling idea if it is unclear or doesn't fit the task, purpose, or audience.
3. **Is my organization logical and easy to navigate?**	▶ **Circle** headings, links, and menu options.	▶ **Group** related paragraphs under boldfaced headings. **Add** links to your menu to allow users to easily move between sections of your article.
4. **Do I use relevant evidence to support my controlling idea?**	▶ **Underline** all quotations, definitions, examples, and facts. **Place a check mark** next to each one that supports your controlling idea.	▶ **Delete** evidence that isn't relevant to your controlling idea. **Add** evidence for any ideas that are not supported.
5. **Do I use multimedia and graphics effectively?**	▶ **Circle** the graphics and multimedia you have included.	▶ **Delete** elements that don't support your controlling idea or that are too distracting.
6. **Does my concluding section support the information I presented?**	▶ **Draw a wavy line** under the restated controlling idea and the sentences that describe the importance of the topic.	▶ **Insert** a restatement of your controlling idea. **Add** a sentence that tells why your topic is important.

 YOUR TURN

PEER REVIEW Review your draft with a partner. Answer each question in the chart and decide how your draft can be improved. Ask: Is my organization easy to follow? Do the multimedia and links add to your understanding?

ANALYZE A STUDENT DRAFT

As you read this draft, notice the comments on its strengths as well as the suggestions for improvement.

COMMON CORE W 2a–b Include formatting, graphics, and multimedia; develop the topic with relevant definitions or other information. **W 5** Develop and strengthen writing by revising, rewriting, or trying a new approach. **SL 5** Integrate multimedia.

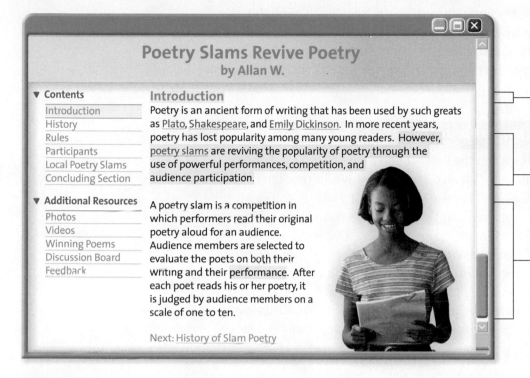

Poetry Slams Revive Poetry
by Allan W.

Contents
Introduction
History
Rules
Participants
Local Poetry Slams
Concluding Section

Additional Resources
Photos
Videos
Winning Poems
Discussion Board
Feedback

Introduction
Poetry is an ancient form of writing that has been used by such greats as Plato, Shakespeare, and Emily Dickinson. In more recent years, poetry has lost popularity among many young readers. However, poetry slams are reviving the popularity of poetry through the use of powerful performances, competition, and audience participation.

A poetry slam is a competition in which performers read their original poetry aloud for an audience. Audience members are selected to evaluate the poets on both their writing and their performance. After each poet reads his or her poetry, it is judged by audience members on a scale of one to ten.

Next: History of Slam Poetry

Allan uses **headings** to logically organize information and help readers navigate his article.

Allan clearly states his **controlling idea.**

Allan could add more depth to his article by providing **links to external Web sites.**

LEARN HOW **Link to External Web Sites** Publishing an online article allows you to link to reliable external sites with more information and multimedia. Allan included links in his first paragraph, but not in his second. Notice how he revised his second paragraph to add a link.

ALLAN'S REVISION TO HIS INTRODUCTION

Audience members are selected to evaluate the poets on both their writing and their <u>performance</u>.

Link to videos of poetry slam performances

 YOUR TURN Use feedback from your peers and teacher as well as the "Learn How" lesson to revise or rewrite parts of your article. Make sure that any links you provide are to reliable sites.

Editing and Publishing

COMMON CORE

W 5 Strengthen writing by editing. L1b, d Use verbs in the active and passive voice; correct inappropriate shifts in verb voice. L 3 a Use verbs in the active and passive voice to achieve effects.

Grammar, spelling, punctuation, and capitalization errors can distract your audience from understanding and appreciating your ideas. In the editing stage, you proofread your article to eliminate such errors, keeping in mind that the spell-check function on your word processor doesn't catch all misspellings. You also need to verify that all of your online features, such as links and multimedia, are working properly. Check that your pages are formatted consistently and are easy to read and navigate.

GRAMMAR IN CONTEXT: VERB VOICE

A verb is in the **active voice** when the subject performs the action. For example: "Mary moved the vase." A verb is in the **passive voice** when the action is received by the subject, as in: "The vase was moved by Mary." You can use both forms of verb voice in your writing, depending on the effect you want to achieve. The active voice is often preferable to the passive voice; sentences with strong active verbs have more energy and interest. However, you can use the passive voice in some instances, such as when you want to emphasize the recipient of the action or when the performer of the action is unknown. Be careful not to mix the active and passive voice in your writing. Having an inconsistent voice can create clumsy sentences that are confusing to readers.

As Allan edited his article, he realized that he shifted from active to passive voice in the same sentence. Here is his revision:

> After each poet reads his or her poetry, ~~it is judged by~~ audience members on a scale of one to ten.
>
> judge it

PUBLISH YOUR WRITING

After you have finished proofreading your article, you are ready to post it online.
- Update your status on social media networks that you participate on to include a link to your article.
- Post a link to your article in forums or online communities that you and your peers frequently visit.
- Send an e-mail or text message to friends and family to notify them that your article is available for viewing.

YOUR TURN Correct any errors in your article. Check that you have avoided awkward shifts in verb voice. After completing these final touches, publish your article for your audience to read and enjoy.

Scoring Rubric

Use this rubric to evaluate your online feature article.

ONLINE FEATURE ARTICLE

SCORE	COMMON CORE TRAITS
6	• **Development** Effectively introduces a topic; states a well-researched controlling idea; develops ideas with varied and relevant evidence; ends powerfully • **Organization** Logically organizes ideas into broader categories; uses varied transitions throughout; effectively uses formatting and multimedia • **Language** Ably uses precise language; maintains a formal style; shows a strong command of conventions
5	• **Development** Competently introduces a topic; states a clear controlling idea; offers relevant evidence; ends capably • **Organization** Logically organizes ideas into categories; effectively uses transitions; uses formatting and multimedia • **Language** Uses precise language; generally maintains a formal style; makes a few errors in conventions
4	• **Development** Adequately introduces a topic; states a controlling idea; includes mostly relevant evidence; ends adequately • **Organization** Is mostly well-organized; could use more transitions, formatting, or multimedia • **Language** Needs more precise words; mostly maintains a formal style; makes some errors in conventions
3	• **Development** States a controlling idea, but the introduction could be more interesting; lacks relevant evidence; has a somewhat weak concluding section • **Organization** Has weaknesses in organization; uses some transitions; has inconsistent formatting or distracting multimedia • **Language** Sometimes uses vague language; has an inconsistent style; makes many errors in conventions
2	• **Development** Has a weak controlling idea and introduction; does not support most ideas; ends abruptly • **Organization** Has serious organizational flaws; often lacks transitions, formatting, and multimedia • **Language** Lacks precise words or uses them incorrectly; uses an informal style; makes many errors in conventions
1	• **Development** Lacks a controlling idea, supporting evidence, and a concluding section • **Organization** Has no organization, formatting, or multimedia • **Language** Uses vague words; has an inappropriate style; shows no command of conventions

Technology Workshop

Updating an Online Feature Article

The World Wide Web is always changing. Content is continually being added, updated, reorganized, or deleted to make way for new information and ideas. As the author of an online feature article, you should maintain your published work and keep it current. In this workshop, you will learn how to effectively update, improve, and enhance your online feature article.

 Complete the workshop activities in your **Reader/Writer Notebook.**

PRODUCE WITH A PURPOSE	COMMON CORE TRAITS
TASK **Update your online feature article** to improve site design and navigation, provide updated information on your topic, and replace dead, or broken, links.	**A SUCCESSFUL UPDATE . . .** • repairs dead links • adds or revises content using current and reliable sources • responds to readers' questions and feedback promptly and in a respectful way • changes the design and organization as needed to improve viewing and navigation • promotes growth in readership by seeking new audiences and encouraging visitors to return

COMMON CORE

W 6 Use technology to publish writing and collaborate with others. **SL 1c** Pose and respond to questions. **SL 5** Integrate multimedia to clarify information and add interest.

Maintaining Your Article

After publishing your article online, visit the site frequently and spend a few minutes maintaining it. Use these guidelines to help you:

• **Update Your Links** The creators of external Web sources you linked to may update the information and structure of their sites. For this reason, it's essential that you regularly check all of your links and ensure that each Web address, or URL, still connects to the correct information. When you locate broken links, update them to reflect the new URL, find suitable replacement links, or delete the links from your article.

• **Respond to Feedback** Politely reply to all appropriate questions and comments posted on your article in a timely manner. Delete inappropriate comments right away. Thoughtful replies can stimulate discussion and promote reader participation.

• **Include a *Last Updated* Date** Provide a line of text that states the date your article was last updated. This note shows readers that they can trust the information and that you are committed to keeping your article up-to-date.

Media Tools

THINK central

Go to **thinkcentral.com.**
KEYWORD: HML8N-676

Modifying and Improving Your Article

As you learn more about your topic and read user feedback, you should modify and improve your online feature article. Regular updates will encourage return visitors and attract new readers. You might modify your article for a variety of reasons, including:

- **To Improve Content** As new information about your topic becomes available, revise your article to include updated content and delete out-of-date information. If you have chosen a topic with aspects that change frequently (such as schedules for local poetry slams), you might consider adding a Recent News or Updates section.

- **To Address User Feedback** Readers may offer feedback on the accuracy of your facts, your navigational features, or your site design. Be willing to revise your work, or even try a new approach, to address valid reader feedback.

- **To Redesign Your Article** A new design could give your article a more contemporary or professional look and keep it visually appealing. Consider reorganizing the navigational features, adding new multimedia and links, or trying a new font. Ensure that any changes make the article look more dynamic and engaging without distracting from the content.

- **To Grow Your Readership** Every time you update content or redesign your article, consider how you can use these changes to attract readers. Try posting a status update on social media networks you participate on, sending e-mail updates to your readers, or posting a link to your article on forums that your audience frequents.

> **Kyrianne** (reader) said . . .
>
> I'd never heard of slam poetry before! This sounds awesome! Do you know if there are any slam poetry events in Oklahoma?
>
> February 17, 10:57 a.m.
>
> **AllanW** (Site Administrator) said . . .
>
> I don't know of any currently scheduled for Oklahoma, but how about trying to organize your own poetry slam? I'm sure you're not the only one in your area who would love to participate. If you decide to organize one, let me know and I'll add it to the schedule!
>
> February 17, 8:16 p.m.

NEWS FEED

AllanW I've updated the **Local Poetry Slams** section with March's schedule of events. I hope you'll participate! I've also added a couple of **new videos** of winning slam poets. Maybe they can help you improve your techniques!

YOUR TURN Visit your online feature article often. Check that your links are still working, and then update, replace, or delete any dead links. Keep your content up-to-date and consider trying new approaches, such as including more images and new text features. Promptly and politely respond to user questions and feedback.

Assessment Practice

DIRECTIONS Read these poems and answer the questions that follow.

An Indian Summer Day on the Prairie

by Vachel Lindsay

IN THE BEGINNING

The sun is a huntress young,
The sun is a red, red joy,
The sun is an Indian girl,
Of the tribe of Illinois.

MID-MORNING

5   The sun is a smoldering fire,
That creeps through the high gray plain,
And leaves not a bush of cloud
To blossom with flowers of rain.

NOON

The Sun is a wounded deer,
10   That treads pale grass in the skies,
Shaking his golden horns,
Flashing his baleful eyes.

SUNSET

The sun is an eagle old,
There in the windless west.
15   Atop of the spirit-cliffs
He builds him a crimson nest.

The Sunflowers *by Mary Oliver*

Come with me
　　　into the field of sunflowers.
　　　　　Their faces are burnished disks,
　　　　　　Their dry spines

5　creak like ship masts,
　　　their green leaves,
　　　　　so heavy and many,
　　　　　　　fill all day with the sticky

sugars of the sun.
10　　　Come with me
　　　　　to visit the sunflowers,
　　　　　　they are shy

but want to be friends;
　　　they have wonderful stories
15　　　　　of when they were young—
　　　　　　the important weather,

the wandering crows.
　　　Don't be afraid
　　　　　To ask them questions!
20　　　　　　Their bright faces,

which follow the sun,
　　　will listen, and all
　　　　　those rows of seeds—
　　　　　　each one a new life!—

25　hope for a deeper acquaintance;
　　　each of them, though it stands
　　　　　in a crowd of many,
　　　　　　like a separate universe,

is lonely, the long work
30　　　of turning their lives
　　　　　into a celebration
　　　　　　is not easy. Come

and let us talk with those modest faces,
　　　the simple garments of leaves,
35　　　　　the coarse roots in the earth
　　　　　　so uprightly burning.

GO ON ➡

Reading Comprehension

Use "An Indian Summer Day on the Prairie" to answer questions 1–8.

1. In the first stanza, the speaker personifies the sun as —

   A. a tribe from Illinois

   B. three red planets

   C. a girl who is hunting

   D. the beginning of the day

2. With each stanza in this poem, the poet develops —

   A. one idea in a single sentence

   B. an unusual appearance on the page

   C. several images in four sentences

   D. a list of unrelated ideas in five lines

3. Which is the best paraphrase of lines 5–8?

   A. The sun's strong rays set the plain on fire during midmorning.

   B. By midmorning, the fiery sun is so hot that it burns away the rain clouds.

   C. The sun at noon is so red that it looks like a fire in the sky.

   D. The midmorning sun is drying up the bushes on the plain.

4. The pattern of rhyming words in every stanza of this poem is —

   A. *abba*   **C.** *abab*

   B. *abcb*   **D.** *abcc*

5. In lines 9–12, the speaker uses an extended metaphor to compare the sun to —

   A. a wounded deer

   B. pale grass

   C. the noon sky

   D. golden horns

6. In lines 13–16, the eagle building his nest is a metaphor for the —

   A. western sky

   B. setting sun

   C. wild deer

   D. prairie hunters

7. Which line from the poem contains an example of assonance?

   A. *The sun is a huntress young.*

   B. *The sun is a smoldering fire.*

   C. *And leaves not a bush of cloud*

   D. *The sun is an eagle old*

8. Which line from the poem contains an example of alliteration?

   A. *The sun is an Indian girl*

   B. *There in the windless west*

   C. *Atop of the spirit-cliffs*

   D. *The sun is an eagle old*

Use "The Sunflowers" to answer questions 9–15.

9. The speaker gives the sunflowers human qualities in order to —

   A. create a humorous image

   B. emphasize human weaknesses

   C. express a connection with nature

   D. make the poem more lyrical

10. The speaker asks readers to —

   A. go along on a visit to the sunflowers

   B. learn about different parts of a sunflower

   C. be strong, like sunflowers in the field

   D. celebrate life, like each seed of a sunflower

11. In lines 1–7, the speaker uses a simile to compare the sound of the sunflower stalks to the —

   A. shape of the human face

   B. sight of burnished disks

   C. noise made by ship masts

   D. smell of green leaves

12. Reread lines 18–19. To whom is this statement directed?

> "Don't be afraid / to ask them questions!"

   A. Crows

   B. Readers

   C. Sun

   D. Sunflowers

13. In lines 26–29, the speaker uses the phrase "a separate universe" to emphasize the sunflower's —

   A. isolation

   B. loyalty

   C. short life

   D. weakness

14. Reread lines 29–32. What is the best paraphrase of these lines?

> "the long work / of turning their lives / into a celebration / is not easy."

   A. Water helps sunflower seeds grow.

   B. Sunflowers are beautiful and useful.

   C. It takes time for seeds to become sunflowers.

   D. Sunflowers can teach us about having fun.

15. Which statement best describes the four-line stanzas in this poem?

   A. The pattern of indented lines connects the ideas from stanza to stanza.

   B. Each stanza contains a single idea that is unrelated to the ideas of the other stanzas.

   C. The stanzas have a simple rhyme scheme that emphasizes the rhythm of the poem.

   D. The length of every line follows the same pattern in each stanza.

> **Use both selections to answer question 16.**

16. To give their descriptions of a bright summer day a musical quality, both poets use —

   A. metaphors and similes

   B. assonance and alliteration

   C. rhyming lines

   D. free verse

SHORT CONSTRUCTED RESPONSE
Write two or three sentences to answer each question.

17. Paraphrase the speakers' invitation in lines 10–17 of "The Sunflowers."

18. What can you tell about the speaker of "The Sunflowers" from the statements made in the poem?

Write a paragraph to answer this question.

19. What do the stanza titles tell you about "An Indian Summer Day on the Prairie"? What story is told by the four stanzas together?

GO ON

Vocabulary

Use your knowledge of context clues and the explanations of word origins to answer the following questions.

1. The word *qirmiz* is the Arabic word for an insect that is used to produce red dye. What word in "An Indian Summer Day on the Prairie" comes from the word *qirmiz*?
   A. Crimson
   B. Golden
   C. Gun
   D. Pale

2. The Old English word *smorian* means "to smoke." What word from "An Indian Summer Day on the Prairie" comes from the word *smorian*?
   A. Flashing
   B. Shaking
   C. Smoldering
   D. Spirit

3. The Old English word *bealu* means "misery." What word from "An Indian Summer Day on the Prairie" comes from the word *bealu*?
   A. Baleful
   B. Bush
   C. Wounded
   D. Young

4. The German word *brun* means "brown." What word from "The Sunflowers" comes from the word *brun*?
   A. Bright
   B. Burning
   C. Burnished
   D. Sunflower

Use your knowledge of Latin words and roots to answer the following questions.

5. The Latin word *accognoscere* means "to know perfectly." In "The Sunflowers," what word comes from the word *accognoscere*?
   A. Acclaim
   B. Acquaintance
   C. Celebration
   D. Visit

6. The Latin word *separare* means "apart." In "The Sunflowers" what word comes from the word *separare*?
   A. Rows
   B. Separate
   C. Uprightly
   D. Wandering

7. The Latin words *unus* and *vertere* mean "one" and "to turn," respectively. In "The Sunflowers" what word comes from *unus* and *vertere*?
   A. Lonely
   B. Rotating
   C. Universe
   D. Wonderful

Revising and Editing

DIRECTIONS Read this passage and answer the questions that follow.

(1) Last winter I read an article about bringing back the prairie. (2) I told my mom dad and brother that I wanted to plant a prairie in our backyard. (3) I hoped to plant yellow foxtail, prairie cordgrass and cattail sedge. (4) My brother offered to build a pond. (5) I knew he would do an excellent job because he is very relyable. (6) He wanted big green bullfrogs to visit our backyard! (7) Before we began planting our small prairie, we became very studyous and read many books about prairies.
(8) We expect to have a joyous, gloryous, and plentiful prairie in our backyard.

1. What is the BEST way to punctuate sentence 2 with commas?
   A. I told, my mom dad and brother that I wanted, to plant a prairie in our backyard.
   B. I told my mom, dad, and brother that I wanted to plant a prairie in our backyard.
   C. I told my mom, dad, and brother, that I wanted to plant a prairie in our backyard.
   D. I told my mom dad and brother that I wanted to plant a prairie, in our backyard.

2. What is the BEST way to punctuate sentence 3 with commas?
   A. I hoped to plant yellow foxtail, prairie cordgrass and cattail, sedge.
   B. I hoped to plant yellow foxtail prairie cordgrass and, cattail sedge.
   C. I hoped to plant, yellow foxtail prairie cordgrass and cattail sedge.
   D. I hoped to plant yellow foxtail, prairie cordgrass, and cattail sedge.

3. What change, if any, should be made in sentence 5?
   A. Change *excellent* to **excelent**
   B. Change *relyable* to **reliable**
   C. Change *because* to **becuase**
   D. Make no change

4. What is the BEST way to punctuate sentence 6 with commas?
   A. He wanted big, green bullfrogs to visit our backyard!
   B. He wanted, big green bullfrogs to visit our backyard!
   C. He wanted big, green, bullfrogs to visit our backyard!
   D. He wanted big green bullfrogs, to visit our backyard!

5. What change, if any, should be made in sentence 7?
   A. Change *planting* to **plantting**
   B. Change *studyous* to **studious**
   C. Change *prairies* to **prairies'**
   D. Make no change

6. What change, if any, should be made in sentence 8?
   A. Change *joyous* to **joious**
   B. Change *gloryous* to **glorious**
   C. Change *plentiful* to **plentyful**
   D. Make no change

683

More Great Reads

Ideas for Independent Reading

Which questions from Unit 5 made an impression on you? Continue exploring them with these books.

COMMON CORE

RL 10 Read and comprehend literature. RI 10 Read and comprehend literary nonfiction.

Does beauty matter?

Uglies
by Scott Westerfeld

In the future, all 16-year-olds have an operation that makes them "beautiful." Most of the younger Uglies can't wait until it's their turn for the operation, but a girl named Shay rebels against being the same as everyone else. Will her friend Tally help her or betray her?

Criss Cross
by Lynne Rae Perkins

Debbie and Hector are 14 years old, and they'd like their appearance to reflect the interesting people they hope they're becoming. How will these important changes happen? It's not always clear, but by the end of the summer, a great deal will be different.

Margaux with an X
by Ronald Koertge

Margaux is dazzlingly beautiful and very popular. She's also miserable. Most of the boys in school have crushes on her, but she's only interested in Danny. A shabby-looking outcast, Danny shares her love of language and helps her cope with problems at home.

Can you be rich without money?

Colibrí
by Ann Cameron

Years ago, a fortune teller told Uncle that Rosa would make him rich. They have been traveling through Guatemala ever since, begging and cheating people to get money and food. Now that Rosa is older, lying to people is harder, and Uncle is getting impatient.

The Black Pearl
by Scott O'Dell

When Ramon finds the Pearl of Heaven, everyone comes to look at it, and his father gives the pearl to the church. Some people think the jewel brings bad luck because it belongs to the Manta Diable. When misfortune hits the village, only Ramon can fix it.

A Year Down Yonder
by Richard Peck

It's the Depression, and people are broke. Mary Alice is sent to live in rural Illinois with her eccentric Grandma Dowdell. Grandma has habits, like "borrowing" the Sheriff's boat or Old Man Nyquist's apples, which seem to make life a little easier.

When do you feel most free?

The Upstairs Room
by Johanna Reiss

Annie is only six when Hitler comes to power in Germany and starts making laws that punish the Jews. Annie is glad she lives in Holland so her family is safe, but as the German army gets stronger, how long will Annie's safety last?

Let Me Play: The Story of Title IX, the Law That Changed the Future of Girls in America
by Karen Blumenthal

Before 1972, many girls weren't able join a soccer team or enter medical school. Finally, the people fighting against this injustice won, and the law was changed.

The Warrior Heir
by Cinda Williams Chima

Every day Jack takes medicine for his heart condition. One day he forgets, and it's the best day of his life. Suddenly, he's faster and stronger. He finds out he's really a magical warrior and his "medicine" was hiding him from people who want to kill him.

Get Novel Wise

THINK central

Go to **thinkcentral.com**.
KEYWORD: HML8-684

A Unique Imprint

STYLE, VOICE, AND TONE

- In Fiction
- In Nonfiction
- In Poetry

Share What You Know

What's in **STYLE?**

How do you decide what clothes to put on in the morning, or how to arrange your hair? You might follow current trends, or you might draw on the fashions of years past to create a unique look. Whatever you choose, your appearance reflects your personal style, the way you express yourself to others. Writers, filmmakers, songwriters, and artists have their own ways of expressing themselves, too. Their style includes the way they use elements of their craft to communicate ideas.

ACTIVITY With a partner, think of an author, actor, singer, or artist whose style you and your partner both like. What about this person's work makes it unique? Answer the following questions:

• What three things come to mind first when you think of this person's creations?

• What sets this person apart?

• What words would you use to describe his or her style?

After answering these questions, discuss whether this person's style has influenced your own style, and how.

Find It Online!

THINK central

Go to **thinkcentral.com** for the interactive version of this unit.

Preview Unit Goals

TEXT ANALYSIS
- Analyze how the structure of a text contributes to its meaning and style
- Compare and contrast style
- Identify and analyze voice, irony, and tone, including the impact of specific word choices on tone

READING
- Use and interpret graphic aids
- Synthesize information

WRITING AND LANGUAGE
- Write a literary analysis
- Write concisely by using appositives and appositive phrases
- Form compound and complex sentences

SPEAKING AND LISTENING
- Present a response to literature

VOCABULARY
- Use context to help determine meaning of idioms and multiple-meaning words
- Understand figurative, connotative, and denotative meanings of words
- Use Latin roots as clues to the meaning of a word

ACADEMIC VOCABULARY
- achieve
- income
- individual
- strategy
- trend

Style, Voice, and Tone

Think about the last time you read an e-mail from a friend. Could you almost "hear" that friend talking to you? Perhaps the e-mail contained phrases your friend often uses, or expressed an attitude that is typical of him or her. The personality that comes across in any piece of writing—whether it's a friend's e-mail or a classic novel—is the **voice**. The voice can belong to the writer or to a narrator. Either way, it is created through the writer's one-of-a-kind style.

COMMON CORE

Included in this workshop:
RL 4 Analyze the impact of specific word choices on tone.
RL 5 Analyze how structure contributes to style.
RI 4 Determine the meaning of words and phrases as they are used in a text, including connotative meanings; analyze the impact of specific word choices on tone.

Part 1: What Is Style?

"The rosy fingertips of dawn spread delicately across the sky." "The sun bounced into view like a giant rubber ball." *How* something is said often affects a reader as much as *what* is being said. In literature, how something is said is called the **style**. A writer's style can be described using such words as *formal*, *conversational*, or *journalistic*. Style is created through a combination of literary elements and devices, such as the following:

ELEMENTS OF STYLE	EXAMPLES	
Word Choice Is the writing packed with conversational words and slang, or elegant, formal phrases? Precise, vivid, casual, formal—the kinds of words a writer uses can help to create style.	**The simple, informal language in this sentence helps to create a conversational style.** I didn't try to shout over the helicopters; they chopped up sound and the air, and whupped up heartbeats. —from *The Fifth Book of Peace* by Maxine Hong Kingston	
Sentence Structure One element of style is **sentence structure**, the lengths and types of sentences a writer uses. Some writers are noted for crafting long, complex sentences. Others are noted for using short, simple ones.	**This long sentence reflects a flowing, descriptive style and gives you a sense of the character's energy.** Miranda gave her mother a quick smile and bounded forward in great skipping leaps up the ramp, across the red and gold carpet in the lobby, down the long side aisle and up the steps onto the stage. —from "Dancing Miranda" by Diane de Anda	
Imagery Words and phrases that appeal to readers' senses create memorable **images**. The kinds and amount of images a writer uses can help to define his or her style.	**This writer layers on image after image, creating a poetic style that reflects the rhythm of the sea.** Beyond the sails stretched the sky itself, as blue as a baby's bluest eyes, while the greenish sea, crowned with lacy caps of foaming white, rushed by with unrelenting speed. —from *The True Confessions of Charlotte Doyle* by Avi	

MODEL 1: COMPARING STYLE

In this excerpt, Rita Williams-Garcia uses a conversational, humorous style to convey the narrator's dread of a family meal. As you read, look closely at the author's word choice—the element that helps to create this style.

from **Food** from the *Outside*

Short story by **Rita Williams-Garcia**

My sister, brother, and I didn't have a dog, but we sure could have used one around dinnertime. Our dog would never have had to beg for table scraps, for we promised sincerely in our mealtime prayers always to feed Rover the main course. It wouldn't have been so much for love of dog, but for survival. You
5 see, our mother, known throughout the neighborhood as "Miss Essie," was still refining her cooking skills. Until we could persuade our parents to let us have a dog, we sat at the dinner table with wax sandwich bags hidden in our pockets, especially when Miss Essie served "Hackensack," our code word for mystery stew.

Close Read

1. Find two examples of words and phrases in this excerpt that sound like casual conversation.

2. Reread the boxed details. Would you describe the narrator's voice as humorous, sincere, sarcastic, or something else? Explain.

MODEL 2: COMPARING STYLE

C. S. Lewis uses a more formal, descriptive style to write about an elaborate feast in the enchanted world of Narnia.

from The Voyage of the *Dawn Treader*

Novel by **C. S. Lewis**

On the table itself there was set out such a banquet as had never been seen, not even when Peter the High King kept his court at Cair Paravel. There were turkeys and geese and peacocks, there were boars' heads and sides of venison, there were pies shaped like ships under full sail or like dragons and elephants,
5 there were ice puddings and bright lobsters and gleaming salmon, there were nuts and grapes, pineapples and peaches, pomegranates and melons and tomatoes. There were flagons[1] of gold and silver and curiously-wrought[2] glass; and the smell of the fruit and the wine blew toward them like a promise of all happiness.

---

1. **flagons:** vessels used for holding wine; flasks.
2. **curiously-wrought:** strangely crafted.

Close Read

1. How would you describe the structure of the author's sentences?

2. One element of Lewis's style is his use of imagery. Two examples have been boxed. Find three more examples.

3. What is the most striking stylistic difference between how the two authors describe a meal? Support your answer.

Part 2: Tone

Another important element of style is **tone**—a writer's attitude toward a subject. The tone of a piece of writing might be described using words such as *humorous, sarcastic, mocking, admiring, serious,* or *sympathetic.* One way to determine a writer's tone is to look at the specific words, phrases, and details he or she chooses to include.

Take a look at these two excerpts. In each, the writer conveys a very specific attitude toward sports.

COMPARING TONE

Walter Dean Myers

By the time I was eleven, basketball had entered my life. I knew I was going to be a star and I could dream about myself playing in the NBA. My strength was my outside shot and in my dreams I always made the last, desperate shot that swished through the net just as the buzzer sounded.

—from "Daydreams"

Myers uses an **optimistic, confident tone** to express his attitude toward his basketball abilities.

- Myers's choice of words reveals his dreamy optimism.
- Details convey the author's confidence.

William Sleator

I was always the last one picked for teams. I was so used to it that it didn't bother me. I was always way out in left field or right field or whichever field it is that balls hardly ever go to, and I lived in fear that a ball would come my way and I'd have to try to catch the thing and it would hit me on the head or I'd drop it. PE was the worst thing about school.

—from "The Masque of the Red Death"

Sleator uses a **negative, yet humorous tone** to express his attitude toward PE class.

- Words and phrases let readers know exactly how Sleator felt about playing baseball in PE class.
- The details reveal the author's sense of humor about his experience, as well as explain *why* PE class was so terrible.

MODEL 1: COMPARING TONE

The narrator of this novel, a teenaged boy, thinks back on helping a neighbor with her lawn. Read on to find out how he felt about this experience.

from
Bird

Novel by **Angela Johnson**

I used to mow old Mrs. Pritchard's lawn when I was eight. She had one of those old mowers that was hard as anything to push through all the grass in her backyard. She said she didn't like the gas mowers because they stunk and scared all the birds away.

5 I wouldn't have done it for anybody else, but she always had lemonade out for me, then she'd feed me the best peach cobbler I ever tasted. I didn't tell her, but I'd have mowed that big yard for nothing but some of that cobbler. I'm easy that way.

Close Read

1. What words and phrases in the boxed lines help you to understand the boy's feelings about helping Mrs. Pritchard?

2. Which word pair best describes the tone revealed in the boxed lines?
   a. warm, nostalgic
   b. resentful, bitter
   c. biting, sarcastic

MODEL 2: COMPARING TONE

In her memoir, Haven Kimmel recalls a time in her childhood when she was strongly encouraged to do good deeds for other people. As you read about Kimmel's first attempt to do something good, think about how you would describe her attitude, or tone.

from A Girl Named **ZIPPY**

Nonfiction by **Haven Kimmel**

I spent every afternoon stalking good works. My first victim was Agnes Johnson who was 164 years old. Her skin, impatient for her to get it over with and die, appeared to be sliding down off her body into a pool around her ankles. She was older than dirt, but feisty. She insisted on cutting her 5 own grass every week with an ancient push mower. For years I'd seen her out there, pushing against the mower as if it were a huge rock, her skinny arms quivering, her lips trembling, a thin film of sweat shining on the place most people had an upper lip. I'd never paid her much mind, but on this particular day I realized I'd hit the jackpot. Ordinarily I'd have rather run naked into 10 a rose bush than cut grass; at my own house I suggested a few times a week that we get a goat or some other furry grazing thing to live in the backyard. (I thought a goat was an especially clever choice because they could also eat our empty tin cans.) So if I mowed Agnes Johnson's yard, I could probably avoid doing any more good deeds until I myself was flat-out old.

Close Read

1. Examine the boxed words. Are these words you would typically associate with doing good deeds? Explain.

2. Identify three details that help you understand Kimmel's feelings about helping Agnes Johnson.

3. What word would you use to describe the author's tone, or attitude, toward doing good deeds?

Part 3: Analyze the Text

Both of the following selections are about romance and the anxiety that it can spark. Though the excerpts share a similar topic, each reveals its writer's distinct personality.

The first excerpt is from an essay Lloyd Alexander wrote about his earliest experience with dating—or, rather, not dating. As you read, look for examples of the elements of style that you have studied in this workshop.

from THE **Truth**
ABOUT
THE
WORLD

Essay by **Lloyd Alexander**

My first date never happened. When I finally built up enough nerve, I dared to ask one of the girls in my ninth-grade class to go to some kind of dance or other—I don't remember exactly; it was long ago. To my amazement, she accepted. For myself, I always thought in large, long-range terms. We
5   would, I imagined, become sweethearts, get engaged, eventually marry, and live happily ever after.

   Friday afternoon, the day before the glorious event, our gym teacher ordered us outdoors to play soccer. I usually preferred loitering around the fringes of the action, but when the ball bounded straight at me, I seized the
10 moment to give it the mightiest kick in school history.

   I noticed a couple of things. For one, I glimpsed the ball rocketing across the field, missing the goal by what looked like about half a mile; for another, I saw an expression of despondency and long suffering on the face of the gym teacher. By then, I was on the grass, trying to hold my left foot in both hands
15 and giving my full attention to learning the nature of agony.

   A couple of classmates hauled me to the nurse's office. My mother had to be summoned. She took me home in our ancient Plymouth and phoned the doctor (they made house calls in those days). He examined my foot, now swollen to the size of a baked ham. He assured me I would live. I was sorry to
20 hear that.

   The date, of course, was off. My mother took charge of canceling it; I hadn't the heart to do it myself. In those days, pain was supposed to build character. After nearly a week of character-building, I limped back to school. I was too ashamed even to look at my might-have-been date. And she, very
25 properly, decided the right thing to do was never to speak to me again.

Close Read

1. One element of Alexander's style is his use of imagery. Find two examples of imagery in the excerpt.

2. The boxed details help to create a humorous, self-mocking tone. Identify two other details that reflect this tone.

3. Based on the voice you "heard" as you read, how would you describe the author's personality?

The following excerpt is from a novel, so the voice you "hear" belongs to the narrator—a teenager named Leo. Here, Leo describes an awkward early encounter with his future girlfriend, who calls herself Stargirl. As you read, consider what elements help to create the author's style.

from

Stargirl

Novel by **Jerry Spinelli**

At first it was enough just to see the house. Then I began to wonder if she was inside. I wondered what she could be doing. Light came from every window I could see. There was a car in the driveway. The longer I hung around, the closer I wanted to be. I crossed the street and practically dashed 5 past the house. As I went by, I scooped up a stone from the yard. I went up the street, turned, and looked at her house in the distance.

I whispered to the salt-sprinkled sky, "That's where Stargirl Caraway lives. She likes me."

I headed back toward the house. The street, the sidewalks were deserted. 10 The stone was warm in my hand. This time I walked slowly as I approached. I felt strange. My eyes fixed on a triangle of light in a curtained window. I saw a shadow on a yellow wall. I seemed to be drifting, footless, into the light.

Suddenly the front door opened. I dived behind the car in the driveway and crouched by the rear fender. I heard the door close. I heard steps. The steps 15 matched the movement of a long shadow cast down the driveway. My breath stopped. The shadow stopped. I felt both ridiculous and weirdly, perfectly placed, as if crouching by that car was precisely what life had in store for me at that moment.

Her voice came from beyond the shadow. "Remember when you followed 20 me into the desert that day after school?"

Absurdly, I debated whether to answer, as if doing so would—what? Give me away? I leaned into the smooth metal of the fender. It never occurred to me to stand, to show myself. Hours seemed to pass before I finally croaked, "Yes."

"Why did you turn around and go back?"

25 Her tone was casual, as if she held conversations every night with people crouching behind the car in the driveway.

Close Read

1. Spinelli's writing Includes rich imagery that helps readers to visualize the setting. Find three examples.

2. Describe the structures of the boxed sentences. What effect do you think Spinelli was trying to achieve through this stylistic choice?

3. Which word pair best describes the tone revealed in lines 7–12 and 16–18?
   a. sarcastic and bitter
   b. romantic and dreamy
   c. sad and serious

4. Compare Spinelli's writing with Alexander's. How are the authors' styles similar or different?

New York Day Women
Short Story by Edwidge Danticat

Who is the REAL you?

COMMON CORE

RL 1 Cite textual evidence to support an analysis of what the text says explicitly. **RL 5** Analyze how the structure of [a] text contributes to its meaning and style.

At first, it might seem silly to wonder who you really are. But do you act the same around your teachers as you do around your friends? And do your grandparents perceive the same person your friends see? We all have different sides to ourselves. In the story you are about to read, a young woman discovers a side of her mother she never knew existed.

QUICKWRITE Think of three or four people who know you in different ways—for example, your best friend, a teacher, a parent, and an enemy. What adjectives would each person use to describe you? How would you describe yourself? Jot down your thoughts about whether anyone perceives the real you.

● TEXT ANALYSIS: STYLE

Each of us has a unique style, or way of dressing, acting, and speaking. In literature, **style** is a writer's way of expressing himself or herself. Style does not refer to what is said, but rather how it is said. Writers show style through the choices they make about the following things:

- Word choice and **imagery**—descriptive words and phrases that appeal to the senses. Notice Edwidge Danticat's descriptions.
- Presentation—the way the story appears on the page. Notice Danticat's use of line spacing, italics, and typographical symbols.
- Sentence structure. Notice Danticat's purposeful use of sentence fragments.

● READING SKILL: IDENTIFY SEQUENCE

Sequence is the order in which events occur in a story. To help yourself keep track of the order, look for signal words and phrases, such as *today, that morning, as, now, an hour later, then,* and *before.*

In the story you are about to read, the narrator relates present-day events while reflecting on conversations and incidents from the past. Keep track of the sequence of present-day events by recording them in a sequence chart like the one shown.

The narrator sees her mother walking down the street.	→	→

▲ VOCABULARY IN CONTEXT

The following boldfaced words help Danticat show how people sometimes don't really understand each other. To see how many words you know, restate each sentence, using a different word or phrase for the boldfaced word.

1. Pablo can **mesmerize** people with his charm, so they forget he isn't reliable.
2. Jenny's only **offense** is that she brags too much.
3. My **pursuit** of the truth only left me more confused.
4. I **contemplate** joining the game, but no one expects me to, so I don't.
5. I doubt that the feisty Emily will **surrender** easily.

Complete the activities in your **Reader/Writer Notebook.**

Meet the Author

Edwidge Danticat
born 1969

A New Home in New York
Writer Edwidge Danticat (ĕd'wēj dăn'tē-kä) emigrated from Haiti to Brooklyn, New York, when she was 12. Danticat had a hard time adjusting to life in New York. Her classmates made fun of her clothing, hairstyle, and Haitian accent. To escape from the loneliness she felt during this time, Danticat wrote stories about her home country. Over her career, Danticat has published several novels and short story collections, most of which involve Haitian culture and characters.

Krik? Krak!
During her childhood, Danticat heard many Haitian stories. Storytellers begin their tales by asking the audience, "Krik?" If the audience is ready, they will respond with an excited "Krak!" This exchange of words became the title of Danticat's first collection of short stories, in which "New York Day Women" appears.

BACKGROUND TO THE STORY
A Haven for Haitians
Danticat's homeland is one of the most densely populated and least developed countries in the Western hemisphere. This small country in the West Indies has been ruled by brutal dictators for much of its history. Hundreds of thousands of Haitians, including Danticat's family, have fled to the United States. Many have settled in Brooklyn, a borough of New York City. According to the 2000 census, over 200,000 Haitians and Haitian Americans live there. In some Brooklyn schools, Haitian children make up 75 percent of the population.

Author Online
THINK central
Go to **thinkcentral.com.**
KEYWORD: HML8-695

NEW YORK DAY WOMEN

Edwidge Danticat

Today, walking down the street, I see my mother. She is strolling with a happy gait, her body thrust toward the DON'T WALK sign and the yellow taxicabs that make forty-five-degree turns on the corner of Madison and Fifty-seventh Street.

I have never seen her in this kind of neighborhood, peering into Chanel and Tiffany's and gawking at the jewels glowing in the Bulgari[1] windows. My mother never shops outside of Brooklyn. She has never seen the advertising office where I work. She is afraid to take the subway, where you may meet those young black militant street preachers who curse black women for straightening their hair.

10 Yet, here she is, my mother, who I left at home that morning in her bathrobe, with pieces of newspapers twisted like rollers in her hair. My mother, who accuses me of random **offenses** as I dash out of the house. **A**

❖

Would you get up and give an old lady like me your subway seat? In this state of mind, I bet you don't even give up your seat to a pregnant lady.

❖

My mother, who is often right about that. Sometimes I get up and give my seat. Other times, I don't. It all depends on how pregnant the woman is and whether or not she is with her . . . husband and whether or not *he* is sitting down. **B**

As my mother stands in front of Carnegie Hall,[2] one taxi driver yells to another, "What do you think this is, a dance floor?"

20 My mother waits patiently for this dispute to be settled before crossing the street.

❖

In Haiti when you get hit by a car, the owner of the car gets out and kicks you for getting blood on his bumper.

❖

offense (ə-fĕns′) *n.* a violation of a moral or social code; a sin

A SEQUENCE
Reread lines 10–12. When did the mother accuse the narrator of "random offenses"? Tell how you know.

B STYLE
Reread lines 10–17. Note any **repetition** of words or phrases. Based on this repetition, what do you think will be the subject of this story?

---

1. **Chanel** (shə-nĕl′); **Tiffany's**; **Bulgari** (bōōl′ gä-rē): very expensive shops that sell luxury goods such as designer clothing, perfume, glassware, and jewelry.
2. **Carnegie Hall** (kär′nə-gē hôl): a famous concert hall in New York City.

The Promenade, Fifth Avenue (1986), Bill Jacklin. Oil on canvas, 243.6 cm × 182.7 cm. Private collection. © Bill Jacklin/Bridgeman Art Library.

My mother who laughs when she says this and shows a large gap in her mouth where she lost three more molars to the dentist last week. My mother, who at fifty-nine, says dentures are okay.

❖

You can take them out when they bother you. I'll like them. I'll like them fine.

❖

Will it feel empty when Papa kisses you?

❖

Oh no, he doesn't kiss me that way anymore.

❖

30 My mother, who watches the lottery drawing every night on channel 11 without ever having played the numbers.

❖

A third of that money is all I would need. We would pay the mortgage, and your father could stop driving that taxicab all over Brooklyn.

❖

I follow my mother, **mesmerized** by the many possibilities of her journey. Even in a flowered dress, she is lost in a sea of pinstripes³ and gray suits, high heels and elegant short skirts, . . . sneakers, dashing from building to building.

My mother, who won't go out to dinner with anyone.

❖

If they want to eat with me, let them come to my house, even if I boil water and give it to them.

❖

My mother, who talks to herself when she peels the skin off poultry.

❖

40 *Fat, you know, and cholesterol. Fat and cholesterol killed your aunt Hermine.* **C**

❖

My mother, who makes jam with dried grapefruit peel and then puts in cinnamon bark that I always think is cockroaches in the jam. My mother, whom I have always bought household appliances for, on her birthday. A nice rice cooker, a blender.

I trail the red orchids in her dress and the heavy faux⁴ leather bag on her shoulders. Realizing the ferocious pace of my **pursuit,** I stop against a wall to rest. My mother keeps on walking as though she owns the sidewalk under her feet.

As she heads toward the Plaza Hotel,⁵ a bicycle messenger swings so close to her that I want to dash forward and rescue her, but she stands dead in her 50 tracks⁶ and lets him ride around her and then goes on.

---

3. **pinstripes:** fabrics with very thin stripes, usually used to make business suits.
4. **faux** (fō): artificial but meant to look genuine.
5. **Plaza Hotel:** a world-renowned hotel located near Central Park in New York City.
6. **dead in her tracks:** perfectly still.

SOCIAL STUDIES CONNECTION

New York City is divided into five boroughs, or municipalities. The family in the story lives in Brooklyn. The narrator and her mother are now in Manhattan.

mesmerize (mĕz′mə-rīz′) *v.* to spellbind; to enthrall

C STYLE
Why do you think Danticat chooses to show the mother's words in italics?

pursuit (pər-sōōt′) *n.* the act of chasing

My mother stops at a corner hot-dog stand and asks for something. The vendor hands her a can of soda that she slips into her bag. She stops by another vendor selling sundresses for seven dollars each. I can tell that she is looking at an African print dress, **contemplating** my size. I think to myself, Please Ma, don't buy it. It would be just another thing I would bury in the garage or give to Goodwill.

❖

Why should we give to Goodwill when there are so many people back home who need clothes? We save our clothes for the relatives in Haiti.

❖

Twenty years we have been saving all kinds of things for the relatives in Haiti. I need the place in the garage for an exercise bike.

❖

60 *You are pretty enough to be a stewardess. Only dogs like bones.*

❖

This mother of mine, she stops at another hot-dog vendor's and buys a frankfurter that she eats on the street. I never knew that she ate frankfurters. With her blood pressure, she shouldn't eat anything with sodium.[7] She has to be careful with her heart, this day woman.[8]

❖

I cannot just swallow salt. Salt is heavier than a hundred bags of shame.

❖

She is slowing her pace, and now I am too close. If she turns around, she might see me. I let her walk into the park before I start to follow again. **D**

My mother walks toward the sandbox in the middle of the park. There a woman is waiting with a child. The woman is wearing a leotard with biker's 70 shorts and has small weights in her hands. The woman kisses the child good-bye and **surrenders** him to my mother, then she bolts off, running on the cemented stretches in the park.

The child given to my mother has frizzy blond hair. His hand slips into hers easily, like he's known her for a long time. When he raises his face to look at my mother, it is as though he is looking at the sky.

My mother gives this child the soda that she bought from the vendor on the street corner. The child's face lights up as she puts . . . a straw in the can for him. This seems to be a conspiracy just between the two of them. **E**

My mother and the child sit and watch the other children play in the sandbox. 80 The child pulls out a comic book from a knapsack with Big Bird on the back. My mother peers into his comic book. My mother, who taught herself to read as a little girl in Haiti from the books that her brothers brought home from school.

My mother, who has now lost six of her seven sisters in Ville Rose[9] and has never had the strength to return for their funerals.

❖

contemplate
(kŏn'təm-plāt') *v.*
to consider carefully
and at length

D SEQUENCE
Reread lines 66–67.
What words help
you understand the
sequence of events?

surrender (sə-rěn'dər) *v.*
to give up possession or
control to another

E STYLE
Reread lines 68–78.
Danticat uses vivid
imagery in this passage.
Which images do you
think best illustrate
the special relationship
between the narrator's
mother and the boy?

---

7. **sodium** (sō'dē-əm): salt.

8. **day woman:** a woman who is employed as a housekeeper or babysitter but does not live in her employer's home.

9. **Ville Rose** (vĭl rōz): a fictional Haitian town.

Many graves to kiss when I go back. Many graves to kiss.

❖

She throws away the empty soda can when the child is done with it. I wait and watch from a corner until the woman in the leotard and biker's shorts returns, sweaty and breathless, an hour later. My mother gives the woman back her child and strolls farther into the park. ◆

90   I turn around and start to walk out of the park before my mother can see me. My lunch hour is long since gone. I have to hurry back to work. I walk through a cluster of joggers, then race to a *Sweden Tours* bus. I stand behind the bus and take a peek at my mother in the park. She is standing in a circle, chatting with a group of women who are taking other people's children on an afternoon outing. They look like a Third World[10] Parent-Teacher Association meeting.

I quickly jump into a cab heading back to the office. Would Ma have said hello had she been the one to see me first? **F**

As the cab races away from the park, it occurs to me that perhaps one day I would chase an old woman down a street by mistake and that old woman

100   would be somebody else's mother, who I would have mistaken for mine.

❖

Day women come out when nobody expects them.

❖

Tonight on the subway, I will get up and give my seat to a pregnant woman or a lady about Ma's age.

My mother, who stuffs thimbles in her mouth and then blows up her cheeks like Dizzy Gillespie[11] while sewing yet another Raggedy Ann[12] doll that she names Suzette after me. **G**

❖

I will have all these little Suzettes in case you never have any babies, which looks more and more like it is going to happen.

❖

My mother, who sews lace collars on my company softball T-shirts when she

110   does my laundry.

❖

Why, you can't look like a lady playing softball?

❖

My mother, who never went to any of my Parent-Teacher Association meetings when I was in school.

❖

You're so good anyway. What are they going to tell me? I don't want to make you ashamed of this day woman. Shame is heavier than a hundred bags of salt. ∾

---

10. **Third World:** the developing nations of Africa, Asia, and Latin America.

11. **Dizzy Gillespie** (dĭz'ē gə-lĕs'pē): an American trumpet player, bandleader, and composer (1917–1993) whose cheeks ballooned out when he played.

12. **Raggedy Ann:** a red-haired rag doll and fictional character who was the subject of several children's books.

◆ **GRAMMAR IN CONTEXT**
In lines 87–88, the narrator uses an appositive phrase to add extra, nonessential information about the woman in biker's shorts.

F SEQUENCE
How long has the narrator been watching her mother? Tell how you know.

G STYLE
Reread lines 104–106. In what way does the structure of this sentence represent Danticat's style?

Comprehension

1. **Recall** What does the narrator's mother do for a living?

2. **Clarify** Why is the narrator, Suzette, surprised to see her mother?

3. **Clarify** Why doesn't Suzette go up to greet her mother?

Text Analysis

4. **Examine Characterization** How does Edwidge Danticat bring the mother's character to life? Using a character map like the one shown, record details from the story that describe the mother's appearance, beliefs and values, and actions.

5. **Examine Sequence** Review the sequence chart you made while reading. Under each square, note what Suzette seems to feel about her mother at that point in the story. In what way does Suzette's perception of her mother change from the beginning to the end of the story?

6. **Draw Conclusions** In the beginning of the story Suzette admits that she might not give up her seat on a bus to an older or pregnant woman. Yet by the story's end, she changes her mind. What do you think causes this change?

7. **Make Judgments** Reread lines 114–115. Do you think Suzette is ashamed of her mother? Why or why not? Support your answer with examples.

8. **Define an Author's Style** Choose a passage from the story that you think is a good example of Danticat's style. You may wish to look for a passage that demonstrates Danticat's unique sentence structures, **imagery,** and way of formatting text, as well as her use of repetition. Copy down the passage. Then identify the important literary devices and other elements in it that are characteristic of Danticat's style.

COMMON CORE

RL 1 Cite textual evidence to support an analysis of what the text says explicitly. **RL 5** Analyze how the structure of [a] text contributes to its meaning and style.

Mother

Appearance   Beliefs and Values   Actions

Extension and Challenge

9. **Readers' Circle** Should Suzette have approached her mother, and if so, what should she have said? Why do you think the mother never told Suzette about her trips to Manhattan? Discuss these questions with a small group.

Who is the **REAL** you?

Describe a situation or relationship in which you act or talk differently than you usually do at home. What is different about your behavior or way of speaking?

Vocabulary in Context

▲ VOCABULARY PRACTICE

Choose the letter of the word or phrase that means the same, or nearly the same, as the boldfaced word or phrase.

1. **contemplate** a decision: (a) disregard, (b) consider, (c) ignore, (d) avoid
2. **mesmerize** an audience: (a) fascinate, (b) bore, (c) puzzle, (d) disappoint
3. **pursuit** of a criminal: (a) arrest, (b) imprisonment, (c) chasing, (d) pardon
4. **surrender** her valuables: (a) purchase, (b) give up, (c) hide, (d) hold
5. a minor **offense:** (a) wrongdoing, (b) injury, (c) argument, (d) accomplishment

contemplate

mesmerize

offense

pursuit

surrender

ACADEMIC VOCABULARY IN WRITING

• achieve   • income   • individual   • strategy   • trend

What do you think you would learn if you followed an **individual** you knew for a day? Write a paragraph explaining your answer. Use at least one Academic Vocabulary word in your paragraph.

VOCABULARY STRATEGY: MULTIPLE-MEANING WORDS

Many English words have more than one meaning. For example, you might know that *offense* is a term used in sports that means "those players whose primary responsibility it is to score." But you might not be familiar with its meaning in this selection: "a violation of a moral or social code."

If a word does not make sense to you, look at the words around it for clues to other possible meanings. For example:

My mother, who accuses me of random offenses as I dash out of the house.

Would the mother be more likely to accuse the narrator of a sports-related move, or of a moral or social mistake? Based on the context of the sentence, you can conclude that the second definition is correct. For further help with multiple-meaning words, check a dictionary.

PRACTICE Define the boldfaced words. Identify context clues that helped you understand the meaning of each.

1. The bus stops suddenly, and the motion **jerks** me out of a deep sleep.
2. Although we were tired, Michael and I decided to play one more **round** of chess.
3. Please **book** me a seat on the next plane to Washington, D.C.
4. I think we need to **table** this issue for now. Let's put it aside until next week.
5. These new circumstances open a **window** of opportunity for us.

:·: **COMMON CORE**

L 4 Clarify the meaning of multiple-meaning words.
L 4a Use context as a clue to the meaning of a word.

Interactive Vocabulary **THINK** central

Go to **thinkcentral.com**.
KEYWORD: HML8-702

Language

◆ **GRAMMAR IN CONTEXT:** Use Appositive Phrases

An **appositive** is a noun or pronoun that identifies or renames another noun or pronoun. An **appositive phrase** is made up of an appositive and its modifiers. You can make your writing more concise by using an appositive or appositive phrase to combine two sentences into one.

> *Original:* The mother works in Manhattan. She is a native of Haiti.
>
> *Revised:* The mother, a native of Haiti, works in Manhattan. (A native of Haiti *is an appositive phrase that adds extra, nonessential information about the* mother.)

Place commas before and after an appositive phrase when it adds extra, nonessential information about the noun or pronoun that precedes it, as in the example above.

PRACTICE In each item, combine the two sentences by changing the second sentence to an appositive phrase.

1. Suzette works in Manhattan. She is a resident of Brooklyn.
2. Suzette doesn't give her subway seat to older passengers. She is the narrator.
3. The mother babysits children. She is a day woman.
4. The mother waits to cross the street. She is a patient woman.

For more help with appositive phrases, see page R61 in the **Grammar Handbook**.

READING-WRITING CONNECTION

YOUR TURN Get to know the characters in "New York Day Women" better by responding to this prompt. Then use the **revising tip** to improve your writing.

WRITING PROMPT	REVISING TIP
Short Constructed Response: Character Sketch What do you learn about Suzette as she pursues her mother? Make inferences about her age, appearance, occupation, and personality. Then write a **one-paragraph character sketch** of her.	Review your character sketch to look for sentences you can combine by using an appositive or an appositive phrase.

Interactive Revision THINK central

Go to **thinkcentral.com**.
KEYWORD: HML8-703

COMMON CORE

L1 Demonstrate command of grammar and usage when writing. **L3** Use knowledge of language when writing.

The Lady, or the Tiger?
Short Story by Frank R. Stockton

 Video link at
thinkcentral.com

The Monty Hall Debate
Newspaper Article by John Tierney

Cartoon
Cartoon by Peter Steiner

VIDEO TRAILER **THINK** central | KEYWORD: HML8-704

How do you make
DECISIONS?

 COMMON CORE

RL 4 Analyze the impact of specific word choices on tone.

How we make decisions depends on the situation. A simple coin toss can help you decide who goes first when playing a video game. But you wouldn't want to flip a coin when making a more important choice, such as which sport to play or which high school to attend. In the story you are about to read, a decision has life-or-death consequences.

The literary selection that follows will explore how people make decisions, the role of laws in society, and what is really fair. After you read "The Lady, or the Tiger?" you'll read an expository selection that explores similar topics and a visual that is partly inspired by the story.

● TEXT ANALYSIS: TONE

Writers often express an attitude, or **tone,** toward the subject, setting, or characters they're writing about. A tone can often be described with one word, such as angry, proud, or playful. Just as knowing a friend's attitude can help you decide whether she's serious or joking, knowing a writer's tone can help you grasp his or her message. To help you determine Frank R. Stockton's tone, pay attention to the words and details he uses to describe

- the **characters**—Do his descriptions of them suggest whether he thinks they're smart or foolish, kind or cruel?
- the **setting**—Does he admire the society's customs?
- the **plot events**—Does his language show that he takes the events seriously, or not?

● READING STRATEGY: PARAPHRASE

One good way to understand and remember what you read is to **paraphrase** it, or restate the writer's language in your own words. To paraphrase, follow these steps:

- Reread the passage, looking for the main ideas.
- Define unfamiliar words using context clues or a dictionary.
- Restate important ideas and details in your own words. A good paraphrase should be about as long as the original text.

As you read, paraphrase difficult sections in your notebook.

Line Numbers	Paraphrase
1–4	Long ago, there lived a rough, cruel king. He had been influenced by forward-thinking cultures, but he was still uncivilized.

▲ VOCABULARY IN CONTEXT

The following words help reveal Stockton's opinion of his characters. In your Reader/Writer Notebook, write a sentence for each of the vocabulary words. Use a dictionary or the definitions in the following selection pages to help you.

WORD LIST		
anguished	conventional	progressiveness
aspire	devious	subordinate
assert	impartial	waver

 Complete the activities in your **Reader/Writer Notebook.**

Meet the Author

Frank R. Stockton
1834–1902

Full of Fairy Tales
Though today Frank R. Stockton's most popular story is "The Lady, or the Tiger?" many of his other works were widely read during his lifetime. Born near Philadelphia, Pennsylvania, Stockton began writing fairy tales as a child, later claiming that he did so because "my mind was full of them."

Literary Sensation
While still in high school, Stockton won a short story contest sponsored by a magazine. Later on in life, Stockton wrote stories for both adults and children. "The Lady, or the Tiger?" caused a sensation among the American public. The ending was debated in high schools, and Stockton received hundreds of letters from people seeking the solution. Unfortunately, Stockton did not like the story as much as his readers did; he felt it did not represent his best work.

BACKGROUND TO THE STORY
Historic Arena
Much of the action in "The Lady, or the Tiger?" takes place in an amphitheater. One of the most famous amphitheaters in history is the Colosseum, built during the Roman empire in the year A.D. 72. Capable of seating 50,000 people, this massive structure featured three levels of seating, wood floors, and an innovative canvas roof that brought in cool air from the outside. The Colosseum was the scene of gruesome "games" involving slaves, prisoners, or animals fighting gladiators (professionally trained swordsmen) to the death. Although lightning and earthquakes destroyed large parts of the Colosseum over the years, much of it still stands today.

Author Online
THINK central
Go to **thinkcentral.com.**
KEYWORD: HML8-705

The *Lady,* or the Tiger?

Frank R. Stockton

In the very olden time, there lived a semi-barbaric king, whose ideas, though somewhat polished and sharpened by the **progressiveness** of distant Latin neighbors, were still large, florid,[1] and untrammeled,[2] as became the half of him which was barbaric.[3] He was a man of exuberant fancy, and, withal, of an authority so irresistible that, at his will, he turned his varied fancies into facts. He was greatly given to self-communing;[4] and, when he and himself agreed upon anything, the thing was done. When every member of his domestic and political systems moved smoothly in its appointed course, his nature was bland and genial; but whenever there was a little hitch, and
10 some of his orbs got out of their orbits, he was blander and more genial still, for nothing pleased him so much as to make the crooked straight, and crush down uneven places. **A**

Among the borrowed notions by which his barbarism had become semifixed was that of the public arena, in which, by exhibitions of manly and beastly valor, the minds of his subjects were refined and cultured.

---

1. **florid** (flôr′ĭd): very ornate; flowery.
2. **untrammeled** (ŭn-trăm′əld): not limited or restricted.
3. **barbaric** (bär-bâr′ĭk): marked by crudeness or lack of restraint in taste, style, or manner.
4. **self-communing:** the act of "talking" things over with oneself only.

Spring (1894), Lawrence Alma-Tadema. Oil on canvas, 70¼″ × 31½″. The J. Paul Getty Museum, Los Angeles. (72.PA.3). © J. Paul Getty Trust.

progressiveness
(prə-grĕs′ĭv-nĭs) *n.* the state of advancing toward better conditions or new policies, ideas, or methods

A TONE
Based on the words he uses to describe the king, how do you think Stockton feels about this character?

Analyze Visuals ▶
What do the details in this painting help you **infer** about the kingdom and its people?

But even here the exuberant and barbaric fancy **asserted** itself. The arena of the king was built, not to give the people an opportunity of hearing the rhapsodies of dying gladiators, nor to enable them to view the inevitable conclusion of a conflict between religious opinions and hungry jaws, but for 20 purposes far better adapted to widen and develop the mental energies of the people. This vast amphitheater, with its encircling galleries, its mysterious vaults, and its unseen passages, was an agent of poetic justice, in which crime was punished, or virtue rewarded, by the decrees of an impartial and incorruptible chance.

When a subject was accused of a crime of sufficient importance to interest the king, public notice was given that on an appointed day the fate of the accused person would be decided in the king's arena—a structure which well deserved its name; for, although its form and plan were borrowed from afar, its purpose emanated solely from the brain of this man, who, every barleycorn 30 a king,[5] knew no tradition to which he owed more allegiance than pleased his fancy, and who ingrafted on every adopted form of human thought and action the rich growth of his barbaric idealism. **B**

When all the people had assembled in the galleries and the king, surrounded by his court, sat high up on his throne of royal state on one side of the arena, he gave a signal, a door beneath him opened, and the accused subject stepped out into the amphitheater. Directly opposite him, on the other side of the enclosed space, were two doors, exactly alike and side by side. It was the duty and the privilege of the person on trial to walk directly to these doors and open one of them. He could open either door he pleased; he was subject to no guidance or 40 influence but that of the aforementioned **impartial** and incorruptible chance. If he opened the one, there came out of it a hungry tiger, the fiercest and most cruel that could be procured, which immediately sprang upon him and tore him to pieces, as a punishment for his guilt. The moment that the case of the criminal was thus decided, doleful iron bells were clanged, great wails went up from the hired mourners posted on the outer rim of the arena, and the vast audience, with bowed heads and downcast hearts, wended slowly their homeward way, mourning greatly that one so young and fair, or so old and respected, should have merited so dire a fate.

But if the accused person opened the other door, there came forth from 50 it a lady, the most suitable to his years and station that his majesty could select among his fair subjects; and to this lady he was immediately married, as a reward for his innocence. It mattered not that he might already possess a wife and family, or that his affections might be engaged upon an object of his own selection: the king allowed no such **subordinate** arrangements to interfere with his great scheme of retribution and reward. The exercises, as in the other instance, took place immediately and in the arena. Another door opened beneath the king, and a priest, followed by a band of choristers

---

5. **every barleycorn a king:** a playful exaggeration of the expression "every ounce a king," meaning "thoroughly kingly." (Grains of barley were formerly used as units of measurement.)

assert (ə-sûrt') *v.* to act forcefully; to take charge

VISUAL VOCABULARY

amphitheater (ăm'fə-thē'ə-tər) *n.* an arena where contests and spectacles are held

B PARAPHRASE
Reread lines 25–32. Paraphrase this passage. Was the amphitheater used in the same way in this kingdom as it was elsewhere? Explain.

impartial (ĭm-pär'shəl) *adj.* not partial or biased; unprejudiced

subordinate (sə-bôr'dn-ĭt) *adj.* secondary; belonging to a lower rank

and dancing maidens blowing joyous airs on golden horns and treading an epithalamic measure,[6] advanced to where the pair stood, side by side; and

60 the wedding was promptly and cheerily solemnized.[7] Then the gay brass bells rang forth their merry peals, the people shouted glad hurrahs, and the innocent man, preceded by children strewing flowers on his path, led his bride to his home.

This was the king's semi-barbaric method of administering justice. Its perfect fairness is obvious. The criminal could not know out of which door would come the lady: he opened either he pleased, without having the slightest idea whether, in the next instant, he was to be devoured or married. On some occasions the tiger came out of one door and on some out of the other. The decisions of this tribunal[8] were not only fair, they were positively

70 determinate: the accused person was instantly punished if he found himself guilty; and, if innocent, he was rewarded on the spot, whether he liked it or not. There was no escape from the judgments of the king's arena. **C**

---

6. **treading an epithalamic** (ĕp′ə-thə-lā′mĭk) **measure:** dancing to wedding music.

7. **solemnized** (sŏl′əm-nīzd′): celebrated or observed with dignity.

8. **tribunal** (trī-byōō′nəl): something that has the power to determine guilt or innocence.

Head Study of a Tiger, Roland Wheelwright. Oil on board, 49.5 cm × 60.9 cm. Private collection. © Roland Wheelwright/Bridgeman Art Library.

Detail of *Study of a Lady,* Frederic Leighton. Oil on canvas, 25.5 cm × 19 cm. Private collection. © Bridgeman Art Library.

THE LADY, OR THE TIGER? **709**

The institution was a very popular one. When the people gathered together on one of the great trial days, they never knew whether they were to witness a bloody slaughter or a hilarious wedding. This element of uncertainty lent an interest to the occasion which it could not otherwise have attained. Thus, the masses were entertained and pleased, and the thinking part of the community could bring no charge of unfairness against this plan; for did not the accused person have the whole matter in his own hands?

80 This semi-barbaric king had a daughter as blooming as his most florid fancies, and with a soul as fervent[9] and imperious[10] as his own. As is usual in such cases, she was the apple of his eye and was loved by him above all humanity. Among his courtiers was a young man of that fineness of blood and lowness of station common to the **conventional** heroes of romance who love royal maidens. This royal maiden was well satisfied with her lover, for he was handsome and brave to a degree unsurpassed in all this kingdom; and she loved him with an ardor that had enough of barbarism in it to make it exceedingly warm and strong. This love affair moved on happily for many months, until one day the king happened to discover its existence. He did not hesitate nor **waver** in

90 regard to his duty in the premises. The youth was immediately cast into prison, and a day was appointed for his trial in the king's arena. This, of course, was an especially important occasion; and his majesty, as well as all the people, was greatly interested in the workings and development of this trial. Never before had such a case occurred; never before had a subject dared to love the daughter of a king. In after-years such things became commonplace enough, but then they were, in no slight degree, novel and startling. **D**

The tiger-cages of the kingdom were searched for the most savage and relentless beasts, from which the fiercest monster might be selected for the arena; and the ranks of maiden youth and beauty throughout the land were

100 carefully surveyed by competent judges, in order that the young man might have a fitting bride in case fate did not determine for him a different destiny. Of course, everybody knew that the deed with which the accused was charged had been done. He had loved the princess, and neither he, she, nor any one else thought of denying the fact; but the king would not think of allowing any fact of this kind to interfere with the workings of the tribunal, in which he took such great delight and satisfaction. No matter how the affair turned out, the youth would be disposed of; and the king would take an aesthetic[11] pleasure in watching the course of events, which would determine whether or not the young man had done wrong in allowing himself to love the princess. **E**

110 The appointed day arrived. From far and near the people gathered, and thronged the great galleries of the arena, and crowds, unable to gain admittance, massed themselves against its outside walls. The king and his court were in their places, opposite the twin doors,—those fateful portals, so terrible in their similarity.

---

9. **fervent** (fûr′vənt): having or showing great emotion or zeal.

10. **imperious** (ĭm-pîr′ē-əs): arrogantly domineering or overbearing.

11. **aesthetic** (ĕs-thĕt′ĭk): concerning the artistic appreciation of beauty.

conventional
(kən-vĕn′shə-nəl) *adj.*
conforming to established practice or accepted standards; traditional

waver (wā′vər) *v.*
to exhibit indecision; to hesitate

D TONE
Reread lines 91–96. Stockton describes the citizens as being "greatly interested" in the "novel and startling" events that are unfolding. In what way might this description be **ironic**, stating the opposite of what Stockton believes?

E PARAPHRASE
Reread lines 102–109. What is the young man's fate? Rewrite this passage in your own words.

All was ready. The signal was given. A door beneath the royal party opened, and the lover of the princess walked into the arena. Tall, beautiful, fair, his appearance was greeted with a low hum of admiration and anxiety. Half the audience had not known so grand a youth had lived among them. No wonder the princess loved him! What a terrible thing for him to be there!

120 As the youth advanced into the arena, he turned, as the custom was, to bow to the king: but he did not think at all of that royal personage; his eyes were fixed upon the princess, who sat to the right of her father. Had it not been for the moiety[12] of barbarism in her nature, it is probable that lady would not have been there; but her intense and fervid[13] soul would not allow her to be absent on an occasion in which she was so terribly interested. From the moment that the decree had gone forth, that her lover should decide his fate in the king's arena, she had thought of nothing, night or day, but this great event and the various subjects connected with it. Possessed of more power, influence, and force of character than any one who had ever before been interested in such a case, she had done what no other person had done—she 130 had possessed herself of the secret of the doors. She knew in which of the two rooms, that lay behind those doors, stood the cage of the tiger, with its open front, and in which waited the lady. Through these thick doors, heavily curtained with skins on the inside, it was impossible that any noise or suggestion should come from within to the person who should approach to raise the latch of one of them; but gold, and the power of a woman's will, had brought the secret to the princess. **F**

And not only did she know in which room stood the lady ready to emerge, all blushing and radiant, should her door be opened, but she knew who the lady was. It was one of the fairest and loveliest of the damsels of the court 140 who had been selected as the reward of the accused youth, should he be proved innocent of the crime of **aspiring** to one so far above him; and the princess hated her. Often had she seen, or imagined that she had seen, this fair creature throwing glances of admiration upon the person of her lover, and sometimes she thought these glances were perceived and even returned. Now and then she had seen them talking together; it was but for a moment or two, but much can be said in a brief space; it may have been on most unimportant topics, but how could she know that? The girl was lovely, but she had dared to raise her eyes to the loved one of the princess; and, with all the intensity of the savage blood transmitted to her through long lines of 150 wholly barbaric ancestors, she hated the woman who blushed and trembled behind that silent door. **G**

When her lover turned and looked at her, and his eyes met hers as she sat there paler and whiter than anyone in the vast ocean of anxious faces about her, he saw, by that power of quick perception which is given to those whose souls are one, that she knew behind which door crouched the tiger, and behind

F TONE
Reread lines 119–136. What is Stockton's attitude toward the princess? Tell what words and details in the passage reveal this attitude.

aspire (ə-spīr') v. to have a great ambition or an ultimate goal; to desire strongly

G TONE
Stockton frequently refers to barbarism in this story. What does this reveal about his attitude toward the characters?

---

12. **moiety** (moi'ĭ-tē): a portion.

13. **fervid** (fûr'vĭd): passionate.

which stood the lady. He had expected her to know it. He understood her nature, and his soul was assured that she would never rest until she had made plain to herself this thing, hidden to all other lookers-on, even to the king. The only hope for the youth in which there was any element of certainty was
160 based upon the success of the princess in discovering this mystery; and the moment he looked upon her, he saw she had succeeded, as in his soul he knew she would succeed.

Then it was that his quick and anxious glance asked the question: "Which?" It was as plain to her as if he shouted it from where he stood. There was not an instant to be lost. The question was asked in a flash; it must be answered in another.

Cleopatra (about 1888), John W. Waterhouse. Oil on canvas, 65.4 cm × 56.8 cm. © 2002 Christie's Images Limited.

◀ **Analyze Visuals**
Does the person in this painting match your idea of the princess in the story? Explain why or why not.

Her right arm lay on the cushioned parapet[14] before her. She raised her hand and made a slight, quick movement toward the right. No one but her lover saw her. Every eye but his was fixed on the man in the arena.

170   He turned, and with a firm and rapid step he walked across the empty space. Every heart stopped beating, every breath was held, every eye was fixed immovably upon that man. Without the slightest hesitation, he went to the door on the right and opened it.

N ow, the point of the story is this: Did the tiger come out of that door, or did the lady?

The more we reflect upon this question, the harder it is to answer. It involves a study of the human heart which leads us through **devious** mazes of passion, out of which it is difficult to find our way. Think of it, fair reader, not as if the decision of the question depended upon yourself, but upon that hot-blooded,
180 semi-barbaric princess, her soul at a white heat beneath the combined fires of despair and jealousy. She had lost him, but who should have him? **H**

How often, in her waking hours and in her dreams, had she started in wild horror, and covered her face with her hands as she thought of her lover opening the door on the other side of which waited the cruel fangs of the tiger!

But how much oftener had she seen him at the other door! How in her grievous reveries[15] had she gnashed her teeth, and torn her hair, when she saw his start of rapturous[16] delight as he opened the door of the lady! How her soul had burned in agony when she had seen him rush to meet that woman, with her flushing cheek and sparkling eye of triumph; when she had seen him lead her forth, his
190 whole frame kindled with the joy of recovered life; when she had heard the glad shouts from the multitude, and the wild ringing of the happy bells; when she had seen the priest, with his joyous followers, advance to the couple, and make them man and wife before her very eyes; and when she had seen them walk away together upon their path of flowers, followed by the tremendous shouts of the hilarious multitude, in which her one despairing shriek was lost and drowned!

Would it not be better for him to die at once, and go to wait for her in the blessed regions of semi-barbaric futurity?

And yet, that awful tiger, those shrieks, that blood!

Her decision had been indicated in an instant, but it had been made after
200 days and nights of **anguished** deliberation. She had known she would be asked, she had decided what she would answer, and, without the slightest hesitation, she had moved her hand to the right.

The question of her decision is one not to be lightly considered, and it is not for me to presume to set myself up as the one person able to answer it. And so I leave it with all of you: Which came out of the opened door—the lady, or the tiger? ೦ೡ

devious (dē′vē-əs) *adj.* departing from the straight or direct course

H PARAPHRASE
Reread lines 176–181. What is Stockton saying to his readers? Paraphrase this passage in your notebook. Remember that to paraphrase well you will need to reread the passage and then restate the most important ideas and details in your own words. If you have paraphrased the passage well, your paraphrase should be about as long as the original text.

anguished (ăng′gwĭsht) *adj.* tormented; distressed

---

14. **parapet** (păr′ə-pĭt): a low railing at the edge of a balcony.
15. **reveries** (rĕv′ə-rēz): daydreams.
16. **rapturous** (răp′chər-əs): filled with great joy; ecstatic.

Comprehension

1. **Recall** How do the citizens of the kingdom feel about the king's method of justice?

2. **Recall** What "crime" has the young man committed?

3. **Represent** Reread lines 21–24 and 33–63. Create a diagram of the arena. Use information from the story to include at least three labels in your diagram.

COMMON CORE

RL 4 Analyze the impact of specific word choices on tone.

Text Analysis

4. **Examine a Story's Ending** What was surprising about the way "The Lady, or the Tiger?" ended? Why did you expect something different?

● 5. **Identify Tone** Consider the way Frank R. Stockton describes the place, time, characters, events, and customs in this kingdom. Then describe his tone with one of these words: *sarcastic, sad, serious, playful, bitter, anxious, sentimental,* or *curious.* Write the word in the top of a chart like the one shown, and support your choice with words and details about the characters, setting, and situation.

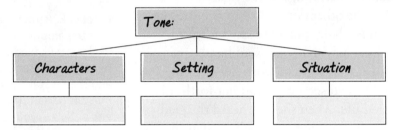

● 6. **Explore Paraphrasing** Choose two of the passages you paraphrased in your notebook. What crucial information did you gain from paraphrasing these passages that helped you understand the story?

7. **Evaluate** Describe the king's system of "justice." Is there anything just, or fair, about it? Explain.

8. **Draw Conclusions** Based on what you know about the princess, which door do you think she **decides** on? Use details from the selection to support your response.

Extension and Challenge

9. **Text Criticism** Frank R. Stockton once said, "If you decide which it was—the lady or the tiger—you find out what kind of person you are yourself." What might your interpretation of the story show you about yourself and your view of human nature?

How do you make DECISIONS?

Create a list of ways people commonly make decisions. Be sure to put on your list both the way the princess makes her decision and the way the man who loves her makes his choice.

Vocabulary in Context

▲ **VOCABULARY PRACTICE**

Choose the word in each group that is most nearly opposite in meaning to the boldfaced word.

1. **impartial:** (a) unbiased, (b) fair, (c) prejudiced, (d) objective
2. **assert:** (a) deny, (b) claim, (c) declare, (d) stress
3. **subordinate:** (a) beneath, (b) second-in-command, (c) presiding, (d) assisting
4. **conventional:** (a) customary, (b) unusual, (c) accepted, (d) traditional
5. **waver:** (a) hesitate, (b) falter, (c) pause, (d) continue
6. **devious:** (a) straightforward, (b) cunning, (c) sneaky, (d) deceitful
7. **aspire:** (a) plan, (b) hope, (c) attempt, (d) fail
8. **anguished:** (a) tormented, (b) pained, (c) miserable, (d) pleased
9. **progressiveness:** (a) narrow-mindedness, (b) forward-thinking, (c) acceptance, (d) tolerance

anguished
aspire
assert
conventional
devious
impartial
progressiveness
subordinate
waver

ACADEMIC VOCABULARY IN WRITING

> • achieve • income • individual • strategy • trend

The young man standing before the two doors has a plan of action In mind. Do you agree with his **strategy?** Explain why or why not in a paragraph, using at least one Academic Vocabulary word.

VOCABULARY STRATEGY: CONNOTATION AND DENOTATION

A **denotation** is the literal meaning of a word—that is, the definition found in a dictionary. A word's **connotation** is a feeling or attitude linked with a word. Connotations have a big impact on the meaning a word conveys. For example, the vocabulary word *conventional* means "traditional." But it also connotes "old-fashioned" or "unimaginative." Recognizing connotations will help you identify the tone of what you read. If you don't recognize the connotations of a word, use context clues to figure them out.

PRACTICE Show the difference in the connotations of the word pairs by writing a sentence for each word.

1. bland/simple
2. youthful/immature
3. fierce/strong
4. disagree/clash
5. cunning/smart
6. adventurous/reckless
7. smell/stench
8. grueling/challenging

:···: **COMMON CORE**

L 5c Distinguish among connotations of words with similar denotations.
L 6 Gather vocabulary knowledge when considering a word important to comprehension.

Interactive Vocabulary **THINK** central

Go to **thinkcentral.com**.
KEYWORD: HML8-715

The Monty Hall Debate

Newspaper Article

What's the Connection?

In "The Lady, or the Tiger?" you read about a man who had to make a life-or-death choice between two doors. The following article is about a similar (though far less serious) decision faced by contestants of "Let's Make a Deal," a television game show popular in the 1960s and 1970s.

Standards Focus: Use a Graphic Aid

"Let's Make a Deal," host Monty Hall became famous for asking contestants to guess which of three doors hid a big prize. After a contestant picked a door, Hall would open one of the other two doors to show that the prize wasn't behind it. Then he'd give the contestants a choice: Do you want to change your guess to the other door or stick to the door you originally picked?

The article you're about to read explains why one choice is better than the other. The explanation is somewhat complicated, but the diagram shown here can help you understand it. Like other **graphic aids,** this diagram provides a visual representation of ideas. Copy it into your notebook, so you can write on it if you want to. Then refer to the diagram as you read the article, and use these tips to help you interpret it:

• Use symbols such as arrows to help you follow the diagram.

• Pay attention to labels that identify specific details, and relate them to what you read in the article.

• Look for patterns in the use of shading. For example, does one type of information always get shaded a certain way?

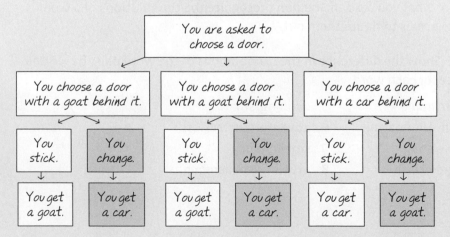

Reprinted from **The New York Times**

SUNDAY, JULY 21, 1991   C3

The Monty Hall Debate

John Tierney

Marilyn vos Savant, a magazine columnist who is listed in the *Guinness Book of World Records* for highest IQ, was once asked this question:

Suppose you're on a game show, and you're given the choice of three doors: Behind one door is a car; behind the others, goats. You pick a
10 door, say No. 1, and the host, who knows what's behind the other doors, opens another door, say No. 3, which has a goat. He then says to you, "Do you want to stick with your original choice or pick door No. 2?" Is it to your advantage to take the switch?

Ms. vos Savant's answer was that you should always change and pick
20 the other door, because the chances are two in three that there will be a car behind that door. Since she gave her answer, Ms. vos Savant estimates she has received 10,000 letters, the great majority disagreeing with her. . . . Of the critical letters she received, close to 1,000 carried signatures with Ph.D.'s, and many were on letterheads of mathematics
30 and science departments. . . . **A**

A GRAPHIC AID Notice how the description in lines 6–13 is represented in the diagram you copied. What do the first and second rows of the diagram show? What do the third and fourth rows show?

Monty Hall hosted "Let's Make A Deal" from 1963 to 1976.

B **GRAPHIC AID**
Reread lines 64–71. What does the shading on the chart on page 716 indicate?

Robert Sachs, a professor of mathematics at George Mason University in Fairfax, Va., expressed the prevailing view that there was no reason to switch doors.

"You blew it!" he wrote. "Let me explain: If one door is shown to be a loser, that information changes the probability of either remaining 40 choice—*neither of which has any reason to be more likely*—to ½. As a professional mathematician, I'm very concerned with the general public's lack of mathematical skills. Please help by confessing your error and, in the future, being more careful.". . .

Monty Hall, the game show host who actually gave contestants this 50 choice on "Let's Make a Deal," said he was not surprised at the experts' insistence that the probability was one out of two. "That's the same assumption contestants would make on the show after I showed them there was nothing behind one door," he said. "They'd think the odds on their door had now gone up to one in two, so they hated to give up the 60 door no matter how much money I offered.[1] By opening one of the other doors we were applying pressure.". . .

Mr. Hall said he realized the contestants were wrong, because the odds on Door 1 were still only one in three even after he opened another door. Since the only other place the car could be was behind Door 2, the 70 odds on that door must now be two in three. **B**

Sitting at his dining room table, Mr. Hall quickly conducted ten rounds of the game as this contestant tried the non-switching strategy. The result was four cars and six goats. Then for the next ten rounds the contestant tried switching doors, and there was a dramatic 80 improvement: eight cars and two goats. A pattern was emerging.

"So her answer's right: you should switch," Mr. Hall said, reaching the same conclusion as the tens of thousands of students who conducted similar experiments at Ms. vos Savant's suggestion. That conclusion was also reached eventually by many of her critics in academia, although most did 90 not bother to write letters of retraction. Dr. Sachs, whose letter was published in her column, was one of the few with the grace to concede his mistake.

"I wrote her another letter," Dr. Sachs said, "telling her that after removing my foot from my mouth I'm now eating humble pie.[2] I vowed as penance to answer all the 100 people who wrote to castigate[3] me. It's been an intense professional embarrassment.". . .

---

1. **how much money I offered:** Monty Hall would sometimes increase the drama of the show by offering contestants money to change their minds about whether to switch doors.

2. **after removing my foot . . . eating humble pie:** after making a careless comment I'm now forced to make an embarrassing apology.

3. **castigate** (kăs′tĭ-gāt′): severely criticize.

Comprehension

1. **Recall** Who is Marilyn vos Savant?

2. **Recall** Did most people who wrote to Ms. vos Savant agree or disagree with her answer to the Monty Hall problem?

3. **Clarify** Reread lines 36–41. According to Robert Sachs, what does Ms. vos Savant fail to realize?

Text Analysis

● 4. **Understand a Graphic Aid** How does the shading on the diagram help you understand that a contestant has a two-in-three chance of getting a car if he or she changes doors? Also explain how the shading reveals what the chance of getting the car is if the contestant sticks with his or her original choice.

Read for Information: Synthesize

WRITING PROMPT

Imagine your best friend is about to go on a game show like "Let's Make a Deal." Since you have seen the show before, you understand that the host knows which door the car is behind. Sometimes he offers contestants money to influence their decision. What advice should you give your friend so that he or she chooses the winning door? Synthesize what you've learned about decision-making from the short story, this article, and your life to answer this question. Then write a letter in which you present your friend with guidelines about making the right decision. Be sure to support your advice with details and examples.

When you **synthesize**, you combine information from various sources to gain a better understanding of a subject. Following these steps can help you synthesize:

1. Reflect on what you learned about decision-making from the story, the article, and your life.

2. Jot down the most important considerations about decision-making that you found in these sources.

3. Write a letter in which you present these considerations as guidelines for choosing the winning door. Support each guideline you offer with an example from your life, the article, or "The Lady, or the Tiger?"

COMMON CORE

RI 1 Cite textual evidence to support inferences drawn from the text. **RI 2** Determine a central idea of a text and analyze its development over the course of the text. **RI 3** Analyze how a text makes connections among ideas (e.g., through categories). **W 8** Gather relevant information from print sources; and quote or paraphrase the data and conclusions of others.

CARTOON One way to create an amusing cartoon is by presenting something familiar in a new, unexpected way. Here, for example, the cartoonist presents the familiar ending to "The Lady, or the Tiger?" in a modern-day context. To get the joke, however, you need to know the story. Now explore other elements that add to the humor of this cartoon by answering the questions below.

COMMON CORE

SL 2 Analyze the purpose of information presented in diverse media and formats.

"Sorry. I was expecting the lady. I can see you're busy. I'll call sometime. We'll do lunch."

1. ANALYZE VISUALS
Why do you suppose the cartoonist chose to draw a salesman on a sales call in place of a tragic hero in a life-or-death moment?

2. INTERPRET
This salesman says what any sales person might say on a routine sales call. Why do you suppose the cartoonist chose to have the salesman react in such a routine way? What might he be implying about sales people? Explain.

Assessment Practice: Short Constructed Response

LITERARY TEXT: "THE LADY, OR THE TIGER?"

Assessments often expect you to answer questions that focus on particular passages from a story. To strengthen your close-reading skills, read the **short constructed response question** on the left and use the strategies on the right to answer it.

> Reread lines 152–173. What do the young man's actions suggest about his character and his love for the princess? Explain your answer and support it with evidence from the text.

◀ **STRATEGIES IN ACTION**

1. Consider what the young man believes the princess will know.

2. Notice what he asks with his glance and what she answers with her gesture.

3. Think about which door the man chooses and how he approaches that door.

4. Consider what his response suggests about the strength of his character and his commitment to the princess.

NONFICTION TEXT: "THE MONTY HALL DEBATE"

Assessments sometimes ask you to answer "change questions" about a nonfiction text as you read. Practice this skill by answering the **short constructed response question** on the left. Use the strategies on the right for help.

> Dr. Sachs's opinion of Ms. vos Savant's math skills changes over time. Describe the way in which his opinion changes and the reason for that shift. Support your answer with evidence from "The Monty Hall Debate."

◀ **STRATEGIES IN ACTION**

1. Review Dr. Sachs's first and last letters. Jot down words in both letters that reveal his attitude toward Ms. vos Savant.

2. Reread the text to find out what occurs to change Dr. Sachs's opinion.

3. Use the evidence you noted in step 1 and what you discovered in step 2 to support your response to the practice question.

COMPARING LITERARY AND NONFICTION TEXTS

Tests sometimes expect you to make thematic connections between literary and nonfiction texts. Using "The Lady, or the Tiger?" and "The Monty Hall Debate" as your two texts, practice this skill by answering the **constructed response question** below.

> Assuming the narrator in "The Lady, or the Tiger?" represents Frank L. Stockton, what opinion might Stockton and Tierney share about the public at large? Support your answer with evidence from **both** texts.

◀ **STRATEGIES IN ACTION**

1. State an opinion about the public that both authors might share.

2. Tell why you think each author might hold this opinion and support your reasons.

Kira-Kira

Coming-of-Age Novel by Cynthia Kadohata

COMMON CORE

RL 10 Read and comprehend literature.

**Other Books by
Cynthia Kadohata**
- *The Floating World*
- *The Glass Mountains*

Meet Cynthia Kadohata

Like the main character's family in *Kira-Kira*, Cynthia Kadohata's family moved often so that her parents could seek work. They lived in Illinois, Arkansas, Georgia, and Michigan before finally settling in California. As a child, Kadohata, a Japanese American, often did not feel like she fit in. "I remember a little girl asking me something like, 'Are you black or white?'" she says. "I really stumbled for an answer. I said, 'I don't know.'" But since then, Kadohata has come to embrace her cultural identity. Today, she is viewed as one of the great voices in Asian-American writing.

Although she majored in journalism in college, in her early 20s Kadohata began to appreciate the power of fiction. "I had always thought that nonfiction represented the 'truth,'" she explains, "but . . . I realized you could say things with fiction that you couldn't say any other way." Kadohata set out to become a fiction writer. She received 25 rejection letters before *The New Yorker* finally published one of her stories, launching her career as an award-winning author. *Kira-Kira* is her first young-adult novel.

Try a Coming-of-Age Novel

At what point do you leave your childhood fears behind and boldly take on greater responsibilities? A novel that centers on a young person's path to greater maturity is called a **coming-of-age novel**. *Kira-Kira*, which follows the life of its young narrator, is an example of this type of novel.

Reading Fluency refers to how easily and well you read. Fluent readers read smoothly, accurately, and with feeling. To improve your reading fluency, it helps to practice reading aloud. When reading aloud, think about your purpose for reading the text. Be sure to group words into meaningful phrases that sound like natural speech.

Read a Great Book

Katie Takeshima thinks her older sister, Lynn, is a genius—
partly because Lynn sees the world in such a unique way.
Lynn finds beauty in ordinary things and teaches Katie to
see them *kira-kira,* or glittering, too. The family business
is far from being a shining success, however; and when
Katie's parents get down to their last $600, they decide
it's time to move on. As the family prepares to leave Iowa
in order for Mr. and Mrs. Takeshima to pursue better job
opportunities in Georgia, Katie wonders how their lives
will change.

cynthia kadohata

from

KIRA-KIRA

kira-kira

We were poor, but in the way Japanese are poor, meaning we never
borrowed money from anyone, period. Meaning once a year we bought
as many fifty-pound bags of rice as we could afford, and we didn't get
nervous again about money until we reached our last bag. Nothing
went to waste in our house. For breakfast my parents often made their
ochazuke—green tea mixed with rice—from the crusty old rice at the
bottom of the pot. For our move to Georgia, Dad and Uncle loaded
up the truck with all the bags of rice that we hadn't sold at the store.
I watched my parents look at the rice in the truck, and I could see that
10 the rice made them feel good. It made them feel safe.

I liked to see them that way, especially my mother, who never seemed
to feel safe. My mother was a delicate, rare, and beautiful flower. Our
father told us that. She weighed hardly more than Lynn. She was so
delicate that if you bumped into her accidentally, you could bruise her.
She fell down a single stair once, and she broke her leg. To her that was
proof even a single stair could present peril. When I would approach
even a single stair, she would call out, "Be careful!"

Our mother didn't like us to run or play or climb, because it was dangerous. She didn't like us to walk in the middle of our empty street, because you never knew. She didn't want us to go to college someday, because we might get strange ideas. She liked peace and quiet. My father used to say, "Shhhh. Your mother is taking a bath." Or, "Quiet down, girls, your mother is drinking tea." We never understood why we couldn't make noise while our mother was doing anything at all. My mother's favorite thing to tell us, in her iron-rimmed singsong voice, was *"Shizukani!"* That means "Hush!"

She never said *"Shizukani!"* to my father. She made him food and rubbed his feet, and for this he let her handle all the money. Lynn said our mother probably knew a special foot-rubbing technique that made men silly. My father loved my mother a lot. That made *me* feel safe.

The night before we moved, my father and uncle sat on a tree stump across the road. Lynn and I peeked out at them before we got in bed. My uncle talked and talked, and my father listened and listened. Sometimes they both laughed loudly.

"What are they talking about?" I said.

"Women," Lynn said knowingly.

"What are they saying about women?"

"That the pretty ones make them giggle."

"Oh. Good night."

"Good night!"

Our mother came into the bedroom in the middle of the night, the way she always did, to make sure we were asleep. As usual, Lynn was asleep and I was awake. If I was awake, I usually pretended to be asleep so as not to get in trouble. But tonight I said, "Mom?"

"It's late, why are you up?"

"I can't sleep without Bera-Bera." Bera-Bera was my favorite stuffed animal, which my mother had packed in a box. Bera-Bera talked too much, laughed too loudly, and sometimes sassed me, but still I loved him.

"Someday you won't even remember Bera-Bera." She said this gently, and as if the thought made her a little sad. The thought made me a little sad too. She kissed my forehead and left. Outside I could hear noises: "Yah! Ooooh-YAH!" Et cetera. Lynn was sound asleep. I got up and watched Uncle Katsuhisa spit. My father no longer sat on the tree stump. It was just Uncle Katsuhisa out there. He was a madman, for sure.

We left Iowa at dusk the next evening. We had meant to leave in the morning but got a little behind schedule for several reasons:

60

1. I couldn't find the box with Bera-Bera, and I was convinced he was lost. Naturally, I had to have hysterics.
2. My parents misplaced their six hundred dollars.
3. Lynn couldn't find her favorite sweater with embroidered flowers. Naturally, she had to have hysterics.
4. Uncle Katsuhisa fell asleep, and we thought it would be rude to wake him.

Uncle woke up on his own. My parents found their money. But Lynn and I didn't find our items, so naturally, we continued our hysterics. Finally, my mother said, "We must leave or I don't know what!" She looked at Lynn and me crying. "Maybe you girls should keep your uncle
70 company while he drives."

"Oh, no," said Uncle. "I wouldn't want to deprive you of their delightful company."

"No," said my mother. "I wouldn't want you to be lonely."

So we climbed into the noisy truck with our noisy uncle. Then we cried so much that our uncle refused to drive with us anymore. He pulled to the side of the highway. Then we got in our parents' car and cried so much that they pulled over and flipped a coin with Uncle Katsuhisa. Uncle lost, so we got back in the truck with him.

Lynn and I were perfectly happy in Iowa. I did not see why we had
80 to move to a new job that my father had told us would be the hardest work he had ever done. I did not see why we had to move to a southern state where my father said you could not understand a word people said

because of their southern accents. I did not see why we had to leave our house for a small apartment.

After awhile Lynn and I ran out of tears and sat glumly in the truck with Uncle Katsuhisa. I knew if I thought of Bera-Bera, I would cry. But I had nothing else to do, so I thought of him. He was half dog, half rabbit, and he had orange fur. He was my best friend next to Lynn. "I want Bera-Bera!" I cried out.

90   Lynn cried out, "I want my sweater!" We both burst into tears.

It was a warm night. Whenever we paused in our crying, the only other sound inside the truck was the sound of my uncle smacking his chewing tobacco. I dreaded to know what would happen when he spit out that tobacco. Now he rolled down the window, and I thought the Great Spit was about to come. Instead, he looked at us slyly.

"I could teach you girls how to spit like a master," he said.

My sister squinted at him. She stopped crying. So did I. I could tell she thought it might be fun to learn how to spit like a master. So did I. Our mother would kill us. Lynn said, "Maybe."

100   He belched very loudly, then glanced at us. I realized his belch was preparation for spitting. I swallowed some air and burped. So did Lynn. Then Uncle Katsuhisa's throat rumbled. The rumbling got louder and louder. Even over the sound of the motor, it seemed like a war was going on in his throat. Lynn and I tried to rumble our throats like him.

"Hocka-hocka-hocka!" he said.

Lynn and I copied him: "Hocka-hocka-hocka!"

"Geh-geh-geh!"

"Geh-geh-geh!"

He turned to his open window, and an amazing wad of brown juice
110 flew from his mouth. The brown juice was like a bat bursting out of a cave. We turned around to watch it speed away. A part of me hoped it would hit the car behind us, but it didn't. I leaned over Lynn and out the passenger window. "Hyaaahhhh!" I said, and a little trickle of saliva fell down my chin.

No one spoke. For some reason the silence made me start crying again. As if Uncle Katsuhisa couldn't restrain himself, he started singing my name over and over, "Katie, Katie, Katie . . ." Then he sang

Katie songs to the tunes of "Row, Row, Row Your Boat," "America the Beautiful," "Kookaburra," and some songs I didn't recognize. For
120 instance, he sang, "Oh, Katie, Kate, for spacious skies, for Katie Katie Kate." He made me giggle. It was almost as if someone were tickling me. For a while I forgot about Bera-Bera.

Lynn smiled with satisfaction. I knew this was because she liked for me to be happy. The wind hit our hair as Uncle Katsuhisa continued to sing Katie songs. I looked outside over a field and tried to find the *Sode Boshi*, the kimono sleeve in the sky where Uncle Katsuhisa said westerners see the constellation Orion. Then my uncle began to sing Lynnie songs.

She laughed and laughed and laughed. ❧

Keep Reading

The Takeshimas are on their way to a new life in a small Georgia town, where there are very few other Japanese Americans. How different will things be for them there? As you continue to read *Kira-Kira*, you will see the family through times of great joy and times of deep sorrow. Through it all, Katie continues to follow her sister's example by looking for beauty in the world around her. Read along as Katie's experiences in Georgia help her to grow into a thoughtful young woman.

from **Roughing It**

Memoir by Mark Twain

Video link at
thinkcentral.com

VIDEO TRAILER **THINK** central   KEYWORD: HML8-728

Why do we
EXAGGERATE?

COMMON CORE

RI 4 Determine the meaning of words and phrases as they are used in a text, including figurative [and] connotative meanings; analyze the impact of specific word choices.

"It takes me forever to walk to school." "I have about a million hours of homework to do." "My backpack must weigh two hundred pounds." Have you ever found yourself saying something like this, even when you know it's not accurate? We all exaggerate at times. In the memoir you are about to read, Mark Twain uses exaggeration not only to make us laugh, but also to make us think.

DISCUSS How good are you at exaggerating? Choose a simple event—your trip to the grocery store, or yesterday's band practice. Tell the story in its basic form, with no exaggeration. Then tell the story again, this time exaggerating the events and descriptive details. Did your exaggeration make the second version more fun to hear? Or did it push the limits of believability too far? Share your stories with your group and let them decide.

Peanuts   by Charles Schulz

Peanuts, Charles Schulz. August 5, 1983. © United Feature Syndicate, Inc.

● TEXT ANALYSIS: VOICE AND STYLE

In literature, **voice** refers to a writer's unique use of language. The way a writer chooses words, constructs sentences, and expresses ideas makes his or her personality come through on the page. As you read, look for places where Mark Twain achieves his humorous voice through these distinctive elements of his style:

- complex sentences containing amusing descriptions
- **hyperbole,** or exaggeration
- **understatement,** or downplaying something's importance

● READING STRATEGY: MONITOR

Twain uses long sentences and old-fashioned vocabulary. To make sure you understand what he's saying, **monitor** yourself, or pause to check your understanding. If you're not clear about what you just read, try these strategies:

- **Adjust your reading rate** by slowing down when you get to long, complicated sentences and passages.
- **Use context clues** or a dictionary to figure out the meaning of archaic (old-fashioned) vocabulary.
- **Note descriptive details** to help you picture characters, events, and settings.
- **Reread difficult passages** to help clarify information.

As you read, use a chart to note the line numbers of difficult passages and the strategies you used to understand them.

Confusing Lines	What They Mean	How I Figured It Out

▲ VOCABULARY IN CONTEXT

Twain uses the following words in a humorous way. To see how many you know, match each word with its synonym.

WORD LIST		
array	legitimate	sensational
conspicuous	livelihood	tolerable
contrive	rigid	yield

1. occupation
2. inflexible
3. shocking
4. surrender
5. assortment
6. valid
7. invent
8. adequate
9. obvious

Complete the activities in your **Reader/Writer Notebook.**

Mark Twain
1835–1910

Growing Up on the River
When Samuel Clemens was four years old, his family moved to Hannibal, Missouri, a small town on the Mississippi River. Clemens grew up fascinated by the river, traveling its waters in homemade rafts, playing in swimming holes, and exploring nearby woods and caves. His carefree childhood days ended at 11, however, when his father died of pneumonia. In order to support his family, Clemens left school and worked for a newspaper and printing firm.

Looking for Adventure
In 1853, Clemens left Hannibal to seek his fortune mining along the Amazon River. But Clemens never made it to the Amazon. On his journey south he befriended a steamboat captain, and for four years he sailed the Mississippi River. After a brief stint in the Confederate Army during the Civil War, Clemens moved to Nevada and began writing for a local paper. It was during this time that he assumed the pen name "Mark Twain," a term that means "two fathoms deep," or water that is deep enough for a riverboat to navigate safely.

The Start of a Legend
Mark Twain made a name for himself traveling around the world and writing newspaper columns about his adventures. His humorous voice captured the hearts of American readers, and before long, Twain was a household name. His book *Roughing It* contains essays about his travels and work experiences, all told in his signature way.

Author Online

THINK central

Go to **thinkcentral.com**.
KEYWORD: HML8-729

ROUGHING IT

Mark Twain

What to do next?

It was a momentous question. I had gone out into the world to shift for myself,[1] at the age of thirteen (for my father had indorsed[2] for friends, and although he left us a sumptuous legacy of pride in his fine Virginian stock and its national distinction, I presently found that I could not live on that alone without occasional bread to wash it down with). **A**
I had gained a **livelihood** in various vocations, but had not dazzled anybody with my successes; still the list was before me, and the amplest liberty in the matter of choosing, provided I wanted to work—which I did not, after being
10 so wealthy. I had once been a grocery clerk, for one day, but had consumed so much sugar in that time that I was relieved from further duty by the proprietor;[3] said he wanted me outside, so that he could have my custom. I had studied law an entire week, and then given it up because it was so prosy and tiresome. I had engaged briefly in the study of blacksmithing, but wasted so much time trying to fix the bellows so that it would blow itself, that the master turned me adrift in disgrace, and told me I would come to no good. I had been a bookseller's clerk for a while, but the customers bothered me so much I could not read with any comfort, and so the proprietor gave me a furlough and forgot

A MONITOR
Why did Twain need to support himself at a young age? Rephrase the information in parentheses to find out.

livelihood (lĭv′lē-hŏŏd′) *n.* a means of support; a way of making a living

Analyze Visuals ▶
What does this image of Mark Twain suggest about his **writing process?**

---

1. **shift for myself:** take care of myself.

2. **indorsed** (ĭn-dôrsd′): endorsed; signed financial documents; perhaps this means that Twain's father backed up friends' unwise financial schemes, and lost all of his own money as a result.

3. **proprietor** (prə-prī′ĭ-tər): one who owns and manages a business.

to put a limit to it. I had clerked in a drug store part of a summer, but my
20 prescriptions were unlucky, and we appeared to sell more stomach-pumps than
soda-water. So I had to go. I had made of myself a **tolerable** printer, under the
impression that I would be another Franklin some day, but somehow had missed
the connection thus far. There was no berth[4] open in the Esmeralda *Union,* and
besides I had always been such a slow compositor[5] that I looked with envy upon
the achievements of apprentices of two years' standing; and when I took a "take,"
foremen were in the habit of suggesting that it would be wanted "some time
during the year." I was a good average St. Louis and New Orleans pilot and by
no means ashamed of my abilities in that line; wages were two hundred and fifty
dollars a month and no board[6] to pay, and I did long to stand behind a wheel
30 again and never roam any more—but I had been making such a fool of myself
lately in grandiloquent letters home about my blind lead and my European
excursion that I did what many and many a poor disappointed miner had done
before; said, "It is all over with me now, and I will never go back home to be
pitied—and snubbed." I had been a private secretary, a silver-miner and a
silver-mill operative, and amounted to less than nothing in each, and now— **B**

W hat to do next?

I **yielded** to Higbie's appeals and consented to try the mining once more.
We climbed far up on the mountainside and went to work on a little rubbishy
claim of ours that had a shaft on it eight feet deep. Higbie descended into it
40 and worked bravely with his pick till he had loosened up a deal of rock and
dirt, and then I went down with a long-handled shovel (the most awkward
invention yet **contrived** by man) to throw it out. You must brace the shovel
forward with the side of your knee till it is full, and then, with a skillful toss,
throw it backward over your left shoulder. I made the toss, and landed the
mess just on the edge of the shaft and it all came back on my head and down
the back of my neck. I never said a word, but climbed out and walked home.
I inwardly resolved that I would starve before I would make a target of myself
and shoot rubbish at it with a long-handled shovel. I sat down, in the cabin,
and gave myself up to solid misery—so to speak. Now in pleasanter days I
50 had amused myself with writing letters to the chief paper of the territory, the
Virginia *Daily Territorial Enterprise,* and had always been surprised when they
appeared in print. My good opinion of the editors had steadily declined; for
it seemed to me that they might have found something better to fill up with
than my literature. I had found a letter in the post-office as I came home from
the hillside, and finally I opened it. Eureka! [I never did know what Eureka
meant, but it seems to be as proper a word to heave in as any when no other
that sounds pretty offers.] It was a deliberate offer to me of Twenty-five Dollars
a week to come up to Virginia and be city editor of the *Enterprise.* **C**

---

4. **berth:** job.
5. **compositor** (kəm-pŏz'ĭ-tər): a worker who sets type for a printing business.
6. **board:** meals.

tolerable (tŏl'ər-ə-bəl)
adj. fairly good; passable

B **VOICE AND STYLE**
Reread lines 19–21.
Where does Twain use
understatement in this
passage?

yield (yēld) *v.* to give in
to another

contrive (kən-trīv') *v.* to
invent or fabricate,
especially by improvisation

(COMMON CORE RI 4
Language Coach
Figures of Speech
When words are used
to express something
other than their usual
meaning, they are
called figures of speech.
The word *solid* usually
describes a firm object
or something without
openings. What does
Twain mean by "solid
misery" in line 49?

C **MONITOR**
How did Twain get a job
offer from the *Enterprise?*
Note the strategy you
used to find this answer.

I would have challenged the publisher in the "blind lead" days—I wanted
60 to fall down and worship him, now. Twenty-five Dollars a week—it looked
like bloated luxury—a fortune, a sinful and lavish waste of money. But
my transports[7] cooled when I thought of my inexperience and consequent
unfitness for the position—and straightway, on top of this, my long **array** of
failures rose up before me. Yet if I refused this place I must presently become
dependent upon somebody for my bread, a thing necessarily distasteful to a
man who had never experienced such a humiliation since he was thirteen years
old. Not much to be proud of, since it is so common—but then it was all I had
to *be* proud of. So I was scared into being a city editor. I would have declined,
otherwise. Necessity is the mother of "taking chances." I do not doubt that
70 if, at that time, I had been offered a salary to translate the Talmud[8] from the
original Hebrew, I would have accepted—albeit with diffidence and some
misgivings—and thrown as much variety into it as I could for the money. **D**

array (ə-rā′) *n.* a large
number of items

D **VOICE AND STYLE**
Reread lines 69–72.
Where is **hyperbole** used
in this passage?

---

7. **transports:** joyful excitement.

8. **Talmud** (täl′mŏŏd): a collection of ancient writings by rabbis; this is the basis of Orthodox Jewish law.

◀ **Analyze
Visuals**
Identify which man in
the illustration is Mark
Twain. How does the
drawing of him **compare**
with your mental
image?

I went up to Virginia and entered upon my new vocation. I was a rusty-looking city editor, I am free to confess—coatless, slouch hat, blue woolen shirt, pantaloons stuffed into boot-tops, whiskered half down to the waist, and the universal navy revolver slung to my belt. But I secured a more
80 conservative costume and discarded the revolver. I had never had occasion to kill anybody, nor ever felt a desire to do so, but had worn the thing in deference to popular sentiment, and in order that I might not, by its absence, be offensively **conspicuous,** and a subject of remark. But the other editors, and all the printers, carried revolvers. I asked the chief editor and proprietor (Mr. Goodman, I will call him, since it describes
90 him as well as any name could do) for some instructions with regard to my duties, and he told me to go all over town and ask all sorts of people all sorts of questions, make notes of the information gained, and write them out for publication. And he added:

"Never say 'We learn' so-and-so, or 'It is reported,' or 'It is rumored,' or 'We understand' so-and-so, but go to headquarters and get the absolute facts,
100 and then speak out and say 'It *is* so-and-so.' Otherwise, people will not put confidence in your news. Unassailable[9] certainty is the thing that gives a newspaper the firmest and most valuable reputation."

It was the whole thing in a nutshell; and to this day, when I find a reporter commencing his article with "We understand," I gather a suspicion that he has not taken as much pains to inform himself as he ought to have done. I moralize well, but I did not always practise well when I was a city editor; I let fancy get the upper hand of fact too often when there was a dearth[10] of news. I can never
110 forget my first day's experience as a reporter. I wandered about town questioning everybody, boring everybody, and finding out that nobody knew anything. At the end of five hours my note-book was still barren. I spoke to Mr. Goodman. He said:

"Dan used to make a good thing out of the hay-wagons in a dry time when there were no fires or inquests. Are there no hay-wagons in from the Truckee?

conspicuous
(kən-spĭk'yōō-əs) *adj.*
easy to notice; obvious

E **MONITOR**
Reread lines 73–95. Do you find any of these sentences difficult to understand? If so, choose a strategy to help you clarify their meaning.

---

9. **unassailable** (ŭn'ə-sā'lə-bəl): impossible to dispute or disprove; undeniable.

10. **dearth** (dûrth): a scarce supply; a lack.

If there are, you might speak of the renewed activity and all that sort of thing, in the hay business, you know. It isn't **sensational** or exciting, but it fills up and looks business-like."

I canvassed the city again and found one wretched old hay-truck dragging in from the country. But I made affluent use of it. I multiplied it by sixteen, brought it into town from sixteen different directions, made sixteen separate items of it, and got up such another sweat about hay as Virginia City had never seen in the world before.

This was encouraging. Two nonpareil[11] columns had to be filled, and I was getting along. Presently, when things began to look dismal again, a desperado killed a man in a saloon and joy returned once more. I never was so glad over any mere trifle before in my life. I said to the murderer:

"Sir, you are a stranger to me, but you have done me a kindness this day which I can never forget. If whole years of gratitude can be to you any slight compensation, they shall be yours. I was in trouble and you have relieved me nobly and at a time when all seemed dark and drear. Count me your friend from this time forth, for I am not a man to forget a favor." **F**

If I did not really say that to him I at least felt a sort of itching desire to do it. I wrote up the murder with a hungry attention to details, and when it was finished experienced but one regret—namely, that they had not hanged my benefactor on the spot, so that I could work him up too.

Next I discovered some emigrant-wagons[12] going into camp on the plaza and found that they had lately come through the hostile Indian country and had fared rather roughly. I made the best of the item that the circumstances permitted, and felt that if I were not confined within **rigid** limits by the presence of the reporters of the other papers I could add particulars that would make the article much more interesting. However, I found one wagon that was going on to California, and made some judicious inquiries of the proprietor. When I learned, through his short and surly answers to my cross-questioning, that he was certainly going on and would not be in the city next day to make trouble, I got ahead of the other papers, for I took down his list of names and added his party to the killed and wounded. Having more scope here, I put this wagon through an Indian fight that to this day has no parallel in history. **G**

My two columns were filled. When I read them over in the morning I felt that I had found my **legitimate** occupation at last. I reasoned within myself that news, and stirring news, too, was what a paper needed, and I felt that I was peculiarly endowed[13] with the ability to furnish it. Mr. Goodman said that I was as good a reporter as Dan. I desired no higher commendation. With encouragement like that, I felt that I could take my pen and murder all the immigrants on the plains if need be, and the interests of the paper demanded it. ∾

---

sensational
(sĕn-sā′shə-nəl) *adj.*
intended to arouse strong curiosity or interest, especially through exaggerated details

F VOICE AND STYLE
Do you think Twain really responded to the murder in this way? Explain your answer.

rigid (rĭj′ĭd) *adj.*
inflexible; strict

G VOICE AND STYLE
Reread lines 137–148. What **amusing descriptions** does Twain use to explain his article about the emigrant-wagons?

legitimate (lə-jĭt′ə-mĭt) *adj.* genuine; authentic

---

11. **nonpareil** (nŏn′pə-rĕl′): unequalled; peerless.
12. **emigrant-wagons** (ĕm′ĭ-grənt): wagons in which pioneers rode on their way to settle in the West.
13. **peculiarly endowed** (pĭ-kyōōl′yər-lē ĕn-doud′): specifically supplied with a talent or quality.

Comprehension

1. **Recall** Why does Mark Twain lose his jobs at the grocery store, bookstore, and drugstore?

2. **Recall** What does Twain decide about mining as an occupation?

3. **Clarify** How does Twain fill up his two newspaper columns?

COMMON CORE

RI 4 Determine the meaning of words and phrases as they are used in a text, including figurative [and] connotative meanings; analyze the impact of specific word choices.

Text Analysis

4. **Make Inferences** Although an **exaggeration** may be misleading, it often contains a grain of truth. Skim the selection for three examples of exaggeration that provide information about the author. In a diagram like the one shown, present the examples and tell what you can infer from each one.

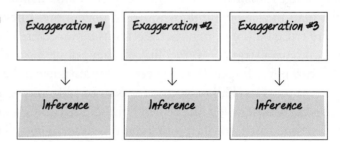

5. **Analyze Voice and Style** Long sentences containing amusing descriptions, hyperbole, and understatement are typical of Twain's unique voice and style. Find three sentences that you think are particularly funny or effective. Then, rewrite each sentence in a more straightforward way. Which version do you like better?

6. **Examine Monitoring** Review the list you kept while reading. Which monitoring strategy helped you best understand and enjoy *Roughing It*? Explain, and give examples.

7. **Draw Conclusions About Style** Reread lines 2–10. Based on what you know about Twain, why do you think he uses such long, complicated sentences?

8. **Make Judgments** A **memoir** is a form of autobiographical nonfiction in which an author shares part of his or her life story. Memoirs are assumed to be based on fact. Given Twain's generous use of exaggeration, do you think it is fair to label *Roughing It* a memoir? Why or why not?

Extension and Challenge

9. **Speaking and Listening** With a partner, create a mock interview with Mark Twain. First, brainstorm a list of questions a reporter would ask Twain, based on the information he provides in *Roughing It*. Then, with one person acting as the reporter and one as Twain, conduct the interview in front of the rest of the class. Try to stay true to the selection, and to Twain's voice, by adding humor and exaggeration to Twain's responses.

Why do we EXAGGERATE?

Now that you have read Twain's exaggerations, how might you change your retelling of the story that you shared at the beginning of this lesson?

Vocabulary in Context

▲ VOCABULARY PRACTICE

Synonyms have a similar meaning, and **antonyms** have opposite or nearly opposite meanings. Decide whether the words in each pair are synonyms or antonyms.

1. rigid/permissive
2. tolerable/acceptable
3. conspicuous/noticeable
4. livelihood/occupation
5. legitimate/wrong
6. yield/resist
7. array/variety
8. sensational/understated
9. contrive/invent

ACADEMIC VOCABULARY IN WRITING

• achieve • income • individual • strategy • trend

Twain tries to earn an **income** from many different kinds of work before he succeeds as a newspaper editor. Think about his explanations for his various dismissals. Then, in a paragraph, explain why you think he fails to **achieve** success in most of these other jobs. Use at least two Academic Vocabulary words in your paragraph.

VOCABULARY STRATEGY: THE LATIN ROOT *leg*

The vocabulary word *legitimate* comes from the Latin root *leg*, which means "law." *Leg* (combined with other word parts) appears in a number of English words. To understand the meaning of a word that contains this root, use context clues and your knowledge of the root's meaning.

PRACTICE Choose the word from the web that best completes each sentence. Then explain how the root *leg* helps to give each word its meaning.

1. The document was written in ____, but I finally figured out what it meant.
2. Each region's voters elect one member of our state ____.
3. Dad e-mailed Representative Lee and asked her to help ____ some tough new environmental laws.
4. Senators are ____ who propose laws in Congress.
5. California abolished the death penalty and then ____ it again.

COMMON CORE

L 4b Use Latin roots as clues to the meaning of a word.
L 6 Acquire and use domain-specific words.

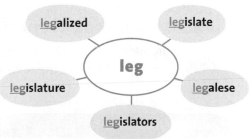

Interactive **THINK** central
Vocabulary

Go to **thinkcentral.com**.
KEYWORD: HML8-737

Language

◯ **COMMON CORE**

L1 Demonstrate command of grammar and usage when writing. **L2a** Use punctuation to indicate a pause or break. **L3** Use knowledge of language when writing.

◆ **GRAMMAR IN CONTEXT:** Form Compound Sentences

A **main clause** is a group of words that contains a subject and a verb and can stand alone as a sentence. A **simple sentence** contains one main clause. A **compound sentence** contains two or more main clauses that are joined either by a comma and a coordinating conjunction, such as *and, but, or, so,* or *yet,* or by a semicolon.

Original: Mark Twain is creative. He's a good writer. (*Each simple sentence contains one main clause.*)

Revised: Mark Twain is creative, and he's a good writer. (*The compound sentence contains two main clauses that are joined by a comma and a coordinating conjunction.*)

PRACTICE Create a compound sentence by joining the two simple sentences with either a comma and a coordinating conjunction or a semicolon.

1. Twain is not interested in hard work. He needs a job to support himself.

2. Twain has an interesting way with words. He tells too many tall tales.

3. Twain will not pass his journalism class. He does not follow the rules of ethical writing.

4. Twain should conduct better research. He should not exaggerate his articles for the sake of selling newspapers.

*For more help with main clauses and simple and compound sentences, see pages R62 and R63 in the **Grammar Handbook**.*

READING-WRITING CONNECTION

YOUR TURN Broaden your understanding of *Roughing It* by responding to this prompt. Then use the **revising tip** to improve your writing.

WRITING PROMPT	REVISING TIP
Extended Constructed Response: Evaluation Imagine that John McCandlish Phillips, author of "The Simple Commandments of Journalistic Ethics" on page 000, is Twain's teacher. How would he evaluate Twain's reporting techniques, including his use of **exaggeration?** Write a **half-page evaluation** of Twain's news articles from Phillips's point of view.	Review your evaluation to find simple sentences that you might combine into compound sentences to make your writing more concise.

▶

Interactive Revision

THINK central

Go to **thinkcentral.com**.
KEYWORD: HML8-738

NEWSPAPER ARTICLE You wouldn't know it from reading about Mark Twain's behavior, but most journalists actually follow a code of ethics, or fairness. In this article, a former *New York Times* writer explains this code to student journalists.

SECTION A   THE STAR JOURNAL   A3

The Simple Commandments of Journalistic Ethics

John McCandlish Phillips

. . . Long after my years in news reporting, I have had repeated occasions to speak to young or aspiring journalists. With rare exceptions, the matter they have wanted most to hear about is reportorial ethics. . . .

Here is the core of what I tell aspiring journalists about the question they so reliably pose:

In journalistic usage, you shall be as accurate and balanced and fair, and as faithful to pinned-down facts, as you possibly can be. The right does not exist to put anything whatever between quotation marks that are not words as they were spoken, to 97 percent word accuracy. Misquotation or fabricated quotation is lying in print—a terrible disservice to those abused by the license taken. It does not help when the act is careless rather than deceitful.

You will not lie. You will not distort. You will not make things up.

You will not embroider your story for effect.

If you get into investigative reporting, never let your suspicions run one-eighth of an inch ahead of your facts—solid, fully ascertained evidence that conclusively verifies the suspicions that promoted the investigation.

Newspapers and broadcast news must—and they do—report accusations made by public figures against other such figures. When the newspaper itself levels the accusation, and presents its supporting case, it is much more deeply hurtful to the accused than the former is.

Always remember that, in public accusation, the irreducible, primary, essential requirement is that it be factually accurate. If it truly is, you have every right to take it to print or on air, and things will likely be better for it.

Students design a school newspaper.

Us and Them
Personal Essay by David Sedaris

What's really NORMAL?

COMMON CORE

RI 4 Analyze the impact of specific word choices on meaning and tone. **L 5a** Interpret figures of speech (e.g. verbal irony) in context.

Imagine a town where everyone dyes his or her hair purple and spends free time either at puppet shows or raising ferrets. If someone moves in who has brown hair and loves video games and soccer, would he or she be considered normal? What we mean by that word often depends on where we are and who we're with. In the selection you are about to read, a young boy is fascinated by a family that doesn't seem normal.

DISCUSS How do you define *normal*? Think about things like the way you and your friends and family dress, the music you listen to, and the activities you participate in. Create a definition for the word *normal* based on these observations, and compare it with classmates' definitions. Is everyone's view of *normal* the same?

TEXT ANALYSIS: IRONY

Have you ever stayed up late to study for a test, only to find out that the test was postponed? Many people would call this turn of events ironic. **Irony** is a contrast between what is expected and what actually exists or happens. Irony can make a piece of literature tragic, thoughtful, or funny, depending upon the writer's goal. Types of irony include

- **situational irony,** which is a contrast between what is expected to happen and what actually does happen
- **verbal irony,** which occurs when someone states one thing and means another
- **dramatic irony,** which happens when readers know more about a situation or a character in a story than the characters do

As you read, record examples of irony in a chart as shown.

Example	Type of Irony	Why It's Ironic

Review: **Tone**

READING SKILL: EVALUATE

When you **evaluate,** you make judgments about the author's opinions, actions, or statements. Asking evaluative questions as you read makes you think about what's right and wrong, and why. As you read, ask yourself whether the young David Sedaris's thoughts and actions seem sensible, fair, and accurate.

▲ VOCABULARY IN CONTEXT

The way Sedaris uses the following boldfaced words helps create the ironic **tone** of his story. Use context clues in each sentence to figure out the meaning of the boldfaced terms.

1. Lucy doesn't **merit** an invitation to my party.
2. Don't **imply** that you believe me if you really don't.
3. Carmen, don't **inflict** your terrible music on me!
4. Although I disagree, I won't **interfere** with your decision.
5. I **attribute** John's grades to hard work and dedication.
6. Taylor tosses her papers **indiscriminately** into her bag.
7. There's no way Mom can **accommodate** all of us in her tiny car.
8. If you **provoke** me, I will likely argue with you.

 Complete the activities in your **Reader/Writer Notebook.**

Meet the Author

David Sedaris
born 1957

A Man of Many Jobs
David Sedaris has had several odd jobs over the years, including apple picking, house painting, performance art, and apartment cleaning. But a humorous essay he wrote about his experiences working as an elf in a department store's holiday display launched his writing career. After reading "The SantaLand Diaries" on National Public Radio, Sedaris became an instant hit, and since then his books have sold millions of copies. His inspiration comes from the diaries he has kept for over 30 years, in which he records his intelligent, funny, and emotional observations on everyday life.

Literary Rock Star
Sedaris frequently tours the U.S. and Europe, reading his essays and short stories to sold-out concert halls. These appearances give Sedaris a chance to meet his fans and also to improve his writing. He often reads unpublished essays, revising them based on the crowd's reaction.

Family Secrets
Many of Sedaris's essays are about the people in his life. His book *Dress Your Family in Corduroy and Denim,* from which this essay was taken, contains thoughts on his family and childhood. In one essay, he writes that his family is afraid to tell him anything important for fear that their stories will end up in his next book. Most of their conversations, he says, begin with the words "You have to swear you will never repeat this." Fortunately for his readers, Sedaris doesn't make those promises.

Author Online
THINKcentral
Go to **thinkcentral.com.**
KEYWORD: HML8-741

Us and THEM

David Sedaris

When my family first moved to North Carolina, we lived in a rented house three blocks from the school where I would begin the third grade. My mother made friends with one of the neighbors, but one seemed enough for her. Within a year we would move again and, as she explained, there wasn't much point in getting too close to people we would have to say good-bye to. Our next house was less than a mile away, and the short journey would hardly **merit** tears or even good-byes, for that matter. It was more of a "see you later" situation, but still I adopted my mother's attitude, as it allowed me to pretend that not making friends was a conscious[1] choice. I could if I 10 wanted to. It just wasn't the right time. **Ⓐ**

Back in New York State, we had lived in the country, with no sidewalks or streetlights; you could leave the house and still be alone. But here, when you looked out the window, you saw other houses, and people inside those houses. I hoped that in walking around after dark I might witness a murder, but for the most part our neighbors just sat in their living rooms, watching TV. The only place that seemed truly different was owned by a man named Mr. Tomkey, who did not believe in television. This was told to us by our mother's friend, who dropped by one afternoon with a basketful of okra.[2] The woman did not editorialize[3]—rather, she just presented her information, leaving her 20 listener to make of it what she might. Had my mother said, "That's the craziest thing I've ever heard in my life," I assume that the friend would have agreed, and had she said, "Three cheers for Mr. Tomkey," the friend likely would have agreed as well. It was a kind of test, as was the okra.

---

1. **conscious:** deliberate.
2. **okra** (ōʹkrə): edible pods used in soups and as a vegetable.
3. **editorialize** (ĕdʹĭ-tôrʹē-əl-īzʹ): to give one's own opinions on a topic.

merit (mĕrʹĭt) *v.*
to deserve

Ⓐ IRONY
Reread lines 6–10. When Sedaris says he could make friends if he wanted to, what does he actually mean?

Analyze Visuals ▶

Note the colors used in this painting. Why do you think the artist chose to **contrast** the inside and outside of the house in this way?

Detail of *Outside In* (2004), Ryan Kapp. Oil on canvas on panel, 18″ × 24″. © Ryan Kapp.

To say that you did not believe in television was different from saying that you did not care for it. Belief **implied** that television had a master plan and that you were against it. It also suggested that you thought too much. When my mother reported that Mr. Tomkey did not believe in television, my father said, "Well, good for him. I don't know that I believe in it, either."

"That's exactly how I feel," my mother said, and then my parents watched
30 the news, and whatever came on after the news. **B**

Word spread that Mr. Tomkey did not own a television, and you began hearing that while this was all very well and good, it was unfair of him to **inflict** his beliefs upon others, specifically his innocent wife and children. It was speculated that just as the blind man develops a keener sense of hearing, the family must somehow compensate for their loss. "Maybe they read," my mother's friend said. "Maybe they listen to the radio, but you can bet your boots they're doing *something*."

I wanted to know what this something was, and so I began peering through the Tomkeys' windows. During the day I'd stand across the street from their
40 house, acting as though I were waiting for someone, and at night, when the view was better and I had less chance of being discovered, I would creep into their yard and hide in the bushes beside their fence.

Because they had no TV, the Tomkeys were forced to talk during dinner. They had no idea how puny their lives were, and so they were not ashamed that a camera would have found them uninteresting. They did not know what attractive was or what dinner was supposed to look like or even what time people were
50 supposed to eat. Sometimes they wouldn't sit down until eight o'clock, long after everyone else had finished doing the dishes. During the meal, Mr. Tomkey would occasionally pound the table and point at his children with a fork, but the moment he finished, everyone would start laughing. I got the idea that he was imitating someone else, and wondered if he spied on us while we were eating.

When fall arrived and school began, I saw
60 the Tomkey children marching up the hill with paper sacks in their hands. The son was one grade lower than me, and the daughter was one grade higher. We never spoke, but I'd pass them in the halls from time to time and attempt to view the world through their eyes. What must it be like to be so ignorant and alone? Could a normal person even imagine it? Staring at an

B **IRONY**
Reread lines 29–30. What's the difference between what the mother says and what she does?

Elmer Fudd[4] lunch box, I tried to divorce myself from[5] everything I already knew: Elmer's inability to pronounce the letter *r*, his constant pursuit of an
70 intelligent and considerably more famous rabbit. I tried to think of him as just a drawing, but it was impossible to separate him from his celebrity. **C**

One day in class a boy named William began to write the wrong answer on the blackboard, and our teacher flailed her arms, saying, "Warning, Will. Danger, danger." Her voice was synthetic and void of emotion, and we laughed, knowing that she was imitating the robot in a weekly show about a family who lived in outer space. The Tomkeys, though, would have thought she was having a heart attack. It occurred to me that they needed a guide, someone who could accompany them through the course of an average day and point out all the things they were unable to understand. I could have done it on weekends, but
80 friendship would have taken away their mystery and **interfered** with the good feeling I got from pitying them. So I kept my distance.[6] **D**

In early October the Tomkeys bought a boat, and everyone seemed greatly relieved, especially my mother's friend, who noted that the motor was definitely secondhand. It was reported that Mr. Tomkey's father-in-law owned a house on the lake and had invited the family to use it whenever they liked. This explained why they were gone all weekend, but it did not make their absences any easier to bear. I felt as if my favorite show had been canceled.

Halloween fell on a Saturday that year, and by the time my mother took us to the store, all the good costumes were gone. My sisters dressed as witches
90 and I went as a hobo. I'd looked forward to going in disguise to the Tomkeys' door, but they were off at the lake, and their house was dark. Before leaving, they had left a coffee can full of gumdrops on the front porch, alongside a sign reading DON'T BE GREEDY. In terms of Halloween candy, individual gumdrops were just about as low as you could get. This was evidenced by the large number of them floating in an adjacent dog bowl. It was disgusting to think that this was what a gumdrop might look like in your stomach, and it was insulting to be told not to take too much of something you didn't really want in the first place. "Who do these Tomkeys think they are?" my sister Lisa said.

100 The night after Halloween, we were sitting around watching TV when the doorbell rang. Visitors were infrequent at our house, so while my father stayed behind, my mother, sisters, and I ran downstairs in a group, opening the door to discover the entire Tomkey family on our front stoop. The parents looked as they always had, but the son and daughter were dressed in costumes—she as a ballerina and he as some kind of a rodent with terry-cloth ears and a tail made from what looked to be an extension cord. It seemed they had spent the previous evening isolated at the lake and had missed the opportunity

---

4. **Elmer Fudd** (ĕl′mər fŭd): a cartoon character who is always chasing after Bugs Bunny; Fudd mispronounces the *r* sound as *w*, as in "wascally wabbit."

5. **divorce myself from:** separate myself from.

6. **kept my distance:** kept myself emotionally distant.

C TONE
Reread lines 43–71. What words and images reveal Sedaris's attitude toward the Tomkeys?

interfere (ĭn′tər-fîr′) *v.* to create an obstacle

D EVALUATE
Do you think Sedaris is right to keep his distance? Explain.

Language Coach

Word Definitions The word *evidence* is usually used as a noun to refer to objects or information that proves something. In line 94, Sedaris uses the word as a verb to mean "demonstrated" or "proved." Reread lines 93–95. What was "evidenced" by "the large number of [gumdrops] floating in an adjacent dog bowl"?

to observe[7] Halloween. "So, well, I guess we're trick-or-treating *now,* if that's okay," Mr. Tomkey said.

110   I **attributed** their behavior to the fact that they didn't have a TV, but television didn't teach you everything. Asking for candy on Halloween was called trick-or-treating, but asking for candy on November first was called begging, and it made people uncomfortable. This was one of the things you were supposed to learn simply by being alive, and it angered me that the Tomkeys didn't understand it. **E**

"Why, of course it's not too late," my mother said. "Kids, why don't you . . . run and get . . . the candy."

"But the candy is gone," my sister Gretchen said. "You gave it away last night."

"Not *that* candy," my mother said. "The other candy. Why don't you run and
120 go get it?"

"You mean *our* candy?" Lisa said. "The candy that we *earned?*"

This was exactly what our mother was talking about, but she didn't want to say this in front of the Tomkeys. In order to spare their feelings, she wanted them to believe that we always kept a bucket of candy lying around the house, just waiting for someone to knock on the door and ask for it. "Go on, now," she said. "Hurry up."

My room was situated right off the foyer, and if the Tomkeys had looked in that direction, they could have seen my bed and the brown paper bag marked MY CANDY. KEEP OUT. I didn't want them to know how much I had, and so I
130 went into my room and shut the door behind me. Then I closed the curtains and emptied my bag onto the bed, searching for whatever was the crummiest. All my life chocolate has made me ill. I don't know if I'm allergic or what, but even the smallest amount leaves me with a blinding headache. Eventually, I learned to stay away from it, but as a child I refused to be left out. The brownies were eaten, and when the pounding began I would blame the grape juice or my mother's cigarette smoke or the tightness of my glasses—anything but the chocolate. My candy bars were poison but they were brand-name, and so I put them in pile no. 1, which definitely would not go to the Tomkeys.

Out in the hallway I could hear my mother straining for something to talk
140 about. "A boat!" she said. "That sounds marvelous. Can you just drive it right into the water?"

"Actually, we have a trailer," Mr. Tomkey said. "So what we do is back it into the lake."

"Oh, a trailer. What kind is it?"

"Well, it's a *boat* trailer," Mr. Tomkey said.

"Right, but is it wooden or, you know . . . I guess what I'm asking is what *style* trailer do you have?"

Behind my mother's words were two messages. The first and most obvious was "Yes, I am talking about boat trailers, but also I am dying." The second,
150 meant only for my sisters and me, was "If you do not immediately step forward

attribute (ə-trĭb'yo͞ot) *v.* to relate to a certain cause

E EVALUATE
Is Sedaris's reaction to the late trick-or-treaters appropriate?

---

7. **observe:** to celebrate.

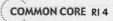

◀ Analyze Visuals

What's the first thing you notice in this photograph? Now look at the photo more carefully and tell what new **details** you see.

with that candy, you will never again experience freedom, happiness, or the possibility of my warm embrace."

I knew that it was just a matter of time before she came into my room and started collecting the candy herself, grabbing **indiscriminately,** with no regard to my rating system. Had I been thinking straight, I would have hidden the most valuable items in my dresser drawer, but instead, panicked by the thought of her hand on my doorknob, I tore off the wrappers and began cramming the candy bars into my mouth, desperately, like someone in a contest. Most were miniature, which made them easier to **accommodate,** but still there was only
160 so much room, and it was hard to chew and fit more in at the same time. The headache began immediately, and I chalked it up to[8] tension. **ⓕ**

My mother told the Tomkeys she needed to check on something, and then she opened the door and stuck her head inside my room. "What . . . are you doing?" she whispered, but my mouth was too full to answer. "I'll just be a moment," she called, and as she closed the door behind her and moved toward my bed, I began breaking the wax lips and candy necklaces pulled from pile no. 2. These were the second-best things I had received, and while it hurt to destroy them, it would have hurt even more to give them away. I had just started to mutilate a miniature box of Red Hots when my mother pried them from my hands, accidentally
170 finishing the job for me. BB-size pellets clattered onto the floor, and as I followed them with my eyes, she snatched up a roll of Necco wafers.

indiscriminately
(ĭn′dĭ-skrĭm′ə-nĭt-lē) *adv.* without making careful distinctions or choices

accommodate
(ə-kŏm′ə-dāt) *v.* to make room for

COMMON CORE RI 4

ⓕ IRONY
What did Sedaris think caused his headache? Remember, dramatic irony occurs when readers know more about a situation or character than the characters do. Tell why this is a good example of **dramatic irony**.

---

8. **chalked it up to:** identified its cause or source as.

"Not those," I pleaded, but rather than words, my mouth expelled chocolate, chewed chocolate, which fell onto the sleeve of her sweater. "Not those. Not those."

She shook her arm, and the mound of chocolate dropped . . . upon my bedspread. "You should look at yourself," she said. "I mean, *really* look at yourself." **G**

Along with the Necco wafers she took several Tootsie Pops and half a dozen caramels wrapped in cellophane. I heard her apologize to the Tomkeys for her 180 absence, and then I heard my candy hitting the bottom of their bags.

"What do you say?" Mrs. Tomkey asked.

And the children answered, "Thank you."

While I was in trouble for not bringing my candy sooner, my sisters were in more trouble for not bringing theirs at all. We spent the early part of the evening in our rooms, then one by one we eased our way back upstairs, and joined our parents in front of the TV. I was the last to arrive, and took a seat on the floor beside the sofa. The show was a Western, and even if my head had not been throbbing, I doubt I would have had the wherewithal[9] to follow it. A posse of outlaws crested a rocky hilltop, squinting at a flurry of dust 190 advancing from the horizon, and I thought again of the Tomkeys and of how alone and out of place they had looked in their dopey costumes. "What was up with that kid's tail?" I asked. ◆

"Shhhh," my family said.

For months I had protected and watched over these people, but now, with one stupid act, they had turned my pity into something hard and ugly. The shift wasn't gradual, but immediate, and it **provoked** an uncomfortable feeling of loss. We hadn't been friends, the Tomkeys and I, but still I had given them the gift of my curiosity. Wondering about the Tomkey family had made me feel generous, but now I would have to shift gears and find pleasure in hating them. 200 The only alternative was to do as my mother had instructed and take a good look at myself. This was an old trick, designed to turn one's hatred inward, and while I was determined not to fall for it, it was hard to shake the mental picture snapped[10] by her suggestion: here is a boy sitting on a bed, his mouth smeared with chocolate. He's a human being, but also he's a pig, surrounded by trash and gorging himself so that others may be denied. Were this the only image in the world, you'd be forced to give it your full attention, but fortunately there were others. This stagecoach, for instance, coming round the bend with a cargo of gold. This shiny new Mustang convertible. This teenage girl, her hair a beatiful mane, sipping Pepsi through a straw, one picture after another, on and on until 210 the news, and whatever came on after the news. ◐ **H**

G EVALUATE
What positive or negative qualities is Sedaris displaying?

◆ GRAMMAR IN CONTEXT
In lines 183–184, Sedaris uses a complex sentence to express how much more trouble his sisters were in than he was.

provoke (prə-vōk′) *v.*
to cause; to bring up

H IRONY
Reread lines 198–210. Why is it ironic for Sedaris to say he felt generous toward the Tomkeys?

---

9. **wherewithal** (wâr′wǐth-ôl′): ability.

10. **mental picture snapped:** an imagined picture brought quickly to mind, like a snapshot, a quickly taken photograph.

Comprehension

1. **Recall** Why did the young Sedaris begin spying on the Tomkeys?

2. **Recall** Why were the Tomkeys unable to trick-or-treat on Halloween?

3. **Clarify** Why did Mrs. Sedaris want to give her children's candy to the Tomkey children?

COMMON CORE

RI 4 Analyze the impact of specific word choices on meaning and tone. **L 5a** Interpret figures of speech (e.g. verbal irony) in context.

Text Analysis

4. **Identify Judgments** The young Sedaris had strong opinions about many things that the Tomkeys did or said. Look through the essay and find at least three places where he makes a positive or negative statement about the family. What do you learn about Sedaris from the judgments he makes? Is his behavior toward the Tomkeys fair? Explain your answer using examples from the selection.

5. **Analyze Irony** This essay was written by an adult looking back on his childhood. Review the chart you made while reading. Which examples of irony show that Sedaris is making fun of himself and his family? Explain.

6. **Draw Conclusions** Reread lines 164–168. Why is it so difficult for Sedaris to share his candy with the Tomkeys? What might have happened if he had chosen to share?

7. **Evaluate Attitudes** Review the passages in which Sedaris mentions television. What are the good and bad things about the role it plays in his and his family's lives? Note them on a scale like the one shown. Then explain whether you think there's anything wrong with the way the Sedarises use TV.

```
3. _____        3. _____
2. _____        2. _____
1. _____        1. _____
```

Good   Bad

Extension and Challenge

8. **Readers' Circle** Comedian Joe Ancis once said, "The only normal people are the ones you don't know very well." Do you think that Sedaris would agree with this quote? Do you agree? Share your conclusions with the class.

What's really **NORMAL?**

Do you think your notion of what's normal might change as you grow up? Why or why not?

Vocabulary in Context

▲ **VOCABULARY PRACTICE**

Show that you understand the meaning of each boldfaced word by deciding *true* or *false* for each statement.

1. A small car can easily **accommodate** six passengers.
2. Moving away can **provoke** homesickness.
3. Winning a competition does not **merit** congratulations.
4. If someone looks tired, we might **attribute** this to lack of sleep.
5. To **imply** that someone is wrong means to tell that person, "You are wrong."
6. Work experience and confidence usually **interfere** with a successful job search.
7. Someone who buys shoes **indiscriminately** may not try them on first.
8. If you **inflict** your views on others, you are forcing people to listen to you.

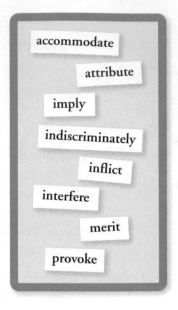

accommodate

attribute

imply

indiscriminately

inflict

interfere

merit

provoke

ACADEMIC VOCABULARY IN WRITING

• achieve • income • individual • strategy • trend

Imagine a future **trend** in fashion or lifestyle. Then write a paragraph to explain why this new trend should become the standard way most people should dress or live. Use at least one Academic Vocabulary word in your explanation.

VOCABULARY STRATEGY: FOREIGN WORDS IN ENGLISH

When you encounter something new, you probably ask what it's called. Then you use the word you've been given to refer to the item. English speakers have done that for centuries as they have encountered new foods, clothing styles, and other items from foreign cultures. As a result, English now includes many words that were once foreign. For example, *silk* and *tea* were originally Chinese; *kangaroo* and *koala* were Australian Aboriginal words; and *cookies*, *skates*, and *sleds* came from the Dutch language. The English use the term *cliché* to identify overused phrases, but the French came up with it. Similarly, *zero* and *algebra* were originally Arabic.

PRACTICE Use your knowledge of other cultures and the options provided in parentheses to figure out the origins of the boldfaced words. If you need help, you can look up the words in a dictionary.

1. If the curry is too spicy, have some **yogurt** with it. (Indian, German)
2. **Chimpanzees** always make me laugh. (French, African)
3. The **delicatessen** serves huge sandwiches and delicious strudel. (Greek, German)
4. This soft **cashmere** shawl always keeps me warm. (Greek, Indian)
5. The **bizarre** new fashions cost a fortune. (French, Arabic)

Interactive Vocabulary

THINK central

Go to **thinkcentral.com**.
KEYWORD: HML8-750

Language

◆ **GRAMMAR IN CONTEXT:** Form Complex Sentences

A **complex sentence** contains one main clause and one or more subordinate clauses. A **main clause** can stand alone as a sentence. A **subordinate clause** is a group of words that contains a subject and a verb but cannot stand alone as a sentence. Subordinate clauses begin with subordinating conjunctions such as *after, because, even though, since, until, where,* and *who.* By adding one of these words or phrases to a main clause, you make it subordinate. The subordinate clause can then be combined with a main clause to form a complex sentence.

> *Original:* We don't own a television. My family still has fun together.
>
> *Revised:* Even though we don't own a television, my family still has fun together. (*This is now one complex sentence.*)

PRACTICE In each item, change one main clause to a subordinate clause. Then combine the clauses to form a complex sentence.

1. My family doesn't have a TV. We spend more time talking to each other.
2. We also spend time at the lake house. My brother catches a lot of fish.
3. Sometimes I wish we had a TV. The kids at school make fun of us.
4. We moved to this neighborhood last year. I've made a few friends.

For more help with subordinate clauses and complex sentences, see page R64 in the Grammar Handbook.

READING-WRITING CONNECTION

YOUR TURN

Continue exploring "Us and Them" by responding to the prompt. Then use the **revising tip** to improve your writing.

WRITING PROMPT	REVISING TIP
Short Constructed Response: Journal Entry Sedaris often wondered what life must have been like for the Tomkeys. What did they do since they didn't watch TV? Write a **one-paragraph journal entry** from the perspective of one of the Tomkey children, describing a normal day in your household.	Review your journal entry to find sentences that you might combine into complex sentences by adding a subordinating conjunction to one of the main clauses.

COMMON CORE

L1 Demonstrate command of grammar and usage when writing. **L3** Use knowledge of language when writing.

Interactive Revision **THINK** central

Go to **thinkcentral.com**.
KEYWORD: HML8-751

O Captain! My Captain!

HISTORY · Video link at thinkcentral.com

I Saw Old General at Bay

Poems by Walt Whitman

What is the COST of victory?

Triumph often comes with consequences. For example, the Union victory in the Civil War preserved the United States and ended slavery, but these outcomes came at a cost. Almost 700,000 people died, countless others suffered, and enormous amounts of property were destroyed. In the two poems you are about to read, Walt Whitman reflects on the great cost of victory in the Civil War.

QUICKWRITE Wars are not the only events in which winning takes a toll. We all have had personal victories that cost us in one way or another. For example, suppose you and your best friend have an argument over an issue that is very important to both of you. You might win the argument, but lose your friend in the process. In your journal, write about a time in your life when victory had a price. Was what you won worth the cost? Explain.

TEXT ANALYSIS: STYLE IN POETRY

Walt Whitman is known for his uniquely American **style,** or way of using language to express ideas. One thing that makes Whitman's style stand out is his unconventional use of language. He often didn't follow traditional rules of line length and rhyme as other poets of his time did. In addition, Whitman often wrote about politics and current events, topics the poets who came before him tended to avoid. The following elements are also part of Whitman's style:

- strong **imagery,** or words and phrases that appeal to the reader's five senses
- **repetition** of a sound, word, phrase, or line for emphasis
- **irony,** or a contrast between what is expected and what actually happens

As you read "O Captain! My Captain!" and "I Saw Old General at Bay," use a chart like the one shown to help you identify these elements of the legendary poet's style.

	"O Captain! My Captain!"	"I Saw Old General at Bay"
Imagery		
Repetition		
Irony		

READING SKILL: UNDERSTAND HISTORICAL CONTEXT

As with other works of literature, Whitman's poems become easier to understand once you know their **historical context,** the real events and people that influenced them. In "O Captain! My Captain!" Whitman uses an extended metaphor that you can only understand if you are aware of the poem's historical context. An **extended metaphor** is a comparison of two seemingly unlike things that develops, or extends, throughout several lines or stanzas, or an entire poem. Whitman wrote "O Captain! My Captain!" and "I Saw Old General at Bay" as a way of expressing his thoughts and feelings about the Civil War. Before you begin the two poems, read the **Background to the Poems** on this page. Then use the information to identify the extended metaphor in "O Captain! My Captain!"

 Complete the activities in your **Reader/Writer Notebook.**

Meet the Author

Walt Whitman
1819–1892

An American Voice
Poet Walt Whitman is considered one of America's most beloved and original writers. The poems in his collection *Leaves of Grass* were the first to be written in free verse, which means they did not contain regular patterns of rhythm and rhyme. Whitman's poetry was praised by a few critics in his lifetime, but many others did not like it. As a result, his work did not become popular until after his death.

BACKGROUND TO THE POEMS
The "Good Gray Poet"
When his brother George, a Union soldier, was injured in battle in 1862, Whitman went to Virginia to care for him. Whitman was moved by the sight of the injured soldiers and decided to stay in Washington, D.C., volunteering in army hospitals. Friends often referred to Whitman as the "Good Gray Poet" because of his charity toward the troops.

A Poet in Mourning
On April 14, 1865, only five days after the end of the Civil War, President Abraham Lincoln was assassinated because of his antislavery beliefs. Whitman was a great admirer of Lincoln's. He wrote "O Captain! My Captain!" to capture the sense of tragedy that overwhelmed the nation upon Lincoln's death. The poem "I Saw Old General at Bay" was published in a collection called *Drum Taps,* which included many poems expressing Whitman's feelings about the war.

Author Online THiNK central
Go to **thinkcentral.com.**
KEYWORD: HML8-753

753

O Captain! My Captain!

Walt Whitman

O Captain! my Captain! our fearful trip is done,
The ship has weather'd every rack,[1] the prize we sought[2] is won, **A**

The port is near, the bells I hear, the people all exulting,
While follow eyes the steady keel,[3] the vessel grim and daring:
5 But O heart! heart! heart!
   O the bleeding drops of red,
    Where on the deck my Captain lies,
     Fallen cold and dead. **B**

O Captain! my Captain! rise up and hear the bells;
10 Rise up—for you the flag is flung[4]—for you the bugle trills,
For you bouquets and ribbon'd wreaths—for you the shores
  a-crowding,
For you they call, the swaying mass, their eager faces turning;
  Here Captain! dear father!
15   This arm beneath your head!
    It is some dream that on the deck,
     You've fallen cold and dead. **C**

My Captain does not answer, his lips are pale and still,
My father does not feel my arm, he has no pulse nor will,
20 The ship is anchor'd safe and sound, its voyage closed and done,
From fearful trip the victor ship comes in with object won;
  Exult O shores, and ring O bells!
   But I with mournful tread,[5]
    Walk the deck my Captain lies,
25   Fallen cold and dead.

---

1. **rack:** a mass of wind-driven clouds.
2. **sought** (sôt): searched for; tried to gain.
3. **keel:** the main part of a ship's structure.
4. **flung:** suddenly put out.
5. **tread** (trĕd): footsteps.

A HISTORICAL CONTEXT
Given what you read in the Background on page 753, who do you think is the captain, and what is his ship?

B STYLE IN POETRY
Reread lines 1–8. In what way does the description of the rejoicing crowds help emphasize the tragedy and **irony** of the captain's death?

C STYLE IN POETRY
Reread lines 9–16. What **imagery** does Whitman use to convey the people's adoration of their leader? Add these images to your chart.

Analyze Visuals ▶
What words would you use to describe the **mood** of this painting?

Lincoln 2, Wendy Allen. Oil on canvas. © Wendy Allen.

I Saw Old General at Bay

Walt Whitman

I saw old General at bay,
(Old as he was, his gray eyes yet shone out in battle like stars,) **D**
His small force was now completely hemm'd[1] in, in his works,
He call'd for volunteers to run the enemy's lines, a desperate
    emergency,
5 I saw a hundred and more step forth from the ranks, but two
    or three were selected,
I saw them receive their orders aside, they listen'd with care,
    the adjutant[2] was very grave,
I saw them depart with cheerfulness, freely risking their lives. **E**

---

1. **hemm'd:** hemmed; surrounded or enclosed.

2. **adjutant** (ăj'ə-tənt): a staff officer who helps a commanding officer with administrative affairs.

D STYLE IN POETRY
Reread line 2. What descriptive words and details help you understand what the general looks like?

E HISTORICAL CONTEXT
Reread the last line. Which of Whitman's experiences best helps you interpret it?

Detail of *Major General John Sedgwick Monument,* Wendy Allen. Oil on canvas, 40″ × 30″. © Wendy Allen.

Comprehension

1. **Recall** What does the speaker of "O Captain! My Captain!" see on the deck of the ship?

2. **Clarify** What "desperate emergency" did the old general face?

3. **Clarify** For what did the general need volunteers?

Text Analysis

4. **Apply Historical Context.** How does knowing about Whitman's life and times help you identify the extended metaphor in "O Captain! My Captain!"? Create a chart to list the elements of the metaphor and what each element represents.

Element	What It Represents
captain	President Lincoln
fearful trip	
ship	
prize	
storm	
arrival of the ship at port	

5. **Make Inferences** Reread the last line of "I Saw Old General at Bay." What do the volunteers' attitudes say about the general?

6. **Understand Elegy** An **elegy** is a poem that is typically written for the purpose of paying tribute to a person who has died recently or to share reflections upon an equally serious subject. Most elegies possess the following characteristics: they are long, thoughtful, and solemn in tone. Of the two poems you just read, which best fits this description? Support your answer with examples from the poem. Then, speculate on why a poem with this purpose might have such characteristics.

7. **Analyze Style** Review the chart you made while reading. Note the places Whitman uses imagery, repetition, and **irony.** How do these elements emphasize both the cost of the war and the greatness of those who led the Union to victory?

Extension and Challenge

8. **SOCIAL STUDIES CONNECTION** Find out more about the Civil War. Create a poster showing the causes, benefits, and cost of the war.

What is the **COST** of victory?

Look back at the Big Question activity you did at the start of this lesson. Then write a journal entry about another time when winning cost you something. If you'd like, you can write your entry as an elegy or another type of poem.

COMMON CORE

RL 2 Determine a central idea of a text and analyze its development over the course of the text. **RL 4** Analyze the impact of specific word choices on meaning and tone. **RL 5** Analyze how the structure of [a] text contributes to its meaning and style.

Writing Workshop
INFORMATIVE TEXT

Literary Analysis

In this unit, you looked closely at style, voice, and other literary elements that make writing distinctive. In this workshop, you will examine literary elements that make a particular text meaningful or enjoyable for you. You'll share your perspective on the text with other readers by writing a literary analysis.

 Complete the workshop activities in your **Reader/Writer Notebook**.

WRITE WITH A PURPOSE

WRITING TASK

Write a **literary analysis** in which you analyze a literary text that you have enjoyed. Assume that your audience includes people who have and have not read the text.

Idea Starters
- a selection from this unit or others in the textbook
- a favorite novel, short story, or play
- a classic fairy tale, fable, or myth
- a children's story
- a biography or an autobiography

THE ESSENTIALS

Here are some common purposes, audiences, and formats for literary analyses.

PURPOSES	AUDIENCES	FORMATS
• to provide information about a literary text • to share an in-depth analysis of a literary text	• classmates and teacher • newspaper readers • readers of a literary magazine • Web users	• essay for class • review for a newspaper or magazine • study guide • oral presentation • blog posting

COMMON CORE TRAITS

1. DEVELOPMENT OF IDEAS
- presents an **engaging introduction** that identifies the title and author of the literary text
- develops a **controlling idea** that offers an **analysis** of one or two literary elements
- supports main points of analysis with **relevant concrete details** and **quotations** from the text
- provides a **concluding section** that supports the analysis

2. ORGANIZATION OF IDEAS
- **organizes** ideas in a logical way
- uses **appropriate transitions** to create cohesion and clarify relationships among ideas

3. LANGUAGE FACILITY AND CONVENTIONS
- establishes and maintains a **formal style**
- includes **precise language** to explain the analysis
- varies **sentence structure**
- employs correct **grammar**, **capitalization**, and **spelling**

Writing Online
THINK central
Go to **thinkcentral.com**.
KEYWORD: HML8N-758

Planning/Prewriting

 COMMON CORE **W 2a–f** Write informative/explanatory texts to examine a topic through the selection, organization, and analysis of relevant content. **W 5** Develop and strengthen writing by planning.

Getting Started

CHOOSE A LITERARY TEXT

Which literary text will you write about? Skim through your textbook's table of contents, use the Idea Starters on page 758, or meet with a partner to discuss possibilities. Make a list, and then circle the selections you know the best. Place a star next to the circled choice that you feel most strongly about.

▶ **WHAT DOES IT LOOK LIKE?**

Possible subjects

("The Lady, or the Tiger?" by Frank Stockton)

"Us and Them" by David Sedaris

The Diary of Anne Frank by Frances Goodrich and Albert Hackett

(*A Year Down Under* by Richard Peck)

(*Roughing It* by Mark Twain)*

NOTE YOUR RESPONSES

After choosing a text, think about your overall reaction to it. Then consider the literary elements —such as characters, style, point of view, theme, or plot— that make the text especially interesting or memorable.

▶ **ASK YOURSELF:**

- How did I react when I read this text? Did I laugh, cry, or have some other reaction?
- How did the text surprise me?
- Which literary elements made this text unique—for example, characters, style, point of view, theme, or plot?
- Why might this text interest my audience?

THINK ABOUT AUDIENCE AND PURPOSE

Before you begin writing, think about who will be reading your response and what they will need to know. Also, identify your **purpose** for writing and how you want your writing to affect your **audience.**

▶ **ASK YOURSELF:**

- Who is my audience? What do I want them to know about this literary text?
- What **domain-specific,** or specialized, **vocabulary** will my audience need to know to understand my analysis?
- What examples from the text can I use to help my audience better comprehend the literary text and my analysis?

DEVELOP A CONTROLLING IDEA

Write a **controlling idea,** or thesis statement, that tells what your essay is about. Your controlling idea should name one or two important literary elements in the text. Developing a controlling idea will help you organize your writing, even if you decide later to try a different approach.

▶ **WHAT DOES IT LOOK LIKE?**

Controlling Idea: Twain exaggerates a lot and uses irony to describe what happened to him, and that makes his memoir a funny story.

Planning/Prewriting *continued*

Getting Started

GATHER EVIDENCE

For each literary element you plan to discuss, you need to provide **relevant facts, concrete details, quotations,** and other examples from the text. Gather this evidence in a chart before you begin drafting your analysis.

▶ **WHAT DOES IT LOOK LIKE?**

Literary Element	Example from Text
irony	says customers "bothered" him in the bookstore; they interrupted his reading
exaggeration	says he was known in the printing business for taking almost a year to set one batch of type

CREATE A WRITING PLAN

Your essay should include several paragraphs organized into an introduction, a body, and a concluding section. Sketch out a plan that includes all of these parts to keep yourself on track as you draft your analysis.

- **Introduction:** Start with an engaging opening, such as an interesting quotation or question. Make sure to identify the type of text you are discussing, the title, and the author. State your controlling idea about the work.
- **Body:** Note your analyses and judgments. Back up your opinions by using well-chosen examples from the text and short quotations.
- **Concluding section:** Restate your controlling idea, but use different words than you did in your introduction. Explain to your readers why you think the literary text is worth reading.

▶ **WHAT DOES IT LOOK LIKE?**

Introduction

Engaging opening: "I let fancy get the upper hand of fact too often."

Work: <u>Roughing It</u> by Mark Twain (memoir)

Controlling idea: Using irony and exaggeration, Twain describes his work experiences in a funny way.

Body

Examples of irony: lost job in a bookstore because the customers disturbed his reading; made customers sick while working in a drug store

Examples of exaggeration: could take up to a year to set one batch of type; described one hay wagon as if it were sixteen

Conclusion

Restatement of controlling idea: mention irony, exaggeration, and humor again

Why work is worthwhile: not only funny but also teaches a lesson about not giving up

PEER REVIEW Share your writing plan with a partner who has also read the literary text. Then ask: Have I provided enough evidence for my controlling idea? What other examples would help convince readers that my analysis is valid?

 YOUR TURN In your *Reader/Writer Notebook*, brainstorm a list of texts that might make a good topic, and then select the one that you feel most strongly about. Develop a controlling idea and gather evidence. Then develop an outline for your introduction, body, and concluding section.

Drafting

COMMON CORE **W 4** Produce clear and coherent writing. **W 9b (RI 1)** Cite textual evidence that most strongly supports an analysis. **L1** Demonstrate command of English grammar and usage.

The following chart shows how to organize a clear and effective literary analysis.

Organizing a Literary Analysis

INTRODUCTION

- Begin with an engaging opening. A **quotation** or a **question** can draw readers in.
- Identify the **title** and **author** of the text as well as its genre.
- Provide a **controlling idea** that states the literary element(s) you will discuss.
- Provide necessary **background information** for readers not familiar with the work.

▼

BODY

- Include **relevant facts, concrete details, quotations,** and other **examples** to support each key point. If necessary, define any **domain-specific vocabulary**.
- Organize your essay in a **logical sequence** and use **transitions** to create cohesion. For example, if the work is a narrative, you might use phrases such as *when the story begins* and *later in the story*.
- Maintain a **formal style** by avoiding contractions and using unbiased, clear language.

▼

CONCLUDING SECTION

- Restate your **controlling idea,** but not in the same words you used in the introduction.
- Explain to your audience why the text is meaningful and worth reading.

GRAMMAR IN CONTEXT: PRONOUNS AND ANTECEDENTS

Whenever you use a **pronoun** (such as *he, she, they,* or *it*), make sure that its antecedent is clear. The **antecedent** is the noun (person, place, or thing) that the pronoun refers to.

Unclear antecedent for "They" (Were the prescriptions unlucky, or the customers?)	▶ *At the drug store, Twain made prescriptions for many customers.* **They** *were unlucky.*
Clear antecedent (The prescriptions were unlucky because they made customers sick.)	▶ *At the drug store, Twain made* **prescriptions.** **They** *were unlucky and made many customers sick.*

 YOUR TURN

Develop a draft of your analysis by following the plan outlined above.
Include examples and quotations from the text to support your analysis.
Check to be sure that all of your pronouns have clear antecedents.

Revising

When you revise, you evaluate the content, organization, and style of your literary analysis. The questions, tips, and strategies in the following chart can help you revise, rewrite, and improve your draft. They can also help you identify when it might be necessary to consider a different approach.

LITERARY ANALYSIS

Ask Yourself	Tips	Revision Strategies
1. Does the introduction identify the title and author? Is there a strong controlling idea?	▶ **Circle** the title and the author's name. **Underline** the controlling idea.	▶ **Double-check** the correct spelling of the author's name and the title of the work. **Add** a controlling idea.
2. Have I included necessary background information?	▶ **Highlight** details that provide background information about the text.	▶ **Add** details about the selection that will help the audience understand the writer's analysis.
3. Do transitional words and phrases create cohesion and clarify relationships among ideas?	▶ **Put a star** next to each appropriate transitional word or phrase.	▶ **Skim** the essay to find places where new ideas are introduced. **Add** transitions to show how each idea fits in with the rest of the essay.
4. Do I maintain a formal style?	▶ **Bracket** contractions, casual slang, or informal language.	▶ **Reword** contractions and **replace** informal language with precise, formal vocabulary.
5. Is the analysis supported by relevant facts, concrete details, quotations, and other examples?	▶ **Draw wavy lines** under examples from the text that support key points and the controlling idea.	▶ **Add** examples from the text to support your analysis.
6. Does the essay end with a satisfying concluding section?	▶ **Draw a box** around the conclusion.	▶ **Expand** upon the controlling idea. **Explain** why the work is recommended to other readers.

YOUR TURN

PEER REVIEW Use these suggestions as you revise with a partner:

- Direct your partner's attention to sections of your draft that you think might need clarification. Discuss what you might add.
- Ask your partner to identify places where it would be helpful to say more about a key point or to add more examples.
- Discuss the questions above, and identify areas where you might try a new approach.

ANALYZE A STUDENT DRAFT

Read this student's draft and the comments about it as a model for revising your own literary analysis.

COMMON CORE

W 2b Develop the topic with relevant examples. **W 5** Strengthen writing by revising, editing, rewriting, or trying a new approach. **W 9b (RI 1)** Cite textual evidence that supports analysis.

Fancy Is Funnier Than Fact

by Ramón Cepero, Oxford Charter School

1   "I let fancy get the upper hand of fact too often," Mark Twain explains in *Roughing It*. What he means is that he likes to tell a few tall tales. He also likes to skip over or change some of the facts, which makes his writing style surprising and funny. The excerpt from his memoir *Roughing It* tells of a period in his life when he was struggling to find a job that he could do well. In this work, Twain uses irony and exaggeration to create a humorous view of a time when he was "down and out."

2   The beginning of the excerpt lists the jobs Twain has already tried and lost. Each failure is funny because he uses irony to describe what happened. He worked in a bookstore. He says he spent all his time there reading. He also was a clerk in a drug store. That didn't work out very well for the customers who got sick.

> Ramón interests his audience by starting with a **quotation**.

> Ramón ends his introduction with a strong **controlling idea**.

> Ramón's first **key point** is about Twain's use of irony. He needs to support it with relevant concrete details, quotations, and other examples.

LEARN HOW Support Key Points In his second paragraph, Ramón says that Twain uses irony to describe his failures in a humorous way. However, he gives no specific examples to support this idea. His audience—especially those who have not read Twain's memoir—may not understand his meaning. When Ramón revised this paragraph, he inserted specific details and direct quotations to support his point.

RAMÓN'S REVISION TO PARAGRAPH ❷

The beginning of the excerpt lists the jobs Twain has already tried and lost. Each failure is funny because he uses irony to describe what happened.

For instance,

, not selling, the books. He adds that the customers "bothered" him so that he "could not read with any comfort."

He worked in a bookstore. He says he spent all his time there reading.

He also was a clerk in a drug store. ~~That didn't work out very well for the customers who got sick.~~

He says that his "prescriptions were unlucky." He says that "we appeared to sell more stomach pumps than soda-water." Obviously, his cures made the customers sicker than they already were.

❸   Another of Twain's job failures was in the printing business. He uses exaggeration to describe just how slow a typesetter he was. He claims that whenever he began setting a batch of type, his bosses would remind him that "it would be wanted 'some time during the year.'" Later in the memoir, Twain uses exaggeration to describe how he kept his job as a reporter. He says that even though only one hay-wagon arrived in the city, he "multiplied [it] by sixteen, brought it into town from sixteen different directions, made sixteen separate items of it, and got up such another sweat about hay as Virginia City had never seen in the world before."

❹   Twain turns his experiences with work into a humorous narrative about failing at jobs, getting fired, inventing "news," and finally finding a "legitimate occupation" as a writer. He uses irony and exaggeration to entertain his readers.

> Ramón's use of quotations and examples supports his **analysis** and shows his **understanding** of the text.

> To make his **concluding section** stronger, Ramón needs to show the significance of the ideas he has presented.

LEARN HOW **Write an Effective Concluding Section** A good concluding section shows the audience why the ideas presented in the essay are important. When Ramón returned to his last paragraph, he realized that he needed to explain why Twain's narrative was more than just a fun read.

RAMÓN'S REVISION TO PARAGRAPH ❹

     Twain turns his experiences with work into a humorous narrative about failing at jobs, getting fired, inventing "news," and finally finding a "legitimate occupation" as a writer. He uses irony and exaggeration to ~~entertain his readers.~~

transform a difficult time in his life into a story that is not only entertaining but also a valuable lesson for readers. Twain shows us that we should never give up or become too discouraged by failure. Having a sense of humor gives us the strength to keep going until better days come along.

YOUR TURN   Use feedback from your peers and your teacher as well as the two "Learn How" lessons to revise your essay. Evaluate how well you have conveyed your analysis and your evaluation of the literary work to your audience.

W 5 Strengthen writing by revising and editing. **L 3** Use knowledge of language and its conventions when writing.

Editing and Publishing

In the editing stage, you proofread your literary analysis to make sure it is free of grammar, usage, spelling, and punctuation errors. You don't want mistakes to distract readers from your analysis.

GRAMMAR IN CONTEXT: SENTENCE VARIETY

Be careful not to use the same sentence structure over and over again. Varying the way you start your sentences can help keep your audience interested. As Ramón reviewed his first draft and the revisions he had already made, he noticed that in the second paragraph, he began several sentences in a similar way. To fix this situation, he rephrased his first sentence and combined the other two.

> *As*
> ~~He also was~~ a clerk in a drug store~~. He says that~~ his "prescriptions were *, he was equally unsuccessful.*
> unlucky." ~~He says that "we~~ *and the store "* appeared to sell more stomach pumps than
> soda-water."

PUBLISH YOUR WRITING

Share your literary analysis with an audience.

- Submit your essay to your school newspaper.
- E-mail your essay to a friend who you think would enjoy the literary text that you wrote about.
- Develop your literary analysis into an oral presentation that you deliver to your audience.
- Post your work on your personal Web page or submit it to an online journal.

YOUR TURN Correct any errors in your essay by carefully proofreading it. Check to see if you have too many sentences in a row with the same structure. If so, add introductory phrases or rearrange word order to make your sentence structures more varied. Then publish your final essay where it is most likely to reach your audience.

Scoring Rubric

Use the rubric below to evaluate your literary analysis from the Writing Workshop or your response to the on-demand writing task on the next page.

LITERARY ANALYSIS

SCORE	COMMON CORE TRAITS
6	• **Development** Has an engaging introduction; includes a controlling idea with an insightful analysis of elements of a literary text; supports main points with relevant evidence; ends powerfully • **Organization** Arranges ideas in an effective, logical order; uses appropriate transitions to create cohesion and link ideas • **Language** Consistently maintains a formal style; uses precise language; shows a strong command of conventions
5	• **Development** Has an effective introduction; provides a controlling idea that offers an original analysis; supports main points with evidence; has a strong concluding section • **Organization** Arranges ideas logically; uses appropriate transitions to link ideas • **Language** Maintains a formal style; uses precise language; has a few errors in conventions
4	• **Development** Has an introduction that could be more engaging; includes a controlling idea that states an analysis of literary elements; could use some more evidence; has an adequate concluding section • **Organization** Arranges ideas logically; could vary transitions more • **Language** Mostly maintains a formal style; needs more precise language at times; has a few distracting errors in conventions
3	• **Development** Has an adequate, though not memorable, introduction; has a controlling idea that makes an obvious statement about literary elements; lacks enough support; has an ordinary concluding section • **Organization** Has some flaws in organization; needs more transitions to link ideas • **Language** Often lapses into an informal style; has some major errors in conventions
2	• **Development** Has a weak introduction and a controlling idea that does not relate to the task; lacks specific, relevant evidence; has a weak concluding section • **Organization** Has organizational flaws; lacks transitions throughout • **Language** Uses an informal style and vague words; has many errors in conventions
1	• **Development** Has no introduction or controlling idea; lacks support; ends abruptly • **Organization** Has no organization or transitions • **Language** Uses an inappropriate style and vague words; has major problems with grammar, mechanics, and spelling

Preparing for Timed Writing

COMMON CORE

W 10 Write routinely over shorter time frames for a range of tasks, purposes, and audiences.

1. ANALYZE THE TASK   5 MIN

Read the task carefully. Then read it again, underlining the words that tell the type of writing, the topic, and the purpose. Circle the audience.

> **WRITING TASK**   *Type of writing*   *Topic*
>
> Write a <u>literary analysis</u> in which you <u>analyze a book or literary selection</u> that you know well. Your response should <u>encourage</u> (other students in your class) to either <u>read</u>
> <u>or not read the text</u>. Use details from the text to support your ideas.   ↖*Purpose*
>
>   *Audience*

2. PLAN YOUR RESPONSE   10 MIN

First, think of some books, stories, or poems that you have read recently. Then choose the piece of literature that you know best. Once you have settled on your subject, list some of the key points you want to make about it. For each point, record evidence from the text that supports it.

Key Points	Evidence

3. RESPOND TO THE TASK   20 MIN

Using the notes you have just made, draft your analysis. It may help to follow these guidelines:

- In the introduction, get your readers' attention with an engaging opening. Provide the title, the author, and the genre (such as short story or poem); a brief description of what the work is about; and a clear controlling idea.
- In the body of your response, use examples and short quotations from the work to support your analysis.
- In the conclusion, tell readers whether you recommend the text and why.

4. IMPROVE YOUR RESPONSE   5–10 MIN

Revising Review your essay to make sure you've done everything the writing task asks. Did you identify the work? Do you have a clear controlling idea? Did you provide evidence to support your key points?

Proofreading Take a few minutes to correct errors in grammar, mechanics, and spelling. Make sure all your edits are neat, and erase any stray marks.

Checking Your Final Copy Before you turn in your response, read it one more time to catch any errors you may have missed.

Presenting a Response to Literature

Throughout life, people will ask for your opinions on various subjects—such as a musician's latest album or a new business strategy at work. When you present an oral response to literature, you share your opinion of a literary text with listeners.

 Complete the workshop activities in your **Reader/Writer Notebook**.

SPEAK WITH A PURPOSE	COMMON CORE TRAITS
TASK Adapt your literary analysis into an **oral response.** After you have rehearsed it, present it to your class.	**A STRONG ORAL RESPONSE . . .** • offers a clear analysis of the literary text • organizes key points and relevant evidence in a way that is easy to follow • explains how the text affects its audience • uses formal English to deliver the message • uses effective verbal and nonverbal techniques to engage the audience

COMMON CORE

SL 4 Present claims and findings, emphasizing salient points in a focused, coherent manner; use eye contact, adequate volume, and clear pronunciation. **SL 6** Adapt speech, demonstrating command of formal English when appropriate.

Adapt Your Literary Analysis

Remember that your audience will be listening to your literary analysis instead of reading it. Your presentation needs to be especially clear, because your listeners can't go back and reread something if they feel confused. Keep these ideas in mind as you adapt your essay for oral presentation:

• **Audience** Use correct formal English, and avoid words that may be unfamiliar to your audience—your classmates. Since this is a formal speech, make sure you maintain the formal tone you used in your essay.

• **Introduction** Grab your audience's attention from the start. For example, you might share an **anecdote** (a brief story) that captures what you like most about the literary text. Then introduce the text by title and author, and preview your main points. State your controlling idea clearly.

• **Evidence** Support your controlling idea with relevant, well-chosen evidence from the text. Write key points and evidence on note cards to help you present your analysis in a focused, coherent way.

• **Literary Elements** Describe literary elements that the author uses especially well (or not so well). Use direct quotations to support your most salient, or important, points.

• **Concluding Section** Restate your controlling idea and expand upon it with additional insights. Tell your audience how you believe this text will affect them as readers.

Speaking & Listening Online

THINK central

Go to **thinkcentral.com**. KEYWORD: HML8-768

Deliver Your Speech

USE VERBAL TECHNIQUES

As you are speaking, you want to make sure that your audience stays engaged and interested in your presentation. These verbal techniques can help you use your voice effectively:

- **Enunciation** Say your words clearly and distinctly so that all your listeners can understand what you are saying.

- **Tempo, or Speaking Rate** If you're nervous about speaking in front of an audience, you might start talking too fast, and your audience will have trouble understanding you. Be sure to practice delivering your response at a natural and unhurried rate. You may want to vary your tempo occasionally to keep your audience engaged.

- **Volume** Speak loudly enough that your voice reaches the back of the room. Add emphasis to important parts of your speech with greater volume.

USE NONVERBAL TECHNIQUES

These nonverbal techniques will also enhance your presentation:

- **Gestures** Use natural hand and arm movements that match what you are saying.

- **Expressions** Use facial expressions (raised eyebrows, grimaces, smiles) that help illustrate and emphasize your points.

- **Eye Contact** Be sure to make eye contact with your audience. Try to let your eyes rest on each member of the audience at least once.

- **Posture** Stand up tall, but try not to look stiff or awkward. If you are relaxed, your audience will be, too.

As a Speaker Deliver your response to a partner, making sure to incorporate the techniques described on this page. Use your partner's feedback to rework your presentation as necessary.

As a Listener Listen carefully to your partner's oral response to assess how clearly the ideas are organized and presented. Note whether your partner's verbal and nonverbal techniques enhance the presentation and are effective for the audience and purpose.

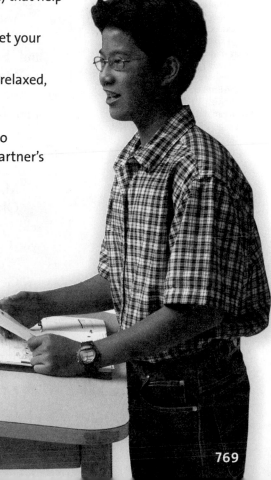

Assessment Practice

DIRECTIONS Read the two selections and the viewing and representing piece. Then answer the questions that follow.

Sam Levenson's narrative is based on his childhood in New York City in the 1920s.

A Hike in New York City

by Sam Levenson

1   At least once each summer we kids went off on a hike, but never without strong opposition from Mama. When it came to the open road, Mama had a closed mind.

2   Her method of discouraging us from venturing into the unknown was to make the entire project appear ridiculous:

3   "You're going on what?"

4   "We're going on a hike."

5   "What's a hike?" Mama would ask.

6   When we started to explain it, the whole idea did in fact become ridiculous.

7   "We go walking, Ma."

8   "Walking? For that you have to leave home? What's the matter with walking right here? You walk; I'll watch."

9   "You don't understand, Ma. We take lunch along."

10   "I'll give you lunch here, and you can march right around the table," and she would start singing a march, clapping her hands rhythmically.

11   "Ma, we climb mountains in the woods."

12   She couldn't understand why it was so much more enjoyable to fall off a mountain than off a fire escape.

13   "And how about the wild animals in the woods?"

14   "Wild animals? What kind of wild animals?"

15   "A bear, for instance. A bear could eat you up."

16   "Ma, bears don't eat little children."

17   "Okay. So he won't eat you, but he could take a bite and spit it out! I'm telling you now, if a wild animal eats you up don't come running to me. And who's going with you?"

18   "Well, there's Georgie—"

19   "Georgie! Not him! He's a real wild animal!" She then went on to list all the conditions for the trip. "And remember one thing, don't tear your pants, and remember one thing, don't eat wild berries and bring me home the cramps, and remember one thing, don't tell me tomorrow morning that you're too tired to go to school, and remember one thing, wear boots, a sweater, warm underwear, and an umbrella, and a hat, and remember one thing, if you should get lost in the jungle, call up so I'll know you're all right. And don't dare come

home without color in your cheeks. I wish I was young and free like you. Take soap."

20   Since the consent was specifically granted for the next day only, that night none of us slept. There was always a chance that it might rain. Brother Albert stayed at the crystal set[1] all night like a ship's radio operator with his earphones on, listening to the weather bulletins and repeating them aloud for the rest of us. "It's clearing in Nebraska. Hot air masses coming up from the Gulf. They say it's good for planting alfalfa. Storm warning off the coast of Newfoundland. It's drizzling in Montreal."

21   At 6:00 A.M. we were ready for Operation Hike, rain or shine, but we had to wait for Papa to get up. We didn't need his permission, but we did need his blanket.

22   Into the valley of Central Park we marched, bowed down with knapsacks, flashlights, a compass-mirror (so you could tell not only where you were lost, but who was lost), a thermos bottle (semi-automatic—you had to fill it but it emptied by itself), and an ax. Onward! Forward! Upward! Philip was always the leader. He was the one to get lost first. Jerry was the lookout. He would yell, "Look out!" and fall off the cliff. None of us knew how long we were supposed to march. We went on because we didn't know what to do if we stopped. One brave coward finally spoke up. "I can't go on anymore. The heat is killing me. Let's start the fire here."

23   No hike was complete without Georgie and his Uncle Bernie's World War I bugle. This kid had lungs like a vacuum cleaner. With him outside the walls of Jericho, they could have sent the rest of the army home. He used to stand on a hill and let go a blast that had the Staten Island ferries running into each other.

24   Lunch, naturally, had been packed in a shoe box—sandwiches, fruit, cheese, and napkins all squashed together neatly. The lid would open by itself every twenty minutes for air.

25   It happened every time, the Miracle of the Sandwiches. One kid always got a "brilliant idea." "Hey, I got a brilliant idea. I'm tired of my mother's sandwiches. Let's everybody trade sandwiches." All the kids exchanged sandwiches and miraculously we all ended up with salami.

26   Albert was the true nature lover. "You know, you can learn a lot about human nature from the ants," he always said as he lifted up rock after rock to study his favorite insects. And he was right. While he was studying the ants, someone swiped his apple.

27   We came home with color in our cheeks—green. To make sure we could go again, we didn't forget Mama. We brought her a bouquet. She took one whiff and broke out in red blotches.

---

1. **crystal set:** a radio.

GO ON ➡

The Heckscher Playground

from **The Park and the People: A History of Central Park**
by Roy Rosenzweig and Elizabeth Blackman

1   The shortage of public space in Manhattan increased the demands placed on Central Park in the twentieth century, especially since new generations did not go to the park just to enjoy its beautiful natural landscape. More and more visitors came to Central Park hoping to play, to be entertained, to see something—a show or spectacle—just as those who could afford it did at Coney Island or the movie house. And park administrators, politicians, and reformers all sought to meet these expectations, to demonstrate that the city's grandest public park had kept pace with the times.

2   Although most progressive reformers regarded playing fields, field houses, and gymnastic equipment as essential park features, before the 1920s, the playground movement had only a limited physical impact on Central Park. In the 1890s reformers had successfully introduced a small sand garden in the shadow of Umpire Rock on the southwest Playground. By 1912 play supervisors ran five summer programs for children in the park, but without equipment. In the spirit of the playground movement, park officials did now permit a number of competitive sports—including soccer, field hockey, and football, as well as the traditional baseball and croquet—on the meadows. Commissioners made only tentative gestures, however, toward building new facilities. As late as the 1920s, only about 9 percent of the park's terrain was devoted to playfields or special programmed events.

3   The Heckscher Playground at 61st Street and Seventh Avenue, added only in 1926, became the sole equipped playground within the park. It was bitterly opposed by several real estate and civic groups, including the League of Women Voters and the Federation of Women's Clubs. The Central Park West and Columbus Avenue Association, which represented West Side property owners, argued that "Central Park was designed as a park where people could go and rest and walk and drive and that it was intended to be maintained with grass and trees." But the area at 61st and Seventh Avenue was designated as a playground in the original Greensward plan of 1858 and had long been in use for children's play and sports. In a political climate sympathetic to the reformers' playground movement, philanthropist August Heckscher used his personal prestige to persuade park officials to ignore the opposition and accept his gift of an equipped playground, 4.5 acres, including swings, merry-go-rounds, spiral slides, jungle gyms, a field house, and a wading pool just south of Umpire Rock.

© Mike Baldwin / Cornered

It's great to get away from it all, except for the crowds.

Reading Comprehension

Use "A Hike in New York City" (pp. 770–771) to answer questions 1–15.

1. When do the children set out on their hike?

   A. Before Albert hears the weather report

   B. At six o'clock in the morning

   C. After they get Papa's blanket

   D. As soon as they eat lunch

2. Which words and phrases from the passage help the reader follow the order of events?

   A. At least, in the woods

   B. On a hike, right here

   C. That night, at 6:00 A.M.

   D. Open road, rain or shine

3. The Latin word *ponere* means "to put." What does the word *opposition* mean in paragraph 1?

   A. Punishment   C. Influence

   B. Resistance   D. Approval

4. The Latin word *ridere* means "to laugh." What does the word *ridiculous* mean in paragraph 2?

   A. Enjoyable   C. Realistic

   B. Silly   D. Unusual

5. Reread the first four sentences in the passage. Which sentence tells you this will be a funny story?

   A. Sentence 1   C. Sentence 3

   B. Sentence 2   D. Sentence 4

6. The author sets the tone by using —

   A. long sentences

   B. ironic comments

   C. specialized vocabulary

   D. detailed descriptions

7. In paragraph 19, Mama says "if you should get lost in the jungle, call up so I'll know you're all right." This statement is ironic because —

   A. it is easy to get lost in a big city park

   B. Mama is afraid that the children will get lost

   C. the children are not all right if they are lost

   D. the New York City park is not a jungle

8. The phrases "Operation Hike" and "the Miracle of the Sandwiches" are funny because they —

   A. express a child's innocent point of view

   B. show Mama's concern for her children

   C. can be interpreted in different ways

   D. make everyday events seem important

9. Which words in the passage help to create an informal style?

   A. Opposition, ridiculous, rhythmically

   B. Kids, swiped, squashed

   C. Hike, walk, marched

   D. Coward, insects, bouquet

10. With the exclamations "Onward! Forward! Upward!" in paragraph 22, the author emphasizes the boys' —

    A. excitement about the hike

    B. fear of getting lost

    C. need for their mother

    D. interest in climbing a hill

11. In paragraph 23, the image that compares Georgie's lungs to a vacuum cleaner shows that he —

    A. has strong lungs

    B. speaks very loudly

    C. likes to play the bugle

    D. has dirt in his lungs

12. In paragraph 25, the quotation marks around "brilliant idea" suggest that this phrase is an example of —

    A. understatement

    B. verbal irony

    C. vivid imagery

    D. symbolism

13. Reread the last paragraph. What is ironic about the children's gift to Mama?

    A. The children bring Mama a gift so that she will let them go hiking again.

    B. The children find flowers in Central Park to bring to Mama.

    C. Mama has an allergic reaction to the bouquet.

    D. Mama is surprised by the children's gift.

14. The word *salami* appears in paragraph 25. Use clues in the following sentence to choose the foreign origin of *salami*.

Maria often serves cubed *salami*, crusty bread, and pasta for lunch.

    A. French   **C.** Italian

    B. German   **D.** English

15. The word *bouquet* appears in paragraph 27. Use clues in the following sentence to choose the foreign origin of *bouquet*.

The artisans at a shop near the Eiffel Tower in Paris fashion flowers into elegant *bouquets*.

    A. French   **C.** Arabic

    B. Greek   **D.** German

> **Use "The Heckscher Playground" (p. 772) to answer questions 16–20.**

16. Which happened first in the development of Central Park?

    A. A philanthropist paid for a playground with equipment.

    B. Reformers built a small sand garden for children.

    C. Play supervisors ran five summer programs for children without equipment.

    D. Sports such as soccer were allowed on the meadows.

17. One element of the authors' style is the use of —

    A. mostly short sentences

    B. mostly long sentences

    C. all short sentences

    D. a mix of long and short sentences

18. Which phrases from the passage help the reader follow the order of events?

    A. More and more, had kept pace

    B. Before the 1920s, as late as

    C. In the park, in the spirit of

    D. In the shadow, on the meadows

19. The word *croquet* appears in paragraph 2. Use clues in the following sentence to choose the foreign origin of *croquet*.

A crude version of what is now *croquet* was first played over a thousand years ago by lonely shepherds in the south of France.

    A. English   **C.** French

    B. Greek   **D.** German

GO ON ➡

20. The Latin root *centrum* means "center." What does *Central* mean in the phrase *Central Park* in paragraph 1?

A. Very large part

B. A colorful thing

C. Near the middle

D. Circular in shape

> **Use "A Hike in New York City" and "The Heckscher Playground" to answer questions 21–23.**

21. Reflect on an adult's attitude about children using Central Park in the 1920s in "A Hike in New York City." How is that attitude reflected in "The Heckscher Playground"?

A. Children were not generally welcome in the park in the 1920s.

B. The park was designed for adults and children to share.

C. A philanthropist wanted to provide a playground in the park.

D. The original plan for the park included a playground.

22. Think about the children's desires in "A Hike in New York City." How did their desires relate to the changes that took place in "The Heckscher Playground"?

A. People stayed away from the park.

B. Organizations added children's activities and equipment to the park.

C. The city decided that the park should remain the same.

D. More organizations began to oppose changes to the park.

23. Which statement from "A Hike in New York City" reflects the reformers' attitude in "The Heckscher Playground"?

A. *There was always a chance that it might rain.*

B. *We went on because we didn't know what to do if we stopped.*

C. *I wish I was young and free like you.*

D. *. . . it was so much more enjoyable to fall off a mountain than off a fire escape.*

> **Use the visual representation on page 773 to answer questions 24 and 25.**

24. The cartoonist creates humor by —

A. placing a crowd where it does not belong

B. showing typical behavior in a park

C. illustrating tall trees

D. including both men and women

25. The cartoonist makes the caption humorous by —

A. writing about how much fun it would be to be in a crowd in the woods

B. claiming that he "gets away" from crowds while being in a crowd at the same time

C. stating that he wants to get away from crowds

D. explaining that he really wants to be in a crowd of people

SHORT CONSTRUCTED RESPONSE
Write a short response to each question, using text evidence to support your response.

26. Find two examples of irony in "A Hike in the Park" and identify each as situational, verbal, or dramatic irony.

27. Find two examples of Sam Levenson's humor, and explain how the words, images, or sentences contribute to the humor.

Revising and Editing

DIRECTIONS Read this passage and answer the questions that follow.

> (1) Central Park occupies 843 acres of land in New York City. (2) It is the most visited park in the nation. (3) When the city bought the land in the mid 1800s, it had to be cleared of farms, livestock, and open sewers. (4) The city held a competition for the new park's design. (5) Officials chose a plan. (6) The completed park looked natural. (7) It consisted of artificial lakes and imported trees and shrubs. (8) Now the park is a popular spot for bird watching. (9) It is an oasis for migrating birds.

1. How might you use an appositive phrase to combine sentences 1 and 2?

    A. Central Park is the most visited park in the nation and occupies 843 acres of land in New York City.

    B. The most visited park in the nation is Central Park, and it occupies 843 acres of land in New York City.

    C. Central Park, the most visited park in the nation, occupies 843 acres of land in New York City.

    D. Occupying 843 acres of land in New York City, Central Park is the most visited park in the nation.

2. How might you combine sentences 4 and 5 to form one compound sentence?

    A. The city held a competition for the new park's design, choosing a plan.

    B. The city held a competition for the new park's design, and officials chose a plan.

    C. After the city held a competition for the new park's design, officials chose a plan.

    D. The city held a competition for the new park's design and chose a plan.

3. How might you combine sentences 6 and 7 to form one complex sentence?

    A. The completed park looked natural, but it consisted of artificial lakes and imported trees and shrubs.

    B. Though the completed park looked natural, it consisted of artificial lakes and imported trees and shrubs.

    C. The completed park looked natural but consisted of artificial lakes and imported trees and shrubs.

    D. The completed park looked natural, consisting of artificial lakes and imported trees and shrubs.

4. How might you use an appositive phrase to combine sentences 8 and 9?

    A. Migrating birds now make the park an oasis and a popular spot for bird watching.

    B. Because it is an oasis for migrating birds, the park is now a popular spot for bird watching.

    C. The park, an oasis for migrating birds, is now a popular spot for bird watching.

    D. The park is an oasis for migrating birds, so now it is a popular spot for bird watching.

STOP

UNIT 6

More Great Reads

Ideas for Independent Reading

Which questions from Unit 6 made an impression on you?
Continue exploring them with these books.

COMMON CORE

RL 10 Read and comprehend literature. **RI 10** Read and comprehend literary nonfiction.

Get Novel Wise

THINK central

Go to **thinkcentral.com**.
KEYWORD: HML8-778

How do you make decisions?

Cheating Lessons
by Nan Willard

Wickham High will finally compete against fancy Pinehurst at the State Quiz Bowl. Bernadette can't wait to crush the other team until she realizes there's no way her school honestly aced the test. She has to decide between telling a lie or hurting friends.

Good Brother, Bad Brother: The Story of Edwin Booth and John Wilkes Booth
by James Cross Giblin

Two brothers grow up together. Both become well-known actors like their father, but one goes on to kill the President of the United States. What happened?

Princess Academy
by Shannon Hale

The king's priests have decreed that the next princess will come from tiny Mount Eskel. Suddenly, all the girls in the village have to go to school. Miri decides she has to be the best student. But what will Miri do if the prince chooses her?

What's really normal?

Act I, Act II, Act Normal
by Martha Weston

Topher has been waiting for three years to be the lead in the 8th grade play. Too bad this year's production is Rumpelstiltskin, the Musical, written by geeky Samantha. Topher takes the role, but will the school bully and the touchy leading lady ruin it for him?

Sweetgrass Basket
by Marlene Carvell

In the early 1900s, Mattie and Sarah are forced to go to a boarding school for Native American children. They're told it's their best chance for a "normal" life. Now far from home, the two girls have to figure out how to survive and keep their traditions.

Hans Christian Andersen: His Fairy Tale Life
by Hjordis Varmer and Lilian Brogger

Everyone knows Andersen's fairy tales, but did you know he was obsessed with fame? He begged rich men, a princess, and even the king, until someone would support his dream to write and act.

What makes a pioneer?

China's Son: Growing Up in the Cultural Revolution
by Da Chen

Da Chen suffers in 1960s China, which is run by communists. His father is often in labor camps and his brothers and sisters work in the fields. Then Da gets the chance to apply for college. Will life finally get better?

Guinea Pig Scientists
by Leslie Dendy and Mel Boring

Scientists who experiment on themselves are brave and sometimes foolhardy. We wouldn't know how the digestive system worked, what animal spread yellow fever, or how to build safer cars without these people.

O Pioneers!
by Willa Cather

Alexandra is only 16 when her father dies and leaves her in charge of their failing homestead on the Nebraska prairies. Her brothers agree to listen to her advice, but will they let her put the farm deeper in debt to chase her father's dream?

778

UNIT 7

Our Place in the World

HISTORY, CULTURE, AND THE AUTHOR

- In Fiction
- In Nonfiction
- In Media
- In Poetry

What SHAPES
who we are?

If you were to write a book about your life, where would you begin? If you're like many authors and artists, what you say would probably reflect the influence of your family, friends, and culture. Although you can't always see it, culture plays an important part in shaping your world. The language you speak, the holidays you celebrate, the games you play, and the music you listen to are all part of your culture.

ACTIVITY What parts of your history and culture influence you the most? Think about the important people, places, and events in your life. Then reflect on your family's traditions and your own taste in entertainment. Make a collage out of images and mementos that symbolize what shapes you.

Find It Online!

THINK central

Go to thinkcentral.com for the interactive version of this unit.

Preview Unit Goals

TEXT ANALYSIS	• Identify and analyze influence of writer's background on plot and theme • Identify and analyze historical and cultural context of selections and their effect on plot and theme • Analyze author's purpose
READING	• Make inferences • Analyze sensory details and their influence on meaning • Compare and contrast
WRITING AND LANGUAGE	• Write a cause-and-effect essay • Combine sentences to form a compound-complex sentence • Use colons and semicolons correctly
SPEAKING AND LISTENING	• Produce a power presentation
VOCABULARY	• Consult reference materials for definitions and pronunciations • Understand analogies
ACADEMIC VOCABULARY	• contribute • culture • interpret • perceive • similar
MEDIA AND VIEWING	• Identify visual aspects of illustrations • Analyze the message and point of view in political cartoons

Media Smart DVD-ROM

Culture Marked by Media

Explore the techniques political cartoonists use to create enduring symbols and reflect changing times. **Page 852**

History, Culture, and the Author

Have you ever heard the lyrics to a song and wondered what motivated the musician to write them? What about a work of literature—do you ever wonder what inspired its creation? In this workshop, you'll learn about different factors that can affect writers. By examining the layers of a writer's experience, you can "read into" literature with far more insight.

Part 1: A Writer's Background

COMMON CORE

Included in this workshop:
RL 1 Cite the evidence that supports what the text says explicitly as well as inferences drawn from the text.
RL 4 Analyze the impact of word choices on meaning and tone.

You are the unique product of many factors, including your heritage, family life, national identity, and economic status. Just as all these factors shape your ideas and beliefs, they influence writers as well. Writers may not consciously realize it, but their heritage, traditions, attitudes, and beliefs are reflected in what they choose to write about and also in how they express their ideas.

For instance, consider "Eating Together," a poem that paints a touching picture of a close-knit family. First, read the poem itself. Then go back and read the background on Li-Young Lee to identify aspects of his heritage and customs that are reflected in the poem. Notice how your knowledge of Lee's personal history deepens your understanding of the poem.

Eating Together

Poem by **Li-Young Lee**

BACKGROUND Li-Young Lee was born to Chinese parents in Jakarta, Indonesia, in 1957. The family moved many times during Lee's childhood—often to avoid anti-Chinese sentiments—before settling in the United States. Lee's poetry frequently focuses on his close-knit, traditional Chinese family, and many poems express the poet's grief over his father's death.

In the steamer is the trout
seasoned with slivers of ginger,
two sprigs of green onion, and sesame oil.
We shall eat it with rice for lunch,
5 brothers, sister, my mother who will
taste the sweetest meat of the head,
holding it between her fingers
deftly, the way my father did
weeks ago. Then he lay down
10 to sleep like a snow-covered road
winding through pines older than him,
without any travelers, and lonely for no one.

QUESTIONS TO ASK

What evidence of the author's heritage and customs do I see?
The Asian family described in the poem seems close-knit and traditional, much like Lee's own family.

What might have been the author's motivation for writing this poem?
Lee may have wanted to express his feelings about his father's death and to reflect on how his father's absence has affected his family.

MODEL 1: ANALYZING A POEM

Read this poem a first time, without knowing anything about the author behind the words and ideas. How would you describe the speaker?

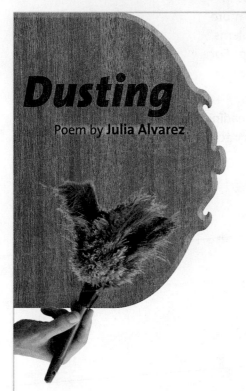

Dusting

Poem by **Julia Alvarez**

Each morning I wrote my name
on the dusty cabinet, then crossed
the dining table in script, scrawled
in capitals on the backs of chairs,
5   practicing signatures like scales
while Mother followed, squirting
linseed[1] from a burping can
into a crumpled-up flannel.

She erased my fingerprints
10 from the bookshelf and rocker,
polished mirrors on the desk
scribbled with my alphabets.
My name was swallowed in the towel
with which she jeweled the table tops.
15 The grain surfaced in the oak
and the pine grew luminous.
But I refused with every mark
to be like her, anonymous.

---

1. **linseed:** yellowish oil made from flax seeds, often used to help preserve the shine of natural wood furniture.

Close Read

1. What images does Alvarez use to help you visualize the actions of the speaker and her mother? Find three examples.

2. Think about what the speaker means by what she says in the boxed lines. How is she different from her mother?

MODEL 2: THE WRITER'S BACKGROUND

Read this background information about Julia Alvarez. Then go back and read the poem a second time.

Julia Alvarez was born in New York in 1950. When she was three months old, her parents returned with her to their native country, the Dominican Republic. However, the family came back to the
5   United States for political reasons when Alvarez was ten years old. Alvarez grew up speaking Spanish, with English as a second language. Her mother worked as a housekeeper and, as a young girl, Alvarez would
10 often go with her mother to work. Alvarez has said, "As I followed my mother cleaning house, washing and ironing clothes, rolling dough, I was using the material of my housebound girl life to claim my woman's legacy." Alvarez later became a writer and continues to share her childhood experiences in her works.

Close Read

1. In what way does the background information help you to better understand the poem?

2. What connection can you draw between the last two lines of the poem and Alvarez's career?

Part 2: Historical and Cultural Contexts

Knowing about a writer's personal background can help you to appreciate his or her work more fully. Similarly, knowing the **historical and cultural contexts** in which the work was written can help you interpret and analyze that work more accurately. **Historical and cultural contexts** refer to the events, social problems, traditions, and values that may have influenced the author and the writing. For example, what events and issues of the time was the author concerned about? How are those concerns reflected in the literature's topic and theme?

Take a look at this excerpt from a story by James Baldwin. Notice how reading the background and answering some questions can give you new insights into Baldwin's writing.

from *Sonny's Blues*

Short story by **James Baldwin**

BACKGROUND In the early 1900s, African Americans were encouraged to move to Manhattan's Harlem neighborhood, partly to shelter them from emerging racial conflicts in other neighborhoods. By 1920, Harlem was populated almost exclusively by African Americans. Though the 1920s became known as the Harlem Renaissance because of the blossoming of jazz music, writing, and art in the African-American community, it was also a time of economic hardship. Since many landlords in other areas refused to rent apartments to African Americans, landlords in Harlem often took advantage of their tenants by charging high rents.

"Sonny's Blues" was published in 1957, reflecting James Baldwin's firsthand knowledge of the neighborhood in which he grew up. Throughout most of the twentieth century, Harlem was known for being troubled by crime and poverty as well as being a prominent African-American cultural community.

The narrator and his brother are returning to the neighborhood of their youth:

Houses exactly like the houses of our past yet dominated the landscape, boys exactly like the boys we once had been found themselves smothering in these houses, came down into the streets for light and air and found themselves encircled by disaster. Some escaped the trap, most didn't. Those
5   who got out always left something of themselves behind, as some animals amputate a leg and leave it in the trap. It might be said, perhaps, that I had escaped, after all, I was a schoolteacher; or that Sonny had, he hadn't lived in Harlem for years. Yet, as the cab moved uptown through streets which seemed, with a rush, to darken with dark people, and as I covertly studied
10 Sonny's face, it came to me that what we both were seeking through our separate cab windows was that part of ourselves which had been left behind.

QUESTIONS TO ASK

What aspects of Baldwin's background are reflected in the writing?
Baldwin uses words and phrases like "smothering," "encircled by disaster," and "the trap" to describe the poverty-stricken Harlem neighborhood of his youth.

What theme might the author have wanted to explore in this story?
Baldwin may have wanted to explore why former residents of Harlem who "escaped the trap" still feel so connected to the neighborhood in which they grew up.

MODEL 1: ANALYZING FICTION

In this story, a British pilot wakes up in a French hospital during World War II. Find out what he's thinking about as a nurse tends to him. First, read this excerpt and answer the **Close Read** questions. Then read the background that follows.

from **Beware of the Dog**

Short story by **Roald Dahl**

"I believe there's someone coming down to see you from the Air Ministry after breakfast," she went on. "They want a report or something. I expect you know all about it. How you got shot down and all that. I won't let him stay long, so don't worry."

5   He did not answer. She finished washing him and gave him a toothbrush and some toothpowder. He brushed his teeth, rinsed his mouth, and spat the water out into the basin.

Later she brought him his breakfast on a tray, but he did not want to eat. He was still feeling weak and sick and he wished only to lie still and think
10 about what had happened. And there was a sentence running through his head. It was a sentence which Johnny, the Intelligence Officer of his squadron, always repeated to the pilots every day before they went out. He could see Johnny now, leaning against the wall of the dispersal hut with his pipe in his hand, saying, "And if they get you, don't forget, just your name, rank, and
15 number. Nothing else. For God's sake, say nothing else."

Close Read

1. What do you learn about the pilot in this passage?

2. The hospital staff is being kind to the pilot, but he believes they are only trying to get information from him. Which words and phrases convey his anxiety?

MODEL 2: HISTORICAL AND CULTURAL CONTEXT

The following background helps to explain why a British pilot would be nervous about waking up in a French hospital.

World War II began with Germany's 1939 invasion of Poland, which caused Britain and France to declare war on Germany. By 1941, German forces had occupied France and much of Western Europe, but Great Britain was still fighting back. Other countries joined the war on both sides of the
5 conflict, dividing into the Axis forces and the Allies. France was not liberated from German occupation until 1944.

Roald Dahl joined the British Royal Air Force in 1939. He became a fighter pilot and flew missions over North Africa, Greece, and the Middle East during the war. After his plane crashed in Egypt, he spent six
10 months in a hospital, recovering from a head injury. When he was asked later to share his experiences, Dahl's career as a writer began. "Beware of the Dog" was published in 1944.

Close Read

1. What exactly is the pilot worried about? Explain how the background helps you to understand his situation.

2. In your opinion, is Dahl's tone in the story sympathetic to the pilot? Explain.

Part 3: Analyze the Text

Before reading "Origami," read the following background information about the author, Susan K. Ito, and the topics mentioned in her story.

BACKGROUND
Crafting Words and Mending Old Wounds

Seeking to Belong
As a child, Susan K. Ito often struggled with her sense of
5 identity. She says, "I felt like I was the only one of my kind: mixed-race, adopted, only child." She often found
10 herself envying women who were full-blooded Japanese, since she was only part Japanese. When she began taking literature and creative writing classes in graduate school, Ito felt like
15 she had found where she belonged: "I was finally immersing myself in the world that I'd longed to be in forever: the world of words." Life as a Japanese American and the struggle for a sense
20 of belonging have been the focus of much of her writing.

Susan K. Ito

Peace Cranes
"Origami" is named after a paper-folding
25 craft that has been practiced for centuries in Japan. Its popularity has now spread to many other countries. One of the
30 most popular paper designs is the crane—a type of bird. In many Asian countries, the crane is a symbol of peace. Many people from around the world send paper cranes to a memorial
35 in Hiroshima, Japan, every year. It is done in memory of those who died there during World War II and as an expression of the senders' wish for world peace.

40 **Japanese Internment** During World War II, nations were divided between the Axis and Allied forces. In 1941 Japan—a member of the Axis powers—bombed the U.S.
45 military base at Pearl Harbor in Honolulu, Hawaii, prompting the United States to declare war on Japan. Four years later, the United States dropped atomic bombs on
50 two Japanese cities: Hiroshima and Nagasaki.

Americans were fearful of another attack within their borders. As a precaution, Japanese immigrants and
55 Americans of Japanese ancestry were sent to and held in facilities called internment camps in order to isolate them from the rest of the American public. The largest camp was the
60 Tule Lake Segregation Center in California. At the time, limiting the rights of one ethnic group was viewed as being done in service of the greater good of the American
65 public. The last internment camp closed in 1948. However, it was not until 1988 that the U.S. government issued its first official apology for its treatment of Japanese Americans
75 during World War II.

Japanese internment camp in Santa Anita, California

The narrator of this short story views herself as an outsider struggling to prove that she belongs. As you read this excerpt, consider how the background information enhances your understanding of the story.

from # ORIGAMI

Short story by **Susan K. Ito**

   I take my place, hesitantly, among the group of Japanese women, smile back at the ones who look up from their task to nod at me. Their words float around me like alphabet soup, familiar, comforting, but nothing that I clearly understand. The long cafeteria table blooms with folded paper birds of all
5 colors: royal purple, light gray, a small shimmering silver one. They're weaving an origami wreath for Sunday's memorial service, a thousand cranes for the souls of those who died at Tule Lake's internment camp.
   I spread the square of sky-blue paper flat under my hands, then fold it in half. So far, this is easy. I'm going to follow all the directions. It's going to be
10 a perfect crane, *tsuru,* flying from my palm. Fold again, then flip that side of the triangle under to make a box. Oh no. What? I didn't get that. I'm lost. The women around me keep creasing, folding, spreading, their fingers moving with easy grace. My thumbs are huge, thick, in the way of these paper wings that are trying to unfold but can't.
15   My heart rises and flutters, beating against its cage in panic, in confusion. I try to retrace my steps, turn the paper upside down, in reverse. It's not working. I want to crumple the paper into a blue ball, an origami rock.
   But instead I unfold the paper with damp, shaking fingers. I persevere. *Gambaro.* Don't give up. I'm going to make this crane if it kills me, I'm going
20 to prove that I can do this thing, this Japanese skill. I'm going to pull the coordination out of my blood, make it flow into my fingers. I have to.
   But what if I can't? Then it only proves the thing that I fear the most, don't want to believe. That I'm not really Japanese. That I'm just an imposter, a fake, a watered-down, inauthentic K-mart version of the real thing.

Close Read

1. Reread the boxed text. How does the background enhance your reading of this passage?

2. Why does the narrator feel insecure in this situation? Support your answer.

3. Does Ito seem to sympathize with the narrator? Explain.

4. Which details show you that the narrator admires people who are Japanese?

5. Which details in the background help you understand why Ito might have chosen to write this story?

The Snapping Turtle
Short Story by Joseph Bruchac

| VIDEO TRAILER | THINK central | KEYWORD: HML8-788 |

Where do we get our
VALUES?

Do you remember where you learned that honesty is the best policy? Or that hard work pays off? We get our values from a patchwork of different sources, including important people in our lives, the communities around us, and mass media. The boy in the story you're about to read gets many of his values from his grandparents, but as you'll see, these values are put to the test.

LIST IT Take one minute to list some of the values that are important to you. Circle the value that most influences how you live your life. Then, as a class, generate a list that reflects the group's responses, and discuss where you learned these values.

1. loyalty
2.
3.

788

TEXT ANALYSIS: CULTURAL CONTEXT

Authors write within a **cultural context**, which includes the events, social problems, traditions, and values in the world around them. This cultural context is often reflected in the themes, or messages about life, that authors share and in the characters they create.

Read the biography on this page to learn more about the cultural context in which Joseph Bruchac writes. Then, as you read "The Snapping Turtle," notice how Bruchac's themes and characters reflect his background.

READING SKILL: COMPARE AND CONTRAST

When you **compare** two or more things, you identify ways in which they are alike. When you **contrast** them, you find ways in which they are different. Thinking about characters' similarities and differences can help you recognize their qualities and values. In "The Snapping Turtle," you will compare and contrast

- the narrator and other boys
- the narrator's grandmother and grandfather

As you read, use Venn diagrams to compare and contrast these characters' attitudes, backgrounds, and values.

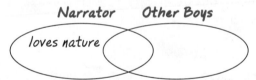

Narrator   Other Boys

loves nature

▲ VOCABULARY IN CONTEXT

Restate each sentence, using a different word or phrase for the boldfaced word.

1. My **philosophy** is "Leave nothing but footprints."
2. The memorial garden seemed to give the hero **immortality.**
3. Amy and I like to **traipse** around the meadow.
4. I have no **inclination** to go indoors when it's nice outside.
5. It takes **craftiness** to successfully trick a raccoon.
6. I **cache** my camping gear behind a tree while I hike.
7. Following their **migration** route, the geese flew north.
8. The thick undergrowth made the forest **impregnable.**
9. The **basking** sunbather enjoyed the afternoon breeze.
10. **Undaunted,** the bird flew on in search of food.

Complete the activities in your **Reader/Writer Notebook.**

Meet the Author

Joseph Bruchac
born 1942

Writer and Storyteller
Joseph Bruchac was raised by his grandparents in the foothills of New York State's Adirondack Mountains, in a house built by his grandfather. After leaving home to study literature, Bruchac returned to his hometown. He and his wife now live in the house where he grew up. Bruchac has published many books of stories and poetry, and he founded his own publishing company, the Greenfield Review Press. In addition to being an author, Bruchac is a well-known professional storyteller, performing the traditional stories of the Native Americans of the Northeast.

Hidden Heritage
Bruchac's grandfather was part Native American. He was descended from the Abenaki (ä'bə-nä'kē), a group that originally lived in New England and southern Canada. Bruchac did not discover this heritage until he was a teenager, because his grandfather feared that he would be discriminated against if he revealed his Native American roots. Although Bruchac did not know it at the time, his grandfather raised him with traditional Abenaki values. The Abenaki believe in honoring their elders, treating the earth with respect by not wasting its resources, and sharing food and possessions with others.

Author Online
THiNK central
Go to **thinkcentral.com.**
KEYWORD: HML8-789

789

The SNAPPING TURTLE

Joseph Bruchac

My grandmother was working in the flower garden near the road that morning when I came out with my fishing pole. She was separating out the roots of iris. As far as flowers go, she and I were agreed that iris had the sweetest scent. Iris would grow about anywhere, shooting up green sword-shaped leaves like the mythical soldiers that sprang from the planted teeth of a dragon. But iris needed some amount of care. Their roots would multiply so thick and fast that they could crowd themselves right up out of the soil. Spring separating and replanting were, as my grandmother put it, just the ticket.[1]

10   Later that day, I knew, she would climb into our blue 1951 Plymouth to drive around the back roads of Greenfield, a box of iris in the back seat. She would stop at farms where she had noticed a certain color of iris that she didn't have yet. Up to the door she would go to ask for a root so that she could add another splash of color to our garden. And, in exchange, she would give that person, most often a flowered-aproned and somewhat elderly woman like herself, some of her own iris.

It wasn't just that she wanted more flowers herself. She had a **philosophy**. If only one person keeps a plant, something might happen to it. Early frost, insects, animals, Lord knows what. But if many have that kind of plant, then it 20   may survive. Sharing meant a kind of **immortality**. I didn't quite understand it then, but I enjoyed taking those rides with her, carrying boxes and cans and flowerpots with new kinds of iris back to the car. **Ⓐ**

"Going fishing, Sonny?" she said now.

Of course, she knew where I was going. Not only the evidence of the pole in my hand, but also the simple facts that it was a Saturday morning in late May and I was a boy of ten, would have led her to that natural conclusion. But she had to ask. It was part of our routine.

---

1. **just the ticket:** the perfect solution.

Analyze Visuals ▶
What **effect** does the artist's use of color have on what you notice in this painting?

philosophy (fĭ-lŏs′ə-fē) *n.* a system of values or beliefs

immortality (ĭm′ôr-tăl′ĭ-tē) *n.* the condition of having an endless life

Ⓐ CULTURAL CONTEXT
What is one attitude or belief expressed in lines 10–22? Tell whether you think this belief reflects the cultural context in which the work was written.

Child Fishing (1989), Lincoln Seligman. Private collection. © Bridgeman Art Library.

"Un-hun," I answered, as I always did. "Unless you and Grampa need some help." Then I held my breath, for though my offer of aid had been sincere
30 enough, I really wanted to go fishing.

Grama thrust her foot down on the spading[2] fork, carefully levering out a heavy clump of iris marked last fall with a purple ribbon to indicate the color. She did such things with half my effort and twice the skill, despite the fact I was growing, as she put it, like a weed. "No, you go on along. This afternoon Grampa and I could use some help, though."

"I'll be back by then," I said, but I didn't turn and walk away. I waited for the next thing I knew she would say.

"You stay off of the state road, now."

In my grandmother's mind, Route 9N, which came down the hill past my
40 grandparents' little gas station and general store on the corner, was nothing less than a Road of Death. If I ever set foot on it, I would surely be as doomed as our four cats and two dogs that met their fates there.

"Runned over and kilt," as Grampa Jesse put it.

Grampa Jesse, who had been the hired man for my grandmother's parents before he and Grama eloped, was not a person with book learning like my college-educated grandmother. His family was Abenaki Indian, poor but honest hill people who could read the signs in the forest, but who had never **traipsed** far along the trails of schoolhouse ways. Between Grama's books and Grampa's practical knowledge, some of which I was about to apply to bring home a
50 mess of[3] trout, I figured I was getting about the best education a ten-year-old boy could have. I was lucky that my grandparents were raising me. **B**

"I'll stay off the state road," I promised. "I'll just follow Bell Brook."

Truth be told, the state road made me a little nervous, too. It was all too easy to imagine myself in the place of one of my defunct pets, stunned by the elephant bellow of a tractor-trailer's horn, looking wild-eyed up to the shiny metal grill; the thud, the lightning-bolt flash of light, and then the eternal dark. I imagined my grandfather shoveling the dirt over me in a backyard grave next to that of Lady, the collie, and Kitty-kitty, the gray cat, while my grandmother dried her eyes with her apron and said, "I told him to stay off
60 that road!"

I was big on knowledge but very short on courage in those years. I mostly played by myself because the other kids my age from the houses and farms scattered around our rural township regarded me as a Grama's boy who would tell if they were to tie me up and threaten to burn my toes with matches, a ritual required to join the local society of pre-teenage boys. A squealer. And they were right.

I didn't much miss the company of other kids. I had discovered that most of them had little interest in the living things around them. They were noisier than Grampa and I were, scaring away the rabbits that we could creep right

---

2. **spading:** digging.

3. **a mess of:** an amount of (food).

COMMON CORE RL 4, L 5

Language Coach

Similes A simile is a comparison using the words *like* or *as*. In lines 33–34, Bruchac uses a simile when he writes, "I was growing . . . like a weed." Does this mean that the narrator was growing quickly or slowly?

traipse (trāps) *v.* to walk or tramp around

B COMPARE AND CONTRAST
Reread lines 44–51. What differences does the narrator point out between Grama and Grampa?

70 up on. Instead of watching the frogs catching flies with their long, gummy tongues, those boys wanted to shoot them with their BB guns. I couldn't imagine any of them having the patience or **inclination** to hold out a hand filled with sunflower seeds, as Grampa had showed me I could, long enough for a chickadee to come and light on an index finger.

Even fishing was done differently when I did it Grampa's way. I knew for a fact that most of those boys would go out and come home with an empty creel. They hadn't been watching for fish from the banks as I had in the weeks before the trout season began, so they didn't know where the fish lived. They didn't know how to keep low, float your line in, wait for that first tap, and 80 then, after the strike that bent your pole, set the hook. And they never said thank-you to every fish they caught, the way I remembered to do. **C**

Walking the creek edge, I set off downstream. By mid-morning, my bait can of moss and red earthworms that Grampa and I had dug from the edge of our manure pile was near empty. I'd gone half a mile and had already caught seven trout. All of them were squaretails, native brook trout whose sides were patterned with a speckled rainbow of bright circles—red, green, gold. I'd only kept the ones more than seven inches long, and I'd remembered to wet my hand before taking the little ones off the hook. Grasping a trout with a dry hand would abrade the slick coat of natural oil from the skin and leave it open 90 for infection and disease.

As always, I'd had to keep the eyes in the back of my head open just as Grampa had told me to do whenever I was in the woods.

"Things is always hunting one another," he'd said.

And he was right. Twice, at places where Bell Brook swung near Mill Road I'd had to leave the stream banks to take shelter when I heard the ominous crunch of bicycle tires on the gravel. Back then, when I was ten, I was smaller than the other boys my age. I made up for it by being harder to catch. Equal parts of **craftiness** and plain old panic at being collared by bullies I viewed as close kin to Attila the Hun[4] kept me slipperier than an eel.

100 From grapevine tangles up the bank, I'd watched as Pauly Roffmeier, Ricky Holstead, and Will Backus rolled up to the creek, making more noise than a herd of hippos, to plunk their own lines in. Both times, they caught nothing. It wasn't surprising, since they were talking like jaybirds, scaring away whatever fish might have been within half a mile. And Will kept lighting matches and throwing them down to watch them hiss out when they struck the water. Not to mention the fact that I had pulled a ten-inch brook trout out of the first hole and an eleven incher out of the second before they even reached the stream. **D**

I looked up at the sky. I didn't wear a watch then. No watch made by man 110 seemed able to work more than a few days when strapped to my wrist. It was a common thing on my Grampa's side of the family. "We jest got too much 'lectricity in us," he explained.

---

4. **Attila the Hun:** a barbarian leader who successfully invaded the Roman Empire in the A.D. 400s.

inclination
(ĭn-klə-nā'shən) *n.* a tendency to prefer one thing over another

VISUAL VOCABULARY

creel: a basket used to carry caught fish

C **CULTURAL CONTEXT**
Reread lines 67–81. What Abenaki customs and attitudes are reflected in this passage?

craftiness (krăf'tē-nĕs) *n.* deviousness or deception

D **COMPARE AND CONTRAST**
Reread lines 100–108. How is the boys' approach to fishing different from that of the narrator?

Without a watch, I could measure time by the sun. I could see it was about ten. I had reached the place where Bell Brook crossed under the state road. Usually I went no further than this. It had been my boundary for years. But somewhere along the way I had decided that today would be different. I think perhaps a part of me was ashamed of hiding from the other boys, ashamed of always being afraid. I wanted to do something that I'd always been afraid to do. I wanted to be brave.

120   I had no need to fish further. I had plenty of trout for our supper. I'd cleaned them all out with my Swiss Army knife, leaving the entrails[5] where the crows and jays could get them. If you did that, the crows and jays would know you for a friend and not sound the alarm when they saw you walking in the woods. I sank the creel under water, wedged it beneath a stone. The water of the brook was deep and cold and I knew it would keep the flesh of the trout fresh and firm. Then I **cached** my pole and bait can under the spice bushes. As I looked up at the highway, Grama's words came back to me:

"Stay off the state road, Sonny."

"*Under*," I said aloud, "is not *on*."

130   Then, taking a deep breath, bent over at the waist, I waded into the culvert[6] that dove under the Road of Death. I had gone no more than half a dozen steps before I walked into a spider web so strong that it actually bounced me back. I splashed a little water from the creek up onto it and watched the beads shape a pattern of concentric circles. The orb-weaver sat unmoving in a corner, one leg resting on a strand of the web. She'd been waiting for the vibration of some flying creature caught in the sticky strands of her net. Clearly, I was much more than she had hoped for. She sat there without moving. Her wide back was patterned with a shape like that of a red and gold hourglass. Her compound eyes, jet black on her head, took in my giant shape. Spiders gave
140   some people the willies.[7] I knew their bite would hurt like blue blazes, but I still thought them graced with great beauty.

"Excuse me," I said. "Didn't mean to bother you."

The spider raised one front leg. A nervous reaction, most likely, but I raised one hand back. Then I ducked carefully beneath the web, entering an area where the light was different. It was like passing from one world into another. I sloshed through the dark culvert, my fingertips brushing the rushing surface of the stream, the current pushing at my calves. My sneakered feet barely held their purchase[8] on the ridged metal, slick with moss. **E**

When I came out the other side, the sunlight was blinding. Just ahead of
150   me the creek was overarched with willows. They were so thick and low that there was no way I could pass without either going underwater or breaking a way through the brush. I wasn't ready to do either. So I made my way up the

---

cache (kăsh) *v.* to store in a hiding place

COMMON CORE RL 2

E **CULTURAL CONTEXT**
The cultural setting of a work refers to the values, beliefs, social problems, and events that are important to the world in which the story takes place. Since many authors write about what they know, the cultural context and the cultural setting of a work can be similar, as they are in this story. How does the cultural setting of this story affect the narrator's values, especially his attitude toward living things such as the spider?

---

5. **entrails** (ĕn'trālz'): the internal organs.

6. **culvert** (kŭl'vərt): a drain that passes under a road.

7. **the willies**: a feeling of fear and/or disgust.

8. **held their purchase**: gripped; refrained from slipping.

Bridge Over Weekeepeemee (1974), Mark Potter. Oil on canvas. Private collection. © Bridgeman Art Library.

bank, thinking to circle back and pick up the creek farther down. For what purpose, I wasn't sure, aside from just wanting to do it. I was nervous as a hen yard when a chicken hawk is circling overhead. But I was excited, too. This was new ground to me, almost a mile from home. I'd gone farther from home in the familiar directions of north and west, into the safety of the woods, but this was different: Across the state road, in the direction of town; someone else's hunting territory. I stayed low to the ground and hugged the edges of the 160 brush as I moved. Then I saw something that drew me away from the creek: The glint of a wider expanse of water. The Rez, the old Greenfield Reservoir.

I'd never been to the Rez, though I knew the other boys went there. As I'd sat alone on the bus, my bookbag clasped tightly to my chest, I'd heard them talk about swimming there, fishing for bass, spearing bullfrogs five times as big as the little frogs in Bell Brook.

I knew I shouldn't be there, yet I was. Slowly I moved to the side of the wide trail that led to the edge of the deep water, and it was just as well that I did: Their bikes had been stashed in the brush down the other side of the path. They'd been more quiet than usual. I might have walked up on them if I 170 hadn't heard a voice. . . .

▲ **Analyze Visuals**

Compare the scene in this painting with the way you picture the culvert in the story. What are the similarities and differences?

I picked up some of the dark mud with my fingertips and drew lines across my cheeks. Grampa had explained it would make me harder to see. Then I slid to a place where an old tree leaned over the bank, cloaked by the cattails that grew from the edge of the Rez. I made my way out on the trunk and looked. . . .

"It's not gonna come up," Ricky said. He picked up something that looked like a makeshift spear. "You lied."

"I did not. It was over there. The biggest snapper I ever saw." Will shaded his eyes with one hand and looked right in my direction without seeing me.

180 "If we catch it, we could sell it for ten dollars to that man on Congress Street. They say snapping turtles have seven different kinds of meat in them."

"Hmph," Pauly said, throwing his own spear aside. "Let's go find something else to do."

One by one, they picked up their fishing poles and went back down the path. I waited without moving, hearing their heavy feet on the trail and then the rattle of their bike chains. . . . All I could think of was that snapping turtle.

I knew a lot about turtles. There were mud turtles and map turtles. There was the smart orange-legged wood turtle and the red-eared slider with its cheeks painted crimson as if it was going to war. Every spring Grama and

190 Grampa and I would drive around, picking up those whose old **migration** routes had been cut by the recent and lethal ribbons of road. Spooked by a car, a turtle falls into that old defense of pulling head and legs and tail into its once **impregnable** fortress. But a shell does little good against the wheels of a Nash or a DeSoto.[9]

Some days we'd rescue as many as a dozen turtles, taking them home for a few days before releasing them back into the wild. Painted turtles, several as big as two hands held together, might nip at you some, but they weren't really dangerous. And the wood turtles would learn in a day or so to reach out for a strawberry or a piece of juicy tomato and then leave their heads out for a

200 scratch while you stroked them with a finger.

Snappers though, they were different. Long-tailed, heavy-bodied and short-tempered, their jaws would gape wide and they'd hiss when you came up on them ashore. Their heads and legs were too big to pull into their shells and they would heave up on their legs and lunge forward as they snapped at you. They might weigh as much as fifty pounds, and it was said they could take off a handful of fingers in one bite. There wasn't much to recommend a snapping turtle as a friend. **F**

Most people seemed to hate snappers. Snappers ate the fish and the ducks; they scared swimmers away. Or I should say that people hated them alive.

210 Dead, they were supposed to be the best-eating turtle of all. *Ten dollars,* I thought. *Enough for me to send away to the mail-order pet place and get a pair of real flying squirrels.* I'd kept that clipping from *Field and Stream* magazine

migration (mī-grā′shən) *n.* the act of changing location seasonally (used here as an adjective)

impregnable (ĭm-prĕg′nə-bəl) *adj.* impossible to enter by force

F CULTURAL CONTEXT
Do you think Bruchac has had experiences similar to those the narrator describes here? Explain your answer.

---

9. **Nash . . . DeSoto:** car brands that were popular during the 1950s.

thumbtacked over my bed for four months now. A sort of plan was coming into my mind. **G**

People were afraid of getting bit by snappers when they were swimming. But from what I'd read, and from what Grampa told me, they really didn't have much to worry about.

"Snapper won't bother you none in the water," Grampa said. If you were even to step on a snapping turtle resting on the bottom of a pond, all it would do would be to move away. On land, all the danger from a snapper was to the front or the side. From behind, a snapper couldn't get you. Get it by the tail, you were safe. That was the way.

And as I thought, I kept watch. And as I kept watch, I kept up a silent chant inside my mind.

Come here, I'm waiting for you.
Come here, I'm waiting for you.

Before long, a smallish log that had been sticking up farther out in the pond began to drift my way. It was, as I had expected, no log at all. It was a turtle's head. I stayed still. The sun's heat beat on my back, but I lay there like a **basking** lizard. Closer and closer the turtle came, heading right into water less than waist deep. It was going right for shore, for the sandy bank bathed in sun. I didn't think about why then, just wondered at the way my wanting seemed to have called it to me.

When it was almost to shore, I slid into the water on the other side of the log I'd been waiting on. The turtle surely sensed me, for it started to swing around as I moved slowly toward it, swimming as much as walking. But I lunged and grabbed it by the tail. Its tail was rough and ridged, as easy to hold as if coated with sandpaper. I pulled hard and the turtle came toward me. I stepped back, trying not to fall and pull it on top of me. My feet found the bank, and I leaned hard to drag the turtle out, its clawed feet digging into the dirt as it tried to get away. A roaring hiss like the rush of air from a punctured tire came out of its mouth, and I stumbled, almost losing my grasp. Then I took another step, heaved again, and it was mine. ◆

Or at least it was until I let go. I knew I could not let go. I looked around, holding its tail, moving my feet to keep it from walking its front legs around to where it would snap at me. It felt as if it weighed a thousand pounds. I could only lift up the back half of its body. I started dragging it toward the creek, fifty yards away. It seemed to take hours, a kind of dance between me and the great turtle, but I did it. I pulled it back through the roaring culvert, water gushing over its shell, under the spider web, and past my hidden pole and creel. I could come back later for the fish. Now there was only room in the world for Bell Brook, the turtle, and me.

The long passage upstream is a blur in my memory. I thought of salmon leaping over falls and learned a little that day how hard such a journey must be.

220

230

240

250

G COMPARE AND CONTRAST
What does the narrator have in common with Will, one of the other boys?

basking (băsk′ĭng) *adj.* warming oneself pleasantly, as in sunlight

◆ GRAMMAR IN CONTEXT
Reread the sentence that begins in line 234. This sentence contains both a **subordinate clause** and a **main clause**. Notice that the subordinate clause cannot stand alone as a sentence. The main clause can.

When I rounded the last bend and reached the place where the brook edged our property, I breathed a great sigh. But I could not rest. There was still a field and the back yard to cross.

My grandparents saw me coming. From the height of the sun it was now mid-afternoon, and I knew I was dreadful late.

260   "Sonny, where have you . . . ?" began Grama.

Then she saw the turtle.

"I'm sorry. It took so long because of . . ." I didn't finish the sentence because the snapping turtle, **undaunted** by his backward passage, took that opportunity to try once more to swing around and get me. I had to make three quick steps in a circle, heaving at its tail as I did so.

undaunted (ŭn-dôn′tĭd) *adj.* not discouraged; courageous

◄ **Analyze Visuals**

What **details** on the snapping turtle do you notice most? What details are difficult to see?

"Nice size turtle," Grampa Jesse said.

My grandmother looked at me. I realized then I must have been a sight. Wet, muddy, face and hands scratched from the brush that overhung the creek.

"I caught it at the reservoir," I said. I didn't think to lie to them about where 270 I'd been. I waited for my grandmother to scold me. But she didn't.

"Jesse," she said, "Get the big washtub."

My grandfather did as she said. He brought it back and then stepped next to me.

"Leave go," he said.

My hands had a life of their own, grimly determined never to let loose of that all-too-familiar tail, but I forced them to open. The turtle flopped down Before it could move, my grandfather dropped the big washtub over it. All was silent for a minute as I stood there, my arms aching as they hung by my side. Then the washtub began to move. My grandmother sat down on it and it 280 stopped.

She looked at me. So did Grampa. It was wonderful how they could focus their attention on me in a way that made me feel they were ready to do whatever they could to help. **H**

"What now?" Grama said.

"I heard that somebody down on Congress Street would pay ten dollars for a snapping turtle."

"Jack's," Grampa said.

My grandmother nodded. "Well," she said, "if you go now you can be back in time for supper. I thought we were having trout." She raised an 290 eyebrow at me.

"I left them this side of the culvert by 9N," I said. "Along with my pole."

"You clean up and put on dry clothes. Your grandfather will get the fish."

"But I hid them."

My grandmother smiled. "Your grandfather will find them." And he did.

An hour later, we were on the way to Congress Street. . . . In the 1950s, Congress Street was like a piece of Harlem[10] dropped into an upstate town. We pulled up in front of Jack's, and a man who looked to be my grandfather's age got up and walked over to us. His skin was only a little darker than my grandfather's, and the two nodded to each other.

300 My grandfather put his hand on the trunk of the Plymouth.

"What you got there?" Jack said.

"Show him, Sonny."

I opened the trunk. My snapping turtle lifted up its head as I did so.

"I heard you might want to buy a turtle like this for ten dollars," I said.

Jack shook his head. "Ten dollars for a little one like that? I'd give you two dollars."

I looked at my turtle. Had it shrunk since Grampa wrestled it into the trunk?

H COMPARE AND CONTRAST
Reread lines 266–283. What similar qualities do Grama and Grampa display?

Language Coach

Homonyms
Homonyms are words with the same spelling and sound but different meanings. The word *trunk* that appears in line 300 is a homonym. *Trunk* can mean either the main stem of a tree or a storage compartment in a car. Which meaning does the word have here?

---

10. **Harlem:** a New York City neighborhood that was and is largely African American.

"That's not enough," I said.

"Three dollars. My last offer."

310 I looked at Grampa. He shrugged his shoulders.

"I guess I don't want to sell it," I said.

"All right," Jack said. "You change your mind, come on back." He touched his hat with two fingers and walked back over to his chair in the sun.

As we drove back toward home, neither of us said anything for a while. Then my grandfather spoke.

"Would five dollars've been enough?"

"No," I said.

"How about ten?"

I thought about that. "I guess not."

320 "Why you suppose that turtle was heading for that sandbank?" Grampa said.

I thought about that, too. Then I realized the truth of it.

"It was coming out to lay its eggs."

"Might be."

I thought hard then. I'd learned it was never right for a hunter to shoot a mother animal, because it hurt the next generation to come. Was a turtle any different? ❶

"Can we take her back?" I asked.

"Up to you, Sonny."

And so we did. Gramp drove the Plymouth right up the trail to the edge of
330 the Rez. He held a stick so the turtle would grab onto it as I hauled her out of the trunk. I put her down and she just stayed there, her nose a foot from the water but not moving.

"We'll leave her," Grampa said. We turned to get into the car. When I looked back over my shoulder, she was gone. Only ripples on the water, widening circles rolling on toward other shores like generations following each other, like my grandmother's flowers still growing in a hundred gardens in Greenfield, like the turtles still seeking out that sandbank, like this story that is no longer just my own but belongs now to your memory, too. ◐

❶ **CULTURAL CONTEXT**
What lesson does the narrator learn? Tell how this lesson reflects Bruchac's values.

Comprehension

1. **Recall** What actions does the narrator take to make sure he fishes responsibly?

2. **Recall** Why does the narrator decide to cross under the state road?

3. **Represent** How does the narrator get the snapping turtle out of the water? Reread lines 234–243, and sketch the scene.

Text Analysis

4. **Visualize** How well does Joseph Bruchac help you visualize the characters, events, and settings in the story? Choose a passage that you find visually descriptive and explain what words and phrases help you picture the scene.

5. **Compare and Contrast Characters** What are the similarities and differences between Grama and Grampa? Consider their backgrounds, values, and traits. Use the notes from one of your Venn diagrams to help you answer the question, and cite evidence from the story.

6. **Analyze Influence of Cultural Context** Reread Bruchac's biography on page 789 to remind you of the culture within which he was raised. In what ways do the themes of "The Snapping Turtle" reflect the values of this culture? In a graphic like the one shown, give examples from the story.

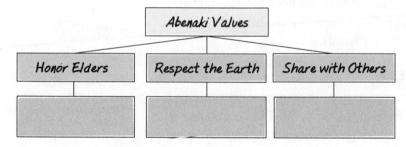

7. **Evaluate the Ending** Reread the last paragraph of the story. How well do you think it wraps up the **plot** and summarizes the **theme**? Refer to specific phrases in the paragraph as you explain your answer.

Extension and Challenge

8. **Inquiry and Research** In Native American cultures, stories are often used to teach children. Find a retelling of a Native American story, perhaps from one of Joseph Bruchac's collections, and present it to the class. Explain what lesson it is meant to teach.

Where do we get our VALUES?

The narrator and the other boys in the story appear to have different values. Describe the values the boys exhibit. Where do you think they get these values? Explain your answer.

COMMON CORE

RL 1 Cite the textual evidence that supports inferences drawn from the text. **RL 2** Determine a theme of a text and analyze its development over the course of the text. **RL 3** Analyze how particular lines of dialogue or incidents in a story or drama reveal aspects of a character.

Vocabulary in Context

▲ VOCABULARY PRACTICE

Choose the word in each group that is closest in meaning to the boldfaced word.

1. **craftiness:** (a) intelligence, (b) slyness, (c) dishonesty
2. **traipse:** (a) stroll, (b) slither, (c) bounce
3. **cache:** (a) spend, (b) waste, (c) conceal
4. **migration:** (a) relocation, (b) nesting, (c) settlement
5. **impregnable:** (a) frightening, (b) unguarded, (c) impenetrable
6. **inclination:** (a) wisdom, (b) desire, (c) strength
7. **basking:** (a) sunbathing, (b) swimming, (c) cooking
8. **undaunted:** (a) unhurt, (b) unafraid, (c) uncaring
9. **immortality:** (a) birth, (b) death, (c) permanence
10. **philosophy:** (a) belief, (b) style, (c) story

basking inclination cache migration craftiness philosophy immortality traipse impregnable undaunted

ACADEMIC VOCABULARY IN SPEAKING

• contribute • culture • interpret • perceive • similar

Imagine that the narrator has been asked to tell his class how the Abenaki **culture** views nature. What might he say? Give a speech from his point of view, using at least one of the Academic Vocabulary words.

VOCABULARY STRATEGY: ANALOGIES

An analogy is a relationship between pairs of words. To complete an analogy, identify the relationship between the words in the first pair. The second pair of words must relate to each other in the same way. One way that words may be related to each other is by function. For example, <u>feet</u> are used for the function of <u>walking</u>, just as <u>wings</u> are used for the function of <u>flying</u>. Another way that words may be related to each other is by description. For example, <u>cold</u> describes <u>snow</u>, just as <u>soft</u> describes a <u>kitten</u>.

Analogies are often written as follows—cold : snow :: soft : kitten. If the analogy is read out loud, you would say, "cold **is to** snow as soft **is to** kitten."

PRACTICE Choose a word from the box to complete each analogy.

sew   rainbow   elephant   dig

1. fork : eat :: shovel : _____
2. wet : rain :: colorful : _____
3. stove : cook :: needle : _____
4. delicate : spider web :: strong : _____

COMMON CORE

L 5b Use the relationship between particular words to better understand each of the words.

Interactive Vocabulary
THINK central
Go to **thinkcentral.com**.
KEYWORD: HML8-802

Language

◆ **GRAMMAR IN CONTEXT:** Form Compound-Complex Sentences

Review the Grammar in Context note on page 797. A **compound-complex sentence** contains two or more main, or independent, clauses and one or more subordinate, or dependent, clauses. (Recall that a subordinate clause cannot stand alone as a sentence and is introduced by words such as *after, because, if,* and *though.*) Compound-complex sentences can help add variety to writing by allowing short, related sentences to be combined.

> *Original:* I did something wrong. You were ready to help. You made me feel safe.
>
> *Revised:* Though I did something wrong, you were ready to help, and you made me feel safe.

PRACTICE In each item, combine the sentences to form one compound-complex sentence. Use the first word in parentheses to join two main clauses. Use the second word to change one sentence to a subordinate clause. In each new sentence, underline the main clauses and double underline the subordinate clause.

1. You wanted to add a new color to both your garden and hers. You'd ask the woman for her iris roots. You'd give her some of your own. (*and, if*)
2. I was going to sell the turtle. I didn't. I remembered your lessons. (*but, after*)
3. We'd catch turtles. Then we'd release them. You didn't want them to die. (*and, because*)
4. The other boys couldn't catch fish. We could. We were quiet. (*but, because*)

For more help with compound-complex sentences, see page R64 in the Grammar Handbook.

READING-WRITING CONNECTION

Demonstrate your understanding of "The Snapping Turtle" by responding to this prompt. Then use the **revising tip** to improve your writing.

WRITING PROMPT	REVISING TIP
Extended Constructed Response: Opinion Do you think that modern American society respects the Native American values described in Joseph Bruchac's story? Explain why or why not in a **two- or three-paragraph response.**	Review your response. Did you include a variety of sentence types? If not, revise your writing. Make sure to include at least one compound-complex sentence.

COMMON CORE

L 1 Demonstrate command of the conventions of standard English grammar and usage when writing or speaking. **L 3** Use knowledge of language and its conventions when writing, speaking, reading, or listening.

Interactive Revision

Go to **thinkcentral.com**.
KEYWORD: HML8-803

Out of Bounds

Short Story by Beverley Naidoo

VIDEO TRAILER **THINK** central KEYWORD: HML8-804

How do you Know what's RIGHT?

COMMON CORE

RL 1 Cite the evidence that supports inferences drawn from the text. **RL 3** Analyze how lines of dialogue or incidents in a story or drama propel the action, reveal aspects of a character, or provoke a decision.

Can you think of a situation when you weren't sure what to do? If so, you know that it's not always easy to tell right from wrong. Sometimes you must rely on your internal compass to guide your behavior. In this story, a boy decides to disobey a rule in order to help someone in need.

DISCUSS What purpose do rules serve in families and society? When might rules have to be changed? Discuss these questions with a small group.

● TEXT ANALYSIS: CULTURAL CONFLICT

When you read a story set in another country, knowing about the area's history and culture can be important background. It can help you to understand the characters' behavior and the cultural conflicts that unfold. A **cultural conflict** is a struggle that arises because of the differing values, customs, or circumstances between groups of people. For example, if a story is set in a place where one religious group has been fighting against another, parents might be angry if their child becomes friends with someone from outside their group.

"Out of Bounds" takes place in South Africa. As you read the selection, notice how the conflicts reflect the history and culture of South Africa. The background on this page will provide you with some of the information you need.

● READING SKILL: MAKE INFERENCES

Fiction writers do not always make direct statements about characters or the cultures in which they live. Instead, writers provide certain details and expect readers to combine these details with their own knowledge to "read between the lines" of a story. This process of forming logical guesses is called **making inferences.** As you read, use a chart like the one shown to record your inferences about the main characters.

Evidence from Story	My Knowledge	Inference
Rohan goes to private school.		

▲ VOCABULARY IN CONTEXT

The boldfaced words help Beverley Naidoo describe a particular society. Using context clues, try to write a definition for each word.

1. The boys **straggle** behind their older brother.
2. The flood could **maroon** many people on rooftops.
3. Members of the newer **sect** didn't agree with people from the orthodox church.
4. The Africans fought **vigorously** for equality.
5. The peace talks gave people a **glimmer** of hope.
6. The evening news was interesting enough to **engross** him.
7. We watched the energized boy **bound** up the hill.
8. Poor communication will **hamper** efforts to get along.

 Complete the activities in your **Reader/Writer Notebook.**

Meet the Author

Beverley Naidoo
born 1943

Writing for Justice
Beverley Naidoo grew up in Johannesburg, South Africa, when the country was racially segregated. It wasn't until she went to college that she recognized the injustice of the laws. After she moved to England, she decided to write children's books that speak honestly about South African society. She published her first book, *Journey to Jo'burg,* in 1984. It was banned in her home country until 1991.

BACKGROUND TO THE STORY

Apartheid
South Africa is the southernmost country on the African continent. The nation is ethnically diverse, with whites forming the smallest group. However, up until 1994, whites ruled the country under a system called apartheid (apartness). Apartheid was based on segregation between the races. The white government classified non-whites into three groups. Africans made up the largest group but had the fewest rights. "Coloureds" (people of mixed race) and those of Indian descent were granted limited rights in 1984. The government decided where each group could live, conduct business, or own land. The effects of apartheid continue to influence South African society today. Africans, on average, remain poorer and have less access to education than other groups.

Storms and Floods
"Out of Bounds" is set in 2000. That year, severe storms devastated southern Africa. Floods swept away schools, roads, crops, and livestock. About 540,000 people were left homeless.

Author Online
THINK central
Go to thinkcentral.com.
KEYWORD: HML8-805

OUT OF BOUNDS

BEVERLEY NAIDOO

Out of bounds.

That's what his parents said as soon as the squatters[1] took over the land below their house. Rohan's dad added another meter of thick concrete bricks to their garden wall and topped it with curling barbed wire. He certainly wasn't going to wait for the first break-in and be sorry later. They lived on the ridge of a steep hill with the garden sloping down. Despite the high wall, from his bedroom upstairs, Rohan could see over the spiked-wire circles down to the place where he and his friends used to play. The wild fig trees under which they had made their hideouts were still there. They had spent hours dragging

10 planks, pipes, sheets of metal and plastic—whatever might be useful—up the hill from rubbish tipped in a ditch below. The first squatters pulled their hideouts apart and used the same old scraps again for their own constructions. Rohan could still see the "ski slope"—the red earth down which he and his friends had bumped and flown on a couple of old garbage can lids. The squatters used it as their road up the hill. Now it looked like a crimson scar cut between the shacks littering the hillside.

"There's only one good thing about this business," Ma said after the back wall was completed. "We won't have to wash that disgusting red dust out of your clothes any more!" **Ⓐ**

Analyze Visuals ▶

Compare the house at the top of the hill with the buildings below. What similarities and differences do you notice?

Ⓐ CULTURAL CONFLICT
In lines 1–19, what do you learn about the family's feelings toward the squatters?

---

1. **squatters:** people who occupy public land in order to gain ownership of it.

20   Rohan said nothing. How could he explain what he had lost?

At first, some of the squatter women and children came up to the houses with buckets asking for water. For a couple of weeks his mother opened the gate after checking that no men were hanging around in the background. She allowed the women to fill their buckets at the outside tap. Most of her neighbors found themselves doing the same. Torrential rains and floods had ushered in the new millennium by sweeping away homes, animals and people in the north of the country. The television was awash with pictures of homeless families and efforts to help them. No one knew from where exactly the squatters had come. But as Ma said, how could you refuse a woman or

30   child some water?

It wasn't long before all that changed. The first complaint of clothes disappearing off the washing line came from their new neighbors. The first African family, in fact, to move in among the Indians on Mount View. No one had actually seen anyone but everyone was suspicious including the neighbor, Mrs. Zuma.

"You can't really trust these people, you know," Mrs. Zuma tutted[2] when she came to ask if Ma had seen anyone hanging around. However, it was when thieves broke into old Mrs. Pillay's house, grabbed the gold thali from around her neck, and left her with a heart attack that views hardened. Young

40   men could be seen hanging around the shacks. Were some of them not part of the same gang? Mrs. Pillay's son demanded the police search through the settlement immediately. But the police argued they would need more evidence and that the thieves could have come from anywhere. **B**

VISUAL
VOCABULARY

thali *n.* necklace given by a groom to his bride at a Hindu wedding ceremony

B MAKE INFERENCES
What ethnicity is Rohan's family?

A new nervousness now gripped the house owners on top of the hill. Every report of theft, break-in, or car hijacking, anywhere in the country, led to another conversation about the squatters on the other side of their garden walls.

At night Rohan peered through the bars of his window before going to sleep. Flickering lights from candles and lamps were the only sign that people

50   were living out there in the thick darkness. In the daytime, when Ma heard the bell and saw that it was a woman or child with a bucket, she no longer answered the call.

All the neighbors were agreed. Why should private house owners be expected to provide water for these people? That was the Council's job. If the squatters were refused water, then perhaps they would find somewhere else to put up their shacks. A more suitable place. Or even, go back to where they came from. **C**

The squatters did not go away. No one knew from where they managed to get their water or how far they had to walk. On the way to school, Rohan

60   and his dad drove past women walking with buckets on their heads.

C MAKE INFERENCES
How does crime affect the residents' attitude toward the squatters?

---

2. **tutted:** made a "tut tut" sound with the tongue to express annoyance.

"These people are tough as ticks! You let them settle and it's impossible to get them out," complained Dad. "Next thing they'll be wanting our electricity."

But Rohan wasn't really listening. He was scanning the line of African children who **straggled** behind the women and who wore the black and white uniform of Mount View Primary, his old school. He had been a pupil there until his parents had moved him to his private school in Durban[3] with its smaller classes, cricket pitch, and its own rugby ground.[4] Most of the African children at Mount View had mothers who cleaned, washed, and ironed for the families on top of the hill. But since the New Year they had been joined by the 70 squatter children and each week the line grew longer.

The queue[5] of traffic at the crossroads slowed them down, giving Rohan more time to find the "wire car" boy. He was looking for a boy who always steered a wire car in front of him with a long handle. He was about his own age—twelve or thirteen perhaps—and very thin and wiry himself. What interested Rohan was that the boy never had the same car for more than two or three days. Nor had he ever seen so many elaborate designs simply made out of wire, each suggesting a different make of car. They were much more complicated than the little wire toys in the African Crafts shop at the mall, **D**

straggle (străg′əl) v. to spread out in a scattered group

D CULTURAL CONFLICT
What differences between Rohan's life and the life of the "wire car" boy are illustrated in lines 63–78?

---

3. **Durban** (dûr′bən): a city in South Africa.

4. **cricket pitch** and **rugby ground**: playing fields for ballgames that originated in England.

5. **queue** (kyoo): a waiting line.

"Hey, cool!" Rohan whistled. "See that, Dad?" The boy must have heard
80 because he glanced toward them. His gaze slid across the silver hood of their
car toward the trunk but didn't rise up to look at Rohan directly.

"It's a Merc[6]—like ours, Dad! What a beaut! Do you think—"

"*Don't* think about it, son! You want us to stop and ask how much he wants,
don't you?"

Rohan half frowned, half smiled. How easily his father knew him!

"No way! If we start buying from these people, we'll be encouraging them!
That's not the message we want them to get now, is it?"

Rohan was quiet. He couldn't argue with his dad's logic. If the squatters
moved away, he and his friends could get their territory back again. **E**

90 **R**ohan returned home early from school. A precious half day. In the past
he would have spent it in his hideout. Instead he flicked on the television.
News. As his finger hovered over the button to switch channels, the whirr of a
helicopter invaded the living room.

"Hey, Ma! Look at this!"

Ma appeared from the kitchen, her hands cupped, white and dusty with
flour. On the screen, a tight human knot swung at the end of a rope above a
valley swirling with muddy water.

"A South African Air Force rescue team today saved a baby from certain
death just an hour after she was born in a tree. Her mother was perched in the
100 tree over floodwaters that have devastated Mozambique. The mother and her
baby daughter were among the lucky few. Many thousands of Mozambicans
are still waiting to be lifted to safety from branches and rooftops. They have
now been **marooned** for days by the rising water that has swallowed whole
towns and villages."

"Those poor people! What a place to give birth!" Ma's floury hands almost
looked ready to cradle a baby.

Rohan was watching how the gale from the rotors[7] forced the leaves and
branches of the tree to open like a giant flower until the helicopter began to
lift. Members of the mother's family still clung desperately to the main trunk.
110 Rohan saw both fear and determination in their eyes.

He and Ma listened to the weather report that followed. Although Cyclone
Eline was over, Cyclone Gloria[8] was now whipping up storms across the Indian
Ocean and heading toward Mozambique. Where would it go next? Durban
was only down the coast. Rohan had seen a program about a **sect** who believed
the new millennium would mark the end of the world. They were convinced
that the floods were a sign that The End was beginning.

"What if the cyclone comes here, Ma?"

---

6. **Merc:** short for Mercedes, a brand of car.
7. **rotors** (rō'tərz): helicopter blades.
8. **Cyclone Eline, Cyclone Gloria:** tropical storms that struck in 2000.

E CULTURAL CONFLICT
Reread lines 83–89. How is Rohan's reason for wanting the squatters to leave different from that of his father?

SOCIAL STUDIES CONNECTION

Racial tension in South Africa and Mozambique affected the response to the flooding.

maroon (mə-roōn') *v.* to leave behind in a place from which there is little hope of escape

sect (sĕkt) *n.* a religious group

"No, we'll be all right son. But that lot out there will get it. The government really should do something." Ma nodded in the direction of the squatters.

120 "Now, let me finish these *rotis*⁹ for your sister!"

Ma returned to her bread making. When she had finished, she wanted Rohan to come with her to his married sister's house. He pleaded to stay behind.

"I've got homework to do, Ma! I'll be fine."

"You won't answer the door unless it's someone we know, will you?"

"No, Ma!" he chanted. Ma said the same thing every time.

Alone in the house, Rohan daydreamed at his desk. He was close enough to the window to see down the hill. What if there was so much rain that a river formed along the road below! As the water rose, people would have to abandon their shacks to climb higher up. They would be trapped between the flood 130 below and the torrents above. In assembly they had heard the story of Noah building the ark. Perhaps it wasn't just a story after all. Perhaps the people had tried to cling on to the tops of trees as tightly as those they had seen on television.

Tough as ticks.

The phrase popped into his mind. Wasn't that what his dad had said about the squatters? Yet the one sure way to get rid of ticks was to cover them in liquid paraffin.¹⁰ Drown them. A terrible thought. He should push it right away. 🅵

Rohan was about to stretch out for his math book when a figure caught his eye on the old ski slope. It was the thin wiry boy, but he wasn't pushing a 140 car this time. He was carrying two large buckets, one on his head, the other by his side. He descended briskly down the slope and turned along the road in the opposite direction to that taken by the women who carried buckets on their heads. Rohan followed the figure until he went out of sight, then forced himself to open his book.

The bell rang just as he was getting interested in the first question. Nuisance! He hurried to the landing. If someone was standing right in front of the gate, it was possible to see who it was from the window above the stairs. He stood back, careful not to be seen himself. It was the same boy, an empty container on the ground each side of him! Didn't he know not to come to 150 the house up here? But he was only a child, and it looked as if he just wanted some water. It would be different if it were an adult or a complete stranger. Rohan's daydream also made him feel a little guilty. He could see the boy look anxiously through the bars, his hand raised as if wondering whether to ring the bell again. Usually when the boy was pushing his wire car on the way to school, he appeared relaxed and calm.

By the time the bell rang a second time, Rohan had decided. He hurried downstairs but slowed himself as he walked outside toward the gate.

🅵 **MAKE INFERENCES**
Note the change in Rohan's attitude toward the squatters. What has caused this change?

Language Coach

Suffixes A suffix is a word part added to the end of a word to form a new word. The word *anxiously* in line 153 contains the suffix *-ly. Anxious* means "nervous." The suffix *-ly* means "in the manner of." What do you think *anxiously* means?

---

9. *rotis* (rō′tēs): Indian flatbreads that are cooked on a griddle.

10. **paraffin** (păr′ə-fĭn): wax.

"What do you want?" Rohan tried not to show that he recognized the boy.

"I need water for my mother. Please." The boy held his palms out in front
160 of him as if asking for a favor. "My mother—she's having a baby—it's bad—
there's no more water. Please."

This was an emergency. Not on television but right in front of him. Still
Rohan hesitated. His parents would be extremely cross that he had put himself
in this situation by coming to talk to the boy. Weren't there stories of adults who
used children as decoys to get people to open their gates so they could storm in?
He should have stayed inside. Should he tell the boy to go next door where there
would at least be an adult? But the boy had chosen to come here. Perhaps he had
seen Rohan watching him from the car and knew this was his house.

"We stay there." The boy pointed in the direction of the squatter camp. "I
170 go to school there." He pointed in the direction of Mount View Primary. He
was trying to reassure Rohan that it would be OK to open the gate. He was
still in his school uniform but wore a pair of dirty-blue rubber sandals. His
legs were as thin as sticks.

"Isn't there a doctor with your mother?" It was such a silly question that as
soon as it was out, Rohan wished he could take it back. If they could afford a
doctor, they wouldn't be squatters on a bare hillside. The boy shook his head
vigorously. If he thought it was stupid, he didn't let it show on his troubled face.

"Wait there!" Rohan returned to the house. The button for the electric gate
was inside the front door. The boy waited while the wrought-iron bars slowly
180 rolled back.

"OK. Bring your buckets over here." Rohan pointed to the outside tap.
The buckets clanked against each other as the boy jogged toward him.

"Thank you," he said quietly.

The unexpected softness in his voice had a strange effect on Rohan.
It sounded so different from his own bossy tone. Suddenly he felt a little
ashamed. This was the same boy whose wire cars he admired! If he were
still at Mount View Primary they would probably be in the same class.
They might even have been friends, and he would be learning how to make
wire cars himself. Why had he spoken so arrogantly? It was really only a
190 small favor that was being asked for. The water in the bucket gurgling and
churning reminded Rohan of the water swirling beneath the Mozambican
woman with her baby. *Her* rescuer had been taking a really big risk but
hadn't looked big headed.[11] He had just got on with the job.

When both buckets were full, the boy stooped to lift one on to his head.
Rohan saw his face and neck muscles strain under the weight. How would he
manage to keep it balanced and carry the other bucket too? **G**

"Wait! I'll give you a hand." Rohan's offer was out before he had time to
think it through properly. If the boy was surprised, he didn't show it. All his
energy seemed to be focused on his task. Rohan dashed into the kitchen to
200 grab the spare set of keys. Ma would be away for another hour at least. He

vigorously (vĭg'ər-əs-lē)
adv. energetically

COMMON CORE RL 1

G MAKE INFERENCES
Paying attention to a
character's thoughts
and actions can help you
make inferences about
his or her qualities. In
turn, you can analyze
how those qualities
affect a story's plot and
theme. What qualities
does Rohan reveal in
lines 184–196? As you
read, consider what
these qualities help
Rohan to discover about
the world.

---

11. **big headed:** conceited.

would be back soon, and she need never know. It was only after the gate clicked behind them that Rohan remembered the neighbors. If anyone saw him, they were bound to ask Ma what he was doing with a boy from the squatter camp. He crossed the fingers of one hand. **H**

At first Rohan said nothing. Sharing the weight of the bucket, he could feel the strain all the way up from his fingers to his left shoulder. When they reached the corner and set off down the hill, the bucket seemed to propel them forward. It was an effort to keep a steady pace. Rohan glanced at the container on the boy's head, marveling at how he kept it balanced. He caught the boy's eye.

210   "How do you do that? You haven't spilled a drop!"

The boy gave a **glimmer** of a smile.

"You learn."

Rohan liked the simple reply. He should ask the boy about the cars. This was his chance, before they turned into the noisy main road and reached the squatter camp.

"I've seen you with wire cars. Do you make them yourself?"

"Yes—and my brother."

"You make them together? Do you keep them all?"

"My brother—he sells them at the beach." The boy waved his free hand in

220 the direction of the sea. "The tourists—they like them." **I**

"Your cars are better than any I've seen in the shops! Do you get lots of money for them?"

"Mmhh!" The boy made a sound something between a laugh and a snort. Rohan realized that he had asked another brainless question. Would they be staying in a shack if they got lots of money? Rohan had often seen his own father bargaining to get something cheaper from a street hawker.[12] He tried to cover his mistake.

"There's a shop in the mall where they sell wire cars. They charge a lot and yours are a hundred times better!"

230   "We can't go there. The guards—they don't let us in."

Rohan knew the security guards at the entrance to the mall. Some of them even greeted his parents with a little salute. Rohan had seen poor children hanging around outside. They offered to push your trolley,[13] to clean your car—anything for a few cents. Sometimes Ma gave an orange or an apple from her shopping bag to a child. Other times she would just say "No thank you" and wave a child away. Ma never gave money. . . . Rohan had never thought what it would be like to be chased away. How did the guards decide who could enter? How could the boy and his brother go and show the lady in the African Crafts shop his cars if they weren't allowed in? **J**

240   Rohan was quiet as they reached the main road and turned toward the squatter camp. The noise of vehicles roaring past was deafening. He never normally walked down here. Not by himself nor with anyone else. His family

---

12. **hawker:** seller.

13. **trolley:** shopping cart.

H **CULTURAL CONFLICT**
What is Rohan's biggest fear about leaving the house to help the boy?

glimmer (glĭm'ər) *n.* a faint sign

I **MAKE INFERENCES**
Reread lines 208–220. What are some of the boy's qualities?

J **CULTURAL CONFLICT**
Reread lines 230–239. How are Rohan and the boy treated differently by the society in which they live?

went everywhere by car. With all the locks down, of course. The only people who walked were poor people. His eyes were drawn to a group of young men walking toward them. They were still some distance away, but already Rohan began to feel uneasy. They were coming from the crossroads that his dad always approached on full alert. Rohan knew how his father jumped the red lights when the road was clear, especially at night. Everyone had heard stories of gangs who hijacked cars waiting for the lights to change.

250   The handle had begun to feel like it was cutting into his fingers. The boy must have sensed something because he signaled to Rohan to lower the bucket. For a few seconds they each stretched their fingers.

    "It's too far? You want to go?" The boy was giving him a chance to change his mind. To leave and go back home. He had already helped carry the water more than half the way. He could make an excuse about the time. But the thought of running back to the house along the road on his own now worried him.

    "No, it's fine. Let's go." Rohan heard a strange brightness in his own voice. He curled his fingers around the handle again. **K**

260   As they drew nearer the men, Rohan felt their gaze on him and suddenly his head was spinning with questions. Why on earth had he offered to help carry the water? What did he think he was doing coming down here? And he hadn't even yet entered the squatter camp itself!

    "We go here." The boy's voice steadied him a little.

    Rohan turned and stared up at his old ski slope. He felt the force of the young men's eyes on his back as he and the boy began to ascend the rough track. Someone behind called out something in Zulu[14] and, without turning, the boy shouted back.

    The words flew so quickly into one another that Rohan didn't pick up any
270 even though he was learning Zulu in school. They must be talking about him, but he was too embarrassed—and frightened—to ask. He could feel his heart pumping faster and told himself it was because of the stiff climb. He needed to concentrate where he put each foot. The track was full of holes and small stones. A quick glance over his shoulder revealed that the young men had also entered the squatter camp but seemed to be heading for a shack with a roof covered in old tires on the lower slope. A couple of them were still watching. He must just look ahead and control his fear. As long as he was with the boy, he was safe, surely? **L**

    A bunch of small children appeared from nowhere, giggling and staring. He
280 couldn't follow their chatter but heard the word *"iNdiya!"* The boy ignored them until a couple of children started darting back and forth in front of them, sweeping up the red dust with their feet.

    "Hambani!" Rohan could hear the boy's irritation as he waved them away. But the darting and dancing continued just out of reach.

K MAKE INFERENCES
What do you think gives Rohan renewed determination to help?

L MAKE INFERENCES
Reread lines 269–278. What is Rohan afraid of?

---

14. **Zulu** (zōō'lōō): the language of the Zulu, a Bantu people of South Africa.

"Hambani-bo!" This time the boy's voice deepened to a threat, and the cluster of children pulled aside with one or two mischievous grins. Beads of sweat had begun trickling down the boy's face. With his own skin prickling with sticky heat, Rohan wondered at the wiry strength of the boy whose back, head, and bucket were still perfectly upright as they mounted the hill.

290   "It's that one—we stay there." The boy, at last, pointed to a structure of corrugated iron,[15] wood, and black plastic a little further up. It was not far from the old fig trees. For a moment Rohan thought he would say something about his hideout which the first squatters had pulled down. But he stopped himself. Maybe the boy had even been one of them!

   As they drew nearer, they heard a woman moaning and a couple of other women's voices that sounded as if they were comforting her. The boy lowered the bucket swiftly from his head and pushed aside a plywood sheet, the door to his home.

▼ **Analyze Visuals**

What do you think life is like in the **setting** pictured?

---

15. **corrugated** (kôr′ə-gā′tĭd) **iron:** sheet iron with parallel ridges.

Rohan wasn't sure what to do. He knew he couldn't follow. The sounds from within scared him. The moans were rapid and painful. . . .

Rohan folded his arms tightly, trying not to show how awkward he felt. The little children were still watching but keeping their distance. They could probably also hear the cries. It would be hard to keep anything private here. The only other people nearby were two gray-haired men sitting on boxes a little lower down the hill. One of them was bent over an old-fashioned sewing machine placed on a metal drum, a makeshift table. Normally Rohan would have been very curious to see what he was stitching, but now he was just grateful that both men were **engrossed** in talking and didn't seem interested in him.

He turned to look up the hill—toward his house and the others at the top protected by their walls with wires, spikes, and broken bottles. When he had hidden in his hideout down here, he had always loved the feeling of being safe yet almost in his own separate little country. But that had been a game and he could just hop over the wall to return to the other side. Surrounded now by homes made out of scraps and other people's leftovers, this place seemed a complete world away from the houses on the hill. In fact, how was he going to get home? If he didn't leave soon, Ma would be back before him. Would the boy at least take him part of the way through the squatter camp? He needed him to come outside so that he could ask him.

"What do you want here?"

Rohan spun around. A man with half-closed eyes and his head tilted to one side stood with his hands on his hips, surveying Rohan from head to foot. His gaze lingered for a moment on Rohan's watch.

"I . . . I brought water with . . . with . . ." Rohan stammered. He hadn't asked the boy his name! Panic-stricken, he pointed to the door of the shack. The man stepped forward, and Rohan stumbled back against the wall of corrugated iron. The clattering brought the boy to the door. The man immediately switched into loud, fast Zulu. The boy spoke quietly at first, but when the man's voice didn't calm down, the boy's began to rise too. Even when he pointed to the bucket and Rohan, the man's face remained scornful. Rohan was fully expecting to be grabbed when a sharp baby's cry interrupted the argument. The boy's face lit up, and the man suddenly fell silent. Rohan's heart thumped wildly as the man's eyes mocked him before he turned and walked away. Ⓜ

Rohan folded his arms tightly, trying not to shake. Before he could say anything, a lady appeared behind the boy, placing a hand on his shoulder.

"You have a little sister!" She smiled at the boy and then at Rohan. She looked friendly but tired. Her cheeks shone as if she too had been perspiring. It was obviously hard work helping to deliver a baby.

"Tell your mother thank you for the water. You really helped us today."

Rohan managed to smile back.

"It's OK." His voice came out strangely small.

"Solani will take you back now—before it gets dark."

Rohan felt a weight lifting. He did not need to ask.

engross (ĕn-grōs') *v.*
to completely occupy

Language Coach

Word Definitions The word *surveying* in line 321 means "to look at carefully." Why do you think the man was surveying Rohan?

Ⓜ **CULTURAL CONFLICT**
Why do you think the man is scornful and mocks Rohan with his eyes?

The sun was getting lower and made long rodlike shadows leap beside them as they scrambled down the slope. Knowing the boy's name made Rohan feel a little easier, and he wondered why he hadn't asked him earlier. He told Solani his own, and the next thing he was telling him about riding on garbage can lids down the ski slope. Solani grinned.

"It's good! But this place—it's a road now. We can't do it. The people will be angry if we knock someone down."

350 Rohan understood that. But what he didn't understand was why the man with scornful eyes had been so angry with him. And why had those other young men looked at him so suspiciously? He decided to ask Solani.

"They don't know you. Sometimes people come and attack us. So if a stranger comes, they must always check first."

When they reached the road, neither spoke. The hometime traffic would have drowned their voices anyway. Rohan thought about what Solani had said about him being a stranger. Surely they knew that he was from one of the houses on top of the hill. The houses that also did not welcome strangers. Like the squatters.

360 They parted at the top of the hill. Rohan was anxious to reach the house before his mother returned, and Solani was eager to see his baby sister. Opening the electronic gates, Rohan was relieved that his mother's car was neither in the yard nor the garage. He dashed upstairs to his room and peered out of the window over to the squatter camp. The evening was falling very rapidly. His mother would be home any minute—and his dad. Neither liked to drive in the dark if they could help it.

▲ **Analyze Visuals**
Note the boy's expression and body language. What can you **infer** about his mood?

Language Coach

Word Root A root is a word part that contains the core meaning of the word. The root for the word *angry* is *angr*, which means "painfully constricted" or "sorrow." Reread lines 348–349. How will the people feel if the boys knock someone down?

Ⓝ **CULTURAL CONFLICT**
What do Rohan's neighborhood and the squatters' camp have in common?

Rohan fixed his eyes on the deep crimson scar, hoping to see Solani climbing the slope. How strange to think that he had been there himself less than half an hour ago. In that other world. Yes! There was Solani! A tiny, wiry figure
370 **bounding** up the hill. Not **hampered** this time with a container of water on his head. Rohan watched Solani weave through other figures traveling more slowly until three quarters of the way up the hill, he darted off and disappeared into the darkening shadow that was his home.

Rohan surprised his parents by joining them for the eight o'clock news. The story about the rescue of mother and baby from the floods in Mozambique was repeated.

"Sophia Pedro and her baby daughter Rositha were among the lucky few. Many thousands of Mozambicans are still waiting to be lifted to safety. . . ."

This time the reporter added their names. Rohan observed the mother
380 more closely. Had she also cried and moaned like Solani's mother? With the roaring waters underneath, how many people had heard her? **O**

"It's nice to see these South African soldiers doing some good," said Ma when the news was finished.

Rohan wished he could say what he too had done that afternoon. But he feared the storm that it would let loose and went upstairs to his bedroom. Before slipping between his sheets, he peered out once again through the bars at the hill swallowed up by the night. He thought he saw a light still flickering in Solani's home and wondered how many people were tucked inside the sheets of iron, plastic, and wood. He prayed that Cyclone Gloria
390 would keep well away.

Next morning, the glint of metal beside the gate caught his eye from the front door. His dad was reversing the car out of the garage. Rohan ran across the drive. There, just inside the gate, was a wire car. A small, perfect Merc! Who could it be from, except Solani? He must have slipped it through the bars of the gate in the early morning. Quickly Rohan pushed it behind a cluster of scarlet gladioli. If his parents saw it, they would want to know from where it had come. They would discover he had gone out of bounds. . . . Well, so had Solani! Each of them had taken a risk. He needed time to think. In the meantime, the car would have to be his secret. Their secret.
400 His and Solani's. ～ **P**

bound (bound) v. to leap forward

hamper (hăm′pər) v. to prevent the free movement of

O MAKE INFERENCES
Why has Rohan become more interested in the news?

P MAKE INFERENCES
Reread lines 384–400. What qualities does Rohan show here? Explain why Rohan's qualities are important to the story's theme, or message about life.

Comprehension

1. **Recall** Why doesn't Rohan go to his hideout anymore?

2. **Recall** Where has Rohan seen Solani before Solani comes to his house?

3. **Represent** Make a sketch showing Rohan's house and the squatters' camp. Think about what these places look like and where they are in relation to one another. Use descriptions in the story to guide you.

COMMON CORE

RL 1 Cite the evidence that supports inferences drawn from the text. **RL 3** Analyze how lines of dialogue or incidents in a story or drama propel the action, reveal aspects of a character, or provoke a decision.

Text Analysis

4. **Make Inferences About Characters** Review your chart of inferences about the characters and their culture. Despite their differences, what qualities do Rohan and Solani share? Name three reasons why these two boys might be drawn together.

5. **Analyze Cultural Conflict** What causes the residents of Mount View to discriminate against the squatters? Consider what you know about the history and culture of South Africa as well as events in the story's plot. Record your response in a diagram like the one shown.

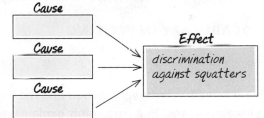

Cause

Cause

Cause

Effect

discrimination against squatters

6. **Evaluate Attitudes** Describe the attitudes of Rohan's mother and father toward the squatters. Do you think they are prejudiced against Africans? Then consider Rohan's experience in the squatters' camp. Do you think the Africans are prejudiced against him? Explain your responses, citing evidence from the story.

7. **Make Judgments** Who do you think took the greater risk by going out of bounds—Rohan or Solani? Explain your answer.

Extension and Challenge

8. **Text Criticism** As a child, Beverley Naidoo didn't notice that she lived in an unfair society. "It was like being brought up to be a horse with blinkers," she has said. "Luckily when I left school, I met people who challenged me . . . and I was able to take off the blinkers." How do Rohan's experiences in "Out of Bounds" reflect the author's background?

9.  **SOCIAL STUDIES CONNECTION** Research Nelson Mandela's role in ending the system of apartheid in South Africa. Why is he considered an inspirational leader?

Nelson Mandela

How do you know what is RIGHT?

Reread lines 162–180. Why did Rohan decide to disregard his mother's instructions and open the gate to Solani?

Vocabulary in Context

▲ VOCABULARY PRACTICE

For each item, choose the word that differs most in meaning from the other words. Refer to a dictionary if you need help.

1. (a) bound, (b) leap, (c) spring, (d) stroll
2. (a) engross, (b) distract, (c) involve, (d) interest
3. (a) glimmer, (b) trace, (c) fraction, (d) excess
4. (a) hamper, (b) free, (c) prevent, (d) hinder
5. (a) maroon, (b) rescue, (c) save, (d) retrieve
6. (a) sect, (b) denomination, (c) group, (d) everyone
7. (a) straggle, (b) lead, (c) scatter, (d) dawdle
8. (a) vigorously, (b) energetically, (c) enthusiastically, (d) weakly

ACADEMIC VOCABULARY IN WRITING

> • contribute • culture • interpret • perceive • similar

Rohan feels a connection between himself and the South African soldiers helping the Mozambicans. In a paragraph, explain whether you think his actions are **similar** to the soldiers'. Use at least one Academic Vocabulary word in your response.

VOCABULARY STRATEGY: USING REFERENCE AIDS

When you encounter a new word, you'll want to learn what it means as well as how to pronounce it. To pronounce long words, it helps to break them into syllables and concentrate on pronouncing one syllable at a time. But if you don't know a word, how can you know what syllables it contains? One way is to look up the word in the dictionary. Not only will you find the definition of the word, but the syllables of each entry will be separated by dots, as shown in the example below:

re•con•nais•sanse (rĭ-kŏn′ə-səns) *n.* An inspection or exploration of an area, especially one made to gather military information.

PRACTICE Look up each word below in a dictionary. Divide the word into syllables and write a simple definition for it.

1. cuneiform
2. hierarchy
3. idiosyncrasy
4. lamentable
5. masticate
6. perpetuate

Interactive Vocabulary THINK central

Go to thinkcentral.com.
KEYWORD: HML8-820

Language

◆ **GRAMMAR IN CONTEXT: Use Colons Correctly**

A **colon** should be placed after a formal greeting in a business letter (*To Whom It May Concern:*) and before a list of items (*I had the following foods for breakfast: eggs, toast, and cereal*). When using a colon to introduce a list, avoid placing it directly after a verb or a preposition. Instead, insert the colon after a noun or after the words *the following*.

Original: The squatters suffer from: poverty, homelessness, and a lack of water.

Revised: The squatters suffer from the following: poverty, homelessness, and a lack of water. (*Inserting* the following *after the preposition* from *makes use of the colon correct.*)

PRACTICE Rewrite the following letter, correcting the colon errors.

> Dear Mount View residents
> To improve our relationship with the squatters, we are recommending that residents provide squatters with: food, water, and blankets. Also, we request that these professionals offer aid to the squatters, doctors, nurses, and teachers. From the walls, please remove: wire, spikes, and broken glass.

*For more help with using colons correctly, see page R50 in the **Grammar Handbook**.*

READING-WRITING CONNECTION

Demonstrate your understanding of "Out of Bounds" by responding to this prompt. Then use the **revising tip** to improve your writing.

WRITING PROMPT	REVISING TIP
Extended Constructed Response: A Plan How could the residents of Mount View Improve their relationship with the squatters? Write a **two- or three-paragraph plan** to help the two communities better understand one another.	Review your plan. Did you introduce any lists of problems or suggestions? If so, make sure you used colons correctly.

Interactive Revision **THINK** central

Go to **thinkcentral.com**.
KEYWORD: HML8-821

COMMON CORE

L 2 Demonstrate command of punctuation. **W 2** Write explanatory texts.

Pecos Bill

 HISTORY

Video link at
thinkcentral.com

Tall Tale Retold by Mary Pope Osborne

What is a
FOLK HERO?

A steel-driving man who defeats a machine through hard work and
perseverance. An outlaw who steals from the rich to give to the poor.
A cowgirl who can circle the moon. Every culture has its folk heroes,
characters whose courage, generosity, or accomplishments inspire
ordinary people. Some folk heroes are real people or are based on the
lives of real people; others are invented to symbolize the values of a
particular culture. In the tall tale you are about to read, you will meet a
fictional American folk hero known for his strength and bravery.

DISCUSS Imagine you were on a committee to select a folk hero to speak
at your school. In small groups, choose a real person or a character
you've read about who would inspire you and your classmates. What
qualities does this person possess that make him or her a folk hero?
What topics would you like to see this person address at your school?

● TEXT ANALYSIS: TALL TALE

Folk heroes often appear in **tall tales,** which are humorous stories about impossible events. Many of these stories originated in the American frontier and were passed down from generation to generation by being told out loud. Some of them even started off with a kernel of truth, but as you'll see, they aren't exactly realistic. Tall tales have these characteristics:

- The hero or heroine is often larger than life, which means he or she is bigger, louder, stronger, or stranger than any real person could be.
- Problems are solved in humorous ways.
- **Hyperbole,** or exaggeration, is used to emphasize the main character's qualities and create humor.

Review the Background on this page to learn more about how the conditions of the frontier affected the stories that were told there. Then, as you read, note how these characteristics apply to "Pecos Bill."

● READING STRATEGY: VISUALIZE

Tall tales are funny and action-packed. To enjoy them fully, it helps to **visualize,** or picture in your mind, the incredible events in the story as you read about them. To visualize, focus on descriptions that appeal to your senses, especially those of sight, sound, and touch. Use these sensory details to form a mental picture of the characters and action. As you read, use a chart like the one shown to note descriptive words and phrases that help you visualize the tall tale.

Character or Event	Descriptive Words or Phrases
Little Bill falls out of the wagon.	"sat there in the dirt" "rattle off in a cloud of dust"

Complete the activities in your **Reader/Writer Notebook.**

Mary Pope Osborne
born 1949

Finding Her Way
After graduating from college, Mary Pope Osborne decided to explore the world. She traveled around Europe, the Middle East, and southern Asia. She slept outdoors and bathed in rivers in Iraq, Afghanistan, and India. And, she says, she was "terrified" almost the whole time. She survived an earthquake and a riot, only to end up sick in a hospital, all alone and far from home. While she rested, she read J. R. R. Tolkien's *The Lord of the Rings* series. She identified with Tolkien's hero, Frodo, whose dangerous journey seemed to resemble her own. Says Osborne, "Ultimately Frodo's courage and powers of endurance became mine," which helped her recover from her illness and make her way home. Eventually, she began writing children's stories for fun and discovered her new career.

BACKGROUND TO THE TALL TALE
Tall Tales and the American Frontier
Tall tales are often set on the American frontier—large parts of the West and Southwest that had small populations in the 19th century. Life on the frontier was often adventurous and free-spirited, and sharing stories became an important social activity. Tall tales may have started as bragging contests held by ranch hands. As the workers tried to outdo each other, they exaggerated stories about their abilities more and more. The achievements described in tall tales often center around the characteristics of courage, determination, and cleverness, all of which were needed to survive on the frontier.

Author Online
THINK central
Go to thinkcentral.com.
KEYWORD: HML8-823

Pecos Bill

RETOLD BY MARY POPE OSBORNE

A sk any coyote near the Pecos River in western Texas who was the best cowboy who ever lived, and he'll throw back his head and howl, "Ah-hooo!" If you didn't know already, that's coyote language for *Pecos Bill*.

When Pecos Bill was a little baby, he was as tough as a pine knot. He teethed on horseshoes instead of teething rings and played with grizzly bears instead of teddy bears. He could have grown up just fine in the untamed land of eastern Texas. But one day his pappy ran in from the fields, hollering, "Pack up, Ma! Neighbors movin' in fifty miles away! It's gettin' too crowded!"

Before sundown Bill's folks loaded their fifteen kids and all their belongings
10 into their covered wagon and started west. **A**

As they clattered across the desolate land of western Texas, the crushing heat nearly drove them all crazy. Baby Bill got so hot and cross that he began to wallop[1] his big brothers. Pretty soon all fifteen kids were going at one another tooth and nail.[2] Before they turned each other into catfish bait, Bill fell out of the wagon and landed *kerplop* on the sun-scorched desert. **B**

The others were so busy fighting that they didn't even notice the baby was missing until it was too late to do anything about it.

Well, tough little Bill just sat there in the dirt, watching his family rattle off in a cloud of dust, until an old coyote walked over and sniffed him.
20 "Goo-goo!" Bill said.

Now it's an amazing coincidence, but "Goo-goo" happens to mean something similar to "Glad to meet you" in coyote language. Naturally the old coyote figured he'd come across one of his own kind. He gave Bill a big lick and picked him up by the scruff of the neck and carried him home to his den.

---

1. **wallop** (wŏl'əp): to beat up.

2. **tooth and nail:** very fiercely.

Analyze Visuals ▶

What **details** make this illustration humorous?

A TALL TALE

Which of young Bill's and his father's qualities are exaggerated?

B VISUALIZE

Reread lines 11–15. What words and phrases help you picture the scene?

Illustrations by Michael McCurdy.

Bill soon discovered the coyote's kinfolk were about the wildest, roughest bunch you could imagine. Before he knew it, he was roaming the prairies with the pack. He howled at the moon, sniffed the brush, and chased lizards across the sand. He was having such a good time, scuttling about naked and dirty on all fours, that he completely forgot what it was like to be a
30 human. **C**

Pecos Bill's coyote days came to an end about seventeen years later. One evening as he was sniffing the sagebrush, a cowpoke[3] came loping by on a big horse. "Hey, you!" he shouted. "What in the world are you?"

Bill sat on his haunches and stared at the feller.

"What *are* you?" asked the cowpoke again.

"Varmint,"[4] said Bill hoarsely, for he hadn't used his human voice in seventeen years.

"No, you ain't!"

"Yeah, I am. I got fleas, don't I?"

40 "Well, that don't mean nothing. A lot of Texans got fleas. The thing varmints got that you ain't got is a tail."

"Oh, yes, I do have a tail," said Pecos Bill.

"Lemme see it then," said the cowpoke.

Bill turned around to look at his rear end, and for the first time in his life he realized he didn't have a tail.

"Dang," he said. "But if I'm not a varmint, what am I?"

"You're a cowboy! So start acting like one!"

Bill just growled at the feller like any coyote worth his salt[5] would. But deep down in his heart of hearts he knew the cowpoke was right. For the last
50 seventeen years he'd had a sneaking suspicion that he was different from that pack of coyotes. For one thing, none of them seemed to smell quite as bad as he did. **D**

So with a heavy heart he said good-bye to his four-legged friends and took off with the cowpoke for the nearest ranch.

Acting like a human wasn't all that easy for Pecos Bill. Even though he soon started dressing right, he never bothered to shave or comb his hair. He'd just throw some water on his face in the morning and go around the rest of the day looking like a wet dog. Ignorant cowpokes claimed Bill wasn't too smart. Some of the meaner ones liked to joke that he wore a ten-dollar hat on a
60 five-cent head.

The truth was Pecos Bill would soon prove to be one of the greatest cowboys who ever lived. He just needed to find the kind of folks who'd appreciate him. One night when he was licking his dinner plate, his ears perked up. A couple of ranch hands were going on about a gang of wild cowboys.

C TALL TALE
Baby Bill gets separated from his family. What's humorous about the way this problem gets solved?

D TALL TALE
Reread lines 39–52. Which lines, if any, are funny to you? Explain why.

---

3. **cowpoke:** cowhand; cattle herder.

4. **varmint:** wild and/or vicious animal.

5. **worth his salt:** worthy of respect.

"Yep. Those fellas are more animal than human," one ranch hand was saying.

"Yep. Them's the toughest bunch I ever come across. Heck, they're so tough, they can kick fire out of flint rock[6] with their bare toes!"

"Yep. 'N' they like to bite nails in half for fun!"

"Who are these fellers?" asked Bill.

70 "The Hell's Gate Gang," said the ranch hand. "The mangiest, meanest, most low-down bunch of low-life varmints that ever grew hair."

"Sounds like my kind of folks," said Bill, and before anyone could holler whoa, he jumped on his horse and took off for Hell's Gate Canyon. **E**

Bill hadn't gone far when disaster struck. His horse stepped in a hole and broke its ankle.

"Dang!" said Bill as he stumbled up from the spill. He draped the lame critter around his neck and hurried on.

After he'd walked about a hundred more miles, Bill heard some mean rattling. Then a fifty-foot rattlesnake reared up its ugly head and stuck out its 80 long, forked tongue, ready to fight.

"Knock it off, you scaly-hided fool. I'm in a hurry," Bill said.

The snake didn't give a spit for Bill's plans. He just rattled on.

Before the cussed varmint could strike, Bill had no choice but to knock him cross-eyed. "Hey, feller," he said, holding up the dazed snake. "I like your spunk. Come go with us." Then he wrapped the rattler around his arm and continued on his way.

After Bill had hiked another hundred miles with his horse around his neck and his snake around his arm, he heard a terrible growl. A huge mountain lion was crouching on a cliff, getting ready to leap on top of him.

90 "Don't jump, you mangy bobtailed[7] fleabag!" Bill said.

Well, call any mountain lion a mangy bobtailed fleabag, and he'll jump on your back for sure. After this one leaped onto Bill, so much fur began to fly that it darkened the sky. Bill wrestled that mountain lion into a headlock, then squeezed him so tight that the big cat had to cry uncle.[8]

When the embarrassed old critter started to slink off, Bill felt sorry for him. "Aw, c'mon, you big silly," he said. "You're more like me than most humans I meet."

He saddled up the cat, jumped on his back, and the four of them headed for the canyon, with the mountain lion screeching, the horse neighing, the rattler 100 rattling, and Pecos Bill hollering a wild war whoop. **F**

When the Hell's Gate Gang heard those noises coming from the prairie, they nearly fainted. They dropped their dinner plates, and their faces turned as white as bleached desert bones. Their knees knocked and their six-guns shook.

"Hey, there!" Bill said as he sidled up to their campfire, grinning. "Who's the boss around here?"

---

6. **flint rock:** a very hard, fine-grained quartz that sparks when struck with steel.

7. **bobtailed:** having a very short tail or one that has been bobbed (cut short).

8. **cry uncle:** give up fighting; admit that one has been beaten.

COMMON CORE RL 3, RL 5

E TALL TALE
When you read a work with a historical setting, you can often learn what was important to the people who lived then by paying attention to the main character. What this character thinks and feels can reflect the attitudes of the general population. Reread lines 55–73. What qualities does Bill seem to value? Consider why these qualities might have been desirable on the frontier.

COMMON CORE L 5a

Language Coach
Figures of Speech
When words are used to express something other than their usual meaning, they are called figures of speech. In line 82, the expression "didn't give a spit" is a figure of speech that means the snake didn't care.

F VISUALIZE
Reread lines 98–100. What words help you see and hear the action?

A nine-foot feller with ten pistols at his sides stepped forward and in a shaky voice said, "Stranger, I was. But from now on, it'll be you."

"Well, thanky, pardner," said Bill. "Get on with your dinner, boys. Don't let me interrupt."

Once Bill settled down with the Hell's Gate Gang, his true genius revealed itself. With his gang's help, he put together the biggest ranch in the southwest. He used New Mexico as a corral and Arizona as a pasture. He invented tarantulas and scorpions as practical jokes. He also invented roping. Some say his rope was exactly as long as the equator; others argue it was two feet shorter. **G**

Things were going fine for Bill until Texas began to suffer the worst drought in its history. It was so dry that all the rivers turned as powdery as biscuit flour. The parched grass was catching fire everywhere. For a while Bill and his gang managed to lasso water from the Rio Grande.[9] When that river dried up, they lassoed water from the Gulf of Mexico.

No matter what he did, though, Bill couldn't get enough water to stay ahead of the drought. All his horses and cows were starting to dry up and blow away like balls of tumbleweed. It was horrible.

Just when the end seemed near, the sky turned a deep shade of purple. From the distant mountains came a terrible roar. The cattle began to stampede, and a huge black funnel of a cyclone appeared, heading straight for Bill's ranch.

The rest of the Hell's Gate Gang shouted, "Help!" and ran.

But Pecos Bill wasn't scared in the least. "Yahoo!" he hollered, and he swung his lariat and lassoed that cyclone around its neck.

Bill held on tight as he got sucked up into the middle of the swirling cloud. He grabbed the cyclone by the ears and pulled himself onto her back. Then he let out a whoop and headed that twister across Texas.

The mighty cyclone bucked, arched, and screamed like a wild bronco. But Pecos Bill just held on with his legs and used his strong hands to wring the rain out of her wind. He wrung out rain that flooded Texas, New Mexico, and Arizona, until finally he slid off the shriveled-up funnel and fell into California. The earth sank about two hundred feet below sea level in the spot where Bill landed, creating the area known today as Death Valley. **H**

"There. That little waterin' should hold things for a while," he said, brushing himself off.

After his cyclone ride, no horse was too wild for Pecos Bill. He soon found a young colt that was as tough as a tiger and as crazy as a streak of lightning. He named the colt Widow Maker and raised him on barbed wire and dynamite. Whenever the two rode together, they back-flipped and somersaulted all over Texas, loving every minute of it.

G **TALL TALE**
Which of Bill's characteristics and achievements are exaggerated in lines 110–115?

H **TALL TALE**
Tall tales sometimes explain how natural phenomena came to be. What do lines 134–139 explain?

---

9. **Rio Grande** (rē′ō gränd′): a river that forms part of the U.S.-Mexican border.

One day when Bill and Widow Maker were bouncing around the Pecos River, they came across an awesome sight: a wild-looking, red-haired woman riding on the back of the biggest catfish Bill had ever seen. The woman looked 150 like she was having a ball, screeching, "Ride 'em, cowgirl!" as the catfish whipped her around in the air. ❶

"What's your name?" Bill shouted.

"Slue-foot[10] Sue! What's it to you?" she said. Then she war-whooped away over the windy water.

Thereafter all Pecos Bill could think of was Slue-foot Sue. He spent more and more time away from the Hell's Gate Gang as he wandered the barren cattle-lands, looking for her. When he finally found her lonely little cabin, he was so love-struck he reverted to some of his old coyote ways. He sat on his haunches in the moonlight and began a-howling and ah-hooing.

---

10. **slue** (slōo): to rotate, turn sharply, or pivot.

❶ **TALL TALE**
What **traits** do Bill and the woman have in common?

160   Well, the good news was that Sue had a bit of coyote in her too, so she completely understood Bill's language. She stuck her head out her window and ah-hooed back to him that she loved him, too. Consequently Bill and Sue decided to get married.

On the day of the wedding Sue wore a beautiful white dress with a steel-spring bustle,[11] and Bill appeared in an elegant buckskin suit.

But after a lovely ceremony, a terrible catastrophe occurred. Slue-foot Sue got it into her head that she just had to have a ride on Bill's wild bronco, Widow Maker.

"You can't do that, honey," Bill said. "He won't let any human toss a leg
170 over him but me."

"Don't worry," said Sue. "You know I can ride anything on four legs, not to mention what flies or swims." **J**

Bill tried his best to talk Sue out of it, but she wouldn't listen. She was dying to buck on the back of that bronco. Wearing her white wedding dress with the bustle, she jumped on Widow Maker and kicked him with her spurs.

Well, that bronco didn't need any thorns in his side to start bucking to beat the band. He bounded up in the air with such amazing force that suddenly Sue was flying high into the Texas sky. She flew over plains and mesas,[12] over
180 canyons, deserts, and prairies. She flew so high that she looped over the new moon and fell back to earth.

But when Sue landed on her steel-spring bustle, she rebounded right back into the heavens! As she bounced back and forth between heaven and earth, Bill whirled his lariat[13] above his head, then lassoed her. But instead of bringing Sue back down to earth, he got yanked into the night sky alongside her!

Together Pecos Bill and Slue-foot Sue bounced off the earth and went flying to the moon. And at that point Bill must have gotten some sort of foothold in a moon crater—because neither he nor Sue returned to earth.
190 Not ever.

Folks figure those two must have dug their boot heels into some moon cheese and raised a pack of wild coyotes just like themselves. Texans'll tell you that every time you hear thunder rolling over the desolate land near the Pecos River, it's just Bill's family having a good laugh upstairs. When you hear a strange ah-hooing in the dark night, don't be fooled—that's the sound of Bill howling *on* the moon instead of *at* it. And when lights flash across the midnight sky, you can bet it's Bill and Sue riding the backs of some white-hot shooting stars. **K**

J TALL TALE
Do you think Sue will succeed in riding Widow Maker? Why or why not?

K VISUALIZE
Reread lines 191–198. Note the descriptive details in this passage. What do they help you picture?

---

11. **bustle** (bŭs'əl): a springy steel framework worn under the back of a woman's skirt to make it puff out.

12. **mesas** (mā'səs): high, flat-topped areas of land.

13. **lariat** (lăr'ē-ət): a rope with a slip-knotted loop at one end that a cowhand throws over an animal's head or body and pulls tight.

Comprehension

1. **Recall** Why does a coyote decide to take care of Bill?

2. **Clarify** How does Bill become the leader of the Hell's Gate Gang?

3. **Summarize** How do Bill and Sue end up leaving Earth and living in the sky?

Text Analysis

● 4. **Examine a Tall Tale** In what ways does "Pecos Bill" exhibit the characteristics of a tall tale? Review the characteristics on page 823. Give examples from the story to support each one.

● 5. **Visualize** Review the chart you filled in as you read. What person or event did you picture most clearly? Tell what descriptions and sensory details helped you. Overall, how well do you think the author helped you visualize the story? Explain.

6. **Analyze Characterization** How does the author help you get to know what Pecos Bill is like? Use a character map to show what you learn about Bill through each of the four methods of characterization.

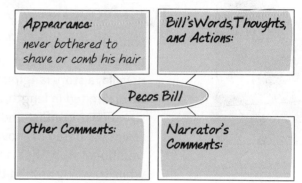

Appearance: never bothered to shave or comb his hair

Bill's Words, Thoughts, and Actions:

Pecos Bill

Other Comments:

Narrator's Comments:

Extension and Challenge

7. **Creative Project: Comic Strip** The incredible characters and events in tall tales have much in common with cartoons. Choose one of the events described in "Pecos Bill." Create a three-to four-panel comic strip that illustrates this event.

8. **SOCIAL STUDIES CONNECTION** What were the lives of cowboys in the 19th century really like? Research the topic, and then compare your findings with the life of Pecos Bill in the story. Are there similarities?

What is a **FOLK HERO?**

Why do you think Pecos Bill became a folk hero in American culture? Consider what his personal characteristics and achievements might represent to people.

COMMON CORE

RL 1 Cite the evidence that supports an analysis of what the text says explicitly as well as inferences drawn from the text. **RL 3** Analyze how particular lines of dialogue or incidents in a story reveal aspects of a character. **RL 5** Analyze how the structure of text contributes to its meaning and style. **L 5a** Interpret figures of speech.

The Pearl

Novella by John Steinbeck

⟨ COMMON CORE

RL 10 Read and comprehend literature.

Other Books by John Steinbeck

- *Cannery Row*
- *The Grapes of Wrath*
- *The Red Pony*
- *Travels with Charley*

Meet John Steinbeck

John Steinbeck grew up in Salinas, California. Some of his earliest jobs were in factories and ranches nearby. He worked alongside many Mexican Americans, and he gained respect for their culture and sympathized with their tough living conditions. Later, he lived in Mexico for a time. Steinbeck won many awards, including the 1962 Nobel Prize in literature. But even after achieving success, he never flaunted his wealth. He lived simply and traveled often.

Try a Novella

Some stories are too short to be called novels but too long to be called short stories. These fall into the category of the **novella,** a story ranging from about 50 to 100 pages in length. Being limited in length, a novella usually focuses on a particular situation or conflict and has fewer characters than a novel. Steinbeck based his novella *The Pearl* on a Mexican parable, a traditional story that is meant to teach a lesson. He heard it while traveling around the Gulf of California, also known as the Sea of Cortez.

Reading Fluency Good readers read smoothly, accurately, and with feeling. To improve your reading fluency, read a passage several times. Your goal in silent reading is to make sense of the writer's words and ideas. When reading aloud, think about the type of text you are reading. You may need to adjust your speed and tone and how you emphasize certain words when reading fiction, nonfiction, or poetry.

Read a Great Book

"If this story is a parable, perhaps everyone takes his own meaning from it and reads his own life into it." So begins the story of Kino, the poor fisherman, his wife, Juana, their baby, Coyotito, and the great pearl that was found and lost again. When Coyotito is stung by a scorpion, Kino and Juana travel from their village to take him to the nearest doctor. However, being poor, they are unable to pay for treatment and are turned away. But once they have a large pearl in their possession, the greedy doctor makes a house call, hoping to get a share of the profits.

from

The *Pearl*

"It is as I thought," he said. "The poison has gone inward and it will strike soon. Come look!" He held the eyelid down. "See—it is blue." And Kino, looking anxiously, saw that indeed it was a little blue. And he didn't know whether or not it was always a little blue. But the trap was set. He couldn't take the chance.

The doctor's eyes watered in their little hammocks. "I will give him something to try to turn the poison aside," he said. And he handed the baby to Kino.

10 Then from his bag he took a little bottle of white powder and a capsule of gelatine. He filled the capsule with the powder and closed it, and then around the first capsule he fitted a second capsule and closed it. Then he worked very deftly. He took the baby and pinched its lower lip until it opened its mouth. His fat fingers placed the capsule far back on the baby's tongue, back of the point where he could spit it out, and then from the floor he picked up the little pitcher of pulque and gave Coyotito a drink, and it was done. He looked again at the baby's eyeball and he pursed his lips and seemed to think.

At last he handed the baby back to Juana, and he turned to Kino.
20 "I think the poison will attack within the hour," he said. "The medicine may save the baby from hurt, but I will come back in an hour. Perhaps I am in time to save him." He took a deep breath and went out of the hut, and his servant followed him with the lantern.

Now Juana had the baby under her shawl, and she stared at it with anxiety and fear. Kino came to her, and he lifted the shawl and stared at the baby. He moved his hand to look under the eyelid, and only then saw that the pearl was still in his hand. Then he went to a box by the wall, and from it he brought a piece of rag. He wrapped the pearl in the rag, then went to the corner of the brush house and dug a little
30 hole with his fingers in the dirt floor, and he put the pearl in the hole and covered it up and concealed the place. And then he went to the fire where Juana was squatting, watching the baby's face.

The doctor, back in his house, settled into his chair and looked at his watch. His people brought him a little supper of chocolate and sweet cakes and fruit, and he stared at the food discontentedly.

In the houses of the neighbors the subject that would lead all conversations for a long time to come was aired for the first time to see how it would go. The neighbors showed one another with their thumbs how big the pearl was, and they made little caressing gestures
40 to show how lovely it was. From now on they would watch Kino and Juana very closely to see whether riches turned their heads, as riches turn all people's heads. Everyone knew why the doctor had come. He was not good at dissembling and he was very well understood.

Out in the estuary a tight woven school of small fishes glittered and broke water to escape a school of great fishes that drove in to eat them. And in the houses the people could hear the swish of the small ones and the bouncing splash of the great ones as the slaughter went on. The dampness arose out of the Gulf and was deposited on bushes and cacti and on little trees in salty drops. And the night mice
50 crept about on the ground and the little night hawks hunted them silently.

The skinny black puppy with flame spots over his eyes came to Kino's door and looked in. He nearly shook his hind quarters loose when Kino glanced up at him, and he subsided when Kino looked away. The puppy did not enter the house, but he watched with frantic interest while Kino ate his beans from the little pottery dish and wiped it clean with a corncake and ate the cake and washed the whole down with a drink of pulque.

60 Kino was finished and was rolling a cigarette when Juana spoke sharply. "Kino." He glanced at her and then got up and went quickly to her for he saw fright in her eyes. He stood over her, looking down, but the light was very dim. He kicked a pile of twigs into the fire hole to make a blaze, and then he could see the face of Coyotito. The baby's face was flushed and his throat was working and a little thick drool of saliva issued from his lips. The spasm of the stomach muscles began, and the baby was very sick.

Kino knelt beside his wife. "So the doctor knew," he said, but he said it for himself as well as for his wife, for his mind was hard and suspicious and he was remembering the white powder. Juana rocked from side to
70 side and moaned out the little Song of the Family as though it could ward off the danger, and the baby vomited and writhed in her arms. Now uncertainty was in Kino, and the music of evil throbbed in his head and nearly drove out Juana's song.

The doctor finished his chocolate and nibbled the little fallen pieces of sweet cake. He brushed his fingers on a napkin, looked at his watch, arose, and took up his little bag.

The news of the baby's illness traveled quickly among the brush houses, for sickness is second only to hunger as the enemy of poor people. And some said softly, "Luck, you see, brings bitter friends."
80 And they nodded and got up to go to Kino's house. The neighbors scuttled with covered noses through the dark until they crowded into Kino's house again. They stood and gazed, and they made little comments on the sadness that this should happen at a time of joy, and they said, "All things are in God's hands." The old women squatted down beside Juana to try to give her aid if they could and comfort if they could not.

Then the doctor hurried in, followed by his man. He scattered the old women like chickens. He took the baby and examined it and felt its head. "The poison it has worked," he said. "I think I can defeat
90 it. I will try my best." He asked for water, and in the cup of it he put three drops of ammonia, and he pried open the baby's mouth and poured it down. The baby spluttered and screeched under the

treatment, and Juana watched him with haunted eyes. The doctor spoke a little as he worked. "It is lucky that I know about the poison of the scorpion, otherwise—" and he shrugged to show what could have happened.

But Kino was suspicious, and he could not take his eyes from the doctor's open bag, and from the bottle of white powder there. Gradually the spasms subsided and the baby relaxed under the doctor's hands. And
100 then Coyotito sighed deeply and went to sleep, for he was very tired with vomiting.

The doctor put the baby in Juana's arms. "He will get well now," he said. "I have won the fight." And Juana looked at him with adoration.

The doctor was closing his bag now. He said, "When do you think you can pay this bill?" He said it even kindly.

"When I have sold my pearl I will pay you," Kino said.

"You have a pearl? A good pearl?" the doctor asked with interest.

And then the chorus of the neighbors broke in. "He has found the Pearl of the World," they cried, and they joined forefinger with thumb
110 to show how great the pearl was.

"Kino will be a rich man," they clamored. "It is a pearl such as one has never seen."

The doctor looked surprised. "I had not heard of it. Do you keep this pearl in a safe place? Perhaps you would like me to put it in my safe?"

Kino's eyes were hooded now, his cheeks were drawn taut. "I have it secure," he said. "Tomorrow I will sell it and then I will pay you."

The doctor shrugged, and his wet eyes never left Kino's eyes. He knew the pearl would be buried in the house, and he thought Kino
120 might look toward the place where it was buried. "It would be a shame to have it stolen before you could sell it," the doctor said, and he saw Kino's eyes flick involuntarily to the floor near the side post of the brush house.

When the doctor had gone and all the neighbors had reluctantly returned to their houses, Kino squatted beside the little glowing coals in the fire hole and listened to the night sound, the soft sweep of the little waves on the shore and the distant barking of dogs, the creeping of the breeze through the brush house roof and the soft speech of his neighbors in their houses in the village. For these people do not sleep

130 soundly all night; they awaken at intervals and talk a little and then go to sleep again. And after a while Kino got up and went to the door of his house.

He smelled the breeze and he listened for any foreign sound of secrecy or creeping, and his eyes searched the darkness, for the music of evil was sounding in his head and he was fierce and afraid. After he had probed the night with his senses he went to the place by the side post where the pearl was buried, and he dug it up and brought it to his sleeping mat, and under his sleeping mat he dug another little hole in the dirt floor and buried the pearl and covered it up again.

140 And Juana, sitting by the fire hole, watched him with questioning eyes, and when he had buried his pearl she asked, "Who do you fear?" ∾

Keep Reading

Is Kino right to fear that something bad is going to happen now that he has the "Pearl of the World"? As you continue to read the novella, you'll follow Kino and Juana as they seek their fortune, dodging danger at every turn. Discover how finding the pearl will change their lives forever.

One Last Time
Memoir by Gary Soto

What can you learn from a JOB?

COMMON CORE

RI 4 Determine the meaning of words and phrases as they are used in a text, including figurative and connotative meanings; analyze the impact of specific word choices on meaning and tone. **RI 6** Determine an author's purpose in a text.

Does the thought of taking out the trash make you groan? Would you rather stay in bed than deliver newspapers on a rainy morning? Lots of times, jobs don't sound fun. But they can teach important lessons and help you figure out your goals for the future. In this memoir, the author discovers that finding out what he doesn't want to do is almost as important as finding out what he does want to do.

QUICKWRITE What have you learned from a job? Whether it was inside or outside your home, describe a job you've had or a chore you've done and the lessons you took away from it.

● TEXT ANALYSIS: AUTHOR'S PURPOSE

Authors usually write for one or more purposes. They might want to express thoughts or feelings, to inform or explain, to persuade, to entertain, or to achieve some combination of these goals. When you understand an author's purpose, it can help you better comprehend what you read.

In this memoir, Gary Soto's purpose is to explore his teenage years working as a field laborer. As you read, look for statements and actions that reveal his thoughts and feelings about this work.

● READING STRATEGY: ANALYZE SENSORY DETAILS

Sensory details are words and phrases that appeal to a reader's five senses. By using such details, a writer helps the reader create vivid mental pictures of settings, people, and events.

For example, in "One Last Time" Soto describes a bus that "started off in slow chugs"—a detail that helps you "hear" the rickety old bus. As you read, look for two or three details that appeal to each sense and record them in a web.

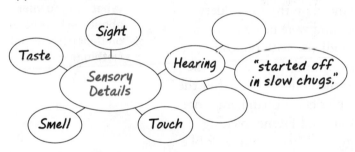

▲ VOCABULARY IN CONTEXT

The words in Column A help Soto describe his jobs. See how many you know by matching each word to the word or phrase in Column B that is closest in meaning.

Column A	Column B
1. ramble	a. weak
2. foreman	b. angry
3. grope	c. workers' boss
4. stoop	d. bend over at the waist
5. contractor	e. unpleasant situation
6. irate	f. awkwardly grab for
7. feeble	g. talk on and on
8. predicament	h. one who provides services for a price

Complete the activities in your **Reader/Writer Notebook**.

ONE LAST TIME

Gary Soto

Yesterday I saw the movie *Gandhi*[1] and recognized a few of the people—not in the theater but in the film. I saw my relatives, dusty and thin as sparrows, returning from the fields with hoes balanced on their shoulders. The workers were squinting, eyes small and veined, and were using their hands to say what there was to say to those in the audience with popcorn. . . . I didn't have any, though. I sat thinking of my family and their years in the fields, beginning with Grandmother who came to the United States after the Mexican revolution[2] to settle in Fresno where she met her husband and bore children, many of them. She worked in the fields around Fresno, picking
10 grapes, oranges, plums, peaches, and cotton, dragging a large white sack like a sled. She worked in the packing houses, Bonner and Sun-Maid Raisin, where she stood at a conveyor belt passing her hand over streams of raisins to pluck out leaves and pebbles. For over twenty years she worked at a machine that boxed raisins until she retired at sixty-five. **A**

Grandfather worked in the fields, as did his children. Mother also found herself out there when she separated from Father for three weeks. I remember her coming home, dusty and so tired that she had to rest on the porch before she trudged inside to wash and start dinner. I didn't understand the complaints about her ankles or the small of her back, even though I had been in the grape
20 fields watching her work. With my brother and sister I ran in and out of the rows; we enjoyed ourselves and pretended not to hear Mother scolding us to sit down and behave ourselves. A few years later, however, I caught on when I went to pick grapes rather than play in the rows.

Analyze Visuals ▶

What can you **infer** about the boys based on their posture and clothing?

A **AUTHOR'S PURPOSE**
What does Soto think about when he sees the working people in the movie? As you continue reading, notice how his family history affects his thoughts and feelings about field work.

---

1. *Gandhi* (gän'dē): a 1982 film biography of Mohandas Gandhi (1869–1948), an Indian spiritual and political leader who, through nonviolent struggle, forced England to grant India's independence.

2. **Mexican revolution** (1910–1920): an armed conflict during which revolutionaries overthrew Mexico's longtime dictator and reformed the government.

Detail of *Los Comaradas del Barrio* (1976), Jesse Treviño. Acrylic on canvas, 36″ × 48″. Collection of the artist.

Mother and I got up before dawn and ate quick bowls of cereal. She drove in silence while I **rambled** on how everything was now solved, how I was going to make enough money to end our misery and even buy her a beautiful copper tea pot, the one I had shown her in Long's Drugs. When we arrived I was frisky and ready to go, self-consciously aware of my grape knife dangling at my wrist. I almost ran to the row the **foreman** had pointed out, but I returned to help Mother with the grape pans and jug of water. She told me to settle down and reminded me not to lose my knife. I walked at her side and listened to her explain how to cut grapes; bent down, hands on knees, I watched her demonstrate by cutting a few bunches into my pan. She stood over me as I tried it myself, tugging at a bunch of grapes that pulled loose like beads from a necklace. "Cut the stem all the way," she told me as last advice before she walked away, her shoes sinking in the loose dirt, to begin work on her own row.

I cut another bunch, then another, fighting the snap and whip of vines. After ten minutes of **groping** for grapes, my first pan brimmed with bunches. I poured them on the paper tray, which was bordered by a wooden frame that kept the grapes from rolling off, and they spilled like jewels from a pirate's chest. The tray was only half filled, so I hurried to jump under the vines and begin groping, cutting, and tugging at the grapes again. I emptied the pan, raked the grapes with my hands to make them look like they filled the tray, and jumped back under the vine on my knees. I tried to cut faster because Mother, in the next row, was slowly moving ahead. I peeked into her row and saw five trays gleaming in the early morning. I cut, pulled hard, and stopped to gather the grapes that missed the pan; already bored, I spat on a few to wash them before tossing them like popcorn into my mouth. **B**

So it went. Two pans equaled one tray—or six cents. By lunchtime I had a trail of thirty-seven trays behind me while Mother had sixty or more. We met about halfway from our last trays, and I sat down with a grunt, knees wet from kneeling on dropped grapes. I washed my hands with the water from the jug, drying them on the inside of my shirt sleeve before I opened the paper bag for the first sandwich, which I gave to Mother. I dipped my hand in again to unwrap a sandwich without looking at it. I took a first bite and chewed it slowly for the tang of mustard. Eating in silence I looked straight ahead at the vines, and only when we were finished with cookies did we talk.

"Are you tired?" she asked.

"No, but I got a sliver from the frame," I told her. I showed her the web of skin between my thumb and index finger. She wrinkled her forehead but said it was nothing.

"How many trays did you do?"

I looked straight ahead, not answering at first. I recounted in my mind the whole morning of bend, cut, pour again and again, before answering a **feeble** "thirty-seven." No elaboration, no detail. Without looking at me she told me how she had done field work in Texas and Michigan as a child. But I had a difficult time listening to her stories. I played with my grape knife, stabbing it

---

ramble (răm′bəl) *v.* to talk at length and aimlessly

foreman (fôr′mən) *n.* the leader of a work crew

grope (grōp) *v.* to reach about with uncertainty

B SENSORY DETAILS
What details in lines 37–48 help you understand the experience of cutting grapes? Add this information to your web.

feeble (fē′bəl) *adj.* weak or faint

into the ground, but stopped when Mother reminded me that I had better not lose it. I left the knife sticking up like a small, leafless plant. She then talked about school, the junior high I would be going to that fall, and then about Rick and Debra, how sorry they would be that they hadn't come out to pick grapes because they'd have no new clothes for the school year. She stopped talking when she peeked at her watch, a bandless one she kept in her pocket. She got up with an *"Ay, Dios,"*[3] and told me that we'd work until three, leaving me cutting figures in the sand with my knife and dreading the return to work.

Finally I rose and walked slowly back to where I had left off, again kneeling under the vine and fixing the pan under bunches of grapes. By that time, 11:30, the sun was over my shoulder and made me squint and think of the pool at the Y.M.C.A. where I was a summer member. I saw myself diving face first into the water and loving it. I saw myself gleaming like something new, at the edge of the pool. I had to daydream and keep my mind busy because boredom was a terror almost as awful as the work itself. My mind went dumb with stupid things, and I had to keep it moving with dreams of baseball and would-be girlfriends. I even sang, however softly, to keep my mind moving, my hands moving. **C**

I worked less hurriedly and with less vision. I no longer saw that copper pot sitting squat on our stove or Mother waiting for it to whistle. The wardrobe that I imagined, crisp and bright in the closet, numbered only one pair of jeans and two shirts because, in half a day, six cents times thirty-seven trays was two dollars and twenty-two cents. It became clear to me. If I worked eight hours, I might make four dollars. I'd take this, even gladly, and walk downtown to look into store windows on the mall and long for the bright madras[4] shirts from Walter Smith or Coffee's, but settling for two imitation ones from Penney's.

That first day I laid down seventy-three trays while Mother had a hundred and twenty behind her. On the back of an old envelope, she wrote out our numbers and hours. We washed at the pump behind the farm house and walked slowly to our car for the drive back to town in the afternoon heat. That evening after dinner I sat in a lawn chair listening to music from a transistor radio while Rick and David King played catch. I joined them in a game of pickle, but there was little joy in trying to avoid their tags because I couldn't get the fields out of my mind: I saw myself dropping on my knees under a vine to tug at a branch that wouldn't come off. In bed, when I closed my eyes, I saw the fields, yellow with kicked up dust, and a crooked trail of trays rotting behind me. **D**

The next day I woke tired and started picking tired. The grapes rained into the pan, slowly filling like a belly, until I had my first tray and started my second. So it went all day, and the next, and all through the following week, so that by the end of thirteen days the foreman counted out, in tens mostly, my pay of fifty-three dollars. Mother earned one hundred and forty-eight dollars. She wrote this on her envelope, with a message I didn't bother to ask her about.

---

3. *Ay, Dios* (ī dē-ōs') *Spanish:* "Oh, God."
4. madras (măd'rəs): cotton cloth, usually with a plaid pattern.

Language Coach

Oral Fluency When English words start with the letters *kn*, the *k* is always silent. Read aloud the sentence that begins in line 76, pronouncing the word *kneeling* correctly.

C AUTHOR'S PURPOSE
What do Soto's statements about work in lines 75 and 81–82 tell you about his attitude toward field work?

D AUTHOR'S PURPOSE
What effect does the author's work environment have on his life away from work?

La Calle Cuatro (2001), Emigdio Vasquez. Oil on canvas, 22″ × 28″. © Emigdio Vasquez.

The next day I walked with my friend Scott to the downtown mall where we drooled over the clothes behind fancy windows, bought popcorn, and sat at a tier of outdoor fountains to talk about girls. Finally we went into Penney's for more popcorn, which we ate walking around, before we returned home without buying anything. It wasn't until a few days before school that I let my fifty-three dollars slip quietly from my hands, buying a pair of pants, two shirts, and a maroon T-shirt, the kind that was in style. At home I tried them on while Rick looked on enviously; later, the day before school started, I tried them on again wondering not so much if they were worth it as who would see me first in those clothes. ◆

Along with my brother and sister I picked grapes until I was fifteen, before giving up and saying that I'd rather wear old clothes than **stoop** like a Mexican. Mother thought I was being stuck-up, even stupid, because there would be no clothes for me in the fall. I told her I didn't care, but when Rick and Debra rose at five in the morning, I lay awake in bed feeling that perhaps I had made a mistake but unwilling to change my mind. That fall Mother bought me two pairs of socks, a packet of colored T-shirts, and underwear. The T-shirts would help, I thought, but who would see that I had new underwear and socks? I wore a new T-shirt on the first day of school, then an old shirt on Tuesday, then another T-shirt on Wednesday, and on Thursday an old Nehru shirt[5] that was embarrassingly out of style. On Friday I changed into the corduroy pants my brother had handed down to me and slipped into my last new T-shirt. I worked like a magician, blinding my classmates, who were all clothes conscious and small-time social climbers, by arranging my wardrobe to make it seem larger than it really was. But by spring I had to do something—my blue jeans were almost silver and my shoes had lost their form, puddling like black ice around my feet. That spring of my sixteenth year,

◂ **Analyze Visuals**

Why might a **setting** like that in the picture be a difficult place for Soto to spend time?

◆ **GRAMMAR IN CONTEXT**

Reread the sentence that begins in line 115 with "At home I tried. . ." Notice how the two main clauses are separated by a **semicolon.**

stoop (sto͞op) *v.* to bend forward and down from the waist or the middle of the back

5. **Nehru** (nā′ro͞o) **shirt:** an Indian-style shirt with a stand-up collar.

Rick and I decided to take a labor bus to chop cotton. In his old Volkswagen, which was more noise than power, we drove on a Saturday morning to West Fresno—or Chinatown as some call it—parked, walked slowly toward a bus, and stood gawking at the . . . blacks, Okies,[6] *Tejanos*[7] with gold teeth, . . .
140 Mexican families, and labor **contractors** shouting "Cotton" or "Beets," the work of spring. **E**

We boarded the "Cotton" bus without looking at the contractor who stood almost blocking the entrance. . . . We boarded scared. . . . We sat . . . looking straight ahead, and only glanced briefly at the others who boarded, almost all of them broken and poorly dressed in loudly mismatched clothes. Finally when the contractor banged his palm against the side of the bus, the young man at the wheel, smiling and talking in Spanish, started the engine, idled it for a moment while he adjusted the mirrors, and started off in slow chugs. Except for the windshield there was no glass in the windows, so as soon as we
150 were on the rural roads outside Fresno, the dust and sand began to be sucked into the bus, whipping about like **irate** wasps as the gravel ticked about us. We closed our eyes, clotted up our mouths that wanted to open with embarrassed laughter because we couldn't believe we were on that bus with those people and the dust attacking us for no reason. **F**

When we arrived at a field we followed the others to a pickup where we each took a hoe and marched to stand before a row. Rick and I, self-conscious and unsure, looked around at the others who leaned on their hoes or squatted in front of the rows, almost all talking in Spanish, joking . . . all waiting for the foreman's whistle to begin work. Mother had explained how to chop cotton by
160 showing us with a broom in the backyard.

"Like this," she said, her broom swishing down weeds. "Leave one plant and cut four—and cut them! Don't leave them standing or the foreman will get mad."

The foreman whistled and we started up the row stealing glances at other workers to see if we were doing it right. But after awhile we worked like we knew what we were doing, neither of us hurrying or falling behind. But slowly the clot of men, women, and kids began to spread and loosen. Even Rick pulled away. I didn't hurry, though. I cut smoothly and cleanly as I walked at a slow pace, in a sort of funeral march. My eyes measured each space of cotton
170 plants before I cut. If I missed the plants, I swished again. I worked intently, seldom looking up, so when I did I was amazed to see the sun, like a broken orange coin, in the east. It looked blurry, unbelievable, like something not of this world. I looked around in amazement, scanning the eastern horizon that was a taut line jutted with an occasional mountain. The horizon was beautiful, like a snapshot of the moon, in the early light of morning, in the quiet of no cars and few people. **G**

---

6. **Okies** (ō′kēz): people from Oklahoma and other midwestern states who moved to California to find work during the Great Depression of the 1930s.

7. *Tejanos* (tā-hä′nōs): Texans of Mexican ancestry.

contractor (kŏn′trăk′tər) *n.* one who agrees to provide services for a specific price

E AUTHOR'S PURPOSE
Reread lines 119–141. What reasons does Soto give for rejecting field work? Tell why his views change.

irate (ī-rāt′) *adj.* very angry

COMMON CORE RI 4

F SENSORY DETAILS
To help readers feel like they are experiencing the events on the page, a writer might describe an unfamiliar sensation by comparing it to something readers have already seen or heard. One way writers do this is by using **similes**, figures of speech that compare two unlike things using the words *like* or *as*. Reread lines 149–151 and identify the simile. What two things are being compared?

G SENSORY DETAILS
What sensory details does Soto use to help you see the beauty of his surroundings?

The foreman trudged in boots in my direction, stepping awkwardly over the plants, to inspect the work. No one around me looked up. We all worked steadily while we waited for him to leave. When he did leave, with a feeble 180 complaint addressed to no one in particular, we looked up smiling under straw hats and bandanas.

By 11:00, our lunch time, my ankles were hurting from walking on clods[8] the size of hardballs. My arms ached and my face was dusted by a wind that was perpetual, always busy whipping about. But the work was not bad, I thought. It was better, so much better, than picking grapes, especially with the hourly wage of a dollar twenty-five instead of piece work. Rick and I walked sorely toward the bus where we washed and drank water. Instead of eating in the bus or in the shade of the bus, we kept to ourselves by walking down to the irrigation canal[9] that ran the length of the field, to open our lunch of 190 sandwiches and crackers. We laughed at the crackers, which seemed like a cruel joke from our Mother, because we were working under the sun and the last thing we wanted was a salty dessert. We ate them anyway and drank more water before we returned to the field, both of us limping in exaggeration. Working side by side, we talked and laughed at our **predicament** because our Mother had warned us year after year that if we didn't get on track in school we'd have to work in the fields and then we would see. We mimicked Mother's whining voice and smirked at her smoky view of the future in which we'd be trapped by marriage and screaming kids. We'd eat beans and then we'd see. **H**

Rick pulled slowly away to the rhythm of his hoe falling faster and 200 smoother. It was better that way, to work alone. I could hum made-up songs or songs from the radio and think to myself about school and friends. At the time I was doing badly in my classes, mainly because of a difficult stepfather, but also because I didn't care anymore. All through junior high and into my first year of high school there were those who said I would never do anything, be anyone. They said I'd work like a donkey and marry the first Mexican girl that came along. I was reminded so often, verbally and in the way I was treated at home, that I began to believe that chopping cotton might be a lifetime job for me. If not chopping cotton, then I might get lucky and find myself in a car wash or restaurant or junkyard. But it was clear; I'd work, and work hard. **I**
210 I cleared my mind by humming and looking about. The sun was directly above with a few soft blades of clouds against a sky that seemed bluer and more beautiful than our sky in the city. Occasionally the breeze flurried and picked up dust so that I had to cover my eyes and screw up my face. The workers were hunched, brown as the clods under our feet, and spread across the field that ran without end—fields that were owned by corporations, not families.

I hoed trying to keep my mind busy with scenes from school and pretend girlfriends until finally my brain turned off and my thinking went fuzzy with boredom. I looked about, no longer mesmerized by the beauty of the

predicament
(prĭ-dĭk′ə-mənt) *n.* an unpleasant situation from which it is difficult to free oneself

H SENSORY DETAILS
Which detail in lines 182–198 most helps you feel what it was like to be with Soto and Rick that day?

I AUTHOR'S PURPOSE
How might Soto's experiences at school and home affect his expectations for himself?

---

8. **clods:** hardened clumps of soil.
9. **irrigation canal:** a ditch that brings water to crops.

landscape, . . . no longer dreaming of the clothes I'd buy with my pay. My
220 eyes followed my chopping as the plants, thin as their shadows, fell with each
strike. I worked slowly with ankles and arms hurting, neck stiff, and eyes
stinging from the dust and the sun that glanced off the field like a mirror.

By quitting time, 3:00, there was such an excruciating pain in my ankles
that I walked as if I were wearing snowshoes. Rick laughed at me and I
laughed too, embarrassed that most of the men were walking normally and I
was among the first timers who had to get used to this work. "And what about
you . . ." I came back at Rick. His eyes were meshed red and his long hippie
hair was flecked with dust and gnats and bits of leaves. We placed our hoes in
the back of a pickup and stood in line for our pay, which was twelve fifty. I
230 was amazed at the pay, which was the most I had ever earned in one day, and
thought that I'd come back the next day, Sunday. This was too good.

Instead of joining the others in the labor bus, we jumped in the back of
a pickup when the driver said we'd get to town sooner and were welcome to
join him. We scrambled into the truck bed to be joined by a heavy-set and
laughing *Tejano* whose head was shaped like an egg, particularly so because the
bandana he wore ended in a point on the top of his head. He laughed almost
demonically as the pickup roared up the dirt path, a gray cape of dust rising
behind us. On the highway, with the wind in our faces, we squinted at the
fields as if we were looking for someone. The *Tejano* had quit laughing but was
240 smiling broadly, occasionally chortling tunes he never finished. I was scared of
him, though Rick, two years older and five inches taller, wasn't. If the *Tejano*
looked at him, Rick stared back for a second or two before he looked away to
the fields. **J**

I felt like a soldier coming home from war when we rattled into Chinatown.
People leaning against car hoods stared, their necks following us, owl-like; . . .
Chinese grocers stopped brooming their storefronts to raise their cadaverous
faces at us. We stopped in front of the Chi Chi Club where Mexican music
blared from the juke box and cue balls cracked like dull ice. The *Tejano,* who
was dirty as we were, stepped awkwardly over the side rail, dusted himself off
250 with his bandana, and sauntered into the club. **K**

Rick and I jumped from the back, thanked the driver who said *de nada*[10]
and popped his clutch, so that the pickup jerked and coughed blue smoke. We
returned smiling to our car, happy with the money we had made and pleased
that we had, in a small way, proved ourselves to be tough; that we worked as
well as other men and earned the same pay.

We returned the next day and the next week until the season was over and
there was nothing to do. I told myself that I wouldn't pick grapes that summer,
saying all through June and July that it was for Mexicans, not me. When August
came around and I still had not found a summer job, I ate my words, sharpened
260 my knife, and joined Mother, Rick, and Debra for one last time. ◗

---

10. **de nada** (də nä′də) *Spanish:* "You're welcome—it's nothing."

Language Coach

Multiple Meaning Words Multiple meaning words have more than one meaning. For example, the word *pay* can mean both "to give money in return for goods or services" or "money given in return for work." Which meaning does the word *pay* have in line 219?

J SENSORY DETAILS
Reread lines 234–243. What details help you understand what the *Tejano* looks like and sounds like as he rides in the truck?

K AUTHOR'S PURPOSE
Reread line 244. What does Soto's statement reflect about his attitude toward the work he's been doing?

HOW THINGS WORK

Gary Soto

Today it's going to cost us twenty dollars
To live. Five for a softball. Four for a book,
A handful of ones for coffee and two sweet rolls,
Bus fare, rosin[1] for your mother's violin.
5 We're completing our task. The tip I left
For the waitress filters down
Like rain, wetting the new roots of a child
Perhaps, a belligerent cat that won't let go
Of a balled sock until there's chicken to eat.
10 As far as I can tell, daughter, it works like this:
You buy bread from a grocery, a bag of apples
From a fruit stand, and what coins
Are passed on helps others buy pencils, glue,
Tickets to a movie in which laughter
15 Is thrown into their faces.
If we buy a goldfish, someone tries on a hat.
If we buy crayons, someone walks home with a broom.
A tip, a small purchase here and there,
And things just keep going. I guess.

---

1. **rosin** (rŏz′ĭn): a substance derived from tree sap that is used
   to increase sliding friction on stringed instruments' bows.

Comprehension

1. **Recall** What does Gary Soto dream of buying his mother?

2. **Recall** What does Soto think about when he is bored at work?

3. **Summarize** Describe Soto's first day chopping cotton.

Text Analysis

4. **Make Inferences** How might Soto's family history affect his thoughts and feelings about working in the fields? Cite evidence from the story and the biography on page 839 to support your response.

5. **Analyze Sensory Details** Review the sensory details you noted in your web. What single detail best captures for you what it was like to pick grapes or chop cotton?

6. **Compare and Contrast** Which does Soto like more, picking grapes or chopping cotton? Note the similarities and differences between the two jobs. Then explain why Soto prefers the one he does.

7. **Examine Author's Purpose** In what ways do Gary Soto's thoughts and feelings toward work change throughout the selection? Consider what happens to Soto's dreams the longer he works in the fields. Track his attitude toward his jobs on a timeline like the one shown. Record his positive feelings above the line and negative feelings below the line.

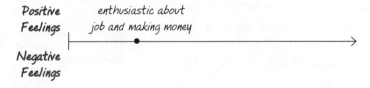

8. **Compare Literary Works** Think about Gary Soto's childhood experiences as a field laborer. What effect might they have had on the view of money he expresses in his poem "How Things Work" on page 848? Explain.

Extension and Challenge

9. **Readers' Circle** Writers choose titles for their selections very carefully. Why do you think Gary Soto titled this memoir "One Last Time"? Reread the last paragraph of the memoir and think about the ideas Soto emphasizes. Then, in small groups, brainstorm other possible titles. Share your best idea with the class.

What can you learn from a JOB?

What might Soto say he learned from his jobs working in the fields? Respond to the Quickwrite activity on page 838 as if you were Soto.

COMMON CORE

RI 4 Determine the meaning of words and phrases as they are used in a text, including figurative and connotative meanings; analyze the impact of specific word choices on meaning and tone. **RI 6** Determine an author's purpose in a text.

Vocabulary in Context

▲ VOCABULARY PRACTICE

Show that you understand the vocabulary words by telling whether each statement is true or false.

1. Someone who **rambles** on about a topic gets right to the point.
2. It is a **foreman**'s job to tell workers what to do.
3. Someone who **gropes** for an item finds it right away.
4. If you drop something on the floor, you can **stoop** to pick it up.
5. **Contractors** supply labor and materials for a project.
6. Most people feel **irate** on their birthdays.
7. A **feeble** voice is difficult to hear.
8. Having two appointments at the same time might be called a **predicament**.

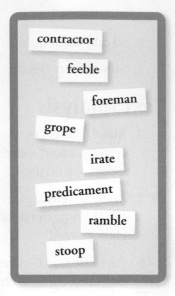

contractor
feeble
foreman
grope
irate
predicament
ramble
stoop

ACADEMIC VOCABULARY IN WRITING

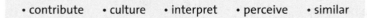

- contribute
- culture
- interpret
- perceive
- similar

What connection does Soto **perceive** between the history of his family and his work in the fields? Try to use at least one Academic Vocabulary word as you explain your answer in a paragraph.

VOCABULARY STRATEGY: SIMILES

Writers sometimes use **similes,** or figures of speech that compare two unlike things using the words *like* or *as.* In "One Last Time," the author says that the dust and sand flying into their moving bus was "whipping around like irate wasps." This simile helps readers imagine what it would feel like to be riding in the bus.

Similes can also provide context clues to help you figure out unfamiliar word meanings. If you know that "whipping around" implies fast, curving motion and that *wasps* move more quickly when they're angered, then you can figure out that *irate* means "very angry."

PRACTICE Use the simile in each sentence as a context clue to help you define the boldfaced word.

1. His **elaborate** story was as layered as a wedding cake.
2. The **idling** engine purred like a lazy kitten.
3. She stared at me as **intently** as a cat watches a bird.
4. The lightning **illuminated** the sky like a fireworks display.
5. Her **excruciating** sense of homesickness felt like physical pain.

COMMON CORE

L 4a Use context as a clue to the meaning of a word or phrase.
L 5 Demonstrate understanding of figurative language.

Interactive Vocabulary **THINK** central

Go to **thinkcentral.com**.
KEYWORD: HML8-850

Language

COMMON CORE

L2 Demonstrate command of punctuation when writing.
W1 Write arguments.

◆ GRAMMAR IN CONTEXT: Use Semicolons Correctly

Review the Grammar in Context note on page 844. Recall that a compound sentence contains two or more main clauses, or word groups that can stand alone as sentences. One way to separate main clauses is to use a semicolon between them. If the clauses are not separated by a **semicolon** or by a comma and a coordinating conjunction (such as *and*), the sentence would be a run-on.

Original: Some children can walk to school other children need to earn money to buy bus tokens.

Revised: Some children can walk to school; other children need to earn money to buy bus tokens.

PRACTICE   In the following sentences, insert semicolons as needed.

1. Not all parents can afford to buy food, clothing, and other necessities children can help by working.
2. Hard work teaches children responsibility parents should allow children to have jobs.
3. Children should be able to work farms are a good place to get work experience.
4. A job harvesting crops teaches children to appreciate their food time spent watching TV or playing video games teaches nothing.

*For more help with semicolons, see page R49 in the **Grammar Handbook**.*

READING-WRITING CONNECTION

YOUR TURN   Deepen your appreciation of "One Last Time" by responding to the prompt. Then use the **revising tip** to improve your writing.

WRITING PROMPT	REVISING TIP
Short Constructed Response: Letter to the Editor Do you think children under the age of 16 should be allowed to work jobs harvesting crops? Write a **one-paragraph letter to the editor** of a newspaper, expressing your opinion.	Review your letter. Have you punctuated your sentences correctly? Make sure you include at least one compound sentence, and separate the main clauses with a semicolon.

Interactive Revision

THINK central

Go to thinkcentral.com.
KEYWORD: HML8-851

Political Cartoons
Image Collection on **Media ◉ Smart** DVD-ROM

Can CARTOONS have a point?

COMMON CORE

RI 2 Determine a central idea of a text. **RI 4** Analyze the impact of specific word choices on meaning and tone, including allusions. **RI 6** Determine an author's point of view. **SL 2** Analyze the purpose of information presented in diverse media and formats and evaluate the motives behind its presentation.

In the United States, everyone can express an opinion, and there are countless ways opinions are expressed. In this lesson, you'll look at how images and words can be carefully combined to make timely statements about American life.

Background

Cartoon Comments A **political cartoon** is a humorous drawing that makes a comment about a political issue or an event. Political cartoons usually appear on the editorial pages of newspapers, alongside writings that express opinions. These cartoons can reflect current topics in a funny or serious way.

　　The following cartoon presents two characters who might look familiar. In political cartoons, the elephant often appears as the symbol of the Republican Party and the donkey stands for the Democratic Party. These characters often represent two sides of an issue. In this case, though, does the cartoonist seem to think that either side is correct?

Media Literacy: Messages in Political Cartoons

For any cartoon, the cartoonist's aim is to include images and details that help you figure out his or her message. One of the most enduring images in political cartoons is the figure of Uncle Sam. Political cartoonists use him as a symbol for the United States. His appearance may vary from cartoon to cartoon. However, he's usually easy to recognize, and the message he communicates is tied to a national issue. Use the following strategies to analyze political cartoons.

STRATEGIES FOR ANALYZING A POLITICAL CARTOON

FRANK EVERS
Courtesy New York Daily News

© Frank Evers/Courtesy New York Daily News.

Identify the subject.

Look for labels. Any words you see might be used to identify people, groups, or events. What label appears in this cartoon?

Identify symbols and specific details.

Almost every detail in a political cartoon is carefully chosen to communicate part of the message. What key symbols, images, and allusions appear in this cartoon?

Look for exaggeration.

Just as in ordinary comics, the humor in political cartoons is delivered often through exaggeration. In this political cartoon, what details appear to be extreme or unusual?

Figure out the point of view.

In any political cartoon, look for clues to the cartoonist's point of view. Are characters portrayed positively or negatively? Are their actions admirable, foolish, or criminal?

Notice how the art elements are used to catch the eye and to create certain effects.

- Political cartoons usually appear in black and white. When you spot any other color, consider what the cartoonist is highlighting and what message he or she is communicating.

- **Lines** convey certain moods. Straight lines can signal an issue is serious. Curvy lines convey playfulness.

- To get your attention, cartoonists exaggerate **shapes,** often making objects appear to be larger than life. Most often, cartoonists exaggerate by changing the **sizes** of familiar objects or of labels.

Viewing Guide for

Political Cartoons

Use the DVD to see larger versions of the political cartoons. As you examine each one, think about when it was created and the issue it comments on. The political cartoon on page 853 was published at a time when the effects of acid rain first became a topic in the news. The cartoon here first appeared in 1890, when the U.S. Congress passed the Sherman Silver Purchase Act. This act called for the government to put more money into circulation by purchasing more silver than ever before.

Think about the way Uncle Sam is drawn in each political cartoon and the images and words each cartoonist uses to make a comment. Use these questions to help you interpret the messages.

NOW VIEW

FIRST VIEWING: Comprehension

1. **Identify** Name any object that appears unusually large in size in the "Acid Rain" political cartoon.

2. **Clarify** Apart from the title, "The Silver Sun of Prosperity," what helps you to understand the subject of this political cartoon?

CLOSE VIEWING: Media Literacy

3. **Identify Exaggeration** In the "Acid Rain" political cartoon, what looks exaggerated about the appearance of Uncle Sam and the rain?

4. **Analyze the Message** In "Acid Rain," Uncle Sam seems to be a bit confused. What comment might the political cartoonist be making by drawing Uncle Sam in this way?

5. **Analyze the Message** The political cartoonist of "The Silver Sun of Prosperity" was in favor of the Sherman Silver Act. What evidence do you see of this in the political cartoon? Think about

   - Uncle Sam's action in the cartoon and what he symbolizes
   - the color choices and the use of text and exaggeration
   - the specific objects the cartoonist chose to depict

Write or Discuss

Compare Political Cartoons You've seen how the image of Uncle Sam has spanned generations. The political cartoons in this lesson were created at different times to address different issues. How else are they alike or different? Write a brief comparison-contrast paragraph that describes at least two more differences. Think about

- whether the political cartoon includes many details or only a few
- the message of each political cartoon
- whether each cartoonist uses color

Produce Your Own Media

Create a Political Cartoon Choose an issue that you think would make a good subject for your own **political cartoon.** This issue may be something that affects your school, your neighborhood, or the entire nation. The basic rule is to choose an issue that's familiar to your audience and that is important enough for them to care about. It may help you to briefly discuss your ideas with your teacher.

HERE'S HOW Use these suggestions in making your political cartoon:

- What details could you use to represent the issue?
- What might you exaggerate in the image to highlight your point?
- Draw attention to the most important part of your image through the use of art elements. For example, make the person or object that matters most larger in size than the other objects.
- Draw or label the people or objects in the political cartoon so that they're easy to recognize. You can also use speech balloons to show what a character is saying. Make sure there are reasons for using any words you include.

STUDENT MODEL

Big Oil Rules

COMMON CORE

RI 2 Determine a central idea of a text. RI 4 Analyze the impact of specific word choices on meaning and tone, including allusions. RI 6 Determine an author's point of view. SL 2 Analyze the purpose of information presented in diverse media and formats and evaluate the motives behind its presentation.

Media Tools — THINK central

Go to **thinkcentral.com**.
KEYWORD: HML8-855

Tech Tip

If available, use a software program to make a slideshow of the cartoons in your class.

I Want to Write

Sit-Ins

Poems by Margaret Walker

HISTORY Video link at
thinkcentral.com

How can we fight
INJUSTICE?

COMMON CORE

RL 1 Cite the evidence that supports an analysis of what the text says explicitly.
RL 2 Determine a theme of a text, including its relationship to setting. **RL 4** Analyze the impact of specific word choices on meaning and tone.

A girl is blamed for someone else's mistake. A boy is accused because of the color of his skin. People are denied rights because of the group they belong to, or they are put into danger because of what they believe. Witnessing injustice can make you feel angry, powerless, or even physically sick. But there are ways to fight back. In the poems you're about to read, Margaret Walker celebrates working for what's right.

LIST IT How can people fight injustice? With a small group, brainstorm a list of ways people can help make the world a fairer place. Then compare your lists with those of other groups. Who came up with the most examples? Who came up with ideas no one else did?

TEXT ANALYSIS: HISTORICAL CONTEXT

Just as a writer's cultural background can affect his or her work, the time period in which a writer lives also can influence his or her subject matter and attitude. When you look at literature in its **historical context,** you consider what was happening in society at the time a piece of writing was created.

Margaret Walker wrote the two poems you are about to read in different decades. She wrote "I Want to Write" in the 1930s and "Sit-Ins" in the 1960s. First study the background on this page, and read the excerpt from *A Dream of Freedom* on page 861. Then, as you read the poems, try to connect historical events with Margaret Walker's words and themes.

READING SKILL: ANALYZE REPETITION

Sound devices can add interest and appeal to all types of poems, whether long, short, funny, or serious. One of the sound devices used in Walker's poems is **repetition,** in which a sound, word, phrase, or line is repeated for emphasis or unity. To understand the effect of repetition in a poem, follow these steps:

- Write down repeated words, phrases, or lines.
- Think about what ideas these repeated elements emphasize.
- Notice how the repetition relates to the poem's overall message.

As you read each poem, record examples of repetition in a chart like the one shown, and describe the effect each has on your understanding of Walker's ideas.

Repetition	Effect

![Reader/Writer Notebook icon] Complete the activities in your **Reader/Writer Notebook.**

Meet the Author

Margaret Walker
1915–1998

Privilege and Pain
Margaret Walker had a middle-class upbringing in the South at a time when many African Americans weren't so lucky. Her parents' jobs provided a nice income, but the family still suffered from discrimination. In an interview, she recalled the effects of racial prejudice: "Before I was 10, I knew what it was to step off the sidewalk to let a white man pass; otherwise he might knock me off...."

For Her People
While Walker was growing up in the 1920s, an African-American cultural movement called the Harlem Renaissance was flourishing in New York City. Walker discovered the works of these new writers when she was 11 years old. Already showing a gift for writing, Walker knew that she, too, wanted to tell the stories of African Americans. Encouraged by poet Langston Hughes, Walker went to college in the North in 1932. Ten years later, Yale University published her first collection of poetry, *For My People*.

BACKGROUND TO THE POEMS
Civil Rights
In the South, "Jim Crow" laws kept blacks and whites separated in public places, such as schools and restaurants. In the 1960s, Martin Luther King Jr. and other leaders organized nonviolent protests against segregation. Tactics included boycotts (refusing to buy products from companies that supported segregation) and sit-ins (peacefully demanding service at segregated businesses).

Author Online

THINK central

Go to **thinkcentral.com.**
KEYWORD: HML8-857

857

Illustration by Jérôme Lagarrigue.

I Want to
Write

Margaret Walker

I want to write
I want to write the songs of my people.
I want to hear them singing melodies in the dark.
I want to catch the last floating strains¹ from their sob-torn throats.
5 I want to frame their dreams into words; their souls into notes.
I want to catch their sunshine laughter in a bowl;
fling dark hands to a darker sky
and fill them full of stars
then crush and mix such lights till they become
10 a mirrored pool of brilliance in the dawn.

▲ **Analyze Visuals**

Look at the image on this page. **Describe** the expression on the girl's face. What do you think her personality is like?

Ⓐ **REPETITION**
Note the phrase in this poem that is repeated. What idea does it emphasize?

---

1. **strains:** tunes.

Illustration by Jérôme Lagarrigue.

Sit-Ins

Margaret Walker

Greensboro, North Carolina, in the Spring of 1960

You were our first brave ones to defy their dissonance of hate
With your silence
With your willingness to suffer
Without violence
5 Those first bright young to fling your names across pages
Of new southern history
With courage and faith, convictions, and intelligence **B**
The first to blaze a flaming path for justice
And awaken consciences
10 Of these stony ones.

Come, Lord Jesus, Bold Young Galilean[1]
Sit Beside this Counter, Lord, with Me! **C**

▲ **Analyze Visuals**

What can you **infer** about why the woman and child might be walking away from the counter?

B **REPETITION**
Reread lines 1–7. What does the repetition help you to understand about the people Walker is describing?

C **HISTORICAL CONTEXT**
What historical details does Walker cite in the poem?

---

1. **Galilean** (găl'ə-lē'ən): According to the Bible, Jesus lived near the Sea of Galilee, in Israel.

Comprehension

1. **Recall** In "I Want to Write," what does the speaker want to write about?

2. **Recall** In "Sit-Ins," what qualities do the people participating in the sit-ins have?

Text Analysis

3. **Understand Imagery** Recall that imagery consists of words and phrases that appeal to readers' senses. In a chart like the one shown, note the images in "I Want to Write" that appeal to the senses of hearing, sight, and touch. What do these images help you to understand about the people Walker wants to write about?

Hearing	Sight	Touch
"singing melodies"		

4. **Examine Historical Context** Margaret Walker writes, "I want to write the songs of my people." Tell what you know about conditions and events that affected African Americans in the 1930s. What is the connection between Walker's theme in "I Want to Write" and the fight against racial injustice? Support your answer with quotations from the poem.

5. **Interpret a Passage** In "Sit-Ins," Walker describes those participating in the sit-ins as "The first to blaze a flaming path for justice/And awaken consciences/Of these stony ones." Who might the "stony ones" be? Think about the qualities the word *stony* suggests.

6. **Compare Texts** What information in the excerpt from *A Dream of Freedom* does the most to help you understand the poem "Sit-Ins"? What details do you get in the poem that help you understand the book excerpt? Explain.

7. **Analyze Repetition** Look at the chart you completed as you read. Decide which poem makes greater use of repetition. What is the overall effect of this repetition on your understanding of Walker's ideas?

Extension and Challenge

8. **SOCIAL STUDIES CONNECTION** Research another major event in the civil rights movement, such as the Montgomery Bus Boycott or the March on Washington. How did people participating in these events hope to achieve justice? In a presentation to the class, explain the event and its significance.

How can we fight INJUSTICE?

Review the list you came up with on page 856. After reading the poems and the book excerpt, do you have anything you want to add to the list? With your group, decide which method you think would be most effective in achieving justice.

COMMON CORE

RL 1 Cite the evidence that supports an analysis of what the text says explicitly.
RL 2 Determine a theme of a text, including its relationship to setting. **RL 4** Analyze the impact of specific word choices on meaning and tone.

BOOK EXCERPT In 1960, four African-American college students decided to protest racial segregation in a new way. This book excerpt describes their bold actions and how the students inspired others to join their cause.

from *A Dream of Freedom*
BY DIANE McWHORTER

Four protesters sit at a whites-only lunch counter at Woolworth's.

On the last day of January 1960, a North Carolina teenager named Ezell Blair Jr. announced to his mother, "Mom, we are going to do something tomorrow that may change history, that might change the world." Blair attended a black college in Greensboro called North Carolina Agricultural and Technical. On Monday afternoon, February 1, he and three A&T classmates, Franklin McCain, David Richmond, and Joseph McNeil, went downtown to Woolworth's department store, took a seat at the lunch counter, and ordered a doughnut and coffee.

"I'm sorry," said the waitress, "we don't serve you here."

Though white-only lunch counters were a fact of southern life, one of the students replied, "We just beg to disagree with you." Before sitting down, they had deliberately bought some school supplies. Holding up a receipt, they pointed out that they had just been served at a nearby cash register. One of the most insulting hypocrisies of segregation was that stores in the South, as Franklin McCain put it, "don't separate your money in this cash register, but, no, please don't step down to the hot dog stand."

The youths sat at the counter for an hour. They were heckled by a black dishwasher, and stared at by a white policeman. An elderly white woman cheered in a loud whisper: "You should have done it ten years ago!"

The store manager turned off the lights at five-thirty, half an hour before closing time. "By then," McCain recalled, "we had the confidence, my goodness, of a Mack truck." In a week, the Greensboro Four had grown to hundreds. Within two months, protests had taken place in 125 cities in nine states. . . .

The sit-ins, as the lunch counter campaign became known, sparked a freedom flame.

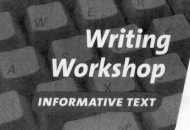

Writing Workshop

INFORMATIVE TEXT

Cause-and-Effect Essay

As you have seen in this unit, history, culture, and life experiences can affect how people act and how events are interpreted. In this workshop, you will write an essay about a cause-and-effect relationship that is significant to you.

 Complete the workshop activities in your **Reader/Writer Notebook.**

WRITE WITH A PURPOSE

WRITING TASK

Write a **cause-and-effect essay** to explain why something happened or to reveal the results of an event or action. Choose a topic that is important to you and will interest your audience.

Idea Starters
- a natural event, such as a hurricane
- a community event, such as building a skate park
- a historical event, such as the Battle of the Alamo
- a problem, such as litter, stray dogs, or noise pollution
- a personal accomplishment, such as getting an award

THE ESSENTIALS

Here are some common purposes, audiences, and formats for cause-and-effect writing.

PURPOSES	AUDIENCES	FORMATS
• to explain why something happened • to inform others about the helpful or harmful effects of something • to persuade an audience to take action	• classmates and teacher • newspaper readers • community members • Web users	• essay for class • letter to the editor of a newspaper • public service announcement (PSA) • blog posting • power presentation

COMMON CORE TRAITS

1. DEVELOPMENT OF IDEAS

- presents an **engaging introduction** that identifies a cause-and-effect relationship
- has a **controlling idea** that offers an **opinion** on the relationship
- develops ideas with **relevant** and **concrete details, quotations,** and **examples**
- provides a **concluding section** that follows from the information presented

2. ORGANIZATION OF IDEAS

- **organizes** ideas in a logical way
- uses **appropriate transitions** to create cohesion and clarify relationships among ideas and concepts

3. LANGUAGE FACILITY AND CONVENTIONS

- establishes and maintains a **formal style** and **tone**
- includes **precise language** and **domain-specific vocabulary**
- uses **appositives** and **complex sentences** correctly
- employs correct **grammar, usage,** and **spelling**

Writing Online

THINK central

Go to **thinkcentral.com**.
KEYWORD: HML8N-862

Planning/Prewriting

COMMON CORE

W 2a–f Write informative/explanatory texts to examine a topic through the selection, organization, and analysis of relevant content. **W 5** Develop and strengthen writing by planning. **W 7** Conduct short research projects to answer a question.

Getting Started

DECIDE ON A TOPIC

Use the Idea Starters on page 862 to help you think of events in your life or in the world that made you ask yourself "What **caused** that to happen?" or "What **effect** did that have?" List the ideas that come to mind. Circle the topic that interests you most.

▶ **WHAT DOES IT LOOK LIKE?**

My World	The Wider World
• Sid's skateboarding accident	• melting glaciers
• Leslie wanting to get a dog	• (noise pollution)
• earning my blue belt in judo	• stereotypes of teenagers

THINK ABOUT AUDIENCE AND PURPOSE

After choosing a subject, think about your **purpose.** In a cause-and-effect essay, the writer often has more than one purpose. For example, you may want to inform your **audience** about an important cause-and-effect relationship and persuade them to take a particular action. Anticipating what your readers know and think about your subject will help you craft a stronger essay.

▶ **ASK YOURSELF:**

- Is my purpose to inform, to explain, or to persuade? Do I have more than one purpose?
- Who is my audience, and what might they want to learn about? What do I want them to know or do?
- What does my audience already know or think about my topic?
- What **domain-specific,** or specialized, **vocabulary** will my audience need to know?

DEVELOP A CONTROLLING IDEA

Your **controlling idea,** or thesis statement, should express a clear and informed judgment, or opinion. An **opinion** is a statement that can't be proved or disproved because it expresses a person's particular point of view. However, a well-supported opinion is more valid, or convincing to readers, than an opinion that has nothing to back it up.

▶ **WHAT DOES IT LOOK LIKE?**

Controlling idea: Loud noise that we hear every day is annoying and can cause hearing problems.

EXPLORE CAUSES AND EFFECTS

Use a chart to map out the causes and effects that support your controlling idea. Make sure there are true cause-and-effect relationships between events. For instance, one event may follow another but not be caused by it, as in "I bought new basketball shoes, and then we lost our game." This is an example of a **false cause.** It is unlikely that one player's shoes caused the team to lose.

▶ **WHAT DOES IT LOOK LIKE?**

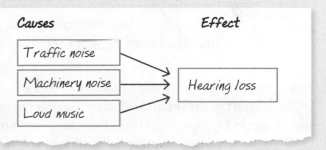

Causes → Effect: Traffic noise, Machinery noise, Loud music → Hearing loss

Planning/Prewriting *continued*

COLLECT EVIDENCE

To make your case, you need to support your opinion with relevant, well-chosen evidence, such as facts, statistics, anecdotes, and quotations from experts. A **fact** is a statement that can be proved. A **statistic** is a fact that includes a number. An **anecdote** is a brief personal story.

▶ ASK YOURSELF:

- What facts and statistics support my controlling idea?
- What makes the person or source I am citing an expert on the subject?
- Where can I look to find additional evidence?
- What anecdotes could I use to illustrate a key point?

ORGANIZE YOUR IDEAS

Writers often organize the body of a cause-and-effect essay in one of the following three ways. Choose the most logical and coherent organizational strategy for your topic.

- **Effect-to-cause organization**—First states the effect of an event or action and then analyzes its causes. Use when your focus is on explaining the causes of something.

- **Cause-to-effect organization**—First states the cause of an action or event and then evaluates its effects. Use when your focus is on explaining the effects of something.

- **Cause-effect chain organization**—Describes a chain of cause-and-effect relationships. Use when you are explaining a complex series of events.

ORGANIZATIONAL PATTERNS FOR A CAUSE-AND-EFFECT ESSAY

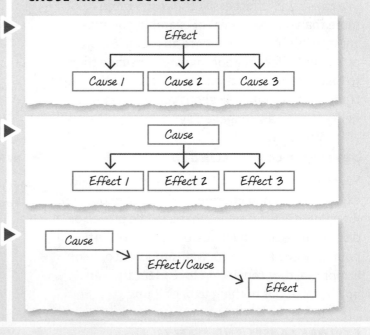

PEER REVIEW Describe your topic to a peer. Then ask if he or she knows any facts or has any anecdotes that could support your controlling idea. Use this information as you plan your essay. If you have trouble supporting your controlling idea, you may need to rework it.

YOUR TURN In your *Reader/Writer Notebook,* record your controlling idea and make a chart of causes and effects, choosing the organizational pattern that works best for your topic. Then, keeping in mind your audience and purpose, make an informal outline of your essay that includes notes on the introduction, body, and concluding section.

Drafting

COMMON CORE

W 4 Produce clear and coherent writing. **W 9b (RI 1)** Cite textual evidence that most strongly supports an analysis. **L1** Demonstrate command of English grammar and usage.

This chart shows how to organize your draft effectively.

Organizing a Cause-and-Effect Essay

INTRODUCTION

- Begin with an **anecdote,** a **question,** or a **striking fact** to engage your readers.
- Using precise language your readers will understand, identify the **cause-and-effect relationship,** and give your opinion on it in a clear **controlling idea.**

▼

BODY

- Decide on a **logical order** for presenting each cause and effect. For example, you might present your most important point first to get your audience's attention. Or, you might save your most important point for last and leave a strong impression.
- Maintain a **formal style,** and support key points with **well-chosen, relevant evidence.**
- Use **transitions** that show cause and effect, such as *because, as a result,* and *therefore.*

▼

CONCLUDING SECTION

- **Summarize** the cause-and-effect relationship you have described in your essay.
- Restate why the topic is important and, if appropriate, **suggest an action** for readers to take.

GRAMMAR IN CONTEXT: APPOSITIVE PHRASES

Appositive phrases are useful for citing facts and evidence. An **appositive** is a noun or pronoun that identifies or renames another noun or pronoun. An **appositive phrase** includes an appositive and modifiers of it. Look at the chart to learn the two kinds of appositive phrases and the correct ways to use them.

Type of Appositive Phrase	Example
essential—provides information that is needed to identify the preceding noun or pronoun; is not set off by commas	▶ The organization **House Ear Institute** focuses its efforts on exploring the science of hearing.
nonessential—adds extra information about a noun or pronoun whose meaning is already clear; is set off by commas	▶ The House Ear Institute, **an organization focused on the science of hearing,** estimates that almost 10 million Americans suffer from hearing loss caused by noise.

YOUR TURN   Develop a draft of your cause-and-effect essay, following the organizational tips in the chart above. Try to include two appositive phrases to add details about the facts and statistics you cite.

Revising

Revising means rereading your draft to look for ways to make your writing more focused, organized, and coherent. You check to see if you have achieved your purpose and addressed your audience in the most effective way. Use the following chart to help you revise, rewrite, and improve your draft.

CAUSE-AND-EFFECT ESSAY

Ask Yourself	Tips	Revision Strategies
1. Does the introduction have a clear controlling idea?	▶ **Underline** the controlling idea.	▶ **Add** a controlling idea that gives an opinion on a cause-and-effect relationship.
2. Is the body of the essay clearly and logically organized?	▶ In the margin, **label** the pattern of organization: cause-to-effect, effect-to-cause, or cause-effect chain.	▶ **Address** each cause or effect in a separate paragraph. If necessary, **rearrange** so that the most important point comes first.
3. Does a variety of relevant, well-chosen evidence support the controlling idea?	▶ Write *F* above any facts, *S* above statistics, and *Q* above quotations.	▶ **Add** details and examples to explain a cause or effect or to show its importance. **Delete** irrelevant details.
4. Are transitions used to link ideas and show causes and effects?	▶ **Put a check mark** next to transitions that show causes and effects.	▶ **Add** transitions, such as *because*, *as a result*, and *therefore*, to show causes and effects.
5. Does precise language help readers understand causes and effects?	▶ **Highlight** precise language that makes causes or effects clear.	▶ **Replace** general language with more exact and vivid words and phrases.
6. Does the concluding section restate the importance of the subject to readers? Does it include a call to action?	▶ **Underline** the restatement of the subject. **Draw brackets** around the call to action.	▶ **Add** a sentence that restates the importance of the controlling idea. **Add** a call to action for the audience, if appropriate.

YOUR TURN *PEER REVIEW* Exchange cause-and-effect essays with a partner. Read through your partner's essay. Discuss which points in the essay were most interesting, surprising, or disturbing, and why. Refer to the strategies above as you identify how the essay could be improved or where a new approach might be necessary.

COMMON CORE

W 2b Develop the topic with examples. **W 5** Strengthen writing by revising, editing, rewriting, or trying a new approach. **W 7** Conduct short research projects to answer a question. **W 9b (RI 1)** Cite textual evidence that supports analysis.

ANALYZE A STUDENT DRAFT

Read this student's draft and the comments about it as a model for revising your own cause-and-effect essay.

Why Is It So Noisy?
by Chris Hawkins, Danvers Intermediate School

1   One afternoon last week, I was sitting in the park, trying to relax. I went there to hear the sound of the wind in the trees and the waves on the shore of the lake. Instead of these soothing natural sounds, though, all I heard was blaring car horns, beeping trucks, squealing bus brakes, and shrieking ambulance sirens. "I can't even hear myself think!" I shouted. This kind of noise pollution is everywhere, and it's not just annoying—it's harmful because it may lead to hearing loss.

> Chris gets the reader's attention with an **anecdote.** His **controlling idea** clearly states a cause-and-effect relationship.

2   Traffic sounds like the ones I heard in the park are the major cause of noise pollution. Just think how much noise a passing car, truck, bus, train, or motorcycle makes. Can you imagine hearing dozens of them at once? In fact, we experience that racket every time we go outside. Don't look up for relief, though. Airplanes make plenty of noise, too.

> Here, Chris provides facts as evidence that noise pollution is a problem. A **statistic** would make the support even stronger.

3   Another cause of noise pollution is machinery like jackhammers, bulldozers, leaf blowers, and lawnmowers. As anyone who lives in the city or suburbs knows, the annoying vibrations from these machines can have immediate and dramatic effects. The noise interrupts our thoughts, makes conversation difficult, and can even be painful to our ears.

> A **transition** indicates that Chris is beginning to discuss a second cause of noise pollution.

LEARN HOW   **Add Statistics as Evidence** In his second paragraph, Chris gives several concrete examples, including buses, motorcycles, and airplanes, to support his point that traffic is a major cause of noise pollution. Providing different types of evidence, such as statistics and quotations, would make his point even stronger. When he revised his essay, he added a statistic from an authoritative source.

CHRIS'S REVISION TO PARAGRAPH **2**

    Traffic sounds like the ones I heard in the park are the major cause of noise pollution. Just think how much noise a passing car, truck, bus, train, or motorcycle makes. Can you imagine hearing dozens of them at once? In fact, we experience that racket every time we go outside. Don't look up for relief, though. Airplanes make plenty of noise, too. *According to the Council on the Environment of New York City, an airplane 2,000 feet away makes a noise as loud as a car blowing its horn just a step away.*

4   When it's loud, music becomes noise, too. The noise level at concerts, arcades, parties, and other events can be almost deafening. We have gotten so used to blaring music that it no longer seems loud. As a result, when we listen to music at home, or even through headphones, we turn the volume way up.

> Specific, relevant **examples** help readers understand what Chris means by loud music.

5   The effects of all this noise are frightening. According to an article in the *Danvers Ledger*, "Loud noises can actually destroy the cells inside our ears." The longer we're exposed to loud noise and the louder it is, the worse the damage is. After this damage, hearing cannot be restored. The House Ear Institute, an organization focused on the science of hearing, estimates that almost 10 million Americans suffer from hearing loss caused by noise.

> Chris supports his **opinion** in the first sentence with **facts** from reliable sources.

6   Understanding what causes noise pollution can prevent its harmful effects. People can avoid noisy environments as much as possible and wear earplugs in construction zones. People can tell others about the harm caused by loud noise and how to prevent it.

> Chris's **concluding section** gives good examples, but it would be more effective if he used a different **tone**.

LEARN HOW **Use an Appropriate Tone** **Tone** is the writer's attitude toward his or her subject. Setting an appropriate tone means choosing words and examples that are suited to your audience and purpose. In a cause-and-effect essay, the writer often adopts a serious but friendly tone. Chris revised his concluding section by using the word *we* throughout the paragraph. This pronoun addresses readers directly and makes a connection with them. He also added another example that better relates to his audience.

CHRIS'S REVISION TO PARAGRAPH ❻

Because we understand what causes noise pollution we can try to prevent its harmful effects. We
   ᴧ ~~Understanding what causes noise pollution can prevent its harmful~~ *^*
~~effects. People~~ *^* can avoid noisy environments as much as possible and wear
         We can turn down our TVs, CD players, computers, and personal music
         players. Finally, we
earplugs in construction zones. ~~People~~ *^* can tell others about the harm caused
   ᴧ
by loud noise and how to prevent it.

YOUR TURN Use comments from your peers and your teacher as well as the two "Learn How" lessons to revise your essay. Evaluate how well your essay fulfills its purpose of clearly explaining a cause-and-effect relationship and why it is important.

COMMON CORE
W 2e Establish and maintain a formal style. **W 5** Strengthen writing by revising and editing. **L 3** Use knowledge of language and its conventions when writing.

Editing and Publishing

During the editing stage, you read your essay again to find and correct errors in grammar, usage, spelling, and punctuation. These kinds of errors are distracting to readers and can even keep them from understanding your writing.

GRAMMAR IN CONTEXT: COMPLEX SENTENCES

Complex sentences can be useful in a cause-and-effect essay because they express a relationship between two actions or events. A **complex sentence** has an independent clause and at least one subordinate clause. The **independent clause,** or main clause, expresses a complete thought and can stand alone as a sentence. The **subordinate clause**

- adds meaning to the main clause.
- begins with a subordinating conjunction, such as *after, because, even though, since, until, where, when, as,* or *if.*
- is followed by a comma when it precedes the main clause.

Here is an example of a complex sentence from Chris's essay:

> *When it's loud, music becomes noise, too.*
>
> [The **subordinate clause** adds meaning to the main clause by telling *when* music becomes noise.]

As Chris was proofreading his essay, he noticed a complex sentence that was incorrectly punctuated. He added a comma after the subordinate clause.

> *Because we understand what causes noise pollution‸we can try to prevent its harmful effects.*

PUBLISH YOUR WRITING

Share your cause-and-effect essay with an audience.
- Publish your essay on a school or community Web site.
- Send your essay to an organization with an interest in your subject or with the power to take the action you want.
- Adapt your essay into a power presentation that includes images and sound, and present it to your audience.

YOUR TURN

Correct any errors in your essay by proofreading It carefully. Clarify your key points by using complex sentences. Make sure you place a comma after any subordinate clause that starts a sentence. Then publish your final essay where it is most likely to reach your audience.

Scoring Rubric

Use the rubric below to evaluate your cause-and-effect essay from the Writing Workshop or your response to the on-demand task on the next page.

CAUSE-AND-EFFECT ESSAY

SCORE	COMMON CORE TRAITS
6	• **Development** Clearly introduces a cause-and-effect relationship; states an effective controlling idea; strongly supports key points with relevant, well-chosen evidence; ends strongly and insightfully • **Organization** Arranges ideas in a clear, logical order; effectively uses appropriate and varied transitions to link ideas and create cohesion • **Language** Consistently maintains a formal style; effectively uses precise language; shows a strong command of conventions
5	• **Development** Competently introduces a cause-and-effect relationship; states a clear controlling idea; supports most key points with relevant, well-chosen evidence; ends strongly • **Organization** Arranges ideas logically; uses appropriate and varied transitions to link ideas • **Language** Maintains a formal style; uses precise language; has a few errors in conventions
4	• **Development** Sufficiently introduces a cause-and-effect relationship; states a controlling idea; could choose better evidence to support key points; has a satisfactory concluding section • **Organization** Arranges ideas fairly logically; uses some transitions that may not make sense • **Language** Mostly maintains a formal style; needs more precise language at times; includes a few distracting errors in conventions
3	• **Development** States a controlling idea but lacks a clear introduction; lacks enough relevant, well-chosen evidence; has an adequate concluding section • **Organization** Has some organizational flaws; needs more transitions to link ideas • **Language** Frequently lapses into an informal style; uses some vague language; has some critical errors in conventions
2	• **Development** Has a weak introduction and controlling idea; lacks relevant, well-chosen evidence; has a weak concluding section • **Organization** Has organizational flaws; lacks transitions throughout • **Language** Uses informal style and vague language; has many errors in conventions
1	• **Development** Has no introduction, controlling idea, and evidence; ends abruptly • **Organization** Has poor organization and no transitions • **Language** Uses an inappropriate style and vague words; has major problems with conventions

Preparing for Timed Writing

W 10 Write routinely over shorter time frames for a range of tasks, purposes, and audiences.

1. ANALYZE THE TASK   5 MIN

Read the writing task carefully. Then read it again, underlining the words that tell the type of writing, the topic, and the purpose.

> **WRITING TASK**   *↙ Type of writing*   *↙ Topic*
>
> Write a <u>cause-and-effect essay</u> about a <u>useful or popular invention</u>, such as the television, the computer, or the microwave oven. State your topic clearly and <u>explain at least three</u> <u>effects of the invention on people's lives.</u> Include relevant examples to support your points. Conclude your essay by telling why your subject is important.
>
> *Purpose*

2. PLAN YOUR RESPONSE   10 MIN

Think of an invention that has a big effect on people's daily lives, including your own. Once you have a topic, use a chart to list three ways that the invention affects how people act or think. Then list facts and details about each effect and why it is important.

Invention: _____	
Effects	Facts and Details

3. RESPOND TO THE TASK   20 MIN

Once you have gathered your ideas and details, draft your essay. As you write, keep these guidelines in mind:

- In the introduction, identify the cause-and-effect relationship you are writing about and why it is important to you and your audience.
- In the body, present each effect of the invention in a logical order. Provide relevant, well-chosen facts and details that will clarify the effects.
- In the concluding section, restate your opinion on the invention's importance based on the effects you have presented.

4. IMPROVE YOUR RESPONSE   5–10 MIN

Revising Go back over key aspects of the essay. Did you clearly state and then explain a cause-and-effect relationship? Did you provide supporting details and examples that help your audience understand the impact of the invention?

Proofreading Neatly correct any mistakes in grammar, usage, spelling, and punctuation.

Checking Your Final Copy Before you turn in your essay, read it one more time to catch any errors you may have missed.

Producing a Power Presentation

Effective presentations often include more than just printed text. They might also include sound, images, animation, and other multimedia elements. Power presentations allow you to present a topic in an exciting and informative way.

 Complete the workshop activities in your **Reader/Writer Notebook.**

PRODUCE WITH A PURPOSE	COMMON CORE TRAITS
TASK Adapt your cause-and-effect essay into a **power presentation.** Your goal is to engage your classmates as you inform them about your topic. Then deliver your presentation to the class.	*A STRONG POWER PRESENTATION . . .* • focuses on an important cause-and-effect relationship • uses a variety of relevant evidence to describe and explain causes and effects • presents key points in a focused, coherent manner • effectively combines text, graphics, images, and sound

Plan Your Presentation

COMMON CORE

W 6 Use technology to produce and publish writing. **SL 4** Present claims and findings in a focused, coherent manner. **SL 5** Integrate multimedia and visual displays. **SL 6** Adapt speech, demonstrating command of formal English.

Your audience will be taking in information in several ways—by looking, listening, and reading. Keep these points in mind as you plan your presentation:

• **Prepare for your presentation.** You will be using computer software to create your presentation, so you may need some assistance from your teacher or school media specialist. Keep the following points in mind as you prepare for your power presentation.

> **Power Presentation**
>
> • You are the speaker and control the flow of information.
>
> • Brief text and simple visuals or sounds highlight key points in your speech.
>
> • Text and visuals are projected on a large screen for the audience to see.
>
> • Text and visuals are arranged in a focused, coherent manner to help you deliver your message in an engaging way.

Media Tools

THiNK central

Go to **thinkcentral.com.**
KEYWORD: HML8-872

• **Think about visuals and audio.** You may be able to present supporting evidence through spoken words, photographs, animations, maps, charts, or graphs. If you decide to add music clips or sound effects, make sure they help to get your message across. Don't forget to get permission for any words, images, or audio that you did not create yourself.

Adapt Your Essay

The multimedia and interactive elements you choose to include in your power presentation will affect how you adapt the text of your cause-and-effect essay.

- Make brief notes on your essay to refer to as you speak. Convert some of your notes into text screens to reinforce key points. Each screen should be brief and to the point—such as a bulleted list, a single important statement, or a simple chart—so that your audience can scan the information quickly and still pay attention to what you're saying.

- Multimedia and interactive elements should be relevant and well chosen. Be sure these elements support your points rather than distract from your message and overall purpose. Use a chart to help you sketch out what your audience will see, hear, and read at the same time.

Text (Spoken or Onscreen)	Sound	Image or Graphic
"What does this sound do to your ears?"	Loud jet engine	Image of airplane flying overhead
"Often, we choose to listen to loud noise."	Music getting louder and louder	Image of young person listening to music on headphones

Share Your Presentation

Deliver your power presentation to an audience. Keep these points in mind:

- Enunciate clearly and speak naturally, but a bit louder and slower than you normally would. Practice advancing to each display screen at the right moment, so you can do this smoothly without disrupting your speech. Remember to maintain eye contact with your audience, and use a tone that is friendly but appropriately formal for your presentation.

- Before you finalize your presentation, review each display screen you've created to support your points. Look for areas where you might try a different approach to improve your presentation.

YOUR TURN Plan, produce, and deliver your power presentation using the guidelines on these pages. Ask those who listen to or use your presentation which parts were most and least effective. Revise your presentation based on their feedback.

Assessment Practice

Practice Test **THINK** central

Take it at thinkcentral.com.
KEYWORD: HML8N-874

DIRECTIONS *Caught by the Sea* is an autobiography, and *The Voyage of the Frog* is a novel. Read these excerpts and answer the questions that follow.

from Caught by the Sea *by Gary Paulsen*

1   The motor suddenly became an intrusion, an ugly sound, and as soon as I was past the jetties and was in open ocean I killed it. For a few seconds, half a minute, we moved on in silence by inertia, coasting from the energy the motor had given us, and then it died and I felt the breeze again on my face as I looked to the rear. It was pushing at the back edge of the sail and I pulled the tiller over to steer off the wind a bit and felt the sail fill. The boat moved differently now, started the dance with the wind and water and moonlight as she heeled slightly and took on life, personality. We glided along in near silence, the only sound the soft gurgle of water along the hull.

2   I did not dare to walk forward in the dark and put up the jib, having never done it before, but she sailed pretty well on the mainsail alone and we kept our course, moving at three or four knots by the speedometer in the cockpit, until daylight some four hours away, when the wind stopped, entirely, and left the dawning ocean as still as a pond and me marooned some twelve miles offshore.

3   I didn't care. I was completely enraptured by what had happened to me. I lowered the mainsail and sat peacefully drifting around in circles, feeling at home, truly at home.

4   For the entire morning there was no wind, and while I might have had enough gas to motor partway back to the harbor, there was something wrong about using it on such a beautiful morning. I made a small pot of oatmeal on the little stove and some instant coffee and ate breakfast in the cockpit, letting the morning sun warm me; then I pulled my sleeping bag out of the cabin and laid it in the cockpit and took a small sleep while the boat rocked gently on the swells.

5   A sound awakened me an hour or so later and I looked over the side to see the boat surrounded by swarms of small fish, maybe anchovies or herring. No sooner did I spot them than pelicans came in and began crash-diving around the boat and then other seabirds arrived, and within minutes a huge pod of dolphins, hundreds of them, showed up. The dolphins began working the school of bait fish, sweeping back and forth like happy wolves, thrashing the water with their tails, perhaps to stun the fish. Then they ate them by the thousands.

6   While I lay in the calm, all around the boat the sea seethed with life. After the dolphins came some sharks, three or four on call to clean up the debris

from the slaughter. In half an hour they were gone, moving off, following the schools of small fish and dolphins and flocks of seabirds.

7   "Amazing," I said aloud. It was amazing that I would be greeted on the sea with such enthusiasm, amazing that on one of the most populated coasts in the world, near a metropolis that stretched nearly two hundred miles from San Diego to Santa Barbara, where nearly eighteen million people jammed the freeways and sidewalks, I would be completely alone with the sea and my boat; amazing that the planet still held such a place.

from The Voyage of the *Frog*
by Gary Paulsen

1   And at two in the morning he saw the light in the water. He saw it first to the stern. In his wake, in the silent bubbles left by the *Frog* moving through the water, there was a rippled, dotted line of eerie light glowing up from the water. It was blue-green, seemed to come from down in the water, and at first it startled and frightened him. But then he remembered hearing about it.

2   Small animals in the water, microscopic organisms, sometimes phosphoresced—gave off light almost like lightning bugs—when disturbed. He must be going through a mass of them. In back of the *Frog* was a long line of blue light, fading as the water settled down again.

3   He tied the tiller off, leaned over the side, and looked toward the front where the bow cut a wave that curled over.

4   "Ohhh . . ." It slipped out of his mouth unbidden, almost a sigh of amazement. The boat was moving through blue fire, blue fire in the night. The bow wave was a rolling curve of blue light, sparkled with bits of green that seemed to crawl up the side of the boat then fold back and over, splashing out in ripples and droplets of light.

5   It could not be as beautiful as it was—not be that beautiful and be real. It was so bright and shining a thing that the *Frog* seemed to be moving through, a lake of cold fire, and as he watched he saw a form move beneath the boat, caught in the blue glow of the bow wave, a torpedo form that shot forward with an incredible burst of speed. He saw first the glowing curved line around the head of the creature and the line showed him that it was the front of a dolphin. All in seconds, in short parts of seconds, he saw the head and the body moving forward beneath the boat and then it exploded—the dolphin blew out of the water in front of the boat.

GO ON ➡

6   It rose in a clean curve just in front of the bowsprit, five, six feet out of the water in a leap of joy that only dolphins can make, carrying with it a shroud of splashing blue-green fire that whirled and spiraled in the darkness to follow the dolphin up, over and down, back into the water and plunging in green light back to the depths beneath the *Frog*.

7   David was frozen with it, did not know how long he stayed with one hand reaching up as if to touch where the dolphin had been, touch the curve of blue fire. It was all there and gone—just as suddenly gone as if it had never been—and his breath burst suddenly into the night.

8   He looked back, expecting to see the dolphin as the boat went over it but there was nothing.

Reading Comprehension

> **Use "Caught by the Sea" to answer questions 1–7.**

1. Reread paragraph 1. To which of your senses do the details in this excerpt appeal?
   A. Sight and hearing
   B. Sight, hearing, and touch
   C. Sight, hearing, touch, and taste
   D. Sight, hearing, touch, taste, and smell

2. Reread paragraph 2. To which of your senses do the details in this excerpt appeal?
   A. Sight
   B. Sight and hearing
   C. Sight and touch
   D. Sight, hearing, and touch

3. The author probably wrote this selection to —
   A. convince readers to become sailors
   B. explain how to fish from a sailboat
   C. provide a description of different fish
   D. describe an experience of sailing at sea

4. Reread paragraph 1. Paulsen turns off the motor of his boat because he —
   A. has to save fuel
   B. is bothered by its noise
   C. senses danger ahead
   D. doesn't want to scare the fish

5. In paragraph 4, Paulsen writes that there is "something wrong" about using the motor on a beautiful morning. What can you infer about him from this statement?
   A. He worries about disturbing others.
   B. He enjoys the peaceful setting.
   C. He is learning how to operate the boat.
   D. He is hiding from someone.

6. You can infer that the seabirds, dolphins, and sharks are attracted to the waters around the boat because of —
   A. Light from the moon
   B. The smell of a human
   C. Swarms of small fish
   D. The sound of the boat's motor

7. Read these lines.

> "I made a small pot of oatmeal on the little stove and some instant coffee and ate breakfast in the cockpit, letting the morning sun warm me; then I pulled my sleeping bag out of the cabin and laid it in the cockpit and took a small sleep while the boat rocked gently on the swells."

What sensations does Paulsen describe?

A. The feeling of being warmed and gently rocked

B. Hearing the slap and splash of the water hitting the sides of the boat

C. The cozy, warming feeling of eating oatmeal and sipping coffee

D. The aromas of oatmeal and coffee

Use "The Voyage of the Frog" to answer questions 8–12.

8. Paulsen's experience as an outdoorsman is reflected in the story's —

A. chronology

B. conflict

C. point of view

D. setting

9. At first the "eerie lights glowing up from the water" in paragraph 1 causes David to feel —

A. alone

B. confused

C. giddy

D. scared

10. Reread paragraph 2. Why are the small animals giving off light?

A. The bright light helps them locate food.

B. The movement of the boat stirs them up.

C. They sense that predators are nearby.

D. They are signaling to other fish in the water.

11. Reread paragraphs 6 and 7. You can infer that David holds his breath when he sees the dolphin because he —

A. plans to capture the dolphin

B. does not want to disturb the dolphin

C. is amazed at the sight of the dolphin

D. thinks that the dolphin might hurt him

12. The author probably wrote this selection to —

A. entertain readers with an amazing experience

B. explain how dolphins swim at night

C. persuade readers that dolphins are dangerous

D. describe what sailing is like at night

Use both selections to answer question 13.

13. The excerpt from *The Voyage of the Frog* reflects which experience in Paulsen's background?

A. Staying up all night to watch the sunrise

B. Getting an unexpected glimpse of sea animals

C. Cooking and sleeping on a boat

D. Learning how to operate a sailboat

SHORT CONSTRUCTED RESPONSE
Write two or three sentences to answer this question.

14. Choose one experience described in *The Voyage of the Frog* that is similar to Paulsen's experiences in *Caught by the Sea*. Explain the similarity between the two.

Write a paragraph to answer this question.

15. Reread paragraphs 1 and 3 in *Caught by the Sea*. What effect does his sailing experience have on Paulsen? Support your answer with examples from the excerpt.

GO ON ➡

Vocabulary

Use the dictionary entries to answer the following questions about the excerpt from *Caught by the Sea.*

1. Read the dictionary entry for the word *swell.*

    swell (swĕl) *n.* **1.** The act or process of swelling. **2.** A long wave on water that moves continuously without breaking. **3.** A rise in the land. **4.** A crescendo followed by a gradual diminuendo.

    Which definition represents the meaning of *swell* as it is used in paragraph 4?

    A. Definition 1

    B. Definition 2

    C. Definition 3

    D. Definition 4

2. Read the dictionary entry for the word *harbor.*

    harbor (här'bər) *n.* **1.** A sheltered part of a body of water. **2.** A place of shelter; a refuge. *v.* **1.** To give shelter to. **2.** To provide a place, home, habitat for.

    Which definition represents the meaning of the word *harbor* as it is used in paragraph 4?

    A. Noun definition 1

    B. Noun definition 2

    C. Verb definition 1

    D. Verb definition 2

3. Read the dictionary entry for the word *knot.*

    knot (nŏt) *n.* **1.** A compact intersection of interlaced material. **2.** A unifying bond. **3.** A tight cluster of persons or things. **4.** A unit of speed, one nautical mile per hour.

    Which definition represents the meaning of the word *knot* as it is used in paragraph 2?

    A. Definition 1

    B. Definition 2

    C. Definition 3

    D. Definition 4

Use context clues and your knowledge of similes to help you determine the meaning of each boldfaced word.

4. The microscopic organisms *phosphoresced* in the water like lightning bugs illuminating a dark night.

    A. Crawled   C. Glowed

    B. Danced   D. Splashed

5. The boat was as *marooned* as a car without wheels.

    A. Abandoned   C. Old

    B. Lifeless   D. Quiet

6. The *commotion* around the boat was like rush hour traffic.

    A. Noisy activity

    B. Peaceful calm

    C. Speedy pursuit

    D. Crashing and churning

Revising and Editing

DIRECTIONS Read this passage and answer the questions that follow.

(1) Dolphins live in water. (2) Many people think of them as fish. (3) They are actually mammals. (4) The following are different types of dolphins the bottle-nosed dolphin, the common dolphin, and the white-sided dolphin. (5) All dolphins share the following characteristics smooth skin, flippers, and a blowhole. (6) Dolphins have no sense of smell. (7) They have a keen sense of hearing. (8) They can detect sounds that humans cannot. (9) Dolphins have been trained to perform in amusement parks, zoos, and aquariums, to retrieve objects, and to guard military ships.

1. What is the BEST way to combine sentences 1, 2, and 3 into one compound-complex sentence?
   A. Dolphins live in water, so many people think of them as fish, but they are actually mammals.
   B. Dolphins live in water, many people think of them as fish, but they are actually mammals.
   C. Because dolphins live in water, many people think of them as fish, but they are actually mammals.
   D. Dolphins are actually mammals, living in water, but many people think of them as fish.

2. In sentence 4, a colon should be placed after which word?
   A. Are   C. Following
   B. Dolphins   D. Of

3. In sentence 5, a colon should be placed after which word?
   A. Characteristics   C. Share
   B. Following   D. Skin

4. What is the BEST way to combine sentences 6, 7, and 8 into one compound-complex sentence?
   A. Though dolphins have no sense of smell, they have a keen sense of hearing, and they can detect sounds that humans cannot hear.
   B. Having no sense of smell but a keen sense of hearing, dolphins can detect sounds that humans cannot.
   C. Dolphins have no sense of smell but a keen sense of hearing, enabling them to detect sounds that humans cannot.
   D. Despite having no sense of smell, dolphins have a keen sense of hearing, detecting sounds that humans cannot.

5. In sentence 9, a semicolon should be placed after which words?
   A. To, aquarium, objects
   B. Parks, zoos, aquariums, objects
   C. Perform, retrieve, guard
   D. Aquariums, objects

Ideas for Independent Reading

Which questions from Unit 7 made an impression on you? Continue exploring them with these books.

COMMON CORE

RL 10 Read and comprehend literature. **RI 10** Read and comprehend literary nonfiction.

Where do we get our values?

Betsy and the Emperor
by Staton Rabin

After years at boarding school, 14-year-old Betsy is back home on St. Helena. Her family is hosting a special "guest": Napoleon, the former emperor of France, is a prisoner at Betsy's house. What can an ex-emperor and a rebellious teenager have in common?

Lizzie Bright and the Buckminster Boy
by Gary D. Schmidt

People in Phippsburg, Maine, don't like it when Turner befriends Lizzie Bright, who lives in a nearby African-American settlement. When the town evicts Lizzie's community, Turner helps fight back.

Part of Me
by Kimberly Willis Holt

Raised in Louisiana during the Great Depression, Rose never goes to college, but she tries to pass on her love of books to her children and grandchildren. Although not all of them follow in her footsteps, the family stories help each generation stay strong.

What can you learn from a job?

Code Talker
By Joseph Bruchac

World War II is raging, and Ned wants to help. He joins the Marines and becomes a secret Navajo code talker. He helps create a code that can't be cracked, and then uses it to send and receive messages in the midst of battle. Will Ned survive the fighting?

Gathering Blue
by Lois Lowry

In the future, when society is in ruins from disasters, a crippled orphan like Kira is often destined to die. But Kira's weaving skills are discovered, and suddenly she's important. If only her new job didn't bring with it serious problems.

Ghost Boy
Iain Lawrence

Harold is an albino, and in his small town he's an outcast. When the circus comes to town, Harold leaves with it, immediately accepted by members of the sideshow. He soon finds out that even in the circus, he and his friends are considered strange.

How can we fight injustice?

Stop The Train!
by Geraldine McCaughrean

In 1893, people came to Florence, Oklahoma, searching for a stake in a new prairie town. Now the Red Rock Railroad Company refuses to stop in Florence. The new town is sure to die unless the settlers can find a way to get the train to stop.

The Outcasts of 19 Schuyler Place
by E.L. Konigsburg

Margaret Rose is happy to be rescued from Camp Talequa by her uncles. But they seem to accept that the town wants to destroy the three beautiful towers they built in the backyard. Someone has to save these works of art.

Warriors Don't Cry
by Melba Pattillo Beals

Melba Pattillo Beals was one of the nine African-American teenagers who integrated the Little Rock Central High School in 1957. In this memoir, she describes both the violent protesters she faced as well as the people and ideals that gave her courage and hope.

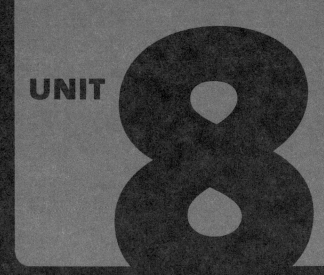

UNIT 8

Believe It or Not

FACTS AND INFORMATION

- In Nonfiction
- In Media

Where do you get your FACTS?

You don't go a single day without needing to gather some facts. With message boards, magazines, books, and directories all offering you information, where do you turn when you need an answer you can count on? It depends on what kind of facts you're looking for, and what you need to know.

ACTIVITY Work with a partner to analyze where you get your information.

- Make a list of five or six facts that you might look for in a typical day.

- Next to each fact, write one or more sources in which you might find it.

- Share your list with others. Do you get most of your facts from printed material, from the Internet, or from somewhere else?

- Discuss which of these sources are most trustworthy and which are easiest to use.

Find It Online! THINK central

Go to thinkcentral.com for the interactive version of this unit.

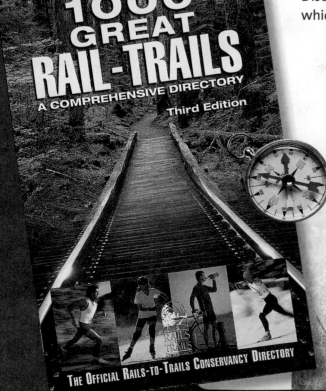

1000 GREAT RAIL-TRAILS
A COMPREHENSIVE DIRECTORY
Third Edition

THE OFFICIAL RAILS-TO-TRAILS CONSERVANCY DIRECTORY

COMMON CORE

Preview Unit Goals

TEXT ANALYSIS	• Determine a central idea of a text and analyze its development over the course of the text • Analyze the structure of a text • Determine an author's point of view or purpose in a text • Distinguish between fact and opinion • Provide an objective summary of a text • Use text features to comprehend and locate information • Read and comprehend technical directions • Interpret and evaluate graphic aids
WRITING AND LANGUAGE	• Write procedural text • Use gerunds and infinitives correctly • Use commas correctly after adverbial clauses
SPEAKING AND LISTENING	• Present and respond to an instructional speech
VOCABULARY	• Use affixes, root words, and context clues to determine the meanings of words • Use word origins to help understand how other languages have influenced English word meaning
ACADEMIC VOCABULARY	• challenge • design • job • method • communicate
MEDIA AND VIEWING	• Analyze the purpose of information presented in diverse media and formats • Compare how different media cover the same event

Media ⬛ Smart DVD-ROM

Facts in the News

Analyze news reports of a NASA space mission to identify the sources behind the news. Page 910

Reading Informational Text

You are living in an age of information. In a matter of minutes, you can find magazine articles, Web sites, and blogs on just about any topic, from global warming to cell-phone technology. But how can you be sure you're getting the most out of what you're reading? What's the best way to wade through all those facts and figures? Learning a few strategies can help you navigate through a sea of information, find answers to your questions, and remember what you've learned.

Part 1: Text Features

COMMON CORE

Included in this workshop:
RI 2 Determine a central idea of a text and analyze its development over the course of the text, including its relationship to supporting ideas; provide an objective summary of the text. **RI 3** Analyze how a text makes connections among and distinctions between ideas (e.g., through categories). **RI 5** Analyze in detail the structure of a specific paragraph in a text, including the role of particular sentences in developing and refining a key concept.

Time is money in the fast-paced, modern world. So, it's important to be able to find information quickly when you're searching through Web sites, books, and magazines. One way to locate useful information at a glance is to notice the text features writers use. **Text features** include titles, subheadings, captions, sidebars, boldfaced words, bulleted lists, and links. These elements allow you to see the most important ideas without having to read every word.

Consider the following article from the back of a "Fun Facts" pamphlet. By scanning the text features, you can anticipate what information the article includes before deciding to read further.

The History of ❶ Hot Dogs

❶ The **title** reveals the topic of the article— the history of hot dogs.

Hot Dogs in Europe ❷

There are several different theories about the origin of the hot dog. Traditionally, Frankfurt-am-Main, Germany, is credited with originating the frankfurter.

❷ **Subheadings** highlight what each section of the article is about.

❸ A **sidebar** provides more information.

Hot Dog Specialties ❸

- In the South, people like their hot dogs "dragged through the garden" with a cole-slaw type topping.
❹
- New Yorkers like their hot dogs served with steamed onions and pale yellow mustard.

- Folks in Kansas City enjoy hot dogs with sauerkraut and Swiss cheese.

❹ A **bulleted list** presents information in an easy-to-read format.

All-American Dogs

Another story points to the Louisiana Purchase Exposition in 1904. A concessionaire sold hot dogs as plain sausages, and provided customers with white gloves for easier eating. After the gloves were not returned, he consulted a baker, who designed the "hot dog bun" to protect eaters' fingers.

One of the more credible stories comes from Barry Popick, a prominent hot dog historian at Roosevelt University. He claims the term began appearing in college magazines in the 1890s. Yale students kept referring to wagons selling hot sausages in buns outside their dorms as "dog wagons." It didn't take long for the use of the word *dog* to become "hot dog."

MODEL: TEXT FEATURES

Skim the text features in this Web article. What information do you think the article will provide? Now read the full article and answer the questions.

File   Edit   View   Tools   Help

Back   Forward   Stop   Refresh   Home   Search   Favorites   Mail   Print

Articles   Games   Fun Facts   Home

DANGER from the Sky

That's not Swiss cheese up there. The <u>craters</u> that cover much of the Moon's surface were caused by collisions with space objects billions of years ago. In 1953 an astronomer even caught on film
5   the bright flash of an object hitting the Moon. With so much evidence of objects hitting our nearest neighbor, scientists wonder when another large object from space will strike our planet.

See More Photos

Impacts on Earth
10   Earth's <u>atmosphere</u> protects us from collisions with small objects, which burn up in the air. However, when a large object strikes Earth, the atmosphere can spread the effects of the impact far beyond the crater. A large collision may throw dust high into the air, where it can be carried around the globe. The dust can block sunlight for months and sharply lower global temperatures.

15   About 65 million years ago, a large space object struck Earth. At about the same time, most species of organisms died out, including the dinosaurs. Many scientists think that the results of this collision caused the global devastation.

Risk of a Meteorite Collision
When will the next space object hit Earth?
20   A collision is probably occurring as you read this sentence. Tiny particles hit Earth's atmosphere all the time. Some of these particles have enough mass to make it through the atmosphere.

Objects that reach Earth's surface are called
25   <u>meteorites.</u> Most meteorites splash harmlessly into the ocean or hit unpopulated areas. However, every few years a meteorite damages a home or other property.

—by Miguel Lopez

TRACKING ASTEROIDS
Although Earth is unlikely to have a major collision with a space object anytime soon, scientists feel the danger is too great to ignore. They are using telescopes to find large, rocky space objects called <u>asteroids</u>. After locating an asteroid, they use computer models to predict its path.

Internet

Close Read

1. If you were doing a report on meteorites, would this article be useful to you? Explain which text feature helped you find the answer.

2. Summarize the information that appears under the subheading "Impacts on Earth." Write another subheading that the author could have used.

3. What additional information does the sidebar provide?

Part 2: Main Idea and Supporting Details

After you preview a text, you're ready to examine it more closely. To do this well, you need to know how to identify main ideas and evaluate texts.

IDENTIFYING MAIN IDEAS

The **topic** of a piece of nonfiction is what the text is about. A topic can usually be stated in a word or two, such as *pets* or *dog training*. The **main idea,** or central idea, is the most important idea that a writer wants to share about a topic. A main idea can usually be stated in a sentence, such as "The key to good dog training is consistency."

Often, the main idea of a paragraph or section of an article is directly stated in a **topic sentence,** which is usually the first or the last sentence in that paragraph or section. Sometimes, however, the main idea is **implied,** which means that it is not actually stated outright; readers must infer the main idea from supporting details. **Supporting details** are facts, examples, and other kinds of information that reinforce or elaborate upon the main idea.

As you read, be on the lookout for the main ideas of paragraphs and sections of text. Then, add up those ideas to identify the text's larger main idea or message.

EVALUATING TEXTS

The next important step in reading informational text is evaluating it. After all, just because the text is about real people, places, and events does not mean that it is true or even well written. To evaluate a text, ask yourself the following questions.

- Is this information accurate, reliable, and trustworthy? If you're not sure, you can learn how to determine **credibility** on pages 1071–1074.

- Does the text have **unity?** In other words, do all the details in each paragraph support its main idea? Do all the paragraphs support a larger main idea?

- Is the writing **coherent?** Specifically, do the sentences connect smoothly and logically? Do text features and the text's structure make it easy to navigate?

- Does the writing have **internal consistency?** Internally consistent text has a clear **structural pattern.** It also uses transitions that make sense together, such as *first, later,* and *afterwards* (as opposed to *first, later,* and *primarily*).

- Is the writing **logical,** or can you spot logical fallacies? If you're not sure, learn more about logical fallacies on page R24.

MODEL 1: MAIN IDEA AND DETAILS

Read this article about a lifelike robot created by a Korean scientist.

Female Android Debuts

Article by **Victoria Gilman**

These school-age tots seem to be making friends with EveR-1, a female android that made her debut in South Korea. The robot was built by
5 Baeg Moon-hong, a senior researcher with the Division for Applied Robot Technology at the Korea Institute of Industrial Technology in Ansan, just south of Seoul.

Children check out Korean android EveR-1.

10 **Meet EveR-1** EveR-1 is designed to resemble a Korean female in her early 20s. Fifteen motors underneath her silicon skin allow her to express a limited range of emotions, and a 400-
15 word vocabulary enables her to hold a simple conversation. The android weighs 110 pounds and would stand 5 feet, 3 inches tall—if she could stand. EveR-1 can move her arms and hands,
20 but her lower half is immobile.

Not Alone Researchers at Osaka University in Japan unveiled their own life-size female android, Repliee Q1. That robot could "speak," and gesture
25 and even appeared to breathe but, like EveR-1, was only mobile from the waist up.

Close Read

1. The main idea of the "Meet EveR-1" section is boxed. Identify the details that support it.

2. What is the main idea of the section with the subheading "Not Alone"?

3. Is there an internal consistency to this article? Explain your answer.

MODEL 2: MAIN IDEA AND DETAILS

This article is about deadly poisons. Skim the title and the subheading, and answer the first **Close Read** question. Then read the article more closely to help you answer the second question.

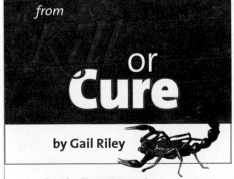

from **Kill or Cure**

by Gail Riley

Night falls in an Israeli desert. A cockroach skitters across the sand. Suddenly, a scorpion grabs the cockroach in its pincers. It
5 injects searing venom into its victim through its stinger. The venom causes paralysis. The cockroach cannot move. It can do nothing to fend off the scorpion's attack.

10 **Toxic Treatments**

It's hard to believe, but the deadly venom that paralyzed the cockroach can be used to heal rather than harm. Scientists are experimenting with the Israeli scorpion's venom. Some of them believe it has the power to shrink brain tumors. For hundreds of years, scientists have been experimenting
15 with poisons extracted from animals and plants. They have found that the same toxins that can injure or kill can also be used to treat health problems.

Close Read

1. Based on the title and the subheading, what do you think the main idea of the article will be?

2. Identify the main idea that the boxed sentences are supporting.

3. Does this article exhibit unity and coherence? Explain your answer.

TAKING NOTES

Have you ever read an article on a fascinating subject—life-saving poisons, for example—and later realized that you couldn't recall a single thing about it? Taking notes as you read can help you prevent that. You can use any number of formats for notes—outline, bulleted list, even a Y-chart. Just use a format that will help you quickly recognize what's most important when you glance back over your notes later. Here are two ways of recording the same information from an article you just read. Notice that the Y-chart emphasizes similarities and differences while the outline captures all the supporting details of each subject.

OUTLINE

I. EveR-1 resembles a Korean female in her 20s.
  A. Made in South Korea
  B. Can show emotion, talk, and move her arms
  C. Can only move the top half of her body

II. Repliee QI is another life-size female android.
  A. Made in Japan
  B. Can talk, move her arms, and looks like she's breathing
  C. Can only move the top half of her body

GRAPHIC ORGANIZER

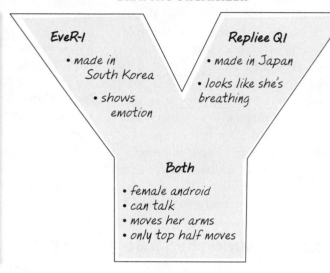

EveR-1
• made in South Korea
• shows emotion

Repliee QI
• made in Japan
• looks like she's breathing

Both
• female android
• can talk
• moves her arms
• only top half moves

SUMMARIZING

Summarizing is the art of briefly retelling in your own words the main ideas and most important details of something you read, heard, or saw. It is a useful way to share your knowledge on a test, in a research report, and in a conversation.

To summarize a text, begin by taking clear and thorough notes—preferably in your own words. Then, restate the main ideas and most important details in two or three complete sentences. Keep in mind that a good summary is always shorter than the text it is summarizing. Here's an example:

The South Korean EveR-1 and the Japanese Repliee QI are both lifesize female androids that can talk and move their arms as well as the top half of their bodies, but only the EveR-1 shows emotions and only the Repliee QI looks as if she's breathing.

Part 3: Analyze the Text

Preview this article and answer the first **Close Read** question. Then read the article more closely, using the other questions to help you take notes. Then use your notes to summarize the article.

THE
Great Chicago Fire
OF 1871

Magazine article
by **Michael Burgan**

RECIPE FOR DISASTER Chicago in 1871 was already a big city, bustling with more than 334,000 residents. Its streets, sidewalks, and most of its buildings were made of wood. Hay and straw were inside every barn. To make the situation worse, people used candles and oil lamps.

5   Fires had been common that year because of the dry weather. The Chicago Fire Department was overworked and underequipped. On Saturday, October 7, firefighters began putting out a fire that wiped out four city blocks. It took them 16 hours. By Sunday evening the men were exhausted. Then around 8:45 P.M., a fire began in the barn of Patrick and Catherine O'Leary.

10 "EVERYTHING WENT WRONG"

Human error then made a bad situation worse. One firefighter later said, "From the beginning of that fatal fire, everything went wrong!" A watchman atop the 15 courthouse saw smoke rising from the O'Leary barn, but he assumed it was coming from the previous fire. When he finally realized a new fire was blazing, he misjudged its location. His assistant 20 sent a message to the fire stations, but he mistakenly directed horse-drawn fire wagons to a location about a mile from the burning barn. When the fire department finally reached the barn, its equipment 25 was no match for the blaze. The new fire raged on.

OUT OF CONTROL

As the fire blazed, there arose a deafening roar—wood crackling as flames devoured 30 it, cries for help, explosions from oil and gas tanks, the crash of falling buildings. The fire department could do nothing to stop the fire. Around 4 A.M. the next day, the fire destroyed the city's waterworks, 35 shutting off water to the fire hydrants. Firefighters had to drag water in buckets from Lake Michigan and the Chicago River. City officials made a desperate call for help to other cities, but their forces 40 arrived too late. The fire kept burning— totally out of control.

THE AFTERMATH

The Great Fire burned until October 10, when rain finally fell. Thousands of 45 buildings had been destroyed. About 300 people had died in the blaze, and more than 100,000 were left homeless.

Close Read

1. Preview the title and subheadings. What information do you think this article will provide?

2. Describe the main idea that the boxed details support. Copy the main idea and details into your notebook. Add letters as necessary.

> I.
>   A.
>   B.

3. The main idea of the second section is listed here. Copy it into your notebook, along with the supporting details.

> II. Human error made a bad situation even worse.
>   A.
>   B.

4. Identify the main idea and details in the third and fourth sections. Add the information to your outline.

> III.
>   A.
>   B. The fire destroyed the city's waterworks.
> IV.
>   A. 300 people died.
>   B.

The Spider Man Behind *Spider-Man*
Feature Article by Bijal P. Trivedi

VIDEO TRAILER THINK central KEYWORD: HML8-890

What is your
DREAM JOB?

COMMON CORE

RI 2 Provide an objective summary of the text.
RI 5 Analyze in detail the structure of a text.

Ever since you were little, people have probably asked you what you want to be when you grow up. Now that you're older and know yourself better, your dream job might be coming into focus. Is it a job that would take you outdoors? Onto a movie set? Into a sports arena? Your ideal career probably reflects your individual talents, interests, and personality. In the following article, you'll read about a man who turned his passion into a dream job.

SURVEY Interview several classmates to find out what their dream jobs would be. Ask these students why they chose the jobs they did. How do their dream careers compare to your own?

Name	Dream Job	Why?
Kayla	Veterinarian	1. Likes taking care of animals 2. Gets good grades in science 3. Enjoys learning about animals

● TEXT ANALYSIS: TEXT FEATURES

Nonfiction articles often utilize **text features,** design elements that highlight the structural patterns of the text and help you identify key ideas. Common text features include

- **headings**—the title of the article
- **subheadings**—headings that signal the beginning of a new topic or section within a written piece
- **sidebars**—additional information set in a box alongside, below, or within an article
- **bulleted lists**—lists of items of equal value or importance. This list of text features is an example of a bulleted list.

As you read "The Spider Man Behind *Spider-Man*," notice how the text features help you locate information on particular topics.

● READING STRATEGY: SUMMARIZE

Have you ever told a friend about a movie you just saw? If so, you probably gave your friend a summary. When you **summarize** a piece of writing, you briefly retell the main ideas or key points in the order in which they appear in the original text. Summarizing is a way to check your understanding, and it can help you remember information. You can also use a summary to clarify relationships among ideas in a text. As you read "The Spider Man Behind *Spider-Man*," use a chart to take notes on the key points. Later, you'll use these notes to summarize the article.

What Steven Kutcher Does	His Training and Background	His Spider-Man Experience

▲ VOCABULARY IN CONTEXT

The boldfaced words help the author describe one man's interesting career. Try using context clues to figure out what each word means.

1. He has the **perseverance** necessary to finish the job.
2. Bill is an **engaging** person whom everyone likes.
3. Maria has the **potential** to become a first-rate scientist.
4. Ashley's watercolor **rendition** of her dream earned praise from her art teacher.

Complete the activities in your **Reader/Writer Notebook.**

Meet the Author

Bijal P. Trivedi
born 1970

A Love of Science
Bijal Trivedi (bĭj′əl trē-vā′dē) became fascinated with dinosaurs at the age of nine. Soon after, she transferred her interest to the space shuttle and astronomy. From an early age, it was clear that Trivedi's dream job would involve science.

Exciting Places and Discoveries
Trivedi studied science in college and earned master's degrees in both biology and science journalism. Because Trivedi didn't want to work in a lab, she became a science writer. She has written for magazines such as *National Geographic, Popular Science,* and *Wired.* She says, "Being a science writer is a bit like being Indiana Jones—you get to travel with lots of smart scientists to exciting places and then write stories about their discoveries." Trivedi has won several awards for her journalism.

BACKGROUND TO THE ARTICLE
The Amazing Spider-Man
In 1962, writer Stan Lee and artist Steve Ditko created the character of Peter Parker, a teenager who gains spider-like powers through the bite of a radioactive spider and becomes Spider-Man. Spider-Man first appeared in an issue of *Amazing Fantasy* by Marvel Comics and then gained a comic book series all his own. *The Amazing Spider-Man* comics have been popular ever since. In the movies about the superhero, CGI, or computer-generated imagery, made it appear that Peter Parker could swing from one tall building to another, stick to walls, and do other incredible feats that only a Spider-Man could do.

Author Online
THINK central
Go to **thinkcentral.com.**
KEYWORD: HML8-891

THE SPIDER MAN BEHIND SPIDER-MAN

Bijal P. Trivedi

Entomologist Steven Kutcher is the spider man behind *Spider-Man*. "He's the guy to call in Hollywood when you need insects—he is the ultimate insect trainer," says Robin Miller, property master for the movie *Spider-Man*.

"I know how to get a cockroach to run across the floor and flip onto its back. I can get cockroaches, beetles, and spiders to crawl to a quarter four feet away on cue. I can make bees swarm indoors and I can repair butterfly wings," says Kutcher. He has even made a live wasp fly into an actor's mouth. "I study insect behavior, and learn what they do and then adapt the behavior to what the director wants," says Kutcher. Ⓐ

10 Passion for Bugs Ⓑ

Kutcher's love of insects began as a toddler when he collected fireflies in New York. But he was also influenced by very "positive early childhood experiences in nature" when his family would spend summers in the Catskills.[1] "Something about seeing fish, catching butterflies, lit a fire within me," says Kutcher.

Kutcher followed his passion for bugs and studied entomology in college, receiving his B.S. from the University of California, Davis, and later an M.A. in biology—with an emphasis on entomology,[2] insect behavior, and ecology[3] from the California State University in Long Beach.
20 He had planned to pursue a Ph.D.,[4] but when he wasn't accepted at the graduate school of his choice he decided to reevaluate his career options.

---

1. **Catskills** (kăt′skĭlz′): the Catskill Mountain region in New York state. It is a popular vacation area.
2. **entomology** (ĕn′tə-mŏl′ə-jē): the study of insects.
3. **ecology** (ĭ-kŏl′ə-jē): the study of relationships among living things and their environment.
4. **B.S.; M.A.; Ph.D.:** Bachelor of Science, an undergraduate degree; Master of Arts, a graduate degree; Doctor of Philosophy, a graduate degree that is usually more time-consuming and difficult to earn than a master's degree.

Ⓐ **SUMMARIZE**
What are some of Kutcher's unique skills? Record them in your chart.

Ⓑ **TEXT FEATURES**
On the basis of this **subheading** and what you've read so far, what information do you expect to find in this section?

◀ **Analyze Visuals**

Based on this photo of Steven Kutcher, what can you **infer** about his interests and personality?

One day he received a call from his former academic advisor asking him to baby-sit 3,000 locusts that were to be used for the movie *Exorcist 2.* Kutcher had to place the locusts wherever they were needed, including on the stars Richard Burton and Linda Blair. That was his first job, and it has been Hollywood creepy crawlies ever since.

After doing a long survey of movies Kutcher found that about one third of all movies had an insect in it. "I saw immediate job **potential**," Kutcher says.

30 Almost 25 years after his first job Kutcher now holds an impressive list of movie, television, music video, and commercial credits that include his biggest movie, *Arachnophobia,* the comedy-thriller in which a California town is overrun with deadly spiders. He also supervised the bug and spider stunts in *Alien, Contact, Jurassic Park, Pacific Heights,* and *Wild Wild West.*

"He is a very observant and **engaging** guy," says Lucinda Strub, a special effects person who worked with Kutcher on *Arachnophobia.* "One of his main goals is to educate the public about how fascinating and interesting insects are. He is really out to teach people about bugs," says Strub, who then . . . clarified that "of course spiders are not bugs, they are arachnids."

potential (pə-tĕn′shəl) *n.* the ability to grow or develop

engaging (ĕn-gāj′ĭng) *adj.* charming; likeable

perseverance (pûr′sə-vîr′əns) *n.* steady persistence in sticking to a course of action

So You Want to Be an Entomologist?

Do you get grossed out when you see a spider or earwig[5] crawling up your wall? Or does the spider's web and the inchworm's movement fascinate you? If the latter question describes you, then entomology could be the perfect career for you.

Entomologists study the classification, life cycle, and habits of insects and related life forms, and plan and implement insect surveys and pest management programs. They also investigate ways to control insect pests and manage beneficial insects such as plant pollinators,[6] insect parasites, and insect predators.

Interests and Skills

Entomologists need the intellect, curiosity, creativity, patience, and **perseverance** required to pursue answers to complex research questions about bugs. Because there are thousands and thousands of insect species, entomologists must also have a good memory. Entomologists must be able to work well both independently and as part of a team.

5. **earwig** (îr-wĭg′): an insect that has two pincers protruding from the rear of its abdomen.

6. **pollinators** (pŏl′ə-nāt′tərs): animals that carry pollen from one plant to another, causing the plants to produce fruit.

40   Even with his busy filmmaking schedule, Kutcher still finds time to teach once a week at a local community college. He also started the annual Insect Fair at the Los Angeles Arboretum. **C**

The Perfect Match

Kutcher's most recent challenge has been finding the perfect spider for the movie *Spider-Man*. . . . The concept designer for the movie produced a computer **rendition** that combined traits of up to four arachnids to create an image of the mutant spider that bites Peter Parker (a.k.a. Spider-Man) and endows him with spider powers. **D**

"I was given this drawing of a spider that didn't exist and told to find
50 a real spider that matched it," says Miller, whose responsibilities include assembling all the props in the entire film. The spider resembled a black widow, which wasn't an option because its bite is too dangerous.

Miller contacted Steven Kutcher and showed him the picture. Kutcher then arranged a "spider Olympics" for *Spider-Man* director Sam Raimi. Kutcher brought in different types of spiders to showcase the talents of each, says Miller, "He literally had the spiders doing tricks." One spider

C SUMMARIZE
Reread lines 22–42. What are two of the most important pieces of information you get from these paragraphs? Add them to your chart.

rendition (rĕn-dĭsh′ən) *n.* a pictorial representation; an interpretation

D TEXT FEATURES
Reread the **subheading** and first sentence of this section. What "perfect match" does the subheading refer to?

Typical Tasks
- Study the evolution of insects
- Discover and describe new species of insects
- Conduct research into the impact and control of insect pest problems
- Conduct field and laboratory tests of pesticides to evaluate their effect on different species of insects under different conditions
- Curate museum insect collections
- Prepare publications that make it possible to identify insect, spider, mite, and tick species
- Coordinate public awareness and education programs **E**

AVERAGE EARNINGS

Maximum Salary:
$71,270

Average Salary:
$47,740

Entry Level Salary:
$29,260

Educational Paths
Students interested in a career working with insects should prepare for college by taking a variety of science classes. Many students get a general undergraduate degree in biology or zoology[7] and then specialize in entomology at the post-graduate level. For those wishing to lead research teams or teach at the university level, a Ph.D. is a requirement. **F**

E TEXT FEATURES
What does this **bulleted list** help you better understand?

F TEXT FEATURES
What does the information presented in the blue **sidebar** add to your understanding of Steven Kutcher and his career?

7. **zoology** (zōō-ŏl′ə-jē): the study of animals.

could jump, another was able to
spin webs very quickly, and yet
another was able to produce a
60 drag line and essentially swing
out of the way—all activities
that Spider-Man can do.

The spider that Raimi
selected was *Steatoda grossa*, a
brown spider with a smooth,
swollen body and thin twiggy
legs. The problem was that the
color was wrong, "we needed
a spider that had metallic blue
70 and a radioactive[8] red-orange
color to it," says Miller.

The answer was spider make-
up. Originally Kutcher wanted
to make an entire costume for
the spider, but the timing came
down to the wire and he finally
settled on body paint. "I had to
find a non-toxic[9] paint, design a
little harness to hold the spider
80 as he was painted, and supervise
the artist painting *Steatoda*."

The *Steatoda grossa* spider

"I need the spider to go from A to B to C and Steve can train it to do
that," says Miller, who has worked with Kutcher on several movies.
"He is very creative; he can figure out how to get the creature to do what
he wants while being very delicate," says Strub.

Why, in this age of computer-generated special effects, did the director
simply not animate the spider? "The real thing always looks best, especially
when it fills the whole movie screen," says Miller. And computer-generated
graphics are very expensive, although the scene where the mutant spider
90 bites Peter Parker is computer-generated.

"People find me, and I'm off on these adventures," says Kutcher,
"problem solving, and exploring, and teaching, and educating people about
insects." But Steven Kutcher's hat best describes his life, his love, and his
philosophy: "Bugs are my business." **G**

◆ **GRAMMAR IN CONTEXT**
Notice in lines 57–59
the author uses the
infinitive forms of the
verbs *spin* and *produce*
to clarify what each
spider was able to do. An
infinitive is a verb form
that usually begins with
the word *to* and acts as
a noun, an adjective, or
an adverb.

Language Coach

Idiom An idiom is
a phrase that has a
meaning different from
its individual words. The
idiom "down to the wire"
in line 76 means "right
up to the deadline."
How does this idiom
help explain why
Kutcher used body paint
on the spider?

G SUMMARIZE
What crucial jobs did
Kutcher perform in
the making of *Spider-
Man*? Add these to the
appropriate section of
your chart.

---

8. **radioactive** (rā′dē-ō-ăk′tĭv): exhibiting radiation emissions that possibly result from a nuclear
   explosion.

9. **non-toxic:** not poisonous or otherwise life-threatening.

Comprehension

1. **Recall** What was Steven Kutcher's first experience on a movie set?

2. **Recall** Why did the makers of the movie *Spider-Man* want to use a real spider instead of a computer-generated spider for most of the spider scenes?

3. **Clarify** Why was it so hard to find the perfect spider for *Spider-Man*?

COMMON CORE

RI 2 Provide an objective summary of the text.
RI 5 Analyze in detail the structure of a text.

Text Analysis

4. **Examine Text Features** Which text features help you find the following pieces of information? Note your answers in a chart like the one shown.

Information	Text Feature That Helps You Find It
Broad focus of the article	
Kutcher's interest in bugs	
Typical tasks performed by entomologists	
General information about entomologists	

5. **Compare Summaries** Using the chart you made as you read, write a summary of the entire article. Next, trade summaries with a classmate. Compare the summary you received with the article to see if the summary accurately captures the main ideas, important details, and underlying meaning of the article. Share your findings with your classmate, and then revise your summary as needed.

6. **Draw Conclusions** Reread lines 11–15 and 35–42. Why do you think Kutcher wants other people to have a better understanding of insects?

7. **Evaluate Text** Now think about the text critically. Does it have unity and coherence? Is its structure easy to identify and follow? Explain why or why not. If you need help recalling what unity and coherence are, see page 886.

Extension and Challenge

8. **Creative Project: Music** Alone or in a small group, create a song or rap from the point of view of an insect who "works" for Steven Kutcher. Look back at the article to help you recall some of the things these creatures have been trained to do and Kutcher's attitude toward what some people call "creepy crawlies." Share your song or rap with the class.

What is your DREAM JOB?

What was your answer to the big question on page 890? Using books or the Internet, find out what skills or education you might need for this career. Present this information in a format similar to the sidebar on pages 894–895.

Vocabulary in Context

▲ **VOCABULARY PRACTICE**

Decide whether the words in each pair are synonyms (words with similar meanings) or antonyms (words with opposite meanings).

1. perseverance/laziness
2. rendition/interpretation
3. engaging/disagreeable
4. potential/promise

ACADEMIC VOCABULARY IN WRITING

> • challenge   • communicate   • design   • job   • method

Imagine that you are applying for a **job** as Steven Kutcher's assistant. What makes you a good candidate? Using at least two Academic Vocabulary words, write a paragraph telling Kutcher why he should hire you.

VOCABULARY STRATEGY: CONTEXT CLUES

Sometimes the context of a word provides clues to its meaning. **Context clues** are words and phrases that surround an unfamiliar, novel, or ambiguous word. For example, a clue to the meaning of *potential* in line 28 of this article comes in the previous sentence, which explains that according to Kutcher's research, "one third of all movies had an insect in it." From this clue, we can figure out that "job potential" is the ability for a career to develop.

⋯ **COMMON CORE**

L 4a Use context (e.g., the overall meaning of a sentence or paragraph) as a clue to the meaning of a word.

PRACTICE Use context clues to determine the definition of each boldfaced word. Then write its definition.

1. If you do not understand an idea, ask your teacher for **clarification**.
2. President Lincoln spoke to a small **assemblage** in the auditorium.
3. My **classification** system is based on size, shape, and color.
4. Hundreds of workers lost their jobs due to the factory closing. Mayor Diaz is concerned that the town's **unemployment** rate will rise dramatically.
5. What **adaptations** help desert plants cope with their environment?

Interactive Vocabulary

Go to thinkcentral.com.
KEYWORD: HML8-898

Language

◆ **GRAMMAR IN CONTEXT:** Use Gerunds and Infinitives

COMMON CORE

L 1a Explain the function of verbals (gerunds, infinitives) in general and their function in particular sentences.

Review the **Grammar in Context** note on page 896. A **verbal** is a word that is formed from a verb and can act as a noun, an adjective, or an adverb. A **verbal phrase** consists of a verbal along with its modifiers and complements.

A **gerund** is a verbal that ends in *ing* and acts as a noun. Gerunds can add a sense of motion or action to a sentence.

> *Example:* Spider-Man had to perform such tricks as **swinging** from tall buildings.

An **infinitive** is a verbal that usually begins with the word *to* and acts as a noun, an adjective, or an adverb. However, sometimes *to* is omitted.

> *Examples:* Originally, Kutcher wanted **to make** an entire costume for the spider. He helped [to] **supervise** the artist painting the spider.

PRACTICE Identify the boldfaced words in each of the following sentences as a gerund or an infinitive form of the verb.

1. Kutcher's first job in the movie industry was **to baby-sit** 3,000 locusts.
2. Until then, he had not realized that **training** insects could be a career.
3. Kutcher still makes time **to teach** at a local community college.
4. His job is really about **solving** problems.
5. He figures out how **to make** bugs do what he wants.

*For more help with verbals and verbal phrases, see page R61 in the **Grammar Handbook**.*

READING-WRITING CONNECTION

YOUR TURN

Explore Steven Kutcher's career further by responding to this prompt. Then use the **revising tip** to improve your writing.

WRITING PROMPT	REVISING TIP
Extended Constructed Response: Job Advertisement Imagine that you are a movie director looking to hire someone to train insects for your next film. What type of person do you want to hire? Write a **two- or three-paragraph advertisement** giving the education, skills, and interests needed for this career. Include a subheading for each section.	Review your advertisement. Check to make sure that you have used verbal phrases where appropriate to make your writing more lively and descriptive.

Interactive Revision **THINK** central

Go to **thinkcentral.com**.
KEYWORD: HML8N-899

Over the Top: The True Adventures of a Volcano Chaser

Magazine Article by Renee Skelton

Video link at
thinkcentral.com

Why do people seek DANGER?

COMMON CORE

RI 1 Cite the textual evidence that supports an analysis of what the text says explicitly. **RI 7** Evaluate the advantages and disadvantages of using different mediums to present a particular topic or idea. **SL 2** Analyze the purpose of information presented in diverse media and formats (e.g., visually).

Most people avoid danger. They buckle their seat belts when they fly on a plane. They take care not to anger mean dogs, not to swim where there are sharks, not to walk on thin ice. But then there are other people—the ones who dream of skydiving and who soar through half-pipes on their skateboards. The man featured in the article you're about to read belongs to this group. He's willing to risk his life to photograph mysteries of the earth.

WEB IT What dangerous activities are also popular pastimes? What is it about these activities that makes people willing to risk their safety? Use a web to explore the reasons why these activities can be viewed as both fun and dangerous.

Feels like you're flying

Parachute might not open

Skydiving

Dangerous Activities

TEXT ANALYSIS: GRAPHIC AIDS

Magazine articles often contain **graphic aids**, which are visual representations of information. Writers use graphic aids to highlight or summarize important concepts and to explain things in fewer words. Common graphic aids include photographs, maps, diagrams, graphs, and timelines.

As you read "Over the Top," use a chart like the one shown to take notes on the article's graphic aids.

Type of Graphic Aid	What It Explains

Review: Text Features

READING STRATEGY: ADJUST READING RATE TO PURPOSE

Effective readers change the speed at which they read to suit their purpose. Try this as you read the following article.

When your purpose is to	Adjust your rate like this
Get an overview of the article	**Skim** before you begin. This involves **quickly** reading the title, subheadings, and any graphic aids.
Find key words or particular information	**Scan** the text. This involves moving your eyes **quickly** over the text, looking for the words or information you need.
Gain a full understanding of something, or clarify information	Read the material at a **slower** pace, and **reread** if necessary.

To use the best strategy for your purpose, stay mindful of why you're reading and whether you need to adjust your rate.

▲ VOCABULARY IN CONTEXT

The following vocabulary words help Renee Skelton tell about a man with a dangerous job. To see how many you know, match each word with its numbered synonym.

WORD LIST	cavernous	pinnacle	searing
	labyrinth	scale	straddle

1. climb
2. vast
3. top
4. span
5. maze
6. hot

 Complete the activities in your **Reader/Writer Notebook.**

Renee Skelton

A Well-Versed Writer
Freelance writer Renee Skelton has written books and articles on topics ranging from American history to climate change. She lives in New Jersey and is a frequent contributor to *National Geographic Kids.*

BACKGROUND TO THE ARTICLE
Sharing Science
National Geographic, first published in 1888, is one of the world's best-known magazines. It's especially known for its colorful, detailed photographs of geographic regions and the people who live there. The photos are taken by some of the world's best photojournalists,

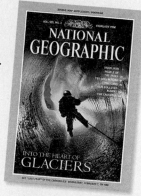

people who present a news story primarily through photographs. These men and women travel the globe with their cameras, seeking out fascinating and sometimes dangerous locations.

Exploring the Unknown
In the article you are about to read, photojournalist Carsten Peter visits an active volcano and chambers beneath glacial ice. No stranger to dangerous situations, Peter has captured stunning images of glaciers, caves, and tornadoes for the pages of *National Geographic.* Why is he so attracted to the dangerous natural wonders he photographs? "I'm most interested in the unknown," he says.

Over the Top

The True Adventures of a Volcano Chaser

Renee Skelton

A ADJUST READING RATE
What can you expect to learn from this article? Take a minute to **skim** the selection and make some predictions about what you'll be reading.

Dangling from a climber's rope, Carsten Peter slowly lowers himself into the fiery throat of Ambrym volcano. One slip, or a direct blast of hot, poisonous gas from the boiling lava lake below, and this descent could be his last. For most people this would have been terror time.

B GRAPHIC AIDS
What does this **photograph** suggest about what the article will focus on?

scale (skāl) *v.* to climb up or over; ascend

C GRAPHIC AIDS
Look carefully at the **map** and its caption. What facts does it offer that you don't get from the text?

But for Peter it was
10 all in a day's work. The daredevil photographer roams the world, <u>scaling</u> mountains and dropping into erupting volcanoes to photograph these fiery mountains at their most frightening—and most beautiful. Does he get scared? "Sure," Peter
20 says. "You wouldn't be normal if you didn't get scared." But volcanoes are a window into Earth's scorching center. And for Peter, peering through that window with his camera is worth the risk.

Peter's adventures keep him globe-trotting. The map shows a few of the places he has explored volcanoes. **C**

Into a Boiling Pit

Ambrym is a tiny South Pacific island that consists of a flat-topped volcano. The volcano erupted violently about 2,000 years ago. The explosion left the

Long Ago
Mount Vesuvius's[1] eruption in A.D. 79 buried two Roman cities, killing 16,000 people.

Loud
The 1883 explosion of Krakatoa, a volcano in Indonesia,[2] was heard 3,000 miles away.

Up There
Mauna Kea, in Hawaii, is the world's tallest volcano. It is 30,000 feet high.

Ring
Most volcanoes are concentrated around the edge of the Pacific Ocean, in the "Ring of Fire."

Blown Away ▶
In mere seconds, whole forests of trees around Mount St. Helens,[3] Washington, were flattened in 1980. Trees 165 feet tall were blown down like toothpicks by the force of the volcano's eruption.

D ADJUST READING RATE
What is the tallest volcano on Earth? **Scan** these captions to find the answer.

Out There ▶
The biggest volcano in our solar system is Olympus Mons on Mars. It is 17 miles high. **D**

1. **Mount Vesuvius** (vĭ-sōō′vē-əs): a volcano located in southern Italy.
2. **Indonesia** (ĭn-dō-nē′zhə): an island nation located in Southeast Asia.
3. **Mount St. Helens:** volcano located in southern Washington state.

seven-and-one-half-mile-wide caldera, or wide crater, that now forms its top. Peter hoped to use one of the vent openings in Ambrym's caldera as a porthole into the volcano's fiery center.

30   When Peter arrived at Ambrym, the volcano was rumbling, its craters belching steam, gas, and ash. He and his group set out right away, hacking through dense jungle and climbing 4,000 feet up the side of the volcano. They emerged from the jungle onto the caldera's rim—a moonscape of boulders and gray-black ash.

After several days of exploring the caldera's surface, Peter decided to descend into Marum, one of Ambrym's pitlike craters. Wearing protective gear, he attached one end of a climbing rope to an anchor hammered into the ground and the other end to his descent device. Peter then disappeared over the edge of Marum's clifflike rim, camera equipment mounted on his helmet and tethered to his back and waist. Peter descended 1,000 feet down the face of the crater's steep walls,
40 as heat rising from the **searing** lava lake blasted him. Pockets of gas and water trapped in the lava expanded and exploded, sending out booms that echoed and shook the crater walls. "The Earth was trembling all around me," Peter says. "And I felt the vibrations all through my body." **E**

Peter had to be careful. A sharp rock could have cut his rope, dropping him into the **cavernous** pit. Tremors[4] could have pried boulders from the cliff above, sending them crashing down on an arm or leg. Peter paused partway down, clutching the rope as volcanic ash stung his eyes and intense heat and sound from the blasting lava rose around him. "If the volcano had exploded then, it would have been the last eruption I ever saw," he says. He drew as close as possible to the spitting, belching lava lake at
50 the bottom. Glowing lava bombs were bursting like fireworks from its surface as Peter snapped photos all night.

---

4. **tremors** (trĕm′ərz): shaking or vibrating of the earth.

Peter captures images of the 2002 eruption of Mount Etna in Sicily.

Language Coach

Personification The word *belching* in line 30 is an example of **personification**, giving human qualities to something that is not human. What human quality does the author use to describe what is happening in the volcano?

searing (sîr′ĭng) *adj.* hot enough to burn, char, or scorch

E   ADJUST READING RATE
What steps did Peter take to safely descend into the crater? Reread lines 34–40 and note Peter's process.

cavernous (kăv′ər-nəs) *adj.* as deep or vast as a cavern, or a large cave

F TEXT FEATURES
Based on this **subheading**, what can you predict about the content of this section?

G GRAPHIC AIDS
What does this **diagram** add to your understanding of the danger Peter faces while photographing Ambrym?

straddle (străd'l) *v.* to be on both sides of

The next morning, exhausted, Peter attached his rope and pulled himself up to safety on Marum's rim. It was time to leave Ambrym for new adventures.

Fire and Ice **F**

60 Half a world away in Iceland,[5] the challenge was more ice than fire. Because of Iceland's location, many volcanoes are hidden below its thick glacial ice. Iceland <u>straddles</u> the mid-Atlantic ridge, where two of the plates that form Earth's crust are pulling apart. The results are frequent tremors and volcanic eruptions. When volcanoes under Iceland's glaciers erupt, they burn through ice at the glacier's base. Escaping heat carves out spectacular formations under the ice.

Signs That "It's Gonna Blow!"

1. In and around a volcano, the frequency and intensity of earthquakes increase.

2. The ground at the eruption site deforms or bulges.

3. The amount of gas released by the volcano increases.

G

---

5. **Iceland:** an island nation located in the North Atlantic Ocean near the Arctic Circle.

H Intense heat from a volcano created this ice cave inside a glacier in Iceland.

H GRAPHIC AIDS
What do these **photos** and captions add to your understanding of Peter's career?

70 Peter's goal was to photograph these underground wonders. After a jolting jeep ride over part of the glacier, Peter continued on foot—leaping crevasses, sloshing through icy rivers of meltwater, and scrambling over jagged ice **pinnacles**. "The heat created chambers inside the ice we were passing over," says Peter. "We had to be very careful." Peter found that out the hard way. Crossing an area of ice that looked solid, Peter stepped on a thin section and crashed through into a hidden river of icy water. He struggled to keep his head and cameras above water. The cameras didn't make it. Luckily Peter did, thanks to two friends who pulled him out of the frigid water.

Exploring the surface ice, Peter discovered a collapsed ice chamber that led to a **labyrinth** of ice caves and tunnels inside the glacier. "It was beautiful, but we

80 were in potential danger because the chamber could have collapsed at any time," Peter says. "Also, we were in a region where earthquakes and floods are common occurrences." But using carbide[6] lights to illuminate the dark tunnels, Peter took incredible photos of the formations in the glacier's frozen heart. **❶**

As you read this, Peter is probably perched on the rim of another volcano, camera in hand. He's withstanding heat from 2,200 degrees Fahrenheit lava flows and dodging deadly clouds of gas to get close to nature at its most extreme. Earth's geology continues to fascinate him. "Volcanoes are very powerful," he says. "When you feel these eruptions, it's the greatest experience you can have."

---

6. **carbide** (kär'bīd'): a very hard material made partly of carbon.

pinnacle (pĭn'ə-kəl) *n.*
a peak; a pointed top

labyrinth (lăb'ə-rĭnth')
n. a maze; an intricate structure of interconnected passages

❶ ADJUST READING RATE
What three things posed a danger to Peter as he explored the ice chamber? **Scan** lines 78–82 to find the answer.

Peter lowers himself through a heat vent in Iceland's Grímsvötn volcano.

Comprehension

1. **Recall** What could have killed or injured Carsten Peter as he photographed inside the Ambrym volcano?

2. **Recall** What did Peter go to Iceland to photograph?

3. **Represent** Using the information provided by the captions on page 904, draw a simple timeline that shows the order in which three famous volcanoes erupted.

COMMON CORE

RI 1 Cite the textual evidence that supports an analysis of what the text says explicitly. **RI 7** Evaluate the advantages and disadvantages of using different mediums to present a particular topic or idea. **SL 2** Analyze the purpose of information presented in diverse media and formats (e.g., visually).

Text Analysis

4. **Analyze Reading Rate** What part of the article did you read most quickly? When did you have to change your reading rate? Explain which strategy you found most useful as you read.

5. **Draw Conclusions** Why do you think Carsten Peter feels it is important to photograph volcanoes in spite of the danger involved?

6. **Compare and Contrast** In what ways are the careers of Steven Kutcher ("The Spider Man Behind *Spider-Man*," page 892) and Carsten Peter alike? In what ways are they different? Complete a Y-chart like the one shown to compare and contrast the two men and their careers. Record the differences in the top part of the Y, and the similarities in the bottom.

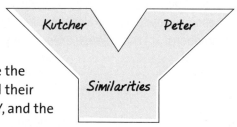

7. **Evaluate Graphic Aids** Look back at the chart you made as you read. What information do you get from the graphic aids? Would this information have been more or less clear if it had been included with the main text but without any visuals? Explain.

Extension and Challenge

8. **Readers' Circle** Carsten Peter obviously believes that the risks he takes are worth the results. Imagine that he is a member of your family, such as your brother, uncle, or father. Would you support his choices, or would you urge him to find a safer career? Discuss your ideas.

9. **SCIENCE CONNECTION** How are volcanoes formed? What causes them to erupt? Research these questions about volcanoes, and ask one additional question of your own. Present your findings to the class in the form of a "slide show," either on paper or the computer.

Why do people seek DANGER?

Now that you have read the selection, what would you add to the web you created about dangerous activities?

Vocabulary in Context

▲ **VOCABULARY PRACTICE**

For each item, choose the word that differs most in meaning from the other words. Refer to a dictionary if you need help.

1. (a) searing, (b) scorching, (c) frigid, (d) sweltering
2. (a) descend, (b) scale, (c) climb, (d) ascend
3. (a) slant, (b) tilt, (c) straddle, (d) lean
4. (a) maze, (b) labyrinth, (c) network, (d) beeline
5. (a) gaping, (b) shallow, (c) deep, (d) cavernous
6. (a) pinnacle, (b) bottom, (c) base, (d) foot

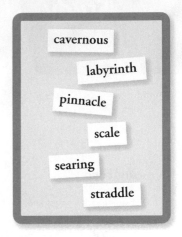

cavernous
labyrinth
pinnacle
scale
searing
straddle

ACADEMIC VOCABULARY IN WRITING

> • challenge • communicate • design • job • method

Write a paragraph about the **challenges** of a daring sport or exciting hobby that interests you. Use at least one of the Academic Vocabulary words in your response.

VOCABULARY STRATEGY: WORD ORIGINS

Many common words in the English language have interesting histories. For example, the vocabulary word *scale* comes from the Latin word *scalae,* meaning "ladder." It makes sense, then, that to scale something means to climb it.

You can find a word's **etymology,** or the history of the word, in most dictionaries. Understanding etymologies can help you connect the word's meaning to something you already know. Here is an example of an etymology:

> **expand** (ĭk-spănd′) *v.* to become greater in size, quantity, volume, or scope [Middle English *expanden,* to spread out, from Latin *expandere: ex-* + *pandere,* to spread]

PRACTICE Look up the etymology of each word in the dictionary. Write the word's origin, and tell how knowing the word's history can help you remember its meaning.

1. intense 3. sparse 5. danger
2. grief 4. glacier

COMMON CORE

L 4c Consult general reference materials (e.g., dictionaries) to determine [a word's] precise meaning.

Interactive Vocabulary **THINK** central

Go to thinkcentral.com.
KEYWORD: HML8-909

News Reports
TV Newscast Clip/Magazine Article on **Media ⬤ Smart** DVD-ROM

What's the SOURCE?

COMMON CORE

RI 7 Evaluate the advantages and disadvantages of using different mediums (e.g., print or video) to present a particular topic or idea. **SL 2** Analyze the purpose of information presented in diverse media and formats (e.g., visually, orally) and evaluate the motives behind its presentation.

Recall a time you watched a TV news report in which someone was making statements to a reporter. What was the circumstance? Did the statements appear to be ones you could trust? In news reporting, it's not just the events that matter but what people have to say about them. In this lesson, you'll see how quotes can help you fully understand a news event.

Background

Fireworks in Space July 4, 2005, was a day of celebration at the National Aeronautics and Space Administration (NASA). As part of a major mission called "Deep Impact," NASA launched a space probe that hit a comet so hard, it burrowed through its surface—then exploded. Scientists and engineers cheered as the probe's nearby mother ship transmitted images of the spectacular event. NASA realized it had gathered a wealth of scientific data about the comet that would help in future research.

To explore how news reporters gather and support their facts, you'll watch a TV newscast and read a magazine article that cover this remarkable event.

Media Literacy: Sources in the News

A **source** is a person who provides information for a news report. A reporter usually uses sources while creating a news report. In printed news, the reporter includes **quotations,** words spoken by the sources to the reporter. In a TV or radio newscast, these statements are called **sound bites,** which are edited from interviews with the sources. Here are the types of sources usually quoted in the news.

TYPES OF SOURCES

Witnesses and Officials

Witnesses are present at the time of an event or are directly affected by it. Officials are people who represent the government, a business, and so on.

Experts

Often experts are quoted after an event occurs. They're qualified to share their knowledge about what happened.

Visual Sources

Photographs or videotape can also be sources. News photographers take still photographs and video footage that are included in news articles and broadcasts.

Sources as Counterpoints

One source may give one side of an event or an issue. In the same report, another source may have a very different view.

STRATEGIES FOR EVALUATING SOURCES

- Identify a source by name and determine his or her role.
- Question why a source is included in a news report. Ask yourself: What is this source helping me to understand about the event?
- Be aware that what you hear or see is not the entire interview. Think about how the sound bites, quotations, or images support certain facts.
- In reports that include countering or opposing sources, check to see that the two sides are **balanced** or are represented equally. It's important that a news report be neutral and fair to all sides.

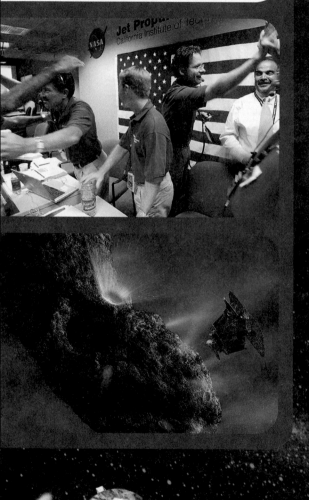

Media ⊚ Smart DVD-ROM

- **News Format 1:** "Deep Impact"
- **Reporter:** Bill Whitaker
- **Genre:** TV newscast
- **Running Time:** 2.5 minutes

- **News Format 2:** "A Grand Slam"
- **Reporter:** Ron Cowen
- **Genre:** Magazine article

Viewing Guide for

News Reports

You'll watch the CBS network news report that first aired at the time of the event. Then you'll read an article that appeared a few days later in the weekly newsmagazine *Science News*. As you examine each one, look for the people who make statements. Take notes about the sources or about any striking feature of each format. Answer these questions to help analyze the news reports.

NOW VIEW

FIRST VIEWING: Comprehension

1. **Clarify** NASA had created an animated model, or simulation, of the comet explosion. According to the TV newscast, what makes the simulation remarkable?

2. **Recall** Which one of the sources is an investigator from Brown University?

CLOSE VIEWING: Media Literacy

3. **Analyze Print Sources** The sources who are quoted in the magazine article are quoted directly or are **paraphrased.** This means the reporter has restated what he was told in his own words. In a science-related article, why might he have chosen to paraphrase?

4. **Interpret TV Sources** The "Deep Impact" report combines **sound bites** of experts with footage of Mission Control technicians celebrating. Why do you think both of these sources were included?

5. **Compare News Sources** Use a chart like this to identify and compare the types of sources of both news reports.

	Sources
"Deep Impact"	
"A Grand Slam"	

Write or Discuss

Evaluate Sources You encountered a number of sources in the TV newscast and in the magazine article. Now choose one of the news reports and make your own statement. In a short paragraph, tell how effectively you think the sources are used. Consider:

- what types of individuals and visuals are used as sources
- your basic impressions of these sources
- what the sources helped you to understand in the news report

Produce Your Own Media

Create an Interview Plan In small groups, brainstorm at least three possible news stories to cover in your school or neighborhood. Once these are determined, imagine you're a team of reporters preparing to interview different sources for the news reports. Use your ideas to help you create an **interview plan.** This plan will help you to determine the most likely people to contact for an interview. It can also help you prepare interview questions.

HERE'S HOW To help you devise your interview plan, use these tips.

- For this planning stage, list the possible sources. Jot down a detail that describes that person's connection to the news story.
- For each source, jot down questions that you think would clearly relate to the news story.
- Try to create questions that are open-ended. The best sound bites start with questions like these. Avoid questions that lead to a simple "yes" or "no" response.

STUDENT MODEL

Possible News Stories:

- the opening of a school's time capsule from 1990
- the new neighborhood garden project

Sources:

Mr. Camacho—He originally installed the time capsule.

Ms. Evans—School principal

Tara Sebring and Jamal Humphrey—They've assembled a new capsule.

Possible Questions:

- Why now for opening the capsule?
- Will there be some sort of ceremony to mark the opening?
- What does the new capsule contain?

Media Tools

Go to **thinkcentral.com**.
KEYWORD: HML8-913

Tech Tip

If available, record your interview plans as electronic files.

Interview with a Songcatcher
Interview by Brian Handwerk

What does MUSIC say about us?

COMMON CORE

RI 4 Determine the meaning of words as they are used in a text, including connotative meanings. **RI 9** Identify matters of fact or interpretation. **RI 10** Read and comprehend literary nonfiction.

Imagine someone you've never met, who knows nothing about you but your three favorite songs. What could she guess about you based on this information? Could she tell what you think is important? what makes you happy? what makes you sad? In the following interview, journalist Brian Handwerk talks to a woman who has made a career of learning about other people through their music.

CHART IT Copy this chart in a notebook. Then decide whether you agree or disagree with each statement. After you read "Interview with a Songcatcher," you'll revisit this chart.

Anticipation Guide		
	Before Reading	After Reading
People with different tastes in music probably don't have much else in common.		
The words of a song are not as important as the melody.		
Politics and social conditions have little impact on a culture's music.		

914

TEXT ANALYSIS: INTERVIEW

If you've ever read an entertainment magazine, you have probably read an interview. An **interview** is a conversation between two people in which one person asks questions and the other responds. An interview

- often includes both the reporter's questions and the interviewee's responses
- typically provides long, uninterrupted quotations that give readers a sense of the person speaking

As you read "Interview with a Songcatcher," notice how the format of the interview helps you follow who is speaking.

READING SKILL: DISTINGUISH FACT AND OPINION

A **fact** is a statement that can be proved true from personal observations, by consulting a reliable source such as an encyclopedia, or even by conducting an experiment. An **opinion** is a statement that cannot be proved because it expresses a person's feelings, thoughts, or beliefs.

Fact: *The Chicago White Sox won the 2005 World Series.*

Opinion: *The Chicago White Sox are a great team.*

When you read nonfiction, it's important to distinguish between facts that you can rely on and opinions about which people could disagree. To practice telling the difference, use a chart to note at least four facts and four opinions as you read this interview.

Statement	Fact or Opinion?

▲ VOCABULARY IN CONTEXT

The words in column A help one woman tell how she's learned about people's music. Match each word with the word in column B that you think is closest in meaning.

Column A	Column B
1. circumstance	a. undeveloped
2. composer	b. innermost
3. informant	c. situation
4. intimate	d. distant
5. primitive	e. songwriter
6. remote	f. speaker

 Complete the activities in your **Reader/Writer Notebook.**

Meet the Author

Brian Handwerk
born 1970

Writing That Travels the Globe
Freelance writers like Brian Handwerk don't work for one particular newspaper or magazine. They get to write for a variety of publications on a range of topics. For example, Handwerk has written articles on the environment, politics, and scientific discoveries. His articles have been printed in publications around the globe. He says, "One of the best parts of the job is being able to interview amazing people like Henrietta Yurchenco ... I'm lucky to be able to meet people like her through my writing."

BACKGROUND TO THE INTERVIEW
Ethnomusicology
Each culture has a unique way of expressing itself through music. The study of ethnomusicology (ĕth′nō-myōō′zĭ-kŏl′ə-jē) is dedicated to preserving the music of all the world's cultures. Ethnomusicologists—also called songcatchers—travel to remote areas to record music from different groups. In addition to studying songs and instruments, songcatchers also study the ideas and methods that lead to the creation of music. For example, Henrietta Yurchenco (hĕn-re-ĕt′ə yûr-chĕn′kō), the songcatcher featured in this interview, spent two years studying and recording music in isolated areas of Mexico and Guatemala. Today, a number of universities and colleges offer courses in ethnomusicology.

Author Online
THINK central
Go to **thinkcentral.com.**
KEYWORD: HML8-915

Interview with a Songcatcher

Brian Handwerk

Ethnomusicologist Henrietta Yurchenco spent over 60 years traveling the world in search of the unrecorded music of small cultural groups. Yurchenco recorded the music of various groups and tribes in Mexico, Central and South America, Spain, and Morocco. Her collection of world music is now housed in the United States Library of Congress, preserved for future generations of music lovers.

(A) INTERVIEW
Who is asking this question? Tell how you know.

circumstance
(sûr′kəm-stăns′) *n.*
a condition that affects or relates to an event or series of events

You've had such an incredible career, how did it all begin? **(A)**

To tell you the truth, I think that most of the things that happened to me in life happened with absolutely no plan whatsoever—just a set of funny **circumstances.**

When I was working at WNYC [radio station] I was introduced to music from around the world, because everyone came to WNYC. I played artists like Woody Guthrie, Leadbelly, Pete Seeger,[1] and I also played music from all around the world. I was curious, you know, just plain curiosity.

One of our friends, the great Mexican painter Rufino Tamayo, called
10 my husband and I and said "We're driving to Mexico, do you want to go?" We did. We drove from New York to Mexico and it changed my life.

---

1. **Woody Guthrie; Leadbelly; Pete Seeger:** American folksingers and composers.

File   Edit   View   Tools   Help

Back   Forward   Stop   Refresh   Home   Search   Favorites   Mail   Print

Henrietta Yurchenco shows off her early recording equipment.

It was in Mexico where you first began field recording of remote tribes?

Yes, because of a chance letter from the Library of Congress. I was doing radio programs for the Inter-American Indian Institute. . . . Dr. [Manuel] Gamio, the head of that institute, said, "We've received a letter from the Library of Congress. They'll send equipment and a little money. Are you interested?" **B**

20   I almost bit his hand off. I said, "I'll do it!" He was telling me about sleeping on the ground, long trips by animals, deadly scorpions, et cetera, but I wasn't listening. I didn't care. That's what I did for the next two years in Mexico and Guatemala.[2]

Were the practical aspects as difficult as advertised? Dealing with cumbersome early equipment, for example?

It was a horror. . . . People have asked me, "You went so far into those **remote** areas with just one recording machine?" One machine? I was thankful

———————————————————————————

2. **Guatemala** (gwä′tə-mä′lə): a country in northern Central America.

Internet

▸**Analyze Visuals**

What do the **details** in this photograph suggest about Henrietta Yurchenco's interests and personality?

B **FACT AND OPINION**
Yurchenco states that the Library of Congress offered money and equipment to the Inter-American Indian Institute to record tribes in Mexico. Is this a fact or an opinion? Explain.

remote (rĭ-mōt′) *adj.* located far away

File Edit View Tools Help

Back | Forward | Stop | Refresh | Home | Search | Favorites | Mail | Print

Yurchenco poses with Tzotzil Maya musicians in 1942.

to have one. . . . At one point the cord broke when we were way into the mountains. My photographer was with me on that trip and he just held it together with his hands. He stayed absolutely still, didn't move an inch, 30 and it was a perfect recording.

On most of the trips we had a big car motor for power. We had to carry gasoline, the machine, and the aluminum or even steel discs. That's all we had so we just hauled it everywhere. The only thing that really terrified me was deadly scorpions. It's not comfortable sleeping on the ground when you know those things are around—but it was a great adventure. **C**

Some places I had help from missionaries,[3] some places I was alone with 200 pounds of equipment. Don't ask me how it worked sometimes. **D**

*How difficult was it for you to understand the culture
of these remote communities?*

40 When I was in Mexico I visited some very **primitive** and isolated people who had had no contact with mainstream society for many years. I swear I saw animal sacrifices and curing ceremonies that were thousands of years old. I discovered what there was of pre-Hispanic[4]

---

3. **missionaries** (mǐsh′ə-nĕr′ēz): people who are sent to do religious work in foreign countries.
4. **pre-Hispanic** (prē-hǐ-spăn′ǐk): related to an era before Spanish conquerors arrived in the Americas.

C INTERVIEW
Reread lines 33–35. What do they reveal about Yurchenco's personality?

D FACT AND OPINION
Reread lines 36–37. What might you do to verify these statements as facts?

primitive (prǐm′ǐ-tǐv) *adj.* of or relating to a nonindustrial, often tribal, culture

Internet

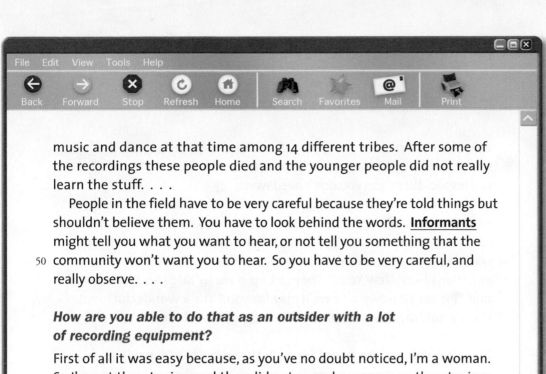

music and dance at that time among 14 different tribes. After some of the recordings these people died and the younger people did not really learn the stuff. . . .

People in the field have to be very careful because they're told things but shouldn't believe them. You have to look behind the words. **Informants** might tell you what you want to hear, or not tell you something that the
50 community won't want you to hear. So you have to be very careful, and really observe. . . .

How are you able to do that as an outsider with a lot of recording equipment?

First of all it was easy because, as you've no doubt noticed, I'm a woman. So I'm not threatening and they did not regard a woman as threatening. Secondly, I never asked direct questions. Anthropologists[5] go into the field with questions. I didn't, I just went with hugs and kisses and asked "Will you please sing for me?" When you ask about music it means, "She's interested, she likes me, she respects me." And I've never met a people
60 who didn't respond to that.

The Yaquis,[6] for example, who were known as a very warlike tribe, were absolutely marvelous. They were poets; their stuff was gorgeous. I said to the chieftain, "I want to get the words for all these songs"; he said, "We'll come together before you leave and we'll write it all down so you get it right." Well, the entire tribe came to this little community center, babies, women, grandparents, everyone. We sweltered in there, it was 100 degrees, but we got it all down. **E**

You had to be a good listener. I've sat on many, many a porch with women of all kinds and colors and just asked "So what happened after that?"

70 *Was the lack of a common language a problem?*

I never found that there was a distance between them and me because I didn't understand their language. To this day I travel to one area of Mexico that has a rich musical heritage. I've been going there since 1942, and the

---

5. **anthropologists** (ăn′thrə-pŏl′ə-jĭsts): scientists who study the origin, behavior, and cultural development of humans.

6. **Yaquis** (yä′kēs): a native people of Sonora, Mexico, who settled mainly along the Yaqui River.

informant (ĭn-fôr′mənt)
n. one who gives
information

E FACT AND OPINION
What two opinions does
Yurchenco express about
the Yaquis? Tell what
words led you to this
conclusion.

composer (kəm-pō′zər)
n. one who creates
musical pieces

F **INTERVIEW**
What does this response
to the question reveal
about Yurchenco's
approach to her work?

COMMON CORE RI 9

G **FACT AND
OPINION**
Statements of opinion
often contain signal
words that suggest a
personal judgment,
such as *good, bad, best,*
or *worst.* Reread the
first sentence in this
paragraph, and identify
whether it expresses
a fact or an opinion.
Explain your answer.

Language Coach

Informal Language
Most interviews
contain informal
language because they
capture the subject's
conversational style.
Which words or phrases
in lines 84–100 are
examples of informal
language?

wife of the main Indian **composer** there doesn't speak Spanish. Every time
she sees me we just hug, and she kisses me and cries. They know whether
you respect them and you don't need words. **F**

   It's better to use music than bombs to win friendships. When we
were in Morocco[7] the last time most of the Jews had left for other
countries. We were sitting in Tangier[8] in a café, and a little ensemble
80 was playing Arabic music. I went up to them and I said, "We are
musicians from New York." They got up, gave us hugs and kisses, and
said, "Please sit down and we'll play for you." It's a wonderful bond.
There's nothing more emotional than the arts and music. **G**

There's a voice to be heard through that emotion as well?

The song to me is the basic human expression. It tells you things, or
avoids telling you things, or disguises things, but you have to look at
what it means.

   There's so much study of folk music and typically there's not much
study of the words. It's like going to the opera for many people, and they
90 don't have the ghost of an idea what it's about. They just hear the music.
But if that's what the composer had meant he would have just written,
you know, "Blah, blah, blah." Music itself tells you things but so do the
words. You have to look at the meaning. . . .

*You've always been attuned to the political aspect
of music as well.*

I'm concerned with more than music. I'm concerned with the society,
with the people more than anything. When I hear popular music I have
to consider the social and political things that are going on in order to
understand it. It's the same with any music around the world, but that
100 fact is very often neglected.

   I'm not a romantic; I'm political. These romantics say "We must
preserve the precious culture." But at the cost of poverty and ignorance?
Is that what you want? That's what it means. Life changes, and with
modern communications, roads, and infrastructure a lot of things will

---

7. **Morocco** (mə-rŏk′ō): a country in northwest Africa. It has coastlines on the Mediterranean
   Sea and the Atlantic Ocean.

8. **Tangier** (tăn-jîr′): a northern Moroccan city.

Internet

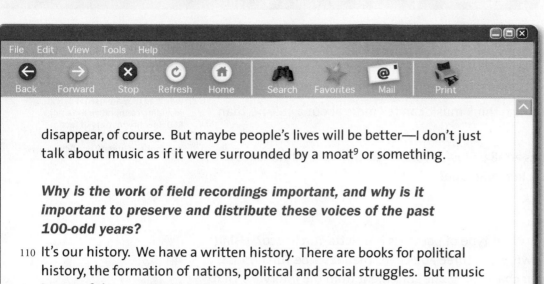

disappear, of course. But maybe people's lives will be better—I don't just talk about music as if it were surrounded by a moat[9] or something.

Why is the work of field recordings important, and why is it important to preserve and distribute these voices of the past 100-odd years?

110　It's our history. We have a written history. There are books for political history, the formation of nations, political and social struggles. But music is one of the most **intimate** expressions. Through music you become knowledgeable of the intimate aspects of life that aren't told in books. It's important because the people themselves tell you; it's not someone's interpretation. History books are written by the victors, but songs are the people's own words and melodies. That's what makes music a very powerful tool to understand people. **H**

---

9. **moat** (mōt): a water-filled ditch that surrounds and protects a castle, fortress, or town.

intimate (ĭn′tə-mĭt) *adj.* relating to one's deepest nature

H **FACT AND OPINION**
Find one fact and one opinion in this paragraph. How were you able to identify each?

◄ **Analyze Visuals**
What can you **infer** from this photo about the way Yurchenco relates to the people she meets?

Comprehension

1. **Recall** How did Henrietta Yurchenco begin recording tribal music?

2. **Clarify** Why does Yurchenco think music can tell more about a culture than history books?

3. **Summarize** Reread lines 70–83. How is Yurchenco able to communicate with people who don't speak her language?

COMMON CORE

RI 4 Determine the meaning of words as they are used in a text, including connotative meanings. **RI 9** Identify matters of fact or interpretation. **RI 10** Read and comprehend literary nonfiction.

Text Analysis

4. **Describe a Songcatcher** What type of person is Henrietta Yurchenco? Using a chart like the one shown, write three adjectives that describe Yurchenco's personality. Expand your chart using one statement from the interview that supports each adjective.

Henrietta Yurchenco

5. **Analyze an Interview** Reread Handwerk's questions to Yurchenco. What do these questions tell you about his interest in or prior knowledge of songcatching?

6. **Identify Fact and Opinion** Look back at the facts and opinions you recorded as you read. Then exchange your list with a partner. Does he or she agree with you about which statements are facts and which are opinions?

7. **Evaluate an Interview** Look again at the questions Handwerk asked Yurchenco. Were they good choices? Why or why not? If you were to continue the interview, what are another two questions you would ask?

Extension and Challenge

8. **Creative Project: Music** Imagine that Henrietta Yurchenco came to your class. What music would you play for her to let her know what it's like to be a student your age in the United States today? With a group, come up with a list of five songs. They can be songs written by recording artists, or songs written by one or all of you. Next to each song, explain why you chose it.

What does MUSIC say about us?

Go back to the anticipation guide you started before reading. Now, fill in the "After Reading" column. Have any of your opinions about music changed after reading this interview? Explain.

Vocabulary in Context

▲ VOCABULARY PRACTICE

Show that you understand the boldfaced vocabulary words by telling whether each statement is true or false.

1. A **remote** village is far away from other communities.
2. A **composer** is someone who writes plays.
3. Most European cultures are **primitive.**
4. An **informant** is the same as a liar.
5. Most people share **intimate** details about their lives with no one but family members and friends.
6. A **circumstance** is a person who bosses others around.

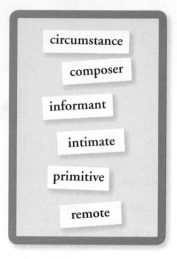

circumstance

composer

informant

intimate

primitive

remote

ACADEMIC VOCABULARY IN WRITING

> • challenge   • communicate   • design   • job   • method

How did Henrietta Yurchenco go about recording the music of ethnic groups in remote places? Write a paragraph about her **methods.** Try to use at least one of the Academic Vocabulary words in your response.

VOCABULARY STRATEGY: DENOTATION AND CONNOTATION

A word's **denotation** is the basic definition found in a dictionary. Its **connotation** is a feeling or attitude linked with that. Connotations can influence the meaning a word conveys. For example, the vocabulary word *primitive* means "of or relating to a nonindustrial, often tribal, culture." But the word has also come to mean "unsophisticated" or "crude." Recognizing connotations can help you understand the opinions of the people you read about. If you are unsure of a word's connotation, look for context clues in the surrounding words and sentences, or consult a dictionary.

⋯ **COMMON CORE**

L 5c Distinguish among the connotations of words with similar denotations.

PRACTICE Replace each boldfaced word with another word with a similar meaning, but a negative connotation.

1. Marcus's dog is **overweight** because the family feeds it too much.
2. Even after she left the room, Lia's perfume left an odd **scent** in the air.
3. The **elderly** woman moved slowly as she crossed the street.
4. Michael is so **clever.** He always gets his way.
5. I can't be friends with Cynthia. Her attitude is **unpleasant.**

Interactive Vocabulary   **THINK** central

Go to **thinkcentral.com.**
KEYWORD: HML8-923

Kabul's Singing Sensation
Magazine Article by Tim McGirk

Why do we SING?

COMMON CORE

RI 2 Determine a central idea of a text and analyze its development over the course of the text, including its relationship to supporting ideas; provide an objective summary of the text. **RI 5** Analyze in detail the role of particular sentences in developing and refining a key concept. **RI 6** Determine an author's point of view or purpose in a text.

Think about the last time you sang. Was it at a birthday party? during choir practice? on the street with a group of friends? Whether it's to celebrate, lift someone's spirits, or express joy, almost everyone belts out a tune at some point or another. In the article you're about to read, you'll meet a boy whose singing helps relieve the suffering of his country.

WEB IT People sing for a variety of reasons. Fill in a web like the one shown with places and events where people sing or hear singing. What do you think is the most common reason to sing?

to entertain · for pleasure · Reasons for Singing · for money · to inspire · in a recording studio

924

● TEXT ANALYSIS: AUTHOR'S PURPOSE

An **author's purpose** is what the writer hopes to achieve in a particular work. For example, the title of Tim McGirk's article suggests that he wants to inform you about a human interest story. In addition to providing information, writers may seek to persuade, to express ideas or feelings, or to entertain. Often a piece of writing will have more than one purpose.

As you read "Kabul's Singing Sensation," look for clues about the author's purpose in the tone of his writing and in his choice of words and details.

● READING SKILL: IDENTIFY MAIN IDEAS AND DETAILS

Nonfiction writers usually organize their writing around **main ideas,** or central ideas, which are the most important ideas they want to share about a topic. Sometimes these main ideas are stated directly, often at the beginning of a section or paragraph. Other times they may merely be implied, or suggested. **Supporting details,** such as facts or examples, help to illustrate main ideas.

The article you are about to read contains several main ideas supported by details. Use an outline like the one shown to record supporting details for each main idea.

> I. Mirwais Najrabi is a talented young Afghan singer.
>   A.
>   B.
> II. Mirwais and his family have suffered hardship.
>   A.
>   B.

▲ VOCABULARY IN CONTEXT

Tim McGirk uses the following words to describe the challenges faced by a young musician. How many words do you know? Make a chart like the one shown, putting each vocabulary word in the appropriate column.

WORD LIST			
edict	immaculate	transcendent	
exile	puritanical	virtuoso	

In your Reader/Writer Notebook, write a sentence for each of the vocabulary words. Use a dictionary or the definitions in the following selection pages to help you.

 Complete the activities in your **Reader/Writer Notebook.**

Meet the Author

Tim McGirk
born 1952

Danger and Determination
Reporters who travel to dangerous areas often have to make difficult decisions. How bold or how careful should they be in order to get information? Tim McGirk, a reporter for *Time* magazine, has had to answer this question himself. In 2001, McGirk had to decide whether to visit an island in the Philippines where rebels held kidnapped tourists and journalists and sometimes killed them. Because of the dangers involved, he chose not to go. However, since 1976, McGirk has covered his share of difficult assignments, including reporting on the people and situations in Latin America and in war-torn areas of the Middle East.

BACKGROUND TO THE ARTICLE
Turbulent Times
The late 20th century saw years of civil unrest in Afghanistan, a landlocked country in southern Asia. The Taliban, a violent Muslim extremist group, captured control of the country in the 1990s. The group imposed strict rules on the Afghan people, based on its extreme interpretation of Islam. Under the Taliban's rule, Afghan girls lost their right to an education, art and sports were outlawed, and even music was banned. Those who violated the Taliban's rules were often brutally punished. The Taliban fell out of power after a 2001 invasion by the United States and its allies. A new government was created, and people in certain parts of the country again enjoyed some of the freedoms they had missed for years.

Author Online THINK central
Go to **thinkcentral.com**.
KEYWORD: HML8-925

Analyze Visuals ▶

This photograph shows Mirwais Najrabi singing at a wedding in Kabul, Afghanistan. How would you describe the expression on his face?

Kabul's Singing *Sensation*

TIM McGIRK

It's midnight, long past bedtime for most children. But in a poor, war-ravaged neighborhood of Kabul,[1] more than 300 men are gathered at a wedding party to listen to the singing of Mirwais Najrabi, a pale, chestnut-haired 13-year-old. He performs in an open courtyard, under the night sky, to an audience that has endured so much suffering and grief over years of oppression, war, and mayhem. Yet for this brief, **transcendent** moment, their burden is lifted by the exquisite purity of the boy's voice. **Ⓐ**

With his jaunty, Bollywood-style[2] haircut and white embroidered
10 tunic, Mirwais looks as though he would warble like a pretty songbird, but his singing is forceful and worldly, as if he has already seen it all. And he has. Tonight, he croons folksongs of impossible love, betrayal, and heroism that flow from the depths of Afghanistan's tragic history. . . . Two men leap up to dance, circling each other like angry cobras. They turn aggressive and are pulled apart. . . . When performances get wild, says Mirwais, he tells himself: "I must not be scared, never."

---

1. **Kabul** (kä'bŏŏl): Afghanistan's capital city.
2. **Bollywood** (bŏl'ē-wŏŏd'): the Indian film industry. The name combines the names *Hollywood* (center of the U.S. film industry) and *Bombay* (the former name for Mumbai, a large Indian city).

transcendent
(trăn-sĕn'dənt) *adj.* being above the material world

Ⓐ AUTHOR'S PURPOSE
Reread lines 1–8. What words and phrases suggest that one of the author's purposes is to express sympathy for the people of Kabul?

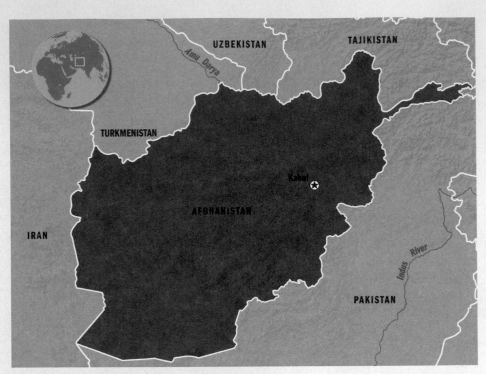

Note that Afghanistan is a mountainous country.

The soulful melancholy in Mirwais's voice is the product of hard times. He may be only 13, but he has already suffered greatly, and this, he says, may have helped him capture the anguish that many Afghans have endured
20 in the last 25 years of scorching battle and **exile.** "I sing what I feel," he says with a child's simplicity. His father was a famous musician who died when Mirwais was only five years old. The family had the misfortune of living in the Char-Deh neighborhood of Kabul on the front line between two warring commanders; as mortars and rockets exploded around them, Mirwais and his brothers risked their lives every day just to draw water from a communal well. **B**

Boy vocalists, long a part of Afghan tradition, were once silenced completely by the **puritanical** Taliban regime, which regarded song as un-Islamic and had many musicians arrested and beaten. When
30 the Taliban seized power, one of their first **edicts** was to ban music. They ransacked the Afghan Radio and Television station, decorating nearby trees and rosebushes with streamers of ripped-out audiotape. (Brave technicians, however, sealed thousands of Afghan records and tapes behind a false wall at the studio, which the Taliban never found.) "We were afraid that the Taliban would kill us," recalls Mirwais's older

brother Nur-ul-Haq, a tabla[3] player who says dozens of artists were beaten in public by Taliban zealots. So the family buried their musical instruments under a chicken coop in the garden. Another brother left to sell flowers in Iran, while Nur-ul-Haq hawked carpets in Pakistan. Mirwais, who was just five years old when the Taliban took over, stayed in Kabul with his mother. **C**

40

As a toddler, Mirwais showed no interest in music. It wasn't until he was six, a year after his father's death, that anyone even heard him sing. According to Nur-ul-Haq, Mirwais had never hummed or whistled until the day when he climbed a pomegranate tree in the garden and sang to his mother. His voice was a revelation. She immediately apprenticed him to a music teacher, Ustaad Amin Jan Mazari, who listened to him and took him on for free. In the South Asian tradition of gurus and disciples,[4] Mirwais lived with his teacher "like a son," recalls Mazari. He did household chores and spent hours each day practicing the broad range of vocal scales found in classical Afghan music. Mirwais came to revere his master. Today, when they meet, the boy's face glows, and he bows to touch his teacher's feet. "He has good talent," says Mazari, "and, by the kindness of Allah, when Mirwais is 40 years old or so, with practice, he will become great."

50

. . . After the Taliban were defeated, singers began wandering back from exile in Europe and the U.S. to a tumultuous welcome, and Kabul's **virtuosos** unearthed the instruments they buried in their gardens. Songs now blast from Kabul shops, and more than a dozen radio stations flourish around the country. Mirwais, one of the first to sing in public after the Taliban's ouster,[5] is at the front of this revival. Despite his youth, he recognizes the enormity of the change. In the old days, he says, "If the Taliban caught me, they would have shaved my head. And only Allah knows what other punishments I would have faced." **D**

60

Remaining a singer until adulthood may be a challenge. Already, Mirwais works punishing hours, often singing until 3:00 A.M. and then rising late to ride his bicycle—whose handlebars have sprouted a bouquet of artificial flowers—to a dirt-floor schoolhouse that has no doors or windows to ward off the icy winter winds. Mirwais sits there with other drably uniformed boys, a bright kid with a sad smile. The schoolyard is full of toughs, and he knows better than to show off his one luxury, a new cell phone in which he's stored dozens of jangling tunes. **E**

70

C MAIN IDEAS
How did the Taliban enforce the ban on music? Note the details that helped you answer this question.

virtuoso (vûr′chŏŏ-ō′sō) *n.* a musician with excellent abilities, techniques, and/ or an attractive personal style

D MAIN IDEAS
Reread lines 56–65. How did Kabul change with the Taliban out of power? Add these details to your outline.

E AUTHOR'S PURPOSE
Which details in this paragraph inform you about what schools are like in Kabul?

◆ **GRAMMAR IN CONTEXT**
Notice that in line 77, the **adverbial clause** "And because he is still a boy" is separated by a comma from the independent clause that follows it.

immaculate (ĭ-măk′yə-lĭt) *adj.* spotless; very clean

F **AUTHOR'S PURPOSE**
What feelings does the author express in lines 81–90?

Young artists like Mirwais have several advantages over their older rivals. The . . . clarity of their voices blends harmoniously with the Afghan rabab, an ancient, 19-stringed instrument that is a cross between a sitar and a mandolin.[6] And because he is still a boy, Mirwais is allowed at weddings to sing for both men and women, whose parties are strictly segregated. This will last until Mirwais turns 15 and is considered a man, no longer to be
80 trusted around unveiled women.[7] ◆

Among the boy singers, Mirwais is tops, though he has a 14-year-old rival, Wali Fateh Ali Khan, a favorite of former King Zahir Shah. But among the common folk, Mirwais is considered the best. He and his three-piece band—a tabla drummer and rabab and harmonium[8] players—were booked every night during the three-month wedding season prior to the holy month of Ramadan, when the partying stops. His crowning achievement came last September, when he won a famous singing contest at Kabul's Park Cinema. That day, Mirwais appeared in an **immaculate** white suit, handling the audience with the casual manner of a mite-sized Sinatra.[9] His performance
90 blew the other contestants off the stage. **F**

---

6. **sitar** (sĭ-tär′); **mandolin** (măn′də-lĭn′): two guitarlike string instruments.
7. **unveiled women:** Some Muslims (followers of Islam) believe that women should wear veils to hide themselves from all men except close family members.
8. **harmonium** (här-mo′nē-əm): an organlike keyboard instrument.
9. **Sinatra** (sə-nä′trə): Frank Sinatra (1915–1998). American singer and actor known for his beautiful voice.

Mirwais practices with his music teacher, Ustaad Mazari (center).

Comprehension

1. **Recall** When did Mirwais first sing?

2. **Recall** From whom did Mirwais receive his musical training?

3. **Recall** What advantages do younger singers have over older singers in Afghanistan?

Text Analysis

4. **Summarize Main Ideas and Details** Look back at the outline you created while reading "Kabul's Singing Sensation." Based on the main ideas and details you noted, summarize the article. Then compare your summary with the article. Decide if you've accurately captured its main ideas, important details, and underlying meaning.

5. **Examine Word Choice** What does Mirwais's voice sound like? Look back at the article and find words and **imagery** that help you "hear" Mirwais's voice.

6. **Analyze Quotations** A quotation is a direct statement made by someone. Lines 16, 20, and 63–65 contain three quotations from Mirwais. What do these quotations tell you about the young singer?

7. **Draw Conclusions About Author's Purpose** Why do you think the author chose Mirwais Najrabi as the subject of his article? What does this choice suggest about his main purpose?

8. **Evaluate Unity** A paragraph has **unity** if all its sentences develop one stated or implied main idea. A piece of writing has unity if each paragraph in it is unified and all the paragraphs together develop one larger main idea or message. Evaluate the unity of this article. Share what you decide and why.

Extension and Challenge

9. **SOCIAL STUDIES CONNECTION** What is the current state of Afghanistan? What is life like for those who live there? Research the social and political climate of Afghanistan. Share your findings with the class.

Why do we SING?

What if singing were banned in this country? How would you react to this decision? What risks would you be willing to take to preserve music? Consider how Mirwais and his family reacted to life under the Taliban as you answer these questions.

COMMON CORE

RI 2 Determine a central idea of a text and analyze its development over the course of the text, including its relationship to supporting ideas; provide an objective summary of the text. **RI 5** Analyze in detail the role of particular sentences in developing and refining a key concept. **RI 6** Determine an author's point of view or purpose in a text.

A family rides on horseback through the mountains of Afghanistan.

Vocabulary in Context

▲ VOCABULARY PRACTICE

Note the letter of the item that you might associate with each boldfaced word.

1. **edict:** (a) a friend's suggestion, (b) a king's order, (c) a polite request
2. **exile:** (a) being sent away, (b) being imprisoned, (c) having to pay a fine
3. **immaculate:** (a) without decorations, (b) without wrinkles, (c) without dirt
4. **puritanical:** (a) like a new school principal, (b) like a group with strict rules, (c) like a popular athletic coach
5. **transcendent:** (a) sinking down, (b) rising above, (c) solving problems
6. **virtuoso:** (a) a beginning violinist, (b) an off-key singer, (c) a musical star

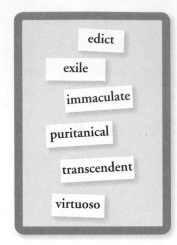

ACADEMIC VOCABULARY IN WRITING

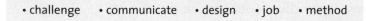

• challenge • communicate • design • job • method

What did you learn about life in Kabul under the Taliban from reading "Kabul's Singing Sensation"? Write a paragraph summarizing the information Tim McGirk **communicates** in the article. Try to use at least one of the Academic Vocabulary words in your response.

VOCABULARY STRATEGY: SUFFIXES THAT FORM ADJECTIVES

A **suffix** is a word part that can be added to a root or base word to form a new word. Some suffixes, such as *-ical* in *puritanical,* can be added to nouns to form adjectives. Others, such as *-ent* in *transcendent,* can be added to verbs to form adjectives. If you can recognize the root or base word in a word with a suffix, you can often figure out the entire word's meaning. Consult the chart for common adjective suffixes and their meanings.

PRACTICE Identify the base word in each boldfaced adjective. Then define the adjective.

1. Yesterday I received the **joyous** news that my grandmother will be coming to visit.
2. Like the earth, the moon is roughly **spherical.**
3. As he waits for his food, our dog wears an **expectant** expression.
4. Can you solve **algebraic** problems?
5. Mrs. Pine is a **considerate** host who makes sure that her guests are comfortable.

:COMMON CORE

L 4b Use Greek affixes as clues to the meaning of a word.

Suffix	Meaning
-ant, -ate, *-ent, -ic,* *-ical, -ous*	like; having to do with; showing; causing

Interactive Vocabulary **THINK** central

Go to thinkcentral.com.
KEYWORD: HML8-932

Language

◆ GRAMMAR IN CONTEXT: Use Commas Correctly

Review the Grammar in Context note on page 930. An **adverbial clause** is a subordinate (dependent) clause that modifies a verb, an adjective, or an adverb. It generally tells how, when, where, why, how much, to what extent, or under what condition the action of a verb takes place. An adverbial clause should be followed by a comma when it comes before an independent clause.

> *Original:* Because the Taliban banned music in Afghanistan musicians had to hide their instruments.

> *Revised:* Because the Taliban banned music in Afghanistan, musicians had to hide their instruments.

Notice that adding a comma, which indicates a pause or break, helps to clarify the original statement's message.

PRACTICE In each sentence, add commas where they are needed.

1. Since the age of four I've played the trumpet.
2. Over the summer my friends and I formed a singing group.
3. After reading the article I wanted to hear your music.
4. When I play music I feel free and happy.

*For more help with commas, see page R49 in the **Grammar Handbook**.*

READING-WRITING CONNECTION

 YOUR TURN Demonstrate your understanding of "Kabul's Singing Sensation" by responding to this prompt. Then use the **revising tip** to improve your writing.

WRITING PROMPT	REVISING TIP
Extended Constructed Response: Letter Music can connect people across distance and culture. Write a **two- or three-paragraph** letter to Mirwais expressing your reactions to the article you just read. Then share with him some of your own experiences and thoughts about singing and music.	Review your letter. If you have used any adverbial clauses, make sure that you have included commas where they are needed.

Interactive Revision **THINK** central

Go to **thinkcentral.com**.
KEYWORD: HML8-933

COMMON CORE

L 2 Demonstrate command of the conventions of standard English punctuation when writing. **L 2a** Use punctuation (comma) to indicate a pause or break.

Robo-Legs

Video link at
thinkcentral.com

Magazine Article by Michel Marriott

Eureka: Scientific Twists of Fate

Online Article

VIDEO TRAILER **THINK** central   KEYWORD: HML8-934

How has SCIENCE changed our lives?

COMMON CORE

RI 2 Determine a central idea of a text and analyze its development over the course of the text, including its relationship to supporting ideas.
RI 5 Analyze in detail the role of particular sentences in developing and refining a key concept.

The next time you answer a cell phone, turn on a light, or take your asthma medicine, think about the knowledge that was needed to create these things. Science has made it possible for doctors, engineers, and inventors to develop technologies and medicines that make our lives healthier and more convenient. In the following articles, you'll read about some of the amazing scientific breakthroughs that have allowed people to lead longer, better lives.

QUICKWRITE What is one scientific development that you feel you could not live without? Think beyond obvious technological gadgets such as your computer or cell phone. Write one paragraph telling what a day might be like if this discovery had never taken place.

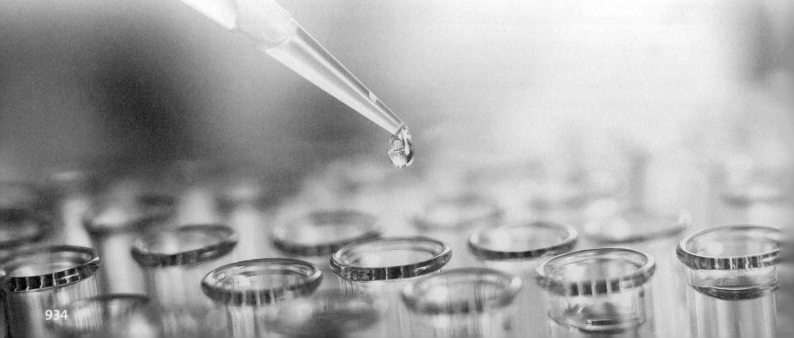

● TEXT ANALYSIS: ORGANIZATION OF IDEAS

Many nonfiction texts are organized in what might be called **part-by-part order.** One idea or group of ideas suggests another, which suggests another, and so on until the end. Each idea is related in some way to the one before it and the one after it, but not necessarily in the same exact way. For example, Michel Marriott begins "Robo-Legs" with Cameron Clapp's personal story. Then he presents information about artificial limb technology. Next he talks about how people's attitudes toward wearing such limbs are changing. Each new idea relates to the one before it—but not in any predictable way. To follow along, you need to pay attention to topic sentences and subheadings, which introduce new parts.

● READING STRATEGY: MONITOR

When you **monitor** your reading, you pause to check your comprehension of the material. To monitor effectively, pause frequently and try the following strategies:

- **Ask questions** about the information presented.
- **Visualize,** or picture, events and details described.
- **Reread** passages that you find confusing.

Use a chart like the one shown to help you monitor.

Where I Paused	What Confused Me	How I Clarified the Information

▲ VOCABULARY IN CONTEXT

How many of the boldfaced words do you know? Use context clues to figure out a definition for each.

1. People who lose an **appendage** can still exercise.
2. The pollution could **contaminate** the water supply.
3. **Infectious** diseases can be transmitted quickly.
4. I need **keener** eyesight to thread the needle.
5. Roberto gains **mobility** by using a wheelchair.
6. The **infection** was **pervasive** throughout her body.
7. Mrs. Blake needed **rehabilitation** following knee surgery.
8. The scientist's **serendipitous** discovery led to a cure.

Complete the activities in your **Reader/Writer Notebook.**

Meet the Author

Michel Marriott
born 1954

A Born Communicator
Michel Marriott says that he was "practically born talking." As a child, he talked all the time, and eventually he began writing out his thoughts on paper. Through his work at his school newspaper, Marriott realized that journalism was a good career choice. Since then, Marriott has worked for the *Washington Post, Newsweek,* and *The New York Times,* covering a variety of topics, including technology, fashion, and urban crime. In 1995, director Spike Lee produced *New Jersey Drive,* a film based on Marriott's series of articles about the desperate lives of young car thieves. The series was nominated for a Pulitzer Prize.

BACKGROUND TO THE ARTICLE
Marvelous Medical Inventions
Throughout history, scientists and inventors have worked to make life better for those with physical disabilities. The first eyeglasses were created in the 1200s. The first hearing aids, called "trumpets," were invented in the early 1800s. Prosthetics, used to replace missing arms and legs, were made of wood or metal as long ago as the days of ancient Rome. In medieval times, a knight who lost an arm could be fitted with a metal prosthetic that held a shield during battle. In the 1800s, wooden legs were fashioned to resemble real legs. They included springs and sockets to allow movement. Today, scientists draw on robotics and a better understanding of the human body to create prosthetics that are very similar to real limbs.

Author Online
THINK central
Go to **thinkcentral.com.**
KEYWORD: HML8-935

Robo-Legs

Michel Marriott

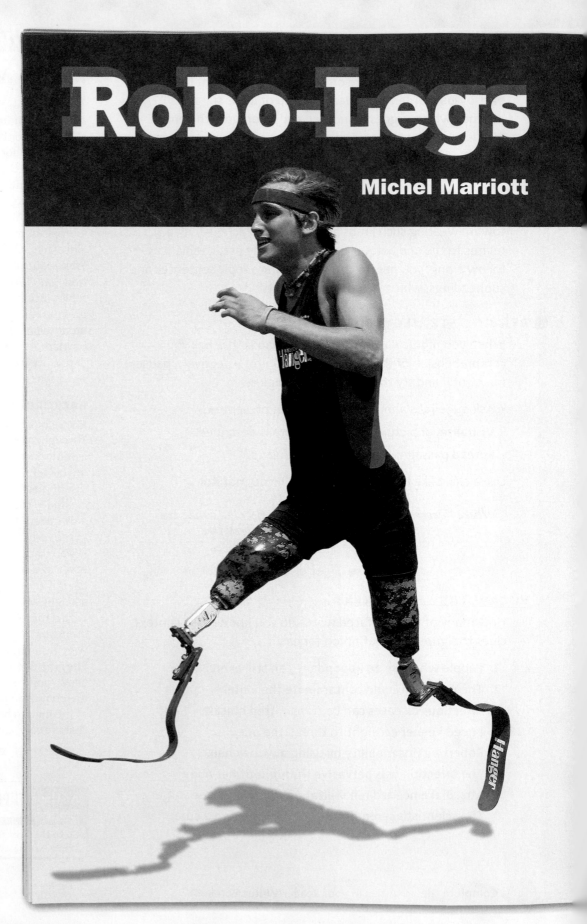

Analyze Visuals ▶

This photo shows Cameron Clapp competing at the 2005 Endeavor Games. Based on his body language and facial expression, what can you **conclude** about Clapp's personality?

New prosthetic limbs[1] are providing increased **mobility** *for many amputees—and blurring the line between humans and machines*

W ith his blond hair, buff torso, and megawatt smile, Cameron Clapp is in many ways the typical California teenager. There are, however, a few things that set him apart: For starters, this former skater boy is now making his way through life on a pair of shiny, state-of-the-art[2] robotic legs. **A**

"I make it look easy," he says.

Clapp, 19, lost both his legs above the knee and his right arm just short of his shoulder after getting hit by a train almost five years ago near his home in Grover Beach, California. Following years of **rehabilitation** and
10 a series of prosthetics, each more technologically advanced than the last, he has become part of a new generation of people who are embracing breakthrough technologies as a means of overcoming their own bodies' limitations.

"I do have a lot of motivation and self-esteem," Clapp says, "but I might look at myself differently if technology was not on my side."

The technology he's referring to is the C-Leg. Introduced by Otto Bock HeathCare, a German company that makes advanced prosthetics, the C-Leg combines computer technology with hydraulics. Sensors monitor how the leg is being placed on the ground, and microprocessors[3] guide the
20 limb's hydraulic system, enabling it to imitate a natural step. It literally does the walking for the walker. The technology, however, is not cheap; a single C-Leg can cost more than $40,000. **B**

The C-Leg is one of the examples of how blazing advancements, including tiny programmable microprocessors, lightweight materials, and **keener** sensors, are restoring remarkable degrees of mobility to amputees, says William Hanson, president of . . . a Massachusetts company that specializes in developing and distributing advanced prosthetic arms and hands.

---

1. **prosthetic limbs** (prŏs-thĕt′ĭk lĭmz): artificial arms and legs.
2. **state-of-the-art:** made using the newest technology available.
3. **microprocessors:** tiny computer parts that operators can program, or give new instructions to.

mobility (mō-bĭl′ĭ-tē) *n.* the capability of moving from place to place

A ORGANIZATION
Reread lines 1–5. To whom are you introduced here? What does Marriot emphasize about him?

rehabilitation
(rē′hə-bĭl′ĭ-tā′shən) *n.* the process of restoring someone to physical capability, usually through exercise and physical therapy

B MONITOR
Examine lines 16–21. What words and phrases help you **visualize** Clapp's legs? Compare your mental image with the photo on page 936.

keener (kēn′ər) *adj.* more acutely sensitive

Clapp's prosthetic legs feature several attachments to suit different purposes.

Three Sets of Legs

For example, Clapp, who remains very involved in athletics despite his
30 condition, has three different sets of specialized prosthetic legs: one for
walking, one for running, and one for swimming. He put all of them to
use at the Endeavor Games in Edmond, Oklahoma—an annual sporting
event for athletes with disabilities—where he competed in events like the
200-meter dash and the 50-yard freestyle swim. **C**

Man or Machine?

But increased mobility is only part of the story. Something more subtle,
and possibly far-reaching, is also occurring: The line that has long
separated human beings from the machines that assist them is blurring,
as complex technologies become a visible part of the people who depend
upon them.
40   Increasingly, amputees, especially young men like Clapp, and soldiers
who have lost limbs in Afghanistan and Iraq, are choosing not to hide their

C MONITOR
What **questions** do you
have after reading this
paragraph? Decide
whether to reread or
read on for answers.

prosthetics under clothing as previous generations did. Instead, some of the estimated 1.2 million amputees in the United States—more than two-thirds of whom are men—proudly polish and decorate their electronic limbs for all to see. . . . **D**

Many young people, especially those who have been using personal electronics since childhood, are comfortable recharging their limbs' batteries in public and plugging their prosthetics into their computers to adjust the software, Hanson says.

50 Nick Springer, 20, a student at Eckerd College in St. Petersburg, Florida, who lost his arms and legs to meningitis when he was 14, recalls doing just that at a party when the lithium-ion batteries[4] for his legs went dead.

"I usually get 30 hours out of them before I have to charge them again," he says. "But I didn't charge them up the day before."

Terminator Legs

When his legs ran out of power, he spent most of his time sitting on a couch talking to people while his legs were plugged into an electrical outlet nearby. According to Springer, no one at the party seemed to care, and his faith in his high-tech **appendages** appears unfazed. "I love my Terminator[5] legs," he says. **E**

60 Springer also remembers going to see *Star Wars: Episode III—Revenge of the Sith* with his father. While he liked the movie, he found the final scenes—in which Anakin Skywalker loses his arms and legs in a light-saber battle and is rebuilt with fully functional prosthetics to become the infamous Darth Vader—a little far-fetched.

70 "We have a long way to go before we get anything like that," he says. "But look how far humanity has come in the past decade. Who knows? The hardest part is getting the ball rolling. We pretty much got it rolling."

Nick Springer plays hockey with the help of specially-made prosthetics. © Dith Pran/New York Times/Redux.

---

4. **lithium-ion batteries** (lĭth′ē-əm–ī′ŏn′ băt′ə-rēz): very light, small batteries with a great deal of energy packed into a small space.

5. **Terminator:** a robotic character in a 1984 film, *The Terminator*.

D ORGANIZATION
Is the topic still Clapp and his sets of legs? If not, what is the new topic? How is it related to the previous topic?

appendage (ə-pĕn′dĭj) *n.* a body part, such as an arm or leg, that is attached to the main part of the body

COMMON CORE RI 5

E ORGANIZATION
In a magazine article, subheads often signal that the writer is shifting to a new idea. But sometimes a subhead is inserted mainly to break up a long block of text. Does the subhead "Terminator Legs" introduce a new idea, or do lines 55–59 support the idea introduced under the previous subhead? Explain your answer.

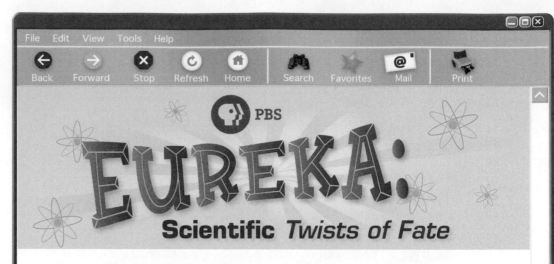

PBS

EUREKA:
Scientific *Twists of Fate*

Ⓐ ORGANIZATION
What main idea is introduced in this paragraph? Based on the last sentence of this paragraph, how do you expect the next part of this article to be related to it?

serendipitous
(sĕr′ən-dĭp′ĭ-təs) *adj.* found by fortunate accident

pervasive (pər-vā′sĭv) *adj.* present throughout

. . . We are all familiar with the tale of Newton's apple. While sitting in his orchard one day in 1665, Isaac Newton's[1] curiosity was sparked by a falling apple, leading him to "discover" the law of gravity. As doubtful as the story sounds, writings by Newton and his contemporaries verify the incident. Though science often seems an orderly and methodical process, history is dotted with surprising discoveries such as these. Were they merely luck? Or the results of a gifted mind? Actually, a bit of both. Sometimes scientific discoveries come from the most unexpected places, when talented people are watching out for them. Here are two examples of similarly **serendipitous** finds. **Ⓐ**

The Smallpox Cure

In the late 1700s, Edward Jenner, a young English doctor-in-training, was told by a local
10 milkmaid that she was safe from smallpox[2] because she had already had cowpox. Like its deadly cousin, cowpox also produced painful blisters, yet doctors had not made a connection between the two diseases. After extensive research, Jenner discovered that what she said was true—milkmaids exposed to a common strain of cowpox almost never contracted smallpox.

Jenner's supervising physicians took little interest in his findings. Then, in 1796, he injected a young boy named James Phipps with tissue taken from a cowpox blister on a milkmaid's hand. He then exposed the boy to the deadly smallpox virus. So **pervasive** and devastating was this disease at the time that the boy's family was willing to take this unimaginable risk. But their gamble paid off. Young James remained completely healthy,
20 and the vaccination process was born.

Jenner's idea opened the door not only to the eradication of smallpox but to the subsequent perfection of the immunization procedure by Louis Pasteur.[3] The modern

---

1. **Isaac Newton:** mathematician and scientist (1642–1727) who developed the theory of gravity.
2. **smallpox:** a highly infectious, often fatal disease characterized by high fevers and blisters that leave pockmarks on the skin.
3. **Louis Pasteur** (lōō′ē păs-tûr′): French chemist (1822–1895) who founded modern microbiology and developed several life-saving vaccines.

Internet

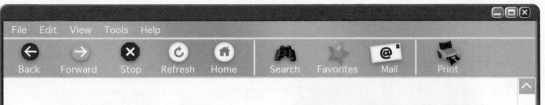

term "vaccine," from the Latin word for "cow," honors Jenner and his life-saving inspiration. . . . **R**

Penicillin

Arguably the most important medical discovery of the 20th century came about purely by accident. Throughout the 1920s, Scottish scientist Alexander Fleming was

30 searching for a cure for **infectious** disease, the major cause of death throughout much of human history. As part of his research, Fleming was cultivating several species of bacteria in separate petri dishes.

Alexander Fleming

One day, Fleming noticed that a mold had **contaminated** the petri dish containing the bacteria *Staphylococcus,* a common microbe responsible for a variety of ailments ranging from the earaches to deadly post-operative infections. But before tossing away the moldy dish, Fleming realized that the intruder had actually killed off much of the bacteria culture.

40 The tiny, wind-born mold spore must have landed in the *Staphylococcus* colony during a brief moment Fleming had uncovered the dish. Fleming isolated the mold and identified it as a member of the genus *Penicillium.* He called the antibiotic substance it secreted penicillin.

Fleming's further investigation found that penicillin killed off several, but not all, strains of the disease-causing microbes he was growing in his lab. Had the penicillium contaminated a different dish, Fleming might never have discovered its medicinal benefits.

Additionally, Fleming found penicillin was non-toxic to humans and animals. Realizing the strategic advantage in possessing the world's first antibiotic, the U.S. and Britain joined forces to mass-produce the drug, and treated thousands of Allied troops wounded

50 in the D-Day invasion of Europe. It has saved countless lives ever since. In 1945, Fleming shared the Nobel Prize in Medicine for his work on the "Wonder Drug" penicillin. . . . **C**

Serendipity or Smarts?

Each of these examples of serendipity helped advance the scope of human knowledge by great leaps and bounds. But these accidents and twists of fate are not quite as random as they seem. Each discovery occurred in the presence of a well-trained intellect. . . . As Louis Pasteur once said, "In the fields of observation, chance favors only the prepared mind."

B MONITOR
Reread the subheading of this section. Based on this, what question about smallpox should you be able to answer? If you can't answer this question for yourself, **reread** lines 9–25.

infectious (ĭn-fĕk′shəs) *adj.* capable of being transmitted by infection

contaminate (kən-tăm′ə-nāt′) *v.* to make impure or unclean through contact

Language Coach

Homonyms Homonyms are words with the same spelling and sound but different meanings. Which context clues help clarify that the word *mold* in line 35 refers to a fungus, not to a container for shaping liquids or plastics as they harden?

C MONITOR
Why is penicillin important? Reread this section if you don't know the answer.

Comprehension

1. **Recall** How does the C-Leg described in "Robo-Legs" work?

2. **Summarize** According to "Robo-Legs," what is different about the way young amputees feel about their prosthetic limbs?

3. **Clarify** James Phipps is mentioned in "Eureka: Scientific Twists of Fate." Why was his family willing to risk his exposure to the smallpox virus?

Text Analysis

4. **Examine the Message** Reread the first paragraph of "Robo-Legs" as well as lines 23–28 and 35–39. Based on the information stated and the descriptive words and phrases used, what do you think is the message the author wants to share about science and technology?

5. **Interpret Quotation** "Eureka: Scientific Twists of Fate" contains this quote from Louis Pasteur: "In the fields of observation, chance favors only the prepared mind." What does he mean? Use examples from the article to support your answer.

6. **Evaluate Monitoring Techniques** Look back at the chart you created as you read. Which strategy best helped you understand the articles? Explain.

7. **Analyze and Compare Organization of Ideas** In a few sentences, describe the part-by-part organization of each article—that is, how each part is related to the next. Then identify one way in which the two authors use part-by-part organization similarly or differently.

8. **Compare Texts** Use a Venn diagram like the one shown to record similarities and differences between the articles. Consider the subject matter, purpose, tone, and organization of ideas in each article. Why do you think these two articles were presented together in a single lesson?

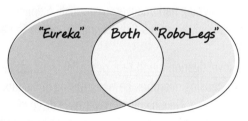

Extension and Challenge

9. **Readers' Circle** Both "Robo-Legs" and "Eureka: Scientific Twists of Fate" describe medical advancements that have helped people lead better lives. What problems would you like science to solve? Discuss your answer with a small group.

10. **SCIENCE CONNECTION** Robotics has become an exciting field of study. Other than prosthetics, what is another way robotics is being used today? Research to find an answer. Then present your findings to the class.

How has SCIENCE changed our lives?

What insights did you gain about science and technology from reading these selections?

COMMON CORE

RI 2 Determine a central idea of a text and analyze its development over the course of the text, including its relationship to supporting ideas. **RI 5** Analyze in detail the role of particular sentences in developing and refining a key concept.

Vocabulary in Context

▲ **VOCABULARY PRACTICE**

Answer each question to show your understanding of the vocabulary words.

1. Which is an **appendage,** a boy's back or his leg?
2. Which can **contaminate** your dinner, bacteria or salt?
3. Which are **infectious,** colds or injuries?
4. If your eyesight gets **keener,** does it get better or worse?
5. Which provides **mobility,** an armchair or a car?
6. If an attitude is **pervasive,** do many people share it or just a few?
7. Would you need **rehabilitation** to recover from a broken leg, or from a cold?
8. If you make a **serendipitous** discovery, are you lucky or unlucky?

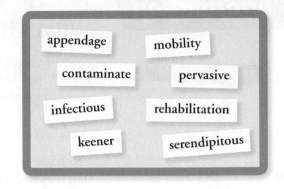

ACADEMIC VOCABULARY IN WRITING

• challenge   • communicate   • design   • job   • method

What technology would you like to **design** to improve people's lives? Write a paragraph describing the invention or improvement of an existing technology. Try to use at least one of the Academic Vocabulary words in your response.

VOCABULARY STRATEGY: THE LATIN ROOT *pend*

The vocabulary word *appendage* contains the Latin root *pend*, which means "hang." Many English words contain this root. To figure out the meaning of words with this root, use context clues and your knowledge of the root's meaning.

PRACTICE Choose the word from the web that best completes each sentence. Then explain how the root *pend* relates to the meaning of the word.

1. If an employee is ____, he will not keep his job very long.
2. Dogs are pack animals, so they hate being left alone; however, cats are fairly ____ creatures.
3. She wore a diamond____ around her neck.
4. The detective has several cases ____, but none of them are resolved.
5. The elephant's trunk swung ____ from side to side.

COMMON CORE

L 4b Use Latin roots as clues to the meaning of a word.

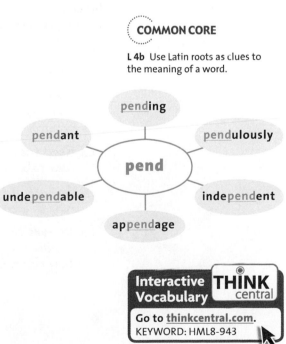

Interactive Vocabulary **THINK** central

Go to **thinkcentral.com.**
KEYWORD: HML8-943

Guide to Computers
Technical Directions

What's the Connection?

In "Robo-Legs," you read about new designs for artificial limbs that are improving the lives of amputees. Now you will read a guide to computers, the invention that made such new designs possible.

Standards Focus: Analyze Technical Directions

You have probably spent a lot of time working on a computer, but would you be able to set one up? If not, you could learn how by following a set of **technical directions.** Technical directions are a type of procedural text, or text that explains how to do something. Specifically, technical directions explain how to assemble or operate a device. Some products, such as computers, game systems, or cameras, are accompanied by instruction manuals that include technical directions. These directions usually contain

- a parts list or glossary of key terms that you will need to know
- illustrations, diagrams, and photos that show key steps
- clearly labeled instructions that appear in a logical sequence

Readers are expected to connect information from all of these elements.

As you read, use this checklist to make sure you analyze the technical directions carefully and avoid mistakes. Remember, if steps are missing, or if you skip steps or perform them out of order, the device may not work.

Use with "Robo-Legs,"
page 936.

COMMON CORE

RI 4 Determine the meaning of words and phrases as they are used in a text, including technical meanings. **RI 5** Analyze in detail the structure of a specific paragraph in a text, including the role of particular sentences in developing and refining a key concept.

> **Checklist**
>
> ☐ **Scan** the heading and any subheadings to learn what process is being explained. Look for numbers or letters that tell you the order in which the steps should be followed.
>
> ☐ **Read** the entire directions through once. Figure out what you need to accomplish.
>
> ☐ **Go back and reread** the instructions one step at a time. After reading each step, do it.
>
> ☐ **Examine** the diagrams or other graphics. They may help you visualize what the written directions are telling you to do, or they may offer other information.

GUIDE TO COMPUTERS

F OCUS ON FORM
"Guide to Computers" is an **instruction manual,** a booklet or electronic file that provides information about a product. Instruction manuals identify basic parts, describe functions, and provide technical directions for assembling or operating a product.

What Is A Computer?

Did a computer help you wake up this morning? You might think of a computer as something you use to send e-mail or surf the Internet, but computers are around you all of the time. Computers are in alarm clocks, cars, phones, and even MP3 players. An MP3 player, like the one in **FIGURE 1**, allows you to build your own music lists and carry thousands of songs with you
10 wherever you go.

A **computer** is an electronic device that performs tasks by processing and storing information. A computer performs a task when it is given a command and has the instructions necessary to carry out that command. Computers do not operate by themselves, or "think." **A**

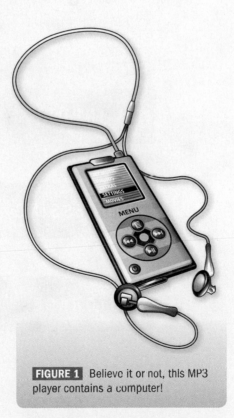

FIGURE 1 Believe it or not, this MP3 player contains a computer!

A INSTRUCTION MANUAL
Reread lines 11–17. What are the basic functions of a computer?

Basic Functions

The basic functions a computer performs are shown in **FIGURE 2**.

   The information you give to a computer is called **input.** Downloading
20 songs onto your MP3 player or setting your alarm clock is a type of
input. To perform a task, a computer **processes** the input, changing it
to the desired form. Processing can mean adding a list of numbers,
executing a drawing, or even moving a piece of equipment. Input
doesn't have to be processed immediately; it can be stored until it is
needed. Computers store information in their **memory.** For example,
your MP3 player stores the songs you have chosen to input. It can
then process this stored information by playing the songs you request.
Output is the final result of the task performed by the computer.
The output of an MP3 player is the music you hear when you put on
30 your headphones! **B**

B **INSTRUCTION MANUAL**

How does the diagram labeled Figure 2 help you understand the functions of a computer described in lines 18–30?

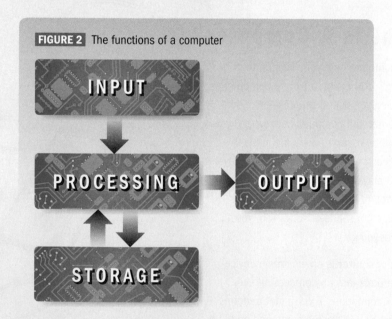

FIGURE 2 The functions of a computer

INPUT

PROCESSING → OUTPUT

STORAGE

The Internet—A Global Network

Thanks to high-speed connections and computer software, it is possible to connect many computers and allow them to communicate with one another. That's what the **Internet** is—a huge computer network consisting of millions of computers that can all share information with one another. **C**

How the Internet Works

Computers can connect to one another on the Internet by using a modem to dial into an Internet service provider, or ISP. A home computer connects to an ISP over a phone or cable line. A school, business, or other group can connect all of its computers to form a local
40 area network (LAN). Then, a single network connection can be used to connect the LAN to an ISP. As depicted in **FIGURE 3**, ISPs are connected globally by satellite. And that's how computers go global!

C INSTRUCTION MANUAL
Reread lines 31–35. What is the purpose of the Internet?

COMMON CORE L 5a

Language Coach

Idiom An **idiom** is a phrase that has a meaning different from its individual words. You can use context clues to figure out the meaning of an idiom. In line 42, what does the idiom "go global" mean?

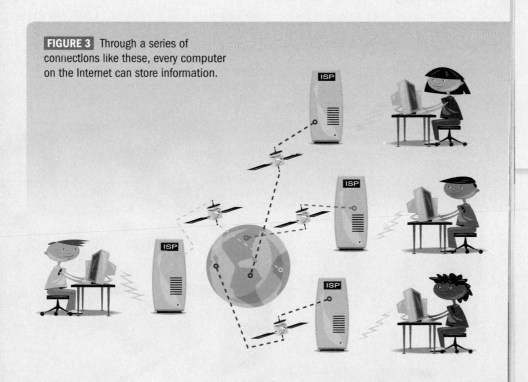

FIGURE 3 Through a series of connections like these, every computer on the Internet can store information.

Computer Hardware

For each function of a computer, there is a corresponding part of the computer where that function occurs. Hardware refers to the parts, or equipment, that make up a computer. As you read about each piece of hardware, refer to **FIGURE 4**.

Input Devices

An **input device** is a piece of hardware that feeds information to the computer. You can enter information into a computer by using a keyboard, mouse, scanner, digitizing pad and pen, or digitizing camera—or even your own voice!

Central Processing Unit

A computer performs tasks within an area called the **central processing unit,** or CPU. In
50 a personal computer, the CPU is a microprocessor. Input goes through the CPU for immediate processing or for storage in memory. The CPU is where the computer does calculations, solves problems, and executes the instructions it is given. Some computers now come with two or more CPUs to process information more effectively.

Memory

Information can be stored in the computer's memory until it is needed. CD-ROMs, DVDs, and flash drives inserted into a computer and hard disks inside a computer have memory

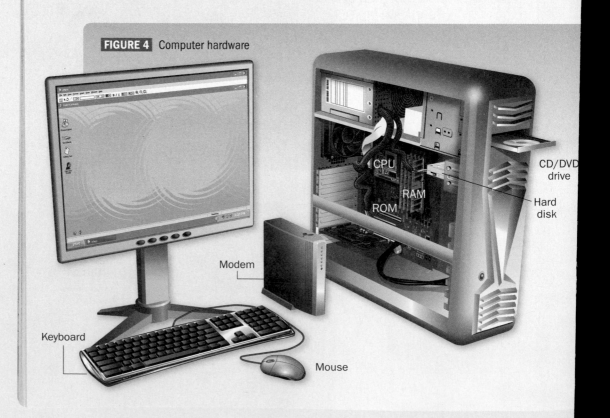

FIGURE 4 Computer hardware

CPU

RAM

ROM

CD/DVD drive

Hard disk

Modem

Keyboard

Mouse

to store information. Two other types of memory are **ROM** (read-only memory) and **RAM** (random-access memory).

ROM is permanent. It handles functions such as computer start-up, maintenance, and hardware management. ROM normally cannot be added to or changed, and it cannot
60 be lost when the computer is turned off. On the other hand, RAM is temporary. It stores information only while that information is being used. RAM is sometimes called working memory. The more RAM a computer has, the more information can be input and the more powerful the computer is. **D**

Output Devices

Once a computer performs a task, it shows the results of the task on an **output device.** Monitors, printers, and speaker systems are all examples of output devices.

Modems

One piece of computer hardware that serves as an input device as well as an output device is a **modem.** Modems allow computers to communicate. One computer can input information into another computer over a telephone or cable line as long as each computer has its own network connection. In this way, modems permit computers to
70 "talk" with each other. **E**

D INSTRUCTION MANUAL
Reread lines 60–63. Why is RAM sometimes called "working memory"?

E INSTRUCTION MANUAL
What piece of hardware serves as both an input and output device? Describe its functions.

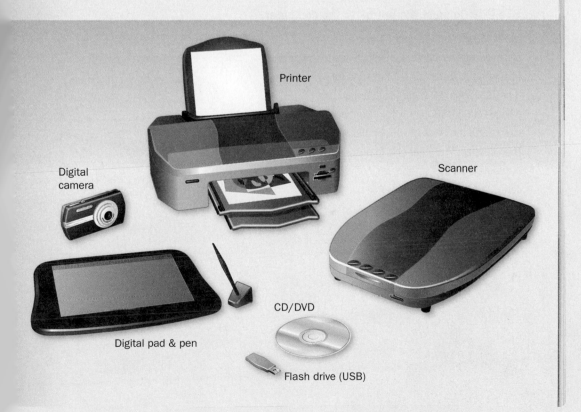

Printer

Digital camera

Scanner

Digital pad & pen

CD/DVD

Flash drive (USB)

How to Set Up a Desktop Computer

STEP 1 Connect the monitor to the computer.

The monitor has two cords. One cord, the monitor interface cable, lets the computer communicate with the monitor. The monitor cable connects to the video port (the port designated for monitors) at the back of the computer. (See **FIGURE 5**.) The connector on this cord is a plug with pins in it; the pins correspond to holes in the video port on the computer. This cable probably has screws to secure the connection. The other cord is the monitor's power cord, which plugs into a wall outlet or surge protector, a plug-in device that protects electronic equipment from high-voltage electrical surges (see Step 5).

80

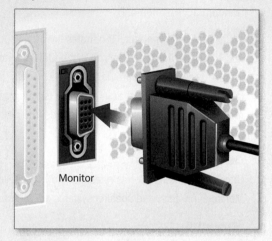

Monitor

STEP 2 Connect the printer to the computer.

The connector on the cable that is attached to your printer is most likely a USB cable. USB ports (USB stands for Universal Serial Bus) can accept any device with a USB connector. Connect one end to the back of your printer. Then connect the other end to an available USB port on the back of your computer. (See **FIGURE 5**.)

90

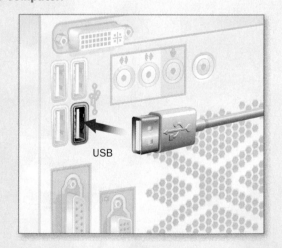

USB

STEP 3 Connect the keyboard and mouse.

Look at the connector on the cord that is
attached to the keyboard or mouse. If this
connector is round, plug the cord into a matching
port on the back of the computer. (See **FIGURE**
100 **5**.) If the connector on the cord is flat, plug it into
any available USB port. (See Step 2 illustration.)
If you are using a cordless keyboard or mouse,
connect it to the computer using the
manufacturer's technical directions.

Cordless mouse

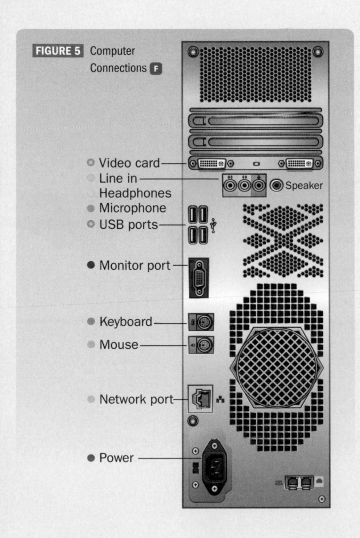

FIGURE 5 Computer
Connections **F**

Video card
Line in
Headphones
Microphone
USB ports

Speaker

Monitor port

Keyboard

Mouse

Network port

Power

F TECHNICAL
DIRECTIONS
When **analyzing
technical directions,**
remember to scan the
headings and study the
graphics. In what way
does Figure 5 differ from
the other graphics on
pages 950–952?

Step 4 Connect the modem to the computer by using a network cable.

Connect the network cable to the network port on the back of your computer. (See **FIGURE 5**.) Connect the other end of the network cable to your modem. As long as you
110 have an active Internet connection, the software should automatically detect that you are connected to the Internet when your computer starts. **G**

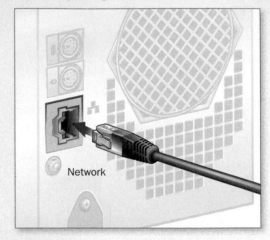

Network

G TECHNICAL DIRECTIONS
Which step should you complete first— connecting the printer or connecting the modem? How do you know?

Step 5 Connect the power cords.

The power cord is a three-pronged, grounded cord that you attach to your computer. First, attach one end of the power cord to the computer; then plug the other end of the cord into a surge protector. (See **FIGURE 5**.) Plug the
120 surge protector into a grounded wall outlet. Turn on the monitor and then the computer, and you are ready to go! **H**

Power cord

H TECHNICAL DIRECTIONS
If you skip Step 5, what will happen?

Comprehension

1. **Recall** What types of memory can be used to store information?

2. **Summarize** Describe the set of connections that must be made for computers to communicate globally.

Text Analysis

● 3. **Examine an Instruction Manual** Why are both diagrams and text included in this manual?

● 4. **Analyze Technical Directions** Choose one of the tips on your checklist (page 944) and explain why it is helpful in following the directions for setting up a desktop computer.

● 5. **Evaluate Technical Directions** Does any information seem to be missing from these directions? Is there information that seems extraneous? Is everything up to date? Explain your answer, citing evidence from the text.

COMMON CORE

RI 4 Determine the meaning of words and phrases as they are used in a text, including technical meanings. **RI 5** Analyze in detail the structure of a specific paragraph in a text, including the role of particular sentences in developing and refining a key concept. **W 9** Draw evidence from informational texts to support analysis.

Read for Information: Evaluate Graphics

WRITING PROMPT

How effective are the graphic elements in "Guide to Computers"? Evaluate the purpose, clarity, and usefulness of the graphics.

To answer the prompt, follow these steps:

1. Review the fourth item on your checklist. Do the graphics fulfill their purpose?

2. Consider whether the graphics are easy to read and understand.

3. Decide whether the graphics would be useful for someone setting up a computer.

4. In a paragraph or two, explain why the graphics are or are not effective. Focus on the purpose, clarity, and usefulness of each.

GRAPHICS	
Purpose	
Clarity	
Usefulness	

An American Plague:

The True and Terrifying Story of the Yellow Fever Epidemic of 1793

COMMON CORE

RI 10 Read and comprehend literary nonfiction.

History Book by Jim Murphy

Meet Jim Murphy

Jim Murphy didn't read much as a child. It wasn't until a high school teacher told his class that they weren't allowed to read a particular novel that Murphy became inspired to read. At first, he did it just to be rebellious. Murphy says that as he continued to read, he developed a love of history, because it enabled him to "visit many different times and places in the past."

Today, Murphy is the award-winning author of over 25 books about American history. "One of my goals in writing about events from the past is to show that children weren't just observers of our history," Murphy says. "They were actual participants and sometimes did amazing and heroic things."

Try a History Book

Sometimes a nonfiction book can be so enthralling, it's almost as though you are reading a suspense novel, wondering what will happen next. History books tell about a series of important events or provide details about one major event, often in chronological order. Some history books start with the outcome, however, and then back up to show readers how it came about.

Reading Fluency Good readers read smoothly, accurately, and with feeling. To improve your reading fluency, read a passage several times. Your goal in silent reading is to make sense of the writer's words and ideas. When reading aloud, think about the type of text you are reading. You may need to adjust your speed and tone and how you emphasize certain words when reading fiction, nonfiction, or poetry.

Other Books by Jim Murphy

- *Blizzard!: The Storm That Changed America*
- *The Great Fire*
- *A Young Patriot: The American Revolution as Experienced by One Boy*

Read a Great Book

In 1793, Philadelphia, Pennsylvania, was the nation's capital. It was also a city at the mercy of an invisible enemy. In this vivid account of the yellow fever epidemic, Jim Murphy highlights some of the conditions in Philadelphia at that time and shows how those conditions contributed to the spread of a deadly disease.

from

An American Plague:

The **True** and **Terrifying** Story of the
Yellow Fever Epidemic of 1793

Saturday, August 3, 1793. The sun came up, as it had every day since the end of May, bright, hot, and unrelenting. The swamps and marshes south of Philadelphia had already lost a great deal of water to the intense heat, while the Delaware and Schuylkill Rivers had receded to reveal long stretches of their muddy, root-choked banks. Dead fish and gooey vegetable matter were exposed and rotted, while swarms of insects droned in the heavy, humid air.

In Philadelphia itself an increasing number of cats were dropping dead every day, attracting, one Philadelphian complained, "an amazing
10 number of flies and other insects." Mosquitoes were everywhere, though their high-pitched whirring was particularly loud near rain barrels, gutters, and open sewers.

These sewers, called "sinks," were particularly ripe this year. Most streets in the city were unpaved and had no system of covered sewers and pipes to channel water away from buildings. Instead, deep holes were dug at various street corners to collect runoff water and anything else that might be washed along. Dead animals were routinely tossed into this soup, where everything decayed and sent up noxious bubbles to foul the air.

Down along the docks lining the Delaware, cargo was being loaded
20 onto ships that would sail to New York, Boston, and other distant ports.
The hard work of hoisting heavy casks into the hold was accompanied
by the stevedores' usual grunts and muttered oaths.

The men laboring near Water Street had particular reason to curse.
The sloop *Amelia* from Santo Domingo had anchored with a cargo
of coffee, which had spoiled during the voyage. The bad coffee was
dumped on Ball's Wharf, where it putrefied in the sun and sent out a
powerful odor that could be smelled over a quarter mile away. Benjamin
Rush, one of Philadelphia's most celebrated doctors and a signer of the
Declaration of Independence, lived three long blocks from Ball's Wharf,
30 but he recalled that the coffee stank "to the great annoyance of the
whole neighborhood."

Despite the stench, the streets nearby were crowded with people that
morning—ship owners and their captains talking seriously, shouting
children darting between wagons or climbing on crates and barrels, well-
dressed men and women out for a stroll, servants and slaves hurrying
from one chore to the next. Philadelphia was then the largest city in
North America, with nearly 51,000 inhabitants; those who didn't
absolutely have to be indoors working had escaped to the open air to
seek relief from the sweltering heat.
40 Many of them stopped at one of the city's 415 shops, whose doors
and windows were wide open to let in light and any hint of a cooling
breeze. The rest continued along, headed for the market on High Street.

Here three city blocks were crowded with vendors calling their wares
while eager shoppers studied merchandise or haggled over weights and
prices. Horse-drawn wagons clattered up and down the cobblestone
street, bringing in more fresh vegetables, squawking chickens, and
squealing pigs. People commented on the stench from Ball's Wharf, but
the market's own ripe blend of odors—of roasting meats, strong cheeses,
days-old sheep and cow guts, dried blood, and horse manure—tended
50 to overwhelm all others.

One and a half blocks from the market was the handsomely
refurbished mansion of Robert Morris, a wealthy manufacturer who
had used his fortune to help finance the Revolutionary War. Morris was
lending this house to George and Martha Washington and had moved
himself into another, larger one he owned just up the block. Washington
was then president of the United States, and Philadelphia was the
temporary capital of the young nation and the center of its federal
government. Washington spent the day at home in a small, stuffy office

seeing visitors, writing letters, and worrying. It was the French problem
60 that was most on his mind these days.

Not so many years before, the French monarch, Louis XVI, had sent
money, ships, and soldiers to aid the struggling Continental Army's
fight against the British. The French aid had been a major reason why
Washington was able to surround and force General Charles Cornwallis
to surrender at Yorktown in 1781. This military victory eventually led
to a British capitulation three years later and to freedom for the United
States—and lasting fame for Washington.

Then, in 1789, France erupted in its own revolution. The common
people and a few nobles and churchmen soon gained complete power
70 in France and beheaded Louis XVI in January 1793. Many of France's
neighbors worried that similar revolutions might spread to their
countries and wanted the new French republic crushed. Soon after
the king was put to death, revolutionary France was at war with Great
Britain, Holland, Spain, and Austria.

Naturally, the French republic had turned to the United States for
help, only to have President Washington hesitate. Washington knew that
he and his country owed the French an eternal debt. He simply wasn't
sure that the United States had the military strength to take on so many
formidable foes.

80 Many citizens felt Washington's Proclamation of Neutrality was
a betrayal of the French people. His own secretary of state, Thomas
Jefferson, certainly did, and he argued bitterly with Treasury Secretary
Alexander Hamilton over the issue. Wasn't the French fight for
individual freedom, Jefferson asked, exactly like America's struggle
against British oppression? . . .

While Washington worried, the city's taverns, beer gardens, and
coffeehouses—all 176 of them—were teeming with activity that
Saturday. There men, and a few women, lifted their glasses in toasts and
singing and let the hours slip away in lively conversation. Business and
90 politics and the latest gossip were the favorite topics. No doubt the heat,
the foul stink from Ball's Wharf, and the country's refusal to join with
France were discussed and argued over at length.

In all respects it seemed as if August 3 was a very normal day, with
business and buying and pleasure as usual.

Oh, there were a few who felt a tingle of unease. For weeks an
unusually large supply of wild pigeons had been for sale at the market.
Popular folklore suggested that such an abundance of pigeons always
brought with it unhealthy air and sickness.

Dr. Rush had no time for such silly notions, but he, too, sensed
100 that something odd was happening. His concern focused on a series of
illnesses that had struck his patients throughout the year—the mumps
in January, jaw and mouth infections in February, scarlet fever in March,
followed by influenza in July. "There was something in the heat and
drought," the good doctor speculated, "which was uncommon, in their
influence upon the human body."

The Reverend J. Henry C. Helmuth of the Lutheran congregation,
too, thought something was wrong in the city, though it had nothing to
do with sickness of the body. It was the souls of its citizens he worried
about. "Philadelphia . . . seemed to strive to exceed all other places in
110 the breaking of the Sabbath," he noted. . . .

Rush and Helmuth would have been surprised to know that their
worries were turning to reality on August 3. For on that Saturday a young
French sailor rooming at Richard Denny's boarding house, over on North
Water Street, was desperately ill with a fever. Eighteenth-century record
keeping wasn't very precise, so no one bothered to write down his name.
Besides, this sailor was poor and a foreigner, not the sort of person who
would draw much attention from the community around him. All we
know is that his fever worsened and was accompanied by violent seizures,
and that a few days later he died.

120 Other residents at Denny's would follow this sailor to the grave—a
Mr. Moore fell into a stupor and passed away, Mrs. Richard Parkinson
expired on August 7, next the lodging house owner and his wife, Mary,
and then the first sailor's roommate. Around the same time, two people
in the house next to Denny's died of the same severe fever.

Eight deaths in the space of a week in two houses on the same
street . . . but the city did not take notice. Summer fevers were
common visitors to all American cities in the eighteenth century, and
therefore not headline news. Besides, Denny's was located on a narrow
out-of-the-way street—really more an alley than a street. "It is much
130 confined," a resident remarked, "ill-aired, and, in every respect, is a
disagreeable street." Things happened along this street all the time—
sometimes very bad things—that went unnoticed by the authorities
and the rest of the population.

So the deaths did not disrupt Philadelphia much at all. Ships came
and went; men and women did chores, talked, and sought relief from
the heat and insects; the markets and shops hummed with activity;
children played; and the city, state, and federal governments went about
their business.

Procedural Text

Fires, spiders, volcanoes—these were just a few of the topics you encountered as you discovered how to dig for information in nonfiction sources. As you master writing a **procedural text** (text that explains how to do something), you will learn how to communicate information in precise ways and in an orderly format.

 Complete the workshop activities in your **Reader/Writer Notebook.**

WRITE WITH A PURPOSE

WRITING TASK

Write a **procedural text** in which you explain to a specific audience how to complete a process.

Idea Starters
- setting up a video game console
- installing a complex device, such as a cable modem
- evacuating a home or school in case of fire
- designing a recycling program for your school
- changing a tire

THE ESSENTIALS

Here are some common purposes, audiences, and formats for a procedural text.

PURPOSES	AUDIENCES	FORMATS
• to communicate information to a specific audience • to explain a complex process in a simple way	• classmates and teacher • parents • product users • community members • Web users	• essay for class • speech • blog posting • poster • podcast • brochure • cable television program

COMMON CORE TRAITS

1. DEVELOPMENT OF IDEAS
- clearly introduces the **topic** and identifies the purpose of the procedure
- develops the steps needed to perform the task with **relevant, well-chosen facts** and **concrete details**
- provides a **concluding section** that follows from the information presented

2. ORGANIZATION OF IDEAS
- **organizes** information in a logical order
- uses appropriate and varied **transitions**
- uses **formatting** to aid comprehension

3. LANGUAGE FACILITY AND CONVENTIONS
- uses **precise language** and **domain-specific vocabulary**
- establishes and maintains a **formal style**
- employs correct **grammar, usage, spelling,** and **punctuation**

Writing Online

THINK central

Go to **thinkcentral.com.**
KEYWORD: HML8N-960

Planning/Prewriting

COMMON CORE

W 2a–f Write informative/explanatory texts to examine and convey ideas, concepts, and information. **W 5** Develop and strengthen writing by planning. **W 7** Conduct short research projects. **W 8** Gather information from multiple sources.

Getting Started

BRAINSTORM A TOPIC

What skills or abilities do you have that could help others? Anything you know how to do well and that others could benefit from is a possible topic for a procedural text. Make a list of such things, and then choose the one you can write about most clearly. Circle the topic you choose.

▶ **WHAT DOES IT LOOK LIKE?**

Possible Topics
- *figure out how to download audiobooks from the library onto an MP3 player*
- *help Dad transfer photos from camera to computer*
- *teach my cousin how to knit a scarf*
- *explain how to start a blog*

THINK ABOUT AUDIENCE AND PURPOSE

As you think about your procedural text, keep your purpose and audience in mind. Make sure that you have a specific **purpose** and that you anticipate the needs of your **audience.**

▶ **ASK YOURSELF:**

- What is my goal in writing these instructions?
- For whom am I writing the instructions?
- How can I make sure that readers cannot misinterpret what I say?

DO THE RESEARCH

Consider the information you will need to write clear and complete directions. Write down some research questions, and then find the answers in books, manuals, and online. Use **search terms**, or key words, to locate useful sources. Make sure the sources you use are **credible**. This means that they are trustworthy because they provide relevant, accurate, and unbiased information.

▶ **WHAT DOES IT LOOK LIKE?**

Research Questions
- *What does Dad's instruction book tell him to do?*
- *Which pictures or information does the book leave out?*
- *Where can I find more information about the process of uploading photos?*

MAP IT OUT

Think about the steps in the procedure you are explaining. Keep in mind the end result you want your audience to reach. Then think of the first thing they need to do in the process of reaching that goal. Follow the procedure in a logical sequence from one step to the next. Use a flowchart to map out the steps.

▶ **WHAT DOES IT LOOK LIKE?**

1. Find the cable.
↓
2. Plug the cable into the camera.
↓
3. Plug the cable into the computer.
↓
4. Turn on the camera.

Planning/Prewriting *continued*

Getting Started

FOCUS ON RELEVANT DETAILS

Your readers need to know more than the steps in the process. You also have to tell them how to complete each step. Review the steps in your flowchart, and write down details to include with each step. Include only those details that the reader will need to complete the procedure, and eliminate any irrelevant information. Be very **precise**, or specific, especially when discussing materials or tools.

Keep in mind that your readers may not know all of the terms that are important to your explanation. Define any **domain-specific**, or specialized, **vocabulary** that your audience will need to know to complete the process.

▶ WHAT DOES IT LOOK LIKE?

> 1. **Find the cable.**
> standard USB connector cable supplied with camera cable; available at electronics store
>
> ↓
>
> 2. **Plug the cable into the camera.**
> use smaller connector on USB cable port on top left side of camera
>
> ↓
>
> 3. **Plug the cable into the computer.**
> use larger connector on USB cable ports on back of computer; icon identifies USB ports
>
> ↓

INCLUDE ALL VARIABLE FACTORS

Think about **factors** that may vary as someone follows your instructions. Try to predict circumstances that would change how someone carries out the procedure.

▶ WHAT DOES IT LOOK LIKE?

> **What if** Dad has lost his USB cable?
> **What if** Dad decides to use Mom's desktop computer instead of his laptop?

PEER REVIEW Share your flowchart with a classmate. Ask if he or she can think of any missing steps or factors that may change how someone carries out the procedure. Be open to changing your topic if the procedure you want to explain is overly complicated.

YOUR TURN In your *Reader/Writer Notebook,* record possible topics and research questions for your procedural text. Then use a flowchart like the one on page 961 to map out the steps you need to explain to your audience. Consider the following tips as you plan your writing:

- Consult multiple print and online sources related to your topic.
- Search for additional information or visuals on reliable and trustworthy Web sites.
- Write notes from your personal experience with the procedure.
- If you quote or paraphrase information from the sources you use, make sure to give credit to the authors.

Drafting

The following chart shows how to organize a draft of a cohesive, or easy-to-follow, procedural text.

W 4 Produce clear and coherent writing appropriate to task, purpose, and audience. **L1** Demonstrate command of the conventions of standard English grammar and usage when writing.

Organizing Your Procedural Text

INTRODUCTION

- Clearly **introduce** your topic and explain the purpose of your procedure.
- List any **materials** or **tools** that the reader will need to complete the process.

▼

BODY

- **Organize** the information in a logical, step-by-step sequence.
- Use **transitions,** such as *first, next, then,* and *finally,* to clarify how the steps are connected.
- Maintain a **formal style** by eliminating casual language and slang.
- Use **formatting,** such as headings, numbers, and bulleted lists, for clarity.
- Consider adding **graphics** or **multimedia** to clarify your instructions.

▼

CONCLUDING SECTION

- State the last thing you want the audience to do to achieve the goal of the instructions.
- Suggest possible next steps or options if appropriate.

GRAMMAR IN CONTEXT: USING ADJECTIVAL CLAUSES

Adjectival clauses are subordinate clauses that modify nouns or pronouns. Adjectival clauses usually begin with *that, which, who, whom,* or *whose.* These **relative pronouns** connect clauses to the words they modify. There are two types of adjectival clauses.

Type of Adjectival Clause	Example
Essential—provides information necessary to identify the preceding noun or pronoun	▶ *A USB cable **that connects the camera and the computer** allows you to upload photos.*
Nonessential—adds additional information about a noun or pronoun whose meaning is already clear (Note that nonessential clauses are set off by commas.)	▶ *The USB cable, **which came with your camera,** is on the table.*

YOUR TURN Develop a first draft of your procedural text, following the structure outlined in the chart above. As you write, correct any grammar and usage errors. Be sure to set off any nonessential clauses with commas.

Revising

Does your draft fulfill your purpose of explaining a procedure for your audience? Your goal as you revise is to look for ways to make your instructions clearer and easier to follow. You may discover that revising, rewriting, or trying a new approach will improve your explanation. The strategies in the chart below can help you.

PROCEDURAL TEXT

Ask Yourself	Tips	Revision Strategies
1. **Does the introduction clearly state the topic and goal?**	▶ **Circle** the topic and goal of the procedure.	▶ **Add or revise** a statement to make your topic and goal clear to the audience.
2. **Are all necessary materials and tools listed in the introduction?**	▶ **Draw a star** next to any materials or tools mentioned in the directions.	▶ **Add** any missing materials or tools to the list in the introduction.
3. **Do the instructions appear in a logical sequence?**	▶ **Number** each step in the procedure.	▶ **Rearrange** steps as necessary, along with their supporting details.
4. **Is information expressed precisely and simply?**	▶ **Bracket** sentences that are wordier or more complicated than they need to be.	▶ **Delete** unnecessary words and replace imprecise words.
5. **Does the format help make the instructions easy to follow?**	▶ **Highlight** headings, numbers, or bulleted lists. **Circle** words that could be emphasized.	▶ **Add** headings, numbers, or bullets to divide your instructions into steps or parts. **Change font styles** to emphasize key words.
6. **Is a formal style maintained throughout the essay?**	▶ **Put a star** next to sentences that sound too casual.	▶ **Rewrite** casual sentences to reflect a formal style.
7. **Does the concluding section contain the final step in the instructions?**	▶ **Underline** the last thing the reader must do to complete the procedure.	▶ **Rearrange** information so that the last step appears in the concluding section.

YOUR TURN **_PEER REVIEW_** Exchange your procedural text with a classmate. As you read and comment on your partner's draft, focus on whether you can follow the instructions easily. Ask questions about steps you don't understand. Give concrete suggestions for improvement, based on the revision strategies suggested in the chart. Discuss any parts that should be reworked or need a new approach.

COMMON CORE W 2d Use precise language. W 5 Develop and strengthen writing as needed by revising, editing, rewriting, or trying a new approach, focusing on how well purpose and audience have been addressed.

ANALYZE A STUDENT DRAFT

Read this student's draft; notice comments on its structure and suggestions for how it could be made even stronger.

How to Upload Photographs
by Daniel Galindo, Woodson Middle School

❶ It is very easy to transfer pictures from your camera to your computer. All you need is a connecting device called a USB cable. Your camera came with one, but if you can't find it, you can buy one at any store that sells computers or other electronic equipment.

❷ **Step 1: Plug the Cable into Your Camera.**

❸ One end of the USB cable is bigger than the other because the holes where it plugs into the camera and the computer are different sizes. You want the smaller end first to plug into the opening on the side of your camera that would be in your left hand if you were getting ready to take a picture. The opening is called a port and you can see it's the same shape as the end of the USB cable. Make sure your camera is turned off, and plug the small end of the USB cable into your camera.

> The introduction states the **goal** and lists materials.

> Daniel uses the **formatting technique** of setting headings in boldface to divide the steps.

> Daniel needs to use more **precise language** to simplify his instructions.

LEARN HOW **Use Precise Language** In the third paragraph, Daniel's sentences are wordier and more complicated than they need to be. By using simple, precise language, Daniel will make his instructions easier for the reader to follow.

DANIEL'S REVISION TO PARAGRAPH ❸

~~One end of the USB cable is bigger than the other because the holes where it plugs into the camera and the computer are different sizes. You want the smaller end first to plug into the opening on the side of your camera that would be in your left hand if you were getting ready to take a picture. The opening is called a port and you can see it's the same shape as the end of the USB cable.~~ Make sure your camera is turned off, and plug the small end of the USB cable into your camera.

The USB cable has two ends. Find the smaller end. Then find the port that the cable plugs into on your camera. (If you hold the camera as if you are ready to shoot, the port is on the top left side.)

④   **Step 2: Plug the Cable into Your Computer.**

⑤   Next, find the port for the USB cable on the back of your computer. There are several ports, so be sure you select the right one. If you are not sure which port to use, refer to your computer manual to learn which icon identifies the USB port. Then plug in the cable.

> Daniel addresses **variable factors** and maintains a **formal style**.

⑥   **Step 3: Upload Your Photos.**

⑦   A box will pop up on your computer screen. Be sure your camera is turned on or this won't happen. What it says will depend on your software, but it may give you the choice of:

> These events are out of order. Daniel needs to improve the **organization**.

- copying the photos to your computer
- organizing and editing your photos
- viewing your photos as a slideshow
- printing your photos

⑧   *Possible next steps* You can burn your photos onto a CD or upload them to photo-sharing sites on the Internet.

> At the end of his instructions, Daniel informs his audience of **possible next steps**.

LEARN HOW Improve Organization In a procedural text, it's especially important to present information in a logical sequence. If the steps appear out of order, it will be difficult for readers to follow the instructions. Daniel improved the organization of his draft by moving the sentence that was out of order and rewriting it with a transition so the ideas flowed more logically and coherently.

DANIEL'S REVISION TO PARAGRAPH ⑦

Now turn on your camera.

⋀ A box will pop up on your computer screen. ~~Be sure your camera is~~ ~~turned on or this won't happen.~~ What it says will depend on your software, but it may give you the choice of:

YOUR TURN   Use the chart on page 964, feedback from your peers and teacher, and the two "Learn How" lessons to revise your draft. Evaluate how well you have succeeded at explaining the procedure simply and clearly so your audience can follow the instructions.

Editing and Publishing

Now that you've researched your procedure and described each step precisely and in logical order, don't let simple mistakes confuse your audience. Review your work and correct any errors in grammar, capitalization, spelling, and punctuation. Do not rely on a spell-checker to find all of your spelling mistakes. Read through your work carefully to find spelling errors.

COMMON CORE

W 5 Develop and strengthen writing as needed by revising and editing. **L 2** Demonstrate command of the conventions of standard English capitalization, punctuation, and spelling. **L 2c** Spell correctly.

GRAMMAR IN CONTEXT: USING COLONS

Writers use the **colon** to introduce a list of items. However, you should not place a colon directly after a verb or a preposition. Instead, place it after a noun or after the words *the following*. When Daniel edited his draft, he realized he had incorrectly used a colon after a preposition.

> What it says will depend on your software, but it may give you
>   *following choices:*
> the ~~choice of~~
> • copying the photos to your computer
> • organizing and editing your photos
> • viewing your photos as a slideshow
> • printing your photos

[Removing the preposition *of* makes the use of the colon correct. It would also be correct to insert *the following* after the preposition.]

Daniel also discovered a place where he needed to add a colon.

> Possible next steps: You can burn your photos onto a CD or upload them to photo-sharing sites on the Internet.

[The colon introduces the options that follow the heading. In this case, the list of two options is written as a complete sentence.]

PUBLISH YOUR WRITING

Share your procedural text with an audience.
- Produce a brochure for people who will find the instructions useful.
- Present the instructions in a speech to your classmates.
- Post the instructions on your personal Web page.

YOUR TURN Correct any errors in your procedural text. As you proofread your work, carefully check your use of punctuation marks, especially colons. Then publish your final text for others to use.

Scoring Rubric

Use the rubric below to evaluate your procedural text from the Writing Workshop or your response to the on-demand task on the next page.

PROCEDURAL TEXT

SCORE	COMMON CORE TRAITS
6	• **Development** Introduces a topic in a clear and engaging way; provides relevant, well-chosen facts and details about each step in the process; ends with a strong concluding section that follows from the explanation • **Organization** Organizes steps in a clear, logical order; effectively uses appropriate and varied transitions to link ideas and create cohesion • **Language** Consistently maintains a formal style; ably uses precise language; shows a strong command of conventions
5	• **Development** Clearly introduces a topic; provides relevant, well-chosen facts and details about most steps in the process; ends with a concluding section that follows from the explanation • **Organization** Arranges steps logically; uses appropriate and varied transitions • **Language** Maintains a formal style; uses precise language; has a few errors in conventions
4	• **Development** Sufficiently introduces a topic; could use more facts and details to explain some steps; has an adequate concluding section • **Organization** Arranges steps in a mostly logical order; uses some transitions • **Language** Mostly maintains a formal style; needs more precise language at times; includes a few distracting errors in conventions
3	• **Development** Introduces a topic and concludes the explanation in an adequate way; lacks enough facts and details in most steps • **Organization** Has some organizational flaws; needs more transitions to link ideas • **Language** Frequently lapses into an informal style; expresses some key ideas in too complex a manner; has some critical errors in conventions
2	• **Development** Has a weak introduction of the topic and concluding section; lacks facts and details in all steps • **Organization** Has organizational flaws; lacks transitions throughout • **Language** Uses an informal style; expresses ideas in too complex a manner; has many errors in conventions
1	• **Development** Lacks an introduction, concluding section, and explanation of steps • **Organization** Has no organization or transitions • **Language** Uses an inappropriate style; expresses ideas in too complex a manner and creates confusion; has major problems with conventions

Preparing for Timed Writing

COMMON CORE

W 10 Write routinely over shorter time frames for a range of tasks, purposes, and audiences.

1. ANALYZE THE TASK   5 MIN

Read the task carefully. Then read it again, underlining or circling the words that tell the type of writing, the purpose, and the audience.

> **WRITING TASK**
>
> ⌐Type of writing
>
> Are you an expert on cell phones? Do you know the rules of a sport or game, or are you good at a craft, such as origami? Write a set of detailed instructions that will help another student do something that you know how to do well.
>
> Audience ↗   ↖ Purpose

2. PLAN YOUR RESPONSE   10 MIN

Think of something that you know how to do well and that you could explain to someone else. Then consider the steps that someone needs to follow in order to complete the procedure. Use a chart to help you plan your instructions.

Goal:
Step 1:
Step 2:
Step 3:
Step 4:

3. RESPOND TO THE TASK   20 MIN

Using your notes about the steps in the procedure, begin writing your instructions. Keep the following points in mind as you write:

- Make the goal clear in the first line. Then present information in a logical sequence to lead your audience step by step through the procedure.
- Use short sentences that are easy to understand. Address any variable factors that your audience might face when following your instructions.
- Use headings or numbers to divide your instructions into parts or steps.

4. IMPROVE YOUR RESPONSE   5–10 MIN

Revising Check your draft against the writing task. Ask yourself: Do my instructions contain all the necessary steps? Is my language precise and simplified? Does the formatting help improve understanding?

Proofreading Review your instructions to correct errors in grammar, spelling, punctuation, and capitalization. Make corrections neatly and legibly.

Checking Your Final Copy Before you turn in your instructions, read through them once more to catch any errors you might have missed.

Presenting and Responding to an Instructional Speech

Have you ever given a friend or family member instructions about how to do something? Just as a writer must provide clear instructions to an audience of readers, speakers also must communicate clearly to a listening audience.

 Complete the workshop activities in your **Reader/Writer Notebook.**

SPEAK WITH A PURPOSE	COMMON CORE TRAITS
TASK Adapt your procedural text into a formal **instructional speech.** Practice your speech, and then present it to your class.	**A STRONG INSTRUCTIONAL SPEECH . . .** • provides step-by-step directions supported by multimedia and visual displays • organizes ideas in a logical sequence • expresses points clearly and simply with well-chosen details • uses formal English to explain the procedure

COMMON CORE

SL 1a, c Come to discussions prepared; pose questions and respond to questions and comments. **SL 4** Present claims and findings. **SL 5** Integrate visual displays into presentations. **SL 6** Adapt speech to a variety of contexts and tasks.

Adapt Your Instructions

Because people will be listening to your instructions instead of reading them, you'll need to adapt your procedural text as you prepare for your speech. Follow these suggestions as you plan your speech:

• **Consider your audience's needs.** Think about what your classmates need to know to successfully achieve the goal of the instructions. Consider their background knowledge of your topic, and plan to address factors that may vary. Though your speech should sound formal, avoid using complex sentences and words that may be unfamiliar to your audience.

• **Identify your goal.** Formulate a clear idea of what you want listeners to be able to do at the end of your speech.

• **Plan your speech.** The formatting techniques that you used in your text can help you organize your speech into logical parts or steps. Make notes about what you want to say about each stage of the procedure.

• **Find or create visuals.** Clarify information and add interest by illustrating important parts or steps on a poster, on transparencies, or in a power presentation. Make your visuals large enough for the audience to see easily. Depending on your topic, you might prepare a handout or include an actual demonstration of what you are explaining.

• **Practice your speech.** Get comfortable with presenting your visuals and words together. Anticipate audience questions, and prepare responses in advance.

THINK central
Speaking &
Listening Online

Go to **thinkcentral.com.**
KEYWORD: HML8-970

Deliver Your Instructional Speech

Here are some tips for presenting your instructions to your audience:

- **Clearly state your purpose.** Begin by telling your audience what they should be able to do at the end of the speech. Then explain the steps in a focused, coherent manner. Include well-chosen details to help your audience understand the procedure.

- **Use appropriate verbal techniques.** Speak clearly, slowly, and distinctly. Pause frequently to let your listeners absorb what you are saying. Maintain an even pitch and an authoritative tone to your voice.

- **Include nonverbal techniques.** Stand up straight, yet in a relaxed way. Maintain eye contact with your audience, and smile. Use gestures to emphasize salient, or key, points or direct attention to visuals.

- **Invite and respond to audience questions and comments.** Tell the audience at the beginning that you will take questions and comments at the end of your speech. Answer questions by restating any points that the listeners missed or by providing additional information to clarify misunderstandings.

Respond to an Instructional Speech

Effective listening requires focus and concentration.

- **Listen and take notes.** Listen attentively to what the speaker is saying. You may want to jot down points that you want to remember or that you want to ask the speaker about.

- **Use the visual aids.** Refer to the visuals to help you follow the instructions.

- **Paraphrase the speech.** Restate the steps of the instructions in your own words to make sure you have understood the main ideas.

- **Ask questions.** Ask the speaker to clarify information that you found confusing or incomplete. You can also pose questions that connect to and extend on what your classmates say about the speech.

- **Practice the instructions.** Try to follow the steps the speaker has outlined. Refer to your notes or to visuals that the speaker provides.

YOUR TURN

As a Speaker Plan your speech and deliver it to a classmate, using the tips on these pages.

As a Listener Evaluate your classmate's delivery. Listen carefully to make sure you can follow the steps in the procedure.

Assessment Practice

ASSESS
Taking this practice test will help you assess your knowledge of these skills and determine your readiness for the Unit Test.

REVIEW
After you take the practice test, your teacher can help you identify any standards you need to review.

COMMON CORE

RI 2 Determine a central idea of a text and analyze its development over the course of the text, including its relationship to supporting ideas; provide an objective summary of the text. **RI 5** Analyze in detail the structure of a specific paragraph in a text, including the role of particular sentences in developing and refining a key concept. **L 2a** Use punctuation (comma) to indicate a pause or break. **L 4a** Use context (e.g., the overall meaning of a sentence or paragraph) as a clue to the meaning of a word.

DIRECTIONS Read this selection and answer the questions that follow.

from Odd Couples   *by Amy Sarver*

1   Living in the wild can be hard. Finding food and staying safe aren't easy. Each day, animals struggle to survive in their habitats. Not all animals get by on their own. Some animals form a close partnership with other kinds of animals. These pairings are called symbiotic relationships.

2   In a symbiotic relationship, the animals depend on each other. One animal helps the other meet its needs. Sounds good, right? Not always. Some animals are not very kind to their partners. In some cases, one animal meets its needs but hurts its partner. Sounds crazy, but it does happen. Take ticks, for example. These insects guzzle blood to live. To get blood, they attach themselves to other kinds of animals. Ticks do not help their hosts. Instead, they can pass germs that cause disease. In other relationships, animals don't treat their partners so poorly. Both animals benefit, or get help, from living with the other animal. Check out how animals pair up to survive.

Keeping Clean

3   Small animals called cleaner shrimps have found a way of helping fish at coral reefs. As their name suggests, the shrimps clean the fish. Here's how it works. The shrimps hang out at what scientists call a cleaning station. A fish stops by. Then a shrimp climbs onto the fish. The shrimp even steps into the fish's mouth. The shrimp uses its tiny claws to pick stuff off the fish's body. That can include dead skin, tiny pieces of food, and wee creatures that can hurt the fish. The fish gets a nice cleaning. The shrimp enjoys a tasty meal of fish trash.

4   Small birds called plovers are also in the cleaning business. They have big customers—crocodiles. Crocs have long snouts filled with sharp teeth. Cleaning them is tricky. That's where the plover comes in. When a croc opens its mouth, the plover hops right in. The croc does not snap its snout shut. Instead, it lets the plover eat small, harmful animals attached to the crocodile's teeth. The plover gets an easy meal. The croc gets clean teeth.

Sweet Success

5   Some animals need each other because they like the same food. Take the honeyguide bird and the ratel. They live on grasslands in Africa. Both animals love honey. Yet each has a problem getting some. The bird can find a beehive, but can't open it. The ratel can open a hive but doesn't know how to find one. So the two animals team up. The bird flies over the grasslands, looking for hives. When it spots one, it swoops down and makes noise. The sound tells the

ratel to come eat. The ratel uses its sharp claws to tear apart the hive. It gobbles up most of the honey-covered mess. Then the honeyguide bird enjoys finishing off the leftovers.

Clowning Around

6   Land and sky animals aren't the only ones that work together. So do some sea animals. One of the oddest couples is made up of the sea anemone and the clownfish. You might think sea anemones look like plants, but they are really hungry animals. They attach themselves to a rock or coral reef. There they wait for a fish to swim by. Then they sting it with their tentacles. The stunned fish is then pulled into the sea anemone's hidden mouth. Still, one daring fish makes its home among sea anemones. It's the clownfish. This orange-and-white fish isn't kidding around. Its body is shielded by a thick layer of mucus. The slime protects the clownfish from the sea anemone's dangerous, stinging tentacles. The clownfish is also a good neighbor. It helps the sea anemone by luring in fish. When a hungry fish spots a colorful clownfish, it darts toward it. The clownfish safely swims under the anemone's tentacles. If the hungry fish follows, it gets stung. Then it becomes the anemone's next meal. The brave clownfish not only reels in fish food, it chases away fish that might eat an anemone. So the clownfish and anemone help keep each other fed and safe.

Instead of searching the sky for insects, the oxpecker bird catches a ride aboard large animals such as the antelope. In return, the bird picks ticks and other pests off the animal's body.

Clownfish live safely among sea anemones. They lure edible fish into the anemones' deadly tentacles and chase away harmful ones.

A Different Way of Life

7   All animals want to do one thing—survive in the wild. Some do that by living alone. Others live in flocks, herds, hives, packs, or schools. Some animals, both large and small, know the best way to stay alive is to live with or near other kinds of animals. At first glance, these teammates don't seem to make sense. If you look more closely, you'll soon learn that these animals help one another find food, shelter, and safety. They make the most of their various differences. These unlikely partners pair up to get the most out of life.

GO ON ➡

SYMBIOTIC INTERACTIONS		
Type of Relationship	**Example**	**Interaction**
Mutualism: both species benefit	bees and flowers	Bees gather nectar from flowers; they spread pollen that the flowers need to reproduce.
	aphids and ants	Aphids provide ants with sweet liquid; ants protect aphids from predators.
Commensalism: one species benefits; the other is not affected	trumpetfish and soft coral	Coral gives the trumpetfish camouflage for hunting; coral is unharmed.
	lichens and trees	Lichens live on trees; trees are unharmed.
Parasitism: one species benefits; the other is harmed	tapeworms and pigs	The tapeworm lives in the intestines of a host, such as a pig; it causes sickness in the host.
	mistletoe and trees	Mistletoe takes food from trees; the trees are damaged.

Reading Comprehension

Use "Odd Couples" to answer questions 1–9.

1. What is the best summary of paragraphs 3 and 4?
   A. Some animals set up cleaning stations where they get food from other animals that stop by.
   B. There isn't much food in the ocean, so shrimp need to eat fish trash.
   C. Birds such as plovers have learned from shrimp how to get food out of another animals' mouth.
   D. Sometimes, one animal gets food by cleaning another animal, so both animals benefit.

2. Reread paragraph 5. The term *sweet success* in the subheading refers to what happens when the —
   A. honeyguide bird finds a beehive
   B. honeyguide bird makes loud noises to attract the ratel
   C. honeyguide bird and the ratel work together to get honey
   D. ratel tears up the beehive and eats most of the honey

3. Which fact in the article does the photograph of the clownfish help you understand?
   A. Sea anemones look like plants.
   B. The clownfish is shielded by a layer of mucus.
   C. A hungry fish gets stung when it darts toward the clownfish.
   D. The clownfish chases away fish that might eat the anemones.

4. Reread the definitions in the chart. Which animal mentioned in the article has a parasitic relationship with another animal?

A. Clownfish

B. Shrimp

C. Ratel

D. Tick

5. According to the article, an unlikely couple can form a relationship that helps both partners. Which two species described in the selection best illustrate that idea?

A. Tick and antelope

B. Tapeworm and pig

C. Trumpetfish and soft coral

D. Plover and crocodile

6. Which detail helps you understand the main idea of the article?

A. The honeyguide bird and the ratel both live on grasslands in Africa.

B. Many animals survive in the wild by living together in flocks or herds.

C. Crocodiles have long snouts with sharp teeth that are difficult to clean.

D. The cleaner shrimp enjoys a meal while removing harmful creatures from a fish.

7. What is the best summary of paragraph 7?

A. Many animals live together in groups of their own species, such as flockes, herds, or schools.

B. The stronger animals survive in the wild by living alone.

C. Wild animal behavior is difficult to predict and often makes little sense.

D. Animals use different survival strategies, including teaming up with unlikely partners.

8. The relationship between the clownfish and the sea anemone supports the idea that —

A. a few animals form partnerships to have fun together

B. in some symbiotic relationships, both animals benefit from forming a partnership

C. animals that form partnerships survive better than those who get by on their own

D. in some symbiotic relationships, one animal meets its needs but hurts its partner

9. Reread the caption with the antelope photograph. Under which subheading would you add a paragraph about the antelope and the oxpecker bird?

A. Keeping Clean

B. Sweet Success

C. Clowning Around

D. A Different Way of Life

SHORT CONSTRUCTED RESPONSE
Write two or three sentences to answer this question.

10. Choose an animal pair from either photograph. Where would you place that pair in the chart: under mutualism, commensalisms, or parasitism? Explain your answer.

Write a paragraph to answer this question.

11. Summarize the key points presented in the chart. Give one example of each type of symbiotic interaction to support your answer.

GO ON

Vocabulary

| Use context clues to answer the following questions. |

1. What does the word *symbiotic* mean in paragraph 1?

   "Some animals form a close partnership with other kinds of animals. These pairings are called <u>symbiotic</u> relationships."

   A. Staying alert in danger

   B. Competing for food

   C. Acting in an aggressive way

   D. Having a close association

2. What does the word *stunned* mean in paragraph 6?

   "The <u>stunned</u> fish is then pulled into the sea anemone's hidden mouth."

   A. Astonished   C. Confused

   B. Bored   D. Paralyzed

3. What does the word *various* mean in paragraph 7?

   "They make the most of their <u>various</u> differences."

   A. Changing   C. Extreme

   B. Consistent   D. Many

4. What does the word *edible* mean in the caption with the clownfish photograph?

   "They lure <u>edible</u> fish into the anemone's deadly tentacles and chase away harmful ones."

   A. Hungry   C. Pleasant tasting

   B. Injured   D. Safe to eat

5. What does the word *creatures* mean in paragraph 3?

   "That can include dead skin, tiny pieces of food, and wee <u>creatures</u> that can hurt the fish."

   A. Domestic animals

   B. Living organisms

   C. Imaginary beings

   D. Artistic life forms

6. What does the word *reproduce* mean as it is used to describe the bee-pollen interaction in the chart?

   ". . . they spread pollen that the flowers need to <u>reproduce</u>."

   A. Do something again

   B. Imitate an action

   C. Begin a process

   D. Generate offspring

7. What does the word *predators* mean as it is used to describe the aphid-ant interaction in the chart?

   ". . . ants protect aphids from <u>predators</u>."

   A. Organisms that live by hunting or catching others

   B. Animals that lived before humans existed

   C. Those that make their presence known in advance

   D. Groups that help each other survive

Revising and Editing

DIRECTIONS Read this passage and answer the questions that follow.

(1) Margaret Bourke-White received her first camera when she was 17. (2) Over the next decades, she would go on to become a renowned photojournalist. (3) During the Great Depression, Bourke-White photographed the South. (4) Her haunting images captured the people and the land and appeared in the book *You Have Seen Their Faces*. (5) When World War II began Bourke-White became the first accredited female war correspondent. (6) She photographed many significant events as she traveled in combat zones. (7) After the war was over Bourke-White spent time in India, Korea, and South Africa. (8) Her photos informed many about the people, the land, and the leaders of those countries.

1. Choose the BEST way to punctuate sentence 1 with a comma.

   A. Margaret Bourke-White, received her first camera when she was 17.

   B. Margaret Bourke-White received her first camera, when she was 17.

   C. Margaret Bourke-White received her first camera when she was 17.

   D. Margaret Bourke-White received her first camera when, she was 17.

2. Choose the BEST way to punctuate sentence 5 with a comma.

   A. When World War II began Bourke-White became the first, accredited female war correspondent.

   B. When World War II began, Bourke-White became the first, accredited female war correspondent.

   C. When World War II began Bourke-White became the first accredited female war correspondent.

   D. When World War II began, Bourke-White became the first accredited female war correspondent.

3. Choose the BEST way to punctuate sentence 6 with a comma.

   A. She photographed many significant events, as she traveled in combat zones.

   B. She photographed many, significant events, as she traveled in combat zones.

   C. She photographed many, significant events as she traveled in combat zones.

   D. She photographed many significant events as she traveled in combat zones.

4. Choose the BEST way to punctuate sentence 7 with a comma.

   A. After the war was over Bourke-White spent time in India, Korea, and South Africa.

   B. After the war was over, Bourke-White spent time in India Korea, and South Africa.

   C. After the war was over, Bourke-White spent time in India, Korea, and South Africa.

   D. After the war was over, Bourke-White spent time in India, Korea, and, South Africa.

STOP

More Great Reads

Ideas for Independent Reading

Which questions from Unit 8 made an impression on you?
Continue exploring them with these books.

COMMON CORE

RL 10 Read and comprehend literature. **RI 10** Read and comprehend literary nonfiction.

What is your dream job?

Dare to Dream! 25 Extraordinary Lives
by *Sandra McLeod Humphrey*

Some of the world's most famous athletes, scientists, artists, and politicians had to overcome serious obstacles to achieve success. This book tells the real-life stories of people who beat the odds.

Come Back to Afghanistan: A California Teenager's Story
by *Said Hyder Akbar and Susan Burton*

After the fall of the Taliban government, Said and his father returned to Afghanistan. Said tells what it was like to be a teenager working to rebuild a country.

Stonecutter
by *Leander Watts*

It's 1835, and 14-year-old Albion is learning to be a stonecutter. His big break comes when he's hired to do the stonework at a new estate. When he gets there, he finds a creepy, half-finished mansion. Something isn't right.

Why do people seek danger?

Mortal Engines
by *Philip Reeve*

What could an assassin, a third-class historian, and a rich man's daughter ever have in common? They are all teenagers who are willing to risk their safety to solve the mystery that threatens to destroy the world.

Eragon
by *Christopher Paolini*

Eragon lives a quiet life on a farm until he finds a dragon's egg. After it hatches, Eragon's peaceful childhood comes to a violent end. He realizes it's his fate to become a dragon rider and join in the war against the evil King Galbatorix.

The Gadget
by *Paul Zindel*

Thirteen-year-old Stephen escapes war-torn London to live with his father, who is a scientist on a secret military base in New Mexico. Stephen is determined to learn all he can about the "gadget" his father is working on, but at what price?

What does music say about us?

The Black Canary
by *Jane Louise Curry*

James's parents think he will become a musician like them, but that is the one thing he knows he doesn't want. His opinion changes when he finds a portal to another time. He's stuck in the 1600s, and he can't go home until he develops his musical gifts.

Mountain Solo
by *Jeanette Ingold*

Tess is a violin prodigy, but after a disastrous concert she vows to give up music. She goes to live with her dad and his new wife in Montana. Can the mystery surrounding a young musician from the pioneer days help her figure out her own truth?

This Land Was Made for You and Me: The Life and Songs of Woody Guthrie
by *Elizabeth Partridge*

Woody Guthrie was a songwriter who traveled the country, singing about people struggling to get by. His own life was difficult, too, but he inspired people from many generations.

Get Novel Wise THINK central

Go to **thinkcentral.com**.
KEYWORD: HML8-978

UNIT

State
Your Case

ARGUMENT AND
PERSUASION

- In Nonfiction
- In Media
- In Literature

979

Whom can you BELIEVE?

As soon as you wake up in the morning, you're surrounded by people, groups, and corporations trying to influence the way you think or act. To persuade you to buy a brand of shoes, a company runs an ad showing a great athlete wearing the same pair as he sinks a jump shot. To encourage you to sell T-shirts for a fundraiser, the class president starts the morning announcements by offering a prize to the student who sells the most. Meanwhile, a friend begs you to work with her instead of with your usual partner. How can you be sure you're doing what's best for you?

ACTIVITY Think about a time when an advertisement persuaded you to buy a product. What influenced your decision to believe that company's claims? Consider the following questions:

• Were you familiar with that company's products?

• What did the advertisement tell you that you did not hear from competing companies' ads?

• Did the company use statistics, celebrity endorsements, or other persuasive techniques to convince you to buy its product?

Find It Online! **THINK** central

Go to **thinkcentral.com** for the interactive version of this unit.

Preview Unit Goals

TEXT ANALYSIS	• Compare arguments in persuasive texts • Identify and analyze persuasive techniques • Analyze reasoning for soundness • Determine an author's purpose • Analyze comparisons and contrasts • Analyze rhetoric • Evaluate the argument in a text • Evaluate evidence for relevance and sufficiency
WRITING AND LANGUAGE	• Write a persuasive essay • Use parallelism to link related ideas • Use punctuation marks correctly
SPEAKING AND LISTENING	• Present a persuasive speech
VOCABULARY	• Use Greek or Latin roots as clues to the meanings of words • Use antonyms as context clues to determine word meaning
ACADEMIC VOCABULARY	• accurate • bias • contrast • convince • logic
MEDIA AND VIEWING	• Analyze and evaluate an ad campaign • Recognize persuasive techniques in media messages

Media Smart DVD-ROM

Believing the Buzz

Examine a movie trailer and posters from the *Star Wars* series to explore how ad campaigns hook you. **Page 1000**

Elements of Persuasive Text

Persuasive messages are everywhere—on buses, billboards, the Web, even cereal boxes. Some tell you what to wear or buy. Others even tell you what to think. So, how do you figure out which ones to believe? You begin by breaking these texts down into their basic elements. Then you examine those elements closely.

○ **COMMON CORE**

Included in this workshop:
RI 1 Cite the textual evidence that supports an analysis of what the text says explicitly.
RI 6 Determine an author's point of view or purpose in a text and analyze how the author acknowledges and responds to conflicting evidence or viewpoints. **RI 8** Delineate and evaluate the argument and specific claims in a text, assessing whether the reasoning is sound and the evidence is relevant and sufficient.

Part 1: The Argument

The word *argument* doesn't always refer to two people having a disagreement. In formal speaking and writing, an **argument** is a claim supported by reasons and evidence. Sound arguments appeal to logic, not to emotions. A strong argument

- presents a **claim,** or the writer's position on a problem or an issue. The claim is often based on a **premise**, or general principle, that most readers would readily agree is true. For example, "Most people want to make a difference" is probably a valid premise.

- provides **support,** or the reasons and evidence that back up the claim. Evidence can include facts, statistics, examples, and quotations from experts.

- anticipates objections that people with the opposing viewpoint might raise and attempts to answer those objections with **counterarguments.**

Look closely at the elements of an argument in this poster.

❶ **Claim:** The subtitle of the poster implies its claim: You want to make a difference, so you should volunteer.

❷ **Support 1:** Giving a few hours of your time will build a stronger community.

❸ **Support 2:** Volunteering will make you feel good and become a better person.

❹ Notice that an opposing viewpoint is addressed and countered: No effort is a wasted effort.

ONE PERSON CAN MAKE A DIFFERENCE!

❶ *Want to make a difference? Volunteer!*

❷ **Public service builds a stronger community.** Consider volunteering a couple of hours each week—as a tutor, activities leader, or coach—to help others.

❸ **Serving others will give you a sense of self-satisfaction.** You'll also grow as an individual. Come see what you can do.

❹ **Don't let anyone convince you that one person can't make a difference.** No effort is a wasted effort!

MODEL: ARGUMENT IN TEXT

The author of this essay makes a case against junk food by focusing on one example. As you read this excerpt, try to identify the author's claim. What reasons and evidence does he provide as support for his position?

from **Why Can't I Live on**
French Fries?

Essay by **Richard J. Roberts**

So what's so bad about stuffing yourself with nothing but French fries all the time, anyway? Simple: Pretty soon you'll be missing important nutrients. Let's start with vitamins. The body does not need much of them, but in most cases, it cannot produce them. Potatoes contain mostly vitamin C and hardly
5 any other vitamin. No vitamin K, for example, which is needed to form a scab when you're bleeding so that the bleeding stops. And no vitamin A, needed for the eyes to function properly. Not enough vitamin A, and you'll see even less well at night than everyone else. Over the long run, a lack of vitamin A can even cause blindness. Many children in Africa suffer from it.
10 If you were to eat only French fries, your teeth would also slowly go bad and your bones would become brittle. That's because potatoes do not contain enough calcium, and your bones need calcium throughout your life, not just while you're growing. Besides, all those mountains of fries would overload you with sodium, because they're often too salty, and salt contains sodium.
15 It's important that your body maintain a good sodium balance, because otherwise, it can't regulate its body temperature very well, but too much sodium causes high blood pressure in some people.

French fries also contain little protein. Proteins are critical. They are the true bearers of life. The cells from which most living creatures are built consist
20 mostly of proteins. Without proteins, for example, you would not have any muscles. . . .

We chemists and doctors still know far too little about nutrition and its effects on health. This is why every person has to find out for him- or herself what's good for each. But one thing I can guarantee: You'll get into trouble
25 if you always eat nothing but French fries. By the way, I myself would love to wolf down French fries every day. But I, too, have to restrain myself and should stick to the advice that I've given you here.

Close Read

1. Reread the title and lines 1–2. What is the author's claim?

2. In the boxed lines, the author explains that a person needs vitamins that are not found in French fries. What examples does he use to support this reason?

3. In lines 10–21, the author offers three other reasons to support his claim. Restate these reasons in your own words.

4. What does the author do in the last paragraph to strengthen his argument?

Part 2: Persuasive Techniques

An argument is the logical part of a persuasive text, but writers often use more than logic to persuade. They also rely on **persuasive techniques** such as appeals to people's needs, values, and feelings. How many of the persuasive techniques on the following chart have influenced you at one time or another?

PERSUASIVE TECHNIQUES	EXAMPLES
Bandwagon Appeal Taps into people's desire to belong	▶ Millions of teens have made City Jeanz part of their wardrobe. What are you waiting for?
Ethical Appeal Tries to gain moral support for a claim by linking the claim to a widely accepted value	▶ If you believe that every child deserves a good education, support the Great Minds Organization.
Appeal to Fear Makes people feel as if their safety, security, or health is in danger	▶ How clean are the hotel rooms you're staying in? You'll be shocked by what our documentary reveals.
Appeal to Pity Taps into people's compassion for others	▶ For the cost of one cup of coffee a day, you could save a life.
Loaded Terms Uses words with strongly positive or negative connotations to stir people's emotions	▶ The alley next to the parking lot is dark and dangerous. Vote to increase the number of street lamps in our neighborhood. Residents deserve to feel safe and protected.

To avoid being influenced by persuasive techniques, look for them. At the same time, also watch out for rhetorical and logical fallacies.

A **rhetorical fallacy** is speech or writing that is false or misleading. For example, it's misleading to describe a corrupt politician as "just an average guy."

A **logical fallacy** is an error in reasoning. "Either I watch TV, or I have nothing to do" is an error in reasoning because it is based on the false assumption that there are only two choices in a situation that really offers more options. Many logical fallacies start with such **false assumptions**, or mistaken beliefs.

Finally, examine the premise—the general principle on which the writer's claim is based—to make sure it's really true. An argument founded on an incorrect premise is flawed from the start. Unfortunately, writers don't always state their premises. Can you spot the claim that is founded on an incorrect premise?

Claim 1: If you don't volunteer, you will never get into a good college.
Claim 2: If you don't volunteer, you'll miss out on a potentially great experience.

Claim 1 is based on the incorrect premise, which is that only people who volunteer get into good colleges.

MODEL 1: PERSUASION IN TEXT

This article challenges the positive concept of competition. What techniques does the author use to persuade you to adopt her position?

from
Against Competition

Newspaper article by **Gayle Heaney**

Our society uses sports metaphors for almost every aspect of life: Gear up, go for the goal, score one for the team! But studies show that the competitive spirit we admire can also have negative effects on a person—especially if the pressure to compete is instilled at a young age.

5   Young children often place excessive value on how they perform and can be emotionally devastated if they fail. Consider, for example, if a boy feels pressured to succeed in a particular sport. If he is unable to improve his skills, his self-esteem will disintegrate. If anyone criticizes his performance, he magnifies the criticism and views himself as a failure in everything.

10   In adults, competition can cause a person's stress levels to skyrocket. High stress levels can have damaging and dangerous consequences because they often lead to high blood pressure or to uncontrollable outbursts of anger. Road rage is turning our nation's highways into battlefields. Sports events often turn into violent fistfights, either on the field or in the crowd.

15   Is this the kind of behavior we should be modeling for our children?

Close Read

1. Notice the highlighted examples of loaded language in the boxed sentence. Find two other examples of loaded language.

2. Reread lines 10–15. To which emotion is the author appealing?

MODEL 2: PERSUASION IN ADVERTISING

Persuasion is a key factor in the advertisements you see on television, in magazines, and on product packaging. What techniques do you notice in this promotional poster?

ANNUAL SPORTS CHALLENGE:
June 20–26

Do *you* have what it takes
to be a champion? Let us show you.

"I DIDN'T HAVE THE NERVE TO TRY OUT FOR THE SOCCER TEAM LAST YEAR. BUT THE SPORTS CHALLENGE PROGRAM HELPED ME BUILD MY SKILLS IN A FUN, CHALLENGING ENVIRONMENT. NOW I HAVE THE CONFIDENCE I NEED TO COMPETE—AND SUCCEED."

JEANNIE, AGE 14

Close Read

1. This poster uses a **testimonial**—the persuasive technique of relying on the backing of a celebrity, an expert, or a satisfied customer to be convincing. Who makes this testimonial?

2. Describe the intended effect of the poster on readers.

Part 3: Analyze the Text

Now you'll apply what you've learned in this workshop as you analyze two texts—an editorial and a poster. Both texts are about the legal driving age. As you read each text, try to identify the claim, the support, and any persuasive techniques that are used. Also analyze the premise of each claim to make sure it is really true.

Should the Driving Age Be Raised to 18?

NO!

Editorial by **Alex Koroknay-Palicz**
National Youth Rights Association

If your neighbor robs a bank, should you go to jail? No. If your classmate gets in an accident, should your driver's license be taken away? Of course not. Neither situation is fair. Raising the driving age will punish all young drivers for the mistakes of a few of their peers.

5   In this country we live by the principle of innocent until proven guilty. Those who want to raise the driving age have labeled teens guilty before they've gotten in an accident or before they've even stepped into a car. They believe that just because of your birth date, you are dangerous and must be punished by having your ability to drive taken from you.

10   Those who favor raising the driving age say that statistics show teenagers are more likely to get into accidents than adults. What they don't say is that statistics also show that men of all ages are 77 percent more likely to kill someone while driving than women. If people want to save lives by raising the driving age, then how about saving lives by allowing only women to drive?

15   Except raising the driving age won't save lives. Studies show that it is inexperience, not age, that causes accidents. Raising the driving age will just create inexperienced, accident-prone drivers at 18 instead of 16.

Teens need the ability to drive just as much as anyone else—to get to school, to get to work, to get to sports or band practice, or just to go out with

20   their friends. Cars are necessary for mobility in this country. Taking that away is a large disruption to the lives of teenagers—for no good reason.

Close Read

1. The title tells you which side of the issue the author falls on, but the claim of his argument is stated in the first paragraph. What is the author's claim?

2. What reasons and evidence does the author provide as support for his claim?

3. The author presents an opposing viewpoint in the boxed lines. In your own words, restate his response to this opposition.

4. Would most readers readily agree with the premise stated in line 20, or is it an incorrect premise? Explain.

The creators of this public-service poster offer a different viewpoint on the same issue. What techniques are used to get you to see their side?

Support Bill 543 to raise the driving age and cut down on needless accidents.

How many more teens need to suffer before we admit that we are putting them behind the wheel too soon? And who's to say you won't be the next victim of an inexperienced teenage driver?

Close Read

1. Examine the text and photograph used in this ad. To which emotion does this ad appeal?

2. Think critically about the premise of this ad: Younger drivers have more accidents than older drivers do. Is this premise correct? Why or why not?

3. Both the editorial and the public-service poster present a position on whether the legal age for driving a car should be raised, but they do so very differently. Identify two major differences in their treatment of the issue.

Zoos: Myth and Reality
Online Article by Rob Laidlaw

Zoos Connect Us to the Natural World
Opinion Piece by Michael Hutchins

VIDEO TRAILER THiNK central KEYWORD: HML8-988

Should WILDLIFE stay wild?

COMMON CORE

RI 1 Cite the textual evidence that supports an analysis of what the text says explicitly. **RI 6** Determine an author's point of view or purpose in a text and analyze how the author acknowledges and responds to conflicting evidence or viewpoints. **RI 8** Evaluate the argument and specific claims in a text, assessing whether the reasoning is sound. **RI 9** Identify where texts disagree on matters of interpretation.

Close your eyes and picture an elephant. Are you picturing it in the zoo or in the wild? As humans inhabit more and more of the earth's land, some species of wildlife are more likely to be found in captivity than in their natural habitat. But is this a good thing? The writers of the selections you're about to read have different views on whether or not zoos are good for humans and animals.

LIST IT With a group, make a list of the good things and bad things about zoos. Do the pros outnumber the cons, or vice versa? Tell whether you think zoos are a good idea.

Pros	Cons
1. They keep animals safe.	1.
2.	2.

● **TEXT ANALYSIS: ARGUMENT**

As you just learned, effective arguments deliver

• a **claim**, or the writer's position on an issue or problem

• **support**, or reasons and evidence that back up the claim.

They also often contain **counterarguments**, arguments made to disprove an opposing viewpoint. For example, the first selection you will read begins by summarizing the zoo industry's argument for having and maintaining zoos, and then argues against it.

As you read each selection, look for the elements of their arguments. Then ask yourself whether the writer's argument is strong enough and broad enough to adequately support the writer's conclusion.

● **READING SKILL: SET A PURPOSE FOR READING**

When you **set a purpose** for reading, you decide what you want to accomplish as you read. In this lesson, your purpose is to compare and contrast two persuasive texts that reach different conclusions about the same topic. Filling in a chart like the one begun here can help. Use line numbers to tell where the elements are.

	"Zoos: Myth and Reality"	*"Zoos Connect Us to the Natural World"*
Claim	lines 4–6: "Most zoos fail to live up to their own propaganda and vast numbers of zoo animals continue to endure lives of misery and deprivation."	
Support		
Conclusion		

▲ **VOCABULARY IN CONTEXT**

In your Reader/Writer Notebook, write a sentence for each of the vocabulary words. Use a dictionary or the definitions in the following selection pages to help you.

WORD LIST		
counterpart	exploit	propaganda
deprivation	futility	sterile
exotic	languish	

Complete the activities in your **Reader/Writer Notebook.**

Rob Laidlaw
born 1959

Wildlife Guardian
Rob Laidlaw has dedicated himself to improving the conditions of animals in captivity. He is co-founder and Executive Director of Zoocheck Canada, an animal protection charity. Laidlaw has inspected close to 1,000 zoos, circuses, and wildlife displays throughout Canada and the United States. He has worked with Canada's government on establishing standards for zoos. Laidlaw also worked on developing a humane stray dog program, and he investigated Canada's role in the international pet reptile trade. Laidlaw shares his knowledge about animals through writing. He has published articles about all kinds of wildlife, from wild horses and polar bears to the red-eared slider and the black rhino.

Michael Hutchins
born 1951

Animal Caretaker
As the executive director of The Wildlife Society, Michael Hutchins has traveled to more than 33 countries. His efforts have involved trapping and tagging mountain goats in the Olympic Mountains, scuba diving with manta rays, and tracking jaguars. He has published many articles, books, and reports on the relationships between animals and their environments and on conservation.

Authors Online
Go to **thinkcentral.com**. KEYWORD: HML8-989

THINK central

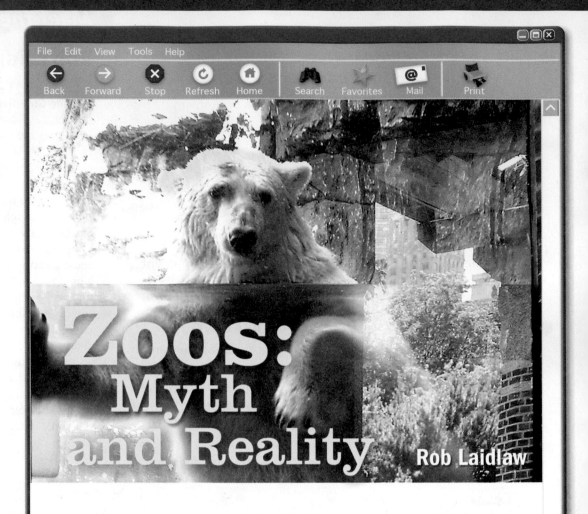

Zoos: Myth and Reality
Rob Laidlaw

propaganda
(prŏp′ə-găn′də) *n.* information that supports a certain cause

deprivation
(dĕp′rə-vā′shən) *n.* the condition of not having one's needs met; a lack of

Ⓐ ARGUMENT
According to Laidlaw, what three benefits do many zoos say they offer? What does Laidlaw claim instead?

In recent years, zoos have become the target of intense public scrutiny and criticism. In response, many have tried to repackage themselves as institutions devoted to wildlife conservation, public education, and animal welfare. But most zoos fail to live up to their own **propaganda** and vast numbers of zoo animals continue to endure lives of misery and **deprivation. Ⓐ**

Nearly every zoo, from the smallest amateur operation to the largest professional facilities, claims to be making important contributions to conservation, usually through participation in endangered species captive 10 propagation initiatives and public education programming. The zoo world buzzword[1] of the moment is "conservation."

Yet, with an estimated 10,000 organized zoos worldwide, representing tens of thousands of human workers and billions of dollars in operating budgets, only a tiny percentage allocate the resources necessary to

---

1. **buzzword:** a word or phrase connected with a specialized field or group that sounds important or technical and is usually used to impress those outside the group.

File Edit View Tools Help

Back Forward Stop Refresh Home Search Favorites Mail Print

participate in captive propagation initiatives, and fewer still provide any real support for the *in situ*[2] protection of wildlife and their natural habitat.

So far, the record on reintroductions to the wild is dismal. Only 16 species have established self-sustaining populations in the wild as a result of captive breeding efforts, and most of those programs were
20 initiated by government wildlife agencies—not zoos. The contribution of zoos in this regard has been minimal, and often involves supplementing existing wild populations with a small number of captive-born individuals who are ill-prepared for life in the wild. **B**

As the **futility** of captive breeding as a major conservation tool becomes evident to those in the industry, many zoos are now turning to education to justify themselves. Yet, zoos claim that they teach visitors about wildlife conservation and habitat protection, and their contention that they motivate members of the public to become directly involved in wildlife conservation work doesn't stand up to scrutiny. The truth is
30 that scant empirical evidence exists to prove that the primary vehicle for education in most zoos—the animal in the cage—actually teaches anyone anything. In fact, viewing animals in cages may be counterproductive educationally by conveying the wrong kinds of messages to the public. Also, the legions[3] of conservationists that zoos should have produced, if their claims were true, have never materialized. **C**

Humane Treatment

But there is one issue about which there appears to be widespread agreement—at least in principle. So long as wild animals are kept in captivity, they ought to be treated humanely.

Studies have shown that animals can suffer physically, mentally, and
40 emotionally. For this reason, captive environments must be complex enough to compensate for the lack of natural freedom and choice, and they must facilitate expression of natural movement and behavior patterns. This principle has been widely espoused by the modern zoo community in various articles, books, and television documentaries. **D**

Yet despite the best of intentions or claims, most animals in zoos in North America are still consigned to lead miserable lives in undersized,

---

2. **in situ** (ĭn sē'tōō): a Latin phrase; in zoology, it refers to studying an animal without removing it from its natural habitat.

3. **legions** (lē'jənz): large numbers.

Internet

B ARGUMENT
Reread lines 17–23.
Identify the opinion and the facts. Do the facts support the author's opinion stated in line 17?

futility (fyoo-tĭl'ĭ-tē) *n.* uselessness

C ARGUMENT
Reread lines 26–35.
What **counterargument** does the author present to disprove the second benefit zoos say they offer?

D ARGUMENT
Reread lines 39–44.
What support does the author cite here? Explain whether this support is convincing to you.

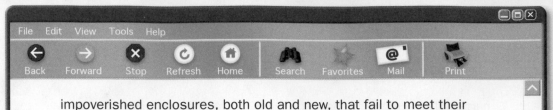
sterile (stĕr′əl) *adj.*
barren; lacking vitality

Language Coach

Figures of Speech When words are used to express something other than their usual meaning, they are called figures of speech. To draw attention to an inaccurate or misleading use of a word, a writer may put the word in quotation marks. Reread lines 53–54. According to Laidlaw, why is it misleading to use the term *advances* to describe recent changes in animal housing and husbandry?

ⓔ ARGUMENT
Reread lines 50–66. What part of the zoo industry's argument does Laidlaw oppose here? In which sentence does he say that this part of the industry's argument is false?

impoverished enclosures, both old and new, that fail to meet their biological and behavioral needs. Many in the zoo industry will bristle[4] at this statement and point to numerous improvements in the zoo field.
50   They'll claim they've shifted from menagerie-style[5] entertainment centers where animals were displayed in barred, **sterile,** biologically irrelevant cages, to kinder, gentler, more scientifically-based kinds of institutions.

But many of the "advances" in zoo animal housing and husbandry are superficial and provide little benefit to the animals. For example, the many new, heavily promoted, Arctic "art deco" polar bear exhibits that are springing up in zoos across the continent consistently ignore the natural biology and behavior of these animals. The artificial rockwork and hard floor surfaces typically resemble a Flintstones movie set more than the natural Arctic ice and tundra habitat of polar bears. These exhibits
60   are made for the public and dupe them into believing things are getting better. What they really achieve is more misery and deprivation.

In addition, many new exhibits are hardly larger than the sterile, barred cages of days gone by. And one look at the prison-like, off-display holding and service areas in most zoos, where many animals spend a good portion of their lives, is proof of the hypocrisy of zoo claims that things are better for the animals than they were in the past. **ⓔ**

Behind the Invisible Bars

If not all is well behind the invisible bars of North America's more luxurious zoos, a more transparent problem is found in the hundreds of substandard roadside zoos that dot the continent. These amateurish
70   operations fall far below any professional standard and do nothing but cause misery and death to thousands of animals.

My own investigations have revealed animals in visible distress lying unprotected from the full glare of the hot summer sun; primates in barren cages with no opportunity to climb; groups of black bears begging for marshmallows as they sit in stagnant moats of excrement-filled water, scarred and wounded from fighting; nocturnal[6] animals kept without shade or privacy; animals without water; and the list goes on and on.

---

4. **bristle** (brĭs′əl): to show annoyance or anger.
5. **menagerie** (mə-năj′ə-rē): a collection of live wild animals on display.
6. **nocturnal** (nŏk-tûr′nəl): habitually active at night and asleep during the daytime.

Internet

Many zoos, including those that meet industry guidelines, also annually produce a predictable surplus in animals that often end up in the hands of
80　private collectors, animal auctions, circuses and novelty acts, substandard zoos, and even "canned hunt" operations where they're shot as trophies.

A look at compliance with the zoo industry's own standards (which in the author's view do not necessarily constitute adequate standards) demonstrates how bad the situation really is. Of the estimated 200 public display facilities in Canada, only 26—slightly more than 10 percent—have been deemed to meet the standards of the Canadian Association of Zoos and Aquariums (CAZA).

In the U.S., out of the 1,800–2,000 licensed exhibitors of wild animals (which includes biomedical research institutions, breeding facilities, small
90　exhibitors, travelling shows, educational programs using live animals, zoos and aquariums), about 175 are accredited by the American Zoo and Aquarium Association (AZA), equivalent to less than 10 percent of all facilities. **F**

Times are changing, and with them, public attitudes. Increasingly, members of the public find the confinement of animals in substandard conditions offensive. Zoos across the continent are feeling the pressure. They have to accept that if wild animals are to be kept in captivity, their needs must be met.

Are there good captive environments where the biological and
100　behavioral needs of animals are being satisfied? The answer is yes. A recent Zoocheck Canada survey of black bear and gray wolf facilities in North America revealed a number of outstanding exhibits where the animals displayed an extensive range of natural movements and behaviors. But they are few and far between.

Can zoos make a useful contribution to conservation and education? Again, the answer is yes. The Durrell Wildlife Conservation Trust (Jersey Zoo) in the U.K., for example, clearly shows that zoos can become leaders in conservation education and wildlife protection. But few actually do.

I can't understand why the more responsible segments of the
110　zoo industry have not come to their senses and acknowledged the obvious—the present state of zoos is untenable. Either zoos can voluntarily adopt humane policies and practices, push for the closure of substandard facilities, and participate in advocating for laws to help wildlife, or they can be dragged kicking and screaming into the new millennium. It's their choice. **G**

F ARGUMENT
Laidlaw has disproved all three benefits that he says accredited zoos offer in their defense. Now he states that these zoos make up only 10 percent of "licensed exhibitors of wild animals." What does this fact help him support? For help, refer to his original claim in lines 4–6.

G ARGUMENT
Reread lines 111–115. Does the evidence Laidlaw has provided support the first part of his conclusion— that "the present state of zoos is untenable"? Does it support the approach toward zoos he recommends taking in the final part of his conclusion? Explain.

Zoos Connect Us to the Natural World

Michael Hutchins

The scene of Little Joe, the curious young gorilla out of his zoo exhibit wandering through Franklin Park,[1] certainly sold papers last month. But less well covered was the very real success that our nation's best zoos have had in nurturing the animals who live within their walls.

At the turn of the last century, gorillas—these strange, human-like creatures from "darkest Africa"—still flourished in the wild and thoroughly captivated the American public. But once relocated from their jungle habitat, gorillas **languished**. Zoos found it impossible to keep the animals alive for more than a few weeks since little was known about the natural history of gorillas. Even as late as the 1960s and '70s, most zoo gorillas were kept singly or in pairs in small, sterile concrete and tile cages and fed inappropriate foods. But things began to change as information from field and zoo biologists brought more understanding of both the physiological and psychological needs of these remarkable creatures.

Gorillas in today's zoos are typically kept in large, naturalistic exhibits, maintained in appropriate social groupings, fed nutritionally appropriate diets, and provided with excellent veterinary care. The result is that zoo gorillas exhibit behavior similar to their wild **counterparts,** reproduce consistently, and live longer on average than they do in nature.

In fact, recent advances in exhibit design, animal nutrition, genetic management, and veterinary medicine have revolutionized animal welfare and care in our zoos. Today, more than 90 percent of mammals housed in accredited[2] facilities were born in zoos and not taken from the wild. They are under the charge of animal curators and caretakers who are trained professionals, with both academic and practical experience. Furthermore, accredited zoos have

---

1. **Franklin Park:** a Boston, Massachusetts, park that has a zoo in it.

2. **accredited** (ə-krĕd'ĭt-əd): meeting certain standards that have been set by a respected authority (in this case, the American Zoo and Aquarium Association).

994   UNIT 9: ARGUMENT AND PERSUASION

ARGUMENT
Based on the title, what is one reason Hutchins will probably give for having and maintaining good zoos?

ARGUMENT
Reread lines 1–8. What point is Hutchins making here?

languish (lăng'gwĭsh) *v.* to lose strength and vitality

counterpart (koun'tər-pärt') *n.* one that has the same functions and traits as another

ARGUMENT
How does Hutchins support the statement that zoos have had some very real successes in nurturing animals?

◀ **Analyze Visuals**
What **conclusions** can you draw about the impact this encounter might have on the girl?

become "learning organizations" that constantly strive to improve the lives and health of the animals
60 in their care.

So why should we have gorillas or any other wild animals in zoos today? Before speculating about the role of these institutions in contemporary society, I must first draw a distinction between accredited zoos and other kinds of facilities that keep wild animals for public display. All of my statements
70 are focused exclusively on the 213 facilities accredited by the American Zoo and Aquarium Association. AZA members undergo a detailed peer-review[3] process, which is more comprehensive than existing local, state, or federal regulations.

At a time when children learn more about the world around them

from television and computers
80 than from personal experience, modern zoos—and aquariums, for that matter—offer fun, safe opportunities to view living wild animals up close and personal. In 2002, over 140 million people visited AZA zoos and aquariums, more than attended all professional baseball, football, basketball, and ice hockey games combined.
90 Modern zoological parks provide us a wonderful opportunity to build awareness and appreciation of wildlife in an increasingly urbanized populace—a group that is becoming progressively disconnected from the natural world.

Only a small percentage of our nation's citizens can afford to travel to **exotic** locations to view wild
100 tigers, elephants, or giant pandas

Language Coach
Oral Fluency When saying the word *zoological*, pronounce the word part *zoo-* as two syllables that sound like *zoo-oh*. Practice this as you read aloud the sentence beginning in line 90.

exotic (ĭg-zŏt′ĭk) *adj.* foreign; unusual; exciting

---

3. **peer-review:** evaluation by equals (in this case, other zoo officials).

or to dive with sharks or moray eels. Zoos provide exhilarating experiences that can't be replicated on two-dimensional television or computer screens. Seeing, smelling, and in some cases even touching real, live animals is a powerful experience.

The best zoos include 110 conservation, education, and science among their core missions,[4] and the animals in their collections can be viewed as ambassadors for their counterparts in the wild. Many species are endangered or threatened and would have little chance of survival without human intervention. Increasingly, zoos are playing an important role in 120 those efforts. Last year alone, AZA member institutions supported 1,400 field conservation[5] and associated educational and scientific projects in over 80 countries worldwide. These ranged from restoring habitat for endangered Karner blue butterflies[6] in Ohio to attempting to curb the illegal, commercial 130 harvest of wildlife for meat in Africa to rehabilitating injured marine mammals and sea turtles and returning them to the sea.

Some critics have characterized zoos and aquariums as "**exploiting**" animals for personal financial gain, but that's not true of the professionals I know. As a curatorial intern at New York's Bronx Zoo/ 140 Wildlife Conservation Society in the late 1980s, I went on rounds with the staff veterinarians as they cared for sick and injured animals. They worked long hours for comparatively little pay, and their dedication was inspiring. I also witnessed animal keepers weeping over the loss of their favorite animals and spending their own money to 150 attend training programs to improve their knowledge and skills. **K**

In my opinion, a society that values wildlife and nature should support our best zoos and aquariums. Habitat conservation is the key to saving endangered species, and professionally managed zoos and aquariums and their expert, dedicated staffs play 160 a vital role by supporting on-the-ground conservation efforts and by encouraging people to care for and learn about wildlife and nature.

Zoos and aquariums are reinventing themselves, but while many are in the process of rebuilding their aging infrastructures, still others retain vestiges of the past or have been hit 170 hard by recent state or local budget cuts. Good zoos and aquariums are invaluable community assets, and they deserve our attention and enthusiastic support. **L**

---

4. **core missions:** central goals and beliefs.

5. **field conservation:** conservation of wild organisms in their natural habitats (not in zoos).

6. **Karner blue butterflies:** endangered butterflies of the northern U.S. and Canada.

K ARGUMENT
Reread lines 134–151. What opposing viewpoint does the author present? What is his **counterargument?**

exploit (ĕk'sploit') *v.* to use for selfish purposes

L ARGUMENT
Reread Hutchins's conclusion in lines 164–174. What kinds of zoos and aquariums does Hutchins propose we should give "our attention and enthusiastic support"? Is his argument broad enough to support this conclusion?

Comprehension

1. **Recall** According to "Zoos: Myth and Reality," what often happens to surplus animals from zoos?

2. **Recall** According to "Zoos Connect Us to the Natural World," how do zoos benefit people?

3. **Clarify** What kind of action does each author call for?

Text Analysis

● 4. **Identify Claim and Support** For each selection, identify the author's claim. Then list three reasons or pieces of evidence the author uses to support his claim.

● 5. **Evaluate Conclusions** Each selection reaches a conclusion about what zoos should do and how people should treat them. Identify each author's conclusion. Then tell whether you think it is adequately supported by his argument. Give reasons for your opinion.

Comparing Persuasive Texts

● 6. **Set a Purpose for Reading** Now that you have read the second persuasive text, finish filling in your chart. Add the final questions and answer them.

	"Zoos: Myth and Reality"	*"Zoos Connect Us to the Natural World"*
Claim	*lines 4–6: "Most zoos fail to live up to their own propaganda and vast numbers of zoo animals continue to endure lives of misery and deprivation."*	
Support		
Conclusion		
In what ways are the persuasive texts similar? In what ways are they different?		

Should WILDLIFE stay wild?

Refer to the list you made of the good and bad things about zoos. What might you add to this list now that you have read these two articles?

COMMON CORE

RI 1 Cite the textual evidence that supports an analysis of what the text says explicitly. **RI 6** Determine an author's point of view or purpose in a text and analyze how the author acknowledges and responds to conflicting evidence or viewpoints. **RI 8** Evaluate the argument and specific claims in a text, assessing whether the reasoning is sound. **RI 9** Identify where texts disagree on matters of interpretation.

Vocabulary in Context

▲ VOCABULARY PRACTICE

For each item, choose the word that differs most in meaning from the other words.

1. (a) suffer, (b) languish, (c) enjoy, (d) endure
2. (a) exploit, (b) aid, (c) help, (d) befriend
3. (a) hope, (b) uselessness, (c) futility, (d) meaninglessness
4. (a) unadorned, (b) desolate, (c) lush, (d) sterile
5. (a) suffering, (b) deprivation, (c) lack, (d) wealth
6. (a) persuasion, (b) truth, (c) propaganda, (d) bias
7. (a) boss, (b) equal, (c) peer, (d) counterpart
8. (a) ordinary, (b) exotic, (c) foreign, (d) extraordinary

ACADEMIC VOCABULARY IN WRITING

> • accurate • bias • contrast • convince • logic

What is your opinion of housing animals in zoos? In a paragraph, state your opinion along with two reasons you might give to **convince** someone to adopt it. Use at least one Academic Vocabulary word in your paragraph.

VOCABULARY STRATEGY: THE GREEK ROOT *exo*

The vocabulary word *exotic* contains the Greek root *exo,* which means "outside" or "external." You can use your understanding of this root along with context clues to help you to figure out the meaning of other words formed from *exo.*

PRACTICE Use a dictionary to look up each word that appears in the web. Then decide which word best completes each sentence. Be ready to explain how the meaning of the root is reflected in each word.

1. The earth's _____ protects it from much of the sun's ultraviolet radiation.
2. A peach's fuzzy _____ holds in the juicy fruit.
3. There was a mass _____ of fans from the stadium after the concert.
4. A beetle's _____ is like armor, protecting it from predators and weather.

COMMON CORE

L 4b Use Greek roots as clues to the meaning of a word.

Interactive Vocabulary THINK central

Go to **thinkcentral.com**.
KEYWORD: HML8-998

Writing for Assessment

COMMON CORE RI 1, RI 6, RI 8, RI 9, W 2, W 2b, W 2f

1. READ THE PROMPT

In writing assessments, you will often be asked to compare and contrast two works that are similar in some way, such as two persuasive texts about the same issue.

> In four or five paragraphs, compare and contrast the arguments in "Zoos: Myth and Reality" with "Zoos Connect Us to the Natural World." Identify the differences in their claims, the nature and strength of their support, and the effectiveness of their conclusions. Use details from the texts to support your ideas.

◄ **STRATEGIES IN ACTION**

1. I need to **identify** each **claim, support,** and **conclusion**.

2. I need to **state the differences** in their claims, the nature and strength of their support, and the strength and soundness of their conclusions.

3. I need to **support my ideas with details from the texts.**

2. PLAN YOUR WRITING

Use your chart to identify the claim, support, and conclusion presented in each text. Write a thesis statement that sums up their major differences. Then consider how to organize your response.

- **Option A:** In one paragraph, describe the claim, nature and strength of the support, and the effectiveness of the conclusion Laidlaw presents in his online article. In the next paragraph, describe the same aspects of Hutchins's opinion piece.

- **Option B:** In one paragraph, contrast each writer's claim. In the next paragraph, contrast their support for their claims. In a third, contrast the effectiveness of their conclusions.

Once you have decided on your approach, create an outline to organize your details.

I. Introduction
II. Claim, support, and conclusion in first article.
III. Claim, support, and conclusion in second piece.
IV. Conclusion

3. DRAFT YOUR RESPONSE

Introduction Provide the titles and authors of both texts, a brief description of each author's position, and your thesis statement.

Body Using your outline as a guide, contrast the claims, nature and strength of support, and effectiveness of the conclusions in the two texts. Include details from the texts to illustrate your statements.

Conclusion Restate your thesis statement, then leave your reader with a final thought about the arguments delivered in each of these texts. For example, you might draw a conclusion about which is the more persuasive text or ask a stirring question.

Revision Make sure you support your thesis statement with the ideas you develop in your body paragraphs and that you illustrate each idea with a detail from the text.

Movie Ad Campaign

Movie Advertisements on **Media ◗ Smart** DVD-ROM

How do ads create BUZZ?

····· COMMON CORE

RI 7 Evaluate the advantages and disadvantages of using different mediums (e.g., print or digital text, video) to present a particular topic or idea. **SL 2** Analyze the purpose of information presented in diverse media and formats (e.g., visually, quantitatively, orally) and evaluate the motives (e.g., social, commercial, political) behind its presentation.

Think about the last movie you just couldn't wait to see. How did you find out about it? Did you watch a preview that made it look exciting? Maybe you saw ads while surfing the Internet or passed billboards on the way to school. In this lesson, you'll explore how advertisers use these marketing techniques to build a sense of anticipation for an upcoming movie release.

Background

Coming Soon . . . Movie studios know that sometimes a commercial is not enough to persuade their target audience to see an upcoming film. They use a series of different types of ads to create excitement, so that not only will you run out to see the movie; you'll also tell your friends about it. In effect, you become part of the studio's ad campaign. This word of mouth is powerful, as people are more likely to trust the opinion of someone they know over the razzle-dazzle of a commercial. A movie is said to have **buzz** around it when it gets people excited enough to spread the word.

You'll look at advertisements for the movie *Star Wars: Episode III—Revenge of the Sith* to see how advertisers try to create buzz.

Media Literacy: Persuasion in Ads

An **ad campaign** is a series of advertisements for a single product or brand. The ads appear over time and in several different forms. Movie studios use carefully chosen visual and sound techniques in each ad to persuade their target audience. The image you see in a **print ad** should evoke the movie's mood as much as the music that plays in a **trailer.** Here are some of the print, trailer, and online advertisements that studios use.

FEATURES OF AN AD CAMPAIGN

Trailers are movie ads that usually appear a few months before the movie opens. They persuade viewers to see the movie by showing the most exciting, funny, or touching moments from the film.

Teaser Trailers are shorter, flashier trailers that come out long before the movie is released. They're designed to make you curious.

Print Ads include billboards, posters, magazine ads, and newspaper ads. Graphic artists and illustrators use images in print ads to give you information and to affect how you feel about a particular subject. For instance, the image of Darth Vader shown here is large, dark, and looming. Print ads can also persuade with a **tagline,** a memorable phrase that sums up the movie.

Promotional Web Sites often include trailers, cast and crew information, and games.

STRATEGIES FOR EVALUATING MOVIE ADS

Whether you're looking at a print ad, a trailer, or a promotional Web site, think about how the ad creates anticipation and excitement about the film.

- Determine the target audience. Think about who is most likely to see the movie and consider how the ad is directed at that group. For example, consider the tone and its level of formality. In your opinion, will an ad with this tone succeed with its target audience?
- Consider the visual and sound techniques used. Think about why each image or sound was chosen and the effect that each has on the viewer.
- Notice how the different ads work together to create an overall feeling about the film. The early ads are usually designed to spark curiosity. The later ads then build on that curiosity, providing more information about the film.

Viewing Guide for

Movie Ad Campaign

View the DVD to examine the ad campaign used for the movie *Star Wars: Episode III—Revenge of the Sith.* You'll examine a **teaser trailer,** a full-length **trailer,** and the visuals and words of **print ads.** As you look at each selection, consider how it attempts to persuade you to see and talk about the film. Jot down the impressions you get of the movie from each selection. Then think about the overall effect of the ad campaign. Use these questions to help you analyze it.

NOW VIEW

FIRST VIEWING: Comprehension

1. **Clarify** What do you learn about the plot of the movie from the **teaser?**

2. **Identify** According to the full-length **trailer,** who are the main characters in *Star Wars: Episode III?*

CLOSE VIEWING: Media Literacy

3. **Analyze Music** What effect does the music in the **teaser** have on you?

4. **Evaluate Images** What information do you get from the images on the **posters?** Which image do you think is strongest, and why? Based on the posters, what is your impression of the movie?

5. **Compare Trailers** Compare and contrast the **teaser** and the full-length **trailer.** How does your response to each differ?

6. **Interpret the Effect** Think about the effect the **ad campaign** may have had on potential moviegoers when the movie was released. Based on the materials you viewed, how do you think these people would have described the movie to their friends?

Write or Discuss

Evaluate the Ad Campaign You've explored how advertisers attempt to create buzz. Think about the ads you examined for *Star Wars: Episode III—Revenge of the Sith*. What parts of the ad campaign did you find effective? Write an opinion statement describing whether or not you think the ad campaign would create buzz among you and your friends today. Think about

- whether the **teaser trailer** sparks your curiosity
- the details you learn about the movie from the full-length **trailer**
- your overall impression of the movie from all of the selections you viewed

Produce Your Own Media

Create Your Own Ad Campaign Imagine your favorite short story or novel has just been made into a movie. You've been asked to plan an **ad campaign** that will get people buzzing about it. Working with one or two other students, draw **storyboards** for a **teaser trailer** and a full-length **trailer,** and draw a **poster** for the film.

HERE'S HOW Use these tips as you create your ad campaign:

- Remember that a storyboard is made up of drawings and brief descriptions of what happens in each shot.
- Think about the most exciting aspects of the story you choose. What will get people talking about the movie?
- For your poster, use an image that represents the overall feeling you want people to get from the film.
- Consider what music you want to play during your teaser trailer.

STUDENT MODEL

Media Tools THINK central

Go to **thinkcentral.com**.
KEYWORD: HML8-1003

Tech Tip

If a camera is available, take photos of classmates dressed as characters and use a computer graphics program to create your poster.

Position on Dodgeball in Physical Education
Position Statement by the National Association
for Sport and Physical Education

The Weak Shall Inherit the Gym
Opinion Piece by Rick Reilly

VIDEO TRAILER **THiNK** central KEYWORD: HML8-1004

Are all GAMES worth playing?

Games are supposed to be fun, right? But have you ever watched a customer at a carnival game spend 20 or 30 dollars trying to win a cheap stuffed animal? Seeing this might make you question not only how fun it is, but also whether or not all games are worth playing. You're about to read two very different opinions on whether the game of dodgeball is fun or torture for those who play it.

LIST IT Work with a group to make two lists. On the first, list five or more games you think are worth playing. On the second, list five or more games you think are not worth the time, money, or risk. Compare your lists with others'. Were there any games that appeared on both the good and not-so-good lists?

● TEXT ANALYSIS: PERSUASION

Writers often rely on more than arguments to be convincing. They may use a tone that encourages readers to take their side or use **persuasive techniques** such as these:

- **Emotional appeals**—the use of words, descriptions, or images that call forth strong feelings, such as pity, fear, or anger. "Innocent puppies are horribly mistreated in puppy mills."

- **Ethical appeals**—attempts to gain moral support for a claim by linking the claim to a widely accepted value. "We need this law because animals deserve decent treatment."

As you read, notice the ways the authors try to convince you.

● READING SKILL: ANALYZE RHETORIC AND REASONING

When reading an argument, look for fallacies. A **rhetorical fallacy** is writing that is false or misleading. A **logical fallacy** is an error in reasoning. Here are three common fallacies:

- **Loaded terms**—words or phrases with strongly positive or negative connotations. Using *immature* to describe a teenager casts the person in a more negative light than using *young*.

- **Leading questions**—questions that contain their answers, such as, "You don't want all the forests to disappear, do you?"

- **Caricatures**—cartoon-like portrayals of opposing arguments, such as, "They want you to go around hugging trees."

As you read the selections, jot down any fallacies you find and note their locations with the text's line numbers on a chart.

	"Position on Dodgeball in Physical Education"	*"The Weak Shall Inherit the Gym"*
Fallacies	*Loaded terms: lines 47–49*	

▲ VOCABULARY IN CONTEXT

The boldfaced words help to convey opinions about playing dodgeball. Try to figure out each word's meaning.

1. If you witness someone cheating, report the **impropriety.**
2. Students are not **adequately** prepared for competition.
3. We were able to **eliminate** the other players one by one.
4. Is dodgeball a safe way to take out **aggression?**
5. The school is going to **ban** the game.

Complete the activities in your **Reader/Writer Notebook.**

Meet the Author

Rick Reilly
born 1958

Funny Man with Serious Talent
Many *Sports Illustrated* readers turn to the last page of their magazine first in order to read Rick Reilly's weekly column "Life of Reilly." The column, along with his novels and essay collections, has earned Reilly the reputation as "one of the funniest humans on the planet." Reilly has written about everything from ice-skating to the Iditarod, the Alaskan dog race. His adventures include facing fastballs from eight-time All-Star pitcher Nolan Ryan, cycling with seven-time Tour de France winner Lance Armstrong, and playing 108 holes of golf in one day. He began his sports writing career as a sophomore at the University of Colorado, taking phoned-in high-school volleyball scores for his hometown newspaper. After graduation, he moved on to stints at the *Denver Post* and the *Los Angeles Times*, eventually landing at *Sports Illustrated* in 1985. He has been voted National Sportswriter of the Year 10 times.

National Association for Sport and Physical Education
The NASPE is made up of gym teachers, coaches, athletic directors, athletic trainers, sport management professionals, researchers, and college faculty. The association provides a way for all of these professionals to help one another to improve physical education in schools. By researching, developing standards, and spreading information, NASPE helps students learn about fitness and stay active all their lives.

Author Online
THINK central

Go to **thinkcentral.com.**
KEYWORD: HML8-1005

Position on Dodgeball in Physical Education

National Association for Sport and Physical Education

With the recent release of both a movie and television show about dodgeball, debate about the game's merits and **improprieties** has escalated in the media and on the NASPE listserv.[1] Thus, the National Association for Sport and Physical Education (NASPE) would like to reiterate its position about including dodgeball in school physical education programs. ◆

NASPE believes that dodgeball is **not** an appropriate activity for K–12 school physical education programs. The purpose of physical education is to provide students with:

- The knowledge, skills, and confidence needed to be physically active for a lifetime
- A daily dose of physical activity for health benefits
- Positive experiences so that kids want to be physically active outside of physical education class and throughout their lifetime

The goals of physical education can be obtained through a wide variety of appropriate physical activities. **A**

Getting and keeping children and adolescents active is one of the biggest challenges facing parents and youth leaders.

- 61.5% of children aged 9–13 years do not participate in any organized physical activity during their non-school hours and 22.6% do not engage in any free-time physical activity.
- One-third of high school students are not **adequately** active and over 10% do not participate in any physical activity at all.
- 16% of U.S. youth aged 6–19 are overweight—triple the proportion of 25 years ago. **B**

According to NASPE's *Appropriate Practices for Elementary School Physical Education* (2000), "in a quality physical education class teachers involve ALL children in activities that allow them to participate actively, both physically and mentally. Activities such as relay races, dodgeball, and

---

1. **listserv** (lĭst-sûrv): an e-mail list that allows a group of people to hold a discussion by writing to each other via the Internet.

impropriety
(ĭm′prə-prī′ĭ-tē) *n.*
an unsuitable or inappropriate act or quality

◆ **GRAMMAR IN CONTEXT**
In line 4, the writer uses parentheses to let you know the abbreviation for the National Association for Sport and Physical Education.

A PERSUASION
What is the NASPE's position on dodgeball in school physical education programs?

adequately
(ăd′ĭ-kwĭt-lē) *adv.*
enough to satisfy a requirement or meet a need

B PERSUASION
Reread lines 18–24. Based on these lines, how would you describe the **tone** of this document?

◀ **Analyze Visuals**
How many people pictured on this dodgeball team appear to be getting exercise?

elimination tag provide limited opportunities for everyone in the class,
30 especially the slower, less agile students who need the activity the most."

The students who are **eliminated** first in dodgeball are typically the ones who most need to be active and practice their skills. Many times these students are also the ones with the least amount of confidence in their physical abilities. Being targeted because they are the "weaker" players, and being hit by a hard-thrown ball, does not help kids to develop confidence.

The arguments most often heard in favor of dodgeball are that it allows for the practice of important physical skills—and kids like it.

- Dodgeball does provide a means of practicing some important physical skills—running, dodging, throwing, and catching.
40 However, there are many activities that allow practice of these skills without using human targets or eliminating students from play.
- Some kids may like it—the most skilled, the most confident. But many do not! Certainly not the student who gets hit hard in the stomach, head, or groin. And it is not appropriate to teach our children that you win by hurting others. **C**

In a recent article about the new GSN (games network) TV show called "Extreme Dodgeball," there is talk of "developing and executing extreme strategies to annihilate opponents" and the use of terms such as "throw-to-kill ratios," and "headshots." NASPE asks, "Is this the type
50 of game that you want children to be exposed to?" **D**

eliminate (ĭ-lĭm'ə-nāt')
v. to remove from consideration by defeating

C PERSUASION
Reread lines 42–45. What kind of **emotional appeal** is being made? What is the **ethical appeal**?

◦◦◦ COMMON CORE RI 4

D ANALYZE RHETORIC AND REASONING
A **leading question** is a question that contains its answer. A **rhetorical question** is one that has such an obvious answer that it does not require a reply. Reread lines 49–50. Is this a leading question or a rhetorical question?

The Weak Shall Inherit the Gym

Rick Reilly

Not to alarm you, but America is going softer than left-out butter. Exhibit 9,137: Schools have started banning dodgeball.

I kid you not. Dodgeball has been outlawed by some school districts in New York, Texas, Utah and Virginia. Many more are thinking about it, like Cecil County, Md., where the school board wants to **ban** any game with "human targets." **E**

Human targets? What's tag? What's a snowball fight? What's a close play at second? Neil Williams, a physical education professor at Eastern
10 Connecticut State, says dodgeball has to go because it "encourages the best to pick on the weak." Noooo! You mean there's weak in the world? There's strong? Of course there is, and dodgeball is one of the first opportunities in life to figure out which one you are and how you're going to deal with it. **F**

We had a bully, Big Joe, in our seventh grade. Must have weighed 225 pounds, . . . We also had a kid named Melvin, who was so thin we could've faxed him from class to class. I'll never forget the dodgeball game in which Big Joe had a ball in each hand and one sandwiched

ban (băn) *v.* to prohibit

E PERSUASION
What words and phrases in the first sentence make Rick Reilly's **tone** immediately clear?

F PERSUASION
Why does Neil Williams object to dodgeball? Describe Reilly's response to this objection.

◀ **Analyze Visuals**

Is the girl in the photo wearing the appropriate amount of protective gear? Why or why not?

between his knees, firing at our side like a human tennis-ball machine,
20 when, all of a sudden, he got plunked. . . . Joe whirled around to see
who'd done it and saw that it was none other than Melvin, all 83 pounds
of him, most of it smile.

Some of these . . . whiners say dodgeball is inappropriate in these
violent times. Are you kidding? Dodgeball is one of the few times in life
when you get to let out your **aggressions,** no questions asked. We don't
need less dodgeball in schools, we need more!

I know what all these . . . parents want. They want their Ambers and
their Alexanders to grow up in a cozy womb of noncompetition, where
everybody shares tofu¹ and Little Red Riding Hood and the big, bad wolf
30 set up a commune.² Then their kids will stumble out into the bright light
of the real world and find out that, yes, there's weak and there's strong
and teams and sides and winning and losing. You'll recognize those kids.
They'll be the ones filling up chalupas.³ Very noncompetitive. **G** **H**

But Williams and his fellow whiners aren't stopping at dodgeball. In
their Physical Education Hall of Shame they've also included duck-duck-
goose and musical chairs. Seriously. So, if we give them dodgeball, you
can look for these games to be banned next:

Tag. Referring to any child as *it* is demeaning and hurtful. Instead
of the child hollering, "You're it!" we recommend, "You're special!"
40 *Baseball.* Involves wrong-headed notions of *stealing, errors* and
gruesome *hit-and-run.* Players should always be safe, never out.

Capture the flag. Mimics war.

Kick the can. Unfair to the can.

If we let these PC twinkies⁴ have their way, we'll be left with:

Duck-duck-duck. Teacher spends the entire hour patting each child
softly on the head.

Upsy down. The entire class takes turns fluffing the gym teacher's
pillow before her nap.

Swedish baseball. Players are allowed free passage to first, second or
50 third, where they receive a relaxing two-minute massage from opposing
players. **I**

---

1. **tofu** (tō′fōō): a protein-rich soybean curd that many vegetarians eat in place of meat.

2. **commune** (kôm′yōōn′): a cooperative community in which a group of people who are not
   necessarily related live and work together.

3. **chalupas** (chə-lū′päs): fried tortillas filled with meat, a Mexican dish similar to tacos that is served
   at several U.S. fast-food chains.

4. **PC twinkies:** Reilly's expression for people who are too concerned (politically correct) with offending
   others by words or actions.

Comprehension

1. **Recall** What reason does the NASPE give for once again announcing its position on dodgeball in school physical education programs?

2. **Clarify** Reread lines 15–22 of "The Weak Shall Inherit the Gym." What did dodgeball do for Melvin?

Text Analysis

3. **Examine Name-Calling** Attempting to discredit a position or idea by attacking people associated with it is **name-calling.** Find examples of name-calling in "The Weak Shall Inherit the Gym." Does it make Reilly's argument more or less convincing? Give reasons for your answer.

4. **Analyze Tone** What is Reilly's tone, or attitude toward opponents of dodgeball? Explain how this tone might persuade readers to adopt his opinion of the game.

5. **Make Judgments** A **stereotype** is an overgeneralization about a person or group. In your opinion, is Reilly guilty of stereotyping? Explain.

6. **Compare Persuasive Texts** Consider the arguments and persuasive techniques that the NASPE and Reilly use to convince readers to adopt their positions. Then explain how each text reaches its conclusion, noting any similarities and differences between them.

7. **Evaluate Rhetoric and Reasoning** Reilly is writing to be funny, but he also has a point to make. Are you convinced by his argument and persuasion? Think about the fallacies you noted on your chart and any you discovered in answering questions 3 and 5. Then support your decision.

Extension and Challenge

8. **Speaking and Listening** Form two teams, one representing the NASPE's viewpoint and one representing Rick Reilly's. Then, with your team, answer the question, "Should opportunities for intense physical competition be provided in middle schools?" from the perspective of your author. Debate the question with the other team, using support from the selections.

Are all GAMES worth playing?

Now that you have read the two selections, revisit the two lists of games you created at the start of this lesson. Would you move any of the games from one list to the other? Why or why not?

COMMON CORE

RI 3 Analyze how a text makes connections among and distinctions between individuals, ideas, or events. **RI 4** Determine connotative meanings; analyze the impact of specific word choices. **RI 8** Evaluate the argument and specific claims, assessing whether the reasoning is sound. **RI 9** Identify where texts disagree on matters of interpretation.

Vocabulary in Context

▲ VOCABULARY PRACTICE

Synonyms are words that have similar meanings, and **antonyms** are words that have opposite meanings. Decide whether the words in each pair are synonyms or antonyms.

1. adequately—insufficiently
2. aggression—ferocity
3. ban—legalize
4. eliminate—banish
5. impropriety—rudeness

adequately

aggression

ban

eliminate

impropriety

ACADEMIC VOCABULARY IN WRITING

- accurate   • bias   • contrast   • convince   • logic

What gym class activity would you like to see either added to or banned from your school? Why? Share your opinion and the **logic** behind it in a paragraph. Use at least one Academic Vocabulary word.

VOCABULARY STRATEGY: THE LATIN WORD *gressus*

The vocabulary word *aggression* comes from the Latin word *gressus*, which means "to go." Many English words have the same origin. To figure out the meaning of words with this history, use context clues and your knowledge of the meaning of *gressus*.

⋮ **COMMON CORE**

L 4b Use Latin roots as clues to the meaning of a word.

PRACTICE Choose the word from the web that best completes each sentence. Then explain how the word *gressus* relates to the meaning of the word.

1. The trainer works with ____ dogs to make them gentler and more obedient.
2. Many dogs will ____ if they don't get constant social interaction.
3. Stealing a car is a serious _____, so car thieves receive harsh penalties.
4. Please stick to the topic and do not _____.
5. The Renaissance was a _____ time period in which the arts flourished and scientists made important discoveries.

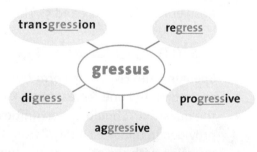

transgression   regress

gressus

digress   progressive

aggressive

Interactive Vocabulary   THINK central

Go to **thinkcentral.com**.
KEYWORD: HML8-1012

Language

◆ **GRAMMAR IN CONTEXT:** Use Punctuation Correctly

⋯ **COMMON CORE**

L 2b Use an ellipsis to indicate an omission when writing.

There are three types of punctuation marks that are especially useful for conveying additional information. **Parentheses** are punctuation marks used in sentences to set off extra information, such as explanations or comments. **Brackets** are punctuation marks used in quotations to set off extra information inserted by the writer (as opposed to the person or source being quoted). An **ellipsis** is a set of three spaced periods (. . . , *not* ...) preceded and followed by a space. Use an ellipsis to show that something has been left out of a quotation. If you use an ellipsis at the end of a sentence, include a period before the ellipsis.

> *Original:* Rick Reilly says, "They want their Ambers and their Alexanders to grow up in a cozy womb of noncompetition, where everybody shares tofu and Little Red Riding Hood and the big, bad wolf set up a commune."

> *Revised:* Rick Reilly says (of these parents), "They want their . . . [children] to grow up in a cozy womb of noncompetition. . . ."

PRACTICE For each item, revise the following sentence according to the instructions given. Use correct punctuation.

Reilly mockingly says, "In their Physical Education Hall of Shame they've also included duck-duck-goose and musical chairs."

1. Insert *of Neil Williams and his supporters* after "says."
2. Insert the abbreviation *PEHS* after "Physical Education Hall of Shame."
3. Leave out "duck-duck-goose and."
4. Leave out "duck-duck-goose and musical chairs" and insert *kindergarten games* in their place.

*For more help with punctuation, see page R50 in the **Grammar Handbook**.*

READING-WRITING CONNECTION

Broaden your understanding of the selections by responding to this prompt. Then use the **revising tip** to improve your writing.

WRITING PROMPT	REVISING TIP
Extended Constructed Response: Letter Write a letter to the NASPE or Rick Reilly in which you identify what you think is presented well and/or in an incorrect, misleading, or unfair way. Use quotations from the piece to illustrate your points.	Review your letter to make sure you have used brackets, parentheses, and ellipses correctly. Where necessary, revise your punctuation.

Interactive Revision THINK central

Go to thinkcentral.com.
KEYWORD: HML8-1013

The Sanctuary of School
Essay by Lynda Barry

Why do we need
SCHOOLS?

COMMON CORE

RI 3 Analyze how a text makes connections among and distinctions between individuals [and] ideas (e.g., through comparisons). **RI 4** Determine figurative meanings. **RI 6** Determine an author's point of view or purpose and analyze how the author acknowledges and responds to conflicting viewpoints.

Traditionally, a school's most basic function was to teach the "three Rs": reading, writing, and 'rithmetic. More recently, Bill Gates, founder of the Microsoft Corporation, suggested that today's schools need to focus on three new "Rs": rigor, relevance, and relationships. In the essay you're about to read, Lynda Barry describes how the relationships made all the difference in her life.

DISCUSS With a small group, discuss what you think are a school's three most important tasks. Write them down and share them with your class. How many ideas have to do with the classroom and lessons? How many are tied to something less academic?

TEXT ANALYSIS: AUTHOR'S PURPOSE

Writers usually have one or more **purposes** when they sit down to write, and they carefully select strategies to achieve these purposes. In this essay, Lynda Barry's purpose is to persuade us to value and support public schools. As you read, analyze the way that Barry uses a personal experience from her childhood to make her larger point. Pay attention to the effect that her words, details, and images have on you.

READING SKILL: IDENTIFY CAUSE AND EFFECT

A **cause** is an event or action that directly results in another event. An **effect** is the direct outcome of an event or action. For example, if your school bus gets a flat tire, that could be the cause of your being late for school. Being late is the effect. Sometimes signal words will alert you to causes (*because, since*) and effects (*as a result, therefore*). Other times, you'll have to make the connection for yourself.

As you read this essay, look for the conditions in Barry's environment that cause her to behave the way she does. Each time you recognize a cause-and-effect relationship, **paraphrase,** or describe in your own words, the cause and effect in a diagram like the one shown.

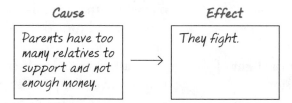

Cause | Effect
| Parents have too many relatives to support and not enough money. | → | They fight. |

▲ VOCABULARY IN CONTEXT

The boldfaced words help Lynda Barry to convey what she felt about school when she was a little girl. To see how many of them you know, restate each sentence, using a different word or phrase for the boldfaced term.

1. A **neglectful** student forgets to do her homework.
2. Children thrive in loving, **secure** homes.
3. Our school doesn't look unique or exciting on the outside, but inside it is anything but **nondescript**.
4. On a hot day, an air-conditioned classroom is a **sanctuary**.

Complete the activities in your **Reader/Writer Notebook.**

Meet the Author

Lynda Barry
born 1956

Difficult Childhood
Lynda Barry never felt that she "fit in"—not with her classmates at school, nor with either side of her parents' Filipino and Norwegian-Irish families. An excellent student, Barry became the first member of her family to attend college. There she began drawing quirky comic strips based on her own life experiences and publishing them in her school's student newspaper.

Comic Strip Success
After college, Barry struggled to decide what to do with her life and how to support herself. Cartoonist and writer Matt Groening (creator of *The Simpsons* television series) had been a college classmate of Barry's. Through Groening, the *Chicago Reader* newspaper learned of Barry's work and hired her to draw a weekly comic strip. Soon, her comic strips "Girls and Boys," "Ernie Pook's Comeek," and "Modern Romance" gained her a nationwide following. She has also published plays and novels, including *The Good Times Are Killing Me* and *Cruddy: An Illustrated Novel.* Her childhood continues to have a big effect on her art. Childhood, she says, is "where all our motivations, feelings, and opinions come from."

Authors Online
Go to **thinkcentral.com.** KEYWORD: HML8-1015

THINK central

Reprinted from **The New York Times**

SUNDAY, JANUARY 5, 1992   A2

The Sanctuary of School

LYNDA BARRY

sanctuary
(săngk′chōo-ĕr′ē) *n.*
a place of refuge

Ⓐ **AUTHOR'S PURPOSE**
What can you **infer** about Barry's reason for walking to school in the dark?

nondescript
(nŏn′dĭ-skrĭpt′) *adj.*
lacking unique qualities

I was seven years old the first time I snuck out of the house in the dark. It was winter and my parents had been fighting all night. They were short on money and long on relatives who kept "temporarily" moving into our house because they had nowhere else to go.

My brother and I were used 10 to giving up our bedroom. We slept on the couch, something we actually liked because it put us that much closer to the light of our lives, our television.

At night when everyone was asleep, we lay on our pillows watching it with the sound off. We watched Steve Allen's[1] mouth moving. We watched Johnny 20 Carson's[2] mouth moving. We watched movies filled with gangsters shooting machine guns into packed rooms, dying soldiers hurling a last grenade and beautiful women crying at windows. Then the sign-off finally came and we tried to sleep.

The morning I snuck out, I woke up filled with a panic about needing to get to school. The sun wasn't 30 quite up yet but my anxiety was so fierce that I just got dressed, walked quietly across the kitchen and let myself out the back door.

It was quiet outside. Stars were still out. Nothing moved and no one was in the street. It was as if someone had turned the sound off on the world.

I walked the alley, breaking 40 thin ice over the puddles with my shoes. I didn't know why I was walking to school in the dark. I didn't think about it. All I knew was a feeling of panic, like the panic that strikes kids when they realize they are lost. Ⓐ

That feeling eased the moment I turned the corner and saw the dark outline of my school at 50 the top of the hill. My school was made up of about 15 **nondescript**

---

1. **Steve Allen:** (1921–2000) actor, comedian, songwriter, and author who hosted popular TV variety shows in the 1950s and 60s.

2. **Johnny Carson:** (1925–2005) comedian who hosted a late-night TV show, *The Tonight Show*, from 1962 to 1992.

◄ **Analyze Visuals**

This illustration by Lynda Barry accompanied the essay when it was originally published in a supplement to *The New York Times*. What can you **conclude** about the young Barry's relationship to school?

portable classrooms set down on a fenced concrete lot in a rundown Seattle[3] neighborhood, but it had the most beautiful view of the Cascade Mountains. You could see them from anywhere on the playfield and you could see them from the windows of my classroom—Room 2. **B**

---

3. **Seattle:** a city in west central Washington state.

B CAUSE AND EFFECT
Reread lines 47–50. What causes Barry to feel less panicked?

Language Coach

Metaphors Writers use metaphors to compare things without using *like* or *as*. In lines 80–81, Barry says that she and her brother were "children with the sound turned off." To what is she comparing her brother and herself? Reread lines 10–17 and 34–38 for help.

C CAUSE AND EFFECT
What causes Barry's parents not to notice she is missing?

D AUTHOR'S PURPOSE
Reread lines 74–86. What link does Barry make between herself, other children, and the importance of school?

E AUTHOR'S PURPOSE
What are your opinions of the janitor and teachers, and of Barry's relationships with them?

secure (sǐ-kyŏŏr') *adj.* safe; protected; free from fear or anxiety

F CAUSE AND EFFECT
Reread lines 119–131. **Paraphrase** the effect that being in school has on Barry.

---

60 I walked over to the monkey bars and hooked my arms around the cold metal. I stood for a long time just looking across Rainier Valley.[4] The sky was beginning to whiten and I could hear a few birds.

In a perfect world my absence at home would not have gone unnoticed. I would have had two parents in a panic to locate me, 70 instead of two parents in a panic to locate an answer to the hard question of survival during a deep financial and emotional crisis. **C**

But in an overcrowded and unhappy home, it's incredibly easy for any child to slip away. The high levels of frustration, depression and anger in my house made my brother and me invisible. 80 We were children with the sound turned off. And for us, as for the steadily increasing number of neglected children in this country, the only place where we could count on being noticed was at school. **D**

"Hey there, young lady. Did you forget to go home last night?" It was Mr. Gunderson, our janitor, 90 whom we all loved. He was nice and he was funny and he was old with white hair, thick glasses and an unbelievable number of keys. I could hear them jingling as he walked across the playfield. I felt incredibly happy to see him.

He let me push his wheeled garbage can between the different portables as he unlocked each 100 room. He let me turn on the lights and raise the window shades and I saw my school slowly come to life. I saw Mrs. Holman, our school secretary, walk into the office without her orange lipstick on yet. She waved.

I saw the fifth-grade teacher, Mr. Cunningham, walking under the breezeway eating a hard roll. 110 He waved.

And I saw my teacher, Mrs. Claire LeSane, walking toward us in a red coat and calling my name in a very happy and surprised way, and suddenly my throat got tight and my eyes stung and I ran toward her crying. It was something that surprised us both. **E**

It's only thinking about it now, 120 28 years later, that I realize I was crying from relief. I was with my teacher, and in a while I was going to sit at my desk, with my crayons and pencils and books and classmates all around me, and for the next six hours I was going to enjoy a thoroughly **secure,** warm and stable world. It was a world I absolutely relied on. Without it, 130 I don't know where I would have gone that morning. **F**

Mrs. LeSane asked me what was wrong and when I said, "Nothing," she seemingly left it at that. But she asked me if I would carry her purse for her, an honor above all honors, and she asked if I wanted to come into Room 2 early and paint.

---

4. **Rainier Valley:** a section of southeast Seattle.

She believed in the natural healing power of painting and drawing for troubled children. In the back of her room there was always a drawing table and an easel with plenty of supplies, and sometimes during the day she would come up to you for what seemed like no good reason and quietly ask if you wanted to go to the back table and "make some pictures for Mrs. LeSane." We all had a chance at it—to sit apart from the class for a while to paint, draw and silently work out impossible problems on 11 × 17 sheets of newsprint.

Drawing came to mean everything to me. At the back table in Room 2, I learned to build myself a life preserver that I could carry into my home. **G**

We all know that a good education system saves lives, but the people of this country are still told that cutting the budget for public schools is necessary, that poor salaries for teachers are all we can manage and that art, music and all creative activities must be the first to go when times are lean.

Before- and after-school programs are cut and we are told that public schools are not made for baby-sitting children. If parents are **neglectful** temporarily or permanently, for whatever reason, it's certainly sad, but their unlucky children must fend for themselves. Or slip through the cracks.[5] Or wander in a dark night alone.

We are told in a thousand ways that not only are public schools not important, but that the children who attend them, the children who need them most, are not important either. We leave them to learn from the blind eye of a television, or to the mercy of "a thousand points of light"[6] that can be as far away as stars.

I was lucky. I had Mrs. LeSane. I had Mr. Gunderson. I had an abundance of art supplies. And I had a particular brand of neglect in my home that allowed me to slip away and get to them. But what about the rest of the kids who weren't as lucky? What happened to them?

By the time the bell rang that morning I had finished my drawing and Mrs. LeSane pinned it up on the special bulletin board she reserved for drawings from the back table. It was the same picture I always drew—a sun in the corner of a blue sky over a nice house with flowers all around it.

Mrs. LeSane asked us to please stand, face the flag, place our right hands over our hearts and say the Pledge of Allegiance. Children across the country do it faithfully. I wonder now when the country will face its children and say a pledge right back. ◐ **H**

5. **slip through the cracks:** become lost or harmed due to negligence.

6. **"a thousand points of light":** volunteers and charities—a metaphor from a 1989 speech by then-President George H. W. Bush.

G AUTHOR'S PURPOSE
Reread lines 156–160. What do you think Barry means when she says she learned to build herself "a life preserver"?

neglectful (nĭ-glĕkt'fəl) *adj.* characterized by a failure to properly care for someone or something

H AUTHOR'S PURPOSE
Reread lines 161–215. Which sentence best sums up Barry's purpose?

Comprehension

1. **Recall** Where does Lynda Barry go after she sneaks out of her house?

2. **Clarify** Why does Barry cry when she sees Mrs. LeSane?

Text Analysis

COMMON CORE

RI 3 Analyze how a text makes connections among and distinctions between individuals [and] ideas (e.g., through comparisons). **RI 6** Determine an author's point of view or purpose and analyze how the author acknowledges and responds to conflicting viewpoints.

3. **Examine Cause and Effect** Look back at the cause-and-effect diagrams you created as you read. Which cause-and-effect relationship do you think is most important to Barry's argument in favor of public schools?

4. **Interpret Imagery** Skim pages 1016 and 1018, and note the three places where Barry describes someone or something as having "the sound turned off." In a graphic like the one shown, tell what she is referring to in each case. Why do you think the image is so powerful to Barry?

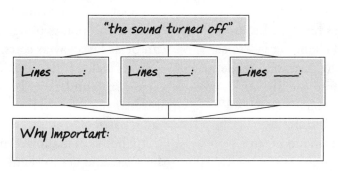

5. **Make Inferences** Reread the last paragraph of the essay. What is the "pledge" that Barry wants Americans to make to schoolchildren?

6. **Analyze Author's Purpose** The evidence Barry offers to persuade the reader comes from a single source—her personal experience. Generalizing from a single experience can be considered **overgeneralization.** Would you say Barry's argument is effective, or is her experience too narrow to achieve her purpose? Explain.

7. **Draw Conclusions** How might Barry's life have been different if she hadn't had creative activities at school?

Extension and Challenge

8. **Inquiry and Research** Lynda Barry's essay encourages us to support public schools for the education and important relationships they offer to all students. Find out about the purpose of public education in the United States. When were public schools established and why? How are they funded? On the basis of what you find out, decide whether Barry's expectations for schools are reasonable.

Why do we need SCHOOLS?

Revisit the notes you took on page 1014. With your group, discuss whether reading Lynda Barry's essay changed your opinion about schools' three most important tasks.

Vocabulary in Context

▲ VOCABULARY PRACTICE

Choose the letter of the term that is most closely related to the boldfaced word.

1. **sanctuary**: (a) playground, (b) forest, (c) refuge
2. **nondescript:** (a) plain, (b) ugly, (c) beautiful
3. **secure:** (a) free, (b) safe, (c) loose
4. **neglectful:** (a) cruel, (b) bossy, (c) inattentive

ACADEMIC VOCABULARY IN SPEAKING

- accurate   - bias   - contrast   - convince   - logic

Do you have a **bias** for a particular place? Using at least one Academic Vocabulary word, describe to your classmates a place you consider a "sanctuary."

VOCABULARY STRATEGY: RELATED WORDS

One strategy that can help you figure out the meaning of an unfamiliar word is to look for a relationship between it and a word you already know. For example, if you don't know the meaning of the word *nondescript*, you might recognize a similarity between that word and the word *descriptive*. You can then guess that *nondescript* has something to do with how much there is to describe.

COMMON CORE

L 5b Use the relationship between particular words to better understand each of the words.

PRACTICE Identify a word you know that relates to each numbered word. Then guess at the definition for the numbered word. Check your definition in a dictionary, and write a sentence using the word.

1. criminology
2. humanitarian
3. logistical
4. inconsolable
5. disenchantment
6. elongation

Interactive Vocabulary THINK central

Go to thinkcentral.com.
KEYWORD: HML8-1021

Educating Sons
Speech by Chief Canasatego

The First Americans
Letter by the Grand Council Fire of American Indians

Who decides what's
IMPORTANT?

COMMON CORE

RI 2 Determine a central idea of a text and analyze its development over the course of the text; provide an objective summary of the text. **RI 4** Determine the meaning of words and phrases as they are used in a text, including figurative [and] connotative meanings; analyze the impact of specific word choices on meaning.

Not everyone agrees on what we should teach or on how it should be taught. Often what is considered important to learn depends on where and when we're living. For example, the speech and letter that follow were written before Native American cultures received much respect from European Americans. Native American leaders have had to argue that their culture, language, history, and way of life are useful knowledge.

SURVEY As a class, make a list of the most important and useful things you've learned in school. Vote on the top four and post them in the four corners of your classroom. Then go stand under the one that you consider most important. Why did you choose what you did? Present your reasons to the class.

PRINCIPAL

TEXT ANALYSIS: RHETORICAL DEVICES

Persuasive writers and speakers often use rhetorical devices such as repetition and parallelism. **Repetition** is the repeated use of the same word or phrase—usually for emphasis. **Parallelism** is the repetition of similar words, phrases, sentences, or grammatical structure. It can show that ideas are related or equally important. It can also help stress a phrase or idea.

As you read the texts that follow, look for these devices and what they help emphasize. Reading the speech aloud can help.

READING SKILL: IDENTIFY COMPARISONS AND CONTRASTS

Writers often make their points by **comparing** and **contrasting** subjects—that is, noting their similarities and differences. For example, in the texts you're about to read, the authors contrast what is taught with what they think should be taught. To keep track of their points, summarize the arguments in each selection in a chart like the one begun for "Educating Sons."

"Educating Sons"	
What Is Taught	What Should Be Taught
sciences	

VOCABULARY IN CONTEXT

The following words help the authors express their views. To see how many you know, use them to complete the sentences.

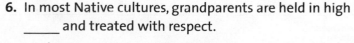

WORD LIST	decline	oratory	savage
	esteem	sacred	treacherous

1. For the Lakota people, the Black Hills region is a _____ place with deep religious significance.
2. Because of his famous speech "I will fight no more forever," Chief Joseph is known for his brilliant _____.
3. To call someone a _____ is to say that he is uncivilized.
4. Because the United States broke so many treaties, most Native Americans viewed the government as _____.
5. Many Cherokees chose to _____ offers to buy their land.
6. In most Native cultures, grandparents are held in high _____ and treated with respect.

Complete the activities in your **Reader/Writer Notebook.**

Meet the Author

A Man of Influence
Chief Canasatego of the Onondaga Tribe was an influential leader in the Iroquois Confederacy, a group of tribes in the upper New York State area. Benjamin Franklin used Canasatego's ideas in his early plans for colonial union.

BACKGROUND TO THE SPEECH AND LETTER

A "No Thank You" Speech
In the 1700s, the British and the French were competing for land and resources in North America. English colonists thought that by offering Iroquois boys the chance to attend the university in Virginia, they would convince the Iroquois to support their side. The Iroquois, however, didn't want to send their sons to the school, for reasons made clear in Chief Canasatego's 1744 speech.

The Grand Council Fire of American Indians
In 1927, Mayor William Hale Thompson of Chicago raised a protest against school textbooks he believed presented history in a way that was prejudiced in favor of Great Britain. The mayor wanted to revise textbooks to be what he called "100 percent American." The members of the Grand Council Fire of American Indians—led by its president Scott H. Peters, a Chippewa Indian—wanted to point out that the British were not the only group portrayed inaccurately in textbooks. They wrote a letter asking the mayor to change texts to reflect the perspectives and accomplishments of Native Americans. They wore full ceremonial dress and war paint when presenting the mayor with their letter.

Author Online
Go to **thinkcentral.com**. KEYWORD: HML8-1023

THINK central

EDUCATING SONS

Chief Canasatego

esteem (ĭ-stēm') *v.* to regard with respect

We know you highly <u>esteem</u> the kind of learning taught in these colleges. And the maintenance of our young men, while with you, would be very expensive to you. We're convinced, therefore, that you mean to do us good by your proposal, and we thank you heartily. But you who are so wise must know that different nations have different conceptions of things. And you will not, therefore, take it amiss[1] if our ideas of this kind of education happens not to be the same with yours.

A RHETORICAL DEVICES
Reread lines 10–15. What phrase is repeated in these lines? What word is repeated in line 14?

10 We have had some experience of it. Several of our young people were formerly brought up in the colleges of the northern province. They were instructed in all your sciences. But when they came back to us, they were bad runners, ignorant of every means of living in the woods, unable to bear either cold or hunger, knew neither how to build a cabin, take a deer, or kill an enemy, spoke our language imperfectly, and therefore were neither fit for hunters nor warriors nor councilors. They were totally good for nothing. **A**

decline (dĭ-klīn') *v.* to politely refuse

We are, however, not the less obliged[2] for your kind offer, though we <u>decline</u> accepting. To show our grateful sense of it, if the gentlemen of Virginia will send us a dozen of their sons, we would take great care in their education, instruct them in all we know, and make men of them.

---

1. **take it amiss:** be offended.
2. **obliged** (ə-blījd'): grateful or indebted.

◀ **Analyze Visuals**

What three **adjectives** best describe the boy in this photograph?

B RHETORICAL DEVICES

Word and phrase choices are important elements of rhetoric, or writing. Realizing this, the Grand Council Fire points out some of the words used in history books that reveal a bias for white men and against Native Americans. For example, "They call all white victories, battles, and all Indian victories, massacres." Reread lines 7–17 to find a second example. Then pick one pair of words and explain the differences in each word's connotations.

treacherous (trĕch′ər-əs) *adj.* not to be relied on; untrustworthy

C COMPARISONS AND CONTRASTS

Reread lines 6–23. According to the Grand Council Fire, what do textbooks teach about Native Americans?

savage (săv′ĭj) *n.* a person regarded as primitive or uncivilized

---

The First Americans

THE GRAND COUNCIL FIRE OF AMERICAN INDIANS

DECEMBER 1, 1927

TO THE MAYOR OF CHICAGO:—

You tell all white men "America First." We believe in that. We are the only ones, truly, that are 100 percent. We therefore ask you while you are teaching school children about America First, teach them truth about the First Americans.

We do not know if school histories are pro-British, but we do know that they are unjust to the life of our people—the American Indian. They call all white victories, battles, and all Indian victories, massacres. The battle with Custer[1] has been taught to school children as a fearful massacre on 10 our part. We ask that this, as well as other incidents, be told fairly. If the Custer battle was a massacre, what was Wounded Knee?[2]

History books teach that Indians were murderers—is it murder to fight in self-defense? Indians killed white men because white men took their lands, ruined their hunting grounds, burned their forests, destroyed their buffalo. White men penned our people on reservations, then took away the reservations. White men who rise to protect their property are called patriots—Indians who do the same are called murderers. **B**

White men call Indians **treacherous**—but no mention is made of broken treaties on the part of the white man. White men say that Indians 20 were always fighting. It was only our lack of skill in white man's warfare that led to our defeat. An Indian mother prayed that her boy be a great medicine man[3] rather than a great warrior. It is true that we had our own small battles, but in the main we were peace-loving and home-loving. **C**

White men called Indians thieves—and yet we lived in frail skin lodges and needed no locks or iron bars. White men call Indians **savages.** What is civilization? Its marks are a noble religion and philosophy, original arts, stirring music, rich history and legend. We had these. Then we were not savages, but a civilized race.

We made blankets that were beautiful that the white man with all 30 his machinery has never been able to duplicate. We made baskets that

---

1. **Custer:** George Armstrong Custer (1839–1876), a U.S. cavalry officer who fought Sioux and Cheyenne warriors at Little Bighorn; Custer was killed and his army was wiped out.

2. **Wounded Knee:** a creek in South Dakota where U.S. troops massacred about 200 Native Americans on December 29, 1890.

3. **medicine man:** a Native-American holy man and healer.

were beautiful. We wove in beads and colored quills, designs that were not just decorative motifs, but were the outward expression of our very thoughts. We made pottery—pottery that was useful and beautiful as well. Why not make school children

40 acquainted with the beautiful handicrafts in which we were skilled? Put in every school Indian blankets, baskets, pottery.

We sang songs that carried in their melodies all the sounds of nature—the running of waters, the sighing of winds, and the calls of the animals. Teach these to your children that they may come to love nature as we love it.

We had our statesmen—and their **oratory** has never been equalled. Teach the children some of these speeches of our people, remarkable for
50 their brilliant oratory.

We played games—games that brought good health and sound bodies. Why not put these in your schools? We told stories. Why not teach school children more of the wholesome proverbs and legends of our people? Tell them how we loved all that was beautiful. That we killed game only for food, not for fun. Indians think white men who kill for fun are murderers. **D**

Tell your children of the friendly acts of Indians to the white people who first settled here. Tell them of our leaders and heroes and their deeds. Tell them of Indians such as Black Partridge,[4] Shabbona,[5] and others who
60 many times saved the people of Chicago at great danger to themselves. Put in your history books the Indian's part in the World War.[6] Tell how the Indian fought for a country of which he was not a citizen, for a flag to which he had no claim, and for a people that have treated him unjustly. **E**

The Indian has long been hurt by these unfair books. We ask only that our story be told in fairness. We do not ask you to overlook what we did, but we do ask you to understand it. A true program of America First will give a generous place to the culture and history of the American Indian.

We ask this, Chief, to keep **sacred** the memory of our people. ॐ

oratory (ôr′ə-tôr′ē) *n.* the art of making speeches

D COMPARISONS AND CONTRASTS
Reread lines 39–54. What does the Grand Council Fire suggest schools should teach?

E RHETORICAL DEVICES
Reread lines 54–63. Identify the phrase that the Grand Council Fire repeats. What does this repetition help emphasize?

sacred (sā′krĭd) *adj.* holy; worthy of religious veneration or respect

---

4. **Black Partridge:** a Potawatomi chief who befriended white settlers.

5. **Shabbona** (shä′bō-nə): a member of the Ottawa people who befriended white settlers.

6. **World War:** World War I (1914–1918), in which Great Britain, France, the United States, and their allies defeated Germany, Austria-Hungary, and their allies.

Comprehension

1. **Recall** Why does Chief Canasatego not want to send Iroquois sons to be educated by the colonists?

2. **Recall** According to the Grand Council Fire of American Indians, how do textbooks refer to "Indian victories"?

Text Analysis

3. **Summarize Underlying Message** Chief Canasatego's speech has an unstated, or underlying, message. Summarize this underlying message.

4. **Summarize Comparisons and Contrasts** Review the chart you completed as you read "The First Americans." Summarize the differences between what was being taught to children and what the Grand Council thought should be taught.

5. **Analyze Irony** Irony occurs when what the speaker says is different from what he or she actually means. Reread lines 16–19 of "Educating Sons." What is the irony in these closing remarks? Explain your answer.

6. **Analyze the Use of Rhetorical Devices** Analyze lines 29–52 in "The First Americans" to identify all the instances of parallelism used by the Grand Council Fire. Think about what the use of this rhetorical device helps to emphasize. Also consider the emotions it stirs. What impact might this rhetorical device have had upon those listening to this speech?

7. **Draw Conclusions About Values** In a Y-chart like the one shown, list three values that Chief Canasatego and the Grand Council each argue are important in their cultures. List the values that are common to both cultures in the stem of the Y. What conclusion can you draw about how Native American values changed over time?

> Chief Canasatego
> 1.
> 2.
> 3.
>
> Grand Council
> 1.
> 2.
> 3.
>
> Common Values

Extension and Challenge

8. **Readers' Circle** With a group, decide what each author would say is the most important thing for young people to learn. Support your views with lines from the texts. Then discuss whether these things are still important today.

9. **SOCIAL STUDIES CONNECTION** Research the Battle of Little Bighorn or the Battle of Wounded Knee. What does this information add to your understanding of the Grand Council's argument?

George Custer, who led American forces at Little Bighorn

Who decides what's IMPORTANT?

In Native cultures, the ability to speak eloquently and persuasively is highly esteemed. Having read the selections, would you add this skill to your list of "important and useful things you've learned in school"? Why or why not?

COMMON CORE

RI 2 Determine a central idea of a text and analyze its development over the course of the text; provide an objective summary of the text. RI 4 Determine the meaning of words and phrases as they are used in a text, including figurative [and] connotative meanings; analyze the impact of specific word choices on meaning.

Vocabulary in Context

▲ VOCABULARY PRACTICE

For each item, choose the word that differs most in meaning from the other words. Refer to a dictionary if you need help.

1. (a) esteem, (b) revere, (c) admire, (d) scorn
2. (a) decline, (b) accept, (c) invite, (d) welcome
3. (a) loyal, (b) treacherous, (c) traitorous, (d) unreliable
4. (a) savage, (b) aristocrat, (c) scholar, (d) intellectual
5. (a) speeches, (b) oratory, (c) proclamations, (d) chitchat
6. (a) holy, (b) sacred, (c) sanctified, (d) profane

decline

esteem

oratory

sacred

savage

treacherous

ACADEMIC VOCABULARY IN SPEAKING

- accurate - bias - contrast - convince - logic

In a discussion with your classmates, **contrast** two versions of the same event or interaction. Use at least one Academic Vocabulary word in your explanation.

VOCABULARY STRATEGY: ANTONYMS AND CONTEXT CLUES

You can often find **context clues** in the words and phrases that surround an unfamiliar word. **Antonyms,** or words with opposite meanings, provide one kind of context clue. For example, a passage in "The First Americans" reads: "White men call Indians savages.... We had [religion, philosophy, arts, music, history, and legend]. Then we were not savages, but a civilized race." The words *not* and *but* signal that *savages* is an antonym for *civilized race*.

PRACTICE In each sentence, identify an antonym for each boldfaced word. Then define the boldfaced word.

1. Although I am **ignorant** of many things, I am very knowledgeable about cats.
2. I should feel **obliged** to her for the invitation, but I'm actually feeling ungrateful.
3. He was certainly not a **patriot**; in fact, he was a **traitor** to his country.
4. Please stop eating unhealthy food; eat something **wholesome** for a change!
5. My parents **overlooked** my untidy bedroom but punished me for lying.

COMMON CORE

L 4a Use context (e.g., the overall meaning of a sentence or paragraph) as a clue to the meaning of a word or phrase.
L 5b Use the relationship between particular words to better understand each of the words.

Interactive Vocabulary **THINK** central

Go to **thinkcentral.com**.
KEYWORD: HML8-1029

What to the Slave Is the Fourth of July?

Speech by Frederick Douglass

VIDEO TRAILER **THiNK** central KEYWORD: HML8-1030

HISTORY Video link at thinkcentral.com

What does
INDEPENDENCE
mean to you?

COMMON CORE

RI 4 Analyze the impact of specific word choices. **RI 5** Analyze in detail the structure of a specific paragraph in a text, including the role of particular sentences. **RI 8** Evaluate the argument and specific claims in a text, assessing whether the reasoning is sound and the evidence is relevant and sufficient. **SL 3** Delineate a speaker's argument, evaluating the reasoning and relevance and sufficiency of the evidence.

In the United States, we celebrate Independence Day on the 4th of July every year. The holiday commemorates our independence from England and the birth of our nation. But what does independence mean to you?

LIST IT With a group, discuss what being independent means to students your age. Make a list of the things you can do or the ideas you can hold as an independent person. For example, perhaps to you independence means being able to choose your own friends or listen to music your parents might not enjoy. Maybe instead it means conquering a skill all on your own. Then consider what independence means in the larger sense—what does it mean to be free?

TEXT ANALYSIS: SPEECH

A **speech** is a talk or public address in which the speaker presents proposals, beliefs, or ideas. In speeches, you will often encounter **rhetorical questions**—questions that do not require a reply. Speech writers use these to prompt listeners to think about an issue or to suggest that the answer is obvious. As you read the following speech, notice how Frederick Douglass uses rhetorical questions and other rhetorical devices to stress his ideas.

READING SKILL: EVALUATE EVIDENCE

To evaluate an argument, you need to understand the writer's claim and the evidence that supports it. Distinguishing between a factual claim and a commonplace assertion will help you determine whether the evidence is adequate.

- **Factual claims** are statements that can be proved by observation, an expert, or other reliable sources. They should not be accepted without evidence to back them up.

  "Students who clean their own school are less likely to litter or vandalize school property."

- **Opinions** are statements of personal belief, feeling, or thought, which do not require proof.

  "It's wrong to make students clean the school."

- **Commonplace assertions** are statements that many people assume to be true but are not necessarily so. Generalizations about life or human nature often fall into this category.

  "One bad apple can spoil the bunch."

As you read Douglass's speech, note examples of factual claims, commonplace assertions, and opinions. Then decide whether he provides enough solid evidence to be convincing.

Factual Claims	Commonplace Assertions	Opinions
Slaves are men.		

▲ VOCABULARY IN CONTEXT

Write a sentence for each of the following words in your Reader/Writer Notebook. Use a dictionary or the definitions in the following selection pages for help.

WORD LIST		
disparity	prosperity	grievous
entitled	sham	fraud

Complete the activities in your **Reader/Writer Notebook**.

Meet the Author

Frederick Douglass
c. 1817–1895

From Slave to Abolitionist
Frederick Douglass endured 21 years of slavery before he escaped to freedom in the North. There, he became an outspoken abolitionist, or antislavery activist. During speeches, he was often attacked by proslavery crowds who hurled insults and even rotten eggs at him, but Douglass carried on. In the years leading up to the Civil War, his powerful speeches encouraged the nation to turn away from slavery.

Dangerous Attention
The publication in 1845 of Douglass's autobiography, *Narrative of the Life of Frederick Douglass, an American Slave*, brought Douglass some dangerous attention. Because he revealed the name of his former owner in his book, Douglass risked being recaptured and returned to slavery. To avoid this, he left the country. When he returned, two friends raised the money to buy his freedom. Douglass then launched an antislavery newspaper and later advised President Lincoln during the Civil War. For Douglass, the end of the war was only a first step towards a greater goal. To the end of his life, he continued working for full and equal rights for African Americans.

BACKGROUND TO THE SPEECH
Douglass delivered this speech on July 5, 1852, nine years before the beginning of the Civil War. It was not until the 13th Amendment was ratified in 1865 that slavery was finally abolished.

Author Online

THINK central

Go to **thinkcentral.com**.
KEYWORD: HML8-1031

1031

What to the Slave Is the Fourth of July?

FREDERICK DOUGLASS

Fellow citizens—Pardon me, and allow me to ask, why am I called upon to speak here today? What have I, or those I represent, to do with your national independence? Are the great principles of political freedom and of natural justice, embodied in that Declaration of Independence, extended to us? And am I, therefore, called upon to bring our humble offering to the national altar, and to confess the benefits, and express devout gratitude for the blessings, resulting from your independence to us? . . .

. . . [S]uch is not the state of the case. I say it with a sad sense of the **disparity** between us. I am not included within the pale[1] of this glorious
10 anniversary! Your high independence only reveals the immeasurable distance between us. The blessings in which you this day rejoice, are not enjoyed in common. The rich inheritance of justice, liberty, **prosperity**, and independence, bequeathed by your fathers, is shared by you, not by me. The sunlight that brought life and healing to you, has brought stripes[2] and death to me. This Fourth of July is *yours*, not mine. You may rejoice, I must mourn. . . .

Fellow citizens, above your national, tumultuous joy, I hear the mournful wail of millions, whose chains, heavy and **grievous** yesterday, are today rendered more intolerable by the jubilant shouts that reach them. . . .
20 My subject, then, fellow citizens, is "American Slavery." I shall see this day and its popular characteristics from the slave's point of view. Standing there, identified with the American bondman,[3] making his wrongs mine, I do not hesitate to declare, with all my soul, that the character and conduct of this nation never looked blacker to me than on this Fourth of July. . . . **A**

What point in the anti-slavery creed[4] would you have me argue? On what branch of the subject do the people of this country need light? Must I

---

1. **within the pale:** within the limits of law or decency.
2. **stripes:** the marks left on the body after a whipping.
3. **bondman:** someone who is enslaved.
4. **creed:** belief.

---

disparity (dĭ-spăr′ĭ-tē) *n.* the condition or fact of being unequal; difference

prosperity (prŏ-spĕr′ĭ-tē) *n.* the condition of having success; flourishing

grievous (grē′vəs) *adj.* causing grief, pain, or anguish

A **EVALUATE EVIDENCE**
Reread lines 20–24. Is this a factual claim or an opinion?

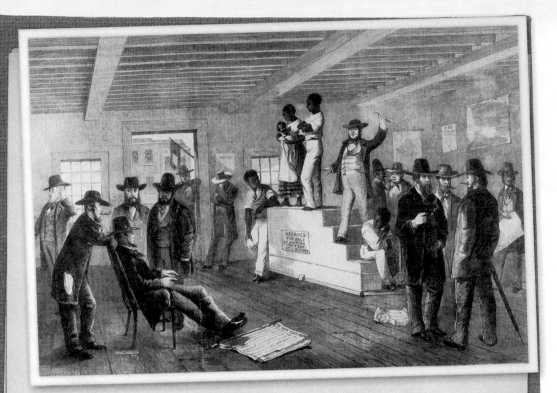

◀ **Analyze Visuals**

What's happening in this image? What might the family on the platform think of the Fourth of July celebration?

undertake to prove that the slave is a man? That point is conceded already. Nobody doubts it. The slaveholders themselves acknowledge it in the enactment of laws for their government. They acknowledge it when they

30 punish disobedience on the part of the slave. There are seventy-two crimes in the state of Virginia, which, if committed by a black man (no matter how ignorant he be), subject him to the punishment of death; while only two of these same crimes will subject a white man to the like punishment. What is this but the acknowledgement that the slave is a moral, intellectual, and responsible being[?] **B**

The manhood of the slave is conceded. It is admitted in the fact that Southern statute[5] books are covered with enactments[6] forbidding, under severe fines and penalties, the teaching of the slave to read or write. When you can point to any such laws, in reference to the beasts of the field, then

40 I may consent to argue the manhood of the slave. When the dogs in your streets, when the fowls of the air, when the cattle on your hills, when the fish of the sea, and the reptiles that crawl, shall be unable to distinguish the slave from a brute, then will I argue with you that the slave is a man!

For the present, it is enough to affirm the equal manhood of the Negro race. Is it not astonishing that, while we are plowing, planting, and reaping, using all kinds of mechanical tools, erecting houses, constructing bridges, building ships, working in metals of brass, iron, copper, silver, and gold; that, while we are reading, writing, and ciphering,[7] acting as clerks,

COMMON CORE RI 4

B SPEECH
Speeches often use the rhetorical device **repetition**—the use of the same word, phrase, or sound over and over. Repetition can help a speaker emphasize certain ideas and even develop a momentum that seizes a crowd's attention and emotions. Identify an example of repetition in lines 27–35.

---

5. **statute:** law.

6. **enactments:** authorized pieces of legislation; laws.

7. **ciphering:** doing arithmetic; working with sums.

entitled (ĕn-tīt′ld) *v.* given
the right to have or do
something

sham (shăm) *n.* something
false or empty that is
presented as genuine; a
fake
fraud (frôd) *n.* a deception
deliberately practiced to
secure unfair or unlawful
gain; a trick

merchants, and secretaries, having among us lawyers, doctors, ministers,
50 poets, authors, editors, orators,[8] and teachers; that, while we are engaged
in all manner of enterprises common to other men—digging gold in
California, capturing the whale in the Pacific, feeding sheep and cattle on
the hillside, living, moving, acting, thinking, planning, living in families as
husbands, wives, and children, and, above all, confessing and worshiping the
Christian's God, and looking hopefully for life and immortality beyond the
grave—we are called upon to prove that we are men! **C**

Would you have me argue that man is **entitled** to liberty? That he is the
rightful owner of his own body? You have already declared it. Must I argue
the wrongfulness of slavery? Is that a question for republicans?[9] Is it to be
60 settled by the rules of logic and argumentation, as a matter beset with great
difficulty, involving a doubtful application of the principle of justice, hard
to be understood? . . . To do so, would be to make myself ridiculous, and
to offer an insult to your understanding. There is not a man beneath the
canopy of heaven that does not know that slavery is wrong for *him*. **D**

What! Am I to argue that it is wrong to make men brutes, to rob them
of their liberty, to work them without wages, to keep them ignorant of their
relations to their fellow men, to beat them with sticks, to flay their flesh
with the lash,[10] to load their limbs with irons,[11] to hunt them with dogs,
to sell them at auction, to sunder their families, to knock out their teeth,
70 to burn their flesh, to starve them into obedience and submission to their
masters? Must I argue that a system, thus marked with blood and stained
with pollution, is wrong? No; I will not. I have better employment for my
time and strength than such arguments would imply. . . .

At a time like this, scorching irony, not convincing argument, is
needed. . . .

What to the American slave is your Fourth of July? I answer, a day that
reveals to him, more than all other days in the year, the gross injustice and
cruelty to which he is the constant victim. To him, your celebration is a
sham; your boasted liberty, an unholy license;[12] your national greatness,
80 swelling vanity; your sounds of rejoicing are empty and heartless; your
denunciations of tyrants, brass-fronted impudence; your shouts of liberty
and equality, hollow mockery; your prayers and hymns, your sermons and
Thanksgivings, with all your religious parade and solemnity, are to him mere
bombast,[13] **fraud**, deception, impiety, and hypocrisy—a thin veil to cover up
crimes which would disgrace a nation of savages. There is not a nation on
the earth guilty of practices more shocking and bloody, than are the people
of these United States, at this very hour. . . . ∾

---

8. **orators:** speakers.
9. **republicans:** people who believe in social equality and oppose aristocracy and privilege.
10. **flay . . . lash:** to strip skin off with a whip.
11. **irons:** metal shackles.
12. **license:** lack of restraint; excessive freedom.
13. **bombast:** high-sounding words.

Comprehension

1. **Recall** What is Douglass's subject?

2. **Recall** The celebration of what holiday spurred Douglass to speak?

3. **Clarify** From whose point of view does Douglass speak?

Text Analysis

4. **Draw Conclusions** Reread lines 1–25. What is one reason that Douglass provides to explain why he will not celebrate the Fourth of July?

● 5. **Analyze a Speech** Identify two or three rhetorical questions in the speech. Explain the points Douglass is trying to make with these questions.

6. **Evaluate an Inference** Once Douglass proves that "the slave is a man," he is able to reason that slaves should be entitled to liberty. Trace the logic Douglass uses to arrive at this inference. Then tell whether you think his inference is accurate and explain why or why not.

● 7. **Evaluate Evidence** Review Douglass's concluding remarks in lines 74–85. In your opinion, does Douglass use sound reasoning and enough reliable support to prove that, to the slave, the Fourth of July is really a cruel sham? Share your conclusions and your reasons for them.

Extension and Challenge

8. **Speaking and Listening** Practice giving this speech aloud to a peer. What rhetorical devices might you emphasize with your tone or pacing? What gestures might you use? What facial expressions and tone of voice?

9. **SOCIAL STUDIES CONNECTION** Find out more about Frederick Douglass's life as a slave and how it inspired him as a speaker. Research his autobiographical writing and summarize what you learn for the class.

What does INDEPENDENCE mean to you?

How different might Frederick Douglass's answer to this question have been from your answer? Explain your thoughts.

COMMON CORE

RI 4 Analyze the impact of specific word choices. **RI 5** Analyze in detail the structure of a specific paragraph in a text, including the role of particular sentences. **RI 8** Evaluate the argument and specific claims in a text, assessing whether the reasoning is sound and the evidence is relevant and sufficient. **SL 3** Delineate a speaker's argument, evaluating the reasoning and relevance and sufficiency of the evidence.

Vocabulary in Context

▲ **VOCABULARY PRACTICE**

Decide whether the words in each pair are synonyms (words that mean the same) or antonyms (words that mean the opposite).

1. disparity / equality
2. prosperity / poverty
3. grievous / terrible
4. entitled / denied
5. sham / genuine
6. fraud / deception

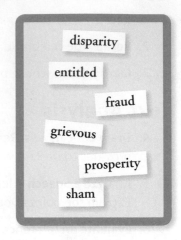

ACADEMIC VOCABULARY IN WRITING

• accurate • bias • contrast • convince • logic

Do you think Douglass's listeners would have trusted Douglass to provide a fair and **accurate** account of the lives of slaves and the laws that govern them? In a paragraph, use at least one Academic Vocabulary word in explaining your thoughts about how they might have regarded Douglass.

VOCABULARY STRATEGY: USING THE DICTIONARY

Frederick Douglass chose his words carefully to convey exactly the message he intended. To be certain you understand his message, it is important to understand his words. You can use a dictionary to determine the meanings of words, as well as their syllabication, pronunciations, alternate word choices, and parts of speech. For example, Douglass calls the celebration of the Fourth of July "mere bombast." Examine this entry:

❶ ❷ ❸
bom•bast (bŏm′bǎst′) *n.*
❹ Grandiloquent, pompous speech or writing.
❺ **syn** POMPOSITY, PRETENTIOUSNESS, BLUSTER, AFFECTATION

❶ Syllabication
❷ Pronunciation
❸ Part of speech
❹ Definition
❺ Alternate word choices

PRACTICE Use a dictionary to answer these questions about the boldfaced words.

1. How many syllables are in the word **prosperity?**
2. What part of speech is the word **fraud?**
3. What is the definition of the word **sham?**
4. What is a synonym for the word **entitled?**
5. How many syllables are in the word **grievous?**

COMMON CORE

L 4c Consult general reference materials (e.g., dictionaries) to find the pronunciation of a word or determine or clarify its precise meaning or its part of speech.
L 4d Verify the preliminary determination of the meaning of a word or phrase (e.g., by checking the inferred meaning in context or in a dictionary).

Interactive Vocabulary
THINK central

Go to **thinkcentral.com**.
KEYWORD: HML8-1036

Language

♦ **GRAMMAR IN CONTEXT:** Use Parallel Structure

COMMON CORE

L 3 Use knowledge of language and its conventions when writing, speaking, [or] reading.

Parallelism is the use of similar grammatical structures to link related ideas. Parts of a sentence that have parallel meanings should have parallel structure. For example, if you're listing various activities, use the same sentence part to describe each activity—nouns with nouns, verbs with verbs, or phrases with phrases. A typical error occurs when *and* is used to join different sentence parts.

> *Original:* Volunteering is fun, easy, and rewards you. (*The construction is not parallel because two adjectives are joined to a verb.*)

> *Revised:* Volunteering is fun, easy, and rewarding. (*The construction is now parallel because three adjectives are joined.*)

PRACTICE Rewrite each of these sentences to make its structure parallel.

1. Volunteers are kind and sympathize with people.
2. Donating clothing, volunteering at a food bank, and work at a homeless shelter are all ways you can help others.
3. Food banks are important for people who are unemployed, disabled, or don't have a home.
4. Don't spend all your time playing video games, watching movies, and at the mall.

*For more help with parallelism, see page R64 in the **Grammar Handbook.***

READING-WRITING CONNECTION

YOUR TURN To better understand how to use the rhetorical devices that Douglass uses so masterfully in his speech, respond to this prompt. Then use the **revising tip** to improve your writing.

WRITING PROMPT	REVISING TIP
Short Constructed Response: Persuasive Speech Think of a practice that you believe is wrong or unfair. Write **one paragraph** to help your classmates recognize how wrong or unjust it is. Use rhetorical questions in your response.	Review your paragraph to make sure you have used parallel structure when listing or linking related ideas.

Interactive Revision **THINK** central

Go to **thinkcentral.com**.
KEYWORD: HML8-1037

Writing Workshop

ARGUMENT

Persuasive Essay

As you have seen in this unit, a skillfully worded argument can persuade readers to agree with you or to do as you ask. In this workshop, you will take a stand on an issue that matters to you by writing a persuasive essay.

 Complete the workshop activities in your **Reader/Writer Notebook.**

WRITE WITH A PURPOSE

WRITING TASK

Write a **persuasive essay** in which you assert a strong claim on an issue and use reasons and evidence to persuade your audience to agree with you.

Idea Starters
- school dress codes
- an extended school year
- leash laws for dogs
- making volunteer work mandatory
- limits on Internet access

THE ESSENTIALS

Here are some common purposes, audiences, and formats for writing arguments.

PURPOSES	AUDIENCES	FORMATS
• to persuade others to agree with your claim • to encourage others to take action	• classmates and teacher • school board • newspaper readers • Web users • school or community groups	• essay for class • editorial • blog posting • letter • speech • power presentation

COMMON CORE TRAITS

1. DEVELOPMENT OF IDEAS
- includes an **introduction** that identifies an issue and states a **claim**
- provides **logical reasons** and **relevant evidence** to support the claim
- anticipates and acknowledges **opposing claims**
- offers a **concluding section** that follows from and supports the claim

2. ORGANIZATION OF IDEAS
- **organizes** reasons and evidence in a **logical way**
- uses **transitions**—words, phrases, and clauses—to create **cohesion** and link ideas

3. LANGUAGE FACILITY AND CONVENTIONS
- maintains a **formal style**
- uses **modifier**s effectively and corrects **run-on sentences**
- employs correct **grammar, usage,** and **spelling**

Writing Online

THiNK central

Go to **thinkcentral.com.**
KEYWORD: HML8N-1038

Planning/Prewriting

COMMON CORE W 1a–e Write arguments to support claims with clear reasons and relevant evidence W 5 Develop and strengthen writing as needed by planning.

Getting Started

CHOOSE AN ISSUE

An **issue** is a subject about which people disagree. For your argument, try to identify an issue that is controversial and important to many people. Brainstorm ideas with a partner or a small group.

▶ **ASK YOURSELF:**

- What are some issues about which I have strong feelings?
- Which issues matter most to people in my school or community?
- What actions do I want people to take?

THINK ABOUT AUDIENCE AND PURPOSE

As you plan your argument, keep your **audience** and **purpose** in mind. Considering your audience's feelings about the issue will help you craft a persuasive argument. Remember, your purpose is to convince readers to agree with you and, perhaps, inspire them to take action.

▶ **ASK YOURSELF:**

- Who is my audience?
- What does my audience care about? How can I get them to agree with my claim, or position?
- What opposing claims might my audience have? How can I respond to their opposing claims?

STATE YOUR CLAIM

Decide where you stand on the issue you have chosen, and state your position in a clear **claim**. A strong claim identifies the issue and makes your position clear. Be sure you can support your claim with solid reasons and evidence.

▶ **WHAT DOES IT LOOK LIKE?**

Issue: whether the school should require student volunteer work	**My viewpoint:** The school should require it.
Claim: The school should require eighth-graders to spend 15 hours during the school year volunteering with the elderly.	

SUPPORT YOUR CLAIM

To be convincing, you'll need to support your claim with logical and relevant **reasons,** or statements that explain or justify your position. Develop at least three logical reasons to support your claim. In addition, anticipate your audience's opposing claims and come up with strong responses to explain why your viewpoint is more valid.

▶ **WHAT DOES IT LOOK LIKE?**

Reason 1	Reason 2	Reason 3
Volunteering with the elderly will be a learning experience.	It is a good way to help others.	It will improve students' people skills.

Opposing claim: Students don't have time.

My response: Fifteen hours isn't much time when it's spread out over the whole school year.

Planning/Prewriting *continued*

Getting Started

GATHER EVIDENCE

Your claim needs to be supported by logical reasons and relevant evidence. Write down at least one piece of evidence for each reason you listed. Kinds of evidence include the following:

- **Anecdote**—a brief personal story that illustrates a point
- **Example**—a specific case that clarifies a general idea
- **Fact**—a statement that can be proven true
- **Statistic**—a fact in numerical form

Your notes can help you organize your argument. Review your evidence and decide which reason has the most convincing support. You might save that reason for the end of your essay, where it will have the most impact on your audience.

▶ WHAT DOES IT LOOK LIKE?

Reasons	Evidence
Volunteering with the elderly will be a learning experience.	I have learned about getting through hard times by talking to people at a nursing home. (anecdote)
It is a good way to help others.	Students can do yard work that some elders can't do for themselves. (example)
It will improve students' people skills.	In a <u>Time</u> poll, 60 percent of nursing students said they gained confidence by talking to elders and their families. (statistic)

USE PERSUASIVE TECHNIQUES

You should strengthen your essay by using **persuasive techniques**—methods writers use to influence people through their feelings and beliefs. One technique is an **emotional appeal,** which relies on strong feelings rather than logic or facts to persuade. Another technique is a **bandwagon appeal**—when the writer taps into people's desire to belong.

▶ ASK YOURSELF:

- What emotions might encourage readers to accept my claim?
- What positive or negative language could I use to stir up these emotions?
- What statements might make people want to join others in acting on my proposal?

PEER REVIEW Share your claim with a peer and ask him or her to review the reasons and evidence you've gathered to support your claim. Then ask: Which evidence is most convincing? What other kinds of evidence could I use to persuade my readers? If the evidence isn't as strong as you might like, ask: What new approach could I take?

YOUR TURN In your *Reader/Writer Notebook,* develop your writing plan. Write a claim about an issue. Then list three reasons that support your claim in a chart like the one on page 1039. Gather supporting evidence, and determine the most effective order in which to present your reasons. Consider how you can use persuasive techniques to strengthen your argument.

Drafting

This chart shows how to effectively structure your argument.

COMMON CORE

W 4 Produce clear and coherent writing.
W 9b (RI 1) Cite textual evidence that most strongly supports an analysis.
L 3 Use knowledge of language and its conventions when writing.

Organizing a Persuasive Essay

INTRODUCTION

- Capture your audience's attention in your opening sentences. For example, you might share a **startling fact,** tell an **interesting anecdote,** or ask a **thought-provoking question.**
- Include a strong **claim** that identifies the issue and your position on it.

▼

BODY

- Provide clear **reasons** in a **logical order** to support your claim.
- Support your reasons with relevant, accurate **evidence.**
- Address possible **opposing claims** and provide responses.
- Use **transitions** (such as *first, another,* and *most important*) to create cohesion.
- Maintain a **formal style** by using a serious tone and thoughtful, persuasive words.

▼

CONCLUDING SECTION

- **Restate your claim,** and remind your audience why their support matters.
- End with a **call to action,** a statement urging your audience to act on your proposal.

GRAMMAR IN CONTEXT: CORRECTING RUN-ON SENTENCES

As you argue for your position, you may get carried away and write a **run-on sentence**—two or more sentences written as if they were one sentence. Study this run-on sentence and two possible strategies for fixing it:

> *Volunteering is a learning experience, students learn how to relate to older people.*

Strategy	Example
Write two sentences instead of one. ▶	*Volunteering is a learning experience.* **Students** *learn how to relate to older people.*
Add a conjunction. ▶	*Volunteering is a learning experience,* **because** *students learn how to relate to older people.*

YOUR TURN Develop a draft of your essay, following the organization in the chart above. As you write, avoid run-on sentences by using one of the strategies shown above.

Revising

Once you've completed your draft, it's time to evaluate the content, organization, and style of what you've written. Use the chart to help you revise, rewrite, and strengthen your argument. Remember, your purpose is to persuade your audience. If necessary, consider trying a new approach to achieve your purpose.

PERSUASIVE ESSAY

Ask Yourself	Tips	Revision Strategies
1. **Does the introduction contain a clear claim?**	▶ **Circle** the sentence that states the issue and the writer's position.	▶ **Add** a claim, or **revise** the existing claim for clarity.
2. **Is the claim supported by solid reasons and evidence?**	▶ **Put a star** next to each reason, and **highlight** the evidence that supports it.	▶ **Add** reasons, or **add** statistics, anecdotes, and other evidence if needed. **Elaborate** to clarify evidence, if necessary.
3. **Does each body paragraph discuss one reason? Are the reasons presented in a logical order?**	▶ **Underline** each reason. **Number** the reasons in order of importance.	▶ **Rearrange** sentences so that each paragraph discusses one reason. **Reorder** paragraphs to present ideas in a logical order.
4. **Have I addressed alternate or opposing claims?**	▶ **List** important opposing claims that have not been addressed.	▶ **Add** persuasive responses to answer possible opposing claims.
5. **Do I maintain a formal style?**	▶ **Bracket** contractions, casual slang, or informal language.	▶ **Reword** contractions and **replace** informal language with precise, formal vocabulary.
6. **Does the concluding section restate my claim? Is there a call to action?**	▶ **Underline** the restatement, and **bracket** the call to action.	▶ **Add** a sentence that restates the claim. **Add** a call to action.

 YOUR TURN

PEER REVIEW Working with a peer, review your drafts. Use the chart to help you identify where and how your draft could be improved or reworked, or where you might try a new approach. Ask for suggestions to help you better persuade your intended audience.

COMMON CORE

W 1b Support claims with relevant evidence. W 5 Strengthen writing by revising, editing, rewriting, or trying a new approach.

ANALYZE A STUDENT DRAFT

Use this student's draft and the comments about it as a model for revising your own argument.

Letter to the School Board

by Teresa Lacey, Franklin Middle School

1   Many young people are eager to help out in their community, but they don't know how. A new proposal by a member of the school board would give every student an opportunity to serve. I am in favor of the proposed requirement that eighth-graders spend fifteen hours during the school year volunteering to help the elderly.

2   One reason this would be a good idea is that it would be a learning experience. Students could learn how to work with and relate to older people.

3   Another reason I think this rule would be magnificent is that it is a good way to help others. Eighth-graders can help people who cannot do things themselves. Students could do yard work or housework, run errands, or just spend time with the elderly so they would not be alone.

> In her introduction, Teresa clearly states her **claim** on the issue.

> Teresa presents her first **reason**. Adding **evidence** and an **emotional appeal** would help convince readers to agree with her.

> Her second reason is supported by **specific examples**.

LEARN HOW   Use Evidence and Persuasive Techniques   Teresa's second paragraph would be more convincing if she supported her reasoning with relevant evidence and used a persuasive technique. When she revised her draft, she added an **anecdote**—a brief personal story—as evidence for her first reason. In describing her experience at a nursing home, she used an **emotional appeal** to stir readers' emotions. Her revised paragraph, shown below, gives logical support for her claim and includes positive language that encourages her audience to feel good about accepting her position.

TERESA'S REVISION TO PARAGRAPH 2

One reason this would be a good idea is that it would be a learning experience. Students could learn how to work with and relate to older people.

My mother works at a nursing home, so I have had the opportunity to help her in the summer. I have learned to help with the residents there by playing games or walking with them, or by reading aloud to them. But it's not just a one-way street! The people there have taught me lessons about getting through tough times and about friendship. I love hearing the stories they tell about their lives.

4   Finally, I think just spending at least fifteen hours a school year with the elderly would improve students' people skills. Students would learn to talk and relate to others. They would learn how to be less shy, too. In a recent *Time* magazine poll, 60 percent of people said they gained confidence by talking to elders who were studying to become nurses.

> A **statistic** backs up Teresa's last reason.

5   For all these reasons, I believe the proposed requirement for volunteering would make a good rule. I hope that you will consider my reasons and vote to accept the proposed requirement.

> Teresa ends with a strong, direct **call to action.** However, she never addresses **possible opposing claims.**

LEARN HOW   **Address Opposing Claims**   A good persuasive essay should anticipate opposing claims the audience might raise. During a peer review of Teresa's draft, one of her classmates made this comment: "I already have so much to do. How could I possibly add volunteering to my busy schedule?" Teresa decided to add a response to address this opposing claim. To do this, she added a new paragraph immediately before her concluding section.

TERESA'S REVISION BEFORE PARAGRAPH 5

     Some students might argue that they already have too much work to do. It's true that we have many obligations, but the proposal is for just fifteen hours per school year. Spread out over nine months, it works out to less than two hours a month. The benefits to both students and community residents would be worth a little rescheduling.

    ∧For all these reasons, I believe the proposed requirement for volunteering would make a good rule. I hope that you will consider my reasons and vote to accept the proposed requirement.

YOUR TURN   Use the two "Learn How" lessons, as well as feedback from your teacher and peers, to revise your argument. Be sure to keep your overall purpose and intended audience in mind as you revise.

Editing and Publishing

COMMON CORE

W 1a Acknowledge and distinguish claim from alternate or opposing claims.
W 5 Strengthen writing by revising and editing. **L 1** Demonstrate command of the conventions of standard English grammar and usage. **L 2c** Spell correctly.

Now it is time to clean up any errors that may distract your audience from the content of your argument. When you edit, you proofread your essay to make sure that it is free of grammar, usage, spelling, and punctuation errors. Carefully read your essay for spelling errors that a word-processing spell checker might have missed.

GRAMMAR IN CONTEXT: PLACING MODIFIERS

Modifiers are words, such as adjectives and adverbs, that change or limit the meanings of other words. Modifying words, phrases, and clauses should be placed as close as possible to the words they modify. While editing her essay, Teresa corrected a misplaced modifier in the following sentence by moving it next to the noun it modifies:

In a recent *Time* magazine poll, 60 percent of people ~~said they gained~~ confidence by talking to elders ~~who were studying to become nurses~~.

[*Who were studying to become nurses* is a clause that modifies *people*. Moving it directly after *people* clarifies the meaning of the sentence.]

A **dangling modifier** does not logically modify any word in a sentence. In the following sentence from Teresa's essay, it's not clear what the phrase *Spread out over nine months* modifies. Here is how Teresa fixed the problem:

the time commitment
Spread out over nine months, ~~it~~ works out to less than two hours a month.

PUBLISH YOUR WRITING

Share your argument with an audience.

- E-mail your essay to a group or organization with an interest in your issue or with the power to make the change you want.
- Present your claim on a class blog, allowing others to comment on and discuss your position and call to action.
- Adapt your argument into a persuasive speech that you deliver to your audience.
- Submit your essay as an editorial to a school or community newspaper.

YOUR TURN Edit your essay to correct any errors. Pay special attention to your modifiers to make sure they are placed correctly. Then publish your final essay where your audience is likely to see it.

Scoring Rubric

Use the rubric below to evaluate your persuasive essay from the Writing Workshop or your response to the on-demand writing task on the next page.

PERSUASIVE ESSAY

SCORE	⦿ COMMON CORE TRAITS
6	• **Development** Effectively introduces the issue and asserts a claim; supports the claim with relevant reasons and evidence; addresses opposing claims; ends with a strong, memorable concluding section • **Organization** Arranges reasons and evidence in a logical order; uses transitions to create cohesion and link ideas • **Language** Consistently maintains a formal style; shows a strong command of conventions
5	• **Development** Competently introduces the issue and states a claim; offers logical reasons and evidence; acknowledges opposing claims; ends with a strong concluding section • **Organization** Organizes reasons and evidence logically; uses transitions to link ideas • **Language** Maintains a formal style; has a few errors in conventions
4	• **Development** Introduces the issue and states a claim; offers mostly relevant support; needs to more thoroughly address opposing claims; has an adequate concluding section • **Organization** Has a logical organization; could use a few more transitions • **Language** Mostly maintains a formal style; includes a few distracting errors in conventions
3	• **Development** States a claim; provides some reasons, but needs more evidence; does not sufficiently address other viewpoints; has a somewhat weak concluding section • **Organization** Reflects some flaws in organization; needs more transitions • **Language** Often lapses into an informal style; has some significant errors in conventions
2	• **Development** Has a weak claim; offers some irrelevant reasons and needs more evidence; fails to acknowledge other viewpoints; has a weak concluding section • **Organization** Has organizational flaws; lacks transitions throughout • **Language** Uses an informal style; has many distracting errors in conventions
1	• **Development** Lacks a clear claim; offers little, if any, support; ignores opposing viewpoints; has no concluding section • **Organization** Has no organization and transitions • **Language** Lacks a formal style; has major problems with grammar, usage, and spelling

Preparing for Timed Writing

COMMON CORE **W 10** Write routinely over shorter time frames for a range of tasks, purposes, and audiences.

1. ANALYZE THE TASK — 5 MIN

Read the task carefully. Underline the type of writing and the purpose. Circle the audience.

WRITING TASK

Students have many choices when deciding how to spend their time after school in extracurricular activities. Write a <u>persuasive essay</u> in which you <u>convince</u> (a friend) to join the activity that you enjoy most. Persuade your friend with logical reasons and relevant evidence, as well as persuasive appeals.

Audience
Purpose
Type of writing

2. PLAN YOUR RESPONSE — 10 MIN

Make a list of your extracurricular activities, such as exercising, playing a sport, volunteering, taking lessons, or tutoring. Circle the one you think would appeal to your friend. Then ask yourself why you enjoy the activity, and decide on two or three reasons to support the position that your friend should join you in this activity. Use a chart to list your reasons and evidence for them.

Join this activity: _____

Reasons	Evidence

3. RESPOND TO THE TASK — 20 MIN

Begin drafting your argument. You may want to start by describing the activity and inviting your friend to join. As you draft, keep the following points in mind:

- In your introduction, state a clear claim on the issue.
- Discuss one reason in each body paragraph. Support each reason with relevant evidence.
- Acknowledge and respond to possible opposing claims.
- End with a call to action.

4. IMPROVE YOUR RESPONSE — 5–10 MIN

Revising Check your draft. Have you addressed the key aspects of the writing task? Did you include persuasive reasons for your friend to join you? Have you supported your ideas with specific examples or anecdotes?

Proofreading Find and correct any errors in grammar, usage, spelling, punctuation, and capitalization. Mark your corrections neatly.

Checking Your Final Copy Before you turn in your essay, read it through one more time to make sure that you have done your best work.

Presenting a Persuasive Speech

Have you ever tried to convince a friend to help you out, or to persuade your parents to let you stay up later and play another video game? When you try to convince others with spoken language, you are giving a persuasive speech.

 Complete the workshop activities in your **Reader/Writer Notebook.**

SPEAK WITH A PURPOSE	COMMON CORE TRAITS
TASK Adapt your persuasive essay into a **persuasive speech.** Practice your speech, and then present it to your class.	*A STRONG PERSUASIVE SPEECH . . .* • makes a clear claim on a specific issue • supports the claim with logical reasons and relevant evidence • uses effective persuasive techniques • uses formal English as well as verbal and nonverbal cues to reinforce the speaker's position

COMMON CORE

SL 3 Delineate a speaker's argument, evaluating the soundness of the reasoning and relevance of the evidence.
SL 4 Present claims and findings in a focused, coherent manner.
SL 6 Adapt speech, demonstrating command of formal English.

Adapt Your Argument

Writing to persuade and speaking to persuade are similar skills. However, to give an effective speech, you will need to do much more than read your persuasive essay directly from the page. You will need to deliver your most salient, or important, points in a solid presentation that will grab the audience's attention. As you adapt your argument, follow these suggestions:

• **Audience** If your listening audience is different from your essay's audience, you will need to reconsider the content of your argument to make sure that it relates to the listeners' backgrounds and interests. Consider what reasons, examples, anecdotes, and facts would appeal to your listening audience.

• **Organization** Begin your speech by clearly stating your claim on an issue. Then you'll need to provide logical reasons and relevant evidence to support your claim. Review your argument and identify the most important points you want to include. Write brief sentences and phrases about those points on note cards or in an outline. Once you have your points listed, number them in the order you want to present them in your speech.

• **Potential Opposing Claims** Think about any concerns your audience is likely to bring up. As you present your argument, your audience may question the soundness, or strength, of your reasoning and the relevance of your evidence. Think about possible opposing claims and include strong responses to them as you adapt your argument.

**Speaking &
Listening Online**

Go to **thinkcentral.com.**
KEYWORD: HML8-1048

Deliver Your Speech

Since the purpose of your speech is to persuade others, your **delivery,** or the way you give the speech, is critical. To ensure that your speech runs smoothly, practice giving it more than once. Keep the following suggestions in mind as you practice:

- **If possible, practice in front of an audience** so that you can get used to speaking in front of a group.
- **Practice using your note cards** or your outline just as you will use it on the day of your speech. Remember to use formal English. Avoid using slang and informal phrasing.
- **Use a timer or watch** to ensure that you stay within the time limit you have been given.
- **Plan your gestures and facial expressions** to match the content of your speech. Practice using eye contact and adjusting your speaking rate, volume, and enunciation to effectively communicate your ideas.
- **Review the evaluation guidelines below.** Knowing how your audience will evaluate your presentation will help you prepare.

GUIDELINES FOR EVALUATING A SPEECH	
Content	Does the speaker clearly state a claim on an issue? Which reasons are sound and which are not? What evidence does the speaker use to support his or her reasons? Does the speaker include unsupported reasons or irrelevant evidence? What are they?
Style	Does the speaker maintain a formal style and use formal English to deliver his or her message? Is the style of the presentation well suited for the audience and purpose?
Delivery	Does the speaker speak clearly and at a good pace? How often does he or she make eye contact? Do the speaker's gestures and facial expressions match his or her message?

YOUR TURN

As a Speaker Deliver your speech to a classmate, using the tips in this workshop to present your ideas clearly and persuasively.

As a Listener Evaluate your classmate's content, style, and delivery. Delineate, or trace, the speaker's argument, listening carefully to make sure you can distinguish between facts and opinions. Identify whether the speaker supports his or her claim with sound reasoning and relevant evidence.

Assessment Practice

DIRECTIONS Read this selection and answer the questions that follow.

Nuclear Energy: Does It Make Sense for the Environment?

After decades of wariness, interest in nuclear power is picking up. Do the benefits outweigh the risks?

YES

1   Nuclear power is the largest source of emission-free energy generation in the United States. One of every five American homes and businesses gets its electricity from a nuclear plant.

2   Meeting tighter limits on air pollution is an ambitious task—one that would be virtually impossible without the clean-air benefits of nuclear power. The Department of Energy recognizes nuclear energy's essential role, identifying it as the single most effective strategy for reducing air pollution.

3   Nuclear power is the only expandable, large-scale energy source that avoids air pollution and can meet the electricity demands of our growing economy. Nuclear plants do not emit carbon dioxide or other greenhouse gases linked to global warming, nor do they emit pollutants that contribute to haze or smog.

4   Here's another way to look at nuclear energy's positive impact: Based on 1999 figures, if nuclear plants had to be replaced with oil- or coal-burning plants, the United States would have to eliminate 135 million passenger cars (about half of all cars!) just to keep our carbon dioxide emissions at current levels.

5   With regard to security, the nation's 103 nuclear power plants are among the best-defended industrial facilities in the United States. And today's nuclear plants have state-of-the-art safety features to prevent accidents.

6   Several notable environmentalists have recently endorsed nuclear energy. They believe global warming is increasingly our most pressing environmental concern, and recognize nuclear energy is a key part of the solution.

—Scott Peterson, Vice President
Nuclear Energy Institute

NO

7   Nuclear energy is not the answer to global warming. It makes no sense to solve one set of environmental problems by creating a bigger and more serious set of problems. And nuclear energy is full of very big and very serious problems.

8   Although new nuclear power plants would certainly be safer than older plants, the consequences of a major accident are still the same: widespread and long-lasting radiation pollution affecting several generations. An explosion at the Chernobyl nuclear reactor in the Soviet Union in 1986 killed 31 people and caused hundreds of thousands of cases of delayed illnesses.

9   In addition, nuclear power plants make attractive targets for terrorists. A disaster caused by sabotage or attack would cause great harm to people and the environment. Another problem for the environment is the spent fuel from nuclear power plants, which remains toxic for thousands of years. The United States still has no operational long-term repository to store the spent fuel safely.

10   The process of turning uranium into fuel for nuclear reactors can be easily modified to produce uranium for nuclear bombs. Pakistan's and India's nuclear bombs were made this way. The potential use of these weapons—possibly by terrorists—would be catastrophic to our environment.

11   Instead of investing in nuclear power, which just trades one set of problems for another, let's invest in renewable energy sources like wind and solar energy. They may cost a little more now, but they don't cause any harm—and they don't run out.

—Kelly Kissock, Associate Professor of Engineering
University of Dayton, Ohio

Reading Comprehension

Use "Nuclear Energy: Does It Make Sense for the Environment?" to answer questions 1–13.

1. The author wrote the "Yes" response most likely to —

    A. warn people about global warming

    B. report on oil- and coal-burning plants

    C. prove that cars emit pollutants

    D. promote the use of nuclear power

2. Which statement from the "Yes" response is an opinion?

    A. *Nuclear power is the largest source of emission-free energy generation in the United States.*

    B. *Meeting tighter limits on air pollution is an ambitious task . . .*

    C. *Nuclear plants do not emit carbon dioxide or other greenhouse gases linked to global warming . . .*

    D. *Several notable environmentalists have recently endorsed nuclear energy.*

3. What claim does the author of the "Yes" response make in paragraph 3?

    A. Nuclear plants are a clean source of energy.

    B. It is impossible to eliminate air pollution.

    C. Nuclear power improves the nation's economy.

    D. All types of energy have risks and benefits.

4. In paragraph 3, the author says that nuclear power plants do not contribute to haze or smog. This is an example of which persuasive technique?

    A. Bandwagon appeal

    B. Ethical appeal

    C. Appeal to fear

    D. Appeal to pity

5. In paragraph 4, the author makes a comparison between —

    A. past and current figures on carbon dioxide emissions

    B. passenger cars and other forms of transportation

    C. nuclear plants and oil- and coal-burning plants

    D. emissions in the United States and other parts of the world

6. What ethical issue does the author raise in the "Yes" response?

    A. Finding an alternative to cars

    B. Cutting energy costs

    C. Protecting the environment

    D. Creating convenient energy sources

7. The "Yes" response claims "today's nuclear plants have state-of-the-art safety features to prevent accidents." Which statement in the "No" response is a counterargument to that claim?

    A. *Another problem for the environment is the spent fuel from nuclear power plants, which remains toxic for thousands of years.*

    B. *In addition, nuclear power plants make attractive targets for terrorists. A disaster caused by sabotage or attack would cause great harm . . .*

    C. *An explosion at the Chernobyl nuclear reactor in the Soviet Union in 1986 killed 31 people and caused hundreds of thousands of cases of delayed illness.*

    D. *Although new nuclear power plants would certainly be safer than older plants, the consequences of a major accident are still the same: widespread and long-lasting radiation pollution . . .*

8. The author wrote the "No" response most likely to —
   A. explain how uranium is converted into fuel for nuclear reactors
   B. document the consequences of the accident at Chernobyl
   C. prove that terrorists can attack nuclear power plants in the United States
   D. convince people that nuclear energy is not worth the risks it presents

9. The author's claim in the "No" response is —
   A. new nuclear power plants are no safer than the old ones
   B. global warming is our most urgent environmental concern
   C. nuclear energy creates as many problems as it solves
   D. scientists are looking for ways to store spent nuclear fuel

10. The first argument in paragraph 9 appeals to the emotion of —
    A. anger
    B. fear
    C. pity
    D. pride

11. In paragraph 11, the author contrasts forms of energy to show that —
    A. it makes sense to use renewable energy sources
    B. nuclear energy costs more than renewable energy
    C. the world has a variety of energy sources
    D. it is possible to run out of nuclear resources

12. Which statement is a factual claim presented in both arguments?
    A. Meeting tighter air pollution limits is virtually impossible without nuclear energy.
    B. Uranium for fuel can easily be turned into uranium for nuclear bombs.
    C. Newer nuclear power plants are safer than older nuclear power plants.
    D. The nation's nuclear power plants are well defended against terror attacks.

13. Which opinion do the authors share?
    A. Global warming is a threat to the environment.
    B. Nuclear energy is a source of serious problems.
    C. The uranium used for fuel can easily be processed for nuclear bombs.
    D. The use of nuclear power effectively reduces air pollution.

SHORT CONSTRUCTED RESPONSE
Write two or three sentences to answer each question.

14. Reread paragraph 3 of the "Yes" response. What evidence does the author cite to support his claim that nuclear plants are a clean source of energy?

15. Reread paragraph 11 of the "No" response. Name two of the comparisons that the author makes between nuclear energy and energy from the wind and the sun.

Write a paragraph to answer this question.

16. Identify the author's purpose in writing the "No" response and discuss the reasons given to support the author's position.

GO ON

Vocabulary

Use context clues and your knowledge of related words to answer the following questions.

1. Use what you know about the word *essence* to define the related word *essential* in paragraph 2.
   A. Enjoyable
   B. Helpful
   C. Lasting
   D. Necessary

2. Use what you know about the word *emit* to define the related word *emissions* in paragraph 4.
   A. Costs of labor and materials
   B. Substances released into the air
   C. Chances of explosion
   D. Dangers to the environment

3. Use what you know about the word *ray* to define the related word *radiation* in paragraph 8.
   A A colorless, odorless gas
   B. A system of pipes for heating or cooling
   C. Waves or particles of radioactive energy
   D. A device that transmits radio signals

4. Use what you know about the word *position* to define the related word *repository* in paragraph 9.
   A. A place to put things
   B. An electrical outlet for a plug
   C. Something hidden for safekeeping
   D. One who acts on behalf of another

Use context clues and the Latin or Greek word root definitions to answer the following questions.

5. The Greek word *oikonomos* means "one who runs a household." In paragraph 3, what does the word *economy* mean?
   A. The system or range of financial activity in a country
   B. A nation's air, water, and other natural resources
   C. A family's management of its resources
   D. The least expensive accommodations for travelers

6. The Latin word *lutum* means "mud." In paragraph 3, what does the word *pollutants* mean?
   A. Areas of low-lying soggy ground
   B. Masses of rocks left by glaciers
   C. Tiny particles that live in swamps
   D. Waste material that contaminates the air

7. The Greek root *kat* means "down," and the Greek word *strephein* means "to turn." What does the word *catastrophe* mean in paragraph 10?
   A. Going against the laws of nature
   B. Producing lower air temperatures
   C. Moving in an opposite direction
   D. Causing great suffering or damage

Revising and Editing

DIRECTIONS Read this passage and answer the questions that follow.

---

(1) The purpose of the Environmental Protection Agency is to protect health and safeguarding the environment. (2) For almost 40 years, the agency has conducted research, set standards, and enforcing activities to prevent pollution. (3) In 1975, the United Nations designated the agency as an information center for environmental data. (4) Its information is reliable, complete, and offers access to everyone. (5) The agency works with organizations such as Habitat for Humanity to make land safe for housing. (6) The agency's mission has always been to give Americans an environment that is clean, healthy, and can be sustained.

---

1. Choose the BEST way to rewrite sentence 1 to make its structure parallel.

   A. The purpose of the Environmental Protection Agency is to protect health and it safeguards the environment.

   B. The purpose of the Environmental Protection Agency is to protect health, safeguarding the environment.

   C. The purpose of the Environmental Protection Agency is to protect health as it is safeguarding the environment.

   D. The purpose of the Environmental Protection Agency is to protect health and safeguard the environment.

2. Choose the BEST way to rewrite sentence 2 to make its structure parallel.

   A. For almost 40 years, the agency has conducted research, set standards, and enforced activities to prevent pollution.

   B. For almost 40 years, the agency has conducted research, set standards, and it enforces activities to prevent pollution.

   C. For almost 40 years, the agency has conducted research, set standards, and to enforce activities to prevent pollution.

   D. For almost 40 years, the agency has conducted research, set standards, and will enforce activities to prevent pollution.

3. Choose the BEST way to rewrite sentence 4 to make its structure parallel.

   A. Its information is reliable, complete, and lacking in secrecy.

   B. Its information is reliable, complete, and accessible.

   C. Its information is reliable, complete, and offering everyone an opportunity to educate himself or herself.

   D. Its information is reliable, complete, and without boundaries in its accessibility.

4. Choose the BEST way to rewrite sentence 6 to make its structure parallel.

   A. The agency's mission has always been to give Americans an environment that is clean, healthy, and that has sustainability.

   B. The agency's mission has always been to give Americans an environment that is clean, healthy, and that won't decay.

   C. The agency's mission has always been to give Americans an environment that is clean, healthy, and wanting to be sustained.

   D. The agency's mission has always been to give Americans an environment that is clean, healthy, and sustainable.

STOP

Ideas for Independent Reading

Which questions from Unit 9 made an impression on you?
Continue exploring them with these books.

COMMON CORE

RL 10 Read and comprehend
literature. **RI 10** Read and
comprehend literary nonfiction.

Should wildlife stay wild?

The Exchange Student
by Kate Gilmore

One hundred years after the
crash, Daria is the youngest
animal breeder working with
endangered animals on Earth.
The last thing she needs is
to host an alien exchange
student named Fen who is
obsessed with Daria's zoo but
who won't say why.

Frightful's Mountain
by Jean Craighead George

Frightful is a peregrine falcon
that has lived with Sam since
she was around 10 days old.
When Sam is forced to let her
go, she must learn to live in
the wild on her own. Will
her instincts be enough to
guide her?

The Wilderness Family: At Home with Africa's Wildlife
by Kobie Krüger

When Kobie moves to
the African bush with her
husband and three daughters,
she becomes a foster mother
to a lion named Leo. Can a
human mother teach a young
lion about life in the wild?

Are all games worth playing?

Heat
by Mike Lupica

Mike's team is sure to make
it to the Little League World
Series until Mike, their best
pitcher, isn't allowed to play.
The authorities want proof of
his age, and they are asking
questions about other things
Mike and his brother don't
want anyone to know about.

Surviving Antarctica: Reality TV 2083
by Andrea White

In 2083, five teens are chosen
to reenact a historic trip to
the South Pole for a television
audience. They might die in
the process, but they have no
other way to improve their
lives. Will society tolerate the
way they're treated?

Game Design for Teens
by Les Pardew and Alpine Studios

How do you create a
computer game? This book
shows you how to take an
idea for a game and make
it a reality. You'll learn the
skills you need and meet
people who have invented
successful games.

Who decides what's important?

Our Eleanor
by Candace Fleming

Until Eleanor Roosevelt came
along, most first ladies didn't
try to affect government
policy. But Eleanor was
different. She persuaded her
husband President Roosevelt
to make the needs of poor
people, women, and children
a priority.

Photo by Brady: A Picture of the Civil War
by Jennifer Armstrong

The Civil War was the first
war to be photographed.
The images captured by the
photographers who went to
the battlegrounds affected
the way those on the home
front viewed the war.

Quicksilver
by Stephanie Spinner

Zeus, the ruler of the Greek
gods, decides the fate of
everyone. This book is told
from the point of view of
Hermes, Zeus' favorite errand
boy. Hermes is quick and
funny, but can he change
Zeus's mind when people's
lives are on the line?

Get Novel Wise

THiNK central

Go to thinkcentral.com.
KEYWORD: HML8-1056

The Power of Research

UNIT

10

RESEARCH WORKSHOPS

- Research Strategies
- Writing Research Papers

1057

Share What You Know

How can RESEARCH help me?

Doing research means locating, analyzing, and understanding information in order to answer a question. You do research every day—for example, when you look up movie times or weather forecasts. Some kinds of research require more effort, such as gathering information for a school report. In this unit, you will learn to find, use, and evaluate sources of information. You will also learn how to improve your ability to search for sources and judge the sources you already use.

ACTIVITY What do you research at school, at home, while shopping, or while doing homework? Work with a partner to list examples.

	What I Research	Where I Find Answers
at school		
at home		
other places		

Find It Online! THINK central

Go to thinkcentral.com for the interactive version of this unit.

COMMON CORE

DEVELOPING RESEARCH SKILLS
- Ask and answer research questions
- Use search terms effectively
- Use library and media center resources to find print and digital sources
- Choose primary and secondary sources
- Evaluate information and sources, including nonfiction books, periodicals, and Web sites
- Conduct your own research

WRITING AND LANGUAGE
- Write a research paper
- Formulate a major research question
- Locate and evaluate sources
- Take notes
- Prepare a source list
- Summarize and paraphrase
- Quote directly and avoid plagiarism
- Document sources
- Prepare a Works Cited list
- Follow a standard format for citation
- Capitalize and punctuate citations correctly

SPEAKING AND LISTENING
- Make a research presentation

ACADEMIC VOCABULARY
- investigate
- publish
- research
- source
- technical

Writing and Research in a Digital Age

KEYWORD: HML8-1059

From online news feeds and electronic archives to podcasts and digital notebooks, technology tools can help you tackle any research project. Find out how.

What is the research PROCESS?

○ **COMMON CORE**

Included in this workshop:
W 7 Conduct short research projects to answer a question, drawing on several sources and generating additional questions. **W 8** Gather information from multiple sources, using search terms effectively; assess the credibility and accuracy of each source.

Researching a fact or two usually isn't challenging. Researching a topic, however, is a complex process that involves using several sources to find many—and sometimes conflicting—facts and opinions. Furthermore, finding the information is only the beginning of the research process. Research also requires you to evaluate the sources you find.

QUICKWRITE In this unit, you will follow a student who is interested in entering a competition for young inventors. If you were this student, how could you find information that would help you accomplish your goals? Try creating a cluster diagram like this one with questions you could ask.

Young Inventors' Competition

What inventions have teens submitted?

Who sponsors contests for young inventors?

CREATIVE THINKING ZONE

invites all teen inventors to a contest for the **BEST NEW INVENTION** by a teenager!

Go to our Web site for details.

Finding and Narrowing Your Topic

Before you begin the research process, take a few minutes to set a research goal and to develop a clearer idea of your topic.

SET RESEARCH GOALS

First, write down a few goals for your research. Here is how one student listed a set of goals related to the topic of competitions for young inventors.

> *General goal:* I want to enter a contest for young inventors.
>
> *Questions:*
>
> - **What are the requirements?** Are the few simple things I've invented suitable to enter in a contest?
> - **What are the contests like?** I'd like a chance to meet other inventors and learn more about inventing in general.
>
> *Specific goals:* I want to learn more about how a young inventor like me can compete in contests, meet other inventors, and learn more about inventing.

LEARN ABOUT YOUR TOPIC

Once you have decided on some specific goals, it's time to start your search. Using a variety of sources will help make your research accurate. Try any or all of these methods.

- **Use the Internet.** Type words related to your topic, such as *teen inventors*, into a search engine. Select one or two Web pages from the search results. Then visit them to get ideas about your topic.
- **Talk with people.** Find someone who knows about your topic or shares your interest in it. Present your research goals and ask for ideas.
- **Use print resources.** Read an article on your topic or skim a nonfiction book.
- **Talk with a librarian.** Ask for suggestions for sources and ways to improve your research focus.

NARROW YOUR TOPIC

A more specific topic is easier to research than a broad topic. Here's how one student narrowed her topic after reading.

Topic	More Specific	Even More Specific
inventions	competitions for young inventors	competitions for young inventors of robots

Research Tools

THINK central

Go to **thinkcentral.com**.
KEYWORD: HML8-1061

DEVELOP RESEARCH QUESTIONS

After you have narrowed the focus of your topic, the next step is to ask research questions about it. Notice how these research questions can't be answered with just yes or no. Instead, they require rich, full answers.

- Which kinds of inventions have teens submitted?
- How do I find a contest that will accept my new game?
- How can I protect my idea?

After you write your research questions, highlight the **keywords,** or words that clearly identify your topic. You will use keywords to search library catalogs and databases and to get information from search engines.

PREPARE TO TAKE NOTES

Getting and staying organized helps you keep track of details, credit sources correctly, and do more in less time. One way to be sure you are organized is to take careful notes. If you are doing research for a report, consider using note cards. See pages 1082–1084 to learn more about this note-taking method.

For other kinds of research, try using lists and charts. Think about what kinds of information you are looking for and which format would be best for that information. Here is how one student kept track of contests she found.

Name of Competition	Type	Requirements	Notes and Important Dates
Creative Thinking Zone	toys	fully working prototype	Grades 6–8 March 1 online registration
Staples Invention Quest	office products	idea described in detailed drawings and itemized specifications	Grades 8–12 October 15 mail-in registration form
Craftsman NSTA Young Inventors Award	tools	description and drawings—no physical prototypes	Grades 6–8 February 15 online registration
Wizardkids.net	all kinds of inventions	working models or drawings	Grades 6–12 March 15 online registration

Many researchers start their searches online. Read on to learn how to find the best sites.

Searching the Internet

The **Internet** is a system of computer networks. The World Wide Web is part of the Internet. The nickname *Web* comes from the hundreds of millions of connections, or links, from site to site. These links can lead users to billions of Web pages. You can access the Internet by using a device called a **modem,** which sends and receives information over phone lines. You can also use a cable or wireless device to access the Internet.

SELECT SEARCH ENGINES

Search engines are Web sites that organize information based on keywords, headings, popularity among Web users, and other criteria. You can choose from many search engines. Each returns different choices because each selects and organizes information in slightly different ways. To get the best results, learn the rules for the specific search engine you are using. You might also try using the advanced search forms that most search engines offer.

USE SPECIFIC KEYWORDS AND SEARCH LIMITERS

Try combining keywords and using search modifiers or limiters like these.

- **Use quotation marks.** A search for *"young inventors"* will give you results that mention both terms, in that order, right next to each other.

- **Combine terms.** Some search engines allow you to use the term AND or a plus sign to combine terms. For example, *"young inventors" AND toys* will return only pages that contain all those terms.

- **Exclude terms.** Some search engines let you exclude terms from your results by typing NOT or a minus sign. For instance, *"inventions by young people"* *–computers* will return all pages with the phrase "inventions by young people" except the ones that also mention computers.

This chart shows how using search limiters can give you more useful results.

TERMS FOR THE INTERNET
You will use these terms when discussing online research:
- Web site
- Web page
- search engine
- keyword
- Web address
- hyperlink

TIP Identifying the best search terms is a multi-step process. Keep changing and refining your terms until you get the results you want.

YOU TYPE IN...	YOU GET...	THIS IS...
young inventors	1,090,000 results	far too many results, so you make your keywords more specific
"young inventor" competition	104 results	much better, but you can tell from the descriptions that many of the results are unrelated to your topic
+"young inventor" +toys +competition	10 results	best, because the results are closest to the research goal

EVALUATE SEARCH ENGINE RESULTS

Searches often return far more results, also called *hits*, than you can examine. Follow these guidelines for deciding which results to click on.

1. **Don't just click on the first result.** It may not be the right one for you.

2. **Focus first on the Web address.** Sites with *.com* and *.net* in their address are usually personal or commercial sites and may contain sales pitches or biased information. Sites with *.org* and *.gov* in their address are usually the work of government agencies or institutions such as museums and nonprofit organizations. Be aware, however, that organizations such as political parties also have *.org* addresses.

3. **Next, read the brief description the search engine provides.** If the address appears promising and the description matches your goal or keywords, click on the result. If not, you can go to the next result or the next page of results. You can also change or refine your search terms and try again.

4. **Read the page.** Print only those pages that provide information that is closely related to your topic and your research goals.

> **TIP** In general, *.gov* and *.org* sites are more reliable than other sites because they are usually the work of large, reputable groups, and their purpose is often only to inform.

YOUR TURN

Choose Search Engine Results

This page shows the first four results from an online search.

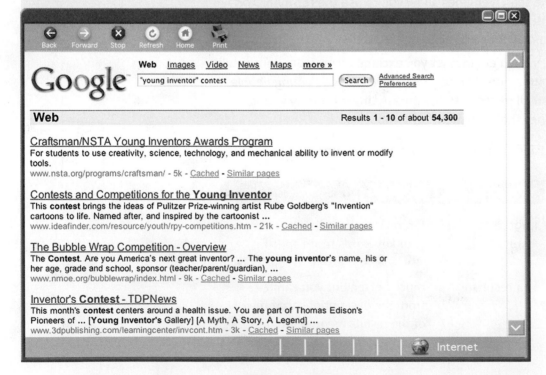

Close Read

1. What terms did the searcher use? How do you know?

2. Do you think these results would be useful to a student searching for contests for young inventors? Explain your answer.

3. How would you modify this search to find out about contests for young inventors of robots? Write your new search terms exactly as you would type them into a search box.

EXPLORE A WEB SITE

When you click on a search result, a Web page will come up.

- **Home page**—A **home page** is the main page of a Web site. It welcomes you to the site and gives a general overview.

- **Menus and Hyperlinks**—**Menus** show the main categories of information on a Web site. Another option for finding information is **hyperlinks,** sometimes referred to simply as links. Hyperlinks and links are underlined or highlighted words, terms, URLs (Web addresses), or Web site names. Click on hyperlinks to move to another page or another site.

- **Icons**—These are small pictures or symbols that you can click on to find information. On the Web site below, clicking on the beanie icon brings up information on Jerome Lemelson's invention of a mechanical beanie.

- **Credits and Sponsor**—The **credits** tell who produced the site, when the site was created, and when it was last updated. A **sponsor** is an organization, agency, or individual that owns the site and controls its content. Knowing about the credits and sponsor helps you evaluate the site for accuracy and reliability. Look for a link that says "About This Site" or "About Us."

 YOUR TURN

Examine a Web Page

This Web page contains the kinds of information shown on many home pages.

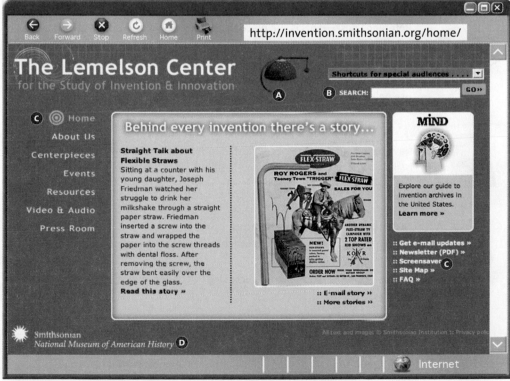

Ⓐ Icon Ⓑ Search Options Ⓒ Menus Ⓓ Sponsor

Close Read

1. Which menu item would you click on if you wanted to be notified of upcoming events at the Lemelson Center?

2. The "Search" option (item B) lets you search for a specific term or terms within the Lemelson Center site. Why is this a useful option?

3. Where would you click to find out more about who owns this site?

4. Based on what you see here, do you judge this site to be reliable? Why or why not?

Using Library Resources

The Internet isn't the only place to find information. Your local public library and your school's media center are also storehouses of information. Furthermore, these places offer access to online information that you cannot get by using most search engines.

Before you start your research, learn how your library or media center is organized and what it offers. Most libraries have different sections for adults, young adults, and children. There may also be special sections devoted to business, local history, or genealogy (tracing your family tree). Many libraries and media centers offer space for quiet study. Computer terminals throughout the library allow you to find out about the library or media center's holdings, use other online sources, send e-mail, and create reports.

LIBRARY AND MEDIA CENTER RESOURCES

BOOKS

Fiction—Novels and short stories are examples of fiction. Fictional works come from the writer's imagination, but they may be based on real people, places, and events.

Nonfiction—Nonfiction works present facts and tell about real people, places, and events. Newspaper and magazine articles, scientific works, essays, speeches, history books, instructional and procedural manuals, and biographies are nonfiction.

REFERENCE

Reference desk—This is the place to ask for help with identifying and locating library materials.

Reference works—The reference section of the library includes almanacs, dictionaries, atlases, encyclopedias, and statistical abstracts. These are for use only in the library—you can't check them out and take them home.

NEWSPAPERS AND PERIODICALS

Newspapers and magazines—Most libraries and media centers carry current issues. Some also have past issues in print, on microfilm, on microfiche, or in a digitized format.

AUDIO AND VIDEO RESOURCES

DVDs—Many libraries lend documentaries, instructional films, and filmed performances.

Audio—Libraries also lend CD recordings of books, music, speeches, poems, and plays.

E-RESOURCES

Electronic collections—You can access and print out articles from databases. You can also download e-books, e-audiobooks, CD-ROMs, podcasts, and MP3s.

TIP To access e-resources from a home or other remote computer, all you need is a library card barcode, which you can get when you apply for a library card.

UNDERSTAND THE LIBRARY CATALOG

The **library catalog** is a complete index of the library's or library network's holdings. Consult the reference librarian or the online search tips for the best and fastest ways to search it.

Library catalogs provide many options for searching. The most common methods are by author, title, and keyword or subject.

- **Author**—Type the author's last name first, like this: *Twain, Mark.* If no results appear, check the spelling, or try the first name first: *Mark Twain.*
- **Title**—Type in the full title or any part of it you know. Leave out unimportant first words such as *the* and *a.*
- **Subject or Keyword**—Type in a word or phrase that names your subject, such as *inventor.* If the results are too broad, then add to your keyword, such as by typing *teen inventor.* Keep in mind that you may need to try several words and phrases before the catalog returns results you can use. For instance, you might find that the phrase *young inventor* or *patent invention* produces better results.

YOUR TURN

Search a Library Catalog

A student typed in the phrase *inventor's contests* to get to the catalog page below.

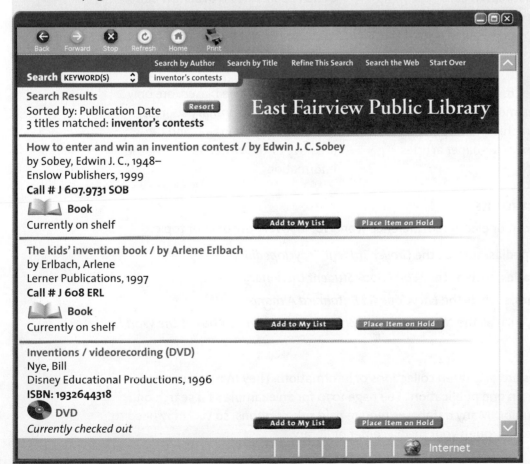

Close Read

1. How are the results on this page arranged?

2. Name five types of information the page gives for each result.

3. Name three options the user has for getting different search results.

Choosing Nonfiction Sources

Understanding different types of nonfiction sources can help you distinguish the nature and value of each and decide which ones to choose.

PRIMARY AND SECONDARY SOURCES

Every nonfiction work is either a primary source or a secondary source.

TYPE OF SOURCE	BENEFITS AND DRAWBACKS
Primary sources: materials written or created by people who took part in or witnessed the events they recorded	**Benefits:** supply interesting firsthand information and details
▼	▼
Examples: autobiographies, public documents such as birth certificates, advertisements, speeches, letters, e-mails, diaries and journals, editorials, political cartoons, first-person newspaper and magazine articles	**Drawbacks:** may be biased because they give just one person's limited point of view; may require specialized knowledge to interpret
Secondary sources: records of events created by people who were not directly involved in or present at the events	**Benefits:** provide an overview or a broad understanding; often synthesize many points of view
▼	▼
Examples: textbooks, encyclopedias, reviews, documentaries, most history books, biographies, third-person magazine and newspaper articles	**Drawbacks:** may be biased; are only as reliable as the primary sources on which they are based and the accuracy of the writer gathering the information

REFERENCE WORKS

Consult print or electronic reference works for an overview of your topic.

- **Encyclopedias,** such as the *Grolier Student Encyclopedia*
- **Dictionaries,** such as the *World Book Student Dictionary*
- **Almanacs,** such as the *Encyclopedia Britannica Almanac*
- **Atlases,** such as the *National Geographic Family Reference Atlas of the World*

DATABASES

Databases are organized collections of information. They may focus on one subject or on one publication. See page 1070 for an example of a search on InfoTrac Junior. Many databases require paid subscriptions, so you may need to access them through your media center or library.

NONFICTION BOOKS

For in-depth information on a topic, be sure to consult nonfiction books. To decide whether a specific book is right for your research goal, follow these steps:

1. Read the **title** and **subtitle** to get a general idea of what the book is about.

2. Examine the **copyright page.** Find the latest copyright date shown. This will tell you how recent the information is.

3. Read the **table of contents.** The titles of parts and chapters will give you an overview of the book's contents. This page also often lists other useful features, such as a **bibliography** (a list of sources used), a list of suggested **further reading,** and a **glossary** (a section that lists and defines specialized terms the author uses).

4. Check the **index** for specific topics or terms that interest you. Single page numbers can signal that there is no more than a brief mention of the topic.

YOUR TURN

Examine the Parts of a Book

Notice the features of the book shown below.

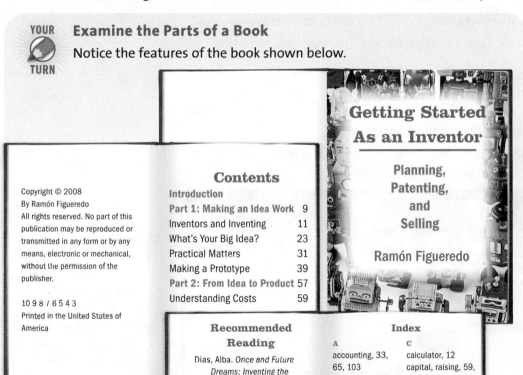

Close Read

1. Is this book recent enough to be helpful? How do you know?

2. Does this book give practical advice about both creating and selling an invention? Explain how you arrived at your answer.

3. Does this book contain information on making a prototype? How about on patent attorneys? Tell where you found this information.

Newspapers and Periodicals

Newspapers are publications that contain news and advertising. Many newspapers include other features as well, such as editorials, letters to the editor, cartoons, and puzzles. Newspapers are published daily, weekly, or very frequently. Most daily newspapers have online versions that are updated throughout the day.

Like newspapers, **periodicals** are publications issued on a regular basis. They contain news, advice, fiction, research findings, or a combination of these. Periodicals called magazines are published for the general public. Periodicals called journals are published for academic and scholarly audiences. Online versions of periodicals often include corrections, updates, and previously published articles.

Researchers often turn to recent newspaper and magazine articles for up-to-date information presented in understandable language. Older newspaper and magazine articles can offer some perspective on a particular time period.

- **Examples of Newspapers:** *Washington Post, San Francisco Chronicle, Denver Post*
- **Examples of Magazines:** *Time, Consumer Reports, Odyssey, Teen Ink, Next Step*

To find articles on your topic, use a database. The page below comes from InfoTrac Junior, a database for students in grades 5 through 12.

YOUR TURN

Examine an Articles Database Search

To see each article listed in the results, the user would have to click on the underlined title of the article or the underlined words *Check Out*.

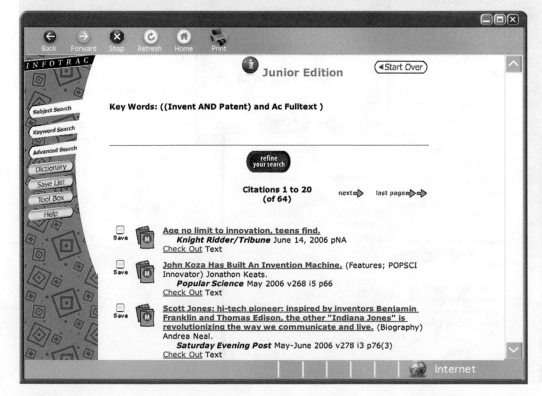

Close Read

1. What three options does this database provide for searching? (Hint: See the menu on the left-hand side of the page.)

2. Which two keywords did the researcher use?

3. Which of these results would you click on first? Explain your answer.

Evaluating Sources

Sources vary widely in purpose, authorship, and the care with which they were created. Therefore, always carefully evaluate the sources you use to see whether their information is **reliable**, or trustworthy. **Evaluating** means asking and answering questions like the ones below about the reliability of every book, magazine, newspaper, Web site, and other source you use. Refer to pages 1072–1074 for questions about specific types of sources.

QUESTION	REASONS TO ASK
What is the publication date?	Up-to-date information is important, especially in medicine, technology, sports, and politics. Even when you are researching an event that happened many years ago, up-to-date sources usually present the latest findings and insights.
Who is the author?	In general, look for sources of information written by people who are experts in their field. The author's profession, other publications, and awards are additional guides to his or her knowledge of the subject.
Who published the source?	Some publishers are more reliable than others. They take care to ensure that the information they present is accurate and objective. Magazines and newspapers that feature articles about fads and celebrities can be unreliable. Instead, look for well-known publishers and university presses. If you're in doubt, ask a librarian for help.
What is the author's or publisher's point of view?	Many Web sites and publications have a political or commercial purpose. Some may present **biased,** or one-sided, views of topics, leaving out information that does not suit their purposes. Determine the source's intended purpose before you decide whether to use it.
Is this information useful to me?	Make sure the source is written at a level that's appropriate for you—not too childish or too scholarly. Also, study the table of contents or menus for your keywords or for other words and phrases that relate specifically to your research goals.

EVALUATE WEB SITES

A book is often the result of teamwork: it has an author as well as editors and reviewers. On the other hand, a Web site may be the work of just one individual. In many cases, no one has checked or reviewed personal Web sites.

To evaluate a Web site, ask and answer these questions:

- **Who created the site?** Is the author an expert? What does the site tell you about the author(s)?

- **Why was the site created?** Consider whether the creators want to sell you something—either a product or an idea.

- **Are there problems on the site?** Watch for mistakes in facts, grammar, or spelling, which may mean that the source is unreliable.

- **Are there credits?** Look for a bibliography of the site's creator, the name of a sponsoring organization, and a "last updated" reference.

- **Could you consult a more reliable source to find coverage of the same topic?** Use a variety of sources, such as encyclopedias, almanacs, magazines, newspapers, documentaries, and interviews with experts.

YOUR TURN

Examine a Personal Web Site

What is useful about this site? What errors or problems do you see?

Close Read

1. What is the purpose of this site?

2. What is missing from this site that could help you evaluate it?

3. Name two other problems with this site.

EVALUATE A NONFICTION BOOK

Once you have found a book with information on your topic, how do you evaluate it? Ask and answer these questions:

- **What is the copyright date?** Look for the most recent date on the copyright page. If you see many dates, that is a good sign because it means that the book has been through many updates and printings. The book jacket may also say *revised, updated,* or *new.*

- **Is the book carefully researched?** Look for a **bibliography,** a list of works the author referred to when writing. Also, look for **footnotes** and **end notes** that help you understand where the author found specific information. Check the back of the book for an **appendix** with additional information, such as maps, charts, or tables.

- **Who is the author?** Look for an author biography on the book jacket or at the end of the book. Use the biography to learn more about the author's education, profession, and other publications.

YOUR TURN

Examine a Nonfiction Book

Decide whether this book is a reliable source for someone who is researching the topic of teen inventors who got patents. Use what you have learned about nonfiction books and about the parts of a book (page 1069).

Kids Create

America's Youngest Inventors

Ilana Brodsky

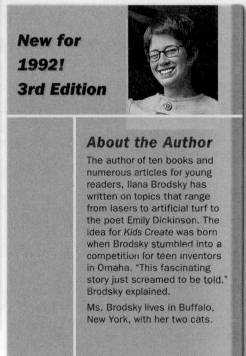

New for 1992! 3rd Edition

About the Author

The author of ten books and numerous articles for young readers, Ilana Brodsky has written on topics that range from lasers to artificial turf to the poet Emily Dickinson. The idea for *Kids Create* was born when Brodsky stumbled into a competition for teen inventors in Omaha. "This fascinating story just screamed to be told," Brodsky explained.

Ms. Brodsky lives in Buffalo, New York, with her two cats.

Close Read

1. What is this book about?

2. Is the author an expert on this topic? What are her qualifications?

3. How up to date is this book? Is it new or revised?

4. What other parts of this book would provide information about its reliability and usefulness? (Hint: See page 1069.)

EVALUATE NEWSPAPERS AND PERIODICALS

Newspapers and periodicals are good sources of recent information. Your library may offer some of them in print and many others online or on microfilm. Once you find a newspaper or periodical article, you should evaluate it before you use it. Ask and answer these questions:

- **Is this magazine or newspaper well-known and respected?** Many national magazines and newspapers with large circulation numbers are reliable. If a publication prints rumors about celebrities, stories about space aliens, or miracle weight-loss cures, avoid it.

- **When was it published?** Up-to-date sources are best unless you're looking for details or insights from a particular period. For example, if you are researching a particular inventor from the past, a magazine or newspaper article from when he or she was alive and inventing could be among your best sources.

- **Who is the author?** Look for information about the writer. Assume that staff writers are as reliable as the publication in which they appear.

- **Can you verify the facts?** You should be able to verify every fact in at least one other source.

YOUR TURN

Examine a Newspaper Article

Ask questions about the periodical, the author, the facts, and other content to evaluate this article.

---

from the **Warren Star**

Warren Teen Wins Inventors' Competition

BY DERONE SANDAGE, STAFF WRITER

Judges at the Young Inventors' Convention in Buffalo have awarded first prize to a local teenager.

"Shoveling snow is nobody's favorite chore," says Warren Middle School student Alex Heisner, "so I thought I would make it a little easier."

Heisner invented the Shovel-L, a sturdy, wheeled shovel that makes snow removal less of a strain on the back and shoulders. "It works on heavy, wet snow and on the dry, powdery kind," explained the 13-year-old, who has applied for a patent. "It isn't so great with leaves, though. They mostly just blow away."

HELP FOR YOUNG INVENTORS

- The Young Inventors Convention will meet in Baltimore next October. Other area and national conventions exist.

- Try calling local colleges and universities and asking for the school of business. Professors, instructors, or business clubs may offer advice.

- The local office of the Small Business Administration can offer tips and contacts.

When Heisner demonstrated his device at the convention, judges agreed that it really did work.

See INVENTOR, page B7

Close Read

1. How well is this article related to the research topic "invention competitions for teens"?

2. Do you think the information in this article is reliable? Why or why not?

3. At the end of this article, the reporter included his e-mail address and the Web address for the Young Inventors' Convention. Why is this information important?

Conducting Your Own Research

The Internet and the library aren't the only places you can find information on your topic. For example, you may be able to gather data by conducting a survey or doing another kind of field research or observation. You may even be able to locate experts to interview.

OBSERVATION AND FIELD RESEARCH

Doing **field research** means observing with a specific research goal in mind. For example, you might attend a young inventors' competition and collect data about the entries and the people who submitted them. Here are the field notes that one student took.

> ### Notes on Visit to Young Inventors' Competition, Austin, 4/26/2009
>
> - 128 participants, 128 inventions
> - participants represent 84 counties in Texas
> - 28 household devices; 61 devices related to computer hardware or software; 4 industrial devices; 6 transportation-related items; 25 miscellaneous
> - Youngest participant: 12 years, 7 months; oldest participant, 17 years, 8 months
> - Sources of inspiration: 16 percent friends; 10 percent parents; 42 percent media (movies, TV, Web sites, radio, books, podcasts); 12 percent teachers or school projects; 20 percent "out of the blue"/don't know

INTERVIEWS

Interviews can yield valuable information from primary sources. You can conduct an interview in person, by telephone, by e-mail, by instant message, or by letter. For the topic of young inventors, you might interview a successful inventor, someone who organizes inventors' competitions, or a patent attorney. Successful interviews depend on excellent preparation and follow-up. At the close of your interview, informally **summarize** what the person said, giving him or her an opportunity to respond to or elaborate on the information you collected. See pages R83–R84 for tips and strategies.

> ### Questions for Competition Participants
>
> - What does your invention do?
> - How did you get the idea for it?
> - What was your development process? Did you build a prototype, make sketches, or talk to experts as you made improvements to your invention?
> - About how much did it cost to develop your invention?
> - I would like to be an inventor. Do you have any advice for me?

Research Tips and Strategies

Library Sleuth

Two basic systems are used to classify nonfiction books. Most high school and public libraries use the Dewey decimal system; university and research libraries generally use the Library of Congress system.

DEWEY DECIMAL SYSTEM

000–099	General works
100–199	Philosophy and psychology
200–299	Religion
300–399	Social sciences
400–499	Language
500–599	Natural sciences and mathematics
600–699	Technology (applied sciences)
700–799	Arts and recreation
800–899	Literature and rhetoric
900–999	Geography and history

LIBRARY OF CONGRESS SYSTEM

A	General works	L	Education
B	Philosophy, psychology, religion	M	Music
C	History	N	Fine arts
D	General and Old World history	P	Language and literature
E–F	American history	Q	Science
G	Geography, anthropology, recreation	R	Medicine
H	Social sciences	S	Agriculture
J	Political science	T	Technology
K	Law	U	Military science
		V	Naval science
		Z	Bibliography and library science

Web Watch

Knowing what search tools to use is crucial to finding information on the World Wide Web.

Search Engines

Search engines differ in speed, size of database, method of searching, and other variables. Never use only one search engine.

- Google
- Yahoo
- Teoma

Metasearch Engines

A metasearch tool can save you time by sending a search to multiple search engines simultaneously.

- Vivismo
- Dogpile
- Metacrawler

Directories

Directories are useful when you are researching a general topic, because they arrange resources into subject categories.

- Galaxy
- About.com
- Yahoo!

Virtual Libraries

At a virtual library, you can look up information in encyclopedias, directories, and indexes. You can even e-mail a question to a librarian.

- Internet Public Library
- Librarians' Index to the Internet

Other Web Resources

Library catalogs: Library of Congress
Encyclopedias: Encyclopaedia Britannica Online
Newspaper archives: New York Times Index
Specialized databases: Medline

Writing and Research in a Digital Age

THINK central

KEYWORD: HML8-1076

Discover a wealth of Web search tools and resources.

Checklist for Evaluating Sources

☑ The information is relevant to the topic you are researching.

☑ The information is up-to-date. (This point is especially important when researching time-sensitive fields such as science, medicine, and sports.)

☑ The information is from someone who is an authority on this topic.

☑ The information is from a trusted source that is updated or reviewed regularly.

☑ The author's or institution's purpose for writing is clear.

☑ The information is written at the right level for your needs. For example, a children's book is probably too simplistic, while a scientific paper may be too complex.

☑ The information has the level of detail you need—neither too general nor too specific.

☑ The facts can be verified in more than one source.

Sharing Your Research

At last you have established your research goal, located sources of information, evaluated the materials, and taken notes on what you learned. Now you have a chance to share the results with the people in your world—and even beyond. Here are some options:

• Use presentation software to create a power presentation for your classmates, friends, or family.

• Publish your research findings on a wiki.

• Develop a newsletter or brochure summarizing your information.

• Explain what you learned in an oral presentation to your classmates or to people in your community.

• Write up your research in a formal research paper. **See the following pages. ▶**

Writing Workshop
INFORMATIVE TEXT

Research Paper

We live in an age of information, and knowing how to find and evaluate sources is essential. In this workshop, you will apply these skills while writing a short research paper that presents information you gather about your topic.

 Complete the workshop activities in your **Reader/Writer Notebook.**

WRITE WITH A PURPOSE

WRITING TASK

Write a **research paper** in which you investigate a topic that interests you.

Idea Starters

- the history of my favorite sport
- how recycling programs work
- an important medical discovery
- how dolphins (or other animals) communicate
- drummer boys in the Civil War

THE ESSENTIALS

Here are some common purposes, audiences, and formats for informative writing.

PURPOSES	AUDIENCES	FORMATS
• to inform readers about a topic you have researched • to express ideas about a topic	• classmates and teacher • people in your community • members of a study group • Web users	• essay for class • encyclopedia article • newspaper or magazine article • informative speech • power presentation • wiki

COMMON CORE TRAITS

1. DEVELOPMENT OF IDEAS

- clearly introduces a topic and states a **controlling idea** that answers the **research question**
- supports the topic with **evidence,** such as **relevant** and **concrete facts, details,** and **quotations**
- draws information from **multiple sources**
- provides a **concluding section** that supports the information

2. ORGANIZATION OF IDEAS

- has a clear and logical **organization**
- includes **formatting** and **graphics** when useful
- uses **appropriate transitions** to create cohesion and connect ideas

3. LANGUAGE FACILITY AND CONVENTIONS

- uses **precise language** and **domain-specific vocabulary**
- maintains a **formal style**
- uses a standard citation **format**
- employs correct **grammar, spelling,** and **punctuation**

Writing Online

THINK central

Go to **thinkcentral.com.**
KEYWORD: HML8N-1078

Planning/Prewriting

COMMON CORE

W 2a–f Write informative/explanatory texts to examine a topic and convey ideas, concepts, and information. **W 5** Develop and strengthen writing as needed by planning. **W 7** Conduct short research projects to answer a question.

Getting Started

CHOOSE A TOPIC

Refer back to the Idea Starters on page 1078. Which topic appeals to you at first glance? What other issues interest you? Meet with a partner or look through your textbooks, current newspapers, or Internet sites to get more ideas for topics. After choosing a possible topic, take a few minutes to freewrite about it. Highlight ideas that you might want to research.

▶ **WHAT DOES IT LOOK LIKE?**

I liked the story we read this year about the Civil War. Where did Ray Bradbury get the idea for it? Were there really boys like Joby in the Civil War? What would it be like to be a young kid in the middle of a war—to know that a big battle is coming and to know that even the general is scared?

NARROW YOUR FOCUS

Visit library databases, general reference works, or Web sites to do some preliminary reading on your topic and evaluate its scope. If entire books are written on it, then you need to focus on one aspect. If it appears at first glance that you will not be able to find enough information on your subject, then you need to broaden your research focus.

▶ **WHAT DOES IT LOOK LIKE?**

Narrowing My Topic

The Civil War (way too broad)
↓
Drummer boys in the Civil War (still seems like a lot for a three-page paper)
↓
What drummer boys did in the Civil War (narrow topic)
↓
Whether drummer boys had music training (too narrow)

THINK ABOUT AUDIENCE AND PURPOSE

As you plan your research paper, keep your purpose and audience in mind. Your general **purpose** is to share information on a topic in an organized way that will provide your **audience** with new insights. Consider what your readers already know and what they need to know to get the most out of your paper.

▶ **ASK YOURSELF:**

- What do my readers already know about my topic?
- What feelings might they have about my topic?
- What additional background information do they need in order to understand what I am saying?
- What **domain-specific,** or specialized, **vocabulary** will I need to include and define?
- What do I want my audience to learn?

Planning/Prewriting *continued*

Getting Started

FORMULATE A RESEARCH QUESTION

To help focus your research, write what you want to learn about your topic in the form of a question. This question should be open-ended—in other words, not one that can be answered in a single word. After formulating your major research question, write some more focused questions related to your topic. These questions will help you locate specific facts and other relevant information to include in your paper.

▶ **WHAT DOES IT LOOK LIKE?**

Topic: drummer boys in the Civil War

Major Research Question: What was the role of drummer boys in the Civil War?

Related Questions:
- How did drummer boys end up in the army?
- Why did armies have drummer boys?
- What were the drummer boys' actual responsibilities?
- Did drummer boys ever fight in battles?

MAKE A RESEARCH PLAN

Your research will go more smoothly if you develop a written plan. This plan should include your major research question, purpose, audience, possible sources, and deadlines. Have your teacher review and approve your plan before you begin your research. Then review the plan periodically to make sure you are on schedule and moving in the right direction.

▶ **TEMPLATE FOR A RESEARCH PLAN**

Name: ....
Major Research Question: ....
....

Purpose: ....
Audience: ....
Possible Sources: ....
....

SCHEDULE
Research Due: ....
First Draft Due: ....
Final Draft Due: ....

Teacher Approval: ....

PEER REVIEW Share your major research question with a partner. Ask: Is it focused enough? What related questions might help me further explore and answer my major question? If the related questions aren't working well, consider reworking your major research question to lead to more effective related questions.

YOUR TURN List several topic ideas in your *Reader/Writer Notebook* and decide which one is the most appropriate for your research paper. Then narrow your topic and formulate a major research question. With your purpose and audience in mind, create a research plan using the template on this page.

Researching

COMMON CORE

W 8 Gather relevant information from multiple sources; assess the credibility and accuracy of each source; quote and paraphrase the work of others and avoid plagiarism. **W 9b (RI 1)** Draw evidence from informational texts to support research.

Following Your Research Plan

FIND SOURCES

Plan to use information from several sources. These can include books, periodicals, newspapers, reference works, Web sites, interviews, or even field research. You can use both primary and secondary sources. **Primary sources** are materials created by people who witnessed or took part in the events they recorded. **Secondary sources** are records made by people who were not directly involved in or present at the events.

You have already listed some possible sources in your research plan. To find others, identify specific **search terms,** or keywords or phrases related to your topic. Search terms will help you locate materials in databases and on the Internet. Keep a list of your sources with comments about each one. Highlight the sources that seem most useful.

TIP Check the bibliographies of your sources to find the titles of other works about your topic.

See pages 1063–1067 for more information about research tools available to you.

▶ WHAT DOES IT LOOK LIKE?

Sources	My Comments
Reference Works "Civil War," *World Book* (print)	nothing about boys who went to war
Library Books *The Boys' War* by Jim Murphy (J973.7 M978)	full of primary source material; has a whole chapter about drummer boys
Callow, Brave and True: A Gospel of Civil War Youth by Jay S. Hoar (973.7 HOAR)	has interesting facts on drummer boys; written by an expert on the Civil War
Web Sites "Young Heroes of the Civil War"	no information about the author and no links to a home page or other sources
"Music of the Civil War" (bookmarked on my computer)	several good facts about my topic, and the sponsor is the National Park Service
Periodicals "Drummer Boys" in *Cobblestone* (December 1999)	great source—all about my topic

EVALUATE EACH SOURCE

Examine each source you find to make sure it is **credible,** or reliable and trustworthy. Ask yourself:

- Is this source **relevant?** Does it focus on the aspect of my topic that I am researching?
- Is the information **accurate?** Can I verify the facts in more than one source?
- What are the author's **qualifications?** Does the author have the necessary background and experience to write about this topic?
- What is the **publication date?** If my topic is current, should I look for a more recent source?

▶ TIPS FOR EVALUATING SOURCES

- Do not use a source if the language is too difficult for you. If you cannot understand the ideas, it will confuse rather than help you.
- Do not use a source that is too childish. You can read it for basic information, but then look for works with more depth.
- Avoid Web sites with errors, broken links, or no visible author or sponsoring organization.
- Be on the lookout for biased viewpoints, or sources that push ideas without considering other viewpoints.

Researching *continued*

PREPARE A SOURCE LIST

After you eliminate unreliable sources, list the sources you plan to use. You can record the information in an electronic file, write the details on index cards, or use note-taking software. Check with your school librarian to see if this special software is available to you.

Whichever method you choose, number your sources and record the following details for each type.

World Wide Web source
- author (if given) and title of Web page or article
- name of site where page or article appears
- name of organization responsible for the site
- date created or posted (if given)
- medium (Web) and date accessed

Book
- author (or editor) and title
- location and publisher
- year of publication
- library call number
- medium of publication (Print)

Encyclopedia article
- author (if given) and title of article
- name and year of encyclopedia
- medium of publication (Print or CD-ROM)

Periodical or newspaper article
- author and title of article
- name of magazine or newspaper
- day, month, and year of publication
- page numbers
- medium of publication (Print)

▶ WHAT DOES IT LOOK LIKE?

World Wide Web source

Source #: 4   **Type:** Article on Web site
Heiser, John. "Music of the Civil War." *Gettysburg National Military Park Kidzpage.* National Park Service. Dec. 2003. Web. 21 Apr. 2010.

Book

Source #: 2   **Type:** Book
Hoar, Jay S. *Callow, Brave and True: A Gospel of Civil War Youth.* Gettysburg, PA: Thomas, 1999. 973.7 HOAR. Print.

Encyclopedia

Source #: 5   **Type:** CD-ROM encyclopedia
"American Civil War." *Encyclopaedia Britannica.* 2004 ed. CD-ROM.

Periodical article

Source #: 1   **Type:** Article in magazine
Currie, Stephen. "Drummer Boys." *Cobblestone.* Dec. 1999: 3–7. Print.

Following Your Research Plan

FORMAT YOUR NOTES

Whether you are recording your notes on a computer or on index cards, the following tips can make the process more efficient:

- Include the number of the source.
- Create a heading that indicates the main idea to which the note is related.
- Record the fact or idea in a way that is easy to read and understand.
- Identify the page number, if there is one.

▶ WHAT DOES IT LOOK LIKE?

Source #: 2
Ages of drummer boys

Some drummer boys were as young as six years old (227).

TAKE ACCURATE NOTES

Skim the relevant parts of the source to get an idea of how the material is organized and what information is most important. Then use one of the following methods to record your notes:

- **Paraphrase** the source by restating it in your own words. Use about the same number of words as the source does.
- **Summarize** the source by recording only the most important ideas in your own words. Use fewer words than the source does.
- **Quote** the source by copying the important phrase, sentence, or paragraph word for word. Enclose the copied words in quotation marks.

TIP Quote secondary sources only when you cannot restate the information as clearly, vividly, or forcefully as the source does. Most of your notes should be summaries and paraphrases.

▶ WHAT DOES IT LOOK LIKE?

Original Source

Many [boys from the North] joined because they wanted to take the defiant South and "set them straight." But most signed up for a simpler reason—to escape the boring routine of farm life and take part in an exciting adventure.

Murphy, Jim. The Boys' War, page 8

Paraphrase

Source #: 3
Reasons boys joined army

Some from the North wanted to punish the South for being rebellious. Many boys simply thought they would have a thrilling life instead of a dull one spent on a farm (8).

Summary

Source #: 3
Reasons boys joined army

Northern boys wanted to defeat the South and to find adventure (8).

Researching *continued*

AVOID PLAGIARISM

Plagiarism occurs when you use someone else's words or ideas without acknowledging it. It is the same as stealing another writer's work, even if it is unintentional. Follow these guidelines to avoid plagiarism:

- **Paraphrase and summarize as you take notes.** Take the time to think through and understand what you read. Put as much information as possible into your own words.
- **Do not rely heavily on a single source.** Even if you find one source that is clearly superior to all others, be sure you blend the facts, ideas, and opinions from at least four sources. By reading a variety of sources, you will see different perspectives on the topic and start to develop your own ideas.
- **Place quotation marks around every significant word, phrase, or sentence that you copy.** Even if you copy just a few key words while paraphrasing the majority of the passage, you must put quotation marks around those words.
- **Put away your sources when you begin your draft.** Do not work from an open book. Never cut and paste passages from an online source. Rely on your notes instead.

TIP In a paraphrase or a summary, you do not have to use quotation marks for common words from your source, such as *Civil War drummer*. However, put quotation marks around specific, descriptive words and phrases, as in this example: *Drummer boys were often "unintended sacrifices," caught in enemy fire.*

▶ WHAT DOES IT LOOK LIKE?

Original Source

When fighting appeared imminent, musicians were often ordered to the rear to assist surgeons and care for the wounded.

Heiser, John. "Music of the Civil War"

Plagiarized Paraphrase

When a battle appeared imminent, musicians were often sent to help surgeons care for the wounded.

Correctly Documented Paraphrase

When a battle was about to start, drummer boys were often sent to help doctors treat the wounded (Heiser).

Original Source

Since Shiloh was significant for the bravery of the young untrained men of the North and South alike, writers frequently wrote about the young . . . soldiers. . . . The drummer boy, often a mere lad who had run away from home to seek adventure in the ranks, became the subject of the most popular literature of the day.

"Shiloh Inspires Writers"

Plagiarized Summary

The drummer boy of Shiloh became the subject of the most popular literature of the time.

Correctly Documented Summary

A legend grew up about the drummer boy of Shiloh ("Shiloh").

Following Your Research Plan

WRITE YOUR CONTROLLING IDEA

Your **controlling idea,** or thesis statement, expresses the main idea of your research paper. It states the most important conclusion you have drawn from your research. All of the details in your paper should relate to and support your controlling idea.

Review your notes and think about how the information answers your major research question. Then consider how you feel about this answer. Combine both ideas in a controlling idea, which you may revise when you write your draft.

▶ WHAT DOES IT LOOK LIKE?

Answers to Some of My Research Questions:
- Many of the boys dreamed of adventure.
- Drummer boys kept time for the troops, which meant marching with big, heavy drums.
- The boys watched soldiers die and sometimes helped care for the wounded.

Controlling Idea:
Most drummer boys were not prepared for their difficult jobs in the Civil War.

ORGANIZE YOUR INFORMATION

One key to a successful research paper is organization. To help you put your information into a logical order, follow these steps:

- Use headings to separate your notes into groups related to similar ideas.
- Arrange these groups in the order that makes the most sense for your paper. For example, you might use chronological order or order of importance.
- Order your notes within each group. Again, choose a logical pattern.
- Create an outline for your paper. Use the main idea of each group of notes as a Roman-numeral heading. List details under each heading in the order you have established.

TIP Instead of an outline, you can organize your details in a graphic organizer, such as a flowchart.

▶ WHAT DOES IT LOOK LIKE?

Drummer Boys in the Civil War
  I. Who the drummer boys were
      A. Too young to be soldiers
      B. Had jobs that were too hard for them
  II. Drummer boys' duties
      A. Acted as human clocks
      B. Drummed the beat of the march
      C. Drummed during battle
      D. Sometimes helped care for wounded
  III. Dying for a cause
      A. Drummer Boy of Shiloh
      B. William Johnston
      C. Clarence McKenzie
      D. Number of deaths
  IV. Last drummer boys
      A. Civil War the last time drummer boys used
      B. Later wars too noisy to hear drums

YOUR TURN Follow your research plan by locating sources that provide answers to your research questions. Take careful notes, paraphrasing and summarizing most of the information. In your *Reader/Writer Notebook,* draft a controlling idea that tells the main idea of your paper. Then put your notes in a logical order and create an outline or a flowchart.

Drafting

The following chart gives a framework for drafting a research paper.

Organizing Your Research Paper

INTRODUCTION

- Capture the attention of your audience with an interesting **statement, quotation, anecdote, question,** or **statistic.**
- Provide necessary **background information.**
- Include a **controlling idea** that identifies your topic and the conclusion you have drawn about it.
- Establish a **formal style** by using precise language and avoiding slang and contractions.

▼

BODY

- Present the main ideas from your outline or graphic organizer. Make sure each idea **supports** your controlling idea.
- Develop your main ideas with **evidence,** including **quotations, summaries,** and **paraphrases.**
- Arrange your main ideas and evidence in a **logical order.** Use **transitions** to show the relationships between ideas.
- **Synthesize** the ideas from your sources by adding your own insights and conclusions to show the significance of the facts you are presenting.
- Use **introductory phrases** that identify the sources of your ideas. For example, you might say "According to Murphy . . ." or "As Wolfe points out. . . ."
- Define **domain-specific,** or specialized, terms that may be unfamiliar.
- **Document the source** of each idea that is not your own in parentheses at the end of the sentence. See the "Learn How" lesson on the next page for help.
- Use **formatting** (bulleted lists, bold heads) and **graphics** (charts, illustrations, diagrams) to help reinforce or clarify important ideas

▼

CONCLUDING SECTION

- **Summarize** your controlling idea and main points.
- Explain the **relevance** of the information you have presented to your audience.

▼

WORKS CITED LIST

- Include a **Works Cited list** as the last page of your paper.
- List the sources you used in **alphabetical order** by the authors' last names. If no author is listed, use the first important word of the title.
- Follow the correct format for **documentation of sources,** depending on your teacher's preference. Two common **style manuals** are the *MLA Handbook for Writers of Research Papers* and *The Chicago Manual of Style.*
- Begin each entry on a **new line**; indent additional lines of an entry by one-half inch.

W 2c Use transitions to clarify relationships among ideas. **W 4** Produce clear and coherent writing. **W 8** Follow a standard format for citation. **L 3** Use knowledge of language and its conventions when writing.

LEARN HOW **Document Your Sources** Each fact, detail, or idea that you have taken from a source must be documented, unless it is common knowledge or found in many sources. Documentation appears in parentheses at the end of the sentence or sentences in which the ideas are found.

Guidelines for Citing Sources in a Research Paper

Source with one author	▶ Author's last name and page number (if any) of the work cited: (Murphy 40)
Author unknown	▶ Shortened title of the work and page number (if any): ("Shiloh")
More than one source supporting an idea	▶ First author's last name (or work title) and page number (if any); second author's name and page number; and so on: ("Shiloh"; Wolfe 745)
Author already mentioned in the sentence	▶ Page number only: (745)

GRAMMAR IN CONTEXT: USING TRANSITIONAL WORDS AND PHRASES

A clear organizational pattern will help readers of your research paper understand the information you present. **Transitional words and phrases** help make your organization clear and establish relationships among ideas.

Type of Transition	Examples
comparison/contrast	▶ however, instead of, yet, but, although, unlike, in contrast to, similarly
cause and effect	▶ because, so, since, therefore, as a result, due to, consequently
chronological	▶ when, later, first, after, before, then, earlier, soon
order of importance	▶ primarily, most important, foremost, least of all
elaboration	▶ in fact, for example, for the most part, also, too

YOUR TURN Develop a draft of your research paper, crediting all sources with parenthetical citations. Be sure to use transitional words and phrases that show the connections between the ideas in your paper.

Revising

An effective research paper is informative, well organized, and clearly written. When you revise, you evaluate these factors and make improvements to your draft. The following chart can help you revise, rewrite, or try a new approach.

RESEARCH PAPER

Ask Yourself	Tips	Revision Strategies
1. Is the controlling idea clearly stated in the introduction? Does it answer the major research question?	**Put a star** next to the controlling idea.	**Add** a controlling idea, if necessary, or **revise** the controlling idea to more clearly answer the research question.
2. Does each body paragraph develop a main idea related to the controlling idea? Is there enough evidence to support each main idea?	**Label** each paragraph with the main idea it develops. **Highlight** facts, examples, and quotations that support the main idea.	**Delete** unrelated ideas, or **rearrange** information into separate paragraphs. If necessary, **add** more facts, examples, and quotations from your notes.
3. Are all sources correctly documented within the paper?	**Place a check mark** next to each parenthetical citation. **Highlight** sentences without citations.	**Review** notes to find the origin of ideas in the sentences you highlighted. **Insert** citations if necessary.
4. Does the concluding section summarize key points and show the significance of the information?	**Circle** the summary of key points. **Draw a wavy line** under sentences that explain why the information in the paper is important.	**Add** a summary of key points in the paper. **Insert** sentences that describe the importance of the topic.
5. Does the paper present information from each source in the Works Cited list?	**Highlight** material from each source with a different color.	**Add** missing source material, or **remove** unused sources from the Works Cited list.
6. Does the Works Cited list correctly document all sources?	**Place a check mark** next to each entry that matches style guidelines.	**Revise** inaccurate entries to reflect style guidelines.

 YOUR TURN

PEER REVIEW Ask a peer to read your paper and use the chart to suggest improvements and identify parts of your paper that need reworking or a new approach. In addition, ask: Have I smoothly integrated direct quotations into my paper? If not, how can I weave them in without interrupting the flow of ideas?

ANALYZE A STUDENT DRAFT

COMMON CORE

W 2a Introduce a topic clearly. **W 5** Strengthen writing as needed by revising, editing, rewriting, or trying a new approach, focusing on how well purpose and audience have been addressed.

Read this student's draft and the comments about it.

Chu 1

Jess Chu
Mr. Kinsella
English 8
6 May 2010

The Difficult Job of a Civil War Drummer Boy

①   When the Civil War broke out, many boys tried to join the army, thinking that war would be an exciting adventure. However, most of them were too young to become soldiers (Murphy 8). In fact, Civil War expert Jay Hoar lists some as young as age six (227). The armies of the North and the South used these young volunteers not as soldiers but as musicians, especially as drummer boys (Murphy 10).

The Drummer Boy's Jobs

②   Drummer boys for the North and South had similar duties. One duty was to be a kind of human clock. Drummers woke the troops up in the morning, called them to roll call and other duties, and sent them to bed (Wolfe 745; Heiser). This part of the job was not too difficult, but the day was very long for a child. It began as early as 5:45 A.M.

> Jess uses the **formats and style** required by her teacher by including page numbers and header information.

> To **capture readers' attention,** Jess presents a startling fact about the ages of some drummer boys. However, her introduction lacks a **controlling idea.**

> The first body paragraph develops one **main idea** with **evidence,** including specific examples and facts.

LEARN HOW Include a Controlling Idea   In a research paper, the **controlling idea** summarizes the writer's conclusion based on information from several sources. When Jess revised her paper, she added a strong controlling idea that clearly reveals her perspective, or view, on the topic of drummer boys and their duties.

JESS'S REVISION TO PARAGRAPH ①

. . . The armies of the North and the South used these young volunteers not as soldiers but as musicians, especially as drummer boys (Murphy 10).

Yet even those jobs had many responsibilities and dangers. For the most part, drummer boys were too young to do the difficult jobs they faced and much too young for war.

3   A more difficult job was keeping time as the troops marched. This job was clearly challenging for many young boys. Hoar points out that at least one drummer boy was just 40 inches tall, so the drums were very big in comparison to the little boys (116). Since marches went on for miles, it's likely that carrying a big drum was exhausting.

4   Drummers also called the men to battle, and some drummed commands during battle. They had to drum with bullets and cannon balls zooming all around them. They watched soldiers die. Sometimes, drummer boys "found themselves the target of enemy fire" (Murphy 40). When drummer boy Delavan Miller was caught in the fighting, he admitted, "I was never so scared in all my life" (quoted in Currie 6).

5   Sometimes drummers had to help care for injured soldiers (Heiser). Drummers suffered in other ways, too. For example, hunger was constant for many Confederates, and some wore ragged clothing (Robertson 1024). Troops also faced bad weather and disease. They had to deal with being bored and homesick, too.

Dying for a Cause

6   Many drummer boys died in the war. According to the legend that has grown up around him, the drummer boy of Shiloh, who kept drumming even when the troops were retreating, smiled and said how proud he was to serve his country just before he died. ("shiloh", Hoar 120) Some, like William Johnston at age 11, were so brave that they won the highest possible medal, the Congressional Medal of Honor (Hoar 24, 234). Others, like 12-year-old Clarence McKenzie, died from a "stray bullet" (Hoar 3).

7   How many drummer boys died during the Civil War? Murphy says that "hundreds were killed and thousands more wounded" (43). Giving their lives was an enormous sacrifice for these children to make.

Jess's original insights and observations convey her **perspective** on the topic.

Most of the evidence is paraphrased or summarized from Jess's sources. Occasionally she includes **quotations** to draw attention to important ideas.

Frequent **transitions** help the audience see the relationships between ideas.

Jess weaves together information from **multiple sources** and uses **parenthetical citations** to credit each source.

Chu 3

The Last Drummer Boys

❽   The Civil War was the last war to use drummer boys on the battlefield. Later wars were noisier, with more rifles and cannons. Therefore, no one could hear the drummer boys anymore (Murphy 41, 43). That seems like one of the few good things to come out of deadlier wars. Drummer boys of the Civil War were too young for the many challenges that they faced. Children today are lucky that this job no longer exists.

> Jess's **concluding section** ends with a final observation that shows the **significance** of the information in her paper.

Chu 4

Works Cited

Currie, Stephen, "Drummer Boys," *Cobblestone*. Dec. 1999: 3–7. Print.

Heiser, John. "Music of the Civil War." *Gettysburg National Military Park Kidzpage*. National Park Service. Dec. 2003. *Web. 21 Apr. 2009.*

Hoar, Jay S. *Callow, Brave and True: A Gospel of Civil War Youth*. Gettysburg, PA: Thomas, 1999. Print.

Murphy, Jim. *The Boys' War*. New York: Clarion, 1990. Print.

Robertson, James I., Jr. "Soldiers." The Confederacy. New York: Simon, 1993. Print.   *(ital.)*

Wolfe, Charles K. "Music." *The Confederacy*. New York: Simon, 1993. Print.

"Shiloh Inspires Writers." *Shiloh*. National Park Service. 2 Dec. 2002. Web. 18 Apr. 2009.

YOUR TURN   Use feedback from your peers and your teacher as well as the two "Learn How" lessons to revise or rewrite parts of your research paper.

LEARN HOW Format a Works Cited List The entries in your Works Cited list must follow the guidelines recommended by your teacher precisely. To correct her Works Cited list, Jess needed to make the following revisions:

- Alphabetize entries according to the author's last name or the first significant word of the title.
- Italicize titles of books.
- Place periods after each part of an entry and at the end.
- Put titles of Web articles in quotation marks.
- Include access date and medium for Web sources.

W 5 Strengthen writing as needed by revising, editing, rewriting, or trying a new approach. L 2 Demonstrate command of the conventions of standard English capitalization, punctuation, and spelling.

Editing and Publishing

In the editing stage, you prepare your research paper for publication by correcting any errors in grammar, usage, spelling, and punctuation. You should also make sure your paper is formatted according to the following guidelines:

- Leave one-inch margins at the top, bottom, and sides of each page (except for page numbers).
- On each page, type your last name and the page number one-half inch from the top, aligned at the right corner.
- At the top left of the first page, type your name, your teacher's name, the class, and the date (as shown on page 1089).
- Double-space all text, including the entries in the Works Cited list.
- Indent paragraphs one-half inch from the left margin.
- Begin your Works Cited list on a separate page.

GRAMMAR IN CONTEXT: CAPITALIZING AND PUNCTUATING CITATIONS

The parenthetical citations in a research paper must be formatted consistently and correctly. Authors' names and the important words in titles must be capitalized. Citations must be placed before the punctuation at the end of a sentence. If more than one work is included in a citation, separate the authors' names or titles with semicolons.

As Jess edited her paper, she found one citation that was not formatted correctly. Her revisions in blue show how she fixed the problem.

. . . the drummer boy of Shiloh, who kept drumming even when the troops were retreating, smiled and said how proud he was to serve his country just before he died ("shiloh"; Hoar 120).

PUBLISH YOUR WRITING

Here are some ideas for sharing your research paper with an audience:

- Find a group interested in the topic of your paper. Arrange to publish your paper in its newsletter or on its Web site.
- With classmates, combine your papers into a resource guide for the classroom.
- Deliver an oral report on your topic to your classmates.

YOUR TURN Correct any errors in your research paper by carefully proofreading it. Be sure all of your parenthetical citations are formatted with correct capitalization and punctuation. Then publish your final paper where it is most likely to reach your audience.

Scoring Rubric

Use the rubric below to evaluate your research paper.

RESEARCH PAPER

SCORE	◌ *COMMON CORE TRAITS*
6	• **Development** Effectively introduces a topic; states an insightful, well-researched controlling idea; develops the topic with varied and relevant evidence; ends powerfully • **Organization** Logically organizes information; includes formatting and graphics to enhance the information; effectively uses varied transitions • **Language** Ably uses precise words; maintains a formal style; shows a strong command of conventions; correctly cites all sources
5	• **Development** Competently introduces a topic; states a well-researched and clear controlling idea; offers relevant evidence; has a strong concluding section • **Organization** Is logically organized; includes formatting and graphics; effectively uses transitions • **Language** Uses precise words; generally maintains a formal style; has a few errors in conventions; correctly cites sources
4	• **Development** Sufficiently introduces a topic; states a clear controlling idea; offers mostly relevant evidence; has an adequate concluding section • **Organization** Is mostly logically organized; could use more formatting and graphics; needs more transitions • **Language** Uses vague words in some places; mostly maintains a formal style; includes a few distracting errors in conventions; incorrectly formats a few source citations
3	• **Development** States a controlling idea, but the introduction could be more engaging; lacks enough evidence; has a somewhat weak concluding section • **Organization** Has some flaws in organization; doesn't include enough formatting or graphics; lacks many transitions • **Language** Needs more precise words; has frequent lapses in style; has some critical errors in conventions; incorrectly formats some source citations
2	• **Development** Has a weak controlling idea; does not support most ideas; ends abruptly • **Organization** Has organizational flaws; lacks formatting or graphics; lacks transitions • **Language** Lacks precise words or uses them incorrectly; uses an informal style; has many errors in conventions; does not cite all sources and cites many incorrectly
1	• **Development** Lacks a controlling idea; offers little, if any, development; has no concluding section • **Organization** Has poor organization, and lacks formatting, graphics, and transitions • **Language** Uses vague words; has an inappropriate style; has major problems in conventions; plagiarizes or does not credit sources

Giving and Listening to an Informative Speech

When you write a research paper, you develop your controlling idea and decide on the best way to convey your information to readers. Preparing an informative speech is similar in many ways, but you also need to consider the specific needs of your listeners.

 Complete the workshop activities in your **Reader/Writer Notebook.**

SPEAK WITH A PURPOSE	COMMON CORE TRAITS
TASK Adapt your research paper into an **informative speech** and present it to the class. When you listen to speeches given by your classmates, summarize the content and evaluate the delivery.	**A STRONG INFORMATIVE SPEECH . . .** • is tailored to listeners' needs • covers the most salient, or important, points from the speaker's research • provides sources for facts and ideas • uses formal English as well as verbal and nonverbal cues to deliver the message

COMMON CORE

SL 4 Present claims and findings, emphasizing salient points in a focused, coherent manner; use appropriate eye contact, adequate volume, and clear pronunciation. **SL 6** Adapt speech to a variety of contexts and tasks.

Give an Informative Speech

Your research paper will form the basis of your oral presentation. However, you'll need to adjust the information for your listeners. Follow these guidelines:

• **Think about the purpose and occasion.** Are you giving an informal speech, or is your speech part of a formal evaluation? The tone of a formal speech should be serious. Avoid casual language and slang. On the other hand, if you are speaking at an informal occasion, make sure your speech doesn't sound overly academic. Choose words and phrases that will put your listeners at ease. Define terms that may be unfamiliar to your audience.

• **Limit your speech to main ideas and supporting evidence.** Review your research paper and highlight your main ideas. These will be the key points that you emphasize in your speech. Order and connect them in a logical way. Keep words and phrases from your paper that tell your audience where you found important facts and ideas. However, do not cite a source for every fact—that would disrupt the flow of your speech.

• **Focus on a strong delivery.** Use appropriate eye contact, adequate volume, and clear pronunciation. Repeat important words or phrases, ask rhetorical questions, and provide **analogies,** or comparisons, to illustrate your points.

• **Use an outline or note cards.** Avoid simply reading your paper aloud. Speaking from an outline or note cards will make your speech sound more natural.

Speaking & Listening Online

THINK central

Go to thinkcentral.com.
KEYWORD: HML8-1094

Listen to an Informative Speech

An informative speech contains a lot of information for listeners to absorb. Use the guidelines in this chart to help you listen actively.

Guidelines for Active Listening	
Before the Speech	• **Determine your purpose for listening.** What do you want to learn from the speech? • **Make predictions.** Identify two or three points that you expect the speaker to cover.
During the Speech	• **Pay attention.** Looking around the room or doing homework will prevent you from learning all you can. Take notes to help you remember key points. • **Listen for cues that signal key points.** Cues can include words and phrases such as *first, second,* and *finally; there are many reasons (or causes); the most important thing is;* and *in conclusion.*
After the Speech	• **Summarize the presentation.** Make sure that you have recorded all the important ideas. • **Ask questions or make comments.** Ask the speaker to elaborate on an interesting concept or clarify points that you found confusing.

Evaluate an Informative Speech

As you listen, use these guidelines to help you evaluate the speech:

- **Examine main ideas and supporting evidence.** Does the speaker offer relevant, well-chosen facts, examples, and other evidence to support his or her main ideas? If not, follow up by asking questions about the evidence.

- **Assess organization.** Is the order of ideas easy to follow and understand?

- **Interpret the speaker's purpose.** Review the content of the speech. Ask yourself if the speaker covered all of the points necessary to fulfill his or her purpose. If not, what did he or she leave out? Ask the speaker to clarify.

- **Distinguish between facts and opinions.** An informative speech should contain more facts than opinions. Listen for phrases such as "I think" or "It is clear to me" that signal the speaker's personal beliefs.

- **Evaluate delivery.** Does the speaker hold your attention and use cues to help you understand his or her meaning?

YOUR TURN

As a Speaker Give your informative speech to a classmate. Be sure to emphasize your key points and supporting evidence in a focused, coherent manner with valid reasoning and well-chosen details.

As a Listener Listen carefully to your partner's speech. Then summarize and evaluate it, using the guidelines above.

Reading any text—whether it is a short story, poem, magazine article, newspaper, or Web page—requires the use of special strategies. For example, you might plot the events of a short story on a diagram, or use text features to spot main ideas in a magazine article. You might also need to identify patterns of organization in the text. Using such strategies can help you read different texts with ease and also help you understand what you're reading.

COMMON CORE

Included in this handbook:
RI 1, RI 2, RI 3, RI 5, RI 6, RI 8

1 Reading Literary and Nonfiction Texts

Literary and Nonfiction texts include short stories, novels, poems, dramas, biographies, autobiographies, and essays. To appreciate and analyze literary and nonfiction texts, you will need to understand the characteristics of each type of text.

1.1 READING A SHORT STORY

Strategies for Reading

- Read the **title.** As you read the story, you may notice that the title has a special meaning.

- Keep track of **events** as they happen. Plot the events on a diagram like this one.

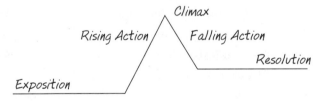

- From the details the writer provides, **visualize** the characters. **Predict** what they might do next.

- Look for specific adjectives that help you visualize the **setting**—the time and place in which events occur.

1.2 READING A POEM

Strategies for Reading

- Notice the **form** of the poem, or the number of its lines and their arrangement on the page.

- Read the poem aloud a few times. Listen for **rhyme** and **rhythm.**

- **Visualize** the images and comparisons.

- **Connect** with the poem by asking yourself what message the poet is trying to send.

- Create a word web or other **graphic organizer** to record your reactions and questions.

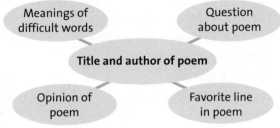

1.3 READING A PLAY

Strategies for Reading

- Read the stage directions to help you **visualize** the setting and characters.

- **Question** what the title means and why the playwright chose it.

- Identify the main conflict (struggle or problem) in the play. To **clarify** the conflict, make a chart that shows what the conflict is and how it is resolved.

- **Analyze** the characters. What do they want? How do they change during the play? You may want to make a chart that lists each character's name, appearance, and traits.

1.4 READING LITERARY NONFICTION

Strategies for Reading

- If you are reading a biography, an autobiography, or another type of biographical writing (such as a diary, a memoir, or letters), use a family tree or word web to keep track of the people mentioned.

- When reading an essay, **evaluate** the writer's ideas. Is there a clear main idea? Does the writer use appropriate details to support a main idea?

2 Reading Informational Texts: Text Features

An **informational text** is writing that provides factual information. Informational materials—such as chapters in textbooks and articles in magazines, encyclopedias, and newspapers—usually contain elements that help the reader recognize their purpose, organization, and key ideas. These elements are known as **text features.**

2.1 UNDERSTANDING TEXT FEATURES

Text features are design elements of a text that indicate its organizational structure or otherwise make its key ideas and information understandable. Text features include titles, headings, subheadings, boldface type, bulleted and numbered lists, and graphic aids, such as charts, graphs, illustrations, and photographs. Notice how the text features help you find key information on the textbook page shown.

A The **title** Identifies the topic.

B A **subheading** indicates the start of a new topic or section and identifies the focus of that section.

C **Questions** may be used to focus your understanding of the text.

D A **bulleted list** shows items of equal importance.

E **Graphic aids,** such as illustrations, photographs, charts, diagrams, maps, and timelines, often make ideas in the text clearer.

F A **caption,** or the text that accompanies a graphic aid, gives information about the graphic aid that isn't necessarily obvious from the image itself.

PRACTICE AND APPLY

1. What is a surplus?

2. What facts do the photograph and caption add to the text?

3. What informational texts do you read outside of class? Why are they informational?

A # The First Communities

D ▶ TERMS & NAMES
- surplus
- specialization
- artisan
- social class
- government

Build on What You Know Do you live in the country, a small town, a city, or a suburb? In the distant past, simple farming villages developed, over hundreds of years, into more complex villages and eventually into cities.

Villages Around the World **B**

C ESSENTIAL QUESTION How did farming villages develop?

When villages prospered, they were able to support more people. Their populations grew. People's skills became more specialized. Village economies became more varied.

Surpluses Boost Development As agricultural techniques improved, farmers sometimes produced **surpluses**—more than what they needed to survive. For example, farmers might grow more grain than their families or village could use. The extra was an economic surplus.

Surpluses in early farming villages were not limited to food. Surpluses also included materials for making cloth and other products. Sheep raisers, for example, may have had surplus wool. Surpluses of food and other materials in good seasons helped villages survive bad seasons.

E

Moroccan Village
This modern village in the Atlas Mountains of Morocco in North Africa continues a way of life that has lasted for thousands of years. ▼ **F**

65

2.2 USING TEXT FEATURES

You can use text features to locate information, to help you understand it, and to take notes. Just use the following strategies when you encounter informational text.

Strategies for Reading

- **Preview** the text by looking at the title, headings, and subheadings to get an idea of the main concepts and the way the text is organized.

- Before you begin reading the text more thoroughly, **skim** it—read it quickly—to get an overview.

- Read any **questions** that appear at the end of a lesson or chapter. Doing this will help you set a purpose for your reading.

- Turn subheadings into questions. Then use the text below the subheadings to answer the questions. Your answers will be a **summary** of the text.

- **Take notes** by turning headings and subheadings into main ideas. You might use a chart like the following.

The First Communities		Main heading
Villages Around the World	1. prosperity means growth 2. specialized skills 3. varied economies	Subheading

- As you read to locate particular facts or details, **scan** the text. Look for key words and phrases as you move slowly down the page.

2.3 TURNING TEXT HEADINGS INTO OUTLINE ENTRIES

After you have read a selection at least once, you can use text features to take notes in outline form. An outline can help you see relationships between ideas in a text and can reveal the logical order of ideas. The following outline shows how one student used text headings from the sample textbook page on page R3. Study the outline and use the strategies that follow to create an outline based on text features.

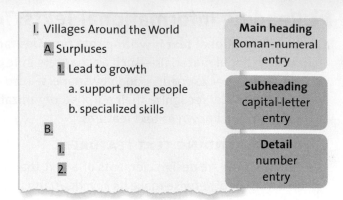

I. Villages Around the World — **Main heading** Roman-numeral entry
 A. Surpluses — **Subheading** capital-letter entry
  1. Lead to growth
   a. support more people
   b. specialized skills
 B.
  1. — **Detail** number entry
  2.

Strategies for Using Text Headings

- Preview the headings and subheadings in the text to get an idea of what different kinds there are and what their positions might be in an outline.

- Be consistent. Note that subheadings that are the same size and color should be used consistently in Roman-numeral or capital-letter entries in the outline. If you decide that a chapter heading should appear with a Roman numeral, then that's the level at which all other chapter headings should appear.

- Write the headings and subheadings that you will use as your Roman-numeral and capital-letter entries first. As you read, fill in numbered details from the text under the headings and subheadings in your outline.

PRACTICE AND APPLY

Reread "So You Want to be an Entomologist?" pages 894–895. Use text features in the selection to take notes in outline form.

Preview the subheadings in the text to get an idea of the different kinds. Write the headings and subheadings you are using as your Roman numeral and capital letter entries first. Then fill in the details.

2.4 GRAPHIC AIDS

Information is communicated not only with words but also with graphic aids. **Graphic aids** are visual representations of information. They can be charts, webs, diagrams, graphs, photographs, or other visual representations of information.

Graphic aids usually make complex information easier to understand. For that reason, graphic aids are often used to organize, simplify, and summarize information for easy reference.

Graphs

Graphs are used to illustrate statistical information. A **graph** is a drawing that shows the relative values of numerical quantities. Different kinds of graphs are used to show different numerical relationships.

Strategies for Reading

Ⓐ Read the title.

Ⓑ Find out what is being represented or measured.

Ⓒ In a circle graph, compare the sizes of the parts.

Ⓓ In a line graph, study the slant of the line. The steeper the line, the faster the rate of change.

Ⓔ In a bar graph, compare the lengths of the bars.

A **circle graph,** or **pie graph,** shows the relationships of parts to a whole. The entire circle equals 100 percent. The parts of the circle represent percentages of the whole.

MODEL: CIRCLE GRAPH

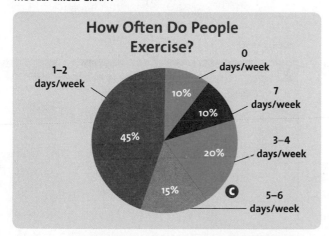

Line graphs show changes in numerical quantities over time and are effective in presenting trends such as changes in temperature. A line graph is made on a grid. Here, the vertical axis indicates degrees Fahrenheit, and the horizontal axis shows dates. Points on the graph indicate data. The line that connects the points highlights a trend or pattern.

MODEL: LINE GRAPH

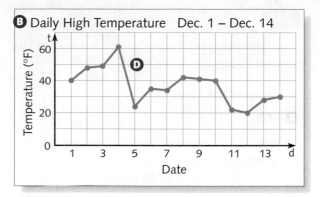

In a **bar graph,** vertical or horizontal bars are used to show or compare categories of information, such as the heights of different buildings. The lengths of the bars in this case indicate height.

MODEL: BAR GRAPH

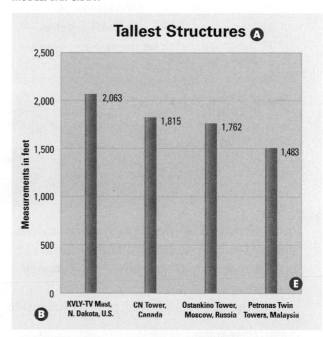

WATCH OUT! Evaluate carefully the information presented in graphs. For example, circle graphs show major factors and differences well but tend to reduce the importance of smaller factors and differences.

Diagrams

A **diagram** is a drawing that shows how something works or how its parts relate to one another. A **picture diagram** is a picture or drawing of the subject being discussed.

Strategies for Reading

Ⓐ Read the title.

Ⓑ Read each label and look at the part it identifies.

Ⓒ Follow any arrows or numbers that show the order of steps in a process, and read any captions.

MODEL: PICTURE DIAGRAM

Ⓐ **Ancient Irrigation**

This model shows how an ancient irrigation system worked.

❶ Gates controlled how much water flowed from the river.

❷ Main canals led from the river. They sloped gently downward to keep the water flowing.

❸ Medium-sized branch canals led away from the main canals.

❹ Small feeder canals led water directly to the fields. Ⓒ

In a **schematic diagram,** lines, symbols, and words are used to help readers visualize processes or objects they cannot normally see. A **cutaway diagram** is a drawing or model of something with part of the outside removed, to show the inside.

MODEL: CUTAWAY DIAGRAM

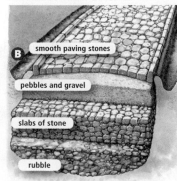

Ⓑ smooth paving stones

pebbles and gravel

slabs of stone

rubble

◀ **Roman Road** Ⓐ **Construction**

Roman roads were constructed in layers. The average width of a road was 15 to 18 feet. Ⓒ

Charts and Tables

A **chart** presents information, shows a process, or makes comparisons, usually in rows or columns.

A **table** is a specific type of chart that presents a collection of facts in rows and columns and shows how the facts relate to one another.

Strategies for Reading

Ⓐ Read the title to learn what information the chart or table covers.

Ⓑ Study column headings and row labels to determine the categories of information presented.

Ⓒ Look down columns and across rows to find specific information.

MODEL: CHART

The Domestication of Animals Ⓐ		
Animal	**Location**	**Use** Ⓑ
llama	South America	transport, meat
turkey	North America	meat
cattle	Europe, Asia, Africa	milk, meat
horse	Asia (southwest steppes)	transport Ⓒ
dog	Asia (possibly China)	guarding, herding, hunting

MODEL: TABLE

Ⓐ

Light Rail Meadowview Route Monday–Friday A.M.			
Meadowview Ⓑ	**City College**	**Arden/ Del Paso**	**Watt/I-80**
6:05	6:14	6:42	6:53
7:05	7:14	7:42	7:53
7:20	7:29 Ⓒ	7:57	8:08
7:50	7:59	8:27	8:38
8:05	8:14	8:42	8:53
8:35	8:44	9:12	9:23
9:05	9:14	9:42	9:53
9:50	9:59	10:27	10:38
10:05	10:14	10:42	10:53
11:05	11:14	11:42	11:53

Maps

A **map** visually represents a geographic region, such as a state or country. It provides information about areas through lines, colors, shapes, and symbols. There are different kinds of maps.

- **Political maps** show political features, such as national borders.
- **Physical maps** show the landforms in areas.
- **Road or travel maps** show roads and highways.
- **Thematic maps** show information on a specific topic, such as climate, weather, or natural resources.

Strategies for Reading

Ⓐ Read the title to find out what kind of map it is.

Ⓑ Read the labels to get an overall sense of what the map shows.

Ⓒ Look at the **key** or **legend** to find out what the symbols and colors on the map stand for.

MODEL: PHYSICAL MAP

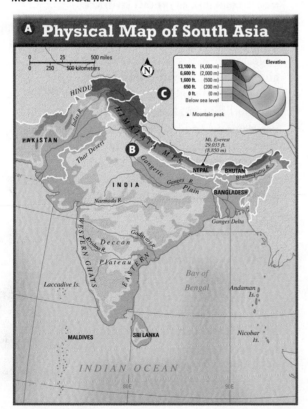

MODEL: THEMATIC MAP

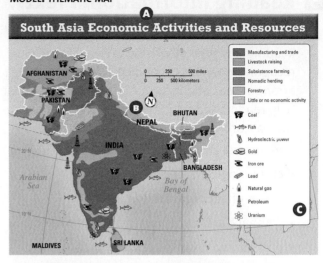

PRACTICE AND APPLY

1. According to the circle graph, how many days a week do most people exercise?

2. On which date was a temperature of 60° F recorded?

3. According to the bar graph, where is the world's tallest structure located?

4. How many kinds of canals were used in ancient irrigation?

5. What material formed the bottom layer of Roman roads?

6. According to the chart, which animal was domesticated in South America?

7. What time would you have to leave City College to get to the Watt/I-80 train station by 11:00?

8. What body of water is on the east coast of India?

9. What is the main economic activity of Afghanistan?

3 Reading Informational Texts: Patterns of Organization

Reading any type of writing is easier once you recognize how it is organized. Writers usually arrange ideas and information in ways that best help readers see how they are related. There are several common patterns of organization:

- main idea and supporting details
- chronological order
- cause-effect organization
- compare-and-contrast organization
- problem-solution organization

Writers also typically present arguments in ways that will help readers follow their reasoning.

*For more about deductive and inductive methods of organization, see **Analyzing Logic and Reasoning**, pages R22–R25.*

3.1 MAIN IDEA AND SUPPORTING DETAILS

Main idea and supporting details is a basic pattern of organization in which a central idea about a topic is supported by details. The **main idea** is the most important idea about a topic that a particular text or paragraph conveys. **Supporting details** are words, phrases, or sentences that tell more about the main idea. The main idea may be directly stated at the beginning and then followed by supporting details, or it may be merely implied by the supporting details. It may also be stated after it has been implied by supporting details.

Strategies for Reading

- To find a stated main idea in a paragraph, identify the paragraph's topic. The topic is what the paragraph is about and can usually be summed up in one or two words. The word, or synonyms of it, will usually appear throughout the paragraph. Headings and subheadings are also clues to the topics of paragraphs.

- Look for the topic sentence, or the sentence that states the most important idea the paragraph conveys. It is often the first sentence in a paragraph; however, it may appear at the end.

- To find an implied main idea, ask yourself: Whom or what did I just read about? What do the details suggest about the topic?

- Formulate a sentence stating this idea and add it to the paragraph. Does your sentence convey the main idea?

Notice how the main idea is expressed in each of the following models.

MODEL: MAIN IDEA AS THE FIRST SENTENCE

On the second day of the heat wave, the temperature soared to a sweltering 110 degrees. [Main idea] The sun melted the tar of the newly paved driveway. It was almost impossible to escape the fumes, which caused him to hold his nose and breathe through his mouth. The air felt like a wet blanket smothering his lungs. Each breath was a struggle. [Supporting details]

MODEL: MAIN IDEA AS THE LAST SENTENCE

His body tried to maintain a healthy temperature by producing large amounts of sweat. Because the air was so humid and there was no breeze, the sweat didn't evaporate and cool him at all. It just dripped unpleasantly, and he grew even hotter as he angrily tried to wipe it away. Despite losing all that water, he wasn't even thirsty. [Supporting details] Though he didn't know it, he was in danger of becoming dehydrated. [Main idea]

MODEL: IMPLIED MAIN IDEA

As he walked along the street looking for something to drink, he began to feel light-headed. He ignored the feeling for a few minutes, but then became so dizzy that he had to sit down. Soon he started to feel sick to his stomach. As he stretched out, he began to shiver. "How can I be cold when it's 110 degrees?" he wondered before he fainted. [Implied main idea: He was dehydrated, which was a serious problem.]

PRACTICE AND APPLY

Read each paragraph, and then do the following:

1. Identify the main idea in the paragraph, using one of the strategies discussed on the previous page. Tell whether it is stated or implied.

2. Evaluate the pattern of organization used in the paragraph. Does it express the main idea effectively?

> The earthquake shook down in San Francisco hundreds of thousands of dollars' worth of walls and chimneys. But the conflagration that followed burned up hundreds of millions of dollars' worth of property. There is no estimating within hundreds of millions the actual damage wrought. Not in history has a modern imperial city been so completely destroyed. San Francisco is gone. Nothing remains of it but memories and a fringe of dwelling houses on its outskirts.
> —Jack London, "The Story of an Eyewitness"

> They never saw him. Now and then they heard whispered rumors to the effect that he was in the neighborhood. The woods were searched. The roads were watched. There was never anything to indicate his whereabouts. But a few days afterward, a goodly number of slaves would be gone from the plantation. Neither the master nor the overseer had heard or seen anything unusual in the quarter. Sometimes one or the other would vaguely remember having heard a whippoorwill call somewhere in the woods, close by, late at night. Though it was the wrong season for whippoorwills.
> —Ann Petry, *Harriet Tubman: Conductor on the Underground Railroad*

3.2 CHRONOLOGICAL ORDER

Chronological order is the arrangement of events in the order in which they happen. This type of organization is used in many short stories and novels, historical writing, biographies, and autobiographies. To show the order of events,

writers use order words such as *after, next,* and *later* and time words and phrases that identify specific times of day, days of the week, and dates, such as *the next morning, Tuesday,* and *March 13, 2007.*

Strategies for Reading

- Scan the text for headings and subheadings that may indicate a chronological pattern of organization.

- Look for words and phrases that identify times, such as *in a year, three hours earlier, in A.D. 1066,* and *the next day.*

- Look for words that signal order, such as *first, afterward, then, during,* and *finally,* to see how events or steps are related.

- Note that a paragraph or passage in which ideas and information are arranged chronologically will have several words or phrases that indicate time order, not just one.

- Ask yourself: Are the events in the paragraph or passage presented in time order?

Notice the words and phrases that signal time order in the first two paragraphs of the following model.

MODEL

The Life of Jack London

Jack London was born in San Francisco, California, in 1876. His family was poor and moved frequently in search of work. In 1881, the family began working on farms. London's dislike of farming drew him to literature as a way "to get beyond the sky lines of my narrow California valley."

The Londons were unlucky in farming. When they lost their land, they moved across the bay to Oakland. To help support his family, the 10-year-old London took his first job. By the time he was 15, he had quit school and was working long hours in a factory. London became a tough teenager who knew how to fight but who never lost his burning passion for books.

Time words and phrases

Events

Living by the sea, London became fascinated by the ships that promised contact with faraway places. At the age of 17, he joined the *Sophia Sutherland* on a seal-hunting voyage to Japan. This trip provided material for his first short story, "Story of a Typhoon off the Coast of Japan," for which he won first prize in a writing contest.

London then returned to California with a passion for travel. The next year, he "hopped a train" heading east and lived as a tramp. However, homelessness persuaded him to return to high school in Oakland. In 1896, with only one year of high school behind him, he passed the entrance exam for the University of California at Berkeley.

Unfortunately, London had to give up his university studies for lack of money. After working for a while in a laundry, he joined the rush north to Canada's Klondike River in search of gold. Although London never struck it rich, his Klondike experiences inspired his later writing.

PRACTICE AND APPLY

Reread the preceding model and then do the following:

1. List three words or phrases in the last three paragraphs that indicate time or order.

2. Describe how London became interested in books.

3. Explain why he returned home after living as a tramp.

3.3 CAUSE-EFFECT ORGANIZATION

Cause-effect organization is a pattern of organization that shows causal relationships between events, ideas, and trends. Cause-effect relationships may be directly stated or merely implied by the order in which the information is presented. Writers often use the cause-effect pattern in historical and scientific writing. Cause-effect relationships may have several forms.

One cause with one effect

One cause with multiple effects

Multiple causes with a single effect

A chain of causes and effects

Strategies for Reading

- Look for headings and subheadings that indicate a cause-effect pattern of organization, such as "Effects of Food Allergies."

- To find the effect or effects, read to answer the question "What happened?"

- To find the cause or causes, read to answer the question "Why did it happen?"

- Look for words and phrases that help you identify specific relationships between events, such as *because, since, had the effect of, led to, as a result, resulted in, for that reason, due to, therefore, if . . . then,* and *consequently.*

- Look closely at each cause-effect relationship. Do not assume that because one event happened before another, the first event caused the second event.

- Use graphic organizers like the diagrams shown to record cause-effect relationships as you read.

Notice the words that signal causes and effects in the following model.

> **MODEL**
> ### We're Destroying Our Rain Forests
> According to a study done by Brazilian scientists, nearly 5 million acres of rain forest are disappearing a year. That's equal to seven football fields a minute.
>
> The cause of this destruction is simple—cutting down trees. Every minute, around 2,000 trees are felled to create highways, railroads, and farms. Some trees, such as mahogany and teak, are harvested for their beautiful hardwood.

Effect

Signal words

Cause

This destruction of the rain forests has wide-ranging effects on living things. About 30,000 plant species live in the Amazon rain forest alone. These plants provide important foods such as bananas, coffee, chocolate, and nuts, as well as medicinal compounds found nowhere else. Just four square miles of a rain forest shelters more than 550 species of birds, reptiles, and amphibians. Almost 100 species worldwide face extinction every day, many due to habitat loss in rainforests.

Rain forests also act as climate regulators, balancing the exchange of oxygen and carbon dioxide in the atmosphere and helping to offset global warming. The earth's well-being will suffer as a result of the rain forests' destruction.

It is crucial that steps be taken immediately to reduce the number of trees being cut down. If this destruction is not reversed, within 50 years, thriving rain forests will be no more than a memory.

PRACTICE AND APPLY

Refer to the preceding model to do the following:

1. Use one of the graphic organizers on page R10 to show the multiple effects of cutting down trees described in the model.

2. List three words or phrases used to signal cause and effect in the last four paragraphs.

3.4 COMPARE-AND-CONTRAST ORGANIZATION

Compare-and-contrast organization is a pattern of organization that provides a way to look at similarities and differences in two or more subjects. A writer may use this pattern of organization to compare the important points or characteristics of two or more subjects. These points or characteristics are called **points of comparison.** There are two ways to develop compare-and-contrast organization:

Point-by-point organization—The writer discusses one point of comparison for both subjects, then goes on to the next point.

Subject-by-subject organization—The writer covers all points of comparison for one subject and then all points of comparison for the next subject.

Strategies for Reading

- Look in the text for headings, subheadings, and sentences that may suggest a compare-and-contrast pattern of organization, such as "Common Behaviors of Different Pets," to help you identify where similarities and differences are addressed.

- To find similarities, look for words and phrases such as *like, all, both, every,* and *in the same way.*

- To find differences, look for words and phrases such as *unlike, but, on the other hand, more, less, in contrast,* and *however.*

- Use a graphic organizer, such as a Venn diagram or a compare-and-contrast chart, to record points of comparison and similarities and differences.

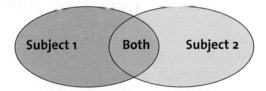

	Subject 1	Subject 2
Point 1		
Point 2		
Point 3		

As you read the following models, use the signal words and phrases to identify the similarities and differences between the subjects and how the details are organized in each text.

MODEL 1

Mr. Frank and Mr. Van Daan

Moving into a tiny apartment with people you have never met is a sure way to discover your differences. In the play *The Diary of Anne Frank,* Mr. Frank and Mr. Van Daan are in a similar situation, but have very different personalities, behaviors, and relationships with their families.

> Subjects

Both men are Jews living in Nazi-occupied Amsterdam during World War II. Both have children: Mr. Frank, two daughters; and Mr. Van Daan, a son. They try to hide

> Comparison words and phrases

their families from the Nazis in the same apartment.

Despite these similarities, there are many differences between the two men. First, they have nearly opposite personalities. Mr. Van Daan is very concerned with appearances and wears expensive clothes. He can be kind, but often loses his temper. He also has strong opinions about the roles of men and women. For example, he acts embarrassed that his son Peter likes his pet cat and disapproves of Anne's outspokenness. He tells her, "A man likes a girl who'll listen to him once in a while."

In contrast, Mr. Frank doesn't seem to care about material things. He always stays calm and has compassion for other people. Even when Mr. Van Daan is caught stealing food, Mr. Frank tries to understand the man's behavior. Mr. Frank's attitude about women differs from Mr. Van Daan's as well. Mr. Frank never criticizes Anne for being unladylike; instead, he encourages her to be herself. He gives her a diary because he knows she loves to write, and he is proud of her creativity when she makes Hanukkah presents for everyone. As Anne says about her father, "He's the only one who's ever given me the feeling that I have any sense."

The two men also respond differently to their situation. Mr. Van Daan is self-centered and believes he suffers more from hunger than the others. He even tries to take Anne's piece of cake. Mr. Frank, on the other hand, always puts the needs of others before his own. For example, he makes the newcomer, Dr. Dussel, feel welcome and gladly offers him food. He also risks his own safety to investigate when a robber enters the downstairs warehouse.

Mr. Frank and Mr. Van Daan relate differently with their families.

> **Comparison words and phrases**

> **Subject**

> **Contrast words and phrases**

> **Subject**

> **Contrast words and phrases**

Although Mr. and Mrs. Van Daan are close, they quarrel often. Mr. Van Daan criticizes his son's slowness and threatens to get rid of his beloved cat. In contrast, Mr. Frank shows only love and respect for his wife and daughters. Even when he scolds Anne, he does it privately and gently. After Anne hurts her mother's feelings, Mr. Frank tells her that parents "can only try to set a good example. The rest you must do yourself."

The differences between Mr. Frank and Mr. Van Daan in *The Diary of Anne Frank* far outnumber their similarities. Mr. Van Daan's selfishness endangers both families, while Mr. Frank's compassion and consideration help them all make the best of a terrible situation.

MODEL 2

Two for Tea

Next to water, tea is the most popular drink worldwide. Served hot or iced, it comes in a variety of flavors to suit every taste. Yerba maté and green tea are two varieties that seem to suit the tastes of increasing numbers of people of all ages and nationalities.

Yerba maté is native to South America. Made from the dried leaves of the yerba maté tree, it is traditionally brewed in hollow gourds, which are themselves called *matés*. The gourd is filled three-quarters full with leaves, and they are then covered with hot water. When the leaves have completely absorbed the moisture, more water is added. The brewed tea is then drunk through a tube with a strainer at one end called a *bombilla*. Yerba maté is sometimes served with milk, sugar, or lemon juice to cut its slight bitterness.

Yerba maté is thought to offer many health benefits. It is loaded with antioxidants that may boost

> **Subjects**

> **Comparison words and phrases**

the immune system and help prevent cancer. It also seems to aid digestion.

Green tea, on the other hand, is native to China and was exported to Japan in about A.D. 800. Unlike yerba maté, green tea usually is brewed in teapots. Only about a teaspoonful of leaves is used per pot. The leaves are steeped for only around two minutes—much less than the soaking time for yerba maté. Green tea has a very mild taste and generally is served plain in ceramic cups so the delicate taste can be savored.

> Contrast words and phrases

Like yerba maté, green tea also is beneficial to health. Similarly rich in antioxidants, it has been reputed to lower cholesterol and blood sugar and also to relieve the pain of arthritis. So, the next time you have tea for two, try one of these two popular drinks— yerba maté and green tea.

> Comparison words and phrases

PRACTICE AND APPLY

Refer to the preceding models to do the following:

1. Find one similarity and one difference in the organization of these two models.

2. For each model, list three words or phrases that signal comparisons or contrasts.

3. Identify two points in each model that the writer compares or contrasts.

4. Make a Venn diagram or compare-and-contrast graphic to show the similarities and differences in one of the models.

3.5 PROBLEM-SOLUTION ORGANIZATION

Problem-solution organization is a pattern of organization in which a problem is stated and analyzed and then one or more solutions are proposed and examined. This pattern of organization is often used in persuasive writing, such as editorials or proposals.

Strategies for Reading

- Look for an explanation of the problem in the first or second paragraph.

- Look for words such as *problem* and *reason* that may signal an explanation of the problem.

- To find the solution, ask: What suggestion does the writer offer to solve the problem?

- Look for words such as *propose, conclude,* and *answer* that may signal a solution.

MODEL

Teachers, administrators, school board members, and parents have begun expressing concerns that the foreign language students aren't getting enough practice using their languages in conversation.

Students read dialogues from their textbooks and respond to questions. They also use the language lab to get more practice speaking the language. The facilities are limited, though, and have to be used after school, which conflicts with other activities. Also, the language lab doesn't give them real-life experience with using the new language to listen to others, either.

One solution to this problem would be to establish language tables in the lunchroom. Students taking a given language would eat lunch at a specific table one day a week. For that time, they would speak only the foreign language.

This plan has several advantages. First, it doesn't require any additional equipment, staff, or materials. Second, it wouldn't take time away from other classes or activities. Language students have to eat lunch just like everyone else, so why not make it an enjoyable learning experience?

Setting up language tables would let students supplement their language skills while nourishing their bodies. That's a recipe for success!

PRACTICE AND APPLY

Reread the model and then answer the following questions:

1. According to the model, what is the cause of the problem?

2. What solution does the writer offer? What words are a clue?

4 Reading Consumer, Public, and Workplace Documents

Informational texts can be grouped into three major categories: consumer, public, and workplace documents. In this section, you will learn strategies for reading these different kinds of texts. At the end of this section, you will also have the chance to use these texts to explain decisions and solve problems.

4.1 READING CONSUMER DOCUMENTS

Consumer documents are printed materials that accompany consumer products and services, such as product care tags, warranties, contracts, schedules, and assembly instructions. Take a moment now to familiarize yourself with the text features and information commonly found in these types of documents, using the strategies provided.

Strategies for Reading

Ⓐ Look for the **product name**, which is usually in the largest type.

Ⓑ Skim **subheadings** to identify the types of product facts you can find.

Ⓒ Don't be swayed by appealing language in a product **description.** Focus on facts rather than feel-good phrases.

Ⓓ A **warranty** explains the rules you must follow to get the item repaired or replaced for free.

Ⓔ Always read the **fine print.** It often tells what the warranty won't cover or what will release the manufacturer from having to keep its promises.

Ⓕ Before throwing anything away, read the warranty to find out what proof(s) of purchase you must provide to qualify for its protection. A **proof of purchase** is a document that verifies you paid for the item. It may be your receipt, a bar code from a box, or the product information tag.

MODEL: PRODUCT INFORMATION TAG

> **Student Traveler Luggage**
>
> **Ⓐ** Deluxe Carry-On
>
> **Ⓒ** Inline skate wheels and a push-button locking handle make this carry-on sized upright easy to roll. It's spacious enough to use for a 2–3 day trip, weighs only 8.9 lbs, and is constructed of sturdy 1680-Denier ballistic nylon.
>
> **PRODUCT CODE**
> 276URX01
>
> **DIMENSIONS**
> 14 x 21 x 8.5 inches
>
> **Ⓑ** COLOR
> Red Ribbon
>
> **PRICE**
> $199.00

MODEL: WARRANTY

> ## Ⓓ GENERAL WARRANTY
>
> If any part of your **Student Traveler Luggage** is *ever* broken or damaged, we will repair it free of charge if you send or bring it to an Authorized Repair Center.
>
> **To locate an Authorized Repair Center** near you, call 888–555–TRAV or go to www.studenttravelerluggage.com.
>
> **NOTE:** You must pay for shipping the bag *to* us, but we'll take care of the cost for its repair and return. Allow 2–3 weeks from your bag's date of arrival for its repair and safe return. **Ⓔ**
>
> **EXCEPTIONS:** Cosmetic damage and cleaning are not covered under this warranty. We are not responsible for the replacement of lost or stolen bags or their contents.
>
> **To qualify for our repair service,** please supply the following items with your luggage:*
> - Warranty certificate (this card) **Ⓕ**
> - Proof of purchase (original receipt *or* product information tag)
>
> *Alternatively, to avoid having to provide paper documentation in the future, register your product online now. Just go to www.studenttravelerluggage.com, click on "activate warranty," and answer the prompts.
>
> **WARRANTY CODE** 276URX-8A

G When reading a consent form or other **contract,** review all the **options** before picking one.

H Notice **write-on lines,** which are lines provided for signatures and handwritten information you may need to supply.

I To figure out what you need to put on a write-on line, look to its left for a question or a **noun phrase followed by a colon.** Also follow any instructions in parentheses.

MODEL: CONTRACT

> ## PARENT/GUARDIAN CONSENT FORM
>
> **G** ___ I hereby **GRANT** permission for my child's photo to be used in school district materials and distributed to local newspapers.
>
> ___ I hereby **DO NOT GRANT** permission for my child's photo to be used in school district materials or to be distributed to local newspapers. (I understand this means photographs of my child in plays, athletic competitions, awards ceremonies, and recitals will not be included in promotional materials or in the local newspaper.)
>
> **Student's Name:** (PLEASE PRINT) _____ **H** _____
> **Name of Parent/Guardian:** (PLEASE PRINT) _____
> **Signature of Parent/Guardian:** (PLEASE SIGN) _____
> **Date: I** _____

PRACTICE AND APPLY

Use the three preceding consumer documents to do the following.

1. Compare the product information tag and the warranty. What purpose and text features do they share? What else do they have in common?

2. Contrast all three documents. What is unique about each document?

MODEL: RULES AND REGULATIONS

4.2 READING PUBLIC DOCUMENTS

Public documents are texts written to provide information that is of interest or concern to the general public. Such documents include speeches, laws, government documents, and posted rules and regulations. For example, the following public document was issued by a school for its eighth grade field trip to Washington, D.C. Study this document, using the strategies provided.

Strategies for Reading

A Read the **heading** to see what the document is about.

B Regard each **numbered item** as important.

C Pay close attention to **verbs** describing actions you should or should not take.

D Pay close attention to **statements that identify the consequences** for breaking or failing to properly follow a rule.

> **B** **A Trip Rules**
>
> 1. Keep your itinerary with you at all times.
> 2. Arrive promptly for departures and report directly to your chaperone.
> 3. Answer promptly whenever a head count is taken.
> **C**
> 4. When out touring, dress and behave with decorum. Unacceptable clothing includes torn jeans, pants that fall 4 inches or more below one's natural waistline, skirts shorter than mid-thigh, tops that expose any part of the midriff, and T-shirts with hostile messages.
> 5. When out touring, do not wear shoes that might bother your feet, including flip flops, clogs, and high heels.
> 6. At the hotel, you are not permitted to order from room service or attach any electronic devices to the hotel television (leave your TV game stations at home).
> 7. By 10 p.m. you must be in your assigned hotel room for the night.
> **D** If you break the 10 p.m. curfew, you will be expelled from the trip.

PRACTICE AND APPLY

Refer to the preceding public document to answer the next questions.

1. On this trip, would you wear a pair of flip flops to tour Washington, D.C.? Why or why not?

2. What will happen if you are discovered in the hall after 10 p.m.?

4.3 READING WORKPLACE DOCUMENTS

Workplace documents are texts produced or used within the workplace, such as memos, business letters, and company policy statements. You can become familiar with some of the conventions used in workplace documents by reading the following business letter, using the strategies provided.

Strategies for Reading

Ⓐ Read the **heading** to find out when the letter was written and by whom.

Ⓑ Read the **inside address** to identify the person for whom the letter is intended.

Ⓒ Notice the **salutation,** or initial greeting. It is usually impersonal (as in "To Whom It May Concern") or formal (as in "Dear").

Ⓓ As you read the **body of the letter,** notice what the sender wants the reader to know or do.

Ⓔ Slow down when reading a **bulleted list,** which is meant to make complex information clearer. Every item on a bulleted list is of equal importance.

Ⓕ In the **closing,** you can find the sender's name, his or her position, and, sometimes, an e-mail address or other contact information.

PRACTICE AND APPLY

Refer to the business letter to answer the following questions.

1. Who is the sender of this letter, and what does he want?

2. By what method are submissions supposed to be made?

MODEL: BUSINESS LETTER

May 5, 2010 **Ⓐ**

Jerry Meyers, Features Editor
Shady Grove Press
1154 Main Street
Shady Grove, VT 05064

Ms. Corinne Anderson **Ⓑ**
Newgate Middle School
Shady Grove, VT 05064

Dear Ms. Anderson: **Ⓒ**

Thank you for informing me of your eighth grade students' upcoming trip to Washington, D.C. On behalf of Shady Grove Press, I would like to invite your students to submit feature articles about their trip for possible publication in our special "back to school" edition. **Ⓓ**

We can only publish one student-written article, but the writer of that article will receive a byline (sorry, no cash payment). Interested students must follow these submission guidelines:

- Articles should be no longer than 750 words.

Ⓔ • Lines must be double-spaced. Type must be 12 pt. Times Roman.

- Article should focus on descriptions of historic sites and personal thoughts about these sites.

- If photos are included, they must come with captions as well as the full names and phone numbers of all students appearing in them.

- All submissions must be made electronically (as e-mail attachments), to the e-mail address provided below *no later than June 15.*

- The writer's contact information must be provided with the article.

I look forward to reading your students' work.

Sincerely,

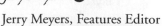 **Ⓕ**

Jerry Meyers, Features Editor
jmeyers@shadygrovepress.com

4.4 USING CONSUMER, PUBLIC, AND WORKPLACE DOCUMENTS TO EXPLAIN A DECISION OR SITUATION OR TO SOLVE A PROBLEM

The information you need to make decisions, handle situations, and solve problems can often be found in consumer, public, or workplace documents. For example, imagine that you are going on a class field trip to Washington, D.C. Use the preceding consumer, public, and workplace documents to tackle the following decisions, situations, and problems.

1. Use the notice from the airlines shown here and the product information tag on page R14 to determine whether you can use the Deluxe Carry-On manufactured by Student Traveler Luggage as your carry-on bag. Then share what you decide and explain how you reached your decision.

    MODEL: AIRLINE REGULATIONS

    ### CARRY-ON BAGGAGE

    For travel worldwide on our airlines, you may carry on one bag and one personal item such as a purse, briefcase, or laptop computer.

    - Carry-on bag dimensions should not exceed 9″ x 14″ x 22″ (length x width x height) or 45 linear inches (the length, height, and width added together).
    - A carry-on bag must fit under your seat or in an overhead bin.

    If your carry-on item cannot be safely stowed on a particular flight, the item will have to travel as checked baggage.

2. What would you do if the zipper on your Deluxe Carry-On broke just 3½ weeks before your flight was scheduled to depart? To solve this problem, consult the warranty on page R14. Then explain your decision.

3. Review the consent form on page R15. What cannot happen if your parent or guardian chooses the second option on that contract?

4. Use the rules and regulations on page R15 to decide whether you would pack any of the following: a TV game station, torn jeans, a T-shirt printed with a controversial message that you use only as a pajama top. Share your decisions and your reasons for them.

5. Imagine that the letter on page R16 was sent to your teacher. Reread it to decide whether you would want to write an article for the paper. State your decision and note details from the letter that led you to make this choice.

5 Reading Technical Directions

Technical directions are a type of procedural text, or text that explains how to do something. Specifically, technical directions are detailed instructions for assembling or operating a product, such as a cell phone. They often can be found in manuals that accompany electronic devices.

Because you need to be able to follow technical directions precisely and locate information within them quickly, you may find it helpful to learn the following strategies for reading technical directions.

Strategies for Reading

🅐 Look at the **heading** to find out the purpose of the document.

🅑 Scan the **subheadings** to see what kinds of information are covered.

🅒 **Examples** may be provided to help you with measurements or calculations.

🅓 **Numbers** will show you the order in which steps should be followed or actions taken.

🅔 As you read the steps, look for **key terms, codes, or parts.** These may be printed in capital letters to make them easier to spot.

🅕 Study any diagrams closely, noticing **labels** that match terms, codes, or parts mentioned in the steps. Then review the steps to better visualize what you will need to do.

PRACTICE AND APPLY

Refer to the technical directions to answer the following questions.

1. What must you do before entering your stride length into the pedometer?

2. Is any information missing from the directions? Do they contain any unnecessary information?

3. How helpful is the diagram to your understanding of the directions?

MODEL: TECHNICAL DIRECTIONS FROM AN INSTRUCTION MANUAL

🅐 PEDOMETER INSTRUCTIONS

Set Your Stride 🅑

1. Measure your stride length by walking 10 steps, then dividing the total distance by 10.

   🅒 **EXAMPLE:** 20 ft ÷ 10 = 2 ft 00 in

2. Press the **MODE (A)** button until **DIST** is displayed on the screen.

🅓 3. Press the **SET (B)** button to enter your stride length. Keep pressing until the correct value is displayed.

4. To enter a new value later, press **RESET (C)** while the unit is in distance mode, then repeat step 3. 🅔

Set Your Weight

1. Press the **MODE (A)** button until **WEIGHT** is displayed.

2. Press the **SET (B)** button to enter your weight. Keep pressing until the correct value is displayed.

3. To enter a new value later, press **RESET (C)** while the unit is in weight mode, then repeat step 2.

Get Going

1. Clip the pedometer to your waist.

2. Press the **MODE (A)** button until **STEP** is displayed.

3. Press **RESET (C)** to reset the display to 0.

4. Close the case and start walking.

Review Your Data

After exercise, press the **MODE (A)** button until **SCAN** is displayed. The screen will show, in sequence:

- the number of steps taken
- the distance covered (in miles)
- the calories consumed (based on weight and distance)

6 Reading Electronic Texts

Electronic text is any text that is in a form that a computer can store and display on a screen. Electronic text can be part of Web pages, CD-ROMs, search engines, and documents that you create with your computer software. Like books, Web pages often provide aids for finding information. However, each Web page is designed differently, and information is not in the same location on each page. It is important to know the functions of different parts of a Web page so that you can easily find the information you want.

Strategies for Reading

Ⓐ Look at the **title** of a page to determine what topics it covers.

Ⓑ For an online source, such as a Web page or search engine, note the **Web address,** known as a **URL** (Universal Resource Locator). You may want to make a note of it in case you need to return to the page later.

Ⓒ Look for a **menu bar** along the top, bottom, or side of a Web page. Clicking on an item in a menu bar will take you to another part of the Web site.

Ⓓ Notice any hyperlinks to related pages. **Hyperlinks** are often underlined or highlighted in a contrasting color. You can click on a hyperlink to get to another page—one that may or may not have been created by the same person or organization.

Ⓔ For information that you want to keep for future reference, save documents on your computer or print them. For online sources, you can pull down the **Favorites** or **Bookmarks** menu and bookmark pages so that you can easily return to them. Printing the pages you need will allow you to highlight key ideas on a hard copy.

MODEL: WEB PAGE

PRACTICE AND APPLY

1. What is the URL of this Web page?

2. Which hyperlinks would you click on to find further information about the photograph?

3. How could you find information about subscribing to *National Geographic* magazine?

7 Reading Persuasive Texts

7.1 ANALYZING AN ARGUMENT

An **argument** expresses a position on an issue or problem and supports it with reasons and evidence. Being able to analyze and evaluate arguments will help you distinguish between claims you should accept and those you should not. A sound argument should appeal strictly to reason. However, arguments are often used in texts that also contain other types of persuasive devices. An argument includes the following elements:

- A **claim** is the writer's position on an issue or problem.

- **Support** is any material that serves to prove a claim. In an argument, support usually consists of reasons and evidence.

- **Reasons** are declarations made to justify an action, decision, or belief. For example: "My reason for walking so quickly is that I'm afraid I'll be late for class."

- **Evidence** consists of the specific references, quotations, facts, examples, and opinions that support a claim. Evidence may also consist of statistics, reports of personal experience, or the views of experts.

- A **counterargument** is an argument made to oppose another argument. A good argument anticipates the opposition's objections and provides counterarguments to disprove or answer them.

Claim	I need a larger allowance.
Reason	I don't have enough money to pay for my school lunches, fees, and transportation.
Evidence	I had to borrow money from my friend two weeks in a row to buy lunch.
Counterargument	My parents say I just need to budget my allowance better, but they don't realize what my expenses are.

Read the following book review and use a chart like the one shown to identify the claim, reason, evidence, and counterargument.

Hatchet
Reviewed by Kristen Loos

What would you do if you suddenly found yourself in the middle of a wilderness with no one else around and only a hatchet to help you survive? That's what happens to Brian Robeson, a boy about my age, in Gary Paulsen's book *Hatchet.* Even if this sounds like a situation you'll never be in, *Hatchet* is worth reading for what it says about facing your fears.

After his parents get a divorce, Brian heads up to northern Canada to spend the summer with his dad. But the pilot flying the airplane has a heart attack, and Brian is forced to crash-land it by himself. From then on, he has to handle everything by himself.

From the beginning all the way to the end of the book, Brian faces big problems just to survive. He's a city kid, so he's used to opening up the refrigerator any time he wants to eat. Now, at the edge of the woods, he has to figure out things like how to be safe from wild animals and how to make a fire without matches. At first, he panics. He doesn't even know what to drink or how to find and prepare food. Even so, he doesn't give up.

One of the things I like about the book is how Brian changes. At first, he hopes he will be rescued very soon. He thinks he can hold out for a few days until his parents or a search party finds him. Then, when a plane flies over without seeing him, he realizes that he is really on his own. He learns to make tools to fish and hunt with and to depend on himself for everything he needs.

Some readers may not like the book because they think this is an unusual situation that most people will never have to face. I don't agree, though, because I think the real message is not just about being lost in the wilderness, but about bravely dealing with whatever challenges we face in our lives.

I'm not going to spoil the book for you by saying how it ends or whether Brian gets rescued. Read it yourself for an exciting adventure and some good lessons about surviving in the wilderness. I hope you enjoy it as much as I did.

7.2 RECOGNIZING PROPOSITION AND SUPPORT PATTERNS

To find an author's claim, support, and counterarguments, it's helpful to identify the author's method for making his or her case. Here are two ways writers often make their cases:

- **Proposition and Support** The writer presents a **proposition**, which is a claim that recommends a policy, and two or three reasons for accepting the policy. For example, "Cigarette smoking should be banned in public places because it's bad for people's health and smelly." Then the writer supports each reason with evidence.

- **Strawman** The writer presents a proposition. Instead of supporting it, though, he or she sums up the other side's position and disproves it. Once that "strawman" has been defeated, the writer declares his or her proposition the best or only option.

Writers usually reveal how they are going to present their cases in the first few paragraphs of their work. Study the following paragraph to see how it signals that the argument to come will use a proposition and support pattern.

MODEL

Have you wanted to ride your bike to school but been frightened off by the car traffic? If so, you're not alone. The city should create bike lanes on busy streets because it would make cycling safer and easier.

Proposition

Support

The next paragraph introduces an editorial in which the writer uses the strawman method.

MODEL

The city should create bike lanes on busy streets. Opponents of bike lanes will tell you that such lanes are a waste of money because drivers just ignore them, but that's not true.

proposition

supposed argument against propostition

PRACTICE AND APPLY

Now use the preceding models and instruction to help you identify the way in which the author of this next introduction plans to persuade her readers to adopt her proposition. Explain how you arrived at your conclusion.

Every neighborhood should have a community garden. If the people in our neighborhood all had the chance to grow their own fruits, flowers, and vegetables in side-by-side garden plots, they would eat better, feel better, and get along better. Of course, not everyone would participate, but those who did would reap the benefits!

7.3 RECOGNIZING PERSUASIVE TECHNIQUES

Persuasive texts typically rely on more than just the **logical appeal** of an argument to be convincing. They also rely on ethical and emotional appeals and other **persuasive techniques**—devices that can convince you to adopt a position or take an action.

Ethical appeals establish a writer's credibility and trustworthiness with an audience. When a writer links a claim to to a widely accepted value, the writer not only gains moral support for that claim but also establishes himself or herself as a reputable, moral person readers can and should trust. For example, with the following appeal, the writer reminds readers of a value they should accept and suggests that if they share this value, then they should support the writer's position: "If you believe that all children deserve a good education, then vote for this legislation."

The chart shown here explains several other means by which a writer may attempt to sway you. Learn to recognize these techniques, and you are less likely to be influenced by them.

Persuasive Technique	Example
Bandwagon appeal Taps into people's desire to belong.	Join the millions of health-conscious people who drink Wonder Water!
Testimonial Relies on endorsements from well-known people or satisfied customers	Send your game over the top with Macon Ace—the racket designed and used by tennis legend Sonja Macon.
Snob appeal Taps into people's desire to be special or part of an elite group	The best deserve only the best—you deserve Beautiful Bubbles bath soap.
Appeals to pity, fear, or vanity Use strong feelings, rather than facts, to persuade	Why go unnoticed when Pretty Face can make you the center of attention?

Sometimes persuasive techniques are misused to create rhetorical fallacies. A **rhetorical fallacy** is writing or speech that is false or misleading. For example, an athlete who endorses a line of athletic shoes would be misleading the public if he or she wears a different kind of shoe in competitions.

PRACTICE AND APPLY

Identify the persuasive techniques used in this model.

A Dry Future?

One of the most talked-about books published this year is *Glass Half Empty.* This informative book paints a frightening picture of our dwindling water resources. In the next few decades, fresh drinking water may become more expensive and harder to find than gasoline! The author warns that competition for water will

cause nations to go to war with each other. Over 40 scientists have spoken in praise of the book. If you care about the planet, rush out and get a copy of *Glass Half Empty.*

7.4 ANALYZING LOGIC AND REASONING

While persuasive techniques may sway you to side with a writer, they should not be enough to convince you that an argument is sound. To determine the soundness of an argument, examine the argument's claim and support and the logic or reasoning that links them. Identifying the writer's mode of reasoning can help.

The Inductive Mode of Reasoning

When a person uses specific evidence to arrive at a generalization, that person is using **inductive reasoning.** Similarly, when a writer presents specific evidence first and then offers a generalization drawn from that evidence, the writer is making an **inductive argument.** Here is an example of inductive reasoning.

SPECIFIC EVIDENCE

Fact 1 Wind and water wear away rocks over time.

Fact 2 Earthquakes and volcanoes create immediate and drastic changes in the land.

Fact 3 The slow movement of the continents and spreading of the sea floor create new landforms.

GENERALIZATION

Natural forces continually change the surface of the earth.

Strategies for Determining the Soundness of Inductive Arguments

Ask yourself the following questions to evaluate an inductive argument:

- **Is the evidence valid and sufficient support for the conclusion?** Inaccurate facts lead to inaccurate conclusions.

- **Does the conclusion follow logically from the evidence?** From the facts listed, the conclusion that Earth's core as well as its surface are constantly changing would be too broad.

- **Is the evidence drawn from a large enough sample?** These three facts are enough to support the claim. If you wanted to claim that these are the *only* forces that cause change, you would need more facts.

The Deductive Mode of Reasoning

When a person uses a **premise,** or general principle, to form a conclusion about a particular situation or problem, that person is using **deductive reasoning.** For example,

To drive a car well, all drivers must give driving their complete attention.	**Premise, or general principle**

Talking on a cell phone takes some of a person's attention.	**The situation being observed or considered**

Drivers shouldn't talk on cell phones while driving.	**Conclusion (also considerd a deduction)**

Similarly, a writer is making a **deductive argument** when he or she begins the argument with a claim that is based on a premise and then presents evidence to support the claim. For example, a writer might begin a deductive argument with the claim "Drivers should not talk on cell phones while they are driving."

Strategies for Determining the Soundness of Deductive Arguments

Ask yourself the following questions to evaluate a deductive argument:

- **Is the premise actually stated, or is it implied?** Writers often present deductive arguments without stating the premises. They just assume that readers will recognize and agree with the premises. So you may want to identify the premise for yourself.

- **Is the premise correct?** Don't assume it is true. Ask yourself whether it is really true.

- **Is the conclusion valid?** To be valid, a conclusion in a deductive argument must follow logically from the premise and the specific situation.

The following chart shows two conclusions drawn from the same premise.

All spiders have eight legs.	
Accurate Deduction	**Inaccurate Deduction**
The black widow is a spider, therefore it has eight legs.	An octopus has eight legs, therefore it is a spider.

An octopus has eight legs, but it belongs to a different category of animals than the spider.

Now, as you read the following model, pay attention to how the author arrives at her conclusion.

The other day when I was waiting at the stoplight on my bike, I noticed that the car in front of me was in the right lane and had its right turn signal on. Wouldn't you have assumed, just like I did, that the driver was going to turn right? Well, I was wrong, and you probably would've been, too. As soon as the light turned green, the car swerved across two lanes and turned left.

Then there was the surprise birthday party the neighborhood kids and I had for one of our friends. We'd managed to keep it a secret, so we all expected her to be really surprised and pleased. Instead, she was upset and embarrassed because she wasn't dressed properly for a party.

It's dangerous to make assumptions about how other people will act. I've learned that the hard way!

PRACTICE AND APPLY

Refer to the preceding model and instruction to do the following:

1. Identify the mode of reasoning used in the model.

2. In your own words, explain the difference between inductively and deductively organizing ideas.

Identifying Faulty Reasoning

Sometimes an argument at first appears to make sense but isn't valid because it is based on a fallacy. A **fallacy** is an error in logic. Learn to recognize these common fallacies.

TYPE OF FALLACY	DEFINITION	EXAMPLE
Circular reasoning	Supporting a statement by simply repeating it in different words	My mother is always busy because **she has too much to do.**
Either/or fallacy	A statement that suggests that there are only two choices available in a situation that really offers more than two options	**Either** I grow two inches this summer **or** I'll never make any friends at my new school.
Oversimplification	An explanation of a complex situation or problem as if it were much simpler than it is	**All you have to do to get good grades** is listen carefully in class.
Overgeneralization	A generalization that is too broad. You can often recognize overgeneralizations by the use of words such as *all, everyone, every time, anything, no one,* and *none.*	**Nobody** has as many chores as I do.
Hasty generalization	A conclusion drawn from too little evidence or from evidence that is biased	I sneezed after taking a bite of the salad, so **I must be allergic to something in it.**
Stereotyping	A dangerous type of overgeneralization. Stereotypes are broad statements about people on the basis of their gender, ethnicity, race, or political, social, professional, or religious group.	**Artists are emotional** and **hard to get along with.**
Attacking the person or name-calling	An attempt to discredit an idea by attacking the person or group associated with it. Candidates often engage in name-calling during political campaigns.	The senator only supports this bill because he is **corrupt.**
Evading the issue	Responding to an objection with arguments and evidence that do not address its central point	I forgot to get the milk, **but dairy products are hard to digest anyway.**
False cause	The mistake of assuming that because one event occurred after another event, the first event caused the second one to occur	It rained this afternoon **because I left my umbrella at home.**
Non sequitur	A conclusion that does not follow logically from the "proof" offered to support it	Mrs. Lewis will make Steve the baseball team captain. **He is already the captain of the volleyball team.**

Look for examples of logical fallacies in the following argument. Identify each one and explain why you identified it as such.

> Store clerks are so rude. A cashier was impatient with me in the supermarket the other day because I bought too much yogurt. They must train the employees to treat customers that way so more people will use the self-checkout lines. I need to budget more money for groceries.

7.5 EVALUATING PERSUASIVE TEXTS

Learning how to evaluate persuasive texts and identify bias will help you become more selective when doing research and also help you improve your own reasoning and arguing skills.

Strategies for Identifying Bias

Bias is an inclination for or against a particular opinion or viewpoint. A writer may reveal a strongly positive or negative bias on an issue by

- **presenting only one way** of looking at it
- **overlooking key information**
- **stacking more evidence on one side** of the argument than the other
- **using unfairly weighted evidence,** which is weak or unproven evidence that a writer treats as if it is more important than it really is
- **using loaded language,** which consists of words with strongly positive or negative connotations

EXAMPLE: *At the* Village Star, *we bring you up-to-the-minute news. That's why so many people read our paper.* (Someone who works for the paper is making the claim. *Up-to-the-minute* has very positive connotations. The writer also fails to mention important information: the paper is free.)

Strategies for Identifying Propaganda

Propaganda is any form of communication that is so distorted that it conveys false or misleading information. Logical fallacies such as name-calling, the either/or fallacy, and false causes are often used in propaganda. The following example shows false cause. The writer uses one fact to support a particular point of view but does not reveal another fact that does not support that viewpoint.

EXAMPLE: *Since Jack Carter was elected mayor, unemployment has decreased by 25%.* (The writer does not mention that it was the previous mayor, not Jack Carter, who was responsible for bringing in the new factory that provides the extra jobs.)

*For more information on logical fallacies, see **Identifying Faulty Reasoning,** page R24.*

Strategies for Evaluating Evidence

It is important to have a set of standards by which you can evaluate persuasive texts. Use the questions below to help you critically assess facts and opinions that are presented as evidence.

- **Are the presented facts verifiable?** A **fact,** or **factual claim,** is a statement that can be proved by consulting a reliable source or doing research.

- **Are the presented opinions and commonplace assertions well informed?** An **opinion** is a statement of personal belief, feeling, or thought that does not require proof. A **commonplace assertion** is a statement that many people assume to be true but isn't necessarily so. When evaluating either type of statement, consider whether the author is knowledgeable about the topic and uses sound reasoning.

- **Is the evidence thorough and balanced?** Thorough evidence leaves no reasonable questions unanswered. Be alert to evidence that is weighted unfairly and contains loaded language or other signs of bias.

- **Is the evidence authoritative?** The people, groups, or organizations that provided the evidence should have credentials that support their authority.

- **Is it important that the evidence be current?** Where timeliness is crucial, as in the areas of medicine and technology, the evidence should reflect the latest developments in the areas.

Read the argument below. Identify the facts, opinions, and elements of bias.

Ultra Bars are the tastiest and most efficient way to get your daily requirement of important nutrients. Our bodies need a well-balanced combination of protein, carbohydrates, fats, vitamins, minerals, and trace elements to function most effectively and make us feel our best. The ingredients in Ultra Bars have been chosen in the perfect proportion to ensure you get the maximum benefit. Best of all, they taste terrific. And they aren't just for athletes—ordinary people should carry these bars with them, too, for a quick boost throughout the day!

Strategies for Determining a Strong Argument

Make sure that all or most of the following statements are true:

- The argument presents a claim or controlling idea.

- The claim is connected to its support by a premise or generalization that most readers would readily agree with. Correct premise: *Doing your best will bring you personal pride.* Incorrect premise: *Doing your best will bring you success.*

- The reasons make sense.

- The reasons are presented in a logical and effective order.

- The claim and all reasons are adequately supported by sound evidence.

- The evidence is adequate, accurate, and appropriate.

- The logic is sound. There are no instances of faulty reasoning.

- The argument adequately anticipates and addresses readers' concerns and counterclaims with counterarguments.

Use the preceding criteria to evaluate the strength of the following proposal.

MODEL
Summary of Proposal
I propose that the city government create a park on the unused plot of land at the edge of town.
Need
We must preserve the natural beauty of the area for all to appreciate and enjoy.
Proposed Solution
The five-acre plot of land on the south side of town is now being considered for improvement.

Some people want to sell the land to a building developer. They say that doing this would be profitable for the town and also provide good housing for new residents.

It's true that the town could make money by developing the land. A park could also be a source of income, however.

The park would generate income in a number of ways. It could charge a small admission fee for summer concerts and other events. It also could lease the space to neighboring communities for their gatherings and to local food concessions and special-interest groups.

The cost of creating and maintaining a park is less than what it would bring in. Community groups already have agreed to donate plants, provide volunteers to landscape and take care of the grounds, create gazebos, and install benches, water fountains, and trashcans.

Without a park, we can't ensure the safety and health of our residents. It would have playgrounds and areas to bike, skate, picnic, and walk or jog. Unlike commercial and even residential buildings, parks do not encourage vandalism and graffiti. The chief of police has confirmed that parks are easier to supervise, too, because it isn't as hard to police them.

No one who cares about our community could fail to see how important it is to create this park.

8 Adjusting Reading Rate to Purpose

You may need to change the way you read certain texts in order to understand what you read. To adjust the way you read, you first need to be aware of what you want to get out of the text. Then you can adjust the speed at which you read in response to your purpose and the difficulty of the material.

Determine Your Purpose for Reading

You read different types of materials for different purposes. You may read a novel for enjoyment. You may read a textbook unit to learn a new concept or to master the content for a test. When you read for enjoyment, you naturally read at a pace that is comfortable for you. When you read for information, you need to read more slowly and thoroughly. When you are being tested on material, you may think you have to read fast, especially if the test is being timed. However, you can actually increase your understanding of the material if you slow down.

Determine Your Reading Rate

The rate at which you read most comfortably is called your **independent reading level.** It is the rate that you use to read materials that you enjoy. To learn to adjust your reading rate to read materials for other purposes, you need to be aware of your independent reading level. You can figure out your reading level by following these steps:

1. Select a passage from a book or story you enjoy.
2. Have a friend or classmate time you as you begin reading the passage silently.
3. Read at the rate that is most comfortable for you.
4. Stop when your friend or classmate tells you one minute has passed.
5. Determine the number of words you read in that minute and write down the number.
6. Repeat the process at least two more times, using different passages.
7. Add the numbers and divide the sum by the number of times your friend timed you.

Reading Techniques for Informational Material

You can use the following techniques to adapt your reading for informational texts, to prepare for tests, and to better understand what you read:

- **Skimming** is reading quickly to get the general idea of a text. To skim, read only the title, headings, graphic aids, highlighted words, and first sentence of each paragraph. Also, read any introduction, conclusion, or summary. Skimming can be especially useful when taking a test. Before reading a passage, you can skim the questions that follow it in order to find out what is expected. This will help you focus on the important ideas in the text.

  When researching a topic, skimming can help you decide whether a source has information related to your topic. This will save time.

- **Scanning** is reading quickly to find a specific piece of information, such as a fact or a definition. When you scan, your eyes sweep across a page, looking for key words that may lead you to the information you want. Use scanning to review for tests and to find answers to questions.

- **Changing pace** is speeding up or slowing down the rate at which you read parts of a particular text. When you come across explanations of familiar concepts, you might be able to speed up without misunderstanding them. When you encounter unfamiliar concepts or material presented in an unpredictable way, however, you may need to slow down to understand the information.

WATCH OUT! Reading too slowly can affect your ability to understand what you read. Make sure you aren't just reading one word at a time. Practice reading phrases.

PRACTICE AND APPLY

Find an article in a magazine or textbook. Skim the article. Then answer the following questions:

1. What did you notice about the organization of the article from skimming it?
2. What is the main idea of the article?

Through writing, you can record your thoughts, feelings, and ideas for yourself alone or you can choose to communicate them to an audience.

COMMON CORE

Included in this handbook:
W 1b, e, W 2a–d, f, W 3a–d, W 4, W 5, W 6

1 The Writing Process

The writing process consists of the following stages: prewriting, drafting, revising and editing, proofreading, and publishing. You may return to an earlier stage at any time to improve your writing.

1.1 PREWRITING

In the prewriting stage, you explore what you want to write about, what your purpose for writing is, whom you are writing for, and what form you will use to express your ideas. Ask yourself the following questions to get started.

Topic	• Is my topic assigned, or can I choose it? • What would I be interested in writing about?
Purpose	• Am I writing to entertain, to inform, to persuade, or for some combination of these purposes? • What effect do I want to have on my readers?
Audience	• Who is the audience? • What might the audience members already know about my topic? • What about the topic might interest them?
Format	• Which format will work best? Letter? Essay? Poem? Speech? Memoir? Short story? Article? Editorial? Review? Research paper? Instructions?

Find Ideas for Writing

• Look at magazines, newspapers, and Web sites.

• Start a log of articles you want to save for future reference.

• With a group, brainstorm as many ideas as you can. Compile your ideas into a list.

• Write down anything that comes into your head.

• Interview someone who is an expert on a particular topic.

• Use a graphic organizer, such as a cluster map, to explore secondary ideas related to a topic.

Organize Ideas

Once you've chosen a topic, you will need to compile and organize your ideas. If you are writing a description, you may need to gather sensory details. For an essay or a research paper, you may need to record information from different sources. To record notes from sources you read or view, use any or all of these methods:

• **Summarize**—Briefly retell the main ideas of a piece of writing in your own words.

• **Paraphrase**—Restate all or almost all of the information in your own words.

• **Quote**—Record the author's exact words.

Depending on what form your writing takes, you may also need to arrange your ideas in a certain pattern.

*For more information, see the **Writing Handbook**, pages R34–R41.*

1.2 DRAFTING

In the drafting stage, you put your ideas on paper and allow them to develop as you write. You don't need to worry about correct grammar and spelling at this stage. There are two ways to draft:

Discovery drafting is a good approach when you are not sure what you think about your subject. Start writing and let your feelings and ideas lead you in developing the topic.

Planned drafting may work better if you know your ideas have to be arranged in a certain way, as in a research paper. Try making a writing plan or an informal outline before you begin drafting.

1.3 REVISING AND EDITING

The revising and editing stage allows you to polish your draft and make changes in its content, organization, and style. Ask yourself:

- Does my writing have a **main idea** or central focus? Is my controlling idea clear?

- Have I used **precise** nouns, verbs, and modifiers?

- Have I included **adequate details** and **evidence?** Where might I add a vivid detail or example?

- Is my writing **unified?** Are all ideas and supporting details relevant to my main idea or controlling impression?

- Have I used a consistent **point of view?**

- Is my writing clear and **coherent?** Do sentences connect to one another smoothly and logically?

- Do I need to add **transitional words, phrases, or sentences** to explain relationships among ideas and improve **coherence?**

- Have I used a **variety of sentence types and sentence openings?** Are they well constructed? What sentences might I combine to improve the rhythm of my writing?

- Have I used a **tone** appropriate for my audience and purpose? Would informal or formal English be more appropriate?

1.4 PROOFREADING

After revising your paper, proofread it for mistakes. Ask the following questions:

- Have I corrected any errors in **subject-verb agreement** and **pronoun-antecedent agreement?**

- Have I checked for errors in **possessive forms** and in the **comparative and superlative forms** of adjectives and adverbs?

- Have I checked for errors in **confusing word pairs,** such as *it's/its, than/then,* and *too/to?*

- Have I corrected any **run-on sentences** and **sentence fragments?**

- Have I followed rules for **correct capitalization** and **punctuation marks?**

- Have I checked the dictionary for the **spellings of unfamiliar words?**

TIP If possible, don't begin proofreading right after you finish writing. Put your work away for at least a few hours. When you return to it, you will find it easier to identify and correct mistakes.

Use the proofreading symbols in the chart to mark changes on your draft.

*For more information, see the **Grammar Handbook** and the **Vocabulary and Spelling Handbook**, pages R46–R77.*

Proofreading Symbols	
⋀ Add letters or words.	/ Make a capital letter lowercase.
⊙ Add a period.	⁋ Begin a new paragraph.
≡ Capitalize a letter.	⌐ Delete letters or words.
⊃ Close up space.	∿ Switch the positions of letters or words.
⋀ Add a comma.	

1.5 PUBLISHING AND REFLECTING

Always consider sharing your finished writing with a wider audience. Reflecting on your writing is another good way to finish a project.

Publishing Ideas

- Post your writing on a Weblog.

- Create a multimedia presentation and share it with classmates.

- Publish your writing in a school newspaper, local newspaper, or literary magazine.

- Present your work orally in a report, speech, reading, or dramatic performance.

Reflecting on Your Writing

Think about your writing process and whether you will add what you have written to your portfolio. You might ask yourself questions like these:

- Which parts of the process did I find easiest?

- What problems did I face during the writing process? How did I solve the problems?

- What changes have occurred in my writing style?

- What features in the writing of published authors or my peers can I apply to my own work?

1.6 PEER RESPONSE

Peer response consists of the suggestions and comments you make about the writing of your peers and also the comments and suggestions they make about your writing. You can ask a peer reader for help at any time in the writing process.

Using Peer Response as a Writer

- Indicate whether you are more interested in feedback about your ideas or about your presentation of them.

- Ask questions that require more than yes-or-no answers. These are more likely to give you specific information you can use as you revise.

- Encourage your readers to be honest, and give them plenty of time to respond thoughtfully to your writing.

Being a Peer Reader

- Respect the writer's feelings. Offer positive reactions first.

- Make sure you understand what kind of feedback the writer is looking for, and then respond accordingly.

For more information on the writing process, see the **Introductory Unit,** *pages 20–23.*

2 Building Blocks of Good Writing

Whatever your purpose in writing, you need to capture your reader's interest and organize your thoughts clearly.

2.1 INTRODUCTIONS

An introduction should capture your reader's attention. It may also include a controlling idea or introduce a main idea.

Kinds of Introductions

There are many different ways to write an introduction. You should choose one based on who the audience is and on your purpose for writing.

Make a Surprising Statement Beginning with a startling statement or an interesting fact can arouse your reader's curiosity about a subject, as in this model.

> **MODEL**
>
> Imagine something only 15 to 20 inches long dropping out of the sky at 200 miles an hour! It would be nothing but a blur. That's exactly what makes the peregrine falcon such an effective bird of prey.

Provide a Description A vivid description sets a mood and brings a scene to life for your reader. Here, details about how a hot air balloon works set the tone for a narrative about a balloon ride.

> **MODEL**
>
> Whoosh! The red and yellow flame shot up into the great nylon cone. The warm air filled the balloon so that the cooler air below held the apparatus aloft. A soft breeze helped to push the balloon and basket along. The four passengers hardly noticed the noise or the heat as they stared in awe at the hilly farmland below.

Ask a Question Beginning with a question can make your reader want to read on to find out the answer. The following introduction asks about the reader's interest in exploring new places.

> **MODEL**
>
> Have you ever wanted to explore uncharted territory? The participants of the Lewis and Clark expedition of 1804–1806 did just that. Their purpose was to map a good water route from St. Louis and the Mississippi River to the Pacific Ocean.

Relate an Anecdote Beginning with an anecdote, or brief story, can hook your reader and help you make a point in a dramatic way. The following anecdote introduces a story about a family trip.

> **MODEL**
>
> When I was in fifth grade, a local bank held a competition with a grand prize of a trip to the Cayman Islands. My parents entered the contest, never dreaming they would win. They also never dreamed that entering a contest would put us all smack in the middle of a hurricane.

Address the Reader Speaking directly to your reader establishes a friendly, informal tone and involves the reader in your topic.

> **MODEL**
>
> Show your concern for our community by supporting the campaign of Jonas Wright. Come to our next meeting at the Community Center Wednesday evening at 6:30—and bring your friends!

Begin with a Controlling Idea A controlling idea expressing a main idea may be woven into both the beginning and the end of a piece of nonfiction writing. The model shown here starts off with a thesis statement comparing two famous leaders and provides some facts to support the statement.

> **MODEL**
>
> There are many similarities between Mahatma Gandhi and Martin Luther King Jr. Both believed in nonviolent resistance to laws they felt were unfair. Both drew millions of people to support their causes and met tragic ends.

TIP To write the best introduction for your paper, you may want to try more than one of the methods and then decide which is the most effective for your purpose and audience.

2.2 PARAGRAPHS

A paragraph is made up of sentences that work together to develop an idea or accomplish a purpose. Whether or not it contains a topic sentence stating the main idea, a good paragraph must have unity and coherence.

Unity

A paragraph has unity when all the sentences support and develop one stated or implied idea. Use the following technique to create unity in your writing:

Write a Topic Sentence A topic sentence states the main idea of the paragraph; all other sentences in the paragraph provide supporting details. A topic sentence is often the first sentence in a paragraph, as shown in the model that follows. However, it may also appear later in a paragraph to reinforce or summarize the main idea.

> **MODEL**
>
> The ability to assemble complex social structures is one of the dolphin's most remarkable qualities. Dolphins live and travel in groupings called pods. These pods often show cooperative behavior and strong social bonding—separated pod-mates will still recognize one another six months later.

TIP Paying attention to topic sentences when you read literature can help you craft your own topic sentences. Notice the use of topic sentences in "Kabul's Singing Sensation" on pages 926–930. For example, the first paragraph on page 928 begins, "The soulful melancholy in Mirwais's voice is the product of hard times." The rest of the paragraph then describes some of those hard times in detail.

Coherence

A paragraph is coherent when all its sentences are related to one another and each flows logically to the next. The following techniques will help you achieve coherence in your writing:

- Present your ideas in the most logical order.
- Use pronouns, synonyms, and repeated words to connect ideas.
- Use transitional words to show relationships among ideas.

In the model shown here, the writer used several techniques to create a coherent paragraph.

> **MODEL**
>
> According to the English colonist John Smith, Pocahontas saved his life. A few years later, she was kidnapped by other colonists. While living with them, she fell in love with John Rolfe, and they were married. Later, Pocahontas, her husband, and their infant son traveled to England, where Pocahontas was introduced to the king.

2.3 TRANSITIONS

Transitions are words and phrases that show connections between paragraphs, passages, and ideas.

Kinds of Transitions

The types of transitions you choose depend on the ideas you want to convey.

Time or Sequence Some transitions help to clarify the sequence of events over time. When you are telling a story or describing a process, you can connect ideas with such transitional words as *first, second, always, then, next, later, soon, before, finally, after, earlier, afterward,* and *tomorrow.*

> **MODEL**
>
> The first thing I did was make sure I wasn't dreaming. That was easy, because I knew my messy room wouldn't appear in anybody's dream. Before I got out of bed, though, I turned on the light and put on my glasses. Only then did I scream.

Spatial Order Transitional words and phrases such as *in front, behind, next to, along, nearest, lowest, above, below, underneath, on the left,* and *in the middle* can help your reader visualize a scene.

> **MODEL**
>
> On my mother's dresser, you can read the history of our family. On the left, a picture shows my parents' wedding. The picture in the middle is of my older brother as a baby, still toothless.

Degree of Importance Transitional words such as *mainly, strongest, weakest, first, second, worst,* and *best* may be used to rank ideas or to show degrees of importance. This example uses parallel structure to help make ideas clear.

> **MODEL**
>
> The most important quality I look for in a friend is whether he or she has interests similar to mine. Second, I want someone who can keep a secret. Least important, my new friend should get along with all my other friends.

Compare and Contrast Words and phrases such as *similarly, likewise, also, like, as, neither . . . nor,* and *either . . . or* show similarity between details. *However, by contrast, yet, but, unlike, instead, whereas,* and *while* show difference. Note how transitions show contrast in the model.

> **MODEL**
>
> Like the lawyer in "The Bet," Jerry in "A Mother in Mannville" spends much of his time alone. Both characters experience loneliness. As an orphan, however, Jerry never chooses to be alone, whereas the lawyer agrees to his solitary confinement.

TIP Both *but* and *however* can be used to join two independent clauses. When *but* is used as a coordinating conjunction, it is preceded by a comma. When *however* is used as a conjunctive adverb, it is preceded by a semicolon and followed by a comma.

EXAMPLE

Water is the best thirst quencher, but it should be cold.

Iced water can be very refreshing; however, drinking it too fast is not good for you and can cause stomach cramps.

Cause-Effect When you are writing about a cause-effect relationship, use transitional words and phrases such as *since, because, thus, therefore, so, due to, for this reason,* and *as a result* to help explain the relationship and make your writing coherent.

MODEL

My notebook might look tattered, but I treasure it because Silvio gave it to me. He was my best friend, and he moved to Texas. Since the notebook is all I have to remember him by, I will never throw it out.

2.4 CONCLUSIONS

A conclusion should be clear and well-supported. It should leave readers with a strong final impression.

Kinds of Conclusions

Good conclusions sum up ideas in a variety of ways. Here are some techniques you might try.

Restate Your Controlling Idea A good way to conclude an essay is by restating your controlling idea, or thesis, in different words. The following conclusion restates the controlling idea introduced on page R31.

MODEL

It is ironic and tragic that the two similar leaders Mahatma Gandhi and Martin Luther King Jr. both inspired the world by preaching and practicing nonviolence, yet both died violent deaths.

Ask a Question Try asking a question that sums up what you have said and gives your reader something new to think about. This question concludes a piece of persuasive writing.

MODEL

So, if you care about your health and want to get in shape, shouldn't you talk to your doctor and begin a fitness program today?

Make a Recommendation When you are persuading your audience to take a position on an issue, you can conclude by recommending a specific course of action.

MODEL

Shawn, Maria, and Katie are real children. The next time you see a homeless person, remember these children and think about what you can do to help.

Offer an Opinion Leave your reader with something to think about by offering your personal opinion on the topic. The following model offers an opinion about homelessness.

MODEL

Any one of us could become homeless at any moment due to events we can't control. Remembering this frightening fact can help us take the problem of homelessness more seriously.

End with the Last Event If you're telling a story, you may end with the last thing that happens. Here, the ending includes the narrator's important realization.

MODEL

By the time the firefighters finally arrived, I had managed to get everyone out of the house and away from danger. Although we all were frightened and in shock, no one was badly hurt. As I watched the flames turn our home into ashes, I knew this was a night I'd never forget.

2.5 ELABORATION

Elaboration is the process of developing an idea by providing specific supporting details that are relevant and appropriate to the purpose and form of your writing.

Facts and Statistics A fact is a statement that can be verified, and a statistic is a fact expressed as a number. Make sure the facts and statistics you supply are from reliable, up-to-date sources.

> **MODEL**
>
> The heat wave this July broke all records. Temperatures rose above 100°F for 11 days in a row, and the scorching 113°F recorded at the airport on Wednesday was the highest reading ever measured here.

Sensory Details Details that show how something looks, sounds, tastes, smells, or feels can enliven a description. Which senses does the writer appeal to in the following model?

> **MODEL**
>
> Opening the cabin door, she felt transported back to her childhood halfway across the country. The crisp air held the promise of frost, and the pine needles on the path were beginning to turn brown and curl up at the edges as if trying to stay warm.

Incidents From our earliest years, we are interested in hearing "stories." One way to illustrate a point powerfully is to relate an incident or tell a story, as shown in the example.

> **MODEL**
>
> Pedestrians, like drivers, should look both ways before crossing the street. I learned how dangerous it can be to break that rule when I was almost hit by a driver who was going the wrong way down a one-way street.

Examples An example can help make an abstract idea concrete or can serve to clarify a complex point for your reader.

> **MODEL**
>
> Narrative poetry tells a story in poetic form. "Paul Revere's Ride" by Henry Wadsworth Longfellow, for example, describes the dramatic events that took place in Massachusetts on April 18, 1775, the night before the battles of Lexington and Concord.

Quotations Choose quotations that clearly support your point, and be sure to copy each quotation word for word. Remember always to credit the source.

> **MODEL**
>
> In his short story "The Tell-Tale Heart," Edgar Allan Poe uses bizarre and frightening details to grip the reader with a sense of horror. "I saw it [the eye] with perfect distinctness—all a dull blue, with a hideous veil over it that chilled the very marrow in my bones . . . ."

3 Writing Description

Descriptive writing allows you to paint word pictures about anything, from events of global importance to the most personal feelings. It is an essential part of almost every piece of writing.

> **CRITERIA: Standards for Writing**
>
> **Successful descriptive writing should**
> - have a controlling impression and sense of purpose
> - use details and precise words to create a vivid image, establish a mood, or express emotion
> - present details in a logical order

3.1 KEY TECHNIQUES

Consider Your Goals What do you want to accomplish with your description? Do you want to show why something is important to you? Do you want to make a person or scene more memorable? Do you want to explain an event?

Identify Your Audience Who will read your description? How familiar are they with your subject? What background information will they need? Which details will they find most interesting?

Think Figuratively What figures of speech might help make your description vivid and interesting? What simile or metaphor comes to mind? What imaginative comparisons can you make? What living thing does an inanimate object remind you of?

Gather Well-Chosen Details Which sights, smells, tastes, sounds, and textures make your subject come alive? Which details stick in your mind when you observe or recall your subject? Which senses does your subject most strongly affect?

You might want to use a chart like the one shown here to collect details about your subject.

Sights	Sounds	Textures	Smells	Tastes

Organize Your Details Details that are presented in a logical order help the reader form a mental picture of the subject. Descriptive details may be organized chronologically, spatially, by order of impression, or by order of importance.

3.2 OPTIONS FOR ORGANIZATION

Option 1: Spatial Order Choose one of these options to show the spatial order of elements in a scene you are describing.

*For more information, see **Transitions,** page R32.*

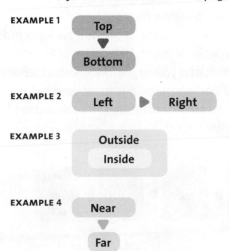

MODEL
Thunder's nostrils quivered as he was led into the barn. How would this be as a place to spend nights from now on? In the stall to the left, the straw smelled fresh. Beyond that stall, a saddle hung from the rough boards. To the right of his stall was another from which a mare looked at him curiously. So far, so good. To the far right, beyond two empty stalls, a cat lay on its side.

Option 2: Order of Impression Order of impression is the order in which you notice details.

TIP Use transitions that help readers understand the order of the impressions you are describing. Some useful transitions are *after, next, during, first, before, finally,* and *then.*

MODEL
As I walked into the planetarium, I was struck by the total darkness. Gradually, my eyes adjusted, and I could see the rows of seats. Finally, daring to raise my eyes from the ground, I gasped in awe at the domed ceiling. Spangled with hundreds of glittering stars, it created the sensation of standing outside on a clear summer night.

Option 3: Order of Importance You can use order of importance as the organizing structure for a description.

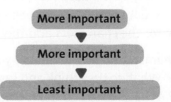

*For more information, see **Transitions,** page R32.*

Option 4: Chronological Order You can use chronological order as the organizing structure for a description. See section 4.2 on this page for an example of how this is done.

4 Writing Narratives

Narrative writing tells a story. If you write a story from your imagination, it is a fictional narrative. A true story about actual events is a nonfictional narrative. Narrative writing can be found in short stories, novels, news articles, personal narratives, and biographies.

> **CRITERIA: Standards for Writing**
>
> **A successful narrative should**
> - begin with an attention-getting introduction
> - present a clear incident, event, or situation
> - include vivid, well-chosen details in describing characters, setting, and action
> - use strategies such as dialogue and comparison/contrast to support descriptions
> - explain the significance of the event for the writer
> - have a logical organization with a clear beginning, middle, and end
> - use language suited to the audience and purpose
> - keep a consistent tone and point of view

*For more information, see **Writing Workshop: Personal Narrative**, pages 148–157, and **Writing Workshop: Short Story**, pages 582–591.*

4.1 KEY TECHNIQUES

Identify the Main Events What are the most important events in your narrative? Is each event needed to tell the story?

Describe the Setting When do the events occur? Where do they take place? How can you use setting to create mood and suspense, and to set the stage for the characters and their actions?

Depict Characters Vividly What do your characters look like? What do they think and say? How do they act? What details can show what they are like?

TIP Dialogue is an effective means of developing characters in a narrative. As you write dialogue, choose words that express your characters' personalities and that show how the characters feel about one another and about the events in the plot.

4.2 OPTIONS FOR ORGANIZATION

Option 1: Chronological Order One way to organize a narrative is to arrange the events in chronological order, as shown.

EXAMPLE

Yukiko's alarm doesn't go off, and she wakes up late on the day of an important English test.

Introduction
Characters and setting

▼

Panic-stricken, she leaps out of bed, throws on her clothes, and grabs her books, ignoring her mother's pleas to eat breakfast.

Event 1

▼

She dashes into the classroom just as the final bell rings. She feels light-headed from running and not having eaten anything.

Event 2

▼

Her mind goes blank, and she can't answer any of the questions. She takes a few minutes to calm down and tells herself she'll just do the best she can.

End
Perhaps showing the significance of the events

Option 2: Flashback In narrative writing, it is also possible to introduce events that happened before the beginning of the story. You may want to hook your reader's interest by opening a story with an exciting event. After your introduction, you can use a flashback to show how past events led up to the present situation or to provide background about a character or event. Use clue words such as *last summer, as a young girl, the previous school year,* and *his earliest memories* to let your reader know that you are interrupting the main action to describe earlier events.

Notice how the flashback interrupts the action in the model.

MODEL

As Yukiko fidgeted in her chair, she remembered a story she once read about a woman with amnesia. The woman wandered around for weeks, not remembering that she had a husband and children. The fact that the woman eventually regained her memory gave Yukiko hope that the material she'd studied so hard eventually would come back to her.

Option 3: Focus on Conflict When a fictional narrative focuses on a central conflict, the story's plot may be organized as in the following example.

EXAMPLE

Yukiko is worried about an important English test and stays up late studying. When she finally goes to bed, she forgets to set her alarm. In the morning, she wakes up in a panic, realizing that school starts in only 20 minutes.

> Describe main characters and setting.

She wonders whether she should try to get to class on time or pretend she is sick and take a make-up test later.

> Present conflict.

- She tells her mother the situation and asks her advice.
- She decides to race to school and take the test, since she's already studied so hard.
- She begins to feel dizzy and weak.

> Relate events that make conflict complex and cause characters to change.

Yukiko gets to class just as the test is beginning. She's nervous and doesn't do as well as she could have, but she is proud of having made the right decision.

> Present resolution or outcome of conflict.

5 Writing Informative Texts

Expository writing informs and explains. You can use it to explain how to cook spaghetti, to explore the origins of the universe, or to compare two pieces of literature. There are many types of expository writing. Think about your topic and select the type that will present the information most clearly.

5.1 COMPARISON AND CONTRAST

Compare-and-contrast writing examines the similarities and differences between two or more subjects. You might, for example, compare and contrast two short stories, the main characters in a novel, or two movies.

> **CRITERIA: Standards for Writing**
>
> **Successful compare-and-contrast writing should**
>
> - hook the reader's attention with a strong introduction
> - clearly identify the subjects that are being compared
> - include specific, relevant details
> - follow a clear plan of organization
> - use language and details appropriate to the audience
> - use transitional words and phrases to clarify similarities and differences

*For more information, see **Writing Workshop: Comparison-Contrast Essay**, pages 438–447.*

Options for Organization

Compare-and-contrast writing can be organized in different ways. The examples that follow demonstrate point-by-point organization and subject-by-subject organization.

Option 1: Point-by-Point Organization

EXAMPLE

I. Similarities between older and newer children's books   **Point 1**

   Subject A. Older books feature children as characters.

   Subject B. Today's books also often include children.

II. Differences between older and newer children's books   **Point 2**

   Subject A. Older books tend to avoid racial and social conflicts.

   Subject B. Today's books are likely to describe realistic racial and social conflicts.

Option 2: Subject-by-Subject Organization

EXAMPLE

I. Older children's books — **Subject A**

    Point 1. They focus on children as main characters.

    Point 2. They avoid discussing racial or social conflicts.

II. Today's children's books — **Subject B**

    Point 1. They focus on children and young people.

    Point 2. They describe realistic racial and social conflicts.

5.2 CAUSE AND EFFECT

Cause-effect writing explains why something happened, why certain conditions exist, or what resulted from an action or a condition. You might use cause-effect writing to explain a character's actions, the progress of a disease, or the outcome of a war.

CRITERIA: Standards for Writing

Successful cause-effect writing should

- identify a true cause-and-effect relationship
- show clear connections between causes and effects
- present causes and effects in a logical order, using parallel structure and transitions
- use facts, examples, and other evidence to illustrate each cause and effect
- differentiate between facts and opinions
- use language and details appropriate to the audience
- be well-balanced, with an introduction, body, and conclusion

*For more information, see **Writing Workshop: Cause-and-Effect Essay**, pages 862–871.*

Options for Organization

Your organization will depend on your topic and your purpose for writing.

Option 1: Effect-to-Cause Organization If you want to explain the causes of an event, such as the risk of not having enough energy to take a test, you might first state the effect and then examine its causes.

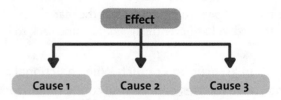

Option 2: Cause-to-Effect Organization If your focus is on explaining the effects of an event, such as the importance of eating a healthy breakfast, you might first state the cause and then explain the effects.

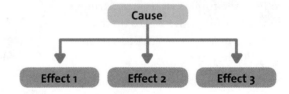

Option 3: Cause-Effect Chain Organization Sometimes you'll want to describe a chain of cause-and-effect relationships to explore a topic such as how to do well on a test.

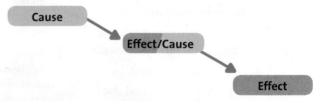

TIP Don't assume that a cause-effect relationship exists just because one event follows another. Look for evidence that the later event could not have happened if the first event had not caused it.

5.3 PROBLEM-SOLUTION

Problem-solution writing clearly states a problem, analyzes the problem, and proposes a solution to the problem. It can be used to identify and solve a conflict between characters, investigate global warming, or tell why the home team keeps losing.

CRITERIA: Standards for Writing

Successful problem-solution writing should

- hook the reader's attention with a strong introduction
- identify the problem and help the reader understand the issues involved
- analyze the causes and effects of the problem
- include anecdotes, quotations, facts, statistics, and other evidence
- explore possible solutions to the problem and recommend the best one(s)
- use language, details, and a tone appropriate to the audience

Options for Organization

Your organization will depend on the goal of your problem-solution piece, your intended audience, and the specific problem you have chosen to address. The organizational methods that follow are effective for different kinds of problem-solution writing.

Option 1: Simple Problem-Solution

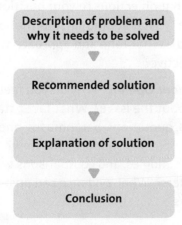

Description of problem and why it needs to be solved
▼
Recommended solution
▼
Explanation of solution
▼
Conclusion

Option 2: Deciding Between Solutions

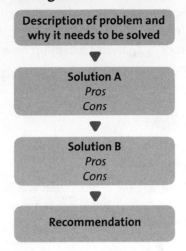

Description of problem and why it needs to be solved
▼
Solution A
Pros
Cons
▼
Solution B
Pros
Cons
▼
Recommendation

5.4 ANALYSIS

In writing an analysis, you explain how something works, how it is defined, or what its parts are.

CRITERIA: Standards for Writing

A successful analysis should

- hook the reader's attention with a strong introduction
- clearly define the subject and its parts
- use a specific organizing structure to provide a logical flow of information
- show connections among facts and ideas through transitional words and phrases
- use language and details appropriate for the audience

Options for Organization

Organize your details in a logical order appropriate to the kind of analysis you're writing. Use one of the following options: process analysis, definition analysis, or parts analysis.

Option 1: Process Analysis A process analysis is usually organized chronologically, with steps or stages in the order in which they occur. You might use a process analysis to explain how to program a cell phone or prepare for a test.

MODEL

Preparing for a test

Doing well on a test requires careful preparation.

Step 1: Reread the material that will be covered on the test and your class notes.
Step 2: Outline the material.
Step 3: Answer any questions in the text and make up and answer your own.
Step 4: Get plenty of sleep the night before.

> Introduce process
>
> Give background
>
> Explain steps

Option 2: Definition Analysis You can organize the details of a definition analysis in order of importance or impression. Use a definition analysis to explain the characteristics of a limerick, the characteristics of insects, or a quality (such as excellence).

MODEL

What is excellence?

Excellence is the quality of being first-rate, exceeding all others, and setting a standard of performance.

Feature 1: being first-rate

Feature 2: exceeding all others

Feature 3: setting a standard of performance

> Introduce term and definition
>
> Explain features

Option 3: Parts Analysis A parts analysis explains a subject by breaking it down into its main pieces.

MODEL

Test preparation consists of three main parts.

Part 1: Getting to know the material

Part 2: Practicing the material

Part 3: Resting and being healthy for the test

> Introduce subject
>
> Explain parts

6 Writing Arguments

Persuasive writing allows you to use the power of language to inform and influence others. It includes speeches, persuasive essays, newspaper editorials, advertisements, and critical reviews.

CRITERIA: Standards for Writing

Successful persuasive writing should

- grab the reader's attention with a strong introduction
- present a well-defined controlling idea, or thesis, that states the issue and the writer's claim
- support arguments with detailed evidence, examples, and reasons
- clearly distinguish between fact and opinion
- anticipate and answer counterarguments, or opposing views, with solid facts and reasons
- use sound logic and persuasive language
- conclude with a summary of points or a call to action

*For more information, see **Writing Workshop: Critical Review**, pages 300–309 and **Writing Workshop: Persuasive Essay**, pages 1038–1047.*

6.1 KEY TECHNIQUES

Clarify Your Claim What do you believe about the issue? How can you express your opinion most clearly?

Know Your Audience Who will read your writing? What do they already know and believe about the issue? What objections to your position might they have? What additional information might they need? What tone and approach would be most effective?

Support Your Opinion Why do you feel the way you do about the issue? What facts, statistics, examples, quotations, paraphrases, anecdotes, or expert opinions support your view? What reasons, analogies, and comparisons will convince your readers? What evidence can answer their objections?

Ways to Support Your Argument	
Statistics	facts that are stated in numbers
Examples	specific instances that explain points
Observations	events or situations you have seen firsthand
Anecdotes	brief stories that illustrate points
Quotations	direct statements from authorities

*For more information, see **Identifying Faulty Reasoning**, page R24.*

Begin and End with a Bang How can you hook your readers and make a lasting impression? What memorable quotation, anecdote, or statistic will catch their attention at the beginning or stick in their minds at the end? What strong summary or call to action can you conclude with?

MODEL

Beginning

Have you ever enjoyed the antics of the orangutans or watched the polar bears swim at Green Park Zoo? Unless we make sure that public funding for the zoo continues, those experiences will be just memories.

End

In addition to being a place for relaxation and fun, Green Park Zoo is a scientific laboratory where professionals work to create educational programs and ensure the survival of endangered species. Don't let the zoo become an endangered species itself. Support public funding today.

6.2 OPTIONS FOR ORGANIZATION

In a two-sided persuasive essay, you want to show the weaknesses of other opinions as you explain the strengths of your own.

Option 1: Reasons for Your Opinion

Introduction states issue and your position on it

▼

Reason 1 with evidence and support

▼

Reason 2 with evidence and support

▼

Reason 3 with evidence and support

▼

Objections to whole argument

▼

Response to objections

▼

Conclusion restates your position and recommends a course of action

Option 2: Point-by-Point Basis

Introduction states issue and your position on it

▼

Reason 1 with evidence and support

▼

Objections and responses for reason 1

▼

Reason 2 with evidence and support

▼

Objections and responses for reason 2

▼

Reason 3 with evidence and support

▼

Objections and responses for reason 3

▼

Conclusion restates your position and recommends a course of action

7 Writing for the Workplace

You might use business writing to ask for information, to complain about a product or service, or as part of a future job or career. Three of the most important and useful kinds of business writing are the business letter, the memo (sometimes called a memorandum), and the job application.

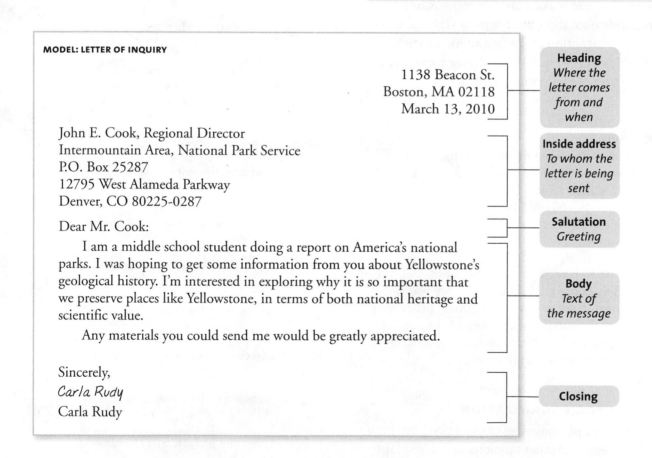

MODEL: LETTER OF INQUIRY

1138 Beacon St.
Boston, MA 02118
March 13, 2010

Heading
Where the letter comes from and when

John E. Cook, Regional Director
Intermountain Area, National Park Service
P.O. Box 25287
12795 West Alameda Parkway
Denver, CO 80225-0287

Inside address
To whom the letter is being sent

Dear Mr. Cook:

Salutation
Greeting

I am a middle school student doing a report on America's national parks. I was hoping to get some information from you about Yellowstone's geological history. I'm interested in exploring why it is so important that we preserve places like Yellowstone, in terms of both national heritage and scientific value.

Any materials you could send me would be greatly appreciated.

Body
Text of the message

Sincerely,
Carla Rudy
Carla Rudy

Closing

MODEL: MEMO

To: Joellen Snipes
From: John Cook
Subject: Informational brochures
Date: March 16, 2010

Joellen, please read the attached letter and send Carla our brochure packet. It's encouraging to receive inquiries from concerned young people, so please add a personal note of thanks for her interest.

Heading
Receiver's name
Sender's name
Topic of memo
Complete date

Body

MODEL: JOB APPLICATION

JIFFY JEANS
EMPLOYMENT APPLICATION

Print clearly in black or blue ink. Answer all questions. Sign and date the form.

Directions
Read carefully

PERSONAL INFORMATION:

Name: Marquell Janek   **Social Security Number:** 555-77-5656

Address: 7218 University Place   **City:** Woodland   **State:** CA   **Zip:** 95659

Phone Number: (530) 661-7814

If you are under age 18, do you have an employment/age certificate? Yes _X_ No __

POSITION/AVAILABILITY:

Position Applied for: Stockroom helper

Days/Hours Available: Monday ____ Tuesday ____ Wednesday 6–8 PM Thursday ____
Friday ____ , Saturday 8 AM–6 PM , Sunday 1 PM–6 PM

What date are you available to start work? June 19, 2010

EDUCATION:

School: Westleigh Middle School   **Highest Grade Completed:** 8

I certify that information contained in this application is true and complete. I understand that false information may be grounds for not hiring me or for immediate termination of employment at any point in the future if I am hired. I authorize the verification of any or all information listed above.

Signature: Marquell Janek   **Date:** 5/31/2010

Information
Fill out accurately and completely

Authorization and signature
Your promise to the employer

PRACTICE AND APPLY

1. Draft a response to the letter of inquiry. Then revise your response as necessary according to the criteria on page R42. Make sure you have included the necessary information and have written in an appropriate tone. Follow the format and spacing shown in the model.

2. Write a memo in response to the memo shown here. Tell the receiver what actions you have taken. Follow the format of the model.

3. Visit a local business and ask for a copy of its job application. Fill it out, then trade with a partner and check each other's work. Which features in your application are also in the model? Which are not?

8 Writing Functional Texts

If you have ever followed a recipe or used a computer manual, you have read a functional text. Functional texts explain rules or give instructions, and they're important for many jobs and careers. The functional text shown on this page is a set of **bylaws** (rules about how to run a group or organization). On the opposite page, you'll see an example of instructions on how to design a system. Other functional texts, such as the example on pages 945–952, tell how to use a device.

CRITERIA: Standards for Writing

Successful functional texts should

- serve a definite purpose, such as designing a system, operating a device, or listing the bylaws of an organization
- clearly identify a sequence of activities
- provide all essential information, such as definitions of unfamiliar terms
- include all factors and variables that need to be considered
- use formatting techniques, such as headings and different fonts, that make the document easier to understand

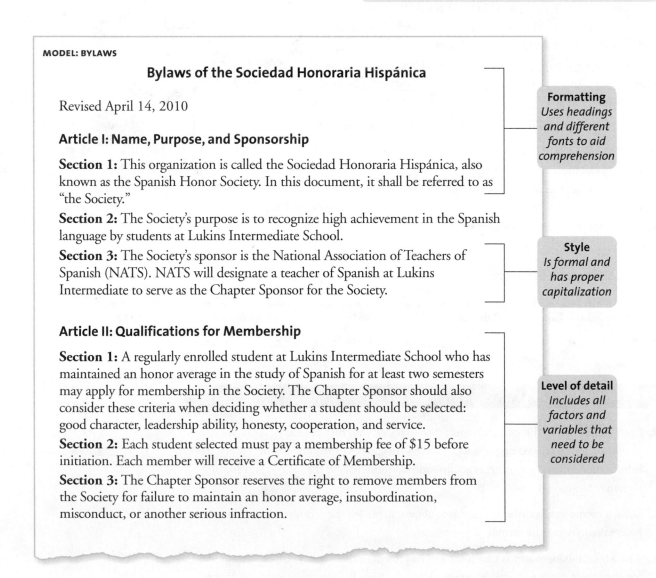

MODEL: BYLAWS

Bylaws of the Sociedad Honoraria Hispánica

Revised April 14, 2010

Article I: Name, Purpose, and Sponsorship

Section 1: This organization is called the Sociedad Honoraria Hispánica, also known as the Spanish Honor Society. In this document, it shall be referred to as "the Society."

Section 2: The Society's purpose is to recognize high achievement in the Spanish language by students at Lukins Intermediate School.

Section 3: The Society's sponsor is the National Association of Teachers of Spanish (NATS). NATS will designate a teacher of Spanish at Lukins Intermediate to serve as the Chapter Sponsor for the Society.

Article II: Qualifications for Membership

Section 1: A regularly enrolled student at Lukins Intermediate School who has maintained an honor average in the study of Spanish for at least two semesters may apply for membership in the Society. The Chapter Sponsor should also consider these criteria when deciding whether a student should be selected: good character, leadership ability, honesty, cooperation, and service.

Section 2: Each student selected must pay a membership fee of $15 before initiation. Each member will receive a Certificate of Membership.

Section 3: The Chapter Sponsor reserves the right to remove members from the Society for failure to maintain an honor average, insubordination, misconduct, or another serious infraction.

Formatting
Uses headings and different fonts to aid comprehension

Style
Is formal and has proper capitalization

Level of detail
Includes all factors and variables that need to be considered

MODEL: SYSTEM DESIGN

Recycling System for Lukins Intermediate School

Introduction: Why Recycle?
Recycling saves trees and reduces waste. According to the Environmental Protection Agency, up to 80 percent of what a typical school throws away can be recycled.

Recycling Paper
- Members of the Recycling Club will set up and maintain sturdy cardboard boxes in the main office, teachers' lounge, library, and south exit.
- Each box will have a label that says "PAPER RECYCLING. No staples, no magazines, no food wrappers."
- When the boxes are almost full, the club president will e-mail Mr. Balderston, the recycling coordinator at the county's Department of Public Works. He will arrange for a pickup.
- Members of the Recycling Club should encourage teachers to photocopy on both sides of the page when possible and to give homework assignments by e-mail instead of on paper.

Recycling Bottles and Cans
- The club members will maintain large plastic bins in the cafeteria, next to the vending machines, and near the north exit.
- Each bin will have a label that says "BOTTLE AND CAN RECYCLING. Glass and plastic only."
- When the bins are more than half full, the club vice-president will call Ms. Fett at Holub Recycling to arrange for a pickup.
- After each pickup, club members should wipe out the bins in case there is spilled soda or juice in them.

Publicity and Motivation
- At the beginning of each school year, club officers will lead a brainstorming session on how to monitor recycling rates and encourage students and staff members to recycle more often.

Formatting
Uses headings and bulleted lists to aid comprehension

Sequence
Identifies a sequence of activities

Style
Is clear and direct; uses proper grammar and spelling

PRACTICE AND APPLY

1. Create a set of bylaws for a club that you are in or one that you would like to start. Consult the "Standards for Writing" checklist to make sure that you have met all the requirements of technical writing. Use a format and spacing similar to the one shown in the model.

2. Show your knowledge of system design by writing a set of instructions. For example, you might explain how to hold student elections, host a sporting event on your school grounds, create a class podcast, or evacuate your home in case of fire. Use the model on this page and the "Standards for Writing" checklist on page R44 as your guides.

Writing Online   THINK central

Go to thinkcentral.com.
KEYWORD: HML8N-R45

Writing that is full of mistakes can confuse or even annoy a reader. Punctuation errors in a letter might lead to a miscommunication and delay a reply. Sentence fragments might lower your grade on an essay. Paying attention to grammar, punctuation, and capitalization rules can make your writing clearer and easier to read.

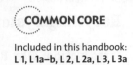

COMMON CORE

Included in this handbook:
L 1, L 1a–b, L 2, L 2a, L 3, L 3a

Quick Reference: Parts of Speech

PART OF SPEECH	FUNCTION	EXAMPLES
Noun	names a person, a place, a thing, an idea, a quality, or an action	
Common	serves as a general name, or a name common to an entire group	shadow, harmonica, paw, mistake
Proper	names a specific, one-of-a-kind person, place, or thing	Chinatown, Switzerland, Jupiter, Herbert
Singular	refers to a single person, place, thing, or idea	earthquake, laboratory, medication, outcome
Plural	refers to more than one person, place, thing, or idea	chemicals, splinters, geniuses, soldiers
Concrete	names something that can be perceived by the senses	calendar, basketball, ocean, snow
Abstract	names something that cannot be perceived by the senses	democracy, authority, beauty, fame
Compound	expresses a single idea through a combination of two or more words	self-esteem, mountaintop, firefighters, light bulb
Collective	refers to a group of people or things	team, family, class, choir
Possessive	shows who or what owns something	Pandora's, Strauss's, Franks', women's
Pronoun	takes the place of a noun or another pronoun	
Personal	refers to the person making a statement, the person(s) being addressed, or the person(s) or thing(s) the statement is about	I, me, my, mine, we, us, our, ours, you, your, yours, she, he, it, her, him, hers, his, its, they, them, their, theirs
Reflexive	follows a verb or preposition and refers to a preceding noun or pronoun	myself, yourself, herself, himself, itself, ourselves, yourselves, themselves
Intensive	emphasizes a noun or another pronoun	(same as reflexives)
Demonstrative	points to one or more specific persons or things	this, that, these, those
Interrogative	signals a question	who, whom, whose, which, what
Indefinite	refers to one or more persons or things not specifically mentioned	both, all, most, many, anyone, everybody, several, none, some
Relative	introduces an adjective clause by relating it to a word in the clause	who, whom, whose, which, that

PART OF SPEECH	FUNCTION	EXAMPLES
Verb	Expresses an action, a condition, or a state of being	
Action	tells what the subject does or did, physically or mentally	find, know, clings, displayed, rises, crave
Linking	connects the subject to something that identifies or describes it	am, is, are, was, were, sound, taste, appear, feel, become, remain, seem
Auxiliary	precedes the main verb in a verb phrase	Be, have, can, do, could, will, would, may, might
Transitive	directs the action toward someone or something; always has an object	She opened the door.
Intransitive	does not direct the action toward someone or something; does not have an object	The door opened.
Adjective	modifies a noun or pronoun	slight groan, dying gladiators, ancient sea, two pigtails
Adverb	modifies a verb, an adjective, or another adverb	always closed, very patiently, more pleasant, ran quickly
Preposition	relates one word to another word	at, by, for, from, in, of, on, to, with
Conjunction	joins words or word groups	
Coordinating	joins words or word groups used the same way	and, but, or, for, so, yet, nor
Correlative	used as a pair to join words or word groups used the same way	both . . . and, either . . . or, neither . . . nor
Subordinating	introduces a clause that cannot stand by itself as a complete sentence	although, after, as, before, because, when, if, unless
Interjection	expresses emotion	wow, ouch, hooray

Quick Reference: The Sentence and Its Parts

The diagrams that follow will give you a brief review of the essentials of a sentence and some of its parts.

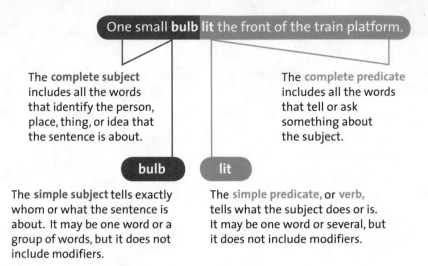

One small **bulb** lit the front of the train platform.

The **complete subject** includes all the words that identify the person, place, thing, or idea that the sentence is about.

The complete predicate includes all the words that tell or ask something about the subject.

bulb

lit

The **simple subject** tells exactly whom or what the sentence is about. It may be one word or a group of words, but it does not include modifiers.

The simple predicate, or verb, tells what the subject does or is. It may be one word or several, but it does not include modifiers.

Every word in a sentence is part of a complete subject or a complete predicate.

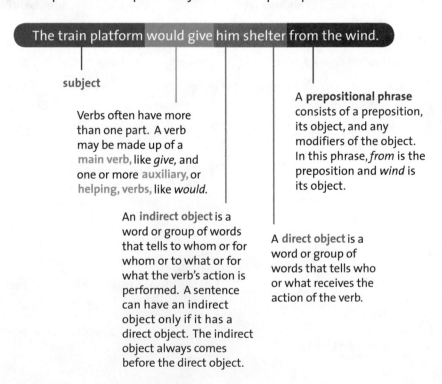

The train platform would give him shelter from the wind.

subject

Verbs often have more than one part. A verb may be made up of a main verb, like *give*, and one or more auxiliary, or helping, verbs, like *would*.

A **prepositional phrase** consists of a preposition, its object, and any modifiers of the object. In this phrase, *from* is the preposition and *wind* is its object.

An **indirect object** is a word or group of words that tells to whom or for whom or to what or for what the verb's action is performed. A sentence can have an indirect object only if it has a direct object. The indirect object always comes before the direct object.

A **direct object** is a word or group of words that tells who or what receives the action of the verb.

Quick Reference: Punctuation

MARK	FUNCTION	EXAMPLES
End Marks period, question mark, exclamation point	ends a sentence	We can start now. When would you like to leave? What a fantastic hit!
period	follows an initial or abbreviation **Exception:** postal abbreviations of states	Mrs. Dorothy Parker, McDougal Littell Inc., C. P. Cavafy, P.M., A.D., lb., oz., Blvd., Dr. NE (Nebraska), NV (Nevada)

period	follows a number or letter in an outline	I. Volcanoes
		  A. Central-vent
		    1. Shield

Comma	separates part of a compound sentence	I had never disliked poetry, but now I really love it.
	separates items in a series	Her humor, grace, and kindness served her well.
	separates adjectives of equal rank that modify the same noun	The slow, easy route is best.
	sets off a term of address	Maria, how can I help you? You must do something, soldier.
	sets off a parenthetical expression	Hard workers, as you know, don't quit. I'm not a quitter, believe me.
	sets off an introductory word, phrase, or dependent clause	Yes, I forgot my key. At the beginning of the day, I feel fresh. While she was out, I was here. Having finished my chores, I went out.
	sets off a nonessential phrase or clause	Ed Pawn, the captain of the chess team, won. Ed Pawn, who is the captain, won. The two leading runners, sprinting toward the finish line, finished in a tie.
	sets off parts of dates and addresses	Mail it by May 14, 2010, to the Hauptman Company, 321 Market Street, Memphis, Tennessee.
	follows the salutation and closing of a letter	Dear Jim, Sincerely yours,
	separates words to avoid confusion	By noon, time had run out. What the minister does, does matter. While cooking, Jim burned his hand.
Semicolon	separates items in a series that contain commas	We spent the first week of summer vacation in Chicago, Illinois; the second week in St. Louis, Missouri; and the third week in Albany, New York.
	separates parts of a compound sentence that are not joined by a coordinating conjunction	The last shall be first; the first shall be last. I read the Bible; however, I have not memorized it.
	separates parts of a compound sentence when the parts contain commas	After I ran out of money, I called my parents; but only my sister was home, unfortunately.

MARK	FUNCTION	EXAMPLES
Colon	introduces a list	Those we wrote to were the following: Dana, John, and Will.
	introduces a long quotation	Abraham Lincoln wrote: "Four score and seven years ago, our fathers brought forth on this continent a new nation . . . ."
	follows the salutation of a business letter	To Whom It May Concern: Dear Leonard Atole:
	separates certain numbers	1:28 P.M., Genesis 2:5
Dash	indicates an abrupt break in thought	I was thinking of my mother—who is arriving tomorrow—just as you walked in.
Parentheses	enclose less important material	It was so unlike him (John is always on time) that I began to worry. The last World Series game (did you see it?) was fun.
Hyphen	joins parts of a compound adjective before a noun	The not-so-rich taxpayer won't stand for this!
	joins parts of a compound with *all-, ex-, self-,* or *-elect*	The ex-firefighter helped rescue him. Our president-elect is self-conscious.
	joins parts of a compound number (to ninety-nine)	Today is the twenty-fifth of November.
	joins parts of a fraction	My cup is one-third full.
	joins a prefix to a word beginning with a capital letter	I'm studying the U.S. presidents pre-1900. It snowed in mid-October.
	indicates that a word is divided at the end of a line	How could you have any reasonable expect- ations of getting a new computer?
Apostrophe	used with *s* to form the possessive of a noun or an indefinite pronoun	my friend's book, my friends' books, anyone's guess, somebody else's problem
	replaces one or more omitted letters in a contraction or numbers in a date	don't (omitted *o*), he'd (omitted *woul*), the class of '99 (omitted *19*)
	used with *s* to form the plural of a letter	I had two A's on my report card.
Quotation Marks	set off a speaker's exact words	"That, I'll do," Lemon said. "That," Lemon said, "I'll do." Did Lemon say, "That I'll do"? Lemon said, "That I'll do!"
	set off the title of a story, an article, a short poem, an essay, a song, or a chapter	I recited Alice Walker's "We Alone" at the assembly. Poe's "The Tell-Tale Heart" and Stockton's "The Lady or the Tiger?" held my interest. I enjoyed Bob Dylan's "Boots of Spanish Leather."
Ellipses	replace material omitted from a quotation	"Her diary tells us that she . . . thought of ordinary things, such as going to school with other kids . . ."
Italics	indicate the title of a book, a play, a magazine, a long poem, an opera, a film, or a TV series, or the name of a ship	*Harriet Tubman: Conductor on the Underground Railroad, The Hitchhiker, TIME, The Magic Flute,* the *Iliad, Star Wars, 60 Minutes,* the *Mayflower*

Quick Reference: Capitalization

CATEGORY	EXAMPLES
People and Titles	
Names and initials of people	Jack London, T.S. Eliot
Titles used before a name	Professor Holmes, Senator Long
Deities and members of religious groups	Jesus, Allah, Buddha, Zeus, Baptists, Roman Catholics
Names of ethnic and national groups	Hispanics, Jews, African Americans
Geographical Names	
Cities, states, countries, continents	Philadelphia, Kansas, Japan, Europe
Regions, bodies of water, mountains	the South, Lake Baikal, Mount Everest
Geographic features, parks	Great Basin, Yellowstone National Park
Streets and roads, planets	318 East Sutton Drive, Charles Court, Jupiter, Mars
Organizations, Events, Etc.	
Companies, organizations, teams	Ford Motor Company, Boy Scouts of America, St. Louis Cardinals
Buildings, bridges, monuments	Empire State Building, Eads Bridge, Washington Monument
Documents, awards	Declaration of Independence, Stanley Cup
Special named events	Mardi Gras, World Series
Government bodies, historical periods and events	U.S. Senate, House of Representatives, Middle Ages, Vietnam War
Days and months, holidays	Thursday, March, Thanksgiving, Labor Day
Specific cars, boats, trains, planes	Porsche, Carpathia, Southwest Chief, Concorde
Proper Adjectives	
Adjectives formed from proper nouns	French cooking, Spanish omelet, Edwardian age, Western movie
First Words and the Pronoun I	
First word in a sentence or quotation	This is it. He said, "Let's go."
First word of sentence in parentheses that is not within another sentence	The spelling rules are covered in another section. (Consult that section for more information.)
First words in the salutation and closing of a letter	Dear Madam, Very truly yours,
First word in each line of most poetry Personal pronoun I	Then am I A happy fly If I live Or if I die.
First word, last word, and all important words in a title	"The Ransom of Red Chief," "Rules of the Game," *Roll of Thunder, Hear My Cry*

1 Nouns

A **noun** is a word used to name a person, a place, a thing, an idea, a quality, or an action. Nouns can be classified in several ways.

For more information on different types of nouns, see Quick Reference: Parts of Speech, page R46.

1.1 COMMON NOUNS

Common nouns are general names, common to entire groups.

1.2 PROPER NOUNS

Proper nouns name specific, one-of-a-kind people, places, and things.

Common	Proper
legend, canyon, girl, city	Pecos Bill, Canyon de Chelly, Anne, Amsterdam

For more information, see Quick Reference: Capitalization, page R51.

1.3 SINGULAR AND PLURAL NOUNS

A noun may take a singular or a plural form, depending on whether it names a single person, place, thing, or idea or more than one. Make sure you use appropriate spellings when forming plurals.

Singular	Plural
diary, valley, revolution, calf	diaries, valleys, revolutions, calves

For more information, see Forming Plural Nouns, page R76.

1.4 POSSESSIVE NOUNS

A **possessive noun** shows who or what owns something.

For more information, see Forming Possessives, page R76.

2 Pronouns

A **pronoun** is a word that is used in place of a noun or another pronoun. The word or word group to which the pronoun refers is called its **antecedent**.

2.1 PERSONAL PRONOUNS

Personal pronouns change their form to express person, number, gender, and case. The forms of these pronouns are shown in the following chart.

	Nominative	Objective	Possessive
Singular			
First person	I	me	my, mine
Second person	you	you	your, yours
Third person	she, he, it	her, him, it	her, hers, his, its
Plural			
First person	we	us	our, ours
Second person	you	you	your, yours
Third person	they	them	their, theirs

2.2 AGREEMENT WITH ANTECEDENT

Pronouns should agree with their antecedents in number, gender, and person.

If an antecedent is singular, use a singular pronoun.

EXAMPLE: *Rachel wrote a **detective story**. It has a surprise ending.*

If an antecedent is plural, use a plural pronoun.

EXAMPLES: *The **characters** have their motives for murder.*

*Javier loves **mysteries** and reads them all the time.*

The gender of a pronoun must be the same as the gender of its antecedent.

EXAMPLE: *The **man** has to use all his wits to stay alive and solve the crime.*

The person of the pronoun must be the same as the person of its antecedent. As the chart in Section 2.1 shows, a pronoun can be in first-person, second-person, or third-person form.

EXAMPLE: *You want a story to grab your attention.*

Rewrite each sentence so that the underlined pronoun agrees with its antecedent.

1. Lawrence Yep, author of "The Great Rat Hunt," had asthma when <u>it</u> was young.

2. The story's suspense keeps readers interested in <u>them</u>.

3. Yep and his father put out rat traps and place bait on <u>it</u>.

4. When the rat shows <u>their</u> teeth, Yep panics.

5. You and <u>her</u> friends should read the story sometime.

2.3 PRONOUN FORMS

Personal pronouns change form to show how they function in sentences. The three forms are the subject form, the object form, and the possessive form. For examples of these pronouns, see the chart in Section 2.1.

A **subject pronoun** is used as a subject in a sentence.

> EXAMPLE: *The poem "Mi Madre" compares the desert to a mother. It was written by Pat Mora.*

Also use the subject form when the pronoun follows a linking verb.

> EXAMPLE: *The person healed by the desert is she.*

An **object pronoun** is used as a direct object, an indirect object, or the object of a preposition.

> SUBJECT   OBJECT
> *We will give them to her.*
>   OBJECT OF PREPOSITION

A **possessive pronoun** shows ownership. The pronouns *mine, yours, hers, his, its, ours,* and *theirs* can be used in place of nouns.

> EXAMPLE: *The desert's gifts are hers.*

The pronouns *my, your, her, his, its, our,* and *their* are used before nouns.

> EXAMPLE: *The poem changed my view of the desert.*

WATCH OUT! Many spelling errors can be avoided if you watch out for *its* and *their*. Don't confuse the possessive pronoun *its* with the contraction *it's*, meaning "it is" or "it has." The homonyms *they're* (a contraction of *they are*) and *there* ("in that place") are often mistakenly used for *their*.

TIP To decide which pronoun to use in a comparison, such as "He tells better tales than (I *or* me)," fill in the missing word(s): *He tells better tales than I tell.*

Write the correct pronoun form to complete each sentence.

1. The thunder and lightning frightens (her, she).

2. Has (him, he) ever eaten prickly pear?

3. The desert sings, but (its, it) songs are mysterious.

4. Raindrops in the desert would surprise (me, I).

5. The desert has lessons for all of (we, us).

2.4 REFLEXIVE AND INTENSIVE PRONOUNS

These pronouns are formed by adding *-self* or *-selves* to certain personal pronouns. Their forms are the same, and they differ only in how they are used.

A **reflexive pronoun** follows a verb or preposition and reflects back on an earlier noun or pronoun.

> EXAMPLES: *He likes himself too much.*
> *She is now herself again.*

Intensive pronouns intensify or emphasize the nouns or pronouns to which they refer.

> EXAMPLES: *They themselves will educate their children.*
> *You did it yourself.*

WATCH OUT! Avoid using *hisself* or *theirselves*. Standard English does not include these forms.

NONSTANDARD: *Colorful desert flowers offer theirselves to the poem's speaker.*

STANDARD: *Colorful desert flowers offer themselves to the poem's speaker.*

2.5 DEMONSTRATIVE PRONOUNS

Demonstrative pronouns point out things and persons near and far.

	Singular	Plural
Near	this	these
Far	that	those

2.6 INDEFINITE PRONOUNS

Indefinite pronouns do not refer to specific persons or things and usually have no antecedents. The chart shows some commonly used indefinite pronouns.

Singular	Plural	Singular or Plural	
another	both	all	none
anybody	few	any	some
no one	many	more	most
neither			

TIP Indefinite pronouns that end in *-one*, *-body*, or *-thing* are always singular.

INCORRECT: *Did everybody play their part well?*

If the indefinite pronoun might refer to either a male or a female, *his or her* may be used to refer to it, or the sentence may be rewritten.

CORRECT: *Did everybody play his or her part well?*
Did all the students play their parts well?

2.7 INTERROGATIVE PRONOUNS

An **interrogative pronoun** tells a reader or listener that a question is coming. The interrogative pronouns are *who, whom, whose, which,* and *what.*

EXAMPLES: *Who is going to rehearse with you?*
From whom did you receive the script?

TIP *Who* is used as a subject; *whom,* as an object. To find out which pronoun you need to use in a question, change the question to a statement.

QUESTION: *(Who/Whom) did you meet there?*
STATEMENT: *You met (?) there.*

Since the verb has a subject (*you*), the needed word must be the object form, *whom.*

EXAMPLE: *Whom did you meet there?*

WATCH OUT! A special problem arises when you use an interrupter, such as *do you think,* within a question.

EXAMPLE: *(Who/Whom) do you think will win?*

If you eliminate the interrupter, it is clear that the word you need is *who.*

2.8 RELATIVE PRONOUNS

Relative pronouns relate, or connect, adjective clauses to the words they modify in sentences. The noun or pronoun that a relative clause modifies is the antecedent of the relative pronoun. Here are the relative pronouns and their uses.

	Subject	Object	Possessive
Person	who	whom	whose
Thing	which	which	whose
Thing/Person	that	that	whose

Often, short sentences with related ideas can be combined by using a relative pronoun to create a more effective sentence.

SHORT SENTENCE: *Louisa May Alcott wrote* Hospital Sketches

RELATED SENTENCE: Hospital Sketches *describes Alcott's experiences as a volunteer nurse.*

COMBINED SENTENCE: *Louisa May Alcott wrote* Hospital Sketches, *which describes her experiences as a volunteer nurse.*

Write the correct form of each incorrect pronoun.

1. Few would have volunteered her services like Alcott did.
2. For who did she risk her own life?
3. Everyone received their care from Alcott.
4. A wounded soldier proved hisself to be respectful.
5. Whom can read her diary without being moved?

2.9 PRONOUN REFERENCE PROBLEMS

The referent of a pronoun should always be clear. Avoid problems by rewriting sentences.

An **indefinite reference** occurs when the pronoun *it, you,* or *they* does not clearly refer to a specific antecedent.

UNCLEAR: *People appreciate it when they learn from an author's experiences.*

CLEAR: *People appreciate learning from an author's experiences.*

A **general reference** occurs when the pronoun *it, this, that, which,* or *such* is used to refer to a general idea rather than a specific antecedent.

UNCLEAR: *I picture myself in the author's situation. This helps me understand her reactions.*

CLEAR: *I picture myself in the author's situation. Putting myself in her position helps me understand her reactions.*

Ambiguous means "having more than one possible meaning." An **ambiguous reference** occurs when a pronoun could refer to two or more antecedents.

UNCLEAR: *Manuel urged Simon to edit his new film review.*

CLEAR: *Manuel urged Simon to edit Manuel's new film review.*

Rewrite the following sentences to correct indefinite, ambiguous, and general pronoun references.

1. Adams kept seeing the hitchhiker as he walked down the road.
2. Adams didn't pick the hitchhiker up, but it made him feel like a fool.
3. The car stalled on the railroad tracks with a train coming. That almost got Adams killed.
4. When Adams tells his story, they think he's crazy.

3 Verbs

A **verb** is a word that expresses an action, a condition, or a state of being.

*For more information, see **Quick Reference: Parts of Speech**, page R47.*

3.1 ACTION VERBS

Action verbs express mental or physical activity.

EXAMPLE: *Otto Frank comforted his family.*

3.2 LINKING VERBS

Linking verbs join subjects with words or phrases that rename or describe them.

EXAMPLE: *They were in hiding during the war.*

3.3 PRINCIPAL PARTS

Action and linking verbs typically have four principal parts, which are used to form verb tenses. The principal parts are the **present,** the **present participle,** the **past,** and the **past participle.**

Action verbs and some linking verbs also fall into two categories: regular and irregular. A **regular verb** is a verb that forms its past and past participle by adding *-ed* or *-d* to the present form.

Present	Present Participle	Past	Past Participle
jump	(is) jumping	jumped	(has) jumped
solve	(is) solving	solved	(has) solved
grab	(is) grabbing	grabbed	(has) grabbed
carry	(is) carrying	carried	(has) carried

An **irregular verb** is a verb that forms its past and past participle in some other way than by adding *-ed* or *-d* to the present form.

Present	Present Participle	Past	Past Participle
begin	(is) beginning	began	(has) begun
break	(is) breaking	broke	(has) broken
go	(is) going	went	(has) gone

3.4 VERB TENSE

The **tense** of a verb indicates the time of the action or the state of being. An action or state of being can occur in the present, the past, or the future. There are six tenses, each expressing a different range of time.

The **present tense** expresses an action or state that is happening at the present time, occurs regularly, or is constant or generally true. Use the present participle.

> NOW: *That snow looks deep.*
> REGULAR: *It snows every day.*
> GENERAL: *Snow falls.*

The **past tense** expresses an action that began and ended in the past. Use the past participle.

> EXAMPLE: *The storyteller finished his tale.*

The **future tense** expresses an action or state that will occur. Use *shall* or *will* with the present participle.

> EXAMPLE: *They will attend the next festival.*

The **present perfect tense** expresses an action or state that (1) was completed at an indefinite time in the past or (2) began in the past and continues into the present. Use *have* or *has* with the past participle.

> EXAMPLE: *Poetry has inspired many readers.*

The **past perfect tense** expresses an action in the past that came before another action in the past. Use *had* with the past participle.

> EXAMPLE: *He had built a fire before the dog ran away.*

The **future perfect tense** expresses an action in the future that will be completed before another action in the future. Use *shall have* or *will have* with the past participle.

> EXAMPLE: *They will have read the novel before they see the movie version of the tale.*

TIP A past-tense form of an irregular verb is not used with an auxiliary verb, but a past-participle main irregular verb is always used with an auxiliary verb.

> INCORRECT: *I have saw her somewhere before.* (*Saw* is the past-tense form of an irregular verb and shouldn't be used with *have*.)

> CORRECT: *I have seen her somewhere before.*

> INCORRECT: *I seen her somewhere before.* (*Seen* is the past participle of an irregular verb and shouldn't be used without an auxiliary verb.)

3.5 PROGRESSIVE FORMS

The progressive forms of the six tenses show ongoing actions. Use forms of *be* with the present participles of verbs.

> PRESENT PROGRESSIVE: *Anne is arguing her case.*
> PAST PROGRESSIVE: *Anne was arguing her case.*
> FUTURE PROGRESSIVE: *Anne will be arguing her case.*
> PRESENT PERFECT PROGRESSIVE: *Anne has been arguing her case.*
> PAST PERFECT PROGRESSIVE: *Anne had been arguing her case.*
> FUTURE PERFECT PROGRESSIVE: *Anne will have been arguing her case.*

WATCH OUT! Do not shift from tense to tense needlessly. Watch out for these special cases.

- In most compound sentences and in sentences with compound predicates, keep the tenses the same.

> INCORRECT: *She defied him, and he scolds her.*
> CORRECT: *She defied him, and he scolded her.*

- If one past action happens before another, do shift tenses.

> INCORRECT: *They wished they started earlier.*
> CORRECT: *They wished they had started earlier.*

GRAMMAR PRACTICE

Rewrite each sentence, using a form of the verb in parentheses. Identify each form that you use.

1. Frederick Douglass (write) a letter to Harriet Tubman in which he (praise) her.

2. He (say) that she (do) much to benefit enslaved people.

3. People (remember) her work with the Underground Railroad forever.

4. Both Douglass and Tubman (appear) in the history books that kids study.

5. They (inspire) seekers of justice for many years to come.

Rewrite each sentence to correct an error in tense.

1. When she went to the plantations, Tubman's signal has been the spiritual "Go Down Moses."

2. She is leading the slaves all the way from Maryland to Canada, and brought them to freedom.

3. Although she never will have been to Canada, she went bravely on.

4. They arrived safe and sound, but Tubman leaves for the South again.

5. Her life's work for the next six years had began.

3.6 ACTIVE AND PASSIVE VOICE

The voice of a verb tells whether its subject performs or receives the action expressed by the verb. When the subject performs the action, the verb is in the **active voice.** When the subject is the receiver of the action, the verb is in the **passive voice.**

Compare these two sentences:

ACTIVE: *Anton Chekhov wrote "The Bet."*

PASSIVE: *"The Bet" was written by Anton Chekhov.*

To form the passive voice, use a form of *be* with the past participle of the verb.

WATCH OUT! Use the passive voice sparingly. It can make writing awkward and less direct.

AWKWARD: *"The Bet" is a short story that was written by Anton Chekhov.*

BETTER: *Anton Chekhov wrote the short story "The Bet."*

There are occasions when you will choose to use the passive voice because

• you want to emphasize the receiver: *The king was shot.*

• the doer is unknown: *My books were stolen.*

• the doer is unimportant: *French is spoken here.*

4 Modifiers

Modifiers are words or groups of words that change or limit the meanings of other words. Adjectives and adverbs are common modifiers.

4.1 ADJECTIVES

Adjectives modify nouns and pronouns by telling which one, what kind, how many, or how much.

WHICH ONE: *this, that, these, those*
EXAMPLE: *This poem uses no capital letters.*

WHAT KIND: *electric, bright, small, open*
EXAMPLE: *An open flame would kill the moth.*

HOW MANY: *one, several, both, none, each*
EXAMPLE: *The moth wants one moment of beauty.*

HOW MUCH: *more, less, enough, as much*
EXAMPLE: *I think the cockroach has more sense than the moth.*

4.2 PREDICATE ADJECTIVES

Most adjectives come before the nouns they modify, as in the examples above. A **predicate adjective,** however, follows a linking verb and describes the subject.

EXAMPLE: *My friends are very intelligent.*

Be especially careful to use adjectives (not adverbs) after such linking verbs as *look, feel, grow, taste,* and *smell.*

EXAMPLE: *The bread smells wonderful.*

4.3 ADVERBS

Adverbs modify verbs, adjectives, and other adverbs by telling where, when, how, or to what extent.

WHERE: *The children played outside.*

WHEN: *The author spoke yesterday.*

HOW: *We walked slowly behind the leader.*

TO WHAT EXTENT: *He worked very hard.*

Adverbs may occur in many places in sentences, both before and after the words they modify.

EXAMPLES: *Suddenly the wind shifted.*

The wind suddenly shifted.

The wind shifted suddenly.

4.4 ADJECTIVE OR ADVERB?

Many adverbs are formed by adding *-ly* to adjectives.

EXAMPLES: *sweet, sweetly; gentle, gently*

However, *-ly* added to a noun will usually yield an adjective.

EXAMPLES: *friend, friendly; woman, womanly*

4.5 COMPARISON OF MODIFIERS

Modifiers can be used to compare two or more things. The form of a modifier shows the degree of comparison. Both adjectives and adverbs have **comparative** and **superlative** forms.

The **comparative form** is used to compare two things, groups, or actions.

EXAMPLES: *His father's hands were stronger than his own.*

My father was more courageous than I am.

The **superlative form** is used to compare more than two things, groups, or actions.

EXAMPLES: *His father's hands were the strongest in the family.*

My father was the most courageous of us all.

4.6 REGULAR COMPARISONS

Most one-syllable and some two-syllable adjectives and adverbs have comparatives and superlatives formed by adding *-er* and *-est*. All three-syllable and most two-syllable modifiers have comparatives and superlatives formed with *more* or *most*.

Modifier	Comparative	Superlative
small	smaller	smallest
thin	thinner	thinnest
sleepy	sleepier	sleepiest
useless	more useless	most useless
precisely	more precisely	most precisely

WATCH OUT! Note that spelling changes must sometimes be made to form the comparatives and superlatives of modifiers.

EXAMPLES: *friendly, friendlier* (Change *y* to *i* and add the ending.)

sad, sadder (Double the final consonant and add the ending.)

4.7 IRREGULAR COMPARISONS

Some commonly used modifiers have irregular comparative and superlative forms. They are listed in the chart. You may wish to memorize them.

Modifier	Comparative	Superlative
good	better	best
bad	worse	worst
far	farther *or* further	farthest *or* furthest
little	less *or* lesser	least
many	more	most
well	better	best
much	more	most

4.8 PROBLEMS WITH MODIFIERS

Study the tips that follow to avoid common mistakes:

Farther and **Further** Use *farther* for distances; use *further* for everything else.

Double Comparisons Make a comparison by using *-er/-est* or by using *more/most*. Using *-er* with *more* or using *-est* with *most* is incorrect.

INCORRECT: *I like her more better than she likes me.*

CORRECT: *I like her better than she likes me.*

Illogical Comparisons An illogical or confusing comparison results when two unrelated things are compared or when something is compared with itself. The word *other* or the word *else* should be used when comparing an individual member to the rest of a group.

> ILLOGICAL: *The cockroach is smarter than any insect.* (implies that the cockroach isn't an insect)
>
> LOGICAL: *The cockroach is smarter than any other insect.* (identifies that the cockroach is an insect)

Bad vs. Badly *Bad,* always an adjective, is used before a noun or after a linking verb. *Badly,* always an adverb, never modifies a noun. Be sure to use the right form after a linking verb.

> INCORRECT: *Ed felt badly after his team lost.*
>
> CORRECT: *Ed felt bad after his team lost.*

Good vs. Well *Good* is always an adjective. It is used before a noun or after a linking verb. *Well* is often an adverb meaning "expertly" or "properly." *Well* can also be used as an adjective after a linking verb when it means "in good health."

> INCORRECT: *Helen writes very good.*
>
> CORRECT: *Helen writes very well.*
>
> CORRECT: *Yesterday I felt bad; today I feel well.*

Double Negatives If you add a negative word to a sentence that is already negative, the result will be an error known as a double negative. When using *not* or *-n't* with a verb, use *any-* words, such as *anybody* or *anything*, rather than *no-* words, such as *nobody* or *nothing*, later in the sentence.

> INCORRECT: *We haven't seen nobody.*
>
> CORRECT: *We haven't seen anybody.*

Using *hardly, barely,* or *scarcely* after a negative word is also incorrect.

> INCORRECT: *They couldn't barely see two feet ahead.*
>
> CORRECT: *They could barely see two feet ahead.*

Misplaced Modifiers Sometimes a modifier is placed so far away from the word it modifies that the intended meaning of the sentence is unclear. Prepositional phrases and participial phrases are often misplaced. Place modifiers as close as possible to the words they modify.

> MISPLACED: *We found the child in the park who was missing.*
>
> CLEARER: *We found the child who was missing in the park.* (The child was missing, not the park.)

Dangling Modifiers Sometimes a modifier doesn't appear to modify any word in a sentence. Most dangling modifiers are participial phrases or infinitive phrases.

> DANGLING: *Looking out the window, his brother was seen driving by.*
>
> CLEARER: *Looking out the window, Josh saw his brother driving by.*

GRAMMAR PRACTICE

Choose the correct word or words from each pair in parentheses.

1. Mark Twain's attempt at studying the law did not go (good, well).

2. That wasn't the (worse, worst) of his many occupations, however.

3. He actually wasn't a (bad, badly) riverboat pilot.

4. He didn't have (no, any) confidence as a newspaper editor.

5. Still, that turned out to be the (more, most) satisfying job he ever had.

GRAMMAR PRACTICE

Rewrite each sentence that contains a misplaced or dangling modifier. Write "correct" if the sentence is written correctly.

1. Mark Twain discovered that he was a good storyteller working as an editor.

2. Twain often added exciting details to his stories.

3. It didn't matter to Twain whether all of the details were true in his articles.

4. He wrote sixteen different articles about a single hay wagon in the paper.

5. When all else failed, he made up events.

5 The Sentence and Its Parts

A **sentence** is a group of words used to express a complete thought. A complete sentence has a subject and a predicate.

*For more information, see **Quick Reference: The Sentence and Its Parts,** page R48.*

5.1 KINDS OF SENTENCES

There are four basic types of sentences.

Type	Definition	Example
Declarative	states a fact, a wish, an intent, or a feeling	This poem is about Abraham Lincoln.
Interrogative	asks a question	Did you understand the metaphor?
Imperative	gives a command or direction	Read it more closely.
Exclamatory	expresses strong feeling or excitement	Whitman really admired Lincoln!

5.2 COMPOUND SUBJECTS AND PREDICATES

A compound subject consists of two or more subjects that share the same verb. They are typically joined by the coordinating conjunction *and* or *or.*

> EXAMPLE: *A short story or novel will keep you engaged.*

A compound predicate consists of two or more predicates that share the same subject. They too are usually joined by a coordinating conjunction: *and, but,* or *or.*

> EXAMPLE: *The class finished all the poetry but did not read the short stories.*

5.3 COMPLEMENTS

A **complement** is a word or group of words that completes the meaning of the sentence. Some sentences contain only a subject and a verb. Most sentences, however, require additional words placed after the verb to complete the meaning of the sentence. There are three kinds of complements: direct objects, indirect objects, and subject complements.

Direct objects are words or word groups that receive the action of action verbs. A direct object answers the question *what* or *whom.*

> EXAMPLES: *Ellis recited the poem.* (Recited what?)
> *His performance entertained the class.* (Entertained whom?)

Indirect objects tell to whom or what or for whom or what the actions of verbs are performed. Indirect objects come before direct objects. In the following examples, the indirect objects are highlighted.

> EXAMPLES: *The teacher gave the speech a good grade.* (Gave to what?)
> *He showed his father the teacher's comments.* (Showed to whom?)

Subject complements come after linking verbs and identify or describe the subjects. A subject complement that names or identifies a subject is called a **predicate nominative.** Predicate nominatives include **predicate nouns** and **predicate pronouns.**

> EXAMPLES: *My friends are very hard workers.*
> *The best writer in the class is she.*

A subject complement that describes a subject is called a **predicate adjective.**

> EXAMPLE: *The pianist appeared very energetic.*

6 Phrases

A **phrase** is a group of related words that does not contain a subject and a predicate but functions in a sentence as a single part of speech.

6.1 PREPOSITIONAL PHRASES

A **prepositional phrase** is a phrase that consists of a preposition, its object, and any modifiers of the object. Prepositional phrases that modify nouns or pronouns are called **adjective phrases.** Prepositional phrases that modify verbs, adjectives, or adverbs are **adverb phrases.**

> ADJECTIVE PHRASE: *The central character of the story is a villain.*

> ADVERB PHRASE: *He reveals his nature in the first scene.*

6.2 APPOSITIVES AND APPOSITIVE PHRASES

An **appositive** is a noun or pronoun that identifies or renames another noun or pronoun. An **appositive phrase** includes an appositive and modifiers of it. An appositive usually follows the noun or pronoun it identifies.

An appositive can be either **essential** or **nonessential**. An **essential appositive** provides information that is needed to identify what is referred to by the preceding noun or pronoun.

> EXAMPLE: *This Greek myth is about the gifted woman Pandora.*

A **nonessential appositive** adds extra information about a noun or pronoun whose meaning is already clear. Nonessential appositives and appositive phrases are set off with commas.

> EXAMPLE: *The story, a myth, describes how evil came into the world.*

7 Verbals and Verbal Phrases

A **verbal** is a verb form that is used as a noun, an adjective, or an adverb. A **verbal phrase** consists of a verbal along with its modifiers and complements. There are three kinds of verbals: **infinitives, participles,** and **gerunds.**

7.1 INFINITIVES AND INFINITIVE PHRASES

An **infinitive** is a verb form that usually begins with *to* and functions as a noun, an adjective, or an adverb. An **infinitive phrase** consists of an infinitive plus its modifiers and complements.

> NOUN: *To keep a promise is difficult.* (subject)
> *Pandora tried to obey the gods.* (direct object)
> *Her chief mistake was to become too curious.* (predicate nominative)
> ADJECTIVE: *That was an error to regret.* (adjective modifying *error*)
> ADVERB: *She opened the box to satisfy her curiosity.* (adverb modifying *opened*)

Because *to* often precedes infinitives, it is usually easy to recognize them. However, sometimes *to* may be omitted.

> EXAMPLE: *Her husband helped her [to] forgive herself.*

7.2 PARTICIPLES AND PARTICIPIAL PHRASES

A **participle** is a verb form that functions as an adjective. Like adjectives, participles modify nouns and pronouns. Most participles are present-participle forms, ending in *-ing,* or past-participle forms ending in *-ed* or *-en.* In the examples below, the participles are highlighted.

> MODIFYING A NOUN: *The dying man had a smile on his face.*
> MODIFYING A PRONOUN: *Frustrated, everyone abandoned the cause.*

Participial phrases are participles with all their modifiers and complements.

> MODIFYING A NOUN: *The dogs searching for survivors are well trained.*
> MODIFYING A PRONOUN: *Having approved your proposal, we are ready to act.*

7.3 DANGLING AND MISPLACED PARTICIPLES

A participle or participial phrase should be placed as close as possible to the word that it modifies. Otherwise the meaning of the sentence may not be clear.

> MISPLACED: *The boys were looking for squirrels searching the trees.*
> CLEARER: *The boys searching the trees were looking for squirrels.*

A participle or participial phrase that does not clearly modify anything in a sentence is called a **dangling participle.** A dangling participle causes confusion because it appears to modify a word that it cannot sensibly modify. Correct a dangling participle by providing a word for the participle to modify.

> DANGLING: *Running like the wind, my hat fell off.* (The hat wasn't running.)
> CLEARER: *Running like the wind, I lost my hat.*

7.4 GERUNDS AND GERUND PHRASES

A **gerund** is a verb form ending in *-ing* that functions as a noun. Gerunds may perform any function nouns perform.

> SUBJECT: *Jogging is my favorite exercise.*
> DIRECT OBJECT: *My sister loves jogging.*

INDIRECT OBJECT: *She gave jogging a try last year.*

SUBJECT COMPLEMENT: *Their real passion is jogging .*

OBJECT OF PREPOSITION: *The effects of jogging .*

Gerund phrases are gerunds with all their modifiers and complements.

SUBJECT: *Creating Pandora was Zeus' idea.*

OBJECT OF PREPOSITION: *She suffered greatly after defying the gods.*

APPOSITIVE: *Her husband, remembering his brother Prometheus' fate, forgave her.*

GRAMMAR PRACTICE

Rewrite each sentence, adding the type of phrase shown in parentheses.

1. I read an excerpt from Anne Frank's diary. (infinitive phrase)

2. Anne was able to maintain her faith in other people. (gerund phrase)

3. Peter Van Daan eventually became Anne's good friend. (appositive phrase)

4. The Nazis found the Franks' hiding place. (prepositional phrase)

5. I know more about World War II. (participial phrase)

8 Clauses

A **clause** is a group of words that contains a subject and a predicate. There are two kinds of clauses: main and subordinate.

8.1 MAIN AND SUBORDINATE CLAUSES

A **main (independent) clause** can stand alone as a sentence.

MAIN CLAUSE: *I enjoyed "Pecos Bill."*

A sentence may contain more than one main clause.

EXAMPLE: *I read it twice, and I gave it to a friend.*

In the preceding example, the coordinating conjunction *and* joins two main clauses.

*For more coordinating conjunctions, see **Quick Reference: Parts of Speech**, page R47.*

A **subordinate (dependent) clause** cannot stand alone as a sentence. It is subordinate to, or dependent on, a main clause.

EXAMPLE: *After I read it, I recommended it to my friends.*

The highlighted clause cannot stand by itself.

8.2 ADJECTIVE CLAUSES

An **adjective clause** is a subordinate clause used as an adjective. It usually follows the noun or pronoun it modifies.

EXAMPLE: *The legend that the story retells is about a cowboy.*

Adjective clauses are typically introduced by the relative pronouns *who, whom, whose, which,* and *that.*

*For more information, see **Relative Pronouns**, page R54.*

EXAMPLE: *Pecos Bill, who was raised by coyotes, lived with them for seventeen years.*

An adjective clause can be either essential or nonessential. An **essential adjective clause** provides information that is necessary to identify the preceding noun or pronoun.

EXAMPLE: *He needed to find people who could appreciate him.*

A **nonessential adjective clause** adds additional information about a noun or pronoun whose meaning is already clear. Nonessential clauses are set off with commas.

EXAMPLE: *He carried his horse, which had broken its ankle, around his neck.*

8.3 ADVERB CLAUSES

An **adverb clause** is a subordinate clause that is used to modify a verb, an adjective, or an adverb. It is introduced by a subordinating conjunction.

*For examples of subordinating conjunctions, see **Noun Clauses**, page R63.*

Adverb clauses typically occur at the beginning or end of sentences.

> MODIFYING A VERB: *When he got bored, Nick told stories.*
>
> MODIFYING AN ADVERB: *Most people study more than Bob does.*
>
> MODIFYING AN ADJECTIVE: *He was excited because a cyclone was forming.*

TIP An adverb clause should be followed by a comma when it comes before a main clause. When an adverb clause comes after a main clause, a comma may not be needed.

8.4 NOUN CLAUSES

A **noun clause** is a subordinate clause that is used as a noun. A noun clause may be used as a subject, a direct object, an indirect object, a predicate nominative, or the object of a preposition. Noun clauses are introduced either by pronouns, such as *that, what, who, whoever, which,* and *whose,* or by subordinating conjunctions, such as *how, when, where, why,* and *whether.*

For more subordinating conjunctions, see **Quick Reference: Parts of Speech,** *page R47.*

TIP Because the same words may introduce adjective and noun clauses, you need to consider how a clause functions within its sentence. To determine if a clause is a noun clause, try substituting *something* or *someone* for the clause. If you can do it, it is probably a noun clause.

> EXAMPLES: *I know whose woods these are.*
>
> ("I know *something.*" The clause is a noun clause, direct object of the verb *know.*)
>
> *Give a copy to whoever wants one.* ("Give a copy to *someone.*" The clause is a noun clause, object of the preposition *to.*)

9 The Structure of Sentences

When classified by their structure, there are four kinds of sentences: simple, compound, complex, and compound-complex.

9.1 SIMPLE SENTENCES

A **simple sentence** is a sentence that has one main clause and no subordinate clauses.

> EXAMPLES: *Sam ran to the theater.*
>
> *Max waited in front of the theater.*

A simple sentence may contain a compound subject or a compound verb.

> EXAMPLES: *Sam and Max went to the movie.* (compound subject)
>
> *They clapped and cheered at their favorite parts.* (compound verb)

9.2 COMPOUND SENTENCES

A **compound sentence** consists of two or more main clauses. The clauses in compound sentences are joined with commas and coordinating conjunctions (*and, but, or, nor, yet, for, so*) or with semicolons. Like simple sentences, compound sentences do not contain any subordinate clauses.

> EXAMPLES: *Sam likes action movies, but Max prefers comedies.*
>
> *The actor jumped from one building to another; he barely made the final leap.*

9.3 COMPLEX SENTENCES

A **complex sentence** consists of one main clause and one or more subordinate clauses.

> EXAMPLES: *One should not complain unless one has a better solution.*
>
> *Mr. Neiman, who is an artist, sketched pictures until the sun went down.*

9.4 COMPOUND-COMPLEX SENTENCES

A **compound-complex sentence** contains two or more main clauses and one or more subordinate clauses. Compound-complex sentences are both compound and complex.

> COMPOUND: *All the students knew the answer, yet they were too shy to volunteer.*
>
> COMPOUND-COMPLEX: *All the students knew the answer that their teacher expected, yet they were too shy to volunteer.*

9.5 PARALLEL STRUCTURE

When you write sentences, make sure that coordinate parts are equivalent, or **parallel,** in structure. For instance, be sure items you list in a series or contrast for emphasis are parallel.

> NOT PARALLEL: *I want to lose weight, becoming a musician, and good grades.* (*To lose weight* is an infinitive phrase, *becoming a musician* is a gerund phrase, and *grades* is a noun.)
>
> PARALLEL: *I want to lose weight, to become a musician, and to get good grades.* (*To lose, to become,* and *to get* are all infinitives.)

> NOT PARALLEL: *I not only want to lose weight, I'm keeping it off, too.* (*To lose weight* is an infinitive phrase; *keeping it off* is a gerund phrase.)
>
> PARALLEL: *I not only want to lose weight, I want to keep it off, too.* (*To lose weight* and *to keep it off* are both infinitive phrases. To make them both infinitive, it is necessary to change *am* to an action verb. Now the contrast set up by *not only* adds emphasis to the second part of the statement.)

Grammar Practice

Revise each sentence to make its parts parallel.

1. Jewell Parker Rhodes wrote "Block Party" about her old neighborhood and to publish a memoir of it.
2. In the story, she mentions many colorful characters, riding her bike with her sister, and watching the world from her front stoop.
3. With her friends, Rhodes played hide and seek in the laundry hanging out to dry, would slide down the banisters in the house, and rode a red tricycle through the kitchen.
4. A block party is when the street is closed off to traffic, hydrants were turned on by the fire department, and the neighbors gather for a picnic.
5. Rhodes went on to earn degrees in drama criticism, English, and a third degree in creative writing.
6. She now writes novels, nonfiction, and even for magazines!

10 Writing Complete Sentences

Remember, a sentence is a group of words that expresses a complete thought. In writing that you wish to share with a reader, try to avoid both sentence fragments and run-on sentences.

10.1 CORRECTING FRAGMENTS

A **sentence fragment** is a group of words that is only part of a sentence. It does not express a complete thought and may be confusing to a reader or listener. A sentence fragment may be lacking a subject, a predicate, or both.

> FRAGMENT: *Worried about not doing well.* (no subject)
>
> CORRECTED: *Laura worried about not doing well.*
>
> FRAGMENT: *Her mother and father.* (no predicate)
>
> CORRECTED: *Her mother and father were both highly successful.*
>
> FRAGMENT: *In a gentle way.* (neither subject nor predicate)
>
> CORRECTED: *They tried to encourage her in a gentle way.*

In your writing, fragments may be a result of haste or incorrect punctuation. Sometimes fixing a fragment will be a matter of attaching it to a preceding or following sentence.

> FRAGMENT: *Laura did her best. But never felt satisfied.*
>
> CORRECTED: *Laura did her best but never felt satisfied.*

10.2 CORRECTING RUN-ON SENTENCES

A **run-on sentence** is made up of two or more sentences written as though they were one. Some run-ons have no punctuation within them. Others may have only commas where conjunctions or stronger punctuation marks are necessary.

Use your judgment in correcting run-on sentences, as you have choices. You can change a run-on to two sentences if the thoughts are not closely connected. If the thoughts are closely related, you can keep the run-on as one sentence by adding a semicolon or a conjunction.

RUN-ON: *She joined more clubs her friendships suffered.*

MAKE TWO SENTENCES: *She joined more clubs. Her friendships suffered.*

RUN-ON: *She joined more clubs they took up all her time.*

USE A SEMICOLON: *She joined more clubs; they took up all her time.*

ADD A CONJUNCTION: *She joined more clubs, but they took up all her time.*

WATCH OUT! When you form compound sentences, make sure you use appropriate punctuation: a comma before a coordinating conjunction, a semicolon when there is no coordinating conjunction. A very common mistake is to use a comma alone instead of a comma and a conjunction. This error is called a **comma splice.**

INCORRECT: *He finished the job, he left the village.*

CORRECT: *He finished the job, and he left the village.*

11 Subject-Verb Agreement

The subject and verb in a clause must agree in number. Agreement means that if the subject is singular, the verb is also singular, and if the subject is plural, the verb is also plural.

11.1 BASIC AGREEMENT

Fortunately, agreement between subjects and verbs in English is simple. Most verbs show the difference between singular and plural only in the third person of the present tense. In the present tense, the third-person singular form ends in -s.

Present-Tense Verb Forms	
Singular	**Plural**
I sleep	we sleep
you sleep	you sleep
she he it sleeps	they sleep

11.2 AGREEMENT WITH *BE*

The verb *be* presents special problems in agreement, because this verb does not follow the usual verb patterns.

Forms of *Be*			
Present Tense		**Past Tense**	
Singular	**Plural**	**Singular**	**Plural**
I am	we are	I was	we were
you are	you are	you were	you were
she he it is	they are	she he it was	they were

11.3 WORDS BETWEEN SUBJECT AND VERB

A verb agrees only with its subject. When words come between a subject and a verb, ignore them when considering proper agreement. Identify the subject and make sure the verb agrees with it.

EXAMPLES: *Whipped cream served with berries is my favorite sweet.*

A study by scientists recommends eating berries.

11.4 AGREEMENT WITH COMPOUND SUBJECTS

Use plural verbs with most compound subjects joined by the word *and*.

EXAMPLE: *My father and his friends play chess every day.*

To confirm that you need a plural verb, you could substitute the plural pronoun *they* for *my father and his friends*.

If a compound subject is thought of as a unit, use a singular verb. Test this by substituting the singular pronoun *it*.

EXAMPLE: *Peanut butter and jelly [it] is my brother's favorite sandwich.*

Use a singular verb with a compound subject that is preceded by *each*, *every*, or *many a*.

> **EXAMPLE:** *Each novel and short story seems grounded in personal experience.*

When the parts of a compound subject are joined by *or, nor*, or the correlative conjunctions *either . . . or* or *neither . . . nor*, make the verb agree with the noun or pronoun nearest the verb.

> **EXAMPLES:** *Cookies or ice cream is my favorite dessert.*
> *Either Cheryl or her friends are being invited.*
> *Neither ice storms nor snow is predicted today.*

11.5 PERSONAL PRONOUNS AS SUBJECTS

When using a personal pronoun as a subject, make sure to match it with the correct form of the verb *be*. (See the chart in Section 11.2.) Note especially that the pronoun *you* takes the forms *are* and *were*, regardless of whether it is singular or plural.

> **WATCH OUT!** *You is* and *you was* are nonstandard forms and should be avoided in writing and speaking. *We was* and *they was* are also forms to be avoided.
>
> **INCORRECT:** *You was a good student.*
> **CORRECT:** *You were a good student.*
> **INCORRECT:** *They was starting a new school.*
> **CORRECT:** *They were starting a new school.*

11.6 INDEFINITE PRONOUNS AS SUBJECTS

Some indefinite pronouns are always singular; some are always plural.

Singular Indefinite Pronouns			
another	either	neither	one
anybody	everybody	nobody	somebody
anyone	everyone	no one	someone
anything	everything	nothing	something
each	much		

> **EXAMPLES:** *Each of the writers was given an award.*
> *Somebody in the room upstairs is sleeping.*

Plural Indefinite Pronouns			
both	few	many	several

> **EXAMPLES:** *Many of the books in our library are not in circulation.*
>
> *Few have been returned recently.*

Still other indefinite pronouns may be either singular or plural.

Singular or Plural Indefinite Pronouns		
all	more	none
any	most	some

The number of the indefinite pronoun *any* or *none* often depends on the intended meaning.

> **EXAMPLES:** *Any of these topics has potential for a good article.* (any one topic)
> *Any of these topics have potential for good articles.* (all of the many topics)

The indefinite pronouns *all, some, more, most*, and *none* are singular when they refer to quantities or parts of things. They are plural when they refer to numbers of individual things. Context will usually provide a clue.

> **EXAMPLES:** *All of the flour is gone.* (referring to a quantity)
> *All of the flowers are gone.* (referring to individual items)

11.7 INVERTED SENTENCES

A sentence in which the subject follows the verb is called an **inverted sentence.** A subject can follow a verb or part of a verb phrase in a question, a sentence beginning with *here* or *there*, or a sentence in which an adjective, an adverb, or a phrase is placed first.

> **EXAMPLES:** *There clearly are far too many cooks in this kitchen.*
> *What is the correct ingredient for this stew?*
> *Far from the frazzled cooks stands the master chef.*

TIP To check subject-verb agreement in some inverted sentences, place the subject before the verb. For example, change *There are many people* to *Many people are there.*

11.8 SENTENCES WITH PREDICATE NOMINATIVES

In a sentence containing a predicate noun (nominative), the verb should agree with the subject, not the predicate noun.

> **EXAMPLES:** *The poems of Henry Wadsworth Longfellow are a unique record of U.S. history.* (*Poems* is the subject—not *record*—and it takes the plural verb *are.*)
>
> *One unique record of U.S. history is the poems of Henry Wadsworth Longfellow.* (The subject is *record*—not *poems*—and it takes the singular verb *is.*)

11.9 *DON'T* AND *DOESN'T* AS AUXILIARY VERBS

The auxiliary verb *doesn't* is used with singular subjects and with the personal pronouns *she, he,* and *it.* The auxiliary verb *don't* is used with plural subjects and with the personal pronouns *I, we, you,* and *they.*

> **SINGULAR:** *Doesn't the poem "Paul Revere's Ride" sound almost like a news report?*
>
> *It doesn't sound like a poem, even though it rhymes.*
>
> **PLURAL:** *People don't know enough about history.*
>
> *Don't they think history is important?*

11.10 COLLECTIVE NOUNS AS SUBJECTS

Collective nouns are singular nouns that name groups of persons or things. *Team,* for example, is the collective name of a group of individuals. A collective noun takes a singular verb when the group acts as a single unit. It takes a plural verb when the members of the group act separately.

> **EXAMPLES:** *Our team usually wins.* (The team as a whole wins.)
>
> *The faculty vote differently on most issues.* (The individual members of the faculty vote.)

11.11 RELATIVE PRONOUNS AS SUBJECTS

When the relative pronoun *who, which,* or *that* is used as a subject in an adjective clause, the verb in the clause must agree in number with the antecedent of the pronoun.

> **SINGULAR:** *The **poem** that affects me most is "Mother to Son."*

The antecedent of the relative pronoun *that* is the singular *poem;* therefore, *that* is singular and must take the singular verb *affects.*

> **PLURAL:** ***Langston Hughes and Gwendolyn Brooks** are African-American poets who write about overcoming life's problems.*

The antecedent of the relative pronoun *who* is the plural compound subject *Langston Hughes and Gwendolyn Brooks.* Therefore *who* is plural, and it takes the plural verb *write.*

GRAMMAR PRACTICE

Locate the subject in each sentence below. Then choose the correct verb form.

1. Daniel Keyes's story "Flowers for Algernon" (describes, describe) a mentally challenged man who takes part in a scientific experiment.

2. (Doesn't, Don't) the doctors treat him like a laboratory mouse?

3. Nobody (realizes, realize) the danger in this experiment.

4. The development of his mental abilities (become, becomes) clear in his growing language skills.

5. His perceptions, as well as his intelligence, (becomes, become) extremely sharp.

6. There (is, are) moments of joy when he falls in love with Miss Kinnian.

7. Everything (progresses, progress) well until he is fired from his job.

8. All of his insights just (makes, make) people withdraw from him.

9. Even the doctors who work with him (treat, treats) him poorly.

10. Neither Algernon's death nor Charlie's own mental failings (seems, seem) sadder than his awareness of what's happening to him.

By learning and practicing vocabulary strategies, you'll know what to do when you encounter unfamiliar words while reading. You'll also know how to refine the words you use for different situations—personal, school, and work. Learning basic spelling rules and checking your spelling in a dictionary will help you spell words that you may not use frequently.

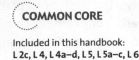

COMMON CORE

Included in this handbook:
L 2c, L 4, L 4a–d, L 5, L 5a–c, L 6

1 Using Context Clues

The context of a word is made up of the punctuation marks, words, sentences, and paragraphs that surround the word. A word's context can give you important clues about its meaning.

1.1 GENERAL CONTEXT

Sometimes you need to determine the meaning of an unfamiliar, ambiguous, or novel word by reading all the information in a passage.

> *Stop teasing me! Just because you are a better tennis player than I am doesn't mean you should belittle my abilities.*

You can figure out from the context that *belittle* means "make something less than it is."

1.2 IDIOMS, SLANG, AND FIGURATIVE LANGUAGE

An **idiom** is an expression whose overall meaning differs from the meaning of the individual words.

> *A nasty case of the flu kept me under the weather. (Under the weather means "tired and sickly.")*

Slang is informal language in which made-up words and ordinary words are used to mean something different from their meanings in formal English.

> *I'm going to jazz up this salad with some walnuts. (Jazz up means "make more interesting.")*

Figurative language is language that communicates meaning beyond the literal meaning of the words.

> *The lone desert monument was like a sentinel standing guard. (Lone and standing guard help describe a sentinel.)*

1.3 SPECIFIC CONTEXT CLUES

Sometimes writers help you understand the meanings of unfamiliar, ambiguous, or novel words by providing specific clues such as those shown in the chart.

Specific Context Clues		
Type of Clue	**Key Words/ Phrases**	**Example**
Definition or restatement of the meaning of the word	or, which is, that is, in other words, also known as, also called	Olympic gymnasts are very *limber,* or **flexible.**
Example following an unfamiliar word	such as, like, as if, for example, especially, including	We collected *kindling,* such as **dry twigs and branches,** to start the fire.
Comparison with a more familiar word or concept	as, like, also, similar to, in the same way, likewise	Kari's face was *luminous,* **like the rays of the sun.**
Contrast with a familiar word or experience	unlike, but, however, although, on the other hand, on the contrary	The summer was *sultry,* but the fall was **dry and cool.**
Cause-and-effect relationship in which one term is familiar	because, since, when, consequently, as a result, therefore	When the *tree fell across the road,* it **obstructed** traffic.

*For more information, see **Vocabulary Strategy: Context Clues,** pages 134 and 898, **Vocabulary Strategy: Similes,** pages 188 and 850, **Vocabulary Strategy: Synonyms as Context Clues,** page 280, **Vocabulary Strategy: Idioms,** page 337.*

2 Analyzing Word Structure

Many words can be broken into smaller parts. These word parts include base words, roots, prefixes, and suffixes.

2.1 BASE WORDS

A **base word** is a word part that by itself is also a word. Other words or word parts can be added to base words to form new words.

2.2 ROOTS

A **root** is a word part that contains the core meaning of the word. Many English words contain roots that come from older languages such as Greek, Latin, Old English (Anglo-Saxon), and Norse. Knowing the meaning of the word's root can help you determine the word's meaning.

Root	Meaning	Example
aud (Latin)	hear	**aud**io, **aud**ition
voc (Latin)	voice	**voc**al, in**voc**e
mem, ment (Latin)	mind	**mem**ory, **ment**al, **ment**ion
chron (Greek)	time	**chron**ic, syn**chron**ize
gram (Greek)	something written	tele**gram**, **gram**mar
gen (Greek)	race, family	**gen**esis, **gen**re, **gen**ius
angr (Old Norse)	painfully constricted, sorrow	**ang**er, **ang**uish

For more information, see Vocabulary Strategy: Word Roots, pages 651, 737, 943, 998, and 1012.

2.3 PREFIXES

A **prefix** is a word part attached to the beginning of a word or word root. Most prefixes come from Greek, Latin, or Old English.

Interactive Vocabulary **THINK** central

Go to **thinkcentral.com**.
KEYWORD: HML8-R69

Prefix	Meaning	Example
mid-	middle, center	**mid**night
pro-	forward	**pro**ceed, **pro**cession
uni-	one	**uni**form, **uni**cycle
tele-	view	**tele**scope
multi-	many, much	**multi**media, **multi**vitamins

For more information, see Vocabulary Strategy: Prefixes, pages 64, 244, and 428.

2.4 SUFFIXES

A **suffix** is a word part that appears at the end of a root or base word to form a new word. Some suffixes do not change word meaning. These suffixes are

- added to nouns to change the number of persons or objects
- added to verbs to change the tense
- added to modifiers to change the degree of comparison

Suffix	Meaning	Examples
-s, -es	to change the number of a noun	lock + s = locks
-d, -ed, -ing	to change verb tense	stew + ed = stewed
-er, -est	to indicate comparison in modifiers	mild + er = milder soft + est = softest

Other suffixes can be added to the root or base to change the word's meaning. These suffixes can also determine a word's part of speech.

Suffix	Meaning	Example
-age	amount	foot**age**
-able, -ible	able, inclined to	read**able**, tang**ible**
-ant, -ent	a specific state or condition	pleas**ant**, differ**ent**

For more information, see Vocabulary Strategy: Suffixes that Form Nouns, page 78, Vocabulary Strategy: Suffixes that Form Adjectives, page 932.

Strategies for Understanding Unfamiliar Words

- Look for any prefixes or suffixes. Remove them so that you can concentrate on the base word or the root.

- See if you recognize any elements—prefix, suffix, root, or base—of the word. You may be able to guess its meaning by analyzing one or two elements.

- Think about the way the word is used in the sentence. Use the context and the word parts to make a logical guess about the word's meaning.

- Look in a dictionary to see whether you are correct.

3 Understanding Word Origins

3.1 DEVELOPMENT OF THE ENGLISH LANGUAGE

During the past 2,000 years or so, English has developed from a language spoken by a few Germanic tribes into a language that is more widely spoken and written than any other in the world. Some experts, in fact, call today's English the first truly global language. Its most valuable characteristic is its ability to change and grow, adopting new words as the need arises. The history of the English language can be divided into three main periods.

Old English About the year A.D. 449, Germanic people who lived on the European continent along the North Sea began a series of invasions into Britain. At that time, Britain was inhabited by the Celts, whose native language was Gaelic. Over a period of years, the raiders conquered and settled in Britain. The conquerors, known today as the Anglo-Saxons, prospered in Britain. In time, Britain became "Engla land," and the Anglo-Saxon languages evolved into "Englisc," or what modern scholars call Old English.

Old English was very different from the English we speak today. It was harsher in sound, had no silent letters, and was written phonetically. Few examples of Old English remain in our current English vocabulary. Those that do exist, however, are common words for people, places, things, and actions.

man (*mann*)	wife (*wif*)	child (*cild*)
house (*hus*)	meat (*mete*)	drink (*drincan*)
sleep (*slæpan*)	live (*libban*)	fight (*feohtan*)

In the sixth and seventh centuries, missionaries from Rome and other Christian cities arrived in England, bringing with them their knowledge of religion and ancient languages. Among the most influential figures was St. Augustine, who converted thousands of Anglo-Saxons, including a king, to Christianity. As the Anglo-Saxons accepted this faith, they also accepted words from Latin and Greek.

Latin	Greek
candle	alphabet
cup	angel
priest	box
noon	demon
scripture	school

During the late 8th century, Viking invaders from Denmark and Norway settled in northeast England. As a result, Scandinavian words became part of Old English.

sky	knife	are
steak	leg	birth
they	skin	seat
window	them	their

Middle English The Norman Conquest brought great changes to England and its language. In 1066, England was defeated by the Normans, a people from an area in France. Their leader, William the Conqueror, staged a successful invasion of England and became the nation's new monarch. With William on the throne of England, Norman French became the language of the English court, government business, nobility, and scholars. Eventually, French words were adopted in everyday vocabulary as well.

The language that evolved is called Middle English. Middle English was not as harsh-sounding as Old English and borrowed many words from Norman French.

attorney	joint	mallet
baron	jolly	marriage
chivalry	laundry	merchandise
gown	lodge	petty

Norman French itself borrowed thousands of words from Latin and Greek, as well as from ancient Indian and Semitic languages. Consequently, Middle English also contained many of these foreign terms.

Latin	Greek	Indian	Semitic
language	circle	ginger	camel
library	hour	jungle	cinnamon
money	lantern	orange	coffee
serpent	leopard	sugar	lion
square	magnet	pepper	syrup

Modern English By the late 1400s, Middle English began to develop into Modern English. The various pronunciations, word forms, and spellings common to Middle English were becoming more uniform. One invention that aided this process was the printing press. Introduced to London around 1476, the printing press allowed printers to standardize the spellings of common English words. As a result, readers and writers of English became accustomed to following "rules" of spelling and grammar.

During this period, the English vocabulary also continued to grow as new ideas and discoveries demanded new words. As the English began to colonize and trade with other areas of the world, they borrowed foreign words. In time, the English vocabulary grew to include words from diverse languages, such as French, Dutch, Spanish, Italian, Portuguese, and Chinese. Many of these words stayed the way they were in their original languages.

French	Dutch	Spanish	Italian
ballet	boss	canyon	diva
beret	caboose	rodeo	carnival
mirage	dock	taco	spaghetti
vague	skate	tornado	studio

Portuguese	Chinese	Japanese	Native American
cashew	chow	kamikaze	caribou
mango	ginseng	karaoke	moccasin
jaguar	kung fu	sushi	papoose
yam	kow tow	tsunami	tomahawk

Today, the English language is still changing and absorbing new words. It is considered the international language of science and technology. It is also widely used in business and politics.

*For more information, see **Vocabulary Strategy: Foreign Words in English,** pages 48 and 750.*

3.2 DICTIONARY AS A SOURCE OF WORD ORIGINS

Many dictionary entries provide information about a word's origin. This information often comes at the end of an entry, as in this example.

ge·om·e·try (jē-ŏm′ĭ-trē) *n., pl.* **-tries 1.** The mathematics of the properties, measurement, and relationships of points, lines, angles, surfaces, and solids. **2.** Arrangement. **3.** A physical arrangement suggesting geometric forms or lines. [from Greek *geōmetriā,* from *geōmetrein,* to measure land].

3.3 WORD FAMILIES

Words that have the same root make up a word family and have related meanings. The charts below show some common Greek and Latin roots. Notice how the meanings of the example words are related to the meanings of their roots.

Latin Root	*circum,* around or about
English	**circumference** the boundary line of a circle
	circumnavigation the act of moving completely around
	circumstance a condition or fact surrounding an event

Greek Root	*monos,* single or alone
English	**monopoly** exclusive control by one group
	monologue a speech delivered by one person
	monotonous sounded or spoken in a single unvarying tone

French Root	*caval,* a horse
English	**calvary** troops trained to fight on horseback
	cavalcade a procession of riders or horse-drawn carriages

TIP Once you recognize a root in one English word, you will notice the same root in other words. Because these words develop from the same root, all words in the word family are similar in meaning.

*For more information, see **Vocabulary Strategy: Researching Word Origins,** page 909.*

4 Synonyms and Antonyms

4.1 SYNONYMS

Positive	Negative
slender	scrawny
thrifty	cheap
young	immature

A **synonym** is a word with a meaning similar to that of another word. You can find synonyms in a thesaurus or a dictionary. In a dictionary, synonyms are often given as part of the definition of the word. The following word pairs are synonyms:

satisfy/please   occasionally/sometimes

rob/steal   schedule/agenda

*For more information, see **Vocabulary Strategy: Synonyms as Context Clues,** page 280.*

4.2 ANTONYMS

An **antonym** is a word with a meaning opposite that of another word. The following word pairs are antonyms:

accurate/incorrect   similar/different

fresh/stale   unusual/ordinary

*For more information, see **Vocabulary Strategy: Antonyms and Context Clues,** page 1029.*

5 Denotation and Connotation

5.1 DENOTATION

A word's dictionary meaning is called its **denotation.** For example, the denotation of the word *thin* is "having little flesh; spare; lean."

5.2 CONNOTATION

The images or feelings you connect to a word add a finer shade of meaning, called **connotation**. The connation of a word goes beyond its basic dictionary definition. Writers use connotations of words to communicate positive or negative feelings.

Make sure you understand the denotation and connotation of a word when you read it or use it in your writing.

*For more information, see **Vocabulary Strategy: Denotations and Connotations,** pages 715 and 923.*

6 Analogies

An **analogy** is a relationship between pairs of words. In an analogy question on a test, the words in one pair relate to each other the same way as the words in a second pair, one of which you have to choose. To complete an analogy, identify the relationship between the words in the first pair. Then choose the word that will cause the words in the second pair to relate to the other in the same way.

Analogies are often written as follows—
    cheap : expensive :: humid : dry

If the analogy is read out loud, you would say, "cheap is to expensive as humid is to dry."

There are various ways the word pairs in an analogy can be related.

- Words can be related because they are opposites, or antonyms, as in the example above.

- Words can be related because they are similar, or synonyms.
    tired : exhausted :: talkative : chatty

- Words can be related by function. If the first pair of words contains a noun and its function, the second pair should also.
    helmet : protection :: lamp : illumination

- Words can be related by description. If the first pair or words contains a noun and a word that describes it, the second pair should also.
    rain : wet :: lettuce : green

*For more information, see **Vocabulary Strategy: Analogies,** pages 260 and 802.*

7 Homonyms, Homographs, and Homophones

7.1 HOMONYMS

Homonyms are words that have the same spelling and sound but have different meanings.

The snake shed its skin in the shed behind the house.

Shed can mean "to lose by natural process," but an identically spelled word means "a small structure."

Sometimes only one of the meanings of a homonym may be familiar to you. Use context clues to help you figure out the meaning of an unfamiliar word.

7.2 HOMOGRAPHS

Homographs are words that are spelled the same but have different meanings and origins. Some are also pronounced differently, as in these examples.

Please close the door. (clōz)
That was a close call. (clōs)

If you see a word used in a way that is unfamiliar to you, check a dictionary to see if it is a homograph.

*For more information, see **Vocabulary Strategy: Homographs,** page 368.*

7.3 HOMOPHONES

Homophones are words that sound alike but have different meanings and spellings. The following homophones are frequently misused:

it's/its	they're/their/there
to/too/two	stationary/stationery

Many misused homophones are pronouns and contractions. Whenever you are unsure whether to write *your* or *you're* and *who's* or *whose*, ask yourself if you mean *you are* and *who is/has*. If you do, write the contraction. For other homophones, such as *fair* and *fare*, use the meaning of the word to help you decide which one to use.

8 Words with Multiple Meanings

Some words have acquired additional meanings over time that are based on the original meaning.

I had to be replaced in the cast of the play because of the cast on my arm.

These two uses of *cast* have different meanings, but both of them have the same origin. You will find all the meanings of *cast* listed in one entry in the dictionary.

*For more information, see **Vocabulary Strategy: Multiple-Meaning Words**, page 289.*

9 Specialized Vocabulary

Specialized vocabulary is special terms suited to a particular field of study or work. For example, science, mathematics, and history all have their own technical or specialized vocabularies. To figure out specialized terms, you can use context clues and reference sources, such as dictionaries on specific subjects, atlases, or manuals.

*For more information, see **Vocabulary Strategy: Specialized Vocabulary**, page 228.*

10 Using Reference Sources

10.1 DICTIONARIES

A **general dictionary** will tell you not only a word's definitions but also its pronunciation, parts of speech, and history and origin, or etymology.

① **tan·gi·ble** (tăn′jə-bəl) *adj.*
1a. Discernible by the touch; palpable. **b.** Possible to touch. **c.** Possible to be treated as fact; real or concrete. **2.** Possible to understand or realize. **3.** Law that can be valued monetarily [Late Latin *tangibilis*, from Latin *tangere*, to touch] **⑤**

①	Entry word
②	Pronunciation
③	Part of speech
④	Definitions
⑤	Etymology

A **specialized dictionary** focuses on terms related to a particular field of study or work. Use a dictionary to check the spelling of any word you are unsure of in your English class and other classes as well.

*For more information, see **Vocabulary Strategy: Using Reference Aids**, pages 89 and 485.*

10.2 THESAURI

A **thesaurus** (plural, *thesauri*) is a dictionary of synonyms. A thesaurus can be especially helpful when you find yourself using the same modifiers over and over again.

10.3 SYNONYM FINDERS

A **synonym finder** is often included in word-processing software. It enables you to highlight a word and be shown a display of its synonyms.

10.4 GLOSSARIES

A **glossary** is a list of specialized terms and their definitions. It is often found in the back of a book and sometimes includes pronunciations. Many textbooks contain glossaries. In fact, this textbook has four glossaries: the **Glossary of Literary and Nonfiction Terms,** the **Glossary of Academic Vocabulary,** the **Glossary of Reading & Informational Terms,** and the **Glossary of Vocabulary in English & Spanish.** Use these glossaries to help you understand how terms are used in this textbook.

11 Spelling Rules

11.1 WORDS ENDING IN A SILENT *E*

Before adding a suffix beginning with a vowel or *y* to a word ending in a silent *e,* drop the *e* (with some exceptions).

> **amaze + -ing = amazing**
> **love + -able = lovable**
> **create + -ed = created**
> **nerve + -ous = nervous**

Exceptions: *change + -able = changeable; courage + -ous = courageous*

When adding a suffix beginning with a consonant to a word ending in a silent *e,* keep the *e* (with some exceptions).

> **late + -ly = lately**
> **spite + -ful = spiteful**
> **noise + -less = noiseless**
> **state + -ment = statement**

Exceptions: *truly, argument, ninth, wholly, awful,* and others

When a suffix beginning with *a* or *o* is added to a word with a final silent *e*, the final *e* is usually retained if it is preceded by a soft *c* or a soft *g*.

bridge + -able = bridgeable
peace + -able = peaceable
outrage + -ous = outrageous
advantage + -ous = advantageous

When a suffix beginning with a vowel is added to words ending in *ee* or *oe*, the final silent *e* is retained.

agree + -ing = agreeing   free + -ing = freeing
hoe + -ing = hoeing   see + -ing = seeing

11.2 WORDS ENDING IN Y

Before adding most suffixes to a word that ends in *y* preceded by a consonant, change the *y* to *i*.

easy + -est = easiest
crazy + -est = craziest
silly + -ness = silliness
marry + -age = marriage

Exceptions: *dryness, shyness,* and *slyness*

However, when you add *-ing,* the *y* does not change.

empty + -ed = emptied but
empty + -ing = emptying

When adding a suffix to a word that ends in *y* preceded by a vowel, the *y* usually does not change.

play + -er = player
employ + -ed = employed
coy + -ness = coyness
pay + -able = payable

11.3 WORDS ENDING IN A CONSONANT

In one-syllable words that end in one consonant preceded by one short vowel, double the final consonant before adding a suffix beginning with a vowel, such as *-ed* or *-ing.* These are sometimes called 1+1+1 words.

dip + -ed = dipped   set + -ing = setting
slim + -est = slimmest   fit + -er = fitter

The rule does not apply to words of one syllable that end in a consonant preceded by two vowels.

feel + -ing = feeling   peel + -ed = peeled
reap + -ed = reaped   loot + -ed = looted

In words of more than one syllable, double the final consonant when (1) the word ends with one consonant preceded by one vowel and (2) when the word is accented on the last syllable.

be•gin'   per•mit'   re•fer'

In the following examples, note that in the new words formed with suffixes, the accent remains on the same syllable:

be•gin' + -ing = be•gin'ning = beginning
per•mit' + -ed = per•mit'ted = permitted

Exceptions: In some words with more than one syllable, though the accent remains on the same syllable when a suffix is added, the final consonant is nevertheless not doubled, as in the following examples:

tra'vel + er = tra'vel•er = traveler
mar'ket + er = mar'ket•er = marketer

In the following examples, the accent does not remain on the same syllable; thus, the final consonant is not doubled:

re•fer' + -ence = ref'er•ence = reference
con•fer' + -ence = con'fer•ence = conference

11.4 PREFIXES AND SUFFIXES

When adding a prefix to a word, do not change the spelling of the base word. When a prefix creates a double letter, keep both letters.

dis- + approve = disapprove
re- + build = rebuild
ir- + regular = irregular
mis- + spell = misspell
anti- + trust = antitrust
il- + logical = illogical

When adding *-ly* to a word ending in *l*, keep both *l*'s. When adding *-ness* to a word ending in *n*, keep both *n*'s.

careful + -ly = carefully
sudden + -ness = suddenness
final + -ly = finally
thin + -ness = thinness

11.5 FORMING PLURAL NOUNS

To form the plural of most nouns, just add -s.

prizes   dreams   circles   stations

For most singular nouns ending in **o**, add -s.

solos   halos   studios   photos   pianos

For a few nouns ending in **o**, add -es.

heroes   tomatoes   potatoes   echoes

When the singular noun ends in **s, sh, ch, x,** or **z,** add -es.

**waitresses   brushes   ditches
axes   buzzes**

When a singular noun ends in **y** with a consonant before it, change the **y** to **i** and add -es.

**army—armies   candy—candies
baby—babies   diary—diaries
ferry—ferries   conspiracy—conspiracies**

When a vowel (**a, e, i, o, u**) comes before the **y**, just add -s.

**boy—boys   way—ways
array—arrays   alloy—alloys
weekday—weekdays   jockey—jockeys**

For most nouns ending in **f** or **fe**, change the **f** to **v** and add -es or -s.

**life—lives   calf—calves   knife—knives
thief—thieves   shelf—shelves loaf—loaves**

For some nouns ending in **f**, add -s to make the plural.

roofs   chiefs   reefs   beliefs

Some nouns have the same form for both singular and plural.

deer   sheep   moose   salmon   trout

For some nouns, the plural is formed in a special way.

**man—men   goose—geese
ox—oxen   woman—women
mouse—mice   child—children**

For a compound noun written as one word, form the plural by changing the last word in the compound to its plural form.

stepchild—stepchildren   firefly—fireflies

If a compound noun is written as a hyphenated word or as two separate words, change the most important word to the plural form.

**brother-in-law—brothers-in-law
life jacket—life jackets**

11.6 FORMING POSSESSIVES

If a noun is singular, add **'s.**

mother—my mother's car   Ross—Ross's desk

Exceptions: The **s** after the apostrophe is dropped after *Jesus', Moses',* and certain names in classical mythology (*Zeus'*). These possessive forms can thus be pronounced easily.

If a noun is plural and ends with **s,** just add an apostrophe.

**parents—my parents' car
the Santinis—the Santinis' house**

If a noun is plural but does not end in **s,** add **'s.**

**people—the people's choice
women—the women's coats**

11.7 SPECIAL SPELLING PROBLEMS

Only one English word ends in -**sede**: *supersede.* Three words end in -**ceed**: *exceed, proceed,* and *succeed.* All other verbs ending in the sound "seed" are spelled with -**cede.**

concede   precede   recede   secede

In words with **ie** or **ei,** when the sound is long **e** (as in *she*), the word is spelled **ie** except after **c** (with some exceptions).

i before *e*	thief	relieve	field
	piece	grieve	pier
except after *c*	conceit	perceive	ceiling
	receive	receipt	
Exceptions:	either	neither	weird
	leisure	seize	

12 Commonly Confused Words

WORDS	DEFINITIONS	EXAMPLES
accept/except	The verb **accept** means "to receive or believe." **Except** is usually a preposition meaning "excluding."	Did the teacher **accept** your report? Everyone smiled for the photographer **except** Jody.
advice/advise	**Advise** is a verb. **Advice** is a noun naming that which an **adviser** gives.	I **advise** you to take that job. Whom should I ask for **advice**?
affect/effect	As a verb, **affect** means "to influence." **Effect** as a verb means "to cause." If you want a noun, you will almost always want **effect**.	How deeply did the news **affect** him? The students tried to **effect** a change in school policy. What **effect** did the acidic soil produce in the plants?
all ready/already	**All ready** is an adjective meaning "fully ready." **Already** is an adverb meaning "before or by this time."	He was **all ready** to go at noon. I have **already** seen that movie.
desert/dessert	**Desert** (dĕz´ərt) means "a dry, sandy, barren region." **Desert** (dĭ-zûrt´) means "to abandon." **Dessert** (dĭ-zûrt´) is a sweet, such as cake.	The Sahara, in North Africa, is the world's largest **desert**. The night guard did not **desert** his post. Alison's favorite **dessert** is chocolate cake.
among/between	**Between** is used when you are speaking of only two things. **Among** is used for three or more.	**Between** ice cream and sherbet, I prefer the latter. Gary Soto is **among** my favorite authors.
bring/take	**Bring** is used to denote motion toward a speaker or place. **Take** is used to denote motion away from such a person or place.	**Bring** the books over here, and I will **take** them to the library.
fewer/less	**Fewer** refers to the number of separate, countable units. **Less** refers to bulk quantity.	We have **less** literature and **fewer** selections in this year's curriculum.
leave/let	**Leave** means "to allow something to remain behind." **Let** means "to permit."	The librarian will **leave** some books on display but will not **let** us borrow any.
lie/lay	To **lie** is "to rest or recline." It does not take an object. **Lay** always takes an object.	Rover loves to **lie** in the sun. We always **lay** some bones next to him.
loose/lose	**Loose** (lo͞os) means "free, not restrained"; **lose** (lo͞oz) means "to misplace or fail to find."	Who turned the horses **loose?** I hope we won't **lose** any of them.
passed/past	**Passed** is the past tense of pass and means "went by." **Past** is an adjective that means "of a former time." **Past** is also a noun that means "time gone by."	We **passed** through the Florida Keys during our vacation. My **past** experiences have taught me to set my alarm. Ebenezer Scrooge is a character who relives his **past**.
than/then	Use **than** in making comparisons. Use **then** on all other occasions.	Ramon is stronger **than** Mark. Cut the grass and **then** trim the hedges.
two/too/to	**Two** is a number. **Too** is an adverb meaning "also" or "very." Use **to** before a verb or as a preposition.	Meg had **to** go **to** town, **too.** We had **too** much reading **to** do. **Two** chapters is **too** many.
their/there/they're	**Their** means "belonging to them." **There** means "in that place." **They're** is the contraction for "they are."	**There** is a movie playing at 9 P.M. **They're** going to see it with me. Sakara and Jessica drove away in **their** car after the movie.

Good speakers and listeners do more than simply talk and hear. They use specific techniques to present their ideas effectively, and they are attentive and critical listeners.

COMMON CORE

Included in this handbook:
SL 1, SL 1a–c, SL 4, SL 6

1 Speech

In school, in business, and in community life, giving a speech can be an effective means of communicating ideas or information.

1.1 ORGANIZING YOUR INFORMATION

Before you write your speech, you will need to know *why* you are making the presentation and to *whom* you are presenting.

- **Know Your Audience** Who will be listening to your speech—classmates, teachers, community members?

- **Consider Your Purpose** What do you want your speech to accomplish? You could inform audience members about an important or exciting topic. You could persuade them to agree with you on a thought-provoking issue. Or you could entertain them with a funny, scary, or dramatic presentation.

- **Think About the Occasion** Will you be the only speaker? If so, you might speak for a longer period than you would if many others gave presentations. Is this a formal or informal event? Adjust the formality or informality of your language accordingly.

- **Match Your Message** For maximum impact, change the message you are sending to fit the audience, purpose, and occasion of your speech.

- **Adjust Your Delivery** Your audience, purpose, and occasion can also affect how you say what you say. You can vary vocabulary, using formal language for a serious occasion and jargon with a group that knows your topic well. You can vary voice modulation, speaking louder or more softly. Your expression can change to reflect the emotions you want your audience to feel. Your tone (attitude) can also change.

1.2 WRITING YOUR SPEECH

Now it's time to get your thoughts on paper. These guidelines will help you as you write:

- **Prepare a Speech Outline** By creating a formal or informal outline, you will give your speech a clear pattern of organization. Most speeches have an introduction, a body, and a conclusion. Include transitions in your outline so listeners understand how the ideas in your speech are related. Preview new information for listeners so they can understand it more easily. Summarize the content of your speech to make sure your main points are clear.

- **Aim for Unity** Each sentence in a paragraph should relate to the key idea of that paragraph. Similarly, each paragraph in your speech should relate to the key idea of your speech. Don't include information that is unrelated to the topic, even if that information is interesting or surprising.

- **Enrich Your Language** Enliven your speech with precise words, strong action verbs, rich sensory details, and colorful yet appropriate modifiers. Use the active voice, not the passive voice, most of the time. Make sure your grammar is correct.

- **Provide Evidence** Include relevant facts, statistics, and incidents; quote experts to support your ideas and opinions. Include specific details and visual or media displays to clarify what you are saying.

- **Arrange Details and Evidence Effectively** In a good presentation, the main thesis statement, or controlling idea, should be supported by clearly stated evidence. The evidence can be presented as details, reasons, descriptions, or examples. Use the following chart to help you arrange your ideas.

Introduction	• Focus on one strong example or statistic.
	• Make sure your introduction is intense or even surprising, so that it grabs the audience's attention.
Body	• Try to provide at least one piece of evidence for every new idea you introduce.
	• Define unfamiliar terms clearly.
	• When possible, include well-labeled diagrams or illustrations.
Conclusion	• Leave your audience with one strong piece of evidence or a powerful detail.

- **Use Figurative Language** To help your audience follow the main ideas of your speech, be sure to draw attention to important points with similes, metaphors, and sensory images.

- **Use Precise Language** Use precise language to convey your Ideas, and vary the structure and length of your sentences. You can keep the audience's attention with a word that brings out strong emotion. You can use a question or side comment to make a personal connection with the audience.

- **Start Strong, Finish Strong** As you begin your speech, consider using a "hook"—an interesting question or statement to capture the audience's attention. At the end of the speech, restate your main ideas simply and clearly. Perhaps conclude with a powerful example or anecdote to reinforce your message.

- **Revise Your Speech** After you write your speech, revise, edit, and proofread it as you would for a written report. Use a variety of sentence structures to achieve a natural rhythm. Check for correct subject-verb agreement and consistent verb tense. Correct run-on sentences and sentence fragments. Use parallel structure to emphasize ideas. Make sure you use complete sentences and correct punctuation and capitalization, even if no one else will see it. Your written speech should be clear and error free. If you notice an error in your notes while you are delivering the speech, you may not remember what you actually wanted to say.

1.3 DELIVERING YOUR SPEECH

Confidence is the key to a successful presentation. Use these techniques to help you prepare and present your speech:

Prepare

- **Review Your Information** Reread your notes and review any background research. This will help you feel more confident during your speech.

- **Organize Your Notes** Some people prefer to write down only key points. Others prefer the entire script. Write each main point, or each paragraph, of your speech on a separate numbered index card. Be sure to include your most important evidence and examples.

- **Plan Your Visual Aids** If you are planning to use visual aids, such as slides, posters, charts, graphs, video clips, overhead transparencies, or computer projections, now is the time to design them and decide how to work them into your speech.

Practice

- **Rehearse** Rehearse your speech several times, possibly in front of a practice audience. Maintain good posture by standing with your shoulders back and your head up. If you are using visual aids, arrange them in the order in which you will use them. Adapt your rate of speaking, pitch, and tone of voice to your audience and setting. Glance at your notes to refresh your memory, but avoid reading them word for word. Your delivery style should express the purpose of your speech. Use the following chart to help you.

Purpose	Pace	Pitch	Tone
To persuade	fast but clear	same throughout	urgent
To inform	using plenty of pauses	same throughout	authoritative
To entertain	usually building to a "punch"	varied to create characters or drama	funny or dramatic

- **Use Audience Feedback** If you had a practice audience, ask them specific questions about your delivery and the content: Did I use enough eye contact? Was my voice at the right volume? Did I stand straight, or did I slouch? Did my tone and inflection fit my purpose? Use the audience's comments to evaluate the effectiveness of your delivery.

- **Evaluate Your Performance** When you have finished each rehearsal, evaluate your performance. Did you pause to let an important point sink in or use gestures for emphasis? Make a list of the aspects of your presentation that you will try to improve for your next rehearsal.

Present

- **Begin Your Speech** Smile, and try to look relaxed.

- **Make Eye Contact** Try to make eye contact with as many audience members as possible. This will establish personal contact and help you determine whether the audience understands your speech.

- **Remember to Pause** Pausing after important points provides emphasis and gives the audience time to think about what you're saying.

- **Enunciate** Speak loud enough to be heard clearly, but not so loud that your voice is overwhelming. Pronounce words properly.

- **Maintain Good Posture** Stand up straight and avoid nervous movements that may distract the audience's attention from what you are saying.

- **Use Expressive Body Language** Use facial expressions to show your feelings toward your topic. Lean forward when you make an important point; move your hands and arms for emphasis. Use your body language to show your own style and reflect your personality.

- **Watch the Audience for Responses** If the audience starts fidgeting or yawning, speak a little louder or get to your conclusion a little sooner. Use what you learn to evaluate your speech and to decide what areas need improvement. Should you make changes to the organization? Do you need to rearrange any words or sentences to clarify your meaning?

Respond to Questions

Depending on the content of your speech, your audience may have questions. Follow these steps to make sure that you answer questions in an appropriate manner:

- Think about what your audience may ask and prepare answers before your speech.

- Tell your audience at the beginning of your speech that you will take questions at the end. This helps avoid audience interruptions during your speech.

- Call on audience members in the order in which they raise their hands.

- Repeat each question before you answer it to ensure that everyone has heard it. This step also gives you time to prepare your answer.

2 Different Types of Oral Presentations

2.1 INFORMATIVE SPEECH

When you deliver an informative speech, you give the audience new information, provide a better understanding of information, or enable the audience to use the information in a new way. An informative speech is presented in an objective way.

Use the following questions to evaluate the presentation of a peer or a public figure, or your own presentation.

Evaluate an Informative Speech

- Did the speaker explain the purpose of the presentation?
- Did the speaker take the audience's previous knowledge into consideration?
- Did the speaker cite a variety of sources for the information?
- Did the speaker communicate the information objectively?
- Did the speaker explain technical terms?
- Did the speaker use visual aids effectively?

2.2 RESEARCH PRESENTATION

An oral research presentation conveys information on a single researched topic. An effective research report will be organized around a controlling idea. It will support that idea with details and evidence from a number of reliable sources.

- **Plan Your Report** Decide on a topic, and then narrow down that topic to find a focus.

- **Consider Your Purpose** Writing down your purpose in sentence or question form will help you develop your controlling idea.

- **Organize Your Material** Choose an order in which to present your information. Be sure that any main points are supported with details and evidence from sources you can cite.

Use the following guidelines to evaluate a research presentation.

Evaluate a Research Presentation
- Did the speaker define a controlling idea?
- Did the speaker support the idea using specific details—such as direct quotations, general concepts, or statistics—from reliable, relevant sources?
- Did the speaker summarize or paraphrase information when necessary?
- Did the speaker include a variety of primary and secondary sources and explain the value of each?
- Did the speaker use charts, maps, and graphs to organize information when appropriate?

2.3 PERSUASIVE SPEECH

When you deliver a persuasive speech, you offer a thesis or controlling idea on a subject, you provide relevant evidence to support your position, and you attempt to convince the audience to accept your point of view.

*For more information, see **Speaking and Listening: Delivering a Persuasive Speech,** page 1048.*

Use the following questions to evaluate the presentation of a peer or a public figure, or your own presentation.

Evaluate a Persuasive Speech
- Did the speaker present a clear, well-defined thesis?
- Did the speaker support the thesis with detailed evidence, relevant examples, and logical reasoning?
- Was it clear which parts of the speech were factual and which were opinions?
- Did the speaker think about audience concerns and counterarguments ahead of time? Did he or she use details, reasons, examples, expert opinions, or other evidence to answer those questions?
- Did the speaker maintain a reasonable tone—calm and confident rather than bored or overemotional?
- Were the speaker's expressions and gestures effective?
- Is your reaction to the speech similar to other audience members'?

2.4 NARRATIVE SPEECH

When you deliver a narrative speech, you tell a story or present a subject using a story-type format. A good narrative keeps an audience informed and entertained. It also allows you to deliver a message in a creative way.

*For more information, see **Speaking and Listening: Presenting an Oral Narrative,** page 158.*

Use the following questions to evaluate a speaker or your own presentation.

Evaluate a Narrative Speech
- Did the speaker describe a single incident, event, or situation clearly and coherently?
- Did the speaker use carefully chosen details?
- Did the speaker reveal why the incident was significant?
- Did the speaker clearly express his or her attitude, or feelings, about the incident?
- Did the speaker keep the audience interested by including dialogue and describing specific actions?
- Did the speaker describe the setting precisely?
- Did the speaker compare or contrast characters effectively?
- Did the speaker provide helpful background information for listeners?
- Is your reaction to the speech similar to other audience members'?

2.5 ORAL READING

When you read a poem, play, or story aloud, your voice can bring the literature to life. An oral reading can be a monologue, during which you assume the voice of a single character, the narrator, or the speaker in a poem. Or it may be a dialogue, during which you take the roles of two or more characters. Use the following techniques when giving an oral reading:

- **Speak Clearly** As you speak, pronounce your words carefully and clearly.

- **Control Your Volume** Make sure that you are loud enough to be heard but not shouting.

- **Pace Yourself** Read at a moderate rate, but vary your pace if it seems appropriate to the emotions of the character or to the action.

- **Vary Your Voice** Use a different voice for each character. Stress important words and phrases. Use your voice to express different emotions.

Evaluate an Oral Reading

- Did the speaker speak clearly and project his or her voice at the proper volume?
- Did he or she maintain eye contact with the audience?
- Did the speaker vary the rate and volume of speech appropriately to express emotion, mood, and action?
- Did the speaker use a different voice for each character?
- Did the speaker use the appropriate tone, inflections, and gestures to enhance meaning?
- What was the interpretation's effect on listeners? Did the speaker seem aware of this effect?

PRACTICE AND APPLY

Listen to an oral reading by a classmate or view a dramatic performance in a theater or on television. Use the preceding guidelines to evaluate it.

2.6 ORAL RESPONSE TO LITERATURE

An oral response to literature is your own personal interpretation of a piece written by someone else. Use the following techniques to help you craft a response:

- **Select Carefully** Think about the assignment, your interest, and the audience.

- **Exhibit Understanding** Direct your audience to specific words, sentences, or paragraphs that are rich with meaning. Discuss why they are important to the piece. Explain the writer's techniques in developing plot, characterization, setting, or theme.

- **Organize Clearly** Construct your response around clear ideas, premises, or images. What elements of the literature are most important? How do they relate to the piece as a whole? Use examples and evidence to show how they provide insight and meaning.

*For more information, see **Speaking and Listening: Presenting a Response to Literature,** page 768.*

Evaluate an Oral Response to Literature

- Did the speaker provide an in-depth analysis of a piece of literature?
- Did the speaker call attention to specific writing techniques and passages that helped to give the piece meaning?
- Did the speaker make inferences about the piece of literature and discuss its effect on him or her as a reader?
- Did the speaker support inferences and judgments with references to the literary work, other literary works, other authors, or personal knowledge?
- Did the speaker present his or her ideas in a clear, well-organized manner?

PRACTICE AND APPLY

Listen as a classmate delivers an oral response to a book or an article. Use the preceding guidelines to evaluate the presentation.

2.7 ORAL INSTRUCTIONS

You give oral instructions any time you are called upon to explain how to do something or how to fix a problem. When you give oral instructions, your goal is to teach the audience how to perform the task you are explaining. Make sure you present steps in order, speak clearly, and explain any terms your audience may not know.

*For more information, see **Speaking and Listening: Presenting and Responding to an Instructional Speech,** page 970.*

Evaluate Oral Instructions

- Did the speaker make it clear what he or she was trying to explain?
- Did the speaker use a rate and volume of speech that helped you to understand him or her?
- Did the speaker relate steps in a logical order?
- Did the speaker stay focused on the topic?
- Did the speaker monitor the audience's understanding by asking for and answering questions?

3 Other Types of Communication

3.1 GROUP DISCUSSION

Successful groups assign a role to each member. These roles distribute responsibility among the members and help keep discussions focused.

Guidelines for Discussion

- Work from an agenda, or a list of things to do.
- Set clear goals, deadlines, and time limits.
- Be informed about the topic.
- Participate in the discussion.
- Ask questions and give appropriate responses.
- Don't talk while someone else is talking.
- Support statements with facts and examples.
- Listen attentively; be respectful of others.
- Stop now and then to informally **summarize** what people have said; be sure to focus on their main ideas.
- Work toward the goal; stay focused on the topic.
- If the group is taking a vote on an issue or action, make sure the process is fair.

Role	Responsibilities
Chairperson	• Introduces topic • Explains goal or purpose • Participates in discussion and keeps it on track • Helps resolve conflicts • Helps group reach goal
Recorder	• Takes notes on discussion • Reports on suggestions and decisions • Organizes and writes up notes • Participates in discussion • Gives an informal verbal summary
Participants	• Contribute relevant facts or ideas • Respond constructively to one another's ideas • Reach agreement or vote on final decision

3.2 INTERVIEW

An **interview** is a formal type of conversation with a definite purpose and goal. To conduct a successful interview, use the following guidelines:

Prepare for the Interview

- Carefully select whom you will interview. Identify who has the kind of knowledge and experience you are looking for.
- Set a time, a date, and a place. Ask permission to record the interview.
- Learn all you can about the person you will interview or the topic you want information on.
- Prepare a list of questions. Create questions that encourage detailed responses instead of yes-or-no answers. Arrange your questions in order from most important to least important.
- Arrive on time with everything you need.

Conduct the Interview

- Ask your questions clearly and listen to the responses carefully. Give the person whom you are interviewing plenty of time to answer.
- Be flexible; follow up on any responses you find interesting.
- Avoid arguments; be tactful and polite.

- Even if you record an interview, take notes on important points.
- Thank the person for the interview, and ask if you can call with any follow-up questions.

Follow Up on the Interview

- Summarize your notes or make a written copy of the recording as soon as possible.
- If any points are unclear or if information is missing, call and ask more questions.
- Think about whether the interviewee was a credible (reliable and trustworthy) source. If the person has a slanted or biased view of things—in other words, if he or she unfairly favors one side over another—you may need to do more research or interview other people.
- If possible, have the person you interviewed review your work to make sure you haven't misrepresented what he or she said.
- Send a thank-you note to the person in appreciation of his or her time and effort.

Evaluate an Interview
- Did you get the type of information you wanted?
- Were your most important questions answered to your satisfaction?
- Were you able to keep the person being interviewed focused on the subject?
- Was the person you interviewed a credible, reliable source?

4 Active Listening

Active listening is the process of receiving, interpreting, evaluating, and responding to a message. When you listen to a class discussion or a formal speech, use the following strategies to get as much as you can from the message.

Before Listening

- Learn what the topic is beforehand. You may need to read background information or learn new terms to understand the speaker's message.
- Think about what you know or want to know about the topic.

- Have a pen and paper to take notes.
- Establish a purpose. Are you listening to learn something new, to make up your mind about a controversial issue, or just to be entertained?

While Listening

- Focus your attention on the speaker. Your facial expressions and body language should demonstrate your interest. Try to ignore uncomfortable room temperature and noise.
- Listen for the speaker's purpose (usually stated at the beginning), which alerts you to main ideas.
- To help you understand the speaker's message, listen for words or phrases that signal important points, such as *to begin with, in addition, most important, finally,* and *in conclusion.*
- Listen carefully for explanations of unfamiliar terms. Use these terms to help you understand the speaker's message.
- Listen for ideas that are repeated for emphasis.
- Take notes. Write down only the most important points.
- If possible, use an outline or list format to organize main ideas and supporting points.
- Note comparisons and contrasts, causes and effects, or problems and solutions.
- As you take notes, use phrases, abbreviations, and symbols to keep up with the speaker.
- To aid your understanding, note how the speaker uses word choice, voice pitch, posture, and gestures to convey meaning.

After Listening

- Ask questions to clarify anything that was unclear or confusing.
- Review your notes right away to make sure you understand what was said.
- Summarize and paraphrase the speaker's ideas.
- You may also wish to compare your interpretation of the speech with the interpretations of others who listened to it.

4.1 CRITICAL LISTENING

Critical listening involves evaluating a spoken message to judge its accuracy and reliability. You can use the following strategies as you listen to messages from public speakers:

- **Determine Purpose and Point of View** Think about the speaker's background knowledge, point of view or perspective on the issue, and possible motives. Separate facts from opinions, and listen carefully to details and supporting evidence. Paraphrasing the speaker's purpose and point of view can help you evaluate the speaker's message.

- **Listen for the Main Idea** Figure out the speaker's main message before allowing yourself to be distracted by seemingly convincing facts and details. To evaluate a speaker's credibility, look for anything that may indicate bias, such as material that is unfairly slanted or contains a hidden agenda.

- **Recognize the Use of Persuasive Techniques** Speakers may present information in a particular way to persuade you to buy a product or accept an idea. Persuasive devices such as bandwagon or snob appeal may provide misleading information.

*For more information, see **Recognizing Persuasive Techniques**, pages R21–R22.*

- **Observe Nonverbal Messages** A speaker's gestures, facial expressions, and tone of voice should reinforce the message. If they don't, you should doubt the speaker's sincerity and his or her message's reliability.

- **Ask Relevant Questions** During or after a presentation, ask questions about the content (what the speaker said), delivery (how he or she said it), and purpose (why he or she said it).

- **Give Appropriate Feedback** An effective speaker looks for verbal and nonverbal cues from you, the listener, to see how the message is being received. For example, if you understand or agree with the message, you might nod your head. If possible, during or after a presentation, ask questions to check your understanding.

4.2 VERBAL FEEDBACK

At times you will be asked to give direct feedback to a speaker. You may be asked to evaluate the way the speaker delivers the presentation as well as the content of the presentation.

Evaluate Delivery

- Did the speaker speak clearly and distinctly?
- Did the speaker pronounce words correctly?
- Did the speaker vary his or her rate of speaking?
- Did the speaker's voice sound natural and not strained?
- Was the speaker's voice loud enough?

Evaluate Content

Here's how to give constructive suggestions for improvement:

Be Specific Instead of vague statements like "Your charts need work," offer concrete suggestions, such as "Please make the type bigger so we can read the chart from the back of the room."

Discuss Only the Most Important Points Don't overload the speaker with too much feedback about too many details. Focus on important points, such as

- Is the topic too advanced for the audience?
- Are the supporting details well organized?
- Is the conclusion strong or weak?

Give Balanced Feedback Tell the speaker not only what didn't work but also what did work: "Consider dropping the last two slides, since you covered those points earlier. The first two slides really got my attention."

Media images and messages—from television, radio, and movies to newspapers and the Internet—are all around us. With so many options, it's important to be a smart media consumer. People who are media literate know what media products are, what they mean, and who created them. They are able to analyze and evaluate the way media messages influence the world. This section introduces some of the tools you'll need to study different forms of media.

COMMON CORE

Included in this handbook:
RI 7, SL 2, SL 3

1 Five Core Concepts in Media Literacy

from The Center for Media Literacy

The five core concepts of media literacy provide you with the basic ideas you can consider when examining media messages.

All media messages are "constructed." All media messages are made by someone. In fact, they are carefully thought out and researched and have attitudes and values built into them. Much of the information that you use to make sense of the world comes from the media. Therefore, it is important to know how a medium is put together so you can better understand the message it conveys.

Media messages are constructed using a creative language with its own rules. Each means of communication—whether it is film, television, newspapers, magazines, radio, or the Internet—has its own language and design. Therefore, the message must use the language and design of the medium that delivers the message. Thus, the medium actually shapes the message. For example, a horror film may use music to heighten suspense, or a newspaper may use a big headline to signal the importance of a story. Understanding the language of each medium can increase your enjoyment of it, as well as help you recognize any subtle attempt to persuade you.

Different people experience the same media messages differently. Personal factors such as age, education, and experience will affect the way a person responds to a media message. How many times has your interpretation of a film or book differed from that of a friend? Everyone interprets media messages differently.

Media messages have embedded values and points of view. Media messages carry underlying values, which are purposely built into them by the creators of the message. For example, a commercial's main purpose may be to persuade you to buy something, but the commercial may also aim to convince you that the product is important to a particular way of life. Understanding not only the main message but also any other points of view will help you decide whether to accept or reject the message.

Most media messages are constructed to gain profit and/or power. The creators of media messages often provide a commodity, such as information or entertainment, in order to make money. The bigger the audience, the more the media outlet can charge for advertising. Consequently, media outlets want to build large audiences in order to bring in more revenue from advertising. For example, a television network will create programming to appeal to the largest audience possible, in the hope that the viewer ratings will attract more advertising dollars.

2 Media Basics

2.1 MESSAGE

When a film or TV show is created, it becomes a media product. Each media product is created to send a **message,** or an expression of a belief or opinion, that serves a specific purpose. In order to understand the message, you will need to deconstruct it.

Deconstruction is the process of analyzing a media presentation. To analyze a media presentation you will need to ask why and how it was created, who created it, and whom it is trying to influence.

2.2 AUDIENCE

A **target audience** is the specific group of people that a product or presentation is aimed at. The members of a target audience usually share certain characteristics, such as age, gender, ethnic background, values, or lifestyle. For example, a target audience may be 11-to-14-year-olds who carry backpacks to school.

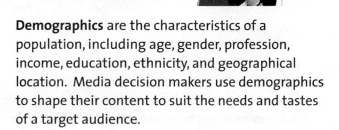

Sturdy-Paks hold EVERYTHING.
Tough and stylish, they're the perfect backpack for busy, busy students

Demographics are the characteristics of a population, including age, gender, profession, income, education, ethnicity, and geographical location. Media decision makers use demographics to shape their content to suit the needs and tastes of a target audience.

2.3 PURPOSE

The **purpose,** or intent, of a media presentation is the reason it was made. All media products—from news programs to video games—are created for a specific purpose. Identifying why a media product was invented is the first step in understanding how it can influence you. The following chart shows purposes of different media products.

Purposes of Media Products	
Purpose	**Example**
Inform	news reports and articles, public service announcements, some Web sites
Persuade	advertisements, editorials, reviews, political cartoons
Entertain	most TV shows, films, recorded music; video games; most talk shows

Most media products have more than one purpose. For example, TV commercials are often entertaining, but their main purpose is to persuade you to buy something. If you aren't aware of all of a media product's purposes, you may become influenced without knowing it. This chart shows some examples.

Main and Other Purposes in Media		
Media Product	**Main Purpose**	**Other Purposes**
News broadcast	to inform	to persuade you that an issue or idea is important
Advertisement	to persuade	to entertain you; to inform you about a product
Sports coverage	to entertain	to inform you about sports or athletes

2.4 TYPES AND GENRES OF MEDIA

The term *media* refers to television, newspapers, magazines, radio, movies, and the Internet. Each is a **medium,** or means for carrying information, entertainment, and advertisements to a large audience.

Media Tools THiNK central

Go to thinkcentral.com.
KEYWORD: HML8-R87

Each type of media has different characteristics, strengths, and weaknesses. The following chart shows how several types of media deliver their messages.

Type of Media	Characteristics
Newspaper article	• Provides detailed information and dramatic photographs • Uses **headlines** and **subheads** to give main ideas • Can't be updated until next edition or next day
Television news report	• Uses an **announcer,** or "anchor," to guide viewers through the news report • Uses **video footage** to bring news to life or clarify what happened • Uses **graphics** to give information at a glance • Can be updated quickly
Documentary	• Tells about historic people and places, major events, and important social, political, or environmental issues • Uses **footage,** or shots of photographs, interviews, news reports, and film clips, to help viewers understand the subject • Features **interviews** of experts or people directly involved with the subject • Uses a **voice-over narrator,** the voice of an unseen speaker, who tells viewers why the subject is important and how the information about the subject is organized
Web site	• Gives in-depth information on specialized subjects • Uses **text, still images,** and **video** • Allows users to select the information they want to receive by clicking on links • Allows users to see when the site was last updated • Can be updated quickly

For more information, see **Types of Media,** *page 10.*

2.5 PRODUCERS AND CREATORS

People who control the media are known as **gatekeepers.** Gatekeepers decide what information to share with the public and the ways it will be presented. This diagram gives some examples.

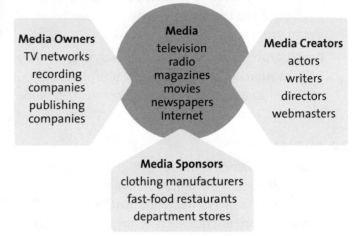

Media sponsors are companies that pay for their products to be advertised. It's important to be aware of sponsors and other gatekeepers, because they control much of what you see and hear. For example, suppose a television network executive disagrees with a particular computer company's business philosophy. As a result, she might decide not to let that company advertise on her network.

2.6 INFLUENCE OF MEDIA

Everywhere you go, you're bombarded by the media—advertisements, newspapers, magazines, radio, and television. Different kinds of media are all competing for your attention, telling you, "Buy this product. Listen to this music. Read this story. Look at this image. Think about this opinion." These media products are usually designed to sell you something. But they may also be sending subtle messages about values that they want you to believe in. Soda ads, for example, are intended to sell soda, but if you examine them closely, you will see that they often try to appeal to a set of values or a certain lifestyle. One message of the ad is that if you drink this soda, you will have as much fun as the people in the ad. The other message is that this lifestyle is good and desirable. TV shows, movies, and news programs also convey values and beliefs.

Media can also shape your opinions about the world. For example, news about crime shapes our understanding about how much and what type of crime is prevalent in the world around us. TV news items, talk show interviews, and commercials may shape what we think of a political candidate, a celebrity, an ethnic group, a country, or a region. As a result, our knowledge of someone or someplace could be completely based on the information we receive from television.

3 Film and TV

Films and television programs come in a variety of types. Films include comedies, dramas, documentaries, and animated features. Televison programs cover dramas, sitcoms, talk shows, reality shows, newscasts, and so on. Producers of films and producers of television programs rely on many of the same elements to make the action and settings seem real and to also affect the emotions of their audiences. Among these elements are scripts, visual and sound elements, special effects, and editing.

3.1 SCRIPT AND WRITTEN ELEMENTS

The writer and editor develop a story for television or film using a script and storyboard. A **script** is the text or words of a film or television show. A **storyboard** is a device used to plan the shooting of a movie or TV show. A storyboard is made up of drawings and brief descriptions of what is happening in each shot of a scene. The drawings of a storyboard help a director visualize how a finished scene might look before the scene is filmed. This storyboard shows some scenes that a student created.

"Runners, take your places at the starting line!"

Medium shot of Squeaky getting ready

*For more information, see **Media Study: Produce Your Own Media**, page 265.*

3.2 VISUAL ELEMENTS

Visual elements in film and television include camera shots and angles. A **camera shot** is a single, continuous view taken by a camera. A **camera angle** is the angle at which the camera is positioned during the recording of a shot or image. Each is carefully planned to create an effect. This chart shows what different shots are used for.

Camera Shot/Angle	Effect
Establishing shot introduces viewers to the location of a scene, usually by presenting a wide view of an area	establishes the setting of a film
Close-up shot shows a close view of a person or object	helps to create emotion and make viewers feel as if they know the character
Medium shot shows a view wider than a close-up but narrower than an establishing or long shot	shows part of an object, or a character from the knees or waist up
Long shot gives a wide view of a scene, showing the full figure(s) of a person or group and the surroundings	allows the viewer to see the "big picture" and shows the relationship between characters and the environment
Reaction shot shows in some way what the subject sees	allows the viewer to see how the subject feels in order to create empathy in the viewer
Low-angle shot looks up at an object or person	makes a character, object, or scene appear more important or threatening
High-angle shot looks down on an object or person	makes a character, object, or scene seem weak or unimportant
Point-of-view (POV) shot shows a part of the story through a character's eyes	helps viewers identify with that character

3.3 SOUND ELEMENTS

Sound elements in film and television include music, voice-over, and sound effects.

Music may be used to set the mood and atmosphere in a scene. Music can have a powerful effect on the way viewers feel about a story. For example, fast-paced music helps viewers feel excited during an action scene.

Voice-over is the voice of the unseen commentator or narrator of a film, TV program, or commercial.

Sound effects are the sounds added to films, TV programs, and commercials during the editing process. Sound effects, such as laugh tracks or the sounds of punches in a fight scene, can create humor, emphasize a point, or contribute to the mood.

3.4 SPECIAL EFFECTS

Special effects include computer-generated animation, manipulated video images, and fast- or slow-motion sequences in films, TV programs, and commercials.

Animation on film involves the frame-by-frame photography of a series of drawings or objects. When these frames are projected—at a rate of 24 per second—the illusion of movement is achieved.

A **split screen** is a special-effects shot in which two or more separate images are shown in the same frame. One example is when two people, actually a distance apart, are shown talking to each other.

3.5 EDITING

Editing is the process of selecting and arranging shots in a sequence. Moviemakers put shots together in ways that help you follow the action of a story. The editor decides which scenes or shots to use, as well as the length of each shot, the number of shots, and their sequence.

Cut is the transition from one shot to another. To create excitement, editors often use quick cuts, which are a series of short shots strung together.

Dissolve is a device in which one scene fades into another.

Fade-in is a device in which a white or black shot fades in to reveal the beginning of a new scene.

Fade-out is a device in which a shot fades to darkness to end a scene.

Jump cut is an abrupt and jarring change from one shot to another. A jump cut shows a break in time.

Pace is the length of time each shot stays on the screen and the rhythm that is created by the transitions between shots. Short, quick cuts create a fast pace in a story. Long cuts slow down a story.

4 News

The **news** is information on events, people, and places in your community, the region, the nation, and the world. It can be found in local newspapers, newscasts, online wire services, magazines, and documentaries. Because it's impossible to publish all the news that happens in one day in any one source, journalists have to decide which stories will appear in newspapers and on newscasts.

4.1 CHOOSING THE NEWS

Newsworthiness is the importance of an event or action that makes it worthy of media reporting. Journalists and their editors often use the following criteria in determining which stories should make the news:

Timeliness is the quality of being very current. Timely events usually take priority over previously reported events. For example, a tornado that strikes a residential area will be timely on the day it occurs. It may be on the front page of a newspaper or may be the lead story on a newscast.

Widespread impact is a characteristic of an event that could affect a large number of people. The more widespread the impact of an event, the more likely it is to be newsworthy.

Proximity measures the nearness of an event to a particular city, region, or country. People tend to be more interested in stories that take place close to where they live and that thus may affect them.

Human interest is a quality of stories that causes readers or listeners to feel emotions such as happiness, anger, or sadness. People are interested in reading stories about other people.

Uniqueness means being the only one of a kind. Unique or uncommon events or circumstances are likely to be interesting to an audience.

Compelling video and **photographs** grab people's attention and stay in their minds. News photographers take photographs and shoot video footage that can provide valuable information and affect your opinions and impressions of an issue.

4.2 REPORTING THE NEWS

While developing a news story, a journalist decides what information to include and how to organize it. The following elements are commonly used in news stories:

5 *W*'s and *H* are the six questions reporters ask—*who, what, when, where, why,* and *how.* It is a journalist's job to answer these questions in any type of news report. These questions also provide a structure for writing and editing a story.

Inverted pyramid is the means of organizing information according to importance. In the diagram below, the most important information (the answers to the 5 *W*'s and *H*) appears at the top. Less important details appear at the bottom. Not all stories are reported using this form. It remains popular, however, because it helps a reader to get the important information without reading the entire story.

A new study suggests that regular exercise is key to keeping cholesterol levels low.

Patients who exercised 30 minutes per day for one year decreased their cholesterol levels significantly.

Researchers also suggested easy ways for people to get 30 minutes of activity daily.

Angle or slant is the point of view from which a story is written. Even an objective report must have an angle.

Consider these two headlines that describe the same crime story.

Painting Stolen from City Museum

Police Fail to Prevent Museum Theft

The first headline focuses on a fact. The second headline focuses on an opinion and has a negative slant.

Standards for News Reporting

The ideal of journalism is to present news in a way that is objective, accurate, and thorough. The best news stories contain the following elements:

- **Objectivity** The story takes a balanced point of view on the issues. It is not biased, nor does it reflect a specific attitude or opinion.
- **Accuracy** The story presents factual information that can be verified.
- **Thoroughness** The story presents all sides of an issue. It includes background information, telling *who, what, when, where, why,* and *how.*

Balanced Versus Biased Reporting

Objectivity in news reporting can be measured by how balanced or biased the story is.

Balanced reporting represents all sides of an issue equally and fairly. A balanced news story

- represents people and subjects in a neutral light
- treats all sides of an issue equally
- does not include inappropriate questions, such as "Why should we take pity on this thief?"
- does not show stereotypes or prejudice toward any particular race, gender, age, or religion
- does not leave out important background information that is needed to establish a context or perspective

Biased reporting is reporting in which one side is favored over another or in which the subject is unfairly represented. Biased reporting may show an overly negative view of a subject, or it may encourage racial, gender, or other stereotypes and prejudices. Sometimes biased reporting is apparent in the journalist's choice of sources.

Hidden agenda means having a concealed interest or preference. If a reporter opposes a local construction project, she may ignore information from property developer on how the company will protect wildlife. Her news story leaves out important information, which means that it is slanted—it unfairly favors one side over the other.

Sources are the people interviewed for the news report and also any written materials and documents the journalist used for background information. From each source, the journalist gets a different point of view. To decide whether news reporting is balanced or biased, you will need to pay attention to the sources. Consider a news story on a new type of diet book. If the only source given in the story is the person who wrote the book, then the report may be biased. But if the journalist also includes the perspective of someone neutral and informed, such as a nutritionist, then the report may be more balanced. This chart shows which sources are generally considered reliable, and which tend to be considered weak.

Sources for News Stories	
Reliable sources	**Weak sources**
• experts in a field • people directly affected by the reported event (eyewitnesses) • published reports that are specifically mentioned or shown	• unnamed or anonymous sources • people who are not involved in the reported event (for example, people who heard about a story from a friend) • research, data, or reports that are not specifically named or are referred to only in vague terms (for example, "Research shows that …")

5 Advertising

Advertising is a sponsor's paid use of various media to promote products, services, or ideas. Some common forms of advertising are shown in the chart.

Type of Ad	Description
Billboard	a large outdoor advertising sign
Print ad	typically appears in magazines and newspapers; uses eye-catching graphics and persuasive copy
Flyer	a print ad that is circulated by hand or mail
Infomercial	an extended ad on TV that usually includes detailed product information, demonstrations, and testimonials
Public service announcement	a message aired on radio or TV to promote ideas that are considered to be in the public interest
Political ad	a broadcast on radio or TV to promote political candidates
Trailer	a short film promoting an upcoming movie, TV show, or video game

Marketing is the process of transferring products and services from producer to consumer. It involves determining the packaging and pricing of a product, how it will be promoted and advertised, and where it will be sold. One way companies market their products is by becoming media sponsors.

Sponsors pay for their products to be advertised. These companies hire advertising agencies to create and produce specific campaigns for their products. They then buy television or radio airtime or magazine, newspaper, or billboard space to feature ads where the target audience is sure to see them. Because selling time and space to advertisers produces much of the income the media need to function, the media need advertisers just as much as advertisers need the media.

Product placement is the intentional and identifiable featuring of brand-name products in movies, television shows, video games, and other media. The intention is to have viewers feel positive about a product because they see a favorite character using it. Another purpose may be to promote product recognition.

5.1 PERSUASIVE TECHNIQUES

Persuasive techniques are the methods used to convince an audience to buy a product or adopt an idea. Advertisers use a combination of visuals, sound, special effects, and words to persuade their target audience. Recognizing the following techniques can help you evaluate persuasive media messages and identify biased, slanted, or otherwise misleading information:

Emotional appeals use strong feelings, such as fear and pity, rather than facts to persuade consumers. An example of an appeal to fear might be, "Is your water safe to drink? Our filter system will help you be sure."

Bandwagon appeals use the argument that a person should believe or do something because "everyone else" does. These appeals take advantage of people's desire to be socially accepted by other people. An example of a bandwagon appeal is "Find out why everyone's talking about the hit film *A Two-Hour Story About Some Funny Characters*."

Slogans are memorable phrases used in advertising campaigns. Slogans substitute catchy phrases for facts.

Logical appeals rely on logic and facts, appealing to a consumer's reason and his or her respect for authority. Two examples of logical appeals are expert opinions and product comparison.

Celebrity ads use one of the following two categories of spokesperson:

- **Celebrity authorities** are experts in a particular field. Advertisers hope that audiences will transfer the admiration they have for the person to the product. For example, a famous athlete might endorse a particular energy drink. The company selling the drink wants people to think it must work, since an athlete wouldn't want an energy drink that didn't help her perform well.

- **Celebrity spokespeople** are famous people who endorse a product. Advertisers hope that audiences will associate the product with the celebrity.

Product comparison is comparing between a product and its competition. Often mentioned by name, the competing product is portrayed as inferior. The intended effect is for people to question the quality of the competing product and to believe the featured product is better.

6 Elements of Design

The design of a media message is just as important as the words are in conveying the message. Like words, visuals are used to persuade, inform, and entertain.

Graphics and images, such as charts, diagrams, maps, timelines, photographs, illustrations, and symbols, present information that can be quickly and easily understood. The following basic elements are used to give meaning to visuals:

Color can be used to highlight important elements such as headlines and subheads. It can also create mood, because many colors have strong emotional or psychological impacts on the reader or viewer. For example, warm colors are often associated with happiness and comfort. Cool colors are often associated with feelings of peace and contentment or sometimes with sadness.

Lines—strokes or marks—can be thick or thin, long or short, and smooth or jagged. They can focus attention and create a feeling of depth. They can frame an object. They can also direct a viewer's eye or create a sense of motion.

Texture is the surface quality or appearance of an object. For example, an object's texture can be rough, wet, or shiny. Texture can be used to create contrast. It can also be used to make an object look "real." For example, wallpaper patterns can create a sense of depth, smoothness, or roughness, even though the texture is only visual and cannot be felt.

Shape is the external outline of an object. Shapes can be used to symbolize living things or geometric objects. They can emphasize visual elements and add interest. Shapes can symbolize ideas.

Notice how this movie poster uses design elements.

Lines Vertical lines guide the reader's eye upward to the lighted windows. This also helps create the visual perspective of a small person looking up at the large building.

Color Dark blues and grays suggest that the film may tell a scary story.

Shape The angular shapes and the placement of the two bright yellow windows combine to make the house look like a face with an evil grin.

The next time you see an advertisement, think about how the graphic artist or illustrator used colors, shapes, and lines to transmit information. Did the visuals affect what you thought or how you felt?

7 Evaluating Media Messages

By looking closely at media products, you can see how their messages influence your opinions and your buying habits. Here are six questions to ask about any media message:

Who made—and who sponsored—this message, and for what purpose? The source of the message is a clue to its purpose. If the source of the message is a private company, that company may be trying to sell you a product. If the source is a government agency, that agency may be trying to promote a program or particular point of view. To discover the purpose, think about why its creator paid for and produced the message.

Who is the target audience, and how is the message specifically tailored to it? Think about the age group, ethnic group, gender, and/or profession the message is targeting. Decide how it relates to you.

What are the different techniques used to inform, persuade, entertain, and attract attention? Analyze the elements, such as humor, music, special effects, and graphics, that have been used to create the message. Think about how visual and sound effects, such as symbols, color, photographs, words, and music, support the purpose behind the message.

What messages are communicated (and/or implied) about certain people, places, events, behaviors, lifestyles, and so forth? The media try to influence who we are, what we believe in, how we view things, and what values we hold. Look or listen closely to determine whether certain types of behavior are being depicted and if judgments or values are communicated through those behaviors. What are the biases or hidden agendas in the message?

How current, accurate, and believable is the information in this message? Think about the reputation of the source. Note the broadcast or publication date of the message and whether the message might change quickly. If a report or account is not supported by facts, authoritative sources, or eyewitness accounts, you should question the message.

What is left out of this message that might be important to know? Think about what the message is asking you to believe. Also think about what questions come to mind as you watch, read, or listen to the message.

Strategies and Practice for State and Standardized Tests

The test items in this section are modeled after test formats that are used on many state and standardized tests. The strategies presented here will help you prepare for these tests. This section offers general test-taking strategies and tips for answering multiple-choice items, as well as short constructed response and extended constructed response questions in critical reading and writing. It also includes guidelines and samples for essay writing. For each test, read the tips in the margin. Then apply the tips to the practice items. You can also apply the tips to Assessment Practice Tests in this book.

1 General Test-Taking Strategies

- Arrive on time and be prepared. Be sure to bring either sharpened pencils with erasers or pens—whichever you are told to bring.

- If you have any questions, ask them before the test begins. Make sure you understand the test procedures, the timing, and the rules.

- Read the test directions carefully. Look at the passages and questions to get an overview of what is expected.

- Tackle the questions one at a time rather than thinking about the whole test.

- Look for main ideas as you read passages. They are often stated at the beginning or the end of a paragraph. Sometimes the main idea is implied.

- Refer back to the reading selections as needed. For example, if a question asks about an author's attitude, you might have to reread a passage for clues.

- If you are not sure of your answer, make a logical guess. You can often arrive at the correct answer by reasoning and eliminating wrong answers.

- As you fill in answers on your answer sheet, make sure you match each test item to its numbered space on the answer sheet.

- Don't look for patterns in the positions of correct choices.

- Only change an answer if you are sure your original choice is incorrect. If you do change an answer, erase your original choice neatly and thoroughly.

- Check your answers and reread your essay.

2 Critical Reading

As you advance into high school, you will be exposed to different types of writing, both fiction and nonfiction. You will read novels, persuasive essays, poems, historical documents, and scientific or technical information. Tests will measure your ability to read and analyze these kinds of writings. Test selections can range in length from 100 words to 500 or 600 words.

> **Directions:** Read the selection and then answer the questions on the following page.

SELECTION

Walt has walked all the fourteen years of his life in suntanned, moose-hide moccasins, and he can go to the Indian camps and "talk big" with the men, and trade calico and beads with them for their precious furs. He can make bread without baking powder, yeast, or hops, shoot a moose at three hundred yards, and drive the wild wolf dogs fifty miles a day on the packed trail.

Last of all, he has a good heart, and is not afraid of the darkness and loneliness, of man or beast or thing. His father is a good man, strong and brave, and Walt is growing up like him.

Walt was born a thousand miles or so down the Yukon, in a trading post
10 below the Ramparts. After his mother died, his father and he came up on the river, step by step, from camp to camp, till now they are settled down on the Mazy May Creek in the Klondike country. Last year they and several others had spent much toil and time on the Mazy May, and endured great hardships; the creek, in turn, was just beginning to show up its richness and to reward them for their heavy labor. But with the news of their discoveries, strange men began to come and go through the short days and long nights, and many unjust things they did to the men who had worked so long upon the creek.

Si Hartman had gone away on a moose hunt, to return and find new
20 stakes driven and his claim jumped. George Lukens and his brother had lost their claims in a like manner, having delayed too long on the way to Dawson to record them. In short, it was the old story, and quite a number of the earnest, industrious prospectors had suffered similar losses.

But Walt Masters's father had recorded his claim at the start, so Walt had nothing to fear now that his father had gone on a short trip up the White River prospecting for quartz. Walt was well able to stay by himself in the cabin, cook his three meals a day, and look after things. Not only did he look after his father's claim, but he had agreed to keep an eye on the adjoining one of Loren Hall, who had started for Dawson to record it.

30 Loren Hall was an old man, and he had no dogs, so he had to travel very slowly. After he had been gone some time, word came up the river that he had broken through the ice at Rosebud Creek and frozen his feet so badly that he would not be able to travel for a couple of weeks. Then Walt Masters received the news that old Loren was nearly all right again, and about to move on afoot for Dawson as fast as a weakened man could.

Tips: Reading Text

❶ Before reading a passage, skim the questions that follow it to help you focus your reading.

❷ Look for key ideas as you read. Competition and fairness are key ideas in this passage.

❸ Make predictions. The passage tells you that Walt is brave, strong, and resourceful. You can predict that he will be all right while his father and Loren Hall are gone.

❹ Pay attention to the connotation of words. For example, the word *stampede* in line 37 suggests something frenzied and out of control. The word is usually applied to a herd of wild animals. Here, its connotation helps describe the ruthless newcomers to the Klondike country.

Walt was worried, however; the claim was liable to be jumped at any moment because of the delay, and a fresh stampede had started in on Mazy May. He did not like the looks of the newcomers, and one day, when five of them came by with crack dog teams and the lightest of camping outfits, he could see they were prepared to make speed, and resolved to keep an eye on them. So he locked up the cabin and followed them, being at the same time careful to remain hidden.

40

④

—from "The King of Mazy May"
by Jack London

Directions: Answer these questions about the selection from "The King of Mazy May."

① stem

1. What can you infer about life in the Klondike from the description in lines 1–18?
   A. People need to use many skills to survive.
   B. The Klondike is a lonely place for most people.
   C. The competition for land makes people dishonest.
   D. Families purchase all of their supplies at trading posts.

2. The author characterizes Walt by presenting **②**
   A. a description of his physical appearance
   B. the narrator's direct comments about him
   C. Walt's thoughts and actions
   D. other characters' opinions of him.

3. The main conflict in this passage involves
   ③ choices
   A. finding a place to trade rare furs
   B. traveling to town in dangerous weather
   C. protecting land from prospecting thieves
   D. hunting for moose along Mazy May Creek

4. Which is an effect of Loren Hall's accident? **④**
   A. Walt must stay alone in the cabin.
   B. Loren is delayed on his way to Dawson.
   C. Loren returns home instead of going to Dawson. **⑤**
   D. The Masters's claim is jumped.

Tips: Multiple Choice

A multiple-choice question consists of a stem and a set of choices. The stem is in the form of a question or an incomplete sentence. One of the choices correctly answers the question or completes the sentence. Many tests offer four answer choices, but no matter how many choices are given, you can use the same strategies to guide you to the best answer.

① Read the stem carefully and try to answer the question before you look at the choices.

② Pay attention to key words in the stem. They may direct you to the correct answer. In question 2, the word *characterizes* tells you to think about how the author develops Walt's character.

③ Read all of the choices before deciding on an answer. In question 3, you might decide to stop at choice B, because Loren Hall falls through the ice on the way to town. The main conflict, however, is about protecting land, not about Hall's difficult trip.

④ Some questions ask you to identify cause-and-effect relationships.

⑤ After reading all of the choices, eliminate any that you know are incorrect. In question 4, you can safely reject choice C, because the passage states that Loren was going to continue on to Dawson.

Answers: 1. C, **2.** B, **3.** C, **4.** B

3 Vocabulary

Most standardized tests include items that ask about the meanings of words. Some questions might refer to a passage you just read, while others might provide a sentence or paragraph followed by the answer choices.

1. Which of the following words from the passage on pages R96–R97 has a negative connotation? ❶
   A. calico (line 3)
   B. toil (line 13)
   C. industrious (line 23)
   D. careful (line 42)

2. Which word from the passage might include the Latin root meaning "hard"?
   A. endured (line 13) ❷
   B. earnest (line 23)
   C. adjoining (line 29)
   D. liable (line 36)

3. In line 28 of the passage, the idiom *keep an eye on* means ❸
   A. report to
   B. think about
   C. watch over
   D. measure

4. Read this dictionary entry for the word *claim*. Which definition represents the meaning of *claim* as used in the passage?

> **DEFINITION**
>
> *v.* **1.** To demand or ask for. **2.** To state to be true; assert. *n.* **1.** A demand for something as due. **2.** Something claimed in a legal manner, especially a tract of public land. **3.** A statement of something as true.

   A. *v.* meaning 1 ❹
   B. *n.* meaning 1
   C. *n.* meaning 2
   D. *n.* meaning 3

Tips: Word Meaning

❶ Connotation is the suggestion or feeling a word carries beyond its literal meaning. *Work* is a neutral word. *Effort* is a more positive word for work, but the word *toil* has a negative connotation.

❷ If you don't know the exact meaning of a word, look for clues in nearby sentences. For the word *endured* in line 13, read the description in the surrounding paragraph. Choice A is the best answer, because the passage is describing hard work and the difficult times the characters lived through.

❸ An idiom is an expression that has a meaning different from the meanings of its individual words. Since Walt is not literally keeping one of his eyes at Loren's claim, you can use context clues to help you figure out the meaning of the idiom *keep an eye on*. Some idioms can be found in the dictionary.

❹ Eliminate any answers that are not the same part of speech as the meaning of the word in the passage. *Claim* is used as a noun in the passsage, so you can rule out answer choice A.

Answers: 1. B, **2.** A, **3.** C, **4.** C

4 Writing and Language

You will be asked to write many essays and research papers in middle school and high school. When it comes to writing, good ideas aren't enough. You need to know how to express them. That requires knowledge of English grammar, sentence structure, and usage. To measure that skill, many standardized tests ask you to identify errors or to improve sentences and paragraphs.

Directions: Read this passage and then answer the questions.

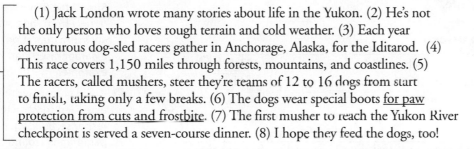

PASSAGE

(1) Jack London wrote many stories about life in the Yukon. (2) He's not the only person who loves rough terrain and cold weather. (3) Each year adventurous dog-sled racers gather in Anchorage, Alaska, for the Iditarod. (4) This race covers 1,150 miles through forests, mountains, and coastlines. (5) The racers, called mushers, steer they're teams of 12 to 16 dogs from start to finish, taking only a few breaks. (6) The dogs wear special boots <u>for paw protection from cuts and frostbite</u>. (7) The first musher to reach the Yukon River checkpoint is served a seven-course dinner. (8) I hope they feed the dogs, too!

1. The correct coordinating conjunction to join sentences 1 and 2 is
   - **A.** but
   - **B.** for
   - **C.** or
   - **D.** so

2. What change, if any, should be made to sentence 5?
   - **A.** Change *steer* to *steers*.
   - **B.** Change *they're* to *their*.
   - **C.** Change *teams* to *team*.
   - **D.** Make no change.

3. What is the best way to rewrite the underlined part of sentence 6?
   - **A.** for cuts and frostbite protection on paws
   - **B.** to protect their paws from cuts and frostbite
   - **C.** for the protection of paws from cuts and frostbite
   - **D.** in order to protect from cuts and frostbite on paws

4. What change, if any, should be made to sentence 7?
   - **A.** Change *reach* to *reaches*.
   - **B.** Change *is* to *are*.
   - **C.** Change *served* to *serving*.
   - **D.** Make no change.

Tips: Grammar

1. Read the entire passage to grasp its overall meaning. Pay particular attention to any underlined parts.

2. If you are asked to combine sentences, think about how the ideas relate to each other. Use the coordinating conjunction *or* to introduce a choice. The words *for* or *so* indicate cause and effect. The word *but* expresses contrasting ideas. When you understand the connection between the two sentences, you will know which word best joins them.

3. Some items will test your knowledge of commonly confused words. Read sentences carefully to determine how each word is used before deciding which choice is best.

4. Before choosing a revision, read through all of the choices to decide which one is best. Your selection should produce a sentence that is grammatically correct.

5. Some items will test your knowledge of language conventions. Make sure that pronouns agree with antecedents and that verbs agree with subjects.

6. In test item 4, choice D says, "Make no change." Choose this answer only if the sentence is correct as it is originally written.

Answers: 1. A, **2.** B, **3.** B, **4.** D

5 Responding to Writing Prompts

Not all tests are multiple choice. Sometimes you have to develop your ideas into a paragraph or a short essay. You might be asked to interpret, summarize, or react to a reading selection.

> **Directions:** Reread the selection from "The King of Mazy May" on pages R96–R97 and follow the directions for the short and extended responses.

SHORT CONSTRUCTED RESPONSE

Write a well-organized paragraph comparing and contrasting the prospectors and the men of the "stampede."

SAMPLE SHORT CONSTRUCTED RESPONSE

The prospectors of Mazy May, such as Walt's father and Loren Hall, ❶ couldn't be more different from the claim-jumping stampeders. The prospectors "spent much toil and time" looking for gold, willing to keep ❷ working for as long as it took. The stampeders, on the other hand, seemed not to arrive until after the prospectors had worked for a year to set up their claims. The stampeders plan to steal the claims and profit from the prospectors' hard work. Walt, who risks danger to protect his neighbor's claim, is the exact opposite of the "unjust" stampeders.

EXTENDED CONSTRUCTED RESPONSE

Discuss in two or three paragraphs the effects of the setting in the selection from "The King of Mazy May."

SAMPLE EXTENDED CONSTRUCTED RESPONSE

The setting in "The King of Mazy May"—Klondike country—affects not only the story's plot, but also its characters and conflict.

❸ Walt is a product of his setting. His whole life, he has lived and worked in the cold weather and lonely conditions of the region. As a result, he's learned to be a good hunter and dog driver. He's become self-reliant because his father must leave on prospecting trips. The skills Walt develops ❹ in the Klondike are what make him able to protect his neighbor's claim.

The setting also presents specific challenges that affect the story's plot ❸ and conflict. For example, the cold water of Rosebud Creek is what delays Loren Hall on his way to Dawson, and the "short days and long nights" seem to encourage the claim jumpers. Finally, the land along the creek is what brings both the prospectors and the thieves to the area in the first place.

Tips: Responding to Writing Prompts

❶ Short constructed response prompts are often fact-based rather than interpretive. Get right to the point in your answer, and stick to the facts.

❷ Make sure that you write about the assigned topic. Support your answer with details from the passage, such as a quotation, a paraphrase, or an example.

❸ When you are writing an extended constructed response, build your paragraphs around clear topic sentences that will pull your ideas together.

❹ If you are asked to interpret a passage, don't just copy the author's words. Try to express the ideas in your own words. Express your ideas clearly so that the reader understands your viewpoint.

❺ Proofread your response for errors in capitalization, punctuation, spelling, or grammar.

6 Writing an Essay

Many tests will ask you to read a prompt and write an essay in response to it. You might be asked to write a narrative, persuasive, or expository essay. You might be asked to write a story, summarize an article, or respond to a piece of writing. It is important to read the prompt carefully and look for direction words that tell you what to write about. Because of the time constraints, an impromptu essay will not be polished. It will represent a first draft. Even so, it should be complete. Essays are scored on the following criteria:

- **Focus** Establish a point of view on your topic in the opening paragraph. Stay with that topic throughout the essay.
- **Organization** Maintain a logical progression of ideas.
- **Support for ideas** Use details and examples to develop an argument or line of thinking.
- **Style/word choice** Use words accurately and vary sentence structure.
- **Grammar** Use standard English and proofread for errors.

Writing Prompt

In 1961, the chairman of the Federal Communications Commission called television programming "a vast wasteland." Many people still feel we would be better off without television. Write a persuasive essay of four or five paragraphs supporting or rejecting this idea.

SAMPLE PERSUASIVE ESSAY

1 I don't agree that television is "a vast wasteland." A wasteland is an ugly place where nothing grows. So, if television were only a wasteland, that would mean that it never offered people anything beautiful or exciting. It would mean that there was no information or entertainment of value that people could get from watching television programs, and that just isn't the case.

It's true that there are many low-quality programs on TV. These programs don't teach us anything. Some shows, such as soap operas, don't show people or their lives the way they actually are. They exaggerate situations and rarely offer a positive or important message.

Other programs, however, offer interesting and important information about nature, science, history, the arts, sports, or current events. These educational and exciting programs can help us grow and improve ourselves. **2**

People who don't agree with me might say that TV turns us into couch potatoes. Many people do just sit in front of the television for hours, watching whatever is on, whether it's good or bad. My answer to that point of view is that we have to be responsible in choosing the programs we watch. If viewers stopped watching bad shows, those shows would eventually be canceled. **3**

In conclusion, TV can be worthwhile if we make good decisions about its use. We just have to use our heads and take charge of the remote control. **4**

Tips: Writing an Essay

Before you begin writing, take a minute or two to gather your thoughts. You don't need to prepare a complete outline, but write the main points you want to make. In the essay here on television, program quality and personal responsibility are key issues.

1 When writing a persuasive essay, state your point of view in the introduction.

2 Facts and examples make your writing come to life. Use them in the body of your essay to clarify your points and to strengthen your arguments. The writer of this essay uses examples to illustrate some possible benefits of television.

3 Try to consider the opposing viewpoint and respond to it. In the sample essay, the student notes that some people think TV "turns us into couch potatoes." Her response is that people should be responsible about what they watch.

4 Make sure your essay has a conclusion, even if it's just a single sentence. A conclusion pulls your ideas together and lets the reader know you have finished.

5 Allow time to reread what you have written. If you have to make a correction, do so neatly and legibly.

Act An act is a major division within a play, similar to a chapter in a book. Each act may be further divided into smaller sections, called scenes. Plays can have as many as five acts. *The Diary of Anne Frank* has two acts.
See page 510.

Adventure Story An adventure story is a literary work in which action is the main element. An adventure novel usually focuses on a main character who is on a mission and is facing many challenges and choices.

Alliteration Alliteration is the repetition of consonant sounds at the beginning of words. Note the repetition of the *s* sound in these lines.

> Say to them,
> say to the down-keepers,
> the sun-slappers,
> the self-soilers,
> —Gwendolyn Brooks, "Speech to the Young:
> Speech to the Progress-Toward"

See page 634.
See also **Consonance.**

Allusion An allusion is a reference to a famous person, place, event, or work of literature. In "The Drummer Boy of Shiloh" by Ray Bradbury, the general makes an allusion to the poet Henry Wadsworth Longfellow.
See page 335.

Analogy An analogy is a point-by-point comparison between two things that are alike in some respect. Often, writers use analogies in nonfiction to explain unfamiliar subjects or ideas in terms of familiar ones.
See also **Extended Metaphor; Metaphor; Simile.**

Anecdote An anecdote is a brief account of an interesting incident or event that is usually intended to entertain or make a point. "Manuscript Found in an Attic" is an example of an anecdote.
See page 62.

Antagonist The antagonist is a force working against the protagonist, or main character, in a story, play, or novel. The antagonist is usually another character but can be a force of nature, society itself, or an internal force within the main character. In Yoshiko Uchida's retelling of "The Wise Old Woman," the cruel young lord is the antagonist.
See page 490.
See also **Protagonist.**

Assonance Assonance is the repetition of vowel sounds within nonrhyming words. An example of assonance is the repetition of the short *a* sound in the following line.

> It's had tacks in it,
> —Langston Hughes, "Mother to Son"

Author's Perspective An author's perspective is the unique combination of ideas, values, feelings, and beliefs that influences the way the writer looks at a topic. Tone, or attitude, often reveals an author's perspective. Gary Soto writes "One Last Time" from a perspective that reflects his family's history of working in the fields and his teenage desire for status and acceptance.
See page 840.
See also **Author's Purpose; Tone.**

Author's Purpose A writer usually writes for one or more of these purposes: to express thoughts or feelings, to inform or explain, to persuade, and to entertain. For example, in "The Sanctuary of School," Lynda Barry's purpose is to persuade Americans to support public schools.
See also **Author's Perspective.**

Autobiography An autobiography is a writer's account of his or her own life. In almost every case, it is told from the first-person point of view. Generally, an autobiography focuses on the most significant events and people in the writer's life over a period of time.
See also **Memoir.**

Ballad A ballad is a type of narrative poem that tells a story and was originally meant to be sung or recited. Because it tells a story, a ballad has a setting, a plot, and characters. Traditional ballads are written in four-line stanzas with regular rhythm and rhyme. Folk ballads were composed orally and handed down by word of mouth. These ballads usually tell about ordinary people who have unusual adventures or perform daring deeds. A literary ballad is a poem written by a poet in imitation of the form and content of a folk ballad. "Boots of Spanish Leather" is an example of a literary ballad.

Blank Verse Blank verse is unrhymed poetry written in iambic pentameter. That is, each line of blank verse has five pairs of syllables. In most pairs, an unstressed syllable is followed by a stressed syllable. The most versatile of poetic forms, blank verse imitates the natural rhythms of English speech. Much of Shakespeare's drama is in blank verse.

Biography A biography is the true account of a person's life, written by another person. As such, biographies are usually told from a third-person point of view. The writer of a biography usually researches his or her subject in order to present accurate information. The best biographers strive for honesty and balance in their accounts of their subjects' lives. Ann Petry's *Harriet Tubman: Conductor on the Underground Railroad* is an example of a biography.
See page 268.

Cast of Characters In the script of a play, a cast of characters is a list of all the characters in the play, usually in order of appearance. It may include a brief description of each character.

Character Characters are the people, animals, or imaginary creatures who take part in the action of a work of literature. Like real people, characters display certain qualities, or character traits, that develop and change over time, and they usually have motivations, or reasons, for their behaviors.

> **Central character:** Central or main characters are the most important characters in literary works. Generally, the plot of a short story focuses on one main character, but a novel may have several main characters.

> **Minor characters:** The less important characters in a literary work are known as minor characters. The story is not centered on them, but they help carry out the action of the story and help the reader learn more about the main character.

> **Dynamic character:** A dynamic character is one who undergoes important changes as a plot unfolds. The changes occur because of the character's actions and experiences in the story. The changes are usually internal and may be good or bad. Main characters are usually, though not always, dynamic.

> **Static character:** A static character is one who remains the same throughout a story. The character may experience events and have interactions with other characters, but he or she is not changed because of them.

See page 247.
See also **Characterization; Character Traits.**

Characterization The way a writer creates and develops characters is known as characterization. There are four basic methods of characterization:

- The writer may make direct comments about a character through the voice of the narrator.
- The writer may describe the character's physical appearance.
- The writer may present the character's own thoughts, speech, and actions.
- The writer may present thoughts, speech, and actions of other characters.

See pages 267, 291.
See also **Character; Character Traits.**

Character Traits Character traits are the qualities shown by a character. Traits may be physical (brown eyes) or expressions of personality (shyness). Writers reveal the traits of their characters through methods of characterization. Sometimes writers directly state a character's traits, but more often readers need to infer traits from a character's words, actions, thoughts, appearance, and relationships. Examples of words that describe traits include *courageous, humble, generous,* and *wild.*

Climax The climax stage is the point of greatest interest in a story or play. The climax usually occurs toward the end of a story, after the reader has understood the conflict and become emotionally involved with the characters. At the climax, the conflict is resolved and the outcome of the plot usually becomes clear. For example, in Toni Cade Bambara's story "Raymond's Run," the climax occurs when Squeaky realizes that she doesn't have to win the race to prove her running skills; she can help her brother Raymond become a great runner.
See pages 30, 38.
See also **Plot.**

Comedy A comedy is a dramatic work that is light and often humorous in tone, usually ending happily with a peaceful resolution of the main conflict.

Conflict A conflict is a struggle between opposing forces. Almost every story has a main conflict—a conflict that is the story's focus. An external conflict involves a character who struggles against a force outside him- or herself, such as nature, a physical obstacle, or another character. An internal conflict is one that occurs within a character. A cultural conflict is a struggle that arises because of differing values, customs, or circumstances between groups of people.

Examples: In O. Henry's "The Ransom of Red Chief," the kidnappers are in conflict with the boy they take captive. In Laurence Yep's memoir "The Great Rat Hunt," the young Yep is torn between wanting to prove his bravery by helping his father and wanting to avoid the rat by staying with his mother. In "Out of Bounds," Rohan's family and neighbors blame the new squatters for robberies, and Rohan's parents tell him not to make contact with the squatters.
See pages 51, 67, 123.
See also **Plot.**

Connotation A word's connotations are the ideas and feelings associated with the word, as opposed to its dictionary definition. For example, the word *mother*, in addition to its basic meaning ("a female parent"), has connotations of love, warmth, and security.

Consonance Consonance is the repetition of consonant sounds within and at the end of words, as in "lonely afternoon." Consonance is unlike rhyme in that the vowel sounds preceding or following the repeated consonant sounds differ. Consonance is often used together with alliteration, assonance, and rhyme to create a musical quality, to emphasize certain words, or to unify a poem.
See also **Alliteration.**

Contemporary Literature Contemporary literature consists of works by authors who are currently writing today or who wrote in the recent past.

Couplet A couplet is a rhymed pair of lines. A couplet may be written in any rhythmic pattern.
See also **Stanza.**

Critical Essay *See* **Essay.**

Denotation A word's denotation is its dictionary definition.
See also **Connotation.**

Description Description is writing that helps a reader to picture events, objects, and characters. To create descriptions, writers often use imagery—words and phrases that appeal to the reader's senses.

Dialect A dialect is a form of a language that is spoken in a particular place or by a particular group of people. Dialects may feature unique pronunciations, vocabulary, and grammar. For example, in "The Treasure of Lemon Brown" by Walter Dean Myers, Lemon Brown speaks in a dialect that reflects his background as an African-American blues musician. His dialect includes informal grammar and nonstandard word forms.

Dialogue Dialogue is written conversation between two or more characters. Writers use dialogue to bring characters to life and to give readers insights into the characters' qualities, traits, and reactions to other characters. In fiction, dialogue is usually set off with quotation marks. In drama, stories are told primarily through dialogue.

Diary A diary is a daily record of a writer's thoughts, experiences, and feelings. As such, it is a type of autobiographical writing. The terms *diary* and *journal* are often used to mean the same thing.
See page 544.

Drama A drama, or play, is a form of literature meant to be performed by actors in front of an audience. In a drama, the characters' dialogue and actions tell the story. The written form of a play is known as a script. A script usually includes dialogue, a cast of characters, and stage directions that give instructions about performing the drama. The person who writes the drama is known as the playwright or dramatist.

Dramatic Irony *See* **Irony.**

Dynamic Character *See* **Character.**

Elegy An elegy is an extended meditative poem in which the speaker reflects on death—often in tribute to a person who has died recently—or on an equally serious subject. Most elegies are written in formal, dignified language and are serious in tone.

Epic An epic is a long narrative poem on a serious subject, presented in an elevated or formal style. It traces the adventures of a great hero whose actions reflect the ideals and values of a nation or race. Epics address universal concerns, such as good and evil, life and death, and sin and redemption. Henry Wadsworth Longfellow's *The Song of Hiawatha* is an example of an epic. The poet Homer was responsible for handing down two famous epics from ancient Greece, the *Iliad* and the *Odyssey*.

Essay An essay is a short work of nonfiction that deals with a single subject. There are many types of essays. An expository essay presents or explains information and ideas. A personal essay usually reflects the writer's experiences, feelings, and personality. A persuasive essay attempts to convince the reader to adopt a certain viewpoint. A critical essay evaluates a situation or a work of art.
See pages 742, 1016.

Exaggeration An extreme overstatement of an idea is called an exaggeration. It is often used for purposes of emphasis or humor. In "Pecos Bill," Mary Pope Osborne exaggerates Bill's toughness and wild behavior in order to create a humorous, memorable impression of the character.

Exposition Exposition is the first stage of a typical story plot. The exposition provides important background information and introduces the setting and the important characters. The conflict the characters face may also be introduced in the exposition, or it may be introduced later, in the rising action.

See pages 30, 37.

See also **Plot.**

Expository Essay *See* **Essay.**

Extended Metaphor An extended metaphor is a figure of speech that compares two essentially unlike things at some length and in several ways. It does not contain the word *like* or *as*. For example, in "O Captain! My Captain!" Walt Whitman compares Abraham Lincoln to a ship's captain and the Civil War to a ship's journey. The comparison begins in the following lines and continues throughout the poem.

> O Captain! my Captain! our fearful trip is done,
> The ship has weather'd every rack, the prize we sought
>   is won,
> The port is near, the bells I hear, the people all
>   exulting,
> While follow eyes the steady keel, the vessel grim and
>   daring;
>   —Walt Whitman, "O Captain! My Captain!"

See also **Metaphor.**

External Conflict *See* **Conflict.**

Fable A fable is a brief tale told to illustrate a moral or teach a lesson. Often the moral of a fable appears in a distinct and memorable statement near the tale's beginning or end.

See also **Moral.**

Falling Action The falling action is the stage of the plot in which the story begins to draw to a close. The falling action comes after the climax and before the resolution. Events in the falling action show the results of the important decision or action that happened at the climax. Tension eases as the falling action begins; however, the final outcome of the story is not yet fully worked out at this stage.

See pages 30, 37.

See also **Climax; Plot.**

Fantasy Fantasy is a type of fiction that is highly imaginative and portrays events, settings, or characters that are unrealistic. The setting might be a nonexistent world, the plot might involve magic or the supernatural, and the characters might have superhuman powers.

Farce Farce is a type of exaggerated comedy that features an absurd plot, ridiculous situations, and humorous dialogue. The main purpose of a farce is to keep an audience laughing. Comic devices typically used in farces include mistaken identity, wordplay (such as puns and double meanings), and exaggeration.

Fiction Fiction is prose writing that tells an imaginary story. The writer of a fictional work might invent all the events and characters or might base parts of the story on real people and events. The basic elements of fiction are plot, character, setting, and theme. Fiction includes both short stories and novels.

See also **Novel; Short Story.**

Figurative Language Figurative language is language that communicates meanings beyond the literal meanings of words. In figurative language, words are often used to symbolize ideas and concepts they would not otherwise be associated with. Writers use figurative language to create effects, to emphasize ideas, and to evoke emotions. Simile, metaphor, extended metaphor, hyperbole, and personification are examples of figurative language.

See pages 608, 611.

See also **Hyperbole; Metaphor; Onomatopoeia; Personification; Simile.**

First-Person Point of View *See* **Point of View.**

Flashback In a literary work, a flashback is an interruption of the action to present events that took place at an earlier time. A flashback provides information that can help a reader better understand a character's current situation.

Example: In "Clean Sweep," Joan Bauer uses flashback to reveal what happened on the day the narrator's father died.

Foil A foil is a character who provides a striking contrast to another character. By using a foil, a writer can call attention to certain traits possessed by a main character or simply enhance a character by contrast. In Joseph Bruchac's "The Snapping Turtle" the boys at the rez provide a foil to the narrator.

Folklore The traditions, customs, and stories that are passed down within a culture are known as its folklore. Folklore includes various types of literature, such as legends, folk tales, myths, trickster tales, and fables.

See also **Fable; Folk Tale; Myth.**

Folk Tale A folk tale is a story that has been passed from generation to generation by word of mouth. Folk tales may be set in the distant past and involve supernatural events. The characters in them may be animals, people, or superhuman beings. "The Wise Old Woman" is an example of a folk tale.

Foreshadowing Foreshadowing occurs when a writer provides hints that suggest future events in a story. Foreshadowing creates suspense and makes readers eager to find out what will happen. For example, in W. W. Jacob's story "The Monkey's Paw," the sergeant-major's warnings about the paw foreshadow the tragedy that wishing upon it brings about.

Form The structure or organization of a work of writing is often called its form. The form of a poem includes the arrangement of its words and lines on the page.

Free Verse Free verse is poetry that does not contain regular patterns of rhythm or rhyme. The lines in free verse often flow more naturally than do rhymed, metrical lines and therefore achieve a rhythm more like that of everyday speech. Although free verse lacks conventional meter, it may contain various rhythmic and sound effects, such as repetitions of syllables or words. Free verse can be used for a variety of subjects. Billy Collins's poem "Introduction to Poetry" is an example of free verse.
See pages 614, 617.
See also **Meter; Rhyme.**

Genre The term *genre* refers to a category in which a work of literature is classified. The major genres in literature are fiction, nonfiction, poetry, and drama.

Hero A hero is a main character or protagonist in a story. In older literary works, heroes tend to be better than ordinary humans. They are typically courageous, strong, honorable, and intelligent. They are protectors of society who hold back the forces of evil and fight to make the world a better place. In modern literature, a hero may simply be the most important character in a story. Such a hero is often an ordinary person with ordinary problems.

Historical Context The historical context of a literary work refers to the social conditions that inspired or influenced its creation. To understand and appreciate certain works, the reader must relate them to particular events in history.
Example: Walt Whitman wrote his poem "O Captain! My Captain!" in 1865 in response to the assassination of Abraham Lincoln.
See pages 753, 784, 857.

Historical Dramas Historical dramas are plays that take place in the past and are based on real events. In many of these plays, the characters are also based on real historical figures. The dialogue and the action, however, are mostly created by the playwright.

Historical Fiction A short story or a novel can be called historical fiction when it is set in the past and includes real places and real events of historical importance. "The Drummer Boy of Shiloh" by Ray Bradbury is an example of historical fiction.
See pages 330, 388.

Humor Humor is a quality that provokes laughter or amusement. Writers create humor through exaggeration, amusing descriptions, irony, and witty and insightful dialogue. In "Roughing It," Mark Twain uses humor to tell about his poor work habits and the job he did as a reporter.
See page 730.

Hyperbole Hyperbole is a figure of speech in which the truth is exaggerated for emphasis or humorous effect.

Idiom An idiom is an expression that has a meaning different from the meaning of its individual words. For example, "to go to the dogs" is an idiom meaning "to go to ruin."

Imagery Imagery consists of descriptive words and phrases that re-create sensory experiences for the reader. Imagery usually appeals to one or more of the five senses—sight, hearing, smell, taste, and touch—to help the reader imagine exactly what is being described. Note the appeals to sight, taste, and touch in the following lines.

> I say feed me.
> She serves me red prickly pear on a spiked cactus.
>
> I say tease me.
> She sprinkles raindrops in my face on a sunny day.
> —Pat Mora, "Mi Madre"

See pages 431, 608, 753.

Internal Conflict *See* **Conflict.**

Interview An interview is a conversation conducted by a writer or reporter, in which facts or statements are elicited from another person, recorded, and then broadcast or published. "Interview with a Song Catcher" is based on a conversation between Brian Handwerk and Henrietta Yurchenco.
See page 916.

Irony Irony is a special kind of contrast between appearance and reality—usually one in which reality is the opposite of what it seems. One type of irony is **situational irony,** a contrast between what a reader or character expects and what actually exists or happens. For example, in O. Henry's "The Ransom of Red Chief," the kidnappers pay to get rid of the boy instead of collecting a ransom for him, as they had planned. Another type of irony is **dramatic irony,** where the reader or viewer knows something that a character does not know. In the myth "Pandora's Box," the readers know that Zeus created Pandora and her box in order to punish Prometheus, but Epimetheus isn't sure. **Verbal irony** exists when someone knowingly exaggerates or says one thing and means another. David Sedaris uses verbal irony in "Us and Them" when he says, "I could make friends if I wanted to. It just wasn't the right time." He actually means that he was unpopular.

See pages 63, 742, 754.

Journal *See* **Diary.**

Legend A legend is a story handed down from the past about a specific person, usually someone of heroic accomplishments. Legends usually have some basis in historical fact.

Limerick A limerick is a short, humorous poem composed of five lines. It usually has the rhyme scheme *aabba*, created by two rhyming couplets followed by a fifth line that rhymes with the first couplet. A limerick typically has a sing-song rhythm.

Limited Point of View *See* **Point of View.**

Line The line is the core unit of a poem. In poetry, line length is an essential element of the poem's meaning and rhythm. Line breaks, where a line of poetry ends, may coincide with grammatical units. However, a line break may also occur in the middle of a grammatical unit, therefore creating a meaningful pause or emphasis. Poets use a variety of line breaks to play with sense, grammar, and syntax and thereby create a wide range of effects.

Lyric Poetry A lyric poem is a short poem in which a single speaker expresses personal thoughts and feelings. Most poems other than dramatic and narrative poems are lyric poems. In ancient Greece, lyric poetry was meant to be sung. Modern lyrics are usually not intended for singing, but they are characterized by strong melodic rhythms. Lyric poetry has a variety of forms and covers many subjects, from love and death to everyday experiences. Langston Hughes's "Mother to Son" is an example of a lyric poem.

Memoir A memoir is a form of autobiographical writing in which a writer shares his or her personal experiences and observations of significant events or people. Often informal or even intimate in tone, memoirs usually give readers insight into the impact of historical events on people's lives. "My First Free Summer" by Julia Alvarez is a memoir.

See page 116.

See also **Autobiography.**

Metaphor A metaphor is a comparison of two things that are basically unlike but have some qualities in common. Unlike a simile, a metaphor does not contain the word *like* or *as*. In "Identity," the speaker of the poem compares himself to a "tall, ugly weed."

See pages 608, 612.

See also **Extended Metaphor; Figurative Language; Simile.**

Meter Meter is a regular pattern of stressed and unstressed syllables in a poem. The meter of a poem emphasizes the musical quality of the language. Each unit of meter, known as a foot, consists of one stressed syllable and one or two unstressed syllables. In representations of meter, a stressed syllable is indicated by the symbol (´); an unstressed syllable by the symbol (˘). The four basic types of metrical feet are the iamb, an unstressed syllable followed by a stressed syllable (˘´); the trochee, a stressed syllable followed by an unstressed syllable (´˘); the anapest, two unstressed syllables followed by a stressed syllable (˘˘´); and the dactyl, a stressed syllable followed by two unstressed syllables (´˘˘). Note the following example of stressed and unstressed syllables.

By the shores of Gitche Gumee,
By the shining Big-Sea-Water,
Stood the wigwam of Nokomis,
Daughter of the Moon, Nokomis.
—Henry Wadsworth Longfellow, *Song of Hiawatha*

See page 660.

See also **Rhythm.**

Minor Character *See* **Character.**

Mood Mood is the feeling or atmosphere that a writer creates for the reader. Descriptive words, imagery, and figurative language all influence the mood of a work. In "The Monkey's Paw," W. W. Jacobs creates a mood of gloom, dread, and desperation.

See pages 324, 374.

See also **Tone.**

Moral A moral is a lesson that a story teaches. A moral is often stated at the end of a fable. Other times, the moral is implied.
See also **Fable.**

Motivation *See* **Character.**

Myth A myth is a traditional story, usually concerning some superhuman being or unlikely event, that was once widely believed to be true. Frequently, myths were attempts to explain natural phenomena, such as solar and lunar eclipses or the cycle of the seasons. For some peoples, myths were both a kind of science and a religion. In addition, myths served as literature and entertainment, just as they do for modern-day audiences. "Pandora's Box" is an example of a myth from ancient Greece.
See page 476.

Narrative Nonfiction Narrative nonfiction is writing that reads much like fiction, except that the characters, setting, and events are based on real life. *An American Plague: The True and Terrifying Story of the Yellow Fever Epidemic of 1793* by Jim Murphy is an example of narrative nonfiction.
See page 954.

Narrative Poetry Poetry that tells a story is called narrative poetry. Like fiction, a narrative poem contains characters, a setting, and a plot. It might also contain such elements of poetry as rhyme, rhythm, imagery, and figurative language. "Paul Revere's Ride" by Henry Wadsworth Longfellow is an example of a narrative poem.

Narrator The narrator is the voice that tells a story. Sometimes the narrator is a character in the story. At other times, the narrator is an outside voice created by the writer. The narrator is not the same as the writer. An unreliable narrator is one who tells a story or interprets events in a way that makes readers doubt what he or she is saying. An unreliable narrator is usually a character in the story. The narrator may be unreliable for a number of different reasons. For example, the narrator may not have all the facts or may be too young to understand the situation.
See also **Point of View.**

Nonfiction Nonfiction is writing that tells about real people, places, and events. Unlike fiction, nonfiction is mainly written to convey factual information. Nonfiction includes a wide range of writing—newspaper articles, letters, essays, biographies, movie reviews, speeches, true-life adventure stories, advertising, and more.

Novel A novel is a long work of fiction. Like a short story, a novel is the product of a writer's imagination. Because a novel is considerably longer than a short story, a novelist can develop the characters and story line more thoroughly.
See also **Fiction.**

Ode An ode is a type of lyric poem that deals with serious themes, such as justice, truth, or beauty. Odes appeal to both the imagination and the intellect, and many commemorate events or praise people or elements of nature. Alexander Pope's example of this poetic form is "Ode on Solitude."

Omniscient Point of View *See* **Point of View.**

Onomatopoeia Onomatopoeia is the use of words whose sounds echo their meanings, such as *buzz, whisper, gargle,* and *murmur.* As a literary technique, onomatopoeia goes beyond the use of simple echoing words. Skilled writers, especially poets, choose words whose sounds intensify images and suggest meaning. In the following lines, onomatopoeia helps the reader imagine the crying infant and the soothing mother.

> Stilled his fretful wail by saying,
> "Hush! the Naked Bear will hear thee!"
> Lulled him into slumber, singing,
> "Ewa-yea! my little owlet!"
> —Henry Wadsworth Longfellow, *Song of Hiawatha*

Oral Literature Oral literature consists of stories that have been passed down by word of mouth from generation to generation. Oral literature includes folk tales, legends, and myths. In more recent times, some examples of oral literature have been written down or recorded so that the stories can be preserved.

Parallel Episodes Parallel episodes occur when elements of a plot are repeated several times in the course of a story. Fairy tales often employ parallel episodes, as in the examples of "Goldilocks and the Three Bears" and "The Three Little Pigs." The short story "Flowers for Algernon" also contains several parallel episodes.

Personal Essay *See* **Essay.**

Personification The giving of human qualities to an animal, object, or idea is known as personification. In "the lesson of the moth," for example, the speaker, a cockroach, and the moth are personified. They have conversations with each other as if they were human.
See also **Figurative Language.**

Persuasive Essay *See* **Essay.**

Play *See* **Drama.**

Playwright *See* **Drama.**

Plot The series of events in a story is called the plot. The plot usually centers on a conflict, or struggle, faced by the main character. The action that the characters take to solve the problem builds toward a climax in the story. At this point, or shortly afterward, the problem is solved and the story ends. Most story plots have five stages: exposition, rising action, climax, falling action, and resolution.

See pages 30, 37, 51.
See also **Climax; Exposition; Falling Action; Rising Action.**

Poetry Poetry is a type of literature in which words are carefully chosen and arranged to create certain effects. Poets use a variety of sound devices, imagery, and figurative language to express emotions and ideas.

See also **Alliteration; Assonance; Ballad; Free Verse; Imagery; Meter; Narrative Poetry; Rhyme; Rhythm; Stanza.**

Point of View *Point of view* refers to the method of narration used in a short story, novel, narrative poem, or work of nonfiction. In a work told from a **first-person point of view,** the narrator is a character in the story, as in "The Tell-Tale Heart" by Edgar Allan Poe. In a work told from a **third-person point of view,** the narrative voice is outside the action, not one of the characters. If a story is told from a **third-person omniscient,** or all-knowing, point of view, as in "The Lady, or the Tiger" by Frank R. Stockton, the narrator sees into the minds of all the characters. If events are related from a **third-person limited point of view,** as in Beverly Naidoo's "Out of Bounds," the narrator tells what only one character thinks, feels, and observes.

See pages 170, 177, 231.
See also **Narrator.**

Prop The word *prop,* originally an abbreviation of the word *property,* refers to any physical object that is used in a drama. In the play *The Diary of Anne Frank,* the props include Anne's diary and Mrs. Van Daan's fur coat.

Prose The word *prose* refers to all forms of writing that are not in verse form. The term may be used to describe very different forms of writing—short stories as well as essays, for example.

Protagonist A protagonist is the main character in a story, play, or novel. The protagonist is involved in the main conflict of the story. Usually, the protagonist undergoes changes as the plot runs its course. In "Flowers for Algernon" by Daniel Keyes, Charlie is the protagonist.

Radio Play A radio play is a drama that is written specifically to be broadcast over the radio. Because the audience is not meant to see a radio play, sound effects are often used to help listeners imagine the setting and the action. The stage directions in the play's script indicate the sound effects. *The Hitchhiker* by Lucille Fletcher is an example of a radio play.

Recurring Theme *See* **Theme.**

Repetition Repetition is a technique in which a sound, word, phrase, or line is repeated for emphasis or unity. Repetition often helps to reinforce meaning and create an appealing rhythm. Note how the use of repetition in the following lines emphasizes the speaker's message about body and soul.

> You are not your body,
> you are not your bones.
> What's essential about you
> Is what can't be owned.
> —Marilyn Nelson, "Not My Bones"

See page 648.
See also **Alliteration; Sound Devices.**

Resolution *See* **Falling Action.**

Rhyme Rhyme is the occurrence of similar or identical sounds at the end of two or more words, such as *suite, heat,* and *complete.* Rhyme that occurs within a single line of poetry is internal rhyme. Rhyme that occurs at the ends of lines of poetry is called end rhyme. End rhyme that is not exact but approximate is called slant rhyme, or off rhyme. Notice the following example of slant rhyme involving the words *sky* and *signed.*

> The willow is like an etching,
> Fine-lined against the <u>sky</u>.
> The ginkgo is like a crude sketch,
> Hardly worthy to be <u>signed</u>.
> —Eve Merriam, "Simile: Willow and Ginkgo"

See pages 606, 612, 640, 642.

Rhyme Scheme A rhyme scheme is a pattern of end rhymes in a poem. A rhyme scheme is noted by assigning a letter of the alphabet, beginning with *a*, to each line. Lines that rhyme are given the same letter. Notice the rhyme scheme of the first stanza of this poem.

There ain't no pay beneath the sun	*a*
As sweet as rest when a job's well done.	*a*
I was born to work up to my grave	*b*
But I was not born	*c*
To be a slave.	*b*
—Maya Angelou, "One More Round"	

See pages 639, 646.

Rhythm Rhythm is a pattern of stressed and unstressed syllables in a line of poetry. Poets use rhythm to bring out the musical quality of language, to emphasize ideas, and to create moods. Devices such as alliteration, rhyme, assonance, and consonance often contribute to creating rhythm.

See pages 606, 657.
See also **Meter.**

Rising Action The rising action is the stage of the plot that develops the conflict, or struggle. During this stage, events occur that make the conflict more complicated. The events in the rising action build toward a climax, or turning point.

See page 37.
See also **Plot.**

Scene In a drama, the action is often divided into acts and scenes. Each scene presents an episode of the play's plot and typically occurs at a single place and time.

See also **Act.**

Scenery Scenery is a painted backdrop or other structures used to create the setting for a play.

Science Fiction Science fiction is fiction in which a writer explores unexpected possibilities of the past or the future, using known scientific data and theories as well as his or her creative imagination. Most science fiction writers create believable worlds, although some create fantasy worlds that have familiar elements. Isaac Asimov, the author of "Hallucination," is a famous writer of science fiction.

See also **Fantasy.**

Screenplay A screenplay is a play written for film.

Script The text of a play, film, or broadcast is called a script.

Sensory Details Sensory details are words and phrases that appeal to the reader's senses of sight, hearing, touch, smell, and taste. Note the use of sensory details that appeal to sight and taste in the following example.

juniper, piñon, or something
with hard, red berries in spring.
You taste them, and they are sweet
and bitter, the berries a delicacy
—Simon Ortiz, "Canyon de Chelly"

See also **Imagery.**

Setting The setting of a story, poem, or play is the time and place of the action. Sometimes the setting is clear and well-defined. At other times, it is left to the reader's imagination. Elements of setting include geographic location, historical period (past, present, or future), season, time of day, and culture.

See pages 322, 329, 345, 395.

Short Story A short story is a work of fiction that centers on a single idea and can be read in one sitting. Generally, a short story has one main conflict that involves the characters and keeps the story moving.

See also **Fiction.**

Simile A simile is a figure of speech that makes a comparison between two unlike things using the word *like* or *as*.

The willow is like a nymph with streaming hair;
—Eve Merriam, "Simile: Willow and Ginkgo"

See pages 608, 611.
See also **Figurative Language; Metaphor.**

Situational Irony *See* **Irony.**

Sonnet A sonnet is a poem that has a formal structure, containing 14 lines and a specific rhyme scheme and meter. A sonnet often consists of three quatrains, or four-line units, and a final couplet. The sonnet, which means "little song," can be used for a variety of subjects. John Keats's "On the Grasshopper and Cricket" is an example of a sonnet.

See also **Couplet; Rhyme Scheme.**

Sound Devices Sound devices, or uses of words for their connection to the sense of hearing, can convey meaning and mood or unify a work. Some common sound devices are **alliteration, assonance, consonance, meter, onomatopoeia, repetition, rhyme,** and **rhythm.** The following poem contains alliteration, repetition, assonance, consonance, rhyme, and rhythm, all of which combine to help convey both meaning and mood.

> It's all I have to bring today—
> This, and my heart beside—
> This, and my heart, and all the fields—
> And all the meadows wide—
> Be sure you count—should I forget
> Some one the sum could tell—
> This, and my heart, and all the Bees
> Which in the Clover dwell.
> —Emily Dickinson, "It's all I have to bring today"

See pages 291, 606, 634, 636, 658, 660.
See also **Alliteration; Assonance; Consonance; Meter; Onomatopoeia; Repetition; Rhyme; Rhythm.**

Speaker In poetry, the speaker is the voice that "talks" to the reader, similar to the narrator in fiction. The speaker is not necessarily the poet. For example, in Langston Hughes's poem "Mother to Son," the speaker is an older woman, not the male poet.
See pages 431, 617.

Speech A speech is a talk or public address. The purpose of a speech may be to entertain, to explain, to persuade, to inspire, or any combination of these purposes. Chief Canasatego's speech "Educating Sons" was delivered in order to explain to the European settlers why the Iroquois were rejecting the offer of a free education.
See page 1024.

Stage Directions In the script of a play, the instructions to the actors, director, and stage crew are called the stage directions. Stage directions might suggest scenery, lighting, sound effects, and ways for actors to move and speak. Stage directions often appear in parentheses and in italic type.
See page 91.

Stanza A stanza is a group of two or more lines that form a unit in a poem. Each stanza may have the same number of lines, or the number of lines may vary. Eve Merriam's poem "Simile: Willow and Ginkgo" is divided into six stanzas.
See also **Couplet; Form; Poetry.**

Static Character *See* **Character.**

Stereotype In literature, characters who are defined by a single trait are known as stereotypes. Such characters do not usually demonstrate the complexities of real people. Familiar stereotypes in popular literature include the absent-minded professor and the busybody.

Structure The structure of a work of literature is the way in which it is put together. In poetry, structure involves the arrangement of words and lines to produce a desired effect. One structural unit in poetry is the stanza. In prose, structure involves the arrangement of such elements as sentences, paragraphs, and events. "The Wise Old Woman," for example, is structured around the three challenges set forth by Lord Higa.

Style A style is a manner of writing. It involves how something is said rather than what is said. For example, "New York Day Women" by Edwidge Danticat is written in a style that makes use of sentence fragments, repetition, and unusual presentation.

Subplot A subplot is an additional, or secondary, plot in a story. The subplot contains its own conflict, which is often separate from the main conflicts of the story.
See pages 67, 68.

Surprise Ending A surprise ending is an unexpected plot twist at the end of a story. The surprise may be a sudden turn in the action or a piece of information that gives a different perspective to the entire story. The short story writer O. Henry is famous for using this device.

Suspense Suspense is a feeling of growing tension and excitement felt by a reader. Suspense makes a reader curious about the outcome of a story or an event within a story. A writer creates suspense by raising questions in the reader's mind. The use of foreshadowing is one way that writers create suspense.
See page 81.
See also **Foreshadowing.**

Symbol A symbol is a person, a place, an object, or an activity that stands for something beyond itself. For example, a flag is a colored piece of cloth that stands for a country. A white dove is a bird that represents peace.
Example: In "Gil's Furniture Bought and Sold" by Sandra Cisneros, the music box represents beauty.
See pages 462, 469, 501.

Tall Tale A tall tale is a humorously exaggerated story about impossible events, often involving the supernatural abilities of the main character. Stories about folk heroes such as Pecos Bill and Paul Bunyan are typical tall tales.

Theme A theme is a message about life or human nature that the writer shares with the reader. In many cases, readers must infer what the writer's message is. One way of figuring out a theme is to apply the lessons learned by the main characters to people in real life. For example, a theme of *The Diary of Anne Frank* is that people are good at heart.

    Recurring themes are themes found in a variety of works. For example, authors from different backgrounds might express similar themes having to do with the importance of family values. Universal themes are themes that are found throughout the literature of all time periods. For example, the folk tales "The Old Grandfather and His Little Grandson" and "The Wise Old Woman" both express the theme that we should treat older people with respect.

See pages 462, 475, 487, 509.

See also **Moral.**

Third-Person Point of View *See* **Point of View.**

Title The title of a piece of writing is the name that is attached to it. A title often refers to an important aspect of the work. For example, the title "Raymond's Run" refers to the climax of the story, when Squeaky realizes she can find fulfillment in helping her brother Raymond improve his skills.

Tone The tone of a literary work expresses the writer's attitude toward his or her subject. Words such as *angry, sad,* and *humorous* can be used to describe different tones. For example, the tone of Mark Twain's essay "Roughing It" is humorous.

See pages 690, 705.

See also **Author's Perspective; Mood.**

Tragedy A tragedy is a dramatic work that presents the downfall of a dignified character or characters involved in historically or socially significant events. The events in a tragic plot are set in motion by a decision that is often an error in judgment on the part of the hero. Succeeding events are linked in a cause-and-effect relationship and lead inevitably to a disastrous conclusion, usually death. William Shakespeare's *Romeo and Juliet* is a famous tragedy.

Traits *See* **Character Traits.**

Turning Point *See* **Climax.**

Understatement Understatement is a technique of creating emphasis by saying less than is actually or literally true. It is the opposite of hyperbole, or exaggeration. Understatement is often used to create a humorous effect.

Universal Theme *See* **Theme.**

Unreliable Narrator *See* **Narrator.**

Verbal Irony *See* **Irony.**

Voice The term *voice* refers to a writer's unique use of language that allows a reader to "hear" a human personality in the writer's work. Elements of style that contribute to a writer's voice can reveal much about the author's personality, beliefs, and attitudes.

See page 729.

Word Choice The success of any writing depends on the writer's choice of words. Words not only communicate ideas but also help describe events, characters, settings, and so on. Word choice can make a writer's work sound formal or informal, serious or humorous. A writer must choose words carefully depending on the goal of the piece of writing. For example, a writer working on a science article would probably use technical, formal words; a writer trying to establish the setting in a short story would probably use more descriptive words.

See also **Style.**

Analogy An analogy is a comparison between two things that are alike in some way. Often, writers use analogies in nonfiction to explain an unfamiliar subject or idea by showing how it is like a familiar one.

Appeal to Authority An appeal to authority is an attempt to persuade an audience by making reference to people who are experts on a subject.

Argument An argument is speaking or writing that expresses a position, or makes a claim, and supports it with reasons and evidence. An argument often takes into account other points of view, anticipating and answering objections that opponents might raise.
See also **Claim; Counterargument; Evidence.**

Assumption An assumption is an opinion or belief that is taken for granted. It can be about a specific situation, a person, or the world in general. Assumptions are often unstated.

Author's Message An author's message is the main idea or theme of a particular work.
See also **Main Idea; Theme,** *Glossary of Literary and Nonfiction Terms, page R112.*

Author's Perspective *See Glossary of Literary and Nonfiction Terms, page R102.*

Author's Position An author's position is his or her opinion on an issue or topic.
See also **Claim.**

Author's Purpose *See Glossary of Literary and Nonfiction Terms, page R102.*

Autobiography *See Glossary of Literary and Nonfiction Terms, page R102.*

Bias In a piece of writing, the author's bias is the side of an issue that he or she favors. Words with extremely positive or negative connotations are often a signal of an author's bias.

Bibliography A bibliography is a list of related books and other materials used to write a text. Bibliographies can be good sources for further study on a subject.
See also **Works Consulted.**

Biography *See Glossary of Literary and Nonfiction Terms, page R103.*

Business Correspondence Business correspondence is written business communications such as business letters, e-mails, and memos. In general, business correspondence is brief, to the point, clear, courteous, and professional.

Cause and Effect Two events are related by cause and effect when one event brings about, or causes, the other. The event that happens first is the **cause;** the one that follows is the **effect.** Cause and effect is also a way of organizing an entire piece of writing. It helps writers show the relationships between events or ideas.
See also **False Cause,** *Reading Handbook, page R24.*

Chronological Order Chronological order is the arrangement of events by their order of occurrence. This type of organization is used in fictional narratives and in historical writing, biography, and autobiography.

Claim In an argument, a claim is the writer's position on an issue or problem. Although an argument focuses on supporting one claim, a writer may make more than one claim in a text.

Clarify Clarifying is a strategy that helps readers understand or make clear what they are reading. Readers usually clarify by rereading, reading aloud, or discussing.

Classification Classification is a pattern of organization in which objects, ideas, and/or information are presented in groups, or classes, based on common characteristics.

Cliché A cliché is an overused expression. "Better late than never" and "hard as nails" are common examples. Good writers generally avoid clichés unless they are using them in dialogue to indicate something about a character's personality.

Compare and Contrast To compare and contrast is to identify the similarities and differences of two or more subjects. Compare and contrast is also a pattern of organizing an entire piece of writing.

Conclusion A conclusion is a statement of belief based on evidence, experience, and reasoning. A valid conclusion is one that logically follows from the facts or statements upon which it is based.

Connect Connecting is a reader's process of relating the content of a text to his or her own knowledge and experience.

Consumer Documents Consumer documents are printed materials that accompany products and services. They usually provide information about the use, care, operation, or assembly of the product or service they accompany. Some common consumer documents are applications, contracts, warranties, manuals, instructions, labels, brochures, and schedules.

Context Clues When you encounter an unfamiliar word, you can often use context clues to understand it. Context clues are the words or phrases surrounding the word that provide hints about the word's meaning.

Counterargument A counterargument is an argument made to oppose another argument. A good argument anticipates opposing viewpoints and provides counterarguments to disprove them.

Credibility Credibility is the believability or trustworthiness of a source and the information it provides.

Critical Review A critical review is an evaluation or critique by a reviewer, or critic. Types of reviews include film reviews, book reviews, music reviews, and art show reviews.

Database A database is a collection of information that can be quickly and easily accessed and searched and from which information can be easily retrieved. It is frequently presented in an electronic format.

Debate A debate is an organized exchange of opinions on an issue. In school settings, debate is usually a formal contest in which two opposing teams defend and attack a proposition.
See also **Argument.**

Deductive Reasoning Deductive reasoning is a way of thinking that begins with a generalization, presents a specific situation, and then moves forward with facts and evidence toward a logical conclusion. The following passage has a deductive argument embedded in it: "All students in the math class must take the quiz on Friday. Since Lana is in the class, she had better show up." This deductive argument can be broken down as follows: generalization—All students in the math class must take the quiz on Friday; specific situation—Lana is a student in the math class; conclusion—Therefore, Lana must take the math quiz.
See also **Analyzing Logic and Reasoning,** *Reading Handbook, page R22.*

Diary *See Glossary of Literary and Nonfiction Terms, page R104.*

Dictionary *See* **Reference Works.**

Draw Conclusions To draw a conclusion is to make a judgment or arrive at a belief based on evidence, experience, and reasoning.

Editorial An editorial is an opinion piece that usually appears on the editorial page of a newspaper or as part of

a news broadcast. The editorial section of the newspaper presents opinions rather than objective news reports.
See also **Op/Ed Piece.**

Either/Or Fallacy An either/or fallacy is a statement that suggests that there are only two choices available in a situation when in fact there are more than two.
See also **Identifying Faulty Reasoning,** *Reading Handbook, page R24.*

Emotional Appeal An emotional appeal is a message that creates strong feelings in order to make a point. An appeal to fear is a message that taps into people's fear of losing their safety or security. An appeal to pity is a message that taps into people's sympathy and compassion for others to build support for an idea, a cause, or a proposed action. An appeal to vanity is a message that attempts to persuade by tapping into people's desire to feel good about themselves.
See also **Recognizing Persuasive Techniques,** *Reading Handbook, page R21.*

Encyclopedia *See* **Reference Works.**

Essay *See Glossary of Literary and Nonfiction Terms, page R104.*

Ethical Appeal In an ethical appeal, a writer links a claim to a widely accepted value in order to gain moral support for the claim. The appeal also creates an image of the writer as a trustworthy, moral person.
See also **Recognizing Persuasive Techniques,** *Reading Handbook, page R21.*

Evaluate To evaluate is to examine something carefully and to judge its value or worth. Evaluating is an important skill. A reader can evaluate the actions of a particular character, for example. A reader can also form opinions about the value of an entire work.

Evidence Evidence is a specific piece of information that is offered to support a claim. Evidence can take the form of a fact, a quotation, an example, a statistic, or a personal experience, among other things.

Expository Essay *See* **Essay,** *Glossary of Literary and Nonfiction Terms, page R104.*

Fact Versus Opinion A **fact** is a statement that can be proved, or verified. An opinion, on the other hand, is a statement that cannot be proved because it expresses a person's beliefs, feelings, or thoughts.
See also **Generalization; Inference.**

Fallacy A fallacy is an error—usually in reasoning. Typically, a fallacy is based on an incorrect inference or a misuse of evidence.

See also **Either/Or Fallacy; Logical Appeal; Overgeneralization.**

See also **Identifying Faulty Reasoning,** *Reading Handbook, page R24.*

Faulty Reasoning *See* **Fallacy.**

Feature Article A feature article is an article in a newspaper or magazine about a topic of human interest or lifestyles.

Generalization A generalization is a broad statement about a class or category of people, ideas, or things based on a study of, or a belief about, only some of its members.

See also **Overgeneralization; Stereotyping.**

Government Publications Government publications are documents produced by government organizations. Pamphlets, brochures, and reports are just some of the many forms these publications take. Government publications can be good resources for a wide variety of topics.

Graphic Aid A graphic aid is a visual tool that is printed, handwritten, or drawn. Charts, diagrams, graphs, photographs, and maps are examples of graphic aids.

See also **Graphic Aids,** *Reading Handbook, page R4.*

Graphic Organizer A graphic organizer is a "word picture"—a visual illustration of a verbal statement—that helps a reader understand a text. Charts, tables, webs, and diagrams can all be graphic organizers. Graphic organizers and graphic aids can look the same. However, graphic organizers and graphic aids do differ in how they are used. Graphic aids help deliver important information to students using a text. Graphic organizers are actually created by students themselves. They help students understand the text or organize information.

Historical Document Historical documents are writings that have played a significant role in human events. The Declaration of Independence, for example, is a historical document.

How-To Book A how-to book explains how to do something—usually an activity, a sport, or a household project.

Implied Main Idea *See* **Main Idea.**

Index The index of a book is an alphabetized list of important topics covered in the book and the page numbers on which they can be found. An index can be used to quickly find specific information about a topic.

Inductive Reasoning Inductive reasoning is the process of logical reasoning that starts with observations, examples, and facts and moves on to a general conclusion or principle.

See also **Analyzing Logic and Reasoning,** *Reading Handbook, page R22.*

Inference An inference is a logical guess that is made based on facts and one's own knowledge and experience.

Informational Text Informational text is writing that provides factual information. It often explains an idea or teaches a process. Examples include news reports, science textbooks, software instructions, and lab reports.

Internet The Internet is a global, interconnected system of computer networks that allows for communication through e-mail, listservs, and the World Wide Web. The Internet connects computers and computer users throughout the world.

Journal A journal is a periodical publication issued by a legal, medical, or other professional organization. The term may also be used to refer to a diary or daily record.

Loaded Language Loaded language consists of words with strongly positive or negative connotations, intended to influence a reader's or listener's attitude.

Logical Appeal A logical appeal is a way of writing or speaking that relies on logic and facts. It appeals to people's reasoning or intellect rather than to their values or emotions. Flawed logical appeals—that is, errors in reasoning—are called logical fallacies.

See also **Fallacy.**

Logical Argument A logical argument is an argument in which the logical relationship between the support and claim is sound.

Main Idea The main idea is the central or most important idea about a topic that a writer or speaker conveys. It can be the central idea of an entire work or of just a paragraph. Often, the main idea of a paragraph is expressed in a topic sentence. However, a main idea may just be implied, or suggested, by details. A main idea is typically supported by details.

Make Inferences *See* **Inference.**

Monitor Monitoring is the strategy of checking your comprehension as you read and modifying the strategies you are using to suit your needs. Monitoring often includes the following strategies: questioning, clarifying, visualizing, predicting, connecting, and rereading.

Narrative Nonfiction *See Glossary of Literary and Nonfiction Terms, page R108.*

News Article A news article is writing that reports on a recent event. In newspapers, news articles are usually brief and to the point, presenting the most important facts first, followed by more detailed information.

Nonfiction *See Glossary of Literary and Nonfiction Terms, page R108.*

Op/Ed Piece An op/ed piece is an opinion piece that typically appears opposite ("op") the editorial page of a newspaper. Unlike editorials, op/ed pieces are written and submitted by readers.

Organization *See* **Pattern of Organization.**

Overgeneralization An overgeneralization is a generalization that is too broad. You can often recognize overgeneralizations by the appearance of words and phrases such as *all, everyone, every time, any, anything, no one,* or *none.* An example is "None of the city's workers really cares about keeping the environment clean." In all probability, there are many exceptions. The writer can't possibly know the feelings of every city worker.
See also **Identifying Faulty Reasoning,** *Reading Handbook, page R24.*

Overview An overview is a short summary of a story, a speech, or an essay.

Paraphrase Paraphrasing is the restating of information in one's own words.
See also **Summarize.**

Part-by-Part Order Part-by-part order is a pattern of organization in which one idea or group of ideas suggests another, which suggests another, and so on until the end.

Pattern of Organization The term *pattern of organization* refers to the way ideas and information are arranged and organized. Patterns of organization include cause and effect, chronological, compare and contrast, classification, part-by-part, and problem-solution, among others.
See also **Cause and Effect; Chronological Order; Classification; Compare and Contrast; Part-by-Part Order; Problem-Solution Order; Sequential Order.**
See also **Reading Informational Texts: Patterns of Organization,** *Reading Handbook, page R8.*

Periodical A periodical is a magazine or other publication that is issued on a regular basis.

Personal Essay *See* **Essay,** *Glossary of Literary and Nonfiction Terms, page R104.*

Persuasion Persuasion is the art of swaying others' feelings, beliefs, or actions. Persuasion normally appeals to both the mind and the emotions of the reader.
See also **Appeal to Authority; Emotional Appeal; Ethical Appeal; Loaded Language; Logical Appeal.**
See also **Recognizing Persuasive Techniques,** *Reading Handbook, page R21.*

Predict Predicting is a reading strategy that involves using text clues to make a reasonable guess about what will happen next in a story.

Primary Source *See* **Source.**

Prior Knowledge Prior knowledge is the knowledge a reader already possesses about a topic. This information might come from personal experiences, expert accounts, books, films, or other sources.

Problem-Solution Order Problem-solution order is a pattern of organization in which a problem is stated and analyzed and then one or more solutions are proposed and examined.

Propaganda Propaganda is any form of communication that is so distorted that it conveys false or misleading information to advance a specific belief or cause.

Public Document Public documents are documents that were written for the public to provide information that is of public interest or concern. They include government documents, speeches, signs, and rules and regulations.
See also **Government Publications.**

Reference Works Reference works are sources that contain facts and background information on a wide range of subjects. Most reference works are good sources of reliable information because they have been reviewed by experts. The following are some common reference works: encyclopedias, dictionaries, thesauri, almanacs, atlases, and directories.

Review *See* **Critical Review.**

Rhetorical Question Rhetorical questions are those that have such obvious answers that they do not require a reply. Writers often use them to suggest that their claim is so obvious that everyone should agree with it.

Scanning Scanning is the process used to search through a text for a particular fact or piece of information. When you scan, you sweep your eyes across a page, looking for key words that may lead you to the information you want.

Scope Scope refers to a work's focus. For example, an article about Austin, Texas, that focuses on the city's history, economy, and residents has a broad scope. An article that focuses only on the restaurants in Austin has a narrower scope.

Secondary Source *See* **Source.**

Sequential Order Sequential order is a pattern of organization that shows the order of steps or stages in a process.

Setting a Purpose The process of establishing specific reasons for reading a text is called setting a purpose.

Sidebar A sidebar is additional information set in a box alongside or within a news or feature article. Popular magazines often make use of sidebars.

Signal Words In a text, signal words are words and phrases that help show how events or ideas are related. Some common examples of signal words are *and, but, however, nevertheless, therefore,* and *in addition.*

Source A source is anything that supplies information. **Primary sources** are materials created by people who witnessed or took part in the event they supply information about. Letters, diaries, autobiographies, and eyewitness accounts are primary sources. **Secondary sources** are those made by people who were not directly involved in the event or even present when it occurred. Encyclopedias, textbooks, biographies, and most news articles are examples of secondary sources.

Speech *See Glossary of Literary and Nonfiction Terms, page R111.*

Stereotyping Stereotyping is a dangerous type of overgeneralization. It can lead to unfair judgments of people based on their ethnic background, beliefs, practices, or physical appearance.

Summarize To summarize is to briefly retell the main ideas of a piece of writing in one's own words. *See also* **Paraphrase.**

Support Support is any information that helps to prove a claim.

Supporting Detail *See* **Main Idea.**

Synthesize To synthesize information means to take individual pieces of information and combine them in order to gain a better understanding of a subject.

Text Feature Text features are elements of a text, such as boldface type, headings, and subheadings, that help organize and call attention to important information. Italic type, bulleted or numbered lists, sidebars, and graphic aids such as charts, tables, timelines, illustrations, and photographs are also considered text features. *See also* **Understanding Text Features,** *Reading Handbook, page R3.*

Thesaurus *See* **Reference Works.**

Thesis Statement A thesis statement is the main proposition that a writer attempts to support in a piece of writing. It serves as the controlling idea of the composition.

Topic Sentence The topic sentence of a paragraph states the paragraph's main idea. All other sentences in the paragraph provide supporting details.

Treatment The way a topic is handled in a work is referred to as its treatment. Treatment includes the form the writing takes as well as the writer's purpose and tone.

Visualize Visualizing is the process of forming a mental picture based on written or spoken information.

Web Site A Web site is a collection of "pages" on the World Wide Web that is usually devoted to one specific subject. Pages are linked together and accessed by clicking hyperlinks or menus, which send the user from page to page within a Web site. Web sites are created by companies, organizations, educational institutions, branches of the government, the military, and individuals.

Workplace Document Workplace documents are materials that are produced or used within a work setting, usually to aid in the functioning of the workplace. They include job applications, office memos, training manuals, job descriptions, and sales reports.

Works Cited The term *works cited* refers to a list of all the works a writer has referred to in his or her text. This list often includes not only books and articles but also Internet sources.

Works Consulted The term *works consulted* refers to a list of all the works a writer consulted in order to create his or her text. It is not limited just to those works cited in the text. *See also* **Bibliography.**

Glossary of Academic Vocabulary in English & Spanish

The Glossary of Academic Vocabulary is an alphabetical list of the Academic Vocabulary words found in this textbook. For each word, the glossary includes the pronunciation, part of speech, and meaning. A Spanish version of each word and definition follows the English version. For more information about the words in the Academic Vocabulary Glossary, please consult a dictionary.

accurate (ăk′yər- ĭt) *adj.* without error, factual; correct and exact
> **preciso** *adj.* sin errores, objetivo; correcto y exacto

affect (ə-fĕkt′) *v.* to have an effect on, to bring about a change
> **afectar** *v.* tener un efecto en algo, provocar un cambio

achieve (ə-chēv′) *v.* to accomplish or to succeed
> **lograr** *v.* alcanzar un objetivo o tener éxito

appropriate (ə-prō′prē-ĭt) *adj.* fitting for the purpose; suitable
> **apropiado** *adj.* adecuado para el propósito; conveniente

assess (ə-sĕs′) *v.* to determine value or significance
> **evaluar** *v.* determinar el valor o la importancia

attitude (ăt′ĭ-tōōd′) *n.* a state of mind or feeling
> **actitud** *sust.* estado de ánimo o sentimiento

bias (bī′əs) *n.* a preference for something or someone that prevents fair decision-making
> **parcialidad** *sust.* preferencia por algo o alguien que impide tomar decisiones de manera justa

circumstance (sûr′kəm-stăns′) *n.* an event or fact having some bearing on a particular situation; a determining factor
> **circunstancia** *sust.* suceso o hecho que tiene relación con una situación en particular; factor determinante

comment (kŏm′ĕnt) *n.* to make a remark, written or spoken
> **comentario** *sust.* observación escrita u oral

communicate (kə-myōō′nĭ-kāt) *v.* to pass along information about; to make known
> **comunicar** *v.* transmitir información; dar a conocer algo

community (kə-myōō′nĭ-tē) *n.* all people living in the same location under the same government
> **comunidad** *sust.* todas las personas que viven en un mismo lugar bajo el mismo gobierno

conclude (kən-klōōd′) *v.* to reach a decision
> **concluir** *v.* tomar una decisión

contrast (kŏn′trăst′) *v.* to show differences in one or more things when compared to each other
> **contrastar** *v.* mostrar las diferencias entre una o más cosas al compararlas entre sí

contribute (kən-trĭb′yōōt) *v.* to give something for a common purpose, to give to an organization
> **contribuir** *v.* dar algo para un propósito común, dar a una organización

convince (kən-vĭns′) *v.* to persuade; to cause one to feel sure about something
> **convencer** *v.* persuadir; hacer sentir seguro de algo

create (krē-āt′) *v.* to cause to exist; to make, form, or bring into being
> **crear** *v.* hacer existir; hacer, formar o dar vida

criteria (krī-tĭr′ē-ə) *n.* standards or rules by which something can be judged; a measure of value
> **criterio** *sust.* norma o estándar según el cual se puede juzgar algo; medida de valor

culture (kŭl′chər) *n.* a society's way of life, including behavior, arts, beliefs, and all other products of work and thought
> **cultura** *sust.* modo de vida de una sociedad, que incluye las conductas, el arte, las creencias y los demás productos del trabajo y el pensamiento

design (dĭ-zīn) *v.* to think up the plans for; to invent
> **diseñar** *v.* planear algo; inventar

emerge (ĭ-mûrj′) *v.* to appear, to come into view or existence
> **surgir** *v.* aparecer, hacerse visible o comenzar a existir

emphasis (ĕm′fə-sĭs) *n.* special attention or effort directed toward something to make it stand out
> **énfasis** *sust.* atención o esfuerzo especial dirigido hacia algo para lograr que se destaque

evident (ĕv′ĭ-dənt) *adj.* easily seen or understood
> **evidente** *adj.* fácil de ver o comprender

challenge (chăl′ənj) *n.* a test of one's abilities
> **desafío** *sust.* prueba de las habilidades de una persona

imply (ĭm-plī′) *v.* to express indirectly
> **implicar** *v.* expresar de manera indirecta

income (ĭn′kŭm) *n.* money one receives as wages, salary, or by other means of profit
> **ingreso** *sust.* dinero que una persona recibe en forma de salario, sueldo u otro medio de compensación

individual (ĭn′də-vĭj′ōō-əl) *adj.* single; relating to one human being or thing
   individual *adj.* simple; relativo a una persona o cosa

initial (ĭ-nĭsh′əl) *adj.* first; happening at the beginning
   inicial *adj.* primero; que ocurre al principio

intelligence (ĭn-tĕl′ə-jəns) *n.* the ability to learn, understand, and solve problems
   inteligencia *sust.* capacidad de aprender, comprender y resolver problemas

interpret (ĭn-tûr′prĭt) *v.* to explain the meaning of
   interpretar *v.* explicar el significado de algo

investigate (ĭn-vĕs′tĭ-gāt) *v.* to examine in detail; to learn the facts
   investigar *v.* examinar en detalle; aprender los datos

job (jŏb) *n.* a position in which one is employed
   trabajo *sust.* puesto laboral que ocupa una persona

logic (lŏj′ĭk) *n.* a system of reasoning
   lógica *sust.* sistema de razonamiento

mental (mĕn′tl) *adj.* of or related to the mind
   mental *adj.* de la mente o relacionado con ella

method (mĕth′əd) *n.* a systematic way of doing something
   método *sust.* manera sistemática de hacer algo

motive (mō′tĭv) *n.* emotion, desire, or need that compels one to take a certain action
   motivo *sust.* emoción, deseo o necesidad que lleva a una persona a realizar una acción determinada

perceive (pər-sēv′) *v.* to become aware of something through one of the senses; to understand
   percibir *v.* tomar conciencia de algo por medio de uno de los sentidos; comprender

perspective (pər-spĕk′tĭv) *n.* a certain point of view; a subjective view of a particular issue
   perspectiva *sust.* punto de vista determinado; visión subjetiva de una cuestión en particular

predominant (prĭ-dŏm′ə-nənt′) *adj.* to have great importance or influence
   predominante *adj.* tener gran importancia o influencia

publish (pŭb′lĭsh) *v.* to prepare printed material for sale or to give out
   publicar *v.* preparar material impreso para su venta o distribución

rely (rĭ-lī′) *v.* to be dependent on for help or support; to have confidence in
   confiar *v.* depender de alguien para recibir ayuda o apoyo; tener confianza en alguien

research (rĭ′-sûrch) *n.* close, careful study
   investigación *sust.* estudio detallado y preciso

role (rōl) *n.* a character or part played by a performer; a function or position
   papel *sust.* personaje o rol que representa un actor; función o posición

similar (sĭm′ə-lər) *adj.* the same, but not identical
   similar *adj.* el mismo pero no idéntico

source (sōrs) *n.* the point at which something comes into being; the point of origin
   fuente *sust.* punto en el que algo comienza a existir; punto de origen

strategy (străt′ə-jē) *n.* following a plan of action to accomplish a certain goal
   estrategia *sust.* sequir un plan de acción para lograr un objetivo

style (stīl) *n.* the unique way in which something is said, done, expressed, or performed
   estilo *sust.* manera especial en que se dice, hace, expresa o representa algo

technical (tĕk-nĭ-kəl) *adj.* having special skill or knowledge, especially in a mechanical or scientfic way
   técnico *adj.* que tiene habilidades o conocimientos especiales, particularmente en el área de la mecánica o las ciencias

technique (tĕk-nēk) *n.* a systematic or especially organized way of completing a task; special skill related to completion of a task
   técnica *sust.* manera sistemática o especial de realizar una tarea; destreza especial relacionada con la realización de una tarea

technology (tĕk-nŏl′ə-jē) *n.* science as it is applied to practical use and work
   tecnología *sust.* ciencia aplicada a la práctica y el trabajo

trend (trĕnd) *n.* the general direction in which something tends to move; current style
   tendencia *sust.* dirección general en la que algo tiende a moverse; estilo actual

Glossary of Vocabulary in English & Spanish

This glossary is an alphabetical list of vocabulary words found in the selections in this book. Use this glossary just as you would use a dictionary—to determine the meanings, syllabication, pronunciations, and parts of speech of words.

Many words in the English language have more than one meaning. The meanings provided here are those that apply to the words as they are used in the selections in this book. When closely related words are listed together in one entry (for instance, *improvised* and *improvise*), the definition given applies to the first form of the word, which is also the entry word.

Each entry word's English pronunciation is given in parentheses. These pronunciations also indicate the syllabication of the words. For help interpreting pronunciation symbols and stress marks, see the Pronunciation Key at the end of this glossary.

The parts of speech are noted with the following abbreviations:
adj. adjective
adv. adverb
n. noun
v. verb

For more information about the words in this glossary, please consult a dictionary.

aberration (ăb′ə-rā′shən) *n.* an abnormal alteration
   aberración *s.* alteración anormal

absurd (əb-sûrd′) *adj.* ridiculously unreasonable
   absurdo *adj.* que va en contra de lo razonable

accommodate (ə-kŏm′ə-dāt) *v.* to make room for
   acomodar *v.* albergar; contener

acute (ə-kyoōt′) *adj.* sharp; keen
   agudo *adj.* fuerte; perspicaz

adequately (ăd′ĭ-kwĭt-lē) *adv.* enough to satisfy a requirement or meet a need
   adecuadamente *adv.* de modo suficiente para cumplir un requisito o necesidad

adorn (ə-dôrn′) *v.* to enhance or decorate
   adornar *v.* embellecer o decorar

adversary (ăd′vər-sĕr′ē) *n.* an opponent
   adversario *s.* oponente

aggression (ə-grĕsh′ən) *n.* hostile or destructive behavior or action
   agresión *s.* conducta o acción hostil o destructiva

ajar (ə-jär′) *adj.* partially open
   entreabierto *adj.* parcialmente abierto

anguished (ăng′gwĭsht) *adj.* tormented; distressed
   angustiado *adj.* atormentado; afligido

appendage (ə-pĕn′dĭj) *n.* a body part, such as an arm or leg, that is attached to the main part of the body
   apéndice *s.* parte del cuerpo pegada al tronco, como un brazo o una pierna

apprehension (ăp′rĭ-hĕn′shən) *n.* nervousness
   aprensión *s.* nerviosismo

array (ə-rā′) *n.* a large number of items
   conjunto *s.* gran cantidad de objetos

arrogant (ăr′ə-gənt) *adj.* displaying a sense of self-importance
   arrogante *adj.* que se las da de importante

askew (ə-skyoō′) *adj.* to one side; awry
   torcido *adj.* que no es recto ni derecho

aspire (ə-spīr′) *v.* to have a great ambition or an ultimate goal; to desire strongly
   aspirar *v.* tener una gran ambición o una meta final; desear con fuerza

assert (ə-sûrt′) *v.* to act forcefully; to take charge
   afirmar *v.* dejar sentado; imponer autoridad

assurance (ə-shoŏr′əns) *n.* a guarantee or pledge
   garantía *s.* compromiso

attribute (ə-trĭb′yoōt) *v.* to relate to a certain cause
   atribuir *v.* relacionar con cierta causa

audacity (ô-dăs′ĭ-tē) *n.* shameless daring or boldness
   audacia *s.* atrevimiento o descaro

authentic (ô-thĕn′tĭk) *adj.* having a verifiable origin; not counterfeit
   auténtico *adj.* de origen comprobado; original

ban (băn) *v.* to prohibit
   prohibir *v.* negar

barricade (băr'ĭ-kād') *n.* a structure that blocks passage
  barricada *s.* estructura que bloquea el paso

basking (băsk'ĭng) *adj.* warming oneself pleasantly, as in sunlight
  asoleado *adj.* expuesto al sol

benefactor (běn'ə-făk'tər) *n.* a person who gives monetary or other aid
  benefactor *s.* persona que da dinero o ayuda

bewilderment (bĭ-wĭl'dər-mənt) *n.* the state of being confused or astonished
  perplejidad *s.* confusión o desconcierto

bound (bound) *v.* to leap forward
  saltar *v.* brincar hacia adelante

brusquely (brŭsk'lē) *adv.* in an abrupt, sudden manner
  bruscamente *adv.* de modo abrupto y repentino

cache (kăsh) *v.* to store in a hiding place
  ocultar *v.* guardar en un escondite

cajole (kə-jōl') *v.* to urge gently; to coax
  persuadir *v.* convencer; engatusar

cavernous (kăv'ər-nəs) *adj.* as deep or vast as a cavern, or a large cave
  cavernoso *adj.* profundo y oscuro como una caverna o cueva grande

circumstance (sûr'kəm-stăns') *n.* a condition that affects or relates to an event or series of events
  circunstancia *s.* situación que rodea a un suceso o serie de sucesos

clutch (klŭch) *v.* to grasp and hold tightly
  agarrar *v.* estrechar y apretar firmemente

collaborate (kə-lăb'ə-rāt') *v.* to work together on a project
  colaborar *v.* trabajar en equipo en un proyecto

commence (kə-mĕns') *v.* to begin
  comenzar *v.* empezar

commend (kə-mĕnd') *v.* to speak highly of; to praise; to recommend
  elogiar *v.* ensalzar; recomendar

commotion (kə-mō'shən) *n.* a disturbance
  conmoción *s.* disturbio

compel (kəm-pĕl') *v.* to pressure by force
  compeler *v.* obligar a la fuerza

compensation (kŏm'pən-sā'shən) *n.* something, such as money, received as payment
  compensación *s.* dinero o cosa recibida en pago

comply (kəm-plī') *v.* to act according to a command or request
  cumplir *v.* seguir una orden o una solicitud

composer (kəm-pō'zər) *n.* one who creates musical pieces
  compositor *s.* persona que crea piezas musicales

conceive (kən-sēv') *v.* to think of
  concebir *v.* idear

concession (kən-sĕsh'ən) *n.* the act of yielding or conceding
  concesión *s.* acción de ceder

conspicuous (kən-spĭk'yōō-əs) *adj.* easy to notice; obvious
  conspicuo *adj.* que salta a la vista; obvio

conspiracy (kən-spîr'ə-sē) *n.* an agreement to perform together an illegal or wrongful act
  conspiración *s.* alianza para preparar una acción ilegal o indebida

contaminate (kən-tăm'ə-nāt') *v.* to make impure or unclean through contact
  contaminar *v.* dañar o alterar la pureza

contemplate (kŏn'təm-plāt') *v.* to consider carefully and at length
  contemplar *v.* considerar cuidadosamente

contractor (kŏn'trăk'tər) *n.* one who agrees to provide services for a specific price
  contratista *s.* persona que se compromete a realizar un servicio por determinado precio

contradiction (kŏn'trə-dĭk'shən) *n.* a denial; an expression that is opposite to
  contradicción *s.* negación de algo que se da por cierto; afirmación de algo contrario a lo ya dicho

contrive (kən-trīv') *v.* to invent or fabricate, especially by improvisation
  ingeniarse *v.* inventar o idear, especialmente de modo improvisado

conventional (kən-vĕn'shə-nəl) *adj.* conforming to established practice or accepted standards; traditional
  convencional *adj.* conforme a la práctica establecida o a estándares aceptados; tradicional

converge (kən-vûrj´) *v.* to come together in one place; meet
converger *v.* unirse en un punto; encontrarse

conviction (kən-vĭk´shən) *n.* a strong belief
convicción *s.* creencia fuerte

cosmic (kŏz´mĭk) *adj.* universal; infinitely large
cósmico *adj.* universal; infinitamente grande

counterpart (koun´tər-pärt´) *n.* one that has the same functions and traits as another
contraparte *s.* el que tiene las mismas funciones y características que otro

craftiness (krăf´tē-nĕs) *n.* deviousness or deception
picardía *s.* astucia o engaño

credulity (krĭ-dōō´lĭ-tē) *n.* a disposition to believe too readily
credulidad *s.* tendencia a creerlo todo

crevice (krĕv´ĭs) *n.* crack
grieta *s.* abertura larga y estrecha

crouch (krouch) *v.* to stoop with bent knees
acuclillarse *v.* agacharse con las rodillas dobladas

deceive (dĭ-sēv´) *v.* to cause to believe what is not true; to mislead
engañar *v.* hacer creer lo que no es cierto; descaminar

decline (dĭ-klīn´) *v.* to politely refuse
declinar *v.* rehusar cortésmente

defy (dĭ-fī´) *v.* to boldly oppose or resist
desafiar *v.* oponerse o resistirse

denounce (dĭ-nouns´) *v.* to condemn; to criticize
denunciar *v.* condenar; criticar

deprivation (dĕp´rə-vā´shən) *n.* the condition of not having one's needs met; a lack of
privación *s.* ausencia o escasez de lo necesario para vivir

derision (dĭ-rĭzh´ən) *n.* ridicule
escarnio *s.* ridículo

descendant (dĭ-sĕn´dənt) *n.* a person whose descent can be traced to an individual or group
descendiente *s.* persona que desciende por línea directa de un individuo o grupo

devious (dē´vē-əs) *adj.* departing from the straight or direct course
tortuoso *adj.* desviado; sinuoso

diatribe (dī´ə-trīb´) *n.* bitter, abusive criticism
diatriba *s.* crítica fuerte y grosera

diminish (dĭ-mĭn´ĭsh´) *v.* to become smaller or less
disminuir *v.* hacerse más pequeño; mermar

dingy (dĭn´jē) *adj.* dirty or discolored
deslucido *adj.* sucio o manchado

disconcert (dĭs´kən-sûrt´) *v.* to ruffle; to frustrate by throwing into disorder
desconcertar *v.* alterar; contrariar

disgruntle (dĭs-grŭn´tl) *v.* to make unhappy
contrariar *v.* enfadar

disheveled (dĭ-shĕv´əld) *adj.* messy; untidy
desarreglado *adj.* desordenado; desaliñado

disparity (dĭ-spăr´ĭ-tē) *n.* the condition or fact of being unequal; difference
discrepancia *sust.* condición o hecho de no ser igual; diferencia

dispel (dĭ-spĕl´) *v.* to drive away
disipar *v.* alejar

edict (ē´dĭkt´) *n.* a command from those in power
edicto *s.* orden de una persona de autoridad

eliminate (ĭ-lĭm´ə-nāt´) *v.* to remove from consideration by defeating
eliminar *v.* quitar, separar o hacer desaparecer

eloquence (ĕl´ə-kwəns) *n.* an ability to speak powerfully and persuasively
elocuencia *s.* eficacia para persuadir o conmover con la palabra

emigrate (ĕm´ĭ-grāt´) *v.* to leave one country and settle in another
emigrar *v.* dejar el país propio y establecerse en otro

engaging (ĕn-gāj´ĭng) *adj.* charming; likeable
agradable *adj.* simpático; encantador

engross (ĕn-grōs´) *v.* to completely occupy
absorber *v.* ocupar por completo

ensnare (ĕn-snâr´) *v.* to take or catch in something
atrapar *v.* alcanzar; coger en una trampa

entitled (ĕn-tīt´l) *v.* given the right to have or do something
autorizado *v.* con derecho a tener o hacer algo

essential (ĭ-sĕn'shəl) *adj.* having the qualities that give something its true identity
   esencial *adj.* que forma parte de la naturaleza de algo

esteem (ĭ-stēm') *v.* to regard with respect
   estimar *v.* apreciar

evoke (ĭ-vōk') *v.* to call forth; to summon
   evocar *v.* traer a la memoria

exile (ĕk'sīl') *n.* enforced removal from one's native country
   exilio *s.* abandono obligatorio de la patria

exotic (ĭg-zŏt'ĭk) *adj.* foreign; unusual; exciting
   exótico *adj.* extranjero; inusual; emocionante

exploit (ĕk'sploit') *v.* to use for selfish purposes
   explotar *v.* usar con fines egoístas

fate (fāt) *n.* a power that is thought to determine the course of events
   destino *s.* fuerza que se cree que determina el curso de los acontecimientos

feeble (fē'bəl) *adj.* weak or faint
   débil *adj.* que tiene poca fuerza o poco vigor

foreboding (fôr-bō'dĭng) *n.* a sense of impending misfortune
   presentimiento *s.* sentimiento de desgracia inminente

foreman (fôr'mən) *n.* the leader of a work crew
   capataz *s.* jefe de una cuadrilla de trabajo

foresight (fôr'sīt) *n.* perception of the significance of events before they have occurred
   previsión *s.* percepción de la importancia de algo antes de que ocurra

fortify (fôr'tə-fī') *v.* to make strong
   fortificar *v.* fortalecer

fraud (frôd) *n.* a deception deliberately practiced to secure unfair or unlawful gain; a trick
   fraude *sust.* engaño deliberado para ganar algo injusta o ilegalmente; trampa

futility (fyōō-tĭl'ĭ-tē) *n.* uselessness
   futilidad *s.* lo que no tiene ninguna importancia

glimmer (glĭm'ər) *n.* a faint sign
   vislumbre *s.* señal vaga

gnarled (närld) *adj.* roughened, as from age or work
   nudoso *adj.* rugoso por la edad o el trabajo

grievous (grē'-vəs) *adj.* causing grief, pain, or anguish
   doloroso *adj.* que causa pena, dolor o angustia

grimace (grĭm'ĭs) *n.* a facial expression of pain or disgust
   mueca *s.* expresión facial de dolor o de asco

grope (grōp) *v.* to reach about with uncertainty
   tantear *v.* andar a tientas

hamper (hăm'pər) *v.* to prevent the free movement of
   dificultar *v.* impedir el libre movimiento

haughtily (hô'tə-lē) *adv.* proudly; scornfully
   altivamente *adv.* orgullosamente; con altanería

hypocritical (hĭp'ə-krĭt'ĭ-kəl) *adj.* false or deceptive
   hipócrita *adj.* falso o engañoso

immaculate (ĭ-măk'yə-lĭt) *adj.* spotless; very clean
   inmaculado *adj.* sin mancha; muy limpio

immortality (ĭm'ôr-tăl'ĭ-tē) *n.* the condition of having an endless life
   inmortalidad *s.* vida eterna

impair (ĭm-pâr') *v.* to weaken; damage
   perjudicar *v.* debilitar; dañar

impart (ĭm-pärt') *v.* to make known; reveal
   impartir *v.* dar a conocer; revelar

impartial (ĭm-pär'shəl) *adj.* not partial or biased; unprejudiced
   imparcial *adj.* neutral; sin prejuicio

imply (ĭm-plī') *v.* to express indirectly
   implicar *v.* expresar indirectamente

impregnable (ĭm-prĕg'nə-bəl) *adj.* impossible to enter by force
   impenetrable *adj.* imposible de penetrar a la fuerza

impropriety (ĭm'prə-prī'ĭ-tē) *n.* an unsuitable or inappropriate act or quality
   incorrección *s.* falta de decoro; falta

improvised (ĭm'prə-vīzd') *adj.* to put together with little preparation or planning **improvise** *v.*
   improvisado *adj.* realizado sin plan previo **improvisar** *v.*

impudent (ĭm'pyə-dənt) *adj.* bold and disrespectful
   insolente *adj.* descarado e irrespetuoso

incarnation (ĭn´-kär-nā´-shən) *n.* a bodily form
encarnación *s.* adopción de forma física

inclination (ĭn-klə-nā´shən) *n.* a tendency to prefer one thing over another
inclinación *s.* tendencia a preferir una de dos cosas

indignantly (ĭn-dĭg´nənt-lē) *adv.* angrily
con indignación *adv.* furiosamente

indiscriminately (ĭn´dĭ-skrĭm´ə-nĭt-lē) *adv.* without making careful distinctions or choices
sin discriminación *adv.* sin criterio o discernimiento

ineptitude (ĭn-ĕp´tĭ-tōōd´) *n.* clumsiness; lack of competence
ineptitud *s.* torpeza; incompetencia

inertia (ĭ-nûr´shə) *n.* resistance to motion, action, or change
inercia *s.* resistencia al movimiento, la acción o el cambio

infectious (ĭn-fĕk´shəs) *adj.* capable of being transmitted by infection
infeccioso *adj.* que se puede contagiar

inflict (ĭn-flĭkt´) *v.* to deal out something unpleasant or burdensome; to impose
infligir *v.* someter a malos tratos o sufrimiento; imponer

informant (ĭn-fôr´mənt) *n.* one who gives information
informante *s.* el que da información

insolent (ĭn´sə-lənt) *adj.* insulting; arrogant
insolente *adj.* insultante; arrogante

instill (ĭn-stĭl´) *v.* to supply gradually
inculcar *v.* infundir gradualmente

interfere (ĭn´tər-fîr´) *v.* to create an obstacle
interferir *v.* crear un obstáculo

intermittently (ĭn´tər-mĭt´nt-lē) *adv.* stopping and starting at intervals
intermitentemente *adv.* que se interrumpe y prosigue a intervalos

interrogation (ĭn-tĕr´ə-gā´shən) *n.* an official or formal questioning
interrogatorio *s.* formulación oficial de preguntas

intimate (ĭn´tə-mĭt) *adj.* relating to one's deepest nature
íntimo *adj.* relacionado con lo más profundo de una persona

intricate (ĭn´trĭ-kĭt) *adj.* elaborate
intrincado *adj.* elaborado

irate (ī-rāt´) *adj.* very angry
airado *adj.* furioso

junction (jŭnk´shən) *n.* a place where two roads meet
cruce *s.* punto de encuentro de dos caminos

keener (kēn´ər) *adj.* acutely sensitive
agudo *adj.* muy sensible

labyrinth (lăb´ə-rĭnth´) *n.* a maze; an intricate structure of interconnected passages
laberinto *s.* estructura formada por caminos cruzados entre sí

languish (lăng´gwĭsh) *v.* to lose strength and vitality
languidecer *v.* perder fuerza y vitalidad

lark (lärk) *n.* a carefree or spirited adventure
travesura *s.* aventura juguetona

lavishly (lăv´ĭsh-lē) *adv.* extravagantly
magníficamente *adv.* con entravagancia

legitimate (lə-jĭt´ə-mĭt) *adj.* genuine; authentic
legítimo *adj.* genuino; auténtico

legitimately (lə-jĭt´ə-mĭt-lē) *adv.* lawfully
legítimamente *adv.* legalmente

liable (lī´ə-bəl) *adj.* likely to
propenso *adj.* que tiene inclinación a algo

linger (lĭng´gər) *v.* to remain or stay longer
quedarse *v.* permanecer o entretenerse un rato

listless (lĭst´lĭs) *adj.* lacking energy
lánguido *adj.* sin energía

livelihood (līv´lē-hŏŏd´) *n.* a means of support; a way of making a living
sustento *s.* medio de ganarse la vida

malodorous (măl-ō´dər-əs) *adj.* having a bad odor
maloliente *adj.* que huele mal

maroon (mə-rōōn´) *v.* to leave behind in a place from which there is little hope of escape
abandonar *v.* dejar a una persona en un lugar de donde no puede salir

meddle (mĕd´l) *v.* to intrude or interfere
entrometerse *v.* inmiscuirse o interferir

melancholy (mĕl′ən-kŏl′ē) *adj.* sad; depressed
  melancólico *adj.* triste; deprimido

menace (mĕn′ĭs) *n.* a possible danger; threat
  amenaza *s.* posible peligro

merit (mĕr′ĭt) *v.* to deserve
  merecer *v.* ser digno de

mesmerize (mĕz′mə-rīz′) *v.* to spellbind; to enthrall
  cautivar *v.* fascinar; embelesar

migration (mī-grā′shən) *n.* the act of changing location seasonally
  migración *s.* cambio de lugar por temporada

minuscule (mĭn′ə-skyool′) *adj.* very small; tiny
  minúsculo *adj.* muy pequeño

mobility (mō-bĭl′ĭ-tē) *n.* the capability of moving from place to place
  movilidad *s.* capacidad de moverse de un lugar a otro

monotony (mə-nŏt′n-ē) *n.* tedious sameness
  monotonía *s.* uniformidad o igualdad tediosa

muted (myoo′tĭd) *adj.* muffled; softened
  apagado *adj.* amortiguado; suave

neglectful (nĭ-glĕkt′fəl) *adj.* characterized by a failure to properly care for someone or something
  negligente *adj.* que no pone cuidado, atención o interés en lo que debe

nondescript (nŏn′dĭ-skrĭpt′) *adj.* lacking unique qualities
  soso *adj.* sin ninguna característica distintiva

offense (ə-fĕns′) *n.* a violation of a moral or social code; a sin
  ofensa *s.* violación de un código moral o social; pecado

ominous (ŏm′ə-nəs) *adj.* threatening
  ominoso *adj.* amenazador

opposition (ŏp′ə-zĭsh′ən) *n.* the act of opposing or resisting
  oposición *s.* acción de oponer u oponerse

oratory (ôr′ə-tôr′ē) *n.* the art of making speeches
  oratoria *s.* arte de dar discursos

pandemonium (păn′də-mō′nē-əm) *n.* wild uproar or noise
  pandemónium *s.* gran ruido y confusión

patronize (pā′trə-nīz′) *v.* to go to as a customer
  frecuentar *v.* ser cliente de

peril (pĕr′əl) *n.* danger
  peligro *s.* riesgo

perpetual (pər-pĕch′oo-əl) *adj.* continuing without interruption
  perpetuo *adj.* sin interrupción

perseverance (pûr′sə-vîr′əns) *n.* steady persistence in sticking to a course of action
  perseverancia *s.* firmeza y constancia en un curso de acción

pervasive (pər-vā′sĭv) *adj.* present throughout
  omnipresente *adj.* que está en todas partes

philosophy (fĭ-lŏs′ə-fē) *n.* a system of values or beliefs
  filosofía *s.* sistema de valores o creencias

pinnacle (pĭn′ə-kəl) *n.* a peak; a pointed top
  pináculo *s.* cumbre; cima

ponder (pŏn′dər) *v.* to think or consider carefully
  considerar *v.* pensar o reflexionar con atención

potential (pə-tĕn′shəl) *n.* the ability to grow or develop
  potenial *s.* capacidad de crecimiento o desarrollo

predicament (prĭ-dĭk′ə-mənt) *n.* an unpleasant situation from which it is difficult to free oneself
  aprieto *s.* situación incómoda de la que es difícil zafarse

primitive (prĭm′ĭ-tĭv) *adj.* of or relating to a nonindustrial, often tribal, culture
  primitivo *adj.* relacionado con una cultura no industrial o tribal

prodigy (prŏd′ə-jē) *n.* a person with an exceptional talent
  prodigio *s.* persona con un talento excepcional

progressiveness (prə-grĕs′ĭv-nĭs) *n.* the state of advancing toward better conditions or new policies, ideas, or methods
  progresismo *s.* avance hacia mejores condiciones, o nuevas medidas, ideas o métodos

propaganda (prŏp′ə-găn′də) *n.* information that supports a certain cause
  propaganda *s.* información que apoya una causa

proportional (prə-pôr′shə-nəl) *adj.* having a constant relation in degree or number
    proporcional *adj.* que tiene una relación constante de grado o cantidad

proposition (prŏp′ə-zĭsh′ən) *n.* a suggested plan
    propuesta *s.* plan sugerido

propriety (prə-prī′ĭ-tē) *n.* the quality of being proper; appropriateness
    corrección *s.* decoro; conveniencia

prosperity (prŏ-spĕr′ĭ-tē) *n.* the condition of having success; flourishing
    prosperidad *sust.* hecho de tener éxito; progreso

provisions (prə-vĭzh′ənz) *n.* necessary supplies; food
    provisiones *s.* suministros necesarios; alimentos

provoke (prə-vōk′) *v.* to cause; to bring up
    provocar *v.* causar; suscitar

pungent (pŭn′jənt) *adj.* sharp or intense
    acre *adj.* agudo o intenso

puritanical (pyŏŏr-ĭ-tăn′ĭ-kəl) *adj.* strictly observant of religious practices; sternly moral
    puritano *adj.* que cumple con rigor las prácticas religiosas; severamente moral

pursuit (pər-sōōt′) *n.* the act of chasing
    persecución *v.* seguimiento

ramble (răm′bəl) *v.* to talk at length and aimlessly
    divagar *v.* hablar sin parar y sin ton ni son

ransom (răn′səm) *n.* payment demanded for the release of a person or property
    rescate *s.* dinero que se pide o se paga por la liberación de una persona o propiedad

rationalize (răsh′ə-nə-līz′) *v.* to make explanations for one's behavior
    justificar *v.* dar explicaciones racionales de la conducta propia

ravage (răv′ĭj) *n.* serious damage or destruction
    devastación *s.* daño o destrucción grave

refrain (rĭ-frān′) *v.* to hold oneself back; to stop
    refrenar *v.* contener, dominar o hacer menos violento; parar

refuge (rĕf′yōōj) *n.* a source of comfort in times of trouble
    refugio *v.* fuente de consuelo en momentos de dificultad

refute (rĭ-fyōōt′) *v.* to prove as false
    refutar *v.* demostrar que es falso

rehabilitation (rē′hə-bĭl′ĭ-tā′shən) *n.* the process of restoring someone to physical capability, usually through exercise and physical therapy
    rehabilitación *s.* proceso de restaurar capacidades físicas con ejercicio y fisioterapia

relay (rē′lā) *n.* a race in which several team members take turns running to complete the race
    carrera de relevos *s.* carrera en que los corredores de cada equipo se van relevando

remorse (rĭ-môrs′) *n.* sorrow; regret
    remordimiento *s.* pesar; arrepentimiento

remote (rĭ-mōt′) *adj.* located far away
    remoto *adj.* lejano

rendition (rĕn-dĭsh′ən) *n.* a pictorial representation; an interpretation
    interpretación *s.* representación pictórica

replete (rĭ-plēt′) *adj.* abundantly supplied
    repleto *adj.* lleno; atiborrado

reserve (rĭ-zûrv′) *n.* self-restraint in the way one looks or acts
    reserva *s.* discreción o comedimiento en la forma de presentarse y de actuar

resignation (rĕz′ĭg-nā′shən) *n.* acceptance of something that is inescapable
    resignación *s.* conformidad para aceptar lo que no tiene remedio

resolute (rĕz′ə-lōōt′) *adj.* firm or determined
    resuelto *adj.* firme o decidido

restrain (rĭ-strān′) *v.* to hold back; to control
    refrenar *v.* contener; controlar

retort (rĭ-tôrt′) *n.* a quick, sharp, witty reply
    réplica *s.* respuesta rápida e ingeniosa

rigid (rĭj′ĭd) *adj.* inflexible; strict
    rígido *adj.* inflexible; estricto

sacred (sā′krĭd) *adj.* holy; worthy of religious veneration or respect
sagrado *adj.* santo; digno de veneración o respeto religioso

sanctuary (săngk′chōō-ĕr′ē) *n.* a place of refuge
santuario *s.* lugar de refugio

savage (săv′ĭj) *n.* a person regarded as primitive or uncivilized
salvaje *s.* persona a quien se considera primitiva o incivilizada

scale (skāl) *v.* to climb up or over; ascend
escalar *v.* subir; ascender

searing (sîr′ĭng) *adj.* hot enough to burn, char, or scorch
abrasador *adj.* que quema o chamusca

sect (sĕkt) *n.* a religious group
secta *s.* grupo religioso

secure (sĭ-kyŏŏr′) *adj.* safe; protected; free from fear or anxiety
seguro *adj.* a salvo; protegido; libre de temores

sensation (sĕn-sā′shən) *n.* a state of great interest and excitement
sensación *s.* estado de gran interés y emoción; furor

sensational (sĕn-sā′shə-nəl) *adj.* intended to arouse strong curiosity or interest, especially through exaggerated details
sensacional *adj.* que llama fuertemente la atención, la curiosidad o el interés, especialmente con detalles exagerados

serendipitous (sĕr′ən-dĭp′ĭ-təs) *adj.* found by fortunate accident
fortuito *adj.* hallado por buena suerte

sham (shăm) *n.* something false or empty that is presented as genuine; a fake
farsa *sust.* algo falso o vacío que se presenta como genuino; mentira

sheepishly (shē′pĭsh-lē) *adv.* meekly; with embarrassment
tímidamente *adv.* mansamente; con vergüenza

sidekick (sīd′kĭk′) *n.* a close friend
compañero *s.* buen amigo

sinister (sĭn′ĭ-stər) *adj.* suggesting or threatening evil
siniestro *adj.* malo o con mala intención

solemn (sŏl′əm) *adj.* deeply serious
solemne *adj.* profundamente serio

specialization (spĕsh′ə-lĭ-za′shən) *n.* a focus on a particular area of study
especialización *s.* preparación en determinada área de estudio

stealthily (stĕl′thə-lē) *adv.* cautiously; secretly
furtivamente *adv.* secretamente; a hurtadillas

sterile (stĕr′əl) *adj.* barren; lacking vitality
estéril *adj.* árido; sin vitalidad

stifled (stī′fəld) *adj.* smothered **stifle** *v.*
sofocado *adj.* ahogado **sofocar** *v.*

stipulation (stĭp′yə-lā′shən) *n.* the act of laying down a condition or agreement
estipulación *s.* acción de definir condiciones o acuerdos

stoop (stōōp) *v.* to bend forward and down from the waist or the middle of the back
encorvarse *v.* doblarse por la cintura o la espalda hacia delante

straddle (străd′l) *v.* to be on both sides of
estar entre dos aguas *v.* estar por ambas partes

straggle (străg′əl) *v.* to spread out in a scattered group
dispersar *v.* separarse en un grupo extendido en distintas direcciones

strew (strōō) *v.* to spread here and there; scatter
esparcir *v.* derramar; dispersar

subordinate (sə-bôr′dn-ĭt) *adj.* secondary; belonging to a lower rank
subordinado *adj.* secundario; de un rango inferior

subtle (sŭt′l) *adj.* slight; difficult to detect
sutil *adj.* leve; imperceptible

sullen (sŭl′ən) *adj.* showing silent resentment; sulky
hosco *adj.* resentido; huraño

summon (sŭm′ən) *v.* to send for; call
llamar *v.* mandar a traer

surrender (sə-rĕn′dər) *v.* to give up possession or control to another
rendir *v.* entregar posesiones o control

tactic (tăk′tĭk) *n.* a maneuver to achieve a goal
  táctica *s.* maniobra para alcanzar una meta

tentatively (tĕn′tə-tĭv-lē) *adv.* uncertainly or hesitantly
  tentativamente *adv.* provisionalmente; con vacilación

tolerable (tŏl′ər-ə-bəl) *adj.* fairly good; passable
  tolerable *adj.* regular; pasable

traipse (trāps) *v.* to walk or tramp around
  recorrer *v.* andar de un lado para otro

transcendent (trăn-sĕn′dənt) *adj.* being above the material world
  trascendente *adj.* por encima del mundo material

treacherous (trĕch′ər-əs) *adj.* not to be relied on; untrustworthy
  traicionero *adj.* traidor; desleal

tremor (trĕm′ər) *n.* nervous trembling
  temblor *s.* estremecimiento nervioso

turmoil (tûr′moil′) *n.* a state of extreme confusion or agitation
  agitación *s.* estado de extrema confusión o caos

unabashed (ŭn′ə-băsht′) *adj.* obvious; bold
  descarado *adj.* desenfadado; sin inmutarse

undaunted (ŭn-dôn′tĭd) *adj.* not discouraged; courageous
  intrépido *adj.* impertérrito; sin desanimarse

unravel (ŭn-răv′əl) *v.* to undo; come apart
  deshilachar *v.* deshacer; desenredar

unseemly (ŭn-sēm′lē) *adj.* inappropriate
  indecoroso *adj.* impropio

valiant (văl′yənt) *adj.* brave
  valiente *adj.* valeroso

vehemently (vē′ə-mənt-lē) *adv.* with intense emotion
  vehementemente *adv.* con intensa emoción

vex (vĕks) *v.* to disturb; to annoy
  irritar *v.* molestar; sacar de quicio

vigilant (vĭj′ə-lənt) *adj.* watchful; alert
  vigilante *adj.* atento; alerta

vigilantly (vĭj′ə-lənt-lē) *adv.* watchfully
  vigilantemente *adv.* con atención

vigorously (vĭg′ər-əs-lē) *adv.* energetically
  vigorosamente *adv.* enérgicamente

vileness (vīl′nəs) *n.* unpleasantness; disgusting quality
  vileza *s.* inmundicia; asquerosidad

virtuoso (vûr′chōō-ō′sō) *n.* a musician with excellent abilities, techniques, and/or an attractive personal style
  virtuoso *s.* músico de excelentes aptitudes, técnicas y/o estilo personal atractivo

waver (wā′vər) *v.* to exhibit indecision; to hesitate
  flaquear *v.* mostrar indecisión; vacilar

wince (wĭns) *v.* to flinch or shrink in pain or distress
  estremecerse *v.* encogerse o contraerse por dolor o malestar

yield (yēld) *v.* to give in to another
  ceder *v.* rendir

Pronunciation Key

Symbol	Examples	Symbol	Examples	Symbol	Examples
ă	at, gas	m	man, seem	v	van, save
ā	ape, day	n	night, mitten	w	web, twice
ä	father, barn	ng	sing, hanger	y	yard, lawyer
âr	fair, dare	ŏ	odd, not	z	zoo, reason
b	bell, table	ō	open, road, grow	zh	treasure, garage
ch	chin, lunch	ô	awful, bought, horse	ə	awake, even, pencil,
d	dig, bored	oi	coin, boy		pilot, focus
ĕ	egg, ten	ŏŏ	look, full	ər	perform, letter
ē	evil, see, meal	ōō	root, glue, through		
f	fall, laugh, phrase	ou	out, cow	**Sounds in Foreign Words**	
g	gold, big	p	pig, cap	KH	*German* ich, auch;
h	hit, inhale	r	rose, star		*Scottish* loch
hw	white, everywhere	s	sit, face	N	*French* entre, bon, fin
ĭ	inch, fit	sh	she, mash	œ	*French* feu, cœur;
ī	idle, my, tried	t	tap, hopped		*German* schön
îr	dear, here	th	thing, with	ü	*French* utile, rue;
j	jar, gem, badge	*th*	then, other		*German* grün
k	keep, cat, luck	ŭ	up, nut		
l	load, rattle	ûr	fur, earn, bird, worm		

Stress Marks

ʹ   This mark Indicates that the preceding syllable receives the primary stress. For example, in the word *language,* the first syllable is stressed: lăngʹgwĭj.

ʹ   This mark is used only in words in which more than one syllable is stressed. It indicates that the preceding syllable is stressed, but somewhat more weakly than the syllable receiving the primary stress. In the word *literature,* for example, the first syllable receives the primary stress, and the last syllable receives a weaker stress: lĭtʹər-ə-chōōrʹ.

Adapted from *The American Heritage Dictionary of the English Language,* fourth edition. Copyright © 2006 by Houghton Mifflin Harcourt Publishing Company. Used with the permission of Houghton Mifflin Harcourt Publishing Company.

INDEX OF FINE ART

Index of Skills

A

Academic vocabulary, 16–19, 27, 48, 64, 78, 89, 121, 134, 169, 188, 228, 244, 280, 289, 321, 337, 368, 386, 408, 428, 461, 485, 498, 603, 651, 687, 702, 715, 737, 750, 781, 802, 820, 850, 883, 898, 909, 923, 932, 943, 981, 998, 1012, 1021, 1029, 1036, 1059, R118–R119. *See also* Specialized vocabulary; Vocabulary.

Act (in a play), 7, R102

Active listening 159, 311, 971, 1095, R84–R85

Active reading, 12–15

Active voice, of verbs, 585, 674, R57

Ad campaigns, 1000–1003
  creating, 1003
  evaluating, 985, 987, 1002–1003
  strategies for viewing, 1001

Adjectival clauses, 403, 963, R62
  essential, 963, R62
  nonessential, 963, R62

Adjectival phrases, R60

Adjectives, R47, R57–R59
  versus adverbs, R58
  comparative forms, 211, 229, R58
  formed from suffixes, 932
  predicate, R57, R60
  proper, R51
  punctuation between, 623, R49
  superlative forms, 229, R58

Adverbial clauses, 930, 933, R62–R63

Adverb phrases, R60

Adverbs, R58–R59. *See also* Modifiers.
  versus adjectives, R58
  comparative forms, R58
  formed from suffixes, 498
  superlative forms, R58

Advertising, 10, 1000–1003, R92–R94
  analyzing, 1000–1003
  billboards, R92
  celebrities in, R93
  demographics, R87
  evaluating, 985, 987, 1002–1003
  flyer, R92
  infomercial, R92
  marketing, R92
  persuasion in, 985, 1001
  political ads, R92
  print ads, 985, 987, 1001, R92
  product comparison, R93

product placement, R92
promotional Web sites, 1001
public service announcements, 987, R87, R92
sponsors, R92
target audience, 1000–1001, R87
teaser trailers, 1001
trailers, 1001, R92

Affixes. *See* Prefixes; Suffixes.

Agreement
  pronoun-antecedent, 103, 445, R52–R53
  subject-verb, 387, 473, R65

Alliteration, 606, 607, 609, 622, 632–637, R102. *See also* Sound devices.

Allusions, 335, R102

Almanacs, 1068. *See also* References.

Analogies, R73, R102, R113. *See also* Rhetorical devices.

Analogies (Vocabulary strategy), 260, 802

Analysis, writing, 65, 113, R39–R40
  criteria for, R39
  options for organization, R39–40

Analyzing Traditional Material in Modern Fiction, FM42

Anecdote, 62, 468–472, R102
  in student writing, 1043, R31, R41

Antecedent-pronoun agreement, 103, 445, R52–R53

Antonyms, 494, 1029, R72

Apostrophes, R50

Appeals, 985, R22. *See also* Arguments; Persuasive techniques.
  to authority, R113
  to reason, 1039, R21, R115
  bandwagon, 984, R22
  emotional, 984–987, 1039, R22, R93, R114
  ethical, 984, R21, R114
  logical, R21, R115
  to pity or fear, 984, R22
  snob appeal, R22

Appositives and appositive phrases, 703, 865, R61

Arguments, 982–983, 988–997, R20, R113. *See also* Appeals; Persuasive essay, writing; Persuasive techniques.
  claims, 982–983, 984, 986, 1031, R20, R113
  counterarguments, 982, 986, 989, 1039, 1044, R20, R26, R40, R114
  deductive, R23, R114

elements of, 982–983, 988–997, R20
evaluating, FM53, 886, 983, 984–987, 1030–1035, R25–R26
evidence, 867, 982–983, 1030–1035, R20, R22–R23, R25–R26, R41, R78, R81, R114
  faulty, 984, R24, R115. *See also* Fallacies.
  inductive, R22–R23, R115
  opposing. *See* counterarguments, *above.*
  premises, 984, 986, 987
  proposition and support, R21
  reasons, 982–983, R20
  strategies for determining strong, R26
  strategies for reading, 982–987, R20–R26
  strawman, R21
  support, 982, R20, R117
  writing, 300–309, R40–R41

Art. *See* Visuals.

Articles (written). *See* Feature articles; History articles; Magazine articles; Newspapers, articles in; Online articles.

Articulation. *See* Speaking strategies.

Artistic effects. *See* Media presentations.

Asking questions. *See* Questioning.

Assertions, commonplace, 1031, 1034

Assessment Practice, 160–165, 312–317, 371, 450–457, 594–599, 678–683, 770–777, 874–879, 972–977, R95–R101
  comparing texts, 344–371, 704–721
  reading comprehension, 160–163, 312–315, 450–456, 594–597, 678–681, 770–776, 874–877, 972–975, R96–R97
  revising and editing, 165, 317, 457, 599, 683, 777, 879, 977
  short constructed response, 163, 315, 371, 456, 597, 681, 721, 776, 877, 975, R100
  visuals, 370, 453, 456, 720, 773, 776
  vocabulary, 164, 316, 598, 682, 878, 976, R98

Assonance, 606, 632–637, R102

Atlases, 1068. *See also* References.

Audience
  media, 111, 113, R86, R87
  speaking and listening, R86
  target, R87

Authority. *See* Appeals; Arguments.

Author's background, 37, 51, 67, 81, 91, 104, 115, 123, 137, 177, 197, 231, 247, 267, 283, 291, 329, 345, 366, 373, 388, 395, 411, 431, 469, 475, 487, 501, 611, 625, 633, 639, 645, 657, 695, 705, 722, 729, 741, 753, 789, 805, 823, 832, 839, 857, 891, 901, 915, 925, 935, 954, 989, 1005, 1015, 1023, 1031
    influence of, 37, 782–787
Author's message, *See* Main ideas; Theme.
Author's perspective, R102
    analysis of, 120
Author's point of view. *See* Author's perspective.
Author's position, R113. *See also* Claims.
Author's purpose, 410–427, 429, 652–655, 838–849, 924–931, 1015–1020, R102
Author's style. *See* Style.
Author's viewpoint. *See* Author's perspective.
Autobiographical narrative, writing, 148–157
    analysis of 153–154
    common core key traits, 148, 156
    options for organization, 151
    preparing for timed writing, 157
    presenting, 158–159
    rubric, 156
Autobiography, 8, R102. *See also* Memoirs.

B

Ballads, 656–666, R102
    analysis of, 657–666
Bandwagon appeal, 984, R22, R85, R93
Bar graphs, R5
Base words, 408, R69. *See also* Word parts; Word roots.
Beliefs, identifying. *See* Values and beliefs, identifying.
Bias, 311, 1026, R25, R113
    identifying, 1026, R25, R85
    in reporting, R92
Bibliography, R113. *See also* Works cited.
    MLA style, 1086
Biographical approach. *See* Author's background, influence of.
Biography, 8, 9, 266–279, 282–288, R103
    analysis and evaluation of, 282–288
Blog, creating, 448–449
Boldface type, as text feature, R3
Book excerpts, 652–655, 861, 954–959
Books, as a resource, 1069
Brainstorming, 372, 430
Bulleted list, as text feature, 891, 895, R3
Business correspondence, R42–R43, R113.

See also Technical and business writing.
    formats for, R43–R45
    key techniques, R42–R43
Bylaws, R44.

C

Camera shots in film and video, R89.
    See also Media elements and techniques.
    close-up, 111, 263, 265, R89
    establishing, R89
    high-angle, R89
    identifying, 264
    long, 263, 264, 265, R89
    low-angle, R89
    medium, 111, R89
    point-of-view, R89
    reaction, 263, 265, R89
Capitalization, 567, R51
    of countries, 567, R51
    of ethnicities, 567, R51
    of languages, 567
    of nationalities, 567, R51
    of political parties, 567
    of religions, 567, R51
    in works cited list, 1092
Captions, R3
Career-related writing. *See* Business correspondence; Workplace and technical writing.
Case, pronoun, R52–R53
    nominative, R52–R53
    objective, R52–R53
    possessive, R52–R53
Catalogs, online, 1067
Cause-and-effect essay, 862–870
    adapting as multimedia presentation, 872–873,
    analysis of, 867–868
    common core key traits, 862
    options for organization, 864
    preparing for timed writing, 871
    rubric, 870
Cause-and-effect organization, 864, R10–R11, R38, R113. *See also* Patterns of organization.
    signal words for, 1015, R10, R33, R68
Cause-and-effect relationships, reading, 114–120, 1014–1020, R10–R11
Cause-effect diagrams, 115, 328, 819, 863, 864, 1015, R10, R38
CD-ROMs, of reference works, 1066
Central idea. *See* Main idea.
Chain of events, R38. *See also* Cause-and-effect organization.

Characterization, 168, 266–279, R103
    analysis of 172–175, 266–279, 288, 701, 831
    in poetry, 290–299
Character motivations, 77, 174, 176–187, 328–336, 344–367, 497
Characters, 5, R103. *See also* Characterization; Character types.
    analysis of, 47, 103, 112, 120, 133, 187, 279
    comparing and contrasting, 47, 102, 243, 246–259, 261, 264, 299, 472, 480, 581, 622, 780–801
    drawing conclusions about, 259
    in films, 111–113, 262–265
    and mood, 324
    motivation of, 77, 174, 176–187, 328–336, 344–367, 497
    in narrative poetry, 136–143
    setting and, 322–323, 794
    theme and, 462, 464
    tone and, 704–714
Character sketch, writing, 281
Character traits, 172, 173, R103
    analysis of, 103, 120, 168, 172–175, 187, 196–223, 227, 812
    evaluation of, 229
Character types
    dynamic, 187, R103
    central, 246–259, R103
    minor, R103
    static, 187, R103
Charts. *See* Graphic aids; Graphic organizers.
Choice of words. *See* Word choice.
Chronological order, 122–133, R9–R10, R36, R113. *See also* Patterns of organization.
    signal words for, 123, R9
Circle graphs, R5
Circular reasoning, R24. *See also* Fallacies; Reasoning.
Citation of sources. *See* Punctuation, of citations; Works cited.
Claims, in argument, 982–983, 984, 986, 988–997, 1031, R20, R113
    commonplace assertions, 1031, 1034
    evaluating an inference, 1030–1035
Clarifying, 47, 63, 77, 88, 102, 112, 120, 133, 147, 187, 195, 227, 243, 264, 279, 288, 299, 336, 367, 385, 407, 427, 472, 484, 506, 545, 580, 622, 655, 666, 701, 719, 736, 757, 831, 897, 922, 942, 997, 1002, 1011, 1035 R113. *See also* Monitoring.
    as reading strategy, 616–622

vocabulary; Specialized vocabulary.
Context clues, 19, 37, 134, 280, 289, 337, 345, 395, 702, 898, 1012, R68, R114. *See also* Vocabulary, in context.
  antonyms as, 1029
  for cause-and-effect, 1015, R68
  for comparison, R68
  for contrast, R68
  for definition or restatement, R68
  examples as, R68
  similes as, 188, 850
  synonyms as, 280
Conventions in myths. *See* Myths.
Correspondence, business, R42–R43, R113. *See also* Technical and business writing; Workplace and technical writing.
Counterarguments, 982, 986, 989, 1039, 1044, R20, R26, R40, R114
Couplets, R104
Credibility, 311, R114. *See also* Sources, evaluating.
Crisis. *See* Climax.
Criteria
  cause-and-effect essay, 870, R38
  comparison-contrast essay, 446, R37
  critical review, 308, R40
  descriptive writing, R34
  literary analysis, 766
  narrative writing, R36
  online feature article, 674
  personal narrative, 156
  persuasive essay, 1046, R40
  problem-solution essay, R39
  procedural text, 968, R44
  research paper, 1093
  short story, 590, R36
  technical writing, 968, R42
Critical listening, R85
Critical reading. *See* Reading skills and strategies; Test-taking strategies.
Critical review, writing, 300–309
Critical thinking. *See* Reading skills and strategies.
Criticism. *See* Text criticism.
Cross-curricular connections. *See also* Cultural context of literature; Historical context of literature.
  science, 70, 77, 622, 652–655
  social studies, 120, 143, 237, 243, 250, 267, 272, 279, 288, 334, 336, 398, 407, 431, 437, 484, 492, 566, 698, 757, 810, 819, 831, 860, 931, 1023, 1028, 1035
Cultural conflict, analysis of, 805–819

Cultural context of literature, 782–787, 789–801, 805, 813, 823,
Currency of sources. *See* Sources, evaluating.

D

Dashes, 409, R50
Data, collecting own, 122, 1075
Databases and database systems, R114. *See also* References.
Debates, 310–311, 1011
Deductive arguments, R23
Deductive reasoning, R23, R114
Delivery. *See* Speaking strategies.
Denotation 413, 715, 923, R72, R104. *See also* Connotation.
Dénouement. *See* Resolution.
Dependent (subordinate) clauses, 271, 281, 869, R62–R63
Derivations of words. *See* Word families; Word parts; Word roots.
  analysis of 305–306
  common core key traits, 300
  preparing for timed writing, 309
  rubric, 308
Descriptive language, R35. *See also* Sensory details.
Descriptive writing, 153, R34–R36.
Details
  descriptive, 153, R35
  sensory, 143, 153, 838–849, 860, R110
  in setting tone, 690, 693
  supporting, 282–288, 886–887, 889, 924–931, R8, R29, R34
Dewey decimal system, 1076
Diagrams, 47, 566, 714, R6. *See also* Graphic aids; Graphic organizers.
  cause-effect, 115, 328, 819, 863, 864, 1015, R10, R38
  cluster, 1034, 1060
  picture diagrams, R6
  schematic diagrams, R6
  Venn, 102, 243, 264, 299, 439, 472, 942, R11
  web, 66, 120, 282, 407, 643, 650, 900, 924, 998
Dialect, R104. *See also* Standard English.
  analysis of, 187, 637
  as element of style, 637
Dialogue, R104
  in drama, 7, 90–102, 509, 545, R104
  in films, 112, 113, 263
  in poetry, 291
  punctuation of, 589
  writing, 79, 240, 473, 587, R36

Diary entry, 544
Diction. *See* Word choice.
Dictionaries 89, 368, 485, 909, 1036, R74. *See also* References.
Digital media. *See* Electronic Media.
Direct objects, R48, R60
Discussion, 26, 279, 288, 367, 474, 656, 740, 822, 856, 908, 922, 1004, R83
  blogs, 448–449
  online discussion rules, 449
  role of chairperson, R83
  role of participants, R83
  role of recorder, R83
  small-group, 80, 88, 90, 122, 136, 187, 196, 336, 372, 385, 545, 632, 701, 804, 849, 856, 942, 1014, R83
Documentaries, 578–581, R88. *See also* Media; Media presentations; Sources.
  strategies for viewing, 579, 580
Documenting sources. *See* Works cited.
Documents
  consumer, R14–R15, R17–R18, R113
  electronic, R19
  historical, R115
  public, R15, R17, R113
  workplace, R16–R17, R42–R43
Double negatives, R59
Drafting techniques, 21, 151, 303, 441, 585, 671, 761, 865, 963, 999, 1041, 1086–1087, R28
Drama, 4, 7, 90–102, 224–227, 508–566, R104
  acts in, 7, R102
  cast of characters, 92, 224, 510, R103
  dialogue, 7, 90–102, R104
  performance, 102, 133, 566
  scenes in, 7, R110
  stage directions, 7, 90–102, R111
  strategies for reading, 90–102, 508–545, 546–566, R2
  theme in, 508–545, 546–566
Drawing conclusions. *See* Conclusions.

E

Editing, of films and video, 263, R90
  analysis of, 264
  cut, R90
  dissolve, R90
  fade-in, R90
  fade-out, R90
  jump cut, R90
  pace, R90
  split screen, R90
Editing, of writing. *See* Revising and editing.

plural, R46, R52
possessive, R46, R52
precise, R29
predicate, R60, R67
proper, R46, R52
singular, R46, R52
Novellas, 5, 832–837
Novels, 5, 166, 318, 458, 600, 684, 778,
        880, 978, 1056
    excerpts from, 104–109, 312, 313,
        388–393, 450–451, 722–727,
        875–876
    historical, 388–393
    mystery, 104–109

O

Objectivity, evaluating, 427
Objections, anticipating, 982, 986, 989,
        1039, 1044, R20, R41
Object pronoun, 303, R52
Objects
    direct, R48, R60
    indirect, R48, R60
    use of *whom* as, 303 R54
Observations as a research source, 1075
Ode, 638–643, R108
Online articles, 145–146, 192–193, 885,
        940–941, 990–993
    maintaining, 676–677
    writing, 668–675
Online catalog, 1067
Online information. *See* Internet; Web sites.
Onomatopoeia, 666, R108
Open-ended response. *See* Extended
        constructed response; Short
        constructed response.
Opinion pieces, 983, 985, 994–996,
        1008–1010
    writing, 1003
Opinions, 915, 1031
    in conclusions, R33
    editorial, 986, R114
    evaluating, R25–R26
    expert, R25, R81, R83–R85
    versus facts, 914–922, R40, R81, R85,
        R114
    identifying, 914–922, 1032, 1034
    in persuasive texts, 1031
    supporting, R20, R41, R83
Opinion statement. *See* Opinion pieces.
Opposing arguments. *See* Counterarguments.
Opposing viewpoints. *See* Counterarguments.
Oral fluency, 75, 127, 181, 843, 995
Oral interpretation, R82
Oral presentations 158–159, 736, 768–769,

970–971, 1011, 1035, 1094–1095,
        R78–R84. *See also* Speaking strategies.
    debate, 310–311, 1011
    descriptive speech, R79
    dramatic performance, 102, 133, 566
    informative speech, 1094–1095, R78
    instructional speech, 970–971
    oral narrative, 158–159
    oral reading, 650
    personal narrative, 158–159
    persuasive speech, 1035, R81
    reciting a poem, R82
    summary, R84
Oral reading, 650
Oral response to literature, 768–769, R82
Oral tradition, 4, R108
    fables, R105
    folk tales, 488–489, 490–496, R106
    myths, 476–479, 480–483, R108
    tall tales, 822–831, R112
Order of events. *See* Sequence.
Organizational patterns. *See* Patterns of
        organization.
Organizing. *See* Graphic organizers; Patterns
        of organization.
Origin of words, 48, 750, R70–R71. *See also*
        Word roots.
Outlines, R4
    for planning writing, 499, 631, 999
    for taking notes, 144, 888, 889, 925
    for research paper, 1085
Overgeneralization, R24, R116
Oversimplification, R24

P

Pace, changing when reading, R27
Pacing. *See* Speaking strategies.
Papers. *See* Research paper, writing.
Paragraphs
    coherence of, R31–R32
    organizing, R31
    response writing, 763–765
    transitions in, R32–R33
    unity of, R31
Parallel episodes, 227, 497, R108
Parallelism, 1022–1028, 1037, R64
Parallel structure, of sentences, 441, R64
Paraphrasing, 136–143, 638–643, 704–714,
        1083–1084, R116. *See also* Plagiarism.
Parentheses, 1006, 1013, R50
Part-by-part order, 935, R116
Participles and participial phrases, 507, R61
    dangling, R59, R61
    misplaced, R61
    past, 507, R61

present, 507, R61
Parts of speech, R46–R47. *See also* specific
        parts of speech.
Passive voice, of verbs, 585, R57
Past tense, 189
    perfect, 128, 135
Patterns of organization
    analyzing, 935–942
    cause-effect, 864, R10–R11, R113
    chronological, 122–133, R9–R10, R113
    classification, R113
    comparison-contrast, 429, 440, 499, 631,
        999, 1023, R11, R113
    deductive, R23, R114
    inductive, R22, R115
    main idea and supporting details, 9,
        283–288, R8–R9, R115
    order of importance, R35, R40
    order of impression, R35
    part-by-part, 935, R116
    point-by-point, 261, 429, 440, 499, 631,
        999, R11
    problem-solution, R13, R116
    proposition and support, R21
    reasons for opinion, R20
    sequential, 963, R117
    spatial order, R35
    subject-by-subject, 261, 429, 440, 499,
        631, 999, R11, R38
Peer review, 23, 150, 152, 302, 304, 440, 442,
        584, 586, 670, 672, 760, 762, 864, 866,
        962, 964, 1040, 1042, 1080, 1088, R30
Performances,
    dramatic, 102, 133, 566
Periodicals, 1070, R116. *See also* Magazines;
        Newspapers.
    evaluation of, 1074
Periods, R49
    in abbreviations, R49
    to correct run-on sentences, 65, 155,
        R64–R65
Personal essays, 366, 740–749, 1014–1020,
        R104
Personal narrative, writing, 148–157
    adapting for speech, 158–159
    analysis of, 153–154
    common core traits, 148, 156
    preparing for timed writing, 157
    rubric, 156
Personification, 141, 608, 905, R108
Perspective, author's. *See* Author's perspective.
Persuasion, 982–987, 1004–1011, R20–R26,
        R116
    in ads, 985
Persuasive essay, writing, 1038–1047

Procedural text, reading, 944–953

Prompts, responding to, 49, 65, 79, 103, 135, 147, 148, 189, 195, 229, 245, 261, 281, 300, 343, 369, 387, 429, 438, 447, 473, 499, 507, 567, 577, 582, 623, 631, 668, 719, 738, 758, 803, 851, 862, 899, 933, 953, 960, 969, 999, 1013, 1037, R100–R101. *See also Preparing for timed writing; Writing for assessment.*

Pronouns, R52–R55

  agreement with antecedent, 103, 445, R52–R53

  capitalization of, R51

  clarity of reference, 761

  case of, R52–R53

  demonstrative, R46, R54

  first-person, R52

  gender of, R52

  indefinite, R46, R54, R66

  intensive, R46, R53

  interrogative, R46, R54

  nominative, R52–R53, R60

  number of, R52, R65

  object, 303, R52–R53

  personal, R46, R52, R53, R54

  person of, R52

  possessive, R52, R53, R54

  predicate, R60

  reference problems, 761, R55

  reflexive, R46, R53

  relative, 403, 963, R46, R54, R62, R67

  second-person, R52

  subject, 303, R52, R53

  third-person, R52

  verb agreement with, R66

Proofreading, 155, 157, 307, 445, 586, 675, 869, R29. *See also* Revising and editing.

  of test responses, 157, R100–R101

Propaganda, R25, R116

Proposition and support, R21

Public documents, R15, R17, R116. *See also* Literary nonfiction, types of; Speeches.

Public service announcements, 987, R87, R92

Publishing, 21, 155, 307, 445, 589, 674, 765, 967, 1045, 1092, R29

Punctuation, 1013, R49–R50

  apostrophes, R50

  brackets, 1013

  of citations, 671

  colons, 821, 967, R50

  commas, 151, 409, 623, 933, R49

  dashes, 409, R50

  of dialogue, 589, R50

  ellipses, 409, 1013, R50

  end marks, 65, R49

  exclamation points, R49, R60

  hyphens, R50

  after introductory words or phrases, R49

  italic type, R50

  parentheses, 1013, R50

  periods, R49

  of possessive forms, R50

  question marks, R49

  quick reference chart, R49–R50

  quotation marks, 589, 992, R50

  semicolons, 56, 65, 155, 851, R49

  of series of items, 151, 623, R49

  works cited, 1092

Purpose for reading, setting, 12, 246–259, 410–427, 486–497, 624–630, 988–997, R117

Q

Questioning, 266–279, R2. *See also* Monitoring.

Question marks, R49

Questions, R30, R33. *See also* Interviews; Research; Sentences.

  in research paper, 1080

  rhetorical, R116

  as text feature, R3

Quick reference charts

  capitalization, R51

  parts of speech, R46–R47

  punctuation, R49–R50

  sentence and its parts, R48

Quickwriting, 36, 47, 114, 230, 290, 394, 468, 508, 610, 624, 644, 694, 752, 838, 934, 1060

Quotation marks, 589, R50

  to designate misleading language, 992

  to enclose Internet search terms, 1063

  to set off speaker's exact words, 589

Quotations, R34. *See also* Plagiarism; Works cited.

  analysis of, 749, 911, 912, 931, 942

  brackets in, 1013

  in elaboration, 763, R34

  ellipses in, 1013, R50

  in news reports, 911

  punctuation with, 671, R50

  when researching, 1083–1084

R

Radio plays, reading, 90–102, R109

Reading comprehension, Assessment Practice, 160–163, 312–315, 450–456, 594–597, 678–681, 770–776,

874–877, 972–975, R95–R97

Reading fluency, 104, 388, 722, 832, 954

Reading for information. 881–959. *See also* Informational texts; Reading skills and strategies.

  anecdotes, 62

  book excerpts, 652–655, 861, 954–959

  citing evidence, R20, R114

  comic strip, 298

  compare and contrast, 147, 410–427, 580, 860, 988–997, 1005–1011, 1023–1028

  diary entry, 544

  electronic texts, R19. *See also* online articles, *below.*

  feature articles, 194, 887, 890–897, R115

  generalizations, making, 577

  history articles, 144–147, 192–193, 889

  information, evaluating, 195, 427, 886–887, 1071–1074, 1077, R25–R26

  informational texts, 884–889, R14–R19

  interview, 571–576, 914–922

  journal, 338–343, 544

  letters, 278, 1026–1027

  magazine articles, 410–427, 902–907, 926–930, 936–939

  maps, R7

  newspaper articles, 569–570, 739

  notes, 144–147, 652–655, 888

  objectivity, evaluating, 427

  online articles, 145–146, 192–193, 885, 940–941, 990–993

  pamphlets, 884

  personal essay, 366, 1014–1020

  political cartoons, 852–855, R87

  primary sources, 338–343, 1081

  sources, evaluating for usefulness, 195, 886, 887, 1071–1074, 1081

  synthesizing, 568–577, 719, R117

  technical directions, 944–953

  text features, using, 884–885, 889, 890–897, R3–R7

  timeline, 191

  treatment, identifying and comparing, 581, 652–655, 855, 912, 986–987, 988–997

Reading rate, adjusting, 729, 900–908, R27

Reading skills and strategies, 11, 12–15

  cause and effect, 114–120, 1014–1020

  chronological order, tracing, 122–133

  clarifying, 47, 63, 77, 88, 102, 112, 120, 133, 147, 187, 195, 227, 243, 264, 279, 288, 299, 336, 367, 385, 407, 427, 472, 484, 506, 580, 616–622, 655,

analogies, R73, R102, R113
parallelism, 1022–1028, 1037, R64
repetition, 630, 650, 1023, 1024, 1027, R109
rhetorical questions, 1007, 1030–1035, 1037, R116
Rhetorical fallacies, 984, 1004–1011. *See also* Fallacies.
Rhyme, 6, 606, R109–R110. *See also* Poetic elements and devices; Sound devices.
    analysis of, 290–297, 299, 605, 606, 607, 638–643
    end, 606, 607, R109
    internal, R109
    soft, 643
Rhyme scheme, 606, R110. *See also* Meter; Poetic elements and devices; Sound devices.
    analysis of, 606, 607, 638–643
Rhythm, 6, 657, R2, R110. *See also* Meter; Poetic elements and devices; Sound devices.
    analysis of, 290–297, 299, 606, 607, 656–666
Rising action, 30, 32–33, 37, 41, 44, 47, R110. *See also* Plot.
Role-playing, 410
Root words. *See* Word roots.
Rubric, 22. *See also* Criteria; Writing rubrics.
Run-on sentences, 56, 65, 155, 851, 1041, R64–R65

S

Scanning, R27, R117
Scene, 7, R110
Schematic diagram, R6
Screenplays, 224–227
Scope, identifying, 190–195, R117
    comparing, 195
Scoring rubrics. *See* Writing rubrics.
Scripts, R110
    for oral presentation, R79
    for video or podcast, 592, R89,
Search engines, 1063, 1076, R19
    evaluating results, 1064
Secondary sources, 1081
Semicolons, 56, 65, 155, 851, R49
Sensory details, R110
    analysis of, 838–849, 860
    in descriptive writing, R34–R35
    elaborating with, 153, R34
    evaluating, 143
    similes and, 845
Sentences, R48
    combining, 65, 738

complements in, R60
complete, 44, R48
complex, 751, 869, R63
compound, 738, R63
compound-complex, 803, R63
declarative, R60
exclamatory, R60
fragments, 44, 49, 281, R64
imperative, R60
incomplete, 49, R64
independent clauses as, 281
interrogative, R60
parallel structure, 441, R64
predicate, complete, R48
predicate, compound, R56, R60
predicate, simple, R48
run-on, 56, 65, 155, R64–R65
simple, R63
structure, 688, 689, R48, R63–R64
subject, compound, 387, R60
subject, simple, R48
topic, R117
variety in, 507, 765, R29
Sequence. *See also* Chronological order.
    flashbacks, 67, 73, 77, R105
    foreshadowing, 90–102, 227, R106
    recognizing, 66–77, 123, 162–163, 694–701
Sequence transitions, 154, 1087, R32
Sequential order, R117
Setting, 5, 322–327, 328–336, R110
    analysis of, 323, 326–327, 328–336, 344–365, 367, 472
    characters and, 322–323, 794
    in creating conflicts, 322–323
    and cultural context, 794
    mood and, creating, 324, 374, 385
    in narrative poetry, 137
    in nonfiction, 394–407
    tone and, 704–714
Short constructed response
    Assessment Practice, 163, 315, 371, 456, 597, 681, 721, 776, 877, 975, R100
    Grammar in Context, 79, 103, 189, 387, 473, 623, 703, 751, 851, 1037
Short stories, 4–5, 31–35, 36–47, 50–63, 66–77, 80–88, 160–163, 176–187, 196–223, 227, 230–243, 246–255, 259, 328–336, 344–365, 367, 372–385, 465–467, 694–701, 788–801, 804–819, R110
    common core traits for writing, 582
    options for organization, 585
    rubric, 590
    strategies for reading, R2

writing, 582–591, 667
Sidebars, 884, 885, 891, 895, R117
Signal words, R117. *See also* Transitions.
    for cause-and-effect organization, 1015, R11, R32
    for chronological order, 123, 126, R9, R32
    for comparison and contrast, R11
    for problem-solution order, R13
    for sequence of events or actions, 67, 70, 71, 73, 695, R9, R32, R36
Similes, 45, 188, 220, 608, 610–615, 792, 845, 1016, R110
Skimming, R27
Slang, 827, R68. *See also* Informal language.
Slogans, R93
Snob appeal, R22
Solutions. *See* Problem-solution essay; Problem-solution order.
Sonnet, 638–643, R110
Sound devices, 291–297, 299, 606–607, R111
    alliteration, 606, 607, 609, 622, 632–637, 673, R102
    assonance, 606, 632–637, R102
    meter, 606, 607, 656–666, R107
    onomatopoeia, 666, R108
    repetition, 291, 295, 296, 299, 606, 607, 630, 645, 649, 650, 856–860, R109
    rhyme, 6, 290–297, 299, 606, 607, R109–R110
    rhyme scheme, 606, 607, 638–643, R110
    rhythm, 6, 290–297, 299, 606, 607, 656–666, R2, R110
Sound elements. *See* Media elements and techniques.
Sources, documenting, 1082, 1086, 1087. *See also* Works cited.
Sources, evaluating, 195, 577, 886–887, 910–913, 1071–1074, 1077, 1081, R25–R26
    bias, 1026, R25, R91, R92, R94
    credibility, 311, 886, 1081, R94
Sources, types of, 1063–1070, R117. *See also* References.
    audio resources, 1066
    databases, 1068, R114
    documentaries, 578–581
    electronic, 1066, R19, R86, R88
    electronic card catalog (online catalog), 1067
    Internet, 1063–1065, R19, R115. *See also* Web sites.
    journals, 338–343, R115
    library resources, 1066–1067
    newspapers, 1066, 1070

T

Page numbers that appear in italics refer to biographical information.

ACKNOWLEDGMENTS

INTRODUCTORY UNIT

Scholastic: Excerpt from *Slam!* by Walter Dean Myers. Copyright © 1996 by Walter Dean Myers. Used by permission of Scholastic Inc.

Arte Público Press: "Teenagers," from Communion by Pat Mora Copyright © 1991 by Pat Mora. Reprinted with permission from the publisher Arte Público Press.

Gary DaSilva: Excerpt from *Brighton Beach Memoirs* by Neil Simon. Copyright © 1984 by Neil Simon. Reprinted by permission of Gary DaSilva, agent for Neil Simon.

Lerner Books: Excerpt from *Steve Jobs: Thinks Different* by Ann Brashares. Copyright © 2001 by The Millbrook Press. Used by permission of Lerner Books.

McIntosh and Otis: Excerpt from "The Winter Hibiscus" by Minfong Ho, from *Join In: Multiethnic Short Stories by Outstanding Writers for Young Adults,* edited by Donald R. Gallo. Copyright © 1993 by Minfong Ho. Reprinted by permission of McIntosh and Otis, Inc.

UNIT 1

Houghton Mifflin Harcourt: Excerpt from *Johnny Tremain* by Esther Forbes. Copyright © 1943 by Esther Forbes Hoskins. Copyright © renewed 1971 by Linwood M. Erskine, Jr., Executor of the Estate of Esther Forbes Hoskins. Reprinted by permission of Houghton Mifflin Harcourt Publishing Company. All rights reserved.

Scovil Chichak Galen Literary Agency: "The Elevator," from *Things That Go Bump in the Night* by William Sleator. Copyright © 1989 by William Sleator. Used by permission of the author and the author's agents, Scovil Chichak Galen Literary Agency, Inc.

Random House: "Raymond's Run," from *Gorilla, My Love* by Toni Cade Bambara. Copyright © 1971 by Toni Cade Bambara. Used by permission of Random House, Inc.

The Carol Mann Agency: "Manuscript Found in the Attic" by Marcus Rosenbaum, from *I Thought My Father Was a God: And Other True Tales from NPR's National Story Project* edited by Paul Auster. Copyright © 2001 by Paul Auster. Reprinted by permission of The Carol Mann Agency.

Sterling Lord Literistic: "Clean Sweep" by Joan Bauer, from *Shelf Life, Stories by the Book* edited by Gary Paulsen. Copyright © 2003 by Joan Bauer. Reprinted by permission of SLL/Sterling Lord Literistic, Inc.

William Morris Agency: "The Hitchhiker," from *Radio's Best Plays* by Lucille Fletcher. Copyright © 1947, 1952, renewed 1980 by Lucille Fletcher. Reprinted by permission of William Morris Agency, LLC, on behalf of the author.

Random House and International Creative Management: Excerpt from *Hoot* by Carl Hiassen. Copyright © 2002 by Carl Hiassen. Used by permission of Alfred A. Knopf, an imprint of Random House Children's Books, a division of Random House, Inc. and International Creative Management.

Susan Bergholz Literary Services: "My First Free Summer" by Julia Alvarez, first published in *Better Homes and Gardens,* August 2003. Copyright © 2003 by Julia Alvarez. Reprinted by permission of Susan Bergholz Literary Services, New York, NY and Lamy, NM. All rights reserved.

Laurence Yep: "The Great Rat Hunt" by Laurence Yep, from *When I Was Your Age: Original Stories about Growing Up,* edited by Amy Ehrlich. Copyright © 1996 by Laurence Yep. Reprinted by permission of the author.

Sternig & Byrne Literary Agency: "The Invaders" by Jack Ritchie, from *Boy's Life,* March 1978. Copyright © 1978 by Jack Ritchie. Reprinted by permission of the Sternig & Byrne Literary Agency.

WGBH: "People & Events: William Dawes (1745-1799)," from American Experience/WGBH Educational Foundation. Copyright © 2002 by WGBH/Boston. Used by permission.

UNIT 2

Houghton Mifflin Harcourt: Excerpt from "Broken Chain," from *Baseball in April and Other Stories* by Gary Soto. Copyright © 1990 by Gary Soto. Reprinted by permission of Harcourt Mifflin Harcourt Publishing Company.

McIntosh and Otis, Inc.: Excerpt from "The Green Armchair," from *First Crossing: Stories About Teen Immigrants* by Minfong Ho. Copyright © 2004 by Minfong Ho. Reprinted with permission of McIntosh & Otis, Inc.

Random House Children's Books and Curtis Brown, Ltd.: Excerpt from "The Moustache," from *Eight Plus One* by Robert Cormier. Copyright © 1975 by Robert Cormier. Used by permission of Random House Children's Books, a division of Random House, Inc. and Curtis Brown, Ltd.

Sheldon Fogelman Agency: Excerpt from *I Go Along* by Richard Peck. Copyright © 1989 by Richard Peck. First published in *Connections,* edited by Donald R. Gallo, by Delacorte Books. All rights reserved. Used by permission of Sheldon Fogelman Agency, Inc.

Miriam Altshuler Literary Agency: "The Treasure of Lemon Brown" by Walter Dean Myers, *Boys' Life,* March 1983. Copyright © 1983 by Walter Dean Myers. Reprinted by permission of Miriam Altshuler Literary Agency, on behalf of Walter Dean Myers.

The New York Times: Excerpts from "Blues Musicians Get Help Overcoming Hard Times" by Andrew Jacobs, from the *New York Times,* March 21, 2004. Copyright © 2004 by the New York Times Co. All rights reserved. Used by permission and protected by the Copyright Laws of the United States. The printing, copying, redistribution, or retransmission of the Material without express written permission is prohibited.

Daniel Keyes: "Flowers for Algernon" by Daniel Keyes, from *The Magazine of Fantasy and Science Fiction.* Copyright © 1959, 1987 by Daniel Keyes. Reprinted by permission of the author. All rights reserved.

G.P. Putnam's Sons: "Rules of the Game," from *The Joy Luck Club* by Amy Tan. Copyright © 1989 by Amy Tan. Used by permission of G.P. Putnam's Sons, a division of Penguin Group (USA) Inc.

Virginia Driving Hawk Sneve: "The Medicine Bag" by Driving Hawk, from *Boy's Life,* March 1975. Copyright © 1975 by Virginia Driving Hawk Sneve. Used by permission of the author.

Scholastic: "Who Are You Today, Maria?" from *Call Me Maria* by Judith Ortiz Cofer. Copyright © 2004 by Judith Ortiz Cofer. Published by Scholastic Inc./Orchard Books. Reprinted by permission.

Russell & Volkening: "The Railroad Runs to Canada" and "Go On or Die," from *Harriet Tubman: Conductor of the Underground Railroad* by Ann Petry. Copyright © 1955 by Ann Petry, renewed 1983 by Ann Petry. Reprinted by permission of Russell & Volkening as agents for the author.

Houghton Mifflin Harcourt: "The Mysterious Mr. Lincoln," from *Lincoln: A Photobiography* by Russell Freedman. Copyright © 1987 by Russell Freedman. Reprinted by permission of Houghton Mifflin Harcourt Publishing Company. All rights reserved.

John Steventon: Excerpt from "Tribute to John Henry" by John Steventon. Used by permission of the author.

Sheldon Fogelman Agency: Excerpt from *A Year Down Yonder* by Richard Peck. Copyright © 2000 by Richard Peck. Published by Dial Books for Young Readers, a division of Penguin Young Readers Group. All rights reserved. Used by permission of Sheldon Fogelman Agency, Inc.

The Curtis Publishing Company: "Luke Baldwin's Vow" by Morley Callaghan as appeared in *The Saturday Evening Post,* March 15, 1947. Copyright © 1947 SEPS: Licensed by Curtis Publishing, Indianapolis, IN. All rights reserved. www.curtispublishing.com

UNIT 3

William Morris Endeavor Entertainment: Excerpt from "Max," from *Zebra and Other Stories* by Chaim Potok. Copyright © 1998 by Chaim Potok. Reprinted by permission of William Morris Endeavor Entertainment, LLC on behalf of the Author.

Bancroft Library: Excerpt from *Journey to Topaz: A Story of the Japanese-American Evacuation* by Yoshiko Uchida. Copyright © 1971 by Yoshiko Uchida. Courtesy of the Bancroft Library, University of California, Berkeley.

Arnold Adoff: Excerpt from *The House of Dies Drear* by Virginia Hamilton. Copyright © 1968 by Virginia Hamilton, renewed © 2008 by The Arnold Adoff Revocable Trust. Used by permission of Arnold Adoff.

Don Congdon Associates: "The Drummer Boy of Shiloh" by Ray Bradbury. Copyright © 1960 by the Curtis Publishing Company, renewed 1988 by Ray Bradbury. Reprinted by permission of Don Congdon Associates, Inc.

Trident Media Group: "Hallucination," from *Gold, The Final Science Fiction Collection* by Isaac Asimov. Copyright © 1995 by Nightfall Inc./The Estate of Isaac Asimov. All rights reserved. Reprinted by the Estate of Isaac Asimov.

Prometheus Books: Excerpt from "Ellis Island and I," from *The Tyrannosaurus Prescription and 100 Other Essays* by Isaac Asimov (Amherst, NY: Prometheus Books). Copyright © 1989 by Isaac Asimov. Reprinted by permission of the publisher.

Dial Books for Young Readers: Excerpt from *Roll of Thunder, Hear My Cry* by Mildred Taylor. Copyright © 1976 by Mildred D. Taylor. Used by permission of Dial Books for Young Readers, A Division of Penguin Young Readers Group, A Member of Penguin Group (USA) Inc., 345 Hudson Street, New York, NY 10014. All rights reserved.

Naomi Shihab Nye: Excerpt from "Thank You in Arabic" by Naomi Shihab Nye. Copyright © 1995 by Naomi Shihab Nye. First published in *Going Where I'm Coming From* by arrangement with the author. Reprinted by permission of the author, Naomi Shihab Nye, 2008.

"My Father and the Figtree," from *19 Varieties of Gazelle: Poems of the Middle East* by Naomi Shihab Nye. Copyright © 1994, 1995, 1998, 2002 by Naomi Shihab Nye. Reprinted by permission of the author, Naomi Shihab Nye, 2008.

The Wylie Agency: Excerpts from "Leaving Desire, The Ninth Ward after the Hurricane" by Jon Lee Anderson, from the *New Yorker,* September 19, 2005. Copyright © 2005 by Jon Lee Anderson. Used by permission of the Wylie Agency, as agents for the author.

Arte Público Press: "Mi Madre," from *Chants* by Pat Mora. Copyright © 1984 by Arte Público Press—University of Houston. Reprinted with permission from Arte Público Press.

Simon J. Ortiz: "Canyon de Chelly" by Simon J. Ortiz, originally published in *Woven Stone,* University of Arizona Press, Tucson, AZ. Copyright © 1992 by Simon J. Ortiz. Permission granted by the author.

Bethlehem Books: Excerpt from *Year of the Black Pony* by Walt Morey. Copyright © 1976 by Walt Morey. Used by permission of Bethlehem Books, Bathgate, North Dakota, 2006.

EQUUS Magazine: "Never Get Lost on the Trail" by Joanne Meszoly, from EQUUS Magazine, August 2001. Copyright © 2001 EQUUS Magazine. Reprinted by permission of EQUUS Magazine.

UNIT 4

HarperCollins Publishers: Excerpt from *The Contender* by Robert Lipsyte. Copyright © 1967 by Robert Lipsyte. Used by permission of HarperCollins Publishers.

Scholastic: "Abuela Invents the Zero," from *An Island Like You: Stories of the Barrio* by Judith Ortiz Cofer. Copyright © 2005 by Judith Ortiz Cofer. Reprinted by permission of Orchard Books/Scholastic Inc.

Susan Bergholz Literary Services: "Gil's Furniture Bought & Sold," from *The House on Mango Street* by Sandra Cisneros. Copyright © 1984 by Sandra Cisneros. Published by Vintage Books, a division of Random House, Inc., and in hardcover by Alfred A. Knopf in 1994. Reprinted by permission of Susan Bergholz Literary Services, New York, NY and Lamy, NM. All rights reserved.

Rowman & Littlefield: "Pandora . . . The Fateful Casket," from *The Firebringer and Other Great Stories, Fifty-Five Legends That*

Will Live Forever by Louis Untermeyer. Copyright © 1968 by Louis Untermeyer. Reprinted by permission of Rowman and Littlefield Publishing, Lanham, MD.

Fulcrum Publishing: "Loo-Wit, the Fire-Keeper," from *Native American Stories* by Joseph Bruchac. Copyright © 1992 by Joseph Bruchac. Reprinted by permission of Fulcrum Publishing.

Little Simon: "The Old Grandfather and His Little Grandson," from *Twenty-Two Russian Tales for Young Children* by Leo Tolstoy, translated by Miriam Morton. Translation copyright © 1969 by Miriam Morton. Reprinted by permission of Little Simon, an imprint of Simon & Schuster Children's Publishing Division.

Bancroft Library: "The Wise Old Woman," from *The Sea of Gold and Other Tales from Japan* adapted by Yoshiko Uchida. Copyright © 1965 by Yoshiko Uchida. Courtesy of the Bancroft Library, University of California, Berkeley.

Teresa Palomo Acosta: "My Mother Pieced Quilts," from *Festival de Flor y Canto: An Anthology of Chicano Literature* by Teresa Palomo Acosta. Copyright © by Teresa Palomo Acosta. Used by permission of the author.

BOA Editions: "quilting," from *Quilting: Poems 1987–1990* by Lucille Clifton. Copyright © 1991 by Lucille Clifton. Reprinted by permission of BOA Editions, Ltd.

Random House: *The Diary of Anne Frank* (Play) by Frances Goodrich and Albert Hackett. Copyright © 1956 by Albert Hackett, Frances Goodrich Hackett, and Otto Frank. Used by permission of Random House, Inc.

Doubleday and Liepman AG: Excerpt from *The Diary of a Young Girl: the Definitive Edition* by Anne Frank. Edited by Otto H. Frank and Mirjam Pressler. Translated by Susan Massotty. Copyright © 1995 by Doubleday. Copyright © 1995 by The Anne Frank-Fonds, Basel, Switzerland. Used by permission of Doubleday, a division of Random House, Inc. and Liepman AG.

Gerda Weissman Klein: Excerpts from "A Diary from Another World" by Gerda Weissman Klein, from *Buffalo News*. Used by permission of the author.

Pantheon Books: Excerpt from *The Last Seven Months of Anne Frank* by Willy Lindwer. Copyright © 1988 by Willy Lindwer. English translation copyright © 1991 by Random House, Inc. Reprinted by permission of Pantheon Books, a division of Random House, Inc.

Cannongate Books Ltd.: "A Blind Man Catches a Bird," from *The Girl Who Married a Lion* by Alexander McCall Smith. First published in Great Britain by Canongate Books, Ltd., 14 High Street, Edinburgh, EH1 1TE. Reprinted by permission of Canongate Books Ltd.

UNIT 5

Sheldon Fogelman Agency: "The Geese" by Richard Peck. Copyright © 1970 by Richard Peck. First published in *Sounds and Silences,* edited by Richard Peck, Donald R. Gallo, by Delacorte Books. All rights reserved. Used with permission of Sheldon Fogelman Agency, Inc.

Rosina M. Albi: Excerpt from "Street Corner Flight" by Norma Landa Flores, from *Sighs and Songs of Aztlan* edited by F. E. Albi and J. G. Nieto. Copyright © 1975 by F. E. Albi and J. G. Nieto. Reprinted by permission of Rosina M. Albi.

The Overlook Press: Excerpt from "That Day," from *I Remember Root River* by David Kherdian. Copyright © 1978 by David Kherdian. Used by permission of the Overlook Press. All rights reserved. www.overlookpress.com

Elizabeth Barnett: "Afternoon on a Hill" by Edna St. Vincent Millay. Copyright © 1931, 1958 by Edna St. Vincent Millay and Norman Millay Ellis. Used by permission of Elizabeth Barnett, Literary Executor. All rights reserved.

Henry Holt and Company: "Stopping by Woods on a Snowy Evening," from *The Poetry of Robert Frost* edited by Edward Connery Lathem. Copyright 1923, 1969 by Henry Holt and Company. Copyright © 1951 by Robert Frost. Reprinted by arrangement with Henry Holt and Company, LLC.

HarperCollins Publishers: Excerpt from "Chrysalis Diary" from *Joyful Noise: Poems for Two Voices* by Paul Fleischman. Copyright © 1988 by Paul Fleischman. Used by permission of HarperCollins Publishers.

Okpaku Communications: "Sunset," from *Sounds of a Cowhide Drum* by Oswald Mbuyiseni Mtshali. Copyright © 1972 by the Third Press, Joseph Okpaku Publishing Company. Used by permission of Okpaku Communication Corporation.

The Estate of May Swenson: Excerpt from "Water Picture," from *Nature: Poems Old and New* by May Swenson. Copyright © 1994 by the Literary Estate of May Swenson. Reprinted by permission of The Estate of May Swenson.

New Directions: "Aware," from *This Great Unknowing: Last Poems* by Denise Levertov. Copyright © 1999 by the Denise Levertov Literary Trust, Paul A. Lacey and Valerie Trueblood Rapport, Co-Trustees. Reprinted by permission of New Directions Publishing Corp.

The University of Georgia Press: "Lineage," from *This Is My Century: New and Collected Poems* by Margaret Walker. Copyright © 1989, by Margaret Walker Alexander. Reprinted by permission of the University of Georgia Press.

Marian Reiner: "Simile: Willow and Ginkgo," from *It Doesn't Always Have to Rhyme* by Eve Merriam. Copyright © 1964, renewed © 1992 by Eve Merriam. All rights reserved. Used by permission of Marian Reiner.

University of Arkansas Press: "Introduction to Poetry," from *The Apple That Astonished Paris* by Billy Collins. Copyright © 1988 by Billy Collins. Reprinted by permission of the University of Arkansas Press.

Doubleday: "The Lesson of the Moth," from *Archy and Mehitabel* by Don Marquis. Copyright © 1927 by Doubleday. Used by permission of Doubleday, a division of Random House, Inc.

Julio Noboa: "Identity" by Julio Noboa. Copyright © by Julio Noboa. Used with permission.

Harvard University Press and the Trustees of Amherst College: "It's all I have to bring today" by Emily Dickinson, from *The Poems of Emily Dickinson,* Thomas J. Johnson, ed., Cambridge, Mass.: The Belknap Press of Harvard University Press. Copyright © 1951,

1955, 1979, 1983 by the President and Fellows of Harvard College. Reprinted by permission of the publishers and the Trustees of Amherst College.

Houghton Mifflin Harcourt: "We Alone," from *Horses Make a Landscape Look More Beautiful: Poems by Alice Walker*. Copyright © 1984 by Alice Walker. Reprinted by permission of Harcourt, Inc.

Brooks Permissions: "Speech to the Young: Speech to the Progress-Toward," from *Blacks* by Gwendolyn Brooks. Copyright © by Gwendolyn Brooks. Reprinted by consent of Brooks Permissions.

Alfred A. Knopf: "Mother to Son," from *The Collected Poems of Langston Hughes* by Langston Hughes. Copyright © 1994 by the Estate of Langston Hughes. Used by permission of Alfred A. Knopf, a division of Random House, Inc.

Random House and Little, Brown Book Group, Ltd.: "One More Round," from *And Still I Rise* by Maya Angelou. Copyright © 1978 by Maya Angelou. Used by permission of Random House, Inc. and Little, Brown Book Group, Ltd.

Boyds Mills Press: "Not My Bones," from *Fortune's Bones, The Manumission Requiem* by Marilyn Nelson. Copyright © 2004 by Marilyn Nelson. Published in Front Street Books, an imprint of Boyds Mills Press. Reprinted by permission.

Excerpt of "Notes" on *Fortune's Bones, The Manumission Requiem* by Marilyn Nelson. Copyright © 2004 by Marilyn Nelson. Published in Front Street Books, an imprint of Boyds Mills Press. Reprinted by permission.

Special Rider Music: "Boots of Spanish Leather" by Bob Dylan. Copyright © 1963; renewed © 1991 by Special Rider Music. All rights reserved. International copyright secured. Reprinted by permission.

Grove/Atlantic: "The Sunflowers," from *Dream Work* by Mary Oliver. Copyright © 1986 by Mary Oliver. Reprinted by permission of Grove/Atlantic, Inc.

UNIT 6

Rita Williams-Garcia: Excerpt from "Food from the Outside" by Rita Williams-Garcia, from *When I Was Your Age: Volume Two-Original Stories About Growing Up*. Copyright © 1999 by Rita Williams-Garcia. Used by permission of the author.

The C. S. Lewis Company: Excerpt from *The Voyage of the Dawn Treader* by C. S. Lewis. Copyright © 1952 by C. S. Lewis Pte. Ltd. Extract reprinted by permission.

Scovil Galen Ghosh Literary Agency, Inc.: From "The Masque of the Red Death," by William Sleator from *Guys Write for Guys Read,* edited by Jon Scieszka. Copyright © 2005 by William Sleator. Reprinted by permission of the author and the author's agents, Scovil Galen Ghosh Literary Agency, Inc.

Brandt & Hochman Literary Agents: Excerpt from "The Truth About the World" by Lloyd Alexander. Copyright © 2005 by Lloyd Alexander. First published in *Guys Write for Guys Read* (Viking, 2005.) Reprinted by permission of Brandt & Hochman Literary Agents, Inc. All rights reserved.

Alfred A. Knopf: From *Stargirl* by Jerry Spinelli. Copyright © 2000 by Jerry Spinelli. Used by permission of Alfred A. Knopf, an imprint of Random House Children's Books, a division of Random House, Inc.

Soho Press: Excerpt from "New York Day Women," from *Krik? Krak!* by Edwidge Danticat. Copyright © 1991, 1992, 1993, 1994, and 1995 by Edwidge Danticat. Reprinted by permission of Soho Press, Inc.

The New York Times: Adaptation of "Behind Monty Hall's Doors: Puzzle, Debate and Answer?" by John Tierney, from the *New York Times*. Copyright © 1991 by the New York Times Co. All rights reserved. Used by permission and protected by the Copyright Laws of the United States. The printing, copying, redistribution, or retransmission of the Material without express written permission is prohibited.

Atheneum Books for Young Readers: Excerpt from *Kira-Kira* by Cynthia Kadohata. Copyright © 2004 by Cynthia Kadohata. Reprinted with the permission of Atheneum Books for Young Readers, an imprint of Simon & Schuster Children's Publishing Division.

John McCandlish Phillips: "The Simple Commandments of Journalistic Ethics" by John McCandlish Phillips, from *Mobile Register,* July 8, 2003. Copyright © John McCandlish Phillips. Used by permission of author.

Little, Brown and Company: Excerpt from *Dress Your Family in Corduroy and Denim* by David Sedaris. Copyright © 2004 by David Sedaris. By permission of Little, Brown and Co., Inc.

Sterling Lord Literistic: "A Hike in New York City" by Samuel Levenson. Copyright © by Esther Levenson, Et Al. Reprinted by permission of Sterling Lord Literistic, Inc.

Carol Mann Agency: Excerpt from *The Park and the People* by Roy Rosenweig and Elizabeth Blackmar. Copyright © 1998 by Roy Rosenweig and Elizabeth Blackmar. Published by Cornell University Press. Reprinted with permission of the Carol Mann Agency.

UNIT 7

BOA Editions: "Eating Together," from *Rose,* by Li-Young Lee. Copyright © 1986 by Li-Young Lee. Reprinted by permission of BOA Editions, Ltd.

Susan Bergholz Literary Services: "Dusting," from *Homecoming: New and Collected Poems* by Julia Alvarez. Copyright © 1984, 1996 by Julia Alvarez. Reprinted by permission of Susan Bergholz Literary Services, New York, NY and Lamy, NM. All rights reserved.

James Baldwin Estate: Excerpt from "Sonny's Blues" by James Baldwin. Copyright © 1957 by James Baldwin; Copyright renewed. Originally published in *Partisan Review*. Collected in *Going to Meet the Man,* published by Vintage Books. Used by arrangement with the James Baldwin Estate.

David Higham Associates: Excerpt from "Beware of the Dog," from *Over to You: 10 Stories of Flyers and Flying* by Roald Dahl. Copyright © 1946 by Roald Dahl. Reprinted by permission of David Higham Associates, Ltd.

Susan Ito: Excerpt from "Origami" by Susan Ito, from *Welcome to Your Life: Writings for the Heart of Young America* edited by David Haynes and Julie Landsman. Copyright © 1998 by Susan K. Ito. Reprinted by permission of the author.

Barbara S. Kouts: "The Snapping Turtle" by Joseph Bruchac, from *When I Was Your Age,* Vol. Two, Candlewick Press, 1999. Copyright © 1999 by Joseph Bruchac. Reprinted by permission of Barbara S. Kouts Literary Agency.

HarperCollins Publishers: Excerpt from *Out of Bounds: Seven Stories of Conflict and Hope* by Beverley Naidoo. Copyright © 1997 by Beverley Naidoo. Used by permission of HarperCollins Publishers.

Alfred A. Knopf: "Pecos Bill," from *American Tall Tales* by Mary Pope Osborne. Copyright © 1991 by Mary Pope Osborne. Used by permission of Alfred A. Knopf, an imprint of Random House Children's Books, a division of Random House, Inc.

Viking Penguin and Penguin Books (UK): Excerpt from *The Pearl* by John Steinbeck. Copyright © 1945 by John Steinbeck. Copyright © renewed 1973 by Elaine Steinbeck, Thom Steinbeck, and John Steinbeck IV. Used by permission of Viking Penguin, a division of Penguin Group (USA) Inc. and Penguin Books (UK).

Gary Soto: "One Last Time," from *Living Up the Street* by Gary Soto. Copyright © 1985 by Gary Soto. Used by permission of the author.

Houghton Mifflin Harcourt: "How Things Work," from *A Fire in My Hands* by Gary Soto. Copyright © 2006, 1999 by Gary Soto. Reprinted by permission of Houghton Mifflin Harcourt Publishing Company. This material may not be reproduced in any form or by any means without the prior written permission of the publisher. All rights reserved.

The University of Georgia Press: "Sit-ins" and "I Want to Write," from *This Is My Century, New and Collected Poems* by Margaret Walker. Copyright © 1989 by Margaret Walker Alexander. Reprinted by permission of the University of Georgia Press.

Scholastic: Excerpt from *A Dream of Freedom: The Civil Rights Movement from 1954 to 1968* by Diane McWhorter. Copyright © 2004 by Diane McWhorter. Reprinted by permission of Scholastic Inc./Nonfiction.

Delacorte Press and Flannery Literary Agency: Excerpt from *Caught by the Sea: My Life On Boats* by Gary Paulsen. Copyright © 2001 by Gary Paulsen. Used by permission of Delacorte Press, an imprint of Random House Children's Books, a division of Random House, Inc. and Flannery Literary Agency.

Franklin Watts: Excerpt from *The Voyage of the Frog* by Gary Paulsen. Copyright © 1989 by Gary Paulsen. Reprinted by permission of Franklin Watts, a division of Scholastic Library Publishing.

UNIT 8

National Geographic Society: "Female Android Debuts in S. Korea" by Victoria Gilman, from *National Geographic News,* May 15, 2006. Copyright © 2006 by National Geographic Society. Reprinted by permission of the National Geographic Society.

Sundance/Newbridge, LLC: Excerpt from "Kill or Cure: Nature's Toxins" by Gail Riley. Copyright © 2006 by Gail Riley. Reprinted by permission of Sundance/Newbridge, LLC.

National Geographic Society: Excerpt from "Escape from the Blaze" by Michael Burgan, from *National Geographic World,* September 1988. Copyright © 1988 by National Geographic Society. Reprinted by permission of the National Geographic Society.

"The Spider Man Behind Spider-Man" by Bijal P. Trivedi, from *National Geographic Today,* May 2, 2002. Copyright © 2002 by National Geographic Society. Reprinted by permission of the National Geographic Society.

The EI Group: Excerpts from "Entomologist," from Career Profiles section of www.schoolsintheusa.com Used by permission of The EI Group.

National Geographic Society: Excerpts from "Over the Top: The True Adventures of a Volcano Chaser" by Renee Skelton, from *National Geographic World,* June 2001. Copyright © 2001 by National Geographic Society. Reprinted by permission of the National Geographic Society.

Excerpt from "Q&A: 'Songcatcher' Pioneer on Musical Heritage" by Brian Handwerk, from *National Geographic News,* June 16, 2003. Copyright © 2003 by National Geographic Society. Reprinted by permission of the National Geographic Society.

Time, Inc.: Adaptation of "Kabul's New Sensation" by Tim McGirk. Copyright © 2010 Time Inc. All rights reserved. Reprinted/Translated from *Time* Magazine with permission.

The New York Times: Excerpt from "Cyberbodies; Robo-Legs" by Michael Marriott, from the *New York Times,* June 20, 2005. Copyright © 2005 by the New York Times Co. All rights reserved. Used by permission and protected by the Copyright Laws of the United States. The printing, copying, redistribution, or retransmission of the Material without express written permission is prohibited.

The Chedd-Angier-Lewis Production Company: "Eureka: Scientific Twist of Fate" from Life's Little Questions II, Scientific American Frontiers, presented by PBS. Used by permission of The Chedd-Angier-Lewis Production Company.

Clarion Books: Excerpt from *An American Plague: The True and Terrifying Story of the Yellow Fever Epidemic of 1793* by Jim Murphy. Copyright © 2003 by Jim Murphy. Reprinted by permission of Clarion Books, an imprint of Houghton Mifflin Harcourt Publishing Company. All rights reserved.

National Geographic Society: "Odd Couples" by Amy Sarver, from *National Geographic Explorer,* Jan-Feb, 2006. Copyright © 2006 by National Geographic Society. Reprinted by permission of The National Geographic Society.

UNIT 9

Atheneum Books for Young Readers: Excerpt from "Why Can't I Live on French Fries?" by Richard J. Roberts, from *The Nobel Book of Answers,* edited by Bettina Stiekel. Copyright © 2001 Wilhelm Heyne Verlag GmbH & Co. KG, Munich. Essay compilation for English language edition copyright © 2003 Ullstein Heyne List GmbH & Co., Munich. English translation copyright © 2003 Simon & Schuster, Inc. Reprinted with the permission of Atheneum Books for Young Readers, an imprint of Simon & Schuster Children's Publishing Division.

Scholastic: Excerpt from "Should the driving age be raised to 18?" by Alex Koroknay-Palicz, National Youth Rights Association, published in *The New York Times Upfront*, May 8, 2006. Copyright © 2006 by Scholastic Inc. Used by permission.

Robert Laidlaw: "Zoos: Myth and Reality" by Rob Laidlaw. Used by permission of the author.

Michael Hutchins: "Zoos connect us to the natural world" by Michael Hutchins, from *The Boston Globe,* November 2, 2003. Copyright © 2003 by Michael Hutchins. Used by permission of the author.

NASPE: "Position on Dodgeball in Physical Education" by NASPE. Reprinted with permission from the National Association for Sport and Physical Education (NASPE), an association of the American Alliance for Health, Physical Education, Recreation, and Dance.

Time, Inc.: Excerpts from "The Weak Shall Inherit the Gym" by Rick Reilly, from *Sports Illustrated,* May 14, 2001. Copyright © 2001 by Time Inc. Reprinted courtesy of Time, Inc. All rights reserved.

Darhansoff Verrill Feldman Literary Agents: "The Sanctuary of School" by Lynda Barry. Copyright © 1992 by Lynda Barry. Originally published in *The New York Times,* January 5, 1992. Used by permission of Darhansoff Verrill Feldman Literary Agents.

Regents University of California: Letter to the Mayor of Chicago from Grand Council Fire of American Indians, from *Textbooks and the American.* Used by permission of California Center for Native Nations, University of California, Riverside.

Scholastic, Inc.: From "Nuclear Energy: Does It Make Sense for the Environment?" by Scott Peterson and Kelly Kissock. Published in *The New York Times Upfront,* October 10, 2005. Copyright © 2005 by Scholastic Inc. Used by permission.

ART CREDITS

CONSULTANTS

Janet Allen © Duane McCubrey; *Arthur Applebee* © Mark Schmidt; *Kylene Beers* © Sam Dudgeon/Houghton Mifflin Harcourt; *Jim Burke* © Bruce Forrester; *Douglas Carnine* © Houghton Mifflin Harcourt; *Carol Jago* Maggie's Photography, Pacific Palisades, CA; *Yvette Jackson* © Howard Gollub; *Robert Jimenez* © Tamra Stallings; *Judith Langer* © Mark Schmidt; *Robert Marzano* © Robert J. Marzano; *Donna Ogle* © Houghton Mifflin Harcourt; *Carol Booth Olson* © Dawson & Associates Photography; *Carol Tomlinson* © Gitchell's Studio; *May Lou McClosky* © Michael Romeo; *Lydia Stack* © Monica Ani; *William McBride* © William McBride; *David Considine* © Bill Caldwell; *Larkin Pauluzzi* © Gabriel Pauluzzi; *Lisa Scheffler* © Steven Scheffler.

TABLE OF CONTENTS

FM9 © Getty Images; **FM12** *top left* Illustration by Howard Simpson; *top right* © er Productions/Getty Images; *bottom* The Newbery Awards are administered by the American Library Service to Children, a division of the American Library Association. Seal image used by permission of American Library Association; **FM13** © PunchStock; **FM14** *top left* From *Harlem* by Walter Dean Myers, illustrated by Christopher Myers. © 1997 by Christopher Myers. Reprinted by permission of Scholastic, Inc; *right* Detail of *Frida* (2004), Maria Sanchez. Acrylic on canvas. C. Perez Collection. © Maria Sanchez; **FM15** © PunchStock; **FM16** *top left* Detail of *Jerusalem* (1984), Tamam Al-akhal. Palestine. Oil on canvas, 50 cm × 70 cm. Private collection; *top right* © Jupiterimages Corporation; *bottom* The Newbery Awards are administered by the American Library Service to Children, a division of the American Library Association. Seal image used by permission of American Library Association; **FM17** © PunchStock; **FM18** *left* Detail of *Crossing Borders* (1995), Deidre Scherer. Fabric and thread. © Deidre Scherer; *right* © Joan Marcus; **FM19** © PunchStock; **FM20** *top left* Detail of *Aspiration* (1936), Aaron Douglas. Oil on canvas, 60″ × 60″. © Fine Arts Museums of San Francisco purchase, the estate of Thurlow E. Tibbs, Jr., the Museum Society Auxiliary, American Art Trust Fund, Unrestricted Art Trust Fund, partial gift of Dr. Ernest A. Bates, Sharon Bell, Jo-Ann Beverly, Barbara Carleton, Dr. and Mrs. Arthur H. Coleman, Dr. and Mrs. Coyness Ennix, Jr., Nicole Y. Ennix, Mr. and Mrs. Gary Francois, Dennis L. Franklin, Mr. and Mrs. Maxwell C. Gillette, Mr. and Mrs. Richard Goodyear, Zuretti L. Goosby, Marion E. Greene, Mrs. Vivian S. W. Hambrick, Laurie Gibbs Harris, Arlene Hollis, Louis A. and Letha Jeanpierre, Daniel and Jackie Johnson, Jr., Stephen L. Johnson, Mr. and Mrs. Arthur Lathan, Lewis and Ribbs Mortuary Garden Chapel, Mr. and Mrs. Gary Love, Glenn R. Nance, Mr. and Mrs. Harry S. Parker III, Mr. and Mrs. Carr T. Preston, Fannie Preston, Pamela R. Ransom, Dr. and Mrs. Benjamin F. Reed, San Francisco Black Chamber of Commerce, San Francisco Chapter of Links, Inc., San Francisco Chapter of the N.A.A.C.P., Sigma Pi Phi Fraternity, Dr. Ella Mae Simmons, Mr. Calvin R. Swinson, Joseph B. Williams, Mr. and Mrs. Alfred S. Wilsey, and the people of the Bay Area, 1997.84; *top right* © Corbis; **FM21** © PunchStock; **FM22** *top left* Detail of *Lincoln 2*, Wendy Allen. Oil on canvas. © Wendy Allen; *top right* Detail of *Californians Catching Wild Horses with Riata* (about 1851), Hugo Wilhelm Arthur Nahl. Oil on canvas mounted on masonite. Courtesy of the Oakland Museum of California Kahn Collection (A65.57). © Laurie Platt Winfrey/Oakland Museum/The Art Archive; *bottom* The Newbery Awards are administered by the American Library Service to Children, a division of the American Library Association. Seal image used by permission of American Library Association; **FM23** © PunchStock; **FM24** *top left* © Steve McCurry/Magnum Photos; *top right* Illustration by Michael McCurdy. © 1991 by Michael McCurdy, from *American Tall Tales* by Mary Pope Osborne. Used by permission of Alfred A. Knopf, an imprint of Random House Children's Boooks, a division of Random House, Inc.; *bottom* AP/Wide World Photos; **FM25** © PunchStock; **FM26** *left* © Science Source/Photo Researchers, Inc.; *right* © Carsten Peter/National Geographic Image Collection; **FM27** © PunchStock; **FM28** *left* © Getty Images; *right* © Steve Bly/Alamy Images; **FM29** © PunchStock; **FM30** *left top* © Gary Walts/Syracuse Newspapers/The Image Works, Inc.; *left, center* © Gregor Schuster/Iconica/Getty Images; *left, bottom left* © Syracuse Newspapers/The Image Works, Inc.; *left, bottom right* Marcio José Sanchez/AP/Wide World Photos; *right* © Getty Images.

STUDENT GUIDE TO ACADEMIC SUCCESS

FM35 © Jupiterimages/Getty Images; **FM36** Maggie's Photography, Pacific Palisades, CA; **FM38** © PunchStock.

THE POWER OF IDEAS

1 *left* Detail of *The Promenade, Fifth Avenue* (1986), Bill Jacklin. Oil on canvas, 243.6 cm × 182.7 cm. Private collection. © Bill Jacklin/Bridgeman Art Library; *top right* © Bill Brooks/Masterfile; *bottom right* Detail of *Harriet Tubman* (1945), William H. Johnson. Oil on paperboard, sheet, 29³⁄₈″ × 23³⁄₈″. Smithsonian American Art Museum, Washington, D.C. © Smithsonian American Art Museum, Washington, D.C./Art Resource, New York; **2** *left* Detail of *The Olive Tree* (2005), Ismail Shammout. Palestine. Oil on canvas, 60 cm × 80 cm. Private collection; *right* Fort Sumter National Monument/National Park Service; **3** *left* © Getty Images; *right* Detail of *Communion*, Joe Geshick. © Joe Geshick; **6** © Stephen Stickler/Getty Images; **8** *1* Library of Congress; *2* © Getty Images; *3* © Hermann J. Knippertz/AP/Wide World Photos; *4* © Carsten Peter/National Geographic Image Collection; *5* Commuter Rail Division of the Regional Transportation Authority, d/b/a/ Metra; **9** © Jerry Cooke/Corbis; **10** *1 Whale Rider* footage provided courtesy of South Pacific Pictures Limited. © South Pacific Pictures Limited and ApolloMedia GmbH & Co. 5 Filmproduktion KG 2002. © Newmarket/Courtesy Everett Collection; *2* © Gary Hershorn/Reuters/Corbis; *3* Photo by Will Hart/© NBC/Courtesy Everett Collection; *4* Footage courtesy of Lucasfilm Ltd. *Star Wars: Episode III-Revenge of the Sith* © 2005 Lucasfilm Ltd. & TM. All rights reserved. Used under authorization. Unauthorized duplication is a violation of applicable law; *5* © James Leynse/Corbis; **13** © Gusto Images/Getty Images; **15** *top* © Brian Hagiwara/Getty Images; *bottom* © Thinkstock/Getty Images; **20** *left* © Comstock Images/Age Fotostock; *center* © SW Productions/Getty Images; *right* Photograph by Sharon Hoogstraten; *right: center cover background* © Bob Gelberg/Sharpshooters; *frontispiece background* The Granger Collection, New York; *Amelia Earhart* © Albert L.

R158 ART CREDITS

Bresnik; *Maya Lin* © 1999 Richard Howard/Black Star; *Juan Seguín* Detail of *Juan Seguín* (1838), Jefferson Wright. Texas State Library and Archives Commission; *Harry S. Truman* White House Collection. © White House Historical Association. Courtesy of the Harry S. Truman Library; *Ida Bell Wells* The Granger Collection, New York; *Abigail Adams* Portrait traditionally said to be Abigail Adams (about 1795), unknown artist. Oil on canvas, 30¼″ × 26½″, N-150.55. Photograph by Richard Walker. Copyright © New York State Historical Association, Cooperstown, New York; *Zitkala-Sa* Negative no. Mss 299, William F. Hansen Collection, Photographic Archives, Harold B. Lee Library, Brigham Young University, Provo, Utah; *Benjamin Franklin* © Joseph-Siffrede Duplessis/Wood River Gallery/PNI; *Abraham Lincoln* The Library of Congress; *Martin Luther King, Jr.* Photograph by Howard Sochrer/Life magazine. Copyright © Time Inc; *right, newspaper* © 2007 The Daily Northwestern; *right, National Geographic Magazine* © Carsten Peter/National Geographic Image Collection; *right, Time Magazine* © Time & Life Pictures/Getty Images; *right, CD with lettering* © Regin Igloria; **23** *left* © ImageSource/Age Fotostock; *center* © Susan Wides/PunchStock; *right* © Corbis/Age Fotostock America, Inc.

UNIT 1

25 *left* Illustration © 2004 by Jan Peng-Wang. From *A Song for Ba*, text © 2004 by Paul Yee. First published in Canada by Groundwood Books, Ltd. Reprinted by permission of the publisher; *right* © Michael Kelley/Getty Images; *right background* © StockAB/Alamy Images; **26–27** © Adam Woolfitt/Corbis; **26** © 20th Century Fox/The Kobal Collection; **28** *left* © Corbis; *center left* © Terje Rakke/Getty Images; *center right* © Dean Conger/Corbis; *right* © Medioimages/Getty Images; **30** © Getty Images; **31** © Vance Lessard/Getty Images; **35** © Getty Images; **36** © 2005 Getty Images; **37** © The New York Public Library/Art Resource, New York; **39** *foreground* © Michael Kelley/Getty Images; *background* © StockAB/Alamy Images; **41** © Lise Gagne/istockphoto.com; **43** © Ingram Publishing Royalty Free Photography/Fotosearch Stock Photography; **46** © er Productions/Getty Images; **50** © Warner Bros./Photofest; **51** © Bettmann/Corbis; **53, 56, 60** Illustrations by Esao Andrews; **62** © Brown Brothers, Sterling, Pennsylvania; **66** Photograph by Sharon Hoogstraten; **67** Photo by Jim Lundquist/Sterling Lord Literistic, Inc., on behalf of Joan Bauer; **69** © Didier Robcis/Getty Images; **70** © Andrew Syred/Photo Researchers, Inc.; **72** © Dennis Novak/Getty Images; **76** © Peter Marlow/Magnum Photos; **80** © Nick Koudis/Getty Images; **81** © Bettmann/Corbis; **82, 86** Illustrations by Howard Simpson; **90** © Louie Psihoyos/Science Faction; **91** © CBS/Landov; **93** © 2006 Gene Laughter; **94** © Ferdinando Scianna/Magnum Photos; **97** © Raymond Depardon/Magnum Photos; **100** © Andreas Feininger/Time & Life Pictures/Getty Images; **104–105** © David R. Frazier Photolibrary, Inc./Alamy Images; **104** *top* © Les Cunliffe/Age Fotostock America, Inc.; *center* © Jerry Bauer; **105** *left* Cover of *Hoot* by Carl Hiaasen. © 2002 by Carl Hiaasen. Cover design and illustration © 2004 by Alfred A. Knopf. Reprinted by permission of Alfred A. Knopf, an imprint of Random House Children's Books, a division of Random House, Inc.; *right* The Newbery Awards are administered by the American Library Service to Children, a division of the American Library Association. Seal image used by permission of American Library Association; **106–107** © Paul Harris/Getty Images; **108–109** © Junichi Kusaka/MIXA Co., Ltd./Alamy; **110, 111** © Warner Brothers/Courtesy Everett Collection; **112** *top, center*

© Warner Brothers Entertainment Inc. All rights reserved; *bottom* © PunchStock; **114** © Reg Charity/Corbis; **115** AP/Wide World Photos; **117** Detail of *The Stillness of an Afternoon* (2003), Bo Bartlett. Oil on panel, 18½″ × 21″. Courtesy of the artist and P.P.O.W. Gallery, New York; **118** © GeoNova LLC; **122** © Getty Images; **123** © Joanne Ryder; **125, 129, 132** Illustrations © 2004 by Jan Peng-Wang. From *A Song for Ba*, text © 2004 by Paul Yee. First published in Canada by Groundwood Books, Ltd. Reprinted by permission of the publisher; **136** © AFP/Getty Images; **137** © Stock Montage; **139** Illustration © 2001 by Christopher Bing. From *The Midnight Ride of Paul Revere* by Henry Wadsworth Longfellow, graved and painted by Christopher Bing. Reprinted by permission of Handprint Books, New York; **140** © Raymond Gehman/Getty Images; **142** © Bill Brooks/Alamy Images; **145** *top* PBS® and the PBS logo are registered trademarks of the Public Broadcasting Service and are used with permission. All rights reserved; *center, William Dawes* (unknown), attributed to John Johnston. Oil on canvas, 35″ × 29″. © Collection of the Evanston Historical Society, Evanston, Illinois; **146** © GeoNova LLC; **148** © Craig Aurness/Corbis; **159** © Larry Williams/Corbis; **166** © Siede Preis/Getty Images.

UNIT 2

167 *left* © Mary Grace Long/Getty Images; *right* Detail of *They Moved Them* (1991), David Behrens. Oil glazing, 9¼″ × 14½″. © David Behrens, www.davidbehrens.com; **168–169** © DreamWorks Animation/Zuma/Corbis; **168** © BBC Films/Photofest; **171** © Jamie Thorpe/ShutterStock; **172** © Digital Vision/PunchStock; **176** © Clarissa Leahy/Getty Images; **177** © Jerry Bauer; **179, 182** From *Harlem* by Walter Dean Myers, illustrated by Christopher Myers. © 1997 by Christopher Myers. Reprinted by permission of Scholastic, Inc.; **191** *top left* The Granger Collection, New York; *top right* © Bettmann/Corbis; *bottom left* © Getty Images; *bottom right* © Bob Adelman/Magnum Photos; **192** *left, right* AP/Wide World Photos; *center left* The Granger Collection, New York; *center right* © Bettmann/Corbis; **194** The New York Times Company; **196** © Paul Eekhoff/Masterfile; **197** *top* © Beth Gwinn, Photographer; *bottom* © CBS/Landov; **199** *Mean Dog* (1998), Sylvia Chesley Smith. © Sylvia Chesley Smith/Corbis; **200** The Granger Collection, New York; **203** © Corbis; **206** © Todd Davidson/Illustration Works; **211** © Images.com/Corbis; **213** © Todd Davidson/Stock Illustration RF/Getty Images; **217** © Todd Davidson PTY Ltd/The Image Bank/Getty Images; **221** © Images.com/Corbis; **225** © Selmur/Cinema Rel. Corp./The Kobal Collection; **230** © Ariel Skelley/Corbis; **231** Jennifer Graylock/AP/Wide World Photos; **233** © Mary Grace Long/Getty Images; **235** © Morton Beebe/Corbis; **238** © Martin Barraud/Getty Images; **242** © Corbis; **246** © Lindsay Hebberd/Corbis; **247** *top* Courtesy of Virginia Driving Hawk Sneve; *bottom* Photo of Judith Ortiz Cofer is reprinted with permission from the publisher Arte Publico Press. © 2005, University of Houston, Houston, Texas; **249** Detail of *They Moved Them* (1991), David Behrens. Oil glazing, 9¼″ × 14½″. © David Behrens, www.davidbehrens.com; **250** © GeoNova LLC; **257** *Frida* (2004), Maria Sanchez. Acrylic on canvas. C. Perez Collection. © Maria Sanchez; **262** *Whale Rider* footage provided courtesy of South Pacific Pictures Limited. © South Pacific Pictures Limited and ApolloMedia GmbH & Co. 5 Filmproduktion KG 2002. © Newmarket/Courtesy Everett Collection; **263** *Whale Rider* footage provided courtesy of South Pacific Pictures Limited. © South Pacific Pictures Limited and ApolloMedia GmbH &

UNIT 3

UNIT 4

Photo © Bridgeman Art Library. © 2007 Estate of Pablo Picasso/ Artists Rights Society (ARS), New York. Reproduction, including downloading of Picasso works is prohibited by copyright laws and international conventions without the express written permission of Artists Rights Society (ARS), New York; **491** *Village Street* (1875), Hiroshige III. From the series *Famous Places on the Tokaido: a Record of the Process of Reform.* © Asian Art & Archaeology, Inc./Corbis; **492** © GeoNova LLC; **493** *The Moon and the Abandoned Old Woman* (1891), Yoshitoshi. © Asian Art & Archaeology, Inc./Corbis; **494** *Moon,* Tsukioka Yoshitoshi. From the *Snow, Moon and Flower* Series. © Christie's Images Ltd.; **500** Photograph by Sharon Hoogstraten; **501** *top* Courtesy Teresa Palomo Acosta; *bottom* © Michael S. Glaser, St. Mary's College of Maryland; **503** *American Childhood* (1995), Jane Burch Cochran. Fabric, beads, buttons, paint, baby dress, gloves. Machine pieced, hand appliqued using beads, hand embellished. 53" × 42". Collection of Pam Monfort; **505** *Crossing Borders* (1995), Deidre Scherer. Fabric and thread. © Deidre Scherer; **506** © Photo by Sharon Hoogstraten; *top left* © Getty Images; *bottom left* © Regin Igloria; *inset, bottom right* © Getty Images; **508** © Getty Images; **509** AP/Wide World Photos; **511, 513, 518, 525, 529, 535, 538** © Joan Marcus; **544** © Getty Images; **547, 551, 557** © Joan Marcus; **565** *The Diary of Anne Frank* (2006), Oregon Shakespeare Festival. Tony De Bruno as Otto Frank. Photo © David Cooper Photography; **569, 570, 571** © Getty Images; **572** *left* Courtesy of Harry Goldsmith (Estate). © United States Holocaust Memorial Museum. The views and opinions expressed in the book and the context in which the images are used, do not necessarily reflect the views or policy of, nor imply approval or endorsement by, the United States Holocaust Memorial Museum; *right* Courtesy of Hannah Kastan Weiss. © United States Holocaust Memorial Museum. The views and opinions expressed in the book and the context in which the images are used, do not necessarily reflect the views or policy of, nor imply approval or endorsement by, the United States Holocaust Memorial Museum; **573** The Granger Collection, New York; **575** Courtesy of Madalae Fraser. © United States Holocaust Memorial Museum. The views and opinions expressed in the book and the context in which the images are used, do not necessarily reflect the views or policy of, nor imply approval or endorsement by, the United States Holocaust Memorial Museum; **578** © Getty Images; **579** *top* Scene from *Anne Frank Remembered* appears courtesy of Sony Pictures Classics, Inc.; *center* © The Everett Collection; *bottom* © Anne Frank Stichting/Allard Bovenberg/2003 Getty Images; **580** *top, center, bottom* © Getty Images; **581** *top left* © Kayte M. Deioma/PhotoEdit; *top center* © Myrleen Ferguson Cate/PhotoEdit; *top right* AP/Wide World Photos; *bottom left* © Michael Newman/PhotoEdit; *bottom center* © Frank Siteman/PhotoEdit; *bottom right* © Michael Newman/PhotoEdit; **582** © Richard Sisk/Jupiter Images; **593** © James Woodson/Getty Images; **600** © Siede Preis/Getty Images.

UNIT 5

601 *left, La Promenade en Mer* (1988), Jean Plichart. Copper engraving. © SuperStock; *right* © Ted Mead/Getty Images; **602–603** Photo by Bac To Trong; **604** *foreground* © Corbis; *background* © Getty Images; **605** © Image Club Graphics; **606** © Getty Images; **607** © Laurie Barr/ShutterStock; **608** *top left* © Corbis; *bottom left* © Merryl McNaughton/ShutterStock; *right* © Robert Blomkvist/ ShutterStock; **609** *top* © Piotr Przeszlo/ShutterStock; *bottom* © Karin Lau/ShutterStock; **610** Designed by Lisa Brennan; **611** *top* © Miriam

Berkley; *bottom* © Christopher Felver/Corbis; **613** *Light – 1* (1992), Atsuko Kato. Oil on board, 100 cm × 70 cm; **614** *Wednesday 6: Rain, slowly clearing eastwards* (2001), Ben McLaughlin. Oil on board, 20.3 cm × 20.3 cm. Private collection. © Bridgeman Art Library; **616** © American Images Inc./Getty Images; **617** *top* © Getty Images; *bottom* Photograph by Norberto E. Martinez/University of Texas at Brownsville and Texas Southmost College; **619** © PIER/Getty Images; **621** *The Mountain* (1991), Albert Herbert. Oil on canvas, 50.8 cm × 61 cm. Private collection. © Bridgeman Art Library; **622** © David Scharf/Science Photo Library/Photo Researchers, Inc.; **624** © Lori Adamski Peek/Getty Images; **625** *top* The Granger Collection, New York; *bottom* © Getty Images; **627** © Paul Edmondson/ Getty Images; **629** © Ted Mead/Getty Images; **632** Designed by Lisa Brennan; **633** *top* © Nancy Crampton; *bottom* © Corbis; **635** *New Dreams,* Ernest Crichlow. Lithograph, 24¾" × 16¾". Photo by Maureen Turci, Mojo Portfolio. Courtesy of the Estate of Ernest Crichlow; **636** *Lady,* Ernest Crichlow. Etching, 22" × 18". Photo by Maureen Turci, Mojo Portfolio. Courtesy of the Estate of Ernest Crichlow; **638** © Just One Productions/Photofest; **639** *top* The Granger Collection, New York; *bottom* Detail of *Alexander Pope* (1740), William Hoare. The Granger Collection, New York; **641** © Corbis; **642** *Barn at Cove, Oregon* (2005), Gary Ernest Smith. Oil on canvas, 30" × 40"; **644** © Mango Productions/Corbis; **645** *top* © Mitchell Gerber/Corbis; *bottom* © Peter Morenus; **647** *Aspiration* (1936), Aaron Douglas. Oil on canvas, 60" × 60". © Fine Arts Museums of San Francisco purchase, the estate of Thurlow E. Tibbs, Jr., the Museum Society Auxiliary, American Art Trust Fund, Unrestricted Art Trust Fund, partial gift of Dr. Ernest A. Bates, Sharon Bell, Jo-Ann Beverly, Barbara Carleton, Dr. and Mrs. Arthur H. Coleman, Dr. and Mrs. Coyness Ennix, Jr., Nicole Y. Ennix, Mr. and Mrs. Gary Francois, Dennis L. Franklin, Mr. and Mrs. Maxwell C. Gillette, Mr. and Mrs. Richard Goodyear, Zuretti L. Goosby, Marion E. Greene, Mrs. Vivian S. W. Hambrick, Laurie Gibbs Harris, Arlene Hollis, Louis A. and Letha Jeanpierre, Daniel and Jackie Johnson, Jr., Stephen L. Johnson, Mr. and Mrs. Arthur Lathan, Lewis and Ribbs Mortuary Garden Chapel, Mr. and Mrs. Gary Love, Glenn R. Nance, Mr. and Mrs. Harry S. Parker III, Mr. and Mrs. Carr T. Preston, Fannie Preston, Pamela R. Ransom, Dr. and Mrs. Benjamin F. Reed, San Francisco Black Chamber of Commerce, San Francisco Chapter of Links, Inc., San Francisco Chapter of the N.A.A.C.P., Sigma Pi Phi Fraternity, Dr. Ella Mae Simmons, Mr. Calvin R. Swinson, Joseph B. Williams, Mr. and Mrs. Alfred S. Wilsey, and the people of the Bay Area, 1997.84; **648** *Fortune* (2001), William B. Westwood. © William B. Westwood; **653** *left, center, right* Facial Reconstruction of Fortune by Frank Bender. © Mattatuck Museum Arts and History Center, Waterbury, Connecticutt; **656** © Paul Panayiotou/Alamy Images; **657** *top* © Getty Images; *bottom* © Stock Montage; **659** *La Promenade en Mer* (1988), Jean Plichart. Copper engraving. © SuperStock; **661** *Communion,* Joe Geshick. © Joe Geshick; **664** *Deer Spirit Helper,* Joe Geshick. Oil. © Joe Geshick; **668** © Daryl Benson/Masterfile; **673** © Hunter Freeman/Getty Images; **677** © Michael Newman/PhotoEdit; **684** © Siede Preis/ Getty Images.

UNIT 6

685 *right* Detail of *The Promenade, Fifth Avenue* (1986), Bill Jacklin. Oil on canvas, 243.6 cm × 182.7 cm. Private collection. © Bill Jacklin/Bridgeman Art Library; *left* © Sherman Hines/Masterfile;

686 *top left* © Pierre Vauthey/Corbis Sygma; *top center left* © The Everett Collection; *top center* © Universal TV/The Kobal Collection; *top right* © Charles Sykes/Rex Features/Courtesy The Everett Collection; *bottom far left* © The Everett Collection; *2nd bottom left* © John Rogers/Getty Images; *bottom center* © John Springer Collection/Corbis; *bottom center right* © The Everett Collection; *bottom right* © Roger Ressmeyer/Corbis; **687** © Bettmann/Corbis; **688** *top* © Robert Kyllo/ShutterStock; *center* © Zina Seletskaya/ShutterStock; *bottom* © ANP/ShutterStock; **690** *top* © Jerry Bauer; *bottom* Reprinted by permission of William Sleator and the author's agents, Scovil Chichak Galen Literary Agency, Inc.; *background* © Albo/ShutterStock; **691** © Paul Maguire/ShutterStock; **692** © Aga and Miko Materne (arsat)/ShutterStock; **694** © Chad Baker/Ryan McVay/Getty Images; **695** © Getty Images; **697** *The Promenade, Fifth Avenue* (1986), Bill Jacklin. Oil on canvas, 243.6 cm × 182.7 cm. Private collection. © Bill Jacklin/Bridgeman Art Library; **698** © GeoNova LLC; **704** © Eyebyte/Alamy Images; **705** © The New York Public Library; **707** *Spring* (1894), Lawrence Alma-Tadema. Oil on canvas, 70¼″ × 31½″. The J. Paul Getty Museum, Los Angeles, (72.PA.3). © J. Paul Getty Trust; **708** © T. Papageorgiou/age fotostock america, inc.; **709** *left*, *Head Study of a Tiger*, Roland Wheelwright. Oil on board, 49.5 cm × 60.9 cm. Private collection. © Roland Wheelwright/ Bridgeman Art Library; *right* Detail of *Study of a Lady*, Frederic Leighton. Oil on canvas, 25.5 cm × 19 cm. Private collection. © Bridgeman Art Library; **712** *Cleopatra* (about 1888), John W. Waterhouse. Oil on canvas, 65.4 cm × 56.8 cm. © 2002 Christie's Images Limited; **717** *top* The New York Times Company; *bottom, Let's Make a Deal,* Host Monty Hall, 1963–1976. © The Everett Collection; **718, 720** © The New Yorker Collection. © 1990 Peter Steiner from cartoonbank.com. All rights reserved; **722–723** © Reuters/Corbis; **722** *top* © Les Cunliffe/Age Fotostock America, Inc.; *center* Reed Saxon/AP/Wide World Photos; **723** *left* Cover of *Kira-Kira* by Cynthia Kadohata. © 2004 by Cynthia Kadohata. Cover photo © Julia Kuskin. Reprinted by permission of Atheneum Books for Young Readers, an imprint of Simon and Schuster Children's Publishing Division, New York; *right* The Newbery Awards are administered by the American Library Service to Children, a division of the American Library Association. Seal image used by permission of American Library Association; **724–725** © Bryan Mullennix/Getty Images; **726–727** © Ken Ross/Getty Images; **728** *Peanuts,* Charles Schulz. August 5, 1983. © United Feature Syndicate; **729** Library of Congress; **731** The Granger Collection, New York; **733** Library of Congress; **734** The Granger Collection, New York; **739** © Michael Newman/PhotoEdit; **740** © Chuck Pefley/Alamy Images; **741** © Hugh Hamrick; **743** Detail of *Outside In* (2004), Ryan Kapp. Oil on canvas on panel, 18″ × 24″. © Ryan Kapp. www.ryankapp.com; **744** © Christopher Stevenson/Getty Images; **747** Photograph by Sharon Hoogstraten; **752** © Kevin Fleming/Corbis; **753** National Archives; **755** *Lincoln 2,* Wendy Allen. Oil on canvas. © Wendy Allen; **756** Detail of *Major General John Sedgwick Monument,* Wendy Allen. Oil on canvas, 40″ × 30″. © Wendy Allen; **758** © J. David Andrews/Masterfile; **769** © Michael Newman/PhotoEdit; **773** © Mike Baldwin/www.CartoonStock.com; **778** © Siede Preis/Getty Images.

UNIT 7

779 *left, Los Comaradas del Barrio* (1976), Jesse Treviño. Acrylic on canvas, 36″ × 48″. Collection of the artist; *right* © Ric Ergenbright/Corbis; **780–781** © PunchStock; **780** © PunchStock; **782** *top* ©

Margaretta Mitchell; *center* © Getty Images; *bottom* © Getty Images; **783** *top foreground* © Getty Images; *top background* © Artbeats; *bottom* AP/Wide World Photos; **784** © Bettmann/Corbis; **785** © Hulton-Deutsch Collection/Corbis; **786** *top* Photo by Christine Lee Zilka; *center* © Ryan McVay/Getty Images; *bottom* © Corbis; **787** © Ryan McVay/Getty Images; **788** © Ariel Skelley/Corbis; **789** Courtesy Joseph Bruchac/Photo by Michael Greenlar; **791** *Child Fishing* (1989), Lincoln Seligman. Private collection. Bridgeman Art Library; **793** © Betsy Cullen/Getty Images; **795** *Bridge Over Weekeepeemee* (1974), Mark Potter. Oil on canvas. Private collection. © Bridgeman Art Library; **798** *foreground* © Georgette Douwma/Photo Researchers, Inc.; *background* © Skye Chalmers/Getty Images; **804** © Richard Wahlstrom/Getty Images; **805** © Colin Izod; **807** © Richard I'Anson/Lonely Planet Images; **808** Marriage necklace or Thali (1800). India (Madras). Golden pendants on black thread. (CT17149). Victoria & Albert Museum, London. © Victoria & Albert Museum, London/Art Resource, New York; **809** © Per-Anders Pettersson/Getty Images; **810** © GeoNova LLC; **815** © Robert Harding Picture Library Ltd/Alamy Images; **817** © Steve McCurry/Magnum Photos; **819** © Gideon Mendel/Corbis; **822** © Will & Deni McIntyre/Corbis; **823** © Paul Coughlin; **825, 829** Illustrations by Michael McCurdy. © 1991 by Michael McCurdy, from *American Tall Tales* by Mary Pope Osborne. Used by permission of Alfred A. Knopf, an imprint of Random House Children's Boooks, a division of Random House, Inc.; **832–833** © Adalberto Rios Lanz/Sexto Sol/Getty Images; **832** *top* © Les Cunliffe/Age Fotostock America, Inc.; *center* © Bettmann/Corbis; **833** *top* AP/Wide World Photos; **834–835** © Danita Delimont/Alamy Images; **836–837** © Kenny Johnson/Getty Images; **838** © Mike Powell/Getty Images; **839** © Gary Soto; **841** Detail of *Los Comaradas del Barrio* (1976), Jesse Treviño. Acrylic on canvas, 36″ × 48″. Collection of the artist; **844** *La Calle Cuatro* (2001), Emigdio Vasquez. Oil on canvas, 22″ × 28″. © Emigdio Vasquez; **848** © Creatas/Superstock; **852** © 2006 Larry Wright. The Detroit News. All rights reserved. Courtesy of Cagle Cartoons, Inc.; **853** *Acid Rain* by Frank Evers © New York Daily News, L.P. Used with permission; **854** *left* The Granger Collection, New York; *bottom* © Corbis; **855** © Jupiterimages Corporation; **856** © Paul Carstairs/Alamy Images; **857** © Tom Roster Photographer; **858** Illustration by Jerome Lagarrigue, from *Going North* by Janice N. Harrington. Pictures © 2005 by Jerome Lagarrigue. Reprinted by permission of Farrar, Straus and Giroux; **859** From *Freedom on the Menu: The Greensboro Sit-ins* by Carole Boston Weatherford. Illustrated by Jerome Lagarrigue. © 2005 by Jerome Lagarrigue, painting. Used by permission of Dial Books for Young Readers, a division of Penguin Young Readers Group, a member of Penguin Group (USA) Inc., 345 Hudson Street, New York 10014. All rights reserved; **861** © Jack Moebes/Corbis; **862** © Jason Ernst/Age Fotostock America, Inc.; **873** © Jeff Greenberg/Age Fotostock; **880** © Siede Preis/Getty Images.

UNIT 8

881 *left* © Carsten Peter/National Geographic Image Collection; *right* © Columbia/Marvel/The Kobal Collection; **882–883** © Corbis; **882** *left* Jacket of *1000 Great Rail-Trails, A Comprehensive Directory.* Cover photos: *woods* © Mark Windom/Index Stock Imagery; *railroad track* © PhotoLink/Getty Images; inset photos: *runner* © Karl Weatherly/Getty Images; *inline skater* © Jules Frazier/Getty Images; *biker* © David Buffington/Getty Images; *skier* © Getty Images; Reprinted by permission of The Globe Pequot Press, Guilford, Connecticut;

compass © Tom Schierlitz/Getty Images; **884** *top left* © Artville/
Royalty-Free; *top right* © Stockfood Creative/Getty Images; *bottom*
© Foodpix/Jupiterimages Corporation; **885** © Denis Scott/Corbis;
886 © Getty Images; **887** *top* © Yonhap - Yonhap does not obtain
releases from subjects, individuals, groups or entities contained in
its photos, that no clearance is obtained from the owners of any
trademarks or copyrighted materials whose marks and materials
are there incidentally in photo; *bottom* © Steve Kaufman/Corbis;
889 *top* © Bettmann/Corbis; *bottom* © Blake Little/Getty Images;
890 © LWA-Dann Tardif/Corbis; **891** Courtesy Bijal Trivedi; **893**
AP/Wide World Photos; *inset* © Columbia/Marvel/The Kobal
Collection; **896** © 2007 © Peter J. Bryant/Biological Photo Service.
All rights reserved; **900** © Corbis; **901, 902–903** © Carsten Peter/
National Geographic Image Collection; **904** *top* © GeoNova LLC;
bottom left Seated man. Victim of the eruption of Mount Vesuvius.
Palestra Grande, Pompeii, Italy. © Scala/Art Resource, New York;
bottom center © Corbis; *bottom right* © Layne Kennedy/Corbis; **905,
906–907** © Carsten Peter/National Geographic Image Collection;
906 Illustration by Richard Bonson/Wildlife Art Ltd.; **907** ©
Carsten Peter/National Geographic Image Collection; **910** NASA
Kennedy Space Center (NASA-KSC); **911** *left* © Jim Ruymen/
Reuters/Corbis; *right: top left* NASA/JPL/University of Maryland/
AP/Wide World Photos; *bottom left* NASA/AP/Wide World Photos;
all other photos NASA Jet Propulsion Laboratory; **912** *top* AP/Wide
World Photos; *center* © NASA/JPL/epa/Corbis; *bottom* © NASA/JPL/
epa/Corbis; **914** © Hugh Sitton/zefa/Corbis; **915** © Alice Handwerk;
917 © Mark Christmas/National Geographic Image Collection;
918 Courtesy Peter and Ingrid Yurchenco; **921** Photo by Joaquin A.
Huerta A./Courtesy Henrietta Yurchenco; **924** © Taili Song Roth/
Corbis; **925** Courtesy Jan McGirk; **926** © Robert Nickelsberg/Getty
Images; **928** © GeoNova LLC; **930** © Robert Nickelsberg/Getty
Images; **931** © Mark Richards/ZUMA/Corbis; **934** © Adam Gault/
Getty Images; **935** © Tony Cenicola/The New York Times; **936,
938** Courtesy of Hanger Prosthetics & Orthotics, Inc. www.hanger.
com; **939** © Dith Pran/New York Times/Redux; **940** PBS® and the
PBS logo are registered trademarks of the Public Broadcasting Service
and are used with permission. All rights reserved; **941** © Science
Source/Photo Researchers, Inc.; **945–952** Illustrations by David
Ballard; **954** *top* © Les Cunliffe/Age Fotostock America, Inc.; *center*
© Arthur Cohen Photography; **955** *right* The Newbery Awards are
administered by the American Library Service to Children, a division
of the American Library Association. Seal image used by permission
of American Library Association; *left* Cover of *An American Plague:
The True and Terrifying Story of the Yellow Fever Epidemic of 1793*
by Jim Murphy. Copyright © 2003 by Jim Murphy. Cover art ©
Houghton Mifflin Company. Reprinted by permission of Clarion
Books, an imprint of Houghton Mifflin Company; **956–957,
958–959** The Granger Collection, New York; **960** © Alain Choisnet/
Getty Images; **971** © Corbis/PunchStock; **975** *top* © Harpe/Peter
Arnold, Inc.; *bottom* © Jeffrey L. Rotman/Corbis; **978** © Siede Preis/
Getty Images.

UNIT 9

979 *left* © Peter Finger/Corbis; *right* © Getty Images; **980–981** ©
Louie Psihoyos/Corbis; **982** © Ronnie Kaufman/Corbis; **983** *top*
© C. Fleurent/photocuisine/Corbis; *bottom* © Artville; **985** © Ken
Kaminesky/Take 2 Productions/Corbis; **987** © David Woods/Corbis;
988 © Steve Bloom/Getty Images; **989** *top* Courtesy Rob Laidlaw;

bottom © Song Hutchins; **990** © Getty Images; **995** © Ali Burafi/
AFP/Getty Images; **1000** *top* © Getty Images; *bottom* Francois
Mori/AP/Wide World Photos; **1001** *top, bottom* Footage courtesy
of Lucasfilm Ltd. *Star Wars: Episode III-Revenge of the Sith* © 2005
Lucasfilm Ltd. & TM. All rights reserved. Used under authorization.
Unauthorized duplication is a violation of applicable law; **1002** *left*
Footage courtesy of Lucasfilm Ltd. *Star Wars: Episode III-Revenge
of the Sith* © 2005 Lucasfilm Ltd. & TM. All rights reserved. Used
under authorization. Unauthorized duplication is a violation of
applicable law; *background* © Getty Images; **1003** *center* © Stockbyte;
right © Getty Images; **1004** © Todd Gipstein/Corbis; **1005** © Peter
Read Miller/Sports Illustrated/Getty Images; **1006** Courtesy of the
National Association for Sport and Physical Education; **1007** © Chris
Clinton/Getty Images; **1008** © Sports Illustrated/Getty Images;
1009 © Peter Finger/Corbis; **1014** © 2004 Twentieth Century
Fox/Photofest; **1015** Courtesy of Darhansoff, Verrill, and Feldman
Agency; **1016** The New York Times Company; **1017** © Lynda Barry;
1022 © Corbis; **1023** © GeoNova LLC; **1025** © Steve Bly/Alamy
Images; **1027** © Saulius T. Kondrotas/Alamy Images, **1028** The
Granger Collection, New York; **1030** © Tom Stewart/Corbis; **1031**
The Granger Collection, New York; **1033** © Corbis; **1038** © Sam
Barricklow/Jupiterimages Corporation; **1049** © Dirk Anschutz/Getty
Images; **1056** © Siede Preis/Getty Images.

UNIT 10

1057 *left* © Getty Images; *right top* © Gary Walts/Syracuse
Newspapers/The Image Works, Inc.; *right, center* © Gregor Schuster/
Iconica/Getty Images; *right, bottom left* © Syracuse Newspapers/
The Image Works, Inc.; *right, bottom right* Marcio Jose Sanchez/AP/
Wide World Photos; **1058–1059** © Robin Sachs/PhotoEdit; **1060**
foreground © CSAImages.com; *background* © Laurent Hamels/Age
Fotostock America, Inc.; **1064** © Google; **1065** Courtesy of the
Smithsonian National Museum of American History, Lemuelson
Center; **1069** © Garry Gay/Getty Images; **1070** From Gale. *InfoTrac.*
© Gale, a part of Cengage Learning, Inc. Reproduced by permission.
www.cengage.com/permissions; **1072** © Bob Brown/Richmond
Times-Dispatch/AP/Wide World Photos; **1073** *left* Marcio José
Sanchez/AP/Wide World Photos; *right* © Rubberball Productions;
1077 © Punchstock/Royalty Free; **1078** © Walter Bibikow/
Jupiterimages Corporation; **1095** © Michael J. Doolittle/The Image
Works, Inc.

STUDENT RESOURCE BANK

R3 © Ben Mangor/SuperStock Inc.; **R5** *Bar graph* © Sense
Interactive Multimedia/Royalty Free; **R6** *top* Ancient irrigation
© Illustration by Gary Hincks; *bottom* Cross-section of a Roman
road. Illustration by Peter Bull; **R7** © GeoNova LLC; **R19** ©
Carsten Peter/National Geographic Image Collection; **R87** *left* ©
Corbis; *right* © Comstock; **R94** © Sony Pictures/Courtesy Everett
Collection.

BACK COVER

top left Photos.com/Jupiter Images; *center* American Childhood
(1995), Jane Burch Cochran. Fabric, beads, buttons, paint, baby
dress, gloves. Machine pieced, hand appliquéd using beads, hand
embellished. 53″ × 42″. Collection of Pam Monfort; *center right*
© Jennifer Graylock/AP/Wide World Photos; *bottom left* © Saulius
T. Kondrotas/Alamy Images.